W9-BIC-527

Invitation to
The
Life Span

Invitation to The Life Span

Second Edition

Kathleen Stassen Berger

Bronx Community College

City University of New York

WORTH PUBLISHERS

A MACMILLAN HIGHER EDUCATION COMPANY

Vice President, Editorial and Production: Catherine Woods

Associate Publisher: Jessica Bayne

Developmental Editor: Tom Churchill

Executive Marketing Manager: Katherine Nurre

Marketing Assistant: Julie Tompkins

Media Editor: Sharon Prevost

Editorial Assistant: Catherine Michaelsen

Associate Managing Editor: Lisa Kinne

Senior Project Editor: Vivien Weiss

Art Director and Cover Designer: Barbara Reingold

Interior Designer: Lyndall Culbertson

Infographic Designer: Charles Yuen

Photo Treatments: Lyndall Culbertson

Layout Designer: Paul Lacy

Photo Editor: Christine Buese

Photo Researchers: Donna Ranieri, Deborah Anderson

Illustrations: Todd Buck Illustrations, MPS Limited, TSI Graphics, Inc.

Production Manager: Barbara Seixas

Composition: MPS Limited

Printing and Binding: RR Donnelley

Cover Art: Sandra Dionisi

Library of Congress Control Number: 2013932603

ISBN-13: 978-1-4292-8352-6

ISBN-10: 1-4292-8352-1

Copyright © 2014, 2010 by Worth Publishers

All rights reserved.

Printed in the United States of America

First printing

Worth Publishers

41 Madison Avenue

New York, NY 10010

www.worthpublishers.com

Credit is given to the following sources for permission to use the photos indicated:

Part Openers

David M. Phillips/Photo Researchers, pp. xxx–1

Scott Hancock/Jupiter Images, pp. vi, 88–89

Craig Pershouse/Getty Images, p. 156

Olaf Krüger/imagebrok/age fotostock, pp. vi, 240–241

Grove Pashley/Corbis, pp. vii, 316

commerceandculturestock/Getty Images, p. 390

Alamy, pp. vii, 496

Chapter Openers

© Erin Moroney LaBelle/The Image Works, p. 2

Jade Brookbank/Getty, pp. viii, 46

Rayes/Getty Images, pp. ix, 90

Nabi Lukic/Getty Images, p. 130

KidStock/Blend Images/Corbis, pp. ix, 166

Daniel Boag/Getty Images, p. 204

Floresco Productions/Corbis, pp. x, 242

Gary John Norman/Getty Images, p. 282

KidStock/Blend Images/Corbis, pp. x, 318

Patrick Sheandell O'Carroll/PhotoAlto/Corbis, pp. xi, 354

Westend61/Getty Images, pp. xi, 392

Patrice Coppee/Getty Images, pp. xii, 426

Yellow Dog Productions Inc./Getty Images, p. 462

punchstock, pp. xii, 498

Ryan McVay/Getty Images, p. 534

Buddhika Weerasinghe/Reuters/Corbis, p. 572

About the Author

Kathleen Stassen Berger received her undergraduate education at Stanford University and Radcliffe College, earned an M.A.T. from Harvard University, and an MS and PhD from Yeshiva University. Her broad experience as an educator includes directing a preschool, serving as chair of philosophy at the United Nations International School, teaching child and adolescent development to graduate students at Fordham University and undergraduates at Montclair State University in New Jersey and at Quinnipiac University in Connecticut, as well as teaching social psychology to inmates at Sing Sing Prison.

Throughout most of her professional career, Berger has taught at Bronx Community College of the City University of New York, first as an adjunct and for the past two decades as a full professor. She has taught introduction to psychology, child and adolescent development, adulthood and aging, social psychology, abnormal psychology, and human motivation. Her students—who come from many ethnic, economic, and educational backgrounds and who have a wide range of ages and interests—consistently honor her with the highest teaching evaluations.

Berger is also the author of *The Developing Person Through the Life Span* and *The Developing Person Through Childhood and Adolescence.* Her developmental texts are currently being used at more than 900 schools worldwide and are available in Spanish, French, Italian, and Portuguese, as well as English. Her research interests include adolescent identity, multigenerational families, immigration, and bullying, and she has published many articles on developmental topics in the *Wiley Encyclopedia of Psychology* and in publications of the American Association for Higher Education and the National Education Association for Higher Education. She continues teaching and learning every semester and in every edition of her books.

Brief Contents

Contents

Preface

My 3-year-old grandson, Asa, talks about good guys and bad guys. He considers himself one of the good guys, destroying the bad guys in his active imagination and in karate kicks in the air.

Oscar, his father, usually sits and watches. He asked me if Asa really believes there are good guys and bad guys, or is that just a cliché. I said that most 3-year-olds believe quite simple opposites.

Undeterred, Oscar told Asa that he knows some adults who were once bad guys but became good guys.

"No," Asa insisted. "That never happens."

Asa is mistaken. As he matures, his body will grow taller but become less active, and his mind will appreciate the nuances of human behavior. This book describes how our thoughts and actions change over the life span, including "what happens" as humans grow older.

COURTESY OF KATHLEEN BERGER

Oscar is not alone in realizing that people change. Many common sayings affirm development over time: People "turn over a new leaf," are "born again"; parents are granted a "do-over" when they become grandparents; today is "the first day of the rest of your life." Adults also recognize that the past never disappears; we say, "The apple does not fall far from the tree," and many other adages that stress past influences.

The complexity, the twists and turns, the endless variety of the human experience at every age is fascinating to me, which is why I wrote this book. We all have echoes of Asa in us: We want life to be simple, and we want to be good guys. But life is not simple. Learning about human growth helps everyone respond to life's complexities, not with imaginary kicks but with wise reactions, as we become closer to good by the end. Knowledge does that. In a vivid example, Steven Pinker (2011) explains that humans kill each other less now than they did in previous centuries; he cites education as one reason.

Education occurs in hundreds of ways. This textbook is only one of them, merely an "invitation" to understand the complexity of your life, my life, and the lives of all the other billions of humans alive now or who have lived. Nonetheless, writing it is my contribution and studying it is yours: Together we might learn how to limit the bad and maximize the good as time goes on.

All this makes me remember again why I study human development. We all need to know more; it will help us, our loved ones, and every person develop with more joy and fulfillment and less harm and despair.

Teaching and writing remain my life's work and passion. I strive to make this text both challenging and accessible to every student, remembering that my students were the inspiration for writing a developmental text in the first place. Students deserve a book that respects their intellect and experiences, without making development seem dull or obscure.

Overall, I believe that a better world is possible because today's students will become tomorrow's leaders. My hope is that the knowledge they gain from reading this book will benefit all their family members—children and adults alike—from one generation to the next.

Family Pride Grandpa Charilaos is proud of his tavern in northern Greece (central Macedonia), but he is even more proud of his talented grandchildren, including Maria Soni (shown here). Note her expert fingering. Her father and mother also play instruments—is that nature or nurture?

To learn more about the specifics of this text, including the material that is new to this edition, read on. Or simply turn to the beginning of Chapter 1 and start your study.

New Material

Every year, scientists discover and explain new concepts and present new research. The best of these are integrated into the text, including hundreds of new references on many topics—among them the genetics of delinquency, infant nutrition, bipolar and autistic spectrum disorders, high-stakes testing, drug use and drug addiction, the importance of attachment and brain development throughout childhood and into the last years of our lives. Cognizant of the interdisciplinary nature of human development, I reflect research in biology, sociology, education, anthropology, political science, and more—as well as in my home discipline, psychology.

Genetics and social contexts are noted throughout. The variations and hazards of infant day care and preschool education are described; the implications of various family structures throughout the life span are explored; the pivotal role of school and the workplace is noted, and so on.

Research on the Brain

Every page of this text reflects new research and theory. Brain development is the most obvious example: Every major section of the book includes a section on the brain, often enhanced with charts and photos to help students understand its inner workings. The following list highlights some of this material:

A View from Science: Implication of low serotonin levels in SIDS, pp. 6–7

The role of neurotransmitters and growth factors such as GDNF in depression, p. 18

PET scans of brains of a depressed and a non-depressed person, p. 19

Effect of the short allele of 5-HTTLPR on stress reactions, p. 22

Prenatal growth of the brain, pp. 60–61; illustrated, p. 62

Teratogenic effects on brain development, p. 73; illustrated, p. 77

Brain development in the first two years, pp. 93–98; illustrated, p. 94

Measurements of brain function applied to evaluate Piaget's sensorimotor intelligence, pp. 116–117

Epigenetic effects on brain development, pp. 119–120

Brain developments that support social emotions, pp. 135–136

The effect of stress on brain development, pp. 136–137

Synchrony and brain maturation, p. 142

Attachment and brain development, p. 145

A View from Science: The effect of lead exposure on brain development, pp. 172–173

Brain development in early childhood (prefrontal cortex, myelination, lateralization, the limbic system), pp. 177–182; illustrated, pp. 177, 178

The effects of physical exercise on the brain, p. 246

Collaboration of cortical regions in selective attention, p. 256

Before Words The infant interpreting a smile is doing what babies do: trying to understand communications.

New Pedagogical Aids

With every edition of my textbooks, I rethink how best to communicate to students—bearing in mind both my experiences with students in the classroom and the most recent research on how students learn. In this edition, I have added a number of new pedagogical features. Learning Objectives appear at the beginning and at the end of each chapter: At the start, "What Will You Know?" questions indicate the big ideas, and at the end, "What Have You Learned?" questions help students assess their learning in detail. Each chapter now has an infographic diagram and a new boxed feature called "Opposing Perspectives" to help students see two sides of an important issue. Critical thinking is encouraged on every page, but these new boxes highlight such thinking by emphasizing that people (including scientists) disagree on key developmental questions. Each of these new features is explained in more detail below.

LEARNING OBJECTIVES

Much of what students learn from this course is a matter of attitude, approach, and perspective—all hard to quantify. In addition, there are specific learning objectives, which supplement the key terms that should also be learned. New to this edition, two sets of objectives are listed for each chapter. Each question asked at the beginning of each chapter ("What Will You Know?") correlates with a major heading in the chapter and focuses on general ideas that students might remember and apply lifelong.

At the end of each chapter are more specific learning objectives ("What Have You Learned?") that also connect to each major heading within the chapter but ask more specific questions about the chapter content. Suggestions and grading rubrics for these questions are available in the test bank that goes along with the book.

Bonded That fathers enjoy their sons is not surprising, but notice the infant's hand reaching for Dad's face. At this age, infants show their trust in adults by grabbing and reaching. Synchrony and attachment are mutual.

BRITTA KASHOLM-TENGVE / GETTY IMAGES

OPPOSING PERSPECTIVES

New to this edition are boxed features on controversial and exciting topics in development—from prenatal sex selection to the right to die. These high-interest sections are introduced in every chapter and provide students with enough information on both sides of an issue so that they can practice assessing arguments, looking at the evidence, and coming up with their own conclusions. A complete list of these new features is included in the table of contents.

VISUALIZING DEVELOPMENT

Also new to this edition are full-page illustrations on key topics in development. Every chapter now includes an infographic display of key data on issues ranging from the biology of twins to the economic benefits of college to where elders spend their last years. Readers will find that many of these infographics often combine global statistics, maps, charts and photographs. Working closely with noted designer Charles Yuen, I have tried to use this visual display of data to reinforce and explain key ideas.

Content Changes to the Second Edition

Life-span development, like all sciences, builds on past learning. Many facts and concepts are scaffolds that remain strong over time: stages and ages, norms and variations, dangers and diversities, classic theories and fascinating applications. However, the study of development is continually changed by discoveries and experiences, so no paragraph in this second edition is exactly what it was in the first edition.

Some major revisions have been made, and hundreds of new examples are cited. Highlights of this updating appear below.

Part I: The Beginning

1. The Science of Human Development

- Scientific method explained at the start of the book, illustrated by research on SIDS—from the mystery of sudden infant death, to hypotheses, to life-saving practices
- Humanism and evolutionary theory now covered in the section "Theories of Human Development"

Eager Eaters Preschoolers generally eat whatever they get. These are the fortunate ones, sharing a fresh fruit snack with a friend.

ZHANG BO / GETTY IMAGES

- The role of neurotransmitters and growth factors such as GDNF in depression
- Effect of the short allele of 5-HTTLPR on stress reactions
- Opposing Perspectives on use of the word *race*
- *Visualizing Development.* Age Structure and Development: Illustrates data on relationship between age structure, economic development, and measures of social well-being worldwide

2. From Conception to Birth

- Section "From Zygote to Newborn" moved up so sequence of normal prenatal development precedes consideration of potential problems
- Opposing Perspectives presents two sides of prenatal sex selection
- A View from Science explores the reasons for the rise in LBW and VLBW babies in the United States
- Revised section on new fathers
- *Visualizing Development.* One Baby or More: Illustrates conception and development of monozygotic and dizygotic twins

Part II: The First Two Years

3. The First Two Years: Body and Mind

- "Perceiving and Moving" section retitled and reorganized so that discussion of perception precedes discussion of movement

- New discussion of pain as an aspect of the sense of touch

- Updated section on immunization; new "Problems with Immunization" subsection discusses parents' reluctance to immunize infants and California's recent whooping cough epidemic

- Brain scan technology applied to test Piaget's theory of infant cognition

- New research on genetic factors in stress reactions

- *Visualizing Development.* Nature, Nurture, and the Brain: Illustrates mechanics of transmission of electrochemical messages in the brain; also illustrates the impact of experience on neural pathways

4. The First Two Years: Psychosocial Development

- New section on brain maturation and its role in the development of emotions in infants and toddlers

- How synchrony and attachment influence brain development

- Expanded section on the effects of maternal employment in infancy

- Addition of humanism and evolutionary theory in "Theories of Infant Psychosocial Development"

- Discussion of proximal and distal parenting reorganized and presented as an Opposing Perspectives feature

- *Visualizing Development.* Developing Attachment: Illustrates the impact of early attachment status throughout the life span

Part III: Early Childhood

5. Early Childhood: Body and Mind

- A View from Science presents new research on the effects of elevated blood lead levels on brain development (illustrated)

- New Opposing Perspectives on the pros and cons of placing restrictions on children's freedom to explore

- Reorganized and expanded section on brain development in early childhood

- Expanded section with new research on intervention programs, including costs of various programs and a cost-benefit analysis (current costs versus projected societal savings)

Idyllic Two 8-year-olds, each with a 6-year-old sister, all four daydreaming or exploring in a very old tree beside a lake in Denmark—what could be better? Ideally, all the world's children would be so fortunate, but most are not.

HENRIK WEIS / CULTURA / CORBIS

- *Visualizing Development.* Developing Motor Skills: Illustrates normal development of motor skills from ages 2 to 6

6. Early Childhood: Psychosocial Development

- Revised discussion of sex differences in emotional regulation, presented as an A View from Science feature

- "Challenges for Adults" section revised to reflect the importance in a child's life of nonparent caregivers

- Opposing Perspectives focuses on the controversy about spanking as a method of punishment

- "Child Maltreatment" section moved from Chapter 5 in the first edition to underscore the psychosocial consequences of maltreatment

- The section "Theories of Sex-Role Development" now includes humanism and evolutionary theory

- *Visualizing Development.* Sex Differences and Similarities: Illustrates sex differences and similarities in weight, psychopathology, and behavior in children

Part IV: Middle Childhood

7. Middle Childhood: Body and Mind

- New section on bipolar disorder in middle childhood

- Activation of different areas of the amygdala in bipolar disorder and ADHD

- New section on educating students who are designated as gifted and talented
- *Visualizing Development.* Childhood Obesity Around the Globe: Illustrates the incidence of childhood obesity around the world as well as the correlation between obesity and TV ads for unhealthy foods

8. Middle Childhood: Psychosocial Development

- New section on cognitive coping—how children's interpretation of potentially stressful events impacts the degree of stress actually experienced
- Substantially revised and updated section on family function and family structure, including the impact of various structures on development
- Opposing Perspectives: Divorce for the Sake of the Children looks at divorce, with up-to-date research on the impact of divorce on family relationships
- Updated research on bullying—causes, consequences, and efforts to combat it
- *Visualizing Development.* A Wedding, or Not? Family Structures Around the World: Illustrates percentage of children living in single-parent households internationally; also compares the influence of family and religion, the likelihood of cohabitation, and the likelihood of a woman in the United States and in Nigeria marrying before age 25

Part V: Adolescence

9. Adolescence: Body and Mind

- Discussion of nutrition in adolescence significantly re-organized and updated
- Attitudes toward racism discussed as an example of the transition from inductive reasoning in childhood to the ability to reason deductively in adolescence
- Comparison of brain scans showing changing proportion of gray matter from childhood through adolescence
- Opposing Perspectives presents issues surrounding high-stakes tests, with recent research on testing and its impact
- New section on motivation in middle school examines the entity approach to intelligence and the incremental approach to intelligence
- *Visualizing Development.* Thinking in Adolescence: Illustrates the differences between inductive and deductive reasoning

10. Adolescence: Psychosocial Development

- Opposing Perspectives offers a multicultural look at the concept of adolescent rebellion

Danger Ahead This boy thinks like the teenager he is. He ignores the risks.

ZAYAN.1904 / GETTY IMAGES

- A View from Science discusses long-term consequences of sexual abuse—cognitive and emotional problems as well as brain changes that can cause distressing flashbacks, impulses, and fears
- *Visualizing Development.* How Many Adolescents Are in School?: Illustrates percentage of 12- to 15-year-olds who are not in school in major regions of the world as well as the U.S. high school dropout rate

Part VI: Adulthood

11. Emerging Adulthood: Body, Mind, and Social World

- New section discusses characteristics of postformal thought, changes in the prefrontal cortex that make it possible, and whether it is really a new stage of thinking
- A greatly expanded and updated section on the effects of college includes discussion of the worldwide expansion of college systems; the ethnic, religious, cultural, and gender diversity now characteristic of most U.S. colleges; and the cognitive benefits of college
- New section on the continuity and plasticity of personality in emerging adulthood
- Revised discussion of linked lives and the effect each family member has on the others; includes recent research on national differences in young adults living with their parents
- *Visualizing Development.* Why Study?: Illustrates percentage of U.S. ethnic groups who are in school, from

elementary school through college; the increase in college enrollment internationally; and the lifetime income impact of an advanced degree

12. Adulthood: Body and Mind

- Substantially reorganized section on the aging process
- A new A View from Science feature presents recent research on breaking bad habits and establishing good ones
- New discussion of the link between fluid intelligence and overall brain health
- Opposing Perspectives considers the factors that make a good mother
- *Visualizing Development.* Adult Overweight Around the Globe: Illustrates the relationship between GNP per person and the incidence of adult overweight in selected countries

13. Adulthood: Psychosocial Development

- Opposing Perspectives discusses the genetic and contextual bases of personality and includes scans of brains of people high in neuroticism
- A View from Science discusses the problem of micro-aggressions in a diverse workforce
- *Visualizing Development.* Partners, or Not: Illustrates percentage of those who are married, widowed, divorced or separated, and never married, by age group (U.S.) as well as average age of marriage in selected countries

Part VI: Late Adulthood

14. Late Adulthood: Body and Mind

- Discussion of the demographic shift, revised and updated with recent research
- Expanded discussion of theories of aging: genetic-clock, wear-and-tear, cellular aging, the Hayflick limit
- Expanded discussion of selective optimization includes examples of individual compensation (sex), social compensation (driving), and technological compensation (sensory aids)
- A View from Science discusses research on the efficacy of elders learning new skills, the resultant improvement in brain function, and crossover of that improvement to other mental activities
- Opposing Perspectives examines the benefits and dangers of prescription drug use by people in late adulthood
- *Visualizing Development.* Social Comparison: Elders Behind the Wheel: Illustrates the U.S. automobile accident rate by incidence and by miles driven (by age group)

Happy Grandfathers No matter where they are, grandparents and grandchildren often enjoy each other partly because conflict is less likely, as grandparents are usually not as strict as parents are. Indeed, Sam Levinson quipped, "The reason grandparents and grandchild get along so well is that they have a common enemy."

15. Late Adulthood: Psychosocial Development

- A View from Science presents new research on the relationship between disappointment, the positivity effect, and brain activation in late adulthood
- Opposing Perspectives discusses advantages and disadvantages of social networking in late adulthood; includes a chart showing the increase in use of social networking sites.
- *Visualizing Development.* Life After 65: Living Independently: Illustrates percentage of those who reach age 65, 75, 85, and 95 who live independently as well as percentage who require varying levels of care; percentage of population who are 65+, by state; and living arrangements of those 65+ (all data for U.S.)

Epilogue: Death and Dying

- New introductory section discusses ancient ideas about death and the afterlife (ancient Egypt and Greece, as well as Mayan, Chinese, and African cultures); also considers contemporary religions and their views on death (Buddhism, Christianity, Hinduism, Islam, Native American religions, and others)
- Expanded discussion in a new section on near-death experiences
- Opposing Perspectives discusses different views on "the right to die," focusing on euthanasia and physician-assisted suicide and policies and practices in various countries

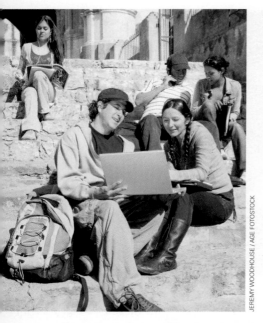

Education in Process These students, checking the Internet on the steps in San Miguel de Allende in Mexico, illustrate why some scholars claim that college students learn more from each other than from their professors.

Ongoing Features

Many characteristics of this book have been acclaimed in the first edition and have been retained in this revision.

Writing That Communicates the Excitement and Challenge of the Field

An overview of the science of human development should be lively, just as real people are. Each sentence conveys tone as well as content. Chapter-opening vignettes bring student readers into the immediacy of development. Examples and explanations abound, helping students make the connections among theory, research, and their own experiences.

Coverage of Diversity

Cross-cultural, international, multiethnic, sexual orientation, wealth, age, gender—all these words and ideas are vital to appreciating how children develop. Research uncovers surprising similarities and notable differences: We have much in common, yet each human is unique. From the discussion of social contexts in Chapter 1 to the coverage of cultural differences in mourning in the Epilogue, each chapter highlights possibilities and variations. New is inclusion of genetic susceptibility, another source of variation.

New research on family structures, immigrants, bilingualism, emerging adults, and ethnic differences in health are among the many topics that illustrate human diversity. Listed here is a smattering of the discussions of culture and diversity in this new edition. Respect for human differences is evident throughout. You will note that examples and research findings from many parts of the world are included, not as add-on highlights, but as integral parts of the description of each age.

Inclusion of all kinds of people in the study of development, p. 4

A View from Science: How cultural differences in infant sleeping practices led to the "back to sleep" movement and a decrease in SIDS deaths worldwide, pp. 6–7

Multicontextual considerations in development (SES, cohort, family configuration, etc.), pp. 9–12

Culture defined; the need to include people of many cultures in developmental study, p. 12

Learning within a culture/cultural transmission (Vygotsky); ethnicity and race defined and discussed (includes Opposing Perspectives), pp. 15–18

Genetic, biochemical, and neurological differences in adults with depression versus adults without depression; international differences in incidence of depression, pp. 18–20

Differential sensitivity defined; example from study of African American boys in rural Georgia, pp. 21–22

Age diversity in cross-sectional research and cohort diversity in cross-sequential research, pp. 37–39

Age, gender, and immigrant/nonimmigrant differences in explanation of correlation, p. 40

Genetic variations among people; male and female chromosomes; alleles (single-gene variants), p. 49

Opposing Perspectives: International differences in sex selection, pp. 52–53

Rates of cesarean births in selected countries, p. 65

Birthing practices in various cultures, p. 66

Sex-chromosome abnormalities, p. 71

Ethnic differences in the allele that causes low folic acid, p. 76

Rates of low birthweight in various countries, p. 80

Biological, gender, ethnic, and age differences in risk of alcoholism; differences in alcohol consumption between Japanese men and women in Japan and those who migrate to the United States, pp. 82–83

Nature–nurture interaction in nearsightedness among children in Britain, Africa, and Asia, pp. 83–84

Opposing Perspectives: Cultural differences in co-sleeping; rates in various countries, pp. 99–100

Infant mortality rates in various countries, p. 107

Breast-feeding and HIV-positive women in Africa, p. 111

Malnutrition: Wasting in developing nations and international rates of stunting, pp. 111–112

Up-to-Date Coverage

My mentors welcomed curiosity, creativity, and skepticism; as a result, I am eager to read and analyze thousands of articles and books on everything from autism to zygosity. The recent explosion of research in neuroscience and genetics has challenged me, once again, first to understand and then to explain many complex findings and speculative leaps. My students continue to ask questions and share their experiences, always providing new perspectives and concerns.

Student Support

This book was designed for today's students. Each chapter begins with a brief real-life vignette to help students connect to the chapter content. Key terms appear in boldface type in the text; they are defined in the margins and again in a glossary at the end of the book. The outline on the first page of every chapter and the system of major and minor subheads facilitate the survey-question-read-write-review (SQ3R) approach. Chapters end with a brief summary, a list of key terms and key questions for review. Then application exercises suggest ways to apply concepts to everyday life.

Each major section of a chapter closes with "Key Points," allowing students to pause and reflect on what they've just read. Active learning is also stressed in "Observation Quizzes" that inspire readers to look more closely at photographs, tables, and graphs, as well as in "Especially for…" questions in the margins. Each "Especially for…" question is addressed to a specific population—such as parents, nurses, educators, psychologists, or social workers—who are asked to apply what they've just read. Furthermore, I chose each photograph and wrote each caption with the expectation that students will learn from it. (This Preface offers a selection of the photographs that appear in the book.)

Critical thinking is encouraged throughout—not just in the Opposing Perspectives boxes. Every chapter challenges myths, research designs, and cultural assumptions. A series of features called "A View from Science" apply the research that shapes theory, practice, and application.

Supplements

As an instructor myself, I know that supplements can make or break a class. Students are now media savvy and instructors use tools that did not exist when they were in college. Many supplements are available for both students and professors.

NEW: Developing Lives: An Interactive Simulation

The study of development fully enters the digital age with *Developing Lives*. Using this interactive program, each student raises his or her own unique "child," makes decisions about common parenting issues (nutrition choices, parenting style, type of schooling), and responds to realistic events (divorce, tempermental variations, and social and economic diversity) that shape a child's physical, cognitive, and social development. At the heart of this program is interactivity, thus *Developing Lives* has a student-friendly "game-like" feel that not only engages students in the program, but also encourages them to learn.

Developing Lives features these helpful resources to reinforce and assess student learning: Integrated links to the eBook version of your Worth text; Readings from *Scientific American;* more than 400 videos and animations, many of them newly filmed for *Developing Lives;* and full integration with the PsychPortal that includes easy-to-implement assessment tools, including assignable quizzes on core topics, discussion threads, and journal questions.

NEW: Learning Curve: Adaptive Quizzing Engine

Developed by a team of psychology instructors with extensive backgrounds in course design and online education, LearningCurve combines adaptive question selection, personalized study plans, and state-of-the-art question analysis reports. LearningCurve is based on the simple yet powerful concept of testing-to-learn, with activities that keep students engaged in the material while helping them learn key concepts. A team of dedicated instructors—including Lisa Hager, Spring Hill College; Jessica Herrick, Mesa State College; Sara Lapsley, Simon Fraser University; Rosemary McCullough, Ave Maria University; Wendy Morrison, Montana State University; Emily Newton, University of California, Davis; Curtis Visca, Saddleback College; and Devon Werble, East Los Angeles Community College—have worked closely to develop more than 5,000 quizzing questions developed specifically for this edition of *Invitation to the Life Span*.

Human Development Videos

In collaboration with dozens of instructors and researchers, Worth has recently produced more than 150 new video clips for classroom or online use in human development. This brings Worth's entire archive of video clips to more than 500—a collection that covers the full range of the course, from classic experiments (like the Strange Situation and Piaget's conservation tasks) to investigations of children's play, adolescent risk taking, or the devastation of Alzheimer disease. Instructors can assign these videos to students through PsychPortal or choose one of 50 popular video activities, which combine videos with short-answer and multiple-choice questions. For presentation purposes, our videos are available in a variety of formats to suit your needs, including download, flash drive, and DVD.

PsychPortal

This is the complete online gateway to all the student and instructor resources available with the textbook. PsychPortal brings together all the resources of the video tool kits, integrated with an eBook and powerful assessment tools to complement your course.

The ready-to-use course template is fully customizable and includes all the teaching and learning resources that go along with the book, preloaded into a ready-to-use course: sophisticated quizzing, personalized study plans for students, and powerful assessment analyses that provide timely and useful feedback on class and individual student performance; and seamless integration of student resources, eBook text, assessment tools, and lecture resources.

For this edition, PsychPortal includes new Launch Pad Assignments for Easy Startup. Sometimes the wealth of online materials in PsychPortal can become daunting. Launch Pad offers a pre-curated set of prebuilt assignments, carefully crafted by a group of instructional designers and instructors. Each assignable unit contains videos, activities, and assessment to build student understanding for each topic.

eBook

The interactive eBook fully integrates the complete text and its electronic study tools in a format that instructors and students can easily customize—at a significant savings on the price of the printed text. It offers easy access from any Internet-connected computer; quick, intuitive navigation to any section or subsection, as well as any printed book page number; a powerful notes feature that allows you to customize any page; a full-text search; text highlighting; and a full, searchable glossary.

Companion Web Site

The companion Web site (at ww.worthpublishers.com/bergerinvitation2e) is an online educational setting for students and instructors. It is free, and tools on the site include a Spanish-language glossary and quizzes. A password-protected Instructor Site offers a full array of teaching resources, including Interactive Presentation slides, an online quiz gradebook, and links to additional tools.

Instructor's Resources

This collection of resources written by Richard O. Straub (University of Michigan, Dearborn) has been hailed as the richest collection of instructor's resources in developmental psychology. The Lecture Guides preview learning objectives, springboard topics for discussion and debate, handouts for student projects, and supplementary readings from journal articles. Course planning suggestions, ideas for term projects, and a guide to audiovisual and software materials are also included.

Study Guide

The *Study Guide* by Richard O. Straub helps students evaluate their understanding and retain their learning longer. Each chapter includes a review of key concepts, guided study questions, and section reviews that encourage students' active participation in the learning process. Two practice tests and a challenge test help them assess their mastery of the material.

Interactive Presentation Slides

A new extraordinary series of "next-generation" interactive presentation lectures give instructors a dynamic yet easy-to-use new way to engage students during classroom presentations of core developmental psychology topics. Each lecture provides opportunities for discussion and interaction and enlivens the psychology classroom with an unprecedented number of embedded video clips and animations from Worth's library of videos. In addition to these animated presentations, Worth also offers a set of prebuilt slide sets with all chapter art and illustrations. These slides can be used as is or can be customized to fit individual needs.

Test Bank and Computerized Test Bank

The test bank, prepared by Jessica Herrick (Colorado Mesa University) and Victoria Van Wie (Lone Star College), includes at least 100 multiple-choice and 70 fill-in, true-false, and essay questions for each chapter. Good test questions are critical to every course and we have gone through each and every one of these test questions with care. Several instructors have consulted with us in reviewing these test questions, including: Cheri Jacobs, Pierce College; Suyin Phillips, University of Hawaii: Kapiolani Community College; Jillene Seiver, Bellevue College; and Jessica Siebenbruner, Winona State University. We have added more challenging questions, and questions are keyed to the textbook by topic, page number, and level of difficulty.

The Diploma computerized test bank, available on a dual-platform CD-ROM for Windows and Macintosh, guides instructors step by step through the process of creating a test. It also allows them to quickly add an unlimited number of questions; edit, scramble, or resequence items; format a test; and include pictures, equations, and media links. The accompanying gradebook enables instructors to record students' grades throughout the course and includes the capacity to sort student records, view detailed analyses of test items, curve tests, generate reports, and add weights to grades.

The CD-ROM is also the access point for Diploma Online Testing, which allows instructors to create and administer secure exams over a network or over the Internet. In addition, Diploma has the ability to restrict tests to specific computers or time blocks. Blackboard-formatted versions of each item in the Test Bank are available on the CD-ROM.

Thanks

I'd like to thank the academic reviewers who have read this book in every edition and who have provided suggestions, criticisms, references, and encouragement. They have all made this a better book. I want to mention especially those who have reviewed this edition:

Shirley Bass-Wright, *St. Philip's College*

Elizabeth Boerger, *Slippery Rock University*

Saundra Boyd, *Houston Community College*

Wanda Clark, *South Plains College*

Ingrid Cominsky, *Onondaga Community College*

Trina Cowan, *Northwest Vista College*

Ernestine Duncan, *Norfolk State University*

Mary Evans, *Los Angeles Community College District*

Lara Fields, *Salt Lake Community College*

Tony Fowler, *Florence-Darlington Technical College*

Daniel Guich, *Mission College*

Nicole Hamilton, *St. Philip's College*

John Haworth, *Chattanooga State Community College*

Jessica Herrick, *Colorado Mesa University*

Pamela Hill, *San Antonio College*

Rosemary Hornak, *Meredith College*

Mildred Huffman, *Virginia Western Community College*

Louise Jarrold, *Dawson College*

David Johnson, *John Brown University*

Diana Joy, *Community College of Denver*

Deena "Amy" Kausler, *Jefferson College*

Cynthia Lofaso, *Central Virginia Community College*

Zena Mello, *University of Colorado, Colorado Springs*

Joseph Miele, *East Stroudsburg University*

Joel Nadler, *Saint Louis Community College–Meramec Campus*

Sherri Palmer, *Truman State University*

Carola Pedreschi, *Miami Dade College*

Patricia Puccio, *College of DuPage*

Linda Rojewski, *Yavapai College*

Bridget Seeley, *Arizona State University*

Peggy Skinner, *South Plains College*

Kathy Trotter, *Chattanooga State Community College*

Angela Zapata, *Marquette University*

Suzi Zoellner, *Community College of Denver*

The editorial, production, sales, and marketing people at Worth Publishers are dedicated to meeting the highest standards of excellence. They devote time, effort, and talent to every aspect of publishing, as is evident on every page. I particularly would like to thank Jessica Bayne, project director, nudge, and inspiration, who also managed to give birth to her fourth child in 2012. Worth Publishers and I are fortunate to have many others who helped with this book: Deborah Anderson, Stacey Alexander, Christine Buese, Tom Chao, Tom Churchill, Lyndall Culbertson, Tom Kling, Tracy Kuehn, Paul Lacy, Katherine Nurre, Sharon Prevost, Donna Ranieri, Babs Reingold, Barbara Seixas, Vivien Weiss, and Catherine Woods, publisher.

Kathleen Stassen Berger
February 2013

The Beginning

The science of human development has many beginnings. Chapter 1 introduces what we study, why, and how, explaining some research strategies and methods used to understand how people grow and change. Pivotal are theories that provide a broad overview of the process of development. Chapter 2 traces development from the genetic interactions that produce all inherited characteristics to the first movements, sounds, and reactions of a newborn.

Throughout these chapters, the interplay of nature (heredity) and nurture (the environment) is illustrated. For instance, whether or not a person will develop type 2 diabetes at age 60 depends on both nature (the person's genetic vulnerability) and nurture (the mother's diet during pregnancy and the person's exercise and eating habits). Similarly, nature and nurture interact to determine whether a 6-year-old will learn to read or a 16-year-old will get drunk. The multicontextual and multicultural aspects of development are apparent throughout the life span.

CHAPTER OUTLINE

THE SCIENCE OF HUMAN
Development

WHAT WILL YOU KNOW?

- What are the complexities of studying all kinds of people?
- Why are theories considered so important in science?
- What special methods do developmentalists use to study change over time?
- Why do scientific conclusions need to be interpreted with caution?

I am holding my daughter's bent right leg in place with all my strength. A nurse holds her left leg while Bethany pulls on a sheet tied to a metal structure over her bed. The midwife commands, "Push . . . push . . . push." Finally, a head is visible, small and wet, but perfect. In a moment, body and limbs emerge, all 4,139 grams of Caleb, perfect as well. Apgar is 9, and every number on the monitor is good. Bethany, smiling, begins to nurse.

Decades of learning, studying, teaching, praying, and mothering have led me to this miracle at 6:11 A.M., my first-born with her first-born. Celestial music is ringing in my ears. The ringing grows louder. Suddenly, I am on the floor, looking up at six medical professionals: I have fainted.

"I am fine," I insist, getting back on the couch where I spent the night. They still stare at me.

"You need to go to triage."

"No, I am fine. Sorry I fainted."

"Hospital policy."

"No. I belong here."

"We must send you to triage, in a wheelchair."

What should I say to make them ignore me and focus on Caleb?

Another nurse wisely adds, "You can refuse treatment."

Of course. I remember now; the law requires patient consent.

So I am wheeled down the hall, wait for the elevator, go to Admitting, explain that I was with my laboring daughter all night with no food or sleep. I fainted, but I am fine. I refuse treatment.

The admitting nurse takes my blood pressure—normal—and checks with her supervisor.

"I refuse treatment," I repeat, standing up to walk back.

Both Blissful One of us rests after an arduous journey, and the other rejoices after crying and fainting.

COURTESY OF KATHLEEN BERGER

"OK. Wait. Sit down. Someone must wheel you back. Hospital policy."

I acquiesce. My immediate priority is my daughter and grandson, not policy change. I return to the delivery room before the placenta is delivered.

I am thankful, but puzzled. Bethany chose me for her birth partner because of my knowledge, experience, and steadiness. I can interpret numbers, jargon, monitors, body language, medical competence, hospital cleanliness, hall noises, and more. I do not panic, and I know that Bethany is strong, healthy, and conscientious. I was grateful but not surprised that Caleb was perfect. I told the triage nurse that I had not slept or eaten all night—true, but I had gone without sleep and food before, never fainting. What happened this time? ●

THIS INCIDENT IS A FITTING INTRODUCTION FOR CHAPTER 1, which begins to explain what we know, what we don't know, and how we learn about human development. Emotions mix with intellect, family bonds with professional competence, contexts with cultures, personal experiences with academic knowledge. Much is known and yet new questions arise, surprises occur. I learned more about physiology, relationships, and cognition because I fainted. I also thought more about my own aging (one reason I fainted) as well as about the effects of genetics and of prenatal care (part of the reason Caleb and Bethany were fine). This chapter, and those that follow, will help you learn as well.

Understanding How and Why

The **science of human development** *seeks to understand how and why people—all kinds of people, everywhere, of every age—change over time.* The goal is to help all 7 billion people on Earth to fulfill their potential: This science is one way to reach that goal.

Developmentalists recognize that growth over the life span is *multidirectional, multicontextual, multicultural, multidisciplinary,* and *plastic,* five terms that will be explained soon. First we need to emphasize that developmental study is a *science.* It depends on theories, data, analysis, critical thinking, and sound methodology, just like every other science. All scientists ask questions and seek answers, to ascertain "how and why."

Science is especially necessary when the topic is human development: Lives depend on the answers. People disagree vehemently about what pregnant women should eat; whether babies should be left to cry; when children should be punished; under what circumstances adults should marry, or divorce, or retire, or die. Opinions are subjective, arising from emotions and culture. Scientists seek to progress from opinion to truth, from subjective to objective, from wishes to evidence.

The Scientific Method

As you surely realize, facts may be twisted, and applications sometimes spring from assumptions, not from data. To avoid unexamined opinions and to rein in personal biases, researchers follow the five steps of the **scientific method** (see Figure 1.1):

1. *Begin with curiosity.* On the basis of theory, prior research, or a personal observation, pose a question.

2. *Develop a hypothesis.* Shape the question into a **hypothesis,** a specific prediction that can be tested.

3. *Test the hypothesis.* Design and conduct research to gather **empirical evidence** (data).

science of human development
The science that seeks to understand how and why people of all ages and circumstances change or remain the same over time.

scientific method
A way to answer questions that requires empirical research and data-based conclusions.

hypothesis
A specific prediction that can be tested.

empirical evidence
Evidence based on data from scientific observation or experiments; not theoretical.

4. *Draw conclusions.* Use the evidence to support or refute the hypothesis.

5. *Report the results.* Share the data, conclusions, and alternative explanations.

As you see, developmental scientists begin with curiosity and then seek the facts, drawing conclusions after careful research. **Replication**—repeating the procedures and methods of a study with different participants—is often a sixth and crucial step (Jasny et al., 2011). Scientists study the reported procedures and results of other scientists. They read publications, attend conferences, send e-mails, and sometimes travel from one nation to another to collaborate. Conclusions are revised, refined, and confirmed after replication.

The implications of those conclusions spread beyond science, often involving religion, politics, and ethics. One of the most famous scientists of all time said, "Science without religion is lame; religion without science is blind" (Einstein, 1954/1994, p. 49). Some of the politics and ethics of scientific research are discussed at the end of this chapter. Every chapter of this book, and every Opposing Perspectives feature, describes the interaction of empirical data with moral values.

The Nature–Nurture Controversy

An easy example of the need for science concerns a great puzzle of development, the *nature–nurture debate.* **Nature** refers to the influence of the genes that people inherit. **Nurture** refers to environmental influences, beginning with the health and diet of the embryo's mother and continuing lifelong, including family, school, community, and society.

The nature–nurture debate has many other names, among them *heredity–environment* and *maturation–learning.* Under whatever name, the basic question is: *How much of any characteristic, behavior, or emotion is the result of genes and how much is the result of specific experiences?* Some people are predisposed to believe that most traits are inborn, that children are innately good or bad, naturally innocent or evil. Other people stress nurture, crediting or blaming parents, or circumstances, or drugs, or food (as in "You are what you eat").

Developmentalists have learned that neither belief is accurate. The question is "how much," not "which," because *both* genes and the environment affect every characteristic: Nature always affects nurture, and then nurture affects nature. Some scientists think that even "how much" is misleading, as it implies that nature and nurture each contribute a fixed amount when actually their explosive interaction is crucial (Gottlieb, 2007; Meaney, 2010; Spencer et al., 2009).

No doubt genes predispose people to be influenced by environment; the impact of a spanking, or a beer, or a marathon depends partly on genetic vulnerability. But the opposite is true as well; a new discipline within genetics is called *epigenetics*—it explores the many ways environmental forces alter genetic expression.

The interaction between nature and nurture is apparent for every topic in this book, as you will see, and in every moment of our lives, as I see in myself. For example, I fainted at Caleb's birth because of the interaction of at least seven factors (low blood sugar, lack of sleep, physical exertion, gender, age, relief, joy), all influenced by both nature and nurture, all combining to land me on the floor.

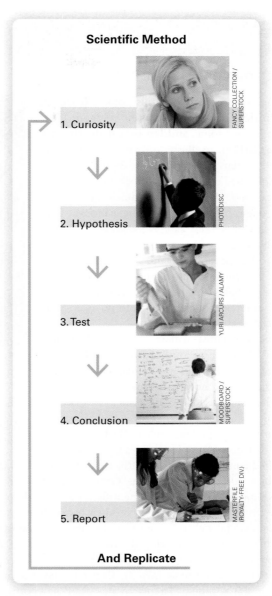

Scientific Method

1. Curiosity

2. Hypothesis

3. Test

4. Conclusion

5. Report

And Replicate

FANCY COLLECTION / SUPERSTOCK

PHOTODISC

YURI ARCURS / ALAMY

MOODBOARD / SUPERSTOCK

MASTERFILE (ROYALTY-FREE DIV.)

FIGURE 1.1 Process, Not Proof
Built into the scientific method—in questions, hypotheses, tests, and replication—is a passion for possibilities, especially unexpected ones.

replication
The repetition of a study, using different participants.

nature
A general term for the traits, capacities, and limitations that each individual inherits genetically from his or her parents at the moment of conception.

nurture
A general term for all the environmental influences that affect development after an individual is conceived.

A VIEW FROM SCIENCE

Sudden Infant Death*

Coverage of every topic in this book is based on research that follows the scientific method. Here we present one topic, **sudden infant death syndrome (SIDS),** to illustrate. Every year until the mid-1990s, tens of thousands of 2- to 6-month-old infants died of SIDS (called *crib death* in North America, *cot death* in England, nameless but nonetheless tragic in many developing nations). Tiny babies smiled at their caregivers, waved at rattles that their small fingers could not yet grasp, went to sleep, but never woke up. For many years, as parents mourned, scientists asked why (*step 1*) and tested hypotheses (the cat? the quilt? unpasteurized honey? homicide? spoiled milk?) to no avail: Sudden infant death was a mystery.

Then a scientist named Susan Beal studied every SIDS death in South Australia, seeking factors that might be causes. She learned that some circumstances did not matter (such as birth order) and others increased the risk (such as maternal smoking and lambskin blankets).

A breakthrough came when Beal noticed an ethnic variation: Australian babies of Chinese descent died far less often of SIDS than did Australian babies of European descent. Genetic? Most experts thought so. But Beal's scientific observation led her to note that Chinese babies slept on their backs, contrary to the Australian (as well as European and American) custom of stomach-sleeping. She developed a new hypothesis (*step 2*): Sleeping position matters.

To test her hypothesis (*step 3*), Beal convinced a large group of non-Chinese parents to put their newborns to

SEAN SPRAGUE / THE IMAGE WORKS

And If I Die Not likely. Death "before I wake" occurred too often in many nations before 1990, but not in Mongolia (shown here) or other Asian countries. The reason, as scientists hypothesized and then confirmed, is that Asian parents put their infants "back to sleep."

OBSERVATION QUIZ

Back-sleeping babies sometimes squirm, making the blankets covering them come loose—another risk factor for SIDS. What detail makes that unlikely here? (see answer, page 8) ➔

sleep on their backs. Almost none of the infants died suddenly. After several years of collecting data, she drew a surprising conclusion (*step 4*): Back-sleeping protected against SIDS. Her published reports (*step 5*) (Beal, 1988) caught the attention of doctors in the Netherlands, where pediatricians for some time had been telling parents that babies should sleep on their stomachs. Two Dutch scientists (Engelberts &

FIGURE 1.2 Before and After Detailed U.S. data on SIDS are available only for the last 25 years, but as best we know the rate was steady at about 1 baby in every 700 throughout most of the twentieth century and has been even lower after 2008, at about 1 baby in 2,000.

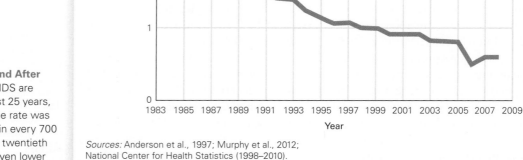

Sources: Anderson et al., 1997; Murphy et al., 2012; National Center for Health Statistics (1998–2010).

de Jonge, 1990) recommended back-sleeping; thousands of parents took heed. SIDS was reduced in Holland by 40 percent in one year—a stunning replication (*step 6*).

By 1994, a "Back to Sleep" campaign in nation after nation cut the SIDS rate dramatically (Kinney & Thach, 2009; Mitchell, 2009). In the United States, SIDS killed 5,245 babies in 1984, 3,050 in 1996. In the twenty-first century, the average is about 2,000 a year (see Figure 1.2). Such results indicate that, in the United States alone, about 40,000 children and young adults are alive today who would otherwise

be dead if they had been born before 1990. The campaign is so successful that babies now crawl later than they used to; physical therapists thus advocate *tummy time*—putting awake infants on their stomachs to develop their muscles (Zachry & Kitzmann, 2011).

Stomach-sleeping is a proven, replicated risk, but it is not the only one: SIDS still occurs. Beyond sleeping position, other risks include low birthweight, a brain-stem abnormality that produces too little serotonin (a neurotransmitter), cigarette smoke in the household, soft blankets or pillows, and bed-sharing (when infants sleep in their parents' bed) (Duncan et al., 2010; Ostfeld et al., 2010). As with almost every development, a combination of nature and nurture produces the outcome.

*Each chapter has an A View from Science feature intended to help readers understand the scientific process as well as to learn details about a topic of interest. For both reasons, don't skip over these boxes.

KEY points

- The study of development is a science that seeks to understand how and why each individual is affected by the changes that occur over the life span.
- As a science, developmental research follows five steps: question, hypothesis, empirical research, conclusions based on data, and publication.
- A sixth step, replication, confirms, refutes, or refines conclusions of a scientific study.
- Both genes and environment affect every human characteristic in an explosive interaction of nature and nurture.

sudden infant death syndrome (SIDS) The term used to describe an infant's unexpected death; when a seemingly healthy baby, usually between 2 and 6 months old, suddenly stops breathing and dies unexpectedly while asleep.

The Life-Span Perspective

The **life-span perspective** (Fingerman et al., 2011; Lerner et al., 2010) takes into account all phases of life, not just the first two decades, which were once the sole focus of developmental study. By including the entirety of life (see Table 1.1), this perspective leads to a new understanding of human development as multidirectional, multicontextual, multicultural, multidisciplinary, and plastic (Baltes et al., 2006; Staudinger & Lindenberger, 2003). Age periods are only a rough guide to "change over time."

The reality that age periods are "only a rough guide" is particularly apparent in adulthood. Emerging adulthood, defined as ages 18 to 25, is not a period accepted by all scholars. Many prefer dividing adulthood into *early adulthood* for ages 20 to 40, *middle adulthood* for ages 40 to 65, and *late adulthood*, said to begin at age 60, 65, or even 70. As you will read in detail, every developmentalist realizes that birthdays are an imperfect measure of the aging process.

Development Is Multidirectional

Multiple changes, in every direction, characterize the life span. If any particular human trait were to be charted over time, it would be apparent that some traits appear and disappear, with increases, decreases, and zigzags (see Figure 1.3).

life-span perspective An approach to the study of human development that takes into account all phases of life, not just childhood or adulthood.

TABLE 1.1 Age Ranges for Different Stages of Development

Infancy	0 to 2 years
Early childhood	2 to 6 years
Middle childhood	6 to 11 years
Adolescence	11 to 18 years
Emerging Adulthood	18 to 25 years
Adulthood	25 to 65 years
Late adulthood	65 years and older

As you will learn, developmentalists are reluctant to specify chronological ages for any period of development, since time is only one of many variables that affect each person. However, age is a crucial variable, and development can be segmented into periods of study. Approximate ages for each period are given here.

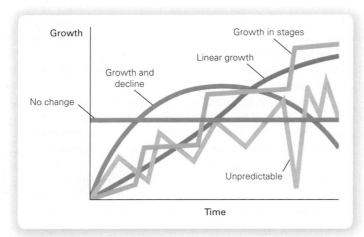

FIGURE 1.3 Patterns of Developmental Growth Many patterns of developmental growth have been discovered by careful research. Although linear (or near-linear) progress seems most common, scientists now find that almost no aspect of human change follows the linear pattern exactly.

critical period
A time when a particular type of developmental growth (in body or behavior) must happen if it is ever going to happen.

sensitive period
A time when a certain type of development is most likely to happen or happens most easily, although it may still happen later with more difficulty. For example, early childhood is considered a sensitive period for language learning.

ANSWER TO **OBSERVATION QUIZ**
(from page 6) The swaddling blanket is not only folded under the baby but is also tied in place. ●

Your Child's Teacher This 19-year-old attending Qang Ninh College in Hanoi, Vietnam, is studying to be a teacher. Emerging adulthood worldwide is a period of exploration and change: He may change professions and locations in the next six years.

The traditional idea—that all development advances until about age 18, steadies, and then declines—has been refuted by life-span research.

Sometimes *discontinuity* is evident: Change can occur rapidly and dramatically, as when caterpillars become butterflies. Sometimes *continuity* is found: Growth can be gradual, as when redwoods grow taller over hundreds of years. Some characteristics do not seem to change at all: Almost every zygote is XY or XX, male or female, and chromosomal sex is lifelong. Of course, the significance of that biological fact changes significantly.

There is simple growth, radical transformation, improvement, and decline as well as stability, stages, and continuity—day to day, year to year, and generation to generation (see Figure 1.3). Not only does the direction of change vary over the life span, but each characteristic follows a distinct pattern: Losses in some specific skills and abilities occur at the same time as gains in others. For example, when babies begin talking, they lose some ability to distinguish sounds from other languages; when adults retire, they may become more creative.

The speed and timing of impairments or improvements vary as well. Some changes are sudden and profound because of a **critical period,** either a time when something *must* occur to ensure normal development or the only time when an abnormality might occur. For instance, the human embryo grows arms and legs, hands and feet, fingers and toes, each over a critical period between 28 and 54 days after conception. After that, it is too late: Unlike some insects, humans never grow replacement limbs.

Tragically, between 1957 and 1961, thousands of newly pregnant women in 30 nations took *thalidomide,* an antinausea drug. This change in nurture (via the mother's bloodstream) disrupted nature (the embryo's genetic program). If an expectant mother ingested thalidomide during the 26 days of that critical period, her newborn's limbs were malformed or absent (Moore & Persaud, 2007). Specifics (e.g., whether arms and legs, or just arms, or only hands were missing) depended on exactly when she swallowed the pill. Surprisingly, if an expectant woman took thalidomide only before day 28 or after day 54, no harm occurred.

Life has very few such critical periods. Often, however, a particular development occurs more easily—but not exclusively—at a certain time. Such a time is called a **sensitive period.** An example is language. If children do not start speaking their first language between ages 1 and 3, they might do so later (hence, the first years are not critical), but their grammar is usually impaired (hence, these years are sensitive). Similarly, childhood is a sensitive period for learning to pronounce a second or third language with a native accent.

As is often the case with development, sweeping generalizations (like those in the preceding sentence) do not apply in every case. Accent-free speech *usually* must be learned before puberty, but some teenagers or adults with exceptional nature and nurture (naturally adept at hearing and then immersed in a new language) master a second language flawlessly (Birdsong, 2006; Muñoz & Singleton, 2011).

Development Is Multicontextual

The second insight from the life-span perspective is that development is multicontextual. It takes place within many contexts, including physical surroundings (climate, noise, population density, etc.) and family configurations (married couple, single parent, cohabiting couple, extended family, etc.). Developmentalists who study the life span take dozens of contexts into account, as explained throughout this book.

ECOLOGICAL SYSTEMS A leading developmentalist, Urie Bronfenbrenner (1917–2005), led the way to considering contexts. Just as a naturalist studying an organism examines the ecology (the multifaceted relationship between the organism and its environment), Bronfenbrenner recommended that developmentalists take an **ecological-systems approach** (Bronfenbrenner & Morris, 2006). He believed that each person is affected by many social contexts and interpersonal interactions.

The ecological-systems approach recognizes three nested levels that surround individuals and affect them (see Figure 1.4). Most obvious are *microsystems,* each person's immediate surroundings, such as family and peer group. Also important are *exosystems* (local institutions such as school and church) and *macrosystems* (the larger social setting, including cultural values, economic policies, and political processes).

Throughout his life, Bronfenbrenner studied people in natural settings, as they actually lived their lives, taking their physical development into account. Before he died, he renamed his approach *bioecological theory* to highlight the important role of biology, recognizing that systems within the body (e.g., the sexual-reproductive system, the cardiovascular system) affect all the external systems (Bronfenbrenner & Morris, 2006).

REUTERS / CLARO CORTES IV CC / DL

Cat, Duck, or Dog? Nine-year-old Sun Minyi must circle the correct animal and then write "cat" in his workbook—not hard at his age. Then why is he listening so attentively? He is one of 32 students in an English class near Shanghai. His first language is Chinese.

OBSERVATION QUIZ
What factors suggest this is not a U.S. classroom? (see answer, page 11) →

ecological-systems approach
The view that in the study of human development, the person should be considered in all the contexts and interactions that constitute a life. (Later renamed *bioecological theory*.)

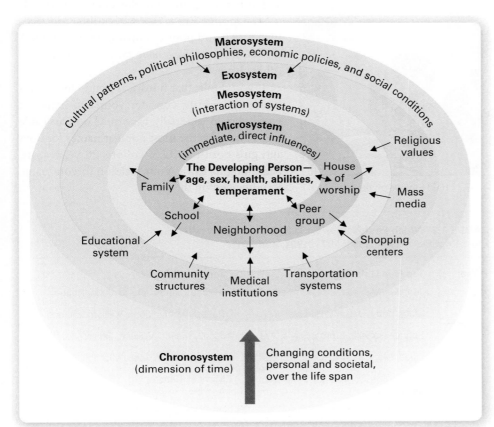

Macrosystem
Cultural patterns, political philosophies, economic policies, and social conditions

Exosystem

Mesosystem
(interaction of systems)

Microsystem
(immediate, direct influences)

The Developing Person—age, sex, health, abilities, temperament

Family
School
Neighborhood
Peer group
House of worship
Religious values
Mass media
Shopping centers
Educational system
Community structures
Medical institutions
Transportation systems

Chronosystem
(dimension of time)

Changing conditions, personal and societal, over the life span

FIGURE 1.4 The Ecological Model Each person is affected by interactions among overlapping systems, which provide the context of development. *Microsystems*—family, peer groups, classroom, neighborhood, house of worship—intimately shape human development. Surrounding and supporting the microsystems are the *exosystems*—external networks, such as local educational, medical, employment, and communications systems—that influence the microsystems. Influencing both of these systems is the *macrosystem*, which includes cultural patterns, political philosophies, economic policies, and social conditions. *Mesosystems* refer to interactions among systems, as when parents and teachers coordinate to educate a child. Bronfenbrenner eventually added a fifth system, the *chronosystem,* to emphasize the importance ● historical time.

What's Under the Bookcase? She may be looking for dust balls, but Bronfenbrenner would see macrosystems in this photo. Gender norms, national culture, and economic status are all evident. If you never vacuum under your bookcase, is that because, unlike this person, you are not a middle-class woman in Sweden?

cohort

A group defined by the shared age of its members, who, because they were born at about the same time, move through life together, experiencing the same historical events and cultural shifts.

"Hey! Elbows off the table."

Twenty-First-Century Manners If he obeyed his father but kept texting, would Emily Post be pleased?

Guess First If your answers, in order from top to bottom, were 1971, 1931, 2011, 1951, and 1991, you are excellent at detecting cohort influences. If you made a mistake, perhaps that's because the data are compiled from applications for Social Security numbers, so the names of those who did not get a Social Security number are omitted.

He also stressed the role of historical conditions and therefore included the *chronosystem* (literally, "time system"). Because he appreciated the dynamic interaction among all the systems, he included a fifth system, the *mesosystem,* consisting of the connections among the other systems.

As you can see, a contextual approach to development is complex; many contexts need to be considered. Two of them, the historical and the socioeconomic contexts, merit explanation now, as they affect people lifelong.

THE HISTORICAL CONTEXT All persons born within a few years of one another are said to be a **cohort,** a group defined by its members' shared age. Cohorts travel through life together, affected by the interaction of their chronological age with the values, events, technologies, and culture of the era. Ages 18 to 25 are a sensitive period for consolidation of social values. For that reason, experiences and circumstances during emerging adulthood have an impact lifelong. One example is that attitudes about war and society differ for the U.S. cohorts who were young adults during World War II; during the conflicts in Vietnam, the Persian Gulf, Iraq, or Afghanistan; or during the wars on poverty, drugs, or terrorism.

Sometimes demographic characteristics rather than political issues reflect the historical context. For example, the cohort born between 1946 and 1964, called the baby-boom generation because it represented a sizable spike in the birth rate, will experience quite a different old age than did earlier cohorts because there are so many of them.

This is especially true in Western nations, where the birth rate was low during the "baby-bust" years of the Great Depression and World War II. The size of this baby-boom cohort is already affecting policies regarding Social Security, Medicare, and other programs for the elderly in developed nations. This is one of the differences between rich and poor countries. As Appendix A shows, some nations have far more elders than others have.

If you doubt that historical trends and events touch individuals, consider your first name—a word chosen especially for you. Look at Table 1.2, which lists the most popular names for boys and girls born into U.S. cohorts 20 years apart, beginning in 1931. Your reaction to your name is influenced by the era.

TABLE 1.2 Which First Names for U.S. Girls and Boys Were Most Popular in 1931, 1951, 1971, 1991, and 2011?

Year	Top Five Girls' Names	Top Five Boys' Names
_____	Jennifer, Michelle, Lisa, Kimberly, Amy	Michael, James, David, John, Robert
_____	Mary, Betty, Dorothy, Barbara, Joan	Robert, James, John, William, Richard
_____	Sophia, Isabella, Emma, Olivia, Ava	Jacob, Mason, William, Jayden, Noah
_____	Linda, Mary, Patricia, Deborah, Barbara	James, Robert, John, Michael, David
_____	Ashley, Jessica, Brittany, Amanda, Samantha	Michael, Christopher, Matthew, Joshua, Andrew

Source: Social Security Administration Web Site (http://www.ssa.gov/OACT/babynames/top5names.html), retrieved August 10, 2012.

THE SOCIOECONOMIC CONTEXT Another influential context of development is the socioeconomic one, reflected in a person's **socioeconomic status,** abbreviated **SES.** Sometimes SES is called *social class* (as in *middle class* or *working class*). SES reflects income and much more, including occupation, education, and neighborhood.

Suppose a U.S. family is composed of an infant, an unemployed mother, and a father who earns $15,000 a year. Their SES would be low if the wage earner is an illiterate dishwasher living in an urban slum, but it would be much higher if the wage earner is a postdoctoral student living on campus and teaching part time.

Obviously, income alone does not define SES, especially when the historical context is considered. In the United States, poverty traditionally relates to food costs and family size: A family of three is below the 2010 poverty threshold if its household income is less than $17,552. A revision of the poverty definition is under way that takes into account housing, medical care, and various subsidies (Short, 2011).

Both methods of calculating poverty find that Americans whose ancestors were Hispanic or African rather than Asian or European are more often poor. Both also show a developmental trend—more poor children than adults. However, when compared to the traditional measures, the revised definition finds increased rates of

Same Situation, Far Apart: Times Are Changing Elders in the twenty-first century live decades longer than did earlier cohorts, affording them opportunities that were previously unavailable. In 1950 in Peru, average life expectancy was 45. Now in Lima, newlyweds Carmen Mercado, age 64, and Jorge de la Cruz, age 74 *(left),* can expect a decade of wedded bliss. While they were courting, Hazel Soares *(right)* was studying, culminating in her graduation from Mills College in Oakland, California, at age 94.

socioeconomic status (SES) A person's position in society as determined by income, wealth, occupation, education, and place of residence. (Sometimes called *social class.*)

ANSWER TO **OBSERVATION QUIZ** (from page 9) Few U.S. third-grade classes have desks set up in rows, and most U.S. teachers expect children to talk as much as listen—especially when learning a new language. In addition, class size is larger in China (an average of 37 students), which seems likely here, given the layout shown. ●

No Fresh Fruit? Many religious groups provide food for low-income families. Lisa Arsa is fortunate to have found this Seventh-Day Adventist food pantry for herself and her son, Isaac. Unfortunately, the food donated to low-income families is usually high in salt, sugar, and fat—among the reasons why the U.S. rates of obesity and diabetes rise as income falls.

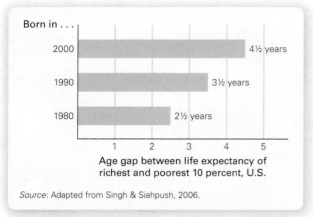

Born in . . .

2000 — 4½ years
1990 — 3½ years
1980 — 2½ years

1 2 3 4 5

Age gap between life expectancy of richest and poorest 10 percent, U.S.

Source: Adapted from Singh & Siahpush, 2006.

FIGURE 1.5 The Rich Live Longer
As you see, the gap in life expectancy between the rich and poor has doubled over the past 30 years in the United States.

culture
A system of shared beliefs, norms, behaviors, and expectations that persist over time and prescribe social behavior and assumptions.

social construction
An idea that is based on shared perceptions, not on objective reality. Many age-related terms, such as *childhood, adolescence, yuppie,* and *senior citizen,* are social constructions.

poverty among people (1) who live in cities, (2) who were born outside the United States, (3) who are Asian, (4) who pay taxes, or (5) who are older than 65.

SES brings advantages and disadvantages, opportunities and limitations—all affecting housing, health, nutrition, knowledge, and habits. Although low income obviously limits a person, other factors are pivotal. Indeed, annual wages are inadequate to measure wealth: One study found that a family's overall financial assets (e.g., a house without a mortgage) affected their children's learning more than the family's current income did (Yeung & Conley, 2008).

Nations differ in their response to SES. For example, in the United States the gap in life expectancy between rich and poor has been increasing over the past decades, as shown in Figure 1.5. The socioeconomic context is also affected by the national and historical contexts, including the proportions of the population in each cohort, as Infographic 1 (page 13) explains.

What to do about cohort, economic, and historical differences is a political rather than a developmental question. Voters choose leaders who decide policies that affect people of various ages and incomes: At best, developmentalists provide data, not prescriptions.

Development Is Multicultural

In order to study "all kinds of people, everywhere, at every age," as developmental science must do, it is essential that people of many cultures be included. For social scientists, **culture** is "the system of shared beliefs, conventions, norms, behaviors, expectations and symbolic representations that persist over time and prescribe social rules of conduct" (Bornstein et al., 2011, p. 30).

Thus, culture is far more than food, clothes, or rituals; it is a set of ideas that people share. This makes culture a powerful **social construction,** a concept constructed, or made, by a society. Social constructions affect how people think and behave and what they value, ignore, and punish. Because culture is so basic to thinking and emotions, people are usually unaware of their cultural values. Fish do not realize that they are surrounded by water; people do not realize that their assumptions about life and death arise from their own culture.

Each family, community, and college has a particular culture, and these cultures may clash. For example, decades ago my friend from a small rural town arrived for

Family Pride Grandpa Charilaos is proud of his tavern in northern Greece (central Macedonia), but he is even more proud of his talented grandchildren, including Maria Soni (shown here). Note her expert fingering. Her father and mother also play instruments—is that nature or nurture?

KUTTIG-RF-KIDS / ALAMY

Age Structure and Development

Children require time and money, which is why a dramatic contrast in age structure is apparent between rich and poor nations. The United Nations clusters nations into three categories: more developed, less developed, and least developed, based on economic growth. As you can see below, a nation's economic status correlates closely with birth rate, which itself correlates with female education. Sadly, when nations have more children, they also have a higher rate of child death.

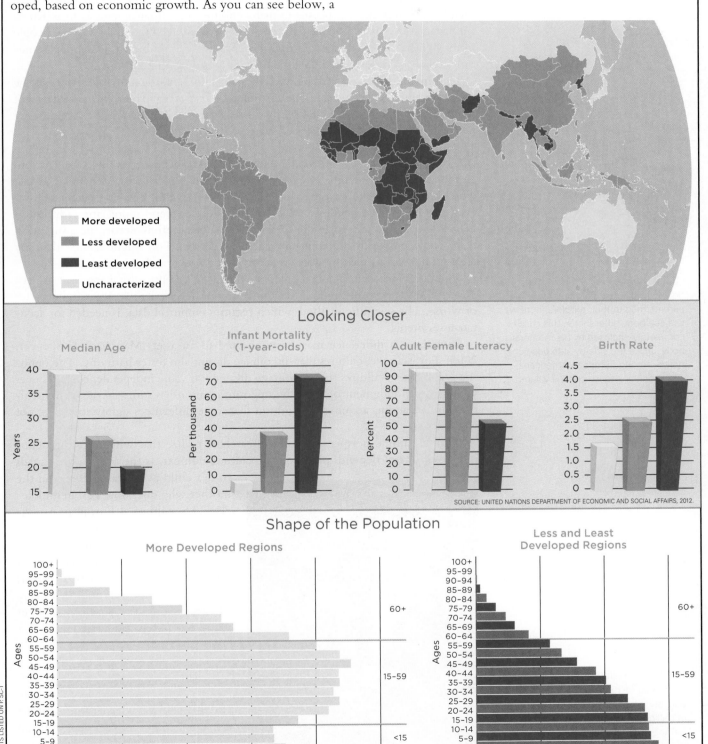

More developed

Less developed

Least developed

Uncharacterized

Looking Closer

Median Age

Infant Mortality (1-year-olds)

Adult Female Literacy

Birth Rate

SOURCE: UNITED NATIONS DEPARTMENT OF ECONOMIC AND SOCIAL AFFAIRS, 2012.

Shape of the Population

More Developed Regions

Less and Least Developed Regions

SOURCES & CREDITS LISTED ON P. SC-1

SOURCE: UNITED NATIONS, DEPARTMENT OF ECONOMIC AND SOCIAL AFFAIRS, POPULATION DIVISION (2011). WORLD POPULATION PROSPECTS: THE 2010 REVISION

difference-equals-deficit error
The mistaken belief that a deviation from some norm is necessarily inferior to behavior or characteristics that meet the standard.

Feet Between Feet The text mentions vocabulary differences when parents read to their toddlers; here we can see body differences. This child is completely enclosed by his mother's body, unlike the side-by-side position typical among European Americans. Both positions teach cultural values.

her first college class wearing her Sunday best: a freshly pressed skirt and blouse with a matching striped jacket. She looked around at her classmates, realized that her community culture was not her college culture, and went directly to a used-clothing store to buy jeans and a T-shirt.

Often people use the word *culture* to refer to large groups of other people, as in "Asian culture" or "Hispanic culture." That invites stereotyping and prejudice, since such large groups include people of many cultures. For instance, people from Korea and Japan are aware of notable cultural differences between themselves, as are people from Mexico and Guatemala. Furthermore, individuals within those cultures sometimes rebel against expected "beliefs, conventions, norms, behaviors."

Culture influences everything we say, do, or think, but the term *culture* needs to be used carefully. Ideally, pride in one's national heritage adds to personal happiness, but sometimes cultural pride is destructive of both the individual and the community (Morrison et al., 2011; Reeskens & Wright, 2011).

DEFICIT OR JUST DIFFERENCE? Humans tend to believe that they, their nation, and their culture are a little better than others. This has benefits: Generally, people who like themselves are happier, prouder, and more willing to help strangers. However, that belief becomes destructive if it reduces respect and appreciation for others. Developmentalists recognize the **difference-equals-deficit error,** the assumption that people unlike us (different) are inferior (deficit). Fish might assume that any creature not surrounded by water is deprived, deficient, and soon dead.

The difference-equals-deficit error is one reason a multicultural approach is necessary. Various ways of thinking or acting are not necessarily wrong or right, better or worse. The scientific method, which requires empirical data, is needed for accurate assessments.

Sometimes a difference may be connected to an asset (Marschark & Spencer, 2003). For example, cultures that discourage dissent also foster harmony. The opposite is also true—cultures that encourage dissent also value independence. Whatever your personal judgment on this, the opposite opinion has some merit. A multicultural understanding requires recognition that some differences signify strengths, not weaknesses.

A multicultural perspective helps researchers realize that whether a difference is an asset or not depends partly on the cultural context. Is the mother who reads

to her child every day better than the mother who does not? Yes, in middle-class U.S. culture. A European American criticism of Mexican Americans is that parents rarely read to their children. But this criticism may reflect the difference-equals-deficit error; cross-cultural research finds that many Mexican American families use other ways to foster language (Hammer et al., 2011).

Affection for Children Vygotsky lived from 1896 to 1934, when war, starvation, and revolution led to the deaths of millions. Throughout this political turmoil, Vygotsky focused on learning. His love of children is suggested by this portrait: He and his daughter have their arms around each other.

LEARNING WITHIN A CULTURE Russian developmentalist Lev Vygotsky (1896–1934) was a leader in describing the interaction between culture and education (Wertsch & Tulviste, 2005). He noticed that adults from the many cultures of the Soviet Union (Asians and Europeans, of many religions) taught their children whatever beliefs and habits they might need as adults.

Vygotsky (discussed in more detail in Chapter 5) believed that *guided participation* is a universal process used by mentors to teach cultural knowledge, skills, and habits. Guided participation can occur via school instruction but more often happens informally, through "mutual involvement in several widespread cultural practices with great importance for learning: narratives, routines, and play" (Rogoff, 2003, p. 285). One example is book reading, as just explained.

Inspired by Vygotsky, Barbara Rogoff studied cultural transmission in Guatemalan, Mexican, Chinese, and U.S. families. Adults always guide children, but clashes occur if parents and teachers are of different cultures. In one such misunderstanding, a teacher praised a student to his mother:

> **Teacher:** Your son is talking well in class. He is speaking up a lot.
> **Mother:** I am sorry.
>
> *[Rogoff, 2003, p. 311; from Crago, 1992, p. 496]*

ethnic group
People whose ancestors were born in the same region and who often share a language, culture, and religion.

What's for Dinner? Markets are universal, but each culture has a unique mix of products, stores, and salespeople. Compare this floating food market in Bangkok, Thailand, with a North American supermarket.

JUPITER IMAGES

ETHNIC AND RACIAL GROUPS It is easy to confuse culture, ethnicity, and race because these terms sometimes overlap (see Figure 1.6). People of an **ethnic group** share certain attributes, almost always including ancestral heritage and usually national origin, religion, and language (Whitfield & McClearn, 2005). As you can see from this definition, ethnic groups often share a culture, but this is not a requirement. Some people of a particular ethnicity differ culturally (consider people of Irish descent in Ireland, Australia, and North America), and some cultures include people of several ethnic groups (consider British culture).

Ethnicity is a social construction, affected by the social context, not a direct outcome of biology. That makes it nurture, not nature. For example, African-born people who live in North America typically consider themselves African, but African-born people living on that continent identify with a more specific ethnic group. (Many Americans may be surprised to realize that, although they may consider participants in civil wars in many parts of the world to be of the same ethnicity, the warring groups themselves do not.)

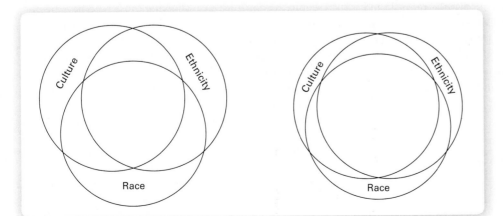

FIGURE 1.6 Overlap—But How Much? Ethnicity, culture, and race are three distinct concepts, but they often—though not always—overlap. Which set of circles do you think is more accurate?

race
A group of people regarded as distinct from other groups on the basis of appearance, typically skin color. Social scientists think race is a misleading concept, as biological differences are not signified by outward appearance.

Ethnic identity becomes strengthened and more specific (Sicilian, not just Italian; South Korean, not just East Asian) when others of the same ethnic group are nearby and when members of other groups emphasize differences. Race is also a social construction—and a misleading one. There are good reasons to abandon the term, and good reasons to keep it, as the following explains.

OPPOSING PERSPECTIVES

Using the Word *Race**

The term **race** has been used to categorize people on the basis of physical differences, particularly outward appearance. Historically, most North Americans believed that race was real, an inborn biological characteristic. Races were categorized by color: white, black, red, and yellow (Coon, 1962).

It is obvious now, but was not a few decades ago, that no one's skin is really white (like this page) or black (like these letters) or red or yellow. Social scientists are now convinced that race is a social construction and that color terms exaggerate minor differences.

Genetic analysis confirms that the concept of "race" is based on a falsehood. Although most genes are identical in every human, those genetic differences that distinguish one person from another are poorly indexed by appearance (Race, Ethnicity, and Genetics Working Group of the American Society of Human Genetics, 2005). Skin color is particularly misleading because dark-skinned people with African ancestors have particularly "high levels of genetic population diversity" (Tishkoff et al., 2009, p. 1035) and because dark-skinned people whose ancestors were not African share neither culture nor ethnicity with Africans.

Race is more than a flawed concept; it is a destructive one. It was used to justify racism, which was expressed in myriad laws and customs, with slavery, lynching, and segregation directly connected to the idea that race was real. Racism continues today in less obvious ways (some highlighted later in this book), undercutting the goal of our science of human development—to help all of us fulfill our potential.

Since race is a social construction that continues to lead to racism, some social scientists believe that the term should be abandoned. Ethnic and cultural differences may be significant for development, but racial differences are not. This realization is embedded in the way the U.S. Census reports differences. Race categories began to be included decades ago, and the original terms *White* and *Black* remain. However, Hispanics, first counted separately in 1980, "may be of any race."

A study of census categories used by 141 nations found that only 15 percent use the word *race* and that almost all of them were once slave-holding nations. The United States is the only nation that separates the racial category from the ethnic one (Morning, 2008), another indication that *race* may be a word of another era.

Cognitively, labels encourage stereotyping, and labeling people by race leads to the notion that superficial differences in appearance are significant (Kelly et al., 2010). Racism may continue partly because the U.S. Census requires everyone to specify race. New in the 2000 census were the categories "More than one race" and "Another race," but even with these, some racial designation is mandated. As one scholar explains:

> The United States' unique conceptual distinction between race and ethnicity may unwittingly support the longstanding belief that race reflects biological difference and ethnicity stems from cultural difference. In this scheme, ethnicity is socially produced but race is an immutable facet of nature. Consequently, walling off race from ethnicity on the census may reinforce essentialist interpretations of race and preclude understanding of the ways in which racial categories are also socially constructed.
>
> *[Morning, 2008, p. 255]*

To avoid racism, one possibility is to avoid using the word *race,* thereby becoming color-blind.

But there is a powerful opposite perspective. In a nation with a history of racial discrimination, reversing that history may require recognizing race, allowing those who have been harmed to be proud of their identity. The fact that race is a social construction, not a biological distinction, does not make it meaningless. Particularly in adolescence, people who are proud of their racial identity are likely to achieve academically, resist drug addiction, and feel better about themselves (Crosnoe & Johnson, 2010).

Furthermore, documenting ongoing racism requires data to show that many medical, educational, and economic conditions—from low birthweight to college graduation, from family income to health insurance—reflect disparities along racial lines. To overcome such disparities, race must first be recognized.

---

*Every page of this text includes information that requires critical thinking and evaluation. In addition, once in each chapter you will find an Opposing Perspectives feature in which an issue that has compelling opposite perspectives is highlighted.

For adults, it may be useful to acknowledge race even when racism is not obvious. An anonymous survey of 4,915 employees found that when most workers endorsed color-blind sentiments, such as "Employees should downplay their racial and ethnic differences," Black employees were less proud and less engaged in their work. By contrast, when workers believed that "policies should support ethnic and racial diversity," Black employees were more committed to their jobs. According to the authors of this study, the entire organization suffered when color blindness was the norm (Plaut et al., 2009).

Similar conclusions are held by many social scientists, who find that to be color-blind is to be subtly racist (e.g., sociologists Marvasti & McKinney, 2011; anthropologist McCabe, 2011). Two political scientists who wrote a book examining the American criminal justice system found that people who claim to be color-blind display "an extraordinary level of naïveté" (Peffley & Hurwitz, 2010, p. 113).

As you see, strong arguments support both sides of this issue. In this book, we refer to ethnicity more often than to race, but we use race or color when the original data are reported that way. Appendix A shows changes in the proportions of people of various races in the United States. Would pride or dismay decrease if data were reported only by national origin? Racial categories may crumble someday, but not yet.

Development Is Multidisciplinary

Scientists often specialize, studying one phenomenon in one species at one age. Such specialization provides a deeper understanding of the rhythms of vocalization among 3-month-old infants, for instance, or of the effects of alcohol on adolescent mice, or of widows' relationships with their grown children. (The results of these studies inform later sections of this book.)

However, human development requires insights and information from many scientists, past and present, in many disciplines. Our understanding of every topic benefits from multidisciplinary research; scientists hesitate to apply conclusions about human life until they are substantiated by several disciplines.

GENETICS AND EPIGENETICS The need for multidisciplinary research became particularly apparent with the onset of genetic analysis. The final decades of the twentieth century witnessed dozens of genetic discoveries, leading to a momentous accomplishment at the turn of the century: The Human Genome Project mapped all the genes that make up a person. To the surprise of many, it is now apparent that every trait—psychological as well as physical—is influenced by genes (see Chapter 2).

At first, it seemed that genes might determine everything, that humans became whatever their genes destined them to be—heroes, killers, or ordinary people. However, research from many disciplines quickly revealed the limitations of genetic research. Yes, genes affect every aspect of behavior. But even identical twins, with identical genes, differ biologically, psychologically, and socially (Poulsen et al., 2007).

The realization that genes alone do not determine development soon led to the further realization that all important human characteristics are **epigenetic.** The prefix *epi-* means "with," "around," "before," "after," "beyond," or "near." The word *epigenetic,* therefore, refers to the environmental factors that surround the genes, affecting genetic expression.

Some "epi" influences occur in the first hours of life as biochemical elements silence certain genes, in a process called *methylation.* The degree of methylation for people changes over the life span, affecting genes (Kendler et al., 2011). In addition, other epigenetic influences occur, including some that impede development (e.g., injury, temperature extremes, drug abuse, and crowding) and some that facilitate it (e.g., nourishing food, loving care, and active play). Research far beyond the discipline of genetics, or even the broader discipline of biology, is needed to discover all the epigenetic effects.

MOODBOARD / CORBIS

What Do You See? Do you first notice their age, their good teeth, their hair? Chances are you first notice their race and wonder whether they really are good friends or whether this is a posed photo. It might be impossible for an English-speaking adult of any ethnicity to be color-blind.

epigenetic
Referring to the effects of environmental forces on the expression of an individual's, or a species', genetic inheritance.

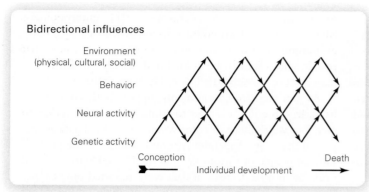

Bidirectional influences

Environment
(physical, cultural, social)

Behavior

Neural activity

Genetic activity

Conception   Death

Individual development

FIGURE 1.7 An Epigenetic Model of Development Notice that there are as many arrows going down as going up, at all levels. Although development begins with genes at conception, it requires that all four factors interact.

The inevitable epigenetic interaction between genes and the environment (nature and nurture) is illustrated in Figure 1.7. That simple diagram, with arrows going up and down over time, has been redrawn and reprinted dozens of times to emphasize that genes interact with environmental conditions again and again in each person's life (G. Gottlieb, 2010).

Epigenetic research is especially important in treating diseases that impair the brain and devastate human development. As one group of researchers explains, "Clearly, the brain contains an epigenetic 'hotspot' with a unique potential to not only better understand its most complex functions, but also to treat its most vicious diseases" (Gräff et al., 2011, p. 603). Genes are always important; some are expressed, affecting development, and some are never noticed, from generation to generation, unless circumstances change. The reasons are epigenetic; factors beyond the genes are crucial (Issa, 2011; Skipper, 2011).

MULTIDISCIPLINARY RESEARCH ON DEPRESSION Consider the importance of many disciplines in understanding depression, which results in 65 million lost years of productive life per year around the world (P. Y. Collins et al., 2011). There is no doubt that depression is partly genetic and neurological—certain brain chemicals make people sad and uninterested in life. There is also no doubt that depression is developmental: Depression increases and decreases throughout the life span (Kapornai & Vetró, 2008; Kendler et al., 2011).

For instance, the incidence of clinical depression suddenly rises in early adolescence, particularly among girls. Throughout life, whether or not a person becomes depressed is affected by chemicals in the brain, not only by neurotransmitters such as dopamine and serotonin but also by growth factors such as GDNF (glial cell line-derived neurotrophic factor), the product of one gene that makes neurons grow or stagnate (Uchida et al., 2011).

Child-rearing practices have an impact as well. Typically, depressed mothers smile and talk to their infants less than other mothers; in turn, the infants become less active and verbal. A researcher who studies mother–infant interaction told nondepressed mothers to do the following with their 3-month-olds for only three minutes:

> to speak in a monotone, to keep their faces flat and expressionless, to slouch back in their chair, to minimize touch, and to imagine that they felt tired and blue. The infants . . . reacted strongly, . . . cycling among states of wariness, disengagement, and distress with brief bids to their mother to resume her normal affective state. Importantly, the infants continued to be distressed and disengaged . . . after the mothers resumed normal interactive behavior.
>
> [Tronick, 2007, p. 306]

Thus, even three minutes of mock-depressive behavior makes infants act depressed. If a mother is actually depressed, her baby will be, too.

As you would expect from the multidirectional and multicontextual nature of development, a child's ongoing depression depends on the mother's ongoing depression and on whether another caregiver is available. Depressed 1-year-olds tend to become much happier by age 6 if their mother's mood has lifted.

One detailed study traced this connection via heart and brain activity as well as social interactions—first when the children were 14 months old and then at ages 2, 3½, 4½, and 6½ (Ashman et al., 2008). Physiological, psychological, and social data showed that the mother's depression throughout early childhood had a major impact. Children of mothers whose depression decreased were less aggressive (as rated by their kindergarten teachers on such observations as "hits other children") than children whose mothers were continually depressed.

The researchers note that "consistent with previous research, contextual risk factors such as low marital satisfaction and high family conflict were found to mediate the relationship between maternal depression and child behavior measures" (Ashman et al., 2008, p. 74). They suggest that the home environment changes the mother, and this affects "children's patterns of brain activity as well as their behavioral outcomes" (p. 73).

Similar conclusions arise from research on adults with depression: Many genetic, biochemical, and neurological factors distinguish them from other adults (Kanner, 2012; Poldrack et al., 2008). However, their moods and behaviors are also powerfully affected by experience and cognition (Huberty, 2012; van Praag et al., 2012). Again, nature is affected by nurture. A person with depressing relationships and experiences is likely to develop the brain patterns characteristic of depression, and vice versa. Overall, at least 12 factors are linked to depression.

- Low serotonin in the brain, as a result of an allele of the gene for serotonin transport *(neuroscience)*
- Childhood caregiver depression, especially postpartum depression with exclusive mother-care *(psychopathology)*
- Low exposure to daylight, as in winter in higher latitudes *(biology)*
- Malnutrition, particularly low hemoglobin *(nutrition)*
- Lack of close friends, especially when entering a new culture, school, or neighborhood *(anthropology)*
- Diseases, including Parkinson's and AIDS, and drugs to treat diseases *(medicine)*
- Disruptive event, such as breakup with a romantic partner *(sociology)*
- Death of mother before age 10 *(psychology)*
- Absence of father during childhood—especially because of divorce, less so because of death or migration *(family studies)*
- Family history of eating disorders (not necessarily of the depressed person) *(genetics)*
- Poverty, especially in a nation where some people are very wealthy *(economics)*
- Low cognitive skills, including illiteracy and lack of exposure to other ideas *(education)*

As you see, each of these factors arises from research in a different discipline (italicized). Of course, disciplines overlap. Lack of close confidants, for instance, is noted by anthropologists, but also by sociologists and psychologists. Furthermore, culture, climate, and politics all have an effect, although the particulars are debatable. For example, consider the national differences in Figure 1.8. There are at least six explanations for the disparity in the incidence of depression between one nation and another—some genetic, some cultural, and some a combination of the two.

A multidisciplinary approach is crucial in alleviating every impairment, including depression: Currently in the United States, a combination of cognitive therapy, family therapy, and antidepressant medication is often more effective than any one of these three alone. International research finds that

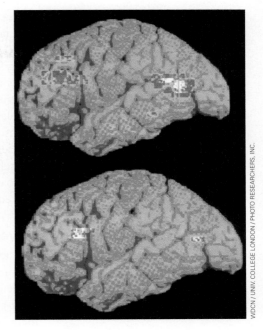

Red Means Stop At top, the red areas on this PET scan show abnormally low metabolic activity and blood flow in a depressed person's brain, in contrast to the normal brain at bottom.

WDCN / UNIV. COLLEGE LONDON / PHOTO RESEARCHERS, INC.

FIGURE 1.8 Why? Interpretation of these data depends on the interpreter's assumption. The low rate in Japan could be caused by something wonderful in Japanese culture—close human bonds, for instance. Or it could be something negative—repression of emotions, perhaps, which would reduce only the rate of diagnosed depression, not the rate of actual depression. As with the results of most research, data often raise new questions.

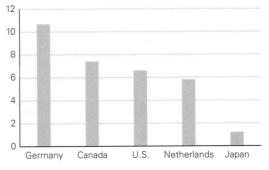

Percent of adults experiencing major depressive episode in past year

Source: Lam, 2012.

depression is quite high in some populations in some places (e.g., half the women in Pakistan) and low in others (e.g., about 3 percent of the non-smoking men in Denmark), again for a combination of reasons (Flensborg-Madsen et al., 2011; Husain et al., 2011; von dem Knesebeck et al., 2011).

As already noted in the discussion of nature and nurture, of SIDS, and of my experience at Caleb's birth, no single factor determines any outcome. In fact, some people who experience one, and only one, of the factors listed above are happy with themselves and their lives. It is a combination of multiple factors that makes a person depressed. As you will now see, for genetic and other reasons, some people are severely affected by circumstances that do not bother others. The multidisciplinary approach to the life span adds a measure of caution to every scientist: No one is able to predict with certainty the future developmental path for anyone.

Development Is Plastic

The term *plasticity* denotes two complementary aspects of development: Human traits can be molded (as plastic can be), and yet people maintain a certain durability of identity (as plastic does). The concept of plasticity in development provides both hope and realism—hope because change is possible, and realism because development builds on what has come before.

dynamic-systems approach
A view of human development as an ongoing, ever-changing interaction between a person's physical and emotional being and between the person and every aspect of his or her environment, including the family and society.

DYNAMIC SYSTEMS The concept of plasticity is basic to the contemporary understanding of human development. This is evident in one of the newest approaches to understanding human growth, an approach called **dynamic systems.** The idea is that human development is an ongoing, ever-changing interaction between the body and mind and between the individual and every aspect of the environment, including all the systems described in the ecological approach. The dynamic-systems approach began in disciplines that focus on changes in the natural world.

> [S]easons change in ordered measure, clouds assemble and disperse, trees grow to a certain shape and size, snowflakes form and melt, minute plants and animals pass through elaborate life cycles that are invisible to us, and social groups come together and disband.
>
> *[Thelen & Smith, 2006, p. 271]*

Note the key word *dynamic:* Physical and emotional influences, time, each person, and every aspect of the environment are always interacting, always in flux, always in motion. This approach builds on many aspects of the life-span perspective already described, including the multidirectional, multicontextual, multicultural, and multidisciplinary nature of development. With any developmental topic, stage, or problem, the dynamic-systems approach urges us to consider all the interrelated aspects, every social and cultural factor, over days and years. In that sense, it is not a theory, and not really new: Focusing on dynamic systems highlights how developmental change has always occurred.

AN EXAMPLE OF INTERACTING SYSTEMS My sister-in-law contracted rubella (also called German measles) early in her third pregnancy, a fact not recognized until her son David was born, blind and dying. Heart surgery two days after birth saved his life, but surgery at 6 months to remove a cataract destroyed that eye. Malformations of his thumbs, ankles, teeth, feet, spine, and brain became evident. David did not walk or talk or even chew for years. Some people wondered why his parents did not place him in an institution.

Yet dire early predictions—from me as well as many others—have proven false. David is a productive adult, and happy. When I questioned him about his life he said, "I try to stay in a positive mood" (personal communication, 2011).

Remember, plasticity cannot erase a person's genes, childhood, or permanent damage. David's disabilities are always with him (he still lives with his parents). But his childhood experiences gave him lifelong strengths. His family loved and nurtured him (consulting the Kentucky School for the Blind when he was a few months old, enrolling him in four preschools and then in public kindergarten at age 6). By age 10, David had skipped a year of school and was a fifth-grader, reading at the eleventh-grade level. He learned a second and a third language. In young adulthood, after one failing semester (requiring family assistance again), he earned several As and graduated from college.

David now works as a translator of German texts, which he enjoys because "I like providing a service to scholars, giving them access to something they would otherwise not have" (personal communication, 2007). As his aunt, I have seen him repeatedly defy predictions. All five of the characteristics of the life-span perspective are evident in David's life, as summarized in Table 1.3.

My Brother's Children Michael, Bill, and David (left to right) are adults now, with quite different personalities, abilities, offspring (4, 2, and none), and contexts (in Massachusetts, Pennsylvania, and California). Yet despite distinct genes, prenatal life, and childhood influences, I see that they shared the influence of Glen and Dot, my brother and sister-in-law—evident here in their similar, friendly smiles.

DIFFERENTIAL SENSITIVITY As just noted, plasticity emphasizes that people can and do change, that predictions are not always accurate. This is sometimes frustrating to scientists, who seek to prevent problems by learning what is particularly risky or helpful for healthy development.

Three insights have improved predictions. Two of them you already know: (1) Nature and nurture always interact, and (2) certain periods of life are sensitive periods, more affected by particular events than others. This was apparent for David: His inherited characteristics affected his ability to learn, and his early-childhood education (a sensitive period for language learning) has helped him lifelong.

The third factor to aid prediction and thus target intervention is a more recent discovery, **differential sensitivity.** The idea is that some people are more vulnerable than others to particular experiences.

Can you remember something you heard in childhood that still affects you, such as a criticism that stung or a compliment that motivated you? Now think of what that same comment meant to the person who uttered it or might have meant to

differential sensitivity
The idea that some people are more vulnerable than others are to certain experiences, usually because of genetic differences.

TABLE 1.3 Five Characteristics of Development

Characteristic	Application in David's Story
Multidirectional. Change occurs in every direction, not always in a straight line. Gains and losses, predictable growth, and unexpected transformations are evident.	David's development seemed static (or even regressive, as when early surgery destroyed one eye) but then accelerated each time he entered a new school or college.
Multidisciplinary. Numerous academic fields—especially psychology, biology, education, and sociology, but also neuroscience, economics, religion, anthropology, history, medicine, genetics, and many more—contribute insights.	Two disciplines were particularly critical: medicine (David would have died without advances in surgery on newborns) and education (special educators guided him and his parents many times).
Multicontextual. Human lives are embedded in many contexts, including historical conditions, economic constraints, and family patterns.	The high SES of David's family made it possible for him to receive daily medical and educational care. His two older brothers protected him.
Multicultural. Many cultures—not just between nations but also within them—affect how people develop.	Appalachia, where David and his family lived, has a particular culture, including acceptance of people with disabilities and willingness to help families in need. Those aspects of that culture benefited David and his family.
Plasticity. Every individual, and every trait within each individual, can be altered at any point in the life span. Change is ongoing, although neither random nor easy.	David's measured IQ changed from about 40 (severely mentally retarded) to about 130 (far above average), and his physical disabilities became less crippling as he matured. Nonetheless, because of a virus contracted before he was born, his entire life will never be what it might have been.

another child. A particular comment stayed with you, but the same words would be forgotten by most other people. That is differential sensitivity.

More generally, many scientists have found genes, or circumstances, that work both ways—they predispose people to being either unusually successful or severely pathological (Belsky et al., 2012; Kéri, 2009). This idea is captured in the folk saying, "Genius is close to madness": The same circumstance (brilliance) can become a gift for an entire society, be a burden for the affected individual, or have little effect.

Here is one example that began with 11-year-old African American boys in rural Georgia, the United States (Brody et al., 2009). Early puberty is a sensitive period when young adolescents seek to rebel against parents, preachers, and teachers and when the allure of alcohol, marijuana, and sexual intercourse is strong. Yet if a boy can resist those hazards until he is more mature, his future is much brighter. A team of researchers hoped they could protect these Georgia boys from harm, and they sought scientific evidence to prove or disprove that hypothesis.

Accordingly, they randomly divided parents and sons into two groups: (1) a group that had no intervention and (2) a group that attended seven seminars designed to increase racial pride, family support, honest communication, and compliance with parents' rules. These features are in keeping with replicated research that finds that pride and parental involvement protect against early sex and drug use.

The first follow-up, five years later, was disappointing. The intervention seemed to have almost no effect. Both groups of boys drank, smoked, or had sex at similar rates.

However, remember that scientists constantly keep up with the work of other scientists, reading published research from many disciplines. By the first follow-up, research on genetics and differential sensitivity had begun appearing in the academic literature, so the Georgia researchers decided to assess (via a saliva test) whether each boy had the short or long version of a particular gene (called 5-HTTLPR).

That small genetic difference turned out to be critical: Those with the long version developed just as well whether they were in the intervention group or not. However, teenagers with the short version who attended the seminars were less likely to have early sex or to use drugs than those who also had the short gene but not the family training (see Figure 1.9). The sensitivity provided by nature (the small difference in the code for 5-HTTLPR) allowed the special nurture (the seminars) to have an impact.

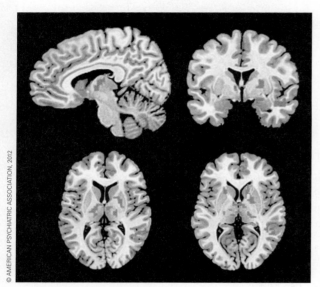

Many Brain Regions More than a dozen brain areas are more reactive to stress when a person has only the short allele of 5-HTTLPR. That is shown in these brain scans from a study of healthy college women who were paid to undergo an experiment involving 12 episodes without shocks, 13 with moderate shocks, and 13 with stronger (painful but not extreme) shocks. Uncertainty increased stress: The women did not know exactly when or how strong the shocks would be. People with only the short version of 5-HTTLPR were much more anxious overall, with more areas of their brains activated (shown here in red), compared to those with the long version.

© AMERICAN PSYCHIATRIC ASSOCIATION, 2012

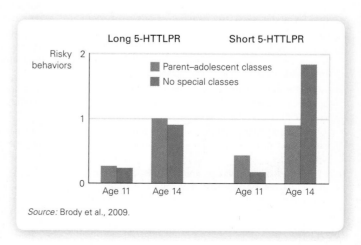

FIGURE 1.9 Differential Sensitivity
The risk score for these boys was a simple 0 to 3, with 1 point for each of the following: drank alcohol, smoked marijuana, had sex. As shown, most had done none of these at age 11, and, by age 14, most had done one (usually drunk beer). However, some of those at genetic risk had done all three, and many had done two. For them, and only them, the seven-session intervention made a difference.

Source: Brody et al., 2009.

KEY points

- Development is multidirectional, with gains and losses evident at every stage.
- Development is multicontextual, with the ecological context from the immediate family to the broad social environment affecting every person. Cohort and socio-economic status have powerful impacts.
- Cultural influences are sometimes unrecognized until another culture is understood. Social constructions, including ethnicity and race, are tangled with cultural values, making culture not only crucial but also complex.
- Many academic disciplines provide insight on how people grow and change over time, as the interaction of all the developmental contexts cannot be fully grasped by any one discipline.
- Each person's development is plastic, with the basic substance of each individual life moldable by contexts and events, sometimes in differential ways, making every person unlike any other person.

Theories of Human Development

As you read earlier in this chapter, the scientific method begins with observations, questions, and theories (step 1). These lead to specific hypotheses that can be tested (step 2). A *theory* is a comprehensive and organized explanation of many phenomena; a *hypothesis* is more limited and may be proven false. Theories are generalities; hypotheses are specific. Data are collected through research (step 3), conclusions are drawn (step 4), and the results are reported (step 5) and replicated.

Although developmental scientists are intrigued by all their observations, theories are crucial to start the scientific process. Theories sharpen researchers' perceptions and organize the thousands of behaviors they observe every day. Each **developmental theory** is a systematic statement of principles and generalizations, providing a framework for understanding how and why people change over the life span. We need theories to "help us describe and explain developmental changes by organizing and giving meaning to facts and by guiding future research" (P. H. Miller, 2011, p. 25). Theories connect facts with patterns, weaving the details of life into a meaningful whole.

Imagine building a house. A person could have a heap of lumber, nails, and other materials, but without a plan and workers, the heap cannot become a home. Likewise, observations of human development are raw materials, but theories put them together. Kurt Lewin (1943) once quipped, "Nothing is as practical as a good theory."

You will encounter dozens of theories throughout this text, each one useful in organizing data and developing hypotheses. Five theories that apply to the entire life span are introduced here; more details about each of them appear later in this text.

Psychoanalytic Theory

Inner drives and motives are the foundation of **psychoanalytic theory.** These basic underlying forces are thought to influence every aspect of thinking and behavior, from the smallest details of daily life to the crucial choices of a lifetime (Dijksterhuis & Nordgren, 2006).

developmental theory
A group of ideas, assumptions, and generalizations that interpret and illuminate the thousands of observations that have been made about human growth. A developmental theory provides a framework for explaining the patterns and problems of development.

psychoanalytic theory
A theory of human development that holds that irrational, unconscious drives and motives, often originating in childhood, underlie human behavior.

Freud at Work In addition to being the world's first psychoanalyst, Sigmund Freud was a prolific writer. His many papers and case histories, primarily descriptions of his patients' bizarre symptoms and unconscious sexual urges, helped make the psychoanalytic perspective a dominant force for much of the twentieth century.

AKG / PHOTO RESEARCHERS, INC.

FREUD'S STAGES Psychoanalytic theory originated with Sigmund Freud (1856–1939), an Austrian physician who treated patients suffering from mental illness. He listened to descriptions of their dreams and fantasies and constructed an elaborate, multifaceted theory.

According to Freud, development in the first six years occurs in three stages, each characterized by sexual pleasure centered on a particular part of the body. Infants experience the *oral stage,* so named because the erotic body part is the mouth, followed by the *anal stage* in early childhood, with the focus on the anus. In the preschool years (the *phallic stage*), the penis becomes a source of pride and fear for boys and a reason for sadness and envy for girls.

In middle childhood comes *latency,* a quiet period that ends when one enters the *genital stage* at puberty. Freud was the most famous theorist who thought that development stopped after puberty and that the genital stage continued throughout adulthood (see Table 1.4).

TABLE 1.4 Comparing Stages: Freud and Erikson

Approximate Age	Freud (Psychosexual)	Erikson (Psychosocial)
Birth to 1 year	*Oral Stage* The lips, tongue, and gums are the focus of pleasurable sensations in the baby's body, and sucking and feeding are the most stimulating activities.	*Trust vs. Mistrust* Babies either trust that others will care for their basic needs, including nourishment, warmth, cleanliness, and physical contact, <u>or</u> develop mistrust about the care of others.
1–3 years	*Anal Stage* The anus is the focus of pleasurable sensations in the baby's body, and toilet training is the most important activity.	*Autonomy vs. Shame and Doubt* Children either become self-sufficient in many activities, including toileting, feeding, walking, exploring, and talking, <u>or</u> doubt their own abilities.
3–6 years	*Phallic Stage* The phallus, or penis, is the most important body part, and pleasure is derived from genital stimulation. Boys are proud of their penises; girls wonder why they don't have one.	*Initiative vs. Guilt* Children either want to undertake many adultlike activities <u>or</u> internalize the limits and prohibitions set by parents. They feel either adventurous <u>or</u> guilty.
6–11 years	*Latency* Not really a stage, latency is an interlude during which sexual needs are quiet and children put psychic energy into conventional activities like schoolwork and sports.	*Industry vs. Inferiority* Children busily learn to be competent and productive in mastering new skills <u>or</u> feel inferior, unable to do anything as well as they wish they could.
Adolescence	*Genital Stage* The genitals are the focus of pleasurable sensations, and the young person seeks sexual stimulation and sexual satisfaction in heterosexual relationships.	*Identity vs. Role Confusion* Adolescents try to figure out "Who am I?" They establish sexual, political, and vocational identities <u>or</u> are confused about what roles to play.
Adulthood	Freud believed that the genital stage lasts throughout adulthood. He also said that the goal of a healthy life is "to love and to work."	*Intimacy vs. Isolation* Young adults seek companionship and love <u>or</u> become isolated from others because they fear rejection and disappointment. *Generativity vs. Stagnation* Middle-aged adults contribute to the next generation through meaningful work, creative activities, and raising a family, <u>or</u> they stagnate. *Integrity vs. Despair* Older adults try to make sense out of their lives, either seeing life as a meaningful whole <u>or</u> despairing at goals never reached.

Freud maintained that at each stage, sensual satisfaction (from stimulation of the mouth, anus, or genitals) is linked to developmental needs, challenges, and conflicts. How people experience and resolve these conflicts—especially those related to weaning (oral), toilet training (anal), male roles (phallic), and sexual pleasure (genital)—determines personality patterns because "the early stages provide the foundation for adult behavior" (Salkind, 2004, p. 125).

ERIKSON'S STAGES Many of Freud's followers became famous theorists themselves. The most notable in human development was Erik Erikson (1902–1994), who described eight developmental stages, each characterized by a challenging developmental crisis (summarized in Table 1.4). Although Erikson's first five stages build on Freud's theory, he also described three adult stages, perhaps because in his own adult life he made several dramatic moves. He was a wandering artist in Italy, a teacher in Austria, and a Harvard professor in the United States.

Erikson named two polarities at each stage (which is why the word *versus* is used in each), but he recognized that many outcomes between these opposites are possible (Erikson, 1963). For most people, development at each stage leads to neither extreme. For instance, the generativity-versus-stagnation stage of adulthood rarely involves a person who is totally stagnant—no children, no work, no creativity. Instead, most adults are somewhat stagnant and somewhat generative.

Erikson, like Freud, believed that adults' problems echo their childhood conflicts. For example, an adult who cannot form a secure, close relationship (intimacy versus isolation) may not have resolved the crisis of infancy (trust versus mistrust). However, Erikson's stages differ significantly from Freud's in that they emphasize family and culture, not sexual urges. He called his theory *epigenetic*, partly to stress that genes and biological impulses are powerfully influenced by the social environment.

Before the emergence of psychoanalytic theory, the first years of life were ignored by most scientists. Both Freud and Erikson noted that psychological conflicts—especially in childhood within families—affect people lifelong, an insight that developmentalists now accept.

A Legendary Couple In his first 30 years, Erikson never fit into a particular local community, since he so frequently changed nations, schools, and professions. Then he met Joan. In their first five decades of marriage, they raised a family and wrote several books. If he had published his theory at age 73 (when this photograph was taken) instead of in his 40s, would he still have described his life as a series of crises?

TED STRESHINSKY / TIME LIFE PICTURES / GETTY IMAGES

MARGO SILVER / GETTY IMAGES

Pink or Purple Hair These adolescents think they are nonconformist, and their short skirts, opaque tights, and hairstyles are certainly unlike those of their mothers or grandmothers. But they are similar to adolescents everywhere—seeking to establish their own distinct identity.

TABLE 1.5 Psychoanalytic Theory vs. Behaviorism

Area of Disagreement	Psychoanalytic Theory	Behaviorism
The unconscious	Emphasizes unconscious wishes and urges, unknown to the person but powerful all the same	Holds that the unconscious not only is unknowable but also may be a destructive fiction that keeps people from changing
Observable behavior	Holds that observable behavior is a symptom, not the cause—the tip of an iceberg, with the bulk of the problem submerged	Looks only at observable behavior—what a person does rather than what a person thinks, feels, or imagines
Importance of childhood	Stresses that early childhood, including infancy, is critical; even if a person does not remember what happened, the early legacy lingers throughout life	Holds that current conditioning is crucial; early habits and patterns can be unlearned, even reversed, if appropriate reinforcements and punishments are used
Scientific status	Holds that most aspects of human development are beyond the reach of scientific experiment; uses ancient myths, the words of disturbed adults, dreams, play, and poetry as raw material	Is proud to be a science, dependent on verifiable data and carefully controlled experiments; discards ideas that sound good but are not proven

ARCHIVES OF THE HISTORY OF AMERICAN PSYCHOLOGY, THE UNIVERSITY OF AKRON

An Early Behaviorist John Watson was an early proponent of learning theory. His ideas are still influential and controversial today.

behaviorism
A theory of human development that studies observable behavior. Behaviorism is also called *learning theory* because it describes the laws and processes by which behavior is learned.

conditioning
According to behaviorism, the processes by which responses become linked to particular stimuli and learning takes place. The word *conditioning* is used to emphasize the importance of repeated practice, as when an athlete *conditions* his or her body to perform well by training for a long time.

Behaviorism

Another influential theory, **behaviorism,** arose in direct opposition to the psychoanalytic emphasis on unconscious, hidden urges (differences are described in Table 1.5). Early in the twentieth century, John B. Watson (1878–1958) argued that scientists should examine only what they could observe and measure. According to Watson, if psychologists focus on behavior, they will realize that anything can be learned. For this reason, behaviorism is also called *learning theory.* Watson wrote:

> Give me a dozen healthy infants, well-formed, and my own specified world to bring them up in and I'll guarantee to take any one at random and train him to become any type of specialist I might select—doctor, lawyer, artist, merchant chief, and yes, even beggar-man and thief, regardless of his talents, penchants, tendencies, abilities, vocations, and race.
>
> *[Watson, 1924/1998, p. 82]*

Many other psychologists, especially in the United States, agreed. They found that the unconscious motives and drives that Freud described were difficult (or impossible) to verify via the scientific method (Uttal, 2000). For instance, researchers discovered that, contrary to Freud's view, the parents' approach to toilet training did not determine a child's later personality.

For every individual at every age, from newborn to centenarian, behaviorists have identified laws to describe how environmental responses shape what people do. All behavior—from reading a book to robbing a bank, from saying "Good morning" to a stranger to "I love you" to a spouse—follows these laws. Every action is learned, step by step.

CONDITIONING The specific laws of learning apply to **conditioning,** the processes by which responses become linked to particular stimuli. There are two types of conditioning: classical and operant.

More than a century ago, Ivan Pavlov (1849–1936), a Russian scientist who won a Nobel Prize for his work on animal digestion, noticed that his experimental dogs drooled not only when they saw and smelled food but also when they heard the footsteps of the attendants who brought the food. This observation led Pavlov to perform experiments in which he conditioned dogs to salivate when they heard a specific noise.

Pavlov began by sounding a tone just be- fore presenting food. After a number of rep- etitions of the tone-then-food sequence, dogs began salivating at the sound, even when there was no food. This simple experiment demon- strated **classical conditioning,** a process in which a person or animal learns to associate a neutral stimulus (the sound) with a meaning- ful stimulus (the food), gradually reacting to the neutral stimulus with the same behavior as to the meaningful one.

The most influential North American behaviorist was B. F. Skinner (1904–1990). He agreed with Watson that psychology should focus on the scientific study of behav- ior and that classical conditioning explains some behavior. However, Skinner stressed another type of conditioning, **operant conditioning.**

In operant conditioning (also called *instrumental conditioning*), animals perform some action and then a response occurs. If the response is useful or pleasurable, the animal is likely to repeat the action; if the response is painful, the animal is not likely to repeat the action. In both cases, the animal has learned.

Pleasant consequences are sometimes called *rewards,* and unpleasant consequences are sometimes called *punishments.* Behaviorists hesitate to use those words, however, because what people commonly think of as a punishment can actually be a reward, and vice versa.

For example, parents punish their children by withholding dessert, by spanking them, by not letting them play, by speaking harshly to them, and so on. But if a particular child dislikes the dessert, being deprived of it is actually a reward, not a punishment. Another child might not mind a spanking, especially if he or she craves parental attention. For that child, the intended punishment (spanking) is actually a reward (attention).

A Contemporary of Freud
Ivan Pavlov was a physiologist who received the Nobel Prize in 1904 for his research on digestive processes. It was this line of study that led to his discovery of classical conditioning.

OBSERVATION QUIZ
In appearance, how is Pavlov similar to Freud, and how do both look differ- ent from the other theorists pictured? (see answer, page 29) →

classical conditioning
A learning process in which a mean- ingful stimulus (such as the smell of food to a hungry animal) gradually comes to be connected with a neutral stimulus (such as a particular sound) that had no special meaning before the learning process began. (Also called *respondent conditioning.*)

operant conditioning
A learning process in which a particular action is followed either by something desired (which makes the person or animal more likely to repeat the action) or by something unwanted (which makes the action less likely to be repeated). (Also called *instrumental conditioning.*)

Rats, Pigeons, and People
B. F. Skinner is best known for his experiments with rats and pigeons, but he also applied his knowledge to human problems. For his daughter (shown here), he designed a glass- enclosed crib in which temperature, humidity, and perceptual stimulation could be controlled to make her time in the crib enjoyable and educational.

reinforcement
A technique for conditioning a particular behavior in which that behavior is followed by something desired, such as food for a hungry animal or a welcoming smile for a lonely person.

social learning theory
An extension of behaviorism that emphasizes that other people influence each person's behavior. The theory's basic principle is that even without specific reinforcement, every individual learns many things through observation and imitation of other people.

Still Social Learning Even in his 80s, Albert Bandura is on the faculty at Stanford University, as might be expected for someone who believes that each person is influenced by hundreds of others.

His Pride and Joy This father is proud of his muscles, but he is even more proud of his son—and didn't want to be photographed showing off his biceps alone. The pride is mutual: The boy hopes to become a man like his dad.

OBSERVATION QUIZ

Behind the posturing, what indicates that this boy models himself after his parent? (see answer, page 30) →

Any consequence that follows a behavior and makes the person (or animal) likely to repeat that behavior is called a positive **reinforcement,** not a reward. Once a behavior has been conditioned, humans and other creatures will repeat it even if reinforcement occurs only occasionally. Similarly, an unpleasant response makes a creature less likely to repeat a certain action. Almost all daily behavior, from combing your hair to joking with friends, is a result of past operant conditioning, according to behaviorists.

This insight has practical application. Early responses are crucial for development because children learn habits that endure. For instance, if parents want their child to share, and their baby offers them a gummy, half-eaten cracker, they should take the gift with apparent delight and then return it, smiling.

The science of human development has benefited from behaviorism. The theory's emphasis on the origins and consequences of observed behavior led to the realization that many actions that seem to be genetic, or to result from deeply rooted emotional problems, are actually learned. And if something is learned, it can be unlearned. No longer are "the events of infancy and early childhood . . . the foundation for adult personality and psychopathology" (Cairns & Cairns, 2006, p. 117), as psychoanalysts believed. People *can* change; plasticity is lifelong.

SOCIAL LEARNING THEORY A major extension of behaviorism is **social learning theory,** which was first described by Albert Bandura (b. 1925), a scientist who continues to study and write. This theory notes that, because humans are social beings, they learn from observing others, even without personally receiving any reinforcement.

Social learning is often called *modeling,* because people learn by observing role models. For example, extensive developmental research finds that children who witness domestic violence are influenced by it. As the multicontextual approach would predict, what they learn varies. For instance, if their father often hits their mother, one son might identify with the abuser and another with the victim. Later in adulthood, because of their past social learning, one man might slap his wife and spank his children, while his brother might be fearful and apologetic at home. They learned opposite lessons. Differential sensitivity may also be evident: A third sibling might not be affected by past memories of domestic violence.

Cognitive Theory

In a third theory, each person's ideas and beliefs are of central importance. According to **cognitive theory,** thoughts and expectations profoundly affect actions. Cognitive theory has dominated psychology since about 1980 and has branched into many versions, each adding insights about human development. The word *cognitive* refers not just to thinking but also to attitudes, beliefs, and assumptions.

The most famous cognitive theorist was a Swiss scientist, Jean Piaget (1896–1980). Unlike other scientists of the early twentieth century, Piaget realized that babies are curious and thoughtful, creating their own interpretations about their world. Piaget began by observing his own three infants; later he studied thousands of older children (Inhelder & Piaget, 1958).

From this work, Piaget developed the central thesis of cognitive theory: How people think (not just what they know) changes with time and experience, and human thinking influences human actions. Piaget maintained that cognitive development occurs in four major age-related periods, or stages: *sensorimotor, preoperational, concrete operational,* and *formal operational* (see Table 1.6).

Intellectual advancement occurs lifelong because humans seek *cognitive equilibrium*— that is, a state of mental balance. An easy way to achieve this balance is to interpret new experiences through the lens of preexisting ideas. For example, infants discover that new objects can be grasped in the same way as familiar objects; adolescents explain the day's headlines as evidence that supports their existing worldviews; older adults speak fondly of the good old days as embodying values that should endure.

cognitive theory
A theory of human development that focuses on changes in how people think over time. According to this theory, our thoughts shape our attitudes, beliefs, and behaviors.

Would You Talk to This Man? Children loved talking to Jean Piaget, and he learned by listening carefully—especially to their incorrect explanations, which no one had paid much attention to before. All his life, Piaget studied the way children think. He called himself a "genetic epistemologist"—one who studies how children gain knowledge about the world as they grow up.

ANSWER TO **OBSERVATION QUIZ** (from page 27) Both are balding, with white beards. Note also that none of the other theorists in this chapter have beards—a cohort difference, not an ideological one. ●

TABLE 1.6 Piaget's Periods of Cognitive Development

Age Range	Name of Period	Characteristics of the Period	Major Gains During the Period
Birth to 2 years	Sensorimotor	Infants use senses and motor abilities to understand the world. Learning is active; there is no conceptual or reflective thought.	Infants learn that an object still exists when it is out of sight (object permanence) and begin to think through mental actions.
2–6 years	Preoperational	Children think magically and poetically, using language to understand the world. Thinking is egocentric, causing children to perceive the world from their own perspective.	The imagination flourishes, and language becomes a significant means of self-expression and of influence from others.
6–11 years	Concrete operational	Children understand and apply logical operations, or principles, to interpret experiences objectively and rationally. Their thinking is limited to what they can personally see, hear, touch, and experience.	By applying logical abilities, children learn to understand concepts of conservation, number, classification, and many other scientific ideas.
12 years through adulthood	Formal operational	Adolescents and adults think about abstractions and hypothetical concepts and reason analytically, not just emotionally. They can be logical about things they have never experienced.	Ethics, politics, and social and moral issues become fascinating as adolescents and adults take a broader and more theoretical approach to experience.

How to Think About Flowers A person's stage of cognitive growth influences how he or she thinks about everything, including flowers. *(a)* At the preoperational stage, flowers fit into the egocentric scheme. This boy wants to touch, smell, and pick the flowers, not realizing how others might perceive such actions. *(b)* At the adult's formal operational stage, flowers can be part of a larger, logical scheme—either to earn money or to cultivate beauty. Thinking is an active process from the beginning of life until the end.

Sometimes, however, a new experience is jarring and incomprehensible. The resulting experience is one of *cognitive disequilibrium,* an imbalance that initially creates confusion. As Figure 1.10 illustrates, disequilibrium leads to cognitive growth because it forces people to adapt their old concepts. Piaget describes two types of adaptation:

- *Assimilation,* in which new experiences are interpreted to fit into, or assimilate with, old ideas
- *Accommodation,* in which old ideas are restructured to include, or accommodate, new experiences

Accommodation requires more mental energy than assimilation, but it is sometimes necessary because new ideas and experiences may not fit into existing cognitive structures. Accommodation produces significant intellectual growth.

Ideally, when people disagree, adaptation is mutual. For example, parents are often startled by their adolescents' strong opinions—say, that heroin should be legalized or that cigarettes should be outlawed. Parents may grow intellectually if they revise their concepts to accommodate such ideas, and adolescents may grow if they incorporate their parents' opinions. Adaptation is lifelong.

ANSWER TO **OBSERVATION QUIZ** (from page 28) The swimsuit—in style and color. You might think it makes more sense for a young boy to have a suit that is shorter and tighter—but then it wouldn't be just like his father's. ●

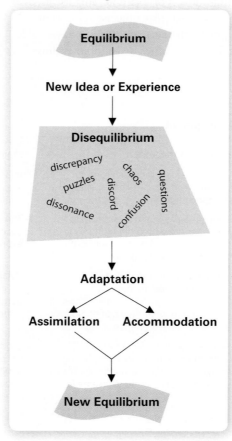

FIGURE 1.10 Challenge Me Most of us, most of the time, prefer the comfort of our conventional conclusions. According to Piaget, however, when new ideas disturb our thinking, we have an opportunity to expand our cognition with a broader and deeper understanding.

Vygotsky's approach to cognition, emphasizing the cultural context, is sometimes considered another cognitive theory. However, Vygotsky's basic emphasis is now shared by almost all developmental scholars, making the sociocultural approach not so much a theory as a corrective to earlier, narrower thinking.

Another influential cognitive theory, called *information processing,* differs from the approaches of Piaget and Vygotsky. Information-processing theory (which is discussed in Chapter 3) is not a stage theory but rather provides a detailed description of the steps of cognition, with attention to perceptual and neurological processes. Many researchers (in addition to those influenced by information-processing theory) now think that some of Piaget's conclusions were mistaken. However, every developmentalist appreciates Piaget's basic insight: Thoughts can influence emotions and actions.

Humanism

Many scientists are convinced that there is something hopeful, unifying, and noble in the human spirit, something ignored by psychoanalytic theory and by behaviorism. The limits of those two major theories were especially apparent to Abraham Maslow (1908–1970), one of the founders of the psychological theory of **humanism.** Maslow believed that all people—no matter what their culture, gender, or background—have the same basic needs and drives. He arranged these needs in a hierarchy (see Figure 1.11):

humanism
A theory that stresses the potential of all human beings for good and the belief that all people have the same basic needs, regardless of culture, gender, or background.

1. Physiological: needing food, water, warmth, and air
2. Safety: feeling protected from injury and death
3. Love and belonging: having loving friends, family, and a community
4. Esteem: being respected by the wider community as well as by oneself
5. Self-actualization: becoming truly oneself, fulfilling one's unique potential

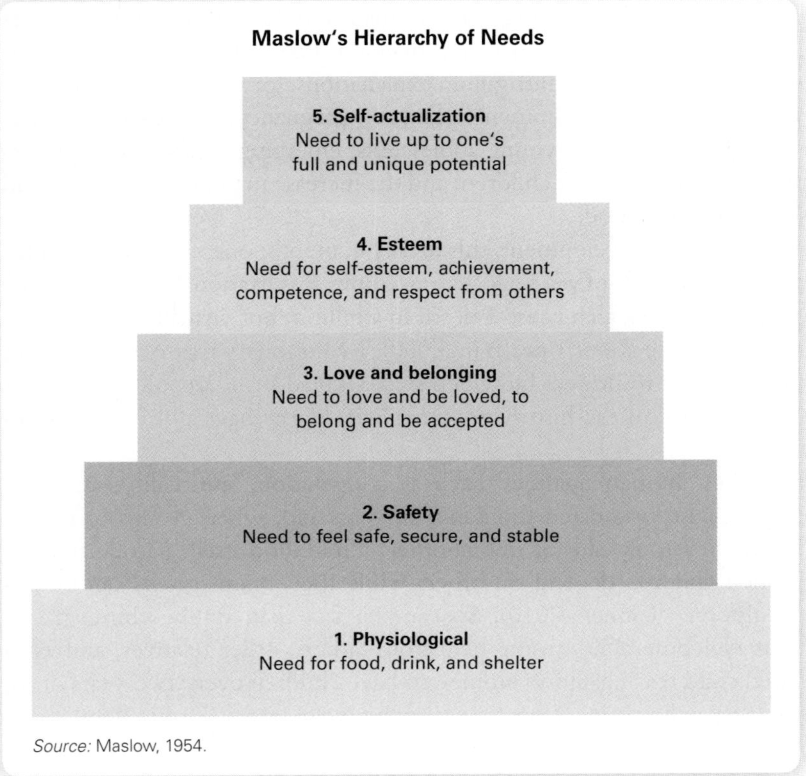

Maslow's Hierarchy of Needs

5. Self-actualization
Need to live up to one's full and unique potential

4. Esteem
Need for self-esteem, achievement, competence, and respect from others

3. Love and belonging
Need to love and be loved, to belong and be accepted

2. Safety
Need to feel safe, secure, and stable

1. Physiological
Need for food, drink, and shelter

Source: Maslow, 1954.

FIGURE 1.11 Moving Up, Not Looking Back
Maslow's hierarchy is like a ladder: Once a person stands firmly on a higher rung, the lower rungs are no longer needed. Thus, someone who has arrived at step 4 might devalue safety (step 2) and be willing to risk personal safety to gain respect.

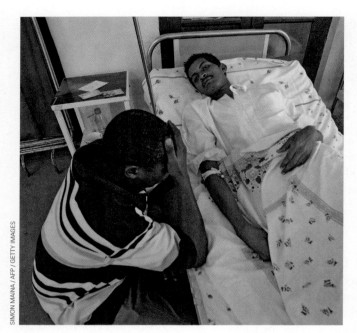

SIMON MAINA / AFP / GETTY IMAGES

Survivor When a ferry off the coast of Zanzibar capsized, 193 people drowned—but not Saleh Omar, shown here in the hospital with his friend. What motivated him to swim four hours to port? One possibility is Maslow's level 3, love and belonging. People do many extraordinary things to be with their friends.

At self-actualization, when all other needs have been met, people can be fully themselves—creative, spiritual, curious, appreciative of nature, able to respect everyone else. The person has "peak experiences" when life is so intensely joyful that time stops and self-seeking disappears.

Maslow contended that everyone must satisfy each lower level before moving higher. A starving man, for instance, may risk his life to secure food (level 1 precedes level 2), or an unloved woman might not care about self-respect because she needs affection (level 3 precedes level 4). People may be destructive and inhumane, not self-actualizing, because of unmet lower needs.

Although humanism does not postulate stages, a developmental application of this theory is that satisfying childhood needs is crucial for later self-acceptance. Thus, when babies cry in hunger, that basic need should be met. People may become thieves or even killers, unable to reach their potential, if they were unsafe or unloved as children.

This theory is prominent among medical professionals because they realize that pain can be physical (the first two levels) or social (the next two) (Majercsik, 2005; Zalenski & Raspa, 2006). Even the very sick need love and belonging (family should be with them) and esteem (the dying need respect).

Evolutionary Theory

Charles Darwin's basic ideas about evolution were first published 150 years ago (Darwin, 1859), but serious research on human development inspired by evolutionary theory is quite recent (Gangestad & Simpson, 2007, p. 2).

According to this theory, nature works to ensure that each species does two things: survive and reproduce. Consequently, many human impulses, needs, and behaviors evolved to help humans survive and thrive over the past 100,000 years (Konner, 2010). Evolutionary theory has intriguing explanations for many phenomena in human development, including women's nausea in pregnancy; 1-year-olds' attachment to their parents; puberty in young adolescents; emerging adults' sexual preferences; parents' investment in their children; and the increase in dementia, cancer, and other diseases in late adulthood.

To understand human development, this theory contends, one needs to recognize what was adaptive thousands of years ago. For example, it is irrational that many people are terrified of snakes (which cause 1 death in a billion) but virtually no one fears automobiles (which cause about 1 death in 5,000). Evolutionary theory suggests that the fear instinct evolved to protect life when snakes killed many people, which was true until quite recently in the history of our species. Fears have not caught up to modern life.

Some of the best human qualities, such as cooperation, spirituality, and self-sacrifice, may have also originated thousands of years ago, when groups of people survived because they took care of one another. Childhood itself, particularly the long period when children depend on others while their brains grow, can be explained via evolution (Konner, 2010). So can the fact that, unlike chimpanzees, human mothers welcome child-raising help from fathers, other relatives, and even strangers. Shared child rearing allows women to have children every two years or so, unlike chimpanzees, who wait at least four years between births (Hrdy, 2009).

KEY points

- Developmental theories provide a crucial framework, enabling people to understand and study life.

- Psychoanalytic theory posits stages of development. Freud emphasized unconscious urges; Erikson stressed eight stages of psychosocial development, from infancy through old age.

- Behaviorism contends that people have learned most of what they do through either association or reinforcement.

- Cognitive theory stresses that how people think affects how they behave. Piaget's stages are one example.

- Humanism recognizes universal human needs that must be met for a person to reach the highest level, self-actualization, becoming the best one can be.

- Evolutionary theory explains emotions and actions by tracing them back through thousands of years of human evolution, describing how they were designed to help the species survive.

scientific observation
A method of testing a hypothesis by unobtrusively watching and recording participants' behavior in a systematic and objective manner—in a natural setting, in a laboratory, or in searches of archival data.

experiment
A research method in which the researcher tries to determine the cause-and-effect relationship between two variables by manipulating one (called the *independent variable*) and then observing and recording the ensuing changes in the other (called the *dependent variable*).

Using the Scientific Method

There are hundreds of ways to design scientific studies and analyze their results, and researchers continually try to make sure that their data are valid and convincing. Often statistical measures help scientists discover relationships between various aspects of the data. (Some statistical perspectives are presented in Table 1.7). Every research design, method, and statistical measure has strengths as well as weaknesses. Now we describe three basic research designs—observation, the experiment, and the survey—and then three ways developmentalists study change over time.

Observation

Scientific observation requires researchers to record behavior systematically and objectively. Observations often occur in a naturalistic setting (such as a home, school, or public park), where people behave as they usually do and where the observer can be ignored or even go unnoticed. Scientific observation can also occur in a laboratory, where scientists record human reactions in various situations, often with wall-mounted video cameras and the scientist in another room.

Observation is crucial in developing hypotheses, as Beal did when she wanted to understand what caused sudden infant death syndrome. However, observation provides issues to explore, not proof. For SIDS, observed differences between Chinese and Australian infants included prenatal care, maternal diet, parental age, breast-feeding, facial features, baby blanket fabrics, and more. An experiment was needed to explore Beal's hypothesis that the crucial difference was sleeping position.

The Experiment

The **experiment** is the usual research method used to establish what causes what. In the social sciences, experimenters typically impose a particular treatment on a group of volunteer participants (formerly referred to as *subjects*) or expose them to a specific condition and then note whether their behavior changes.

Can They See Her? No, and they cannot hear one another. This scientist is observing three deaf boys through a window that is a mirror on the other side. Her observations will help them learn to communicate.

ALAMY

<table>
<tr><td colspan="2">**TABLE 1.7 Statistical Measures Often Used to Analyze Research Results**</td></tr>
<tr><td>Measure</td><td>Use</td></tr>
<tr><td>Effect size</td><td>Indicates how much one variable affects another. Effect size ranges from 0 to 1: An effect size of 0.2 is called small, 0.5 moderate, and 0.8 large.</td></tr>
<tr><td>Significance</td><td>Indicates whether the results might have occurred by chance. A finding that chance would produce the results only 5 times in 100 is significant at the 0.05 level. A finding that chance would produce the results once in 100 times is significant at 0.01; once in 1,000 times is significant at 0.001.</td></tr>
<tr><td>Cost-benefit analysis</td><td>Calculates how much a particular independent variable costs versus how much it saves. This is particularly useful for analyzing public spending. For instance, one cost-benefit analysis showed that an intensive preschool program cost $15,166 per child (in 2000 dollars) but saved $215,000 by the time that child reached age 40, in reduced costs of special education, unemployment, prison, and other public expenses (Belfield et al., 2006).</td></tr>
<tr><td>Odds ratio</td><td>Indicates how a particular variable compares to a standard, set at 1. For example, one study found that, although less than 1 percent of all child homicides occurred at school, the odds were similar for public and private schools. The odds of such deaths occurring in high schools, however, were 18.47 times that of elementary or middle schools (set at 1.0) (MMWR, January 18, 2008).</td></tr>
<tr><td>Factor analysis</td><td>Hundreds of variables could affect any given behavior. In addition, many variables (such as family income and parental education) may overlap. To take this into account, analysis reveals variables that can be clustered together to form a factor, which is a composite of many variables. For example, SES might become one factor, child personality another.</td></tr>
<tr><td>Meta-analysis</td><td>A "study of studies." Researchers use statistical tools to synthesize the results of previous, separate studies. Then they analyze the accumulated results, using criteria that weight each study fairly. This approach improves data analysis by combining the results of studies that were too small, or too narrow, to lead to solid conclusions.</td></tr>
</table>

Sources: Alasuutari et al., 2008; Duncan & Magnuson, 2007; Hubbard & Lindsay, 2008.

Who Participates? For all these measures, the characteristics of the people who participate in the study (formerly called the subjects, now called the participants) are important, as is the number of people who are studied.

✦ **ESPECIALLY FOR Nurses** In the field of medicine, why are experiments conducted to test new drugs and treatments? (see response, page 37) →

independent variable
In an experiment, the variable that is introduced to see what effect it has on the dependent variable. (Also called *experimental variable*.)

dependent variable
In an experiment, the variable that may change as a result of whatever new condition or situation the experimenter adds. In other words, the dependent variable *depends* on the independent variable.

survey
A research method in which information is collected from a large number of people by interviews, written questionnaires, or some other means.

In technical terms, the experimenters manipulate an **independent variable,** which is the imposed treatment or special condition (also called the *experimental variable*; a *variable* is anything that can vary). They note whether this independent variable affects whatever they are studying, called the **dependent variable** (which *depends* on the independent variable).

Thus, the independent variable is the new, special treatment; any change in the dependent variable is the result. In Beal's research, convincing some European Australian parents to put their infants to sleep on their backs (the independent variable) was crucial to connect cause (sleeping position) and effect (survival).

The purpose of an experiment is to find out whether an independent variable affects the dependent variable. In a typical experiment (as diagrammed in Figure 1.12), two groups of participants are studied. One group, the *experimental group*, gets a particular treatment (the independent variable). The other group, the *comparison group* (also called the *control group*), does not.

Another example of an experiment in this chapter was the study involving 11-year-old African American boys and their parents. As you remember, half of them (the experimental group) attended special seminars, while the other half (the comparison group) did not. Having that comparison was crucial in showing that the seminars made a difference for the boys with the short version of the 5-HTTLPR gene.

The Survey

A third research method is the **survey.** Information is collected from a large number of people by interview, questionnaire, or some other means. This is a quick, direct way to obtain data.

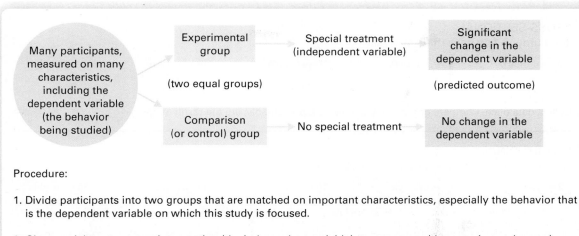

Procedure:

1. Divide participants into two groups that are matched on important characteristics, especially the behavior that is the dependent variable on which this study is focused.

2. Give special treatment, or intervention (the independent variable), to one group (the experimental group).

3. Compare the groups on the dependent variable. If they now differ, the cause of the difference was probably the independent variable.

4. Publish the results.

FIGURE 1.12 How to Conduct an Experiment The basic sequence diagrammed here applies to all experiments. Many additional features, especially the statistical measures listed in Table 1.7 and various ways of reducing experimenter bias, affect whether publication occurs. (Scientific journals reject reports of experiments that were not rigorous in method and analysis.)

Unfortunately, although surveys may be quick and direct, they are not necessarily accurate. When pollsters try to predict elections, they survey thousands of potential voters. They hope that the people they survey will vote as they say they will, that undecided people will follow the trends, and that people who refuse to give their opinion, or who are not included, will be similar to those surveyed. None of this is certain. Some people lie, some change their minds, some (especially those who don't have phones or who never talk to strangers) are never counted.

Furthermore, survey answers are influenced by the wording and the sequence of the questions. For instance, "climate change" and "global warming" are two ways to describe the same phenomenon, according to many scientists, yet many people believe in climate change but not in global warming (McCright & Dunlap, 2011). For that reason, surveys that seem to be about the same issue may reach opposite conclusions.

Additionally, survey respondents present themselves as they would like to be perceived. For instance, every two years since 1991, high school students in the United States have been surveyed. The participants are carefully chosen to be representative of all students in the nation. The most recent survey included 15,503 students from all 50 states and from schools large and small, public and private (MMWR, June 8, 2012).

Students are asked whether they had sexual intercourse *before* age 13. Every year, compared to the twelfth-grade boys, about twice as many ninth-grade boys say they had sex before age 13 (see Figure 1.13). Do seniors forget or do ninth-graders lie? Or are some 13-year-olds proud of early sexual experience, but ashamed by age 17?

FIGURE 1.13 I Forgot? If these were the only data available, you might conclude that 12-year-olds have suddenly become more sexually active. But we have 20 years of data—half of those ninth-graders who say yes now will say no in three years.

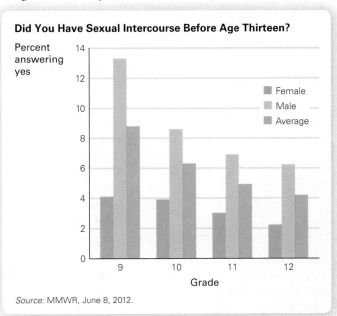

Source: MMWR, June 8, 2012.

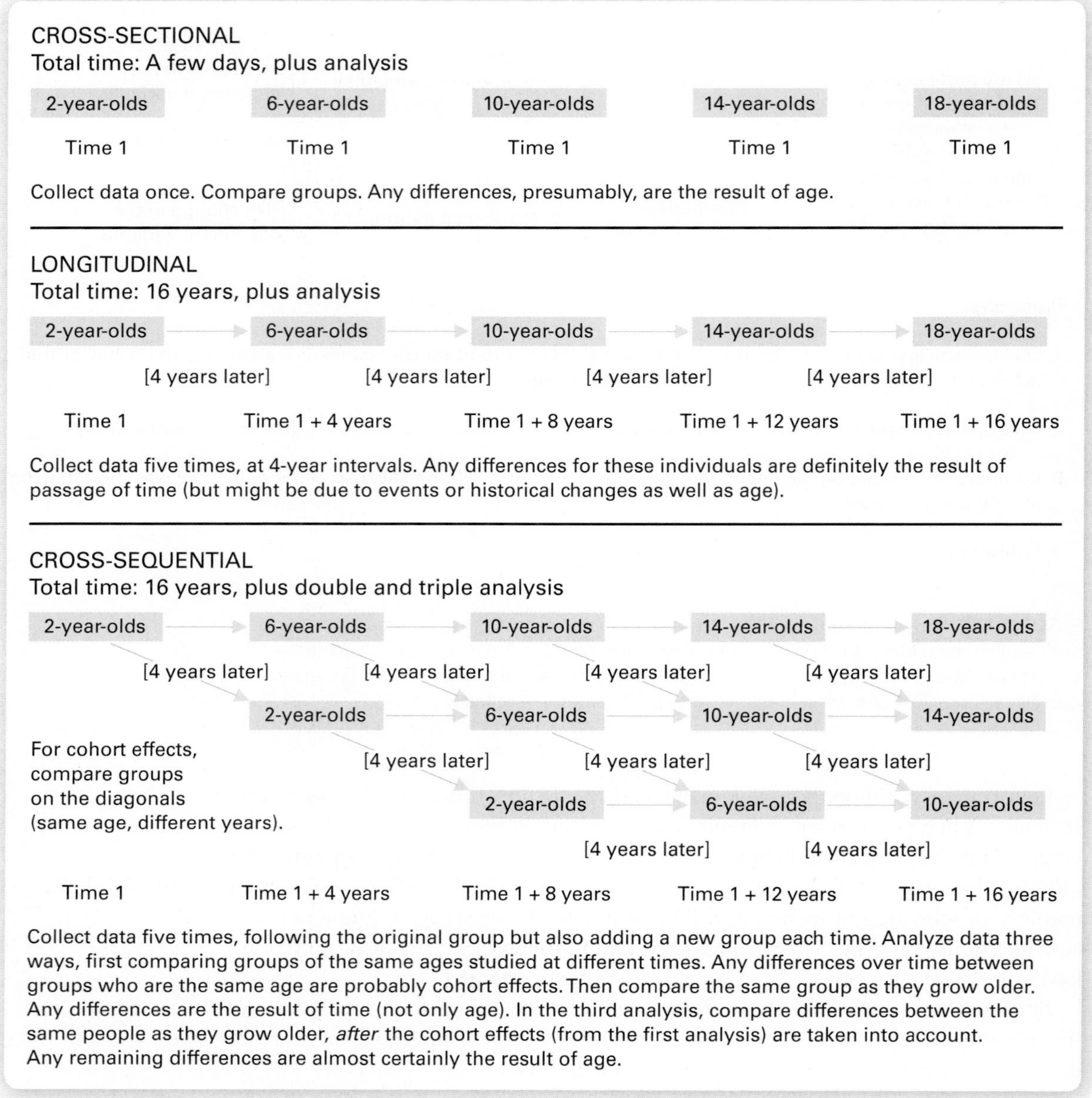

CROSS-SECTIONAL
Total time: A few days, plus analysis

2-year-olds	6-year-olds	10-year-olds	14-year-olds	18-year-olds
Time 1	Time 1	Time 1	Time 1	Time 1

Collect data once. Compare groups. Any differences, presumably, are the result of age.

LONGITUDINAL
Total time: 16 years, plus analysis

2-year-olds	→	6-year-olds	→	10-year-olds	→	14-year-olds	→	18-year-olds
	[4 years later]		[4 years later]		[4 years later]		[4 years later]	
Time 1		Time 1 + 4 years		Time 1 + 8 years		Time 1 + 12 years		Time 1 + 16 years

Collect data five times, at 4-year intervals. Any differences for these individuals are definitely the result of passage of time (but might be due to events or historical changes as well as age).

CROSS-SEQUENTIAL
Total time: 16 years, plus double and triple analysis

2-year-olds	6-year-olds	10-year-olds	14-year-olds	18-year-olds
[4 years later]	[4 years later]	[4 years later]	[4 years later]	
	2-year-olds	6-year-olds	10-year-olds	14-year-olds
	[4 years later]	[4 years later]	[4 years later]	
		2-year-olds	6-year-olds	10-year-olds
		[4 years later]	[4 years later]	
Time 1	Time 1 + 4 years	Time 1 + 8 years	Time 1 + 12 years	Time 1 + 16 years

For cohort effects, compare groups on the diagonals (same age, different years).

Collect data five times, following the original group but also adding a new group each time. Analyze data three ways, first comparing groups of the same ages studied at different times. Any differences over time between groups who are the same age are probably cohort effects. Then compare the same group as they grow older. Any differences are the result of time (not only age). In the third analysis, compare differences between the same people as they grow older, *after* the cohort effects (from the first analysis) are taken into account. Any remaining differences are almost certainly the result of age.

FIGURE 1.14 Which Approach Is Best? Cross-sequential research is the most time-consuming and complex, but it yields the best information. One reason that hundreds of scientists conduct research on the same topics, replicating one another's work, is to gain some advantages of cross-sequential research without waiting for decades.

To understand responses in more depth, another method can be used—the **case study,** which is an in-depth study of one person. Case studies usually require personal interviews, background information, test or questionnaire results, and more. Although in some ways case studies seem more accurate than more superficial measures, in other ways they are not: The assumptions and interpretations of the researcher are more likely to bias the results than would a survey that has been validated on hundreds of participants.

Even if accurate, the case study applies only to one person, who may be quite unlike other people. For instance, my report on my nephew David is a case study, but David is unique: Other embryos exposed to rubella may have quite different lives than David's.

case study
An in-depth study of one person, usually requiring personal interviews to collect background information and various follow-up discussions, tests, questionnaires, and so on.

Studying Development over the Life Span

In addition to conducting observations, experiments, and surveys, developmentalists must measure how people *change or remain the same over time,* as our definition of the science of human development stresses. Remember that systems are dynamic, ever-changing. To capture that dynamism, developmental researchers use one of three basic research designs: cross-sectional, longitudinal, or cross-sequential (see Figure 1.14).

CROSS-SECTIONAL RESEARCH The quickest and least expensive way to study development over time is with **cross-sectional research,** in which groups of people of one age are compared with people of another age. For instance, in the United States in 2011, 82 percent of men aged 25 to 29 were in the labor force, but only 55 percent of those aged 60 to 64 were (U.S. Bureau of Labor Statistics, 2011). It seems that one-third of all men stop working between age 30 and 60. Younger adults might imagine them golfing in the sun, happy with their pensions and free time.

Cross-sectional design seems simple. However, it is difficult to ensure that the various groups being compared are similar in every way except age. In this example, the younger U.S. men, on average, had more education than the older ones. Thus, what seems to be the result of age might actually have to do with schooling: Perhaps education, not age, accounted for the higher employment rates of the younger adults. Or perhaps age discrimination was the problem: The older adults may have wanted jobs but been unable to get them.

LONGITUDINAL RESEARCH To help discover whether age itself rather than cohort or economic differences causes a developmental change, scientists undertake **longitudinal research.** This requires collecting data repeatedly on the same individuals as they age. Longitudinal research is particularly useful in tracing development over many years (Elder & Shanahan, 2006).

However, longitudinal research has several drawbacks. Over time, participants may withdraw, move to an unknown address, or die. These losses can skew the final results if those who disappear are unlike those who stay, as is often the case. Another problem is that participants become increasingly aware of the questions or the goals of the study—knowledge that could change them in ways unlike most other people.

Probably the biggest problem comes from the historical context. Science, popular culture, and politics alter life experiences, and those changes limit the current relevance of data collected on people born decades ago. Results from longitudinal studies of people born in 1900, as they made their way through childhood, adulthood,

Compare These with Those These diverse groups seem ideal for cross-sectional research. The younger ones *(left)* have their hands all over each other and express open-mouth joy—but with age, even smiling classmates, like these graduating high school seniors *(right),* are more restrained. However, with cross-sectional research, it is not certain whether such contrasts are the direct result of chronological age or the result of other variables—perhaps income, cohort, or culture.

✦ **ESPECIALLY FOR Future Researchers** What is the best method for collecting data? (see response, page 39) →

RESPONSE FOR Nurses (from page 34) Experiments are the only way to determine cause-and-effect relationships. If we want to be sure that a new drug or treatment is safe and effective, an experiment must be conducted to establish that the drug or treatment improves health. ●

cross-sectional research
A research design that compares groups of people who differ in age but are similar in other important characteristics.

longitudinal research
A research design in which the same individuals are followed over time and their development is repeatedly assessed.

Five Stages of Life These photos show Sarah-Maria, born in 1980 in Switzerland, in infancy (age 1), early childhood (age 3), adolescence (age 15), emerging adulthood (age 19), and adulthood (age 29). Continuity (that smile) and discontinuity (her hair) are both evident in longitudinal research.

cross-sequential research
A hybrid research design in which researchers first study several groups of people of different ages (a cross-sectional approach) and then follow those groups over the years (a longitudinal approach). (Also called *cohort-sequential research* or *time-sequential research*.)

Protecting Canadians Two ministers of the Canadian government (Environment, John Baird; Health, Tony Clement) hand baby bottles, made without BPA, to a puzzled infant. Canada has banned BPA in baby products—a move that aims to protect children and certainly pleases mothers.

and old age, may not be relevant to people born in 2000. Regarding male employment, voluntary retirement before age 60 has been less common over the past decade, not because people have changed but because the exosystem has.

Furthermore, longitudinal research requires years of data. For example, alarm about possible future harm caused by ingesting *phthalates* and *bisphenol A* (BPA) (chemicals used in manufacturing) from plastic baby bottles and infant toys leads many parents to use glass baby bottles. But perhaps the risk of occasional shattered glass causes more harm than the chemicals in plastic, or perhaps the mother's use of cosmetics, which puts phthalates in breast milk, is a much greater source of the chemicals than any bottles (Wittassek et al., 2011). Could breast-feeding harm infants? The benefits of breast milk probably outweigh the dangers, but we want answers now, not in decades.

CROSS-SEQUENTIAL RESEARCH Scientists have discovered a third strategy, combining cross-sectional and longitudinal research. This combination is called **cross-sequential research** (also referred to as *cohort-sequential* or *time-sequential research*). With this design, researchers study several groups of people of different ages (a cross-sectional approach) and follow them over the years (a longitudinal approach).

A cross-sequential design lets researchers compare findings for a group of, say, 18-year-olds with findings for the same individuals at age 8, as well as with findings for groups who were 18 a decade or two earlier and with findings for groups who are currently 8 years old (see Figure 1.14). Cross-sequential research is the most complicated, in recruitment and analysis, but it lets scientists disentangle age from history.

One well-known cross-sequential study (the *Seattle Longitudinal Study*) found that some intellectual abilities (vocabulary) increase even after age 60, whereas others (speed) start to decline at age 30 (Schaie, 2005). This confirms the multidirectional nature of development. This study also discovered that declines in math ability are more closely related to education than to age, a finding that neither cross-sectional nor longitudinal research alone could reveal.

Some more recent cross-sequential research focuses on the mental health of children. Cross-sequential studies find that many factors are influential throughout childhood but that some harm schoolchildren more than babies. Father absence or unemployment is one of them (Sanson et al., 2011).

KEY Points

- Scientists use many methods because none is perfect.
- Careful and systematic observation can discover phenomena that were unnoticed before.
- Experiments uncover what causes what; specifically, how the independent variable affects the dependent variable.
- Surveys are quick, and case studies are detailed, but both are vulnerable to bias and lies.
- To study change over time, cross-sectional, longitudinal, and cross-sequential designs are used, each with advantages and disadvantages.

RESPONSE FOR Future Researchers (from page 37) There is no best method for collecting data. The method used depends on many factors, such as the age of participants (infants can't complete questionnaires), the question being researched, and the time frame. ●

Cautions and Challenges from Science

There is no doubt that the scientific method illuminates and illustrates human development as nothing else does. Facts, hypotheses, and possibilities have all emerged that would not be known without science—and people of all ages are healthier, happier, and more capable than people of previous generations because of it.

For example, infectious diseases in children, illiteracy in adults, depression in late adulthood, and racism and sexism at every age are much less prevalent today than a century ago. Science deserves credit for all these advances. Even violent death is less likely, with scientific discoveries and education likely reasons (Pinker, 2011).

Developmental scientists have also discovered unexpected sources of harm. Video games, cigarettes, television, shift work, and asbestos are all less benign than people first thought.

Although the benefits of science are many, so are the pitfalls. We now discuss three potential hazards: misinterpreting correlation, depending too heavily on numbers, and ignoring ethics.

correlation
A number that indicates the degree of relationship between two variables, expressed in terms of the likelihood that one variable will (or will not) occur when the other variable does (or does not). A correlation indicates only that two variables are related, not that one variable causes the other to occur.

For each of these three pairs of variables, indicate whether the correlation between them is positive, negative, or nonexistent. Then try to think of a third variable that would determine the direction of the correlation. The correct answers are printed upside down below.

Correlation and Causation

Probably the most common mistake in interpreting research is the confusion of correlation with causation. A **correlation** exists between two variables if one variable is more (or less) likely to occur when the other does. A correlation is *positive* if both variables tend to increase together or decrease together, *negative* if one variable tends to increase while the other decreases, and *zero* if no connection is evident.

To illustrate: From birth to age 9, there is a positive correlation between age and height (children grow taller as they grow older), a negative correlation between age and amount of sleep (children sleep less as they grow older), and zero correlation between age and number of toes (children do not have more or fewer toes as they grow older). (Now try taking the quiz on correlation in Table 1.8.)

TABLE 1.8 Quiz on Correlation

Two Variables	Positive, Negative, or Zero Correlation?	Why? (Third Variable)
1. Ice cream sales and murder rate	_____	_____
2. Learning to read and number of baby teeth	_____	_____
3. Child gender and sex of parent	_____	_____

Expressed in numerical terms, correlations vary from +1.0 (the most positive) to −1.0 (the most negative). Correlations are almost never that extreme; a correlation of +0.3 or −0.3 is noteworthy; a correlation of +0.8 or −0.8 is astonishing.

Many correlations are unexpected. For instance, first-born children are more likely to develop asthma than are later-born children, teenage girls have higher rates of mental health problems than do teenage boys, and newborns of immigrants weigh more than do newborns of nonimmigrants. (All these correlations are discussed later.) At this point, the important caution to remember is *correlation is not causation*. Just because two variables are correlated does not mean that one causes the other—even if it seems logical that it does. It proves only that the variables are connected somehow. Many mistaken and even dangerous conclusions are drawn because people misunderstand correlation.

Quantity and Quality

A second caution concerns how heavily scientists should rely on data produced by **quantitative research** (from the word *quantity*). Quantitative research data can be categorized, ranked, or numbered and thus can be easily translated across cultures and for diverse populations. One example of quantitative research is the use of children's school achievement scores to measure the effectiveness of education.

Since quantities can be easily summarized, compared, charted, and replicated, many scientists prefer quantitative research. Statistics require numbers. Quantitative data are easier to replicate and less open to bias, although researchers who choose this method have some implicit beliefs about evidence and verification (Creswell, 2009).

When data are presented in categories and numbers, some nuances and individual distinctions are lost. Many developmental researchers thus turn to **qualitative research** (from *quality*)—asking open-ended questions, reporting answers in narrative (not numerical) form. Qualitative researchers are "interested in understanding how people interpret their experiences, how they construct their world . . ."

quantitative research
Research that provides data that can be expressed with numbers, such as ranks or scales.

qualitative research
Research that considers qualities instead of quantities. Descriptions of particular conditions and participants' expressed ideas are often part of qualitative studies.

Answers:
1. Positive; third variable: heat
2. Negative; third variable: age
3. Zero; each child must have a parent of each sex; no third variable

(Merriam, 2009, p. 5). Qualitative research reflects cultural and contextual diversity, but it is also more vulnerable to bias and harder to replicate.

Developmentalists use both quantitative and qualitative methods (Creswell, 2009). Sometimes they translate qualitative research into quantifiable data; sometimes they use qualitative studies to suggest hypotheses for quantitative research.

One caution applies especially to qualitative research: Scientists must not leap to conclusions on the basis of one small study. In the same way, personal experiences may suggest topics and hypotheses, but the particulars of our lives are no substitute for empirical research on hundreds of other people. Another caution applies to quantitative research: The accuracy of conclusions depends on exactly how the numbers are defined and collected—a truth that is obvious when you realize that a score (4.0) that yields an A in one class is easier to get than a score (3.0) that yields a B in another.

Ethics

The most important caution for all scientists, especially for those studying humans, is to uphold ethical standards in their research. Each academic discipline and professional society involved in the study of human development has a *code of ethics* (a set of moral principles) and specific practices within a scientific culture to protect the integrity of research.

Ethical standards and codes are increasingly stringent. Most educational and medical institutions have an *Institutional Review Board* (IRB), a group that permits only research that follows certain guidelines. Although IRBs often slow down scientific study, some research conducted before they were established was clearly unethical, especially when the participants were children, members of minority groups, prisoners, or animals (Blum, 2002; Washington, 2006).

PROTECTION OF RESEARCH PARTICIPANTS Researchers must ensure that participation is voluntary, confidential, and harmless. In Western nations, this entails the *informed consent* of the participants—that is, the participants must understand and agree to the research procedures and know what risks are involved.

If children are involved, consent must be obtained from the parents as well as the children, and the children must be allowed to end their participation at any time. In some other nations, ethical standards require consent of the village elders and heads of families, in addition to that of the research participants themselves (Doumbo, 2005).

Historically, shocking examples of unethical practices—from not treating syphilis to neglecting babies—include some "studies carried out by respected psychologists and published in the finest journals of the day. We've come a long way since then, baby. And babies are grateful" (Stephen L. Black, personal communication, 2005).

Protection of participants may conflict with the goals of science. The Canadian Psychological Association suggests four guiding principles as follows:

1. Respect for the dignity of persons
2. Responsible caring
3. Integrity in relationships
4. Responsibility to society

All four should be followed, if possible, but they are ranked in order of importance: Respect for individuals is most important (Canadian Psychological Association, 2000).

✦ **ESPECIALLY FOR People Who Have Applied to College or Graduate School** Is the admissions process based on quality or quantity? (see response, page 42) →

A crucial question for all scientists is whether their research is ethical and will help solve human problems.

✦ **ESPECIALLY FOR Future Researchers and Science Writers** Do any ethical guidelines apply when an author writes about the experiences of family members, friends, or research participants? (see response, page 43) →

RESPONSE FOR People Who Have Applied to College or Graduate School (from page 41) Most institutions of higher education emphasize quantitative data—the SAT, GRE, GPA, class rank, and so on. Decide for yourself whether this is fairer than a more qualitative approach. ●

IMPLICATIONS OF RESEARCH RESULTS Once a study has been completed, additional issues arise. Scientists are obligated to "promote accuracy, honesty, and truthfulness" (American Psychological Association, 2010).

Deliberate falsification is rare. When it does occur, it leads to ostracism from the scientific community, dismissal from a teaching or research position, and, sometimes, criminal prosecution. Another obvious breach of ethics is to "cook" the data, or distort one's findings, in order to make a particular conclusion seem to be the only reasonable one. This is not as rare as it should be. Tenure, promotion, and funding all encourage scientists to publish, and publishers seek remarkable findings. Researchers recognize the "file-drawer" problem—studies without significant findings that are relegated to personal files rather than publication. Awareness of this danger is leading to increased calls for replication (Carpenter, 2012).

Insidious dangers include unintentionally slanting the conclusions and withholding publication of a result, especially when there is "ferocious . . . pressure from commercial funders to ignore good scientific practice" (Bateson, 2005, p. 645). Similarly, nonprofit research groups and academic institutions pressure scientists to produce publishable results.

Ethical standards cannot be taken for granted. As stressed in the beginning of this chapter, researchers, like all other humans, have strong opinions, which they expect research to confirm. Therefore, they might try (sometimes without even realizing it) to achieve the results they want. As one team explains:

> Our job as scientists is to discover truths about the world. We generate hypotheses, collect data, and examine whether or not the data are consistent with those hypotheses . . . [but we] often lose sight of this goal, yielding to pressure to do whatever is justifiable to compile a set of studies we can publish. This is not driven by a willingness to deceive but by the self-serving interpretation of ambiguity . . .
>
> *[Simmons et al., 2011, pp. 1359, 1365]*

Obviously, collaboration, replication, and transparency are essential ethical safeguards for all scientists.

What Should We Study?

Finally, the most important ethical concern for developmentalists is to study issues that will help "all kinds of people, everywhere, of every age" live satisfying and productive lives. Consider these questions, for instance:

● Do we know enough about prenatal drug abuse to protect every fetus?

● Do we know enough about poverty to enable everyone to be healthy?

● Do we know enough about same-sex relationships, or polygamy, or single parenthood, or divorce to make sure all people develop well no matter what their family structure?

● Do we know enough about dying to enable everyone to die with dignity?

The answer to all these questions is a resounding *NO*. The reasons are many, but a major one is that these topics are controversial. Some researchers avoid them, fearing unwelcome and uninformed publicity (Kempner et al., 2005). Few funders are eager to support scientific studies of drug abuse, poverty, nonstandard families, or death, partly because people have strong opinions on these issues that may conflict with scientific findings and conclusions. Religion, politics, and ethics shape scientific research, sometimes stopping investigation before it begins. Yet developmentalists must study whatever benefits the human family.

The next cohort of developmental scientists will build on what is known, mindful of what needs to be explored. Remember that the goal is to help all 7 billion people on Earth fulfill their potential. Much more needs to be learned. The next 14 chapters are only a beginning.

> ## KEY points
>
> - Correlation is not causation. Two variables may be related, not because one causes the other but because a third variable affects both.
> - Quantitative research is easier to analyze and compare, but qualitative study captures more nuances.
> - Research ethics require that participants be respected; they must give informed consent and confidentiality must be assured.
> - Scientists need to study and report data on many issues that are crucial for the optimal development of all people.

RESPONSE FOR Future Researchers and Science Writers (from page 41) Yes. Anyone you write about must give consent and be fully informed about your intentions. They can be identified by name only if they give permission. For example, family members gave permission before anecdotes about them were included in this text. My nephew David read the first draft of his story (see pages 20–21) and is proud to have his experiences used to teach others. ●

SUMMARY

Understanding How and Why

1. The study of human development is a science that seeks to understand how people change or remain the same over time. A scientist begins with questions and hypotheses, then gathers empirical data, and finally draws conclusions that are shared (usually published) with other scientists, who replicate the study to confirm, modify, or refute the conclusions.

2. Nature and nurture always interact. Each human characteristic is affected by both genes (nature) and environment (nurture) and by their interaction. Epigenetically, genes are affected by the environment.

The Life-Span Perspective

3. Development is multidirectional, multicontextual, and multicultural. That means that gains and losses are apparent throughout life, that an ecological approach that considers the immediate contexts (family, school) as well as broader contexts (historical conditions, socioeconomic status) is essential, and that each culture embraces values and assumptions about human life.

4. Culture, ethnicity, and race are social constructions, concepts created by society. Culture includes beliefs about life and patterns of behavior; ethnicity refers to ancestral heritage. The social construction of "race" has been misused, so some social scientists want to abandon it, while others want to use it to combat racism.

5. Development needs to be understood using the methods and viewpoints of many disciplines. For example, to understand the cause of psychological depression, at least a dozen factors from a dozen disciplines are helpful.

6. Development is plastic, which means that, although inborn traits and childhood experiences affect later development, patterns and possibilities can change lifelong.

Theories of Human Development

7. Psychoanalytic theory, as developed by Freud, emphasizes that human actions and thoughts originate from unconscious impulses and childhood conflicts. Erikson went beyond Freud: He described eight stages of psychosocial development, each reflecting the age, culture, and context of the individual.

8. Behaviorism, or learning theory, stresses the impact of the environment on the individual. People of all ages develop according to the associations and reinforcements that accompany their actions.

9. Cognitive theory emphasizes that thought processes affect all human behaviors and assumptions. Piaget described how these change with age; information-processing theory stresses the step-by-step advances in cognition.

10. Humanism contends that all humans have basic needs that must be met for people to reach their full potential, becoming self-actualized.

11. Evolutionary theory traces the inborn impulses that arise from past millennia of human life and that enable humans to survive and reproduce successfully. This perspective explains some irrational fears as well as some noble human traits.

Using the Scientific Method

12. Several specific research designs help scientists understand human development. Scientific observation, the experiment, and the survey each provide insights and discoveries that were not apparent before the research. Each also has liabilities; before a conclusion is accepted by the scientific community, several methods are typically used.

13. An additional challenge for developmentalists is to study change over time. Two traditional research designs are often used:

cross-sectional research (comparing people of different ages) and longitudinal research (studying the same people over time). A third method, cross-sequential research (combining the two other methods) is more complicated but also provides more reliable conclusions.

Cautions and Challenges from Science

14. A correlation shows that two variables are related. However, it does not prove that one variable *causes* the other: The relationship of variables may be opposite to the one expected, or both may be the result of a third variable.

15. Quantitative research provides numerical data; thus, it is often used to compare people in different contexts and cultures. By contrast, qualitative research captures the nuance of individual lives. Both approaches are needed.

16. Ethical behavior is crucial in all the sciences. Not only must participants be protected and data be kept confidential (primary concerns of IRBs), but results must be fairly reported, honestly interpreted, and replicated. Scientists must be mindful of the implications of their research.

17. Appropriate application of scientific research depends partly on the training and integrity of the scientists. The most important ethical question is whether scientists are designing, conducting, analyzing, publishing, and applying the research that is most critically needed to help the entire human family develop well.

KEY TERMS

behaviorism (p. 26)
case study (p. 36)
classical conditioning (p. 27)
cognitive theory (p. 29)
cohort (p. 10)
conditioning (p. 26)
correlation (p. 40)
critical period (p. 8)
cross-sectional research (p. 37)
cross-sequential research (p. 38)
culture (p. 12)
dependent variable (p. 34)

developmental theory (p. 23)
difference-equals-deficit error (p. 14)
differential sensitivity (p. 21)
dynamic-systems approach (p. 20)
ecological-systems approach (p. 9)
empirical evidence (p. 4)
epigenetic (p. 17)
ethnic group (p. 15)
experiment (p. 33)
humanism (p. 31)

hypothesis (p. 4)
independent variable (p. 34)
life-span perspective (p. 7)
longitudinal research (p. 37)
nature (p. 5)
nurture (p. 5)
operant conditioning (p. 27)
psychoanalytic theory (p. 23)
qualitative research (p. 40)
quantitative research (p. 40)
race (p. 16)
reinforcement (p. 28)
replication (p. 5)

science of human development (p. 4)
scientific method (p. 4)
scientific observation (p. 33)
sensitive period (p. 8)
social construction (p. 12)
social learning theory (p. 28)
socioeconomic status (SES) (p. 11)
sudden infant death syndrome (SIDS) (p. 6)
survey (p. 34)

WHAT HAVE YOU LEARNED?

1. What are the five steps of the scientific method?

2. What basic question is at the heart of the nature–nurture controversy?

3. Give an example of *discontinuity* and of *continuity* as it relates to your development.

4. What does it mean to say that development is multicontextual?

5. How does the exosystem affect your life today?

6. What are some cohort differences between you and your parents?

7. What factors comprise a person's socioeconomic status?

8. Give an example of a social construction. Why is it a construction, not a fact?

9. Explain the concept of *guided participation,* as described by Vygotsky.

10. What is the difference between race and ethnicity?

11. How do both specialization and multidisciplinary research add to our understanding of a topic?

12. What is the difference between "genetics" and "epigenetics"?

13. In what two ways is human development plastic?

14. What is implied about human development when it is described as dynamic?

15. Give an example that explains the concept of "differential sensitivity."

16. What main idea underlies Freud's psychoanalytic theory?

17. What is the main difference between Erikson's theory of human development and Freud's?

18. How can behaviorism be seen as a reaction to psychoanalytic theory?

19. How do classical and operant conditioning differ?

20. Why is social learning also called modeling?

21. What is the basic idea of cognitive theory?

22. According to Maslow, what is the five-step hierarchy of people's basic needs and drives?

23. How does the theory of evolution help explain human development?

24. Explain the following concept: "Observation provides issues to explore, not proof."

25. Why do experimenters use a control (or comparison) group as well as an experimental group?

26. What are the strengths and weaknesses of the survey method?

27. Why would a scientist conduct a cross-sectional study?

28. What are some advantages and disadvantages of longitudinal research?

29. Explain the following statement: Cross-sequential research combines cross-sectional and longitudinal research.

30. Why does correlation not prove causation?

31. Why do some researchers prefer quantitative research while others prefer qualitative research?

32. Why is it important for academic disciplines and professional societies to follow codes of ethics?

33. What is one additional question about development that should be answered?

APPLICATIONS

1. It is said that culture is pervasive but that people are unaware of it. List 30 things you did today that you might have done differently in another culture.

2. How would your life be different if your parents were much higher or lower in SES than they are? What if you had been born in another cohort?

3. Design an experiment to answer a question you have about human development. Specify the question and the hypothesis and then describe the experiment, including the sample size and the variables. (Look first at Appendix B.)

>>ONLINE CONNECTIONS

To accompany your textbook, you have access to a number of online resources, including quizzes for every chapter of the book, flashcards (in English and Spanish), critical thinking questions, and case studies. For access to any of these links, go to www.worthpublishers.com/bergerinvitation2e. In addition to these free resources, you'll also find links to podcasts, video clips, diagnostic quizzing with personalized study advice, and an ebook. Some of the videos and activities available online include:

■ *Ethics in Human Research: Violating One's Privacy?* This video introduces the controversies around a research project in Iceland that collects genetic and health information about private citizens.

■ *What's Wrong with This Study?* This activity allows you to review some of the pitfalls in various research designs.

CHAPTER OUTLINE

FROM CONCEPTION
to Birth

WHAT WILL YOU KNOW?

- How do genes affect each individual?
- What birth practices are best for father, mother, and newborn?
- How can serious birth disorders be avoided?
- Is alcoholism genetic or cultural?

"She needs a special school. She cannot come back next year," Elissa's middle school principal told us.

Martin and I were dumbfounded. Could the principal be right that our wonderful daughter was learning-disabled, specifically, "severely spatially disorganized"? We knew she often misplaced homework and got lost—but we thought that insignificant compared to her intelligence and social skills.

What could be wrong? It wasn't something I did during pregnancy: She was my third baby, and by then I knew what to avoid. Perhaps it was genetic. Both Martin and I were naturally disorganized, but we had learned to compensate: He did not hesitate to ask strangers for directions; I kept my students' papers at my office, in clearly marked folders. Despite our genes, we were both successful; we thought Elissa was fine.

I also knew that nurture works with nature. Accordingly, we began to focus on a learning problem that we had not recognized (perhaps because we had the same disabilities?). For instance, we taught Elissa to list her assignments, check them off when done, put them carefully in her backpack. Fearful she might have to leave her friends, Elissa began to study diligently. Success! She aced her final exams, and the principal allowed her back. She became a master organizer as well as a brilliant professional. ●

- -

THIS CHAPTER BEGINS WITH GENES, continues through prenatal development, and ends with nurture. The goal here is to help you understand the dynamic interaction among these long before you have a seventh-grade daughter.

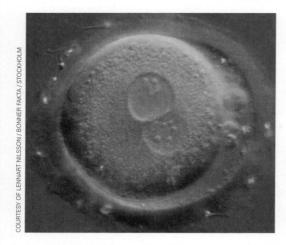

The Moment of Conception This ovum is about to become a zygote. It has been penetrated by a single sperm, whose nucleus now lies next to the nucleus of the ovum. Soon, the two nuclei will fuse, bringing together about 20,000 genes to guide development.

zygote
The single cell that is formed from the fusing of two gametes, a sperm and an ovum.

DNA (deoxyribonucleic acid)
The molecule that contains the chemical instructions for cells to manufacture various proteins.

chromosome
One of the 46 molecules of DNA (in 23 pairs) that each cell of the human body contains and that, together, contain all the genes. Other species have more or fewer chromosomes.

gene
A small section of a chromosome; the basic unit for the transmission of heredity. A gene consists of a string of chemicals that provide instructions for the cell to manufacture certain proteins.

gamete
A reproductive cell; that is, a sperm or an ovum that can produce a new individual if it combines with a gamete from the other sex to form a zygote.

The Beginning of Life

Every person starts life as a single cell, called a **zygote.** Each zygote is distinct from any other human cell ever created, yet that cell contains genes that have been passed down for thousands of years. The first hours of development are a compelling example of both the universal and the unique characteristics of each human.

Genes and Chromosomes

First, the universal. All living things are composed of cells that promote growth and sustain life according to instructions in their molecules of **DNA (deoxyribonucleic acid)** (see Figure 2.1). Each molecule of DNA is called a **chromosome.** Chromosomes contain units of instructions called **genes,** with each gene located on a particular chromosome.

Additional DNA and RNA (another molecule) surround each gene. In a process called *methylation,* this material enhances, transcribes, connects, empowers, silences, and alters genes (Shapiro, 2009). This nongenetic material used to be called *junk*—but no longer. Thousands of scientists now seek to discover exactly what these molecules do (Wright & Bruford, 2011). Methylation continues throughout life, and it can alter a gene's expression even after a person is born. This is part of epigenetics, explained in Chapter 1.

With one important exception, every cell of each human being normally has copies of that person's 46 chromosomes, arranged in 23 pairs. That one exception is the reproductive cell, called a **gamete.** Each gamete—*sperm* in a man and *ovum* in a woman—has only 23 chromosomes, one from each of a person's 23 pairs of chromosomes.

Generally, at conception the genes on each chromosome of the sperm match with the genes on the same chromosome of the ovum. For instance, the eye-color gene from the father on chromosome 15 matches with an eye-color gene from the mother on the zygote's other chromosome 15.

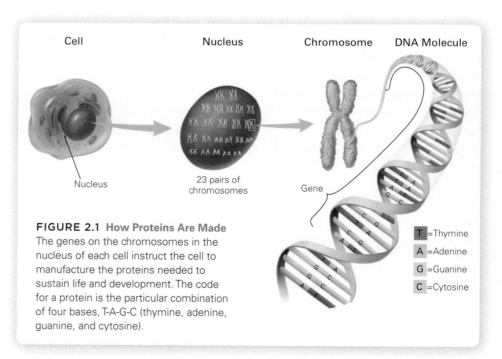

FIGURE 2.1 How Proteins Are Made
The genes on the chromosomes in the nucleus of each cell instruct the cell to manufacture the proteins needed to sustain life and development. The code for a protein is the particular combination of four bases, T-A-G-C (thymine, adenine, guanine, and cytosine).

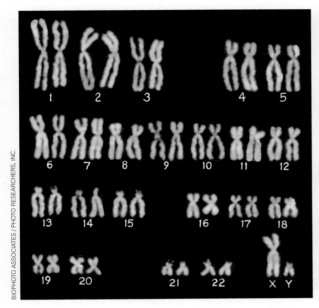
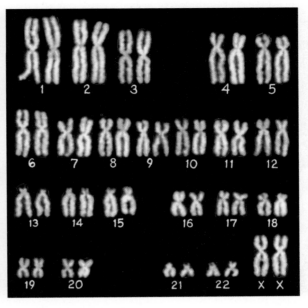

BIOPHOTO ASSOCIATES / PHOTO RESEARCHERS, INC.

Uncertain Sex Every now and then, a baby is born with "ambiguous genitals," meaning that the child's sex is not abundantly clear. When this happens, a quick analysis of the chromosomes is needed, to make sure there are exactly 46 and to see whether the 23rd pair is XY or XX. The karyotypes shown here indicate a normal baby boy *(left)* and girl *(right)*.

Variations Among People

Now, the unique. Since each gamete has only one of each person's pair of chromosomes, each man or woman can produce 2^{23} different gametes—more than 8 million versions of their chromosomes (actually 8,388,608). When a sperm and an ovum combine, they create a new cell in which one of those 8 million possible gametes from the father interacts with one of the 8 million possible gametes from the mother. Your parents could have given you an astronomical number of siblings, each unique.

More variations occur because the DNA code contains 3 billion pairs of chemicals organized in triplets (sets of three pairs), each of which specifies production of one of 20 possible amino acids. Those amino acids combine to produce proteins, and those proteins combine to produce a person. Small variations or repetitions (called *copy number* variations) in the base pairs or triplets could make a notable difference in the proteins and thus, eventually, in the person.

And that is what happens. Some triplets on some genes have transpositions, deletions, or repetitions not found in other versions of the same gene. Each of these variations is called an **allele** of that gene. Genes that have various alleles are called *polymorphic* (literally, "many forms"), and each variation is a *single-nucleotide polymorphism* (abbreviated SNP).

Most alleles cause only minor differences (such as the shape of an eyebrow); some seem to have no effect; some are notable, even devastating. Alleles make one person unlike any other. One difference in a triplet could make a person tall, or artistically talented, or red-haired (see Figure 2.2).

Every zygote inherits many alleles from its sperm or ovum, which means that many gene pairs do not exactly match in every triplet. In addition, mutations occur as the gametes form. That makes each person a little bit unusual. As one expert said, "What's cool is that we are a mosaic of pieces of genomes. None of us is truly normal" (Eichler, quoted in Cohen, 2007, p. 1315).

● **UNDERSTANDING THE NUMBERS**
With only two possibilities at each chromosome site, and with the chromosomes of every full sibling coming directly from the same two parents, it seems as if all brothers and sisters should be quite similar genetically. Why aren't they?

Answer They share only half their genes, so the possible combinations are in the millions. Remember how rapidly the power of 2 builds ($2^4 = 16, \ldots,$ $2^{10} = 1,024, \ldots, 2^{20} = 1,098,576, \ldots,$ and $2^{23} = 8,388,608$). Those numbers are for gametes from only one parent. With both parents contributing genes, the possibilities seem astronomical.

allele
Any of the possible forms in which a gene for a particular trait can occur.

THIRD FROM TOP: GETTY IMAGES / HEMERA /THINKSTOCK; OTHERS: PHOTODISC

Phenotype	Allele 1	Allele 2	Allele 3
 Long	×	—	—
 Short	—	—	—
 Curly	×	—	×
 Wire	—	×	—

FIGURE 2.2 One Species, A Billion Variations Dogs immediately recognize other dogs, even from a distance, despite dramatic differences in size, shape, coloring (of tongues and eyes as well as coats), and, as shown here, in hair. Minor code variations become marked fur differences—long or short, curly or straight, wiry or limp.

genotype
An organism's entire genetic inheritance, or genetic potential.

phenotype
The observable characteristics of a person, including appearance, personality, intelligence, and all other traits.

genome
The full set of genes that are the instructions to make an individual member of a certain species.

For each individual, the collection of his or her genes is called the **genotype.** It was once thought that the genotype led directly to facial characteristics, body formation, intelligence, personality, and so on, but this is much too simplistic.

Because of numerous epigenetic effects, as well as the interactions among the genes themselves, the **phenotype,** which is a person's actual appearance and behavior, reflects much more than the genotype. The genotype is the beginning of diversity; the phenotype is the actual manifestation of it.

Genetic diversity not only distinguishes each person (you can immediately spot a close friend in a crowd) but also allows adaptation. We are the only species that thrives on every continent, from the poles to the equator. One of the best parts of our adaptation is that we teach each other. If you or I suddenly found ourselves in a climate we had never experienced, we would quickly learn how to dress, where to sleep, and what to eat by observing the other people who had already adapted to that place.

Thanks to our genetic diversity, even devastating diseases have not killed us all. For instance, a few people have alleles that defend them from HIV, the virus that causes AIDS (Aouizerat et al., 2011). Similarly, genotype differences allowed some of our ancestors to survive tuberculosis, malaria, the Black Death, and other scourges.

More on Shared and Divergent Genes

The entire packet of instructions that make a living organism is called the **genome.** There is a genome for every species, from *Homo sapiens* to the smallest insect, even for every kind of plant. A worldwide effort to map all the human genes led to the *Human Genome Project,* which was virtually completed in 2003 and which continues to reveal surprises today.

The first surprise was that any two men or women, of whatever ethnicity, share 99.5 percent of their genetic codes. Similarly, codes for humans and chimpanzees are 98 percent the same (although chimp genes are on 48, not 46, chromosomes). The genomes for humans and every other mammal are at least 90 percent the same. All these shared genes allow scientists to learn about human genetics from other creatures, especially mice, by transposing, deactivating, enhancing, and duplicating their genes.

The more scientists experiment, the more they are amazed. Until 2001, scientists thought humans had about 100,000 genes, but that turned out to be a gross overestimate. The Human Genome Project found only about 20,000 to 23,000 genes. Genomes from other creatures led to more surprises: Dogs and mice have more genes than humans, and mice have several times more. The precise count is still unknown, partly because of another surprise: It is not always clear where one gene ends and another begins (Pennisi, 2007).

A more recent international project, called the HapMap, aims to spot all the variations in the human genome. HapMap has found 11 million differences among the 3 billion possible chemical pairs in humans (Hinds et al., 2005). Some genes are exactly identical for every person, but some have dozens of alleles—though this is rare. Humans are all alike, all one species, yet because of those 11 million differences, each of us is unique.

Applications of HapMap research are problematic: Much remains to be understood about the connection between alleles in the genotype and actual characteristics of the phenotype. The sheer number of variations is daunting. Scientists know that "genomics is not destiny. Indeed, if genomic sequence 'determines' anything behaviorally, it determines diversity" (Landis & Insel, 2008, p. 821).

THE 23RD PAIR The difference between one person and another—and between one species and another—begins with the genes, but it is much more epigenetic than genetic. The material surrounding a gene can halt, or expand, the instructions from that gene. Hormones, or proteins, or other factors that shape the phenotype begin with a gene but do not end there. Consider sex differences: They originate from one gene (SRY) on one chromosome, as the following explains.

In 22 of the 23 pairs of human chromosomes that each person inherits, the chromosomes of each pair are closely matched. They are called *autosomes,* and they could be inherited by a male or female.

The 23rd pair of chromosomes is a special case. In females, it is composed of two large X-shaped chromosomes. Accordingly, it is designated **XX.** In males, the 23rd pair has one large X-shaped chromosome with many genes and one quite small chromosome, with only a few genes, which is Y-shaped. That 23rd pair is called **XY.**

Because a female's 23rd pair is XX, every ovum that her body creates contains either one X or the other—but always an X. Because a male's 23rd pair is XY, when his body splits his 46 chromosomes to make gametes, half of his sperm carry an X chromosome and half carry a Y.

The Y chromosome has the SRY gene that directs the developing fetus to make male organs. Thus, the sex of the developing organism depends on which sperm penetrates the ovum—either an X sperm, which creates a girl (XX), or a Y sperm, which creates a boy (XY) (see Figure 2.3).

That SRY gene not only directs the embryo to grow a penis, it also directs hormone production that affects the brain, skeleton, body fat, muscles, and much else from the moment of conception to the last breath in old age. At conception, there are about 120 males for every 100 females, perhaps because Y sperm swim faster and reach the ovum first (remember, they carry fewer genes, so they are lighter than the X sperm).

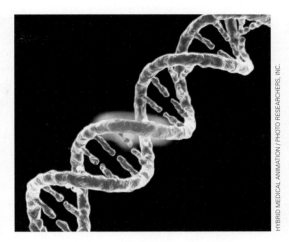

Twelve of 3 Billion Pairs This is a computer illustration of a small segment of one gene, with several triplets. Even a small difference in one gene, such as a few extra triplets, can cause major changes in a person's phenotype.

XX
A 23rd chromosome pair that consists of two X-shaped chromosomes, one each from the mother and the father. XX zygotes become females.

XY
A 23rd chromosome pair that consists of an X-shaped chromosome from the mother and a Y-shaped chromosome from the father. XY zygotes become males.

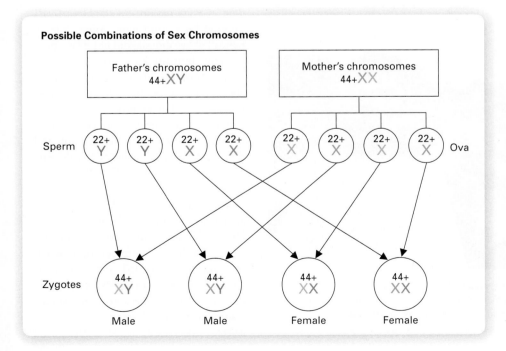

FIGURE 2.3 Determining a Zygote's Sex Any given couple can produce four possible combinations of sex chromosomes; two lead to female children and two to male. In terms of the future person's sex, it does not matter which of the mother's Xs the zygote inherited. All that matters is whether the father's Y sperm or X sperm fertilized the ovum. However, for X-linked conditions it matters a great deal because typically one, but not both, of the mother's Xs carries the trait.

However, male embryos are more vulnerable than female ones (because of fewer genes, again?), so they are less likely to survive prenatally: At birth the boy/girl ratio is about 105:100. When conditions are stressful (as in famine), male embryos suffer more: In many African nations (including South Africa, the Congo, Ghana, Nigeria, Kenya, and Ethiopia), the ratio at birth is 102 males per 100 females. In several Asian nations, the current ratio is more than 110 boys to 100 girls—as soon explained.

But first note that all the male–female differences—from the toy trucks given to 1-day-old boys to the survival rates of older women—begin with that one gene and influence every part of the body and every aspect of the culture. In turn, the culture affects the expression of that gene.

Obviously, the impact of that SRY gene is much more than the quantitative fact that it is only one of about 20,000 genes, or only .00005 of the genotype. The SRY gene, via epigenetic factors, affects thousands of other genetic and environmental influences that make for more sex differences than might be expected from .00005 of the genome. Likewise, many other genes are similarly enhanced, promoted, and guided by other genetic material and myriad cultural forces.

✦ **ESPECIALLY FOR Biologists** Many people believe that the differences between the sexes are primarily sociocultural, not biological. Is there any prenatal support for that view? (see response, page 57) ➔

OPPOSING PERSPECTIVES

Choosing a Boy

Historically, most couples believed that only chance, or God, or fate determined whether a newborn was male or female. If nurture had any role, people thought it occurred via the mother, particularly her diet, prayers, or sleeping position. Although boys were often preferred, most parents accepted whatever came.

For many couples, "whatever came" was more than accepted: Healthy newborns were welcomed. I have four daughters and no sons. I am convinced this is for the best,

and I bristle when anyone implies otherwise. Among my reasons: My children did not suffer from boy–girl rivalry; same-sex siblings more easily share the same room, the same chores, and the same clothes; my husband and I are better parents for girls than boys. (I probably would have created a different list of reasons if I'd had a boy.)

But some human history is appalling: Female infanticide was once accepted in almost every culture. In fact, it became so common in the Arab world that Muhammad explicitly forbade it. Wife blaming was also evident in every nation and era: Henry VIII ordered his second wife, Anne Boleyn, beheaded because she did not bear a boy.

Now humans know better than to blame mothers. But knowing more about conception has allowed couples to select sex before birth by (1) inactivating X or Y sperm before conception, (2) undergoing in vitro fertilization and then inserting only male or female embryos, or (3) aborting XX or XY fetuses. Should that be legal?

In China, a one-child policy initiated in 1979 cut the birth rate in half and lifted millions of families out of poverty. But it also led to more abortions when amniocentesis revealed a female fetus and to more newborn girls being available for adoption because their parents wanted to try for a boy.

AP PHOTO / MANISH SWARUP

My Strength, My Daughter That's the slogan these girls in New Delhi are shouting at a demonstration against abortion of female fetuses in India. The current sex ratio of children in India suggests that this campaign has not convinced every couple.

The Chinese have discovered problems with having too many boys. One is that far more young men than young women die in China, perhaps because they cannot find wives (Kruger & Polanski, 2011).

Not only in China but in every nation, unmarried young men take foolish risks to show their bravery, part of the competition for women. Compared with married men, unmarried men also have higher rates of depression and drug addiction. Other problems with male-heavy societies include more learning disabilities, schizophrenia, violence, wars, and heart attacks but fewer nurses, day-care centers, or close family bonds.

The Chinese are now allowed to have two children, but prenatal sex selection still occurs (Greenhalgh, 2008). The most recent Chinese census reports 118 male newborns for every 100 girls (Hvistendahl, 2011). Many other Asian nations also have more young boys than girls.

National governments recognize problems with an imbalance of males and females. Consequently, in many nations, including China and India, prenatal sex determination is illegal. That seems logical, but now consider the opposite view.

Most Americans approve of personal choice, including choice in sexual matters. For example, if a couple wants four or more children even though that means a greater financial burden on other Americans, they are not stopped—no one-child or two-child policy interferes.

Similarly, most U.S. fertility doctors believe that sex selection is a reproductive right (Puri & Nachtigall, 2010). As one fertility doctor said, "Reproductive choice, as far as I'm concerned, is a very personal issue. If it's not going to hurt anyone, we go ahead and give them what they want" (Steinberg, quoted in Grady, 2007).

In the United States, there is no evidence that this opinion has affected many births. Although the birth rate has decreased by 45 percent since 1960, the sex ratio remains 105 boys for every 100 girls.

Freedom of individual choice—not just in the sex of a baby but also in sexual activity, sexual partner, contraception, prenatal care, and abortion—often clashes with social values, expressed by governments, religious groups, and many individuals. Balancing personal freedom and community needs has never been easy. As you see, there are two opposing perspectives and each seems valid.

TWINS There is one major exception to genetic diversity. Although every zygote is genetically unique, not every newborn is.

About once in every 250 human conceptions, the zygote not only duplicates but splits apart completely, creating two, or four, or even eight separate zygotes, each genetically identical to that first single cell. If each separate cell implants and grows, multiple births occur. One separation results in **monozygotic twins,** also called *identical twins,* from one *(mono)* zygote. Two or three separations create monozygotic quadruplets or octuplets. (An incomplete split creates *conjoined twins,* formerly called Siamese twins.)

monozygotic twins
Twins who originate from one zygote that splits apart very early in development. (Also called *identical twins.*)

Same Birthday, Same (or Different?) Genes Twins who are of different sexes are dizygotic, sharing only half of their genes. Many same-sex twins are dizygotic as well. One of these twin pairs is dizygotic; the other is monozygotic.

OBSERVATION QUIZ
Can you tell which pair is monozygotic?
(see answer, page 57) →

dizygotic twins
Twins who are formed when two separate ova are fertilized by two separate sperm at roughly the same time. (Also called *fraternal twins.*)

additive gene
A gene that adds something to some aspect of the phenotype. Its contribution depends on additions from the other genes, which may come from either the same or the other parent.

dominant–recessive pattern
The interaction of a pair of alleles in such a way that the phenotype reveals the influence of one allele (the dominant gene) more than that of the other (the recessive gene).

carrier
A person whose genotype includes a gene that is not expressed in the phenotype. Such an unexpressed gene occurs in half the carrier's gametes and thus is passed on to half the carrier's children, who will most likely be carriers, too. Generally, the characteristic appears in the phenotype only when such a gene is inherited from both parents.

Hidden Husband Shyness is inherited, but this mother seems not to have the gene. Her husband is probably the shy one—unless nurture has taught the daughter to be shy and the mother to be outgoing.

Because monozygotic multiples originate from the same zygote, they have the same genotype, with identical genetic instructions for physical appearance, psychological traits, vulnerability to diseases, and everything else. However, because nurture always affects nature, even before birth, identical twins do not have exactly the same phenotype.

Usually, monozygotic twins develop their own identities while enjoying twinship. They might both have inherited athletic ability, for instance, but one chooses basketball and the other, soccer. One monozygotic twin writes:

> Twins put into high relief *the* central challenge for all of us: self-definition. How do we each plant our stake in the ground, decide how sensitive, callous, ambitious, cautious, or conciliatory we want to be every day? . . . Twins come with a built-in constant comparison, but defining oneself against one's twin is just an amped-up version of every person's life-long challenge: to individuate, to create a distinctive persona in the world.
>
> *[Pogrebin, 2010, p. 9]*

Dizygotic twins, also called *fraternal twins,* occur about twice as often as monozygotic twins. They began life as two zygotes created by two ova fertilized by two sperm. (Usually, the ovaries release only one ovum per month, but sometimes two or more ova are released.) Dizygotic twins, like any other siblings, have half their genes in common. Their phenotypes may differ in obvious ways (about half are male–female pairs) or they can look quite similar, again like other siblings.

The tendency to ovulate more than one ovum is influenced by genes, so if a woman has one set of twins, she is more likely to have another set (Painter et al., 2010). Her daughters also have a 50/50 chance of inheriting her twin-producing X. A son from that family is not particularly likely to have twins because he is not the one who ovulates, but his daughter is, because she has an X from his mother, and half the time it happens to be the multiple-ovulation X (see Infographic 2 on page 55).

Genetic Interactions

No gene functions alone. Thus, almost every trait is *polygenic* (affected by many genes) and *multifactorial* (influenced by many factors). Almost daily, researchers describe new complexities in polygenic and multifactorial interaction. It is apparent that "phenotypic variation . . . results from multiple interactions among numerous genetic and environmental factors" (Nadeau & Dudley, 2011, p. 1015). Here we describe a few of the complexities that occur at conception.

Some genes are **additive genes.** Their effects *add up* to make the phenotype. When genes interact additively, the phenotype reflects all the genes that are involved. Height, hair curliness, and skin color, for instance, are influenced by additive genes. Indeed, height is probably influenced by 180 genes, each contributing a very small amount (Enserink, 2011).

Less common are *nonadditive* genes, which do not contribute equal shares. In one nonadditive form of heredity, alleles interact in a **dominant–recessive pattern,** in which one allele, the *dominant gene,* is far more influential than the other, the *recessive gene.* When someone inherits a recessive gene that is not expressed in the phenotype, that person is said to be a **carrier** of that gene: The recessive gene is *carried* on the genotype.

Most recessive genes are harmless. For example, blue eyes are determined by a recessive allele and brown eyes by a dominant one, which means that a child conceived by a blue-eyed person and a brown-eyed person will usually have brown eyes. "Usually" is accurate, because sometimes a brown-eyed person is a carrier of the blue-eye gene. In that case, in a blue-eye/brown-eye

MARCO C. PEREIRA / SARA WONG / 4SEE / REDUX

One Baby or More

Humans usually have one baby at a time, but sometimes (especially in Africa) twins are born. Most often they are from two ova fertilized by two sperm (right), resulting in dizygotic twins. Sometimes, however, one zygote splits in two (left), resulting in monozygotic twins; if each of these zygotes splits again, the result is monozygotic quadruplets.

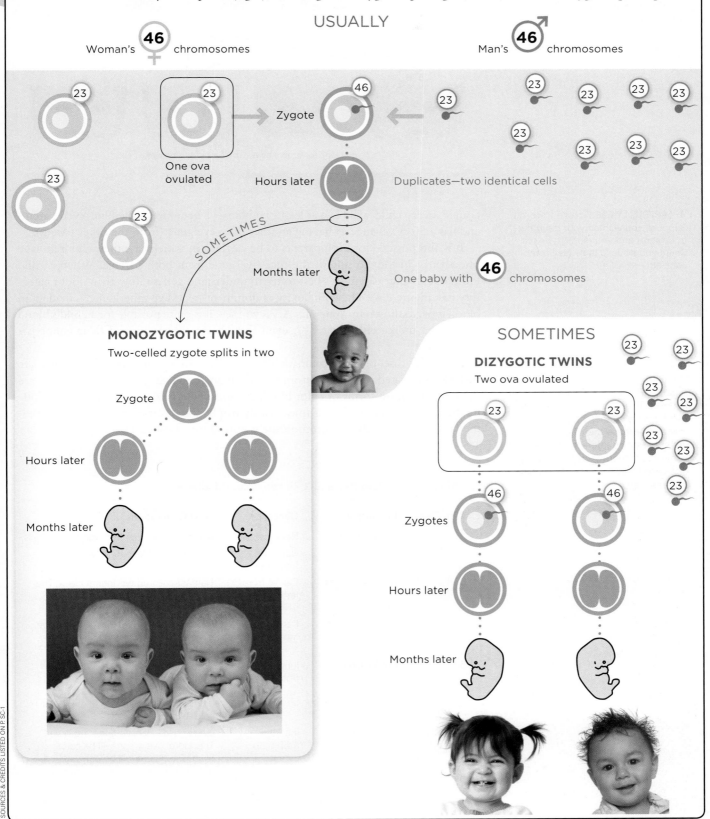

USUALLY

Woman's **46** chromosomes   Man's **46** chromosomes

One ova ovulated

Zygote

Hours later — Duplicates—two identical cells

SOMETIMES

Months later — One baby with **46** chromosomes

MONOZYGOTIC TWINS
Two-celled zygote splits in two

Zygote

Hours later

Months later

SOMETIMES

DIZYGOTIC TWINS
Two ova ovulated

Zygotes

Hours later

Months later

SOURCES & CREDITS LISTED ON P. SC-1

FIGURE 2.4 Changeling? Not a changeling. If two brown-eyed parents both carry the blue-eye gene, they have one chance in four of having a blue-eyed child. Other recessive genes include those for red hair, Rh-negative blood, and many genetic diseases.

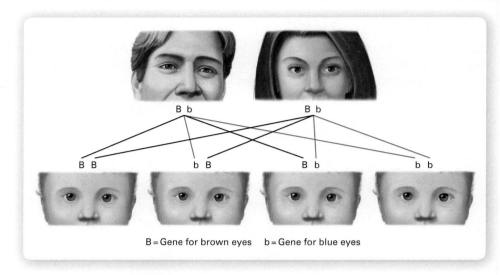

B = Gene for brown eyes   b = Gene for blue eyes

✦ **ESPECIALLY FOR Future Parents**
Suppose you wanted your daughters to be short and your sons to be tall. Could you achieve that? (see response, page 58) →

X-linked
A gene carried on the X chromosome. If a male inherits an X-linked recessive trait from his mother, he expresses that trait because the Y from his father has no counteracting gene. Females are more likely to be carriers of X-linked traits but are less likely to express them.

couple, every child will have at least one blue-eye gene (from the blue-eyed parent) and has a 50/50 chance of having another blue-eye gene (from the other parent).

It is also possible for both parents to be carriers, in which case their children have one chance in four to inherit the recessive gene from both parents. When a child looks like neither parent, it's best to try to understand genes rather than doubt paternity (see Figure 2.4). The complexity of dominant–recessive inheritance is evident in blood type, as shown in Appendix A. As you see, it is quite possible for a child's blood type to be unlike either parent's, even though the interactions of their genotypes produced it.

A special case of the dominant–recessive pattern occurs with genes that are **X-linked** (located on the X chromosome). If an X-linked gene is recessive—as are the genes for most forms of color blindness, many allergies, several diseases (including hemophilia and Duchenne muscular dystrophy), and some learning disabilities—the fact that it is on the X chromosome is critical (see Table 2.1).

TABLE 2.1 The 23rd Pair and X-Linked Color Blindness

23rd Pair	Phenotype	Genotype	Next Generation
1. XX	Normal woman	Not a carrier	No color blindness from mother
2. XY	Normal man	Normal X from mother	No color blindness from father
3. XX	Normal woman	Carrier from father	Half her children will inherit her X. The girls with her X will be carriers; the boys with her X will be color-blind.
4. XX	Normal woman	Carrier from mother	Half her children will inherit her X. The girls with her X will be carriers; the boys with her X will be color-blind.
5. XY	Color-blind man	Inherited from mother	All his daughters will have his X. None of his sons will have his X. All his children will have normal vision, unless their mother also had an X for color blindness.
6. XX	Color-blind woman (rare)	Inherited from both parents	Every child will have one X from her. Therefore, every son will be color-blind. Daughters will be only carriers, unless they also inherit an X from the father, as their mother did.

Since the Y chromosome is much smaller than the X, an X-linked recessive gene almost never has a dominant counterpart on the Y. Therefore, recessive traits carried on the X affect the phenotypes of sons more often than those of daughters because the daughters are protected by their other X chromosome, which usually will have the dominant gene. This explains why males with an X-linked disorder inherited it from their mothers, not their fathers. Because of their mothers, 20 times more boys than girls are color-blind (McIntyre, 2002).

Thousands of disabilities begin with genes and chromosomes, as described at the end of this chapter. First, however, we consider the more usual case: the development of a healthy embryo, fetus, and baby.

RESPONSE FOR Biologists (from page 52) Only one of the 46 human chromosomes determines sex, and the genitals develop last in the prenatal sequence. Sex differences are apparent before birth, but they are relatively minor. ●

KEY points

- Each person's 46 chromosomes and 20,000 or so genes are inherited from their parents; diversity and commonality are normal parts of the process.
- The 23rd pair of chromosomes produces a male (XY) or female (XX), with the father's gamete the determining factor.
- Monozygotic twins are genetically identical; dizygotic twins share half of their genes, like other siblings.
- Genes interact with each other in an additive or dominant–recessive manner, always affected by epigenetic factors.

ANSWER TO **OBSERVATION QUIZ** (from page 53) The Japanese American girls are the monozygotic twins. If you were not sure, look at their teeth, their eyebrows, and the shape of their faces, compared with the boys' head shapes and personality. ●

From Zygote to Newborn

The most dramatic and extensive transformation of the entire life span occurs before birth. To make it easier to study, prenatal development is often divided into three main periods. The first two weeks are called the **germinal period;** the third through the eighth week is the **embryonic period;** the ninth week until birth is the **fetal period** (see Table 2.2 for alternative terms).

germinal period
The first two weeks of prenatal development after conception, characterized by rapid cell division and the beginning of cell differentiation.

embryonic period
The stage of prenatal development from approximately the third through the eighth week after conception, during which the basic forms of all body structures, including internal organs, develop.

fetal period
The stage of prenatal development from the ninth week after conception until birth, during which the fetus grows in size and matures in functioning.

TABLE 2.2 Timing and Terminology

Popular and professional books use various phrases to segment pregnancy. The following comments may help to clarify the phrases used.

- *Beginning of pregnancy:* Pregnancy begins at conception, which is also the starting point of *gestational age.* However, the organism does not become an embryo until about two weeks later, and pregnancy does not affect the woman (and cannot be confirmed by blood or urine testing) until implantation. Paradoxically, many obstetricians date the onset of pregnancy from the date of the woman's last menstrual period (LMP), about 14 days *before* conception.

- *Length of pregnancy:* Full-term pregnancies last 266 days, or 38 weeks, or 9 months. If the LMP is used as the starting time, pregnancy lasts 40 weeks, sometimes referred to as 10 lunar months (a lunar month is 28 days long).

- *Trimesters:* Instead of *germinal period, embryonic period,* and *fetal period,* some writers divide pregnancy into three-month periods called *trimesters.* Months 1, 2, and 3 are called the *first trimester;* months 4, 5, and 6, the *second trimester;* and months 7, 8, and 9, the *third trimester.*

- *Due date:* Although doctors assign a specific due date (based on the woman's LMP), only 5 percent of babies are born on that exact date. Babies born between three weeks before and two weeks after that date are considered "full term" or "on time." Babies born earlier are called *preterm;* babies born later are called *post-term.* The words *preterm* and *post-term* are more accurate than *premature* and *postmature.*

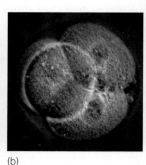
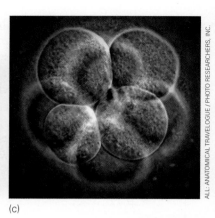

(a)   (b)   (c)

ALL: ANATOMICAL TRAVELOGUE / PHOTO RESEARCHERS, INC.

First Stages of the Germinal Period
The original zygote as it divides into
(a) two cells, *(b)* four cells, and *(c)* eight
cells. Occasionally at this early stage,
the cells separate completely, forming
the beginning of monozygotic twins,
quadruplets, or octuplets.

RESPONSE FOR Future Parents
(from page 56) Yes, but you wouldn't
want to. You would have to choose one
mate for your sons and another for
your daughters, and you would have
to use sex-selection methods. Even so,
it might not work, given all the genes
of your genotype. More importantly,
the effort would be unethical, unnatu-
ral, and possibly illegal. ●

stem cells
Cells from which any other specialized
type of cell can form.

implantation
The process, beginning about 10 days
after conception, in which the developing organism burrows into the tissue
that lines the uterus, where it can be
nourished and protected as it continues to develop.

embryo
The name for a developing human
organism from about the third through
the eighth week after conception.

Germinal: The First 14 Days

Within hours after conception, the zygote begins *duplication* and *division*. First, the 23
pairs of chromosomes carrying all the genes duplicate, forming two complete sets of
the genome. These two sets move toward opposite sides of the zygote, and the single
cell splits neatly down the middle into two cells, each containing the original genetic
code. These two cells duplicate and divide, becoming four, which themselves duplicate and divide, becoming eight, and so on.

If the two-celled organism is split apart (either naturally or artificially, which is
illegal for humans but successful with mice), and each cell is allowed to develop, that
creates monozygotic twins. Every cell of both would have the same DNA.

Those first cells are **stem cells,** able to direct production of any other cell and thus
to become a complete person. After about the eight-cell stage, duplication and division continue and a third process, *differentiation*, begins. Soon cells specialize, taking
different forms and reproducing at various rates, depending on where they are located.
They are no longer omnipotent stem cells (some cells in adults can also take on other
functions, but they are not nearly as adaptable as early stem cells) (Slack, 2012).

For instance, even though every cell carries the complete genetic code, differentiation means that some cells become part of an eye, others part of a finger, still others
part of the brain. As one expert explains, "We are sitting with parts of our body that
could have been used for thinking" (Gottlieb, 1992/2002, p. 172).

About a week after conception, the multiplying cells (now numbering more than
100) separate into two distinct masses. The outer cells form a shell that will become
the *placenta* (the organ that surrounds and protects the developing creature), and the
inner cells form a nucleus that will become the embryo.

The first task of the outer cells is **implantation**—that is, to embed themselves
in the nurturing lining of the uterus. This is far from automatic; about 50 percent
of natural conceptions and an even larger percentage of in vitro conceptions never
implant (see Table 2.3). Most new life ends before an embryo begins (Sadler, 2009).

Embryo: From the Third Through the Eighth Week

The start of the third week after conception initiates the *embryonic period*, during
which the formless mass of cells becomes a distinct being—not yet recognizably
human but worthy of a new name, **embryo.** (The word *embryo* is often used loosely,
but each stage of development has a particular name; here, embryo refers to the developing human from day 14 to day 56.)

At about day 14, a thin line (called the *primitive streak*) appears down the middle
of the embryo, becoming the neural tube 22 days after conception; it eventually
develops into the central nervous system, brain, and spinal column (Sadler, 2010).
The head appears in the fourth week, as eyes, ears, nose, and mouth start to form.

TABLE 2.3 Vulnerability During Prenatal Development

The Germinal Period
An estimated 60 percent of all zygotes do not grow or implant properly and thus do not survive the germinal period. Many of these organisms are abnormal; few women realize they were pregnant.

The Embryonic Period
About 20 percent of all embryos are aborted spontaneously, most often because of chromosomal abnormalities. This is usually called an early miscarriage.

The Fetal Period
About 5 percent of all fetuses are aborted spontaneously before viability at 22 weeks or are stillborn, defined as born dead after 22 weeks. This is much more common in poor nations.

Birth
Because of all these factors, only about 31 percent of all zygotes grow and survive to become living newborn babies. Age is crucial. One estimate is that less than 3 percent of all conceptions after age 40 result in live births.

Sources: Bentley & Mascie-Taylor, 2000; Corda et al., 2012; Laurino et al., 2005.

● **UNDERSTANDING THE NUMBERS**
If the numbers in the table are added up (60 + 20 + 5 = 85), it appears that only 15 percent of zygotes survive. Why does the table say 31 percent?

Answer The later rates are percentages of those who have already survived to that point. The 5 percent of fetal deaths refer to the 36 percent that have reached week 8.

Also in the fourth week, a minuscule blood vessel that will become the heart begins to pulsate.

By the fifth week, buds that will become arms and legs emerge. The upper arms and then forearms, palms, and webbed fingers grow. Legs, knees, feet, and webbed toes, in that order, are apparent a few days later, each having the beginning of a skeletal structure. Then, 52 and 54 days after conception, respectively, the fingers and toes separate (Sadler, 2009).

As you can see, prenatally, the head develops first, in a *cephalocaudal* (literally, "head-to-tail") pattern, and the extremities form last, in a *proximodistal* (literally, "near-to-far") pattern. This is true for all living creatures, part of universal genetic instructions.

At the end of the eighth week after conception (56 days), the embryo weighs just one-thirtieth of an ounce (1 gram) and is about 1 inch (2½ centimeters) long. It has all the organs and body parts (except sex organs) of a human being, including elbows and knees. It moves frequently, about 150 times per hour, but such movement is random and imperceptible to the woman, who may not even realize that she is pregnant.

The Embryonic Period *(a)* At 4 weeks past conception, the embryo is only about ⅛ inch (3 millimeters) long, but already the head has taken shape. *(b)* By 7 weeks, the organism is somewhat less than an inch (2½ centimeters) long. Eyes, nose, the digestive system, and even the first stage of finger and toe formation can be seen.

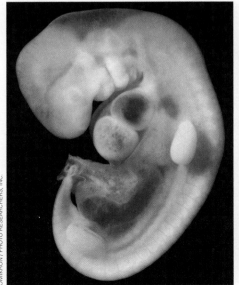
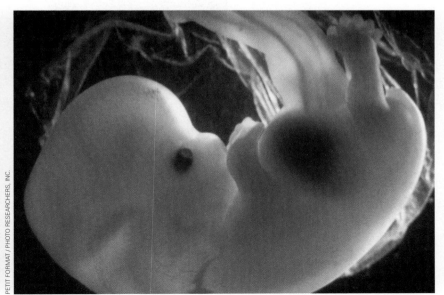

(a)   (b)

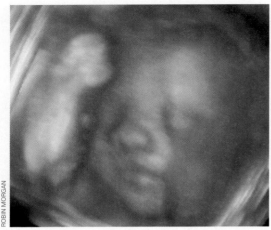

ROBIN MORGAN

There's Your Baby For many parents, their first glimpse of their future child is an ultrasound image. This is Alice Morgan, 63 days before birth.

fetus
The name for a developing human organism from the start of the ninth week after conception until birth.

ultrasound
An image of a fetus (or an internal organ) produced by using high-frequency sound waves. (Also called *sonogram*.)

age of viability
The age (about 22 weeks after conception) at which a fetus may survive outside the mother's uterus if specialized medical care is available.

Fetus: From the Ninth Week Until Birth

The organism is called a **fetus** from the ninth week after conception until birth. The fetal period encompasses dramatic change, from a tiny, sexless creature smaller than the final joint of your thumb to a boy or girl about 20 inches (51 centimeters) long.

In the ninth week, sex organs develop, soon visible via **ultrasound** (also called *sonogram*). The male fetus experiences a rush of the hormone testosterone, affecting the brain (Morris et al., 2004; Neave, 2008).

By 3 months, the fetus weighs about 3 ounces (87 grams) and is about 3 inches (7.5 centimeters) long. Those numbers—3 months, 3 ounces, 3 inches—are rounded off for easy recollection, but growth rates vary— some 3-month-old fetuses do not quite weigh 3 ounces and others already weigh 4 (Sadler, 2009).

As prenatal growth continues, the cardiovascular, digestive, and excretory systems develop. The brain increases about six times in size from the fourth to the sixth month, developing many new neurons (*neurogenesis*) and synapses (*synaptogenesis*). Indeed, up to half a million brain cells per minute are created at peak growth during mid-pregnancy (Dowling, 2004).

This brain growth is critical because it enables regulation of all the body functions, including breathing (Johnson, 2011). That allows the fetus to reach the **age of viability,** when a preterm newborn might survive. Thanks to intensive medical care, the age of viability decreased dramatically in the twentieth century, but it now seems stuck at about 22 weeks (Pignotti, 2010) because even the most advanced technology cannot maintain life without some brain response.

As the brain matures and axons connect, the organs of the body begin to work in harmony, fetal movement as well as heart rate quiet down during rest, and the heart beats faster during activity (which may be when the mother is trying to sleep).

Attaining the age of viability simply means that life outside the womb is *possible* (see Figure 2.5). Each day of the final three months improves the odds, not only of survival but also of life without disability (Iacovidou et al., 2010).

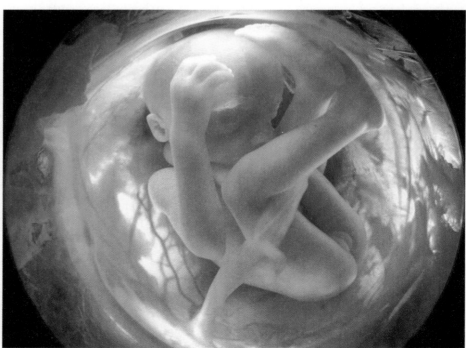

LENNART NILSSON SCANPIX

Viability This fetus is in mid-pregnancy, a few weeks shy of viability. As you can see, the body is completely formed. Unseen is the extent of brain and lung development, which will take at least another month to become sufficiently mature to allow for survival.

A preterm infant born in the seventh month is a tiny creature requiring intensive care for each gram of nourishment and every shallow breath. The care and complications of preterm infants are discussed at the end of this chapter.

Usually, however, after nine months or so, newborns are ready to thrive at home on mother's milk—no expert help, oxygenated air, or special feeding required. The fetus typically gains at least 4½ pounds (2.1 kilograms) in the third trimester, increasing to almost 7½ pounds (about 3.4 kilograms) at birth (see At About This Time).

By full term, human brain growth is so extensive that the *cortex* (the brain's advanced outer layers) forms several folds in order to fit into the skull (see Figure 2.6). Although some large mammals (e.g., whales) have bigger brains than humans, no other creature needs as many folds as humans do, because the human cortex contains much more material than the brains of nonhumans. Those mammals that have bigger brains than humans also have far bigger bodies; proportionally, human brains are largest.

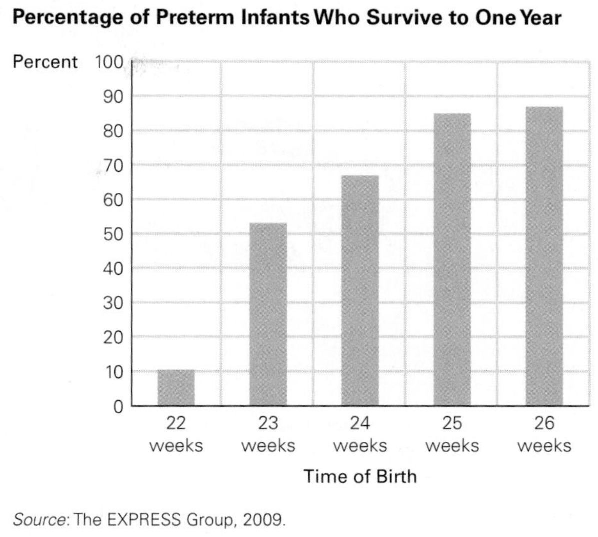

Finally, a Baby

About 38 weeks (266 days) after conception, the fetal brain signals the release of hormones, specifically *oxytocin,* which prepares the fetus for delivery and starts labor. The average baby is born after about 12 hours of active labor for first births and 7 hours for subsequent births (Moore & Persaud, 2003), although labor may take twice or half as long. The definition of "active" labor varies, which is one reason some women believe they are in active labor for days and others say 10 minutes.

Percentage of Preterm Infants Who Survive to One Year

Source: The EXPRESS Group, 2009.

FIGURE 2.5 **Each Critical Day** Even with advanced medical care, survival of extremely preterm newborns is in doubt. These data come from a thousand births in Sweden, where prenatal care is free and easily obtained. As you can see, the age of viability (22 weeks) means only that an infant *might* survive, not that it will. By full term (not shown), the survival rate is almost 100 percent.

AT ABOUT THIS TIME
Average Prenatal Weights*

Period of Development	Weeks Past Conception	Average Weight (nonmetric)	Average Weight (metric)	Notes
End of embryonic period	8	1/30 oz	1 g	Most common time for spontaneous abortion (miscarriage).
End of first trimester	13	3 oz	85 g	
At viability (50/50 chance of survival)	22–25	20–32 oz	565–900 g	A birthweight less than 2 lb, 3 oz (1,000 g) is extremely low birthweight (ELBW).
End of second trimester	26–28	2–3 lb	900–1,400 g	Less than 3 lb, 5 oz (1,500 g) is very low birthweight (VLBW).
End of preterm period	35	5½ lb	2,500 g	Less than 5½ lb (2,500 g) is low birthweight (LBW).
Full term	38	7½ lb	3,400 g	Between 5½ lb and 9 lb (2,500–4,000 g) is considered normal weight.

*To make them easier to remember, the weights are rounded off (hence the imprecise correspondence between metric and nonmetric). Actual weights vary. For instance, normal full-term infants weigh between 5½ and 9 pounds (2,500 and 4,000 grams); viable preterm newborns, especially twins or triplets, weigh less than shown here.

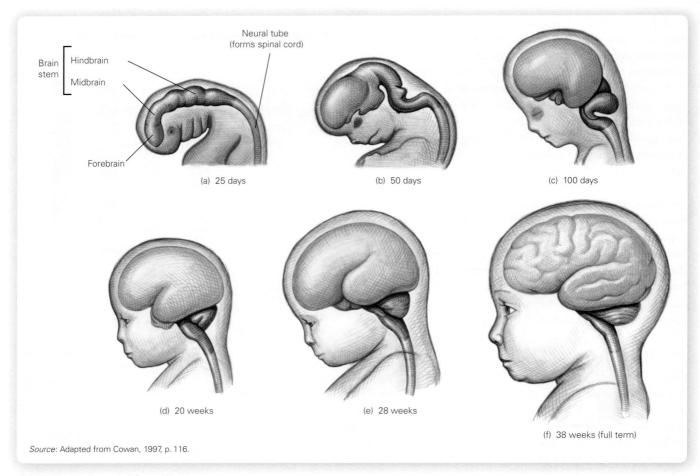

Brain stem {
Hindbrain
Midbrain
}
Neural tube (forms spinal cord)
Forebrain
(a) 25 days
(b) 50 days
(c) 100 days
(d) 20 weeks
(e) 28 weeks
(f) 38 weeks (full term)

Source: Adapted from Cowan, 1997, p. 116.

FIGURE 2.6 Prenatal Growth of the Brain Just 25 days after conception *(a)*, the central nervous system is already evident. The brain looks distinctly human by day 100 *(c)*. By the 28th week of gestation *(e)*, the various sections of the brain are recognizable. When the fetus is full term *(f)*, all the parts of the brain, including the cortex (the outer layers), are formed, folding over one another and becoming more convoluted, or wrinkled, as the number of brain cells increases.

Apgar scale
A quick assessment of a newborn's body functioning. The baby's heart rate, respiratory effort, muscle tone, color, and reflexes are given a score of 0, 1, or 2 twice—at one minute and five minutes after birth—and each time the total of all five scores is compared with the ideal score of 10 (which is rarely attained).

Women's birthing positions also vary—sitting, squatting, lying down. Some women give birth while immersed in warm water, which helps the woman relax (the fetus continues to get oxygen via the umbilical cord). However, some physicians believe water births increase the rate of infection, and the underwater emergence of the head is difficult for the medical team to monitor (Tracy, 2009).

Preferences and opinions on birthing positions (as on almost every other aspect of prenatal development and birth) are partly cultural and partly personal. In general, physicians find it easier to see the head emerge if the woman lies on her back. However, many women find it easier to push the fetus out if they sit up. Neither of these generalities is true for every individual. (Figure 2.7 shows the stages of birth.)

THE NEWBORN'S FIRST MINUTES Newborns usually breathe and cry on their own. Between spontaneous cries, the first breaths of air bring oxygen to the lungs and blood, and the infant's color changes from bluish to pinkish. (Pinkish refers to blood color, visible beneath the skin, and applies to newborns of all hues.) Eyes open wide; tiny fingers grab; even tinier toes stretch and retract. The full-term baby is instantly, zestfully, ready for life.

One assessment of newborn health is the **Apgar scale** (see Table 2.4), first developed by Dr. Virginia Apgar. When she earned her MD in 1933, Apgar wanted to work in a hospital but was told that only men did surgery. Consequently, she became an anesthesiologist.

Apgar saw that "delivery room doctors focused on mothers and paid little attention to babies. Those who were small and struggling were often left to die" (Beck,

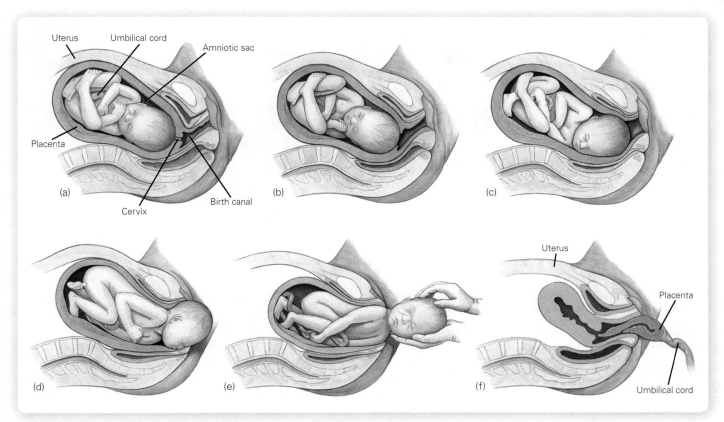

FIGURE 2.7 A Normal, Uncomplicated Birth *(a)* The baby's position as the birth process begins. *(b)* The first stage of labor: The cervix dilates to allow passage of the baby's head. *(c)* Transition: The baby's head moves into the "birth canal," the vagina. *(d)* The second stage of labor: The baby's head moves through the opening of the vagina ("crowns") and *(e)* emerges completely, followed by the rest of the body about a minute later. *(f)* The third stage of labor is the expulsion of the placenta. This usually occurs naturally, but it is crucial that the whole placenta be expelled, so birth attendants check carefully. In some cultures, the placenta is ceremonially buried, to commemorate the life-giving role it plays.

TABLE 2.4 Criteria and Scoring of the Apgar Scale

		Five Vital Signs			
Score	Color	Heartbeat	Reflex Irritability	Muscle Tone	Respiratory Effort
0	Blue, pale	Absent	No response	Flaccid, limp	Absent
1	Body pink, extremities blue	Slow (below 100)	Grimace	Weak, inactive	Irregular, slow
2	Entirely pink	Rapid (over 100)	Coughing, sneezing, crying	Strong, active	Good; baby is crying

Source: Apgar, 1953.

2009, p. D-1). To save those young lives, Apgar developed a simple rating scale of five vital signs—color, heart rate, cry, muscle tone, and breathing—to alert doctors when a newborn was in crisis.

Since 1950, birth attendants worldwide have used the Apgar (often using the name as an acronym: Appearance, Pulse, Grimace, Activity, and Respiration) at one minute and again at five minutes after birth, assigning each vital sign a score of 0, 1, or 2. If the five-minute Apgar is 7 or higher, all is well.

One of the Tiniest Rumaisa Rahman was born after 26 weeks and 6 days, weighing only 8.6 ounces (244 grams). Nevertheless, she has a good chance of living a full, normal life. Rumaisa gained 5 pounds (2,270 grams) in the hospital and then, six months after her birth, went home. Her twin sister, Hiba, who weighed 1.3 pounds (590 grams) at birth, had gone home two months earlier. At their one-year birthday, the twins seemed normal, with Rumaisa weighing 15 pounds (6,800 grams) and Hiba 17 pounds (7,711 grams) (CBS News, 2005).

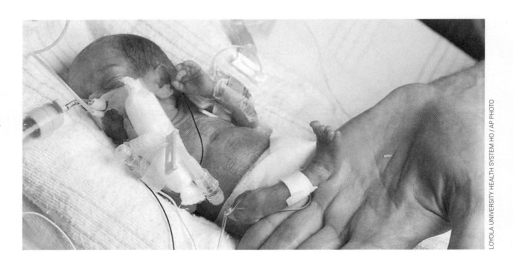

✦ ESPECIALLY FOR Conservatives and Liberals Do people's attitudes about medical intervention at birth reflect their attitudes about medicine at other points in the life span, in such areas as assisted reproductive technology (ART), immunization, and life support? (see response, page 67) →

cesarean section (c-section)
A surgical birth, in which incisions through the mother's abdomen and uterus allow the fetus to be removed quickly, instead of being delivered through the vagina.

MEDICAL ASSISTANCE AT BIRTH The specifics of birth depend on the parents' preparation, the position and size of the fetus, and the customs of the culture. In developed nations, births almost always include sterile procedures, electronic monitoring, and drugs to dull pain or speed contractions. In addition, many aspects of birth depend on who delivers the baby—doctor, midwife, or the parents themselves.

Midwives are as skilled at delivering babies as physicians are, but in most nations only medical doctors perform surgery. More than one-third of U.S. births occur via **cesarean section** (**c-section,** or simply *section*), whereby the fetus is removed through incisions in the mother's abdomen. A new endeavor in Africa to teach midwives to perform cesareans is projected to save a million lives per year.

Cesareans are usually safe for mother and baby and have many advantages for hospitals (easier to schedule, quicker, and more expensive than vaginal deliveries), but they also bring more complications after birth and reduce breast-feeding (Malloy, 2009).

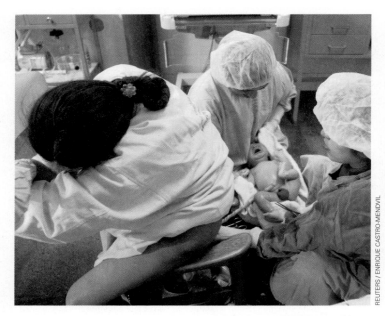

Choice, Culture, or Cohort? Why do it that way? Both these women (in Peru on the left, in England on the right) chose methods of labor that are unusual in the United States, where birthing stools and birthing pools are uncommon. However, in all three nations, most births occur in hospitals—a rare choice a century ago.

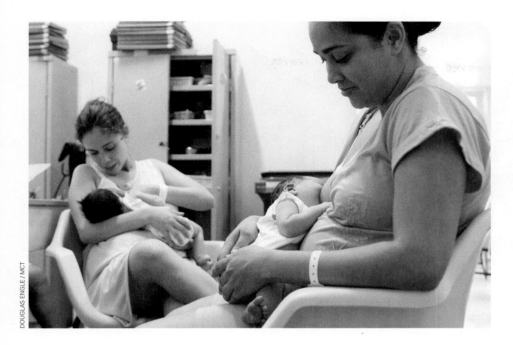

From Day One For various reasons, some countries have much higher rates of cesarean deliveries than others. These new mothers in Brazil, which has a high cesarean rate, have safely delivered their babies and, with the encouragement of the hospital, are breast-feeding them from the very beginning.

FIGURE 2.8 Too Many Cesareans or Too Few? Rates of cesarean deliveries vary widely from nation to nation. The underlying issue is whether some women who should have cesareans do not get them, while other women have unnecessary cesareans.

Given that, it is not surprising that cesareans are controversial. The World Health Organization suggests that they are medically indicated in 15 percent of births. In some nations, there are far fewer than that; in others, many more (see Figure 2.8).

For example, rates in China increased from 5 percent in 1991 to 46 percent in 2008 (Guo et al., 2007; Juan, 2010). In the United States, the rate rose every year between 1996 and 2009 (from 21 percent to 34 percent, with notable state variations, from 22 percent in Utah to 39 percent in Florida) (Menacker & Hamilton, 2010).

Less studied is the *epidural,* an injection in a particular part of the spine of the laboring woman to alleviate pain. Epidurals are often used in hospital births, but they increase the rate of cesarean sections and decrease the readiness of newborn infants to suck immediately after birth (A. F. Bell et al., 2010).

Another medical intervention is *induced labor,* in which labor is started, speeded, or strengthened with a drug. The rate of induced labor in many developed nations has more than doubled since 1990, up to 20 or 25 percent. The reasons are sometimes medically warranted (such as when a woman develops eclampsia, which could kill the fetus), sometimes not (Grivell et al., 2012). Induced labor increases the rate of complications, including cesareans.

ALTERNATIVES TO HOSPITAL TECHNOLOGY Questions of costs and benefits abound. For instance, c-section and epidural rates vary more by doctor, hospital, day of the week, and region than by medical circumstances. This is partly an economic issue; in the United States, the c-section rate increases when the birth is fully covered by insurance. But c-sections are also increasing in Sweden, where obstetric care is paid for by the government (Schytt & Waldenström, 2010).

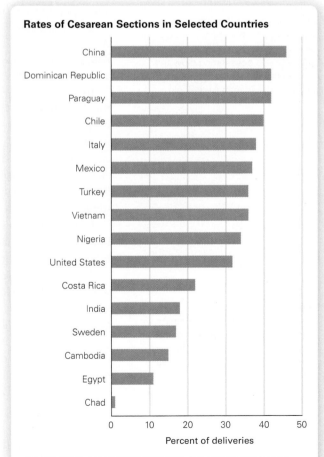

Rates of Cesarean Sections in Selected Countries

Sources: Various sources from 2000–2012. Since data change by year and sources provide different rates, this chart is approximate.

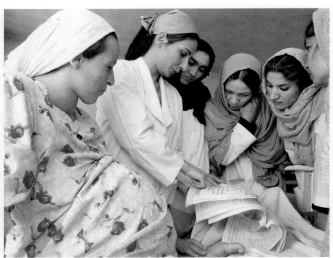

Same Situation, Far Apart: Getting Ready There are many similarities here: Six adults and three fetuses on the left and six adults and two fetuses (twins) on the right. But the differences are tragic, evident in the face of the expectant mother on the right. The husbands in the Netherlands are learning how to help their wives give birth at home, as most Dutch couples do. The Afghan doctor on the right, however, is explaining why this woman's labor will be induced, with neither baby expected to survive—a devastating blow this woman has already faced, having twice lost a baby less than a week old.

doula
A woman who helps with the birth process. Doulas are trained to offer support to new mothers, including massage and suggestions for breast-feeding positions.

A rare complication (uterine rupture), which sometimes happens when women give birth vaginally after a previous cesarean, has caused most doctors to insist that after one cesarean, subsequent births also be cesarean. However, some people disagree (Malloy, 2009). One reason for the high rate of c-sections may be the fear of legal action. Juries blame doctors for inaction more than action; to avoid lawsuits, doctors operate.

Most U.S. births now take place in hospital labor rooms with high-tech facilities and equipment nearby. Another 5 percent of U.S. births occur in *birthing centers* (not in a hospital), and less than 1 percent occur at home (illegal in some jurisdictions). About half of the home births are planned and half are unexpected because labor happened too quickly. The latter situation is hazardous if no one is nearby to rescue a newborn in distress (Tracy, 2009).

In some European nations, many births occur at home by plan (30 percent in the Netherlands). In Europe, home births have fewer complications than those in hospitals—perhaps because pregnant women requesting home births are screened to disallow those at risk (such as an older woman having twins), or perhaps because the women are more relaxed at home. In the Netherlands, special ambulances called *flying storks* speed mothers and newborns to hospitals if needed. Dutch research finds home births better for mothers and no worse for infants than hospital births (de Jonge et al., 2009).

In most hospitals during most of the twentieth century, women giving birth labored alone. Fathers and other family members were kept away and the moment of birth was attended only by nurses and doctors. No longer.

Almost everyone now agrees that other people should always be with a laboring woman. Relatives or friends are often present, midwives often replace doctors, and sometimes a **doula** (a woman trained to support women in labor) provides practical as well as emotional support for the mother and other family members.

Many studies have found that doulas benefit anyone giving birth—rich or poor, married or not (Vonderheid et al., 2011). For example, in one study 420 middle-class married women who arrived at a hospital in labor with their husbands were randomly assigned a doula or not. Those with doulas had fewer cesareans (13 versus 25 percent) or epidurals (65 versus 76 percent) (McGrath & Kennell, 2008).

The New Family

The fact that mothers are now less lonely during labor stems in part from the recognition that humans are social creatures, seeking support from their families and their societies. Each family member—newborn, mother, and father—responds to every other person.

THE NEWBORN Before birth, developing humans already contribute to their families in many ways, including via fetal movements and hormones that cause protective impulses in the mother early in pregnancy and nurturing impulses at the end (Konner, 2010). The appearance of the newborn (big hairless head, tiny feet, and so on) stirs the human heart, as is evident in adults' brain activity and heart rate when they see a baby.

Newborns are responsive social creatures—listening, staring, sucking, cuddling. In the first day or two after birth, a professional might administer the **Brazelton Neonatal Behavioral Assessment Scale (NBAS),** which records 46 behaviors, including 20 reflexes. Parents watching the NBAS are amazed at their newborn's competence—and this fosters early parent–child connection (Hawthorne, 2009).

Technically, a **reflex** is an involuntary response to a particular stimulus. Humans of every age reflexively seek to protect themselves (the eyeblink is an example). The speed and strength of reflexes varies, even among newborns, who have three sets of protective reflexes:

- *Reflexes that maintain oxygen supply.* The *breathing reflex* begins even before the umbilical cord, with its supply of oxygen, is cut. Additional reflexes that maintain oxygen are reflexive *hiccups* and *sneezes,* as well as *thrashing* (moving the arms and legs about) to escape something that covers the face.

- *Reflexes that maintain constant body temperature.* When infants are cold, they *cry, shiver,* and *tuck their legs* close to their bodies. When they are hot, they try to *push away* blankets and then stay still.

- *Reflexes that manage feeding.* The *sucking reflex* causes newborns to suck anything that touches their lips—fingers, toes, blankets, and rattles, as well as natural and artificial nipples of various textures and shapes. The *rooting reflex* causes babies to turn their mouths toward anything that brushes against their cheeks—a reflexive search for a nipple—and start to suck. *Swallowing* is another reflex that aids feeding, as is *crying* when the stomach is empty and *spitting up* when it's full.

Each of these 13 reflexes (in italics) normally causes a caregiving reaction, as the new parents do what seems necessary to protect their newborn. Thus, reflexes affect

RESPONSE FOR Conservatives and Liberals (from page 64) Yes, some people are much less likely than others to want nature to take its course. However, personal experience often trumps political attitudes about birth and death: Several of those who advocate hospital births are also in favor of spending one's final days at home. ●

Brazelton Neonatal Behavioral Assessment Scale (NBAS)
A test often administered to newborns that measures responsiveness and records 46 behaviors, including 20 reflexes.

reflex
An unlearned, involuntary action or movement in response to a stimulus. A reflex occurs without conscious thought.

Never Underestimate the Power of a Reflex
For developmentalists, newborn reflexes are mechanisms for survival, indicators of brain maturation, and vestiges of evolutionary history. For parents, they are mostly delightful and sometimes amazing. Both of these viewpoints are demonstrated by three star performers: a newborn boy sucking peacefully on the doctor's finger, a newborn grasping so tightly that his legs dangle in space, and a 1-day-old girl stepping eagerly forward on legs too tiny to support her body.

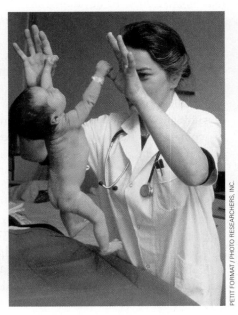

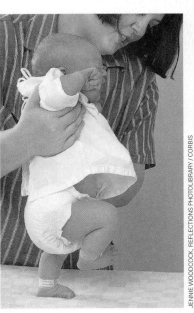

A Good Beginning The apparent joy and bonding between this expectant couple and their unborn child is a wonderful sign. Although this couple in Germany may experience social discrimination—one reason the divorce rate is higher among multiracial couples than monoracial ones—their own parental alliance is crucial for their child. Many multiracial children become adults with higher achievement, greater self-understanding, and more tolerance than others.

couvade
Symptoms of pregnancy and birth experienced by fathers.

postpartum depression
The sadness and inadequacy felt by some new mothers in the days and weeks after giving birth.

human interaction. In addition, a newborn's senses are also responsive to people: New babies listen more to voices than to traffic, for instance, and they stare at faces more than at machines. Typically, when a baby stares at a new parent, he or she talks and the baby listens.

NEW FATHERS Fathers affect development from conception on. Fathers-to-be help mothers-to-be stay healthy, nourished, and drug-free. Mothers have an easier birth when their partners are beside them. Fathers are often enraptured by their scraggly newborns and protective of their exhausted wives, who may appreciate their husbands more than at other times.

Currently, about 40 percent of all U.S. women are not married when their baby is born (U.S. Census Bureau, 2011). Sometimes their partners are present at the birth, and, even if not, they may be named on the birth certificate.

A study of all live single births in Milwaukee from 1993 to 2006 (151,869 babies!) found that medical complications correlated with several expected variables (e.g., maternal cigarette smoking) and one unexpected one—no father listed on the birth record. This was especially apparent for European American births: When the mother did not list the father, she was more likely to have long labor, a cesarean section, or other complications (Ngui et al., 2009).

Pregnancy and birth may be biologically (not just psychologically) experienced by fathers. For example, levels of stress hormones correlate between expectant fathers and mothers, probably because they reflect each other's emotions (Berg & Wynne-Edwards, 2002). Beyond that, many fathers experience weight gain and indigestion during pregnancy and pain during labor. Indeed, among some Latin American Indians, fathers go through the motions of labor when their wives do, to help ensure an easy birth.

Paternal experiences of pregnancy and birth are called **couvade,** expected in some cultures, a normal variation in many, and considered pathological in others (M. Sloan, 2009). In developed nations, couvade is unnoticed and unstudied, but researchers find that fathers are often intensely involved with pregnancy and birth (Brennan et al., 2007).

NEW MOTHERS About half of all women experience physical problems after giving birth, such as incisions from a c-section, or painfully sore nipples, or problems with urination (Danel et al., 2003). However, worse than any physical problems are psychological ones. When the birth hormones decrease, between 8 and 15 percent of women experience **postpartum depression,** a sense of inadequacy and sadness (called *baby blues* in the mild version and *postpartum psychosis* in the most severe form) (Perfetti et al., 2004). With postpartum depression, baby care (feeding, diapering, bathing) feels very burdensome.

Sometimes the first sign that something is amiss is that the mother seems euphoric after birth. She cannot sleep, or stop talking, or keep from worrying about the newborn. Some of this is normal, but family members and medical personnel need to be alert, as a crash might follow the high.

Maternal depression can have a long-term impact on the child, one of the many reasons why postpartum depression should be quickly recognized and treated. Fathers are usually the first responders; they may be instrumental in getting the help the mother and baby need (Cuijpers et al., 2010; Goodman & Gotlib, 2002). This is easier said than done, however, as fathers may become depressed as well; in such cases, other people need to step in.

From a developmental perspective, causes of postpartum depression (such as marital problems) sometimes predate pregnancy; others (such as financial stress) occur during pregnancy; others correlate with birth (especially if the mother is alone); still others (health, feeding, or sleeping problems) are specific to the particular infant. Successful breast-feeding may mitigate maternal depression, in part by increasing levels of oxytocin, a bonding hormone. This is one of the many reasons a lactation counselor (who helps with breast-feeding techniques) may be a crucial member of the new mother's support team.

BONDING To what extent are the first hours crucial for the **parent–infant bond,** the strong, loving connection that forms as parents hold, examine, and feed their newborn? It has been claimed that this bond develops in the first hours after birth when a mother cradles her naked baby, just as sheep and goats must immediately smell and nuzzle their newborns if they are to nurture them (Klaus & Kennell, 1976).

Although the concept of early contact was welcomed a few decades ago because it reduced the impersonal medicalization of hospital births, early skin-to-skin contact is *not* essential for human bonding (Eyer, 1992; Lamb, 1982). Nonetheless, the active involvement of both parents in pregnancy, birth, and newborn care benefits everyone. Factors that encourage parents (biological or adoptive) to nurture their newborns have lifelong benefits, proven with mice, monkeys, and humans (Champagne & Curley, 2010).

The importance of early mothering has recently become apparent with **kangaroo care,** in which the newborn lies between the mother's breasts, skin-to-skin, listening to her heartbeat and feeling her body heat. Many studies find that kangaroo-care newborns sleep more deeply, gain weight more quickly, and spend more time alert than do infants with standard care (Ludington-Hoe, 2011).

SHEHZAD NOORANI / PETER ARNOLD, INC.

A Teenage Mother This week-old baby, born in a poor village in Myanmar (Burma), has a better chance of survival than he might otherwise have had because his 18-year-old mother has bonded with him.

parent–infant bond
The strong, loving connection that forms as parents hold, examine, and feed their newborn.

kangaroo care
A child-care technique in which a new mother holds the baby between her breasts, like a kangaroo that carries her immature newborn in a pouch on her abdomen.

✦ **ESPECIALLY FOR Scientists**
Research with non-human animals can benefit people, but it is sometimes used too quickly to support conclusions about humans. When does that happen? (see response, page 70) →

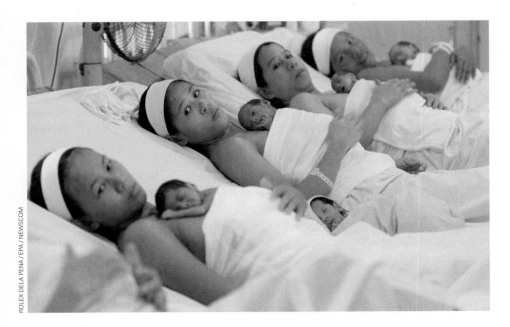

ROLEX DELA PENA / EPA / NEWSCOM

A Beneficial Beginning These new mothers in a maternity ward in Manila are providing their babies with kangaroo care.

RESPONSE FOR **Scientists** (from page 69) Animal research tends to be used too quickly whenever it supports an assertion that is popular but has not been substantiated by research data, as in the social construction about physical contact being crucial for parent–infant bonding. ●

Kangaroo care was first used with low-birthweight newborns, but it also benefits healthy newborns. Fathers also can provide kangaroo care, benefiting babies and themselves (Thomas, 2008). Months after being given kangaroo care, infants tend to flourish, either because of improved infant adjustment to life outside the womb or because of increased parental sensitivity and effectiveness. Probably both. Oxytocin is released during kangaroo care, and that benefits everyone (Ludington-Hoe, 2011).

KEY points

- The germinal period ends two weeks after conception with implantation, followed by the development of the embryo, as the creature takes shape.
- At eight weeks after conception, fetal life begins. This is the longest stage of pregnancy, normally with seven more months of brain and body maturation.
- Full-term birth is a natural event, assisted by drugs and other medical measures in developed countries.
- Human social interaction begins even before birth, as mothers, fathers, and babies respond to each other.

Problems and Solutions

The early days of prenatal life place the developing person on a path toward health and success—or not. Fortunately, resilience is apparent from the beginning; healthy newborns are the norm, not the exception.

From the moment of conception to the days and months after birth, many biological and psychological factors protect each new life. We now look at specific problems that may occur and how to prevent or minimize them. Always remember dynamic systems—every hazard is affected by dozens of factors.

As one scientist stresses, "genes and their products almost never act alone, but in networks with other genes and proteins and in the context of the environment. . . . [C]omplex disorders arise from an accumulation of genetic defects" that may erupt in disorders that seem alike but in fact have many different origins and cures (Chakravarti, 2011, p. 15).

Abnormal Genes and Chromosomes

Perhaps half of all zygotes have serious abnormalities of their chromosomes or genes. Most of them never grow or implant—an early example of the protection built into nature. However, some newborns with serious genetics problems do survive and can lead a close-to-normal life—especially if protective factors are present (Nadeau & Dudley, 2011).

Down syndrome
A condition in which a person has 47 chromosomes instead of the usual 46, with three rather than two chromosomes at the 21st position. People with Down syndrome typically have distinctive characteristics, including unusual facial features (thick tongue, round face, slanted eyes), heart abnormalities, and language difficulties. (Also called *trisomy-21*.)

CHROMOSOMAL MISCOUNTS About once in every 200 births, an infant is born with 45, 47, or even 48 or 49 chromosomes instead of the usual 46. Each of these produces a recognizable *syndrome,* a cluster of distinct characteristics that occur together. The variable that most often correlates with an odd number of chromosomes is the age of the mother, presumably because her ova become increasingly fragile by midlife. The father's age is also relevant, again probably because of his gametes (Brenner et al., 2009).

The most common extra-chromosome condition that results in a surviving child is **Down syndrome,** also called *trisomy-21* because the person has three (tri) copies of chromosome 21. No individual with Down syndrome is identical to another, but most have specific observable characteristics—a thick tongue, round face, slanted eyes, distinctive body proportions.

Many also have hearing problems, heart abnormalities, muscle weakness, and short stature. They are usually slower to develop intellectually, especially in language, and they reach their maximum intellectual potential at about age 15 (Rondal, 2010). Some are severely retarded; others are of average or above-average intelligence. That extra chromosome affects the person lifelong, but family context, educational efforts, and possibly medication can improve the person's prognosis (Kuehn, 2011).

Another common problem occurs at the 23rd pair. Not every person has two, and only two, sex chromosomes. About 1 in every 500 infants is born with only one sex chromosome (no Y) or with three or more (not just two) (Hamerton & Evans, 2005). Such children are impaired in many ways, especially in sexual maturation and fertility. The specifics depend on the particular configuration as well as on other genetic factors (Mazzocco & Ross, 2007).

GENE DISORDERS Everyone is a carrier of genes or alleles that *could* produce serious diseases or handicaps in the next generation. Given that most disorders are polygenic and that the mapping of the human genome is recent, the exact impact of each allele is not yet known (Couzin-Frankel, 2011a). It is likely that "common complex disorders arise from an accumulation of genetic defects in many genes" (Chakravarti, 2011, p. 15). Although most disorders result from many genes, single-gene disorders have been studied for decades. Our accumulated knowledge of them can help us understand more complex disorders.

Most of the 7,000 *known* single-gene disorders are dominant and easy to identify as such: Half the offspring of parents with a dominant disorder will also have the disorder (in other words, it will be expressed in their phenotype) and half will escape the gene, and hence the disorder, completely.

If the condition is fatal in childhood, it will, of course, never be transmitted. Thus, all common dominant disorders either begin in adulthood (Huntington disease and early-onset Alzheimer disease, for instance) or have relatively mild symptoms.

Universal Happiness All young children delight in painting brightly colored pictures on a big canvas, but this scene is unusual for two reasons: Daniel has trisomy-21, and this photograph was taken at the only school in Chile where normal and special-needs children share classrooms.

She Laughs Too Much No, not the smiling sister, but the 10-year-old on the right, who has Angelman syndrome. She inherited it from her mother's chromosome 15. Fortunately, her two siblings inherited the mother's other chromosome 15 and are normal. If she had inherited the identical deletion on her father's chromosome 15, she would have developed Prader-Willi syndrome, which would cause her to be overweight as well as always hungry and often angry. With Angelman syndrome, however, laughing, even at someone's pain, is a symptom.

One disorder once thought to be dominant is *Tourette syndrome,* which may cause a person to have uncontrollable tics and explosive verbal outbursts. But most people with Tourette syndrome have milder symptoms, such as an occasional twitch or a controllable impulse to speak inappropriately. Recent research finds complex inheritance: probably multiple genes and epigenetic factors rather than a single dominant gene (Woods et al., 2007).

The number of *recessive disorders* is probably in the millions, most of them rare. However, cystic fibrosis, thalassemia, and sickle-cell anemia are common recessive conditions; about 1 in 12 North Americans is a carrier for one of them. The reason these three are common is that carriers are protected from lethal diseases.

For example, carriers of the sickle-cell trait are unlikely to die of malaria, a deadly killer in central Africa. As a result, over the centuries, African carriers were more likely than noncarriers to survive. Similarly, the single cystic fibrosis gene is more common among people whose ancestors came from northern Europe because carriers of that gene may have been protected against cholera. Prenatal and even preconception tests can detect many disorders (see Table 2.5).

Teratogens

Possible problems can occur after conception as well because many toxins, illnesses, and experiences can harm a fetus. Every week scientists discover an unexpected

TABLE 2.5 Methods of Prenatal and Preconception Testing*

Method	Description	Risks, Concerns, and Indications
Preconception blood tests	Test for nutrients (especially iron); for diseases (syphilis, HIV, herpes, hepatitis B); for carrier status (cystic fibrosis, sickle-cell anemia, Tay-Sachs disease, thalassemia, etc.).	Might require postponement of pregnancy for counseling, treatment.
Pre-implantation testing	After in vitro fertilization, one cell is removed from each zygote at the four- or eight-cell stage and analyzed.	Not entirely accurate; requires in vitro fertilization and rapid assessment, delaying implantation. Used when couples are at high risk of known, testable disorders.
Tests for pregnancy-associated plasma protein A (PAPPA) and human chorionic gonadotropin	Blood tests are usually done at about 11 weeks to indicate levels of these substances.	Low levels correlate with chromosomal miscounts and slow prenatal growth, but false-positive or false-negative results can occur.
Alpha-fetoprotein assay	Blood is tested for alpha-fetoprotein (AFP) level, often combined with other blood tests and repeat sonogram.	High AFP indicates neural-tube defects or multiple embryos; low AFP indicates Down syndrome. Normal levels change weekly; accurate conception dating required.
Sonogram (ultrasound)	High-frequency sound waves produce a "picture" of the fetus, often done several times, from 6 to 38 weeks. Detects many problems, anticipates complications.	Reveals head or body malformations, excess brain fluid, Down syndrome (via fetal neck measurement), and several diseases. Estimates fetal age and growth, reveals multiple fetuses and placental position. No known risks, unlike the X-rays that it has replaced.
Chorionic villus sampling (CVS)	A sample of the chorion (part of the placenta) obtained (via sonogram and syringe) at 10 weeks and analyzed. Cells of placenta are genetically identical to fetal cells, so CVS indicates genetic conditions.	Can cause spontaneous abortion (rare).
Amniocentesis	Some fluid inside the placenta is withdrawn (via sonogram and syringe) at 16 weeks; cells cultured and analyzed.	Can cause spontaneous abortion (rare). Detects abnormalities later in pregnancy than other tests but is very accurate.

*Many newer tests are experimental, soon to be offered to the general public. Therefore, this list is partial, to illustrate that many tests are used at various times during pregnancy to indicate possible problems.

teratogen, which is anything—drugs, viruses, pollutants, malnutrition, stress, and more—that increases the risk of prenatal abnormalities. Many abnormalities can be avoided, many potential teratogens do no harm, and much damage can be remedied.

Some teratogens cause no physical defects but rather affect the brain, making a child hyperactive, antisocial, or learning-disabled. These are **behavioral teratogens.** About 20 percent of all children have difficulties that *could* be connected to behavioral teratogens, although the link is not straightforward: The cascade is murky, in part because the impact of the environment varies (A. M. Bell & Robinson, 2011).

One of my students described her little brother as follows:

> I was nine years old when my mother announced she was pregnant. I was the one who was most excited. . . . My mother was a heavy smoker, Colt 45 beer drinker. . . . I asked, "Why are you doing it?" She said, "I don't know."
>
> During this time, I was in the fifth grade and we saw a film about birth defects. My biggest fear was that my mother was going to give birth to a fetal alcohol syndrome infant. . . . My baby brother was born right on schedule. The doctors claimed a healthy newborn. . . . Once I heard "healthy," I thought everything was going to be fine. I was wrong, then again I was just a child. . . . My baby brother never showed any interest in toys . . . he just cannot get the right words out of his mouth . . . he has no common sense . . .
>
> *[J., personal communication]*

My student wrote: "Why hurt those who cannot defend themselves?" J. blames her mother for drinking beer, although genes, postnatal experiences, and lack of information and services to prevent harm (e.g., some drug rehab programs do not accept pregnant women) may have contributed to her brother's lack of "common sense." Just as every teratogen can be mitigated by other circumstances, each one can be made even worse. An understanding of risk is crucial.

Risk Analysis

Risk analysis discerns which chances are worth taking and how risks are minimized. To pick an easy example: Crossing the street is a risk, yet it would be worse to avoid all street crossing. Knowing this, we cross carefully, making sure to look both ways.

Although all teratogens increase the *risk* of harm, none *always* cause damage. The impact of teratogens depends on the interplay of many factors, both destructive and protective, an example of the dynamic-systems perspective.

THE CRITICAL TIME One crucial factor in the effect of a teratogen is *timing*—the age of the developing embryo or fetus when it is exposed to the teratogen (Sadler, 2009). Some teratogens cause damage only during a *critical period* (see Chapter 1) (see Figure 2.9).

Obstetricians recommend that *before* pregnancy occurs, women should avoid drugs (especially alcohol), supplement a balanced diet with extra folic acid and iron, and update their immunizations. Indeed, preconception health is at least as important as health during pregnancy. Unfortunately, almost half the births in the United States are unplanned, often to women who are not in the best of health before conception (D'Angelo et al., 2007) (see Figure 2.10).

The first days and weeks after conception (the germinal and embryonic periods) are critical for body formation, but the entire fetal period is a sensitive time for brain development. Furthermore, preterm birth is a risk factor that is affected by nutrition and drugs throughout pregnancy.

Timing may be important even before conception. When pregnancy occurs soon after a previous pregnancy, risk increases, perhaps because a woman's body may need time to recover from birth. For example, second-born children are twice as likely to

teratogen
Any agent or condition, including viruses, drugs, and chemicals, that can impair prenatal development, resulting in birth defects or complications.

behavioral teratogens
Agents and conditions that can harm the prenatal brain, impairing the future child's intellectual and emotional functioning.

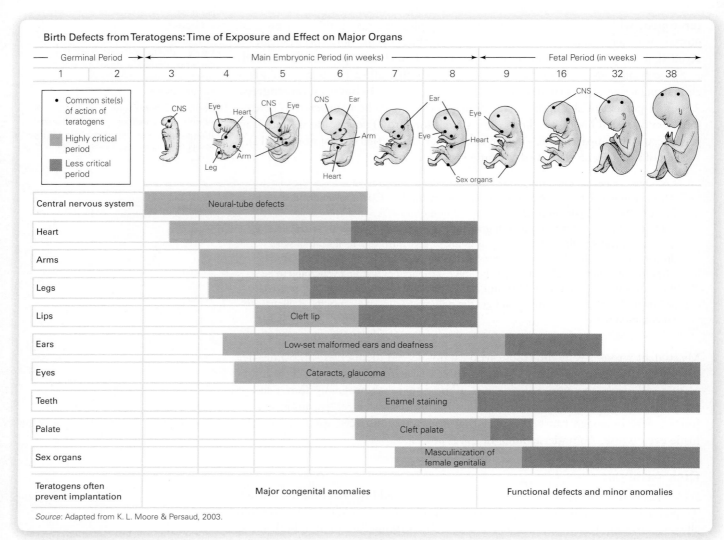

Birth Defects from Teratogens: Time of Exposure and Effect on Major Organs

Source: Adapted from K. L. Moore & Persaud, 2003.

FIGURE 2.9 Critical Periods in Human Development The most serious damage from teratogens (green bars) is likely to occur early in prenatal development. However, significant damage (purple bars) to many vital parts of the body can occur during the last months of pregnancy as well. Behavioral teratogens also affect the fetus throughout development.

cerebral palsy
A disorder that results from damage to the brain's motor centers. People with cerebral palsy have difficulty with muscle control, so their speech and/or body movements are impaired.

anoxia
A lack of oxygen that, if prolonged, can cause brain damage or death.

be autistic if they are born within a year of the first-born child than if they are born several years later (Cheslack-Postava et al., 2011). Mothers who are under age 16 or over age 40 have higher rates of genetic, prenatal, and birth complications.

The concept of critical and sensitive periods is helpful in understanding **cerebral palsy** (difficulties with movement control resulting from brain damage), which was once thought to be caused solely by birth procedures (excessive medication, slow breech birth, or use of forceps to pull the fetal head through the birth canal). We now know that cerebral palsy results from genetic vulnerability, teratogens, and maternal infection (J. R. Mann et al., 2009), not only from insufficient oxygen to the fetal brain at birth.

A lack of oxygen, called **anoxia,** often occurs for a second or two during birth, indicated by a slower fetal heart rate. To prevent prolonged anoxia, the fetal heart rate is monitored during labor. The danger of anoxia is the reason that two of the five Apgar ratings indicate oxygen level. How long anoxia can continue without harming the brain depends on genes, birthweight, gestational age (preterm newborns are more vulnerable), drugs (either taken by the mother before birth or given during birth), and many other factors.

Insufficient oxygen may begin long before birth. Thus, anoxia is part of a cascade that may cause cerebral palsy or other problems. Inadequate oxygen during pregnancy is a serious condition, which is why listening to the fetal heartbeat is part of every prenatal visit.

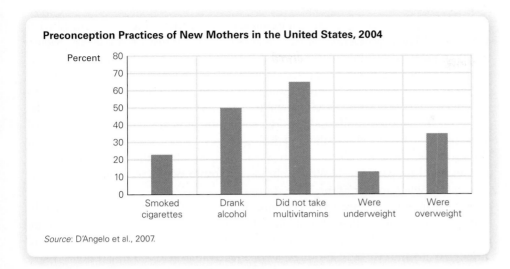

Preconception Practices of New Mothers in the United States, 2004

Source: D'Angelo et al., 2007.

FIGURE 2.10 **No One is Perfect**
Blaming pregnant women is easy, but almost no one avoids all drugs and stresses, sleeps and eats well, weighs just the right amount, exercises at least an hour each day, and completely avoids fried or salty foods. If you are the exception, could you keep it up for a year, while gaining 35 pounds; sometimes feeling nauseous; coping with stares and the questions of friends, relatives, and strangers; and going to the doctor every few weeks?

HOW MUCH IS TOO MUCH? A second factor affecting the harm from any teratogen is the dose and/or frequency of exposure. Some teratogens have a **threshold effect;** they are virtually harmless until exposure reaches a certain level, at which point they "cross the threshold" and become damaging. This threshold is not a fixed boundary: dose, timing, frequency, and other teratogens affect when the threshold is crossed (O'Leary et al., 2010).

Thresholds are difficult to set because one teratogen may increase the harm from another. Consider alcohol. Early in pregnancy, an embryo exposed to heavy drinking can develop **fetal alcohol syndrome (FAS),** which distorts the facial features (especially the eyes, ears, and upper lip). Later in pregnancy, alcohol is a behavioral teratogen, the cause of *fetal alcohol effects (FAE),* leading to hyperactivity, poor concentration, impaired spatial reasoning, and slow learning (Niccols, 2007; Streissguth & Connor, 2001).

However, some pregnant women drink alcohol with no evident harm to the fetus. FAS is more apparent when women are poorly nourished and cigarette smokers (Abel, 2009). If occasional drinking during pregnancy always caused FAS, almost everyone born in Europe before 1980 would be affected. As for FAE, hyperactivity and slow learning are so common that FAE cannot be blamed for every case.

Currently, U.S. women hoping to become pregnant are advised to avoid all alcohol. By contrast, women in the United Kingdom receive conflicting advice about drinking an occasional glass of wine (Raymond et al., 2009), and French women are told to abstain but many have not heard that message (Toutain, 2010). Total abstinence requires that all women who might become pregnant avoid a legal substance that most adults use routinely. Wise? Probably. Necessary? Maybe not.

INNATE VULNERABILITY Genes are a third influential factor in every aspect of conception, pregnancy, and birth. Consider what happens when a woman carrying dizygotic twins drinks alcohol, for example. The alcohol in the mother's bloodstream reaches the placenta and then the embryos via the umbilical cord. Thus, the twins' blood alcohol levels are equal. However, one twin may be more severely affected than the other because their alleles for the enzyme that metabolizes alcohol may differ.

threshold effect
A situation in which a certain teratogen is relatively harmless in small doses but becomes harmful once exposure reaches a certain level (the threshold).

fetal alcohol syndrome (FAS)
A cluster of birth defects, including abnormal facial characteristics, slow physical growth, and intellectual disabilities, that may occur in the child of a woman who drinks alcohol while pregnant.

Swing High and Low Adopted by loving parents but born with fetal alcohol syndrome, Philip, shown here at age 11, sometimes threatens to kill his family members. His parents sent him to this residential ranch in Eureka, Montana, a temporary home (non-profit, tuition $3,500 a month) for children like him. This moment during recess is a happy one; it is not known whether he learned to control his fury.

✦ **ESPECIALLY FOR Judges and Juries** How much protection, if any, should the legal system provide for fetuses? Should alcoholic women who are pregnant be jailed to prevent them from drinking? What about people who enable them to drink, such as their partners, their parents, bar owners, bartenders? (see response, page 76) ➡

RESPONSE FOR Judges and Juries (from page 75) The law punishes women who jeopardize the health of their fetuses, but a developmental view would consider the micro-, exo-, and macrosystems. ●

Genetic vulnerability is a particular example of differential sensitivity, as described in Chapter 1. Genetic protections or hazards are suspected for many birth defects (Sadler, 2012). A protective factor seems to be the X chromosome; male fetuses (only one X) are more vulnerable to teratogens than are females (XX) (Lewis & Kestler, 2012).

Since fathers provide 23 chromosomes, they are almost as likely as mothers to provide genetic protection or vulnerability. Maternal genes have an additional role: They affect a mother's body and thus the environment of the womb. One maternal allele results in low levels of folic acid during pregnancy. Via the umbilical cord, that can produce *neural-tube defects*—either *spina bifida,* in which the tail of the spine is not enclosed properly (in healthy embryos, enclosure occurs at about week 7), or *anencephaly,* wherein part of the brain is missing.

Neural-tube defects are more common in certain ethnic groups (Irish, English, and Egyptian) than in others. For them, folic acid supplements before pregnancy are strongly recommended. The allele that causes low folic acid in the woman is rare among Asians and Africans, although supplemental folic acid is not harmful.

A 1998 U.S. law requires that folic acid be added to packaged cereal, to protect every woman, even if she does not expect to become pregnant. That regulation is credited with reducing neural-tube defects by 26 percent (MMWR, September 13, 2002).

However, some women rarely eat cereal or take vitamins. Either diet or genes may be the reason that the U.S. rates of neural-tube defects are much higher in Appalachia. In 2010, in the mountainous areas of Kentucky, West Virginia, and Pennsylvania, about 1 newborn in 1,000 had a neural-tube defect (Rochat et al., 2011).

APPLYING THE RESEARCH Risk analysis cannot precisely predict the results of genetic vulnerability, teratogenic exposure, or birth complications in individual cases. However, much is known about what individuals and society can do to reduce the risks. Table 2.6 lists some teratogens and their possible effects, as well as preventive measures.

TABLE 2.6 Teratogens: Effects of Exposure and Prevention of Damage*

Teratogens	Effects of Exposure on Fetus	Measures for Preventing Damage
Diseases		
Rubella (German measles)	In embryonic period, causes blindness and deafness; in first and second trimesters, causes brain damage.	Get immunized before becoming pregnant.
Toxoplasmosis	Brain damage, loss of vision, intellectual disabilities.	Avoid eating undercooked meat and handling cat feces, garden dirt during pregnancy.
Measles, chicken pox, influenza	May impair brain functioning.	Get immunized before getting pregnant; avoid infected people during pregnancy.
Syphilis	Baby is born with syphilis, which, untreated, leads to brain and bone damage and eventual death.	Early prenatal diagnosis and treatment with antibiotics.
AIDS	Baby may catch the virus. Without treatment, illness and death are likely during childhood.	Prenatal drugs and cesarean birth make AIDS transmission rare.
Other sexually transmitted infections, including gonorrhea and chlamydia	Not usually harmful during pregnancy but may cause blindness and infections if transmitted during birth.	Early diagnosis and treatment; if necessary, cesarean section, treatment of newborn.
Infections, including infections of urinary tract, gums, and teeth	May cause premature labor, which increases vulnerability to brain damage.	Get infection treated, preferably before becoming pregnant.
Pollutants		
Lead, mercury, PCBs (polychlorinated biphenyls); dioxin; and some pesticides, herbicides, and cleaning compounds	May cause spontaneous abortion, preterm labor, and brain damage.	Most common substances are harmless in small doses, but pregnant women should avoid regular and direct exposure, such as drinking well water, eating unwashed fruits or vegetables, using chemical compounds, and eating fish from polluted waters.

TABLE 2.6 (Continued)

Teratogens	Effects of Exposure on Fetus	Measures for Preventing Damage
Radiation		
Massive or repeated exposure to radiation, as in medical X-rays	In the embryonic period, may cause abnormally small head (microcephaly) and intellectual disabilities; in the fetal period, suspected but not proven to cause brain damage. Exposure to background radiation, as from power plants, is usually too low to have an effect.	Get sonograms, not X-rays, during pregnancy; pregnant women who work directly with radiation need special protection or temporary assignment to another job.
Social and Behavioral Factors		
Very high stress	Early in pregnancy, may cause cleft lip or cleft palate, spontaneous abortion, or preterm labor.	Get adequate relaxation, rest, and sleep; reduce hours of employment; get help with housework and child care.
Malnutrition	When severe, may interfere with conception, implantation, normal fetal development, and full-term birth.	Eat a balanced diet (with adequate vitamins and minerals, including, especially, folic acid, iron, and vitamin A); achieve normal weight before getting pregnant, then gain 25–35 lbs (10–15 kg) during pregnancy.
Excessive, exhausting exercise	Can affect fetal development when it interferes with pregnant woman's sleep, digestion, or nutrition.	Get regular, moderate exercise.
Medicinal Drugs		
Lithium	Can cause heart abnormalities.	Avoid all medicines, whether prescription or over-the-counter, during pregnancy unless they are approved by a medical professional who knows about the pregnancy and is aware of the most recent research.
Tetracycline	Can harm teeth.	
Retinoic acid	Can cause limb deformities.	
Streptomycin	Can cause deafness.	
ACE inhibitors	Can harm digestive organs.	
Phenobarbital	Can affect brain development.	
Thalidomide	Can stop ear and limb formation.	
Psychoactive Drugs		
Caffeine	Normal use poses no problem.	Avoid excessive use: Drink no more than three cups a day of beverages containing caffeine (coffee, tea, cola drinks, hot chocolate).
Alcohol	May cause fetal alcohol syndrome (FAS) or fetal alcohol effects (FAE).	Stop or severely limit alcohol consumption during pregnancy; especially dangerous are three or more drinks a day or four or more drinks on one occasion.
Tobacco	Reduces birthweight, increases risk of malformations of limbs and urinary tract, and may affect the baby's lungs.	Stop smoking before becoming pregnant; if already pregnant, stop smoking immediately.
Marijuana	Heavy exposure may affect the central nervous system; when smoked, may hinder fetal growth.	Avoid or strictly limit marijuana consumption.
Heroin	Slows fetal growth and may cause premature labor; newborns with heroin in their bloodstream require medical treatment to prevent the pain and convulsions of withdrawal.	Get treated for heroin addiction before becoming pregnant; if already pregnant, gradual withdrawal on methadone is better than continued use of heroin.
Cocaine	May cause slow fetal growth, premature labor, and learning problems in the first years of life.	Stop using cocaine before pregnancy; babies of cocaine-using mothers may need special medical and educational attention in their first years of life.
Inhaled solvents (glue or aerosol)	May cause abnormally small head, crossed eyes, and other indications of brain damage.	Stop sniffing inhalants before becoming pregnant; be aware that serious damage can occur before a woman knows she is pregnant.

* The field of toxicology advances daily. Research on new substances begins with their effects on nonhuman species, which provides suggestive (though not conclusive) evidence. This table is a primer; it is no substitute for careful consultation with a professional who knows the recent research.

Sources: Gupta, 2011; Mann & Andrews, 2007; O'Rahilly & Müller, 2001; Reece & Hobbins, 2007; Sadler, 2012; Shepard & Lemire, 2004.

low birthweight (LBW)
A body weight at birth of less than 5½ pounds (2,500 grams).

very low birthweight (VLBW)
A body weight at birth of less than 3 pounds, 5 ounces (1,500 grams).

extremely low birthweight (ELBW)
A body weight at birth of less than 2 pounds, 3 ounces (1,000 grams).

preterm birth
A birth that occurs three or more weeks before the full 38 weeks of the typical pregnancy have elapsed—that is, at 35 or fewer weeks after conception.

small for gestational age (SGA)
Having a body weight at birth that is significantly lower than expected, given the time since conception. For example, a 5-pound (2,265-gram) newborn is considered SGA if born on time but not SGA if born two months early. (Also called *small-for-dates*.)

Remember that the outcomes vary. Many fetuses are exposed with no evident harm. The opposite occurs as well: About 20 percent of all serious defects occur for reasons unknown. Women are advised to maintain good nutrition and avoid teratogens, especially drugs and chemicals (pesticides, cleaning fluids, and many cosmetics contain teratogenic chemicals). Some medications are necessary (e.g., for women who have epilepsy, diabetes, severe depression) and should be continued, but caution should begin *before* pregnancy is confirmed.

Sadly, the cascade of teratogens is most likely to begin with women who are already vulnerable. For example, cigarette smokers are more often drinkers (as was my student J.'s mother); those whose jobs involve chemicals and pesticides are more often malnourished; women of low socioeconomic status (SES) are more likely to give birth early, less likely to get prenatal care, and less likely to be admitted to modern hospitals (Ahmed & Jaakkola, 2007; Bryant et al., 2011; Hougaard & Hansen, 2007).

The benefits of early prenatal care are many: Women can be told which substances to avoid, they can learn what to eat and what to do, and they may be diagnosed and treated for some conditions (syphilis and HIV among them) that harm the fetus only if early treatment does not occur. As noted earlier, prenatal tests (of blood, urine, and fetal heart rate, as well as ultrasound) and even preconception tests can identify many disorders (see Table 2.5 on page 72).

When possible complications (such as twins, gestational diabetes, infections) arise, early recognition increases the chance of a healthy birth. One obvious effect of early prenatal care is that the risk of low birthweight is reduced. As you will now see, an underweight newborn is vulnerable in dozens of ways. Indeed, the U.S. rate of infant death is higher than that of many other nations largely because of more underweight babies.

Low Birthweight

Some newborns are small and immature. With modern hospital care, tiny infants usually survive, but it would be better for everyone—mother, father, baby, and society—if all newborns were in the womb for at least 35 weeks and weighed more than 2,500 grams (5½ pounds).

Low birthweight (LBW) is defined by the World Health Organization as weight under 2,500 grams. LBW babies are further grouped into **very low birthweight (VLBW),** under 1,500 grams (3 pounds, 5 ounces), and **extremely low birthweight (ELBW),** under 1,000 grams (2 pounds, 3 ounces).

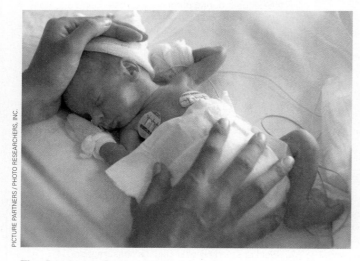

PICTURE PARTNERS / PHOTO RESEARCHERS, INC.

Tiny Dutchman Survival is uncertain for extremely low-birthweight newborns, such as Kareem. However, his chances are excellent, partly because he was in the womb for 29 weeks (each week after 22 aids survival) and partly because he was born in the Netherlands (where rates of preterm survival are among the best in the world).

MATERNAL BEHAVIOR Fetal weight normally doubles in the last three months of a full-term pregnancy, with 900 grams (about 2 pounds) of that gain occurring in the final three weeks. Thus, a baby born **preterm** (three or more weeks early; no longer called *premature*) is usually LBW.

Preterm birth correlates with many of the teratogens already mentioned, an example of the cascade that leads to newborns with evident problems. The prenatal environment itself may cause early labor as well. Indeed, when the environment of the womb is harmful, as when multiples reduce nourishment to each fetus, hormones precipitate labor.

Early birth is only one cause of low birthweight. Some fetuses gain weight slowly throughout pregnancy and are **small for gestational age (SGA).** For example, a full-term baby weighing only 2,500 grams and a 30-week-old fetus weighing 1,000 grams are both SGA (also called *small-for-dates*). The former is one gram shy of LBW and the latter, if born, is ELBW *and* SGA.

Maternal or fetal illness might cause SGA, but maternal drug use before and during pregnancy is the most common underlying cause. Every psychoactive drug slows fetal growth; tobacco is implicated in 25 percent of all low-birthweight births worldwide.

Another common reason for slow fetal growth is maternal malnutrition. Women who begin pregnancy underweight, who eat poorly during pregnancy, or who gain less than 3 pounds (1.3 kilograms) per month in the final six months are likely to have an underweight infant. Malnutrition (not age) is the primary reason teenagers often have small babies. Unfortunately, many of the risk factors just mentioned—underweight, undernutrition, underage, and smoking—tend to occur together (see Figure 2.10).

FATHERS AND OTHERS The causes of low birthweight just mentioned focus on the pregnant woman (see Table 2.7). If she takes drugs or is undernourished, her fetus suffers. However, the more we learn about birth problems, the more important fathers—and grandmothers, neighbors, and communities—are discovered to be, before as well as during pregnancy.

As an editorial in a journal for obstetricians explains: "Fathers' attitudes regarding the pregnancy, fathers' behaviors during the prenatal period, and the relationship between fathers and mothers . . . may indirectly influence risk for adverse birth outcomes" (Misra et al., 2010, p. 99).

Not only fathers—the entire social network is crucial (Lewallen, 2011). This is most apparent in what has been called the **Hispanic paradox.** In general, low SES correlates with low birthweight, with the LBW rate increasing in every nation as income falls. Immigrants to the United States, especially those from Spanish-speaking nations, average much lower SES than the native-born.

Logically, then, babies born to immigrants should weigh less than those born to native-born women. But, paradoxically, U.S. babies born to immigrants are generally healthier in every way, including birthweight, than are those of U.S.-born women of the same ethnicity. One explanation is that these newborns benefit from their mothers, who are supported by their husbands, their mothers, and their culture.

This surprise was first documented among Mexican Americans. Prenatal development is also better than expected among U.S. immigrants from other Spanish-speaking nations, from the Caribbean, and from eastern Europe. Indeed, throughout childhood, children born to low-SES immigrants seem to do better in health and cognition than native-born children of the same ancestry and income (García Coll & Marks, 2012).

His Baby, Too Thanks to her husband, this Latina mother-to-be is likely to eat well, avoid drugs, and rest when she is tired. The Hispanic paradox might more aptly be named the paternal paradox, since without any direct biological connection after conception, fathers have a powerful impact on fetal health.

Hispanic paradox
The surprising discovery that, although low SES usually correlates with poor health, this is not true for Hispanics in the United States. For example, when compared with the U.S. average LBW rate, Hispanic newborns are less often of low birthweight.

TABLE 2.7 Before Pregnancy

What Prospective Mothers Should Do	What Prospective Mothers Really Do (U.S. data)
1. Plan the pregnancy.	1. About 60 percent of pregnancies are intended.
2. Take a daily multivitamin with folic acid.	2. About 40 percent of women aged 18 to 45 take vitamins.
3. Avoid binge drinking (defined as four or more drinks in a row).	3. One-eighth of all women who might become pregnant binge-drink.
4. Update immunizations against all teratogenic viruses, especially rubella.	4. Because of laws regarding school admission, most young women in the United States are well immunized. This is not true in most developing nations.
5. Gain or lose weight, as appropriate.	5. Babies born to underweight women are at risk for low birthweight. Babies born to obese women have three times the usual rate of birth complications. Only half of all women begin pregnancy at an appropriate weight.
6. Reassess use of prescription drugs.	6. Eighty-five percent of pregnant women take prescription drugs (not counting vitamins).
7. Develop exercise habits.	7. Many women do not exercise, yet daily exercise improves health, with benefits to the embryo, fetus, and newborn.

Sources: Downs & Hausenblas, 2007; Suellentrop et al., 2006; Tsai et al., 2007.

FIGURE 2.11 Getting Better Some public health experts consider the rate of low birthweight to be indicative of national health, since both are affected by the same causes. If that is true, the world is getting healthier, since the LBW world average was 28 percent in 2009 but 16 percent in 2012. When all nations are included, 47 report LBW at 6 per 100 or lower, which suggests that many nations (including the United States and United Kingdom) could improve.

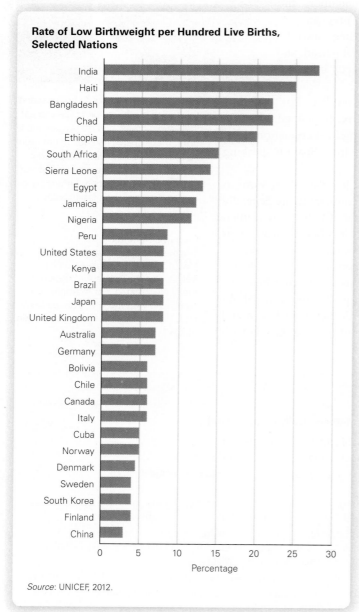

Rate of Low Birthweight per Hundred Live Births, Selected Nations

Source: UNICEF, 2012.

Newborns of Chinese descent are an interesting case. If their mothers' socioeconomic status is low, these newborns weigh more and are less likely to die *if* their mothers were born in China, not in the United States; the same is true for other immigrant groups. However, babies born to college-educated Chinese Americans (high SES) are less likely to be LBW or to die in the first year if their mothers were born in the United States, not China (Li & Keith, 2011).

This suggests that both education and social support are protective of prenatal health; ideally, newborns of every ethnicity have both. Among other things, pregnant women need to nourish themselves well (no drugs) and avoid exhaustion, often with the help of expectant fathers.

CONSEQUENCES OF LOW BIRTHWEIGHT Early death is the most obvious hazard of low birthweight. But problems do not end after surviving birth. When compared with newborns conceived at the same time but born later, very-low-birthweight infants are later to smile, to hold a bottle, to walk, and to talk.

As months go by, cognitive, visual, and hearing impairments emerge. High-risk newborns become infants and children who cry more, pay attention less, disobey, and experience language delays (Aarnoudse-Moens et al., 2009; Spinillo et al., 2009).

Longitudinal research studies find that, compared with the average child in middle childhood, formerly SGA children have smaller brain volume, and those who were preterm have lower IQs (van Soelen et al., 2010). Even in adulthood, risks persist: Adults who were LBW are more likely to have heart disease and diabetes.

However, remember that risk analysis gives odds, not certainties—and remember that many factors (including the genes and prenatal care already described and the caregiving explained in the following chapters) affect each child. Although low birthweight is a risk to be avoided if possible, some tiny newborns, by age 4, are normal in brain development and in every other way (Claas et al., 2011; Spittle et al., 2009).

COMPARING NATIONS Ranking worse than most developed nations—and similar to Poland and Malaysia—the United States has a low-birthweight rate of about 8 percent. In some northern European nations, such as Sweden, only 4 percent of newborns weigh less than 2,500 grams; in several South Asian nations, including India, more than 20 percent do (see Figure 2.11).

Worldwide, far fewer low-birthweight babies are born today than 20 years ago, and neonatal deaths have been reduced by one-third as a result (Rajaratnam et al., 2010). Some nations, China and Chile among them, have shown dramatic improvement. In 1970, about half of Chinese newborns were LBW; recent estimates put that number at 4 percent (UNICEF, 2012). By contrast, in other nations, notably in sub-Saharan Africa, the LBW rate is steady or rising because global warming, AIDS, food shortages, wars, and other problems affect pregnancy.

A VIEW FROM SCIENCE

Why More Tiny Newborns?

Why did the frequency of low birthweight in the United States decrease steadily throughout most of the twentieth century, reaching a low of 7 per 100 in 1990, but then rise again, with the 2008 rate at 8.2 percent (Figure 2.12)? This is unrelated to ethnicity: In every racial group, more underweight newborns are recorded today than was the case 30 years ago (U.S. Census Bureau, 2011).

Adding to the puzzle is the fact that several changes in maternal ethnicity, age, and health since 1990 should have decreased LBW, not increased it. For instance, maternal obesity and diabetes are increasing; both lead to heavier babies, not lighter ones.

Furthermore, African Americans have LBW newborns twice as often as the national average (almost 14 percent), and younger teenagers have smaller babies than do women in their 20s (e.g., 12 percent for 15-year-old mothers). However, the birth rate among African Americans and teens has been declining dramatically, so the LBW rate should be going down, not up.

Many scientists have developed hypotheses. One early explanation was increasing rates of assisted reproduction (ART, explained in Chapter 10), which often leads to twins and triplets. However, LBW rates are rising even for natural conceptions (Pinborg et al., 2004), so the ART hypothesis cannot be the only explanation.

Something else must be amiss. Another possibility is nutrition. Nations with many small newborns are also nations where hunger is prevalent, and increasing hunger correlates with increasing LBW. In both Chile and China, LBW fell dramatically as nutrition improved.

As for the United States, the Department of Agriculture found an increase in *food insecurity* (measured by skipped meals, use of food stamps, and outright hunger) in the past decade. Food insecurity directly affects LBW, and it also increases chronic illness, which itself correlates with LBW (Seligman & Schillinger, 2010).

In 2008, about 15 percent of U.S. households were considered food-insecure, with rates higher among women in their prime reproductive years than among middle-aged women or men of any age. These rates increased with the economic recession of 2008–2010; if the food-insecurity hypothesis is accurate, rates of LBW will continue to increase.

Another possibility is drug use. As you will see in Chapter 10, the rates of smoking, drinking, and other drug use among high school girls reached a low in 1992, then increased, then decreased. Most U.S. women now giving birth are in a cohort that experienced rising drug use; they may still be suffering the effects.

If smoking cigarettes and so on is the reason for the rise in low birthweight, then the decrease in drug use since the mid-1990s should mean that LBW should fall again in the United States. Sadly, in developing nations, more young women are smoking and drinking than a decade ago, including in China, where LBW decreased dramatically. Will rates rise in China soon?

The latest data suggest that LBW may finally be holding steady or even decreasing in the United States—welcome news, but we need several more years to see a trend. Scientists, and everyone reading this book, will check the rates in 2013 and beyond in order to draw empirical conclusions.

As you remember from Chapter 1, scientists welcome data, even when it does not confirm their hypotheses. Perhaps neither food insecurity nor rates of drug abuse cause the high rates of babies born too small in the United States. Once we know the reason, we will be better able to reverse the trend.

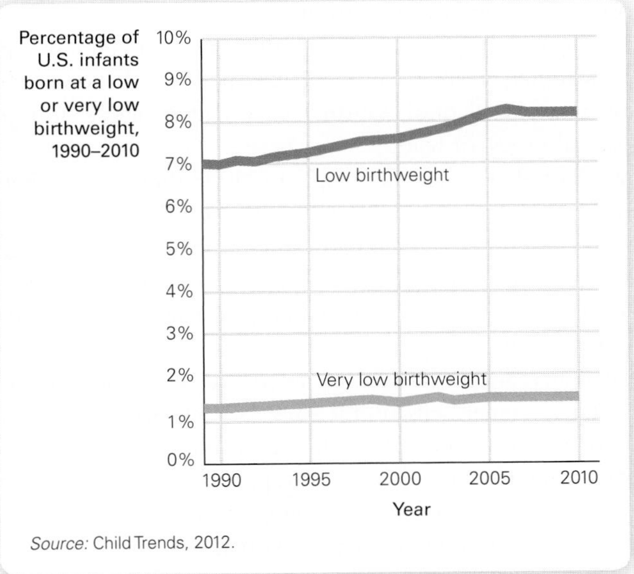

Percentage of U.S. infants born at a low or very low birthweight, 1990–2010

Low birthweight

Very low birthweight

Year

Source: Child Trends, 2012.

FIGURE 2.12 Something Wrong Here From 1990 to 2010, most nations have experienced marked reductions in newborns weighing less than 2,500 grams. The United States is an exception. Hypotheses include food insecurity, lack of health insurance for young adults, more twins, and fewer births to high-SES women.

KEY points

- Zygotes with abnormal chromosomes and genes are common; most are spontaneously aborted soon after conception. Survivors (e.g., those with Down syndrome) benefit from good care.
- Although hundreds of teratogens can harm the fetus, many future babies are protected by genes, timing (late), dose (small), and frequency (rare).
- Fathers, future grandparents, and cultures reduce risks, making sure that pregnant women are well fed, not tired, and drug-free.
- Newborns born early and small for gestational age are at risk for many problems, at birth and lifelong.

Nature and Nurture Connected

We close this chapter with a detailed look at two phenomena—alcoholism and nearsightedness—that illustrate the connections among genes, prenatal care, developmental age, and culture. The interaction is dynamic, not simple, but understanding it has many practical applications for parents, professionals, and everyone else.

Alcoholism

At various times, people have considered drug abuse to be a moral weakness, a social scourge, or a personality defect. Attention has been on alcohol, in part because fermentation is natural and universal, present in every culture and era, and in part because alcoholism is a far more common addiction than any other and may be as destructive, if not more so.

In various times and places, alcoholics were locked up, doused with cold water, or burned at the stake. Alcohol has been declared illegal (as in the United States from 1919 to 1933), condemned as sinful (in Islam, Mormonism, and many other religions), and considered sacred (as in many Jewish and Catholic rituals). Science has now learned that the human reaction to alcohol is affected by dozens of alleles as well as by diverse cultural practices, so any universal prohibition or veneration will affect individuals in opposite ways. Differential sensitivity again.

As you might expect, alcoholism begins with genes that create an addictive pull that can be overpowering, extremely weak, or somewhere in between. To be specific, each person's biochemistry reacts to alcohol, causing sleep, nausea, aggression, joy, relaxation, forgetfulness, sexual urges, or tears.

How bodies metabolize alcohol allows some people to "hold their liquor" better and therefore drink too much, whereas others (including many East Asians) sweat and become red-faced after just a few sips, an embarrassing response that may lead to abstinence. Candidate genes and alleles for alcoholism have been identified on every chromosome except the Y chromosome (ironic, since, internationally, more men than women are alcoholics) (Epps & Holt, 2011).

Inherited psychological traits affect alcoholism as much as biological ones (Macgregor et al., 2009). A quick temper, sensation seeking, or high anxiety encourage drinking. It is impossible to specify how much alcoholism is genetic or cultural because these influences are "inexorably intertwined" (Dick, 2011, p. 225); the relationship between nature and nurture varies by age and context (Young-Wolff et al., 2011).

For example, some contexts (such as fraternity parties) make it hard to avoid alcohol; other contexts (a church social in a "dry" county) make it difficult to swallow anything stronger than lemonade. Age is also pivotal. Adolescents experience more pleasure, and less pain, from being drunk than do people who are older or younger

(Spear, 2011). Consequently, they get drunk more often—and have higher rates of car accidents, temper tantrums, and unprotected sex while drinking.

Biological sex (XX or XY) and gender (cultural) also affect the risk of alcoholism. For biological reasons (body size, fat composition, metabolism), women become drunk on less alcohol than men, but how much a woman drinks depends on her social context.

For instance, in Japan, both sexes inherit the same genes for metabolizing alcohol, yet Japanese men—not women—drink more alcohol than their peers elsewhere. When Japanese women migrate to the United States, their alcohol consumption is said to increase about fivefold (Higuchi et al., 1996; Makimoto, 1998). Their alcoholism increases as well. For all immigrants, alcohol consumption is related to the original culture, the stress of immigration, and U.S. norms—increasing or decreasing depending on specifics (Szaflarski et al., 2011).

As you have read, prenatal exposure to alcohol may seriously impair the fetus, but it also is more likely that a baby born to a drinking mother will become an alcoholic later on. Is that a genetic, prenatal, or childhood effect—or all three?

Nearsightedness

Age, genes, and culture affect vision as well. First consider age. Newborns focus only on things within 2 feet of their eyes; vision improves steadily until about age 10. At puberty, the eyeball changes shape, which increases nearsightedness; eyeball shape changes again in middle age, decreasing nearsightedness (myopia) but increasing farsightedness.

Now consider genes. A study of British twins found that the gene that governs eye formation (Pax6) has many alleles that increase nearsightedness (Hammond et al., 2004). This research found *heritability* of almost 90 percent, which means that if one monozygotic twin was nearsighted, the other twin was almost always nearsighted, too.

However, **heritability** is a statistic that indicates only how much of the variation in a particular trait *within a particular population* in a particular context and era can be traced to genes. For example, the heritability of height is very high (about 95 percent) when children receive good medical care and ample nourishment, but it is low (about 20 percent) when children are malnourished. Thus, the 90 percent heritability of nearsightedness among the British children may not apply elsewhere.

Instead, visual problems may be caused by the environment. In some African nations, heritability of vision is close to zero because severe vitamin A deficiency is the main reason some children see less well than others. Scientists are working to develop a strain of maize (the local staple) that is high in vitamin A. If they succeed, heritability will increase and overall vision will improve (Harjes et al., 2008).

But what about children who are well nourished? Is their vision entirely inherited? Cross-cultural research suggests not.

One report claims that "myopia is increasing at an 'epidemic' rate, particularly in East Asia" (Park & Congdon, 2004, p. 21). The first published research on this phenomenon appeared in 1992, when scholars noticed that, in army-mandated medical exams of all 17-year-old males in Singapore, 26 percent were nearsighted in 1980 but 43 percent were nearsighted in 1990 (Tay et al., 1992).

Further studies found nearsightedness increasing from 12 to 84 percent between ages 6 and 17 in Taiwan, with increases in myopia during middle childhood also in Singapore and Hong Kong (cited in Grosvenor, 2003). One author claims "very strong environmental impacts" on Asian children's vision (Morgan, 2003, p. 276). What could that be?

Bright-Eyed and Nearsighted These are star students from Beijing, China, waiting in line for visas to the United States. If they had spent less time studying, would they be here?

heritability
A statistic that indicates what percentage of the variation in a particular trait within a particular population, in a particular context and era, can be traced to genes.

One clue is that, unlike earlier generations or children in other nations, since 1980 East Asian children have become amazingly proficient in math and science because they study intensely, in school and after school. As their developing eyes focus on the print in front of them, those with a genetic vulnerability to myopia may lose acuity for objects far away—which is exactly what nearsightedness means.

A study of Singaporean 10- to 12-year-olds found a correlation between nearsightedness (measured by optometric exams) and high achievement, especially in language (presumably reflecting more reading). Correlation is not causation, but statistics (odds ratio of 2.5, significance of 0.001) strongly suggest a link (Saw et al., 2007).

Ophthalmologists believe that the underlying cause is not time spent studying but inadequate time spent in daylight. An editorial in a leading U.S. journal for opthalmologists explains:

> The probability of becoming myopic by the eighth grade is about 60% if a child has two myopic parents and does less than 5 hours per week of sports/outdoor activity. . . . [It is] about 20% if a two-myopic-parent child does 14 hours or more per week of sports/outdoor activity.
>
> *[Mutti & Zadnik, 2009, p. 77]*

Between the early 1970s and the early 2000s, nearsightedness in the U.S. population increased from 25 to 42 percent (Vitale et al., 2009). Urbanization, video games, homework, and fear of strangers have kept many contemporary U.S. children indoors, doing close work much of the time, unlike earlier generations who played outside for hours each day. The correlation between nearsightedness and outside play is striking.

A vision scientist from Ohio State University says: "We're kind of a dim indoors people nowadays. . . . If you ask me, I would say modern society is missing the protective effect of being outdoors" (Mutti, quoted in Holden, 2010, p. 17). See Figure 2.13.

However, correlation is not cause. To prove a causal link, a longitudinal experiment would require some children to stay indoors while others from the same families (to control for genes) play outside. Since that is hypothesized to harm those who stay inside, such research would be unethical (see Chapter 1) as well as impossible. Nonetheless, many applications arise from this and many other ideas from this chapter.

FIGURE 2.13 Go Out and Play!
If both your parents are nearsighted, chances are you will be, too—but not if you play sports at least six hours a week. The dramatic correlation between childhood myopia and playing sports does *not* prove causation: Some children who wear glasses choose to avoid sports. Nonetheless, parents and schools should encourage children to play outside every day. Currently, only about half of all parents of preschoolers make sure children do so.

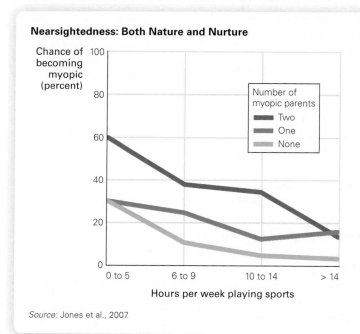

Source: Jones et al., 2007.

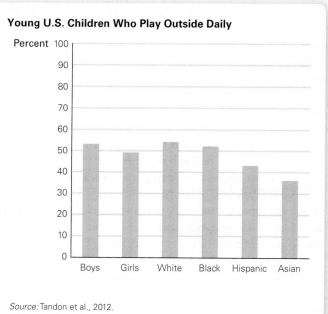

Source: Tandon et al., 2012.

Practical Applications

Since genes affect every disorder, no one should be blamed or punished for inherited problems. However, knowing that genes do not act in isolation can lead to preventive measures before, during, and after prenatal development.

For instance, if alcoholism is in their genes, women can avoid alcohol before, during, and after pregnancy. Furthermore, parents can keep alcohol out of their home, hoping their children become cognitively and socially mature before drinking. (If alcohol is available at home, most children taste it before age 10.) Similarly, if nearsightedness runs in the family, parents can make sure that children play outdoors every day.

Of course, outdoor play and abstention from alcohol are recommended for every child, as are dozens of other behaviors, such as flossing the teeth, saying "please," getting enough sleep, eating vegetables, and writing thank-you notes. However, no parent can enforce every recommendation.

Awareness of genetic risks alerts parents to set priorities and act on them, and it helps professionals advise pregnant women. Some recommendations should be routine (e.g., prenatal vitamins including folic acid) because it is impossible to know who is at risk. Others are tailored to the individual, such as weight gain for underweight women.

Care must be taken to keep pregnancy and birth from being an anxious time, filled with restrictions and fears about diet, diseases, drugs, and other possible dangers. Anxiety itself may reduce sleep, impair digestion, and raise blood pressure—all of which hinder development—which in turn may make birth complicated and postpartum depression likely.

Indeed, stress reduces the chance of conception, increases the chance of prenatal damage, and slows down the birth process. A conclusion from every page of this chapter is that risks are apparent in every moment of conception, pregnancy, and birth. But those risks can be minimal if everyone—fathers as well as mothers, professionals as well as community members—does what is needed to ensure that newborns begin life eager and able to live 80 more healthy years.

KEY points

- Nature and nurture always interact. Whether a particular genetic vulnerability becomes a lifelong problem depends a great deal on the environment.
- Alcoholism is affected by genes for metabolism and personality, but also by the social context.
- Nearsightedness has increased in the past decades, particularly in East Asia but also in North America. Less time spent playing outdoors is the suspected reason.
- Knowing genetic risks helps parents avoid triggers for problems and hopefully reduces generalized anxiety, which itself can be a teratogen.

SUMMARY

The Beginning of Life

1. Genes are the foundation for all development. Human conception occurs when two gametes (an ovum and a sperm, each with 23 chromosomes) combine to form a zygote, 46 chromosomes in a single cell.

2. Every cell of every human being has a unique genetic code made up of about 20,000 to 23,000 genes, some in variations called alleles. The environment interacts with the genetic instructions for every trait.

3. The sex of an embryo depends on the sperm: A Y sperm creates an XY (male) embryo; an X sperm creates an XX (female) embryo. Twins occur if a zygote splits in two (monozygotic, or identical, twins) or if two ova are fertilized by two sperm (dizygotic, or fraternal, twins).

4. Genes interact in various ways: sometimes additively, with multiple genes contributing to a trait, and sometimes in a dominant–recessive pattern. While the genotype of each person is always determined by the combined genotypes of the parents, the phenotype (apparent characteristics) may be quite different from the genotype.

From Zygote to Newborn

5. The first two weeks of prenatal growth are called the germinal period. The cells differentiate, and the developing organism implants itself in the lining of the uterus.

6. The period from the third through the eighth week after conception is called the embryonic period. The heart begins to beat, and the eyes, ears, nose, and mouth form. By the eighth week, the embryo has the basic organs and features of a human, with the exception of the sex organs.

7. The fetal period extends from the ninth week until birth. By the 12th week, all the organs and body structures have formed. The fetus attains viability at 22 weeks, when the brain is sufficiently mature to regulate basic body functions.

8. The average fetus gains approximately 4½ pounds (2,000 grams) during the last three months of pregnancy. Maturation of brain, lungs, and heart ensures survival of virtually all full-term babies.

9. Medical intervention can speed contractions, dull pain, measure infant health via the Apgar scale, and save lives. However, some measures seem unnecessary. The goal is a balance, protecting the baby but also allowing parental involvement and control.

10. Some women feel unhappy, incompetent, or unwell after giving birth. Postpartum depression gradually disappears with appropriate help; fathers are particularly crucial to the well-being of mother and child, although they, too, are vulnerable to depression.

Problems and Solutions

11. Often a zygote has more or fewer than 46 chromosomes. Such zygotes usually do not develop; the main exceptions are those with three chromosomes at the 21st location (Down syndrome, or trisomy-21) or an odd number of sex chromosomes.

12. Thousands of teratogens, especially drugs and alcohol, have the potential to harm the embryo or fetus. Actual harm occurs because of a cascade: Genes, critical periods, dose, and frequency all have an impact.

13. Birth complications, such as an unusually long and stressful labor that includes anoxia (a lack of oxygen to the fetus), have many causes. Low birthweight (less than 5½ pounds, or 2,500 grams) may result from multiple fetuses, placental problems, maternal illness, genes, malnutrition, smoking, drinking, and drug use.

Nature and Nurture Connected

14. Alcoholism is partly genetic, but not completely. It is particularly crucial that children who are genetically vulnerable avoid early exposure to alcohol.

15. Nearsightedness is also partly genetic, but understanding heritability (the impact of genes within a population, not necessarily within an individual) helps show that the relatively recent increase in nearsightedness is affected by the childhood environment.

16. Nature and nurture interact to cause virtually all human problems; understanding genes, prenatal development, birth, and childhood increase the odds that a newborn will have a long and healthy life.

KEY TERMS

additive gene (p. 54)	dizygotic twins (p. 54)	gamete (p. 48)	postpartum depression (p. 68)
age of viability (p. 60)	DNA (deoxyribonucleic acid) (p. 48)	gene (p. 48)	preterm birth (p. 78)
allele (p. 49)		genome (p. 50)	reflex (p. 67)
anoxia (p. 74)	dominant–recessive pattern (p. 54)	genotype (p. 50)	small for gestational age (SGA) (p. 78)
Apgar scale (p. 62)	doula (p. 66)	germinal period (p. 57)	stem cells (p. 58)
behavioral teratogens (p. 73)	Down syndrome (p. 70)	heritability (p. 83)	teratogen (p. 73)
Brazelton Neonatal Behavioral Assessment Scale (NBAS) (p. 67)	embryo (p. 58)	Hispanic paradox (p. 79)	threshold effect (p. 75)
	embryonic period (p. 57)	implantation (p. 58)	ultrasound (p. 60)
carrier (p. 54)	extremely low birthweight (ELBW) (p. 78)	kangaroo care (p. 69)	very low birthweight (VLBW) (p. 78)
cerebral palsy (p. 74)	fetal alcohol syndrome (FAS) (p. 75)	low birthweight (LBW) (p. 78)	X-linked (p. 56)
cesarean section (c-section) (p. 64)		monozygotic twins (p. 53)	XX (p. 51)
chromosome (p. 48)	fetal period (p. 57)	parent–infant bond (p. 69)	XY (p. 51)
couvade (p. 68)	fetus (p. 60)	phenotype (p. 50)	zygote (p. 48)

WHAT HAVE YOU LEARNED?

1. What is the relationship among DNA, chromosomes, and genes?

2. Use the concept of gametes to explain why your parents could have given you millions of different siblings.

3. What surprises came from the *Human Genome Project*?

4. How is the sex of a zygote determined?

5. What are the differences among monozygotic twins, dizygotic twins, and other siblings?

6. When talking about genes, what is meant by a "dominant–recessive pattern"?

7. What are three major developments in the germinal period?

8. What body parts develop during the embryonic period?

9. What major milestone is reached about halfway through the fetal period?

10. What role does the hormone oxytocin play in birth?

11. What five vital signs does the Apgar scale measure?

12. What are some advantages and disadvantages of cesarean sections?

13. In what ways do doulas support women before, during, and after labor?

14. What three sets of protective reflexes are typically seen in newborns? Give three examples of reflexes from each set.

15. How do fathers experience pregnancy?

16. What are the signs of postpartum depression?

17. What are the results of kangaroo care?

18. What are the consequences if an infant is born with trisomy-21?

19. Why are a few recessive traits (such as sickle-cell) quite common?

20. What teratogens harm the developing baby, and what types of harm can they cause?

21. How does the timing of exposure to a teratogen affect the risk of harm to the fetus?

22. What are the potential consequences of drinking alcohol during pregnancy?

23. What factors increase or decrease the risk of spina bifida?

24. What are the benefits of prenatal care?

25. What are the differences among LBW, VLBW, and ELBW?

26. List at least four reasons why a baby might be born LBW.

27. What are some potential consequences of low birthweight?

28. In what ways do biology, psychology, and culture influence the risk of alcoholism?

29. In what ways do age, genes, and culture affect vision?

30. How might an awareness of genetic risks influence parents' behavior before, during, and after pregnancy?

APPLICATIONS

1. Pick one of your traits, and explain the influences that both nature *and* nurture have on it. For example, if you have a short temper, explain its origins in your genetics, your culture, and your childhood experiences.

2. Draw a genetic chart of your biological relatives, going back as many generations as you can, listing all serious illnesses and causes of death. Include ancestors who died in infancy. Do you see any genetic susceptibility? If so, how can you overcome it?

3. Go to a nearby greeting-card store and analyze the cards about pregnancy and birth. Do you see any cultural attitudes (e.g., variations depending on the sex of the newborn or of the parent)? If possible, compare those cards with cards from a store that caters to another economic or cultural group.

4. Interview three mothers of varied backgrounds about their birth experiences. Make your interviews open-ended—let them choose what to tell you, as long as they give at least a 10-minute description. Then compare and contrast the three accounts, noting especially any influences of culture, personality, circumstances, or cohort.

>>ONLINE CONNECTIONS

To accompany your textbook, you have access to a number of online resources, including quizzes for every chapter of the book, flashcards (in English and Spanish), critical thinking questions, and case studies. For access to any of these links, go to www.worthpublishers.com/bergerinvitation2e. In addition to these free resources, you'll also find links to podcasts, video clips, diagnostic quizzing with personalized study advice, and an ebook. Some of the videos and activities available online include:

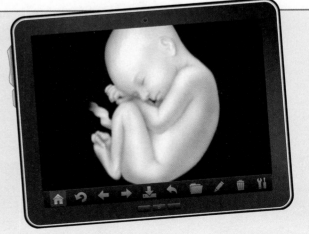

- *Brain Development: In the Beginning.* Three-dimensional animation follows brain development from the formation of the neural tube until birth. Animations of microscopic changes in the brain include synaptic pruning.

- *Periods of Prenatal Development.* A series of detailed animations show the stages of prenatal development from fertilization to birth.

- CHAPTER 3
- CHAPTER 4

The First Two Years

Adults don't change much in a year or two. They might have longer, grayer, or thinner hair; they might gain or lose weight; they might learn something new. But if you saw friends you hadn't seen for two years, you'd recognize them immediately.

Imagine caring for a newborn 24 hours a day for a month and then leaving for two years. On your return, you might not recognize him or her. The baby would have quadrupled in weight, grown a foot taller, and sprouted a new head of hair. Behavior and emotions change, too—less crying, but new laughter and fear—including fear of you.

A year or two is not much compared with the 80 or so years of the average life. However, in their first two years humans reach half their adult height, learn to talk in sentences, and express almost every emotion—not just joy and fear but also love, jealousy, and shame. The next two chapters describe these radical and awesome changes.

CHAPTER OUTLINE

THE FIRST TWO YEARS
Body and Mind

WHAT WILL YOU KNOW?

■ What part of an infant grows most in the first two years?

■ How are newborn humans the opposite of newborn kittens?

■ Does immunization protect or harm babies?

■ If a baby doesn't look for an object that disappears, what does that mean?

■ Why talk to babies who are too young to understand words?

Our first child, Bethany, was born when I was in graduate school. I studiously memorized developmental norms, including sitting at 6 months, walking and talking at 12. But at 14 months, Bethany had not yet taken her first step. Instead of worrying, I told my husband that genes were more influential than anything we did. I had read that babies in Paris are among the latest walkers in the world, and my grandmother was French. My speculation was bolstered when our next two children, Rachel and Elissa, were also slow to walk. The genetic hypothesis was confirmed by my students, all devoted parents. Those with ancestors from Guatemala and Ghana had infants who walked before a year, unlike those with East Asian or European heritage.

Fourteen years after Bethany, Sarah was born. I could afford a full-time caregiver, Mrs. Todd, from Jamaica. She thought Sarah was the most advanced baby she had ever known, except for her own daughter, Gillian. I told her that Berger children walk late.

"She'll be walking by a year," Mrs. Todd told me. "Gillian walked at 10 months."

"We'll see," I graciously replied, confident of my genetic explanation.

I underestimated Mrs. Todd. She bounced my delighted baby on her lap, day after day, and spent hours giving her "walking practice." Sarah took her first step at 12 months, late for a Todd, early for a Berger, and a humbling lesson for me. ●

My Youngest at 8 Months When I look at this photo of Sarah, I see evidence of Mrs. Todd's devotion. Sarah's hair is washed and carefully brushed, her jumper and blouse are clean and pressed, and the carpet and stepstool are perfect equipment for standing practice. Sarah's legs—chubby and far apart—indicate that she is not about to walk early; but, given all these signs of Mrs. Todd's attention to caregiving, it is not surprising, in hindsight, that my fourth daughter was my earliest walker.

HAZEL HANKIN

AS A SCIENTIST, I KNOW THAT A SINGLE CASE PROVES NOTHING. Sarah shares only half her genes with Bethany. My daughters are only one-eighth French, a fraction I had ignored when they were infants.

Nonetheless, as you read about development, remember that caregiving enables babies to grow, move, and learn. Development is not as straightforward and automatic, nor as genetically determined, as it once seemed. It is multidirectional and multicontextual, multicultural and plastic. Parents express their devotion in many ways, some massaging infant bodies every day, some talking in response to every noise. No wonder babies vary.

Growth in Infancy

In infancy, growth is so rapid and the consequences of neglect are so severe that gains are closely monitored. Medical checkups, including measurement of height, weight, and head circumference, occur often in developed nations because these measurements provide the first clues as to whether an infant is progressing as expected—or not.

Body Size

Weight gain is dramatic. Newborns lose a few ounces in the first three days and then gain an ounce a day for several months. Birthweight typically doubles by 4 months and triples by a year. An average 7-pound newborn will be 21 pounds at 12 months (9,525 grams, up from 3,175 grams at birth).

Physical growth in the second year is slower but still rapid. By 24 months, most children weigh almost 28 pounds (13 kilograms). They have added more than a foot in height—from about 20 inches at birth to about 34 inches at age 2 (from 51 to 86 centimeters). This means that 2-year-olds are half their adult height and about one-fifth their adult weight, four times heavier than they were at birth (see Figure 3.1).

Each of these numbers is a **norm,** which is an average, or standard, for a particular population. The "particular population" for the norms just cited is North American infants. Remember, however, that genetic diversity means that some perfectly healthy newborns are smaller or larger than these norms.

At each well-baby checkup (monthly at first), a doctor or nurse measures the baby's growth and compares it to that baby's previous numbers. Often measurements

norm
An average, or standard, measurement, calculated from the measurements of many individuals within a specific group or population.

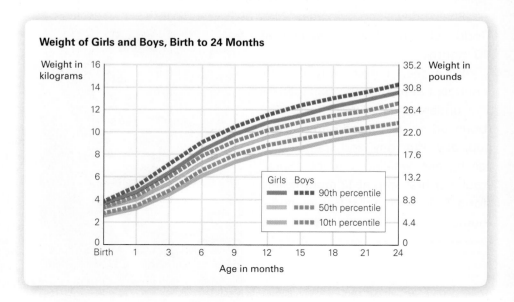

FIGURE 3.1 Eat and Sleep The rate of increasing weight in the first weeks of life makes it obvious why new babies need to be fed day and night.

Same Boy, Much Changed All three photos show Riley, first at 3 months, then at 12 months, and finally at 24 months. Note the rapid growth in the first two years, especially apparent in head proportions and use of the legs.

are expressed in percentiles, from 0 to 100. (Percentiles express where a particular baby ranks on a specific measure compared with other babies of the same age.) Thus, weight at the 30th percentile means that 30 percent of all babies weigh less, and 70 percent weigh more.

For a baby who has always ranked in the average range (50th percentile), the situation becomes worrisome if the percentile changes a lot, either up or down. Abnormal growth may signify a problem; that's why early checkups are vital.

Prenatal and postnatal brain growth (measured by head circumference) is crucial for later cognition (Gilles & Nelson, 2012). If teething or a stuffed-up nose temporarily slows weight gain, nature slows growth of the body but not the brain, a phenomenon called **head-sparing.** Sadly, prolonged malnutrition affects the brain as well, as explained later.

From two weeks after conception to two years after birth, the brain

In Just the First Two Years . . .

grows more rapidly than any other organ, being about 25 percent of adult weight at birth and almost 75 percent at age 2 (see Figure 3.2). Over the same period, brain circumference increases from about 14 to 19 inches.

Brain Development

The brain is essential lifelong; it is discussed in every chapter of this book. We begin now with the basics—neurons, axons, dendrites, neurotransmitters, synapses, and the cortex, especially the prefrontal cortex.

BRAIN BASICS Communication within the central nervous system (CNS)—the brain and spinal cord—begins with nerve cells, called **neurons.** At birth, the human brain has billions of neurons, most of them (about 70 percent) in the **cortex,** the

FIGURE 3.2 Growing Up
Two-year-olds are totally dependent on adults, but they have already reached half their adult height and three-fourths of their adult brain size.

● **UNDERSTANDING THE NUMBERS**
Does the 5-inch increase in brain circumference (from 14 to 19 inches) from birth to age 2 mean a 35 percent increase in brain volume?

Answer No, much more. Sphere volume is calculated by squaring the circumference, which means an increase of 84 percent. Actually, the brain is not a sphere, so volume normally more than doubles over the first two years.

head-sparing
A biological mechanism that protects the brain when malnutrition disrupts body growth. The brain is the last part of the body to be damaged by malnutrition.

neuron
One of billions of nerve cells in the central nervous system, especially in the brain.

cortex
The outer layers of the brain in humans and other mammals. Most thinking, feeling, and sensing involve the cortex.

prefrontal cortex
The area of the cortex at the very front of the brain that specializes in anticipation, planning, and impulse control.

axon
A fiber that extends from a neuron and transmits electrochemical impulses from that neuron to the dendrites of other neurons.

dendrite
A fiber that extends from a neuron and receives electrochemical impulses transmitted from other neurons via their axons.

synapses
The intersection between the axon of one neuron and the dendrites of other neurons.

neurotransmitter
A brain chemical that carries information from the axon of a sending neuron to the dendrites of a receiving neuron.

synaptic gap
The pathway across which neurotransmitters carry information from the axon of the sending neuron to the dendrites of the receiving neuron.

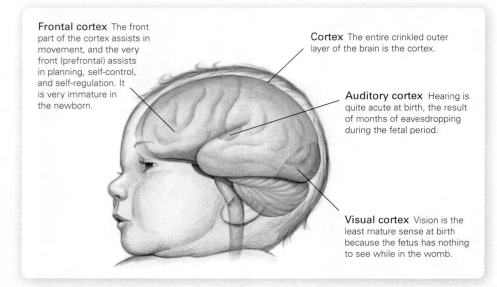

Frontal cortex The front part of the cortex assists in movement, and the very front (prefrontal) assists in planning, self-control, and self-regulation. It is very immature in the newborn.

Cortex The entire crinkled outer layer of the brain is the cortex.

Auditory cortex Hearing is quite acute at birth, the result of months of eavesdropping during the fetal period.

Visual cortex Vision is the least mature sense at birth because the fetus has nothing to see while in the womb.

FIGURE 3.3 The Developing Cortex The infant's cortex consists of four to six thin layers of tissue that cover the brain. It contains virtually all the neurons that make conscious thought possible. Some areas of the cortex, such as those devoted to the basic senses, mature relatively early. Others, such as the prefrontal cortex, mature quite late.

How Two Neurons Communicate
The infant brain actually contains billions of neurons, each with one axon and many dendrites. Every electrochemical message to or from the brain causes thousands of neurons to fire, each transmitting the message across the synapse to neighboring neurons. This electron micrograph shows neurons greatly magnified, with their tangled but highly organized and well-coordinated sets of dendrites and axons.

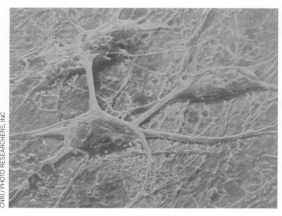

CNRI / PHOTO RESEARCHERS, INC

brain's six outer layers (see Figure 3.3). The cortex is crucial: Most thinking, feeling, and sensing occur in the cortex (Johnson, 2010). The final part of the brain to mature is the **prefrontal cortex,** the area for anticipation, planning, and impulse control. It is virtually inactive in the first months of infancy and gradually becomes more efficient in childhood, adolescence, and early adulthood (Wahlstrom et al., 2010).

Areas of the brain specialize. Some regions deep within the skull maintain breathing and heartbeat, some in the midbrain underlie emotions and impulses, and some in the cortex allow perception and cognition. For instance, there is a visual cortex, an auditory cortex, and an area dedicated to the sense of touch for each body part—including for each finger of a person or each whisker of a rat (Barnett et al., 2006).

Within and between areas of the central nervous system, neurons are connected to other neurons by intricate networks of nerve fibers called **axons** and **dendrites** (see Infographic 3, page 95). Each neuron has a single axon and numerous dendrites, which spread out like the branches of a tree. The axon of one neuron meets the dendrites of other neurons at intersections called **synapses,** which are critical communication links within the brain.

To be more specific, neurons communicate by sending electrochemical impulses through their axons to synapses, to be picked up by the dendrites of other neurons. The dendrites bring messages to the cell bodies of their neurons, which, in turn, convey the messages via their axons to the dendrites of other neurons.

Axons and dendrites do not touch at synapses. Instead, the electrical impulses in axons typically cause the release of chemicals called **neurotransmitters,** which carry information from the axon of the sending neuron, across the **synaptic gap,** to the dendrites of the receiving neuron.

EXPERIENCES AND PRUNING At birth, the brain contains at least 100 billion neurons, more than a person needs. However, the newborn's brain has far fewer dendrites and synapses than the person will

Nature, Nurture, and the Brain

The mechanics of neurological functioning are varied and complex; neuroscientists hypothesize, experiment, and discover more each day. Adults have an estimated 86 billion neurons, millions firing at once; obviously, this diagram shows only a tiny part of the whole.

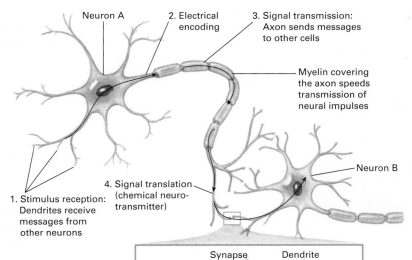

- Neuron A
- 2. Electrical encoding
- 3. Signal transmission: Axon sends messages to other cells
- Myelin covering the axon speeds transmission of neural impulses
- 1. Stimulus reception: Dendrites receive messages from other neurons
- 4. Signal translation (chemical neuro-transmitter)
- Neuron B

- Synapse
- Dendrite
- Axon
- Neuron B
- Neuron A
- Neurotransmitters

NATURE

The link between one neuron and another is shown in this simplified diagram. The infant brain contains billions of neurons, each with one axon and many dendrites. Every electro-chemical message to or from the brain causes thousands of neurons to fire simultaneously, each transmitting the message across the synapse to neighboring neurons.

NURTURE

Every experience that a person has—especially in the early days and months—activates and prunes neurons, such that the firing patterns from one axon to another dendrite reflect the past. This was first shown dramatically with baby mice: Some were licked and nuzzled by their mothers almost constantly and some were neglected. Social scientists now believe that every aspect of early life affects brain pattern.

The biology of neuron activity is shown above, but research now finds that experience affects development of neural pathways. Neglected newborn mice will be anxious all their lives because of early brain programming.

THE BRAIN

To be more specific, when a mother mouse licks her newborn babies, that reduces methylation of a gene (called Nr3c1), allowing increased serotonin to be released by the hypothalamus. That serotonin not only increases momentary pleasure (mice love being licked) but also starts a chain of epigenetic responses that reduce stress hormones from many parts of the brain and body, including the adrenal glands. The effects are lifelong, as proven many times in mice. In humans, a mother's gentle stroking and cuddling of her newborn seem to affect the baby similarly.

Early epigenetic effects on the brain

Low maternal licking and grooming	High licking maternal and grooming
High stress hormone levels	Low stress hormone levels
High anxiety	Low anxiety
Low licking or grooming	High licking or grooming

SOURCES & CREDITS LISTED ON P. SC-1

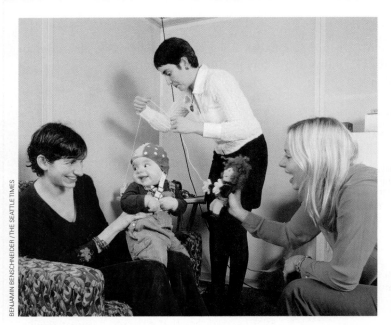

Electric Excitement Milo's delight at his mother's facial expressions is visible, not just in his eyes and mouth but also in the neurons of the outer layer of his cortex. Electrodes map his brain activation, region by region and moment by moment. Every month of life up to age 2 shows increased electrical excitement.

transient exuberance
The great but temporary increase in the number of dendrites that develop in an infant's brain during the first two years of life.

pruning
When applied to brain development, the process by which unused connections in the brain atrophy and die.

eventually possess. During the first months and years, rapid growth and refinement in axons, dendrites, and synapses occur, especially in the cortex. Dendrite growth is the major reason that brain weight triples from birth to age 2 (Johnson, 2010).

An estimated fivefold increase in dendrites in the cortex occurs in the 24 months after birth, with about 100 trillion synapses being present at age 2. According to one expert, "40,000 new synapses are formed every second in the infant's brain" (Schore & McIntosh, 2011, p. 502).

This extensive postnatal brain growth is highly unusual for mammals. Why does it occur in humans? Although prenatal brain development is remarkable, it is limited by the simple fact that the human pelvis is relatively small, so the baby's head must also be relatively small in order to make birth possible. Thus, there is an acceleration of growth after birth. In fact, unlike other species, humans must nurture and protect their offspring for more than a decade as children's brains continue to develop (Konner, 2010).

Early dendrite growth is called **transient exuberance:** *exuberant* because it is so rapid and *transient* because some of it is temporary. The expansive growth of dendrites is followed by **pruning.** Just as a gardener might prune a rose bush by cutting away some growth to enable more, or more beautiful, roses to bloom, unused brain connections atrophy and die (Stiles & Jernigan, 2010).

The specifics of brain structure and growth depend on genes and maturation but even more on experience (Stiles & Jernigan, 2010). Some dendrites wither away because they are never used—that is, no experiences have caused them to send a message to other neurons. Expansion and pruning of dendrites occur for every aspect of early experience, from noticing musical rhythms to understanding emotions (Scott et al., 2007).

Strangely enough, this loss of dendrites increases brainpower. The space between neurons in human brains, for instance—especially in regions for advanced, abstract thought—is far greater than the space in chimpanzee brains (Miller, 2010). The densely packed neurons of chimps make them less intelligent than people, probably because humans have more space for dendrite formation, allowing more synapses and thus more complex thinking.

Some children with intellectual disabilities have "a persistent failure of normal synapse pruning" (Irwin et al., 2002, p. 194). That makes thinking difficult. And one sign of autism is more rapid brain growth, suggesting too little pruning (Hazlett et al., 2011).

Yet just as too little pruning creates problems, so does too much pruning. Brain sculpting is attuned to experience: The appropriate links in the brain need to be established, protected, and strengthened while inappropriate ones are eliminated. One group of scientists speculates that "lack of normative experiences may lead to overpruning of neurons and synapses, both of which may lead to reduction of brain activity" (Moulson et al., 2009, p. 1051).

Another group suggests that infants who are often hungry, or hurt, or neglected may develop brains that compensate—and cannot be reprogrammed even if circumstances change. The hungry baby becomes the obese adult, the neglected child rejects attention, and so on, always with the interaction of nature and nurture (van IJzendoorn et al., 2012).

A VIEW FROM SCIENCE

Face Recognition

Unless you have prosopagnosia (face blindness, relatively uncommon), the *fusiform face area* of your brain is astonishingly adept at face recognition. This area is primed among newborns, although it has yet to reflect experience: Newborns stare at pictures of monkey faces and human ones, at pictures and toys with faces, as well as at live faces.

Soon, experiences (such as seeing mother or father again and again) refine perception (De Heering et al., 2010). By 3 months, most babies smile more readily at familiar people and are more accurate at differentiating faces from their own ethnic group (called the *own-race effect*).

The own-race effect is the result of limited multiethnic experience, not innate prejudice. Children of one ethnicity, adopted and raised exclusively among people of another ethnicity, recognize differences among people of their adopted group more readily than differences among people of their biological group.

The importance of early experience is further evidenced in two studies. In one, 6-month-old infants were repeatedly (more than 30 times) shown a book of pictures of six monkey faces, each with a name written on the page, over a three-month period (see photo).

For one-third of the babies, the parents read the names while showing the pictures; another one-third of the parents said only "monkey" as they turned each page; and the final one-third simply turned pages. At 9 months, all the infants viewed pictures of six *unfamiliar* monkeys. The infants who had repeatedly seen named monkeys were better at distinguishing one new monkey from another than were the infants who saw the same picture book but did not hear each monkey's name (Scott & Monesson, 2010).

The second example begins with the fact that many children and adults do not notice the individuality of newborns. Some even claim that "all babies look alike." However, one study found that 3-year-olds with younger siblings were much better at recognizing differences between photos of unfamiliar newborns than were 3-year-olds with no younger brothers or sisters (Cassia et al., 2009). This shows that experience matters, contributing to development of dendrites in the fusiform face area.

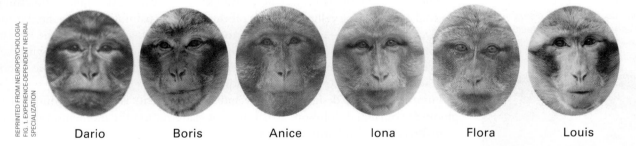

REPRINTED FROM NEUROPSYCHOLOGIA, FIG. 1 EXPERIENCE-DEPENDENT NEURAL SPECIALIZATION

| Dario | Boris | Anice | Iona | Flora | Louis |

Iona Is Not Flora If you heard that Dario was quite different from Louis or Boris, would you stare at unfamiliar monkey faces more closely in the future? For 6-month-olds, the answer is yes.

HARM AND PROTECTION Most infants develop well within their culture, and head-sparing usually ensures that baby brains are sufficiently nourished. For brain development, it does not matter whether a baby hears French or Farsi, or sees emotions displayed dramatically or subtly (e.g., throwing oneself to the floor or merely pursing the lips, a cultural difference). However, infant brains do not develop well without certain experiences that all humans need.

To begin with, infants need stimulation. Playing with a young baby, allowing varied sensations, and encouraging movement (arm waving in the early months, walking later on) are all fodder for brain connections. Severe lack of stimulation (e.g., no talking at all) stunts the brain. As one review of early brain development explains, "enrichment and deprivation studies provide powerful evidence of . . . widespread effects of experience on the complexity and function of the developing system" (Stiles & Jernigan, 2010, p. 345).

This does not mean that babies require spinning, buzzing, multitextured, and multicolored toys. In fact, such toys may be a waste of time and money since infants

✦ **ESPECIALLY FOR Parents of Grown Children** Suppose you realize that you seldom talked to your children until they talked to you and that you often put them in cribs and playpens. Did you limit their brain growth and their sensory capacity? (see response, page 99) →

shaken baby syndrome
A life-threatening injury that occurs when an infant is forcefully shaken back and forth, a motion that ruptures blood vessels in the brain and breaks neural connections.

self-righting
The inborn drive to remedy a developmental deficit; literally, to return to sitting or standing upright after being tipped over. People of all ages have self-righting impulses, for emotional as well as physical imbalance.

REM (rapid eye movement) sleep
A stage of sleep characterized by flickering eyes behind closed lids, dreaming, and rapid brain waves.

Protective Sleeping It matters little what infants sleep in—bassinet, cradle, crib, or Billum bag made from local plants in Papua New Guinea, as shown here. In fact, this kind of bag is very useful since babies can easily be carried in it. It can also be used for carrying food, tools, and much else. What does matter is the infant's sleeping position—always on the back, like this healthy infant.

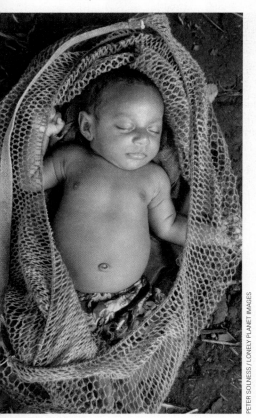

PETER SOLNESS / LONELY PLANET IMAGES

can be overstimulated by them; babies usually cry or go to sleep when that happens, to avoid bombardment. Infants are fascinated by simple objects and facial expressions; however, there is no evidence that overstimulation harms the brain.

A simple application of what has been learned about the prefrontal cortex is that hundreds of objects, from the very simple to the quite elaborate, can capture an infant's attention. There is also a tragic implication: The brain is not yet under thoughtful control, since the prefrontal cortex is not well developed. Unless adults understand this, they might get angry if an infant keeps crying. Infants cry as a reflex to pain (usually digestive pain); they are too immature to *decide* to stop crying, as adults do.

If a frustrated caregiver reacts to crying by shaking the baby, that can cause **shaken baby syndrome,** a life-threatening condition that occurs when infants are shaken back and forth sharply and quickly. Because the brain is still developing, shaking stops the crying because blood vessels in the brain rupture and fragile neural connections break. Pediatricians consider shaken baby syndrome an example of *abusive head trauma* (Christian et al., 2009). Death is the worst possible result; lifelong intellectual impairment is the more likely one.

The fact that infant brains respond to their circumstances suggests that waiting until evidence that a young child is mistreated is waiting too long. In the first months of life, babies adjust to their world, becoming withdrawn and quiet if their caregivers are depressed or becoming loud and demanding if they need to do so to get fed. In both cases, they learn patterns that are destructive later on. Thus, understanding development as dynamic and interactive means helping caregivers from the start, not waiting until destructive systems are established (Tronick & Beegly, 2011).

The word *systems* is crucial here. Almost every baby experiences something stressful—a caregiver yelling, or a fall off the bed, or a painful stomachache. Fortunately, **self-righting**—an inborn drive to remedy deficits—is built into the human system. For example, infants with no toys develop their brains by using whatever objects are available, and infants with neglectful mothers may develop close bonds with someone else who provides daily stimulation.

Human brains are designed to grow and adapt; plasticity is apparent from the beginning (Tomalski & Johnson, 2010). It is the patterns, not the moments, of neglect or maltreatment that harm the brain.

Sleep

One consequence of brain maturation is the ability to sleep through the night. Newborns cannot do this. Normally, they sleep 15 to 17 hours a day, in one- to three-hour segments. Hours of sleep decrease rapidly with maturity: The norm per day for the first 2 months is 14¼ hours; for the next 3 months, 13¼ hours; for 6 to 17 months, 12¾ hours.

Variation is particularly apparent in the early weeks. As reported by parents (who might exaggerate), 1 new baby in 20 sleeps 9 hours or fewer per day and 1 in 20 sleeps 19 hours or more (Sadeh et al., 2009).

Sleep specifics vary not only because of biology (age and genes) but also because of the social environment. With responsive parents, full-term newborns sleep more than low-birthweight babies, who are hungry every two hours. Babies who are fed cow's milk and cereal sleep more soundly—easier for parents but not ideal for the baby. Social environment has a direct effect: If parents respond to predawn cries with food and play, babies wake up early each morning (Sadeh et al., 2009).

Over the first months, the relative amount of time in various stages of sleep changes. Babies born preterm may always seem to be dozing. About half of the sleep of full-term newborns is **REM (rapid eye movement) sleep**, with flickering eyes and rapid brain waves. That indicates dreaming. REM sleep declines over the early weeks, as does "transitional sleep," the dozing, half-awake stage. At 3 or 4 months, quiet sleep (also called *slow-wave sleep*) increases, as does time alert and wide awake.

Overall, 25 percent of children under age 3 have sleeping problems, according to parents surveyed in an Internet study of more than 5,000 North Americans (Sadeh et al., 2009). Sleep problems are more troubling for parents than for infants. This does not render them insignificant, however; overtired parents may be less patient and responsive (Bayer et al., 2007). Patience is needed to ensure the baby's sleep position is properly "back to sleep," to protect against sudden infant death syndrome (see Chapter 1).

One problem for parents is that advice about where infants should sleep varies, from contending that infants should sleep beside their parents—who must immediately respond to every cry (Nicholson & Parker, 2009)—to advising that infants need their own room, should be allowed to "cry it out" so they will not be spoiled, and can learn to soothe themselves. Both sets of advice make sense, as the following explains.

> **RESPONSE FOR Parents of Grown Children** (from page 97) Probably not. Brain development is programmed to occur for all infants, requiring only the stimulation that virtually all families provide—warmth, reassuring touch, overheard conversation, facial expressions, movement. Extras such as baby talk, music, exercise, mobiles, and massage may be beneficial but are not essential. ●

co-sleeping
A custom in which parents and their children (usually infants) sleep together in the same room.

OPPOSING PERSPECTIVES

Where Should Babies Sleep?

Traditionally, most middle-class U.S. infants slept in cribs in their own rooms; it was feared that they would be traumatized by the parents' sexual interactions. By contrast, infants in Asia, Africa, and Latin America slept with their parents, a practice called **co-sleeping.** People in those cultures believed that parent–child separation at night was cruel.

Even today, at baby's bedtime, Asian and African mothers worry more about separation, whereas European and North American mothers worry more about lack of privacy. A study in 19 nations confirms that parents act on their fears: The extremes were 82 percent of babies in Vietnam sleeping with their parents compared with 6 percent in New Zealand (Mindell et al., 2010) (see Figure 3.4).

At first, this may seem to be a matter of income: Families of low socioeconomic status (SES) are less likely to have an extra room. But even wealthy Japanese families often co-sleep, and many poor Western families find a separate space for their children to sleep. Co-sleeping is a matter of custom, not merely income (Kohyama et al., 2011).

The argument for co-sleeping is that it is easier to respond to infants in the middle of the night, especially if a baby is hungry or scared. When parents opt for co-sleeping, they are less exhausted since they can reach over to feed or comfort their baby. Breast-feeding, often done every hour or two at first, is easier with co-sleeping—one reason many high-SES North Americans now practice it.

Yet the argument against co-sleeping rests on a chilling statistic: Sudden infant death is more common when babies sleep beside their parents (Gettler & McKenna, 2010; Ruys et al., 2007). Although everyone knows that drugs are destructive, many young fathers and mothers occasionally go to sleep after drinking or drugging. If their baby is beside them, that is dangerous.

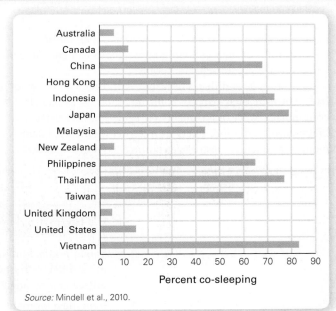

Source: Mindell et al., 2010.

FIGURE 3.4 Awake at Night Why the disparity between Asian and non-Asian rates of co-sleeping? It may be that Western parents use a variety of gadgets and objects—monitors, night lights, pacifiers, cuddle cloths, sound machines—to accomplish the same things Asian parents do by having their infant next to them.

Furthermore, adult beds, unlike cribs, are often soft, with comforters, mattresses, and pillows that increase the risk of suffocation (Alm, 2007). A commercial solution is a "co-sleeper," which is a baby bed designed to be next to the parents' bed but not in it. That way, the dangers of *bed-sharing* are avoided. Privacy issues remain, however.

One reason for opposing views is that every adult is affected by early experiences and seeks to avoid the mistakes of his or her parents. This phenomenon is called *ghosts in the*

YAGI STUDIO / GETTY IMAGES

Infant at Risk? Sleeping in the parents' bed is a risk factor for SIDS in the United States, but don't worry about this Japanese girl. In Japan, 97 percent of infants sleep next to their parents, yet infant mortality is only 3 per 1,000—compared with 7 per 1,000 in the United States. Is this bed, or this mother, or this sleeping position protective?

nursery because the parents bring decades-old memories into the bedrooms of their children. Those ghosts can encourage either co-sleeping or separate rooms.

One study found that, compared with Israeli adults who had slept near their parents as infants, those who had slept communally with other infants (as sometimes occurred on kibbutzim) were more likely to interpret their own infants' nighttime cries as distress, requiring comfort (Tikotzky et al., 2010). That is a ghost from the past that affects current behavior; when parents think their crying babies are frightened, lonely, and distressed, they want to respond quickly. Quick responses are more possible with co-sleeping. On the other hand, if parents' only private place is in their bedroom at night, the marriage may suffer if the baby sleeps there.

A developmental perspective begins with what we know: Infants learn from their earliest experiences. If babies become accustomed to bed-sharing, they will crawl into their parents' bed when they are long past infancy. Parents might lose sleep for years because they wanted more sleep when their babies were small.

Of course, that concern reflects a cultural norm as well. According to an ethnographic study, by the time Mexican Mayan children are 5 years old, they choose "when, how long, and with whom to sleep" (Gaskins, 1999, p. 40), a practice that bewilders many other North Americans.

Developmentalists hesitate to declare any particular pattern best (Tamis-LeMonda et al., 2008) because the issue is "tricky and complex" (Gettler & McKenna, 2010, p. 77). Sleeping alone may encourage independence and individuality—traits appreciated in some cultures, abhorred in others. Past experiences (ghosts in the nursery) affect us all: Should some ghosts be welcomed and others banned?

✦ **ESPECIALLY FOR New Parents** You are aware of cultural differences in sleeping practices, which raises a very practical issue: Should your newborn sleep in bed with you? (see response, page 102) →

KEY points

- Weight and height increase markedly in the first two years; the norms are three times a baby's birthweight by age 1 and 12 inches (30 centimeters) taller than birth height by age 2.
- Brain development is rapid during infancy, particularly development of the axons, dendrites, and synapses within the cortex.
- Experience shapes the infant brain, as pruning eliminates unused connections.
- Where and how much infants sleep is shaped by brain maturation and family practices.

Perceiving and Moving

People who don't know infants might think they are passive creatures at first, unable to do much. But that is far from the truth: Developmentalists have traced the immediate and rapid development of every skill.

The Senses

Every sense functions at birth. Newborns have open eyes; sensitive ears; and responsive noses, tongues, and skin. Indeed, very young babies seem to attend to everything without much judgment. For instance, in the first months of life, they smile at strangers and suck almost anything in their mouths (Adolph & Berger, 2005).

Why are new infants not more cautious? Because sensation precedes perception, and perception leads to cognition. In order to learn, babies need to begin by responding to every sensation that might be significant.

Sensation occurs when a sensory system detects a stimulus, as when the inner ear reverberates with sound or the retina and pupil of the eye intercept light. Thus, sensations begin when an outer organ (eye, ear, nose, tongue, or skin) meets anything that can be seen, heard, smelled, tasted, or touched.

Sensation at birth is affected by genetic selection over more than 100,000 years. Humans cannot hear what mice hear, or see what bats see, or smell what puppies smell; humans do not need those sensory abilities. However, survival requires people to respond to other people, and newborns innately do so (Konner, 2010; Lloyd-Fox et al., 2009).

Perception occurs when the brain processes a sensation. This happens in the cortex, usually as the result of a message from one of the sensing organs, such as from the eye to the visual cortex. If a particular sensation occurs often, it connects with past experience, making a particular sight worth interpreting (M. E. Diamond, 2007).

Some sensations are beyond comprehension at first. A newborn has no idea that the letters on a page might have significance, that Mother's face should be distinguished from Father's, or that the smells of roses and garlic have different connotations. Perceptions require experience.

Infants' brains are especially attuned to their own repeated social experiences, and that is how perception occurs. Thus, a newborn named Emily has no concept that *Emily* is her name. However, she is born with crucial sensations, including the brain and auditory capacity to hear sounds in the usual speech range (not the high sounds that only dogs can hear) and an inborn preference for repeated patterns and human speech.

By about 4 months, when her auditory cortex is rapidly creating and pruning dendrites, the repeated word *Emily* is perceived as well as sensed, especially because that sound emanates from the people Emily has come to love (Saffran et al., 2006). By 6 months, Emily may open her eyes and turn her head when her name is called. It will take many more months before she says "Emmy" and still longer before she knows that *Emily* is indeed her name.

Thus, perception follows sensation, when senses are noticed by the brain. Then cognition follows perception, when people think about what they have perceived. (Later, cognition no longer requires sensation: People imagine, fantasize, hypothesize.) The sequence from sensation to perception to cognition requires that an infant's sense organs function. No wonder the parts of the cortex dedicated to the senses develop rapidly: That is the prerequisite for human intellect. Now some specifics.

HEARING AND SEEING The sense of hearing develops during the last trimester of pregnancy, which means that fetuses hear sounds in the womb. Familiar, rhythmic sounds, such as a heartbeat, are soothing—one reason kangaroo care reduces newborn stress (see Chapter 2). Newborn hearing is routinely checked because the sense of hearing is normally quite acute: If a newborn seems deaf, early remediation may allow language to develop normally.

By 4 months after birth, infants have developed perceptions of speech, as is evident in the Emily example above. Babies expect the rhythms, segmentation, and cadence of the words they hear long before they understand their meaning (Minagawa-Kawai et al., 2011).

Vision is the least mature sense at birth. Although the eyes open in mid-pregnancy and are sensitive to bright light (if the pregnant woman is sunbathing in a bikini, for

sensation
The response of a sensory system (eyes, ears, skin, tongue, nose) when it detects a stimulus.

perception
The mental processing of sensory information when the brain interprets a sensation.

✦ **ESPECIALLY FOR Nurses and Pediatricians** The parents of a 6-month-old have just been told that their child is deaf. They don't believe it because, as they tell you, the baby babbles as much as their other children did. What do you tell them? (see response, page 103) →

Before Leaving the Hospital As mandated by a 2004 Ohio law, 1-day-old Henry has his hearing tested via vibrations of the inner ear in response to various tones. The computer interprets the data and signals any need for more tests—as is the case for about 1 baby in 100. Normal newborns hear quite well; Henry's hearing was fine.

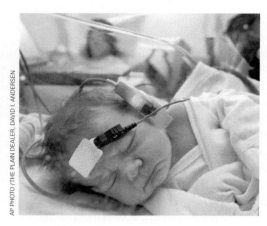

AP PHOTO / THE PLAIN DEALER, DAVID I. ANDERSEN

binocular vision
The ability to focus the two eyes in a coordinated manner in order to see one image.

MARK RICHARDS / PHOTOEDIT

Depth Perception This toddler in a laboratory in Berkeley, California, is crawling on the experimental apparatus called a visual cliff. She stops at the edge of what she perceives as a drop-off.

RESPONSE FOR New Parents (from page 100) From the psychological and cultural perspectives, babies can sleep anywhere as long as the parents can hear them if they cry. The main consideration is safety: Infants should not sleep on a mattress that is too soft, nor beside an adult who is drunk or drugged. Otherwise, each family should decide for itself. ●

instance), the fetus has nothing much to see. Newborns are legally blind; they focus only on things between 4 and 30 inches (10 and 75 centimeters) away (Bornstein et al., 2005).

Almost immediately, experience combines with maturation of the visual cortex to improve the ability to see shapes and then notice details. Vision improves so rapidly that researchers are hard-pressed to describe the day-by-day improvements (Dobson et al., 2009). By 2 months, infants not only stare at faces but also, after perception and then cognition, smile. (Smiling can occur earlier, but not because of perception.)

As perception builds, visual scanning improves. Thus, 3-month-olds look closely at the eyes and mouth, smiling more at smiling faces than at angry or expressionless ones. They pay attention to patterns, colors, and motion (Kellman & Arterberry, 2006).

Because **binocular vision** (coordinating both eyes to see one image) is impossible in the womb (nothing is far enough away to need two eyes), many newborns seem to use their two eyes independently, momentarily appearing wall-eyed or cross-eyed. Normally, visual experience leads to rapid development of focus and binocular vision; usually between 2 and 4 months, both eyes can focus on a single thing (Wang & Candy, 2010). This aids in the development of depth perception, which has been demonstrated in 3-month-olds, although it was once thought to develop much later due to infants' reactions on an experimental apparatus called the visual cliff (see photo).

TASTING AND SMELLING As with vision and hearing, smell and taste function at birth and rapidly adapt to the social world. Infants learn to appreciate what their mothers eat, first through the breast milk and then through smells and spoonfuls of whatever the family has for dinner.

Some herbs and plants contain natural substances that are medicinal. The foods of a particular culture may aid survival: For example, bitter foods provide some defense against malaria, hot spices help preserve food and thus work against food poisoning, and so on (Krebs, 2009). Thus, developing a taste for family food may be life-saving.

Adaptation also occurs for the sense of smell. When breast-feeding mothers used a chamomile balm to ease cracked nipples during the first days of their baby's lives, those babies preferred that smell almost two years later, compared with babies whose mothers used an odorless ointment (Delaunay-El Allam et al., 2010).

As babies learn to recognize each person's scent, they prefer to sleep next to their caregivers, and they nuzzle into their caregivers chests—especially when the adults are shirtless. One way to help infants who are frightened of the bath (some love bathing, some hate it) is for the parent to get in the tub with the baby. The smells of the adult's body mix with the smell of soap, making the experience comforting.

TOUCH AND PAIN The sense of touch is acute in infants, with wrapping, rubbing, and cradling all soothing to many new babies. Some infants relax when held by their caregivers, even when their eyes are closed. The ability to be comforted by touch is one of the skills tested in the Brazelton Neonatal Behavioral Assessment Scale (NBAS, described in Chapter 2).

Although all newborns respond to being securely held, soon they prefer specific, familiar touches. Caressing, swaddling, kissing, massaging, tickling, bouncing, and rocking are each comforting to some infants.

Learning About a Lime As with every other normal infant, Jacqueline's curiosity leads to taste and then to a slow reaction, from puzzlement to tongue-out disgust. Jacqueline's responses demonstrate that the sense of taste is acute in infancy and that quick brain reactions are still to come.

Pain and temperature are not among the five senses, but they are often connected to touch. Some babies cry when being changed because sudden coldness on their skin is distressing. Some touches seem to be intrusive and produce crying.

Scientists are not certain about infant pain. Some experiences that are painful to adults (circumcision, setting of a broken bone) are much less so to newborns. For many newborn medical procedures, from a pinprick to minor surgery, a taste of sugar right before the event is an anesthetic. An empirical study, with an experimental group and a control group, found that newborns typically cry lustily when their heel is pricked (routine after birth), but not if they have had a drop of sucrose beforehand (Harrison et al., 2010).

Some people assume that even the fetus can feel pain; others say that the sense of pain does not mature until months or years later. Many young infants cry for 10 minutes or more, with no obvious reason or effective consolation: Digestive pain is the usual explanation. Many infants fuss or cry before their first tooth erupts: Teething is said to be painful. However, these explanations are unproven; infant crying may not indicate pain (nor does adult crying, necessarily).

Many physiological measures, including stress hormones, erratic heartbeats, and rapid brain waves, are now studied to assess pain in preterm infants, who typically undergo many procedures that would be painful to an adult (Holsti et al., 2011). But infant brains are immature: We cannot assume that they do, or do not, feel pain.

RESPONSE FOR Nurses and Pediatricians (from page 101) Urge the parents to begin learning sign language and investigate the possibility of cochlear implants. Babbling has a biological basis and begins at a specified time, in deaf as well as hearing babies. If their infant can hear, sign language does no harm. If the child is deaf, however, noncommunication may be destructive. ●

Motor Skills

The most dramatic **motor skill** (any movement ability) is independent walking; this is one reason I was concerned about my daughters' late walking (see the beginning of this chapter). Walking and all other motor skills, from the newborn's head-lifting to the toddler's stair-climbing, develop gradually over the first two years. The first evidence is in reflexes, already explained in Chapter 2.

Caregiving and culture matter. Reflexes become skills if they are practiced and encouraged. As you saw in the chapter's beginning, the foundation for Sarah's walking was laid by Mrs. Todd's culture and caregiving when Sarah was only a few months old, long before her first step.

motor skills
The learned abilities to move some part of the body, in actions ranging from a large leap to a flicker of the eyelid. (The word *motor* here refers to movement of muscles.)

GROSS MOTOR SKILLS Deliberate actions that coordinate many parts of the body, producing large movements, are called **gross motor skills.** These emerge directly from reflexes and proceed in a cephalocaudal (head-down) and proximodistal (center-out) direction. Infants first control their heads, lifting them up to look around.

gross motor skills
Physical abilities involving large body movements, such as walking and jumping. (The word *gross* here means "big.")

AT ABOUT THIS TIME
Age Norms (in Months) for Gross Motor Skills

Skill	When 50% of All Babies Master the Skill	When 90% of All Babies Master the Skill
Sit, head steady	3	4
Sit, unsupported	6	7
Pull to stand (holding on)	9	10
Stand alone	12	14
Walk well	13	15
Walk backward	15	17
Run	18	20
Jump up	26	29

Note: As the text explains, age norms are affected by culture and cohort. These are U.S. norms, mostly for European Americans. Mastering skills a few weeks earlier or later does not indicate health or intelligence. Being very late, however, is a cause for concern.

Source: Coovadia & Wittenberg, 2004; based on Denver II (Frankenburg et al., 1992).

OBSERVATION QUIZ
Which of these skills has the greatest variation in age of acquisition? Why? (see answer, page 106) →

CATHARINA VAN DEN DIKKENBERG / ISTOCKPHOTO

Young Expert This infant is an adept crawler. Note the coordination between hands and knees as well as the arm and leg strength needed to support the body in this early version of push-ups. This boy will probably become an expert walker and runner.

fine motor skills
Physical abilities involving small body movements, especially of the hands and fingers, such as drawing and picking up a coin. (The word *fine* here means "small.")

Then they control their upper bodies, their arms, and finally their legs and feet (see At About This Time).

Sitting develops gradually, a matter of developing the muscles to steady the top half of the body. By 3 months, most babies can sit propped up in someone's lap. By 6 months, they can usually sit unsupported. Standing and then walking take longer.

Crawling is another example of this head-down and center-out direction of skill mastery. When placed on their stomachs, many newborns reflexively try to lift their heads and move their arms as if they were swimming. As they gain muscle strength, infants wiggle, attempting to move forward by pushing their arms, shoulders, and upper bodies against whatever surface they are lying on.

Usually by 5 months, infants use their arms, and then legs, to inch forward (or backward) on their bellies. Exactly when this occurs depends partly on how much "tummy time" the infant has had, which is affected by culture (Zachry & Kitzmann, 2011).

Between 8 and 10 months after birth, most infants lift their midsections and crawl (or *creep*, as the British call it) on "all fours," coordinating the movements of their hands and knees. Crawling depends on experience as well as maturation. Some normal babies never do it, especially if the floor is cold, hot, or rough or if they have always lain on their backs (Pin et al., 2007). It is not true that babies *must* crawl to develop normally.

All babies figure out some way to move before they can walk (inching, bear-walking, scooting, creeping, or crawling), but many resist being placed on their stomachs to play (Adolph & Berger, 2005). Overweight babies master gross motor skills later than thinner ones: Practice is harder when the body is heavy (Slining et al., 2010).

The dynamic systems underlying motor skills have three interacting elements, each illustrated here with an example related to walking.

1. *Muscle strength.* Newborns with skinny legs and 3-month-olds buoyed by water make stepping movements, but 6-month-olds on dry land do not; their legs are too chubby for their underdeveloped muscles.

2. *Brain maturation.* The first leg movements—kicking (alternating legs at birth and then both legs together or one leg repeatedly at about 3 months)—occur without much thought. As the brain matures, deliberate leg action becomes possible.

2. *Practice.* Unbalanced, wide-legged, short strides become a steady, smooth gait.

This last item, *practice,* is powerfully affected by caregiving before the first independent step. Some adults spend hours helping infants walk (holding their hands or the back of their shirts) or providing walkers (dangerous if not supervised).

Once toddlers can walk by themselves, they practice obsessively, barefoot or not, at home or in stores, on sidewalks or streets, on lawns or in mud. They fall often, but that does not stop them—"they average between 500 and 1,500 walking steps per hour so that by the end of each day, they have taken 9,000 walking steps and traveled the length of 29 football fields" (Adolph et al., 2003, p. 494).

FINE MOTOR SKILLS Small body movements are called **fine motor skills.** Finger movements are fine motor skills, enabling humans to write, draw, type, tie, and so on. Movements of the tongue, jaw, lips, and toes are fine movements, too.

Actually, mouth skills precede finger skills by many months (newborns can suck; chewing precedes drawing by a year or more). Every culture encourages finger dexterity, so children practice finger movements. By contrast, skilled spitting or chewing is not praised; even blowing bubble gum is admired only by other children.

Regarding hand skills, newborns have a strong reflexive grasp but lack control. During their first 2 months, babies excitedly stare and wave their arms at objects dangling within reach. By 3 months, they can usually touch such objects, but they cannot yet grab and hold on unless an object is placed in their hands, partly because their eye–hand coordination is limited.

By 4 months, infants sometimes grab, but their timing is off: They close their hands too early or too late. Finally, by 6 months, with a concentrated, deliberate stare, most babies can reach, grab, and grasp almost any object that is of the right size. Some can even transfer an object from one hand to the other. Almost all can hold a bottle, shake a rattle, and yank a sister's braids. Once grabbing is possible, babies practice it enthusiastically: "[F]rom 6 to 9 months, reaching appears as a quite compulsive behaviour for small objects presented within arm's reach" (Atkinson & Braddick, 2003, p. 58).

Toward the end of the first year and throughout the second, finger skills improve as babies master the pincer movement (using thumb and forefinger to pick up tiny objects) and self-feeding (first with hands, then fingers, then utensils) (Ho, 2010).

As with gross motor skills, fine motor skills are shaped by culture and opportunity. For example, infants given "sticky mittens" (with Velcro) that allow grabbing master hand skills sooner than usual. Their perception advances as well (Libertus et al., 2010; Soska et al., 2010).

In the second year, grasping becomes more selective. Toddlers learn when *not* to pull at a sister's braids, or Mommy's earrings, or Daddy's glasses. However, as explained later in this chapter, the curiosity of the "little scientist" may overwhelm this caution.

Dynamic Sensory-Motor Systems

The entire package of sensations and motor skills furthers three goals:

1. Social interaction
2. Comfort
3. Learning

Young human infants are, physiologically, an unusual combination of motor immaturity (they cannot walk for many months), sensory acuteness (all senses function at birth), and curiosity (Konner, 2010). What a contrast to kittens, for instance, who are born deaf, with eyes sealed shut, and who stay beside their mother although they can walk.

Human newborns listen and look from day 1, eager to practice every motor skill as soon as possible. An amusing example is rolling over. At about 3 months, infants can roll over from their stomach to their back, but not vice versa. Many a baby rolls over, fusses until someone puts him or her stomach down again, and then immediately rolls over again, only to fuss once more.

The most important experiences are perceived with interacting senses and skills, in dynamic systems (see Chapter 1). Breast milk, for instance, is a mild sedative, so the newborn literally feels happier at Mother's breast, connecting that pleasure with taste, touch, smell, and sight. But in order for all those joys to occur, the infant must actively suck at the nipple (an inborn motor skill, which becomes more efficient with practice).

Bossa Nova Baby? This boy in Brazil demonstrates his joy at acquiring the gross motor skill of walking, which quickly becomes dancing whenever music plays.

RICK GOMEZ / MASTERFILE

Sensory Exuberance Human animals are unusual in that all the senses function at birth, but motor skills develop slowly. This Toronto boy loves to taste and bite the toy designed for looking at (that bull's eye) and grabbing (those plastic rings), even though he cannot yet sit up unsupported.

RADIUS IMAGES / GLOW IMAGES

ANSWER TO **OBSERVATION QUIZ**
(from page 104) Jumping up, with a
three-month age range for acquisition.
The reason is that the older an infant
is, the more impact both nature and
nurture have. ●

Similarly, 6-month-olds coordinate their senses and skills, expecting lip movements to synchronize with speech, for instance (Lewkowicz, 2010), and making responsive noises themselves. For toddlers, crawling and walking are part of dynamic systems; they are used to explore, and thus sensations lead to perception and cognition.

Piaget named the first two years of cognitive development "sensorimotor" for good reason, as you will soon see. But first, one obvious prerequisite for all the growth already described—staying alive.

KEY points

- All the senses function at birth, with hearing the most acute sense and vision the least developed.

- Every sense allows perception to develop and furthers social understanding. Caregivers are recognized by sight, touch, smell, and voice.

- Gross motor skills follow a genetic timetable for maturation; they are also affected by practice and experience.

- Fine motor skills also develop with time and experience, combining with the senses as part of dynamic systems.

Surviving in Good Health

Although precise worldwide statistics are unavailable, at least 10 billion children were born between 1950 and 2010. More than 2 billion of them died before age 5. Although 2 billion is far too many, twice that many would have died without recent public health measures. As best we know, in earlier centuries more than half of all newborns died in infancy.

Better Days Ahead

In the twenty-first century in developed nations, 99.9 percent of newborns who survive the first month (when the sickest and smallest die) live to adulthood. Even in the poorest nations, where a few decades ago many infants died, now about 93 per-

Well Protected Disease and early death are common in Africa, where this photo was taken, but neither is likely for 2-year-old Salem. He is protected not only by the nutrition and antibodies in his mother's milk but also by the large blue net that surrounds them. Treated bed nets, like this one provided by the Carter Center and the Ethiopian Health Ministry, are often large enough for families to eat, read, as well as sleep in together, without fear of malaria-infected mosquitos.

LOUISE GUBB / CORBIS

cent live (see Figure 3.5a). Some nations have seen dramatic improvement. For instance, Chile's rate of infant mortality was almost 4 times higher than the rate in the United States in 1970; now it is even (see Figure 3.5b).

The world death rate in the first five years of life has dropped about 2 percent per year since 1990 (Rajaratnam et al., 2010). Public health measures (clean water, nourishing food, immunization) are the main reasons for the higher rate of survival, which has led to many other benefits—lower birth rates, less starvation, and more education.

When women realize that each newborn is likely to survive to adulthood, they have fewer babies, and that advances the national economy. Infant survival and maternal education are the two main reasons the world's 2010 fertility rate is half what the rate was in 1950 (Bloom, 2011; Lutz & K.C., 2011).

If doctors and nurses were available in underserved areas, the current infant death rate would be cut in half

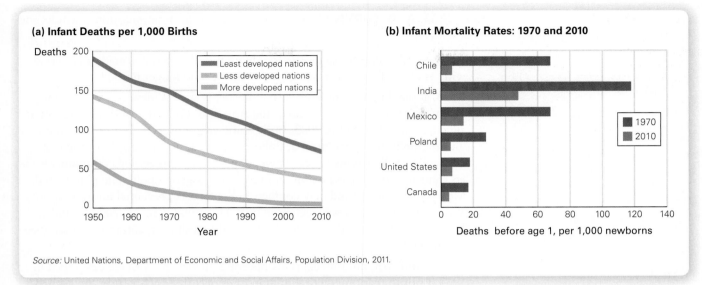

FIGURE 3.5 More Babies Are Surviving Improvements in public health—better nutrition, cleaner water, more widespread immunization—over the past three decades have meant millions of survivors.

Source: United Nations, Department of Economic and Social Affairs, Population Division, 2011.

Note: in graph *(a)*:

Least developed nations: Haiti, Cambodia, Yemen, Bangladesh, Nepal, Afghanistan, all nations of sub-Saharan Africa (except those listed in "Less developed nations")

Less developed nations: Kenya, Mauritania, Zimbabwe, Cameroon, Nigeria, Ghana, Korea, Gabon, Mexico, all Northern Africa, all Asia (except Japan and those listed in "Least developed nations"), all Caribbean (except Haiti), all Central America

More developed nations: Japan, all Europe, Australia, New Zealand, United States

again—immediately by newborn survival and widespread immunization, and soon via measures to help the whole population, such as better food distribution, less violence, more education, and clean water (Farahani et al., 2009).

For example, every year in Africa 1 million people die of malaria, most of them undernourished children. Immediate drug treatment can save lives, but many victims live far from medical help, and some anti-malaria drugs are expensive or no longer effective (Kun et al., 2010).

One innovation has cut the malaria death rate in half: bed nets treated with insect repellant that mothers drape over sleeping areas (Roberts, 2007) (see photo). Over the long term, however, systemic prevention means making mosquitoes sterile—a promising research effort now entering clinical trials (James et al., 2011).

Immunization

Immunization primes the body's immune system to resist a particular disease. Immunization (also called *vaccination*) is said to have had "a greater impact on human mortality reduction and population growth than any other public health intervention besides clean water" (J. P. Baker, 2000, p. 199).

No immunization is yet available for malaria. Thousands of scientists are working to develop one, and some clinical trials seem promising (Vaughan & Kappe, 2012). However, immunization has been developed for measles, mumps, whooping cough, smallpox, pneumonia, polio, and rotavirus, which no longer kill hundreds of thousands of children each year.

It used to be that the only way to become immune to these diseases was to catch them, sicken, and recover. The immune system would then produce antibodies to prevent recurrence. Beginning with smallpox in the nineteenth century, doctors discovered that giving a vaccine—a small dose of the virus—to healthy people who have not had the disease stimulates the same antibodies. (Immunization schedules, with U.S. recommendations, appear in Appendix A. Most of the vaccines listed reduce the risk of child death in every nation. However, specifics vary; caregivers need to heed local health authorities.)

immunization
A process that stimulates the body's immune system to defend against attack by a particular contagious disease. Immunization may be accomplished either naturally (by having the disease) or through vaccination (often by having an injection). (Also called *vaccination.*)

✦ **ESPECIALLY FOR Nurses and Pediatricians** A mother refuses to have her baby immunized because she wants to prevent side effects. She wants your signature for a religious exemption, which in some jurisdictions allows the mother to refuse vaccination because she says it is for religious reasons. What should you do? (see response, page 109) ➡

SUCCESS AND SURVIVAL Stunning successes in immunization include the following:

● Smallpox, the most lethal disease for children in the past, was eradicated worldwide as of 1971. Vaccination against smallpox is no longer needed.

● Polio, a crippling and sometimes fatal disease, is rare. Widespread vaccination, begun in 1955, eliminated polio in the Americas. Only 784 cases were reported anywhere in the world in 2003. In the same year, however, rumors halted immunization in northern Nigeria. Polio reappeared, sickening 1,948 people in 2005, almost all in West Africa. Then public health workers and community leaders campaigned to increase immunization, and Nigeria's polio rate plummeted. Meanwhile, poverty and new conflicts in South Asia prevented immunization: Worldwide, 650 cases were reported in 2011, primarily in Afghanistan, India, Nigeria, and Pakistan (De Cock, 2011; World Health Organization, 2012). (See Figure 3.6.)

● Measles (rubeola, not rubella) is disappearing, thanks to a vaccine developed in 1963. Prior to that time, 3 to 4 million cases occurred each year in the United States alone (Centers for Disease Control and Prevention, 2007). In 2010 in the United States, only 61 people had measles, most of them born in nations without widespread immunization (MMWR, January 7, 2011).

Immunization protects children not only from temporary sickness but also from complications, including deafness, blindness, sterility, and meningitis. Sometimes the damage from illness is not apparent until decades later. Childhood mumps, for instance, can cause sterility and doubles the risk of schizophrenia in adulthood (Dalman et al., 2008).

Some people cannot be safely immunized, including the following:

● Embryos, who may be born blind, deaf, and brain-damaged if their pregnant mother contracts rubella (German measles)

● Newborns, who may die from a disease that is mild in older children

● People with impaired immune systems (HIV-positive, aged, or undergoing chemotherapy), who can become deathly ill

Fortunately, each vaccinated child stops transmission of the disease and thus protects others, a phenomenon called *herd immunity*. Although specifics vary by disease, usually if 90 percent of the people in a community (a herd) are immunized, the

FIGURE 3.6 Not Yet Zero Many public health advocates hope polio will be the next infectious disease to be eliminated worldwide, as is the case in almost all of North America. The number of cases has fallen dramatically worldwide (a). However, there was a discouraging increase in polio rates from 2003 to 2005 (b).

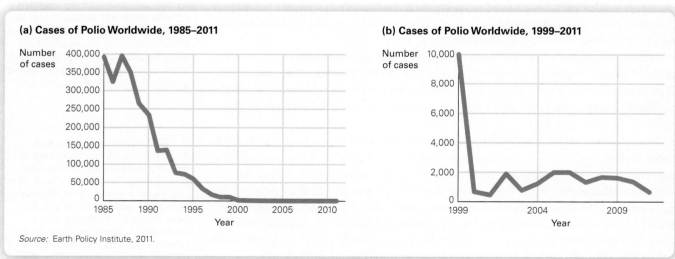

(a) Cases of Polio Worldwide, 1985–2011

(b) Cases of Polio Worldwide, 1999–2011

Source: Earth Policy Institute, 2011.

disease does not spread to those who are vulnerable. Without herd immunity, some community members die of a "childhood" disease.

PROBLEMS WITH IMMUNIZATION Infants may react to immunization by being irritable or even feverish for a day or so, to the distress of their parents. However, parents do not notice if their child does *not* get polio, measles, or so on. Before the varicella (chicken pox) vaccine, more than 100 people in the United States died each year from that disease, and 1 million were itchy and feverish for a week. Now almost no one dies of varicella, and far fewer get chicken pox.

Many parents are concerned about potential side effects. Whenever something seems to go amiss with vaccination, the media broadcasts it, which frightens parents. As a result, the rate of missed vaccinations in the United States has been rising over the past decade. This horrifies public health workers, who, taking a longitudinal and society-wide perspective, are convinced that the risks of the diseases are far greater than the risks from immunization. A hypothesis that the MMR (measles-mumps-rubella) vaccine causes autism has been repeatedly disproved (Mrozek-Budzyn et al., 2010; Shattuck, 2006). (More on autism in Chapter 7.)

Doctors agree that vaccines "are one of the most cost-effective, successful interventions in the history of public health" and lament that that success has made parents, physicians, and governments less vigilant (Hannan et al., 2009, p. S571). For example, lack of immunization is blamed for a spike in infant whooping cough deaths in 2010 in California, which declared a whooping cough epidemic (McKinley, 2010).

Nutrition

Infant mortality worldwide has plummeted in recent years. Several reasons have already been mentioned: fewer sudden infant deaths (explained in Chapter 1), advances in prenatal and newborn care (explained in Chapter 2), and immunization (as you just read). One more measure has made a huge difference: better nutrition.

BREAST IS BEST Ideally, nutrition starts with *colostrum,* a thick, high-calorie fluid secreted by the mother's breasts at birth. After about three days, the breasts begin to produce milk. Compared with formula based on cow's milk, human milk is sterile; always at body temperature; and rich in iron, vitamins, and other newly discovered nutrients for brain and body (Drover et al., 2009).

Babies who are exclusively breast-fed are less often sick. In infancy, breast milk provides antibodies against any disease to which the mother is immune and decreases allergies and asthma. Disease protection continues lifelong because babies who are exclusively breast-fed for six months are less likely to become obese (Huh et al., 2011) and thus less likely to develop diabetes or heart disease.

Breast milk is especially protective for preterm babies; if a preterm baby's mother cannot provide breast milk, physicians recommend milk from another woman (Schanler, 2011). (Once a woman has given birth, her breasts produce milk for decades if they continue to be stimulated.)

The specific fats and sugars in breast milk make it more digestible and better for the brain than any substitute (Drover et al., 2009; Riordan, 2005). The composition of breast milk adjusts to the age of the baby, with milk for premature babies distinct

True Dedication This young Buddhist monk lives in a remote region of Nepal, where, until recently, measles was a fatal disease. Fortunately, a UNICEF porter carried the vaccine over mountain trails for two days so that this boy—and his whole community—could be immunized.

RESPONSE FOR Nurses and Pediatricians (from page 107) It is difficult to convince people that their method of child rearing is wrong, although you should try. In this case, listen respectfully and then describe specific instances of serious illness or death from a childhood disease. Suggest that the mother ask her grandparents if they knew anyone who had polio, tuberculosis, or tetanus (they probably did). If you cannot convince this mother, do not despair: Vaccination of 95 percent of toddlers helps protect the other 5 percent. If the mother has religious reasons, talk to her clergy adviser. ●

ALAIN EVRARD / PHOTOLIBRARY

SELECTSTOCK / GETTY IMAGES

Same Situation, Far Apart: Breast-Feeding Breast-feeding is universal. None of us would exist if our fore-mothers had not successfully breast-fed their babies for millennia. Currently, breast-feeding is practiced worldwide, but it is no longer the only way to feed infants, and each culture has particular practices.

OBSERVATION QUIZ

(see answer, page 112) What three differences do you see between these two breast-feeding women—one in the United States and one in Laos? →

from that for older infants. Quantity increases to meet the demand: Twins and even triplets can grow strong while being exclusively breast-fed for months.

In fact, breast milk appears to have so many advantages over formula (see Table 3.1) that one might question the validity of the research: Are breast-feeding mothers better for their babies in ways not measured?

Formula-feeding is preferable only in unusual cases, such as when the mother is HIV-positive or uses toxic or addictive drugs. Even then, however, breast milk without supplementation may be advised, depending on the risks and the alternatives.

TABLE 3.1 The Benefits of Breast-Feeding

For the Baby
Balance of nutrition (fat, protein, etc.) adjusts to age of baby

Breast milk has micronutrients not found in formula

Less infant illness, including allergies, ear infections, stomach upsets

Less childhood asthma

Better childhood vision

Less adult illness, including diabetes, cancer, heart disease

Protection against many childhood diseases, since breast milk contains antibodies from the mother

Stronger jaws, fewer cavities, advanced breathing reflexes (less SIDS)

Higher IQ, less likely to drop out of school, more likely to attend college

Later puberty, less teenage pregnancy

Less likely to become obese or hypertensive by age 12

For the Mother
Easier bonding with baby

Reduced risk of breast cancer and osteoporosis

Natural contraception (with exclusive breast-feeding, for several months)

Pleasure of breast stimulation

Satisfaction of meeting infant's basic need

No formula to prepare; no sterilization

Easier travel with the baby

For the Family
Increased survival of other children (because of spacing of births)

Increased family income (because formula and medical care are expensive)

Less stress on father, especially at night

Sources: Beilin & Huang, 2008; Riordan & Wambach, 2009; Schanler, 2011; U.S. Department of Health and Human Services, 2011.

For example, in some African nations, HIV-positive women are encouraged to breast-feed because their infants' risk of catching HIV from their mothers is lower than the risk of dying from infections, diarrhea, or malnutrition as a result of bottle-feeding (Cohen, 2007; Kuhn et al., 2009).

For all these reasons, doctors worldwide recommend breast-feeding with no other foods—not even juice. Some pediatricians suggest adding foods (rice cereal and bananas) at 4 months; others want mothers to wait until 6 months (Fewtrell et al., 2011). For breast milk to meet the baby's nutritional needs, the mother must be well fed and hydrated (especially important in hot climates) and should avoid alcohol, cigarettes, and other drugs.

Breast-feeding was once universal, but by the middle of the twentieth century many mothers thought formula was better because it was more modern. Fortunately, that has changed again. In the United States, 77 percent of infants are breast-fed at birth, 48 percent at 6 months (most with other food as well), and 25 percent at a year (virtually all with other food and drink) (see Figure 3.7) (U.S. Department of Health and Human Services, 2011). Worldwide, about half of all 2-year-olds are still nursing, usually at night.

How long a mother breast-feeds is strongly affected by her experiences in the first weeks (DiGirolamo et al., 2005). Successful breast-feeding involves some learning for both baby and mother (e.g., how to latch on and off), and many women quit when they experience pain. Bottle-feeding can be done by anyone.

Since formula-feeding may seem easier for the mother, particularly in the early weeks, encouragement of, and help with, breast-feeding from family members, especially new fathers, are crucial. Since the quantity of milk increases to meet demand, in the beginning some babies need to nurse every two hours—almost impossible if the mother has to return to work. Ideally, nurses visit new mothers weekly at home; such visits (routine in some nations, rare in others) increase the likelihood that breast-feeding will continue.

MALNUTRITION **Protein–calorie malnutrition** occurs when a person does not consume enough food to sustain normal growth. That form of malnutrition occurs for roughly one-third of the world's children in developing nations: They suffer from **stunting,** being short for their age because chronic malnutrition kept them from

✦ **ESPECIALLY FOR New Parents**
When should parents decide whether to feed their baby only by breast, only by bottle, or using some combination? When should they decide whether or not to let their baby use a pacifier? (see response, page 113) →

protein-calorie malnutrition
A condition in which a person does not consume sufficient food of any kind. This deprivation can result in several illnesses, severe weight loss, and even death.

stunting
The failure of children to grow to a normal height for their age due to severe and chronic malnutrition.

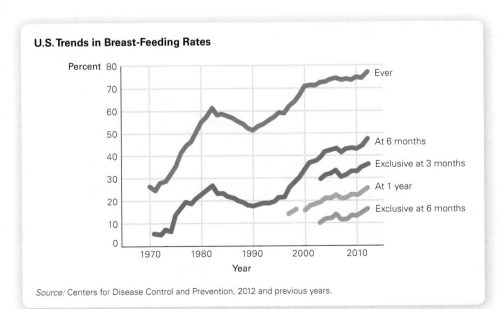

U.S. Trends in Breast-Feeding Rates

Source: Centers for Disease Control and Prevention, 2012 and previous years.

FIGURE 3.7 **A Smart Choice** In 1970, educated women were taught that formula was the smart, modern way to provide nutrition—but no longer. Today, more education for women correlates with more breast milk for babies. About half of U.S. women with college degrees now manage three months of *exclusive* breast-feeding—no juice, no water, and certainly no cereal.

FIGURE 3.8 Genetic? The data show that basic nutrition is still unavailable to many children in the developing world. Some critics contend that Asian children are genetically small and therefore that Western norms make it appear as if India and Africa have more stunted children than they really do. However, children of Asian and African descent born and nurtured in North America are as tall as those of European descent. Thus, malnutrition, not genes, accounts for most stunting worldwide.

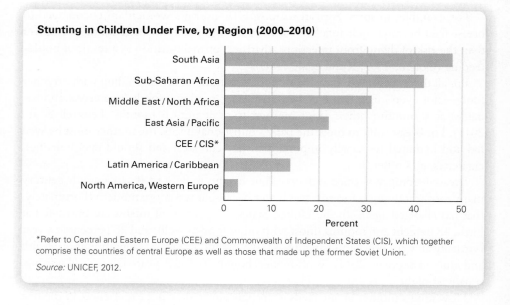

Stunting in Children Under Five, by Region (2000–2010)

*Refer to Central and Eastern Europe (CEE) and Commonwealth of Independent States (CIS), which together comprise the countries of central Europe as well as those that made up the former Soviet Union.

Source: UNICEF, 2012.

wasting
The tendency for children to be severely underweight for their age as a result of malnutrition.

ANSWER TO **OBSERVATION QUIZ**
(from page 110) The babies' ages, the settings, and the mothers' apparent attitudes. The U.S. mother *(right)* is at home and seems attentive to whether she is feeding her 5-month-old infant the right way. The mother in Laos *(left)* seems content as she feeds her 2-year-old outside, confident that the child needs no special attention. ●

growing (World Bank, 2010). Stunting is most common in the poorest nations (see Figure 3.8).

Even worse is **wasting,** when children are severely underweight for their age and height (2 or more standard deviations below average). Many nations, especially in East Asia, Latin America, and central Europe have seen improvement in child nutrition in the past decades, with an accompanying decrease in wasting and stunting.

In some other nations, primarily in Africa, wasting has increased. And in several nations in South Asia, about half the children over age 5 are stunted and half of them also wasted, at least for a year (World Bank, 2010). In terms of development, the worst effect is that energy is reduced and normal curiosity is absent (Osorio, 2011).

One common way to measure a particular child's nutritional status is to compare weight and height with the norms presented in Figure 3.1 and Figure 3.9 (and in Appendix A). Remember that some children may simply be genetically small, but all children should grow rapidly in the first two years.

Length of Girls and Boys, Birth to 24 Months

FIGURE 3.9 Gender Differences
Boys and girls grow at almost the same rate throughout childhood—until age 11 or so, when girls temporarily grow faster than boys.

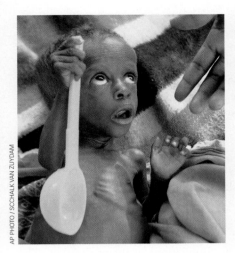 

AP PHOTO / SCCHALK VAN ZUYDAM

DANG NGO / ZUMA PRESS / NEWSCOM

Same Situation, Far Apart: Children Still Malnourished Infant malnutrition is common in nations at war (like Afghanistan, at right) or with crop failure (like Niger, at left). UNICEF relief programs reach only half the children in either nation. The children in these photographs are among the lucky ones who are being fed.

Chronically malnourished infants and children suffer in three ways (World Bank, 2010):

1. Their brains may not develop normally. If malnutrition has continued long enough to affect height, it may also have affected the brain.

2. Malnourished children have no body reserves to protect them against common diseases. About half of all childhood deaths occur because malnutrition makes a childhood disease lethal.

3. Some diseases result directly from malnutrition—both **marasmus** during the first year, when body tissues waste away, and **kwashiorkor** after age 1, when growth slows down; hair becomes thin; skin becomes splotchy; and the face, legs, and abdomen swell with fluid (edema).

Prevention, more than treatment, stops childhood malnutrition. In fact, some children hospitalized for marasmus or kwashiorkor die even after feeding because their digestive systems are already failing. Ideally, prevention starts with ample prenatal nutrition for the mother and then breast-feeding on demand, with supplemental iron and vitamin A for mother and child.

A study of two of the poorest African nations (Niger and Gambia) found several specific factors that reduced the likelihood of wasting and stunting: breast-feeding, both parents at home, water piped to the house, a tile (not dirt) floor, a toilet, electricity, immunization, a radio, and the mother's secondary education (Oyekale & Oyekale, 2009). Overall, "a mother's education is key in determining whether her children will survive their first five years of life" (United Nations, 2011, p. 26).

marasmus
A disease of severe protein-calorie malnutrition during early infancy, in which growth stops, body tissues waste away, and the infant eventually dies.

kwashiorkor
A disease of chronic malnutrition during childhood, in which a protein deficiency makes the child more vulnerable to other diseases, such as measles, diarrhea, and influenza.

KEY points

- Various public health measures have saved billions of infants in the past half-century.

- Immunization protects those who are inoculated and also halts the spread of contagious diseases (via herd immunity).

- Breast milk is the ideal infant food, improving development for decades and reducing infant malnutrition and death.

- Although most newborns are breast-fed, as are many 2-year-olds in developing nations, only one-third of North American 3-month-olds are exclusively breast-fed.

RESPONSE FOR New Parents (from page 111) Both decisions should be made within the first month, during the stage of reflexes. If parents wait until the infant is 4 months or older, they may discover that they are too late. It is difficult to introduce a bottle to a 4-month-old who has been exclusively breast-fed or a pacifier to a baby who has already adapted the sucking reflex to a thumb. ●

Infant Cognition

The rapid physical growth of the human infant, just described, is impressive, but intellectual growth during infancy is even more awesome. Concepts, memories, and sentences—nonexistent in newborns—are evident by age 1 and consolidated by age 2. We begin with Jean Piaget, "arguably the most influential researcher of all time within the area of cognitive developmental psychology" (Birney et al., 2005, p. 328).

Sensorimotor Intelligence

sensorimotor intelligence
Piaget's term for the way infants think—by using their senses and motor skills—during the first period of cognitive development.

Piaget called cognition in the first two years **sensorimotor intelligence** because infants learn through their senses and motor skills. He subdivided this period into six stages (see Table 3.2).

STAGES ONE AND TWO Stage one, called the *stage of reflexes,* lasts only a month. It includes senses as well as motor reflexes, the foundations of infant thought. The newborn's reflexes evoke some brain reactions. Soon sensation leads to perception, which ushers in stage two, *first acquired adaptations* (also called the *stage of first habits*).

For example, newborns reflexively suck anything that touches their lips. By about 1 month, they have adapted this reflex to bottles or breasts, pacifiers or fingers, each requiring specific types of tongue-pushing. This adaptation is a sign that infants have begun to interpret their perceptions; as they accommodate to pacifiers, they are thinking.

STAGES THREE AND FOUR In stages three and four, reactions are no longer confined to the infant's body; they are an *interaction* between the baby and something else. During stage three (4 to 8 months), infants attempt to produce exciting experiences, *making interesting sights last.*

Actually, the word *sights* includes more than what babies see: At this stage of cognitive advancement, babies try to continue any pleasing event. Realizing that rattles make noise, for example, they wave their arms and laugh whenever someone puts a rattle in their hand. The sight of something delightful—a favorite book, a smiling parent—can trigger active efforts for interaction.

Time for Adaptation Sucking is a reflex at first, but adaptation begins as soon as an infant differentiates a pacifier from her mother's breast or realizes that her hand has grown too big to fit into her mouth. This infant's expression of concentration suggests that she is about to make that adaptation and suck just her thumb from now on.

Next comes stage four (8 months to 1 year), *new adaptation and anticipation,* also called the *means to the end* because babies have goals that they try to reach. Often they ask for help (fussing, pointing, gesturing) to accomplish what they want. Thinking is more innovative because adaptation is more complex. For instance, instead of always smiling at Daddy, an infant might first assess Daddy's mood and then try to engage. Stage-three babies know how to continue an experience; stage-four babies initiate and anticipate.

That initiation is *goal-directed,* not random. For instance, babies who are breast-fed indicate that they are hungry by lifting up their mother's shirt. They also indicate when they do not want to eat, keeping their mouths firmly shut if they are full or if the food on the spoon is not what they want. If the caregivers have been using sign language, among the first signs learned before age 1 are "eat" and "all done."

object permanence
The realization that objects (including people) still exist even if they can no longer be seen, touched, or heard.

OBJECT PERMANENCE Piaget thought that, at about 8 months, babies first understand **object permanence**—the concept that objects or people continue to exist when they are no longer in sight. As he described, beginning at about 8 months, infants search for toys that have fallen from the crib, rolled under a couch, or disappeared under a blanket. Blind babies also acquire object permanence toward the end of their first year, reaching for an object that they hear nearby (Fazzi et al., 2011).

TABLE 3.2 The Six Stages of Sensorimotor Intelligence

For an overview of the stages of sensorimotor thought, it helps to group the six stages into pairs. The first two stages involve the infant's responses to its own body.

Primary Circular Reactions

Stage One (birth to 1 month)   *Reflexes:* sucking, grasping, staring, listening

Stage Two (1–4 months)   *The first acquired adaptations:* accommodation and coordination of reflexes
Examples: sucking a pacifier differently from a nipple; grabbing a bottle to suck it

The next two stages involve the infant's responses to objects and people.

Secondary Circular Reactions

Stage Three (4–8 months)   *Making interesting sights last:* responding to people and objects
Example: clapping hands when mother says "patty-cake"

Stage Four (8–12 months)   *New adaptation and anticipation:* becoming more deliberate and purposeful in responding to people and objects
Example: putting mother's hands together in order to make her start playing patty-cake

The last two stages are the most creative, first with action and then with ideas.

Tertiary Circular Reactions

Stage Five (12–18 months)   *New means through active experimentation:* experimentation and creativity in the actions of the "little scientist"
Example: putting a teddy bear in the toilet and flushing it

Stage Six (18–24 months)   *New means through mental combinations:* considering before doing, which provides the child with new ways of achieving a goal without resorting to trial-and-error experiments
Example: before flushing, remembering that the toilet overflowed and mother was angry the last time, and hesitating

Piaget developed a basic experiment to measure object permanence: An adult shows an infant an interesting toy and then covers it with a lightweight cloth. The results are as follows:

- Infants under 8 months do not search for the object (by removing the cloth).

- At about 8 months, infants will search immediately, removing the cloth after the object is covered but not if they have to wait a few seconds.

- By 2 years, children fully comprehend object permanence, progressing through several stages of ever-advanced cognition (Piaget, 1954).

Piaget believed that failure to search before 8 months was evidence that the baby had no concept of object permanence—that "out of sight" literally means "out of mind." However, researchers who track infants' eye movements and brain activity find Piaget was mistaken. Indeed, some scientists believe that "infants as young as 2 and 3 months of age can represent fully hidden objects" (Cohen & Cashon, 2006, p. 224). Other scientists are not convinced (Kagan, 2008).

Added to the puzzle is the fact that many other creatures (cats, monkeys, dogs, birds) develop object permanence at younger ages than Piaget found in children. Does this reflect slower development of the human brain or simply slower maturation of the motor skill required to grab a cloth to uncover a toy (Bruce & Muhammad, 2009)?

Where's Grandma? Experienced caregivers everywhere know that peek-a-boo captures infants' attention when they're beginning to understand object permanence.

RUTH JENKINSON / GETTY IMAGES

Exploration at 15 Months One of the best ways to investigate food is to squish it in your hands, observe any changes in color and texture, and listen for any sounds. Taste and smell are primary senses for adults when eating, but it looks as if Jonathan has already had his fill of those.

✦ **ESPECIALLY FOR Parents of Toddlers** One parent wants to put all the breakable or dangerous objects away because a toddler is now able to move around independently. The other parent says that the baby should learn not to touch certain things. Who is right? (see response, page 120) →

little scientist
The stage-five toddler (age 12 to 18 months) who experiments without anticipating the results, using trial and error in active and creative exploration.

deferred imitation
A sequence in which an infant first perceives something done by someone else and then performs the same action hours or even days later.

ARIEL SKELLEY / AGE FOTOSTOCK

STAGES FIVE AND SIX In their second year, infants start experimenting in thought and deed—or, rather, in the opposite sequence: deed and thought. They act first (stage five) and think later (stage six).

Stage five (12 to 18 months) is called *new means through active experimentation,* when goal-directed anticipation (stage four) becomes more expansive and creative. Toddlers delight in squeezing all the toothpaste out of the tube, taking apart an alarm clock, or uncovering an anthill. These actions are all creative, in that the children have never seen an adult undertake such exploration. Piaget referred to the stage-five toddler as a **little scientist** who "experiments in order to see." Their devotion to discovery is familiar to every adult scientist—and to every parent.

Finally, in the sixth stage (ages 18 to 24 months), toddlers enter the stage of *new means through mental combinations.* Thankfully, the stage-six infant uses thought and memory, which deters the little scientist somewhat. Stage-six infants can even pretend. For instance, at 22 months my grandson gave me "shoe ice cream" and laughed as I pretended to eat it.

Piaget describes another stage-six intellectual accomplishment, **deferred imitation,** when mental combinations allow children to copy behavior they noticed hours or even days earlier (Piaget, 1945/1962). He wrote about his daughter, Jacqueline, who observed another toddler

> who got into a terrible temper. He screamed as he tried to get out of a playpen and pushed it backward, stamping his feet. Jacqueline stood watching him in amazement, never having witnessed such a scene before. The next day, she herself screamed in her playpen and tried to move it, stamping her foot lightly several times in succession.

[Piaget, 1945/1962, p. 63]

PIAGET REEVALUATED As detailed by hundreds of developmentalists, many infants reach the stages of sensorimotor intelligence earlier than Piaget predicted (Oakes et al., 2011). Not only do 5-month-olds show surprise when objects seem to disappear (evidence of object permanence before 8 months, as described earlier); some babies younger than 1 year pretend and defer imitation (both stage-six abilities, according to Piaget).

A major limitation of Piaget's method for determining what infants could think is that it relied only on direct observation of behavior, such as noticing whether or not a baby pulled away a cloth to search for a hidden object. Scientists now have many ways of measuring brain activity long before any observable evidence is apparent (see Table 3.3) (Johnson, 2010).

Some require millisecond video analysis, such as whether an infant stares at a disappearing object for 20 or 30 milliseconds. Before any conclusions are drawn, data from dozens of infants need to be analyzed statistically.

Other techniques involve brain scans. For example, in functional magnetic resonance imaging (fMRI), a burst of electrical activity measured by blood flow within the brain is recorded, indicating that neurons are firing. This leads researchers to conclude that a particular stimulus has been noticed and processed, even if the infant takes no action.

TOOGA PRODUCTIONS, INC. / GETTY IMAGES

No More Playpens Much has changed since Jacqueline watched a temper tantrum in a playpen. Little scientists still "experiment in order to see," but this 14-month-old uses a digital tablet and might protest if it is taken away.

TABLE 3.3 Some Techniques Used by Neuroscientists to Understand Brain Function

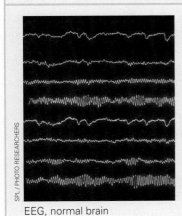

Technique
EEG (electroencephalogram)

Use
Measures electrical activity in the top layers of the brain, where the cortex is.

Limitations
Especially in infancy, much brain activity of interest occurs below the cortex.

EEG, normal brain

Technique
ERP (event-related potential)

Use
Notes the amplitude and frequency of electrical activity (as shown by brain waves) in specific parts of the cortex in reaction to various stimuli.

Limitations
Reaction within the cortex signifies perception, but interpretation of the amplitude and timing of brain waves is not straightforward.

ERP when listening

© 2001 UNIVERSITY OF WASHINGTON, INSTITUTE FOR LEARNING AND BRAIN SCIENCES

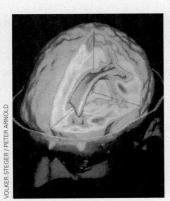

Technique
fMRI (functional magnetic resonance imaging)

Use
Measures changes in blood flow anywhere in the brain (not just the outer layers).

Limitations
Signifies brain activity, but infants are notoriously active, which can make fMRIs useless.

fMRI when talking

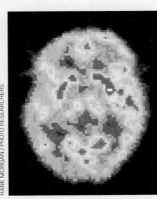

Technique
PET (positron emission tomography)

Use
PET (like fMRI) reveals activity in various parts of the brain. Locations can be pinpointed with precision, but PET requires injection of radioactive dye to light up the active parts of the brain.

Limitations
Many parents and researchers hesitate to inject radioactive dye into an infant's brain unless a serious abnormality is suspected.

PET scan of sleep

For both practical and ethical reasons, these techniques have not been used with large, representative samples of normal infants. One of the challenges of neuroscience is to develop methods that are harmless, easy to use, and comprehensive for the study of normal children. A more immediate challenge is to depict the data in ways that are easy to interpret and understand.

Brain scans are one way to investigate **mirror neurons,** an astonishing discovery that arose from careful research on monkeys—something not done in Piaget's day. About two decades ago, scientists were surprised to discover that a particular region of a macaque monkey's brain responded to actions the monkey had merely observed as if it had actually performed those actions itself (Gallese et al., 1996).

For example, when one macaque saw another reach for a banana, the same brain areas were activated (lit up in brain scans) in both monkeys. Mirror neurons in the F5 area of the observing macaque's premotor cortex responded to what was observed. Using increasingly advanced technology, neuroscientists have now found mirror neurons in several parts of the human brain (Keysers & Gazzola, 2010).

Many scientists are particularly interested in the implications for infant cognition. Perhaps the avid watching and listening that babies do enable them to learn long before Piaget realized. Because of mirror neurons, their understanding of objects, language, or human intentions might be far more advanced than researchers have demonstrated (Diamond & Amso, 2008; Rossi et al., 2011; Virji-Babul et al., 2012).

Scientists are now convinced that infants have memories, goals, deferred imitation, and mental combinations well in advance of the timing that Piaget proposed for his stages (Bauer et al., 2010; Morasch & Bell, 2009). Piaget was correct to describe babies as eager learners. He simply underestimated how rapidly that learning occurs.

mirror neurons
Cells in an observer's brain that respond to an action performed by someone else in the same way they would if the observer had actually performed that action.

Goals and Cognition Much of infant intellectual development is about goal-directed behavior. At 18 months, Leila has already learned that grabbing will result in a push from her brother and punishment from her mother. Now, at the beginning of mental combinations, she knows a more effective way to make her wishes clear—gathering sympathy. Will that get her the ice cream her mirror neurons indicate she's already licking?

information-processing theory A perspective that compares human thinking processes, by analogy, to computer analysis of data, including sensory input, connections, stored memories, and output.

Information Processing

As mentioned in Chapter 1, Piaget's sweeping overview of four periods of cognition contrasts with **information-processing theory,** a perspective originally modeled after computer functioning, involving input, memory, programming, calculation, and output.

Information-processing research has found that many concepts and categories develop in very young brains. Even math concepts may begin as early as 3 months, advancing throughout the first year (Libertus & Brannon, 2009). For instance, 6-month-olds can detect the difference between a display of 8 dots and one of 16 dots, but not until 9 months of age can they distinguish between 8 and 12 dots (Lipton & Spelke, 2003).

The information-processing perspective has uncovered many notable aspects of infant cognition. Babies are now thought to be little scientists in the first year of life. As one researcher summarizes, "Rather than bumbling babies, they are individuals who . . . can learn surprisingly fast about the patterns of nature" (Keil, 2011, p. 1023).

The term *infant amnesia* refers to the belief that infants remember nothing until about age 2. Information processing has revealed otherwise. We now focus on one specific aspect of the information-processing perspective—memory.

MEMORY A series of experiments reveals that very young infants *can* remember, even if they cannot later put memories into words. Memories are particularly evident when:

● Experimental conditions are similar to those of real life.
● Motivation is high.
● Retrieval is strengthened by reminders and repetition.

The most dramatic evidence for infant memory comes from innovative experiments in which 3-month-olds were taught to make a mobile move by kicking their legs (Rovee-Collier, 1987, 1990). The infants lay on their backs, in their own cribs, connected to a mobile by means of a ribbon tied to one foot (see photo, top right).

Virtually all the infants began making some occasional kicks (as well as random arm movements and noises) and realized, after a while, that kicking made the mobile move. They then kicked more vigorously and frequently, sometimes laughing at their accomplishment. So far, this is no surprise—self-activated movement is highly reinforcing to infants, a part of dynamic perception.

Selective Amnesia As we grow older, we forget about spitting up, nursing, crying, and almost everything else from our early years. However, strong emotions (love, fear, mistrust) may leave lifelong traces.

When some infants had the mobile-and-ribbon apparatus reinstalled in their cribs *one week later,* most started to kick immediately. Their quick reaction indicated that they remembered their previous experience. But when other 3-month-old infants were not retested until *two weeks later,* they began with only random kicks. Apparently they had forgotten.

Then the lead researcher, Carolyn Rovee-Collier, developed another experiment. Two weeks after the initial training, the infants watched the mobile move but were *not* tied to it and were positioned so that they could *not* kick. This experience of looking, but not kicking, was a **reminder session.** The next day, when they were again connected to the mobile and positioned so that they could move their legs, they kicked as they had learned to do two weeks earlier.

Apparently, watching the mobile move on the previous day had revived their faded memory. The information about making the mobile move was stored in their brains, but they needed processing time to retrieve it. The reminder session provided that time.

Other research finds that repeated reminders are more powerful than single reminders and that context is crucial, especially for infants younger than 9 months old: Being tested with the same mobile in the same room as the initial experience aids memory (Rovee-Collier & Cuevas, 2009a).

THE ACTIVE BRAIN The crucial insight from information processing is that the brain is a very active organ, even in early infancy, so the particulars of experiences and memory are critically important in determining what a child knows or does not know. Soon generalization is possible. In another study, after 6-month-olds had had only two half-hour sessions with a novel puppet, a month later they remembered the experience—an amazing feat of memory for babies who could not talk or even stand up (Giles & Rovee-Collier, 2011).

Other research finds that toddlers transfer learning from one object or experience to another. They learn from many people and events—from parents and strangers, from other babies and older siblings, from picture books and family photographs (Hayne & Simcock, 2009). The dendrites and neurons of the brain change to reflect

MICHAEL NEWMAN/ PHOTOEDIT

He Remembers! In this demonstration of Rovee-Collier's experiment, a young infant immediately remembers how to make the familiar mobile move. (Unfamiliar mobiles do not provoke the same reaction.) He kicks his right leg and flails both arms, just as he learned to do several weeks ago.

OBSERVATION QUIZ
How and why is this mobile unlike those usually sold for babies? (see answer, page 120) →

reminder session
A perceptual experience that is intended to help a person recollect an idea, a thing, or an experience, without testing whether the person remembers it at the moment.

MARINA RAITH / PHOTO LIBRARY

The Next Move These infants are intrigued by things and people, as would be expected. However, they have much to learn about how to grab a ball or play with a friend. It would not be surprising if, a minute later, the ball rolled away, one child cried, and the wide-eyed redhead hit her playmate.

Memory Aid Personal motivation and action are crucial to early memory, which is why Noel has no trouble remembering which shape covers the photograph of herself as a baby.

early experiences and memories. Infants do not simply imagine doing what someone else does (mirror neurons) or copy what they have seen; they think about it.

For example, 15-month-old infants were shown an adult playing with a toy in a particular way. A day later, they were given another toy, one they had never seen. They tried to play with it as they remembered from the day before. This was especially true if, on the previous day, the toddler had also been allowed to play with the toy (Yang et al., 2010). Action strengthens memory.

Many studies show that infants remember not only specific events and objects but also patterns and general goals (Keil, 2011). Some examples come from research, such as memory of what syllables and rhythms are heard and how objects move in relation to other objects. Additional examples arise from close observations of babies at home, such as what they expect from Mommy as compared to Daddy or what details indicate bedtime. Every day of their young lives, infants are processing information and storing conclusions.

> ## KEY points
>
> - Infants demonstrate cognitive advances throughout their first years.
> - Piaget described cognition in the first two years as sensorimotor development, a period that has six stages, from reflexes to new exploration and deferred imitation.
> - Piaget said that object permanence begins at 8 months, but more recent research finds that it starts earlier.
> - Information-processing theory traces the step-by-step learning of infants. Each advance is seen as the accumulation of many small advances, not as a new stage.
> - Very young infants can store memories, especially if they are given reminder sessions.

RESPONSE FOR Parents of Toddlers (from page 116) It is easier and safer to babyproof the house because toddlers, being little scientists, want to explore. However, both parents should encourage and guide the baby. A couple may leave out a few untouchable items if that will prevent a major conflict between them. ●

Language

No other species has anything approaching the neurons and networks that support the 6,000 or so human languages. The human ability to communicate, even at age 2, far surpasses that of full-grown adults of every other species. This includes dolphins, ravens, and chimpanzees, all with much better communication mechanisms than was formerly believed.

Here we describe the specific steps in human language learning, "from burp to grammar" as one scholar put it (Saxton, 2010, p. 2). We then ask: How do babies do it?

The Universal Sequence

The timing of language acquisition varies; the most advanced 10 percent of 2-year-olds speak more than 550 words, and the least advanced 10 percent speak fewer than 1[...] fivefold diff[e]rence (Merriman, 1999). But although timing varies, the se[...] same w[or]ldwide (see At About This Time). Even deaf children who become able to hear before age 3 (thanks to cochlear implants) follow the sequence (Ertmer et al., 2007).

ANSWER TO OBSERVATION QUIZ (from page 119) It is black and white, with larger objects dangling—designed to be particularly attractive to infants, not to adult shoppers. ●

LISTENING AND RESPONDING Hearing infants begin learning language before birth, via brain connections. They prefer the language their mother speaks over an unheard language; newborns of bilingual mothers respond to both languages and differentiate between them (Byers-Heinlein et al., 2010).

Newborns look closely at facial expressions, apparently trying to connect words and expressions to understand what is being communicated. By 6 months, infants can distinguish whether or not a person is speaking their native language just by looking at the person's mouth movements (no sound) (Weikum et al., 2007). The ability to distinguish sounds and gestures in the language (or languages) of caregivers improves over the first year, whereas the ability to hear sounds never spoken in the native language deteriorates (Narayan et al., 2010).

Adults everywhere use higher pitch, simpler words, repetition, varied speeds, and exaggerated emotional tones when they speak to infants (Bryant & Barrett, 2007). This special language form is sometimes called *baby talk,* since it is talk directed toward babies, and sometimes called *motherese,* since mothers universally speak it. Nonmothers speak it as well. In fact, both these terms may be misleading; scientists prefer the more formal designation: **child-directed speech.** No matter what term is used, child-directed speech captures infants' attention and thus fosters learning.

Sounds are preferred over content. Infants like alliteration, rhymes, repetition, rhythm, and varied pitch (Hayes & Slater, 2008; Saxton, 2010; Schön et al., 2008). Think of your favorite lullaby (itself an alliterative word). All infants listen to whatever they can and appreciate the sounds they hear. Even music is culture-specific: 4- to 8-month-olds seem to like their own native music best (Soley & Hannon, 2010).

BABBLING At first, babies mostly listen. By 6 months, they start practicing sounds, repeating certain syllables (*ma-ma-ma, da-da-da, ba-ba-ba*), a phenomenon referred to as **babbling.** Responses from other people encourage babbling (this is the age of "making interesting events last").

Toward the end of the first year, babbling begins to sound like the infant's native language; infants imitate what they hear in accents, cadence, consonants, and so on. Gestures also become more specific, as all babies (deaf as well as hearing) express concepts with gestures sooner than with speech (Goldin-Meadow, 2006).

One early gesture is pointing, typical in human babies at 10 months. An advanced social gesture, pointing requires understanding another person's perspective. Most animals cannot interpret pointing; most 10-month-old humans can look toward whatever another person is pointing at and can also point themselves—even to where an object is expected to be but no longer is (Liszkowski et al., 2009).

FIRST WORDS Finally, at about 1 year, the average hearing baby utters a few words, although some normal babies do not begin to talk until about 18 months. Caregivers usually understand the first words before strangers do, which makes it hard for researchers to pinpoint exactly what a 12-month-old can say.

Spoken vocabulary increases gradually (perhaps one new word a week). However, 6- to 15-month-olds learn meanings rapidly; they understand about 10 times more words than they can say (Schafer, 2005; Snow, 2006). Initially, the first words are merely labels for familiar things (*mama* and *dada* are common), but each can convey many messages. Imagine meaningful sentences encapsulated in "Dada!" "Dada?" and "Dada." Each is a **holophrase,** a single word that expresses an entire thought.

Careful tracing of early language from the information-processing perspective finds periods when vocalization seems to slow down before a burst of new talking erupts, as perception and action are interdependent (Pulvermüller & Fadiga, 2010).

JANEK SKARZYNSKI / AFP / GETTY IMAGES

KIDSTOCK / GETTY IMAGES

Same Situation, Far Apart: Before Words The Polish babies learning sign language *(top)* and the New York infant interpreting a smile *(bottom)* are all doing what babies do: trying to understand communications long before they are able to talk.

child-directed speech
The high-pitched, simplified, and repetitive way adults speak to infants. (Also called *baby talk* or *motherese.*)

babbling
The extended repetition of certain syllables, such as *ba-ba-ba,* that begins when babies are between 6 and 9 months old.

holophrase
A single word that is used to express a complete, meaningful thought.

✦ **ESPECIALLY FOR Caregivers**
A toddler calls two people "Mama." Is this a sign of confusion? (see response, page 124) →

AT ABOUT THIS TIME
The Development of Spoken Language in the First Two Years

Age*	Means of Communication
Newborn	Reflexive communication—cries, movements, facial expressions.
2 months	A range of meaningful noises—cooing, fussing, crying, laughing.
3–6 months	New sounds, including squeals, growls, croons, trills, vowel sounds.
6–10 months	Babbling, including both consonant and vowel sounds repeated in syllables.
10–12 months	Comprehension of simple words; speechlike intonations; specific vocalizations that have meaning to those who know the infant well. Deaf babies express their first signs; hearing babies also use specific gestures (e.g., pointing) to communicate.
12 months	First spoken words that are recognizably part of the native language.
13–18 months	Slow growth of vocabulary, up to about 50 words.
18 months	Naming explosion—three or more words learned per day. Much variation: Some toddlers do not yet speak.
21 months	First two-word sentence.
24 months	Multiword sentences. Half the toddler's utterances are two or more words long.

*The ages of accomplishment in this table reflect norms. Many healthy children with normal intelligence attain these steps in language development earlier or later than indicated here.

naming explosion
A sudden increase in an infant's vocabulary, especially in the number of nouns, that begins at about 18 months of age.

Who Is Babbling? Probably both the 6-month-old and the 27-year-old. During every day of infancy, mothers and babies communicate with noises, movements (notice the hands), and expressions.

ARIEL SKELLEY / GETTY IMAGES

This means that sometimes, with a new perceptual understanding, it takes time for verbal output to reflect that neurological advance. This slowdown before a language spurt is not evident in every infant, but many seem temporarily quieter before a burst of new words (Parladé & Iverson, 2011).

CULTURAL DIFFERENCES Once vocabulary reaches about 50 *expressed* words (understood words are far more extensive), it builds rapidly, at a rate of 50 to 100 words per month, with 21-month-olds saying twice as many words as 18-month-olds (Adamson & Bakeman, 2006). This language spurt is called the **naming explosion** because many early words are nouns—although the word *noun* is a linguistic category that may not include all the words that infants use as names (Waxman & Lidz, 2006).

Early sequence and uttered sounds are universal, but differences soon emerge. For instance, about 30 languages of the world use a click sound as part of the spoken words; infants in those communities become adept at clicking. Similarly, the rolled *r*, the enunciated *l* or *th*, the difference between *b* and *v* are mastered by infants in some languages but not others, depending on what they hear.

Although all new talkers say more nouns than any other parts of speech, the ratio of nouns to verbs varies from place to place. For example, by 18 months, English-speaking infants use relatively more nouns but fewer verbs than Chinese or Korean infants do. Why?

One explanation goes back to the language itself. Mandarin, Cantonese, and Korean are "verb-friendly" in that verbs are placed at the beginning or end of sentences, which makes them easier to learn. In English, verbs occur in various positions within sentences, and their forms change in illogical ways (e.g., *go, gone, will go, went*). This irregularity makes English verbs harder to learn than nouns.

An alternative explanation considers the entire social context: Playing with a variety of toys and learning about dozens of objects are crucial in North American culture, whereas East Asian cultures emphasize human interactions—specifically, how one person responds to another.

Accordingly, North American infants are expected to name many objects, whereas Asian infants are expected to act on objects (as explained in Chapter 1) and respond to people. Thus, Chinese toddlers might learn the equivalent of *come, play, love, carry, run,* and so on before Canadian ones. (This is the result of experience, not genes. A toddler of Chinese ancestry, growing up in an English-speaking Canadian home, has the learning patterns of other English-speaking toddlers.)

A simpler explanation is that young children are sensitive to the sounds of words, with some sounds more salient than others. Verbs are learned more easily if they sound like the action (Imai et al., 2008), and such verbs may be more common in some languages than others.

In English, most verbs are not onomatopoeic, although perhaps *jump, kiss,* and *poop*—all learned relatively early in life—are exceptions. The infant preference for sounds may be one reason why many English-speaking toddlers who have never been on a farm nonetheless know that a cow says "moo" and a duck says "quack."

Show Me Where Pointing is one of the earliest forms of communication, emerging at about 10 months.

IMAGE SOURCE / GETTY IMAGES

PUTTING WORDS TOGETHER Grammar can be defined as including all the methods that languages use to communicate meaning. Word order, prefixes, suffixes, intonation, verb forms, pronouns and negations, prepositions and articles—all of these are aspects of grammar, all varying by whatever language the infant hears (Saxton, 2010).

Grammar can be discerned in holophrases but becomes obvious between 18 and 24 months, when two-word combinations begin. For example, in English, "Baby cry" and "More juice" follow the proper word order. No child asks, "Juice more," and already by age 2 children know that "cry baby" has an entirely different meaning. Soon the child combines three words, usually in subject–verb–object order in English (e.g., "Mommy read book"), rather than any of the five other possible sequences of those words.

Young children can master two languages, not just one. The crucial variable is how much speech in both languages the child hears. Listening to two languages does not necessarily slow down the acquisition of grammar, rather "development in each language proceeds separately and in a language-specific manner" (Conboy & Thal, 2006, p. 727).

Indeed, some evidence suggests that children are statisticians: They implicitly track the number of words and phrases and learn those expressed most often. That is certainly the case when children are learning their mother tongue; it is probably true when learning a second language as well (Johnson & Tyler, 2010).

Bilingual toddlers soon realize differences between languages, adjusting tone, pronunciation, cadence, and vocabulary when speaking to a monolingual person. Most bilingual children have parents who are also bilingual; hence, these children mix languages because they know their parents will understand.

Note that mixing languages is a cultural adaptation, not a sign of mental deficiency. In fact, bilingual children and adults seem to have a cognitive advantage over monolingual people, as noted in Chapter 5.

grammar
All the methods—word order, verb forms, and so on—that languages use to communicate meaning, apart from the words themselves.

✦ **ESPECIALLY FOR Educators**
An infant day-care center has a new child whose parents speak a language other than the one the teachers speak. Should the teachers learn basic words in the new language, or should they expect the baby to learn their language? (see response, page 124) ➔

RESPONSE FOR Caregivers (from page 122) Not at all. Toddlers hear several people called "Mama" (their own mother, their grandmothers, their cousins' and friends' mothers) and experience mothering from several people, so it is not surprising if they use "Mama" too broadly. They will eventually narrow the label down to the one correct person. ●

How Do They Do It?

Worldwide, people who are not yet 2 years old already speak their native tongue. They continue to learn rapidly: Some teenagers compose lyrics or deliver orations that move thousands of their co-linguists. How is language learned so easily and so well? Answers come from three schools of thought, one emphasizing learning, one emphasizing culture, and the third stressing evolution.

THEORY ONE: INFANTS NEED TO BE TAUGHT The seeds of the first perspective were planted more than 50 years ago, when the dominant theory in North American psychology was behaviorism, or learning theory (see Chapter 1). The essential idea was that all learning is acquired, step-by-step, through association and reinforcement. Just as Pavlov's dogs learned to associate the sound of a tone with the presentation of food, behaviorists believe that infants associate objects with words they have heard often, especially if reinforcement occurs.

B. F. Skinner (1957) noticed that spontaneous babbling is usually reinforced. Typically, every time the baby says "ma-ma-ma-ma," a grinning mother appears, repeating the sound as well as showering the baby with attention, praise, and perhaps food. Skinner believed that most parents are excellent instructors, responding to their infants' gestures and sounds, thus reinforcing speech (Saxton, 2010).

The core ideas of this theory are as follows:

- Parents are expert teachers, although other caregivers help.
- Frequent repetition is instructive, especially when linked to daily life.
- Well-taught infants become well-spoken children.

Behaviorists note that some 3-year-olds converse in elaborate sentences; others just barely put one simple word with another. Such variations correlate with the amount of language each child has heard. Parents of the most verbal children teach language throughout infancy—singing, explaining, listening, responding, and reading to them every day, even before age 1 (Forget-Dubois et al., 2009) (see Figure 3.10).

THEORY TWO: CULTURE FOSTERS INFANT LANGUAGE The second theory arises from the sociocultural reason for language: communication. According to this perspective, infants communicate because humans have evolved as social beings, dependent on one another for survival and joy. Each culture has practices that further social interaction; talking is one of those practices.

RESPONSE FOR Educators (from page 123) Probably both. Infants love to communicate, and they seek every possible way to do so. Therefore, the teachers should try to understand the baby and the baby's parents, but they can also teach another language. ●

FIGURE 3.10 Maternal Responsiveness and Infants' Language Acquisition Learning the first 50 words is a milestone in early language acquisition, as it predicts the arrival of the naming explosion and the multiword sentence a few weeks later. Researchers found that the 9-month-old infants of highly responsive mothers (top 10 percent) reached this milestone as early as 15 months. The infants of nonresponsive mothers (bottom 10 percent) lagged significantly behind.

OBSERVATION QUIZ

Why does the blue line end at 18 months? (see answer, page 126) →

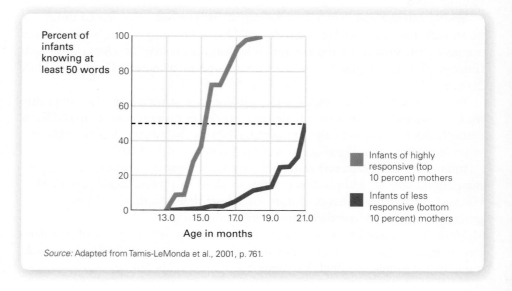

Source: Adapted from Tamis-LeMonda et al., 2001, p. 761.

It is the emotional messages of speech, not the words, that are the focus of early communication, according to this perspective. In one study, Shuar hunter-gatherers, living in isolation near the Andes mountains and never having heard English, listened to tapes of North American mothers talking to their babies. The Shuar successfully distinguished speech conveying comfort, approval, attention, and prohibition, without knowing any of the words (Bryant & Barrett, 2007). Thus, the social content of speech is universal, which is why babies learn whatever their culture provides.

For example, many 1-year-olds enjoy watching television and videos, but the evidence implies that they learn from it only when adults are actively involved in teaching. In a controlled experiment, 1-year-olds learned vocabulary much better when someone directly taught them than when the same person taught on a video (Roseberry et al., 2009). This suggests personal, social, language acquisition, not impersonal learning.

According to theory two, then, social impulses, not explicit teaching, lead infants to learn language "as part of the package of being a human social animal" (Hollich et al., 2000, p. 11). Those same impulses are evident in all the ways infants learn: According to this theory, people differ from the great apes in that they depend on others within their community and thus learn whatever way their culture uses to communicate.

Thus, all infants (and no chimpanzees) master words and grammar to join the social world in which they find themselves (Tomasello & Herrmann, 2010). Cultures vary not only in the languages they speak but also in how they communicate—some using gestures and touch more than words. A learning theorist might consider the quieter, less verbal child to be developmentally delayed, but this second perspective contends that the crucial aspect of language is social communication and that the quieter child may simply be communicating in another way. Language is not necessarily spoken.

THEORY THREE: INFANTS TEACH THEMSELVES A third theory holds that language learning is innate; adults need not teach it, nor is it a by-product of social interaction. It arises from the universal human impulse to imitate. As already explained in the research on memory, infants and toddlers observe what they see and apply it—not slavishly but according to their own concepts and intentions. This may be what they do with the language they hear as well (Saxton, 2010).

The seeds of this perspective were planted soon after Skinner proposed his theory of verbal learning. Noam Chomsky (1968, 1980) and his followers felt that language is too complex to be mastered merely through step-by-step conditioning. Although behaviorists focus on variations among children in vocabulary size, Chomsky focused on similarities in language acquisition—the universals, not the differences.

Noting that all young children master basic grammar at about the same age, Chomsky cited this *universal grammar* as evidence that humans are born with a mental structure that prepares them to seek some elements of human language—for example, the use of a raised tone at the end of an utterance to indicate a question. Chomsky labeled this hypothesized mental structure the **language acquisition device (LAD),** which enables children to derive the rules of grammar quickly and effectively from the speech they hear every day, regardless of whether their native language is English, Thai, or Urdu.

Other scholars agree with Chomsky that infants are innately ready to use their minds to understand and speak whatever language is offered. All babies are eager learners, and language may be considered one more aspect of neurological maturation (Wagner & Lakusta, 2009).

This idea does not strip languages and cultures of their differences in sounds, grammar, and almost everything else. Chomsky called those "surface" language. However, the basic idea is that "language is a window on human nature, exposing

✦ **ESPECIALLY FOR Social Workers** Some parents never speak to their infants. When is this silence a deficit, and when is it merely a difference? (see response, page 127) →

✦ **ESPECIALLY FOR Nurses and Pediatricians** Bob and Joan have been reading about language development in children. Because they are convinced that language is "hardwired," they believe they don't need to talk to their 6-month-old son. How do you respond? (see response, page 127) →

language acquisition device (LAD) Chomsky's term for a hypothesized mental structure that enables humans to learn language, including the basic aspects of grammar, vocabulary, and intonation.

WOLFGANG KAEHLER / CORBIS

Cultural Values If they are typical of most families in the relatively taciturn Otavalo culture of Ecuador, these three children hear significantly less conversation than children elsewhere. In most Western cultures, that might be called maltreatment. However, each culture encourages the qualities it values, and verbal fluency is not a priority in this community. In fact, people who talk too much are ostracized and those who keep secrets are valued, so encouragement of talking may constitute maltreatment in the Otavalo culture.

hybrid theory
A perspective that combines various aspects of different theories to explain how language, or any other developmental phenomenon, occurs.

ANSWER TO **OBSERVATION QUIZ**
(from page 124) By 18 months, every one of the infants of highly responsive mothers (top 10 percent) knows 50 words. Not until 30 months do all the infants with quiet mothers reach the naming explosion. ●

deep and universal features of our thoughts and feelings" (Pinker, 2007, p. 148).

The various languages of the world are all logical, coherent, and systematic. Infants are primed to grasp the particular language they are exposed to, making caregiver speech "not a 'trigger' but a 'nutrient'" (Slobin, 2001, p. 438). There is no need for a trigger, according to theory three, because the developing brain quickly and efficiently connects neurons and dendrites to support whichever language the infant hears.

Research supports this perspective as well. As you remember, newborns are primed to listen to speech (Vouloumanos & Werker, 2007), and all infants babble *ma-ma* and *da-da* sounds (not yet referring to mother or father). No reinforcement or teaching is required; all infants need is for dendrites to grow, mouth muscles to strengthen, synapses to connect, and speech to be heard.

ALL TRUE? Which of these three perspectives is correct? Perhaps all of them. In one monograph that included details and results of 12 experiments, the authors presented a *hybrid* (which literally means "a new creature, formed by combining other living things") of previous theories (Hollich et al., 2000).

Since infants learn language to do numerous things—such as indicate intention, call objects by name, put words together, talk to family members, sing to themselves, express their wishes, remember the past, and much more—some aspects of language learning might be best explained by one theory at one age while other aspects are better explained by another theory at another age. Although originally developed to explain acquisition of first words, mostly nouns, this **hybrid theory** also explains learning verbs: Perceptual, social, and linguistic abilities combine to make that learning possible (Golinkoff & Hirsh-Pasek, 2008).

After intensive study, another group of scientists also endorsed a hybrid theory, concluding that "multiple attentional, social and linguistic cues" contribute to early language (Tsao et al., 2004, p. 1081). It makes logical and practical sense for nature to provide several paths toward language learning, for various theorists to emphasize one or another of them (Sebastián-Gallés, 2007), and for some children to learn better in one way while others learn better in a different way (Goodman et al., 2008).

Some scholars, inspired by evolutionary theory, think that language is the crucial trait that makes humans unlike any other species—that "language is entwined with human life" (Pinker, 2007, p. viii). If that is true, then there must be many paths to language learning, to ensure that every human learns.

Adults need to talk often to infants (theory one), encourage social connections (theory two), and appreciate the innate abilities of the child (theory three). As one expert concludes:

> In the current view, our best hope for unraveling some of the mysteries of language acquisition rests with approaches that incorporate multiple factors, that is, with approaches that incorporate not only some explicit linguistic model, but also the full range of biological, cultural, and psycholinguistic processes involved.
>
> *[Tomasello, 2006, pp. 292–293]*

The idea that every theory is correct in some way may seem uncritical, naive, and idealistic. However, a similar conclusion was arrived at by scientists extending and interpreting research on language acquisition. They contend that language learning is neither the direct product of repeated input (behaviorism) nor the result of a specific human neurological capacity (LAD).

Rather, "different elements of the language apparatus may have evolved in different ways," and thus a "piecemeal and empirical" approach is needed (Marcus & Rabagliati, 2009, p. 281). In other words, a single theory that explains how babies learn language does not reflect the data: Humans accomplish this feat in many ways.

Infants are active learners not only of language (as just outlined) and of perceptions and motor skills (as explained in the first half of this chapter) but also of everything else in their experience. Active and interactive social and emotional understanding is described in the next chapter.

RESPONSE FOR Social Workers (from page 125) Not talking to an infant would be a deficit in developed nations, where verbal expression, reading, and writing are skills every child needs. If parents are not convinced that infant speech is important, they may still be excellent and loving caregivers. The social worker should find another person (e.g., sibling or teacher) to provide language so that the child can function well in a developed nation. ●

RESPONSE FOR Nurses and Pediatricians (from page 125) While much of language development is indeed hardwired, many experts assert that exposure to language is required. You don't need to convince Bob and Joan of this point, though—just convince them that their baby will be happier if they talk to him. ●

KEY points

- Infants pay close attention to the sounds and rhythms of speech, comprehending far more than they can say.

- Infants learn rapidly to communicate, starting with cries in the first weeks and progressing to words by 1 year and sentences before age 2.

- Some experts emphasize the importance of adult reinforcement of early speech; others suggest that language learning is innate; still others believe it is a by-product of social impulses.

- A hybrid explanation suggests that language learning occurs in many ways, depending on the specific age, culture, and goals of the infant.

SUMMARY

Growth in Infancy

1. In the first two years of life, infants grow taller, gain weight, and increase in head circumference—all indicative of development. Birthweight doubles by 4 months, triples by 1 year, and quadruples by 2 years, when toddlers weigh about 30 pounds (13½ kilograms).

2. Brain size increases even more dramatically, from about 25 to 75 percent of adult weight in the first two years. Complexity increases as well, with cell growth, development of dendrites, and formation of synapses. Both growth and pruning aid cognition. Experience is vital for brain development.

3. Sleep gradually decreases over the first two years. As with all areas of development, variations in sleep patterns are normal, caused by both nature and nurture. Bed-sharing is the norm in many developing nations, and co-sleeping is increasingly common in developed ones.

Perceiving and Moving

4. At birth, the senses already respond to stimuli. Prenatal experience makes hearing the most mature sense. Vision is the least mature sense at birth, but it improves quickly. Infants use all their senses to strengthen their early social interactions.

5. Infants gradually improve their motor skills as they begin to grow and brain maturation increases. Gross motor skills are soon

evident, from rolling over to sitting up (at about 6 months), from standing to walking (at about 1 year), from climbing to running (before age 2).

6. Babies gradually develop the fine motor skills to grab, aim, and manipulate almost anything within reach. Experience, time, and motivation allow infants to advance in all their motor skills.

Surviving in Good Health

7. About 2 billion infant deaths have been prevented in the past half-century because of improved health care. One major innovation is immunization, which has eradicated smallpox and virtually eliminated polio and measles. More medical professionals are needed to prevent, diagnose, and treat the diseases that still cause many infant deaths in poor nations.

8. Breast-feeding is best for infants, partly because breast milk helps them resist disease and promotes growth of every kind. Most babies are breast-fed at birth, but in North America only one-third are exclusively breast-fed for three months, as doctors worldwide recommend.

9. Severe malnutrition stunts growth and can cause death, both directly through marasmus or kwashiorkor and indirectly through vulnerability if a child catches measles, an intestinal disorder, or some other illness.

Infant Cognition

10. Piaget realized that very young infants are active learners, seeking to understand their complex observations and experiences. Sensorimotor intelligence develops in six stages, beginning with reflexes and ending with mental combinations.

11. Infants gradually develop an understanding of objects. As shown in Piaget's classic experiment, infants understand object permanence and begin to search for hidden objects at about 8 months. Other research finds that Piaget underestimated infant cognition in the timing of object permanence and in many other ways.

12. Another approach to understanding infant cognition is information-processing theory, which looks at each step of the thinking process, from input to output. Each week, infants understand more about numbers, objects, patterns of speech, and so on.

13. Infant memory is fragile but not completely absent. Reminder sessions help trigger memories, and young brains learn motor sequences long before they can remember with words.

Language

14. Language learning may be the most impressive cognitive accomplishment of infants, distinguishing the human species from other animals. Eager attempts to communicate are apparent in the first weeks and months. Infants babble at about 6 to 9 months, understand words and gestures by 10 months, and speak their first words at about 1 year.

15. Vocabulary begins to build very slowly until the infant knows approximately 50 words. Then the naming explosion begins. Toward the end of the second year, toddlers put words together, showing that they understand the rudiments of grammar.

16. Various theories explain how infants learn language as quickly as they do. The three main theories emphasize different aspects of early language learning: that infants must be taught, that their social impulses foster language learning, and that their brains are genetically attuned to language. Each theory seems true for some aspects of language acquisition.

KEY TERMS

axons (p. 94)
babbling (p. 121)
binocular vision (p. 102)
child-directed speech (p. 121)
co-sleeping (p. 99)
cortex (p. 93)
deferred imitation (p. 116)
dendrites (p. 94)
fine motor skills (p. 104)
grammar (p. 123)
gross motor skills (p. 103)
head-sparing (p. 93)

holophrase (p. 121)
hybrid theory (p. 126)
immunization (p. 107)
information-processing theory (p. 118)
kwashiorkor (p. 113)
language acquisition device (LAD) (p. 125)
little scientist (p. 116)
marasmus (p. 113)
mirror neurons (p. 117)
motor skill (p. 103)

naming explosion (p. 122)
neurons (p. 93)
neurotransmitters (p. 94)
norm (p. 92)
object permanence (p. 114)
perception (p. 101)
prefrontal cortex (p. 94)
protein-calorie malnutrition (p. 111)
pruning (p. 96)
REM (rapid eye movement) sleep (p. 98)

reminder session (p. 119)
self-righting (p. 98)
sensation (p. 101)
sensorimotor intelligence (p. 114)
shaken baby syndrome (p. 98)
stunting (p. 111)
synapses (p. 94)
synaptic gap (p. 94)
transient exuberance (p. 96)
wasting (p. 112)

WHAT HAVE YOU LEARNED?

1. In what ways does a baby's weight and height change in the first two years?

2. Describe the process of communication within the central nervous system.

3. Why is pruning an essential part of brain development?

4. What should caregivers remember about brain development when an infant cries?

5. How do a baby's sleep patterns change over the first 18 months?

6. What is the relationship among perception, sensation, and cognition?

7. How does an infant's vision change over the first three months?

8. Give examples to describe how an infant's gross motor skills develop over the first year.

9. Describe how a baby's hand skills develop over the first two years.

10. Why has there been a decrease in infant mortality rates? What other measures could lead to a further decrease?

11. What is the purpose of immunization?

12. In what ways does herd immunity save lives?

13. Why has the rate of immunization decreased over the past decade?

14. What are the reasons for and against breast-feeding until a child is at least 1 year old?

15. In what ways does malnutrition affect infants and children?

16. Why did Piaget call cognition in the first two years "sensorimotor intelligence"?

17. Describe the first two stages of sensorimotor intelligence.

18. In sensorimotor intelligence, what is the difference between stages three and four?

19. Why is the concept of object permanence important to an infant's development?

20. What does the active experimentation of the stage-five toddler suggest for parents?

21. Why did Piaget underestimate how rapidly early cognition occurs?

22. What conditions help 3-month-olds remember something?

23. What have researchers discovered about the way adults talk to babies?

24. How would a caregiver who subscribes to the behaviorist theory of language learning respond when an infant babbles?

25. What is typical of the rate and nature of the first words that infants speak?

26. What indicates that toddlers use some grammar?

27. According to behaviorism, how do adults teach infants to talk?

28. According to sociocultural theory, why do infants try to communicate?

29. What is Chomsky's theory about how young children learn language?

30. What does the hybrid model of language learning suggest to caregivers?

APPLICATIONS

1. Immunization regulations and practices vary, partly for social and political reasons. Ask at least two faculty or administrative staff members what immunizations students at your college must have and why. If you hear, "It's the law," ask why.

2. Observe three infants (whom you do not know) in public places such as a store, playground, or bus. Look closely at body size and motor skills, especially how much control each baby has over legs and hands. From that, estimate the age in months, then ask the caregiver how old the infant is.

3. Many educators recommend that parents read to babies even before the babies begin talking. How would advocates of each of

the three hypotheses about language development respond to this advice?

4. Test an infant's ability to search for a hidden object. Ideally, the infant should be about 7 or 8 months old, and you should retest over a period of weeks. If the infant can immediately find the object, make the task harder by pausing between the hiding and the searching or by secretly moving the object from one hiding place to another. Describe this experiment in detail.

>> ONLINE CONNECTIONS

To accompany your textbook, you have access to a number of online resources, including quizzes for every chapter of the book, flashcards (in English and Spanish), critical thinking questions, and case studies. For access to any of these links, go to www.worthpublishers.com/bergerinvitation2e. In addition to these free resources, you'll also find links to podcasts, video clips, diagnostic quizzing with personalized study advice, and an ebook. Some of the videos and activities available online include:

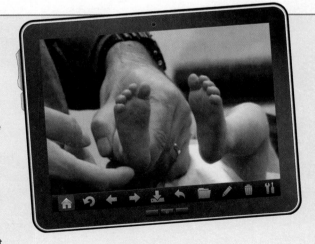

- *Nutritional Needs of Infants and Children.* Including video footage from UNICEF of children around the world, this activity provides an overview of the nutritional needs and challenges children face in both developed and developing countries.

- *Language Development in Infancy.* How easy is it to understand a newborn's coos? Or a 6-month-old's babbling? But we can almost all make out the voice of a toddler singing "Twinkle, Twinkle." Video clips from a variety of real-life contexts bring to life the development of children's language.

CHAPTER OUTLINE

Psychosocial Development

WHAT WILL YOU KNOW?

- How do smiles, tears, anger, and fear change from birth to age 2?
- Does a baby's temperament predict lifelong personality?
- What are the signs of a healthy parent–infant relationship?
- Do the five major theories and the hundreds of human cultures differ in their understanding of infant emotions and caregiving practices?

My 1-week-old grandson cried. Often. Again and again. Day and night. For a long time. Again. He and his parents were living with me while they looked for an apartment. I was the dog walker and dinner cooker, not caregiver, so I didn't mind the crying for myself. But I did mind for my sleep-deprived daughter.

"Give him a pacifier," I told her.

"No, that causes 'nipple confusion,'" she said.

"I never heard of that. What have you been reading? Give him a pacifier."

My daughter knows that I value research and evidence, not hearsay or anecdote. She replied, "The American Academy of Pediatrics says no pacifiers for breast-fed babies in the first month. Here it is on their Web site."

That quieted me, but soon I developed another worry—that my son-in-law would resent fatherhood. He spent many hours, day and night, carrying my grandson while my daughter slept.

"It seems to me that you do most of the baby comforting," I told him.

"That's because Elissa does most of the breast-feeding," he answered with a smile.

I learned in those months. In the decades since my children were infants, pediatricians have developed new recommendations, and fathers have become more active partners. ●

COURTESY OF KATHLEEN BERGER

131

THIS CHAPTER OPENS BY TRACING INFANTS' EMOTIONS as their brains mature and their experiences accumulate, noting temperamental and cultural differences. This leads to an exploration of caregiver–infant interaction, particularly *synchrony, attachment,* and *social referencing.* For every aspect of caregiving, fathers as well as mothers are included.

Then we apply each of the five theories introduced in Chapter 1. After the theories are explained, we apply them to a controversial topic in infant psychosocial development: Who should provide daily care?

Many specifics vary depending on culture and cohort, but some universal psychosocial needs are apparent. With or without pacifiers or patient fathers, most infants (including my now-happy grandson) thrive, as long as their basic physical and emotional needs are met.

Emotional Development

In the first two years, infants progress from reactive pain and pleasure to complex patterns of social awareness (see At About This Time) (Lewis, 2010). This is a period of "high emotional responsiveness" (Izard et al., 2002, p. 767), expressed in speedy, uncensored reactions—crying, startling, laughing, raging—and, by toddlerhood, in complex responses, from self-satisfied grins to mournful pouts.

Early Emotions

At first, there is pleasure and pain. Newborns are happy and relaxed when fed and drifting off to sleep. They cry when they are hurt or hungry, tired or frightened (as by a loud noise or a sudden loss of support). Some infants have bouts of uncontrollable crying, called *colic*—probably the result of immature digestion. About 20 percent of babies cry "excessively," defined as more than three hours a day, for more than three days a week, for more than three weeks (J. S. Kim, 2011).

SMILING AND LAUGHING Soon, additional emotions become recognizable (Lavelli & Fogel, 2005). Curiosity is evident as infants (and people of all ages) respond to objects and experiences that are new but not too novel. Happiness is expressed by the

AT ABOUT THIS TIME
Ages When Emotions Emerge

Birth	Crying; contentment
6 weeks	Social smile
3 months	Laughter; curiosity
4 months	Full, responsive smiles
4–8 months	Anger
9–14 months	Fear of social events (strangers, separation from caregiver)
12 months	Fear of unexpected sights and sounds
18 months	Self-awareness; pride; shame; embarrassment

As always, culture and experience influence the norms of development. This is especially true for emotional development after the first eight months.

Smiles All Around Joy is universal when an infant smiles at her beaming grandparents—a smile made even better when the tongue joins in. This particular scene takes place in Kazakhstan in central Asia, an independent nation only since 1991.

CHRISTOPHER HERWIG / LONELY PLANET IMAGES

social smile, evoked by a human face at about 6 weeks. Preterm babies smile a few weeks later because the social smile is affected by age since conception.

Infants worldwide express social joy, even laughter, between 2 and 4 months (Konner, 2007; Lewis, 2011). Among the Navajo, whoever brings forth that first laugh gives a feast to celebrate the baby's becoming a person (Rogoff, 2003). Laughter builds as curiosity does; a typical 6-month-old laughs loudly upon discovering new things, particularly social experiences that have the right balance between familiarity and surprise, such as Daddy making a funny face.

ANGER AND SADNESS The positive emotions of joy and contentment are soon joined by negative emotions, more frequent in infancy than later on (Izard, 2009). Anger is evident at 6 months, usually triggered by frustration, such as when infants are prevented from moving or grabbing.

For instance, to see how infants responded to frustration, researchers "crouched behind the child and gently restrained his or her arms for 2 minutes or until 20 seconds of hard crying ensued" (Mills-Koonce et al., 2011, p. 390). "Hard crying" is not infrequent: Infants hate to be strapped in, caged in, closed in, or even just held in place when they want to explore.

Indeed, in infancy, anger is a healthy response to frustration, unlike sadness, which also appears in the first months. Sadness indicates withdrawal and is accompanied by an increase in the body's production of **cortisol,** the primary stress hormone.

This is one conclusion from experiments in which 4-month-olds were taught to pull a string to see a picture, which they enjoyed—not unlike the leg-kicking study to move the mobile, described in Chapter 3. Then the string was disconnected. Most babies reacted by angrily jerking the string. Some, however, quit trying and looked sad (Lewis & Ramsay, 2005); their cortisol increased. This suggests that anger relieves stress but that some babies learn, to their sorrow, to repress their anger.

Since sadness produces physiological stress (e.g., cortisol), sorrow negatively impacts the infant. All social emotions, particularly sadness and fear, probably shape the brain (Fries & Pollak, 2007; M. H. Johnson, 2011). As you learned in Chapter 3, experience matters. Too much sadness early in life correlates with depression later.

FEAR Fear in response to some person, thing, or situation (not just being startled in surprise) is evident at about 9 months and soon becomes more frequent and obvious (Witherington et al., 2004). Two kinds of social fear are typical:

- **Separation anxiety**—clinging and crying when a familiar caregiver is about to leave
- **Stranger wariness**—fear of unfamiliar people, especially when they move too close, too quickly

Separation anxiety is normal at age 1, intensifies by age 2, and usually subsides after that. Fear of separation interferes with infant sleep. For example, infants who fall asleep next to familiar people may wake up terrified if they are alone (Sadeh et al., 2010). Some babies become accustomed to a "transitional object," such as a teddy bear or blanket that comforts them as they transition from sleeping in their parents' arms to sleeping alone.

Transitional objects are not pathological; they are the infant's way to cope with anxiety. However, if separation anxiety remains strong after age 3, it is considered an emotional disorder and is accompanied by physiological signs of distress (Kossowsky et al., 2011).

social smile
A smile evoked by a human face, normally first evident in infants about 6 weeks after birth.

cortisol
The primary stress hormone; fluctuations in the body's cortisol level affect human emotion.

separation anxiety
An infant's distress when a familiar caregiver leaves, most obvious between 9 and 14 months.

stranger wariness
An infant's expression of concern—a quiet stare while clinging to a familiar person, or a look of fear—when a stranger appears.

Developmentally Correct Both Santa's smile and Olivia's grimace are appropriate reactions for people of their age. Adults playing Santa must smile no matter what, and if Olivia smiled that would be troubling to anyone who knows about 7-month-olds. But why did someone scare this infant by putting her in the grip of an oddly dressed, bearded stranger?

Strangers—especially those who do not resemble or move like familiar caregivers—merit stares, not smiles, at age 1. This is a good sign: Infant memory is active and engaged.

Many 1-year-olds fear not only strangers but also anything unexpected, from the flush of the toilet to the pop of a jack-in-the-box, from closing elevator doors to the tail-wagging approach of a dog. With repeated experience and reassurance, older infants might enjoy flushing the toilet (again and again) or calling the dog (and might in fact cry if the dog does *not* come).

Every aspect of early emotional development interacts with cultural beliefs, expressed in parental actions. There seems to be more separation anxiety and stranger wariness in Japan than in Germany because Japanese infants "have very few experiences with separation from the mother," whereas in German towns, "infants are frequently left alone outside of stores or supermarkets" while their mothers shop (Saarni et al., 2006, p. 237).

Toddlers' Emotions

Emotions take on new strength during toddlerhood (Izard, 2009). For example, throughout the second year and beyond, anger and fear become less frequent but more focused, targeted toward infuriating or terrifying experiences. Similarly, laughing and crying are louder and more discriminating.

The new strength of emotions is apparent in temper tantrums. Toddlers are famous for fury, when something angers them so much that they yell, scream, cry, and do something physical—throw a chair, throw a punch, throw themselves on the floor. Logic is beyond them; if adults respond with anger or teasing, that makes it worse. Soon sadness comes to the fore, and then comfort (not acquiescence or punishment) is helpful (Green et al., 2011).

SOCIAL AWARENESS Temper can be seen as an expression of selfhood. So can new emotions: pride, shame, embarrassment, disgust, and guilt (Stevenson et al., 2010; Thompson, 2006). These emotions require social and self awareness, which emerges from family interactions, shaped by the culture (Mesquita & Leu, 2007).

For example, many North American parents encourage toddler pride (saying, "You did it yourself"—even when that is untrue), but Asian families typically discourage pride. Instead, they cultivate modesty and shame (Rogoff, 2003). Such differences may still be apparent in adult personality and judgment, as some criticize people who brag but others criticize those who are too self-deprecating.

Disgust is also strongly influenced by other people and age. Many 18-month-olds (but not younger infants) express disgust at touching a dead animal. None, however, are yet disgusted when a teenager curses at an elderly person—something that parents and older children often find disgusting (Stevenson et al., 2010).

By age 2, most children display the entire spectrum of emotions, and they begin to regulate their reactions, with more fear or boldness, depending on experience (Saarni et al., 2006). For example, many toddlers hide behind their mothers when friendly dogs approach. Some mothers teach fear by protectively picking up the child; others teach joy as they happily pet the dog. In that case, toddlers are likely to peek out and perhaps pet the dog themselves.

SELF-AWARENESS In addition to social awareness, another foundation for emotional growth is **self-awareness,** the realization that one's body, mind, and activities are distinct from those of other people (Kopp, 2011). Closely following the new mobility that results from walking, an emerging sense of "me" and "mine" leads to a new consciousness of others at about age 1.

✦ **ESPECIALLY FOR Nurses and Pediatricians** Parents come to you concerned that their 1-year-old hides her face and holds onto them tightly whenever a stranger appears. What do you tell them? (see response, page 136) ➜

self-awareness
A person's realization that he or she is a distinct individual whose body, mind, and actions are separate from those of other people.

Very young infants have no sense of self—at least of *self* as most people define it (Harter, 2006). In fact, the prominent psychoanalyst Margaret Mahler theorized that for the first 4 months infants see themselves as part of their mothers. They "hatch" at about 5 months and spend the next several months developing self-awareness (Mahler et al., 1975).

Some aspects of selfhood emerge before age 1, but

> more complex self-representations are reflected [in] . . . self-referential emotions. . . . By the end of the second year and increasingly in the third [ages 1 and 2], the simple joy of success becomes accompanied by looking and smiling to an adult and calling attention to the feat; the simple sadness of failure becomes accompanied either by avoidance of eye contact with the adult and turning away or by reparative activity and confession . . .
>
> *[Thompson, 2006, p. 79]*

In a classic experiment (M. Lewis & Brooks, 1978), 9- to 24-month-olds looked into a mirror after a dot of rouge had been surreptitiously put on their noses. If they reacted by touching their noses, that meant they knew the mirror showed their own faces. None of the babies younger than 12 months old showed that self-recognition, although they sometimes smiled and touched the dot on the "other" baby in the mirror.

However, between 15 and 24 months, babies became self-aware, touching their noses with curiosity and puzzlement. Self-recognition in the mirror/rouge test (and in photographs) usually emerges at about 18 months, along with two other advances: pretending and using first-person pronouns *(I, me, mine, myself, my)* (Lewis, 2010).

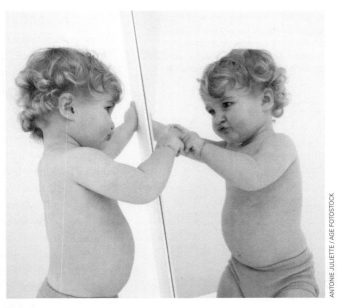

Who Is That? At 18 months, he is at the beginning of self-awareness, testing to see whether his mirror image will meet his finger.

ANTONIE JULIETTE / AGE FOTOSTOCK

KEYpoints

- A newborn's emotions are distress and contentment, expressed by crying or looking relaxed.
- Older babies exhibit curiosity, laughter, anger (when they are kept from something they want), and fear (when something unexpected occurs).
- Toddlers express many emotions that indicate awareness of themselves and others.
- Cultural expectations and parental actions influence emotions.

Brain and Emotions

Brain maturation is involved in the emotional developments just described because all emotional reactions begin in the brain (Johnson, 2010). Experience and culture promote specific connections between neurons and emotions.

Links between expressed emotions and brain growth are complex and thus difficult to assess and describe (Lewis, 2011). Compared with the emotions of adults, discrete emotions during early infancy are murky and unpredictable. For instance, an infant's cry can be triggered by pain, fear, tiredness, surprise, or excitement; laughter can quickly turn to tears. Furthermore, infant emotions may erupt, increase, or disappear for unknown reasons (Camras & Shutter, 2010). Growth of synapses and dendrites is a likely explanation, the result of past experiences and ongoing maturation.

RESPONSE FOR Nurses and Pediatricians (from page 134) Stranger wariness is normal up to about 14 months. This baby's behavior actually sounds like secure attachment! ●

Growth of the Brain

Many specific aspects of brain development support social emotions (Lloyd-Fox et al., 2009). For instance, the social smile and laughter appear as the cortex matures (Konner, 2010). The same is probably true for fear, self-awareness, and anger. The maturation of a particular part of the cortex (the anterior cingulate gyrus) is directly connected to emotional self-regulation, allowing a child to express or hide feelings (Posner et al., 2007).

Cultural differences may become encoded in the infant brain, called "a cultural sponge" by one group of scientists (Ambady & Bharucha, 2009, p. 342). It is difficult to measure how infant brains are molded by their context, but one study (Zhu et al., 2007) of adults—half of whom were born in the United States and half in China—found that in both groups, a particular area of the brain (the medial prefrontal cortex) was activated when the adults judged whether certain adjectives applied to them. However, only in the Chinese was that area also activated when they were asked whether those adjectives applied to their mothers.

Researchers consider this to be "neuroimaging evidence that culture shapes the functional anatomy of self-representation" (Zhu et al., 2007, p. 1310). They speculate that brain activation occurs because the Chinese participants learned, as babies, that they are closely aligned with their mothers, whereas the Americans learned to be independent. (A related cultural difference is explored in the Opposing Perspectives feature of proximal and distal parenting later in this chapter.)

MEMORY All emotional reactions, particularly those connected to self-awareness, depend partly on memory (Harter, 2006; Lewis, 2010). As already explained in Chapter 3, memory is fragile at first and gradually improves as dendrites and axons connect over the first year. No wonder toddlers are more quickly angered than younger babies when teased by an older sibling, as well as more likely to resist entering the doctor's office. Unlike young infants, they have vivid memories of the previous time a sibling frustrated them or the doctor gave them a shot.

Memory for events and places is evident, but memory for people is even more powerful. Particular people (typically those the infant sees most often) arouse strong emotions. Even in the early weeks, faces are connected to sensations. For example, a breast-feeding mother's face is connected to sucking and relief of hunger.

The tentative social smile at every face, which occurs naturally as the brain reaches six weeks of maturity, soon becomes a much quicker and fuller smile when an infant sees a familiar, loving caregiver. This occurs because the neurons that fire together become more closely and quickly connected to each other (via dendrites and neurotransmitters) with repeated experience.

Social preferences form in the early months and are connected with an individual's face, voice, touch, and smell. This is one reason adopted children are placed with their new parents in the first days of life whenever possible—a change from 100 years ago, when adoptions began after age 1. It is also a reason to respect an infant's reaction to a babysitter: If a 6-month-old screams and clings to the parent when the sitter arrives, another caregiver probably needs to be found. (Do not confuse this with separation anxiety at 12 months—a normal, expected reaction.)

STRESS Emotions are connected to brain activity and hormones, but the connections are complicated—affected by genes, past experiences, and additional hormones and neurotransmitters not yet understood (Lewis, 2011). One link is clear: Excessive stress (which increases cortisol) harms the developing brain (Adam et al., 2007). The hypothalamus (discussed further in Chapter 5), in particular, grows more slowly if an infant is often frightened.

The impact of infant abuse on the brain is difficult to prove experimentally, for obvious reasons. No researcher would deliberately abuse one group of infants and later compare their brains to those of another group. If abuse is apparent in a particular infant, the ethical reaction is to intervene immediately, not to allow the abuse to continue in order to study the brain years later.

However, brain scans of children who were discovered to have been maltreated in infancy show abnormal responses to stress, anger, and other emotions—and even to photographs of frightened people (Gordis et al., 2008; Masten et al., 2008). This research has led many developmentalists to suspect that abnormal neurological responses are caused by early abuse.

The likelihood that early caregiving affects the brain lifelong leads to obvious applications (Belsky & de Haan, 2011). Since infants learn emotional responses, caregivers need to be consistent and reassuring. This is not always easy—remember that some infants cry inconsolably in the early weeks. As one researcher notes:

> An infant's crying has 2 possible consequences: it may elicit tenderness and desire to soothe, or helplessness and rage. It can be a signal that encourages attachment or one that jeopardizes the early relationship by triggering depression and, in some cases, even neglect or abuse.

> [J. S. Kim, 2011, p. 229]

Sometimes mothers are blamed, or blame themselves, when their infant keeps crying. This is not helpful: A mother who feels guilty or incompetent may become angry at her baby, which may lead to unresponsive parenting, an unhappy child, and a hostile mother. But a negative relationship between difficult infants and their mothers is not inevitable. Some colicky babies have loving parents and, when the colic subsides, a warm, reciprocal bond develops.

However, if parental hostility continues, toddlers who are mobile and talkative often become defiant and stubborn, thereby causing their parents to blame them. This perpetuates a mutually destructive pattern. Years later, first-grade classmates and teachers are likely to consider such children disruptive and aggressive (Lorber & Egeland, 2011).

Temperament

This chapter began by describing universals of infant emotions and then explained that brain maturation undergirds those universals. You just read that mothers should not blame themselves. Who, then, is to blame when a baby cries often and rarely sleeps? When my friend had a difficult infant, she laughingly said that she and her husband wanted to exchange her for another model. And my daughter with my crying grandson (in the opening of this chapter) was upset when I said my babies were all easy. She felt I was bragging or forgetful, not sympathetic.

GENES AND EMOTIONS Certainly not all babies are easygoing. Infant emotions are affected by alleles and prenatal events; the uniqueness of each person means that some babies are difficult from the moment they are born. I do not write this to comfort my friend and my daughter; I write this because all developmentalists recognize the impact of genes and prenatal experiences. Some devote their lives to discovering alleles that affect specific emotions (M. H. Johnson & Fearon, 2011).

For example, researchers have found that the 7-repeat allele of the DRD4 VNTR gene, when combined with the 5-HTTLPR genotype, results in 6-month-olds who are difficult—they cry often, are hard to distract, and are slow to laugh (Holmboe et al., 2011). You need not remember the letters of these alleles, but remember that infant emotions vary, often for genetic reasons.

Temperament is defined as the "biologically based core of individual differences in style of approach and response to the environment that is stable across time and situations" (van den Akker et al., 2010, p. 485). "Biologically based" means that these

✦ **ESPECIALLY FOR Nurses** Parents come to you with their fussy 3-month-old. They say they have read that temperament is "fixed" before birth, and they are worried that their child will always be difficult. What do you tell them? (see response, page 138) →

temperament
Inborn differences between one person and another in emotions, activity, and self-regulation. It is measured by the person's typical responses to the environment.

RESPONSE FOR Nurses (from page 137) It's too soon to tell. Temperament is not truly "fixed" but variable, especially in the first few months. Many "difficult" infants become happy, successful adolescents and adults. ●

traits originate with nature, not nurture. Confirmation that temperament arises from the inborn brain comes from an analysis of the tone, duration, and intensity of infant cries after the first inoculation, before much experience outside the womb. Cry variations at this every early stage correlated with later temperament (Jong et al., 2010).

Temperament is not the same as personality, although temperamental inclinations may lead to personality differences. Generally, personality traits (e.g., honesty and humility) are learned, whereas temperamental traits (e.g., shyness and aggression) are genetic.

Of course, heredity and experience always interact. Although temperament originates with genes, the expression of emotions over the life span is modified by experience—the result of child-rearing methods, culture, and learning (Rothbart & Bates, 2006). How this happens will be clearer with examples.

RESEARCH ON TEMPERAMENT In laboratory studies of temperament, infants are exposed to events that are frightening or attractive. Four-month-olds might see spinning mobiles or hear unusual sounds. Older babies might confront a noisy, moving robot or a clown who quickly moves close. At such experiences, some children laugh, some cry, others are quiet, and still others exhibit some combination of these—reactions that help classify them in one of four categories ("easy," "difficult," "slow to warm up," or "hard to classify").

These categories come from the *New York Longitudinal Study* (NYLS). Begun in the 1960s, the NYLS was the first large study to recognize that each newborn has distinct inborn traits (Thomas & Chess, 1977). According to the NYLS, by 3 months, infants manifest nine traits that cluster into the four categories just described. The proportion of infants in each category was as follows:

● Easy (40 percent)
● Difficult (10 percent)
● Slow to warm up (15 percent)
● Hard to classify (35 percent)

Later research confirms again and again that newborns differ temperamentally and that some are unusually difficult. However, although the NYLS began a rich research endeavor, its nine dimensions have not held up in large, later studies (Caspi & Shiner, 2006; Zentner & Bates, 2008). Generally, only three (not nine) dimensions of temperament are clearly present in early childhood (Else-Quest et al., 2006; van den Akker et al., 2010). Although each study uses somewhat different terms, the following three dimensions of temperament are apparent:

● Effortful control (able to regulate attention and emotion, to self-soothe)
● Negative mood (fearful, angry, unhappy)
● Surgency (active, social, not shy, exuberant)

KEYpoints

- Brain maturation underlies much of emotional development in the first two years.
- The stress of early maltreatment probably affects the brain, causing abnormal responses later.
- Temperament is inborn, with some babies much easier than others.
- Difficult or fearful babies sometimes become successful, confident children.

A VIEW FROM SCIENCE

The Long Reach of Temperament

As noted, thousands of scientists have studied infant temperament. One particularly impressive longitudinal study analyzed temperament in the same children at 4, 9, 14, 24, and 48 months; again in middle childhood; and again at adolescence. Each time, the researchers reevaluated their past data and considered related cross-sectional and international studies (Fox et al., 2001, 2005; Hane et al., 2008; L. R. Williams et al., 2010).

These researchers used many methods, as a multidisciplinary perspective would suggest. They designed laboratory experiments with specifics appropriate for the age of the children; collected detailed reports from the mothers and later from the participants themselves; and gathered observational data and physiological evidence, including brain scans.

Half of the participants did not change much from 4 months to 4 years, reacting the same way and having similar brain-wave patterns when confronted with frightening experiences every time they were tested. The other half did change. Curiously, the ones most likely to change were the inhibited, fearful ones. Least likely to change were the exuberant ones (see Figure 4.1). That speaks to the influence of child-rearing methods in the United States: Adults coax frightened infants to be brave but encourage exuberant children to stay happy.

The researchers found unexpected gender differences as well. As teenagers, the formerly inhibited boys were more likely than the average adolescent to use drugs, but the inhibited girls were less likely to do so (L. R. Williams et al., 2010). The most likely explanation is cultural: Shy boys try to become less anxious by using drugs, but shy girls are more accepted as they are.

Continuity and change were also found in another study that described temperament using three traits (expressive, typical, and fearful). Fearful infants again were most likely to change. Only about one-third (5 percent overall) who were earlier fearful still seemed afraid at age 3 (van den Akker et al., 2010). Parental attitudes and actions influenced these changes.

Other studies also find that difficult infants often become easier—*if* their parents provide excellent, patient care (Belsky & Pluess, 2009). How could this be? Some scientists suggest that, since fussy and scared children come to the parents often for comfort or reassurance, they are particularly likely to flourish with responsive parenting but wither if their parents are rejecting (Stupica et al., 2011). This is differential sensitivity (see Chapter 1).

Here is one example. Researchers selected 32 very difficult newborns (they were highly irritable, as indicated by their crying quickly and loudly when an examiner tested their reflexes) and 52 moderately difficult ones. The quality of their caregiving and bonding was measured (via attachment, soon described) at age 1. These 84 infants were assessed at 18 and 24 months on their ability to explore new objects and respond to strangers—two skills that promote learning in toddlerhood.

Highly irritable infants who received responsive parenting (secure attachment) were *more* social, and no less adept at exploration, than the other toddlers. By contrast, all the infants with less good care (insecure) were markedly less social and less skilled than average at exploring. Impairment was especially strong for the ones who were very irritable newborns (Stupica et al., 2011).

The two patterns evident in all these studies—continuity and improvement—have been replicated in many longitudinal studies of infant temperament, especially for antisocial personality traits. Difficult babies tend to become difficult children, but family and culture sometimes mitigate negative outcomes (Kagan et al., 2007; Zentner & Bates, 2008).

Many factors, from both nature and nurture, affect temperament and personality. This is good news: Although some infants are markedly less easy and cheerful than others, early child rearing turns many of them into accomplished, successful children. The social context is always influential (see Infographic 4, page 140).

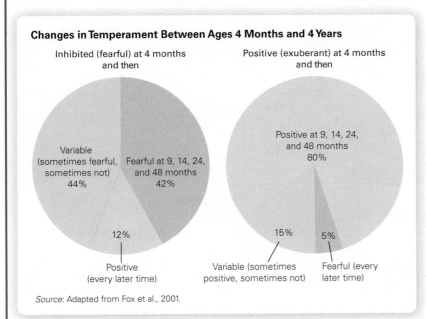

Changes in Temperament Between Ages 4 Months and 4 Years

Inhibited (fearful) at 4 months and then

Variable (sometimes fearful, sometimes not) 44%

Fearful at 9, 14, 24, and 48 months 42%

12%

Positive (every later time)

Positive (exuberant) at 4 months and then

Positive at 9, 14, 24, and 48 months 80%

15%

Variable (sometimes positive, sometimes not)

5%

Fearful (every later time)

Source: Adapted from Fox et al., 2001.

FIGURE 4.1 Do Babies' Temperaments Change? Sometimes. Especially if they were fearful. Adults who are reassuring help children overcome an innate fearfulness. If fearful children do not change, it is not known whether that's because their parents are not sufficiently reassuring (nurture) or because they are temperamentally more fearful (nature).

SOURCES & CREDITS LISTED ON P SC-1

VISUALIZING DEVELOPMENT

Developing Attachment

Attachment may begin with bonding at birth, affected by newborn appearance, maternal hormones, and skin-to-skin contact. Attachment patterns in infancy echo in later life, but they are not determinative. Insecure infants may become secure adults who have healthy and supportive relationships with partners and children. As this shows, however, attachment styles are often carried from one life stage to another. Each cloud includes factors proven to affect development. The size of circles indicates approximate population distribution of attachment statuses.

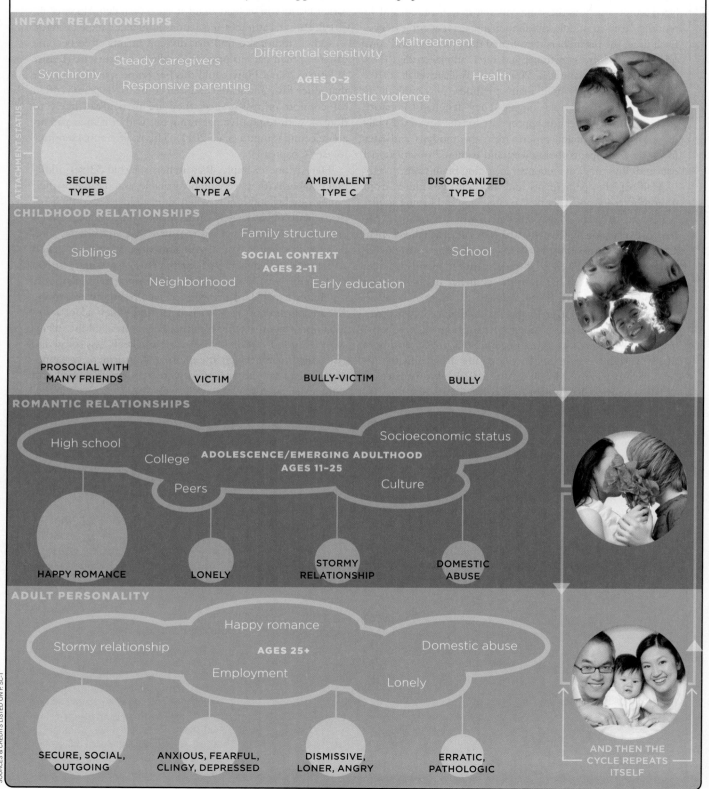

INFANT RELATIONSHIPS

ATTACHMENT STATUS

Maltreatment
Differential sensitivity
Steady caregivers
Synchrony
Responsive parenting
AGES 0–2
Health
Domestic violence

SECURE TYPE B
ANXIOUS TYPE A
AMBIVALENT TYPE C
DISORGANIZED TYPE D

CHILDHOOD RELATIONSHIPS

Family structure
Siblings
SOCIAL CONTEXT AGES 2–11
School
Neighborhood
Early education

PROSOCIAL WITH MANY FRIENDS
VICTIM
BULLY-VICTIM
BULLY

ROMANTIC RELATIONSHIPS

Socioeconomic status
High school
College
ADOLESCENCE/EMERGING ADULTHOOD AGES 11–25
Peers
Culture

HAPPY ROMANCE
LONELY
STORMY RELATIONSHIP
DOMESTIC ABUSE

ADULT PERSONALITY

Happy romance
Stormy relationship
AGES 25+
Domestic abuse
Employment
Lonely

SECURE, SOCIAL, OUTGOING
ANXIOUS, FEARFUL, CLINGY, DEPRESSED
DISMISSIVE, LONER, ANGRY
ERRATIC, PATHOLOGIC

AND THEN THE CYCLE REPEATS ITSELF

The Development of Social Bonds

As you see, the social context has a powerful impact on development. So does the infant's age, via brain maturation. Regarding emotional development, how old the baby is determines specific social interactions that lead to growth—first synchrony, then attachment, then social referencing.

Synchrony

Early parent–child interactions are described as **synchrony,** a mutual exchange that requires split-second timing. Synchrony is evident in the first three months, becoming more frequent and elaborate as the infant matures (Feldman, 2007).

synchrony
A coordinated, rapid, and smooth exchange of responses between a caregiver and an infant.

BOTH PARTNERS ACTIVE Detailed research reveals the symbiosis of the adult–infant partnerships. Adults rarely smile at young infants until the infants smile at them, several weeks after birth. Then adults usually grin broadly and talk animatedly (Lavelli & Fogel, 2005).

Synchrony is evident not only in direct observation, as when watching a caregiver play with an infant too young to talk, but also via computer calculation of the millisecond timing of smiles, arched eyebrows, and so on (Messinger et al., 2010). Synchrony is a joy for both participants and is also a powerful learning experience. In every episode, infants learn to read others' emotions and develop social skills, such as taking turns and watching expressions.

One study found that those mothers who took longer to bathe, feed, and diaper their infants were also most responsive. Apparently, some parents combine caregiving with emotional play, which takes longer but also allows more synchrony.

Synchrony usually begins with adults imitating infants (not vice versa) (Lavelli & Fogel, 2005), with split-second timing and also with tone and rhythm (Van Puyvelde et al., 2010). Metaphors for synchrony are often musical—a waltz, a jazz duet—to emphasize that each partner must be attuned to the other. Adults respond to nuances of infant facial expressions and body motions. This helps infants connect their internal state with external expressions understood within their culture. Synchrony is particularly apparent in Asian cultures, perhaps because of a cultural focus on interpersonal sensitivity (Morelli & Rothbaum, 2007).

In Western cultures as well, parents become partners with their infants. This is especially crucial when the infant is at medical risk; the need for time-consuming physical care might overwhelm a nurse's or doctor's awareness of psychosocial needs, yet those needs are as important for long-term health as are the more immediate physical needs (Newnham et al., 2009).

Same Situation, Far Apart: Sweet Synchrony Differences in gender and nation (England, left, and Cuba, right) are obvious but superficial. The essence of early parent–infant interaction is synchrony.

still-face technique
An experimental practice in which an adult keeps his or her face unmoving and expressionless in face-to-face interaction with an infant.

NEGLECTED SYNCHRONY Is synchrony necessary? If no one plays with an infant, what will happen? Experiments involving the **still-face technique** have addressed these questions (Tronick, 1989; Tronick & Weinberg, 1997).

In these experiments, an infant faces an adult who responds normally while two video cameras simultaneously record their interpersonal reactions. Frame-by-frame analysis reveals that parents instinctively synchronize their responses to the infants' movements, with exaggerated tone and expression. Babies reciprocate with smiles and flailing limbs.

To be specific, long before they can reach out and grab, infants respond excitedly to caregiver attention by waving their arms. They are delighted if the adult moves closer so that a waving arm touches the face or, even better, a hand grabs hair. You read about this eagerness for interaction in Chapter 3, when infants try to "make interesting sights last" or when they babble in response to adult speech. Meanwhile, adults open their eyes wider, raise their eyebrows, smack their lips, emit nonsense sounds—all in response to tiny infant actions.

In still-face experiments, on cue, the adult does not move closer but instead erases all facial expression, staring quietly with a "still face" for a minute or two. Sometimes by 2 months, and clearly by 6 months, infants are upset by still faces, especially from their parents (less so from strangers). Babies frown, fuss, drool, look away, kick, cry, or suck their fingers. By 5 months, they also vocalize, as if to say, "Pay attention to me" (Goldstein et al., 2009).

Many studies reach the same conclusion: Synchrony is vital. Responsiveness aids psychosocial and biological development, evident in heart rate, weight gain, and brain maturation (Moore & Calkins, 2004; Newnham et al., 2009). Particularly in the first year, babies of depressed mothers suffer unless someone else is a sensitive partner (Bagner et al., 2010).

Attachment

Toward the end of the first year, such face-to-face synchrony almost disappears. Once infants can move around, they are no longer content to respond, moment by moment, to adult facial expressions and vocalizations. Another connection, called *attachment,* overtakes synchrony. Thousands of researchers on every continent have focused on attachment, all inspired by British theorist John Bowlby and then by the seminal research of one young woman, Mary Ainsworth, who described mother–infant relationships in central Africa 50 years ago (Ainsworth, 1967).

Attachment is a lasting emotional bond. Although it is most evident at about age 1, attachment begins before birth and influences relationships throughout life (see At About This Time). Adults' attachment to their parents, formed decades earlier, affects their behavior with their own children as well as their relationship with their partners (Grossmann et al., 2005; Kline, 2008; Simpson & Rholes, 2010; Sroufe et al., 2005).

attachment
According to Ainsworth, "an affectional tie" that an infant forms with a caregiver—a tie that binds them together in space and endures over time.

SIGNS OF ATTACHMENT Infants show their attachment through *proximity-seeking* (such as approaching and following their caregivers) and through *contact-maintaining* (such as touching, snuggling, and holding). Proximity-seeking is evident when a baby cries if the mother wants privacy when she goes to the bathroom or if a back-facing car seat prevents the baby from seeing the parent. Some parents in the front passenger seat reach back to give a hand, which sometimes reassures the baby. Contact-maintaining need not be physical: Visual or verbal connections are often sufficient.

Caregivers show their own urge to remain attached. They keep a watchful eye on their baby and maintain contact by initiating and responding to expressions, gestures, and vocalizations. Many parents, awakening in the middle of the night, tiptoe to the crib to gaze fondly at their sleeping infant. This is evidence of proximity-

AT ABOUT THIS TIME
Stages of Attachment

Birth to 6 weeks	*Preattachment.* Newborns signal, via crying and body movements, that they need others. When people respond positively, the newborn is comforted and learns to seek more interaction. Newborns are also primed by brain patterns to recognize familiar voices and faces.
6 weeks to 8 months	*Attachment in the making.* Infants respond preferentially to familiar people by smiling, laughing, babbling. Their caregivers' voices, touch, expressions, and gestures are comforting, often overriding the infant's impulse to cry. Trust (Erikson) develops.
8 months to 2 years	*Classic secure attachment.* Infants greet the primary caregiver, play happily when the caregiver is present, show separation anxiety when the caregiver leaves. Both infant and caregiver seek to be close to each other (proximity) and frequently look at each other (contact). In many caregiver–infant pairs, physical touch (patting, holding, caressing) is frequent.
2 to 6 years	*Attachment as launching pad.* Young children seek their caregiver's praise and reassurance as their social world expands. Interactive conversations and games (hide-and-seek, object play, reading, pretending) are common. Children expect caregivers to comfort and entertain.
6 to 12 years	*Mutual attachment.* Children seek to make their caregivers proud by learning whatever adults want them to learn, and adults reciprocate. In concrete operational thought (Piaget), specific accomplishments are valued by adults and children.
12 to 18 years	*New attachment figures.* Teenagers explore and make friendships on their own, using their working models of earlier attachments as a base. With more advanced, formal operational thinking (Piaget), shared ideals and goals become more influential.
18 years on	*Attachment revisited.* Adults develop relationships with others, especially relationships with romantic partners and their own children, influenced by earlier attachment patterns. Past insecure attachments from childhood can be repaired rather than repeated, although this does not always happen.

Source: Adapted from Grobman, 2008.

seeking. During the day, in contact-maintaining, caregivers sometimes absentmindedly smooth their toddler's hair or caress their child's hands.

Research on attachment has occurred in dozens of nations, with people of many ages. Attachment seems to be universal, part of the inborn social nature of the human species, but specific manifestations vary.

For instance, Ugandan mothers never kiss their infants but often massage them, contrary to Western custom. Adults who are securely attached to each other might remain in contact via daily phone calls, e-mails, or texts and keep in proximity by sitting in the same room as each reads quietly. Some scholars believe that attachment, not only of mother and infant but also of fathers, grandparents, and non-relatives, is the reason that *Homo sapiens* thrived when other species became extinct (Hrdy, 2009).

SECURE AND INSECURE ATTACHMENT Attachment is classified into four types: A, B, C, and D (see Table 4.1). Infants with **secure attachment** (type B) feel comfortable and confident. The caregiver is a *base for exploration*, providing assurance, enabling exploration. A toddler might, for example, scramble down from the caregiver's lap to play with an intriguing toy but periodically look back and vocalize (contact-maintaining) or bring the toy to the caregiver for inspection (proximity-seeking).

secure attachment
A relationship in which an infant obtains both comfort and confidence from the presence of his or her caregiver.

TABLE 4.1 Patterns of Infant Attachment

Type	Name of Pattern	In Play Room	Mother Leaves	Mother Returns	Toddlers in Category (%)
A	Insecure-avoidant	Child plays happily.	Child continues playing.	Child ignores her.	10–20
B	Secure	Child plays happily.	Child pauses, is not as happy.	Child welcomes her, returns to play.	50–70
C	Insecure-resistant/ ambivalent	Child clings, is preoccupied with mother.	Child is unhappy, may stop playing.	Child is angry; may cry, hit mother, cling.	10–20
D	Disorganized	Child is cautious.	Child may stare or yell; looks scared, confused.	Child acts oddly— may scream, hit self, throw things.	5–10

insecure-avoidant attachment
A pattern of attachment in which an infant avoids connection with the caregiver, as when the infant seems not to care about the caregiver's presence, departure, or return.

insecure-resistant/ambivalent attachment
A pattern of attachment in which an infant's anxiety and uncertainty are evident, as when the infant becomes very upset at separation from the caregiver and both resists and seeks contact on reunion.

disorganized attachment
A type of attachment that is marked by an infant's inconsistent reactions to the caregiver's departure and return.

Strange Situation
A laboratory procedure for measuring attachment by evoking infants' reactions to the stress of various adults' comings and goings in an unfamiliar playroom.

By contrast, insecure attachment (types A and C) is characterized by fear, anxiety, anger, or indifference. Some insecure children play independently without maintaining contact; this is **insecure-avoidant attachment** (type A). The opposite reaction, called **insecure-resistant/ambivalent attachment** (type C), is also insecure: Such children are unwilling to leave the caregiver's lap or are angry at being left.

Ainsworth's original schema differentiated only types A, B, and C. Later researchers discovered a fourth category (type D), **disorganized attachment.** Type D infants may shift suddenly from hitting to kissing their mothers, from staring blankly to crying hysterically, from pinching themselves to freezing in place.

Among the general population (not among infants with special needs), almost two-thirds are secure (type B). Their mothers' presence gives them courage to explore; her departure causes distress; her return elicits positive social contact (such as smiling or hugging) and then more playing. A balanced reaction, being concerned but not overwhelmed by comings and goings, indicates security. (Reference here to the mother is deliberate, as most early research was on mother–infant attachment; later research includes fathers, siblings, and other caregivers.)

About one-third of infants are insecure, either indifferent (type A) or unduly anxious (type C). About 5 to 10 percent of infants fit into none of these categories and are thus labeled disorganized (type D). Disorganized infants have no evident strategy for social interaction (even an avoidant or resistant one, type A or C). Sometimes they become hostile and aggressive, difficult for anyone to relate to (Lyons-Ruth et al., 1999). Unlike the first three types, disorganized infants have elevated levels of cortisol in reaction to stress (Bernard & Dozier, 2010).

MEASURING ATTACHMENT Ainsworth (1973) developed a now-classic laboratory procedure called the **Strange Situation** to measure attachment. In a well-equipped playroom, an infant is observed for eight episodes, each lasting three minutes. First, the child and mother are together. Next, according to a set sequence, the mother and then a stranger come and go. Infants' responses to their mother indicate which type of attachment they have formed.

Researchers are rigorously trained to distinguish types A, B, C, and D. They focus on the following:

● *Exploration of the toys.* A secure toddler plays happily.

● *Reaction to the caregiver's departure.* A secure toddler notices when the caregiver leaves and shows some sign of missing him or her.

● *Reaction to the caregiver's return.* A secure toddler welcomes the caregiver's reappearance, usually seeking contact, and then plays again.

The Attachment Experiment In this episode of the Strange Situation, Brian shows every sign of secure attachment. *(a)* He explores the playroom happily when his mother is present; *(b)* he cries when she leaves; and *(c)* he is readily comforted when she returns.

Attachment is not always measured via the Strange Situation; surveys and interviews are also used. Sometimes parents answer 90 questions about their children's characteristics, and sometimes adults are interviewed extensively (according to a detailed protocol) about their relationships with their own parents, again with various specific measurements (Fortuna & Roisman, 2008).

Research measuring attachment has revealed that some behaviors that might seem normal are, in fact, a sign of insecurity. For instance, an infant who clings to the caregiver and refuses to explore the toys in the new playroom might be type A. Likewise, adults who say their childhood was happy and their mother was a saint, especially if they provide few specific memories, might be insecure. And young children who are immediately friendly to strangers may never have formed a secure attachment (Tarullo et al., 2011).

Assessments of attachment, developed and validated for middle-class North Americans, may not be culturally appropriate elsewhere. Infants who seem dismissive or clingy may not always be insecure, as cultures differ. Everywhere, however, parents and infants are attached to each other, and everywhere secure attachment predicts academic success and emotional stability (Erdman & Ng, 2010; Molitor & Hsu, 2011; Rothbaum et al., 2011).

Insecure Attachment and Social Setting

At first, developmentalists expected secure attachment to "predict all the outcomes reasonably expected from a well-functioning personality" (R. A. Thompson & Raikes, 2003, p. 708). But this expectation turned out to be naive.

Securely attached infants *are* more likely to become secure toddlers, socially competent preschoolers, high-achieving schoolchildren, and capable parents (R. A. Thompson, 2006) (see Table 4.2). Attachment affects early brain development, one reason these later outcomes occur (Diamond & Fagundes, 2010). Yet type A, B, C, or D status may shift with family circumstances, such as divorce, abuse, or income loss.

Harsh contexts, especially the stresses of poverty, reduce the incidence of secure attachment (Seifer et al., 2004; van IJzendoorn & Bakermans-Kranenburg, 2010), and insecure attachment correlates with many later problems. However, correlation is not causation, and thus insecure attachment may be a sign but may not be the direct cause of those problems.

Many aspects of low SES make low school achievement, hostile children, and fearful adults more likely. The underlying premise—that responsive early parenting leads to secure attachment, which buffers stress and encourages exploration—seems valid, but attachment behaviors in the Strange Situation constitute only one indication of the quality of the parent–child relationship.

TABLE 4.2 Predictors of Attachment Type

Secure attachment (type B) is more likely if:

- The parent is usually sensitive and responsive to the infant's needs.
- The infant–parent relationship is high in synchrony.
- The infant's temperament is "easy."
- The parents are not stressed about income, other children, or their marriage.
- The parents have a working model of secure attachment to their own parents.

Insecure attachment is more likely if:

- The parent mistreats the child. (Neglect increases type A; abuse increases types C and D.)
- The mother is mentally ill. (Paranoia increases type D; depression increases type C.)
- The parents are highly stressed about income, other children, or their marriage. (Parental stress increases types A and D.)
- The parents are intrusive and controlling. (Parental domination increases type A.)
- The parents are active alcoholics. (Alcoholic father increases type A; alcoholic mother increases type D.)
- The child's temperament is "difficult." (Difficult children tend to be type C.)
- The child's temperament is "slow to warm up." (This correlates with type A.)

INSIGHTS FROM ROMANIA No scholar doubts that close human relationships should develop in the first year of life and that the lack of such relationships has dire consequences. Unfortunately, thousands of children born in Romania are proof.

When Romanian dictator Nicolae Ceausesçu forbade birth control and abortions in the 1980s, illegal abortions became the leading cause of death for Romanian women aged 15 to 45 (Verona, 2003), and more than 100,000 children were abandoned to crowded, impersonal, state-run orphanages. The children experienced severe deprivation, including virtually no normal interaction, play, or conversation (Rutter et al., 2007).

In the two years after Ceausesçu was ousted and killed in 1989, thousands of those children were adopted by North American, western European, and Australian families. Those who were adopted before 6 months of age fared best; synchrony was established via play and caregiving. Most of them developed normally.

For those adopted after 6 months, and especially after 12 months, early signs were encouraging: Skinny infants gained weight and grew faster than other 1-year-olds, developing motor skills they had lacked (H. Park et al., 2011). However, their early social deprivation soon became evident in their emotions and cognition. Many were overly friendly to strangers throughout childhood, a sign of insecure attachment (Tarullo et al., 2011). At age 11, they scored an average of only 85 on the WISC IQ test, 15 points below normal (Rutter et al., 2010).

These children are now young adults, many with serious emotional or conduct problems. The cause is more social than biological. Even those who were relatively well nourished at adoption, or who caught up to normal growth, often became impulsive and angry teenagers. Apparently, the stresses of adolescence and emerging adulthood exacerbate the cognitive and social strains on these young people and their families (Merz & McCall, 2011).

Danger Ongoing Look closely and you can see danger. That bent crib bar could strangle an infant, and that chipped paint could contain lead (is that why a child is biting it?). Fortunately, these three Romanian infants (photographed in 1990) escaped those dangers to be raised in loving adoptive homes. Unfortunately, the damage of social isolation (note the sheet around the crib) could not be completely overcome: Some young adults who spent their first year in an institution like this still carry emotional scars.

©JOSEF POLLEROSS/THE IMAGE WORKS

Romanian infants are no longer available for international adoption, but some are still abandoned. Research confirms that early emotional deprivation, not genes or nutrition, is their greatest problem. Romanian infants develop best in their own families, second best in foster families, and worst in institutions (Nelson et al., 2007). As best we know, this applies to infants everywhere: Families usually care for their babies better than strangers.

Fortunately, institutions have improved somewhat; more recent adoptees are not as impaired as those 1990 Romanian orphans (Merz & McCall, 2011). Unfortunately, though, some infants in every nation are still deprived of healthy interactions, and the early months seem to be a sensitive period for emotional development. Children need responsive parents, biological or not (McCall et al., 2011).

PREVENTING PROBLEMS All infants need love and stimulation; all seek synchrony and then attachment—secure if possible, insecure if not. Without some adult support, infants become disorganized and adrift, emotionally troubled. Extreme early social deprivation is very difficult to overcome.

Since synchrony and attachment develop over the first year, and since more than one-third of all parents have difficulty establishing secure attachments, many developmentalists seek to discover what particularly impairs these parents and what can be done. We know that secure attachment is more difficult when the parents were abused as children, when families are socially isolated, when mothers are young adolescents, or when infants are unusually difficult (Zeanah et al., 2011). If biological parents cannot care for their newborns, foster or adoptive parents need to be found quickly so that synchrony and attachment can develop (McCall et al., 2011).

Some birth parents know they cannot provide responsive parenting, and they choose adoptive parents for their newborns. If high-risk birth parents believe they can provide good care, early support may avoid later problems. Success has been reported when skilled professionals come to the home to nurture secure relationships between infant and caregiver (Lowell et al., 2011). In fact, if a professional helps parents in the first days after birth, perhaps by using the Brazelton Neonatal Behavioral Assessment Scale (mentioned in Chapter 2) to encourage bonding, problems need never start (e.g., Nugent et al., 2009).

Social Referencing

Social referencing refers to seeking emotional responses or information from other people, much as a student might consult a dictionary or other reference work. Someone's reassuring glance or cautionary words; a facial expression of alarm, pleasure, or dismay—those are social references.

After age 1, when infants can walk and are little scientists, their need to consult others becomes urgent. Social referencing is constant, as toddlers search for clues in gazes, faces, and body position, paying close attention to emotions and intentions. They focus especially on their familiar caregivers, but they also use relatives, other children, and even strangers to help them assess objects and events. They are remarkably selective: Even at 16 months, they notice which strangers are reliable references and which are not (Poulin-Dubois & Chow, 2009).

Social referencing has many practical applications. Consider mealtime. Caregivers the world over smack their lips, pretend to taste, and say "yum-yum," encouraging toddlers to eat their first beets, liver, or spinach. For their part, toddlers become astute at reading expressions, insisting on the foods that the adults *really* like.

social referencing
Seeking information about how to react to an unfamiliar or ambiguous object or event by observing someone else's expressions and reactions. That other person becomes a social reference.

Rotini Pasta? Look Again. Every family teaches their children to relish delicacies that other people avoid. Examples are bacon (not in Arab nations), hamburgers (not in India), and, as shown here, a witchetty grub. This Australian aboriginal boy is about to swallow an insect larva.

BILL BACHMAN / ALAMY

Through this process, some children may develop a taste for raw fish or curried goat or smelly cheese—foods that children in other cultures refuse. Similarly, toddlers use social cues to understand the difference between real and pretend eating (Nishida & Lillard, 2007), as well as to understand which toys, emotions, and activities are encouraged or forbidden.

Fathers as Social Partners

Fathers enhance their children's social and emotional development in many ways (Lamb, 2010). Synchrony, attachment, and social referencing are all apparent with fathers, sometimes even more than with mothers. This was doubted until research found that some infants are securely attached to their fathers but not to their mothers (Bretherton, 2010). Furthermore, fathers elicit more smiles and laughter from their infants than mothers do.

Close father–infant relationships can teach infants (especially boys) appropriate expressions of emotion (Boyce et al., 2006), particularly anger. The results may endure: Teenagers are less likely to lash out at friends and authorities if, as infants, they experienced a warm, responsive relationship with their father (Trautmann-Villalba et al., 2006). Close relationships with infants help the men, too, reducing the risk of depression (Borke et al., 2007; Bronte-Tinkew et al., 2007).

In most cultures and ethnic groups, fathers spend much less time with infants than mothers do (Parke & Buriel, 2006; Tudge, 2008). National culture and parental attitudes are influential: Some women believe that child care is their special domain (Gaertner et al., 2007) and exclude fathers (perhaps indirectly, saying, "You're not holding her right"). Some fathers think it unmanly to dote on an infant.

That is not equally true everywhere. For example, Denmark has high rates of father involvement. At birth, 97 percent of Danish fathers are present, and five months later, most Danish fathers say that *every day* they change diapers (83 percent), feed (61 percent), and play with (98 percent) their infants (Munck, 2009).

Less rigid sex roles seem to be developing among parents in every nation. One example of historical change is the number of married mothers who are employed

Same Situation, Far Apart: Bonded That fathers enjoy their sons is not surprising, but notice the infants' hands—one clutching Dad's hair tightly and the other reaching for Dad's face. At this age, infants show their trust in adults by grabbing and reaching. Synchrony and attachment are mutual, in Ireland *(left)*, Kenya *(right)*, and everywhere.

in the United States, with children under age 6. In 1970, 30 percent of mothers were employed; in 2009, 70 percent were (U.S. Bureau of the Census, 2011b). These statistics include many mothers of young children.

Note the reference to "married" mothers: About half the mothers of infants in the United States are not married, and their employment rates are higher. As detailed later in this chapter, often fathers—not necessarily married to the mothers—help care for infants when mothers are at the workplace.

One sex difference seems to endure: "Mothers engage in more caregiving and comforting, and fathers in more high intensity play" (Kochanska et al., 2008, p. 41). When asked to play with their baby, mothers typically caress, read, sing, or rely on traditional games such as peek-a-boo. Fathers are more exciting: They move their infant's limbs in imitation of walking, kicking, or climbing, or they swing the baby through the air, sideways, or even upside down.

Mothers might say, "Don't drop him"; fathers and babies laugh with joy. In this way, fathers tend to help children become less fearful. Over the past 20 years, father–infant research has tried to answer three questions:

1. Can men provide the same care as women?

2. Is father–infant interaction different from mother–infant interaction?

3. How do fathers and mothers cooperate to provide infant care?

Many studies over the past two decades have answered yes to the first two. A baby fed, bathed, and diapered by Dad is just as happy and clean as when Mom does it. Gender differences are sometimes found in specifics, but they are not harmful.

On the third question, the answer depends on the family (Bretherton, 2010). Usually, mothers are caregivers and fathers are playmates, but not always—each couple, given their circumstances (which might include being immigrant, low-income, or same-sex parents), finds their own way to complement each other to help their infant thrive (Lamb, 2010).

A constructive parental alliance can not be assumed, whether or not the parents are legally wed. Sometimes neither parent is happy with their infant, with themselves, or with each other. One study reported that 7 percent of fathers of 1-year-olds were depressed, and they were four times as likely to spank as were nondepressed fathers (40 percent versus 10 percent) (Davis et al., 2011) (see Figure 4.2).

Family members are affected by each other's moods: Paternal depression correlates with maternal depression and with sad, angry, and disobedient toddlers. Cause and consequence are intertwined. When infants are depressed, or anxious, or hostile, all members of the family triad (mother, father, baby) need help.

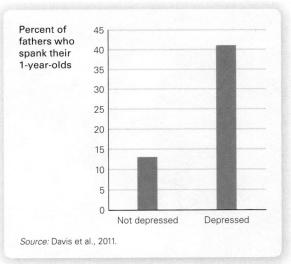

Source: Davis et al., 2011.

FIGURE 4.2 Shame on Whom? Not on the toddlers, who are naturally curious and careless, but maybe not on the fathers, either. Both depression and spanking are affected by financial stress, marital conflict, and cultural norms—who is responsible for those?

KEYpoints

- Caregivers and young infants engage in split-second interaction, evidence of synchrony.
- Attachment between people is universal, apparent in infancy with contact-maintaining and proximity-seeking as 1-year-olds play.
- Toddlers use other people as social references, to guide them in their exploration.
- Fathers are as capable as mothers in social partnerships with infants, although they may favor physical, creative play more than mothers do.

trust versus mistrust
Erikson's first crisis of psychosocial development. Infants learn basic trust if
the world is a secure place where their
basic needs (for food, comfort, attention, and so on) are met.

autonomy versus shame and doubt
Erikson's second crisis of psychosocial
development. Toddlers either succeed
or fail in gaining a sense of self-rule
over their actions and their bodies.

✦ ESPECIALLY FOR Nursing Mothers
You have heard that if you wean your
child too early, he or she will overeat
or become an alcoholic. Is it true? (see
response, page 153) →

Theories of Infant Psychosocial Development

We now consider again the theories discussed in Chapter 1. As you will see, theories lead to insight and applications, preparing us for the final topic of this chapter, infant day care.

Psychoanalytic Theory

Psychoanalytic theory connects biosocial and psychosocial development. Sigmund Freud and Erik Erikson each described two distinct stages of early development. Freud (1935, 1940/1964) wrote about the *oral stage* and the *anal stage*. Erikson (1963) called his first stages *trust versus mistrust* and *autonomy versus shame and doubt*.

FREUD: ORAL AND ANAL STAGES According to Freud, the first year of life is the *oral stage,* so named because the mouth is the young infant's primary source of grati-fication. In the second year, with the *anal stage,* the infant's main pleasure comes from the anus—particularly from the sensual pleasure of bowel movements and, eventually, the psychological pleasure of controlling them.

Freud believed that the oral and anal stages are fraught with potential conflicts that have long-term consequences. If a mother frustrates her infant's urge to suck—weaning the infant too early, for example, or preventing the child from sucking a thumb or a pacifier—the child may become distressed and anxious, eventually becoming an adult with an *oral fixation.* Such a person is stuck (fixated) at the oral stage and therefore eats, drinks, chews, bites, or talks excessively, in quest of the mouth-related pleasure denied in infancy.

All Together, Now Toddlers in an employees' day-care program at a flower
farm in Colombia learn to use the potty
on a schedule.

Similarly, if toilet training is overly strict or if it begins before the infant is mature enough, parent and infant may become locked in a conflict over the toddler's refusal, or inability, to comply. The child develops an anal personality and becomes an adult who seeks self-control, with an unusually strong need for regularity in all aspects of life.

ERIKSON: TRUST AND AUTONOMY According to Erikson, the first crisis of life is **trust versus mistrust,** when infants learn whether the world can be trusted to satisfy basic needs. Babies feel secure when food and comfort are provided with "con-sistency, continuity, and sameness of experience" (Erikson, 1963, p. 247). If social interaction inspires trust, the child (later the adult) confidently explores the social world.

The second crisis is **autonomy versus shame and doubt,** beginning at about 18 months, when self-awareness emerges. Toddlers want autonomy (self-rule) over their own actions and bodies. Without it, they feel ashamed and doubtful. Like Freud, Erikson believed that problems in early infancy could last a lifetime, creating adults who are suspicious and pessimistic (mistrusting) or easily shamed (lacking autonomy). (See Chapter 1.)

Erikson was aware of cultural variations. He knew that mistrust and shame could be destructive or not, depending on norms and expectations. Some cultures encour-age independence and autonomy; in others, "shame is a normative emotion that develops as parents use explicit shaming techniques" to encourage children's loyalty and harmony within their families (Mascolo et al., 2003, p. 402).

REUTERS / JOSE MIGUEL GOMEZ / LANDOV

JOSE LUIS PELEAZ, INC. / CORBIS

A Mother's Dilemma Infants are wonderfully curious, as this little boy demonstrates. Parents, however, must guide as well as encourage the drive toward autonomy. Notice this mother's expression as she makes sure her son does not crush or eat the flower.

Westerners expect toddlers to go through the stubborn and defiant "terrible twos"; parents elsewhere expect toddlers to be docile and obedient. Because of dozens of cues, guidelines, and norms, toddlers tend to manifest the traits their culture values.

Behaviorism

From the perspective of behaviorism, emotions and personality are molded as parents reinforce or punish a child. Behaviorists believe that parents who respond joyously to every glimmer of a grin will have children with a sunny disposition. The opposite is also true:

> Failure to bring up a happy child, a well-adjusted child—assuming bodily health— falls squarely upon the parents' shoulders. [By the time the child is 3] parents have already determined . . . [whether the child] is to grow into a happy person, whole-some and good-natured, whether he is to be a whining, complaining neurotic, an anger-driven, vindictive, over-bearing slave driver, or one whose every move in life is definitely controlled by fear.
>
> *[Watson, 1928, pp. 7, 45]*

Later behaviorists recognized that infants' behavior also has an element of **social learning,** through which infants learn from the people around them. Albert Bandura conducted a classic experiment (Bandura, 1977) in which young children were frus-trated by being told they could not play with some attractive toys. They were then left alone with a mallet and a rubber toy clown (Bobo) after seeing an adult hit the toy. Both boys and girls pounded and kicked Bobo as the adult had done, indicating that they had learned from observation.

Since that experiment, developmentalists have demonstrated that social learning occurs throughout life (Morris et al., 2007; Nielsen, 2006). In many families, toddlers

social learning
The acquisition of behavior patterns by observing the behavior of others.

Hammering Bobo These images are stills from the film of Bandura's original study of social learning, in which frus-trated 4-year-olds imitated the behavior they had observed an adult perform. The children used the same weapon as the adult, with the same intent— whether that involved hitting the doll with a hammer, shooting it with a toy gun, or throwing a large ball at it.

COPYRIGHT ALBERT BANDURA

express emotions in various ways—from giggling to cursing—just as their parents or older siblings do.

A boy might develop a hot temper if his father's outbursts seem to win his mother's respect; a girl might be coy, or passive-aggressive, if that is what she has seen. These examples are deliberately sexist: Social learning theories hold that gender roles, in particular, are learned.

Social learning theorists acknowledge inborn temperament but stress that children follow the role models they see. Shyness may be inborn, for instance, but parents who model social interaction, greeting their many friends warmly, will help a withdrawn child become more outgoing (Rubin et al., 2009). Often parents unwittingly encourage certain traits in their children by how they respond to their infants. This is evident in the effects of proximal versus distal parenting, explained below.

proximal parenting
Caregiving practices that involve being physically close to the baby, with frequent holding and touching.

distal parenting
Caregiving practices that involve remaining distant from the baby, providing toys, food, and face-to-face communication with minimal holding and touching.

OPPOSING PERSPECTIVES

Proximal and Distal Parenting

Should parents carry infants most of the time, or will that spoil them? Should babies have many toys, or will that make them too materialistic?

These questions refer to the distinction between **proximal parenting** (being physically close to a baby, often holding and touching) and **distal parenting** (keeping some distance—providing toys, feeding by putting finger food within reach, talking face-to-face instead of communicating by touch). Caregivers tend to behave in proximal or distal ways very early, when infants are only 2 months old (Kärtner et al., 2010).

The research finds notable cultural differences, not only with newborns but also with older children (Keller et al., 2010). For example, a longitudinal study comparing child-rearing methods of the Nso people of Cameroon with those of Greeks in Athens found marked differences in proximal and distal parenting (H. Keller et al., 2004). In that study, 78 mothers were videotaped as they played with their 3-month-olds. Coders (who did not know the study's hypothesis) counted frequency of proximal play (e.g., carrying, swinging, caressing, exercising the child's body) and distal play (e.g., face-to-face talking) (see Table 4.3). The Nso mothers were proximal, holding their babies all the time and almost never

using toys or bottles. The Greek mothers were relatively distal, using objects almost half the time.

The researchers hypothesized that proximal parenting would result in toddlers who were less self-aware but more compliant—traits needed in an interdependent and cooperative society such as that of rural Cameroon. By contrast, distal parenting might produce children who were self-aware but less obedient, as needed when a culture values independence and self-reliance.

The predictions were accurate. At 18 months, these same infants were tested on self-awareness (via the mirror/rouge test) and obedience to their parents. The African toddlers (proximal) didn't recognize themselves in the mirror but were compliant; the opposite was true of the Greek toddlers (distal).

Replicating their own work, these researchers studied a dozen mother–infant pairs in Costa Rica. In that Central American nation, caregiver–infant distance was midway between the Nso and the Greeks, as was later toddler behavior (H. Keller et al., 2004).

The researchers then reanalyzed all their data, child by child. They found that, even apart from culture, proximal or distal play at 3 months was highly predictive: Greek mothers who, unlike most of their peers, were proximal parents had more obedient toddlers. Further research in several other nations confirmed the consequences of these two forms of parenting (Borke et al., 2007; Kärtner et al., 2011).

TABLE 4.3 Infants in Rural Cameroon and Urban Greece

	Cameroon	Athens, Greece
I. Infant–mother play at 3 months		
Percent of time held by mother	100%	31%
Percent of time playing with objects	3%	40%
II. Toddler behavior at 18 months		
Self-recognition	3%	68%
Immediate compliance with request	72%	2%

Source: Adapted from Keller et al., 2004.

✦ **ESPECIALLY FOR Statisticians** Note the sizes of the samples: 78 mother–infant pairs in Cameroon and Greece and 12 pairs in Costa Rica. Are these samples large enough to draw conclusions? (see answer, page 154) ➙

TOM PRETTYMAN / PHOTO EDIT

DAWN DELANEY / LONELY PLANET / GETTY IMAGES

Not Just a Snapshot Proximal and distal patterns are pervasive, affecting every moment of infant care. How often do you think the infant in the stroller is strapped to her mother's body, and how often does the infant on the right travel without seeing who is pushing her? Probably never.

✦ **ESPECIALLY FOR Pediatricians** A mother complains that her child refuses to stay in the car seat, spits out disliked foods, and almost never does what she says. How should you respond? (see response, page 155) ➙

For every aspect of infant care, cultural attitudes have some impact, but for the proximal/distal response, culture is especially pivotal. Is independence valued over dependence? Is autonomy more important than compliance? Cultures differ in their answers. If a mother asks her toddler to put away some toys that he or she did not use (a test sometimes used to measure compliance), and the toddler puts them away without protest, is that wonderful or disturbing?

Answers may depend on whether rebellious independence or law-abiding morality is the quality most needed in a particular society. If you have an answer that you believe is best, you can figure out whether to pick up your baby (proximal) or give her a pacifier (distal) when she cries and whether to breast-feed her (proximal) until she is 2 or switch her to bottle-feeding as soon as possible (distal). Of course, as detailed in Appendix A, many other factors influence whether or not a woman will breast-feed in the United States; but worldwide, those cultures that are proximal tend also to be those where breast-feeding continues for months and even years.

Cognitive Theory

Cognitive theory holds that thoughts and values determine a person's perspective. Early experiences are important because beliefs, perceptions, and memories make them so, not because they are buried in the unconscious (psychoanalytic theory) or burned into the brain's patterns (behaviorism).

According to many cognitive theorists, early experiences help infants develop a **working model,** a set of assumptions that become a frame of reference for later life (Johnson et al., 2010). It is a "model" because early relationships form a prototype, or blueprint, for later interactions; it is "working" because, although it is used, it is not necessarily fixed or final.

Ideally, infants develop "a working model of the self as valued, loved, and competent" and "a working model of parents as emotionally available, loving, sensitive and supportive" (Harter, 2006, p. 519). However, reality does not always conform to this ideal. A 1-year-old girl might develop a model, based on her parents' inconsistent responses to her, that people are unpredictable. She will continue to apply that model to everyone: Her childhood friendships will be insecure and her adult relationships will be guarded.

To use Piaget's terminology, such a girl develops a cognitive *schema* to organize her perceptions. A schema is an organized conception of something. Usually, schemas are not as comprehensive as the example above, the assumption that people are not

working model
In cognitive theory, a set of assumptions that the individual uses to organize perceptions and experiences. For example, a person might assume that other people are trustworthy and be surprised by an incident that this working model of human behavior was erroneous.

RESPONSE FOR Nursing Mothers
(from page 150) Freud thought so, but there is no experimental evidence that weaning, even when ill timed, has such dire long-term effects. ●

BILL BACHMANN / DANITADELIMONT.COM

Stranger Danger Some parents teach their children to be respectful of any adult; others teach them to fear any stranger. No matter what their culture or parents say, each of these two sisters in Nepal reacts according to her inborn temperament.

RESPONSE FOR Statisticians (from page 152) Probably not. These studies are reported here because the results were dramatic (see Table 4.3) and because the two studies pointed in the same direction. Nevertheless, replication by other researchers is needed. ●

to be trusted. A more likely schema is object permanence, as explained in Chapter 3—that an object no longer visible nonetheless continues to exist somewhere. Working models are similar to schemas, in that they are comprised of thoughts and assumptions, but they are more elaborate and more difficult to change.

The crucial idea, according to cognitive theory, is that an infant's early experiences themselves are not necessarily pivotal, but the interpretation of those experiences is (Olson & Dweck, 2009). Children may misinterpret their experiences, or parents may offer inaccurate explanations, and these form ideas that affect later thinking and behavior.

In this way, working models formed in childhood echo lifelong. A hopeful message from cognitive theory is that people can rethink and reorganize their thoughts, developing new models. Our mistrustful girl might marry a faithful and loving man and gradually develop a new working model.

Humanism

Remember from Chapter 1 that Maslow described a hierarchy of needs (physiological, safety/security, love/belonging, success/esteem, and self-actualization), with the lower levels being prerequisites for higher ones. Infants begin at the first level: Their emotions serve to ensure that physiological needs are met. That's why babies cry when they are hungry or hurt, as adults usually do not. Basic survival needs must be satisfied to enable the person to reach higher levels (Silton et al., 2011).

Humanism reminds us that caregivers also have needs, and their needs influence how they respond to infants. Self-actualized people are no longer needy for themselves, so they can nurture an infant well. But most young parents are at level 3 or 4, seeking love or respect. They may be troubled by "ghosts in the nursery" (first mentioned in Chapter 3 in the discussion of infant sleep). Their own babyhood experiences often include unmet needs, and that interferes with their ability to nurture.

For example, while all experts endorse breast-feeding as the best way to meet infants' physiological needs, many mothers quit breast-feeding after trying for a few days, and many fathers feel excluded if the mother spends most of her time and attention on nursing. This may puzzle the experts but not the humanist theorists, who realize that a parent's needs may clash with the infant's needs (Mulder & Johnson, 2010).

For example, one mother of a 1-year-old said:

> My son couldn't latch so I was pumping and my breasts were massive and I'm a pretty small woman with big breasts and they were enormous during pregnancy. It has always been a sore spot for me and I've never loved my breasts. And that has been hard for me in not feeling good about myself. And I stopped pumping in January and slowly they are going back and I'm beginning to feel some confidence again and that definitely helps. Because I felt overweight, your boobs are not your own and you are exhausted and your body is strange it's just really hard to want to share that with someone. They think you are beautiful, they love it and love you the way you are but it is not necessarily what you feel.
>
> *[quoted in Shapiro, 2011, p. 18]*

This woman's need for self-respect was overwhelming, causing her to stop breast-feeding in order to feel some confidence about her shape. Her husband's love of her body, or her son's need for breast-feeding, did not help, because she was not past level 3 (love and belonging). Her "strange" body attacked her self-esteem (level 4).

Her personal needs may have been unmet since puberty (she says, "I've never loved my breasts"). She blames her husband for not understanding her feelings and her son who "couldn't latch." Since all babies learn to latch with time and help, this woman's saying that her son couldn't latch suggests something amiss in synchrony and attachment—unmet baby needs because of unmet mother needs.

By contrast, some parents understand their baby's need for safety and security (level 2) even if they themselves are far beyond that stage. Kevin is an example.

> Kevin is a very active, outgoing person who loves to try new things. Today he takes his 11-month-old daughter, Tyra, to the park for the first time. Tyra is playing alone in the sandbox, when a group of toddlers joins her. At first, Tyra smiles and eagerly watches them play. But as the toddlers become more active and noisy, Tyra's smiles turn quickly to tears. She . . . reaches for Kevin, who picks her up and comforts her. But then Kevin goes a step further. After Tyra calms down, Kevin gently encourages her to play near the other children. He sits at her side, talking and playing with her. Soon Tyra is slowly creeping closer to the group of toddlers, curiously watching their moves.
>
> *[Lerner & Dombro, 2004, p. 42]*

Evolutionary Theory

Remember that evolutionary theory stresses two needs: survival and reproduction. Humans are extraordinarily adept at those tasks. We have much bigger brains, proportionally, than any other creature, which allows us to use our genetic diversity to aid our own survival and that of our children, in every climate and on every continent.

It takes about 20 years of maturation before the human brain is fully functioning. A child must be nourished, protected, and taught by adults for much longer than offspring of any other species. Infant and parent emotional development help ensure such lengthy protection (Hrdy, 2009).

EMOTIONS FOR SURVIVAL Infant emotions are part of the evolutionary mandate. All the emotions described in the first part of this chapter—from the hunger cry to the temper tantrum—can be seen from this perspective (Konner, 2010).

For example, newborns are extraordinarily dependent, unable to walk or talk or even sit up and feed themselves for months after birth. They must attract adult devotion—and they do. That first smile, the sound of infant laughter, and their role in synchrony are all powerfully attractive to adults—especially to parents.

Adults call their hairless, chinless, round-faced, small-limbed creatures "cute," "handsome," "beautiful," "adorable," and willingly spend hours carrying, feeding, changing, and cleaning them. Adaptation is evident: In some cultures, fathers are equal partners in child care, whereas in others they are disengaged. Men have the genetic potential to be caregivers, but circumstances dictate what they do.

If humans were motivated merely by objective reward, caregiving would make no sense, but many adults think that parenting is worth every sacrifice. Children are costly, from birth on. Food (even breast milk requires the mother to eat more), diapers, clothes, furniture, medical bills, toys, and child care (whether paid or unpaid) are just a start. Before a child becomes financially independent, many parents have paid for a bigger house, for education, for vacations, and much more. These are just the financial costs; the emotional costs are even greater.

Reproductive nurturance depends on years of self-sacrificing investment, and humans have evolved to provide it. Hormones—specifically, oxytocin—do much more than trigger birth and promote breast-feeding; they increase the impulse to bond with others, especially one's children. Both men and women have oxytocin in their blood and saliva, and this hormone continues to be produced as needed for caregiving (Feldman et al., 2011).

Evolutionary theory holds that, over human history, proximity-seeking and contact-maintaining fostered species survival by keeping toddlers near their caregivers and keeping caregivers vigilant. Infants fuss at the still face, fear separation, and laugh

RESPONSE FOR Pediatricians (from page 153) Consider the origins of the misbehavior—probably a combination of the child's inborn temperament and the mother's distal parenting. That could contribute to the child's being stubborn and independent. Acceptance is more warranted than anger. Perhaps this mother is expressing hostility toward the child—a sign that intervention may be needed. Find out. ●

allocare
Literally, "other-care"; the care of children by people other than the biological parents.

Same Situation, Far Apart: Safe-keeping Historically, grandmothers were sometimes crucial for child survival. Now even though medical care has reduced child mortality, grandmothers still do their part to keep children safe, as shown by these two—in the eastern United States *(top)* and western China *(bottom)*.

when adults play with them, all to sustain parent–child interdependence. We inherited these emotional reactions from our great-great- . . . grandparents, who would have died without them.

As explained in Chapter 2, human bonding is unlike that of goats and sheep—a mother does not need to nuzzle her newborn immediately to bond with him or her. Bonding, and then synchrony, and then attachment are greater and more durable for humans than for other animals. Toddlers attend to nuances of adult expressions (social referencing) to establish the relationships between self and others.

The dependence is mutual. It is almost impossible not to dote on a baby who grins at the sight of your face and pays attention when you frown. Thus, it is part of human nature for babies to evoke caregiving and for caregivers to attend to babies. That's why most infants live long enough to become parents themselves.

ALLOCARE Evolutionary social scientists note that if mothers were the exclusive caregivers of each child until children were adults, able to provide for themselves and their own children, a given woman could rear only one or two offspring—not enough for the species to survive. Instead, the interval between births for humans is two to four years (much less than the interval for our nearest primate relative, the chimpanzee). The reason humans can do this—and essential for species survival—is **allocare,** the care of children by people other than the biological parents (Hrdy, 2009).

Compared with many other species, human mothers are surprisingly willing to let other people help with child care, and other people are eager to do so (Kachel et al., 2011). Throughout the centuries, the particular person to provide allocare has varied by culture and ecological conditions. Evolutionary theorists believe that the flexibility of allocare is necessary, since someone has to do it, and infants and mothers need to adapt to the specifics of their situation.

Often fathers helped, but not always: Some men were far away, fighting, or hunting, or seeking work; some had several wives and a dozen or more children. In those situations, other women (daughters, grandmothers, sisters, friends) and sometimes other men provided allocare.

In several cultures, infants were breast-fed by several lactating women, especially in the beginning, before the mother's milk became plentiful. In some cultures, grandmothers provide extensive care, as is true today in many families, especially in developing nations. All this can be explained by evolutionary theory. Of course, as you just read, other theories are plausible as well.

Infant Day Care

Cultural variations in allocare are vast, and each theory can be used to justify or criticize certain variations. This makes infant day care a controversial topic, and no theory directly endorses any particular position. Nonetheless, theories are made to be useful, so we include in this discussion some speculation as to which theory might favor which practices.

It is estimated that about 134 million babies will be born each year from 2010 to 2021 (United Nations, 2011). Most newborns will be cared for primarily or exclusively by their mothers, with allocare increasing from ages 1 to 20. Some infants, even in the first months of life, are cared for by relatives, typically fathers in the United States and grandmothers in most other nations (Leach, 2009). Worldwide,

FABRICE TROMBERT PHOTOGRAPHY INC. / GETTY IMAGES

TOM SALYER

only about 15 percent of infants (birth to age 2) receive daily care from a nonrelative who is paid and trained to provide it.

Statistics on the precise incidence and consequences of various forms of infant care in each nation are difficult to find or interpret because "informal in-family arrangements speak to the ingenuity of parents trying to cope but bedevil child care statistics" (Leach, 2009, p. 44). Furthermore, patterns of infant care are part of a complex web of child rearing: It is difficult to connect any one particular pattern with one particular outcome.

Many people believe that their own family's or culture's practices are best and that other patterns harm either the infant or the mother. This is another example of the difference-equals-deficit error. Without evidence, assumptions flourish.

INTERNATIONAL COMPARISONS Center-based care is common in France, Israel, China, and Sweden, where it is heavily subsidized by the governments, and scarce in South Asia, Africa, and Latin America, where it is not. North America is in between these extremes, but variation from place to place is apparent.

Involvement of relatives in infant care also varies. Worldwide, fathers are increasingly involved in baby care. Some nations provide paid leave at birth for fathers as well as mothers; several nations provide paid family leave that can be taken by either parent or shared between them; some nations mandate that a job be held for a woman who takes an unpaid maternity leave; most developing nations provide limited paid leave for mothers (India does not allow women to be employed in the first six weeks after birth) but no paid leave for fathers (see Figure 4.3).

Note that these are policies, not always practices. In many nations, parents have intense, unregulated employment and take off only a day or two for birth. Also note that underlying such policies are theories about what is best for infants. When nations mandate paid leave, the belief is that infants need maternal care and that employers should encourage that to occur.

In the United States, marked variations are apparent by state and by employer (some more generous than the law requires). Federal policy mandates that a job be held for a parent who takes unpaid leave of up to 12 weeks unless the company has fewer than 50 employees. Almost no company pays for paternal leave, with one exception: The U.S. military allows 10 days of paid leave for fathers.

In the United States, only 20 percent of infants are cared for *exclusively* by their mothers (no other relatives or babysitters) throughout their first year. This is in contrast to Canada, which is similar in ethnic diversity but has lower rates of maternal employment: 70 percent of Canadian infants are cared for only by their mothers (Côté et al., 2008). Obviously, these differences are affected by culture more than by universal psychosocial needs of babies and parents, and changes occur through economic and political pressures—which means that data on infant care in 2014 will differ from the numbers reported here.

One might hope that centuries of maternal, paternal, and allocare would provide clear conclusions about the best practices. Unfortunately, the evidence is mixed. In most nations and centuries, infants were more likely to survive if their grandmothers

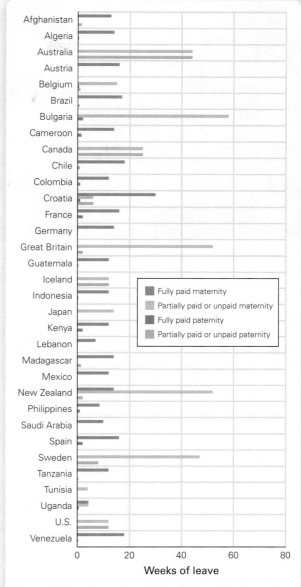

Source: ILO Database on Conditions of Work and Employment Laws, 2011.

Note: In some cases, leave can be shared between parents or other family members.

FIGURE 4.3 A Changing World No one was offered maternity leave a century ago because the only jobs that mothers had were unregulated ones. Now, virtually every nation has a maternity leave policy, revised every decade or so. Note, however, that as of 2012 only Australia, Iceland, and Canada offered policies reflecting gender equality. That may be the next innovation in many nations.

● **UNDERSTANDING THE NUMBERS**
How would you express the odds of a U.S. infant receiving nonmaternal care?

Answer A calculation of odds is a comparison. Compared with Canadian infants, the odds are 80/30 = 2.7.

Same Situation, Far Apart: Instead of Mothers Casper, Wyoming *(left),* is on the opposite side of the earth from Dhaka, Bangladesh *(right),* but day care is needed in both places, as shown here.

OBSERVATION QUIZ
What three cultural differences do you see? (see answer, page 160) →

family day care
Child care that includes several children of various ages and usually occurs in the home of a woman who is paid to provide it.

center day care
Child care that occurs in a place especially designed for the purpose, where several paid adults care for many children. Usually, the children are grouped by age, the day-care center is licensed, and providers are trained and certified in child development.

were nearby, especially during the time immediately after weaning (Sear & Mace, 2008). This is thought to have been because the grandmothers provided essential nourishment and protection.

However, in at least one community (northern Germany, 1720–1874), having a living grandmother, especially a paternal grandmother, had a negative effect on infant survival (Beise & Voland, 2002). Speculation is that mothers-in-law increased the stress on their pregnant daughters-in-law and diminished some of the expectant fathers' protective devotion, which led to more frequent preterm births.

TYPES OF NONMATERNAL CARE In the twenty-first century, most mothers prefer that their baby's father become the chief alternate caregiver. This is probably in keeping with psychoanalytic, behaviorist, and cognitive theory, all of which focus on the parents. In the United States, many couples coordinate their work schedules so one or the other parent is always present—an arrangement that may help the infant and the budget but not the romantic relationship, as parents have much less time together (Meteyer & Perry-Jenkins, 2010). Grandmothers, too, are often caregivers in the first year, less so as children become more mobile and social (Leach, 2009).

When parents turn to paid nonrelatives, wealthier families may hire someone to come to the home, but most parents find **family day care,** in which one caregiver looks after a small group of young children in her (almost never his) home. The quality of family day care varies; sometimes it is excellent, but often infants and toddlers get less attention than 3- and 4-year-olds (Kryzer et al., 2007).

As you know, providing physical care and ensuring safety are only the beginning of quality caretaking, although those factors tend to be the focus when parents seek allocare. Evolutionary theory notes that the survival of infants was far from guaranteed in earlier centuries, so parents still focus on safety when they seek nonmaternal care, perhaps to the detriment of other aspects of good care. Ideally, each baby experiences many hours each day of personalized social interaction. Finding a family-day-care provider who offers excellent emotional care is difficult.

A better option may be **center day care,** in which licensed and specially educated adults care for several infants in a place expressly designed for them. Most centers separate infants from older children, a good strategy for ensuring that everyone's developmental needs are met, as humanists would prioritize. Preschoolers are not yet able to ignore their own needs when infants need care.

Ideally, an infant day-care center has ample safe space, appropriate equipment, and trained providers whose own needs are sufficiently satisfied that they devote themselves to their charges (humanism again).

There should be two adults for a group of five or fewer infants (de Schipper et al., 2006; NAEYC, 2012) (see Table 4.4). Such a setting advances both cognitive and social skills: Babies are intrigued by other babies, and they learn from them.

No matter what form of care is chosen, or what theory is endorsed, responsive, individualized care with stable caregivers seems best (Morrissey, 2009). Caregiver change is especially problematic for infants because each simple gesture or sound that a baby makes not only merits an encouraging response but also requires interpretation by someone who knows that particular baby well. "Baba" could mean bottle, baby, blanket, banana, or some other word that does not even begin with *b*. This example is an easy one, relevant for some 12-month-olds but not for younger infants. If you have any doubts, remember the importance of synchrony and the troubled lives of the Romanian orphans who received excellent care after adoption but not in their first year.

> **TABLE 4.4 High-Quality Day Care**
>
> High-quality day care during infancy has five essential characteristics:
>
> 1. *Adequate attention to each infant.* A small group of infants (no more than five) needs two reliable, familiar, loving caregivers. Continuity of care is crucial.
> 2. *Encouragement of language and sensorimotor development.* Infants need language—songs, conversations, and positive talk—and easily manipulated toys.
> 3. *Attention to health and safety.* Cleanliness routines (e.g., handwashing), accident prevention (e.g., no small objects), and safe areas to explore are essential.
> 4. *Professional caregivers.* Caregivers should have experience and degrees/certificates in early-childhood education. Turnover should be low, morale high, and enthusiasm evident.
> 5. *Warm and responsive caregivers.* Providers should engage the children in active play and guide them in problem solving. Quiet, obedient children may indicate unresponsive care.

THE EFFECTS OF INFANT DAY CARE The evidence is overwhelming that good preschool education (discussed in Chapter 5) benefits children, especially in cognition. However, when it comes to infants, "disagreements about the wisdom (indeed, the morality) of nonmaternal child care for the very young remain" (NICHD Early Child Care Research Network, 2005, p. xiv). A major problem is that quality varies a great deal. Some caregivers with no training look after many infants, and the result is inadequate care.

Some babies seem far more affected than others by the quality of their care (Phillips et al., 2011; Pluess & Belsky, 2009). The main concern is that some infants with extensive nonmaternal care will become more aggressive later on (Jacob, 2009).

As one review explained: "This evidence now indicates that early nonparental care environments sometimes pose risks to young children and sometimes confer benefits" (Phillips et al., 2011). Differential sensitivity is evident: For genetic and familial reasons, the choice about how best to provide care for an infant varies from case to case.

Consider three examples of this "evidence" in detail.

First, in England, one study found that infants who were not exclusively in their mothers' care were less advanced emotionally at age 5 (Fergusson et al., 2008). Most of those infants were cared for by grandmothers, especially when the mothers were young and poor. As you know from your understanding of correlation, however, low SES itself is associated with several variables, in addition to nonmaternal care, that might account for the delayed emotional development reported in this study.

In this case, the relevant variables may include the grandmothers' low SES, the mothers' immaturity, and the households' financial stress. Any of those could be the reason for the 5-year-olds' emotional immaturity. Or their behavior could be the direct result of nonmaternal infant care; the data show us correlation, not cause.

Second, a large study in Canada found that infant girls seemed to develop equally well in various care arrangements. However, boys were more complex. Boys from high-income families with infant allocare fared less well than did similar boys in exclusive maternal care: By age 4, they were slightly more assertive or aggressive and had more emotional problems (e.g., a teacher might note that a boy "seems unhappy").

ANSWER TO **OBSERVATION QUIZ**
(from page 158) The Bangladeshi children are dressed alike, are the same
age, and are all seated around toy
balls in a net—there's not a book in
sight, unlike the Wyoming setting. ●

✦ **ESPECIALLY FOR Day-Care
Providers** A mother who brings her
child to you for day care says that she
knows she is harming her baby, but
economic necessity compels her to
work. What do you say? (see response,
page 161) →

The opposite was true for boys from low-income families: On average, they ben-efited from nonmaternal care in infancy, again according to teacher reports. The re-searchers insist that no policy implications can be derived from this study, partly because care varied so much in quality, location, and provider (Côté et al., 2008). Research in the United States on low-income families also finds that center care is beneficial for low-SES families (Peng & Robins, 2010).

The third study may be the most solid research, in that it is longitudinal and began with a large and diverse sample. The Early Child Care Network of the National In-stitute of Child Health and Human Development (NICHD) has followed the devel-opment of more than 1,300 children from birth to age 11. Researchers found many cognitive benefits of early day care, especially in language development. Attachment to mothers seemed as secure for babies in day care as for babies with exclusive ma-ternal care. Some babies in infant care were also securely attached to their caregivers, a good sign.

Like other, smaller studies, the NICHD research confirms that the mother–child relationship is pivotal. The NICHD study and the consensus of many researchers in the United States is that infant day care, even for 40 hours a week before age 1, has much less influence on child development than does the warmth of the mother–infant relationship (Phillips et al., 2011).

However, the NICHD study also found that infant day care is detrimental when the mother is insensitive *and* the infant spends more than 20 hours a week in a poor-quality program (McCartney et al., 2010). In particular, boys who experienced extensive nonmaternal care became more quarrelsome as they matured, having more conflicts with their teachers than did the girls or other boys with a different mix of maternal traits and day-care experiences.

What can be concluded from these three studies? There are no simple answers. Each study is complex: International variations, uncertainty about the quality and extent of care (both at home and elsewhere), and the fact that choices are not ran-dom (e.g., maternal employment—and hence allocare—is more likely in families with educated parents but less likely if the parents are married and financially secure) make general conclusions elusive.

Family income, culture, religion, and education affect choice of care, and those same variables affect child development. The fact that boys are more affected than girls may indicate something about biological sex, or that difficult boys are more often placed in day care, or that cultures encourage traits in boys that are discouraged in girls. Indeed, not every study finds that boys are more affected—again, there are many possible reasons to explain a lack of gender differences, just as there are many reasons to explain gender differences.

MATERNAL EMPLOYMENT IN INFANCY Closely tied to the issue of infant day care is the issue of maternal employment. Once it was assumed that mothers should stay home with their children. That is what was recommended by psychoanalytic and behaviorist theory. That assumption has been challenged, partly by the idea that mothers have needs that merit attention (humanism) and by historical evidence that exclusive maternal care was far from typical over the centuries (evolutionary theory).

A summary of the longitudinal outcomes of nonmaternal infant care finds "exter-nalizing behavior is predicted from a constellation of variables in multiple contexts . . . and no study has found that children of employed mothers develop serious emo-tional or other problems *solely* because their mothers are working outside the home" (McCartney et al., 2010, pp. 1, 16).

Indeed, research from the United States indicates that children generally benefit if their mothers are employed (Goldberg et al., 2008). The most likely reasons are that maternal income reduces parental depression and increases family wealth, both of which correlate with happier and more successful children.

A time-use study found that mothers who worked full time outside the home spent almost as much time playing with their babies (14½ hours a week) as did mothers with no outside jobs (16 hours a week) (Huston & Aronson, 2005). To make more time for their babies, they spent half as much time on housework, less time with their husbands, and almost no time on leisure. The study concludes:

> There was no evidence that mothers' time at work interfered with the quality of their relationship with their infants, the quality of the home environment, or children's development. In fact, the results suggest the opposite. Mothers who spent more time at work provided slightly higher quality home environments.
>
> *[Huston & Aronson, 2005, p. 479]*

That is a comforting conclusion for employed mothers, but, again, other interpretations are possible. It may be that the women who were able to find worthwhile work were more capable of providing a "quality home environment" than the women who were unemployed. Furthermore, the fact that they spent less time with their husbands does not bode well for the child's future.

Marital relationships benefit from shared activities, so couples who rarely spend time together are likely to be less dedicated to each other. This may be particularly problematic as regards the men because husbands who are devoted to their wives are more likely to be active and involved fathers. Father involvement correlates with child happiness and success. The opposite is also true.

As you see, every study reflects many variables, just as every theory has a different perspective on infant care. Given that, and given divergent cultural assumptions, it is not surprising that researchers find mixed evidence on infant care and caregivers. Many factors are relevant: infant sex and temperament, family income and education, and especially the quality of care at home and elsewhere.

Thus, as with many topics in child development, questions remain. What is definite is that each infant needs personal responsiveness from at least one person—ideally from both mother and father, but another relative or even a nonrelative can suffice. Someone should be a partner in the synchrony duet, a base for secure attachment, and a social reference who encourages exploration. If the baby has that, infant emotions and experiences—cries and laughter, fears and joys—will ensure that development goes well.

KEYPoints

- All theories recognize that infant care is crucial: Psychosocial development depends on it.
- Psychoanalytic theory stresses early caregiving routines, with Freud and Erikson differing in specifics.
- Behaviorists emphasize early learning, and cognitive theories emphasize early thinking. In both cases, lifelong patterns are said to begin in infancy.
- Humanists recognize that we all—adults as well as infants—have basic needs we seek to fulfill.
- According to evolutionary theory, inborn impulses provide the interdependence that humans need for survival.
- Infant day care and maternal employment are now common in the United States, but worldwide they remain controversial.

RESPONSE FOR Day-Care Providers (from page 160): Reassure the mother that you will keep her baby safe and will help to develop the baby's mind and social skills by fostering synchrony and attachment. Also tell her that the quality of mother–infant interaction at home is more important than anything else for psychosocial development; mothers who are employed full time usually have wonderful, secure relationships with their infants. If the mother wishes, you can discuss ways to be a responsive mother. ●

SUMMARY

Emotional Development

1. Two emotions, contentment and distress, appear as soon as an infant is born. Smiles and laughter are evident in the early months. Anger emerges in reaction to restriction and frustration, between 4 and 8 months of age, and becomes stronger by age 1.

2. Reflexive fear is apparent in very young infants. Fear of something specific, including fear of strangers and of separation, appears toward the end of the first year.

3. In the second year, social awareness produces more selective fear, anger, and joy. As infants become increasingly self-aware, emotions emerge that encourage an interface between the self and others—specifically, pride, shame, and affection. Self-recognition (on the mirror/rouge test) emerges at about 18 months.

Brain and Emotions

4. Stress impedes early brain and emotional development. Some infants are particularly vulnerable to the effects of early mistreatment.

5. Temperament is a set of genetic traits whose expression is influenced by the context. Inborn temperament is linked to later personality, although plasticity is also evident.

The Development of Social Bonds

6. Sometimes by 2 months, and clearly by 6 months, infants become more responsive and social, and synchrony begins. Infants are disturbed by a still face because they expect and need social interaction.

7. Attachment, measured by the baby's reaction to the caregiver's presence, departure, and return in the Strange Situation, is crucial. Some infants seem indifferent (type A attachment—insecure-avoidant) or overly dependent (type C—insecure-resistant/ambivalent), instead of secure (type B). Disorganized attachment (type D) is the most worrisome. Secure attachment provides encouragement for infant exploration.

8. As they play, toddlers engage in social referencing, looking to other people's facial expressions and body language to detect what is safe, frightening, or fun.

9. Infants frequently use fathers as partners in synchrony, attachment figures, and social references, developing emotions and exploring their world via father caregiving.

Theories of Infant Psychosocial Development

10. According to all major theories, caregiver behavior is especially influential in the first two years. Freud stressed the mother's impact on oral and anal pleasure; Erikson emphasized trust and autonomy.

11. Behaviorists focus on learning; parents teach their babies many things, including when to be fearful or joyful. Cognitive theory holds that infants develop working models based on their experiences.

12. Humanism notes that some adults are stuck in their own unfinished development, impairing their ability to give infants the loving responses that they need.

13. Evolutionary theorists recognize that both infants and caregivers have impulses and emotions, developed over the centuries, that foster the survival of each new member of the human species.

14. The impact of nonmaternal care depends on many factors; it varies from one nation to another and probably from one child to another. Although each theory focuses on a different aspect of this controversy, all agree that quality of care (responsive, individualized) is crucial, no matter who provides that care.

KEY TERMS

allocare (p. 156)
attachment (p. 142)
autonomy versus shame and doubt (p. 150)
center day care (p. 158)
cortisol (p. 133)
disorganized attachment (p. 144)

distal parenting (p. 152)
family day care (p. 158)
insecure-avoidant attachment (p. 144)
insecure-resistant/ambivalent attachment (p. 144)
proximal parenting (p. 152)

secure attachment (p. 143)
self-awareness (p. 134)
separation anxiety (p. 133)
social learning (p. 151)
social referencing (p. 147)
social smile (p. 133)
still-face technique (p. 142)

Strange Situation (p. 144)
stranger wariness (p. 133)
synchrony (p. 141)
temperament (p. 137)
trust versus mistrust (p. 150)
working model (p. 153)

WHAT HAVE YOU LEARNED?

1. What are the first emotions to appear in infants?

2. What experiences trigger anger and sadness in infants?

3. What do 1-year-olds fear?

4. How do emotions differ between the first and second year of life?

5. How do family interactions and culture shape toddler's emotions?

6. What is known and unknown about the impact of brain maturation on emotions?

7. How are memory and emotion connected?

8. How does stress affect early brain development?

9. Why are temperamental traits more apparent in some people than others?

10. How might synchrony affect early emotional development?

11. Give examples of how infants and caregivers demonstrate proximity-seeking and contact-maintaining behaviors.

12. Describe the four types of attachment. How might each affect later life?

13. How do negative circumstances (e.g., divorce, abuse, low SES) affect attachment?

14. What can be done to improve the parent–child bond?

15. How is social referencing important in infancy?

16. How does father involvement affect infants?

17. What might happen if a person is stuck in the oral or anal stage of development?

18. How might the crisis of "trust versus mistrust" affect later life?

19. How might the crisis of "autonomy versus shame and doubt" affect later life?

20. How do behaviorists explain the development of emotions and personality?

21. Why does "working model" arise from cognitive theory instead of from the other theories?

22. According to humanism, how might caregivers' needs affect their response to an infant?

23. How does evolution explain the parent–child bond?

24. Why is allocare necessary for survival of the human species?

25. What are the advantages and disadvantages of nonmaternal infant care?

26. Compare costs and benefits of infant care by relatives versus center day care.

27. Why is it difficult to draw conclusions about infant day care?

28. What are the benefits and problems for infants if their mothers are employed?

APPLICATIONS

1. One cultural factor influencing infant development is how infants are carried from place to place. Ask four mothers whose infants were born in each of the past four decades how they transported them—front or back carriers, facing out or in, strollers or carriages, in car seats or on mother's laps, and so on. Why did they choose the mode(s) they chose? What are their opinions and yours on how that cultural practice might affect infants' development?

2. Observe synchrony for three minutes. Ideally, ask the parent of an infant under 8 months of age to play with the infant. If no infant is available, observe a pair of lovers as they converse. Note the sequence and timing of every facial expression, sound, and gesture of both partners.

3. Telephone several day-care centers to try to assess the quality of care they provide. Ask about such factors as adult/child ratio, group size, and training for caregivers of children of various ages. Is there a minimum age? Why or why not? Analyze the answers, using Table 4.4 as a guide.

>> ONLINE CONNECTIONS

To accompany your textbook, you have access to a number of online resources, including quizzes for every chapter of the book, flashcards (in English and Spanish), critical thinking questions, and case studies. For access to any of these links, go to www.worthpublishers.com/bergerinvitation2e. In addition to these free resources, you'll also find links to podcasts, video clips, diagnostic quizzing with personalized study advice, and an ebook. Some of the videos and activities available online include:

- *Attachment Behaviors in the Strange Situation*. You'll get a chance to watch—and take your best guess about attachment states—as some infants are left in the company of strangers.

- *Child Care*. A variety of videos showcase different types of early child care and different strategies for best practices.

Early Childhood

From ages 2 to 6, young children spend most of their waking hours discovering, creating, laughing, and imagining, as they acquire the skills they need. They chase each other and attempt new challenges (developing their bodies); they play with sounds, words, and ideas (developing their minds); they invent games and dramatize fantasies (learning social skills and morals)—all under the guidance of their families and communities.

These years have been called the *preschool years*, but that has become a misnomer. School no longer means sitting at desks in rows. Although still called preschoolers, many 2- to 6-year-olds are in "school," learning and playing. Indeed, they learn while playing—imagination and fantasy make these years prime time for new ideas, language advances, and informal education. Consequently, this period is best called *early childhood*, a joyful time not only for young children but also for anyone who joins them.

CHAPTER OUTLINE

EARLY CHILDHOOD
Body and Mind

WHAT WILL YOU KNOW?

- Why do some young children get too fat?
- Should left-handed toddlers become right-handed adults?
- How should adults answer when children ask, "Why?"
- Does it confuse young children if they hear two or more languages?
- What do children learn in preschool?

Asa, not yet 3 feet tall, held a large rubber ball. He said I should play basketball with him.

"We can't play basketball; we don't have a hoop," I told him.

"We can imagine a hoop," he answered, throwing up the ball.

"I got it in," he said happily. "You try."

I did. "You got it in, too," he announced, and did a little dance.

Soon I was tired, and sat down.

"I want to sit and think my thoughts," I told him.

"Get up," he urged. "You can play basketball and think your thoughts."

I laughed and stood up to play. ●

- -

ASA IS TYPICAL. Imagination comes easily to him, and he aspires to the skills of older, taller people in his culture. He thinks by doing, and his vocabulary is impressive, but he does not yet understand that my feelings are not identical to his, that I would rather sit than throw imaginary baskets. He does know, however, that I am likely to respond to his requests.

This chapter describes those characteristics of the young child—imagination, motor skills, active learning, vocabulary. I hope it also conveys the joy that adults can find if they understand early childhood, and then get up to play.

Body Changes

In early childhood, as in infancy, the body and brain develop according to powerful epigenetic forces. Biology works with culture as children eat, grow, and play.

Growth Patterns

Comparing a toddling, unsteady 1-year-old with a cartwheeling 6-year-old makes some differences obvious. During early childhood, children slim down as the legs and arms lengthen and fat turns to muscle. The average body mass index (BMI, the ratio of weight to height) is lower at ages 5 and 6 than at any other time of life.

KATRINA WITTKAMP / GETTY IMAGES

Size and Balance These cousins are only four years apart, but note the doubling in leg length and marked improvement in balance. The 2-year-old needs to plant both legs on the sand, while the 6-year-old cavorts on one foot.

Victory! Well, maybe not quite yet, but he's on his way. This boy participates in a British effort to combat childhood obesity; mother and son exercising in Liverpool Park is part of the solution. Harder to implement are dietary changes—many parents let children eat as much as they want.

HOWARD BARLOW / ALAMY

Gone are the toddler's protruding belly, round face, short limbs, and large head.

The center of gravity moves from the breast to the belly, enabling cartwheels, somersaults, and many other motor skills. The joys of dancing, gymnastics, and pumping a swing become possible. Toddlers often tumble, unbalanced—fortunately, they are close to the floor and thus don't have too far to fall. Kindergartners race and rarely slip.

Increases in weight and height accompany this growth (see Appendix A). Over each year of early childhood, well-nourished children gain about 4½ pounds (2 kilograms) and grow almost 3 inches (about 7 centimeters). By age 6, the average child in a developed nation:

- Weighs between 40 and 50 pounds (18 to 22 kilograms)
- Is at least 3½ feet tall (more than 100 centimeters)
- Has adultlike body proportions (legs constitute about half the total height)

Nutrition

Although they rarely starve, 2- to 6-year-olds may be at greater nutritional risk than children of any other age because they eat too much of the wrong foods. Over the centuries, families encouraged eating, protecting children against famine. Even today in the poorest nations, infant and early-childhood malnutrition contributes to one-third of all child deaths (UNICEF, 2012) and slows later growth, including growth of the brain.

OVERWEIGHT The cultural practice of encouraging children to eat has turned from protective to destructive. One example is Brazil, where 30 years ago the most common nutritional problem was undernutrition; now it is overnutrition (Monteiro et al., 2004), with low-income Brazilians particularly vulnerable (Monteiro et al., 2007). In almost every nation, 4-year-olds are more often overweight than 2-year-olds. This suggests that habits, not genetics, are the problem.

Heart disease and diabetes are becoming epidemic because overfed children often grow up to become overweight adults (Saul, 2008). An article in *The Lancet* (the leading medical journal in England) predicts that by 2020, 228 million adults worldwide will have diabetes (more in India than in any other nation) because of unhealthy eating habits acquired in childhood. The author writes, "U.S. children could become the first generation in more than a century to have shorter life spans than their parents if current trends of excessive weight and obesity continue" (Devi, 2008, p. 105).

Appetite decreases between ages 1 and 6. Young children need fewer calories per pound, and they get less exercise than their grandparents did, moving less, not more, as they grow older. They rarely help on the farm, walk to school, or play in empty lots. Instead, in developed nations, 2- to 6-year-olds are old enough to open the refrigerator and climb up to the cabinets but not wise enough to choose carrots over cake.

Nonetheless, many adults still fret, threaten, and bribe their young children to overeat ("Eat your dinner and you can have dessert"). Most parents falsely think that relatively thin children are less healthy than relatively heavy ones (Laraway et al., 2010). In fact, as long as they have enough energy to run and play, preschool children rarely lack food unless the entire family is starving.

NUTRITIONAL DEFICIENCIES Although most children consume enough calories, they do not always obtain adequate iron, zinc, and calcium. For example, North American children drink less milk than did their peers a few decades ago, which means weaker bones later on. Another problem is sugar; many customs entice children to eat sweets—in birthday cake, holiday candy, desserts, and other treats. Such food quickly fills a small stomach.

Products advertised as containing 100 percent of daily vitamin requirements are a poor substitute for a balanced, varied diet, partly because some nutrients have not yet been identified, much less listed on food labels. The lack of micronutrients is severe in poor nations, but vitamin pills and added supplements do not always help (Ramakrishnan et al., 2011).

In developed nations as well, fresh food is the best source of nutrition. Compared with the average child, those who eat more vegetables and fewer fried foods usually gain bone mass but not fat, according to a study that controlled for many factors, including ethnicity (some groups are naturally thinner than others), gender (girls have more body fat), and income (poor children have worse diets) (Wosje et al., 2010).

ALLERGIES AND OBSESSIONS Unfortunately, it is not easy to feed children well, even if they do not fill up with empty calories. Allergies are one complication. Between 3 and 8 percent of all young children have a food allergy, usually to a healthy, common food. Cow's milk, eggs, peanuts, tree nuts, soy, wheat, and shellfish are frequent culprits.

Diagnostic standards for assessing allergies vary (which explains why estimates range greatly). Treatment varies even more (Chafen et al., 2010). Some experts advocate avoiding the offending food completely: There are peanut-free schools, where even nonallergic children are not allowed to bring a peanut-butter sandwich for lunch. Others suggest building up tolerance, such as by giving babies a tiny bit of peanut butter (Reche et al., 2011).

Feeding young children a varied diet is also complicated by the strong preferences that many of them have for routines. A child might insist that bedtime be preceded by brushing teeth, reading a book, and saying prayers—or by eating a snack, sitting on the toilet, and singing a song. Whatever the routine, children are upset if someone strays from it when putting them to bed.

Similarly, some children insist on certain foods, prepared and served in a particular way. This rigidity, known as **just right,** might signify an obsessive-compulsive disorder in older children. However, a passion for continuity and sameness is normal at about age 3 (Evans & Leckman, 2006; Pietrefesa & Evans, 2007). Even familiar foods may be rejected if presented in a new way.

By age 6, rigidity fades (see Figure 5.1). As one team wrote: "Most, if not all, children exhibit normal age-dependent obsessive-compulsive behaviors [that are] usually gone by middle childhood" (March et al., 2004, p. 216). The best reaction may be patience: A young child's insistence on a particular routine, a favorite cup, or a preferred cereal can be accommodated for a year or two. Remember that adults also have routines, although they usually keep their obsessions private or can at least modify them with rational thinking (Evans & Leckman, 2006). For

"I'm not hungry. I ate with Rover."

Eat Your Veggies On their own, children do not always eat wisely.

◆ **ESPECIALLY FOR Nutritionists** A parent complains that she prepares a variety of vegetables and fruits, but her 4-year-old wants only French fries and cake. What should you advise? (see response, page 172) →

just right The tendency of children to insist on having things done in a particular way. This can include clothes, food, bedtime routines, and so on.

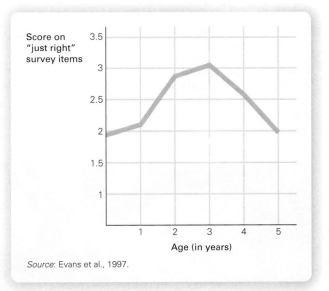

Source: Evans et al., 1997.

FIGURE 5.1 Young Children's Insistence on Routine This chart shows the average scores of children (who are rated by their parents) on a survey indicating the child's desire to have certain things—including food selection and preparation—done "just right." Such strong preferences for rigid routines tend to fade by age 6.

Same Situation, Far Apart: Eager Eaters Preschoolers generally eat whatever they get. These are the fortunate ones, enjoying chicken, grapes, celery, and whole wheat bread at a Latin American Community Center *(left)*, and sharing a fresh fruit snack with a friend *(right)*.

✦ **ESPECIALLY FOR Early-Childhood Teachers** You know that young children are upset if forced to eat a food they hate, but you have eight 3-year-olds with eight different preferences. What do you do? (see response, page 174) →

Same Situation, Far Apart: Finger Skills Children learn whatever motor skills their culture teaches. Some master chopsticks, with fingers to spare; others cut sausage with a knife and fork. Unlike these children in Japan *(left)* and Germany *(right)*, some never master either, because about one-third of adults worldwide eat directly with their hands.

children, routines need to be simple, clear, and healthy; then they can be accommodated until the child is ready to change.

ORAL HEALTH Too much sugar and too little fiber cause another common problem, tooth decay, which affects more than one-third of all young U.S. children (Brickhouse et al., 2008). Soda and punch are prime causes; even diet soda contains acid that makes decay likely (Holtzman, 2009).

Fortunately, permanent teeth replace "baby" teeth between ages 6 and 10. But severe early decay harms the formation of permanent teeth and the jaw, impairing speech. This is a particular hazard for children of young parents, who themselves tend to have poor oral health and to avoid dentists (Niji et al., 2010). All health habits are best learned early in life.

Many young and poor parents are overwhelmed with work and child care and do not realize that tooth brushing and dentist visits should begin before age 3 (Mofidi et al., 2009). Sometimes access, not ignorance, is the problem. In the United States, free dentistry is scarce: Most low-income parents "want to do better" for their children's teeth than they did for their own (Lewis et al., 2010), but they find it difficult to instill habits—especially ones that require daily effort and costly dentist visits—that were not part of their own childhood.

Improved Motor Skills

As the body gains strength, children develop motor skills, both gross motor skills (such as skipping) and fine motor skills (such as drawing). Mastery depends on maturation and practice; some 6-year-olds can ice-skate or print legibly—but most cannot (see Infographic 5, page 171).

Developing Motor Skills

Obviously, much depends on culture and practice, but maturation is also crucial, and every child can do much more with every passing year. Here are examples that might be accurate for one child from ages 2 to 6—but each child is unique.

2 YEARS
- Run without falling
- Climb out of cribs
- Walk up stairs
- Feed self with spoon
- Draw spirals

3 YEARS
- Kick and throw a ball
- Jump with both feet
- Pedal a tricycle
- Copy simple shapes
- Walk down stairs
- Climb ladders

4 YEARS
- Catch a beach ball
- Use scissors
- Hop on either foot
- Feed self with fork
- Dress self
- Copy most letters
- Pour juice without spilling
- Brush teeth

5 YEARS
- Skip and gallop in rythmn
- Clap, bang, sing in rythmn
- Copy difficult shapes and letters
- Climb trees, jump over things
- Use a knife to cut
- Tie a bow
- Throw a ball
- Wash face, comb hair

6 YEARS
- Draw and paint recognizable images
- Write simple words
- Scan a page of print
- Ride a bicycle
- Do a cartwheel
- Tie shoes
- Catch a baseball

All, however, love to move, practicing whatever skills their culture and their friends value. (Asa wanted to play basketball partly because many taller boys in his neighborhood did so. He was not troubled that he was so short or that I wanted to sit). If adults provide safe spaces, time, and playmates, skills develop. Children learn best from peers who do whatever the child is ready to try—from catching a ball to climbing a tree.

ENVIRONMENTAL HAZARDS Safety and supervision are crucial for young children—they might chase that ball into the street or climb a branch that breaks. Realistic assessment of risk is aided by the prefrontal cortex, soon to be explained, which does not fully mature until adulthood.

Less obvious dangers come from pollutants that harm young, growing brains and bodies more than older, developed ones. For that, supervision is not enough: Regulation makes a difference. For example, in India, one city of 14 million (Kolkata, formerly Calcutta) has such extensive air pollution that childhood asthma rates are soaring and lung damage is prevalent. In another Indian city (Mumbai, formerly Bombay), air pollution has been reduced and children's health improved through several measures, including an extensive system of public buses that use clean fuels (Bhattacharjee, 2008).

Research on lower animals suggests that hundreds of substances in the air, food, and water affect the brain and impede balance, finger dexterity, and motivation. The data are not conclusive, however. The administrator of environmental public health for the state of Oregon says, "We simply do not know—as scientists, as regulators, as health professionals—the health impacts of the soup of chemicals to which we expose human beings" (Shibley, quoted in T. D. Johnson, 2011).

A careful study of air pollution in western Canada (N. A. Clark et al., 2010) aimed to jumpstart the attainment of such knowledge. Some suspected pollutants, such as car and truck exhausts, were proven to be harmful to children, whereas others, such as wood smoke, were not. Much more research on pollutants in food and water, in other nations, is needed.

Same Situation, Far Apart: Could Your Child Do This? Probably. If acrobatics was your family's profession and passion, you might encourage your toddler to practice headstands, and years later, your child could balance on your head. Everywhere, young children try to do whatever their parents do.

OBSERVATION QUIZ

Was this photo taken in the United States? (see answer, page 175) →

RESPONSE FOR Nutritionists (from page 169) The nutritionally wise advice would be to offer only fruits, vegetables, and other nourishing, low-fat foods, counting on the child's eventual hunger to drive him or her to eat them. However, centuries of cultural custom make it almost impossible for parents to be wise in such cases. A physical checkup, with a blood test, may be warranted, to make sure the child is healthy. ●

A VIEW FROM SCIENCE

Eliminating Lead

Lead was targeted as a poison a century ago (Hamilton, 1914). The symptoms of *plumbism,* as lead poisoning is called, were obvious—intellectual disability, hyperactivity, and even death if the level reached 70 micrograms per deciliter of blood.

The lead industry defended the heavy metal as an additive, arguing that low levels were harmless and that parents needed to prevent their children from eating chips of lead paint (which tastes sweet). Developmental scientists noted that correlation (between lead exposure and the symptoms mentioned above) does not prove causation. Children with high levels of lead in their blood were often from low-SES families: Malnutrition, inadequate schools, family conditions, or a host of other causes not related to lead could have been the reason for their reduced IQ (Scarr, 1985).

Consequently, lead remained a major ingredient in paint (it speeds drying) and in gasoline (it raises octane) for most of the twentieth century. The fact that babies in lead-painted cribs, that preschoolers living near traffic, and that children in lead-painted homes were often intellectually impaired and hyperactive was claimed to be correlation, not causation.

Finally, chemical analysis of blood and teeth, more accurate intelligence tests, and careful longitudinal and replicated research proved that lead was indeed a poison, even at relatively low levels (Needleman et al., 1990; Needleman & Gatsonis, 1990). The United States banned the use of lead in paint (in 1978) and automobile fuel (in 1996). Thankfully, children now have much lower blood lead levels than did children in those earlier decades. Pediatricians have set

JEFFREY L. ROTMAN / CORBIS

the acceptable level, formerly 40 micrograms per deciliter of blood, at 10 micrograms or fewer. The U.S. Centers for Disease Control and Prevention declares levels above 10 "unsafe."

Although it is tragic that it took so long for science to recognize and set policy to protect against the danger of lead, it is heartening that children today rarely have high lead levels in their blood, bodies, or brains. In the United States in 1997, 8 percent of children under age 6 had higher than 10 micrograms of lead per deciliter of blood. In 2010, less than 1 percent had levels that high (see Figure 5.2).

Yet some lead sources are still unregulated, including in drinking water and jet fuel. That may be harmless, but one team contends that even 5 micrograms per deciliter is too much (Cole & Winsler, 2010), especially in a young child whose brain is rapidly developing.

In some states (e.g., Colorado and Wyoming), average lead levels for young children are close to zero. In other states that once had extensive lead-based manufacturing, young children are still at risk, probably because of lead in the soil and dust. In 2010, Pennsylvania documented 509 children under age 6 with more than 20 micrograms per deciliter in their blood; Ohio had 417; Michigan had 254 (National Center for Environmental Health, 2012).

Sadly, of the 25 million U.S. children under age 6, it is probable that many more than the 1,180 children in the states just mentioned are affected. Only 15 percent of U.S. children are tested even once, and two tests are required before a high concentration is reported (National Center for Environmental Health, 2012). Repeated testing is required because if a child's lead level is high and the source (old paint, dirt, glazed dishes, home medicines) is identified and eliminated, blood lead levels fall and the brain recovers. However, scientists want to know how often the first test is above average; unfortunately, those data are unavailable.

Exposure to lead must be reduced by laws and policies, but parents can take action as well. Specifics include increasing children's consumption of calcium, wiping window ledges clean of dust, testing drinking water, replacing old window frames, and making sure no child swallows peeling chips of lead-based paint (still found in old buildings) (Dilworth-Bart & Moore, 2006; Nevin et al., 2008). Every young

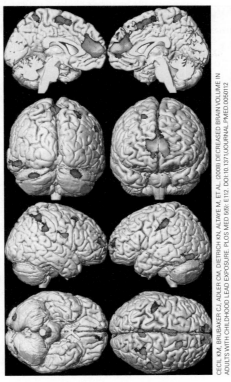

Toxic Shrinkage A composite of 157 brains shows reduced volume because of high lead levels. The red and yellow hotspots are all areas that are smaller than in a normal brain. No wonder lead-exposed children have multiple intellectual and behavioral problems.

CECIL KM, BRUBAKER CJ, ADLER CM, DIETRICH KN, ALTAYE M, ET AL. (2008) DECREASED BRAIN VOLUME IN ADULTS WITH CHILDHOOD LEAD EXPOSURE. PLOS MED 5(5): E112. DOI:10.1371/JOURNAL.PMED.0050112

child should be tested—only a pinprick of blood is needed.

Remember from Chapter 1 that scientists use data collected for other reasons to draw new conclusions. This is the case with lead. About 15 years after the sharp decline in the number of preschool children with high lead levels, the rate of violent crime committed by teenagers and young adults fell sharply. Year-by-year correlations are apparent.

A scientist comparing these two trends concluded that some teenagers commit impulsive, violent crimes because their brains were poisoned by lead when they were preschoolers. The correlation is found not only in the United States but also in every nation that has reliable data on lead and crime—Canada, Germany, Italy, Australia, New Zealand, France, and Finland (Nevin, 2007). Not everyone is convinced, but the research shows that, although correlation does not prove causation, correlations can raise hypotheses no one imagined before.

FIGURE 5.2 Got the Lead Out! Everyone merits praise—legislators for changing the ingredients in gas, parents for keeping children away from paint chips, landlords for removing lead paint, pediatricians for taking blood samples, and others. Now the children think more clearly because the adults finally acted.

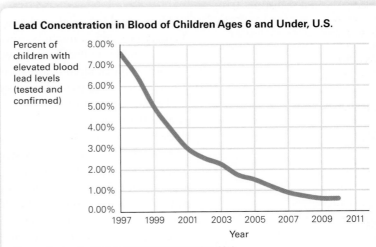

Lead Concentration in Blood of Children Ages 6 and Under, U.S.

Source: Centers for Disease Control and Prevention, 2012.

RESPONSE FOR Early-Childhood Teachers (from page 170) Remember to keep food simple and familiar. Offer every child the same food, allowing refusal but no substitutes—unless for all eight. Children do not expect school and home routines to be identical; they eventually taste whatever other children enjoy. ●

injury control/harm reduction
Practices that are aimed at anticipating, controlling, and preventing dangerous activities; these practices reflect the beliefs that accidents are not random and that injuries can be made less harmful if proper controls are in place.

primary prevention
Actions that change overall background conditions to prevent some unwanted event or circumstance, such as injury, disease, or abuse.

secondary prevention
Actions that avert harm in a high-risk situation, such as stopping a car before it hits a pedestrian or installing traffic lights at dangerous intersections.

tertiary prevention
Actions, such as immediate and effective medical treatment, that are taken after an adverse event (such as illness, injury, or abuse) occurs and that are aimed at reducing the harm or preventing disability.

AVOIDABLE INJURY Worldwide, injuries cause millions of premature deaths among adults as well as children: Not until age 40 does any specific disease overtake accidents as a cause of mortality (World Health Organization, 2010). Everywhere, 2- to 6-year-olds are at greater risk than are slightly older children. In the United States, for instance, twice as many children are seriously hurt before age 6 as after because their new mobility (described earlier) is not yet controlled by brain maturity (soon to be discussed).

Those injuries are not deliberate, but public health experts prefer not to call them "accidents." The word *accident* implies that an injury is random and unpredictable. If anyone is at fault, it's a careless parent or an accident-prone child, not public policies. This is the "accident paradigm"—as if "injuries will occur despite our best efforts" (Benjamin, 2004, p. 521).

Instead of *accident prevention,* health workers prefer the term **injury control** (or **harm reduction**). Minor injuries are inevitable during a normal, active childhood, but serious injury is unlikely if a fall is on a safety surface instead of on concrete, if a car seat protects the body in a crash, if a bicycle helmet cracks instead of a skull, if pills are in a tiny bottle with a child-resistant cap.

Less than half as many 1- to 5-year-olds in the United States were fatally injured in 2010 as in 1980, thanks to community awareness and policies regarding poisons, fires, and cars. New hazards have emerged, however. For instance, as more homes have private swimming pools, drowning has become a leading cause of unintentional death among 1- to 4-year-olds.

PREVENTION Three levels of harm reduction apply to every childhood health and safety issue:

- **Primary prevention** occurs in the macrosystem to make harm less likely, reducing the risk of sickness, injury, or death for everyone of any age. Universal immunization and reduced pollution are examples of primary prevention.
- **Secondary prevention** is more specific, averting harm in high-risk situations or for vulnerable individuals. For children who are genetically predisposed to obesity, secondary prevention might mean exclusive breast-feeding for 6 months, no soda or sweets available in the home or at school, and frequent play outside.
- **Tertiary prevention** begins after harm has occurred, limiting the damage. If a child falls and breaks an arm, a speedy ambulance and a sturdy cast are tertiary prevention.

How would these three levels apply to preventing child deaths from drowning? Tertiary prevention might be immediate mouth-to-mouth resuscitation when a submerged child is pulled from the water, secondary prevention would have parents put life jackets on children before taking them onto motor boats, and primary prevention might be laws that swimming pools be enclosed by a locked fence on all four sides.

Tertiary prevention is most dramatic; primary prevention is most effective (Cohen et al., 2010) because it begins long before any particular child, parent, or politician does something foolish.

For developmentalists, a systems approach helps pinpoint effective prevention. Thus, when a child is seriously injured, analysis seeks causes in the microsystem, exosystem, and macrosystem. If a child is hit by a car, for instance, the analysis would note the age and gender of the child (young boys are victims more often than older girls); the family structure and supervision (microsystem); the local speed limit, sidewalks, traffic lights (all exosystem); and national policies and customs regarding drivers, cars, and roadways (macrosystem).

Empirical data are sought in any scientific approach. For example, the rate of childhood poisoning has decreased since pill manufacturers implemented the use of

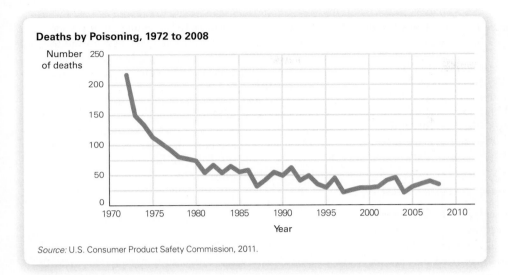

Deaths by Poisoning, 1972 to 2008

Source: U.S. Consumer Product Safety Commission, 2011.

FIGURE 5.3 Dramatic Improvement U.S. data shown here reveal that child poison deaths plummeted when safety caps on prescription medicine were mandated. However, today illegal drugs are more often fatal to young children than they were 30 years ago. Should there be laws about packaging cocaine?

bottles with safety caps—a useful statistic when anyone complains about the inconvenience (see Figure 5.3).

Some adults say that children today are overprotected, with fewer swings and jungle gyms, more safety surfaces and mandated car seats, and so on. Statistics, not anecdotes and memories ("I loved the metal monkey bars, and I am still alive"), are needed because otherwise cultural assumptions may overtake effective injury control. Without evidence, people disagree as to when protection becomes overprotection, as the following explains.

ANSWER TO **OBSERVATION QUIZ** (from page 172) No—not because of ethnicity (many U.S. citizens are of Indian descent) but because of child labor laws. This duo is part of a circus (note the rigging), and no child in North America is allowed to perform such feats for pay. ●

OPPOSING PERSPECTIVES

Freedom Versus Caution

Children need to grab, run, and explore to develop their motor skills as well as their minds, yet they also need to be prevented from falling down stairs, choking on pebbles, or running into the street—as many are inclined to do. Where is the line between independence and restraint?

Consider what one mother wrote about her flight on a U.S. airline from Australia to California:

> I traveled with my 10-month-old daughter and was absolutely and thoroughly disappointed in the treatment we received from the flight crew captain at the time. I was told or more like instructed that I was to "restrain" my child for the whole flight, which was 13 hours.
>
> I said that other people were able to move around the plane freely, why wasn't she? I was told that due to turbulence she would have to be restrained for the whole trip. On several occasions the flight crew captain would make a point of going out of his way to almost scold me for not listening to him when I would put her down to crawl around.
>
> *[Retrieved April 3, 2011, from Complaints.com]*

This same mother praised other long flights, on Asian airlines, when her child was allowed to move more freely and

Dangerous? Maybe. Is the seat belt sign on? Where are the parents?

the crew was helpful. Which culture is better? I sided with the mother and the Asians until I read this response:

Consider the laws in the U.S. regarding child safety in an automobile. Nobody thinks a child should be free to crawl around in a car. No parent thinks their rights have been violated because their child is prevented from free flight inside a car when it impacts. Why not just put the child in the bed of a truck and drive around? . . . Her child could get stepped on, slammed against a seat leg, wedged under a seat, fallen on, etc.

[Comment from Complaints.com, April 3, 2011]

Both sides in this dispute make sense, yet both cannot be right. The data prove that safety seats in cars save lives, but "impact" in planes is unlike that in a car crash. Statistical analysis is needed. Do airplane passengers step on crawling children? If so, is that controllable harm or a serious hazard?

Here is another example, from a fellow grandmother:

I took my 5-year-old granddaughter and my 3-year-old grandson to a children's play. As we settled in our seats, we chatted with friendly people on both sides of us, who were also grandparents with grandchildren. Once the curtain rose, my granddaughter was mesmerized, but my grandson became bored. He said he had to pee again [I had taken him before the show].

I told my granddaughter to come with us, but she said, "No." I asked her again, she said she was sure she would be fine without me. I thought she would cry if I made her come. So I asked the grandmother next to me to keep an eye on her, and took my grandson to the bathroom. We returned quickly; she didn't seem to notice that we ever left.

When we came home, I told my son and daughter-in-law. They were livid, forbidding me to ever take my grandchildren out of the house again. I explained to my son that I would have done the same with him, when he was little. But he sided with his wife. The most he grudgingly acknowledged was, "Maybe years ago, in your small Kentucky town, it might have been okay, but not now in Boston."

[personal communication]

These parents were terrified of abduction, and this grandmother was heartbroken. I sympathize with both generations, each with opposing perspectives. When does protection become overprotection? Is the grandmother oblivious to danger or is she modeling healthy socialization?

There are hundreds of similar dilemmas. I fed my grandson processed cheese until my daughter read the ingredients; the swings from a nearby playground were removed after a child knocked over a toddler; I know a mother who won't let her child play in the sandbox because it might contain worm eggs. Opinions on these issues are influenced by cohort, culture, and personality; the best answers for the children are not clear.

Same Situation, Far Apart: Keeping Everyone Safe Preventing child accidents requires action by adults and children. In the United States *(left)*, adults passed laws and bought safety seats—and here two sisters have taught each other how to buckle themselves in. In France *(right)*, teachers stop cars while children hold hands to cross the street—so no daydreaming or rebellious partners running off.

DAVID YOUNG-WOLFF / PHOTO EDIT

DAVID R. FRAZIER / DANITADELIMONT.COM

KEYpoints

- Young children continue to grow and develop motor skills, eating enough and playing actively.
- Hazards include eating too much of the wrong foods, as childhood obesity correlates with diabetes and other health problems later on.
- Young children's natural energy and sudden curiosity make them vulnerable to injury.
- Primary and secondary prevention of harm begin long before injury, with restrictions on lead and other pollutants (primary) and measures to reduce harm to young children (secondary).

Brain Development

As with motor skills, the brains of young children show impressive growth but are not nearly as developed as they will be later on. By age 2, most neurons are connected to other neurons and substantial pruning has occurred, as described in Chapter 3. The 2-year-old's brain is already 75 percent of adult weight; the 6-year-old's brain is 90 percent of adult weight. (The major structures of the brain are diagrammed in Figure 5.4.)

FIGURE 5.4 Connections A few of the dozens of named parts of the brain are shown here. Although each area has particular functions, the entire brain is interconnected. The processing of emotions, for example, occurs primarily in the limbic system, where many brain areas are involved, including the amygdala, hippocampus, and hypothalamus.

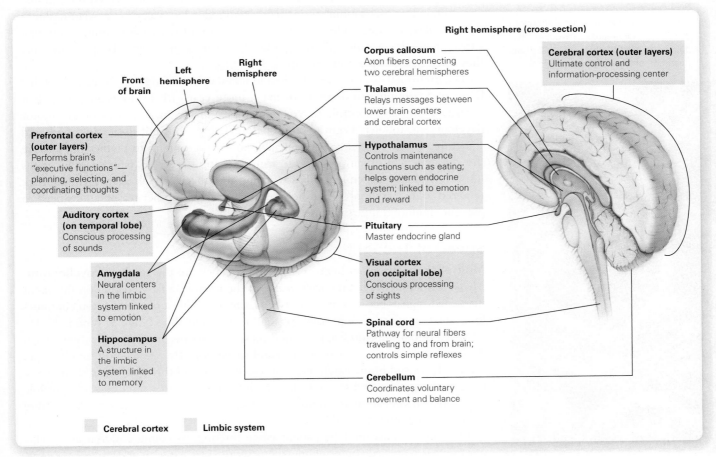

Right hemisphere (cross-section)

Corpus callosum
Axon fibers connecting two cerebral hemispheres

Cerebral cortex (outer layers)
Ultimate control and information-processing center

Thalamus
Relays messages between lower brain centers and cerebral cortex

Front of brain — **Left hemisphere** — **Right hemisphere**

Prefrontal cortex (outer layers)
Performs brain's "executive functions"—planning, selecting, and coordinating thoughts

Hypothalamus
Controls maintenance functions such as eating; helps govern endocrine system; linked to emotion and reward

Auditory cortex (on temporal lobe)
Conscious processing of sounds

Pituitary
Master endocrine gland

Amygdala
Neural centers in the limbic system linked to emotion

Visual cortex (on occipital lobe)
Conscious processing of sights

Hippocampus
A structure in the limbic system linked to memory

Spinal cord
Pathway for neural fibers traveling to and from brain; controls simple reflexes

Cerebellum
Coordinates voluntary movement and balance

Cerebral cortex   Limbic system

prefrontal cortex
The area of the cortex at the front of the brain that specializes in anticipation, planning, and impulse control.

myelination
The process by which axons become coated with myelin, a fatty substance that speeds the transmission of nerve impulses from neuron to neuron.

FIGURE 5.5 Faster and Faster
Myelination is a lifelong process. Shown here is a cross section of an axon (dark middle) coated with many layers of Schwann cells, as more and more myelin wraps around the axon throughout childhood. Age-related slowdowns in adulthood are caused by gradual disappearance of myelin layers.

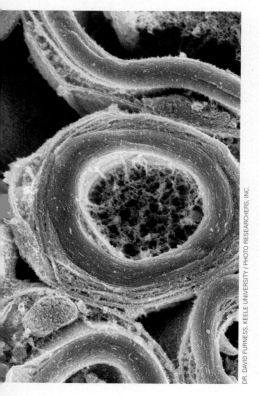

DR. DAVID FURNESS, KEELE UNIVERSITY / PHOTO RESEARCHERS, INC.

The Maturing Cortex

Since most of the brain is already present and functioning by age 2, what remains to develop? The most important parts!

Although the 2-year-olds of other primates are more developed than human children in some ways (they climb trees better, walk sooner, etc.), and although many animals have abilities that people lack (e.g., dogs' sense of smell), young humans have intellectual capacities far beyond those of any other animal. Human brains continue to develop at least until early adulthood (Konner, 2010).

Considered from an evolutionary perspective, human brains allowed the species to develop "a mode of living built on social cohesion, cooperation and efficient planning. . . . [S]urvival of the smartest" seems more accurate than survival of the fittest (Corballis, 2011, p. 194). Those functions of the brain that make us human, not merely apes, begin in infancy but develop primarily after age 2, enabling quicker, better-coordinated, and more reflective thought (M. H. Johnson, 2011; Kagan & Herschkowitz, 2005).

Between ages 2 and 6, neurological increases are especially notable in the areas of the cortex, where planning, thinking, social awareness, and language occur. Elephants, crows, chimpanzees, and dolphins have all surprised researchers with their intelligence, but none come close to *Homo sapiens* in the relative size of the cortex or its capacity for social understanding (Corballis, 2011).

For example, researchers gave a series of tests to 106 chimpanzees, 32 orangutans, and 105 human 2½-year-olds. The young humans were "equivalent . . . to chimpanzees on tasks of physical cognition but far outstripped both chimpanzees and orangutans on tasks of social cognition" such as pointing or following someone's gaze (Herrmann et al., 2007, p. 1365).

The **prefrontal cortex,** a brain area right above the eyes, is called the *executive* of the brain because planning, prioritizing, and reflection occur there. Maturation of this area allows young children to begin to plan ahead as well as to think about past experiences—for instance, deciding who they want at their birthday party or what they liked best about a summer trip.

The prefrontal cortex is very limited in infancy, begins to function in early childhood, and continues to develop for many more years (M. H. Johnson, 2011). It is crucial for impulse control. As you remember, in the final stage of sensorimotor development, toddlers begin to think before acting—but not until adulthood (and sometimes not even then) are people able to use their brains to predict and analyze the consequences of various actions, from crossing the street (which is why adults insist on holding the child's hand) to going to college (which is why children are required to go to school). Neurological immaturity is another reason adults need to prevent childhood injury, as just explained.

Speed of Thought

Most of the increases in brain weight after infancy are the result of **myelination.** *Myelin* (sometimes called the *white matter* of the brain) is a fatty coating on the axons that speeds signals between neurons (see Figure 5.5). Although myelination continues for years, the effects are especially apparent in early childhood (Silk & Wood, 2011).

Speed of transmission from one neuron to another becomes pivotal when several thoughts and actions must occur in rapid succession. By age 6, most children can see an object and immediately name it, catch a ball and throw it, write their ABCs in proper sequence, and so on. In fact, rapid naming of letters and objects—possible only when myelination is extensive—is a crucial indicator of later reading ability (Shanahan & Lonigan, 2010).

Of course, adults must be patient when listening to young children talk, helping them get dressed, or watching them write each letter of their names. Everything is done more slowly by 6-year-olds than by 16-year-olds because the younger children's brains have less myelination, which slows information processing. However, thanks to myelination, older preschoolers are much quicker than toddlers, who sometimes forget what they were doing before they finish.

IMPULSIVENESS AND PERSEVERATION The young child's inability to speedily combine thoughts is evident when both action and reflection are needed. Neurons have only two kinds of impulses: on–off (activate–inhibit). Each is signaled by biochemical messages in the brain. A balance of activation and inhibition is needed for thoughtful adults, who neither leap too quickly nor hesitate too long.

Many young children have not yet found the balance. They are impulsive, flitting from one activity to another. That explains why many 3-year-olds cannot stay quietly on one task, even in "circle time" in preschool, where each child is told to sit in place, not talking or touching anyone else. Others persevere in, or stick to, one thought or action. That is called **perseveration,** evident when children are furious when told to stop what they are doing. Impulsiveness and perseveration are opposite manifestations of a prefrontal cortex that is too immature to check activation or halt inhibition.

SHAPES AND COLORS Perseveration gradually declines in every child. Consider a series of experiments in which 3-year-olds consistently make a stunning mistake that disappears by age 5. Children are given a set of cards with clear outlines of trucks or flowers, some red and some blue. They are asked to "play the shape game," putting trucks in one pile and flowers in another. Three-year-olds do this correctly.

Then they are asked to "play the color game," sorting the cards by color. Most fail. Instead they sort by shape, as they had done before. This basic test has been replicated in many nations; 3-year-olds usually perseverate, getting stuck in their initial sorting pattern.

When this result was first obtained, researchers thought that 3-year-olds might not know colors. To test this possibility, some other 3-year-olds were asked to sort by color. Most did that correctly. Then, when asked to play "the shape game," they still sorted by color. Even with a new set of cards, such as yellow and green or rabbits and boats, 3-year-olds sort as they did originally, either by color or shape. Most 5-year-olds can make the switch.

Researchers are looking into many possible explanations for this result (Marcovitch et al., 2010; Müller et al., 2006; Yerys & Munakata, 2006). All agree, however, that something in the brain matures between ages 3 and 5 to enable children to switch their way of sorting objects.

Connecting Hemispheres

One part of the brain that grows and myelinates rapidly during early childhood is the **corpus callosum,** a long, thick band of nerve fibers that connects the left and right sides of the brain. Growth of the corpus callosum makes communication between hemispheres more efficient, allowing children to coordinate the two sides of the brain or body. Failure of the corpus callosum to mature results in serious disorders: This is one of several possible causes of autism (Frazier & Hardan, 2009), discussed in Chapter 7.

The two sides of the body and of the brain are not identical. Typically, the brain's left half controls the body's right side as well as areas dedicated to logical reasoning, detailed analysis, and the basics of language; the brain's right half controls the body's left side, with areas dedicated to emotions, creativity, and appreciation of music, art, and poetry. However, this left–right distinction has been exaggerated (Hugdahl & Westerhausen, 2010); both sides of the brain are normally involved in almost every skill.

✦ **ESPECIALLY FOR Early-Childhood Teachers** You know you should be patient, but you feel your frustration rising when your young charges dawdle as they walk to the playground a block away. What should you do? (see response, page 182) →

perseveration
The tendency to persevere in, or stick to, one thought or action for a long time.

corpus callosum
A long, thick band of nerve fibers that connects the left and right hemispheres of the brain and allows communication between them.

STOCKBYTE / GETTY IMAGES

Smarter than Most? Beware of stereotypes. Obviously, this student is a girl, Asian, left-handed, attending a structured school (note the uniform). Each of these four characteristics leads some to conclude that she is more, or less, intelligent than other 7-year-olds. But all children have brains with the potential to learn: Specific teaching, not innate characteristics, is crucial.

lateralization
Literally, "sidedness," referring to the specialization in certain functions by each side of the brain, with one side dominant for each activity. The left side of the brain controls the right side of the body, and vice versa.

limbic system
The major brain region crucial to the development of emotional expression and regulation; its three main areas are the amygdala, the hippocampus, and the hypothalamus, although recent research has found that many other areas of the brain are involved with emotions.

amygdala
A tiny brain structure that registers emotions, particularly fear and anxiety.

hippocampus
A brain structure that is a central processor of memory, especially memory for locations.

hypothalamus
A brain area that responds to the amygdala and the hippocampus to produce hormones that activate other parts of the brain and body.

Nonetheless, each side specializes, being dominant for certain functions—the result of **lateralization**—literally, "sidedness"—which advances with maturation of the corpus callosum (Boles et al., 2008). Lateralization is genetic, present at birth, but practice as well as time are needed before children can efficiently coordinate both hands, feet, ears, and so on.

Some research a decade ago found that, relatively speaking, the corpus callosum was thicker in females than in males, a finding that led to speculation about women's superior emotional understanding and men's logic. However, research using more advanced techniques now finds that this sex difference is far from universal. Some individual males and females have notably thicker corpus callosa than others, but reliable sex differences are not found (Savic, 2010).

Although gender does not seem to affect thickness of the corpus callosa, handedness might. Left-handed people tend to develop thicker corpus callosa than right-handed people, perhaps because they need to vary the interaction between the two sides of their bodies, depending on the task. For example, most left-handed people brush their teeth with their left hand because that is easier, but they shake hands with their right hand because that is what the social convention requires. Left-handed children need to learn when their nondominant hand is to be used—with scissors that are not specially designed for left-handed people, for instance.

Often cultures assume everyone should be right-handed, an example of the *difference-equals-deficit* error. For example, many letters and languages are written from left to right, easier for right-handed people, especially in the days when fresh ink would smear. In some Asian and African cultures, it is an insult to give someone anything with the left hand. Fortunately, acceptance of left-handedness is more widespread now than a century ago: About 10 percent of adults in Great Britain and the United States now claim to be left-handed, compared to only 3 percent in 1900 (McManus et al., 2010).

Developmentalists advise against switching a left-handed child, not only because this causes adult–child conflicts and brain confusion, but also because left-handed people may have an advantage in creativity and rapid use of the entire brain. Michelangelo, Seal, Jimi Hendrix, Paul McCartney, Larry Bird, and Sandy Koufax, as well as four of the past six U.S. presidents (Ronald Reagan, Jimmy Carter, Bill Clinton, and Barack Obama) were/are lefties.

Emotions and the Brain

Now that we have considered the prefrontal cortex and the corpus callosum, we turn to the major brain region for emotions, sometimes called the **limbic system.** Emotional expression and emotional regulation advance during early childhood (more about that in the next chapter). Crucial to that advance are three major areas of the limbic system—the amygdala, the hippocampus, and the hypothalamus.

The **amygdala** is a tiny structure deep in the brain, named after the Greek word for almond because it is about the shape and size of an almond. It registers emotions, both positive and negative, especially fear. Increased amygdala activity is one reason some young children have terrifying nightmares or sudden phobias, overwhelming the prefrontal cortex and disrupting reason. A child may refuse to enter an elevator or may hide when it thunders. Specifics depend on the child's innate temperament as well as on past social experiences (Tarullo et al., 2011).

Another structure in the brain's limbic system, the **hippocampus,** is located right next to the amygdala. A central processor of memory, especially memory for locations, the hippocampus responds to the anxieties of the amygdala by summoning memory.

A child can remember, for instance, whether previous elevator riding was scary or fun. Memories of location are fragile in early childhood because the hippocampus is still developing. Nonetheless, deep emotional memories from early childhood can interfere with rational thinking: In adulthood, a person might have a panic attack on an elevator but not know why.

The interaction of the amygdala and the hippocampus is sometimes helpful, sometimes not; fear can be constructive or destructive (LaBar, 2007). Studies performed on some animals show that when the amygdala is surgically removed, the animals are fearless in situations that should scare them; for instance, a cat will stroll nonchalantly past monkeys—something no normal cat would do (Kolb & Whishaw, 2008). With humans, if the amygdala is less connected to the other parts of the brain, young children are likely to be depressed, presumably because emotions are more overwhelming when the rest of the brain is disengaged (Luking et al., 2011).

A third part of the limbic system, the **hypothalamus,** responds to signals from the amygdala (arousing) and from the hippocampus (usually dampening) by producing cortisol and other hormones that activate parts of the brain and body. Ideally, this hormone production occurs in moderation (Tarullo & Gunnar, 2006).

As the limbic system develops, young children watch their parents' emotions closely, an example of the social referencing described in Chapter 4. If a parent looks worried when entering an elevator, the child may fearfully cling to the parent when the elevator moves. If this sequence recurs often enough, the child's amygdala may become hypersensitive, as fear is connected to the memory of a specific location (hippocampus), resulting in increased cortisol (hypothalamus). If, instead, the parent calmly makes elevator riding fun (letting the child push the buttons, for instance), initial feelings of fear will diminish and the child might run to the elevator, happily pushing buttons.

Knowing the varieties of fear and joy is helpful if a teacher takes a group of young children on a trip. To stick with the elevator example, one child might be terrified while another might rush forward, pushing the "close" button before the teacher enters. Every experience (elevators, fire engines, animals at the zoo, a police officer) is likely to trigger a range of emotions, without much reflection, in a group of 3-year-olds: A trip needs several adults, ready to activate or inhibit young brains and bodies, as need be.

ZUMA PRESS PHOTOS VIA NEWSCOM

Ashes to Ashes, Dust to Dust Many religious rituals have sustained humans of all ages for centuries, including listening quietly in church on Ash Wednesday —as Nailah Pierre tries to do. This is developmentally difficult for young children, but for three reasons she probably will succeed: (1) gender (girls mature earlier than boys), (2) experience (she has been in church many times), and (3) social context (she is one of 750 students in her school attending a special service at Nativity Catholic church).

✦ ESPECIALLY FOR Neurologists
Why do many experts think that identifying the limbic system as the regulator of emotions is an oversimplified explanation of brain function? (see response, page 182) →

©THE NEW YORKER COLLECTION 2010 BARBARA SMALLER FROM CARTOONBANK.COM. ALL RIGHTS RESERVED.

B. Smaller

"I would share, but I'm not there developmentally."

Good Excuse It is true that emotional control of selfish instincts is difficult for young children because the prefrontal cortex is not yet mature enough to regulate some emotions. However, family practices can advance social understanding.

RESPONSE FOR Early-Childhood Teachers (from page 179) One solution is to remind yourself that the children's brains are not yet myelinated enough to enable them to quickly walk, talk, or even button their jackets. Maturation has a major effect, as you will observe if you can schedule excursions in September and again in November. Progress, while still slow, will be a few seconds faster. ●

RESPONSE FOR Neurologists (from page 181) The more we discover about the brain, the more complex we realize it is. Each part has specific functions and is connected to every other part. ●

> ## KEY Points
>
> - The prefrontal cortex develops in early childhood and beyond, allowing the planning and analyzing that comprise executive processing.
> - Myelination speeds mental processing, which eventually reduces impulsivity and perseveration.
> - Emotional regulation requires coordination of several brain areas, including the amygdala, the hippocampus, and the hypothalamus.
> - Brain maturation of young children is more advanced, especially in social understanding, than in other animals, but each child's particular culture and experience have a notable impact.

Thinking During Early Childhood

You have just learned that every year of early childhood advances motor skills, brain development, and impulse control. Each of these affects cognition, as first described by Jean Piaget and Lev Vygotsky, already mentioned in Chapter 1.

Piaget: Preoperational Thought

preoperational intelligence
Piaget's term for cognitive development between the ages of about 2 and 6; it includes language and imagination (which involve symbolic thought), but logical, operational thinking is not yet possible.

symbolic thought
The concept that an object or word can stand for something else, including something pretend or something not seen. Once symbolic thought is possible, language becomes much more useful.

animism
The belief that natural objects and phenomena are alive.

Early childhood is the time of **preoperational intelligence,** the second of Piaget's four periods. He called early childhood thinking *pre*operational because children do not yet use logical operations (reasoning processes) (Inhelder & Piaget, 1964).

However, preoperational children are past sensorimotor intelligence because they can think in symbols, not just via senses and motor skills. In **symbolic thought,** an object or word can stand for something else, including something pretend or something not seen.

The word *dog,* for instance, is at first only the family dog sniffing at the child; but when the word becomes a symbol, it can refer to a remembered dog, or a plastic dog, or an imagined dog. Symbolic thought allows for the language explosion (detailed later in this chapter), when children can talk about thoughts and memories.

Symbolic thought helps explain **animism,** the belief of many young children that natural objects (such as a tree or a cloud) are alive and that nonhuman animals have the same characteristics as the child. Many children's stories include animals or objects that talk and listen (Aesop's fables, Winnie the Pooh, *Goodnight Moon*). Preoperational thought is symbolic and magical, not logical and realistic. Animism gradually disappears as the mind becomes more mature (Kesselring & Müller, 2011).

OBSTACLES TO LOGIC Piaget described symbolic thought as characteristic of preoperational thought. He also described four limitations that make logic difficult until about age 6: centration, focus on appearance, static reasoning, and irreversibility.

centration
A characteristic of preoperational thought whereby a young child focuses (centers) on one idea, excluding all others.

egocentrism
Piaget's term for young children's tendency to think about the world entirely from their own personal perspective.

Centration is the tendency to focus on one aspect of a situation to the exclusion of all others. Young children may, for example, insist that Daddy is a father, not a brother, because they center on the role that he fills for them.

The daddy example illustrates a particular type of centration that Piaget called **egocentrism**—literally, "self-centeredness." Egocentric children contemplate the world exclusively from their personal perspective.

Egocentrism is not selfishness, however. Consider, for example, a 3-year-old who chose to buy a model car as a birthday present for his mother: His "behavior was not selfish or greedy; he carefully wrapped the present and gave it to his mother with an expression that clearly showed that he expected her to love it" (Crain, 2005, p. 108).

A second characteristic of preoperational thought is a **focus on appearance** to the exclusion of other attributes. For instance, a girl given a short haircut might worry that she has turned into a boy. In preoperational thought, a thing is whatever it appears to be—evident in the joy young children have in wearing the hats or shoes of a grown-up.

Third, preoperational children use **static reasoning,** believing that the world is unchanging, always in the state in which they currently encounter it. For instance, many children cannot imagine that their own parents were ever children. If they are told that Grandma is their mother's mother, they still do not understand how people change with maturation. One preschooler told his grandmother to tell his mother to never spank him because "she has to do what her mother says."

The fourth characteristic of preoperational thought is **irreversibility.** Preoperational thinkers fail to recognize that reversing a process sometimes restores whatever existed before. A young child might cry because her mother put lettuce on her sandwich. Overwhelmed by her desire to have things "just right," she might reject the food even after the lettuce is removed because she believes that what is done cannot be undone.

CONSERVATION AND LOGIC Piaget highlighted several ways in which preoperational intelligence overlooks logic. A famous set of experiments involved **conservation,** the notion that the amount of something remains the same (is conserved) despite changes in its appearance.

Suppose two identical glasses contain the same amount of milk, and the milk from one of these glasses is poured into a taller, narrower glass. If young children are asked whether one glass contains more or both glasses contain the same amount, they will insist that the narrower glass (with the higher level) has more. (See Figure 5.6 for other examples.)

All four characteristics of preoperational thought are evident in this mistake. Young children fail to understand conservation because they focus (*center*) on what they see (*appearance*), noticing only the immediate (*static*) condition. It does not occur to them that they could reverse the process and re-create the level of a moment earlier (*irreversibility*).

Piaget's original tests of conservation required children to respond verbally to an adult's questions. Later research has found that when the tests of logic are simplified

focus on appearance
A characteristic of preoperational thought whereby a young child ignores all attributes that are not apparent.

static reasoning
A characteristic of preoperational thought whereby a young child thinks that nothing changes. Whatever is now has always been and always will be.

irreversibility
A characteristic of preoperational thought whereby a young child thinks that nothing can be undone. A thing cannot be restored to the way it was before a change occurred.

conservation
The principle that the amount of a substance remains the same (i.e., is conserved) even when its appearance changes.

✦ **ESPECIALLY FOR Early-Childhood Teachers** How might research on conservation help adults when feeding young children? (see response, page 184) ➜

COURTESY OF KATHLEEN BERGER

Demonstration of Conservation My youngest daughter, Sarah, here at age 5¾, demonstrates Piaget's conservation-of-liquids experiment. First, she examines both short glasses to be sure they contain the same amount of milk. Then, after the contents of one are poured into the tall glass and she is asked which has more, she points to the tall glass, just as Piaget would have expected. Later she added, "It looks like it has more because it's taller," indicating that some direct instruction might change her mind.

Tests of Various Types of Conservation

Type of Conservation	Initial Presentation	Transformation	Question	Preoperational Child's Answer
Volume	Two equal glasses of liquid.	Pour one into a taller, narrower glass.	Which glass contains more?	The taller one.
Number	Two equal lines of checkers.	Increase spacing of checkers in one line.	Which line has more checkers?	The longer one.
Matter	Two equal balls of clay.	Squeeze one ball into a long, thin shape.	Which piece has more clay?	The long one.
Length	Two sticks of equal length.	Move one stick.	Which stick is longer?	The one that is farther to the right.

FIGURE 5.6 Conservation, Please
According to Piaget, until children grasp the concept of conservation at (he believed) about age 6 or 7, they cannot understand that the transformations shown here do not change the total amount of liquid, checkers, clay, and wood.

or made playful, young children may succeed. In many ways, children indicate that they know something via eye movements or gestures before they can say it in words (Goldin-Meadow, 2009).

As with sensorimotor intelligence in infancy, Piaget underestimated what preoperational children could understand. Nonetheless, he was a pioneer in recognizing several crucial ways in which children's thought patterns are unlike those of adults.

Vygotsky: Social Learning

For decades, the magical, illogical, and self-centered aspects of early-childhood cognition dominated research; scientists were understandably awed by Piaget. His description of egocentrism was confirmed daily by anecdotes of young children's behavior.

Vygotsky emphasized another side of early cognition—that thinking is shaped by other people's wishes and goals. He emphasized the social aspects of development, a contrast to Piaget's emphasis on the individual. That led Vygotsky to notice the power of culture, acknowledging that "the culturally specific nature of experience is an integral part of how the person thinks and acts," as several developmentalists explain (Gauvain et al., 2011).

CHILDREN AND MENTORS Vygotsky believed that every aspect of children's cognitive development is embedded in a social context (Vygotsky, 1934/1987). Children are curious and observant. They ask questions—about how machines work, why weather changes, where the sky ends—and seek answers from more knowledgeable mentors. These answers are affected by the mentors' perceptions and assumptions—that is, their culture.

As you remember from Chapter 1, children learn through *guided participation*, as older and more skilled mentors teach them. Parents are the first guides, although many teachers, other family members, and peers are mentors as well. For example,

RESPONSE FOR Early-Childhood Teachers (from page 183) Since appearance is crucial, when you are giving drinks to more than one child, all the cups should be the same size. Children will also be happier with two very small crackers rather than one bigger one or with a scoop of ice cream in a small bowl rather than the same-sized scoop in a large one. ●

the verbal proficiency of children in day-care centers is affected by the language of their playmates, who teach vocabulary without consciously doing so (Mashburn et al., 2009).

According to Vygotsky, children learn because their mentors do the following:

● Present challenges

● Offer assistance (without taking over)

● Add crucial information

● Encourage motivation

Overall, the ability to learn from mentors indicates intelligence, according to Vygotsky: "What children can do with the assistance of others might be in some sense even more indicative of their mental development than what they can do alone" (1934/1987, p. 5).

SCAFFOLDING Vygotsky believed that all individuals learn within their **zone of proximal development (ZPD),** an intellectual arena where new ideas and skills can be mastered. *Proximal* means "near," so the ZPD includes the ideas children are close to understanding as well as the skills they can almost master but are not yet able to demonstrate independently. How and when children learn depends, in part, on the wisdom and willingness of mentors to provide **scaffolding,** or temporary sensitive support, to help them within their developmental zone.

Good mentors provide plenty of scaffolding, encouraging children to look both ways before crossing the street (while holding the child's hand) or letting them stir the cake batter (perhaps while covering the child's hand on the spoon handle, in guided participation).

Sometimes scaffolding is inadvertent, when children observe something said or done and then try to do likewise—even if it is something that adults would rather the child not do. Young children curse, kick, and do even worse things because someone else has shown them how.

More benignly, children imitate habits and customs that are meaningless, a trait called **overimitation,** evident in humans but not in other animals. This stems from the child's eagerness to learn from mentors, allowing "rapid, high-fidelity intergenerational transmission of cultural forms" (Nielsen & Tomaselli, 2010, p. 735).

Overimitation was demonstrated in an experiment with 2- to 6-year-olds, 61 from Bushman communities in South Africa and Botswana and 16 from Australia. Australian adults often scaffold with words and actions, but Bushman adults rarely do. The researchers expected the Australian children to follow adult demonstrations, as they had been taught. They did not expect the Bushman children to do so (Nielsen & Tomaselli, 2010).

One by one, some children observed an adult perform irrelevant actions, such as waving a red stick above a box three times and then using that stick to push down a knob to open the box, which could be easily and more efficiently opened by merely pulling a knob. Then children were given the stick and the box. No matter what their cultural background, the children followed the adult example, waving the stick three times.

Other children did not see the demonstration. When they were given the stick and the box, they simply pulled the knob. Then they observed an adult do the stick-waving opening—and copied those inefficient actions, even though they already knew the easy way to open the box.

CORBIS / AGE FOTOSTOCK

Words, Don't Fail Me Now Could you describe how to tie shoes? The limitations of verbal tests of cognitive understanding are apparent in many skills.

OBSERVATION QUIZ
What three sociocultural factors make it likely that this child will learn? (see answer, page 187) →

zone of proximal development (ZPD)
Vygotsky's term for the skills—cognitive as well as physical—that a person can exercise only with assistance, not yet independently.

scaffolding
Temporary support that is tailored to a learner's needs and abilities and aimed at helping the learner master the next task in a given learning process.

overimitation
The tendency of children to copy an action that is not a relevant part of the behavior to be learned; common among 2- to 6-year-olds when they imitate adult actions that are irrelevant and inefficient.

✦ **ESPECIALLY FOR Teachers**
Sometimes your students cry, curse, or quit. How would Vygotsky advise you to proceed? (see response, page 187) →

Apparently, children everywhere learn from others via observation, even if not deliberately taught. Thus, scaffolding occurs via observation as well as explicit guidance. Across cultures, "similarity of performance is profound" (Nielsen & Tomaselli, 2010, p. 734), as Vygotsky explained.

Children's Theories

Piaget and Vygotsky recognized that children work to understand their world. No contemporary developmental scientist doubts that. The question now is: When and how do children acquire their impressive knowledge? Part of the answer is that children do more than gain words, skills, and concepts—they develop theories to help them understand and remember.

theory-theory
The idea that children attempt to explain everything they see and hear.

THEORY-THEORY Humans of all ages want explanations. **Theory-theory** refers to the idea that children naturally construct theories to explain whatever they see and hear. In other words, the theory about how children think is that they construct a theory. All people

> search for causal regularities in the world around us. We are perpetually driven to look for deeper explanations of our experience, and broader and more reliable predictions about it. . . . Children seem, quite literally, to be born with . . . the desire to understand the world and the desire to discover how to behave in it.
>
> [Gopnik, 2001, p. 66]

According to theory-theory, the best explanation for cognition is that humans seek reasons, causes, and underlying principles to make sense of their experience. That requires curiosity and thought, connecting bits of knowledge and observations, which is what young children do.

Exactly how do children seek explanations? They ask questions, and, if not content with the answers, they develop their own theories. This is particularly evident in children's understanding of God and religion. One child thought his grandpa died because God was lonely; another thought thunder occurred because God was rearranging the furniture.

In one study, Mexican American mothers kept detailed diaries of every question their 3- to 5-year-olds asked and also what they themselves responded (Kelemen et al., 2005). Most of the questions were about human behavior and characteristics (see Figure 5.7); for example, "Why do you give my mother a kiss?" "Why is my brother bad?" "Why do women have breasts?" "Why are there Black kids?" Fewer questions were about nonliving things ("Why does it rain?") or objects ("Why is my daddy's car white?").

Children seem to wonder about the underlying purpose of whatever they observe, although parents usually respond as if children were seeking scientific explanations. An adult might interpret a child's "Why?" to mean "What causes X to happen?" when the child intended "Why?" to mean "Tell me more about X" (Leach, 1997).

For instance, if a child asks why women have breasts, adults might talk about hormones and maturation, but a child-centered response would be that breasts are for feeding babies. From a child's egocentric perspective, any query includes, "How does this relate to me?" Accordingly, an adult might add that the child was nourished from the mother's breasts.

A series of experiments that explored when and how 3-year-olds imitate others provides some support for theory-theory (Williamson et al., 2008). Children seem to figure out *why* adults act as they do before deciding to copy those actions. If an adult intended to accomplish something and succeeded, a

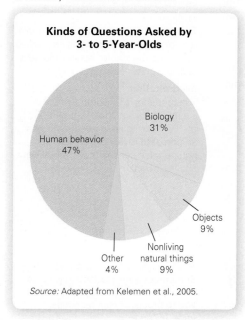

FIGURE 5.7 Questions, Questions Parents found that most of their children's questions were about human behavior—especially the parents' behavior toward the child. Children seek to develop a theory to explain things, so the question "Why can't I have some candy?" is not satisfactorily answered by "It's almost dinnertime."

Kinds of Questions Asked by 3- to 5-Year-Olds

Biology 31%
Human behavior 47%
Objects 9%
Nonliving natural things 9%
Other 4%

Source: Adapted from Kelemen et al., 2005.

child is likely to follow the example, but if the same action and result seemed inadvertent or accidental, the child is less likely to copy it.

Indeed, even when asked to repeat something ungrammatical that an adult says, children are likely to correct the grammar based on their theory that the adult intended to speak grammatically but failed to do so (Over & Gattis, 2010). This is another example of a general principle: Children develop theories about intentions before they employ their impressive ability to imitate; they do not mindlessly copy whatever they observe. For instance, in the example in which the adult waved the stick before opening the box, the children theorized that, since the adult did it deliberately, stick waving was somehow important.

THEORY OF MIND Mental processes—thoughts, emotions, beliefs, motives, and intentions—are among the most complicated and puzzling phenomena that humans encounter every day. Adults wonder why people fall in love with the particular persons they do, or why they vote for the candidates they do, or why they make foolish choices—from taking on a huge mortgage to buying an overripe cucumber. Children are puzzled about a playmate's unexpected anger, a sibling's generosity, or an aunt's too-wet kiss.

To know what goes on in another's mind, people develop a *folk psychology,* which includes ideas about other people's thinking, called **theory of mind.** Theory of mind is an emergent ability, slow to develop but typically beginning in most children at about age 4 (Sterck & Begeer, 2010).

Realizing that thoughts do not mirror reality is beyond very young children, but that realization dawns on them sometime after age 3. It then occurs to them that people can be deliberately deceived or fooled—an idea that requires some theory of mind.

In one of several false-belief tests that researchers have developed, a child watches a doll named Max put a puppy into a red box. Then Max leaves and the child sees the puppy taken out of the red box and put in a blue box. When Max returns, the child is asked, "Where will Max look for the puppy?" Most 3-year-olds confidently say, "In the blue box"; most 6-year-olds correctly say, "In the red box," a pattern found in a dozen nations (Wellman et al., 2001).

Indeed, 3-year-olds almost always confuse what they recently learned with what they once thought and what someone else might think. Another way of describing this is to say that they are "cursed" by their own knowledge (Birch & Bloom, 2003), too egocentric to grasp others' perspectives. Asa did that in the vignette at the start of this chapter when he failed to understand that I was tired of throwing imaginary baskets and wanted to sit.

The development of theory of mind can be seen when young children try to escape punishment by lying. Their facial expression often betrays them. Parents sometimes say, "I know when you are lying," and, to the consternation of most 3-year-olds, parents are usually right.

In one experiment, 247 children, aged 3 to 5, were left alone at a table that had an upside-down cup covering dozens of candies (Evans et al., 2011). The children were told not to peek, but 142 (57 percent) did, spilling the candies onto the table. There were far too many spilled candies for them to put them back to hide the fact that they'd peeked. The examiner returned, asking how the candies got on the table. Only one-fourth of the participants (more often the younger ones) told the truth.

The rest lied, with increasing skill. The 3-year-olds typically told hopeless lies (e.g., "The candies got out by themselves"); the 4-year-olds told unlikely lies (e.g., "Other children came in and knocked over the cup"). Some of the 5-year-olds, however, told plausible lies (e.g., "My elbow knocked over the cup accidentally").

ANSWER TO **OBSERVATION QUIZ** (from page 185) Motivation (in Spain, boys like yellow running shoes); human relationships (note the physical touching of father and son); and materials (the long laces make tying them easier). ●

theory of mind
A person's theory of what other people might be thinking. In order to have a theory of mind, children must realize that other people are not necessarily thinking the same thoughts that they themselves are. That realization is seldom achieved before age 4.

✦ **ESPECIALLY FOR Social Scientists** Can you think of any connection between Piaget's theory of preoperational thought and 3-year-olds' errors in this theory-of-mind task? (see response, page 189) →

RESPONSE FOR Teachers (from page 185) Use guided participation and scaffold the instruction so your students are not overwhelmed. Be sure to provide lots of praise and days of practice. If emotion erupts, do not take it as an attack on you. ●

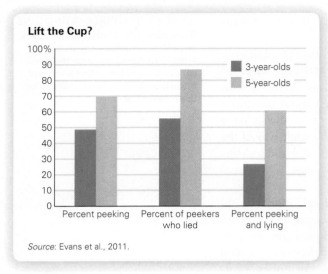

Lift the Cup?

Source: Evans et al., 2011.

FIGURE 5.8 Better with Age?
Could an obedient and honest 3-year-old become a disobedient and lying 5-year-old? Apparently yes, as the proportion of peekers and liars in this study more than doubled over those two years. Does maturation make children more able to think for themselves or less trustworthy?

This particular study was done in Beijing, China, but the results seem universal: Older children are better liars. Beyond the age differences, the experimenters found that the more logical liars were also more advanced in theory of mind and executive functioning (Evans et al., 2011), which indicates a more mature prefrontal cortex (see Figure 5.8).

Brain and Context

Many scientists have found that a child's ability to develop theories correlates with the maturity of the prefrontal cortex and with advances in executive processing (Mar, 2011). The brain connection was further suggested by research on 8- to 16-year-olds. Their readiness to lie did *not* correlate with age or brain maturation (they were old enough to realize that a lie was possible, but whether they actually lied depended on their expectations and values); yet if they did lie, their executive abilities correlated with the sophistication of their lies (Evans & Lee, 2011).

Context and experience are relevant as well (Sterck & Begeer, 2010). Language proficiency correlates with all aspects of learning, especially if mother–child conversations involve thoughts and wishes (Ontai & Thompson, 2008). Vygotsky particularly stressed the role of language to advance thought. He wrote that *private speech,* which is talking to oneself either out loud or in one's mind, is an important road to cognitive development. That seems to be true in early childhood (Al-Namlah et al., 2012).

Siblings promote cognition as well. As brothers and sisters argue, agree, compete, and cooperate, and as older siblings fool younger ones, it dawns on 3-year-olds that not everyone thinks as they do. Egocentrism is somewhat modified.

By age 5, children with siblings know what words and actions will gain parental sympathy to protect themselves against their older siblings, as well as how to persuade their younger brothers and sisters to give them a toy. As one expert quipped regarding theory of mind, "Two older siblings are worth about a year of chronological age" (Perner, 2000, p. 383).

Finally, culture and context matter. A meta-analysis of 254 studies done in China and North America reported that Chinese children were about six months ahead of U.S. children in development of theory of mind (Liu et al., 2008), and a Canadian study found that children were slower by a few months if they often watched television (Mar et al., 2010). Everywhere, however, sometime between ages 2 and 6, children realize that not everyone knows what they know.

KEYpoints

- Preoperational children, according to Piaget, can use symbolic thought but are illogical and egocentric, limited by appearance and immediate experience.
- Vygotsky realized that children are influenced by their social contexts, including their mentors and the cultures in which they live.
- In the zone of proximal development, children are ready to move beyond their current understanding, especially if deliberate or inadvertent scaffolding occurs.
- Children use their cognitive abilities to develop theories about their experiences, as is evident in theory of mind, which appears between ages 3 and 5.
- In all of cognitive development, family interactions guide and advance learning.

Language Learning

Language is the premier cognitive accomplishment of early childhood. Two-year-olds use short, telegraphic sentences (like a telegram: "Want cookie," "Where Daddy go?"), but 6-year-olds seem able to understand and discuss almost anything (see At About This Time).

A Sensitive Time

Brain maturation, myelination, scaffolding, and social interaction make early childhood ideal for learning language. As you remember from Chapter 1, scientists once thought that early childhood was a *critical period* for language learning—the *only* time when a first language could be mastered and the best time for learning a second or third language. It is true that children organize words and sounds into meaning (theory-theory). For that reason teachers and parents should speak and listen to children many hours each day. However, many people learn languages after age 6; the critical-period hypothesis is false (Singleton & Munoz, 2011).

Instead, early childhood is a *sensitive period* for language learning—for rapidly and easily mastering vocabulary, grammar, and pronunciation. Young children are called "language sponges" because they soak up every drop of language they encounter.

Language learning is an example of dynamic systems, in that every part of the developmental process influences every other part. To be specific, there are "multiple sensitive periods . . . auditory, phonological, semantic, syntactic, and motor systems, along with the developmental interactions among these components" (Thomas & Johnson, 2008, p. 2). All of these facilitate language learning.

One of the valuable (and sometimes frustrating) traits of young children is that they talk a lot—to adults, to each other, to themselves, to their toys—unfazed by misuse, mispronunciation, stuttering, or other impediments to fluency.

Language comes easily for young children partly because they are not self-critical about what they say. Egocentrism has advantages; this is one of them. Children believe they know more than they do (Marazita & Merriman, 2011), and they readily and confidently talk about it. Asa said a toy lion was a mother; I said it couldn't be a mother because it had a mane. Rather than recognizing that I knew more about sex differences in lions than he did, he advised me that this particular lion was a mother with a mane.

The Vocabulary Explosion

The average child knows about 500 words at age 2 and more than 10,000 at age 6 (Herschensohn, 2007). That's more than 6 new words a day. Precise estimates of vocabulary size vary; some children learn four times as many words as others. Always, however, vocabulary builds quickly and comprehension is more extensive than speech. Every child could become bilingual.

FAST-MAPPING After painstakingly learning one word at a time between 12 and 18 months of age, children develop an interconnected set of categories for words,

AT ABOUT THIS TIME	
Language in Early Childhood	
Approximate Age	Characteristic or Achievement in First Language
2 years	*Vocabulary:* 100–2,000 words *Sentence length:* 2–6 words *Grammar:* Plurals; pronouns; many nouns, verbs, adjectives *Questions:* Many "What's that?" questions
3 years	*Vocabulary:* 1,000–5,000 words *Sentence length:* 3–8 words *Grammar:* Conjunctions, adverbs, articles *Questions:* Many "Why?" questions
4 years	*Vocabulary:* 3,000–10,000 words *Sentence length:* 5–20 words *Grammar:* Dependent clauses, tags at sentence end (". . . didn't I?" ". . . won't you?") *Questions:* Peak of "Why?" questions; many "How?" and "When?" questions
5 years	*Vocabulary:* 5,000–20,000 words *Sentence length:* Some seem unending (". . . and . . . who . . . and . . . that . . . and . . .") *Grammar:* Complex, depending on what the child has heard. Some children correctly use the passive voice ("Man bitten by dog") and subjunctive ("If I were . . ."). *Questions:* Some about social differences (male–female, old–young, rich–poor) and many other issues

RESPONSE FOR Social Scientists (from page 187) According to Piaget, preschool children focus on appearance and on static conditions (so they cannot mentally reverse a process). Furthermore, they are egocentric, believing that everyone shares their point of view. No wonder they believe that Max would look for the puppy in the blue box instead of the red one. ●

fast-mapping
The speedy and sometimes imprecise way in which children learn new words by tentatively placing them in mental categories according to their perceived meaning.

a kind of grid or mental map, which makes speedy vocabulary acquisition possible. The process is called **fast-mapping** (Woodward & Markman, 1998) because, rather than figuring out the exact definition after hearing a word used in several contexts, children hear a word once and quickly stick it into a category in their mental language grid. That quick-sticking is fast-mapping, similar to theory-theory except the map is for words, not concepts.

Language mapping is not precise. For example, children rapidly connect new animal names close to already-known animal names, without knowing all the details. Thus, *tiger* is easy to map if you know *lion*, but a leopard might be called a tiger. A trip to the zoo facilitates fast-mapping of animal names if zoos scaffold learning by placing similar animals near each other. So does a picture book, if a mentor points to the tiger's stripes and the leopard's spots.

Fast-mapping begins even before age 2, and it accelerates over childhood, as each new word makes it easier to map other words (Gershkoff-Stowe & Hahn, 2007). Generally, the more linguistic clues children have, the better their fast-mapping is (Mintz, 2005).

An experiment in teaching the names of parts of objects (e.g., the spigot of a faucet) found that children learned much better if the adults named the object that had the part and then spoke of the object in the possessive (e.g., "See this butterfly? Look, this is the butterfly's *thorax*") (Saylor & Sabbagh, 2004). It is easier to map a new word when it is connected to a familiar one.

Horse or Dromedary? These children might fast-map and call it a horse since it is horse-sized, horse-colored, and has a horselike head and legs. Fast-mapping can be misleading. However, if you think this is a dromedary, you made a similar mistake. All dromedaries are camels, but not all camels are dromedaries. This one is not.

OBSERVATION QUIZ
Is this scene set in the United States or some other country? (see answer, page 192) →

WORDS AND THE LIMITS OF LOGIC Closely related to fast-mapping is a phenomenon called *logical extension:* After learning a word, children use it to describe other objects in the same category. One child told her father she had seen some "Dalmatian cows" on a school trip to a farm. He remembered that she had petted a Dalmatian dog the weekend before.

Bilingual children who don't know a word in the language they are speaking often insert a word from the other language. Soon they know who understands which language—and make no substitutions when speaking to a monolingual person.

Some words are particularly difficult—*who/whom, have been/had been, here/there, yesterday/tomorrow.* More than one child has awakened on Christmas morning and asked, "Is it tomorrow yet?" A child told to "stay there" or "come here" may not follow instructions because the terms are confusing. It might be better to say "Stay on that bench" or "Come hold my hand."

Extensive study of children's language abilities finds that fast-mapping is only one of many techniques that children use to learn language: When a word does not refer to an object on the mental map, children find other ways to master it (Carey, 2010). If a word does not refer to anything the child can see or otherwise sense or act on, it may be ignored. Always, however, action helps. A hole is to dig; love is hugging; hearts beat.

LISTENING, TALKING, AND READING Because literacy is crucial in the United States, a meta-analysis of about 300 studies analyzed which activities in early childhood aided reading a few years later in elementary school. Both vocabulary and attention to the sounds of words (phonics) predicted fluent reading (Shanahan & Lonigan, 2010). Five specific strategies and experiences were particularly effective for young children of all income levels and ethnicities:

1. *Code-focused teaching.* In order for children to learn to read, they must "break the code" from spoken to written words. It is helpful for children to learn the letters and sounds of the alphabet (e.g., "*A*, alligators all around" or, conventionally, "*B* is for baby").

2. *Book reading.* Vocabulary as well as familiarity with pages and print increase when adults read to children, allowing questions and conversation.

3. *Parent education.* When teachers and other professionals teach parents how to stimulate cognition (as in the book reading of the previous item), children become better readers.

4. *Language enhancement.* Within each child's zone of proximal development, mentors can expand vocabulary and grammar, based on what the child knows and experiences.

5. *Preschool programs.* Children learn from teachers, songs, excursions, and other children.

ACQUIRING BASIC GRAMMAR We noted in Chapter 3 that the *grammar* of language includes the structures, techniques, and rules that communicate meaning. By age 2, children understand the basics. For example, English-speaking children know word order (subject/verb/object), saying, "I eat apple," not any of the five other possible sequences of those words. They use plurals; tenses (past, present, and future); and nominative, objective, and possessive pronouns (*I, me,* and *mine* or *my*).

Some 3-year-olds use articles (*the, a, an*) correctly, although proper article use in English is bewilderingly complex, as non–English speakers can attest. Every language has both easy and difficult aspects that native speakers eventually learn. Learning each aspect of language (grammar, vocabulary, pronunciation, etc.) follows a particular developmental path.

One reason for variation in language learning is that several parts of the brain are involved, each myelinating at a different rate. Furthermore, many genes and alleles affect comprehension and expression. In general, genes affect *expressive* (spoken or written) language more than *receptive* (heard or read) language. Thus, some children are relatively talkative or quiet because they inherit that tendency, but experience (not genes) determines what they understand (Kovas et al., 2005).

Children are eager to apply rules of grammar as soon as they learn them. For example, English-speaking children quickly learn to add an *s* to form the plural: Toddlers follow that rule when they ask for two cookies or more blocks.

Soon they add an *s* to make the plural of words they have never heard before, even nonsense words. If preschoolers are shown a drawing of an abstract shape, are told it is called a *wug,* and are then shown two of these shapes, they say there are two *wugs.* In keeping with the distinction between reception and expression, very young children realize words have a singular and a plural before they can express it (Zapf & Smith, 2007).

However, sometimes children apply the rules of grammar when they should not, an error called **overregularization.** By age 4, many children overregularize that final *s,* talking about *foots, tooths,* and *mouses.* This is actually evidence of increasing knowledge: Many children first say words correctly (*feet, teeth, mice*), repeating what they have heard. Later, when they grasp the grammar and try to apply it, they overregularize, assuming that all constructions follow the regular path (Ramscar & Dye, 2011).

overregularization
The application of rules of grammar even when exceptions occur, making the language seem more "regular" than it actually is.

Learning Two Languages

Language-minority children (who speak a language that is not their nation's dominant one) suffer if they do not also speak the majority language. In the United States, those who are not proficient in English have lower school achievement, diminished self-esteem, and inadequate employment, as well as many other problems. Fluency in English can erase these liabilities; fluency in another language then becomes an asset.

In the United States in 2010, 21 percent of schoolchildren spoke a language other than English at home, with most of them (75 percent) also speaking English well

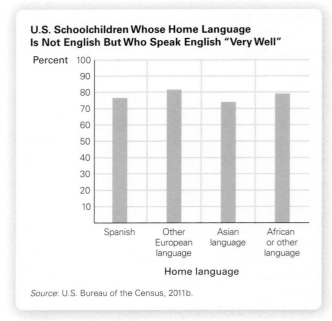

U.S. Schoolchildren Whose Home Language Is Not English But Who Speak English "Very Well"

Source: U.S. Bureau of the Census, 2011b.

FIGURE 5.9 Mastering English: The Younger, the Better Of all the schoolchildren whose home language is not English, this is the proportion who, according to their parents, speak English well. Immigrant children who attend school almost always master English within five years.

✦ **ESPECIALLY FOR Immigrant Parents** You want your children to be fluent in the language of your family's new country, even though you do not speak that language well. Should you speak to your children in your native tongue or in the new language? (see response, page 194) ➜

ANSWER TO OBSERVATION QUIZ (from page 190) It is not in the United States. Some clues are the boys' haircuts, the girl's headscarf, and the clothes on all three—each possible in the United States, but unlikely on three U.S. children together. Another clue is that camels with two humps are rare in U.S. zoos. But one thing is definitive: the fence. By law and custom, no U.S. zoos have fences children can crawl through. Is this cultural scaffolding, leading U.S. preschoolers to fear camels more than these Italians do? ●

(U.S. Bureau of the Census, 2011b) (see Figure 5.9). The percentage of bilingual children is higher in many other nations: In Canada and many African, Asian, and European nations, by sixth grade many children are bilingual, and some are trilingual. Language learning is aided by school instruction, but generally, the earlier a child learns a second language, the more easily and quickly the learning occurs.

HOW AND WHY Is national unity threatened by language-minority speakers? Would having all citizens speak one and only one language increase national pride? Is international understanding crucial, and would speaking several languages accomplish that?

Should a nation have one official language, several, or none? (Switzerland has three official languages, Canada has two; India has one national language [Hindi], but many states of India also have their own, for a total of 28 official languages; the United States has none, although the ability to read, write, and speak English is required for citizenship.) There is disagreement about the answers to all of these questions.

Some worry that young children taught two languages might become semilingual, not bilingual, "at risk for delayed, incomplete, and possibly even impaired language development" (Genesee, 2008, p. 17). Others argue that "there is absolutely no evidence that children get confused if they learn two languages" (Genesee, 2008, p. 18). This second position has more research support: Soon after the vocabulary explosion, children who have heard two languages since birth usually master two distinct sets of words and grammar, along with each language's pauses, pronunciations, intonations, and gestures (Genesee & Nicoladis, 2007).

No doubt early childhood is the best time to learn a language or languages. Neuroscience finds that young bilingual children site both languages in the same areas of their brains yet manage to keep them separate. This separation allows them to activate one language and temporarily inhibit the other, experiencing no confusion when they speak to a monolingual person (Crinion et al., 2006). They may be a millisecond slower to respond if they must switch languages, but their brains overall function better. Being bilingual in childhood may even provide some resistance to Alzheimer dementia in old age (Bialystok et al., 2009).

Pronunciation is particularly hard to master after childhood, in any language. However, do not mistake pronunciation for comprehension, and do not assume that someone who speaks with an accent lacks knowledge (difference is not deficit). From infancy on, hearing is more acute than vocalization. Almost all children have pronunciation difficulties in their first language, but they are blithely unaware of mistakes and gradually echo precisely whatever accent they hear.

In early childhood, children transpose sounds (*magazine* becomes *mazagine*), drop consonants (*truck* becomes *ruck*), and convert difficult sounds to easier ones (*father* becomes *fadder*). Mispronunciation does not impair fluency primarily because young children are more receptive than expressive—they hear better than they talk. For instance, when 4-year-old Rachel asked for a "yeyo yayipop," her father repeated, "You want a yeyo yayipop?" She replied, "Daddy, sometimes you talk funny."

To speak well, young children need to be "bathed in language," as some early-childhood educators express it. They need to listen and speak in every situation, just as a person taking a bath is surrounded by water. Television is a poor teacher because children need personalized, responsive instruction in their zone of proximal development. In fact, young children who watch the most television tend to be delayed in language learning (Harrison & McLeod, 2010).

LANGUAGE LOSS AND GAINS Schools in all nations stress the dominant language, and language-minority parents fear that their children will make a *language shift*, becoming more fluent in the school language than in their home language. Language shift occurs everywhere—some Mexican language-minority children shift to Spanish (Messing, 2007), some First Nations children in Canada shift to English (Allen, 2007), as do some Chinese-speaking children in the United States—but not always (Zhang, 2010). The attitudes and practices of parents and the community are crucial.

Remember that young children are preoperational: They center on the immediate status of their language (not on its future global usefulness or past glory) and on appearance more than substance. No wonder many shift toward the language of the dominant culture. Since language is integral to culture, if a child is to become fluently bilingual, everyone who speaks with the child should show evident appreciation of both cultures (Pearson, 2008; Snow & Kang, 2006).

Becoming a **balanced bilingual,** speaking two languages so well that no audible hint suggests the other language, is accomplished by millions of young children in many nations. This benefits their intellectual flexibility (Bialystok & Viswanathan, 2009; Pearson, 2008).

balanced bilingual
A person who is fluent in two languages, not favoring one over the other.

Yet language loss is a valid fear. Millions of children either abandon their first language or do not learn the second as well as they might. Although skills in one language can be transferred to benefit acquisition of another, "transfer is neither automatic nor inevitable" (Snow & Kang, 2006, p. 97). Scaffolding is needed.

The basics of language learning—the naming and vocabulary explosions, fast-mapping, overregularization, extensive practice—apply to every language children learn. Young children's vocabulary in two languages is directly connected to how much they hear. If a child is to become a balanced bilingual, that child needs to hear twice as much talk as usual (Hammer et al., 2011).

The same practices can make a child fluently trilingual, as some 5 year-olds are. One parent might talk and read to a child in French, for instance, another in English, while the child plays with friends at a Spanish-speaking preschool.

Bilingual children and adults are advanced in theory of mind and executive functioning, probably because they need to be more reflective and strategic when they speak. However, sheer linguistic proficiency does not necessarily lead to cognitive advances (Bialystock & Barac, 2011). Simply learning new words and grammar (many preschools teach songs in a second language) does not guarantee a child will learn to understand and appreciate other cultures.

Smiling Faces, Usually Everyone in this group is an immigrant, born far from his current home in Burlington, Vermont. Jean Luc Dushime escaped the 1994 genocide in Rwanda, central Africa, when he was 14. He eventually adapted to his new language, climate, surroundings, and culture. Today he helps immigrant children make the same transition.

KEYpoints

- Children learn language rapidly and well during early childhood.
- Fast-mapping is one way children learn. Errors in precision, overregularization, and mispronunciation are common and are not problematic at this age.
- Vocabulary advances, particularly if a child is "bathed in language," hearing many words and concepts.
- Young children can learn two languages almost as easily as one, if adults talk frequently, listen carefully, and value both languages.

RESPONSE FOR Immigrant Parents
(from page 192) Children learn by
listening, so it is important to speak
with them often. You might prefer to
read to your children, sing to them,
and converse with them primarily in
your native language and find a good
preschool where they will learn the
new language. The worst thing you
could do would be to restrict speech in
either tongue. ●

Tricky Indeed Young children are
omnivorous learners, picking up certain
habits, curses, and attitudes that adults
would rather not transmit. Deciding
what to teach—by actions more than
words—is essential.

© THE NEW YORKER COLLECTION 1991 ROBERT WEBER FROM CARTOONBANK.COM. ALL RIGHTS RESERVED.

"We teach them that the world can be an unpredictable,
dangerous, and sometimes frightening place, while being careful
not to spoil their lovely innocence. It's tricky."

Early-Childhood Education

A hundred years ago, children had no formal education until first grade, which is why it was called "first" and why young children were "*pre*schoolers." Today, virtually every nation has some program of early-childhood education (Britto et al., 2011). In some countries, most 3- to 6-year-olds are in school (see Figure 5.10 for U.S. trends) not only because of changing family and economic patterns but also because research "documents the rapid development and great learning potential of the early years" (Hyson et al., 2006, p. 6).

Homes and Schools

A robust research conclusion is that quality matters. If the home educational environment is poor, a good preschool program aids health, cognition, and social skills (Hindman et al., 2010). However, if a family provides extensive learning opportunities and encouragement, the quality of the preschool is less crucial. It is better for the young children to be at such a home than in a stressful, overcrowded preschool.

It is difficult to judge the quality of homes and schools in the United States because of the "stunning variability and fragmentation" of public and private schools (Pianta et al., 2009, p. 50) and the changing configuration of home care. It is a mistake to conclude that care by the mother is better than care by another relative or nonrelative—or vice versa.

Educational institutions for young children are referred to by various names (preschool, nursery school, day care, pre-primary, pre-K) or structures (public, private, center, family), but these labels do not reliably indicate quality (A.S. Fuligni et al., 2009). Each early-childhood educational program (and sometimes each teacher) emphasizes different skills, goals, and methods (Chambers et al., 2010; Walsh & Petty, 2007).

We will now consider two general categories of early-childhood education: child-centered and teacher-directed. Remember, however, that the quality of the home and the effectiveness of the teachers have more impact on young children than does the label or professed philosophy of the program.

Child-Centered Programs

Many programs are called *developmental,* or *child-centered,* because they stress each child's development and growth. Teachers in such programs believe children need to follow their own interests rather than adult directions. For example, they agree that "children should be allowed to select many of their own activities from a variety of learning areas that the teacher has prepared" (Lara-Cinisomo et al., 2011). The physical space and the materials (such as dress-up clothing, art supplies, puzzles, blocks, other toys) are arranged to allow self-paced exploration.

Most child-centered programs encourage artistic expression (Lim, 2004). Some educators argue that young children "are all poets" in that they are gifted in seeing the world more imaginatively than older people do. According to advocates of child-centered programs, this peak of creative vision should be encouraged; children are given many opportunities to tell stories, draw pictures, dance, and make music for their own delight.

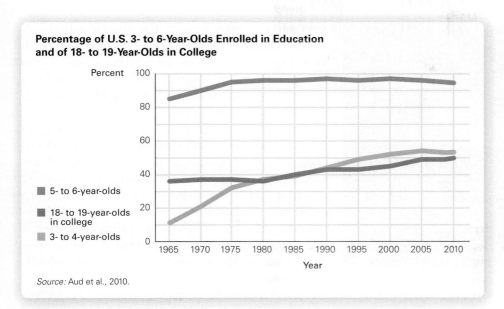

Percentage of U.S. 3- to 6-Year-Olds Enrolled in Education and of 18- to 19-Year-Olds in College

5- to 6-year-olds

18- to 19-year-olds in college

3- to 4-year-olds

Source: Aud et al., 2010.

FIGURE 5.10 Changing Times As research increasingly finds that preschool education provides a foundation for later learning, most young children are enrolled in educational programs. Note the contrast with 18- to 19-year-olds in college (not shown are the 18- to 19-year-olds still in high school—about 15 percent).

● **UNDERSTANDING THE NUMBERS**

Often, accurate interpretation of numbers requires knowing exactly what definition is used to decide what the count should include. To say that most 3- to 6-year-olds are "in school" reflects a broad definition of school. Can you elaborate?

Answer As the figure shows, most U.S. 3- to 6-year-olds are in some kind of organized group setting where they are learning. However, if school is defined more traditionally, as the place of instruction in the "three R's" (reading, writing, and arithmetic), then only about 10 percent of 3- to 6-year-olds in the United States are in school.

OBSERVATION QUIZ

At what point did the percentage of 3- to 4-year-olds in school exceed that of 18- to 19-year-olds in college? (see answer, page 197) ➞

Child-centered programs are often influenced by Piaget, who emphasized that each child will discover new ideas, and by Vygotsky, who thought that children learn from other children, with adult guidance (Bodrova & Leong, 2005). Trained teachers are crucial: A child-centered program requires appropriate activities for each child and teachers who guide and scaffold so that each child advances (Dominguez et al., 2010).

MONTESSORI SCHOOLS One type of child-centered school began more than 100 years ago, when Maria Montessori opened nursery schools for poor children in Rome. She believed that children needed structured, individualized projects to give them a sense of accomplishment. They completed puzzles, used sponges and water to clean tables, traced shapes, and so on.

Contemporary **Montessori schools** still emphasize individual pride and achievement, presenting many literacy-related tasks (e.g., outlining letters and looking at books) to young children (Lillard, 2005). Specific materials differ from those that Montessori developed, but the underlying philosophy is the same. Children seek out learning tasks; they do not sit quietly in groups while a teacher instructs them. That makes Montessori programs child-centered.

This philosophy seems to work. A study of 5-year-olds in inner-city Milwaukee who were chosen by lottery to attend Montessori programs found that the children were advanced in prereading (such as recognizing letters), math, and theory of mind, compared with their peers in other schools (Lillard & Else-Quest, 2006). The probable explanation: Their Montessori tasks seem to lead to self-confidence, curiosity, and exploration, which transferred to more academic tasks.

REGGIO EMILIA Another form of early-childhood education is **Reggio Emilia,** named after the town in Italy where it began. In Reggio Emilia, children are encouraged to master skills that are not usually taught in North American schools until age 7 or so, such as writing and using tools (hammers, knives, and so on).

In Reggio schools, there is no large-group instruction, with lessons in, say, forming letters or cutting paper. Instead, "Every child is a creative child, full of potential"

Montessori schools

Schools that offer early-childhood education based on the philosophy of Maria Montessori (an Italian educator more than a century ago); it emphasizes careful work and tasks that each young child can do.

Reggio Emilia

A famous program of early-childhood education that originated in the town of Reggio Emilia, Italy; it encourages each child's creativity in a carefully designed setting.

INFOCUSPHOTOS.COM / ALAMY

Tibet, China, India, and . . . Italy?
Over the past half-century, as China increased its control of Tibet, thousands of refugees fled to northern India. Tibet traditionally had no preschools, but young children adapt quickly, as here in Ladakh, India. This Tibetan boy is working a classic Montessori board.

(Gandini et al., 2005, p. 1), with personal learning needs and artistic drive. Measurement of achievements, such as standardized testing to see whether children have learned their letters, is not part of the core belief that each child should explore and learn in his or her own way (Lewin-Benham, 2008).

Appreciation of the arts is evident. Every Reggio Emilia school has a studio, an artist, and space to encourage creativity. Consequently, Reggio Emilia schools have a large central room with many hubs of activity and a low child/adult ratio. Children's art is displayed on white walls and hung from high ceilings, and floor-to-ceiling windows open to a spacious, plant-filled playground. Big mirrors are part of the schools' décor—again, with the idea of fostering individuality and self-expression.

The curious little scientist is encouraged with materials to explore. One analysis of Reggio Emilia in the United States found "a science-rich context that triggered and supported preschoolers' inquiries and effectively engaged preschoolers' hands, heads, and hearts with science" (Inan et al., 2010, p. 1186).

Teacher-Directed Programs

Unlike child-centered programs, teacher-directed preschools stress academics, often taught by one adult to the entire group. The curriculum includes learning the names of letters, numbers, shapes, and colors according to a set timetable; every child naps, snacks, and goes to the bathroom on schedule as well. Children learn to sit quietly and listen to the teacher. Praise and other reinforcements are given for good behavior, and time-outs (brief separation from activities) are imposed to punish misbehavior.

In teacher-directed programs, the serious work of schooling is distinguished from the unstructured play of home. According to a study of preschool educators, some teachers endorse ideas that indicate their teacher-directed philosophy, such as that children should form letters correctly before they are allowed to create a story (Lara-Cinisomo et al., 2011).

The goal of teacher-directed programs is to make all children "ready to learn" when they enter elementary school. For that reason, basic skills are stressed, including precursors to reading, writing, and arithmetic, perhaps via teachers asking questions that children answer together.

Child-Centered Pride How can Rachel Koepke, a 3-year-old from a Wisconsin town called Pleasant Prairie, seem so pleased that her hands (and cuffs) are blue? The answer arises from northern Italy—Rachel attends a Reggio Emilia preschool that encourages creative expression.

Children practice forming letters, sounding out words, counting objects, and writing their names. If a 4-year-old learns to read, that is success. (In a child-centered program, that might arouse suspicion that there was too little time to play or socialize.) Good behavior, not informal social interaction, is rewarded—leading one critic to suggest that "readiness" is too narrowly defined (Winter, 2011).

Many teacher-directed programs were inspired by behaviorism, which emphasizes step-by-step learning and repetition, with reinforcement (praise, gold stars, prizes) for accomplishment. Another inspiration for teacher-directed programs comes from research indicating that children who have not learned basic vocabulary and listening skills by kindergarten often fall behind in primary school. Many state legislatures mandate that preschoolers learn particular concepts, an outcome best achieved by teacher-directed learning (Bracken & Crawford, 2010).

ELIZABETH FLORES KRT / NEWSCOM

Head Start

Millions of young children in the United States were thought to need a "head start" on their formal education to help foster better health and cognition before first grade. Consequently, since 1965 the federal government has funded a massive program for 4-year-olds called **Head Start.**

The goals for Head Start have changed over the decades, from lifting families out of poverty to promoting literacy, from providing dental care and immunizations to teaching Standard English. Although initially most Head Start programs were child-centered, they have become increasingly teacher-directed as waves of legislators have approved and shaped them. Children have benefited, learning whatever their teachers and curricula emphasize. For example, many low-income 3- and 4-year-olds in the United States are not normally exposed to math. One Head Start program engaged children in a board game with numbers; their mathematical understanding advanced significantly (Siegler, 2009).

A recent congressional authorization of funding for Head Start included a requirement for extensive evaluation to answer two questions:

1. What difference does Head Start make to key outcomes of development and learning (in particular, school readiness) for low-income children? How does Head Start affect parental practices?

2. Under what circumstances and for whom does Head Start achieve the greatest impact?

The answers were not as dramatic as either advocates or detractors had hoped (U.S. Department of Health and Human Services, 2010). Head Start improved literacy and math skills, oral health, and parental responsiveness. However, many academic benefits faded by first grade. One reason might be that, unlike when Head Start began, in the twenty-first century many of the non–Head Start children in the comparison group were enrolled in other early-childhood programs—sometimes excellent ones, sometimes not.

Head Start
The most widespread early-childhood-education program in the United States, begun in 1965 and funded by the federal government.

ANSWER TO **OBSERVATION QUIZ**
(from page 195) Between 1985 and 1990.
The exact year (not shown) was 1988. ●

PAUL CHESLEY / STONE / GETTY IMAGES

Learning from One Another Every nation creates its own version of early education. In this scene at a nursery school in Kuala Lumpur, Malaysia, note the head coverings, uniforms, bare feet, and absence of boys. None of these elements would be found in most early-childhood education classrooms in North America or Europe.

OBSERVATION QUIZ
What seemingly universal aspects of childhood are visible in this photograph? (see answer, page 199) →

ELLEN B. SENSI / IMAGE WORKS

Disaster Recovery The success of Head Start led to Early Head Start, for children such as this 2-year-old in Biloxi, Mississippi. When Hurricane Katrina destroyed most of the community, it was the first program to reemerge there. Small children recover from disasters more easily if their parents can reestablish a normal life—which is why this Head Start program is helping entire families.

✦ **ESPECIALLY FOR** Teachers In trying to find a preschool program, what should parents look for? (see response, page 200) ⟶

Certain children benefited more than others did, with benefits most apparent for children with the lowest family incomes, those living in rural areas, and those with disabilities (U.S. Department of Health and Human Services, 2010). These were also the children least likely to find other sources of early education, which supports the notion that Head Start is better than no program at all. The strongest overall benefits were advances in language and social skills during early childhood, but by elementary school, other children had caught up, with one exception: Head Start children were still ahead in vocabulary.

That also supports what you have just read about early childhood as a sensitive period for language learning. Any good preschool is bound to introduce children to words they would not learn at home. The result is that the children fast-map those words, gaining a linguistic advantage that makes it easier to expand their vocabulary.

THE NEED FOR STRUCTURE Many developmentalists resist legislative prescriptions (such as those in some current Head Start regulations) regarding what 3- and 4-year-olds should learn. Some teachers want to do whatever they believe is best, resulting in a happy hodgepodge of strategies. However, this may confuse children and parents. Differences may reflect culture, not what is best for children or what is consistent based on theory and research.

This was apparent in a detailed study in the Netherlands, where native-born Dutch teachers emphasized individual achievement (child-centered) more than did the teachers from the Caribbean or Mediterranean, who stressed proper behavior and group learning (teacher-directed) (Huijbregts et al., 2009). Teachers of either background who had worked together for years shared more beliefs and practices than new teachers did (Huijbregts et al., 2009). Hopefully, they had learned from one another.

As many studies have shown, children can learn whatever academic and social skills are taught to them; those who attended preschool are usually advanced in cognitive skills because such skills are emphasized (Camilli et al., 2010; Chambers et al., 2010). But no matter what the curriculum, all young children need personal attention, consistency, and continuity: It does not help when every adult applies idiosyncratic rules and routines. This is one of many reasons that parents and teachers should communicate and cooperate in teaching young children, a strategy Head Start has emphasized from the early days.

BILINGUAL EDUCATION The need for a coherent strategy is apparent in bilingual education. Successful strategies need to vary depending on the child, the home background, and national values. As one review concludes, "It is highly unlikely that one approach will be equally effective for all DLLs [dual language learners]" (Hammer et al., 2011), but some strategy is needed.

U.S. research has focused on the approximately 25 percent of the country's young children who are of Hispanic heritage. In general, programs that combine English and Spanish instruction, sometimes with half a day for each, are more successful at teaching English while advancing Spanish than are programs that simply immerse the Spanish-speaking children in an English-only setting (Barnett et al., 2007) or keep Spanish as the sole language of instruction.

Unfortunately, for political and cultural reasons, the young children who are least likely to attend preschool in the United States are those from Spanish-speaking homes—only about one-third of them are in preschool (see Figure 5.11). These data are for 4-year-olds; the proportions of 3-year-olds from Spanish-speaking homes who are in preschools is even lower, perhaps 15 percent. As discussed earlier, learning a second language is easiest before age 4; most Spanish-speaking children do not have that opportunity.

Head Start now requires that children be from low-income families. Many Hispanic children qualify and hence could take advantage of free early education. However, even in Head Start, Hispanic children are not likely to be enrolled (see Figure 5.11).

One reason for the low attendance of young Spanish-speaking children (most of whom are citizens) is their parents' fear of deportation if anyone in the extended family is undocumented. Another reason is custom: The evidence that young children benefit from preschool is familiar to most English-speaking adults, but not to most immigrants.

An added problem is that many Head Start programs are limited to three hours a day, and relatively few teachers are native Spanish speakers. Since adult women who speak only Spanish are more likely than bilingual mothers to be unemployed, or employed with long hours, many families opt for the mother or other relative to provide child care, not realizing the impact of Spanish-only learning on later education.

The percentage of Hispanic children in preschool programs would be even lower if the statistics included all children now living in the United States who were born elsewhere. Almost none of them are in preschool, although all of them (whether citizens, documented immigrants, or undocumented immigrants) are eligible for public education once they reach age 6. Each year, almost a million children enter first grade in the United States with poor English skills, primarily because they had no early education that included learning English.

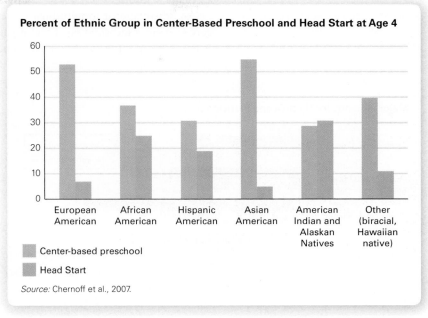

Percent of Ethnic Group in Center-Based Preschool and Head Start at Age 4

■ Center-based preschool
■ Head Start

Source: Chernoff et al., 2007.

FIGURE 5.11 The Other Half Many research studies find that 4-year-olds who attend preschool are more competent in kindergarten—they have better language skills and are more likely to make friends. However, it is not known why half of all 4-year-olds are not in prekindergarten programs of any kind.

Long-Term Gains from Intensive Programs

This discussion of various programs, with fluctuating philosophies, practices, and child participation, may give the impression that the research is mixed. That is the wrong impression. It is true that specifics are debatable, but empirical evidence and longitudinal evaluation have convinced most developmentalists that preschool education has many benefits if it is sufficiently intensive and employs effective teachers.

The best evidence comes from three longitudinal programs that enrolled children full time for years, sometimes beginning with home visits in infancy, sometimes continuing in after-school programs through first grade. One program, called *Perry* (or *High/Scope*), was spearheaded in Michigan (Schweinhart & Weikart, 1997); another, called *Abecedarian*, got its start in North Carolina (Campbell et al., 2001); a third, called *Child–Parent Centers*, began in Chicago (Reynolds, 2000). Because of the political context when these programs began, all were focused on children from low-SES families.

All three programs compared experimental groups of children with matched control groups, and all reached the same conclusion: Early education can have substantial long-term benefits that become most apparent when children are in the third grade or later. By age 10, children who had been enrolled in one of these three programs scored higher on math and reading achievement tests than did

ANSWER TO **OBSERVATION QUIZ**
(from page 197) Three aspects are readily apparent: These girls enjoy their friendships; they are playing a hand-clapping game (some version of which is found in every culture); and, most important, they have begun the formal education that their families want for them. ●

other children from the same backgrounds, schools, and neighborhoods. They were less likely to be placed in special classes for slow or disruptive children or to repeat a year of school.

An advantage of longitudinal research from these studies is that adults who received early education can be compared to adults who did not. For all three programs, benefits continue. In adolescence, the children who had undergone intensive preschool education had higher aspirations, possessed a greater sense of achievement, and were less likely to have been abused. As young adults, they were more likely to attend college and less likely to go to jail, more often paying taxes rather than being on welfare (Reynolds & Ou, 2011; Schweinhart et al., 2005). Early education affected every aspect of their adult life, as "early cognitive and scholastic advantages lead to social and motivational gains that culminate in enhanced well-being" (Reynolds & Ou, 2011, p. 578) (see Figure 5.12).

All three research projects found that providing direct cognitive training (rather than simply letting children play), with specific instruction in various school-readiness skills, was useful as long as each child's needs and talents were considered—a circumstance made possible because the child/adult ratio was low. The curricular approach was a combination of child-centered and teacher-directed, with teachers all trained in a specific structure, so children were not confused. Furthermore, teachers were encouraged to involve parents in their children's education, and each program included strategies to ensure this home–school connection.

These programs were expensive (ranging from $5,000 to $17,000 annually per young child in 2010 dollars). From a developmental perspective, the decreased need for special education and other social services eventually made such programs a wise investment, perhaps saving $4 for every dollar spent (Barnett, 2007). The benefits to society over the child's lifetime, including increased employment, taxes, and reduced crime, are much more than that.

In fact, the greatest lifetime return came from boys from high-poverty neighborhoods in the Chicago preschool program, with a social benefit over the boys' lifetime more than 12 times the cost (Reynolds et al., 2011). The political problem is that the costs are immediate and the benefits long term; without a developmental perspective, some legislators and voters are unwilling to fund expensive intervention programs that do not pay off until a decade or more later.

Fortunately, that is changing: 40 states sponsor public education for young children—although usually only for low-income 4-year-olds. In 2009–2010, more than a million children (1,292,310) attended state-sponsored preschools—double the number a decade earlier (Barnett et al., 2010). Since 4 million (actually, 4,268,000) children were born in 2006, that is slightly more than one child in three.

From a developmental perspective, the leading state is Oklahoma, which provides full-day kindergarten and preschool education for all children. Attendance is voluntary, but most children are enrolled. The data showed more gains than in Head Start, which usually offers only a half-day program (Gormley et al., 2008). The Oklahoma curriculum emphasizes literacy and math; benefits are particularly strong for children whose home language is Spanish (Phillips et al., 2009).

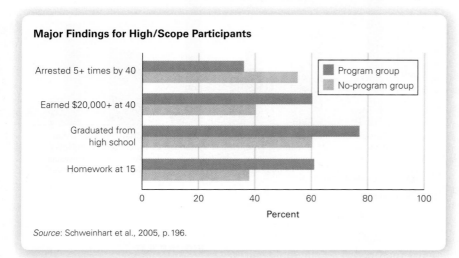

Major Findings for High/Scope Participants

Program group
No-program group

Source: Schweinhart et al., 2005, p. 196.

FIGURE 5.12 And in Middle Age
Longitudinal research found that two years in the intensive High/Scope preschool program changed the lives of dozens of children from impoverished families. The program had a positive impact on many aspects of their education, early adulthood, and middle age. (This graph does not illustrate another intriguing finding: The girls who attended High/Scope fared much better than the boys.)

RESPONSE FOR Teachers (from page 198) Tell parents to look at the people more than the program. Parents should see the children in action and note whether the teachers show warmth and respect for each child. ●

Although developmentalists are pleased that the public finally recognizes the benefits of early education, the message that quality matters does not seem to be understood. For the 40 states that sponsor early education, the average funding is less than $5,000 per year per student. That is obviously not enough to support a program with a low child/adult ratio; teachers who have college degrees; and professional mentoring in a safe, well-equipped space.

Only four states (Alabama, Alaska, North Carolina, and Rhode Island) have programs that developmentalists consider to be of high quality, and those four states enroll only a tiny fraction of young children (Barnett et al., 2010). Developmentalists agree that increasing the number of participants and improving the quality of preschool programs is a prime goal; the only problem is finding out how to convince legislators and the public that it must be done.

Note also that the initial research was on low-income children. Most developmentalists think that the findings apply to all children, but that is controversial—especially when funding for education at all levels is diminishing.

Indeed, the same dilemma is apparent for many aspects of early cognition. Much more is known now than formerly about what children can learn, and there is no doubt that 2- and 3-year-olds are capable of learning languages, concepts, and much else. A hundred years ago, that was not understood. Piaget was a leader in recognizing the abilities of the child. Now Piaget's work has been eclipsed by new research: What a child learns before age 6 is pivotal for later schooling and adult life, yet many children do not learn what they need to know.

This theme continues in the next chapter, on the interaction between children and all the systems that surround them.

KEY Points

- Young children can learn a great deal before kindergarten, either in a child-centered or teacher-directed preschool, or in an excellent home setting.
- Montessori and Reggio Emilia schools advance children's learning. Both emphasize individual accomplishments and child development.
- Teacher-directed programs stress readiness for school, emphasizing letters and numbers that all children should understand.
- Head Start and other programs advance learning for low-income children. Longitudinal research finds that some of the benefits are evident in adulthood.
- Unfortunately, relatively few Spanish-speaking children are enrolled in good preschool education.

SUMMARY

Body Changes

1. Children continue to gain weight and add height during early childhood. Many adults overfeed children, not realizing that young children are naturally quite thin.

2. Many young children consume too much sugar and too little calcium and other nutrients. One consequence is poor oral health. Children need to brush their teeth and visit the dentist years before their permanent teeth erupt.

3. Gross motor skills continue to develop; clumsy 2-year-olds become agile 6-year-olds who move their bodies well, guided by their culture. By playing with other children in safe places, they practice the skills needed for formal education.

4. Accidents cause more preventable deaths than diseases do. Young children are more likely to suffer a serious injury or premature death than are older children. Close supervision and public safeguards can protect young children from their own eager,

impulsive curiosity. Pollutants hamper development, with lead proven to impair the brain and motor skills.

5. Injury control occurs on many levels, including long before and immediately after each harmful incident. Primary prevention protects everyone. Secondary and tertiary prevention also save lives.

Brain Development

6. The brain continues to grow in early childhood, reaching 75 percent of its adult weight at age 2 and 90 percent by age 5. Lateralization becomes evident.

7. Myelination is substantial during early childhood, speeding messages from one part of the brain to another. The corpus callosum becomes thicker and functions much better. Maturation of the prefrontal cortex, known as the executive of the brain, reduces both impulsivity and perseveration.

8. The expression and regulation of emotions are fostered by several brain areas collectively called the limbic system, including the amygdala, the hippocampus, and the hypothalamus.

Thinking During Early Childhood

9. Piaget stressed the egocentric and illogical aspects of thought during the play years; he called thinking at this stage preoperational because young children often cannot yet use logical operations. They sometimes focus on only one thing (centration) and see things only from their own viewpoint (egocentrism), remaining stuck on appearances and current reality.

10. Vygotsky stressed the social aspects of childhood cognition, noting that children learn by participating in various experiences, guided by more knowledgeable adults or peers who scaffold to aid learning. Such guidance assists learning within the zone of proximal development.

11. Children develop theories to explain human behavior. One theory about children's thinking is called *theory-theory*—the hypothesis that children develop theories because people innately seek explanations for everything they observe.

12. In early childhood, children develop a theory of mind—an understanding of what others may be thinking. Notable advances in theory of mind occur at around age 4. Theory of mind is partly the result of brain maturation, but culture and experiences also have an impact.

Language Learning

13. Language develops rapidly during early childhood, a sensitive period but not a critical one for language learning. Vocabulary increases dramatically, with thousands of words added between ages 2 and 6. In addition, basic grammar is mastered.

14. Many children learn to speak more than one language, gaining cognitive as well as social advantages. Ideally, children become balanced bilinguals, equally proficient in two languages, by age 6.

Early-Childhood Education

15. Organized educational programs during early childhood advance cognitive and social skills. Many child-centered programs are inspired by Piaget and Vygotsky. Behaviorist principles led to many specific practices of teacher-directed programs.

16. Many types of preschool programs are successful. It is the quality of early education—whether at home or at school—that matters.

KEY TERMS

amygdala (p. 180)
animism (p. 182)
balanced bilingual (p. 193)
centration (p. 182)
conservation (p. 183)
corpus callosum (p. 179)
egocentrism (p. 182)
fast-mapping (p. 190)
focus on appearance (p. 183)
Head Start (p. 197)

hippocampus (p. 180)
hypothalamus (p. 181)
injury control/harm reduction (p. 174)
irreversibility (p. 183)
just right (p.169)
lateralization (p. 180)
limbic system (p.180)
Montessori schools (p.195)

myelination (p. 178)
overimitation (p.185)
overregularization (p. 191)
perseveration (p. 179)
prefrontal cortex (p.178)
preoperational intelligence (p. 182)
primary prevention (p. 174)
Reggio Emilia (p. 195)

scaffolding (p. 185)
secondary prevention (p. 174)
static reasoning (p. 183)
symbolic thought (p.182)
tertiary prevention (p. 174)
theory of mind (p. 187)
theory-theory (p. 186)
zone of proximal development (ZPD) (p. 185)

WHAT HAVE YOU LEARNED?

1. How are growth rates, body proportions, and motor skills related during early childhood?

2. Why might lower-income children be more vulnerable to nutritional problems?

3. What factors help children develop their motor skills?

4. Why do public health workers prefer to speak of "injury control" rather than "accident prevention"?

5. What are the differences among the three levels of harm reduction?

6. What changes in the brain's functioning are evident between ages 2 and 6?

7. Why is myelination important for thinking and motor skills?

8. How does the prefrontal cortex affect impulsivity and perseveration?

9. What is the function of the corpus callosum?

10. Why might left-handed children have thicker corpus callosa than right-handed children?

11. What role do the amygdala, hippocampus, and hypothalamus play in the expression and regulation of emotions?

12. In what way does symbolic thought advance cognition?

13. What barriers to logic exist at the preoperational stage? How might these affect children's thinking?

14. According to Vygotsky, what should parents and other caregivers do to encourage children's learning?

15. How does scaffolding increase a child's zone of proximal development?

16. What does the idea of theory-theory suggest about how children think?

17. What factors spur the development of theory of mind?

18. In what ways do theory-theory and theory of mind help explain why older children lie with greater skill than younger children do?

19. What is the evidence that early childhood is a sensitive time for learning language?

20. How does fast-mapping aid the language explosion?

21. Explain how code-focused teaching, book reading, parent education, language enhancement, and preschool programs each contribute to children's literacy.

22. How does overregularization signify a cognitive advance?

23. Why is early childhood the best time to learn a second (or third) language?

24. In child-centered programs, what do the teachers do?

25. Why are Montessori schools still functioning, 100 years after the first such schools opened?

APPLICATIONS

1. Keep a food diary for 24 hours, writing down what you eat, how much, when, how, and why. Then think about nutrition and eating habits in early childhood. Did your food habits originate in early childhood, in adolescence, or at some other time? Explain.

2. Go to a playground or other place where young children play. Note the motor skills that the children demonstrate, including abilities and inabilities, and keep track of age and sex. What differences do you see among the children?

3. Replicate one of Piaget's conservation experiments. The easiest one is conservation of liquids (illustrated in Figure 5.6). Work with a child under age 5 who tells you that two identically shaped glasses contain the same amount of liquid. Then ask the child to carefully pour one glass of liquid into a taller, narrower glass. Ask the child which glass now contains more or if the glasses contain the same amount.

>>ONLINE CONNECTIONS

To accompany your textbook, you have access to a number of online resources, including quizzes for every chapter of the book, flashcards (in English and Spanish), critical thinking questions, and case studies. For access to any of these links, go to www.worthpublishers.com/bergerinvitation2e. In addition to these free resources, you'll also find links to podcasts, video clips, diagnostic quizzing with personalized study advice, and an ebook. Some of the videos and activities available online include:

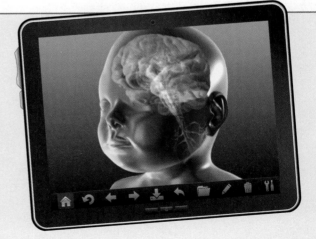

- *Brain Development in Early Childhood.* Animations illustrate the macroscopic and microscopic changes as children's brains grow.

- *Stolen Childhoods.* Some children, because of poverty or abuse, never have the opportunities for schooling and nurture that many of us take for granted. Children in a variety of difficult circumstances, from sex work to work in carpet factories, tell their stories in a variety of video clips.

CHAPTER OUTLINE

EARLY CHILDHOOD
Psychosocial Development

WHAT WILL YOU KNOW?

- Why do 2-year-olds have more sudden tempers, tears, and terrors than 6-year-olds?

- If a child never plays, is that a problem?

- What happens if parents let their children do whatever they want?

- What are the long-term effects of spanking children?

- Do maltreated children always become abusive adults?

t was a hot summer afternoon. My thirsty 3- and 4-year-olds were with me in the kitchen, which was in one corner of our living/dining area. The younger one opened the refrigerator and grabbed a bottle of orange juice. The sticky bottle slipped, shattering on the floor. My stunned daughters looked at me, at the shards, at the spreading juice with extra pulp. I picked them up and plopped them on the couch.

"Stay there until I clean this up," I shouted.

They did, wide-eyed at my fury. As they watched me pick, sweep, and mop, I understood how parents could hit their kids. By the end of the chapter, I hope you also realize how a moment like this—in the summer heat, with two small children, and unexpected and difficult work—can turn a loving, patient parent into something else. It is not easy, day after day, being the guide and model that parents should be. ●

- -

FORTUNATELY, MANY SAFEGUARDS prevented serious maltreatment—the girls stayed on the couch, my belief about not hitting children kept me from laying a hand on them, my finances made it easy to buy more juice. Many aspects of psychosocial development—as children learn to manage their emotions, as parents learn to guide their children, as the macrosystem and microsystem (beliefs and income) influence adult–child interaction—affect how well children develop from ages 2 to 6. This chapter describes all that.

Emotional Development

Children gradually learn when and how to express emotions, becoming more capable in every aspect of their lives (Buckley & Saarni, 2009; Denham et al., 2003; Morrison et al., 2010). Controlling the expression of emotions, called **emotional regulation,** is the preeminent psychosocial task between ages 2 and 6 (N. Eisenberg et al., 2004).

Such regulation is virtually impossible in infancy, but when the emotional hot spots of the limbic system connect to the prefrontal cortex, children become more aware of their reactions and better able to control them. By age 6, children can usually be angry but not explosive, frightened but not terrified, sad but not inconsolable, anxious but not withdrawn, proud but not boastful. Emotional regulation is a lifelong necessity and no one does it perfectly all the time.

Initiative Versus Guilt

During Erikson's third developmental stage, **initiative versus guilt,** children acquire many skills and competencies. *Initiative* can mean several things—saying something new, expanding an ability, beginning a project. Depending on the outcome (especially reactions from other people), children feel proud or guilty.

Usually, North American parents encourage enthusiasm, effort, and pride in their 2- to 6-year-olds. If, instead, parents ignore rather than guide emotions, a child may not learn emotional regulation (Morris et al., 2007).

emotional regulation
The ability to control when and how emotions are expressed.

initiative versus guilt
Erikson's third psychosocial crisis, in which children undertake new skills and activities and feel guilty when they do not succeed at them.

A Poet and We Know It She is the proud winner of a national poetry contest. Is she as surprised, humbled, and thankful as an adult winner would be?

ENIGMA / ALAMY

PROTECTIVE OPTIMISM Children's beliefs about their worth are connected to parental confirmation, especially when parents remind their children of their positive accomplishments ("You helped Daddy sweep the sidewalk. You made it very clean.") (Reese et al., 2007).

Remember that Erikson described autonomy at ages 1 and 2, often expressed as stubbornness and nicknamed "the terrible twos." By age 3, autonomy is better regulated and soon becomes initiative, as children are eager to learn new skills (Rubin et al., 2009). Indeed, the opening anecdote of this chapter is an example: My daughter was learning to get things from the refrigerator. Both autonomy and initiative are much more prized in Western cultures than in Eastern ones, where children learn to be socially attuned and interdependent (Keller & Otto, 2011).

Children in North America and Europe develop a strong **self-concept,** an understanding of themselves. For example, young children are given choices: "Water or juice?" "Blue pajamas or red ones?" Choosing makes people believe they are independent agents (Kim & Chu, 2011). In the United States, self-concept quickly includes gender and size. Girls are usually happy to be girls; boys to be boys; both are glad they aren't babies. "Crybaby" is an insult; praise for being "a big kid" is welcomed.

Erikson recognized that young children are not realistic. They believe that they are strong, smart, and good-looking—and thus that any goal is achievable. Whatever they are (self-concept) is thought to be good.

For instance, young children believe that their nation and religion are best; they feel sorry for children who do not belong to their country or church. At this age, a

self-concept
A person's understanding of who he or she is, incorporating self-esteem, physical appearance, personality, and various personal traits, such as gender and size.

positivity bias encourages children to try unfamiliar activities, make friends, begin school, and so on (Boseovski, 2010). They learn to pour juice, zip pants, or climb trees, undeterred by overflowing juice, stuck zippers, or a perch too high. Faith in themselves helps them persist. My daughter dropped the bottle, but at least she tried to get the juice.

BRAIN MATURATION The new initiative that Erikson describes benefits from myelination of the limbic system, growth of the prefrontal cortex, and a longer attention span—all made possible by the neurological maturation described in Chapter 5. Emotional and cognitive maturation develop together, each enabling the other to advance (Bell & Calkins, 2011).

Normally, neurological advances in the prefrontal cortex at about age 4 or 5 make children less likely to throw a temper tantrum, provoke a physical attack, or burst into giggles during prayer (Kagan & Herschkowitz, 2005). Throughout early childhood, violent outbursts, uncontrolled crying, and terrifying phobias (irrational, crippling fears) diminish. The capacity for self-control—such as not opening a present immediately if asked to wait and not expressing disappointment at an undesirable gift—becomes more evident (Carlson, 2003; Grolnick et al., 2006).

For example, in one study researchers asked children to wait 8 minutes while their mothers did some paperwork before opening a wrapped present that was in front of them (Cole, Tan et al., 2011). The children used strategies, including distractions and private speech. Keisha was one of the study participants:

Tejano (aka Texas) Pride Nations, states, and ethnic groups all celebrate their heroes, and preschoolers believe what they are told—that George Washington never lied, for instance. No wonder this 4-year-old is beaming: He is in an Austin parade honoring the contributions of Spanish-speaking settlers in Texas 300 years ago.

> "Are you done, Mom?" . . . "I wonder what's in it" . . . "Can I open it now?"
>
> Each time her mother reminds Keisha to wait, eventually adding, "If you keep interrupting me, I can't finish and if I don't finish . . ." Keisha plops in her chair, frustrated. "I really want it," she laments, aloud but to herself. "I want to talk to mommy so I won't open it. If I talk, Mommy won't finish. If she doesn't finish, I can't have it." She sighs deeply, folds her arms, and scans the room. . . . The research assistant returns. Keisha looks at her mother with excited anticipation. Her mother says, "OK, now." Keisha tears open the gift.
>
> [Cole, Armstrong et al., 2011, p. 59]

Motivation

Motivation (the impulse that propels someone to act) comes either from a person's own desires or from the social context.

Intrinsic motivation occurs when people do something for the joy of doing it: A musician might enjoy making music even when no one else hears it. **Extrinsic motivation** comes from outside the person, when people do something to gain praise (or some other reinforcement): A musician might play for applause or money.

Encouraging intrinsic motivation is crucial in teaching young children (Cheng & Yeh, 2009). Preschool children are often intrinsically motivated, eager to play and practice, whether or not someone else wants them to. Praise and prizes might be appreciated, but that's not why children work at what they do. When playing a game, they might not keep score; the fun is in the activity (intrinsic), not the winning.

IMAGINARY FRIENDS Intrinsic motivation is apparent when children invent dialogues for their toys, concentrate on creating a work of art or architecture, and converse with **imaginary friends** who exist only in the child's imagination. The latter are rarely encouraged by adults (i.e., there is no extrinsic motivation), but imaginary friends are nonetheless increasingly common with age over the years of early

intrinsic motivation
A drive, or reason to pursue a goal, that comes from inside a person, such as the need to feel smart or competent.

extrinsic motivation
A drive, or reason to pursue a goal, that arises from the need to have one's achievements rewarded from outside, perhaps by receiving material possessions or another person's esteem.

imaginary friends
Make-believe friends who exist only in a child's imagination; increasingly common from ages 3 through 7, they combat loneliness and aid emotional regulation.

✦ ESPECIALLY FOR Teachers One of your students tells you about playing, sleeping, and talking with an imaginary friend. Does this mean that that child is emotionally disturbed? (see response, page 212) →

childhood. Children know their imaginary friends are invisible and pretend, but conjuring them up meets various psychosocial needs (Taylor et al., 2009).

Some imaginary friends help with emotional regulation: Children use them to control their fears and temper as well as to provide comfort and companionship. One girl's imaginary friend named Elephant was "7 inches tall, gray color, black eyes, wears tank top and shorts . . . sometimes is mean" (Taylor et al., 2004, p. 1178). By having an imaginary friend who "sometimes is mean," this girl was developing strategies to deal with mean people.

AN EXPERIMENT IN MOTIVATION In a classic experiment, preschool children were given markers and paper and assigned to one of three groups who received, respectively: (1) no award, (2) an expected award (they were told *before* they had drawn anything that they would get a certificate), and (3) an unexpected award (*after* they had drawn something, they heard, "You were a big help," and got a certificate) (Lepper et al., 1973).

Later, observers noted how often children in each group chose to draw on their own. Those who received the expected award were less likely to draw than those who were unexpectedly rewarded. The interpretation was that extrinsic motivation (condition #2) undercut intrinsic motivation.

This research triggered a flood of studies seeking to understand whether, when, and how positive reinforcement should be given. The consensus is that praising or paying a person after an accomplishment sometimes encourages that behavior. However, if payment is promised in advance, that extrinsic reinforcement may backfire (Cameron & Pierce, 2002; Deci et al., 1999; Gottfried et al., 2009).

Praise is effective if connected to the particular production, not to a general trait ("You did a good drawing," not "You are a great artist") because then the child believes that effort paid off, which motivates a repeat performance (Zentall & Morris, 2010).

✦ ESPECIALLY FOR College Students Is extrinsic or intrinsic motivation more influential in your study efforts? (see response, page 212) →

Culture and Emotional Control

Although there is considerable variation within as well as among cultures, national emphases regarding which emotions to regulate seem to include the following (Chen, 2011; Harkness et al., 2011; J. G. Miller, 2004; Stubben, 2001):

● Fear (United States)
● Anger (Puerto Rico)
● Pride (China)
● Selfishness (Japan)
● Impatience (many Native American communities)
● Disobedience (Mexico)
● Erratic moods (the Netherlands)

Control strategies vary as well (Matsumoto, 2004). Peers, parents, and strangers sometimes ignore emotional outbursts, sometimes deflect them, sometimes punish them. Shame is used when social reputation is a priority. Indeed, in some cultures, "pride goeth before a fall" and people who "have no shame" are considered mentally ill (Stein, 2006).

Cultural differences are also apparent in emotional expression: Children may be encouraged to laugh/cry/yell or, the opposite, to hide their emotions (H. S. Kim et al., 2008). Some adults guffaw, slap their knees, and stomp their feet for joy; others cover their mouths with their hands if a smile spontaneously appears. Children learn to do the same.

Finally, temperaments vary, which makes people within the same culture unlike one another. "Cultures are inevitably more complicated than the framework that is supposed to explain them" (Harkness et al., 2011, p. 92). Nonetheless, parents everywhere teach emotional regulation as their context expects. And everywhere, one sad consequence for children of parents with schizophrenia, bipolar disorder, or depression is that they are less able to regulate their emotions (Kovacs et al., 2008).

Seeking Emotional Balance

At every age, in all cultures and cohorts, caregivers try to prevent **psychopathology,** an illness or disorder (*-pathology*) of the mind (*psycho-*). Although symptoms and diagnoses are influenced by culture (rebellion is expected in some cultures and pathological in others), impaired emotional regulation universally signals mental imbalance. Parents guide young children toward "an optimal balance" between emotional expression and emotional control (Blair & Dennis, 2011; Trommsdorff & Cole, 2011).

Without adequate regulation, emotions can be overwhelming. Intense reactions can occur in opposite ways, as you might expect from the activate/inhibit nature of neurons. Some people have **externalizing problems:** Their powerful feelings burst out uncontrollably. They externalize rage, for example, by lashing out or breaking things. Without emotional regulation, an angry child might flail at another person or lie down screaming and kicking. By age 5, children usually have learned more self-control, perhaps pouting or cursing, not hitting and screaming.

Other people have **internalizing problems:** They are fearful and withdrawn, turning distress inward. Emotions may be internalized via headaches or stomachaches. Although the cause is psychological, the ache is real.

Again, with maturity, the extreme fears of some 2-year-olds (e.g., terror of the bathtub drain, of an imagined tidal wave, of a stranger on crutches) diminish. The fear isn't gone, but expression is regulated: A child might be afraid of kindergarten, for instance, but bravely lets go of Mother's hand anyway.

psychopathology
An illness or disorder of the mind.

externalizing problems
Difficulty with emotional regulation that involves expressing powerful feelings through uncontrolled physical or verbal outbursts, as by lashing out at other people or breaking things.

internalizing problems
Difficulty with emotional regulation that involves turning one's emotional distress inward, as by feeling excessively guilty, ashamed, or worthless.

Same Situation, Far Apart: Overwhelming Emotions The days of early childhood are filled with terrors and tantrums because children have not yet learned how to use their words and logic to control their world. The result is futile protest: The U.S. mother *(left)* is not about to let her son do what he wants, and this Japanese big brother (age 4, *right*) is moving his book away. Both children are likely to keep crying.

A VIEW FROM SCIENCE

Sex Differences in Emotional Regulation

Biologically, the differences between males and females are minor, at least until puberty. Only one gene causes the difference in genitals. Most aspects of physical and cognitive growth are the same for all children. Except for the sex organs, when differences appear they are in averages, not absolutes. For example, as you read in Chapter 5, girls average slightly more body fat than boys, but many boys are fatter than the average girl (see Infographic 6, page 211).

This overlapping of characteristics is one of two crucial points that scientists stress when they consider sex differences. Beyond anatomy, it is never true that all the boys have one trait, and none of the girls do. The sexes overlap; they are not opposites.

The second crucial point is that both nature and nurture are connected to every difference that is found between boys and girls. For instance, even the fact that girls have more body fat than boys may seem to be nature, but among poor families in India, girls have less fat than boys, on average. The reason is cultural: When food is scarce, boys are better fed.

Now to emotional regulation: *On average,* young girls are advanced in controlling their emotions, particularly anger, compared with boys.

One study traced externalizing and internalizing emotions from early to middle childhood. Researchers gave 5-year-olds two toy figures and told them the beginning of a story (Zahn-Waxler et al., 2008): The two toy children (named Mark and Scott for the boys, Mary and Sarah for the girls) were said to start yelling at each other. The 5-year-olds were asked to show what happened next.

Many boys showed Mark and Scott hitting and kicking each other. Boys whose externalizing behavior worsened between ages 5 and 9 (as rated by teachers and parents) were the most likely to dramatize such attacks at age 5. They became aggressive 9-year-olds.

By contrast, 5-year-old girls often had Mary and Sarah discuss the conflict or change the subject. Curiously, however, those 5-year-old girls who immediately had Mary and Sarah engage in "reparative behavior" (repairing the relationship, such as having Mary hug Sarah and say, "I'm sorry")

were more likely to be disruptive at age 9 than the other girls were. Their quickness to repair the conflict may have signaled too much guilt or shame, which would sometimes erupt later on.

The authors of the study wrote:

> Gender-role stereotypes or exaggerations of masculine qualities (e.g., impulsive, aggressive, uncaring) and feminine qualities (submissive, unassertive, socially sensitive) are reflected not only in the types of problems males and females tend to develop but also in different forms of expression.
>
> *[Zahn-Waxler et al., 2008, p. 114]*

These researchers suggest that extreme externalization or extreme internalization predicts future psychopathology. Because of gender differences, mistreated boys are likely to externalize and mistreated girls to internalize. By age 5, without emotional regulation, maltreated boys throw and hit, and maltreated girls sob uncontrollably or hide.

Later you will read that men are generally more likely to become antisocial or schizophrenic; women are more likely to be overwhelmed by anxiety or depression. Furthermore, females *attempt* suicide more often, but males are more likely to kill themselves—typically without the warnings (a note, uncontrolled crying, a despairing comment) that suicidal females often provide. Is that culture or hormones?

In this study of 5-year-olds, why didn't more boys have Mark and Scott discuss their conflict? Does emotional regulation appear more readily in young girls because their parents teach them to restrain their impulse to hit? Or does prenatal testosterone shape those boys' brains, making them more violent at age 5? Both hypotheses are possible; scientists have yet to reach a consensus.

FLORESCO PRODUCTIONS CULTURA / NEWSCOM

Cute or Too Shy? Cute, of course. Universally, girls and women are expected to be reticent. They cling more to their mothers in kindergarten, they wait to be asked to dance or date, they talk less in co-ed groups. If she were a he, would he be considered too shy?

VISUALIZING DEVELOPMENT

Sex Differences and Similarities

Humans tend to exaggerate differences and forget how much we have in common. Despite the common phrase "opposite sex," most of our biological characteristics except sex organs are the same. We all have two eyes, two ears, and two legs.

MALES AND FEMALES

 ALMOST NEVER OPPOSITES

 SOMETIMES NO DIFFERENCE

 AND OFTEN OVERLAPS

For example, at age 3, the average boy is slightly heavier than the average girl, but 98 percent of 3-year-olds of either sex weigh between 27 and 37 pounds.

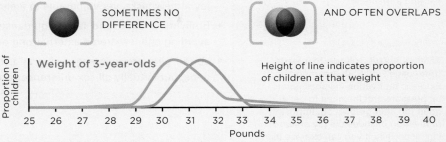

Weight of 3-year-olds

Height of line indicates proportion of children at that weight

Proportion of children

25 26 27 28 29 30 31 32 33 34 35 36 37 38 39 40
Pounds

DIFFERENCES IN PSYCHOPATHOLOGY

For children under age 10, boys have higher rates of psychopathology, although specific ratios vary by cohort and location. Researchers find the following approximate sex ratios.

Autism spectrum disorders

Conduct disorder

Attention-deficit/ hyperactivity disorder

Oppositional defiant disorder

SOME COMPLICATIONS

Every study that details sex differences in children's behavior reports a complex picture.

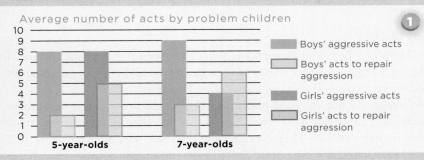

Average number of acts by problem children

10 9 8 7 6 5 4 3 2 1 0

5-year-olds   7-year-olds

■ Boys' aggressive acts

■ Boys' acts to repair aggression

■ Girls' aggressive acts

■ Girls' acts to repair aggression

1 Perhaps between ages 5 and 10, boys *learn* to become more aggressive and girls *learn* to apologize more often. In one study teachers and parents judged the behavior of children from ages 5 to 9 (Zahn-Wexler et al., 2008). Most improved over those 4 years, but some (called "problem children") did not. All the children, at age 5 and 7, used dolls to show what might happen in several conflict situations. The "problem children" were more aggressive. Most boys continued to be aggressive, but girls were more likely to try to repair the situation.

2 Many adults generalize that boys have externalizing problems (they act out by hitting, breaking things, etc.) while girls have internalizing problems (they withdraw, cry, blame themselves). But, as you see here, the actual picture is more complex, with many children having both kinds of problems. Also note that mothers, fathers, and teachers rated the same children but often did not agree.

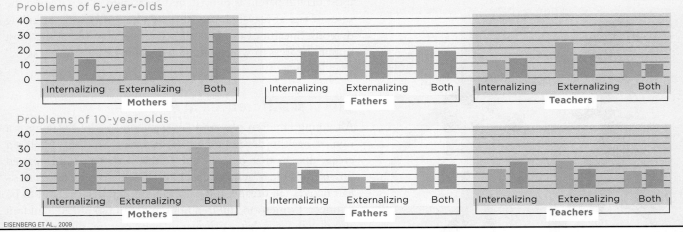

Problems of 6-year-olds

40 30 20 10 0

Internalizing Externalizing Both
Mothers

Internalizing Externalizing Both
Fathers

Internalizing Externalizing Both
Teachers

Problems of 10-year-olds

40 30 20 10 0

Internalizing Externalizing Both
Mothers

Internalizing Externalizing Both
Fathers

Internalizing Externalizing Both
Teachers

EISENBERG ET AL., 2009

CONCLUSION

These studies are complex, but the bottom line is the same as the top: Whenever sex differences appear, be cautious— remember, sex similarities are more apparent than differences, and every study shows overlap. The two sexes are never opposites.

SOURCES & CREDITS LISTED ON P. SC-1

RESPONSE FOR Teachers (from page 208) No, unless the student is over age 10. In fact, imaginary friends are quite common, especially among creative children. The child may be somewhat lonely, though; you could help him or her find a friend. ●

RESPONSE FOR College Students (from page 208) Both are important. Extrinsic motivation includes parental pressure and the need to get a good job after graduation. Intrinsic motivation includes the joy of learning, especially if you can express that learning in ways others recognize. Have you ever taken a course that was not required and was said to be difficult? That was intrinsic motivation. ●

> ## KEY ϸoints
>
> - Emotional regulation is the crucial psychosocial task in early childhood.
> - Erikson thought young children are naturally motivated to take initiative, with joy at new tasks, yet vulnerable to feeling guilty.
> - Brain maturation and family guidance help children regulate their emotions, avoiding either extreme externalizing or internalizing reactions.
> - Young girls are less aggressive and more advanced in controlling their emotions, but virtually all sex differences are in averages, not absolutes.

Play

Play is timeless and universal—apparent in every part of the world for thousands of years. Many developmentalists believe that play is the most productive as well as the most enjoyable activity that children undertake (Elkind, 2007; Frost, 2009; P. K. Smith, 2010). Whether play is essential for normal growth or is merely a fun activity that has development benefits is "a controversial topic of study" (Pelligrini, 2011, p. 3).

There are echoes of this controversy in the variations in preschool education that were explained in Chapter 5. Some educators want children to focus on reading and math skills; others predict emotional and academic problems for children who rarely play (Hirsh-Pasek et al., 2009; Pelligrini, 2009; Rubin et al., 2009).

Playmates

Young children play best with *peers,* that is, people of about the same age and social status. Although even infants are intrigued by other small children, some maturation is required for social play.

Two-year-olds are not yet good playmates: One might throw a ball and expect a peer to throw it back, but most other 2-year-olds will keep it. By contrast, most 6-year-olds are quite skilled: They can not only play ball, they can gain entry to a peer group, manage conflict, take turns, find friends, and keep playmates. Over those years, social play with peers teaches emotional regulation, empathy, and cultural understanding (Göncü & Gaskins, 2011).

There is an obvious task for parents: Find playmates for their children. Even the most playful parent is outmatched by a child at negotiating the rules of tag, at play-fighting, at pretending to be sick, at killing dragons. Specifics vary, but "play with peers is one of the most important areas in which children develop positive social skills" (Xu, 2010, p. 496).

Cultural Differences in Play

All young children play and "everywhere, a child playing is a sign of healthy development" (Gosso, 2010, p. 95). Children create dramas that reflect their culture and play games passed down from older generations. Chinese children fly kites, Alaskan natives tell dreams and stories, Lapp children pretend to be reindeer, Cameroon children hunt mice, and so on. All children also play in ways that are similar in every culture, such as throwing and catching; pretending to be adults; drawing with chalk, markers, sticks, or what have you. Everywhere, play is the prime activity of young children, as illustrated in Figure 6.1.

Play Ball! In every nation, young children play with balls, but the specific games they play vary with the culture. Soccer is the favorite game in many countries, including Brazil, where these children are practicing their dribbling on Copacabana Beach in Rio de Janeiro.

REUTERS / SERGIO MORAES

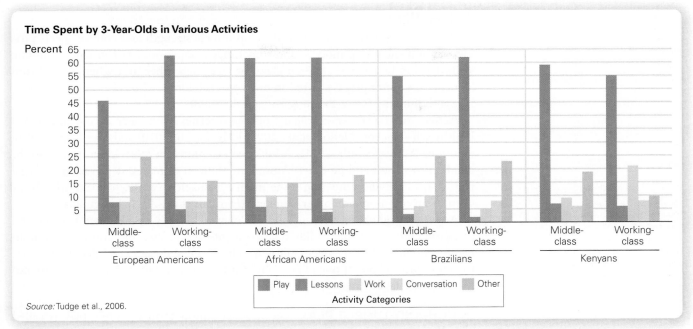

Time Spent by 3-Year-Olds in Various Activities

Percent

Source: Tudge et al., 2006.

Activity Categories: Play Lessons Work Conversation Other

FIGURE 6.1 Mostly Playing When researchers studied 3-year-olds in the United States, Brazil, and Kenya, they found that, on average, the children spent more than half their time playing. Note the low percentages of both middle- and working-class Brazilian children in the Lessons category, which included all intentional efforts to teach children something. There is a cultural explanation: Unlike parents in Kenya and the United States, most Brazilian parents believe that children of this age learn without instruction.

Although play is universal, not only do specifics differ but so do playmates: When adults are concerned with basic survival, they rarely play with their children. Children play with each other instead, and spend more time on chores than do children in less impoverished communities (Kalliala, 2006; Roopnarine, 2011).

As children grow older, play becomes more social, influenced not only by the availability of playmates but also by the physical setting (a small playroom, a large park, a wild hillside). One developmentalist bemoans the twenty-first century's "swift and pervasive rise of electronic media" and adults who lean "more toward control than freedom" (Chudacoff, 2011, p. 108). He praises children who find places to play independently and "conspire ways to elude adult management."

This opinion may be extreme, but it is echoed in more common concerns. As you remember, one dispute in preschool education is how much unstructured, creative play versus how much teacher-directed learning should occur. Television, videos, and computer screens present a challenge for parents—soon, we'll explain how.

Before the electronic age, young children played outside with neighborhood children, often of both sexes and several ages. The youngest children learned from the older ones. The development of social play from ages 1 to 6 was described by the American sociologist Mildred Parten in 1932. She distinguished five kinds of play, each more advanced than the previous one:

1. *Solitary play:* A child plays alone, unaware of any other children playing nearby.
2. *Onlooker play:* A child watches other children play.
3. *Parallel play:* Children play with similar objects in similar ways, but not together.
4. *Associative play:* Children interact, sharing material, but their play is not reciprocal.
5. *Cooperative play:* Children play together, creating dramas or taking turns.

As already mentioned, play is affected by culture and context, and both of these have changed since Parten's day. Many Asian parents teach 3-year-olds to take turns, share, and otherwise cooperate—and they do. On the other hand, many North American children, at age 6 and older, engage in parallel play, especially in schools where each child has a desk. Given all the social, political, and economic changes over the past century, many forms of social play (not necessarily in Parten's sequence) may be age-appropriate (Xu, 2010).

Active Play

Children need physical activity to develop muscle strength and control. Peers provide an audience, role models, and sometimes competition. For instance, running skills develop best when children chase or race each other, not when a child runs alone. Gross motor play is favored among young children, who enjoy climbing, kicking, and tumbling (Case-Smith & Kuhaneck, 2008).

Active social play—not solitary play—correlates with peer acceptance and a healthy self-concept (Nelson et al., 2008; P. K. Smith, 2010) and may help regulate emotions (Sutton-Smith, 2011). Adults need to remember this when they wish for children to sit still and be quiet. Among nonhuman primates, deprivation of social play warps later life, rendering some monkeys unable to mate, to make friends, or even to survive alongside other monkeys (Herman et al., 2011; Palagi, 2011).

Active play advances planning and self-control. Two-year-olds merely chase and catch each other, but older children keep the interaction fair, long-lasting, and fun. In tag, for instance, they set rules (adjusted to location) and each child decides how far to venture from base. If one child is "It" for too long, another child (often a friend) makes it easy to be caught.

ROUGH-AND-TUMBLE PLAY The most common form of active play is called **rough-and-tumble** because it looks quite rough and because the children seem to tumble over one another. The term was coined by British scientists who studied primates in East Africa (Blurton-Jones, 1976). They noticed that monkeys often chased, attacked, rolled over in the dirt, and wrestled quite roughly, but without hurting one another.

If a young monkey wanted to engage in rough-and-tumble play, it would simply come close, catch the eye of a peer, and then run a few feet away. The invitation was almost always accepted, with a *play face* (smiling, not angry). Puppies, kittens, and chimps behave similarly.

When the scientists returned to London, they saw that human youngsters, like baby monkeys, also enjoy rough-and-tumble play (Pellegrini & Smith, 2005). They chase, wrestle, and grab each other and develop games like tag and cops-and-robbers, all with play faces and lots of chasing, as well as various conventions, expressions, and gestures that children use to signify "just pretend."

Rough-and-tumble play happens everywhere (although cops-and-robbers can be "robots-and-humans" or many other iterations). It is particularly common among young male friends (human and otherwise) playing in ample space with minimal supervision (Berenbaum et al., 2008; Hassett et al., 2008).

Many scientists think that rough-and-tumble play helps the prefrontal cortex develop, as children learn to regulate emotions, practice social skills, and strengthen their bodies (Pellegrini et al., 2007; Pellis & Pellis, 2011). Indeed, some believe that play in childhood, especially rough-and-tumble between a boy and his father, may prevent antisocial behavior (even murder) later on (Wenner, 2009).

DRAMA AND PRETENDING Another major type of active play is **sociodramatic play,** in which children act out various roles and plots. Through sociodramatic play, children:

- Explore and rehearse social roles
- Learn how to explain their ideas and convince playmates to agree
- Practice emotional regulation by pretending to be afraid, angry, brave, and so on
- Develop self-concept in a nonthreatening context

Sociodramatic play builds on pretending, which emerges in toddlerhood. But preschoolers do more than pretend; they combine their imagination with their friends'

rough-and-tumble play
Play that mimics aggression through wrestling, chasing, or hitting, but in which there is no intent to harm.

sociodramatic play
Pretend play in which children act out various roles and themes in stories that they create.

imaginations, advancing in theory of mind (Kavanaugh, 2011). The beginnings of sociodramatic play are illustrated by the following pair, a 3-year-old girl and a 2-year-old boy. The girl wanted to act out the role of a baby, and she persuaded a boy in her nursery school to join her.

Boy: Not good. You bad.
Girl: Why?
Boy: 'Cause you spill your milk.
Girl: No. 'Cause I bit somebody.
Boy: Yes, you did.
Girl: Say, "Go to sleep. Put your head down."
Boy: Put your head down.
Girl: No.
Boy: Yes.
Girl: No.
Boy: Yes. Okay, I will spank you. Bad boy. *[Spanks her, not hard]*
Girl: No. My head is up. *[Giggles]* I want my teddy bear.
Boy: No. Your teddy bear go away.
[At this point she asked if he was really going to take the teddy bear away.]

[from Garvey, reported in Cohen, 2006, p. 72]

Note the social interaction in this form of play. The girl directed and played her part, sometimes accepting what the boy said and sometimes not. The boy took direction yet also made up his own dialogue and actions ("Bad boy").

Older children are much more elaborate than these two in their sociodramatic play, evident in four boys, about age 5, in a day-care center in Finland. Joni plays the role of the evil one who menaces the other boys; Tuomas directs the drama and acts in it as well.

Tuomas: And now he [Joni] would take me and would hang me. . . . This would be the end of all of me.
Joni: Hands behind.
Tuomas: I can't help it. I have to. *[The two other boys follow his example.]*
Joni: I would put fire all around them.

A Toy Machine Gun These boys in Liberia are doing what young children everywhere do—following adult example. Whenever countries are at war, children play soldiers, rebels, heroes, or spies. From their perspective, there is only one problem with such play—no one wants to be the enemy.

[All three brave boys lie on the floor with hands tied behind their backs. Joni piles mattresses on them, and pretends to light a fire, which crackles closer and closer.]

Tuomas: Everything is lost.

[One boy starts to laugh.]

Petterl: Better not to laugh, soon we will all be dead. . . . I am saying my last words.

Tuomas: Now you can say your last wish. . . . And now I say I wish we can be terribly strong.

[At that point, the three boys suddenly gain extraordinary strength, pushing off the mattresses and extinguishing the fire. Good triumphs over evil, but not until the last moment, because, as one boy explains, "Otherwise this playing is not exciting at all."]

[adapted from Kalliala, 2006, p. 83]

Good versus evil is a favorite theme of boys' sociodramatic play. In contrast, girls often act out domestic scenes. Such gender differences are found in many cultures. In the same day-care center where Joni piles mattresses on his playmates, the girls say their play is "more beautiful and peaceful . . . [but] boys play all kinds of violent games" (Kalliala, 2006, p. 110).

Although gender differences in sociodramatic play are found universally, the prevalence of such play varies. Some cultures find it frivolous and discourage it; in other cultures, parents teach toddlers to be lions, or robots, or ladies drinking tea, and then children develop elaborate and extensive play based on those themes (Kavanaugh, 2011).

KEYⲣoints

- All children everywhere in every era play during early childhood, which makes some developmentalists think play is essential for healthy development.
- The specific forms of play vary by culture, gender, and parental example.
- Playmates of the same age foster emotional regulation.
- Rough-and-tumble play and sociodramatic play both help children with socialization, with boys and girls often creating distinct imaginary dramas.

Challenges for Caregivers

We have seen that young children's emotions and actions are affected by many factors, including brain maturation, culture, and peers. Now we focus on another primary influence on young children: their caregivers.

All children need parents who care about them because, no matter what the parenting style, "parental involvement plays an important role in the development of both social and cognitive competence" (Parke & Buriel, 2006, p. 437). As more and more children spend long hours during early childhood with other adults, alternate caregivers become pivotal as well.

Caregiving Styles

Although thousands of researchers have traced the effects of parenting on child development, the work of one person, 50 years ago, continues to be influential. In her original research, Diana Baumrind (1967, 1971) studied 100 preschool children, all from California, almost all middle-class European Americans. (The cohort and cultural limitations of this sample were not obvious at the time.)

Baumrind found that parents differed on four important dimensions:

1. *Expressions of warmth.* Some parents are warm and affectionate; others, cold and critical.
2. *Strategies for discipline.* Parents vary in how they explain, criticize, persuade, and punish.
3. *Communication.* Some parents listen patiently; others demand silence.
4. *Expectations for maturity.* Parents vary in how much responsibility and self-control they expect.

BAUMRIND'S THREE STYLES OF CAREGIVING On the basis of the dimensions listed above, Baumrind identified three parenting styles (summarized in Table 6.1).

- **Authoritarian parenting.** The authoritarian parent's word is law, not to be questioned. Misconduct brings strict punishment, usually physical. Authoritarian parents set down clear rules and hold high standards. They do not expect children to offer opinions; discussion about emotions is especially rare. (One adult from such a family said that "How do you feel?" had only two possible answers: "Fine" and "Tired.") Authoritarian parents seem cold, rarely showing affection.

- **Permissive parenting.** Permissive parents (also called *indulgent*) make few demands, hiding any impatience they feel. Discipline is lax, partly because they have low expectations for maturity. Permissive parents are nurturing and accepting, listening to whatever their offspring say.

- **Authoritative parenting.** Authoritative parents set limits, but they are flexible. They encourage maturity, but they usually listen and forgive (not punish) if the child falls short. They consider themselves guides, not authorities (unlike authoritarian parents) and not friends (unlike permissive parents).

Other researchers describe a fourth style, called **neglectful/uninvolved parenting,** which may be confused with permissive but is quite different (Steinberg, 2001). The similarity is that neither permissive nor neglectful parents use physical punishment. However, neglectful parents are oblivious to their children's behavior; they seem not to care. By contrast, permissive parents care very much: They defend their children, arrange play dates, and sacrifice to buy coveted toys.

The following long-term effects of parenting styles have been reported, not only in the United States but in many other nations as well (Baumrind, 2005; Baumrind et al., 2010; Chan & Koo, 2011; Huver et al., 2010; Rothrauff et al., 2009).

- *Authoritarian* parents raise children who become conscientious, obedient, and quiet but not especially happy. Such children tend to feel guilty or depressed, internalizing their frustrations and blaming themselves when things don't go well. As adolescents, they sometimes rebel, leaving home before age 20.

authoritarian parenting
An approach to child rearing that is characterized by high behavioral standards, strict punishment of misconduct, and little communication.

permissive parenting
An approach to child rearing that is characterized by high nurturance and communication but little discipline, guidance, or control.

authoritative parenting
An approach to child rearing in which the parents set limits and enforce rules but are flexible and listen to their children.

neglectful/uninvolved parenting
An approach to child rearing in which the parents are indifferent toward their children and unaware of what is going on in their children's lives.

TABLE 6.1 Characteristics of Parenting Styles Identified by Baumrind

Style	Warmth	Discipline	Expectations of Maturity	Communication Parent to Child	Child to Parent
Authoritarian	Low	Strict, often physical	High	High	Low
Permissive	High	Rare	Low	Low	High
Authoritative	High	Moderate, with much discussion	Moderate	High	High

- *Permissive* parents raise unhappy children who lack self-control, especially in the give-and-take of peer relationships. Inadequate emotional regulation makes them immature and impedes friendships, which is the main reason for their unhappiness. They tend to continue to live at home, still dependent on their parents, in early adulthood.

- *Authoritative* parents raise children who are successful, articulate, happy with themselves, and generous with others. These children are usually liked by teachers and peers, especially in cultures that value individual initiative (e.g., the United States).

- *Neglectful/uninvolved* parents raise children who are immature, sad, lonely, and at risk of injury and abuse in early childhood and lifelong.

PROBLEMS WITH BAUMRIND'S STYLES Baumrind's classification schema is often criticized. Problems include the following:

- Her participants were not diverse in SES, ethnicity, or culture.
- She focused more on adult attitudes than on adult actions.
- She overlooked children's temperamental differences.
- She did not recognize that some "authoritarian" parents are also affectionate.
- She did not realize that some "permissive" parents provide extensive verbal guidance.

We now know that a child's temperament and the culture's standards powerfully affect caregivers, as do the consequences of one style or another (Cipriano & Stifter, 2010). This is as it should be.

Fearful or impulsive children require particular styles (reassurance for the fearful ones and restraint for the impulsive ones). Every child needs guidance and protection, but not too much—overprotection seems to be both a cause and a consequence of childhood anxiety (McShane & Hastings, 2009). Much depends on the particular characteristics of the child, as the concept of differential sensitivity makes clear.

A study of parenting at age 2 and children's competence in kindergarten (including emotional regulation and friendships) found "multiple developmental pathways," with the best outcomes dependent on the child and the adult (Blandon et al., 2010). Such studies suggest that simplistic advice from a book, a professional, or a neighbor who does not know the child may be misguided: Scientific observation of parent–child interactions is needed before determining that an adult provides guidance without being overly controlling.

Cultural Variations

The significance of the context is particularly obvious when children of various ethnic groups are compared. It may be that certain alleles are more common in children of one group or another, and that affects their temperament. However, much more influential are the attitudes and actions of adult caregivers.

PARENTAL INFLUENCE U.S. parents of Chinese, Caribbean, or African heritage are often stricter than those of European backgrounds, yet their children develop better than if the parents were easygoing (Chao, 2001; Parke & Buriel, 2006). Latino parents are sometimes thought to be too intrusive, other times too permissive—but their children seem to be happier than the children of European American parents who behave the same way (García & Gracia, 2009; Ispa et al., 2004). A three-way interaction seems to influence the outcome of any parenting style: the child's temperament, the parent's personality, and the social context.

In a detailed study of 1,477 instances in which Mexican American mothers of 4-year-olds tried to get their children to do something they were not doing, most of the time the mothers simply uttered a command and the children complied (Livas-Dlott et al., 2010). This simple strategy, with the mother asserting authority and the children obeying without question, might be considered authoritarian.

However, almost never did the mothers use physical punishment or even harsh threats when the children did not immediately do as they were told—which happened 14 percent of the time. For example,

> Hailey [the 4-year-old] decided to look for another doll and started digging through her toys, throwing them behind her as she dug. Maricruz [the mother] told Hailey she should not throw her toys. Hailey continued to throw toys, and Maricruz said her name to remind her to stop. Hailey continued her misbehavior, and her mother repeated "Hailey" once more. When Hailey continued, Maricruz raised her voice but calmly directed, "Hailey, look at me." Hailey continued but then looked at Maricruz as she explained, "You don't throw toys; you could hurt someone." Finally, Hailey complied and stopped.
>
> *[Livas-Dlott et al., 2010, p. 572]*

Note that the mother's first three efforts failed, and then a look accompanied by an explanation (albeit inaccurate in that setting, as no one could be hurt) succeeded. The researchers explain that these Mexican American families do not fit any of Baumrind's categories; respect for adult authority does not mean a cold mother–child relationship. Instead, the relationship shows evident *cariono* (caring) (Livas-Dlott et al., 2010).

Given a multicultural and multicontextual perspective, developmentalists hesitate to recommend any particular parenting style (Dishion & Bullock, 2002; J. G. Miller, 2004). That does not mean that all families function equally well—far from it. Signs of trouble, including a child's anxiety, aggression, and inability to play with others, are indicative. Ineffective, abusive, and neglectful parents are one cause of such trouble, but not the only one. (Another cause, child maltreatment, is discussed at the end of this chapter.)

"He's just doing that to get attention."

Pay Attention Children develop best with lots of love and attention. They shouldn't have to ask for it!

© THE NEW YORKER COLLECTION 2001 PAT BYRNES FROM CARTOONBANK.COM. ALL RIGHTS RESERVED.

WHAT ABOUT THE TEACHERS? When Baumrind did her original research, 2- to 5-year-olds were cared for, almost exclusively, by their parents. Now most young children have teachers and other caregivers who can likewise be authoritative, authoritarian, permissive, or neglectful (Ertesvåg, 2011).

Although all four styles are possible for caregivers who watch only one child, almost no teacher is permissive or neglectful. They couldn't be. Allowing a group of 2- to 5-year-olds to do whatever they want would result in chaos, conflict, and perhaps danger. Young children are not sufficiently adept at emotional regulation and impulse control that several of them can safely play together, unguided or unsupervised, for long.

However, teachers can be authoritarian, enforcing rules with no exceptions, or authoritative, setting flexible guidelines. Teachers with more education tend to be authoritative, responding to each child, listening and encouraging language, and so on. This fosters more capable children. For that reason, a teacher's education (such as college classes in human development and degrees in early childhood) is one measure used to indicate the quality of educational programs (Barnett et al., 2010; Norris, 2010).

In general, young children learn more from authoritative teachers because the teachers are perceived as warmer and more loving. In fact, one study found that, compared with children who had authoritarian teachers, those children whose teachers were child-centered, noncontrolling, and very supportive scored higher on school-readiness measures (Barbarin et al., 2010).

In that same study, however, a surprising result was reported for African American children who had authoritarian parents (Barbarin et al., 2010). If their teachers were also authoritarian, they learned less than if their teachers were authoritative.

This result is surprising because usually children are confused when their teachers have one style and their parents another. That was not the case for these children. Did these children feel personally rejected (recall egocentrism) when their teacher was strict? African American children with authoritarian parents may recognize their parents' affection despite the authoritarian style, but they may not have seen warmth in their strict teachers.

The New Media

New challenges confront each generation. One of today's great challenges is the influence of electronic media. All media—television, the Internet, electronic games, and so on—*can* be harmful, especially when the content is violent (Anderson et al., 2007, 2008; Bailey et al., 2010; Gentile et al., 2007; Smyth, 2007).

Media technologies for young children have become a multimillion-dollar industry, seeking profit through the education and entertainment of billions of young viewers (Steemers, 2010). Some children learn from educational videos, especially if adults watch with them and reinforce the lessons. However, children on their own rarely select educational programs over fast-paced cartoons, in which characters hit, shoot, and kick.

Six major organizations (the American Psychological Association, the American Academy of Pediatrics, the American Medical Association, the American Academy of Child and Adolescent Psychiatry, the American Academy of Family Physicians, and the American Psychiatric Association) recommend no electronic media at all for children under age 2 and strict limitations after that.

Average Daily Exposure to Video, U.S. Children

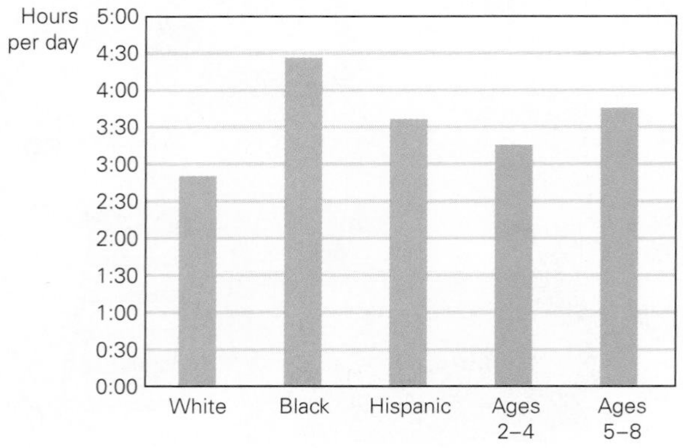

Source: Common Sense Media, 2011.

FIGURE 6.2 Learning by Playing Fifty years ago, the average child spent three hours a day in outdoor play. Video games and television have largely replaced that, especially in cities. Children seem safer if parents can keep an eye on them, but what are they learning? The long-term effects on brain and body may be dangerous.

The problem is not only that violent media teach aggression but also that even nonviolent media take time from constructive interaction and creative play (see Figure 6.2). Social interaction among family members is reduced when a TV is on, whether or not anyone is watching (Kirkorian et al., 2009).

Becoming Boys and Girls

Biology determines whether a child is male or female. As you remember from Chapter 2, at about 8 weeks after conception, the SRY gene directs the reproductive organs to develop externally, and then male hormones exert subtle control over the brain, body, and later behavior. Without that gene, the fetus develops female organs, which produce female hormones that also affect the brain and behavior.

It is possible for sex hormones to be unexpressed prenatally, in which case the child does not develop like the typical boy or girl (Hines, 2010). That is very rare; most children are male or female in all three ways: chromosomes, genitals, and hormones. That is their nature, but obviously nurture affects their sexual development from birth until death.

During early childhood, sex patterns and preferences become important to children and apparent to adults. At age 2, children apply gender labels (*Mrs., Mr., lady, man*) consistently. By age 4, children are convinced that certain toys (such as dolls or trucks) and roles (not just Daddy or Mommy, but also nurse, teacher, police officer, soldier) are "best suited" for one sex or the other. Dynamic-systems theory helps us realize that such preferences are affected by many developmental aspects of biology and culture, changing as humans grow older (Martin & Ruble, 2010).

Playing in the Sand What do you need at the beach? Depending on gender, either a man-sized shovel or a flowery raincoat. Already by age 4, girls are more likely to hold hands and boys much more likely to use construction tools.

SEX AND GENDER Scientists distinguish **sex differences,** which are biological differences between males and females, from **gender differences,** which are culturally prescribed roles and behaviors. In theory, this seems straightforward, but, as with every nature–nurture distinction, the interaction between sex and gender makes it hard to separate the two (Hines, 2004).

Young children are often confused about sexual differences. One little girl said she would grow a penis when she got older, and one little boy offered to buy his mother one. Ignorance about biology was demonstrated by a 3-year-old who went with his father to see a neighbor's newborn kittens. Returning home, the child told his mother that there were three girl kittens and two boy kittens. "How do you know?" she asked. "Daddy picked them up and read what was written on their tummies," he replied.

In recent years, sex and gender issues have become increasingly complex—to the outrage of some and the joy of others. Adults may be lesbian, gay, bi, trans, "mostly straight," or totally heterosexual (Thompson & Morgan, 2008, p. 15).

Despite the increasing acceptance of sexual diversity, many preschoolers become remarkably rigid in their ideas of male and female. Already by age 3, boys reject pink toys and girls prefer them (LoBue & DeLoache, 2011). If young boys need new shoes, but the only ones that fit them are pink, most would rather go barefoot.

In early-childhood programs, girls tend to play with other girls and boys with other boys. Despite their parents' and teachers' wishes, children say, "No girls [or boys] allowed." Most older children consider ethnic discrimination immoral, but they are more likely to accept sex discrimination (Møller & Tenenbaum, 2011). Why?

A dynamic-systems approach reminds us that attitudes, roles, and even the biology of gender differences and similarities change from one developmental period to the next; theories about how and why this occurs change as well (Martin & Ruble, 2010). Nonetheless, it is useful to review the five theories described in Chapter 1, to understand the range of explanations for the apparent sexism of many 5-year-olds.

PSYCHOANALYTIC THEORY Freud (1938) called the period from about ages 3 to 6 the **phallic stage,** named after the *phallus,* the Greek word for penis. At about 3 or 4 years of age, said Freud, boys become aware of their male sexual organ. They masturbate, fear castration, and develop sexual feelings toward their mother.

sex differences
Biological differences between males and females, in organs, hormones, and body shape.

gender differences
Differences in the roles and behaviors that are prescribed by a culture for males and females.

phallic stage
Freud's third stage of development, when the penis becomes the focus of concern and pleasure.

Same Situation, Far Apart: Culture Clash? He wears the orange robes of a Buddhist monk and she wears the hijab of a Muslim girl. Although he is at a week-long spiritual retreat led by the Dalai Lama and she is in an alley in Pakistan, both carry universal toys—a pop gun and a bride doll, identical to those found in any town in the United States.

DIPTENDU DUTTA / AFP / GETTY IMAGES

ILYAS DEAN / THE IMAGE WORKS

Oedipus complex
The unconscious desire of young boys to replace their fathers and win their mothers' exclusive love.

superego
In psychoanalytic theory, the judgmental part of the personality that internalizes the moral standards of the parents.

Electra complex
The unconscious desire of girls to replace their mothers and win their fathers' exclusive love.

identification
An attempt to defend one's self-concept by taking on the behaviors and attitudes of someone else.

This makes every young boy jealous of his father—so jealous, according to Freud, that he wants to replace his dad. Freud called this the **Oedipus complex,** after Oedipus, son of a king in Greek mythology. Abandoned as an infant and raised in a distant kingdom, Oedipus returned to his birthplace and, without realizing it, killed his father and married his mother. When he discovered the horror, he blinded himself.

Freud believed that this ancient story dramatizes emotions that all boys feel about their parents—both love and hate. Every male feels guilty about his unconscious incestuous and murderous impulses. In self-defense, he develops a powerful conscience called the **superego,** which is quick to judge and punish.

That marks the beginning of morality, according to psychoanalytic theory, which contends that a boy's fascination with superheroes, guns, kung fu, and the like arises from his unconscious impulse to kill his father. An adult man's homosexuality; homophobia; or obsession with guns, sins, and guilt signals problems at the phallic stage.

Freud offered several descriptions of the moral development of girls as well. One centers on the **Electra complex** (also named after a figure in classical mythology). The Electra complex is similar to the Oedipus complex in that the little girl wants to eliminate the same-sex parent (her mother) and become intimate with the opposite-sex parent (her father). That may also lead girls to develop a superego.

According to psychoanalytic theory, at the phallic stage children cope with guilt and fear through **identification;** that is, they try to become like the same-sex parent. Consequently, young boys copy their fathers' mannerisms, opinions, actions, and girls copy their mothers'. Both sexes exaggerate the male or female role.

Since the superego arises from the phallic stage, and since Freud believed that sexual identity and expression were crucial for mental health, his theory suggests that parents encourage boys and girls to accept and follow appropriate sex roles. Many social scientists disagree. They contend that the psychoanalytic explanation of sexual and moral development "flies in the face of sociological and historical evidence" (David et al., 2004, p. 139).

Accordingly, I learned in graduate school that Freud was unscientific. However, as explained in Chapter 1, developmental scientists seek to connect research, theory, and experience. My own experience has made me rethink my rejection of Freud.

It began with a conversation with my eldest daughter, Bethany, when she was about 4 years old:

Bethany: When I grow up, I'm going to marry Daddy.
Me: But Daddy's married to me.
Bethany: That's all right. When I grow up, you'll probably be dead.
Me: *[Determined to stick up for myself]* Daddy's older than me, so when I'm dead, he'll probably be dead, too.
Bethany: That's OK. I'll marry him when he gets born again.

I was dumbfounded, without a good reply. I had no idea where she had gotten the concept of reincarnation. Bethany saw my face fall, and she took pity on me:

Bethany: Don't worry, Mommy. After you get born again, you can be our baby.

The second episode was a conversation I had with my daughter Rachel when she was about 5:

Rachel: When I get married, I'm going to marry Daddy.
Me: Daddy's already married to me.
Rachel: *[With the joy of having discovered a wonderful solution]* Then we can have a double wedding!

The third episode was considerably more graphic. It took the form of a "valentine" left on my husband's pillow on February 14th by my daughter Elissa (see figure).

Finally, when Sarah turned 5, she also said she would marry her father. I told her she couldn't, because he was married to me. Her response revealed one more hazard of watching TV: "Oh, yes, a man can have two wives. I saw it on television."

As you remember from Chapter 1, a single example (or four daughters from one family) does not prove that Freud was correct. I still think Freud was wrong on many counts. But his description of the phallic stage seems less bizarre than I once thought.

Pillow Talk Elissa placed this artwork on my husband's pillow. My pillow, beside it, had a less colorful, less elaborate note—an afterthought. It read "Dear Mom, I love you too."

OTHER THEORIES OF SEX-ROLE DEVELOPMENT Although the psychoanalytic theory of early sex-role development is the most elaborate, many other theories differ in their explanation of the young child's sex and gender awareness. We describe here the four other theories, first mentioned in Chapter 1.

Behaviorists believe that virtually all roles, values, and morals are learned. To behaviorists, gender distinctions are the product of ongoing reinforcement and punishment, as well as social learning.

Parents, peers, and teachers all reward behavior that is "gender appropriate" more than behavior that is "gender inappropriate" (Berenbaum et al., 2008). For example, "adults compliment a girl when she wears a dress but not when she wears pants" (Ruble et al., 2006, p. 897), and a boy who asks for a train and a doll for his birthday is more likely to get the train. Boys are rewarded for boyish requests, not for girlish ones.

According to social learning theory, children model themselves after people they perceive to be nurturing, powerful, and yet similar to themselves. For young children, those people are usually their parents. As it happens, adults are the most sex-typed of their entire lives when they are raising young children. If ever a working woman is going to leave the labor market to take care of her home and children, it is when her children are infants and preschool age.

Furthermore, although national policies (e.g., subsidizing preschool) impact gender roles and many fathers are involved caregivers, women in every nation nonetheless do much more child care, house cleaning, and meal preparation than do men (Hook, 2010). Children follow those examples, unaware that the examples they see

gender schema
A child's cognitive concept or general belief about sex differences, which is based on his or her observations and experiences.

are caused partly by their very existence: Before children are born, many couples share domestic work.

Cognitive theory offers an alternative explanation for the strong gender identity that becomes apparent at about age 5. Remember that cognitive theorists focus on how children understand various ideas. A **gender schema** is the child's understanding of sex differences (Kohlberg et al., 1983; Martin et al., 2011; Renk et al., 2006).

Young children have many gender-related experiences but not much cognitive depth. They tend to see the world in simple terms. For this reason, their gender schema categorize male and female as opposites. Nuances, complexities, exceptions, and gradations about gender (as well as about everything else) are beyond them.

Furthermore, as children try to make sense of their culture, they encounter numerous customs, taboos, and terminologies that enforce the gender norms. Remember that for preoperational children, appearance is crucial. When they see men and women cut their hair, use cosmetics, and dress in distinct, gender-typed ways, static preoperational thinking makes them conclude that what they see is permanent, irreversible.

Humanism stresses the hierarchy of needs, beginning with survival, then safety, then love and belonging. The final two needs—respect and self-actualization—are not priorities for people until the earlier ones have been satisfied.

Ideally, babies have all their basic needs met, and toddlers learn to feel safe, which puts preschoolers at the love and belonging stage. They seem to strive for admiration from a group of peers they belong to even more than for the love of their parents. Therefore, the girls want to be one of the girls and the boys to be one of the boys.

In a study of slightly older children, participants wanted to be identified as male or female, not because they disliked the other sex, but because same-sex groups satisfied their need to belong (Zosuls et al., 2010).

This theory explains cultural differences in the strength of sexism, in that male/female divisions are much more dominant in some places than others. Specifics vary (a man holding the hand of another man is taboo or expected, depending on local customs) but everywhere young children try to belong by conforming to gender norms.

Evolutionary theory holds that sexual attraction is crucial for humankind's most basic urge, to reproduce. For this reason, males and females try to look attractive to the other sex, walking, talking, and laughing in gendered ways. If girls see their mothers wearing make-up and high heels, they want to do likewise. According to evolutionary theory, the species' need to reproduce is part of everyone's genetic impulses, so young boys and girls practice becoming attractive to the other sex. This ensures that they will be ready after puberty to find each other, and a new generation will be born.

WHAT IS BEST? Each of the major developmental theories strives to explain the sex and gender roles that young children express, but no consensus has been reached (as we saw was the case with emotional regulation in this chapter and language development in Chapter 5). The theories all raise important questions: What gender patterns *should* parents and other caregivers teach? Should every child learn to combine the best of both sexes (called *androgyny*), thereby causing gender stereotypes to eventually disappear as children become more mature, as happens with their belief in Santa Claus and the Tooth Fairy? Or should male–female distinctions be encouraged as essential for the human family?

Answers vary among developmentalists as well as among parents and cultures. This section refers to "challenges" for caregivers. Determining how to raise children to become happy with their own sex and gender is certainly one such challenge.

KEY points

- Parenting styles vary, from very strict, cold, and demanding to very lax, warm, and permissive.
- In general, a middle ground—neither strict nor lax—seems best, but cultural differences in specific patterns are apparent.
- Young children are powerfully influenced by television, videos, and other electronic devices, creating a dilemma for parents.
- Young children develop ideas and stereotypes about male and female behavior. Parents, cultures, and theorists sometimes conflict in their responses.

Moral Development

Children develop increasingly complex moral values, judgments, and behaviors as they mature. Social bonds (Chapter 4), theory of mind (Chapter 5), and the emotional and social maturation just described, are the foundations for morality.

Piaget thought that moral development began when children learned games with rules, which he connected with concrete operational thought at about age 7 (Piaget, 1932/1997). We now know that Piaget was mistaken: Games with rules and moral development are both evident much earlier. Some precursors of morality appear in infancy (Narvaez & Lapsley, 2009).

Many developmentalists believe that children's attachment to their parents, and then to others, is the beginning of morality. According to evolutionary theory, humans protect, cooperate, and even sacrifice for one another precisely because

> our bodies are rather defenseless against the elements and even more vulnerable against possible predators. Thus, to survive, people have long needed to rely on co-ordination and cooperation.
>
> *[Dunning, 2011, pp. 1–2]*

With maturity and adult guidance, children develop guilt (as Erikson explained) and self-control. That helps them behave in ethical ways (Kochanska et al., 2009; Konner, 2010).

Nature and Nurture

Many parents, teachers, and other adults consider moral development more important than any other advancement already described (physical strength, motor skills, intelligence, language, etc.). Perhaps for this reason, debate rages over how children internalize standards, develop virtues, and avoid vices. Conflicting perspectives are held by scholars in many social sciences.

- The "nature" perspective suggests that morality is genetic, an outgrowth of natural bonding, attachment, and cognitive maturation. That would explain why young children help and defend their parents, no matter what the parents do, and punish other children who violate moral rules. Even infants have a sense of what is fair and not, expecting adults to reward effort (Sloane et al., 2012).

- The "nurture" perspective contends that culture is crucial to the development of morality. That would explain why young children emulate people who follow the rules of their community, even if the actual behavior is not innately good or bad. Some children believe that people who eat raw fish, or hamburgers, or bacon, or dogs are immoral.

Both nature and nurture are always influential, but developmentalists disagree about which is more important for morality (Killen & Smetana, 2007; Krebs, 2008; Narvaez & Lapsley, 2009; Turiel, 2006). That debate cannot be settled here; readers are encouraged to explore the issue further.

However, here we explore two moral issues that arise from age 2 to age 6: children's aggression and adults' disciplinary practices. Nature and nurture are evident in both.

Empathy and Antipathy

Moral emotions are evident as children play with one another. With increasing social experiences and decreasing egocentrism, children develop **empathy,** an understanding of other people's feelings and concerns, and **antipathy,** dislike or even hatred.

PROSOCIAL ACTIONS Scientists studying young humans and other primates report spontaneous efforts to help others who are hurt, crying, or in need of help: That is evidence of empathy, which then leads to **prosocial behavior,** extending helpfulness and kindness without any obvious benefit to oneself (Warneken & Tomasello, 2009).

Expressing concern, offering to share, and including a shy child in a game or conversation are examples of prosocial behavior among young children. Jack, age 3, showed empathy when he "refused to bring snacks with peanuts to school because another boy had to sit alone during snack because he was allergic to nuts. Jack wanted to sit with him" (Lovecky, 2009, p. 161). Prosocial behavior seems to result more from empathy than from cognition, more from emotional understanding than from theory of mind (Eggum et al., 2011).

However, prosocial reactions are not automatic. Some children protect their own emotions by "avoiding contact with the person in need . . ." which illustrates "the importance of emotion development and regulation in the development of prosocial behavior" and the critical influence of cultural norms (Trommsdorff & Cole, 2011, p. 136). Feeling distress may be part of nature; responding to distress may be nurture.

ANTISOCIAL ACTIONS Antipathy can lead to **antisocial behavior,** deliberately hurting another person, including people who have done no harm. Antisocial actions include verbal insults, social exclusion, and physical assaults (Calkins & Keane, 2009). An antisocial 4-year-old might look another child in the eye, scowl, and then kick him hard without provocation.

empathy
The ability to understand the emotions and concerns of another person, especially when they differ from one's own.

antipathy
Feelings of dislike or even hatred for another person.

prosocial behavior
Actions that are helpful and kind but that are of no obvious benefit to the person doing them.

antisocial behavior
Actions that are deliberately hurtful or destructive to another person.

Pinch, Poke, or Pat Antisocial and prosocial responses are actually a sign of maturation: Babies do not recognize the impact of their actions. These children have much more to learn.

Toddlers hit, grab, and pull hair, seemingly unaware that they are hurting someone. By age 4 or 5—as a result of brain maturation, theory of mind, emotional regulation, and interactions with caregivers—children are aware. Some are deliberately prosocial, others antisocial.

Emotional regulation, moral development, and the emergence of empathy are nowhere more apparent than in the way children learn to deal with their anger at other people. Rough-and-tumble play, for instance, teaches children not to hurt their playmates. Concern for helping other people, or not, is also apparent in the fantasies of domination and submission acted out in sociodramatic play, in taking turns, and in the sharing of art supplies, construction materials, and toys (Peterson & Flanders, 2005; Utendale & Hastings, 2011).

Even letting another child use a crayon that a child has already used is hard at age 2; most 5-year-olds can do it. Much depends on the child's family and preschool education: Children learn the balance between giving and taking. The result is more prosocial and fewer antisocial actions as children mature (Ramani et al., 2010).

Not surprisingly, given the moral sensibilities of young children, 5-year-olds already judge whether another child's aggression is justified (Etchu, 2007). As with adults, self-defense is more readily forgiven than is a deliberate, unprovoked attack. However, do not assume that bullies realize when they are wrong: At every age, aggressors feel they had a reason to do what they did.

Researchers recognize four general types of aggression, all evident in early childhood (see Table 6.2). **Instrumental aggression** is common among 2-year-olds, who often want something they do not have and simply try to take it. An aggressive reaction from the other child—crying, hitting, and resisting the grab of the instrumentally aggressive child—is also more typical at age 2 than earlier or later.

Reactive aggression is therefore common among young children; almost every child reacts when attacked. Children are less likely to respond with physical aggression as they develop emotional control and theory of mind (Olson et al., 2011).

Relational aggression (usually verbal) destroys another child's self-esteem and disrupts the victim's social networks, becoming more hurtful as children mature. A young child might tell another, "You can't be my friend" or "You are fat," hurting another's feelings. That is relational aggression.

The fourth and most ominous type is **bullying aggression,** done to dominate someone else. It is not rare among young children but should be stopped before school age, when it becomes particularly destructive. Not only does it destroy the self-esteem of victims, it impairs the later development of the bullies, who learn patterns that will harm them in adulthood (see in-depth discussion of bullying in Chapter 8).

instrumental aggression
Hurtful behavior that is intended to get something that another person has and to keep it.

reactive aggression
An impulsive retaliation for another person's intentional or accidental action, verbal or physical.

relational aggression
Nonphysical acts, such as insults or social rejection, aimed at harming the social connection between the victim and other people.

bullying aggression
Unprovoked, repeated physical or verbal attack, especially on victims who are unlikely to defend themselves.

TABLE 6.2 The Four Forms of Aggression

Type of Aggression	Definition	Comments
Instrumental aggression	Hurtful behavior that is aimed at gaining something (such as a toy, a place in line, or a turn on the swing) that someone else has	Often increases from age 2 to 6; involves objects more than people; quite normal; more egocentric than antisocial.
Reactive aggression	An impulsive retaliation for a hurt (intentional or accidental) that can be verbal or physical	Indicates a lack of emotional regulation, characteristic of 2-year-olds. A 5-year-old can usually stop and think before reacting.
Relational aggression	Nonphysical acts, such as insults or social rejection, aimed at harming the social connections between the victim and others	Involves a personal attack and thus is directly antisocial; can be very hurtful; more common as children become socially aware.
Bullying aggression	Unprovoked, repeated physical or verbal attack, especially on victims who are unlikely to defend themselves	In both bullies and victims, a sign of poor emotional regulation; adults should intervene before the school years. (Bullying is discussed in Chapter 8.)

All forms of aggression usually become less common from age 2 to 6, as the brain matures and empathy increases. Parents, peers, and preschool teachers are pivotal mentors in this process. It is a mistake to expect children to regulate their emotions without guidance because they may develop destructive patterns. It is also a mistake to punish the aggressor too harshly because that may remove them from their zone of proximal development, where they can learn to regulate their anger.

Discipline

Adult values, temperament, and experiences affect children's own responses when they misbehave. Of course, adult values depend partly on culture. Discipline does as well.

Ideally, adults guide children toward good behavior and internalized standards of morality so that children behave well and never need to be disciplined. But this ideal is not realistic: Misbehavior cannot always be prevented.

Lest anyone imagine that, with benevolent parents, children will always be good, consider a study of mothers and 3-year-olds during late afternoon (a stressful time). Conflicts (including verbal disagreements) arose about every two minutes (Laible et al., 2008). Here is one example that began with an activity recommended for every parent; the mother was about to take her daughter for a walk:

> **Child:** I want my other shoes.
> **Mother:** You don't need your other shoes. You wear your Pooh sandals when we go for a walk.
> **Child:** Noooooo.
> **Mother:** *[Child's name]*! You don't need your other shoes.
> **Child:** *[Cries loudly]*
> **Mother:** No, you don't need your other shoes. You wear your Pooh sandals when we go for a walk.
> **Child:** Ahhhh. Want pretty dress. *[Crying]*
> **Mother:** Your pretty dress!
> **Child:** Yeah.
> **Mother:** You can wear them some other day.
> **Child:** Noooooo. *[Crying]*
>
> *[from Laible et al., 2008, pp. 442–443]*

✦ **ESPECIALLY FOR Parents of 3-Year-Olds** How could a parent compromise with a child who wants to wear "other shoes"? (see response, page 230) →

In this study, those 3-year-olds who had been securely attached at age 1 (an indication of responsive parenting) had as many conflicts as those who had been insecurely attached. Obviously, good parenting does not always produce good children, if the latter is defined as children who are peaceful and obedient.

However, unlike in the snippet above, the mothers of securely attached children were more likely to compromise and explain (Laible et al., 2008). Is that the best response? Should the mother have offered reasons why the other shoes were not appropriate, or should she have let her daughter wear them? Alternatively, should she have slapped the child for crying, or said "I don't want to walk with you if you fuss"?

PHYSICAL PUNISHMENT In the United States, young children are slapped, spanked, or beaten more often than are infants or older children, and more often than children in Canada or western Europe. Adults in many nations remember receiving physical punishment and think it works. In some ways, they are correct: Physical punishment (called *corporal punishment* because it hurts the body) succeeds at the moment—spanking stops misbehavior.

However, longitudinal research finds that children who are physically punished are more likely to become bullies, delinquents, and then abusive adults. They are also less likely to learn quickly in school or attend college (Straus & Paschall, 2009).

In several nations of Europe, corporal punishment is illegal; in many nations on other continents, it is the norm. In the United States, it is legal and often used by parents, but illegal (though sometimes used anyway) in most schools. Although some adults believe that physical punishment will "teach a lesson" of obedience, the lesson that children learn is that "might makes right." When they become bigger and stronger, they use corporal punishment on others. Parents who hit were usually hit themselves.

Many studies of children from all family constellations find that physical punishment of young children correlates with delayed theory of mind and increased aggression (Olson et al., 2011). To prove cause without a doubt would require parents of monozygotic twins to raise them identically, except that one twin would be spanked often and the other never. Of course, that is unethical as well as impossible.

Nonetheless, many developmentalists wonder why parents would take the chance. The best argument in favor of spanking is that alternative punishments are often worse (Larzelere et al., 2010). Let us consider some of those alternatives.

PSYCHOLOGICAL CONTROL Another common method of discipline is called **psychological control,** in which children's shame, guilt, and gratitude are used to control their behavior (Barber, 2002). Psychological control may reduce academic achievement and emotional intelligence, just as spanking is thought to do (Alegre, 2011).

Consider the results of a study of an entire cohort (the best way to obtain an unbiased sample) of children born in Finland (Aunola & Nurmi, 2004). Their parents were asked 20 questions about their approach to child rearing. The following four items, which the parents rated from 1 ("Not at all like me") to 5 ("Very much like me"), measured psychological control:

1. "My child should be aware of how much I have done for him/her."
2. "I let my child see how disappointed and shamed I am if he/she misbehaves."
3. "My child should be aware of how much I sacrifice for him/her."
4. "I expect my child to be grateful and appreciate all the advantages he/she has."

The higher the parents scored on these four measures of psychological control, the lower the children's math scores were—and this connection grew stronger over time. Surprisingly, math achievement suffered most if parents were also high in affection (e.g., they frequently hugged their children) (Aunola & Nurmi, 2004). One explanation is that affection increased the child's fear of disappointing the parent, which slowed down their willingness to learn new ideas.

Other research also finds that psychological control can depress children's achievement, creativity, and social acceptance (Soenens & Vansteenkiste, 2010). Compared with corporal punishment, children punished with psychological control seem less likely to be physical bullies but more likely to be relationally aggressive (Kuppens et al., 2009), depressed, and anxious (Gershoff et al., 2010).

SOCIAL EXCLUSION The disciplinary technique most often used with young children in North America is the **time-out,** in which an adult requires a misbehaving child to sit quietly, without toys or playmates, for a short time (Barkin et al., 2007). Time-out is favored by many experts in the United States. For example, in the large, longitudinal evaluation of the Head Start program highlighted in Chapter 5, an increase in time-outs and a decrease in

✦ **ESPECIALLY FOR Parents** Suppose you agree that spanking is destructive, but you sometimes get so angry at your child's behavior that you hit him or her. Is your reaction appropriate? (see response, page 231) →

psychological control
A disciplinary technique that involves threatening to withdraw love and support and that relies on a child's feelings of guilt and gratitude to the parents.

time-out
A disciplinary technique in which a child is separated from other people and activities for a specified time.

Bad Boy or Bad Parent? For some children and in some cultures, sitting alone is an effective form of punishment; for others, it produces an angry child.

SW PRODUCTIONS / AGE FOTOSTOCK

RESPONSE FOR Parents of 3-Year-Olds (from page 228) Remember, authoritative parents listen but do not usually give in. A parent could ask why the child did not want the Pooh sandals (ugly, too tight, old?) and explain why the "other shoes" were not appropriate (raining, save for special occasions, hard to walk in). A promise for the future (e.g., "Let's save your other shoes and pretty dress for the birthday party tomorrow") might stop the "Noooo." ●

spankings were considered signs of improved parental discipline (U.S. Department of Health and Human Services, 2010).

However, research on the effectiveness of time-out is confounded by the many ways it is used. Some parents angrily put the child in a corner, yelling at him or her to stay there until the parent is no longer angry. The effect is similar to corporal punishment: The child feels rejected. To be effective, time-out must be brief; one minute for each year of the child's age is suggested. As with every form of discipline, the parents' own emotional state and the child's temperament need to be considered.

EXPLANATION Another alternative to physical punishment and psychological control is *induction,* in which the parents talk extensively with the offender, helping the children understand why their behavior was wrong. Ideally, parents listen as children articulate their emotions and then encourage the children to imagine what they might have done instead of what they did.

Conversation helps children internalize standards, but induction takes time and patience. Since 3-year-olds confuse causes with consequences, they cannot answer an angry "Why did you do that?" or appreciate a lengthy explanation of why the behavior was wrong. Simple induction ("You made him sad") may be more appropriate.

OPPOSING PERSPECTIVES

Is Spanking OK?

Worldwide, cultural differences in child discipline are apparent. For example, only half as many Canadian parents as U.S. parents slap, pinch, or smack their children (Oldershaw, 2002). Although many U.S. school districts forbid corporal punishment in schools, the U.S. Supreme Court decided in 2004 that teachers and parents could use "reasonable force" to punish children (Bugental & Grusec, 2006).

By contrast, physical punishment by anyone—parent, teacher, sibling, stranger—is illegal in many other developed nations (including Austria, Croatia, Cyprus, Denmark, Finland, Germany, Israel, Italy, Norway, New Zealand, and Sweden). It is considered a violation of human rights (Bitensky, 2006).

Opinions about spanking are influenced by past experiences and cultural norms, making it hard for opposing perspectives to be understood by people on the other side. For that reason, consider why a person might or might not put hot sauce on a child's tongue. Then see if those reasons apply to other forms of corporal punishment.

In a book titled *Creative Correction* (Whelchel, 2005), an evangelical Christian suggests hot sauce (which burns) as punishment for forbidden speech, such as curses or sexual slang. (Many other methods, including spanking, are also suggested therein.)

Readers seem to be strongly for or against this suggestion. Of the 198 comments on the book that were posted on Amazon.com through November 2012, half were highly favorable (97 readers rated it 5), 34 percent were highly un-

favorable (71 rated it 1), and only 15 percent were in between (at 2, 3, or 4). One woman wrote:

> Putting hot sauce on your child's tongue? I bet the author wouldn't ever dare to do that to herself & look at all the hate spewing out of her mouth. As a born-again believer & mother, I'd never follow anything in this book. It's so unchristlike that it's sickening. There's nothing "creative" about her correction ideas—it's just plain mean & a newer version of old abuse tactics that our parents used to do.

An opposing perspective came from another woman:

> I haven't had the need for the Tabasco trick yet, but I'm not above using it. It would make a strong impression and wouldn't require a repeat dose, I'm quite sure. Child abuse? Hardly. Giving a child free reign over the TV, internet and the house IS child abuse. Ask any elementary school teacher who her problem child is and it'll be the kid with no discipline at home. A well-behaved child grows into a well-behaved adult. This world certainly needs more of those.

Back to spanking: If both the above comments seem extreme, consider whether your attitudes about spanking are also more extreme than they might be. The research finds that many methods of discipline, including spanking, affect the child's later level of anxiety and aggression (Gershoff et al., 2010). Developmentalists themselves suggest many opposing strategies.

The parents' underlying attitude may be crucial. One study of African American mothers found that if they disapproved of spanking but did it nonetheless, their children were likely to be depressed. However, their children were not harmed if spanking mothers were convinced that spanking was the correct thing to do (McLoyd et al., 2007). Similarly, Chinese American parents who used physical punishment and shame raised children who were relatively happy and well-adjusted *if* the parents used those methods because they agreed with the Chinese ideology that led to them (Fung & Lau, 2009).

What might be wrong with spanking? One problem is not only the attitudes but also the emotions of the adult. Angry spankers might become abusive. Another problem is the child's thoughts, as he or she may not understand the reasoning behind the spanking. Parents assume the transgression is obvious, but many children think the parents' emotions, not the child's actions, triggered the spanking (Harkness et al., 2011).

Further complications can occur. Children vary in temperament; some may suffer from spanking and some may not care. Parents vary in personality; some spank while out of control. Cultures differ as well. Harmful effects are reduced, but do not necessarily disappear, if children believe the punishment is fair because similar punishments happen to every child they know (Vittrup & Holden, 2010).

A U.S. study of parents who attend religiously conservative Protestant churches found that, as expected, they spanked their children more often than other parents did. However, unexpectedly, children spanked during early (but not middle) childhood did not seem to develop the lower self-esteem and increased aggression that has been found with other spanked children (Ellison et al., 2011). Indeed, the opposite was more likely.

Smack Will the doll learn never to disobey her mother again?

The authors of the study suggest that, since spanking was the norm and since most religious leaders also tell parents to explain transgressions (induction), to assure children that they are loved, and never to spank in anger, then

it is less likely that conservative Protestant children will perceive this practice as stigmatizing or demeaning. To the contrary, they may well come to view mild-to-moderate corporal punishment as legitimate, appropriate, and even an indicator of parental involvement, commitment, and concern.

[Ellison et al., 2011, p. 957]

As I write these words, I realize that the opposing perspective is mine. As you saw in the opening of this chapter, I believe that children should never be hit. I am one of many developmentalists convinced that alternatives to spanking are better for the child as well as a safeguard against abuse. But a dynamic-systems view considers discipline as one aspect of a complex web. I know I am not always right.

KEY Points

- Children often advance in moral development during early childhood, usually gaining empathy as their theory of mind advances and emotions become better regulated.
- New empathy usually helps a child act prosocially, able to share, take turns, and so on.
- Children can also increasingly develop antipathy, which leads some to be aggressive without a self-protective reason (i.e., bullies), unlike those with instrumental or reactive aggression.
- Parents, guided by their culture, teach morality in many ways, including the strategies they choose for discipline.
- Every means of punishment may have long-term effects, with physical punishment especially criticized for encouraging aggression.

RESPONSE FOR Parents (from page 229) No. The worst time to spank a child is when you are angry. You might seriously hurt the child, and the child will associate anger with violence. You would do better to learn to control your anger and develop other strategies for discipline and for prevention of misbehavior. ●

Child Maltreatment

We have saved for the end of this chapter the most disturbing topic: child maltreatment. The assumption throughout has been that parents and other adults seek the best for young children and that their disagreements (e.g., what to feed, how to discipline, what kind of early education to provide) arise from contrasting theories about what is best.

However, the sad fact is that not everyone seeks the best for children. Sometimes parents harm their own offspring. Often the rest of society ignores the preventive and protective measures that could stop maltreatment. Lest we become part of the problem, not part of the solution, we first need to recognize child neglect and abuse.

Maltreatment Noticed and Defined

Until about 1960, people thought child maltreatment was a rare, sudden attack by a disturbed stranger. Today we know better, thanks to a pioneering observation of the "battered child syndrome" in a Boston hospital (Kempe & Kempe, 1978). Maltreatment is neither rare nor sudden; the perpetrators are usually one or both of the child's parents. That makes it worse: Ongoing maltreatment, with no protector, is much more damaging than a single incident, however injurious.

With this recognition came a broader definition: **Child maltreatment** now refers to all intentional harm to, or avoidable endangerment of, anyone under 18 years of age. Thus, child maltreatment includes both **child abuse,** which is deliberate action that is harmful to a child's physical, emotional, or sexual well-being, and **child neglect,** which is failure to meet a child's basic physical or emotional needs.

Reported maltreatment means that the authorities have been informed. Since 1993, the number of children *reported* as maltreated in the United States has ranged from about 2.7 million to 3.6 million per year (Children's Bureau, 2010). The overall rate of maltreatment has decreased over the past decade, but the number of neglect victims has increased, far surpassing the number abused (U.S. Bureau of the Census, 2011b).

Substantiated maltreatment means that a reported case has been investigated and verified (see Figure 6.3). The U.S. rate was about 700,000 in 2011, almost 200,000 of them during the preschool years. About 1 in every 90 young children, aged 2 to 5 years old, is substantiated as a maltreatment victim, more often neglected than abused.

---

child maltreatment
Intentional harm to or avoidable endangerment of anyone under 18 years of age.

child abuse
Deliberate action that is harmful to a child's physical, emotional, or sexual well-being.

child neglect
Failure to meet a child's basic physical, educational, or emotional needs.

reported maltreatment
Harm or endangerment about which someone has notified the authorities.

substantiated maltreatment
Harm or endangerment that has been reported, investigated, and verified.

● **UNDERSTANDING THE NUMBERS**
Accurate statistics on maltreatment are impossible to confirm, as many cases are not reported and substantiated. So how can these numbers best be applied to developmental research?

Answer The rate in this text (1 preschool child in 90) is based on dividing the total number of U.S. children aged 2 to 5 (about 17 million) by the total number of children that age who were substantiated victims of maltreatment, according to U.S. statistics (about 190,000; all numbers have been rounded off here). The hope is that readers will remember that most children are *not* abused, but more than one preschooler in 100 does suffer serious harm.

FIGURE 6.3 **Still Far Too Many**
The number of substantiated cases of maltreatment of children under age 18 in the United States is too high, but there is some good news: The rate has declined significantly from its peak in 1993.

OBSERVATION QUIZ
The data point for 2010 is close to the bottom of the graph. Does that mean it is close to zero? (see answer, page 234) ➞

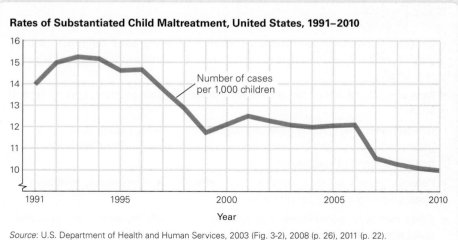

Rates of Substantiated Child Maltreatment, United States, 1991–2010

Number of cases per 1,000 children

Source: U.S. Department of Health and Human Services, 2003 (Fig. 3-2), 2008 (p. 26), 2011 (p. 22).

Why are there four times as many reports as substantiated cases? The main reason is that the same child is often reported several times, leading to one substantiated case. In addition, substantiation requires proof, either physical evidence (broken bones, severe malnutrition) or reliable witnesses.

Noticing children who are maltreated is only part of the task; we need to also notice the conditions and contexts that make abuse or neglect more likely (Daro, 2009). Poverty, social isolation, and inadequate support (public and private) for caregivers are among them. From a developmental perspective, immaturity of the caregiver is a risk factor: Maltreatment is more common if parents are younger than 20 or if families have several children under age 6.

Abuse Victim? Fair-skinned Anna, age 5, told the school nurse she was sunburned because her mommy, Patricia, took her to a tanning salon. Patricia said Anna was gardening in the sun; Anna's father and brother (shown here) said all three waited outside the salon while Patricia tanned inside. The story led to an arrest for child endangerment, a court trial, and a media frenzy. Is the media abusive, the nurse intrusive, or are some too quick to defend harmful mothers? If your child sunburns, is it your fault?

CHRISTOPHER SADOWSKI / SPLASH NEWS / NEWSCOM

Frequency of Maltreatment

How common is maltreatment? No one knows. Not all cases are noticed; not all noted cases are reported; not all reports are substantiated. Reports have increased since 1950, but substantiated rates have decreased every year since 1990 (see Figure 6.4). One reason for lower rates may be that fewer households have many small children: In 1965, 22 percent of family households had more than 3 children under age 18, but in 2010 only 9 percent did (U.S. Bureau of the Census, 2011a and previous years).

That is good news. However, official reports leave room for doubt. For example, Pennsylvania and Maine reported almost identical numbers of child maltreatment victims in 2009 (4,073 and 4,084), but the child population of Pennsylvania is 10 times that of Maine (U.S. Bureau of the Census, 2011b). It is unlikely that Maine

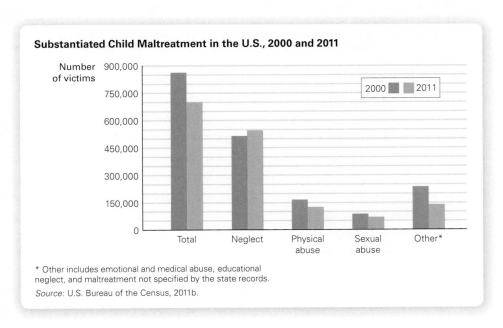

Substantiated Child Maltreatment in the U.S., 2000 and 2011

* Other includes emotional and medical abuse, educational neglect, and maltreatment not specified by the state records.
Source: U.S. Bureau of the Census, 2011b.

FIGURE 6.4 Getting Better? As you can see, the number of victims of child maltreatment in the United States has declined in the past decade. The legal and social-work response to serious maltreatment has improved over the years, which is a likely explanation for the decline. Other, less sanguine, explanations are possible, however.

OBSERVATION QUIZ
Have all types of maltreatment declined since 2000? (see answer, page 235) →

ANSWER TO **OBSERVATION QUIZ**
(from page 232) No. The number is
actually 10.0 per 1,000. Note the little
squiggle on the graph's vertical axis
below the number 10. This means that
numbers between 0 and 9 are not
shown. ●

✦ **ESPECIALLY FOR Criminal Justice
Professionals** Over the past decade,
the rate of sexual abuse has gone
down by almost 20 percent. What
are three possible explanations? (see
response, page 236) ➝

✦ **ESPECIALLY FOR Nurses** While
weighing a 4-year-old, you notice several bruises on the child's legs. When
you ask about them, the child says
nothing and the parent says the child
bumps into things. What should you
do? (see response, page 237) ➝

children suffer maltreatment 10 times more than Pennsylvania ones; something in
the process of reporting and substantiating must differ between those two states.

Furthermore, some professionals in particular jurisdictions are more likely to
notice and report maltreatment than others. For example, the percent of maltreatment reports from educators is 10 times higher in Minnesota than in North Carolina (24 percent versus 2.5 percent) (Children's Bureau, 2010). There are many
plausible reasons for that, but no one thinks Minnesota schoolchildren are much
more often abused.

In a confidential nationwide survey of young adults in the United States, 1 in 4
said they had been physically abused ("slapped, hit, or kicked" by a parent or other
adult caregiver) before sixth grade, and 1 in 22 had been sexually abused ("touched
or forced to touch someone else in a sexual way") (Hussey et al., 2006). Almost never
had their abuse been reported. The authors of this study think these rates are *underestimates* (Hussey et al., 2006)!

One reason for the high rates in this survey is that the respondents were asked
if they had *ever* been mistreated; most other sources report annual rates. Even these
retrospective reports may be inaccurate.

Some adults who were slapped, hit, or kicked do not consider that abuse; other
adults do not realize they were abused until they reanalyze their early experiences;
still others remember abuse that did not actually happen (McNally & Geraerts, 2009).
Each of these alternatives would change the rate of remembered abuse, but it is hard
to know how often each of these occurs.

More useful than trying to determine the rates of child maltreatment decades ago
is to spot it and stop it now. Often the first sign of maltreatment is delayed development, such as slow growth, immature communication, lack of curiosity, or unusual
social interactions. Anyone familiar with child development can observe a young
child and notice such problems.

Often maltreated children seem fearful, startled by noise, defensive and quick to
attack, and confused between fantasy and reality. Table 6.3 lists signs of child maltreatment, both neglect and abuse. None of these signs is proof that a child has been
abused, but whenever any one of them occurs, it signifies trouble.

TABLE 6.3 Signs of Maltreatment in Children Aged 2 to 10

Injuries that do not fit an "accidental" explanation, such as bruises on both sides of the
face or body; burns with a clear line between burned and unburned skin; "falls" that result
in cuts, not scrapes

Repeated injuries, especially broken bones not properly tended (visible on X-ray)

Fantasy play, with dominant themes of violence or sexual knowledge

Slow physical growth, especially with unusual appetite or lack of appetite

Ongoing physical complaints, such as stomachaches, headaches, genital pain, sleepiness

Reluctance to talk, to play, or to move, especially if development is slow

No close friendships; hostility toward others; bullying of smaller children

Hypervigilance, with quick, impulsive reactions, such as cringing, startling, or hitting

Frequent absence from school

Frequent changes of address

Turnover in caregivers who pick up child, or caregiver who comes late, seems high

Expressions of fear rather than joy on seeing the caregiver

Consequences of Maltreatment

The impact of any child-rearing practice is affected by the cultural context. Certain customs (e.g., circumcision, pierced ears, and spanking) are considered abusive in some cultures but not in others; their effects vary accordingly. Children suffer most if their parents seem to love them less when compared with the love they witness in neighborhood families.

If a parent forbids something other children have (from candy to cell phones) or punishes more severely or not at all, children might feel unloved. Nonetheless, severe abuse or neglect is never benign, even if it is common (Gershoff, 2010). Although culture is always relevant, as more longitudinal research is published the effects of maltreatment are proven to be devastating and long-lasting.

The biological and academic impairment from maltreatment is relatively easy to notice—a nurse sees that a child is bruised and broken, a teacher sees that a child is hungry, sleepy, or failing despite ability. However, when researchers follow maltreated children over the years, enduring deficits in social skills seem even more crippling than biological or academic ones.

To be specific, many studies have found that mistreated children typically regard other people as hostile and exploitative; hence, these children are less friendly, more aggressive, and more isolated than other children. The earlier abuse starts and the longer it continues, the worse children's peer relationships become (Scannapieco & Connell-Carrick, 2005).

Not only is child neglect three times more common than overt abuse (see Figure 6.4), but research shows that children who were neglected also experience greater social deficits than abused ones because they were unable to relate to anyone, even in infancy (Stevenson, 2007). The best cure for a mistreated child is a warm and enduring friendship, but maltreatment makes this unlikely.

Adults who were severely maltreated (physically, sexually, or emotionally) often abuse drugs or alcohol, enter unsupportive relationships, become victims or aggressors, sabotage their own careers, eat too much or too little, and engage in other self-destructive behaviors. They also have a much higher risk of emotional disorders and suicide attempts, even after other risk factors (e.g., poverty) are considered (Afifi et al., 2008).

In the current economic climate, finding and keeping a job is a critical aspect of adult well-being; adults who were maltreated suffer in this way as well. One study (Currie & Widom, 2010) carefully matched 807 children who had experienced substantiated maltreatment with other children from the same neighborhood, of the same sex, ethnicity, and SES. About 35 years later, the employment rate for those who had been mistreated was 14 percent lower than the rate for those who had not been mistreated.

The researchers concluded that "abused and neglected children experience large and enduring economic consequences" (Currie & Widom, 2010, p. 111). In this study, the women were more impaired than the men: It may be that self-esteem, emotional stability, and social skills are even more important for female than for male employees.

Three Levels of Prevention, Again

Just as with injury control, there are three levels of prevention of maltreatment. The ultimate goal is *primary prevention* that focuses on the macrosystem and exosystem. Examples of primary prevention include increasing stable neighborhoods and family cohesion, and decreasing financial instability, family isolation, and teenage parenthood.

ANSWER TO **OBSERVATION QUIZ** (from page 233) Most types of abuse are declining, but not neglect. This kind of maltreatment may be the most harmful because the psychological wounds last for decades. ●

RESPONSE FOR Criminal Justice Professionals (from page 234) Perhaps more adults or children are aware of sexual abuse and stop it before it starts. A second possibility is that sexual abuse is less often reported and substantiated because the culture is more accepting of teenage sex (most victims of sexual abuse are between ages 10 and 18). A third possible explanation is that the increase in single mothers means that fathers have less access to children (fathers are the most frequent sexual abusers).

permanency planning
An effort by child-welfare authorities to find a long-term living situation that will provide stability and support for a maltreated child. A goal is to avoid repeated changes of caregiver or school, which can be particularly harmful to the child.

kinship care
A form of foster care in which a relative of a maltreated child, usually a grandparent, becomes the approved caregiver.

Mother–Daughter Love, Finally After a difficult childhood, 7-year-old Alexia is now safe and happy in her mother's arms. Maria Luz Martinez was her foster parent and has now become her adoptive mother.

Secondary prevention involves spotting warning signs and intervening to keep a risky situation from getting worse (Giardino & Alexander, 2011). For example, insecure attachment, especially of the disorganized type (described in Chapter 4), is a sign of a disrupted parent–child relationship. Secondary prevention includes home visits by helpful nurses or social workers, as well as high-quality day care that gives vulnerable parents a break while teaching children how to make friends and resolve conflicts.

When there are several young children in the family, they are at particular risk of maltreatment, especially when the family head is a single parent with money problems. If a nation offers health care for every child, nurses can spot and protect vulnerable children before serious harm occurs—that's secondary prevention.

Tertiary prevention includes everything that limits harm after maltreatment has already occurred. Reporting and substantiating abuse are only the first steps. Often the caregiver needs help to provide better care. Sometimes the child needs another home. If hospitalization is required, that signifies failure: Intervention should have begun much earlier. At that point, treatment is very expensive, harm has already been done, and hospitalization itself further strains the parent–child bond (Rovi et al., 2004).

Children need caregivers they trust, in safe and stable homes, whether they live with their biological parents, a foster family, or an adoptive family. Whenever a child is legally removed from an abusive or neglectful home and placed in foster care, **permanency planning** must begin in order to find a family to nurture that child until adulthood.

Permanency planning is a complex task because adults may disagree about the appropriate solution. Parents are reluctant to give up their rights to the child; foster parents hesitate to take a child who is hostile and frightened; maltreated children need intensive medical and psychological help, but foster care agencies are slow to pay for such services, and the payment is far less than insurance providers charge private clients.

The most common type of foster care in the United States is **kinship care,** in which a relative (usually the grandmother) takes over child rearing from a parent convicted of maltreatment. Kinship care is no worse for children than other forms of foster care, but it typically receives fewer services and adds stress to the lives of the adults involved, a topic further discussed in Chapter 15 (Sakai et al., 2011). While adults argue about parental rights, criminal charges, and cultural differences, the immediate needs of the child may be ignored.

A good treatment plan requires cooperation among social workers, judges, and psychologists as well as the caregivers themselves (Edwards, 2007). Sometimes the child's original family can become better; sometimes a relative can be found who will provide good kinship care; sometimes an outsider is the best caregiver.

As detailed many times in these chapters, caring for young children—from getting them to brush their teeth to guiding their emotions—is not easy. Parents shoulder most of the burden, and their love and protection usually result in strong and happy children. Sadly, parents do not always get the help they need, and children sometimes suffer.

KEY points

- The source of child maltreatment is often the family system and the cultural context, not a deranged stranger.
- Child maltreatment includes both abuse and neglect, with neglect more common and perhaps more destructive.
- Maltreatment can have long-term effects on cognitive and social development, depending partly on the child's personality and on cultural values.
- Prevention can be primary (laws and practices that protect everyone), secondary (protective measures for high-risk situations), and tertiary (reduction of harm after maltreatment has occurred).

RESPONSE FOR Nurses (from page 234) Any suspicion of child maltreatment must be reported, and these bruises are suspicious. Someone in authority must find out what is happening so that the parent as well as the child can be helped. ●

SUMMARY

Emotional Development

1. Learning to regulate and control emotions is crucial during early childhood. Emotional regulation is made possible by maturation of the brain, particularly of the prefrontal cortex, as well as by experiences with parents and peers.

2. In Erikson's psychosocial theory, the crisis of initiative versus guilt occurs during early childhood. Children normally feel pride, sometimes mixed with feelings of guilt. Shame is also evident, particularly in some cultures.

3. Both externalizing and internalizing problems indicate impaired self-control. Some emotional problems that indicate psychopathology are first evident during these years, with boys more often manifesting externalizing behaviors and girls exhibiting internalizing behaviors.

Play

4. All young children enjoy playing—preferably with other children of the same sex, who teach them lessons in social interaction that their parents do not.

5. Active play takes many forms, with rough-and-tumble play fostering social skills and sociodramatic play developing emotional regulation.

Challenges for Caregivers

6. Three classic styles of parenting have been identified: authoritarian, permissive, and authoritative. Generally, children are more successful and happy when their parents express warmth and set guidelines.

7. A fourth style of parenting, neglectful/uninvolved, is always harmful. The particulars of parenting reflect the culture as well as the temperament of the child.

8. Children are prime consumers of many kinds of media. The problems that arise from media exposure include increased aggression and less creative play.

9. Even 2-year-olds correctly use sex-specific labels. Young children become aware of gender differences in clothes, toys, playmates, and future careers.

10. Freud emphasized that children are attracted to the opposite-sex parent and eventually seek to identify, or align themselves, with the same-sex parent. Behaviorists hold that gender-related behaviors are learned through reinforcement and punishment (especially for males) and social modeling.

11. Cognitive theorists note that simplistic preoperational thinking leads to gender schemas and therefore stereotypes. Humanists stress the powerful need of all humans to belong to their group. Evolutionary theory contends that sex and gender differences are crucial for the survival and reproduction of the species.

12. All five theories of sex-role development are plausible, which poses a challenge for caregivers.

Moral Development

13. The sense of self and the social awareness of young children become the foundation for morality, influenced by both nature and nurture.

14. Prosocial emotions lead to caring for others; antisocial behavior includes instrumental, reactive, relational, and bullying aggression.

15. Parental punishment can have long-term consequences, with both corporal punishment and psychological control teaching lessons that few parents want their children to learn.

Child Maltreatment

16. Child maltreatment includes ongoing abuse and neglect, usually by a child's own parents. Physical abuse is the most obvious form of maltreatment, but neglect is more common and may be more harmful.

17. Health, learning, and social skills are all impeded by abuse and neglect, not only during childhood but also decades later.

18. Tertiary prevention may include placement of a child in foster care, including kinship care. Permanency planning is needed.

KEY TERMS

antipathy (p. 226)
antisocial behavior (p. 226)
authoritarian parenting (p. 217)
authoritative parenting (p. 217)
bullying aggression (p. 227)
child abuse (p. 232)
child maltreatment (p. 232)
child neglect (p. 232)
Electra complex (p. 222)
emotional regulation (p. 206)
empathy (p. 226)

externalizing problems (p. 209)
extrinsic motivation (p. 207)
gender differences (p. 221)
gender schema (p. 224)
identification (p. 222)
imaginary friends (p. 207)
initiative versus guilt (p. 206)
instrumental aggression
    (p. 227)
internalizing problems (p. 209)
intrinsic motivation (p. 207)

kinship care (p. 236)
neglectful/uninvolved
    parenting (p. 217)
Oedipus complex (p. 222)
permanency planning (p. 236)
permissive parenting (p. 217)
phallic stage (p. 221)
prosocial behavior (p. 226)
psychological control (p. 229)
psychopathology (p. 209)
reactive aggression (p. 227)

relational aggression (p. 227)
reported maltreatment (p. 232)
rough-and-tumble play
    (p. 214)
self-concept (p. 206)
sex differences (p. 221)
sociodramatic play (p. 214)
substantiated maltreatment
    (p. 232)
superego (p. 222)
time-out (p. 229)

WHAT HAVE YOU LEARNED?

1. How might positivity bias lead to a child's acquisition of new skills and competencies?

2. What are examples of intrinsic versus extrinsic motivations for reading a book?

3. What is the connection between psychopathology and emotional regulation?

4. In what ways might playing with peers teach emotional regulation, empathy, and cultural understanding?

5. How is the development of social play affected by culture?

6. Why might children's muscle strength and control develop better when playing with peers than when playing alone?

7. What do children learn from rough-and-tumble play?

8. What do children learn from sociodramatic play?

9. Describe the characteristics of the parenting style that seems to promote the happiest, most successful children.

10. Why might American child professionals advise no or limited electronic media for young children?

11. What did Piaget believe about the moral development of children? How might evolutionary theory explain moral development?

12. What is the nature perspective on how people develop morals? What is the nurture perspective?

13. How might children develop empathy and antipathy as they play with one another?

14. What is the connection between empathy and prosocial behavior?

15. What are the similarities and differences of the four kinds of aggression?

16. How does moral development relate to discipline?

17. Why have many nations made corporal punishment illegal?

18. When is time-out an effective punishment and when is it not?

19. What are the advantages and disadvantages of using induction as punishment?

20. What does psychoanalytic theory say about the origins of sex differences and gender roles?

21. What do behaviorists say about the origins of sex differences and gender roles?

22. How does evolutionary theory explain why children follow gender norms?

23. Why might poverty, isolation of parents, and lack of good child care contribute to child maltreatment?

24. Why is it difficult to know exactly how often childhood maltreatment occurs?

25. What are the short-term and long-term consequences of childhood maltreatment?

26. What are the three levels of prevention of maltreatment? Give examples of each.

APPLICATIONS

1. Children's television programming is rife with stereotypes about ethnicity, gender, and morality. Watch an hour of children's TV, especially on a Saturday morning, and describe the content of both the programs and the commercials. Draw some conclusions about stereotyping in the material you watched, citing specific evidence (rather than merely reporting your impressions).

2. Gender indicators often go unnoticed. Go to a public place (park, restaurant, busy street) and spend at least 10 minutes recording examples of gender differentiation, such as articles of clothing, mannerisms, interaction patterns, and activities. Quan-

tify what you see, such as baseball hats on eight males and two females. Or (better, but more difficult) describe four male–female conversations, indicating gender differences in length and frequency of talking, interruptions, vocabulary, and so on.

3. Ask three parents about punishment, including their preferred type, at what age, for what misdeeds, and by whom. Ask your three informants how they were punished as children and how that affected them. If your sources all agree, find a parent (or a classmate) who has a different view.

>>ONLINE CONNECTIONS

To accompany your textbook, you have access to a number of online resources, including quizzes for every chapter of the book, flashcards (in English and Spanish), critical thinking questions, and case studies. For access to any of these links, go to www.worthpublishers.com/bergerinvitation2e. In addition to these free resources, you'll also find links to podcasts, video clips, diagnostic quizzing with personalized study advice, and an ebook. Some of the videos and activities available online include:

- *Children at Play.* Watch video clips of children at play, identify the types of play you see, and review how each type contributes to children's development.

- *Bullying.* With video clips of bullying, this activity covers physical and relational aggression, gender differences in bullying, and the impact on victims. It presents causes and preventive measures.

Middle Childhood

Every age has joys and sorrows, gains and losses. But if you were pushed to choose one best time, you might select ages 6 to 11, when most children experience good health and steady growth as they master new athletic skills, learn thousands of words, become less dependent on families. Usually they appreciate their parents, make new friends, and proudly learn about their nation and religion. Life is safe and happy; the dangers of adolescence (drugs, sex, violence) are not yet on the horizon.

Yet some adults remember these years as the worst, not the best. Some children hate school, some live in destructive families, some have no permanent home. Many contend with obesity, asthma, learning disabilities, or bullies. The next two chapters celebrate the joys and discuss the difficulties of ages 6 to 11.

CHAPTER OUTLINE

MIDDLE CHILDHOOD
Body and Mind

WHAT WILL YOU KNOW?

- Whose fault is it if a child is obese?
- Why are math concepts difficult at age 4 but much easier at age 8?
- What is the best way to teach a child a new language?
- Are schools in the United States similar to schools in other nations?
- What causes a child to have autism?

n the middle of the second grade, my family and I moved a thousand miles across the country. I entered a new school, where my accent was odd and the teachers criticized my behavior. My nose was sometimes runny from allergies not yet diagnosed; I was self-conscious and lonely. Cynthia had a friendly smile, freckles, and red hair. More important, she talked to me. I asked her to be my friend.

"We cannot be friends," she said, "because I am a Democrat."

"So am I," I answered. (I knew my family believed in democracy.)

"No, you're not. You are a Republican," she said.

I was stunned and sad. We never became friends.

Neither Cynthia nor I realized that all children are unusual in some way (perhaps because of appearance, culture, or family) and yet capable of friendship with children unlike themselves. Cynthia and I could have been good friends, but neither of us knew it. Her parents had told her something about my parents that I did not understand. Cynthia left school after that year, friendless; I stayed and made other friends.

THIS CHAPTER DESCRIBES NOT ONLY THE SIMILARITIES among children but also differences—in size, health, learning ability, and more. At the end of this chapter, we focus on children with special needs—who particularly need friends but have trouble finding them. ●

Health and Sickness

Genetic and environmental factors safeguard **middle childhood** (about ages 6 to 11), the period after early childhood and before adolescence. One explanation comes from the evolutionary perspective: Genes protect children who have already survived the hazards of birth and early childhood, so they can live long enough to reproduce (Konner, 2010). This evolutionary explanation may not be

middle childhood
The period between early childhood and early adolescence, approximately from ages 6 to 11.

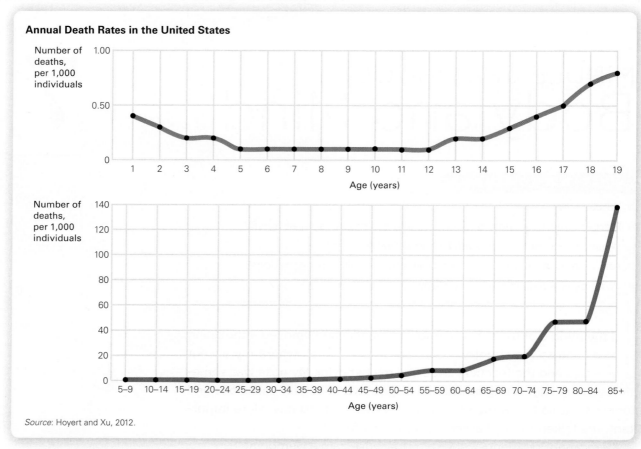

Annual Death Rates in the United States

Source: Hoyert and Xu, 2012.

FIGURE 7.1 Death at an Early Age? Almost Never! Schoolchildren are remarkably hardy, as measured in many ways. These charts show that death rates for 6- to 11-year-olds are lower than those for children younger than 6 or older than 11 and are about 100 times lower than those for adults.

accurate, but for whatever reason, fewer fatal diseases or accidents occur from ages 6 to 11 than at any other period of life (see Figure 7.1).

Slower Growth, Greater Strength

Unlike infants or adolescents, school-age children's growth is slow and steady. Self-care is easy: from brushing their new teeth to dressing themselves, from making their own lunch to walking with friends to school. Once at school, brain maturation soon allows most of them to sit at their desks or tables and learn without breaking their pencils, tearing their papers, or elbowing their classmates.

Muscles, including the heart and lungs, become strong. With each passing year, children run faster and exercise longer (Malina et al., 2004). As long as their entire community is not starving, school-age children get enough food, continuing to grow 2 inches (5 centimeters) or more each year.

Medical Care

Immunization has reduced deaths dramatically, and throughout childhood lethal accidents and fatal illnesses are far less common than a few decades ago. For example, in the United States, 70 per 100,000 5- to 14-year-olds died in 1950; in 2010, only 15 per 100,000 did (see Figure 7.1).

Furthermore, better medical care (diagnostic and preventative) has meant fewer children suffer with chronic conditions such as hearing impairments or anemia, both now half as frequent in middle childhood as they were two decades ago, partly because those problems are diagnosed and treated earlier. In addition, fewer children breathe secondhand smoke: Cotinine (a biomarker that reveals inhaled nicotine) in children's blood declined by 28 percent in just one decade (1994 to 2004) (MMWR, July 11, 2008).

Children themselves also have better habits than they did a few generations ago: They more often wash their hands and cover their sneezes. Those with chronic diseases can attend special camps and programs that show them they are not alone as they learn self-care.

Establishing good health habits is vital before adolescence. If teenage rebellion leads those with serious, chronic conditions (e.g., diabetes, phenylketonuria, epilepsy, cancer, asthma, and sickle-cell anemia) to ignore special diets, pills, warning signs, and doctors, they get sicker (Dean et al., 2010; Suris et al., 2008).

For all children, childhood protects later health. Unfortunately, children in poor health for economic or social reasons are vulnerable lifelong. For low-income children in particular, having a parent who is attentive and responsive (not only regarding health) makes a decided difference for their health in childhood, adolescence, and adulthood (G. E. Miller et al., 2011).

Physical Activity

Beyond the sheer fun of playing, some benefits of physical activity—especially games with rules—are immediate. For example, a Canadian study found that 6- and 7-year-olds who felt victimized nonetheless improved academically if they played sports (Perron et al., 2011).

Active play contributes to the following:

- Better overall health
- Less obesity
- Appreciation of cooperation and fair play
- Improved problem-solving abilities
- Respect for teammates and opponents of many ethnicities and nationalities

Expert Eye–Hand Coordination The specifics of motor-skill development in middle childhood depend on the culture. These flute players are carrying on the European Baroque musical tradition that thrives among the poor, remote Guarayo people of Bolivia.

Playing sports during middle childhood also poses risks, however:

- Loss of self-esteem (teammates and coaches are sometimes cruel)
- Injuries (sometimes serious, including concussions)
- Reinforcement of prejudice (especially against the other sex)
- Increased stress (evidenced by altered hormone levels, insomnia)

Where can children reap the benefits and avoid the hazards of active play? There are three possibilities: neighborhoods, schools, and sports leagues.

NEIGHBORHOOD GAMES Neighborhood play is flexible. Rules and boundaries are adapted to the context (out of bounds is "past the tree" or "behind the parked truck"). Stickball, touch football, tag, hide-and-seek, and dozens of other running and catching games go on forever—or at least until dark. The play is active, interactive, and inclusive—ideal for children of both sexes and several ages. It also teaches ethics. As one scholar notes:

> Children play tag, hide and seek, or pickup basketball. They compete with one another but always according to rules, and rules that they enforce themselves without recourse to an impartial judge. The penalty for not playing by the rules is not playing, that is, social exclusion . . .

[Gillespie, 2010, p. 298]

HENRIK WEIS / CULTURA / CORBIS

Idyllic Two 8-year-olds, each with a 6-year-old sister, all four day-dreaming or exploring in a very old tree beside a lake in Denmark—what could be better? Ideally, all the world's children would be so fortunate, but most are not.

Unfortunately, "not playing" is not only a consequence of ignoring the rules but also of not having the time or a place to play. Vacant lots and empty fields are increasingly scarce. A century ago, 90 percent of the world's children lived in rural areas; now most live in crowded cities or at the city's edge.

To make matters worse, many parents keep their children inside because they fear "stranger danger"—although one expert writes that "there is a much greater chance that your child is going to be dangerously overweight from staying inside than that he is going to be abducted" (quoted in Layden, 2004, p. 86). Homework and video games compete with outdoor play, especially in the United States. According to an Australian scholar:

> Australian children are lucky. Here the dominant view is that children's after school time is leisure time. In the United States, it seems that leisure time is available to fewer and fewer children. If a child performs poorly in school, recreation time rapidly becomes remediation time. For high achievers, after school time is often spent in academic enrichment.
>
> *[Vered, 2008, p. 170]*

The United States is not the worst-offending nation in terms of using after-school time as study time instead of play time. South Korea in particular is known for the intensity of "shadow education," which is extra tutoring that parents find for their children, hoping to improve their test grades later on (Lee & Shouse, 2011).

EXERCISE IN SCHOOL Active play during school hours has also declined. A study of 10,000 third-graders throughout the United States found that about one-third had less than 15 minutes of recess daily, with city-dwellers in low-SES families most likely to have no recess at all (Barros et al., 2009).

Paradoxically, school exercise may actually improve academic achievement (Carlson et al., 2008). How could this be? A review of the research suggests several possible mechanisms that involve the brain, including direct benefits of increased blood flow and increased release of neurotransmitters, as well as the indirect results of better mood and thus better ability to concentrate (Singh et al., 2012). The Centers for Disease Control recommends that children be active (e.g., not sit on the sidelines awaiting a turn) for at least half the duration of their physical education classes (Khan et al., 2009). Many schools do not reach this goal.

Several schools have after-school sports teams, which do provide exercise but also increase injuries. National organizations are developing practices that may prevent concussions among 7- and 8-year-olds in football practice as well as halt full-body impact among children playing ice hockey, but the fact that regulations are needed to protect children from serious harm is sobering (Toporek, 2012).

ATHLETIC CLUBS AND LEAGUES Private or nonprofit clubs and organizations offer additional opportunities for activity, with culture and family affecting specifics: Some children learn golf, others tennis, others boxing. Cricket, baseball, and soccer are each practiced by most boys in some nations, by almost none in others.

Unfortunately, children from low-SES families or with disabilities are less likely to belong to local clubs and teams (e.g., Little League), yet they would benefit most from the strength, activity, and teamwork of organized play.

✦ **ESPECIALLY FOR Physical Education Teachers** A group of parents of fourth- and fifth-graders has asked for your help in persuading the school administration to sponsor a competitive sports team. How should you advise the group to proceed? (see response, page 250) →

THE NEW YORKER COLLECTION 2001 PAT BYRNES FROM CARTOONBANK.COM. ALL RIGHTS RESERVED.

P. BYRNES.

"Just remember, son, it doesn't matter whether you win or lose— unless you want Daddy's love."

JIM WEST / AGE FOTOSTOCK

Why Helmets? Sports organized by adults, such as this football team of 7- to 8-year-old boys sponsored by the Detroit Lions and Police Athletic League of Detroit, may be harmful to children. The best games are those that require lots of running and teamwork—but no pushing or shoving.

Even when joining is free, these children are less likely to be involved in extracurricular activities of any kind, and they suffer because of it (Dearing et al., 2009).

Health Problems

Although few children are seriously ill during middle childhood, many have at least one chronic condition that might interfere with school, play, or friendship. Individual, family, and contextual influences interact with one another in the causes and treatments of every illness. To illustrate the dynamic interactions of every health condition, we focus on two examples: obesity and asthma.

CHILDHOOD OBESITY **Body mass index (BMI)**, as mentioned in Chapter 5, is the ratio of weight to height. **Childhood overweight** is usually defined as a BMI above the 85th percentile, and **childhood obesity** is defined as a BMI above the 95th percentile of children that age (Barlow et al., 2007). In 2010, 18 percent of 6- to 9-year-olds were obese (Ogden et al., 2012).

Childhood obesity is increasing worldwide, having more than doubled since 1980 in all three nations of North America (Mexico, the United States, and Canada) (Ogden et al., 2011). U.S. data from the twenty-first century find obesity rates are no longer rising in children, but the current plateau is far too high. About one-third (32.6 percent) of 6- to 11-year-old children are overweight, more than half of whom are obese (Ogden et al., 2012) (see Figure 7.2).

The World Health Organization uses another set of statistics, with lower cutoffs between healthy and excess weight, and thus some international statistics report even more childhood obesity (Shields & Tremblay, 2010). No matter what standards are used, however, childhood obesity is far too high.

Childhood overweight correlates with asthma, high blood pressure, and elevated cholesterol (especially LDL, the "lousy" cholesterol). As excessive weight builds, school achievement often decreases, self-esteem falls, and loneliness rises (Harrist et al., 2012). If obese children stay heavy, they become adults who are less likely to marry, attend college, or find work that reflects their ability (Han et al., 2011; Sobal & Hanson, 2012).

There are "hundreds if not thousands of contributing factors" for childhood obesity, from the cells of the body to the norms of the society (Harrison et al., 2011, p. 51). More than 200 genes affect weight by influencing activity level, food

● UNDERSTANDING THE NUMBERS
How could 18 percent of the children be in the top 5 percent?

Answer Mathematically, of course, only the top 5 percent of any group are above the 95th percentile (that's what percentile means). But the children's weight and height percentiles were set by the BMIs of U.S. children from 1975 to 1980. Today, for 6- to 11-year-olds, 20 percent of the boys and 16 percent of the girls are as heavy as only 5 percent were then (see BMI table in Appendix A).

body mass index (BMI)
A person's weight in kilograms divided by the square of height in meters.

childhood overweight
In a child, having a BMI above the 85th percentile, according to the U.S. Centers for Disease Control's 1980 standards for children of a given age.

childhood obesity
In a child, having a BMI above the 95th percentile, according to the U.S. Centers for Disease Control's 1980 standards for children of a given age.

FIGURE 7.2 Fatter and Fatter As you see, obesity (defined here as the 95th percentile or above, per the Centers for Disease Control and Prevention 2000 growth charts) increases as children grow older. Not shown is the rate in infancy, which is significantly lower for every group. The "All Groups" rate includes children of groups not shown separately, such as biracial, Asian, Hawaiian, Alaskan native, and American Indian.

OBSERVATION QUIZ

Generally, rates of obesity increase every year from ages 2 to 19, but boys and girls in one group here seem *less* likely to be overweight in adolescence than in middle childhood. Which group, and why? (see answer, page 250) →

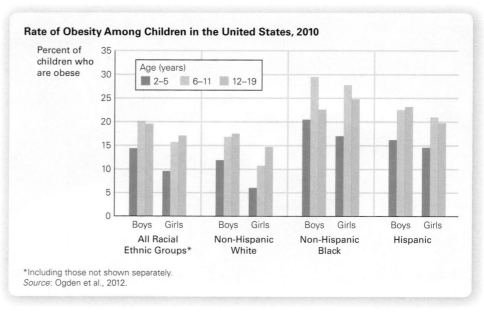

Rate of Obesity Among Children in the United States, 2010

*Including those not shown separately.
Source: Ogden et al., 2012.

✦ **ESPECIALLY FOR Teachers** A child in your class is overweight, but you are hesitant to say anything to the parents, who are also overweight, because you do not want to insult them. What should you do? (see response, page 252) →

Same Situation, Far Apart: Not Chips or Cookies Children have high energy but small stomachs, so they enjoy frequent snacks more than big meals. Yet snacks are typically poor sources of nutrition. Who is healthier, the Bangladeshi American children eating cotton candy at a state fair in Texas or the Japanese children eating takoyaki (an octopus dumpling) as part of a traditional celebration near Tokyo?

preferences, body type, and metabolism (Gluckman & Hanson, 2006). Having two copies of an allele called FTO (inherited by 16 percent of all European Americans) increases the likelihood of both obesity and diabetes (Frayling et al., 2007).

But do not blame genes for today's increased obesity, since genes change little from one generation to the next (Harrison et al., 2011). Family practices, however, have changed. Obesity is more common in infants who are not breast-fed; in preschoolers who watch TV and drink soda; and in school-age children who are driven to school, sleep too little, and rarely play outside (Hart et al., 2011; Institute of Medicine, 2006; Rhee, 2008).

During middle childhood, children themselves contribute to their weight gain. They have *pester power*—the ability to get adults to do what they want (Powell et al., 2011). Usually, they pester their parents to provide calorie-dense foods, but children who learn about health from their teacher or nurse can pester in the opposite direction—to play outside, to join a sports team, and so on.

All these family contexts changed for the worse toward the end of the twentieth century. For instance, pester power increases as family size decreases. No wonder childhood obesity has increased dramatically, worldwide (see Infographic 7, page 249).

Childhood Obesity Around the Globe

Obesity now causes more deaths worldwide than malnutrition. There are more than 42 million overweight children around the world. Obesity is caused by factors in every system—biological, familial, social, and cultural. One specific example is advertisements for unhealthy foods, often marketed directly to children (see below).

Percentage of Overweight 5- to 17-Year-Olds

- No data
- Less than 10%
- 10–15%
- 15–20%
- 20–25%
- 25–30%
- Over 30%

ADS AND OBESITY

Nations differ not only in obesity rates but also in children's television ads. The amount of advertising of unhealthy foods on television correlates with childhood obesity—except in nations where few children watch TV.

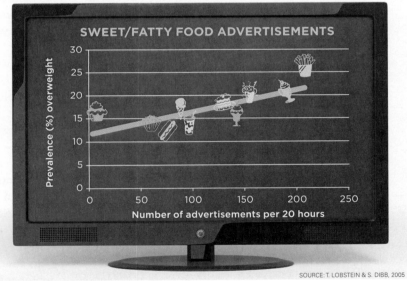

SWEET/FATTY FOOD ADVERTISEMENTS

Prevalence (%) overweight

Number of advertisements per 20 hours

SOURCE: T. LOBSTEIN & S. DIBB, 2005

WHO RECOMMENDATIONS FOR PHYSICAL ACTIVITY

1 Children ages 5 to 17 should be active for at least an hour a day.

2 More than an hour of exercise brings additional benefits.

3 Most physical activity should be aerobic. Vigorous activities should occur 3 times per week or more.

SOURCES & CREDITS LISTED ON P. SC-1

RESPONSE FOR Physical Education Teachers (from page 246) Discuss with the parents their reasons for wanting the team. Children need physical activity, but some aspects of competitive sports are better suited to adolescents and adults than to children. ●

ANSWER TO OBSERVATION QUIZ (from page 248) Non-Hispanic Blacks. The reasons are not known, but one possibility is that African American teenagers become more aware of the larger society and more able to make their own food choices. Note, however, that children and adolescents of every group carry more excess weight than is healthy. ●

asthma
A chronic disease of the respiratory system in which inflammation narrows the airways from the nose and mouth to the lungs, causing difficulty in breathing. Signs and symptoms include wheezing, shortness of breath, chest tightness, and coughing.

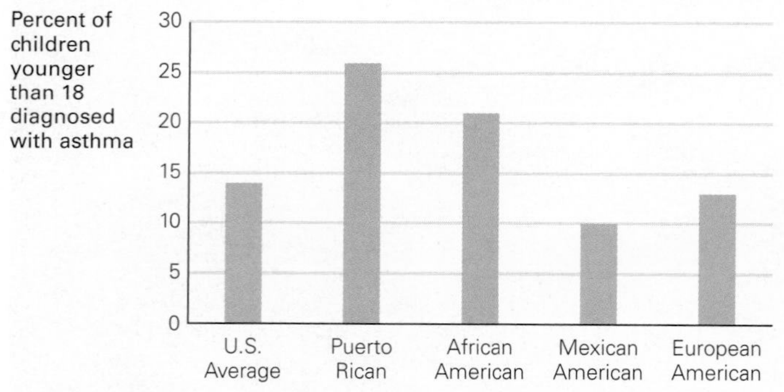

Source: Bloom et al., 2009; National Center for Health Statistics, 2011.

FIGURE 7.3 Not Breathing Easy Of all U.S. children younger than 18, 14 percent have been diagnosed at least once with asthma. Why are Puerto Rican and African American children more likely to have asthma? Is that nature or nurture, genetics or pollution?

Finally, social practices and policies have an impact (Branca et al., 2007), sometimes positive, sometimes not. Communities and nations determine: the quality of school lunches; the location of vending machines and fast food restaurants; the prevalence of parks, bike paths, and sidewalks; the subsidies for corn oil and sugar.

One particular culprit is advertising for candy, cereal, and fast food (Linn & Novosat, 2008). Such advertising is illegal or limited on children's television in some nations—and the rate of childhood obesity correlates with how often children see food commercials (Lobstein & Dibb, 2005).

Since every system (bio-, micro-, macro-, and exo-) is relevant, it is not surprising that parents blame genes or outsiders, while medical professionals and political leaders blame parents. The media contend that advertisements are only suggestions and parents or children are to blame if they follow harmful suggestions.

Rather than trying to zero in on any single factor, a dynamic-systems approach is needed: Many factors, over time, make a child overweight (Harrison et al., 2011). Changing each one makes a difference, although no single change is sufficient. The answer to the first "What Will You Know?" question at the beginning of this chapter is that everyone is at least a tiny bit at fault.

ASTHMA **Asthma** is a chronic inflammatory disorder of the airways that makes breathing difficult. Although asthma affects people of every age, rates are highest among school-age children and have been increasing worldwide for decades (Cruz et al., 2010).

In the United States, child asthma rates have tripled since 1980. Parents report that 10 percent of U.S. 5- to 9-year-olds currently have asthma; 6 percent have had an attack within the past year (National Center for Health Statistics, 2011) (see Figure 7.3).

Curiously, although U.S. children classified as Hispanic have high rates of asthma, those born in Mexico have half the rate of asthma as those of Mexican heritage who are born in the United States; yet for those of Puerto Rican heritage, asthma is *more* likely if they were born in Puerto Rico than in New York (Lara et al., 2006). Obviously, ethnicity and birthplace are both influential; experts do not agree as to why.

Many researchers seek the causes of asthma. A few alleles have been identified as contributing factors, but none acts in isolation (Akinbami et al., 2010; Bossé & Hudson, 2007). Several aspects of modern life—carpets, pollution, house pets, airtight windows, parental smoking, cockroaches, less outdoor play—contribute to the increased rates of asthma (Tamay et al., 2007), but again no single factor is the cause.

Some experts suggest a *hygiene hypothesis,* proposing that "the immune system needs to tangle with microbes when we are young" (Leslie, 2012, p. 1428). Children may be overprotected from viruses and bacteria. Because parents are worried about hygiene, young children are not exposed to minor infections and diseases that would strengthen their immunity. This hypothesis is supported by data showing that (1) first-born children develop asthma more often than later-born ones; (2) farm children have less asthma and other allergies; (3) children born by cesarean delivery (very sterile) have more asthma.

However, none of those *prove* the hygiene hypothesis. Perhaps farm children are protected by drinking unpasteurized milk, by outdoor chores, or by genes that are more common in farm families, rather than by being more often exposed to a range of bacteria (von Mutius & Vercelli, 2010).

The incidence of asthma increases as nations get richer, as seen dramatically in Brazil and China. Better hygiene for wealthier children is one explanation, but so is increasing urbanization, which correlates with more cars, more pollution, more allergens, and better medical diagnoses (Cruz et al., 2010). One review of the hygiene hypothesis notes that "the picture can be dishearteningly complex" (Couzin-Frankel, 2010, p. 1168).

PREVENTION OF HEALTH PROBLEMS The three levels of prevention (discussed in Chapters 5 and 6) apply to every health problem, including the two just reviewed, obesity and asthma.

Primary prevention requires changes in the entire society. Better ventilation of schools and homes, less pollution, fewer cockroaches, fewer antibiotics, and more outdoor play would benefit everyone. Michelle Obama's "Let's Move" initiative is an example of primary prevention if it makes everyone more likely to be active.

Secondary prevention decreases illness among high-risk children. If asthma or obesity runs in the family, then breast-feeding for a year, regular and sufficient sleep, and low-fat diets would prevent some illness. Annual check-ups by the same pediatrician—who tests vision, hearing, weight, posture, blood pressure and more—can spot potential problems while secondary prevention is still possible.

Finally, *tertiary prevention* treats problems after they appear. For child overweight, that means more exercise and less junk food (not a strict diet). For asthma, prompt use of injections and inhalers prevents hospitalization. Hypoallergenic materials (e.g., for mattress covers) also reduce asthma attacks—but not by much, probably because such measures begin too late (MMWR, January 14, 2005). But even if tertiary prevention does not halt a condition, it can reduce the burden, as the following illustrates.

Pride and Prejudice In some city schools, asthma is so common that using an inhaler is a sign of prestige, as suggested by the facial expressions of these two boys. The "prejudice" is more apparent beyond the walls of this school nurse's room, in a society that allows high rates of childhood asthma to occur.

A VIEW FROM SCIENCE

Asthma in Two 8-Year-Old Girls

A team of social scientists analyzed statistics to produce *The Measure of America,* which compares development in the United States and elsewhere (Burd-Sharps et al., 2008; Lewis & Burd-Sharps, 2010). Their statistical analysis considered data from hundreds of thousands of people. They also presented case studies to illustrate the impact of SES, like this one of Sophie and Alexa, both 8-year-old girls with asthma.

Sophie is a vibrant eight-year-old who was diagnosed with severe asthma when she was two. She lives in a house in a New York City suburb with a park down the street and fresh air outside—an environment with few asthma triggers.

Her family has private health insurance, a benefit of her father's job, with extensive provisions for preventative care and patient education. Her parents' jobs have personal and sick days that give them time off from work

to take her to the doctor. After some early difficulty finding a suitable medication regime, she has settled into a routine of daily-inhaled medication (at a cost of $500 per month, fully covered by insurance), annual flu shots, and a special medication she takes only when she is sick with a cold. Sophie sees her pediatrician regularly and a top-flight asthma specialist yearly, to monitor her progress; has a nebulizer for quick relief in case of a serious attack; and can rely on nebulizers in her school and after-school program as well.

Sophie has never had to go to the emergency room for an attack, almost always participates in gym, and misses about two or three days of school a year due to asthma-related problems.

Alexa is also eight years old and was first diagnosed with severe asthma at age three. She lives with her mother in a Brooklyn apartment three blocks from a waste transfer station that receives, sorts, and dispatches thirteen thousand tons of garbage each weekday. In addition to the acrid smell of garbage, the cockroaches that frequent her apartment also trigger Alexa's asthma attacks through allergens in their droppings. Her mother works at a minimum-wage job; she loses income when she takes Alexa to the doctor, fills emergency prescriptions, or stays home with Alexa when she is sick.

Alexa's mother could qualify for SCHIP, which would provide health insurance for Alexa, but she has never heard of it. Instead, Alexa is officially listed as living with her grandmother, whose Medicaid coverage extends to Alexa. Alexa sees a doctor annually, though her grandmother fears Alexa is not benefitting from the latest advances in asthma care.

Alexa misses twelve to fifteen days of school each year, does not participate in gym, and spends up to eight fearful nights each year in a hospital emergency room. When she misses consecutive days of school, she struggles with schoolwork. She wishes she could run around like her classmates.

[Burd-Sharps et al., 2008, p. 67]

These cases highlight economic disparities in prevention. However, as with obesity, severe asthma in childhood can be blamed on genes, parents, schools, doctors, and neighborhoods, as well as on public policies regarding poverty and health care. Who is to blame is a political dispute, and people disagree about the target for prevention—primary, secondary, and tertiary. But no one wants Alexa to spend "eight fearful nights" in the hospital each year.

The scientists studying asthma have found a multitude of causes. They have documented increases in every nation, which is disheartening. But, recently, researchers are restoring hope, because they have found that some efforts make a difference. We conclude this A View from Science with one encouraging study.

One hundred caregivers for children with asthma agreed to allow a Spanish-speaking counselor to come repeatedly to their homes to help their children (Borrelli et al., 2010). These adults were addicted to smoking: They did not necessarily want to quit.

The counselor placed a smoke monitor in the child's bedroom. A week later, she showed the caregiver how much smoke exposure the child had experienced. Then, in three sessions, she provided specific counseling on quitting, based on the best research on addiction, with particular sensitivity to Latino values.

Three months later, one-fourth of the caregivers had quit smoking. Many of the rest had cut down. The average child's exposure to smoke was reduced by half, and asthma attacks were less frequent (Borrelli et al., 2010).

Note that precise knowledge and personal encouragement were provided here—which not all parents have. Other research confirms that most adults, including those who are neither parents nor Latino, want to protect children but lack specific knowledge. As proven with hearing and vision impairments, with measles and malnutrition, many professionals can help reduce childhood illness, if research shows them how to do it.

RESPONSE FOR Teachers (from page 248) Speak to the parents, not accusingly (because you know that genes and culture have a major influence on body weight), but helpfully. Alert them to the potential social and health problems their child's weight poses. Most parents are very concerned about their child's well-being and will work with you to improve the child's snacks and exercise level. ●

KEY points

- Most 6- to 11-year-olds are healthy and capable of self-care, with less disease than at any other time of life.
- Active play is crucial at this age, for learning as well as for health.
- Unfortunately, obesity and asthma are increasingly common among school-age children.
- Health problems among children are partly genetic, partly familial, and partly the result of laws and values in the society.

Cognition in Middle Childhood

Learning is rapid in childhood. Some children, by age 11, beat their elders at chess, play music that adults pay to hear, publish poems, solve complex math problems in their heads. Others survive on the streets or fight in civil wars, learning lessons that no child should know. In fact, during these years children can learn almost anything. Adults need to decide how and what to teach. Theories and practices differ, as you will see.

Piaget and Middle Childhood

Piaget called the cognition of middle childhood **concrete operational thought,** characterized by concepts that enable children to use logic. *Operational* comes from the Latin word *operare*, "to work; to produce."

By calling this period operational, Piaget emphasized productive thinking. The 6- to 11-year-old school-age child, no longer limited by egocentrism and static reasoning, performs logical operations. However, thinking at this stage is *concrete*—that is, logic is applied to visible, tangible, real things, not to abstractions, which are understood at the next stage, formal operations.

A HIERARCHY OF CATEGORIES One concrete example is **classification,** the organization of things into groups (or *categories* or *classes*), according to some characteristic that they share. For example, *family* is a category that includes parents, siblings, and cousins. Other common classes are people, animals, toys, and food. Each class includes some elements and excludes others, and each is part of a hierarchy.

Piaget devised many experiments to reveal children's understanding of classification. For example, an examiner shows a child a bunch of nine flowers—seven yellow daisies and two white roses (revised and published in Piaget et al., 2001). The examiner makes sure the child knows the words *flowers, daisies,* and *roses.* Then comes the pivotal question: "Are there more daisies or more flowers?"

Until about age 7, most children say, "More daisies." Young children seem unable to justify their answers, but some 6- or 7-year-olds can do so. They explain that "there are more yellow ones than white ones" or that "because daisies are daisies, they aren't flowers" (Piaget et al., 2001). By age 8, most children can classify correctly: "More flowers than daisies," they say, and they can explain why they think so.

MATH CONCEPTS Another logical concept is *seriation,* the understanding that things can be arranged in a logical series. Seriation is crucial for using the alphabet or the number sequence (not merely memorizing, which younger children can do). For example, while most 5-year-olds can count up to 100, few can correctly estimate where any particular two-digit number would be placed on a line that starts at 0 and ends at 100. Generally, children can do this by age 8 (Meadows, 2006).

Concrete operational thinking allows children to understand math operations. For example, once children understand conservation (explained in Chapter 5), they realize that $12 + 3 = 3 + 12$, and that 15 is always 15. Reversibility allows the realization that if $5 \times 3 = 15$, then 15 divided by 3 must be 5.

Although logic connects to math concepts, you will learn later in this chapter that research finds more continuity than discontinuity in number skills. Thus, Piaget was mistaken: There is no sudden shift between preoperational and concrete operational logic.

Nonetheless, Piaget's experiments revealed that after about age 6, children use mental categories and subcategories more flexibly and inductively. They are less egocentric and more advanced thinkers, becoming operational in ways that younger children are not (Meadows, 2006).

Vygotsky and Middle Childhood

Like Piaget, Vygotsky felt that educators should consider thought *processes*, not just the outcomes. He recognized that younger children are confused by some concepts that older children understand because they have not yet learned to process the ideas.

concrete operational thought
Piaget's term for the ability to reason logically about direct experiences and perceptions.

classification
The logical principle that things can be organized into groups (or categories or classes) according to some characteristic they have in common.

AP PHOTO /THE AUGUSTA CHRONICLE, CHRIS THELEN

His Science Project Concrete operational 10-year-olds like Daniel, shown here with some of his family's dairy cows, can be logical about anything they see, hear, or touch. Daniel's science experiment, on the effect of music on milk production, won first place in a Georgia regional science fair.

✦ **ESPECIALLY FOR Teachers** How might Piaget's and Vygotsky's ideas help in teaching geography to a class of third-graders? (see response, page 256) →

THE ROLE OF INSTRUCTION Unlike Piaget, however, Vygotsky regarded instruction as crucial (Vygotsky, 1934/1994). He thought that peers and teachers provide the bridge between developmental potential and needed skills and knowledge, via guided participation, scaffolding, and the zone of proximal development, as explained in Chapters 1 and 5.

Confirmation of the role of social interaction and instruction comes from children who, because of their school's entry-date cutoff, begin kindergarten when they are relatively young or old, not quite 5 or almost 6. Achievement scores of those 6-year-olds who began school relatively young, and thus already had a year of first grade, far exceed those of 6-year-olds who were born only one month later but had just completed kindergarten (Lincove & Painter, 2006; NICHD, 2007).

This proves that children learn a great deal from time in school. This comparison doesn't necessarily mean that it is best to enter kindergarten at age 4, since as first-graders they may not be as proficient as their classmates who are almost a year older. But it does mean that school advances abilities that mere maturation does not.

Remember that Vygotsky believed education occurs everywhere, not only in classrooms. Children mentor one another as they play together. They learn from watching television, from eating with their families, from observing people on the street, and from every other daily experience. This education—which includes things adults may wish children not learn—accumulates from infancy on.

An example of knowledge acquired from the social context comes from children in the northeast Indian district of Varanasi. Some of them have an extraordinary sense of spatial orientation—such as knowing whether they are facing north or south, even when they are inside a room with no windows.

In one experiment, after Varanasi children were blindfolded, spun around, and led to a second room, many of them knew which direction (north, south, east, west) they were currently facing (Mishra et al., 2009). They learned that skill because people in their culture refer to the compass orientation to name the location of objects and so on. (Although the specifics differ, a cultural equivalent might be to say that the dog is sleeping southeast, not that the dog is sleeping by the door).

This amazing sense of direction, or any other skill learned in childhood, does not automatically transfer from one context to another. The blindfolded children retained their excellent sense of direction in this experiment, but a child from Varanasi might become disoriented in a tangle of mega-city streets—still knowing where north is, but not knowing how to get downtown. A child who is logical about math may not be logical about family relationships.

In the United States, adults are particularly concerned that 6- to 11-year-olds learn academic skills and knowledge. For this, Vygotsky's emphasis on mentoring is insightful. For instance, a large study of reading and math ability in third- and fifth-grade children found that high-scoring children usually had had three sources of cognitive stimulation:

● Their families (parents read to them daily when they were toddlers)

● Preschool programs (classmates were involved in a variety of learning activities)

● First grade (teachers emphasized literacy, with sensitivity to individual needs).

Although low-SES children were less likely to have all three experiences, the achievement scores of those few low-SES children who did have these mentoring advantages were higher than the average of high-SES children who did not have all three advantages (Crosnoe et al., 2010). In other words, active mentoring trumped socioeconomic status.

DAVID R. FRAZIER PHOTOLIBRARY, INC. / ALAMY

He Knows His Stuff Many child vendors, like this boy selling combs and other grooming aids on the streets of Manaus, Brazil, understand basic math and the give-and-take of social interaction; but, deprived of formal education, they know little or nothing about history and literature.

Culture affects mentors and methods. This was evident in a study of 80 Mexican American children in California (Silva et al., 2010). Half were from families in which indigenous Indian learning was the norm: Children from that culture are expected to learn by watching others and to help one another if need be.

The other half were from families more acculturated to U.S. norms; the children were accustomed to direct instruction, not observational learning. They expected to learn from adults and then to work on their own, without collaborating with their peers. (Indeed, in some classrooms, children are seated at separate desks and told to keep their eyes on their own papers, not to look at other children.)

Researchers compared children from both backgrounds in a study in which children waited passively while a teacher taught their sibling how to make a toy. If they tried to help their brother or sister (more common among the indigenous children), they were prevented from doing so. A week later, the children were surprised to have an opportunity to make the toy themselves. The children from indigenous Indian backgrounds were better at it. This shows that they learned more from observation than did the children who were more used to U.S. learning methods.

Information Processing and the Brain

As you learned in Chapter 1, the *information-processing perspective* is more recent than either Piaget's or Vygotsky's theories. Information processing benefits from technology, which allows for more detailed data and analysis than was possible 50 years ago, particularly in neuroscience (P. H. Miller, 2011).

Rather than describing broad stages (Piaget) or social contexts (Vygotsky), this perspective was inspired by the knowledge of how computers work. This leads many information-processing researchers to describe each small increment of input, processing, and output.

CONNECTING PARTS OF THE BRAIN Recall that the maturing corpus callosum connects the hemispheres of the brain, enabling balance and two-handed coordination, while myelination speeds up thoughts and behavior. The prefrontal cortex—the executive part of the brain—plans, monitors, and evaluates. All of these neurological developments are evident in early childhood, and they continue in middle childhood and beyond.

Increasing maturation results "by 7 or 8 years of age, in a massively interconnected brain" (Kagan & Herschkowitz, 2005, p. 220). Such connections are crucial for the complex tasks that children must master (M. H. Johnson et al., 2009). One example is learning to read. Reading is not instinctual: Our ancestors never did it. Consequently, the brain has no areas dedicated to reading, the way it does for talking, gesturing, or face recognition (Gabrieli, 2009).

How do humans read without brain-specific structures? The answer is "massive interconnections" between the parts of the brain that deal with sounds, vision, comprehension, and so on—all coordinated by the prefrontal cortex.

Interconnections are needed for many social skills as well—deciding whom to trust, figuring out what is fair, interpreting ambiguous gestures and expressions. Younger children are not proficient at this. That's why they are told, "Don't talk to strangers," whereas adults use judgment to decide which strangers merit what kinds of interactions. Adults ask strangers for directions, for the time, for weather predictions—but adults know that some strangers should not be queried.

During middle childhood, various parts of the brain connect to enable reading, writing, logic, and social decisions (Crone & Westenberg, 2009). For many activities, children use more parts of their brains than adults do, thus requiring more connections (M. H. Johnson et al., 2009).

reaction time
The time it takes to respond to a stimulus, either physically (with a reflexive movement such as an eyeblink) or cognitively (with a thought).

selective attention
The ability to concentrate on some stimuli while ignoring others.

RESPONSE FOR Teachers (from page 254) Here are two of the most obvious ways. (1) Use logic. Once children can grasp classification and class inclusion, they can understand cities within states, states within nations, and nations within continents. Organize your instruction to make logical categorization easier. (2) Make use of children's need for concrete and personal involvement. You might have the children learn first about their own location, then about the places where relatives and friends live, and finally about places beyond their personal experience (via books, photographs, videos, and guest speakers). ●

SPEED OF THOUGHT **Reaction time** is how long it takes the brain to respond to a stimulus; specifically, how quickly an impulse travels from one neuron to another to allow thinking to occur. Reactions are quicker with each passing year of childhood because increasing myelination and repeated sequences of action reduce reaction time. Speedy reactions allow faster and more efficient learning. For example, school achievement requires quick coordination of multiple messages within the brain. The result is a child who can read a sentence fluently, write a paragraph, or even answer a multiple-choice question.

Indeed, reaction time relates to every intellectual, motor, and social skill, in school or not. A simple example is being able to kick a speeding soccer ball toward a teammate; a more complex example is being able to calculate when to utter a witty remark and when to stay quiet. Young children find both impossible; fast-thinking older children sometimes succeed.

By early adolescence, reaction time is quicker than at any later time—few adults can beat a teenager at a video game. Teenage emotions also rise or fall quickly, as described in Chapter 9.

PAY ATTENTION Neurological advances allow children to do more than think quickly. As the brain matures, it allows children to pay special heed to the most important elements of their environment. A crucial step in information processing occurs before conscious awareness, as the brain responds to input by deciding if it merits consideration.

Selective attention is the ability to concentrate on some stimuli while ignoring others. This improves markedly at about age 7. Older children learn to notice various stimuli (which is one form of attention) that younger children do not (such as the small difference in the appearance of the letters *b, p,* and *d*) and to select the best response when several possibilities conflict (such as whether a *c* sounds like an *s* or a *k*) (Rueda et al., 2007).

In the classroom, selective attention allows children to listen, take concise notes, and ignore distractions (all difficult at age 6, easier by age 10). In the din of the cafeteria, children comprehend one another's gestures and expressions and react. On the baseball diamond, older batters ignore the other team's attempts to distract them, and older fielders start moving into position as soon as a ball is hit their way.

Indeed, selective attention underlies all the abilities that gradually mature during the school years. "Networks of collaborating cortical regions" (M. H. Johnson et al., 2009, p. 151) are required because attention involves not just one brain function but three: alerting, orienting, and executive control (Posner et al., 2007).

LEARNING MATH One of the leaders of the information-processing perspective is Robert Siegler, who has studied the day-by-day details of children's understanding of math (Siegler & Chen, 2008). Remember that some logical ideas explained by Piaget relate to math understanding, but information-processing research finds that those ideas (such as conservation and seriation) do not necessarily lead to proficient calculations.

Siegler has shown that a child attempts, ignores, half-uses, abandons, and finally adopts new and better strategies to solve math problems. Siegler compares the acquisition of knowledge with *waves* on a beach when the tide is rising. There is substantial ebb and flow as information is processed (Thompson & Siegler, 2010).

A practical application of the idea that knowledge comes in waves is that children need lots of practice in order to master a new idea or strategy. Just because a child says a correct answer on one day does not mean that the achievement is permanent. Lapses, earlier mistakes, momentary insights are all part of the learning process—and adults need to be patient as well as consistent in what they teach.

Since brains develop connections in response to experience, teachers should never give up on a child. Similarly, sex differences in the brain are mostly the result of experience, not hormones, so both boys and girls need extensive practice reading, calculating, and so on (Jordan-Young, 2010).

MEMORY One foundation of new learning appears to be memory, which allows children to connect various aspects of past knowledge. Memory is now often studied with an information-processing approach. Input, storage, and retrieval underlie the increasing cognitive abilities of the schoolchild. Each of the three major steps in the memory process—sensory memory, working memory, and long-term memory—is affected by maturation and experience.

Sensory memory (also called the *sensory register*) is the first component of the human information-processing system. It stores incoming stimuli for a split second after they are received, with sounds retained slightly longer than sights. To use terms explained in Chapter 3, *sensations* are retained for a moment, and then some become *perceptions*. This first step of memory is already quite good in early childhood, improves slightly until about age 10, and remains adequate until late adulthood.

Once some sensations become perceptions, the brain selects those perceptions that are meaningful and transfers them to working memory for further analysis. This is selective memory, the result of selective attention as just described. It is in **working memory** (formerly called *short-term memory*) that current, conscious mental activity occurs. Processing, not mere exposure, is essential for getting information into working memory, which is why working memory improves markedly in middle childhood (Cowan & Alloway, 2009) (see Table 7.1).

As Siegler's waves metaphor suggests, memory strategies do not appear suddenly. Gradual improvement occurs from toddlerhood through adolescence (Schneider & Lockl, 2008). Children develop strategies to increase working memory (Camos & Barrouillet, 2011), and they use these strategies occasionally at first, then consistently.

Cultural differences are evident here, with children learning ways to master whatever their culture expects. For example, many Muslim children are taught to

sensory memory
The component of the information-processing system in which incoming stimulus information is stored for a split second to allow it to be processed. (Also called the *sensory register.*)

working memory
The component of the information-processing system in which current conscious mental activity occurs. (Formerly called *short-term memory.*)

✦ **ESPECIALLY FOR Teachers** How might your understanding of memory help you teach a 2,000-word vocabulary list to a class of fourth-graders? (see response, page 259) →

TABLE 7.1 Advances in Memory from Infancy to Age 11

Child's Age	Memory Capabilities
Under 2 years	Infants remember actions and routines that involve them. Memory is implicit, triggered by sights and sounds (an interactive toy, a caregiver's voice).
2–5 years	Words are now used to encode and retrieve memories. Explicit memory begins, although children do not yet use memory strategies. Children remember things by rote (their phone number, nursery rhymes) without truly understanding them.
5–7 years	Children realize that some things should be remembered, and they begin to use simple strategies, primarily rehearsal (repeating an item again and again). This is not a very efficient strategy, but with enough repetition, automatization occurs.
7–9 years	Children use new strategies if they are taught them. Children use visual clues (remembering how a particular spelling word looks) and auditory hints (rhymes, letters), evidence of brain functions called the visual–spatial sketchpad and phonological loop. Children now benefit from the organization of things to be remembered.
9–11 years	Memory becomes more adaptive and strategic as children become able to learn various memory techniques from teachers and other children. They can organize material themselves, developing their own memory aids.

Source: Based on Meadows, 2006.

Verbs and Adverbs Erin, Ally, Paige, and Sabrina perform rap lyrics they wrote to review key concepts for an upcoming assessment test. Such mnemonic devices are beyond younger children but may be very helpful in middle childhood.

long-term memory
The component of the information-processing system in which virtually limitless amounts of information can be stored indefinitely.

knowledge base
A body of knowledge in a particular area that makes it easier to master new information in that area.

control processes
Mechanisms (including selective attention, metacognition, and emotional regulation) that combine memory, processing speed, and knowledge to regulate the analysis and flow of information within the information-processing system. (Also called *executive processes*.)

metacognition
"Thinking about thinking," or the ability to evaluate a cognitive task in order to determine how best to accomplish it, and then to monitor and adjust one's performance on that task.

memorize all 80,000 words of the Quran, and they develop strategies to remember long passages—strategies that non-Muslim children do not know. The ability to draw a face is not particularly valued in many Muslim families, but it is valued among some other groups—and those children develop strategies to improve their work, such as learning the ratio of distance of forehead, eyes, mouth, and chin.

Finally, information from working memory may be transferred to **long-term memory,** to store it for minutes, hours, days, months, or years. The capacity of long-term memory—how much can be crammed into one brain—is very large by the end of middle childhood. Together with sensory memory and working memory, long-term memory organizes ideas and reactions, with more effective brain functioning over the years of middle childhood (Wendelken et al., 2011).

Crucial to long-term memory is not merely *storage* (how much material has been deposited) but also *retrieval* (how readily past learning can be brought into working memory). For everyone, at every age, retrieval is easier for some memories (especially memories of vivid, emotional experiences) than for others. And for everyone, long-term memory is imperfect: We all forget and distort memories.

KNOWLEDGE As information-processing researchers have found, the more people know, the more they can learn. Having an extensive **knowledge base,** or a broad body of knowledge in a particular subject, makes it easier to master new, related information.

Three factors facilitate increases in the knowledge base: past experience, current opportunity, and personal motivation. The third one is crucial. Because of motivation, children's knowledge base is not always what their parents or teachers would like. Lack of motivation helps explain why some students don't remember what they learned in science class but do remember the scores of local athletic contests.

Specific examples of the results of motivation on the knowledge base include that many U.S. schoolchildren memorize words and rhythms of hit songs, know plots and characters of television programs, and can recite the names and histories of baseball players—yet they may not know whether World War I occurred in the nineteenth or twentieth century, or whether Afghanistan is in Asia or Africa.

This provides a clue for teachers: New concepts are learned best if they are connected to personal and emotional experiences (Schneider & Lockl, 2008; Wittrock, 1974/2010). Parents likewise need to do more than tell children what they want them to know; they need to actively involve them. This understanding led to the idea of "take your child to work day" in order to teach children about future employment.

CONTROL PROCESSES The mechanisms that combine memory, processing speed, and the knowledge base are **control processes;** they regulate the analysis and flow of information within the system. Control processes include *emotional regulation* (part of impulse control, explained in Chapter 9) and *selective attention,* explained earlier on page 256.

Equally important is **metacognition,** sometimes defined as "thinking about thinking." Metacognition is the ultimate control process because it allows a person to evaluate a cognitive task, determine how to accomplish it, monitor performance, and then make adjustments.

Metacognition and other control processes improve with age and experience. For instance, in one study, children took a fill-in-the-blanks test and indicated how confident they were of each answer. Then they were allowed to delete some questions, making the remaining ones count more. By age 9, the children were able to estimate correctness; by age 11, they were skilled at knowing what to delete (Roebers et al., 2009). That is metacognition, knowing which of one's ideas are solid and which are shaky.

You learned that long-term memory is imperfect. Gradually children become more adept at differentiating what they know with certainty from what they only imagine. Unlike younger children, older children use control processes to know whether a certain thought was just a hope, fantasy, or dream.

Control processes can allow knowledge in one domain to transfer to another domain. This is the case for bilingual children, who learn to inhibit one language while using another. They are advanced not only in language but also in other measures of executive control (Bialystok, 2010).

Information processing improves spontaneously during childhood, but children can learn explicit strategies and memory methods, with cultural differences as mentioned earlier. Table 7.1 notes memory improvements from birth to age 11. How much of this improvement involves metacognition?

Sometimes teaching of memory strategies is explicit, more so in some nations (e.g., Germany) than in others (e.g., the United States) (Bjorklund et al., 2009). Often children with special needs require help learning control processes (Riccio et al., 2010). Genes matter as well. Children with the long allele of dopamine D4 benefit from knowing how well they are doing in each learning task—that seems to help them control their effort. Children without that allele are not affected by immediate feedback (Kegel et al., 2011).

RESPONSE FOR Teachers (from page 257) Children this age can be taught strategies for remembering by making links between working memory and long-term memory. You might break down the vocabulary list into word clusters, grouped according to root words, connections to the children's existing knowledge, applications, or (as a last resort) first letters or rhymes. Active, social learning is useful; perhaps groups of students could write a story each day that incorporates 15 new words. Each group could read its story aloud to the class. ●

KEY points

- Piaget recognized concrete operational thought, when children can use logic regarding their actual (concrete) experiences.
- Vygotsky stressed the social instruction that helps schoolchildren learn.
- Information-processing theorists note children's step-by-step learning.
- Brain advances during middle childhood allow for faster reactions, selective attention, broader knowledge base, and development of control processes.
- All aspects of memory (sensory register, working, and long-term) improve in middle childhood, making metacognition possible.

Language Advances

By age 6, children have mastered the basic vocabulary and grammar of their first language. Many also speak a second language fluently. These linguistic abilities form a strong knowledge base, enabling some school-age children to learn up to 20 new words a day and to apply complex grammar rules. Here are some specifics.

Vocabulary

By age 6, children know the names of thousands of objects, and they use many parts of speech—adjectives and adverbs, as well as nouns and verbs. As Piaget recognized, they soon become more flexible and logical; they can understand prefixes, suffixes, compound words, phrases, metaphors, and figures of speech. This is a major accomplishment.

RADIUS IMAGES / PHOTOLIBRARY

Homework Despite first appearances, this is not teacher and student but father and daughter, as Dad becomes excited about his 7-year-old's science project. Actually, if she is as intrigued as she appears to be, he is teacher as well as father. Children learn most of their vocabulary with friends and family, not in class.

The humorist James Thurber remembered:

> the enchanted private world of my early boyhood. . . . In this world, businessmen who phoned their wives to say they were tied up at the office sat roped to their swivel chairs, and probably gagged, unable to move or speak except somehow, miraculously, to telephone. . . . Then there was the man who left town under a cloud. Sometimes I saw him all wrapped up in the cloud and invisible. . . . At other times it floated, about the size of a sofa, above him wherever he went. . . . [I remember] the old lady who was always up in the air, the husband who did not seem able to put his foot down, the man who lost his head during a fire but was still able to run out of the house yelling.
>
> *[Thurber, 1999, p. 40]*

Adults may not realize that figures of speech are culture-specific. A book written by an American who lived in China for decades cites many metaphors having to do with baseball that U.S. children know: such as "drop the ball," "throw a curve," "strike out" (Davis, 1999). If a teacher wants a class to pay attention and says, "Keep your eye on the ball," some immigrant children might find their attention wandering as they try to see where the ball might be.

Because school-age children are able to create as well as understand metaphors, asking them to do so reveals emotions that might not be expressed in other ways. For instance, one 11-year-old said that his asthma is like

> a jellyfish, which has a deadly sting and vicious bite and tentacles which could squeeze your throat and make your bronchioles get smaller and make breathing harder. Or like a boa constrictor squeezing life out of you.
>
> *[quoted in Peterson & Sterling, 2009, p. 97]*

That boy felt that he alone had to fight his disease, which he considered evil and dangerous—and beyond help from his parents. Other children in the same study had more benign metaphors. This suggests a strategy for teachers who want to know how a child feels about something—ask for a metaphor.

Adjusting to the Context

pragmatics
The practical use of language that includes the ability to adjust language communication according to audience and context.

One aspect of language that advances markedly in middle childhood is **pragmatics,** the practical use of language, which includes the ability to use words and other devices to communicate well with varied audiences in different contexts. As children master pragmatics, they become more adept in all domains. Shy 6-year-olds cope far better with the social pressures of school if they use pragmatics well (Coplan & Weeks, 2009).

LEARNING THE CODES Mastery of pragmatics allows children to change styles of speech, or "codes," depending on their audience. Each code includes many aspects of language—tone, pronunciation, gestures, sentence length, idioms, vocabulary, and grammar. Sometimes the switch is between *formal code* (used in academic contexts) and *informal code* (used with friends); sometimes it is between standard (or proper) speech and dialect or vernacular (used on the street). Many children use code in text messaging, with numbers (411), abbreviations (LOL), and emoticons (:-D), as well as spelling that teachers might mark wrong but that is pragmatic (r u ok?).

Children need instruction from teachers to become fluent in the formal code because the logic of grammar (whether *who* or *whom* is correct or when a sentence is incomplete) is almost impossible to deduce. Peers teach the informal code, with curses, slang, gestures, and alternate grammar.

Code changes are obvious when children speak one language at home and another at school. Every nation includes many such children; most of the world's 6,000 languages are not school languages.

✦ **ESPECIALLY FOR Parents** You've had an exhausting day but are setting out to buy groceries. Your 7-year-old son wants to go with you. Should you explain that you are so tired that you want to make a quick solo trip to the supermarket this time? (see response, page 262) →

For instance, English is the language of instruction in Australia, but 17 percent of Australian children speak one of 246 other languages at home (Centre for Community Child Health, 2009). In the United States, 23 percent of all 5- to 17-year-olds speak a language other than English at home, though most of them also speak English well. In addition, some children speak an English dialect at home that is quite different from the pronunciation and grammar codes of the English taught at school.

LEARNING A SECOND LANGUAGE The questions of when, how, to whom, and even whether schools should provide second-language instruction are answered in different ways from nation to nation. Some schools teach several languages throughout childhood, while others punish children who utter any word that is not in the majority language.

Almost every European child speaks two languages by age 10, as does almost every Canadian child, although many of these children are not equally fluent in both languages. African children who are talented and fortunate enough to reach high school often understand three languages. In the United States, less than 5 percent of children under age 11 study a language other than English in school, although most have some exposure to a second language in songs or phrases (Robelen, 2011).

What about children who do not speak the school language? One approach is **immersion,** in which children are placed in the regular class, with native speakers. As the name implies, immersed students either sink or swim. Another approach is the opposite: Children are taught in their first language for several years, and then the second language is taught as a foreign tongue.

Between these extremes lie **bilingual schooling,** with instruction in two languages, and, in North America, **ESL (English as a second language),** in which all non-English speakers are placed in a special class where they are taught intensively and exclusively in English.

Children sometimes successfully master a second language and sometimes fail: The research is not clear as to which approach is best (Gandara & Rumberger, 2009).

Typical Yet Unusual Not unusual that these children are texting in French—they live in Bordeaux, and typically children everywhere text their friends. The oddity is that a girl and a boy are lying head-to-head, which rarely occurs in middle childhood. The explanation? They are siblings. Like dogs and cats that grew up in the same household, familiarity overtakes hostility.

immersion
A strategy in which instruction in all school subjects occurs in the second (usually the majority) language that a child is learning.

bilingual schooling
A strategy in which school subjects are taught in both the learner's original language and the second (majority) language.

ESL (English as a second language)
An approach to teaching English in which all children who do not speak English are placed together in an intensive course to learn basic English so that they can be educated in the same classroom as native English speakers.

All the Same These five children all speak a language other than English at home and are now learning English as a new language at school. Although such classes should ideally be taught to true English-language learners (ELLs), children who already speak English are sometimes mistakenly included in such classes (like 8-year-old Elana, from Mexico).

RESPONSE FOR Parents (from page 260) Your son would understand your explanation, but you should take him along if you can do so without losing patience. You wouldn't ignore his need for food or medicine; don't ignore his need for learning. While shopping, you can teach vocabulary (does he know pimientos, pepperoni, polenta?), categories (root vegetables, freshwater fish), and math (which size box of cereal is cheaper?). Explain in advance that you need him to help you find items and carry them and that he can choose only one item that you wouldn't normally buy. Seven-year-olds can understand rules, and they enjoy being helpful. ●

As you remember, motivation is crucial for learning in middle childhood. Children need to feel they are accepted and appreciated for who they are and that their original language is accepted and respected, in order to want to learn another language.

Success is also affected by personality, ability, and background. Home literacy (frequent reading, writing, and listening in any language) and cultural values have an effect. As explained in Chapter 5, ideally parents themselves encourage language development in two languages. If that is impossible, it is better for the child's family to listen and talk frequently in at least one language than not to speak at all.

Although cognitive research leaves no doubt that a second language can be learned in middle childhood if taught logically in a step-by-step fashion, whether that happens is affected by factors beyond cognitive research: SES, expectations, and national policies.

> ## KEY points
>
> - Language continues to develop rapidly during middle childhood.
> - Because children are now more logical, they can understand metaphors, prefixes, suffixes, and formal codes.
> - Social acceptance is crucial; pragmatics is evident as children learn the informal code.
> - Children advance in two languages if motivation is high and instruction is individualized.

Teaching and Learning

As we have just described, 6- to 11-year-olds are great learners. They use logic, develop strategies, accumulate knowledge, and expand vocabulary. Throughout history and worldwide, children are given new responsibilities and knowledge in middle childhood because that is when the human brain is ready.

Traditionally, children learned at home: Girls were taught to cook, clean, and care for babies while boys learned to hunt and herd animals. Now more than 95 percent of the world's 7-year-olds are instructed in academics at school (Cohen & Malin, 2010). This is true even in poor nations. In 2010, for instance, India passed a law providing free education (no more school fees) for all 6- to 14-year-olds, regardless of caste. India now has over 100 million young children in school. Internationally, quality and content vary markedly, but most 7-year-olds have some formal education.

International Schooling

Specifics of national education reveal that cultures differ in what they value. Although literacy and numeracy (reading and math) are goals for all children almost everywhere, many aspects of curricula vary by nation, by community, and by subject. In France in 2000, for example, children had physical education for three hours and arts instruction for more than two hours each week (Marlow-Ferguson, 2002). By contrast, half of all U.S. 18- to 24-year-olds say they had no arts education in childhood, either in school or anywhere else (Rabkin & Hedberg, 2011).

Educational practices differ radically even between nations that are geographically close. For example, in Germany the average schoolchild studies science three times more often than in the Netherlands (Snyder & Dillow, 2010).

"The path to becoming an astronaut is rougher than I thought."

CARTOONSTOCK.COM

WILL & DENI MCINTYRE / CORBIS

OLIVIER CIRENDINI / LONELY PLANET / GETTY IMAGES

THE HIDDEN CURRICULUM Variation is even greater in aspects of the **hidden curriculum,** which refers to implicit values and assumptions evident in course selection, schedules, tracking, teacher characteristics, discipline, settings, teaching methods, sports competition, student government, extracurricular activities, and so on. Even within nations, such practices differ. When I changed from one school to another (as described in this chapter's opening anecdote), I was punished for making a joke during a math lesson—which would not have happened in my old school.

Whether students should be quiet or talkative is part of the hidden curriculum, taught to students from kindergarten on. This was especially apparent to me when I taught high school students at the United Nations school. One student newly arrived from India not only was quiet in class discussions but also stood up when I called on him—to the surprise of his classmates. Within a week, he learned to stay in his seat, but he never spoke spontaneously.

More generally, if teachers differ from their students in gender, ethnicity, or economic background, the hidden message may be that education is irrelevant for these children's daily lives. If some students are in gifted classes, the message may be that they are more capable of learning and that less is expected of the other students.

A curriculum of social values is expressed in the school's physical setting, which might include spacious classrooms, wide hallways, and large, grassy playgrounds— or cramped, poorly equipped rooms and cement play yards or play streets. In some nations, school is outdoors, with no chairs, desks, or books, where a downpour cancels class. What is the hidden curriculum there?

Same Situation, Far Apart: Spot the Hidden Curriculum Literacy is central to the curriculum for schoolchildren everywhere, no matter how far apart they live. However, in the U.S. classroom at the left, boys and girls learn together, clothes are casual, history books are paperback and illustrated, and children of every background read the same stories with the same patriotic—but not religious—themes. All these aspects of the hidden curriculum are absent from the boy memorizing his holy book on the right.

hidden curriculum
The unofficial, unstated, or implicit rules and priorities that influence the academic curriculum and every other aspect of learning in a school.

Coming and Going Two U.S. elementary schools—one in Los Angeles, California *(left),* the other in Wayzata, Minnesota *(right)*—illustrate differences in hidden curriculum. Political leaders and taxpayers often disagree with parents and teachers as to whether this affects classroom learning.

MICHAEL NEWMAN / PHOTOEDIT

© ANDREA RUGG / BEATEWORKS / CORBIS

INTERNATIONAL TESTING Over the past two decades, more than 50 nations have participated in at least one massive test of educational achievement. Results are studied by political leaders because, if achievement rises, the national economy advances—a sequence that seems causal, not merely correlational (Hanushek & Woessmann, 2009). Better-educated adults become more productive, as well as healthier, workers.

Science and math are tested in the **Trends in Math and Science Study (TIMSS)**. The main test of reading is the **Progress in International Reading Literacy Study (PIRLS)**. Both of these tests have been given several times, with East Asian nations usually at the top and the United States rising, but not as high as other nations (see Tables 7.2 and 7.3). Most developing nations do not give these tests, but when they do, scores are low, with Yemen at the bottom.

Many experts wonder what factors produce higher achievement. Teachers are often thought to be crucial. After a wholesale reform of the educational system, scores of children in Finland recently increased dramatically (Sahlberg, 2011). Teachers may be one crucial component. Only the top 3 percent of high school graduates in Finland are admitted to teachers' colleges, where they receive five years of free college education, including a master's degree in education theory and practice, and advanced training in an academic discipline.

Then Finnish teachers are granted more autonomy within their classrooms than is typical in other systems, and they have time and are encouraged to work with col-

Trends in Math and Science Study (TIMSS)
An international assessment of the math and science skills of fourth- and eighth-graders. Although the TIMSS is very useful, different countries' scores are not always comparable because sample selection, test administration, and content validity are hard to keep uniform.

Progress in International Reading Literacy Study (PIRLS)
Inaugurated in 2001, a planned five-year cycle of international trend studies in the reading ability of fourth-graders.

TABLE 7.2 TIMSS Ranking and Average Scores of Math Achievement for Fourth-Graders, 2011

Rank*	Country	Score
1.	Singapore	606
2.	Korea	605
3.	Hong Kong	602
4.	Chinese Taipei	591
5.	Japan	585
6.	N. Ireland	562
7.	Belgium	549
8.	Finland	545
9.	England	542
10.	Russia	542
11.	United States	541
12.	Netherlands	540
	Canada (Quebec)	533
	Germany	528
	Canada (Ontario)	518
	Australia	516
	Italy	508
	Sweden	504
	New Zealand	486
	Iran	431
	Yemen	248

*The top 12 groups are listed in order, but after that not all the jurisdictions that took the test are listed. Some nations have improved over the past 15 years (notably, Hong Kong, England) and some have declined (Austria, Netherlands), but most continue about where they have always been.

Source: Provasnik et al., 2012; TIMSS 2011 International Mathematics Report.

TABLE 7.3 PIRLS Distribution of Reading Achievement

Country	Score
Hong Kong	571
Russia	568
Finland	568
Singapore	567
N. Ireland	558
United States	556
Denmark	554
Chinese Taipei	553
Ireland	552
England	552
Canada	548
Italy	541
Germany	541
Israel	541
New Zealand	531
Australia	527
Poland	526
France	520
Spain	513
Iran	457
Colombia	448
Indonesia	428
Morocco	310

Source: Adapted from Mullis et al., 2012.

leagues (Sahlberg, 2011). Buildings are designed to foster collaboration, with comfortable teacher's lounges (Sparks, 2012). Teachers might be the reason for Finland's success, or it may be something more basic regarding Finland's size, population, culture, or history.

TIMSS experts videotaped 231 math classes in three nations—Japan, Germany, and the United States (Stigler & Hiebert, 1999/2009). The U.S. teachers presented math at a lower level than did their German and Japanese counterparts, with more definitions but less connection to what the students had already learned. Few students were engaged because in math, "teachers seem to believe that learning terms and practicing skills is not very exciting" (p. 89).

By contrast, the Japanese teachers were excited about math instruction, working collaboratively and structuring lessons so that the children developed proofs and alternative solutions, alone and in groups. Teachers used social interaction and followed an orderly sequence (lessons built on previous knowledge). Such teaching reflected all three theories of cognition: problem solving from Piaget, collaborative learning from Vygotsky, and sequencing from information processing. Remember that Japanese students excel on the TIMSS, which suggests that all three theories may be relevant.

"Big deal, an A in math. That would be a D in any other country."

© THE NEW YORKER COLLECTION 1998 MIKE TWOHY FROM CARTOONBANK.COM. ALL RIGHTS RESERVED.

GENDER DIFFERENCES IN SCHOOL PERFORMANCE In addition to marked national, ethnic, and economic differences, gender differences in achievement scores are reported. The PIRLS results find girls ahead of boys in verbal skills in every nation and, traditionally, boys scored ahead of girls in math and science.

In recent TIMSS, however, gender differences in math have narrowed or disappeared. Boys were slightly higher (10 points) than girls overall; the differences were even smaller (6 points) in the United States. Fourth-grade girls scored higher in math than did boys in Russia, Singapore, Algeria, and Iran (Gonzales et al., 2009). Such results lead to a *gender-similarities hypothesis,* that males and females are similar in cognition, with "trivial" exceptions (Hyde et al., 2008, p. 494).

Academic achievement also shows gender differences. During middle childhood, girls have higher grades overall, including in math and science. Then, at puberty, girls' achievement dips, especially in science.

Many reasons for these gender differences have been suggested (Halpern et al., 2007). For instance, girls are ahead in physiological maturation (bones, teeth, etc.), which may make it easier for them to sit at desks and concentrate. Then, at puberty, sexual thoughts may interfere with academic ones.

Alternatively, social prejudice may favor young girls but not young women. Since most elementary school teachers are women, girls in the early grades may feel (or be) encouraged. Then, when girls begin to prepare for adulthood, they seek the skills that women seem to need, which they conclude from personal observation do not include the expertise in calculus that would prepare them to be engineers or physicists (Weisgram et al., 2010). For that reason, their motivation may falter in science and math.

Research on fifth-graders with high IQs found an intriguing gender difference: When academic material became confusing, girls were less likely to persevere, but boys enjoyed the challenge (Dweck, 2007). Such discrepancies could be explained by nature or nurture.

However, do not make too much of either explanation for gender differences in school achievement. When scores are compared, gender differences are tiny compared with SES or national ones. The 443-point difference between Hong Kong and Yemen (667 and 224) dwarfs the 10-point gender divide. International differences are

AP PHOTO / JAE C. HONG

How Many Fingers? It looks as if teacher Alvin Yardley and fourth-grader Matthew are fully engaged in figuring out a math problem. However, U.S. fourth-graders score far below those in East Asia. Some critics blame the teachers, some the students, others the schools, and still others the culture.

No Child Left Behind Act
A U.S. law enacted in 2001 that was intended to increase accountability in education by requiring states to qualify for federal educational funding by administering standardized tests to measure school achievement.

National Assessment of Educational Progress (NAEP)
An ongoing and nationally representative measure of U.S. children's achievement in reading, mathematics, and other subjects over time; nicknamed "the Nation's Report Card."

usually explained as rooted in educational practices, national values, and economic wherewithal. Such factors are relevant within nations as well, as we will now see.

In the United States

Although some national tests find improvements, when U.S. children are compared with children in other nations, not much has changed in reading or math scores in the past two decades. A particular concern is that a child's achievement seems more influenced by income and ethnicity in the United States than in other nations.

Although many educators and political leaders have attempted to overcome disparities linked to a child's background, the gap between fourth-grade European Americans and their Latino and African American peers is as wide as it was 15 years ago. Furthermore, the gap between low- and high-income U.S. students is widening, as is the gap between American Indians and other groups (Maxwell, 2012; National Center for Education Statistics, 2012).

NATIONAL STANDARDS These international comparisons and ethnic disparities led President Bush to pass the **No Child Left Behind Act** of 2001 (NCLB), a federal law promoting high standards for public schools, with frequent testing to measure achievement. Low-scoring schools could be forced to close, with teachers reassigned or dismissed.

Most parents and teachers agree with the goals of NCLB (accountability and achievement), but many disagree with the strategies. Strong conflicting opinions are expressed by politicians, educators, and scholars, such as those expressed in a single issue of *Science* magazine (Hanushek, 2009; Koretz, 2009). To prevent massive school closings, half the states have been granted waivers from some aspects of NCLB.

Many states developed tests that allowed most of their schools to progress (and thus get federal funds). State tests typically assess students as more proficient than does a particular federally sponsored test, the **National Assessment of Educational Progress (NAEP),** which most educators believe is a more valid assessment (Applegate et al., 2009).

Doubts about state assessments led the governors of all 50 states to develop a *Common Core* of high standards, finalized in 2010, with a dozen or more specific expectations in each subject for every grade (Table 7.4 provides a sample). As of 2012, 46 states had adopted this *Common Core.*

CHOOSING SCHOOLS An underlying issue is the role of community control and parental choice in education. This is probably the major difference between the United States, where choice and variability are evident everywhere, and other nations, where matters regarding public education—including curriculum, funding, teacher training, and so on—are set by the central governments. In most nations, every child attends his or her local school, which is similar in resources and standards to schools elsewhere in the nation.

In the United States, because local jurisdictions provide most of the funds and guidelines, wealthy communities have a very different hidden curriculum than do poorer communities. Differences are also apparent between the states, and even between one school and another in the same region.

Most children attend their local public school, but that school is affected by the child's parents, who communicate with their child's teacher, become active in

TABLE 7.4 The Common Core: Sample Items for Each Grade

Grade	Reading and Writing	Math
Kindergarten	Pronounce the primary sound for each consonant	Know number names and the count sequence
First	Decode regularly spelled one-syllable words	Relate counting to addition and subtraction (e.g., by counting 2 more to add 2)
Second	Decode words with common prefixes and suffixes	Measure the length of an object twice, using different units of length for the two measurements; describe how the two measurements relate to the size of the unit chosen
Third	Decode multisyllabic words	Understand division as an unknown-factor problem; for example, find 32 ÷ 8 by finding the number that makes 32 when multiplied by 8
Fourth	Use combined knowledge of all letter–sound correspondences, syllable patterns, and morphology (e.g., roots and affixes) to read accurately unfamiliar multisyllabic words in context and out of context	Apply and extend previous understandings of multiplication to multiply a fraction by a whole number
Fifth	With guidance and support from peers and adults, develop and strengthen writing as needed by planning, revising, editing, rewriting, or trying a new approach	Graph points on the coordinate plane to solve real-world and mathematical problems

Source: National Governors Association, 2010.

parent–teacher associations, move to a particular school zone, and lobby for funds, often secured via public votes on bond issues. Almost one-third of parents do not send their child to the zoned public school. Instead, an increasing number choose a public charter school, a private school, a religious school, or home schooling.

Charter schools are public schools, funded and licensed by states or local districts. Typically, they also have private money and sponsors. They are exempt from some regulations, especially those negotiated by unions, and they have some control over admissions and expulsions. For that reason, they often are more ethnically segregated and enroll fewer children with special needs. On average in charter schools, teachers are younger and work longer hours, and school size is smaller than traditional public schools.

Some charter schools are remarkably successful; others are not (Peyser, 2011). A major criticism is that not every child who enters a charter school stays to graduate—

charter school
A public school with its own set of standards that is funded and licensed by the state or local district in which it is located.

Chance or Design? These third-graders are using dice to play a game that may teach them multiplication.

OBSERVATION QUIZ
This is a charter school in New Jersey. What three signs are visible here that few typical public schools share? (see answer, page 269) →

AP PHOTO / MIKE DERER

one scholar says "the dropout rate for African American males is shocking" (Miron, quoted in Zehr, 2011, p. 1). Overall, children and teachers leave charter schools more often than they leave regular public schools, a disturbing statistic. However, since teachers and parents actively choose charter schools, they may be more selective by nature and thus more willing to leave if their expectations are not met.

Private schools are funded by tuition, endowments, and church sponsors. Traditionally in the United States, most private schools were **parochial schools,** organized by the Catholic Church, that included religion in the curriculum. Tuition was relatively low since many teachers were nuns who earned little pay. In the past decades, many parochial schools have closed, but more independent private schools have opened.

Some U.S. jurisdictions issue **vouchers,** money that parents can use to pay some or all of the tuition at a private school, including a church-sponsored one. This practice is controversial, not only because it decreases public school support but also because public funds go to religious institutions, which is contrary to the U.S. principle of separation of church and state. Advocates say that vouchers increase competition and improve all schools, public and private. Critics say it weakens public schools and is costly to taxpayers.

Home schooling occurs when parents avoid both public and private schools by educating their children at home. This solution is becoming more common, but only about 1 child in 35 (more Whites than Blacks, more girls than boys, more preadolescent) is home-schooled (Snyder & Dillow, 2012). A prerequisite is an adult at home (usually the mother in a two-parent family) who is willing to teach the children. Authorities set standards for what a child must learn, but home-schooling families decide specifics of curriculum, schedules, and discipline.

The major problem with home schooling is not academic (some mothers are demanding teachers and some home-schooled children score high on achievement tests) but social, since children miss the interaction of the classroom. To compensate, many home-schooling parents plan activities with other home-schooling families. This practice reflects local culture: Home schooling is more common in some parts of the United States than others (higher rates in the south and the northwest than in the northeast or midwest), which affects how readily parents can find other home-schooled children.

MORE RESEARCH NEEDED On many educational issues, research clashes with parental emotions. Parents choose schools based on other parents' opinions, which may not be valid. Furthermore, small class size and nightly homework are more attractive to parents than beneficial to children.

Consider class size. Parents sometimes opt for private schools because fewer children are in each class. Yet nations whose children score high on international tests sometimes have large student/teacher ratios (Korea's average is 28 to 1) and sometimes small (Finland's is 14 to 1, the same as for public schools in the United States—where small classes for children with special needs reduce the average ratio). These facts do not prove that class size is irrelevant (there are many differences between Asian and U.S. schools and cultures), but they do raise the question.

In another example, fourth-graders with no homework averaged higher achievement scores than those with homework (Snyder & Dillow, 2010). Again, do not jump to conclusions too quickly: Perhaps weaker students are assigned more homework.

Who should decide what children should learn and how? Every developmental theory can lead to suggestions for teaching and learning (Farrar & Al-Qatawneh, 2010), but none endorse one curriculum or method to the exclusion of all others. Parents, politicians, and developmental experts all agree that children should be taught, that some children learn much more than others, and that some teachers

private school
A school funded by parents and sponsoring institutions. Such schools have control over admissions, hiring, and specifics of curriculum, although some regulations apply.

parochial school
Non-public schools organized by a religious group, often Roman Catholic but sometimes Jewish, Muslim, and so on. The curriculum, discipline, and many instructors in parochial schools reflect the beliefs of the religious body, which often provides substantial financial support.

voucher
A monetary commitment by the government to pay for the education of a child. Vouchers vary a great deal from place to place, not only in amount and availability, but in restrictions as to who gets them and what schools accept them. Typically, the voucher goes to whatever school the child attends.

home schooling
Education in which children are taught at home, usually by their parents, instead of attending any school, public or private.

✦ ESPECIALLY FOR Parents Suppose you and your school-age children move to a new community that is 50 miles from the nearest location that offers instruction in your faith or value system. Your neighbor says, "Don't worry, they don't have to make any moral decisions until they are teenagers." Is your neighbor correct? (see response, page 270) →

are more skilled than others, but adults certainly do not agree on curriculum—hidden or overt.

More quantitative and qualitative research is needed to determine what works best. A 19-member panel of experts seeking the best math curricula for the United States examined 16,000 studies but "found a serious lack of studies with adequate scale and design for us to reach conclusions" (Faulkner, quoted in Mervis, 2008, p. 1605).

Similarly, a review of home schooling, charter schools, and vouchers complains of "the difficulty of interpreting the research literature on this topic, most of which is biased and far from approaching balanced social science" (Boyd, 2007, p. 7). Every educational issue would benefit from large-scale, controlled studies.

There are no simple answers. Apparently "high-performing schools are the result of a hundred 1 percent solutions. Not only is there no silver bullet, but there is not even a secret sauce. The key to success is an unflagging attention to detail" (Peyser, 2011, p. 8).

Although critics seek the one magic bullet that would improve education for all children, and many adults believe they have found it, researchers have yet to prove that any particular method of teaching reading, or training teachers, or designing curriculum, is a dramatic improvement for every child. From a developmental perspective, all educators need to understand that age, motivation, and culture vary in ways that affect learning. Evidence from children in schools, not from laboratories, is needed.

Measuring the Mind

An underlying question is: Who should be taught in which way? Some children are ahead of others even before they enter school. Such early advantages typically increase with age. Differential sensitivity and individual capacity mean that strategies, pacing, and curriculum details need to be tailored to the particular nature of the child (Kegel et al., 2011).

One example is that reading scores rise with early phonic instruction for low-scoring children, but not for high-scoring ones (Sonnenschein et al., 2009). Another example is special education (discussed soon), which may be needed when a child's ability seems greater than achievement. But how should cognitive ability be assessed?

APTITUDE, ACHIEVEMENT, AND IQ *In theory,* **aptitude** is the potential to master a specific skill or to learn a certain body of knowledge. Intellectual aptitude is often measured by **IQ (intelligence quotient) tests.**

Originally, an IQ score was literally a quotient: Mental age (the age of a typical child who had reached the tested child's intellectual level) was divided by chronological age (the tested child's actual age), and the result of that division (the quotient) was multiplied by 100. If mental age was the same as chronological age, the quotient would be 1, and the child's IQ would be 100, exactly average. The current method of calculating IQ is more complicated, but an IQ of 100 is still considered average.

In theory, achievement is learning that has occurred, not learning potential (aptitude). **Achievement tests** compare scores to norms established for each grade. For example, children of any age whose reading is typical of the average third-grader are said to be at the third-grade level in reading achievement.

In 1904, a Frenchman named Alfred Binet developed IQ tests because he saw that children who did not achieve in school were beaten, shamed, and excluded. He wondered if their aptitude rendered them unable to achieve at grade level. IQ tests protected those children. Binet's tests were revised and published as the Stanford-Binet IQ tests, now in their fifth edition, used in more than 1,000 published studies in 2012.

ANSWER TO **OBSERVATION QUIZ**
(from page 267) Carpets and rugs, students lying down to do schoolwork, clipboards, and dice—all are highly unusual for traditional schools. ●

PHOTO COURTESY OF JESSICA BAYNE / WECHSLER ADULT INTELLIGENCE SCALE, FOURTH EDITION (WAIS-IV). COPYRIGHT © 2008 NCS PEARSON, INC. REPRODUCED WITH PERMISSION. ALL RIGHTS RESERVED

Trial and Understanding This youngster completes one of the five performance tests of the Wechsler Intelligence Scale for Children (WISC). If her score is high, is that because of superior innate intelligence? ["Wechsler Adult Intelligence Scale" and "WAIS" are trademarks, in the U.S. and/or other countries, of Pearson Education, Inc. or its affiliate(s).]

aptitude
The potential to master a specific skill or to learn a certain body of knowledge.

IQ (intelligence quotient) test
A test designed to measure intellectual aptitude, or ability to learn in school. Originally, intelligence was defined as mental age divided by chronological age, times 100—hence the term *intelligence quotient,* or *IQ.*

achievement test
A measure of mastery or proficiency in reading, mathematics, writing, science, or some other subject.

RESPONSE FOR Parents (from page 268) No. In fact, these are prime years for moral education. You might travel those 50 miles once or twice a week or recruit other parents to organize a local program. Don't skip moral instruction. Discuss and demonstrate your moral and religious values, and help your children meet other children who share those values. ●

multiple intelligences
The idea that human intelligence is comprised of a varied set of abilities rather than a single, all-encompassing one.

✦ **ESPECIALLY FOR Teachers**
What are the advantages and disadvantages of using Gardner's idea of multiple intelligences to guide your classroom curriculum? (see response, page 273) →

The words *in theory* precede the definitions of aptitude and achievement because, although potential and accomplishment are supposed to be distinct, IQ and achievement scores are strongly correlated for individuals, for groups of children, and for nations (Lynn & Mikk, 2007). Binet assumed that some children did not achieve much *because* of their low IQ, but perhaps low achievement was a cause (not just a result) of low IQ. Or some third factor (malnutrition?) could decrease both IQ and achievement.

Moreover, people once thought that aptitude was a fixed characteristic, present at birth—but this is not the case. Children with a low IQ can become above average, or even gifted, like my nephew David (discussed in Chapter 1). Indeed, the average IQ scores of entire nations have risen substantially—a phenomenon called the Flynn effect, named after the researcher who first described this increase in nation after nation. At first Flynn's conclusion was doubted, but the data have convinced the skeptics. The rise in intelligence may be one result of worldwide improvements in education and nutrition (Flynn, 1999, 2007). Social scientists agree that the IQ score is only a snapshot, a static view of a dynamic, developing brain.

MULTIPLE INTELLIGENCES Beyond the fact that IQ scores change, a fundamental question is whether any single test can measure the complexities of cognitive development. This criticism has been targeted particularly at IQ tests, because the underlying assumption is that there is one general thing called *intelligence* (often referred to as *g*, for general intelligence).

Children may instead inherit a set of abilities, some high and some low, rather than general intellectual ability (e.g., Q. Zhu et al., 2010). Two leading developmentalists (Sternberg and Gardner) are among those who believe that humans have **multiple intelligences,** not just one (Furnham, 2012).

Robert Sternberg (1996) described three distinct types of intelligence: *academic,* measured by IQ and achievement tests; *creative,* evidenced by imaginative endeavors; and *practical,* seen in everyday problem solving.

Howard Gardner (1983) originally described seven intelligences: *linguistic, logical-mathematical, musical, spatial, bodily-kinesthetic* (movement), *interpersonal* (social understanding), and *intrapersonal* (self-understanding)—each associated with a region of the brain. He has since added two more: *naturalistic* (understanding nature, as in biology or farming) and *existential* (thinking about life and death) (Gardner, 1999, 2006; Gardner & Moran, 2006).

Although every normal (not severely brain-damaged) person has some of all nine intelligences, Gardner believes each individual has highs and lows. For example, someone might be gifted spatially but not linguistically (a visual artist who cannot describe her work) or might have interpersonal but not naturalistic intelligence (an astute clinical psychologist whose houseplants die).

Gardner's theory has been influential in education, especially the education of children (e.g., Armstrong, 2009; Rettig, 2005), when teachers allow children to demonstrate knowledge in their own ways—illustrating history with a drawing rather than an essay, for instance. Some children may learn by listening, others by looking, others by doing—an idea that led to research on learning styles.

Similarly, Sternberg believes that matching instruction to a person's analytic, creative, or practical ability advances his or her comprehension. However, these applications may not be supported by scientific research (Almeida et al., 2010; Pashler et al., 2008).

Debate continues about whether intelligence is general or multiple, whether learning styles are relevant to achievement, and what the educational implications of test scores might be (Furnham, 2012).

CULTURAL VARIATIONS One final criticism of IQ testing arises from two aspects of the life-span perspective: multicultural and multicontextual understanding. Every test reflects the culture of the people who create, administer, and take it. On achievement tests, a child may score low because of the school, the teacher, the family, or the culture, not because of ability. Indeed, one reason IQ tests are still used is that achievement tests do not necessarily reflect aptitude.

Some experts try to use aptitude tests that are culture-free, such as by asking children to identify shapes, draw people, repeat stories, hop on one foot, name their classmates, sort objects, and much more. However, even with such tests, culture is relevant. One group reports that Sudanese children averaged 40 points lower when IQ testing required them to write with pencils, which they had not done before (Wicherts et al., 2010).

Beyond such specifics, though, most tests assume that scores are characteristic of an individual. Consequently, the IQ tests considered most accurate (the WISC [Wechsler Intelligence Scale for Children] and the Stanford-Binet) rely on one professional testing one child. The professional has been trained to encourage without giving answers, and the report includes any specifics (e.g., that this particular child was not feeling well) that might affect the score.

Yet remember that children reflect the hidden curricula. In some cultures, individuals are taught to consider themselves part of a group, and the intellectually gifted are particularly adept at working with others. In such cultures, a child's intellect might be more evident in social interaction, not in isolation. In Africa, for instance, testing an isolated child's IQ might not indicate potential (Nsamenang, 2004).

Furthermore, if children have been taught to be quiet and respectful, they might not readily answer questions posed by an unfamiliar professional. Then their IQ would not reflect their potential. They might mistakenly be assigned to special education, a topic we explain next.

KEY points

- Children worldwide attend school, but curricula, teaching methods, settings, and much else differ from one nation to another.
- International tests of achievement usually find children in East Asian nations scoring far above U.S. children and above children in many other nations.
- Attempts to improve the achievement of U.S. children, such as the No Child Left Behind Act or the *Common Core* standards, have not yet succeeded.
- School choice and local funding characterize U.S. education; different families opt for public, private, parochial, charter, or home schooling.
- IQ tests are designed to measure aptitude and other tests measure achievement, but both are affected by culture and by assumptions about intelligence.

Children with Special Needs

Many children have learning patterns that respond best to targeted education. Although some differences among children are harmless, others indicate disorders that need to be recognized in order to help children learn. Before leaping from diagnosis to special education, however, three concepts—*comorbidity, multifinality,* and *equifinality*—should be considered (Cicchetti & Toth, 2009).

comorbid
Refers to the presence of two or more disease conditions at the same time in the same person.

multifinality
A basic principle of developmental psychopathology that holds that one cause can have many (multiple) final manifestations.

equifinality
A basic principle of developmental psychopathology that holds that one symptom can have many causes.

Many disorders are **comorbid,** which means that several problems occur in the same person. A child may need special help to overcome one problem, but every intervention needs to take into account other problems that the child might have.

Multifinality means that one cause can have many (multiple) final manifestations. The same genes or past trauma may produce a child who is easily angered (conduct disorder) or quick to cry (major depression). That is multifinality.

Equifinality (equal in final form) means that one symptom can have many causes. For instance, a 6-year-old who does not talk may be autistic, hard of hearing, developmentally disabled, or electively mute. Comorbidity, multifinality, and equifinality are reasons to be cautious before leaping from symptom to cure.

To illustrate all three concepts, we focus here only on attention-deficit and bipolar disorders, learning disabilities, and autism spectrum disorders. (Readers interested in any of the hundreds of specific disorders of childhood should study relevant research.)

Attention-Deficit and Bipolar Disorders

These two disorders are discussed together because they are often comorbid and confused with one another (Miklowitz & Cicchetti, 2010). Childhood attention-deficit and bipolar disorders both manifest in explosive rage and then deep regret (equifinality).

attention-deficit/hyperactivity disorder (ADHD)
A condition in which a person not only has great difficulty concentrating for more than a few moments but also is inattentive, impulsive, and overactive.

ATTENTION-DEFICIT DISORDER Perhaps 10 percent of all young children have an *attention-deficit disorder* (ADD), which means they have difficulty paying attention. Often ADD is accompanied by an uncontrollable urge to be active, in which case it is called **attention-deficit/hyperactivity disorder (ADHD).**

Children with ADHD are inattentive, impulsive, and overactive and are thus disruptive when adults want them to be still (Barkley, 2006). About twice as many boys as girls have ADHD (National Center for Health Statistics, 2011).

A typical child with ADHD, when made to sit down to do homework, might look up, ask questions, think about playing, get a drink, fidget, squirm, tap the table, jiggle his or her legs, and go to the bathroom—and then start the whole sequence again. Not surprisingly, such children tend to have academic difficulties; they are less likely to graduate from high school and college (Loe & Feldman, 2007).

The number of children diagnosed with ADHD has increased in the United States from about 5 percent in 1980 to about 10 percent currently. Rates are affected by ethnicity, with more European American children than Latino ones thought to have ADHD—at least as measured by medication use. The rate has doubled in Europe as well, although more U.S. children than European ones are diagnosed with the problem (e.g., Hsia & Maclennan, 2009; van den Ban et al., 2010).

Diagnosis itself is a problem since some adults are quick to blame children (especially boys) for normal activity. Experts say that ADHD should be diagnosed only when it is apparent in at least two places (e.g., home and school) and when hyperactivity does not improve with consistent structure and guidance. A first step is for parents and teachers to learn how to provide that guidance (Subcommittee on ADHD, 2011).

SACRAMENTO BEE / LEZLIE STERLING / ZUMA PRESS

Almost Impossible The concentration needed to do homework is almost beyond Clint, age 11, who takes medication for ADHD. Note his furrowed brow, resting head, and sad face.

✦ **ESPECIALLY FOR Health Workers** Parents ask that some medication be prescribed for their kindergartener, who they say is much too active for them to handle. How do you respond? (see response, page 275) →

bipolar disorder
A condition characterized by extreme mood swings, from euphoria to deep depression, not caused by outside experiences.

BIPOLAR DISORDER **Bipolar disorder** is characterized by extreme mood swings, from euphoria to deep depression. Children with this disorder usually experience at least one episode of grandiosity. They might believe, for instance, that they are the smartest person in school, a genius destined to save the world. At other times, they might be severely depressed, unwilling or unable to read, play, or go to school. They are far more irritable than the typical child; the younger a child is, the more difficult the diagnosis (Miklowitz & Cicchetti, 2010).

One U.S. study reports that medical visits for those younger than 18 with a primary diagnosis of bipolar disorder (one-third of them comorbid with attention-deficit disorder) increased 40-fold between 1995 and 2003, a period when adult diagnosis of bipolar disorder merely doubled (Moreno et al., 2007).

That rapid increase led some to suggest that childhood bipolar disorder was a fad, a popular diagnosis in the mind of the observer, not in the moods of the child. However, it is now thought that the rise was more the result of earlier misdiagnoses than current overdiagnoses (Miklowitz & Cicchetti, 2010; Santosh & Canagaratnam, 2008).

DISTINGUISHING BETWEEN DISORDERS Bipolar disorder "remains notoriously difficult to differentiate from other psychiatric illnesses in youth" (Phillips, 2010, p. 4). Many children diagnosed with either ADHD or bipolar disorder may be more accurately diagnosed with the other.

Both disorders are more common in children with a parent who suffers from psychopathology of some sort. Some parents have the same disorder as the child. When the parent's disorder is unlike the child's, children with ADHD often have a parent with learning disabilities, whereas children with bipolar disorder often have a parent with mood disturbances, such as depression. This suggests a genetic link as well as multifinality.

Both disorders correlate with unusual brain patterns. Children with either disorder are less able than the average child to distinguish emotions when looking at faces. That is true for both disorders, but activation of distinct parts of the amygdala differs between the two (Brotman et al., 2008, 2010).

Treatment involves (1) counseling and training for the family and the child, (2) showing teachers how to direct attention and increase structure to help the children learn, and, if that does not help, (3) medication to stabilize moods for bipolar children and to calm children with ADHD. Ongoing monitoring is crucial because some drugs help children with ADHD but harm children with bipolar disorder. Even with an accurate diagnosis, each child responds differently to each drug, and responses change with time. Giving psychoactive medication to children is controversial, as the following explains.

MARC ASNIN / REDUX

Go Team Remember that abnormality is normal. Which of these boys has been diagnosed with a serious disability? Michael, second from the right, has bipolar disorder.

RESPONSE FOR Teachers (from page 270) The advantages are that all the children learn more aspects of human knowledge and that many children can develop their talents. Art, music, and sports should be an integral part of education, not just a break from academics. The disadvantage is that they take time and attention away from reading and math, which might lead to less proficiency in those subjects on standard tests and thus to criticism from parents and supervisors. ●

OPPOSING PERSPECTIVES

Drugs for Children

In the United States, more than 2 million children and adolescents younger than 18 take prescription drugs to regulate their emotions and behavior. The rate has leveled off in recent years but remains high, with more than 1 in 20 children taking psychoactive drugs in middle childhood, usually for ADHD (Rabin, 2011; Scheffler et al., 2009; Zuvekas et al., 2006). In many other nations as well, drug use in middle childhood is increasing (Hsia & Maclennan, 2009; van den Ban et al., 2010).

The drug most commonly prescribed in middle childhood is Ritalin (for ADHD), but at least 20 other psychoactive drugs treat ADHD, depression, anxiety, developmental delay, autism, bipolar disorder, and many other conditions.

Children aged 2 to 5 also take psychoactive drugs more often than was the case a decade ago, although that rate (about 1 child in 600) is far lower than the rate for older children (Olfson et al., 2010).

Because they have been inadequately tested in children, many drugs are prescribed "off label"—they have not been approved for patients of that age or for the particular condition for which they are prescribed. Much of the American public is suspicious of any childhood psychiatric medicine (dosReis & Myers, 2008; McLeod et al., 2004; Rose, 2008).

That suspicion affects drug use. One small study of parents whose children were diagnosed with ADHD found that about 20 percent believed drugs should *never* be used for children (dosReis et al., 2009). A larger study found that only about half (56 percent) of the parents of U.S. children who are diagnosed with ADHD give them medication every day (Scheffler et al., 2009). African American children have more ADHD symptoms but are less often medicated, for reasons that include fragmented medical care and distrust of doctors (T. W. Miller et al., 2009).

The opposite perspective comes from professionals who find that medication helps schoolchildren with emotional or behavioral problems, particularly ADHD (Epstein et al., 2010; King et al., 2009; Scheffler et al., 2009). Many educators and psychiatrists consider it tragic that only 56 percent of the children diagnosed with ADHD take the corresponding medication regularly (National Center for Health Statistics, 2011). They argue that if a child had type 1 diabetes, parents would give insulin; so, logically, when a child has an emotional illness, parents should give medicine if it helps.

Some parents agree with that perspective. The same study that found 20 percent of parents always opposed to drugs also found 29 percent who believed that drugs were necessary. They blamed doctors for waiting too long to prescribe (dosReis et al., 2009).

Although many drugs help children with their immediate problems, the long-term effects of drug use are a major concern. Three questions are often raised:

1. Will children who take drugs become adolescent addicts?
2. Will height be stunted?
3. Will medication cause other psychiatric disorders?

The answer to all three is *no,* according to scientific longitudinal studies. In fact, childhood medication for children who are unable to function normally reduces the risk of later illegal drug use and of other disorders, and it does not make children shorter than their genes destined them to be (Biederman et al., 2009, 2010; Faraone & Wilens, 2003).

The rate of developing another psychiatric disorder is compared not with the overall average but with the rate in children who have the same initial psychological problems but are not medicated. This is important because the incidence of pathology for young children who have special needs is higher than average, no matter what treatment they are given (Geller et al., 2008; Loe & Feldman, 2007; Molina et al., 2009). It is a mistake to blame earlier medication for emotional problems in adolescence.

There is another issue, however. As more drugs are prescribed, more abuse of those drugs occurs. Ritalin in particular is sometimes taken by teenagers who want an extra boost (Setlik et al., 2009). Either they get the drug from someone who actually has ADHD, or they pretend to have ADHD themselves, or they buy it illegally.

Finally, although harmful effects are not evident, and many children benefit from drug use in the short term, there is scant evidence that long-term use has any benefits (Sroufe, 2012).

As you see, neither side has all the evidence in their favor. Since psychoactive drugs, taken daily from childhood on, add to the profits of drug manufacturers, some people suspect that money contaminates the research. Everyone agrees that, when children have special needs, parents and teachers need support and training. People on both sides agree that drugs are not a lifelong solution. Whether short-term use in childhood is a benefit depends on many specifics, about which adults disagree.

Learning Disabilities

Many children have some specific **learning disability** that leads to difficulty in mastering a particular skill that other people acquire easily. Indeed, according to Gardner's view of multiple intelligences, almost everyone has a specific inadequacy or two. Perhaps one person is clumsy (low in kinesthetic intelligence), while another sings loudly but off key (low in musical intelligence).

Most such learning disabilities are not debilitating (the off-key singer learns to be quiet in chorus), but every schoolchild is expected to learn reading and math. Disabilities in either of these two subjects often undercut academic achievement and make a child feel inadequate, ashamed, and stupid.

The most commonly diagnosed learning disability is **dyslexia,** unusual difficulty with reading. No single test accurately diagnoses dyslexia (or any learning disability) because every academic achievement involves many specifics (Riccio & Rodriguez, 2007). As you remember, many brain areas are involved in reading: If a child is impaired in one area, the others might be intact.

Early theories hypothesized that visual difficulties—for example, reversals of letters (reading *was* instead of *saw*) and mirror writing (*b* instead of *d*)—were the cause of dyslexia. It now seems that more often dyslexia originates with speech and hearing difficulties (Gabrieli, 2009).

learning disability
A marked delay in a particular area of learning that is not caused by an apparent physical disability, by another disorder, or by an unusually stressful home environment.

dyslexia
Unusual difficulty with reading; thought to be the result of some neurological underdevelopment.

dyscalculia
Unusual difficulty with math, probably originating from a distinct part of the brain.

A decade ago, dyslexia was diagnosed when a child's reading achievement was far below that child's intellectual potential—that is, scores on achievement tests were lower than IQ. Now fMRI brain scans reveal that children of all intellectual levels (from genius to disabled) can have neurological problems that make reading difficult (Tanaka et al., 2011). It is not necessary to wait until tests reveal low achievement.

Dyscalculia is unusual difficulty with math. Dyslexia and dyscalculia are often comorbid, but each is a separate disorder originating from a distinct part of the brain, and each requires targeted education (Butterworth et al., 2011). Often computer programs as well as various auditory and visual treatments help, but simply waiting for a child to outgrow a learning disability is a dangerous strategy. Many children who have learning problems develop behavior problems as well.

Say Ooo Most children teach themselves to talk clearly, but some need special help—as this 5-year-old does. Mirrors, mentoring, and manipulation may all be part of speech therapy.

Autism Spectrum Disorders

Early on, autism was diagnosed only when a child was severely impaired—perhaps unable to talk at all, crying at a human touch, completely self-absorbed. Now we realize that many children have less severe autistic symptoms. They have an **autism spectrum disorder,** which characterizes about 1 in every 110 children in the United States (three times as many boys as girls and more European Americans than Latino, Asian, or African Americans) (Lord & Bishop, 2010).

DIAGNOSIS There are three signs of an autism spectrum disorder: (1) delayed language, (2) impaired social responses, and (3) unusual, repetitive play. Children with any form of autism find it difficult to understand emotions. That makes them feel alien, like "an anthropologist on Mars," as Temple Grandin, an educator and writer with autism, expressed it (quoted in Sacks, 1995). Consequently, they do not want to talk, play, or otherwise interact with anyone, and they are slow to develop a theory of mind (Senju et al., 2010).

Some children with autism spectrum disorders never speak, rarely smile, and often play for hours with one object (such as a spinning top or a toy train). Others are called "high-functioning" or have *Asperger syndrome.* Such children are extremely talented in some specialized area, such as drawing or geometry, and their speech is close to normal. Many are brilliant in unusual ways (Dawson et al., 2007), as is Grandin, a well-respected expert on animal care (Grandin & Johnson, 2009). However, social interaction is always impaired. Grandin was bewildered by romantic love.

Far more children are diagnosed with an autism spectrum disorder now than in 1990, either because the incidence has increased or because more children receive the diagnosis. You read that currently about 1 child in 110 has an autism spectrum disorder. Some other estimates put the number even higher—perhaps 1 child in 40. Underlying that range is the reality that no measure diagnoses autism definitively: Many people are socially inept—do they all have autism?

TREATMENT Some children with autism are on special diets, take vitamin supplements, or are on medication. One drug in particular, risperidone, relieves some symptoms (although research reports side effects, including weight gain), but no biochemical treatment has proven successful at relieving the disorder itself. As you already know, medication use is controversial: Whether a child takes risperidone depends on many factors other than symptoms (Arnold et al., 2010; Rosenberg et al., 2010).

● **UNDERSTANDING THE NUMBERS**
The reported incidence of autism has increased. The rate in this text, 1 in 110, is generally accepted, but one 2012 report suggested a rate of 1 in 88 and the draft of the DSM-5 (not yet published) has stricter criteria, probably reducing the rate to 1 in 150. Why do these variations occur?

Answer These variations occur because no laboratory test is definitive; consequently, parents, hospitals, school systems, and clinicians differ in their assessments (Atladóttir et al. 2012; Davidovitch et al., 2012; J. S. Miller et al., 2013).

autism spectrum disorder
Any of several disorders characterized by inadequate social skills, impaired communication, and unusual play.

RESPONSE FOR Health Workers (from page 272) Medication helps some hyperactive children, but not all. It might be useful for this child, but other forms of intervention should be tried first. Compliment the parents on their concern about their child, but refer them to an expert in early childhood for an evaluation and recommendations. Behavior-management techniques geared to the particular situation, not medication, will be the first strategy ●

Many parents first noticed their infants' lack of social responses after vaccinations and believe that thimerosal, an antiseptic containing mercury that was once used in immunizations, was the cause. No scientist who examines the evidence agrees: Extensive research has disproven this hypothesis many times (Offit, 2008). Thimerosal was removed from most vaccines a decade ago, but the rate of autism is still rising.

Doctors fear that parents who cling to this hypothesis are not only wrong but are harming millions of other children. Indeed, in the United States, the 2012 rate of whooping cough was higher than in any year since 1960. Babies younger than 2 months have died of whooping cough because they are too young to be immunized and because older children whose parents do not vaccinate them spread contagious diseases.

One popular treatment for autism is putting the child in a hyperbaric chamber to breathe more concentrated oxygen than is found in everyday air. Two studies of hyperbaric treatments—both with randomized participant selection and with control groups—reported contradictory results, either benefits (Rossignol et al., 2009) or no effect (Granpeesheh et al., 2010). Part of the problem may be multifinality and equifinality: Children with autism spectrum disorders share core symptoms (equifinality), but they differ in causes—from genes to birth trauma, from prenatal toxins to postnatal chemicals—and those same causes sometimes have other outcomes (multifinality).

Many behavioral methods to improve talking and socialization have been tried, with mixed results (Granpeesheh et al., 2009; Hayward et al., 2009; Howlin et al., 2009). Early and individualized education of the child and parents sometimes succeeds, although special education is not a panacea, as you will now see.

Precious Gifts Many children with autism are gifted artists. This boy attends a school in Montmoreau, France, that features workshops in which children with autism develop social, play, and learning skills.

PHANIE / PHOTO RESEARCHERS, INC.

Special Education

Developmentalists are well aware that physical, cognitive, and psychosocial development interact to affect each child's behavior. That means doctors, parents, teachers, and policy-makers need to work collaboratively for each child. However, this does not necessarily occur. Special education is one example.

CHANGING POLICIES In the United States, a series of reforms in the treatment and education of children with special needs began with the 1975 Education of All Handicapped Children Act, which stipulated that children with special needs must be educated in the **least restrictive environment (LRE).**

Most of the time, LRE has meant educating children with special needs in a regular class, sometimes called *mainstreaming.* Sometimes children are sent to a *resource room,* with a teacher who provides targeted tutoring. Other times, students attend an *inclusion class,* which means that children with special needs are "included" in the general classroom, with "appropriate aids and services" (Kalambouka et al., 2007).

A recent strategy is called **response to intervention (RTI)** (Fletcher & Vaughn, 2009; Shapiro et al., 2011). All children who are below average are given some special intervention. Most of them improve. For those who do not, more intervention occurs. Only if repeated intervention fails is the child referred for testing.

Professionals use a battery of tests (not just IQ or achievement tests) to decide whether a child needs special education. If so, they discuss an **individual education plan (IEP)** with the parents to specify educational goals for the child.

COHORT AND CULTURE Developmentalists consider a child's biological and brain development as the starting point for whatever special assistance will allow each child to reach full potential. Then home and school practices are crucial.

least restrictive environment (LRE) A legal requirement that children with special needs be assigned to the most general educational context in which they can be expected to learn.

response to intervention (RTI) An educational strategy that uses early intervention to help children who demonstrate below-average achievement. Only children who are not helped are designated for more intense measures.

individual education plan (IEP) A document that specifies educational goals and plans for a child with special needs.

All Together Now Kiemel Lamb (top center) leads autistic children in song, a major accomplishment. For many of them, music is soothing, words are difficult, and hand-holding in a group is almost impossible.

However, as Table 7.5 shows, among all the children in the United States who are recognized as having special needs, cohort changes are notable, and some basic categories (e.g., attention–deficit disorder) are missing. The number of 3- to 21-year-olds served by special education increased from 8 percent in 1980 to 13 percent in 2010.

About 6 percent of children with educational disabilities are now designated as autistic and almost 6 percent as developmentally delayed (Aud et al., 2012). Neither of those two categories existed in 1977. Most children who were considered "mentally retarded" in the 1970s would be called autistic or developmentally delayed if they were diagnosed today. Labels change more quickly than children do.

These are U.S. designations. Other nations have quite different policies. For instance, in Finland almost every child is recognized as having some special educational

TABLE 7.5 Percent of Children with Special Education Needs* by Specific Designation

	1980		2000		2010	
Learning disabilities	35.3	(**3.6)	45.7	(6)	37.5	(4.9)
Speech impairment	28.2	(2.9)	17.4	(2.3)	21.8	(2.9)
Mentally retarded	20	(2)	9.7	(1.3)	7.1	(0.9)
Emotionally disturbed	8.4	(0.8)	7.6	(1)	6.3	(0.7)
Deafness and hearing loss	1.9	(0.2)	1.1	(0.2)	1.2	(0.2)
Blindness and low vision	0.7	(0.1)	0.4	(0.1)	0.4	(0.1)
Developmental delay	—	—	0.3	(0)	5.7	(0.7)
Autism spectrum	—	—	1	(0.1)	5.8	(0.8)
Orthopedic handicap	1.4	(0.1)	1.1	(0.2)	1	(0.1)
Other health problems†	2.4	(0.2)	4.1	(0.5)	10.6	(1.4)

* Those aged 3–21 served under Individuals with Disabilities Act, Part B, by type of disability.
** Numbers in parentheses are percentages of children enrolled in public schools.
† Other health problems include having limited strength, vitality, or alertness due to chronic or acute health problems such as heart condition, tuberculosis, rheumatic fever, nephritis, asthma, sickle cell anemia, hemophilia, epilepsy, lead poisoning, leukemia, or diabetes.

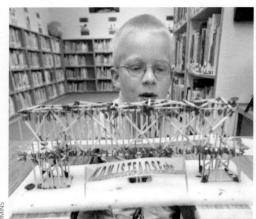

AP PHOTO / MOSCOW-PULLMAN DAILY NEWS, GEOFF CRIMMINS

Fourth-Grade Challenge How much weight can a bridge hold? Thirty-three students in gifted classes at an Idaho elementary school designed and built toothpick bridges and then tested them. David Stubbens (shown here) added 61 pounds to the bucket before his bridge collapsed.

needs, but almost no child is labeled or removed from the class for that reason. Instead, every teacher works to help each child, with his or her special needs (Sahlberg, 2011).

GIFTED AND TALENTED The impact of cohort and culture is also apparent when children are unusually gifted. They are not covered by the federal special education laws, but every U.S. state selects and then educates them. How they do it varies tremendously. Should such children be accelerated, skipped, segregated, enriched, or left alone?

At one time, such children were simply put ahead a grade or more, but that left them socially isolated. As one such gifted student remembers:

> Nine-year-old little girls are so cruel to younger girls. I was much smaller than them, of course, and would have done anything to have a friend. Although I could cope with the academic work very easily, emotionally I wasn't up to it. Maybe it was my fault and I was asking to be picked on. I was a weed at the edge of the playground.
>
> *[Rachel, in Freeman, 2010, p. 27]*

Lifelong problems occurred for this girl partly because she skipped two grades. She still thinks it might have been her fault that she was a weed not a flower.

Currently, the most common solution for gifted and talented children is to teach all such children together. Ideally, the children are neither bored nor lonely because each is challenged and appreciated. Their brains develop as well. As you know, a child's brain is quite plastic, and all children learn whatever their context teaches. Thus, talents may be developed, not wasted, with special education.

However, if the gifted designation occurs at age 5 (as it often does), children of lower-SES families, or those from less privileged ethnic groups, may be unfairly excluded. Bias against girls, or boys, may be problematic as well.

This concern is not abstract. Consider data from the United States in 2006 (Snyder & Dillow, 2011). Of every 150 schoolchildren in Kentucky, 23 are designated gifted and talented; only 1 in 150 in Massachusetts is designated as such. Obviously, something in the culture or politics of those states, not in the nature of the children, influences this determination.

Most states have 10 percent more girls than boys in gifted classes (sexism or biology?), yet three states (Kansas, New Mexico, and South Dakota) have about 10 percent more boys than girls in such classes. In most states, the proportion of European American children in gifted-and-talented classes is twice as high as the proportion of minority groups (economics or biology?), but proportions are almost equal in Utah. Why? In most states, higher proportions of African Americans than Hispanics are designated as gifted, but the opposite is true in Texas (racism or genetics?).

DIFFERENCE AS THE RULE Scholars all find "much heterogeneity and diversity of high human potential in terms of varied developmental niches, trajectories, and pathways" (Dai, 2010, p. 121). With so many complexities, many nations avoid special education of the gifted, or of any child with special needs, at least until high school or college.

China insists that effort, not innate ability, leads to excellence, and thus all children are educated together. In many nations of Asia and Africa, every child is expected to help his or her classmates, so separating out the gifted or the disabled would undercut education. In Scotland, too, all children are educated together (Smith, 2006).

This sometimes occurs in the United States as well. For instance, the school board in Montgomery County, Maryland (known for high-achieving students), abolished the designation of gifted beginning in 2009 (Sternberg et al., 2011). A leading U.S. educator suggests that we

> give up the notions of "the normal," "the disabled," and "the gifted" as they are typically applied in schools, especially for the purposes of classification and grouping, and simply accept difference as the rule.
>
> *[Borland, 2003, p. 121]*

Considering development in body and mind during middle childhood, differences abound—in size, health, skill, logic, intelligence, language, and more. The next chapter describes other major differences in family structures and social contexts. What are the implications? Answers are suggested at the end of Chapter 8.

KEYpoints

- Emotional and behavioral disorders in childhood are difficult to diagnose and treat, in part because of multifinality and equifinality.
- In diagnosis of special needs, bipolar disorder is often confused with attention-deficit/hyperactivity disorder, although the treatment for the two differs.
- Learning disabilities are common, with dyslexia and dyscalculia problematic in school.
- Children with autism spectrum disorders have difficulty with social interaction, language, and creative play.

SUMMARY

Health and Sickness

1. Middle childhood is a time of steady growth and few serious illnesses, thanks to genes and medical advances.

2. Physical activity aids health and joy. However, current social and environmental conditions make informal neighborhood play scarce, school physical education less prevalent, and sports leagues less welcoming.

3. Childhood obesity and asthma are increasing worldwide. Although genes are part of the cause, public policies (e.g., food advertising, pollution standards) and family practices also have an impact.

Cognition in Middle Childhood

4. According to Piaget, middle childhood is the time of concrete operational thought, when egocentrism diminishes and logical thinking begins. School-age children can understand classification and conservation.

5. Vygotsky stressed the social context of learning, including the specific lessons of school and learning from peers and adults. Culture affects not only what children learn but also how they learn.

6. An information-processing approach examines each step of the thinking process, focusing especially on brain processes, which continue to mature. Notable advances occur in reaction time, allowing faster and better coordination of many parts of the brain.

7. Memory begins with information that reaches the brain from the sense organs. Then selection processes allow some information to reach working memory. Finally, long-term memory stores images and ideas indefinitely.

8. Selective attention, a broader knowledge base, logical strategies for retrieval, and faster processing advance every aspect of memory and cognition. Control processes, including metacognition, are crucial.

Language Advances

9. Language learning advances in many practical ways, including expansion of vocabulary and understanding of metaphors.

10. Children excel at pragmatics, often using one code with their friends and another in school. Many children become fluent in the school language while speaking their first language at home.

Teaching and Learning

11. Nations and experts agree that primary education should be universal. Reading is assessed internationally with the PIRLS, math and science with the TIMSS. On both, children in East Asia excel.

12. The United States has many types of locally controlled primary schools. The *Common Core* has been adopted by almost all U.S. states, with the hope of raising national standards and improving accountability.

13. IQ tests are designed to quantify intellectual aptitude. Most such tests emphasize language and logic and predict school achievement. Critics contend that traditional IQ tests assess too narrowly because people have multiple types of intelligence.

14. Achievement tests measure accomplishment, often in specific academic areas. Aptitude and achievement are correlated, both for individuals and for nations.

Children with Special Needs

15. Many children have special educational needs. Among the more common causes are attention-deficit/hyperactivity disorder (ADHD), in which children have problems with inattention, impulsiveness, and overactivity; bipolar disorder, characterized by marked mood swings; specific learning disabilities; and autistic spectrum disorders.

16. All special needs are partly genetic, but family and school factors can make the problems better or worse. Treatments include medication, targeted education, and family training—all controversial.

17. In the United States, about 13 percent of school-age children receive special education services, with an individual education plan (IEP) and assignment to the least restrictive environment (LRE), usually the regular classroom.

KEY TERMS

achievement test (p. 269)
aptitude (p. 269)
asthma (p. 250)
attention-deficit/hyperactivity disorder (ADHD) (p. 272)
autism spectrum disorder (p. 275)
bilingual schooling (p. 261)
bipolar disorder (p. 272)
body mass index (BMI) (p. 247)
charter school (p. 267)
childhood obesity (p. 247)
childhood overweight (p. 247)
classification (p. 253)
comorbid (p. 272)

concrete operational thought (p. 253)
control processes (p. 258)
dyscalculia (p. 274)
dyslexia (p. 274)
equifinality (p. 272)
ESL (English as a second language) (p. 261)
Flynn effect (p. 270)
hidden curriculum (p. 263)
home schooling (p. 268)
immersion (p. 261)
individual education plan (IEP) (p. 276)
IQ (intelligence quotient) test (p. 269)

knowledge base (p. 258)
learning disability (p. 274)
least restrictive environment (LRE) (p. 276)
long-term memory (p. 258)
metacognition (p. 258)
middle childhood (p. 243)
multifinality (p. 272)
multiple intelligences (p. 270)
National Assessment of Educational Progress (NAEP) (p. 266)
No Child Left Behind Act (p. 266)
parochial school (p. 268)
pragmatics (p. 260)

private school (p. 268)
Progress in International Reading Literacy Study (PIRLS) (p. 264)
reaction time (p. 256)
response to intervention (RTI) (p. 276)
selective attention (p. 256)
sensory memory (p. 257)
Trends in Math and Science Study (TIMSS) (p. 264)
voucher (p. 268)
working memory (p. 257)

WHAT HAVE YOU LEARNED?

1. How does the physical growth of the school-age child compare with that of the younger child? What abilities emerge as a result of these changes?

2. How have children's medical care and health habits changed over the past few decades?

3. What are the main advantages and disadvantages of physical play during middle childhood?

4. What are the short-term and long-term effects of childhood obesity?

5. What roles do nature and nurture play in childhood asthma?

6. Why did Piaget call cognition in middle childhood concrete operational thought?

7. According to Vygotsky, where and how does cognitive development occur?

8. Why does quicker reaction time improve the ability to learn?

9. How might a lack of selective attention affect a child's ability to learn?

10. What aspects of memory improve markedly during middle childhood?

11. Why might having an extensive knowledge base make it easier for children to learn new, related information?

12. How might metacognitive skills help a student?

13. How is the understanding of vocabulary and metaphors affected by a child's age?

14. Why would a child's linguistic code be criticized by teachers but admired by friends?

15. How might a hidden curriculum affect how well a child learns in school?

16. What are the two most common international tests of achievement? Why are these tests given?

17. What gender differences are found in educational tests and school grades?

18. What are the main goals and criticisms of No Child Left Behind?

19. What are the differences among charter schools, private schools, and home schooling?

20. What is the difference between aptitude and achievement? Why might this difference be in theory only?

21. Why might it be important for teachers to know about the theory of multiple intelligences?

22. In what ways might a child's culture affect the results of an IQ test?

23. Why might a child with ADHD have difficulty learning?

24. What are the signs of bipolar disorder?

25. What are dyslexia and dyscalculia?

26. What are the signs of autistic spectrum disorders?

27. Describe LRE and RTI. How might each of these strategies help students with special needs?

28. How and why might SES and ethnic group affect a child being designated as gifted?

29. Why might boards or governments choose not to separate gifted or disabled children from other students?

APPLICATIONS

1. Developmental psychologists believe that every teacher should be skilled at teaching children with a wide variety of needs. Does the teacher-training curriculum at your college or university reflect this goal? Should all teachers take the same courses or should some teachers be specialized? Give reasons for your opinions.

2. Internet sources vary in quality on any topic, but this may be particularly true of Web sites designed for parents of children with special needs. Pick one childhood disability or disease and find several Web sources devoted to that condition. How might parents evaluate the information provided?

3. Visit a local elementary school and look for the hidden curriculum. For example, do the children line up? Why or why not, when and how? Does gender, age, ability, or talent affect the grouping of children or the selection of staff? What is on the walls? Are parents involved? If so, how? For everything you observe, speculate about the underlying assumptions.

4. Interview a 7- to 11-year-old child to find out what he or she knows *and understands* about mathematics. Relate both correct and incorrect responses to the logic of concrete operational thought.

>>ONLINE CONNECTIONS

To accompany your textbook, you have access to a number of online resources, including quizzes for every chapter of the book, flashcards (in English and Spanish), critical thinking questions, and case studies. For access to any of these links, go to www.worthpublishers.com/bergerinvitation2e. In addition to these free resources, you'll also find links to podcasts, video clips, diagnostic quizzing with personalized study advice, and an ebook. Some of the videos and activities available online include:

■ *Autism.* This activity explores the symptoms of autism and the importance of early diagnosis. Video clips give a glimpse into the world of parents and autistic children.

■ *Motivation and Learning.* Are children really "little scientists," as Piaget believed? This video explores intrinsic motivation and classroom strategies that inspire it.

CHAPTER OUTLINE

MIDDLE CHILDHOOD
Psychosocial Development

WHAT WILL YOU KNOW?

- Why do children collect worthless things, like pebbles or unusable stamps?
- Do children always suffer if their parents divorce?
- Why are friends (more than teachers or parents) the best defense against bullies?
- How is it moral for a child to lie to protect another child who has done something wrong?

student of mine drove to a gas station to get a flat tire fixed. She wrote:

> As I pulled up, I saw a very short boy sitting at the garage door. I imagined him to be about 8 or 9 years old and wondered why he was sitting there by himself. He directed me to park, and summoned a man who looked at my tire and spoke to the boy in a language I did not understand. This little boy then lifted my car with a jack, removed all the bolts, and fixed the flat. I was in shock. When I paid the man (who was his father), I asked how long his son had been doing this. He said about three years.
>
> *[adapted from Tiffany, personal communication, 2008]*

Adults like Tiffany are shocked to learn that many of the world's children are forced to work, in defiance of the United Nations' declaration that children have the right

> to be protected from economic exploitation and from performing any work that is likely to be hazardous or to interfere with the child's education, or to be harmful to the child's health or physical, mental, spiritual, moral, or social development.
>
> *[Convention on the Rights of the Child, 1990, ratified by 190 nations as of 2012]*

The International Labour Organization (ILO) of the United Nations estimated that this right is violated for 153 million 5- to 14-year-olds worldwide, with 115 million of them (4.3 percent of all children) engaged in hazardous work (Diallo et al., 2010).

Changing tires is not considered hazardous, but did it "interfere with the child's education" or harm him? The answer is not obvious. As with almost every aspect of middle childhood, the details are crucial. ●

ALL CHILDREN NEED FRIENDS, families, and skills, but specifics matter: Some peers are destructive, some families are dysfunctional, and some skills should not be learned. This chapter describes specifics that affect children's "physical, mental, spiritual, moral, or social development." You will learn that child labor, peer culture, bullying, single-parent families, poverty, and divorce are often harmful, but much depends on context. For instance, a child might be poor, sharing a bedroom with siblings and rarely eating meat for dinner, but be unscathed. We begin with the children themselves and then discuss families, peers, and morality.

The Nature of the Child

As explained in the previous chapter, steady growth, brain maturation, and intellectual advances make middle childhood a time when children gain independence and autonomy (see At About This Time). They acquire an "increasing ability to regulate themselves, to take responsibility, and to exercise self-control" (Huston & Ripke, 2006, p. 9)—all strengths that make this a period of positive growth.

One result is that school-age children can care for themselves. They not only feed themselves but also make their dinner, not only dress themselves but also pack their suitcases, not only walk to school but also organize games with friends. They venture outdoors alone. Boys are especially likely to put some distance between themselves and their home, engaging in activities without their parents' awareness or approval (Munroe & Romney, 2006). This budding independence fosters growth.

Industry and Inferiority

Although adults have always taught 6- to 11-year-olds the skills they would need later on, it was not until developmentalists focused on the characteristics of these children that it became clear why they are such great learners. More than people of any other age, children of this age are naturally industrious, practicing whatever skills their culture values, or are busy with their own childhood concerns. At the same time, they are far more vulnerable to criticism than are younger children.

ERIKSON'S INSIGHTS The tension between productivity and incompetence is the fourth psychosocial crisis, **industry versus inferiority,** as described by Erik Erikson. He noted that during these years, the child "must forget past hopes and wishes, while his exuberant imagination is tamed and harnessed to the laws of impersonal things," and he becomes "ready to apply himself to given skills and tasks" (Erikson, 1963, pp. 258, 259).

Think of learning to read and add—painstaking and sometimes boring processes. For instance, slowly sounding out "Jane has a dog" or writing "3 + 4 = 7" for the hundredth time is not exciting. Yet children busily practice reading and math: They are intrinsically motivated to read a page, finish a worksheet, memorize a spelling word, color a map, and so on. Similarly, they enjoy collecting, categorizing, and counting whatever they accumulate—perhaps stamps, stickers, stones, or seashells. That is industry.

AT ABOUT THIS TIME
Signs of Psychosocial Maturation over the Years of Middle Childhood

Children responsibly perform specific chores.

Children make decisions about a weekly allowance.

Children can tell time, and they have set times for various activities.

Children have homework, including some assignments over several days.

Children are less often punished physically than when they were younger.

Children try to conform to peers in clothes, language, and so on.

Children voice preferences about their after-school care, lessons, and activities.

Children are responsible for younger children, pets, and, in some places, work.

Children strive for independence from parents.

---

industry versus inferiority
The fourth of Erikson's eight psychosocial crises, during which children attempt to master many skills, developing a sense of themselves as either industrious or inferior, competent or incompetent.

Overall, children judge themselves as either *industrious* or *inferior*—deciding whether they are competent or incompetent, productive or useless, winners or losers. Being productive is intrinsically joyous, and it fosters the self-control that is a crucial defense against emotional problems (Bradley & Corwyn, 2005).

A sense of industry may be a defense against early substance use as well. In a longitudinal study in Arizona of 509 third- and fourth-graders, over a five-month period, an increasing number had tried, or were expecting to try, alcohol (from 58 percent to 72 percent) and cigarettes (from 18 to 23 percent) (Jones, 2011).

These children were aged 9 and 10, yet many already wanted the drugs that adolescents use. But here is the crucial finding: The children most likely to anticipate smoking or drinking were those who increasingly felt inferior, not industrious (Jones, 2011). For example, they did not agree that they "stick with things until they are finished" and they were not proud of what they did.

FREUD ON LATENCY Sigmund Freud described this period as **latency,** a time when emotional drives are quiet and unconscious sexual conflicts are submerged. Some experts complain that "middle childhood has been neglected at least since Freud relegated these years to the status of an uninteresting 'latency period' " (Huston & Ripke, 2006, p. 7).

But in one sense, at least, Freud was correct: Sexual impulses are quiet. Even when children were betrothed before age 12 (rare today, but not uncommon in earlier centuries), the young husband and wife had little interaction. Everywhere, boys and girls choose to be with others of their own sex. Indeed, boys who scrawl "Girls stay out!" on their clubhouses, and girls who complain that "boys stink," are typical.

Self-Concept

As children mature, they develop their self-concepts, which are their ideas about themselves—including their intelligence, personality, abilities, gender, and ethnic background. As you remember, the very notion that they are individuals is a discovery in toddlerhood, and a positive, global self-concept is typical in early childhood.

That global self-acceptance changes in middle childhood. The self-concept gradually becomes more specific and logical, as one might expect, given increases in cognitive development and social awareness. As one group explains, "The cognitive ability to combine specific behavioral features of the self (I can run fast and throw far) into higher-order generalizations . . . (I am athletic) appears in middle childhood . . ." (Pfeifer et al., 2010, p. 144).

Yet as the self-concept becomes more specific and logical, it also becomes less optimistic, incorporating influences from peers and the overall society. For example, some 6-year-olds from minority ethnic groups are refreshingly unaware of prejudice against their group; by age 11, they are aware, usually taking pride in their self-concept as, say, Latino, in defense against specific insults they have heard (Garcia Coll & Marks, 2009).

COMPARED WITH OTHERS The schoolchild's self-concept no longer mirrors the parents' perspective. Every theory and every observer notes that children become more concerned with the opinions of their peers as they age from 6 to 11.

LINDSEY HEBBARD / WOODFIN CAMP & ASSOCIATES

Celebrating Spring No matter where they live, 7- to 11-year-olds seek to understand and develop whatever skills are valued by their culture. They do so in active, industrious ways, as described in every theory. This is illustrated here, as four friends in Assam, northeastern India, usher in spring with a Bihu celebration. Soon they will be given sweets and tea, which is the sociocultural validation of their energy, independence, and skill.

latency
Freud's term for middle childhood, during which children's emotional drives and psychosexual needs are quiet (latent). Freud thought that sexual conflicts from earlier stages are only temporarily submerged, bursting forth again at puberty.

During preadolescence, "the peer group exerts an increasingly salient socializing function" (Thomaes et al., 2010, p. 812). This does not mean that parents are irrelevant. Increasingly, children regulate their own emotions, but *co-regulation* (regulating with their parents) is more accurate than independence (regulating alone). In middle childhood, emotional regulation is influenced by parents as well as peers, with parental attachment still mitigating low self-esteem at age 10 and 12 (Kerns et al., 2011).

However, not only parents but also peers, older children, and even strangers become potential critics. Children depend on **social comparison,** comparing themselves with other people, as they develop their self-concept (Carpendale & Lewis, 2004; Davis-Kean et al., 2009). Ideally, social comparison helps them value themselves and abandon the imaginary, rosy self-evaluation of preschoolers.

social comparison
The tendency to assess one's abilities, achievements, social status, and other attributes by measuring them against those of other people, especially one's peers.

Yet some children—especially those from minority ethnic or religious groups—become newly aware of prejudices they need to overcome (Kiang & Harter, 2008; McKown & Strambler, 2009). Children also compare themselves with peers of the other sex and become aware of gender discrimination; for example, girls complain that they are not allowed to play tougher sports, and boys complain that teachers favor the girls (Brown et al., 2011).

For all children, increasing self-understanding and social awareness come at a price. Self-criticism and self-consciousness rise from ages 6 to 11, and "by middle childhood this [earlier] overestimate of their ability or judgments decreases" (Davis-Kean et al., 2009, p. 184) while self-esteem falls. Children's self-concept becomes influenced by the opinions of others, even of children they do not know (Thomaes et al., 2010).

In addition, partly because children think concretely during middle childhood, materialism increases and appearances matter. Attributes that adults might find superficial become important to children, which makes self-esteem more fragile and more dependent on externals (Chaplin & John, 2007). For instance, insecure 10-year-olds might covet the latest shoes, smart phones, and so on. They also might criticize the way their parents dress, or talk, or style their hair.

CULTURE AND SELF-ESTEEM Ideally, "children develop feelings of self-esteem, competence, and individuality during middle childhood as they begin comparing themselves with peers" (Ripke et al., 2006, p. 261). Research in many nations has

Same Situation, Far Apart: Helping at Home Sichuan, in China, and Virginia, in the United States, provide vastly different contexts for child development. For instance, in some American suburbs, laws require recycling and forbid hanging laundry outside—but not in rural China. Nonetheless, everywhere children help their families with household chores, as these two do.

© CORBIS

TAO IMAGES LIMITED / GETTY IMAGES

found that teaching anxious children to confide in friends as well as to understand their own emotions helps them develop a better self-concept (Siu, 2007). After-school activities, particularly sports, can provide a foundation for friendship and realistic self-esteem.

Although many North American parents praise their children and want them to be proud of themselves, this is a cultural view, not a universal one (Yamaguchi et al., 2007). Many other cultures expect children to be modest, not prideful.

For example, Australians say that "tall poppies" are cut down, and the Japanese discourage social comparison aimed at making oneself feel superior. Even among American children, researchers have found that very high self-esteem in middle childhood can undercut effort and empathy and thus work against healthy development (de Castro et al., 2011; Menon et al., 2007).

Culture seems to be more relevant to a child's self-concept than is the child's objective accomplishment. For instance, Japanese children excel at math on the TIMSS, but only 17 percent are confident of their math ability. In the United States, 53 percent of those taking the TIMSS are confident, yet they score significantly lower than the Japanese children do (Snyder & Dillow, 2010). In Estonia, low self-esteem correlates with high academic achievement (Pullmann & Allik, 2008).

Resilience and Stress

Before age 6, children depend on their immediate families for food, learning, and life itself. Then "experiences in middle childhood can sustain, magnify, or reverse the advantages or disadvantages that children acquire in the preschool years" (Huston & Ripke, 2006, p. 2).

Supportive families continue to be protective, but 6- to 11-year-old children may escape destructive family influences by finding their own niche in the larger world. Some children break free, seemingly unscathed by early experiences. They have been called "resilient" or even "invincible."

Resilience has been defined as "a dynamic process encompassing positive adaptation within the context of significant adversity" (Luthar et al., 2000, p. 543). Note the three parts of this definition:

resilience
The capacity to adapt well to significant adversity and to overcome serious stress.

1. Resilience is *dynamic,* not static: It may be evident at one age but not another.

2. Resilience is a *positive adaptation* to stress. For example, if a child escapes home problems via academic involvement and school friends, it is positive adaptation.

3. Adversity must be *significant.* Some adversities are comparatively minor (large class size, poor vision) and some are major (victimization, neglect). Children cope with both, but only major coping is called resilient.

Current thinking about resilience (see Table 8.1), with insights from dynamic-systems theory, suggests that, although some children cope better than others, none are unaffected by their past (Jenson & Fraser, 2006; Luthar et al., 2003). Sensitivity is affected by genes, early child rearing, preschool education, and sociocultural values. Some children are hardy, "dandelions" not "orchids" (Ellis & Boyce, 2008).

CUMULATIVE STRESS One important discovery is that accumulated stresses over time, including minor ones (called "daily hassles"), are more devastating than an isolated major stress. Almost every child can withstand a single stressful, momentary event, but repeated stresses make resilience difficult (Jaffee et al., 2007).

One example comes from children who experienced Hurricane Katrina at the end of August 2005. Years afterward, about half the children were resilient, but the other half (especially those in middle childhood at the time of the hurricane) were still traumatized. The incidence of serious psychological problems was affected

TABLE 8.1 Dominant Ideas About Resilience, 1965—Present

1965	All children have the same needs for healthy development.
1970	Some conditions or circumstances—such as "absent father," "teenage mother," "working mom," and "day care"—are harmful for every child.
1975	All children are *not* the same. Some children are resilient, coping easily with stressors that cause harm in other children.
1980	Nothing inevitably causes harm. Both maternal employment and preschool education, once thought to be risks, are often helpful.
1985	Factors beyond the family, both in the child (low birthweight, prenatal alcohol exposure, aggressive temperament) and in the community (poverty, violence), can be very risky for children.
1990	Risk–benefit analysis finds that some children are "invulnerable" to, or even benefit from, circumstances that destroy others.
1995	No child is invincibly resilient. Risks are always harmful—if not in education, then in emotions; if not immediately, then long term.
2000	Risk–benefit analysis involves the interplay among many biological, cognitive, and social factors, some within the child (genes, disability, temperament), the family (function as well as structure), and the community (including neighborhood, school, church, and culture).
2008	Focus on strengths, not risks. Assets in child (intelligence, personality), family (secure attachment, warmth), community (schools, after-school programs), and nation (income support, health care) must be nurtured.
2010	Strengths vary by culture and national values. Both universal ideals and local variations must be recognized and respected.
2012	Genes as well as cultural practices can be either strengths or weaknesses; differential sensitivity means identical stressors can benefit one child and harm another.

more by their later repeated stresses—frequent moves, new caregivers, disruption of schooling—than by the hurricane itself (Kronenberg et al., 2010; Viadero, 2007).

An international example comes from Sri Lanka, where many children were exposed to civil war, the 2004 tsunami, poverty, deaths of relatives, and relocation. The accumulated stresses, more than any single adversity, increased pathology and decreased achievement. Researchers point to "the importance of multiple contextual, past, and current factors in influencing children's adaptation" (Catani et al., 2010, p. 1188).

COGNITIVE COPING Coping measures reduce the impact of repeated stress. One factor is the child's own interpretation of events. Cortisol increased in low-income children *if* they interpreted events connected to their family's poverty as a personal threat and *if* the family lacked order and routines (thus increasing daily hassles) (E. Chen et al., 2010). When low-income children did not take things personally and their family was not chaotic, more were resilient, with less cortisol.

The effects are lifelong. Many adults who did not consider themselves poor as children were nonetheless from very low-income families. But because they did not know they were poor, they were not burdened by their poverty. As you remember from Chapter 7, low income in childhood is less likely to harm later health if the child's mother was affectionate and supportive (Miller et al., 2011). This applies to psychosocial health as well as physical health.

In general, a child's interpretation of a family situation (poverty, divorce, etc.) impacts how that situation affects him or her (Olson & Dweck, 2008). Some children consider the family they were born into a temporary hardship; they look forward to the day when they can leave childhood behind. Children who endured Hurricane Katrina were affected by their thoughts, both positive and negative, even more than by factors one might expect, such as caregiver distress (Kilmer & Gil-Rivas, 2010).

Some children experience *parentification*: They act as parents, trying to take care of everyone, including their actual parents (Byng-Hall, 2008). They experience the burdens and worries of adulthood, which undercuts their experience of play and friendships in childhood.

ESCAPING HOME Children may develop their own friends, activities, and skills, blossoming once they are old enough, becoming "increasingly autonomous and industrious" (Pagani et al., 2006, p. 132). Many activities—from 4-H to midnight basketball, from choir to Little League—help children develop a self-concept as industrious, not inferior.

A 40-year study in Hawaii began with children born into poverty, often to parents who were alcoholic or mentally ill. Not surprisingly, many of these children showed signs of deprivation when they were infants (low weight, medical problems, etc.). Experts predicted a troubled future for them, but that did not necessarily happen.

One such infant was Michael, born preterm, weighing less than 5 pounds. His parents were low-income teenagers; his father was absent for the first years of his life, returning only to impregnate Michael's mother again and again and again. When Michael was 8 years old, both parents left him and his three younger siblings with their grandparents. Yet Michael ultimately became a successful, happy, loving adult (E. Werner, 1979).

Michael was not the only resilient one. Amazingly, about one-third of the high-risk Hawaiian babies coped well. By middle childhood, they had discovered ways to avoid family stresses, to achieve in school, to make good friends, and to find adult mentors. As adults, they left family problems behind (many moved far away) and established their own healthy relationships (E. Werner & Smith, 1992, 2001).

As was true for many of these children, attending school and then heading to college can be an escape. Although an easygoing temperament and a high IQ help children cope with adversity, those qualities are not essential. For the Hawaiian children, "a realistic goal orientation, persistence, and 'learned creativity' enabled . . . a remarkable degree of personal, social, and occupational success," even for those with learning disabilities (E. Werner & Smith, 2001, p. 140).

Learning as Lifeline Originally from Libya—where bombs, guns, and death were common—this boy's family escaped to a refugee camp in Tunisia. The adults suffer from crowding and deprivation, but some children are resilient—especially with the help of a caring teacher and regular schooling, as seems to be the case here.

SOCIAL SUPPORT AND RELIGIOUS FAITH Social support is a major factor that strengthens the ability to deal with stress, especially for minority children who are aware of prejudice against them (Gillen-O'Neel et al., 2011). Compared with the homebound lives of younger children, the expanding social world of middle childhood allows new possibilities.

Relatives, teachers, peers, pets, community programs (even libraries and concerts) all help children cope with stress (Bryant & Donnellan, 2007). That means anyone might be on the rescue team for children. One study concludes:

> When children attempt to seek out experiences that will help them overcome adversity, it is critical that resources, in the form of supportive adults or learning opportunities, be made available to them so that their own self-righting potential can be fulfilled.

> *[Kim-Cohen et al., 2004, p. 664]*

A specific example is children's use of religion, which often provides support via adults from the same faith group. Many studies find that religious involvement particularly helps African American children in communities rife with drugs, early sex,

JONKMANNS / LAIF / REDUX

NAFTALI HILGER / LAIF / REDUX

Same Situation, Far Apart: Praying Hands Differences are obvious between the Northern Indian girls entering their Hindu school and the West African boy in a Christian church, even in their clothes and hand positions. But underlying similarities are more important. In every culture, many 8-year-olds are more devout than their elders.

and racial prejudice. The help occurs in three ways: practical (a church or temple becomes a second home, with many activities), social (children use slightly older believers as role models), and cognitive (concepts of sin, grace, and salvation help children make sense of what they see) (Mattis & Mattis, 2011). Faith is psychologically protective when it guides children to reinterpret their experiences (Crawford et al., 2006).

Prayer may also foster resilience. In one study, adults were required to pray for a specific person for several weeks. Their attitude about that person changed (Lambert et al., 2010). Ethics precludes such an experiment with children, but it is known that children often pray, expecting that prayer will make them feel better, especially when they are sad or angry (Bamford & Lagattuta, 2010). As you now know, expectations and interpretations can be powerful.

> ## KEY points
>
> - In middle childhood, children seek to be industrious, actively mastering various skills.
> - Social comparison helps children refine their self-concept.
> - Resilient children cope well with major adversities.
> - Schools, churches, and many other institutions help children escape from difficult family conditions.

Families and Children

No one doubts that genes affect personality as well as ability, that peers are vital, and that schools and cultures influence what, and how much, children learn as well as how they feel about themselves.

It has been suggested that these three—genes, peers, and communities—have so much influence that parenting has little impact unless it is grossly abusive (Harris, 1998, 2002; McLeod et al., 2007). This suggestion arose from research on the effect of the environment on child development.

Shared and Nonshared Environments

Environmental influence on any two children comes either from factors that are shared (both children experience the same environment) or are not shared. For example, all the children raised in one home might be said to share the same parents, and children who grow up in separate nations might have nonshared cultural influences.

Many studies have found that children are less affected by *shared environment* than by *nonshared environment.* A formula for the influences on a child is *G + Shared E + Nonshared E,* a formula that is read as: genes plus home environment plus non-home environment.

Careful research that applied this formula to twins, full and half siblings, and stepchildren found that most personality traits and intellectual characteristics are the product of genes plus nonshared environments, with little left over for the shared influences, such as those for siblings growing up together.

Even psychopathology (Burt, 2009) and sexual orientation (Långström et al., 2010) arise primarily from genes and non-shared environment. Parenting does not make a child heterosexual or homosexual: Identical twins usually have the same sexual orientation, but if they do not, it seems to be because of nonshared factors.

Since shared environment has little impact, does this mean that parents merely provide basic care (food, shelter), with little influence on children's personality, intellect, and so on, no matter what rules, routines, or responses they provide? No!

Recent findings reassert parent power. The formula and calculation of shared and nonshared influences was correct, but the definition of Shared E was based on a false assumption. Siblings raised together do *not* share the same environment.

For example, if relocation, divorce, unemployment, or a new job occurs in a family, the impact on each child depends on that child's age, genes, resilience, and gender. Thus, moving to another town might disturb a 9-year-old-girl more than her baby brother because she must leave friends behind; divorce generally harms boys more than girls because it weakens connection with their father; poverty may hurt children of one age more than another.

The variations just mentioned do not apply equally to all children: *Differential sensitivity* means that one child is more affected, for better or worse, than another (Pluess & Belsky, 2010). Even if siblings are raised together, the mix of parental personality and children's genes, age, and gender may lead one sibling to become antisocial, another to have a personality disorder, and a third to be resilient (Beauchaine et al., 2009). One of my friends grew up fatherless and poor, but he is a gifted and respected city councilman. His brother was a drug addict killed by gunfire. You probably know other families with divergent children.

In addition to variations within the home, parents choose for their children many outside, nonshared influences, such as school and neighborhood. Those choices affect the children, sometimes differently for each child (Simpkins et al., 2006). Perhaps the oldest child attended the nearby public school and then family income or values shifted so that a younger sibling attended a religious school 10 miles away. School would be a nonshared influence on these two children, but the parents played pivotal roles.

Even identical twins, with the same genes, age, sex, and home, may not share their home or school environment (Caspi et al., 2004). For example, one mother spoke of her monozygotic daughters:

Family Unity Thinking about any family—even a happy, wealthy family like this one—makes it apparent that each child's family experiences differ. For instance, would you expect this 5-year-old boy to be treated the same way as his two older sisters? And how about each child's feelings toward the parents? Even though the 12-year-olds are twins, one may favor her mother while the other favors her father.

✦ **ESPECIALLY FOR** Scientists How would you determine whether parents treat all their children the same way? (see response, page 293) →

Susan can be very sweet. She loves babies . . . she can be insecure . . . she flutters and dances around. . . . There's not much between her ears. . . . She's exceptionally vain, more so than Ann. Ann loves any game involving a ball, very sporty, climbs trees, very much a tomboy. One is a serious tomboy and one's a serious girlie girl. Even when they were babies I always dressed one in blue stuff and one in pink stuff.

[quoted in Caspi et al., 2004, p. 156]

By dressing these girls differently from infancy, this mother created different environments for them. It would have been harder for Ann to climb trees if she wore pink, frilly dresses.

Family Structure and Family Function

Family structure refers to the legal and genetic connections among people living in the same household. **Family function** refers to how a family cares for its members.

The data affirm that parents are crucial for family function, determining non-shared as well as shared environments. Does it matter what structure the family has? Are some family structures more supportive of parents, enabling well-functioning families? What is a dysfunctional, or a well-functioning, family?

Part of the answer is known. No matter what the structure, one family function is crucial: People need family love and encouragement. Beyond that, needs vary by age. As you have seen, infants need responsive caregiving, frequent exposure to language, and social interaction; preschoolers need encouragement and guidance. Later chapters of this text describe the needs of adolescents and adults.

During middle childhood, children need five things from their families:

1. *Physical necessities.* Although children in middle childhood eat, dress, and go to sleep without help, families furnish food, clothing, and shelter.

2. *Learning.* These are prime learning years: Families choose schools, help with homework, encourage education.

3. *Self-respect.* Families give each child a way to shine. Especially if academic success is elusive, opportunities in sports, the arts, and so on are crucial.

4. *Peer relationships.* Families foster friendships, via play dates, group activities, school choice, classroom support.

5. *Harmony and stability.* Families provide protective, predictable routines within a home that is a safe haven for everyone.

CONTINUITY AND CHANGE No family always functions perfectly, but children worldwide fare better in families than in other institutions (such as group residences) and best if families provide the five functions listed above. Item five, harmony and stability, is especially crucial in middle childhood: Children like continuity, not change; peace, not conflict.

To some degree, this is unique to middle childhood. Indeed, a decade or so later, emerging adults enjoy new places, seek challenges, and provoke arguments with friends and family. College students sometimes study in other nations or stay up all night debating issues with friends—not something young children do.

Adults may not recognize a child's wish for continuity. Parents often move to a "better" neighborhood during these years, thinking they are securing a better life for their children when, instead, the children may feel vulnerable, not protected. To be specific, in one year (2010), 19 percent of U.S. 5- to 9-year-olds changed residences, a rate five times that of adults older than 65 (U.S. Bureau of the Census, 2011a).

A surprising study revealed the value of continuity (Tanaka & Nakazawa, 2005). The researchers began with the knowledge that children benefit from living with their fathers. Father absence also correlates with poverty and divorce, both also harmful.

---

family structure
The legal and genetic relationships among relatives living in the same home; includes nuclear family, extended family, stepfamily, and so on.

family function
The way a family works to meet the needs of its members. Children need families to provide basic material necessities, to encourage learning, to help them develop self-respect, to nurture friendships, and to foster harmony and stability.

● UNDERSTANDING THE NUMBERS
Since the annual moving rate for each of the five years from ages 5 to 9 is 0.19, what is the average moving rate for each child for the entire 5-year period?

Answer The average for each child is 5 × 0.19, which equals 0.95—about one move during middle childhood. As with all quantitative averages, individual variations are lost. Some children move a dozen times (for instance, if they are homeless) and others stay put. The latter are less stressed.

Given that, these researchers wanted to learn how children would be affected if the father's absence did *not* correlate with low income and hostile mother–father interaction. Accordingly, they sought to replicate prior father-absence investigation by studying children of happily married couples in which the fathers were gainfully employed and supporting the family.

An opportunity for such research arose naturally in Japan. Many Japanese corporations transfer employees temporarily from one location to another to help them understand how the entire company functions. Some families move if the father is the employee and some families do not, so researchers were able to find two similar groups of children, with only one major difference between the groups: whether the father was present or absent every day.

The hypothesis was that children who moved with their fathers would benefit because his daily presence would help them with self-esteem, homework, and therefore school achievement. However, the opposite turned out to be true. Although the mothers who moved with their husbands were happier, the schoolchildren who moved were more depressed and their school achievement suffered. It seems that the benefit of father presence was undermined by the stress of change.

Other international research also finds that the *reason* for father absence is significant. In a Mexican study, children who remained at home when their fathers emigrated to support the family were compared with children whose fathers were absent because of divorce; the former group seemed to function much better (Nobles, 2011). However, if the whole family emigrated, school-age children were more stressed than younger ones.

Such findings raise a similar question regarding children living in the United States for years, but whose mother or father is being deported. How are these children affected if they go back with their parent (it is estimated that 300,000 such children now live in Mexico) and how are they affected if they stay? Objective research has not yet been published that compares these two eventualities, but it is by no means established that following the father is always best (Cave, 2012).

What Must She Leave Behind? In every nation, children are uprooted from familiar places as a result of adult struggles and/or aspirations for a better life. This girl is leaving a settlement in the Gaza Strip, due to the Israeli–Palestinian conflict that has disrupted millions of lives. Worldwide, it's the children who suffer most from relocation.

MILITARY FAMILIES A notable example of family functioning occurs for U.S. children in military families. On the first four points on the list of family functions, such children are advantaged compared with children whose parents have similar backgrounds but are not in the service. On average, enlisted parents tend to have higher incomes, better health care, and more education than do civilians from the same backgrounds; in addition, military bases tend to have better schools and more after-school activities. Furthermore, military housing makes it easier for children to have friends because of the proximity of similar families.

However, stability is virtually nonexistent. Military parents repeatedly depart and return, and families typically relocate every few years (Riggs & Riggs, 2011; Titus, 2007). Generally speaking, adults are happy when a soldier comes home, but even a safe return may disrupt the children's lives. Military children (dubbed "military brats," a telling nickname) experience emotional problems and decreased achievement with each change (Hall, 2008). For that reason, the U.S. Army encourages caregivers to avoid changes in the child's life: no new homes, rules, family members, or schools (Lester et al., 2011).

The same underlying principles apply to nonmilitary families. Remember that children crave stability. If an out-of-work parent finds a job far away, or if changing circumstances make it easier to leave a destructive neighborhood, an inferior school, or a crowded extended family, most family members may rejoice—but not necessarily the 6- to 11-year-olds. This, of course, does not preclude such moves, but disrupted children need special attention and support.

RESPONSE FOR Scientists (from page 291) Proof is very difficult when human interaction is the subject of investigation, since random assignment is impossible. Ideally, researchers would find identical twins being raised together and would then observe the parents' behavior over the years. ●

DIVERSITY OF STRUCTURES Worldwide, two cohort factors—more single-parent households (see Infographic 8, page 296) and fewer children per family—have changed childhood from what it was a few decades ago. Most of our discussion here focuses on the United States in about 2012. However, the advantages and disadvantages of each family structure are similar in every culture.

In middle childhood, about two-thirds of U.S. children live in two-parent homes (see Table 8.2), most often with both biological parents—an arrangement called a **nuclear family.** In U.S. nuclear families, the parents are usually married, although in many other nations nuclear families are headed by couples who are not legally wed. Other two-parent structures include adoptive parents, foster parents, grandparents without parents, a biological parent with a stepparent, and same-sex couples. Strictly speaking, these are not nuclear families, but some observers consider them as such.

In the United States, about 31 percent of 6- to 11-year-olds currently live in a **single-parent family.** Far more live in a single-parent family at some point between birth and age 18 because (1) their mother was neither married nor cohabiting when they were born (true for 41 percent in 2011), (2) their parents separated or divorced (about 30 percent), and/or (3) one parent died (about 5 percent). Sometimes two or even all three of these occur for the same child, thus the percentage who experience single parenthood at some point is less than 76 (41 + 30 + 5) percent, but more than half, perhaps 60 percent.

Two-parent and single-parent structures are often contrasted with the **extended family,** a family that includes nonparental adults, usually grandparents and often aunts, uncles, and cousins, all under one roof. In 2010, about one in six U.S. families was an extended family—an increase from 1980 (one in eight) and a decrease from 1940 (one in five) (Pew Social Trends, 2010). Infants are more likely to live in extended families than older children are. Extended families save on housing costs and child care, which makes them more common among low-income households and nations.

The distinction between one-parent, two-parent, and extended families is not as simple in practice as on paper. Many young parents live near relatives who provide meals, emotional support, money, and child care, functioning as an extended family. Similarly, extended families can function like nuclear families, especially in developing nations: Some families are considered extended because they share a roof, but they create separate living quarters for each set of parents and children (Georgas et al., 2006).

In many nations, the **polygamous family** (one husband with two or more wives) is an acceptable structure. Generally in polygamous families, income per child

---

nuclear family
A family that consists of a father, a mother, and their biological children under age 18.

single-parent family
A family that consists of only one parent and his or her biological children under age 18.

extended family
A family of three or more generations living in one household.

polygamous family
A family consisting of one man, several wives, and their children.

Same Situation, Far Apart: Happy Families The boys in both photos are about 4 years old. Roberto *(left)* lives with his single mother in Chicago. She pays $360 a month for her two children to attend a day-care center. The youngest child in the Balmedina family *(right)* lives with his nuclear family—no day care needed—in the Philippines. Which boy has the better life? The answer is not known; family function is more crucial than family structure.

TABLE 8.2 Family Structures (percent of U.S. 6- to 11-year-olds in each type)*

Two-Parent Families (69%)

1. **Nuclear family** (55%). Named after the nucleus (the tightly connected core particles of an atom), the nuclear family consists of a man and a woman and their biological offspring under 18 years of age. About half of all school-age children live in nuclear families. About 10 percent of such families also include a grandparent, and often an aunt or uncle, living under the same roof and hence are extended families.

2. **Stepparent family** (9%). Divorced fathers usually remarry; divorced mothers remarry about half the time. When children from a former relationship live with the new couple it makes a stepparent family. If the stepparent family includes children born to two or more couples (such as children from the spouses' previous marriages and/or children of the new couple), that is called a *blended family*.

3. **Adoptive family** (2%). Although as many as one-third of infertile married couples adopt children, few adoptable children are available and so most adoptive couples have only one or two children. Thus, only 2 percent of children are adopted, although the overall percentage of adoptive families is higher than that.

4. **Grandparents alone** (2%). Grandparents take on parenting for some children when biological parents are absent (dead, imprisoned, sick, addicted, etc.).

5. **Two same-sex parents** (1%). Some two-parent families are headed by a same-sex couple, whose legal status (married, step-, adoptive) varies.

Single-Parent Families (31%)

One-parent families are increasing, but they average fewer children than two-parent families, so in middle childhood, only 31 percent of children have a lone parent.

1. **Single mother—never married** (13%). In 2010, 41 percent of all U.S. births were to unmarried mothers; but when children are school age, many mothers who were unmarried are now married or have entrusted their children to their parents' care. So only about 13 percent of 6- to 11-year-olds, at any given moment, are in single-mother homes.

2. **Single mother—divorced, separated, or widowed** (12%). Although many marriages end in divorce (almost half in the United States, fewer in other nations), many divorcing couples have no children. Others remarry. Thus, only 12 percent of school-age children currently live with single, formerly married mothers.

3. **Single father** (4%). About 1 father in 25 has physical custody of his children and raises them without their mother or a new wife. This category increased at the start of the twenty-first century but has decreased since 2005.

4. **Grandparent alone** (2%). Sometimes a single grandparent (usually the grandmother) becomes the sole caregiving adult for a child.

More Than Two Adults (15%) [Also listed as two-parent or one-parent family]

1. **Extended family** (15%). Some children live with a grandparent or other relatives, as well as with one (5 percent) or both of their parents (10 percent). This pattern is most common with infants (20 percent) but occurs in middle childhood as well.

2. **Polygamous family** (0%). In some nations (not the United States), men can legally have several wives. This family structure is more favored by adults than children. Everywhere, polyandry (one woman, several husbands) is rare.

*Less than 1 percent of U.S. children live without any caregiving adult; they are not included in this table.

Source: The percentages on this table are estimates, based on data in U.S. Bureau of the Census, 2011b, *Statistical Abstract* and Current Population Reports, *America's Families and Living Arrangements,* 2011; and Pew reports, 2011. The category "extended family" in this table is higher than most published statistics, since some families do not tell official authorities about relatives living with them.

is reduced and education, especially for girls, is limited (Omariba & Boyle, 2007). Polygamy is illegal in the United States, although some say that repeated divorce and remarriage is similar to polygamy. In nations where polygamy is legal, divorce is less common but rates of polygamy are declining. In Ghana, for example, men with several wives and a dozen children were once common but now are rare (Heaton & Darkwah, 2011).

SOURCES & CREDITS LISTED ON P. SC-1

VISUALIZING DEVELOPMENT

A Wedding, or Not? Family Structures Around the World

Children fare best when both parents actively care for them every day. This is most likely to occur if the parents are married, although there are many exceptions. Many developmentalists now focus on the rate of single parenthood, shown on this map. Some single parents raise children well, but the risk of neglect, poverty, and instability increases the chances of child problems.

RATES OF SINGLE PARENTHOOD

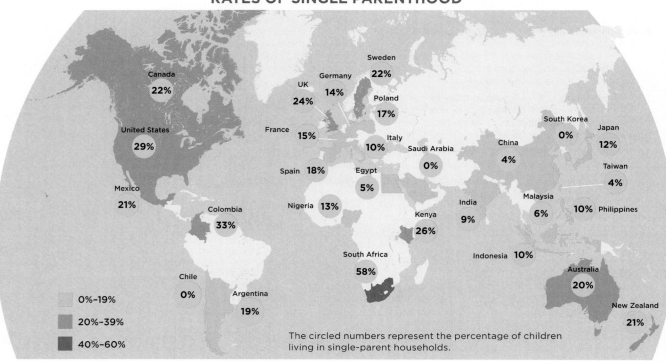

Canada 22%
United States 29%
Mexico 21%
Colombia 33%
Chile 0%
Argentina 19%
UK 24%
France 15%
Spain 18%
Germany 14%
Sweden 22%
Poland 17%
Italy 10%
Egypt 5%
Saudi Arabia 0%
Nigeria 13%
Kenya 26%
South Africa 58%
China 4%
India 9%
South Korea 0%
Japan 12%
Taiwan 4%
Malaysia 6%
Philippines 10%
Indonesia 10%
Australia 20%
New Zealand 21%

0%–19%
20%–39%
40%–60%

The circled numbers represent the percentage of children living in single-parent households.

A young couple in love and committed to each other—what next?

IN THE UNITED STATES:

Influence of family and religion:
relatively weak

Likelihood of cohabitation:
70%

Likelihood of woman's marriage before age 25:
40%

IN NIGERIA:

influence of family and religion:
relatively strong

(Islam in Northern Nigeria, evangelical Christianity in Eastern Nigeria)

Likelihood of cohabitation:
1%

Likelihood of woman's marriage before age 25:
80%

Cohabitation and marriage rates change from year to year and from culture to culture. These two are illustrative and approximate. The crucial issue is whether a couple stays together over the decades in a strong parental alliance. Family-structure statistics often focus on marital status, making it seem as if Nigerian children are more fortunate than American children. However, the actual household functioning is more complex than that.

Connecting Family Structure and Function

Structure influences but does not determine function. Which structures make it more likely that the five family functions (necessities, learning, self-respect, friendship, harmony/stability) will occur?

FUNCTION OF NUCLEAR FAMILIES In general, nuclear families function best; children in the nuclear structure tend to achieve higher grades in school with fewer psychological problems. A scholar who summarized dozens of studies concludes: "Children living with two biological married parents experience better educational, social, cognitive, and behavioral outcomes than do other children" (Brown, 2010, p. 1062).

Does this mean that parents should all marry and stay married? Developmentalists are not that prescriptive because some of the benefits are correlates, not causes.

To be specific, many advantages of nuclear families begin before the wedding because education, earning potential, and emotional maturity all increase the chance that people will marry, have children, and stay married. Thus, brides and grooms bring personal assets to their new family.

In other words, there is a correlation between child success and married parents partly because of who marries, not because of the legality of the union. If all the immature, unmarried parents were forced to wed, their children would not fare as well as children of married parents now do.

However, to some extent, marriage itself benefits children. The selection effects noted in the previous paragraph are not the entire story (Amato, 2005; Brown, 2010). Ideally, mutual affection between spouses encourages them to become wealthier and healthier than either would be alone, and that helps their children. Furthermore, the *parental alliance,* in which mother and father support each other in their commitment to the child, decreases neglect and abuse and increases the likelihood that children have someone to read to them, check homework, invite friends over, buy new clothes, and save for their future.

In fact, a broad survey of parental contributions to college tuition found that the highest contributions came from nuclear families. These results might be expected when two-parent families are compared with single and divorced parents because one-parent families average less income. However, even when the income of remarried parents is comparable with that of nuclear parents, they contribute less, on average, to the college tuition of stepchildren (Turley & Desmond, 2011). This and other research suggests that the benefits of nuclear families continue for decades, even after children are grown.

FUNCTION OF OTHER TWO-PARENT FAMILIES Although nuclear families may be the ideal, they certainly are not the only way to raise healthy and happy children. The advantages of two-parent families are not limited to biological parents, whose genetic connection to their children partially explains their commitment. No type of two-parent family guarantees good functioning, but the fact that two adults are involved nudge it in the right direction.

Adoptive and same-sex parents typically function very well for children, often better than the average nuclear family. Some stepparent families function well also. When children are younger than 2 and a new stepparent forms a happy relationship with the biological parent, the children usually thrive (Ganong et al., 2011). Now some details.

A topic of considerable controversy—how same-sex couples function for children—has been a focus of recent developmental research. Small studies are reassuring, but because same-sex marriage is relatively recent and not available in many states and nations, the ideal studies—longitudinal research on a large sample, with valid

DAVID MAXWELL / THE NEW YORK TIMES / REDUX

Middle American Family This seems to be a typical breakfast in Brunswick, Ohio—Cheerios for 1-year-old Carson, pancakes that 7-year-old Carter does not finish eating, and family photos crowded on the far table. The one apparent difference, that both parents are women, does not necessarily create or avoid children's problems.

Cherish the Moment Tom and Jakey expect a happy future as husband and wife. They plan to wed in three months, move into their new house (behind them) and lead a happy, blended family with his smiling daughters, Simone (17) and Shayla (12), now swinging her son, Nathaniel (5). Unfortunately, stepchildren pose unanticipated challenges: Many second marriages end with a second divorce.

KIMBERLY P. MITCHELL / DETROIT FREE PRESS / MCT / NEWSCOM

comparisons to male/female families of the same age, marital status, and education—have not yet been published.

Fortunately, for decades some female/female couples have raised children, usually the biological child of one mother who has custody after divorce. In general, their offspring develop well, emotionally and intellectually (Biblarz & Stacey, 2010). Same-sex and other-sex partnerships seem to have similar problems: Such families are sometimes dysfunctional, sometimes not.

The *stepparent structure* also has advantages and disadvantages. The primary advantage is financial, especially when compared with the average single-parent family. However, some biological fathers who do not have custody and some stepfathers who are not genetically related to their stepchildren are reluctant to provide the formal and informal support that children need (Meyer et al., 2011). Furthermore, the other biological parent, as well as the children themselves, may make it difficult for the noncustodial or stepparent to develop a parental relationship with the child.

Income and intimacy aside, another disadvantage of stepfamilies is in meeting the fifth family function listed earlier—providing harmony and stability. Instability is typical: Not only does remarriage usually entail moving to a new home, but also older stepchildren leave home sooner than older biological children, new babies arrive more often, and marriages are more likely to dissolve (Teachman, 2008).

Harmony may also be absent, especially if the child's loyalty to both biological parents is undermined by ongoing disputes between them. A solid parental alliance is more difficult to form when it includes three adults—two of whom disliked each other enough to divorce, and a third who is a newcomer to the child's life.

Another version of a two-parent family occurs when grandparents are full-time caretakers for children without parents present (called a *skipped-generation family*, the most common form of foster care). The hope is that grandparents provide excellent care since they are experienced, mature, and devoted to their grandchildren. Those characteristics may be present, but skipped-generation families average lower incomes, more health problems, and less stability than other two-parent families (Arber & Timonen, 2012).

Adequate health care and schooling for the children is particularly difficult in skipped-generation families, partly because schools and insurance plans create barriers and partly because many of these children have special needs due to the circumstances that led them to live with their grandparents in the first place. Thus, skipped-generation families need extra help, but they may not get it (Baker & Mutchler, 2010).

Finally, adoptive and foster-parent families vary tremendously in their ability to meet the needs of children. Many of the children in such families pose special challenges, particularly at puberty and later. Again, agencies and communities are not always helpful.

FUNCTION OF SINGLE-PARENT FAMILIES On average, the single-parent structure functions less well because income and stability are lower. Most single parents fill many roles in addition to parent—including wage earner, daughter or son (single parents often depend on their own parents), and lover (many seek a new partner)—which makes it hard to provide steady emotional and academic support for their children. If they are depressed (and many are), they are less available to meet their children's needs.

One case study provided the example of Neesha, who had been late or absent for more than one-third of her fourth-grade year, although she read at the seventh-grade level (reported in Wilmshurst, 2011). Her mother was a single parent, depressed and worried about paying the rent on the tiny apartment she moved into when Neesha's father left three years earlier to live with his girlfriend, now raising his baby.

Neesha showed signs of resilience—her academic achievement was far above grade level and she tried to care for her mother. But her family situation made her fragile; she often fell asleep in school and was teased because of it. The school counselor reported:

> The school principal received a call from Neesha's mother, who asked that her daughter not be sent home from school because she was going to kill herself. She . . . did not want Neesha to come home and find her dead. . . . [T]he school contacted the police, who apprehended mom while she was talking on her cell phone . . . a loaded gun was on her lap. . . .
> Neesha said, "Sometimes it's hard being a kid."
>
> *[Wilmshurst, 2011, pp. 154–155]*

Neesha is an extreme example. In fact, some single parents are not depressed and do an excellent job with their children. However, the emotional and financial stresses of being a single parent often make it "hard being a kid" for many school-age children.

Community support for single parents makes a difference. In this case, the school and then the police probably saved this single mother's life, as she was then taken to a psychiatric hospital where she was treated for depression. The report does not say what happened with Neesha, however. Her father did not want her. Ideally, another family would provide good care, but no relatives were ready to do so. In general, single parents who need help the most seem least likely to receive it (Harknett & Hartnett, 2011).

Neesha's story illustrates the problems that might occur in a single-parent household, but we should also add that millions of children raised by single parents are well loved and nurtured. Remember that difference is not always deficit; good caregiving is more difficult in the single-parent structure, but it is far from impossible.

CULTURE AND FAMILY STRUCTURE Cultural variations in the support provided for various family structures make it hard to conclude that a particular structure is always best. For example, many French parents are unmarried; U.S. surveys would have classified such women as single parents until recently. However, French unmarried mothers generally live with their children's fathers. French cohabiting parents separate less often than do married parents in the United States, which suggests more stability in the average French cohabiting family than in the average married structure in the United States. An analysis of 27 nations found that for women in particular, the social context had a major impact on their happiness (Lee & Ono, 2012), which probably would affect their ability to parent successfully.

In the United States, the cohabiting structure is worse for children than the marriage structure because cohabiting parents separate more often than married parents do (Musick & Bumpass, 2012). This is one example of a general truth: Function is affected by national mores.

✦ **ESPECIALLY FOR Single Parents** You have heard that children raised in one-parent families will have difficulty in establishing intimate relationships as adolescents and adults. What can you do about this possibility? (see response, page 300) →

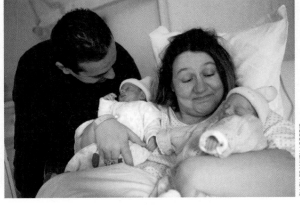

French Bliss Healthy twins (Layanne and Rayanne) born in Paris to thrilled parents—what could be better? Perhaps a wedding: These parents are not married.

OWEN FRANKEN / CORBIS

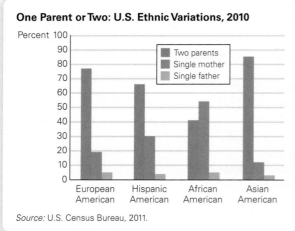

One Parent or Two: U.S. Ethnic Variations, 2010

Source: U.S. Census Bureau, 2011.

FIGURE 8.1 Diverse Families The fact that family structure is affected partly by ethnicity has implications for everyone in the family. It is easier to be a single parent if there are others of the same background who are also single parents.

RESPONSE FOR Single Parents (from page 299) Do not get married mainly to provide a second parent for your child. If you were to do so, things would probably get worse rather than better. Do make an effort to have friends of both sexes with whom your child can interact. ●

Ethnic norms matter as well. Single parenthood is more accepted among African Americans (60 percent of African American 6- to 11-year-olds live with only one parent). Consequently, relatives and friends routinely help single parents, who would be more isolated and dysfunctional if they were of another ethnicity (Cain & Combs-Orme, 2005; Taylor et al., 2008).

By contrast, single parents head less than 15 percent of Asian American families (see Figure 8.1). Thus, most Asian American children benefit from two caregiving parents, but those with single parents are more vulnerable. Similarly, Latino couples are more likely to marry than non-Latinos, which benefits children, but one result is that unmarried Latino mothers are less happy and more likely to be hostile toward their children than Latino mothers who are married (Gibson-Davis & Gassman-Pines, 2010).

Mexican American families are especially likely to be nuclear or extended, but some of the usual advantages of such families may be absent. If the fathers consider their neighborhood dangerous and value family cohesion (familism), they may be especially strict; their children are likely to consider them cold and punitive (authoritarian). One result is more child anxiety and depression—which means that the two-parent family structure may undercut healthy development (White & Roosa, 2012).

All these are generalities; individuals, contexts, and cultures always matter. In the study of Mexican American families just cited, the researchers stress context and culture. The fathers were very strict parents *because* they reflected the strong Latino emphasis on family support and wanted to protect their children from problems in a low-income, hostile U.S. community (White & Roosa, 2012). The same men, in less dangerous neighborhoods, might have been warm and supportive fathers.

When analyzing family structure, always remember variations and do not be too quick to conclude that one structure is better than another. Contrary to the averages, thousands of nuclear families are destructive, thousands of stepparents provide excellent care, thousands of cohabiting couples are great parents, and thousands of single-parent families are wonderful. Structure and culture tend to protect or undercut healthy function, but many parents overcome structural problems and many families of all types provide school-age children with the support and encouragement they need.

OPPOSING PERSPECTIVES

Divorce for the Sake of the Children

Opposing perspectives on divorce begin with three facts.

1. The United States leads the world in rates of divorce and remarriage. Almost half of all marriages end in divorce.

2. On average, children fare best, emotionally and academically, with married parents.

3. On average, divorce impairs children's academic achievement and psychosocial development for years, even decades.

One might conclude from these three facts that every couple should marry before they have children and that no married couple should divorce. Many adults, including some political leaders, share this view. But the opposite side—that divorce often benefits children—has proponents as well, who begin by pointing out that any statistic reported as an overall average correlation dismisses variability and does not consider causes.

Opinions are strongly influenced by each person's past history and culture. For example, married parents who stay together are much more negative about divorce than are divorced adults. Adults whose parents divorced tend to have a much more positive take on divorce than adults whose parents stayed together (Michelle Moon, 2011).

Some say that marriage, not divorce, is the root of the problem (Cherlin, 2009). U.S. culture idolizes both marriage and personal freedom. As a result, if parents disapprove of a future mate, young adults in the United States sometimes assert their independence by marrying "for love." Later, if they are overwhelmed by child care and financial stress while passion fades, the marriage becomes strained, and their parents are not supportive. Divorce seems the best solution. That may be why divorce rates are higher for people who marry soon after they meet or who are relatively young.

Because marriage remains the ideal, divorced adults blame their former mate or their own poor decision for the break-up. They seek another spouse—which may lead to another divorce; if they have children in each relationship, the children in particular suffer. From this perspective, a shift in cultural mores is needed, from an individualistic focus to a collectivist one. If adults were more cognizant of their communities, including their responsibility to their parents and their children, they might avoid risky marriages and thus avoid divorce. Children would thrive.

This has important policy implications, but not simple ones. Persuading unmarried parents to wed may be short-sighted because such marriages are at high risk of divorce (Brown, 2010). Indeed, at least one longitudinal study of unwed mothers found that those who married were eventually worse off than those who did not (Lichter et al., 2006). Research on unwed parents finds that many consider marriage a much riskier commitment than childbearing (Gibson-Davis, 2011). For their children, it may be.

Scholars now describe marriage and divorce as a process, with transitions and conflicts before and after the formal events (Magnuson & Berger, 2009; Potter, 2010). As you remember, resilience is difficult when children must contend with repeated changes and ongoing hassles—yet this is what divorce brings. Coping is particularly hard if divorce occurs during a developmental transition, such as when a child enters first grade or begins puberty, and if parents draw children into marital conflict.

Looking internationally, it is noteworthy that in some nations (especially in the Middle East, Africa, and Asia) divorce is rare. In those regions, adults expect marriages to endure, so in-laws help troubled couples stay together. Are children better off because of that? Maybe not. In fact, more child abuse and less child education characterize low-divorce nations. But again, linking these outcomes is a leap, not supported by data.

By contrast, in the United States and other nations, marriage partners expect each other to be soul mates, providing great sex, financial support, and intellectual stimulation. This is difficult, and when it does not occur, couples divorce because they are "incompatible" (Wilcox & Dew, 2010). Even sexual compatibility is partly cultural, as infidelity is grounds for divorce in some places, but not in others—especially when the unfaithful spouse is the man, another cultural difference.

Given all this, many U.S. young adults avoid marriage in order to avoid divorce. This strategy is working—the age at first marriage in the United States is increasing, which is one reason the divorce rate is falling even faster than the marriage rate (Amato, 2010). Is this a problem or a solution?

The research leads to opposite conclusions. For instance, marriages need not be satisfying to the adults in order to function well for the children—an argument against divorce. But a pro-divorce argument arises from other research. If a marriage is harmful to family harmony, then divorce may help the children. This is especially true if both divorced parents are warm, attentive, and involved with their children, separating their interpersonal relationship from their parenting roles (Vélez et al., 2011).

Another finding from developmental research is that marital bliss depends partly on the circumstances of the family at the time. Often the happiest time is right after the wedding, before children are born; the least happy time is when the children are infants or young teenagers. Financial and caregiving strains are greatest when children are younger than 5. Many couples meet that challenge by alternating working shifts, so one parent is always home. That solution has one hazard: Divorce is more common in such families.

Knowledge about the developmental path of marriage might help parents through the hard patches. For example, when children are small, couples can make sure they spend time together doing what they both enjoy—dancing, traveling, praying, and so on. Otherwise, infant care not only sucks up time, it also undercuts love.

A life-span view provides some perspective: Marriage happiness dips during infancy and rises when all the children are self-sufficient adults. This is a hopeful generality—but like all generalities, it is not always true. Some couples divorce after their children are grown. There is no easy answer, which is why both opposing perspectives thrive.

Children are harmed when they live in a home where their parents actively fight, but not if the parents are merely compatible roommates (Amato, 2010). Indeed, some believe that even when spouse abuse makes parents separate, children may benefit if parents make peace and reunite (Holtzworth-Munroe, 2011). This is a minority perspective, but the fact that anyone would advocate it illustrates the problem—people disagree about the effects of divorce on children.

Beyond highlighting these opposing perspectives, can any conclusion be drawn by developmental study? As emphasized in the beginning of this discussion, marriage should not occur impulsively. Now we can add that childbearing and divorce should not be impulsive, either. Whether divorce is good for the children depends on careful analysis, case by case.

Family Trouble

Two factors interfere with family function in every structure, ethnic group, and nation: low income and high conflict. Many families experience both poverty and acrimony because financial stress increases conflict and vice versa (McLanahan, 2009).

POVERTY Suppose a 6-year-old boy spills his milk, as every 6-year-old sometimes does. In a well-functioning, two-parent family, one parent guides him to mop up the spill while the other parent pours more milk, perhaps encouraging family harmony by saying, "Everyone has an accident sometimes."

What if the 6-year-old lives with a single parent struggling with overdue rent, unemployment, and an older child who wants money for a school trip? What if the last of the food stamps bought that milk? Shouting, crying, and accusations are almost inevitable (perhaps the sibling claims, "He did it on purpose," to which the 6-year-old responds, "You pushed me," and a visitor adds, "You should teach him to be careful"). As in this example, poverty makes anger spill over when the milk does.

Family income correlates with structure. Many low-income adults are reluctant to marry until both spouses have good jobs, so the married structure is less common as income falls. Since conflicts about money are a major reason for divorce, if such parents do marry, then low income makes divorce more likely.

Family function is also affected by income: Obviously money is needed for the first of the five functions listed earlier—physical necessities—and it has an influence on functions 2 through 5 as well. Since most funds for U.S. schools come from local property taxes, *learning* is affected by neighborhood affluence. Since *self-esteem* may benefit from costly sports and arts programs, poverty reduces that as well. *Friendship* is limited if children have many tasks to do at home, and poor families *move* more often.

The effects of poverty on children are cumulative; most children are resilient if income drops for a year, but an entire childhood in poverty is difficult to overcome. Low SES may be especially damaging during middle childhood (Duncan et al., 2010).

Several researchers have developed the *family-stress model,* which holds that the crucial question about any risk factor (e.g., low income, divorce, single parenthood, unemployment) is whether it increases stress. Thus, poverty is less stressful *if* low income is temporary and the family's net worth (home ownership, investments, etc.) buffers the strain (Yeung & Conley, 2008). However, ongoing economic hardship increases stress, and adults may become tense and hostile (Conger et al., 2002; Parke et al., 2004). Thus, the *reaction* to poverty, not the sheer monthly income, is crucial.

Reaction to wealth may also be harmful. Children in high-income families develop more than their share of developmental problems, such as depression, eating disorders, and drug addiction. One reason may be parental pressure, causing children to develop externalizing and internalizing problems (see Chapter 6) (Ansary & Luthar, 2009).

Some intervention programs aim to teach parents to be more encouraging and patient (McLoyd et al., 2006). In low-income families, however, this focus may be misplaced. Poverty itself—with attendant problems such as inadequate schools, poor health, and the threat of homelessness—causes stress (Duncan et al., 2010).

Remember the dynamic-systems perspective described in Chapter 1? That perspective applies to poverty: Multigenerational research finds that poverty is both a cause and a symptom—parents with less education and immature emotional control are more likely to have difficulty finding employment and raising their children, and then low income adds to those difficulties (Schofield et al., 2011).

If that is so, more income might improve family functioning. Some support for this idea comes from research indicating that children in single-mother households do much better if their father pays child support, even if he is not actively involved in the child's daily life (Huang, 2009).

Nations that subsidize single parents (e.g., Austria and Iceland) also have smaller achievement gaps between low- and middle-SES children on the TIMSS. This is suggestive, but controversial and value-laden. Some developmentalists report that raising income does *not,* by itself, improve parenting (L. M. Berger et al., 2009).

CONFLICT There is no controversy about conflict. Every researcher agrees that family conflict harms children, especially when adults fight about child rearing. Such fights are more common in stepfamilies, divorced families, and extended families. Of course, nuclear families are not immune: Children suffer especially if their parents abuse each other or if one parent walks out, leaving the other distraught.

The impact of genes on children's reaction to conflict was explored in a longitudinal study of family conflict in 1,734 married parents, each with a twin who was also a parent and part of the research. The twins' husbands or wives, and an adolescent from each family, were also studied. Genetics as well as conflict could be analyzed, since 388 of the pairs of twins were monozygotic and 479 were dizygotic. Each adolescent was compared with a cousin, who had half (if the parent was monozygotic) or a quarter (if the parent was dizygotic) of the same genes (Schermerhorn et al., 2011).

Participants were 5,202 individuals, one-third of them adult twins, one-third married to a twin, and one-third adolescents with a twin parent. Conflict was assessed with a questionnaire that included items such as, "We fight a lot in our family."

The researchers found that although genes had some effect, conflict itself was the main influence on the child's well-being. For example, whether teenagers became delinquent depended less on the genes they inherited than on the conflict in their families. Open conflict was especially detrimental, leading to externalizing problems in the boys and internalizing problems in the girls.

Simple disagreement (assessed by both members of each couple) did not much harm the child—unless the dispute erupted in open conflict (such as yelling in front of the children) or divorce (Schermerhorn et al., 2011).

The general conclusion was that conflict had a greater impact than genes. However, one measure did show genetic influence—the adolescents' (not the parents') estimate of how much conflict the family had. From this, the researchers suggest that some teenagers, for temperamental reasons, are more sensitive to conflict than others.

KEYpoints

- Parents influence their children's development primarily in nonshared ways that differ for each child.
- During middle childhood, families ideally provide basic necessities and foster learning opportunities, self-respect, friendships, harmony, and stability.
- Every family structure can support child development, but children from nuclear families, on average, are most likely to develop well.
- Family poverty and conflict are usually harmful to 6- to 11-year-olds, although genes and culture can provide some protection.
- When parents are stressed, by poverty, divorce, or anything else, they are less likely to nurture children well.

child culture
The particular habits, styles, and values that reflect the set of rules and rituals that characterize children as distinct from adult society.

The Peer Group

Peers become increasingly important in middle childhood. Younger children learn from their friends, but egocentrism buffers them from rejection. By age 8, however, children are painfully aware of their classmates' opinions, judgments, and accomplishments. Social comparison, already explained at the beginning of this chapter, is one consequence of concrete operational thought.

The Culture of Children

Peer relationships, unlike adult–child relationships, involve partners who negotiate, compromise, share, and defend themselves as equals. Consequently, children learn social lessons from one another that grown-ups cannot teach. Adults sometimes command obedience, sometimes are playfully docile, but they are always much older and bigger, with the values and experiences of their own cohort, not the child's.

Child culture includes the particular rules and behaviors that are passed down to younger children from slightly older ones; it includes not only fashions and gestures but also values and rituals. Jump-rope rhymes, insults, and superstitions are often part of the peer culture. Even nursery games echo child culture.

How to Play Boys teach each other the rituals and rules of engagement. The bigger boy shown here could hurt the smaller one, but he won't; their culture forbids it in such situations.

One example is "Ring around the rosy/Pocketful of posy/Ashes, ashes/We all fall down." A popular interpretation is that it originated with children coping with the bubonic plague (the Black Death), which killed about one-third of the population of Europe in the middle of the fourteenth century (Kastenbaum, 2006). (*Rosy* may be short for *rosary; posies* may be the herbs people carried to ward off the plague.)

However, that may not be the origin at all, since "Ring around the Rosy" was not published (and presumably not said) until 500 years later. Instead that rhyme may have been a nonsense saying that gave devout children a chance to hold hands and fall on each other in the nineteenth century, when dancing was forbidden for them. In any case, children enjoy rhymes, and adults try to figure out what they mean.

Throughout the world, the child culture encourages independence from adults. Classmates pity those (especially boys) whose parents kiss them ("mama's boy"), tease those who please the teachers ("teacher's pet," "suck-up"), and despise those who betray children to adults ("tattletale," "grasser," "snitch," "rat"). Keeping secrets is always part of the culture of children, and parents always want to know about their children's lives (Gillis, 2008).

Pity the Teacher The culture of children encourages pranks, jokes, and the defiance of authorities at school. At the same time, as social cognition develops, many children secretly feel empathy for their teachers.

A clash thus develops between the generations. In another example, many children refuse to wear the clothes their parents buy for them because they are too loose, too tight, too long, too short, or wrong in color, style, brand, or some other aspect that adults ignore. Such cohort differences may be multiplied if grandparents are involved, who may be shocked at what their grandchildren wear, say, or do.

The culture of children is not always benign. For instance, because children seek to communicate with their peers, immigrant parents proudly note that their children speak a second language and that they depend on their children for translation. However, sometimes children's quickness to pick up their peers' language is less welcome. Parents of every group may be distressed when their children spout their peers' curses, accents, and slang.

In seeking independence from parents, children find friends who defy authority (J. Snyder et al., 2005), sometimes harmlessly (passing a note during class), sometimes not (shoplifting, cigarette smoking).

WELCOME BACK CLASS!

IT'S AN ESPRESSO LATTE, I THOUGHT YOU MIGHT NEED IT.

FRIENDSHIP AND SOCIAL ACCEPTANCE Children want to be liked; they learn faster and feel happier when they have friends. Indeed, if they had to choose between being friendless but popular (looked up to by many peers) or having close friends but being unpopular (ignored by most classmates), most would prefer having friends. This is particularly true for children younger than 10; in early adolescence, popularity may become the priority (LaFontana & Cillessen, 2010).

Friendships become more intense and intimate as social cognition and effortful control advance. By the end of middle childhood, friends demand more of one another, including loyalty. It can be devastating when a friendship ends, partly because making new friends is difficult. Gender differences persist in activities (girls converse more, boys play active games), but both boys and girls want best friends. Having no close friend at age 11 predicts depression at age 13 (Brendgen et al., 2010).

Most children learn how to be a good friend. For example, when fifth-graders were asked how they would react if other children teased their friend, almost all said they would ask their friend to do something fun with them and would reassure the friend that "things like that happen to everyone" (Rose & Asher, 2004).

Older children tend to choose best friends whose interests, values, and backgrounds are similar to their own. By the end of middle childhood, close friendships are almost always between children of the same sex, age, ethnicity, and socioeconomic status. This occurs not because children become more prejudiced over the course of middle childhood (they do not) but because they seek friends who understand and agree with them. Remember: Harmony, not conflict, is sought.

Academic achievement is also valued in middle childhood. From ages 7 to 10, one longitudinal study found that higher-achieving children have more friends, as well as classmates who want to be their friends. They are not necessarily the most popular children, but their friends are themselves high achievers (Véronneau et al., 2010).

POPULAR AND UNPOPULAR CHILDREN It seems universally true that children seek close friends, yet it is also true that culture and cohort affect which qualities are desirable. Academic achievement is less admired if a particular child is the only one who attains it. In North America, shy children are not popular, but a 1990 school survey in Shanghai found that shy children were respected and often well liked (X. Chen et al., 1992).

That is a cultural difference, but a cohort difference occurred over 12 years in Shanghai. As assertiveness became more valued in Chinese culture, a survey from the same schools found that shy children were less popular than their shy predecessors had been (X. Chen et al., 2005). A later third study found that, in rural China, shyness was still valued and predicted adult adjustment (X. Chen et al., 2009). Obviously, cohort and context matter.

At least in the United States, over the years of middle childhood two types of popular children and three types of unpopular children become apparent (see Figure 8.2). Throughout childhood, children who are "kind, trustworthy, cooperative" are well liked. The second type of popular children emerges around fifth grade, when children who are "athletic, cool, dominant, arrogant, and . . . aggressive" are sometimes popular (Cillessen & Mayeux, 2004a, p. 147; Rodkin & Roisman, 2010).

As for the three types of unpopular children, some are *neglected,* but not actively rejected by peers. They are ignored, but not shunned. The neglected child does not enjoy school but is psychologically unharmed, especially if the child has a supportive family and outstanding talent (e.g., in music or the arts) (Sandstrom & Zakriski, 2004).

The other two types of unpopular children may be psychologically harmed. Specifically, they are at increased risk of depression and uncontrolled anger over the years of middle childhood. One type is **aggressive-rejected,** disliked because they are antagonistic and confrontational; the other type is **withdrawn-rejected,** disliked

aggressive-rejected
Rejected by peers because of antagonistic, confrontational behavior.

withdrawn-rejected
Rejected by peers because of timid, withdrawn, and anxious behavior.

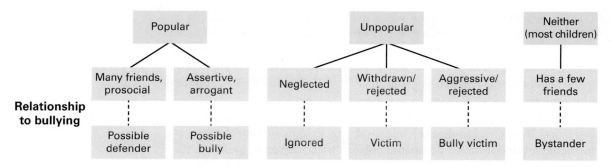

Popular		Unpopular			Neither (most children)
Many friends, prosocial	Assertive, arrogant	Neglected	Withdrawn/rejected	Aggressive/rejected	Has a few friends

Relationship to bullying

Possible defender	Possible bully	Ignored	Victim	Bully victim	Bystander

FIGURE 8.2 Popularity Most children are neither popular nor unpopular, and the arrogant popular type is not usually evident until the end of middle childhood. The relationship to bullying is shown as a dotted line because these types are not always involved in bullying—it depends on the school culture.

bullying
Repeated, systematic efforts to inflict harm through physical, verbal, or social attack on a weaker person.

because they are timid and anxious. Children of these two types have much in common, often misinterpreting social situations, lacking emotional regulation, and experiencing mistreatment at home. They may become bullies or victims, a topic discussed next.

Bullying

From a developmental perspective, childhood bullying is connected to many other aspects of aggression, including maltreatment at home and delinquency in the community (discussed in Chapters 6 and 10). Here we focus on bullies and victims in school.

Bullying is defined as repeated, systematic attacks intended to harm those who are unable or unlikely to defend themselves. It occurs in every nation, in every community, and in every kind of school (religious or secular, public or private, progressive or traditional, large or small). Although adults are often unaware of it, children recognize it as common. As one girl said, "There's a little bit of bully in everyone" (Guerra et al., 2011, p. 303).

Bullying may be of four types:

1. *Physical* (hitting, pinching, or kicking)
2. *Verbal* (teasing, taunting, or name-calling)
3. *Relational* (destroying peer acceptance and friendship)
4. *Cyberbullying* (using electronic means to harm another)

The first three are common in primary school and begin even earlier, in preschool. Cyberbullying is a particularly devastating form of relational bullying, more common in secondary school than in primary school, and is discussed in Chapter 9.

A key word in the definition of bullying is *repeated*. Almost everyone experiences an isolated attack or is called a derogatory name at some point in middle childhood. Victims of bullying, however, endure shameful experiences again and again—being forced almost daily to hand over lunch money, laugh at insults, drink milk mixed with detergent, and so on—with no one defending them. Victims tend to be "cautious, sensitive, quiet . . . lonely and abandoned at school. As a rule, they do not have a single good friend in their class" (Olweus et al., 1999, p. 15).

Some adults think that victims are particularly ugly or odd, but this is not usually true. Victims are chosen because of their personality and isolation; they may be teased about their appearance, but it is their emotional vulnerability that attracts the bully. As one boy said:

> You can get bullied because you are weak or annoying or because you are different. Kids with big ears get bullied. Dorks get bullied. You can also get bullied because you think too much of yourself and try to show off. Teacher's pet gets bullied. If you say the right answer too many times in class you can get bullied. There are lots of popular groups who bully each other and other groups, but you can get bullied

within your group too. If you do not want to get bullied, you have to stay under the radar, but then you might feel sad because no one pays attention to you.

[quoted in Guerra et al., 2011, p. 306]

Remember the three types of unpopular children? Neglected children are not victimized; they are ignored, "under the radar." But if their family is supportive, they may be emotionally strong (Bowes et al., 2010).

Rejected children, however, often have trouble at home as well. Most of them are withdrawn-rejected, but some are aggressive-rejected. The latter are **bully-victims** (or *provocative victims*) (Unnever, 2005), "the most strongly disliked members of the peer group," with neither friends nor sympathizers (Sandstrom & Zakriski, 2004, p. 110). One study found that teachers tend to mistreat bully-victims, making their problems worse (Khoury-Kassabri, 2009).

Unlike bully-victims, most bullies are *not* rejected. Although some have low self-esteem, others are proud; they bully because they are pleased with themselves and they find bullying cool (Guerra et al., 2011). Often bullies have a few admiring friends, more as they refine their social perception. Typically, bullying is a social event, as bullies show off their power (not true for cyberbullying but very true for physical bullying).

Bullies usually pick victims who are already rejected by most classmates (Veenstra et al., 2010), who have no friends to stick up for them, and who cannot alone fight back effectively. That is true for all forms of bullying, relational as well as physical, for both sexes, but there are some sex differences in bullying type. Boy bullies are often big; they use physical aggression on smaller, weaker boys. By contrast, girl bullies are sharp-tongued, preferring verbal aggression. They mock or spread rumors about shyer, more soft-spoken girls.

Remember the latency period, in which children are involved with others of their own sex, both as friends and as victims. Bullies generally turn on their own, seeking admiration from other boys or other girls. Occasionally, boys accept other boys who bully girls, but girls almost never bully boys in middle childhood. This changes at puberty: Boys are no longer admired for bullying girls, but girls are allowed to bully boys as a defense against (or expression of?) sexual feelings (Veenstra et al., 2010).

CAUSES AND CONSEQUENCES OF BULLYING Bullying may originate with a genetic predisposition or a brain abnormality. When a toddler is aggressive, parents, teachers, and peers usually teach that child to rein in those impulses, developing emotional regulation (Chapter 6) and effortful control. However, the opposite may occur (Granic & Patterson, 2006). Young children become more aggressive if their families create insecure attachment, provide a stressful home life, are ineffective at discipline, or include hostile siblings.

Peers are influential as well. Some peer groups approve of bullying, and children in those groups entertain their classmates by mocking, excluding, punching, and insulting one another (N. E. Werner & Hill, 2010). On the other hand, when students themselves disapprove of bullying, its incidence is reduced (Guerra & Williams, 2010).

Young bullies and victims sometimes escape serious depression or other harm. Both bullies and victims can be identified in first grade and "need active guidance and remediation" before their behavior patterns become truly destructive (Leadbeater & Hoglund, 2009, p. 857). Unless bullies are deterred, they and their victims risk lower school achievement and relationship difficulties later on. Bystanders suffer, too (Ma et al., 2009; Monks & Coyne, 2011; Nishina & Juvonen, 2005; Rivers et al., 2009).

CAN BULLYING BE STOPPED? Most victimized children find ways to halt ongoing bullying—by ignoring, retaliating, defusing, or avoiding. A study of older children who were bullied one year but not the next indicated that finding new friends was

bully-victim
Someone who attacks others and who is attacked as well. (Also called *provocative victims* because they do things that elicit bullying.)

PETER TITMUSS / ALAMY

HENRY KING / GETTY IMAGES

Who Suffers More? The 12-year-old girl and the 10-year-old boy both seem to be bullying younger children, but their attacks differ. Some developmentalists think a verbal assault is more painful than a physical one because it lingers for years.

Buddies, Not Bullies Within the past two decades, virtually every U.S. state has passed laws against bullying, and many schools have specific anti-bullying curricula. Positive demonstrations by the children themselves (as shown here by Noel Rodriguez and Jonathan Almendarez, who have just acted out a skit showing how to stop a bully) are better than adult lectures, laws, or punishments.

OBSERVATION QUIZ

These boys share a characteristic that might make them particularly vulnerable to bullying. What is it? (see answer, page 310) →

✦ ESPECIALLY FOR Parents of an Accused Bully Another parent has told you that your child is a bully. Your child denies it and explains that the other child doesn't mind being teased. What should you do? (see response, page 311) →

crucial (P. K. Smith et al., 2004). Friendships help individual victims, but what can be done to halt bullying altogether?

We know what does *not* work: increasing students' awareness, instituting zero tolerance for fighting, or putting troubled students together in a therapy group or a classroom (Baldry & Farrington, 2007; Monks & Coyne, 2011). This last measure tends to make daily life easier for some teachers, but it increases aggression.

We also know that each specific school, with their teachers, students, and practices, can make much more difference than the macrosystem can (such as a state policy against bullying, or a national value). For example, a study of over a thousand schools in Colombia (where guerilla and paramilitary troops have fought for decades) found that regional poverty, population density, and homicide rate did *not* correlate with bullying nearly as much as did hostility and lack of empathy within each school (Chaux et al., 2009).

Empathy can be taught via cooperative learning, friendship encouragement, and school pride. A "whole school" approach—including all teachers and bystanders, parents and aides, bullies and victims—seems to be most effective. For example, a Colorado study of children with high self-esteem found that when the overall school climate seemed to encourage learning, friendship, and cooperation, children with high self-esteem were unlikely to be bullies; yet when the school climate was hostile, those with high self-esteem were often bullies (Gendron et al., 2011).

Peers are crucial: If they are taught to notice bullying, become aware, and yet do nothing (some antibullying programs don't teach them what to do), that is no help. However, if peers empathize with victims and refuse to admire bullies, that reduces classroom aggression (Salmivalli, 2010).

Efforts to change the entire school are credited for recent successes in decreasing bullying in 29 schools in England (e.g., Cross et al., 2010), throughout Norway, in Finland (Kärnä et al., 2011), and often in the United States (Allen, 2010; Limber, 2011). A review of all research on successful ways to halt bullying finds the following (Berger, 2007):

● Everyone in the school must change, not just the identified bullies.
● Intervention is more effective in the earlier grades.
● Evaluation is critical: Programs that seem good on paper might not work.

This final point merits special emphasis. Longitudinal research finds that some programs reduce bullying and others increase it. Results depend on the age of the children, the strategies employed, and the outcome measures used (peer reports, teacher reports, suspensions, etc.). Objective follow-up suggests that, although well-intentioned efforts sometimes fail, bullying can be reduced.

KEYpoints

● Schoolchildren want and need friends to encourage and support them and to convey the culture of children.
● Some children are popular, others not, primarily for their behavior and degree of conformity.
● Bullying is common in middle childhood, occurring in every school, in every nation.
● Bullying can be reduced by an effort that engages everyone in a school—children, teachers, parents, principals—to change the school culture so that empathy and friendship increase.

Children's Moral Values

Although the origins of morality are debatable (see Chapter 6), there is no doubt that middle childhood is prime time for moral development. These are:

> years of eager, lively searching on the part of children . . . as they try to understand things, to figure them out, but also to weigh the rights and wrongs. . . . This is the time for growth of the moral imagination, fueled constantly by the willingness, the eagerness of children to put themselves in the shoes of others.
>
> *[Coles, 1997, p. 99]*

That optimistic assessment seems validated by detailed research. In middle childhood, children are quite capable of making moral judgments, differentiating universal principles from mere conventional norms (Turiel, 2008). Empirical studies show that throughout middle childhood, children readily suggest moral arguments to distinguish right from wrong (Killen, 2007).

Many forces drive children's growing interest in such issues. Three of them are: (1) peer culture, (2) personal experience, and (3) empathy. As already explained, part of the culture of children involves moral values, such as being loyal to friends and protecting children from adults. A child's personal experiences also matter. For example, children in multiethnic schools are better able to use principles to argue against prejudice than are children who attend ethnically homogeneous schools (Killen et al., 2006).

Empathy becomes stronger in middle childhood because children are more aware of one another. This increasing perception can backfire, however. One example was just described: Bullies become adept at picking victims who are rejected by classmates, and then others admire the bullies (Veenstra et al., 2010). However, the increase in empathy during middle childhood at least allows the *possibility* of moral judgment that notices, and defends, children who are unfairly rejected.

Obviously, ethical advances are not automatic. Children who are slow to develop theory of mind—which, as you remember from Chapter 5, is affected by family and culture—are also slow to develop empathy (Caravita et al., 2010).

The authors of a study of 7-year-olds conclude that "moral *competence* may be a universal human characteristic, but that it takes a situation with specific demand characteristics to translate this competence into actual prosocial performance" (van IJzendoorn et al., 2010, p. 1). In other words, school-age children can think and act morally, but they do not always do so.

Empathy Building Look at their facial expressions, not just their matching hats and gloves. For this 9-year-old sister and 7-year-old brother, moral development is apparent. This is not necessarily the case for all siblings, however; imagine the same behavior but with angry expressions.

Moral Reasoning

Much of the developmental research on children's moral thinking began with Piaget's descriptions of the rules used by children as they play (Piaget, 1932/1997). This led to Lawrence Kohlberg's description of cognitive stages of morality (Kohlberg, 1963).

KOHLBERG'S LEVELS OF MORAL THOUGHT Kohlberg described three levels of moral reasoning and two stages at each level (see Table 8.3), with parallels to Piaget's stages of cognition (see also Table 1.6).

- **Preconventional moral reasoning** is similar to preoperational thought in that it is egocentric; children seek pleasure and avoid pain rather than focusing on social concerns.

- **Conventional moral reasoning** parallels concrete operational thought in that it relates to specific practices; children try to follow what parents, teachers, and friends do.

- **Postconventional moral reasoning** uses formal operational thought; people use logic, questioning "what is" in order to decide "what should be."

preconventional moral reasoning Kohlberg's first level of moral reasoning, emphasizing rewards and punishments.

conventional moral reasoning Kohlberg's second level of moral reasoning, emphasizing social rules.

postconventional moral reasoning Kohlberg's third level of moral reasoning, emphasizing moral principles.

> **TABLE 8.3 Kohlberg's Three Levels and Six Stages of Moral Reasoning**
>
> **Level I: Preconventional Moral Reasoning**
> The goal is to get rewards and avoid punishments; this is a self-centered level.
>
> - *Stage one: Might makes right* (a punishment-and-obedience orientation). The most important value is to maintain the appearance of obedience to authority, avoiding punishment while still advancing self-interest. Don't get caught!
>
> - *Stage two: Look out for number one* (an instrumental and relativist orientation). Each person tries to take care of his or her own needs. The reason to be nice to other people is so that they will be nice to you.
>
> **Level II: Conventional Moral Reasoning**
> Emphasis is placed on social rules; this is a parent- and community-centered level.
>
> - *Stage three: Good girl and nice boy.* Proper behavior pleases other people. Social approval is more important than any specific reward.
>
> - *Stage four: Law and order.* Proper behavior means being a dutiful citizen and obeying the laws set down by society, even when no police are nearby.
>
> **Level III: Postconventional Moral Reasoning**
> Emphasis is placed on moral principles; this level is centered on ideals.
>
> - *Stage five: Social contract.* Obey social rules because they benefit everyone and are established by mutual agreement. If the rules become destructive or if one party doesn't live up to the agreement, the contract is no longer binding. Under some circumstances, disobeying the law is moral.
>
> - *Stage six: Universal ethical principles.* Universal principles, not individual situations (level I) or community practices (level II), determine right and wrong. Ethical values (such as "life is sacred") are established by individual reflection and may contradict egocentric (level I) or social and community (level II) values.

According to Kohlberg, cognitive development advances morality. During middle childhood, children's answers shift from being preconventional to conventional: Concrete thought and peer experiences help children move past the first two stages (level I) to the next two (level II). Postconventional reasoning does not appear until later, if at all.

Kohlberg posed moral dilemmas to school-age boys (and eventually girls, teenagers, and adults). The story of a poor man named Heinz, whose wife was dying, was one such dilemma. A local druggist sold the only cure for 10 times what it cost to make.

> Heinz went to everyone he knew to borrow the money, but he could only get together about half of what it cost. He told the druggist that his wife was dying and asked him to sell it cheaper or let him pay later. But the druggist said "no." The husband got desperate and broke into the man's store to steal the drug for his wife. Should the husband have done that? Why?
>
> *[Kohlberg, 1963, p. 19]*

That "why?" is crucial. Kohlberg judged moral development not by the answers but by the *reasons* for the answers. For instance, someone might say that the husband should steal the drug because he needs his wife to care for him (preconventional), or because people will blame him if he lets his wife die (conventional), or because human life is more important than obeying the law (postconventional).

CRITICISMS OF KOHLBERG Kohlberg has been criticized for not appreciating cultural or gender differences. For example, he valued abstract justice more than family or cultural loyalty: Not every culture agrees (Sherblom, 2008). Furthermore, his original participants were all boys, which may have led him to discount female values of nurturance and relationships (Gilligan, 1982).

Another criticism arises from a developmental perspective: Kohlberg did not recognize that although children's morality differs from that of adults, the children's distinct values may be equally valid. Children question adult rules that seem unfair (Turiel, 2006, 2008)—one example of their moral and postconventional thought.

In one respect, however, Kohlberg was undeniably correct. Children use their intellectual abilities to justify their moral actions.

The role of cognition was evident when trios of 8- to 18-year-olds (each trio about the same age) were asked to decide how to divide a sum of money with another trio of children. Some groups chose to share equally; other groups were more selfish. There were no age differences in the actual decisions, but there were age differences in the arguments voiced. Older children suggested more complex rationalizations for their choices, both selfish and altruistic (Gummerum et al., 2008).

What Children Value

Many lines of research have shown that children develop their own morality, guided by peers, parents, and culture (Turiel, 2006). Some prosocial values are evident long before middle childhood. Among these are caring for close family members, cooperating with other children, and not hurting anyone intentionally (Eisenberg et al., 2006).

As children become more aware of themselves and others in middle childhood, they realize that one person's values may conflict with another's. Concrete operational

ANSWER TO **OBSERVATION QUIZ** (from page 308) They are both Latino, but that is not it. They are also both deaf. Although any child in any school could become a bully, those who are disabled in some way are more likely to be victims.

cognition, which gives children the ability to use logic about what they see, propels them to think and act ethically (Turiel, 2006), to recognize immorality in their peers (Abrams et al., 2008) and, later, in their parents, themselves, and their culture.

When child culture conflicts with adult morality, children often align themselves with peers. A child might lie to a teacher in order to protect a friend, for instance. On a broader level, one study found that 98 percent of a group of children believed that no child should be excluded from a sports team because of gender or race, even when adult society was less tolerant. Some of the same children, however, justified excluding another child from a friendship circle for such reasons (Killen et al., 2002).

The conflict between the morality of children and that of adults is evident in the value that children place on education. Adults usually prize school, but children may encourage one another to play hooky, cheat on tests, or, later, to drop out. If a child sees another child cheating, he or she is unlikely to tell the teacher—for moral reasons! Three common values among 6- to 11-year-olds are the following:

1. Protect your friends.
2. Don't tell adults what is happening.
3. Don't be too different from your peers.

These three values can explain both apparent boredom and overt defiance, as well as standards of dress that mystify adults (such as jeans so loose that they fall off or so tight that they impede digestion—both styles worn by my children, who grew up in different cohorts).

Given what is known about middle childhood, it is no surprise that children do not echo adult morality. This discrepancy broadens as puberty begins, when some boys wear their pants so low that their underwear shows, and some girls wear transparent blouses that show their bras—to the horror of their grandparents.

Fortunately, peers help one another develop morals. You have already seen this in the discussion of bullies. The best way to stop a bully is for bystanders to take action, defending the victim and isolating the bully. This is exactly what occurs when the whole-school approach is effective: The adults do not lecture (that can backfire), but everyone—children, parents, and school staff alike—works together to stop bullying.

Since bullies lack empathy, they need peers to teach them that their actions are not appreciated (many bullies believe their actions are admired). During middle childhood, morality can be scaffolded just as cognitive skills are, with mentors—peers or adults—structuring moral dilemmas to advance moral understanding (Nucci & Turiel, 2009; Turner & Berkowitz, 2005).

RESPONSE FOR Parents of an Accused Bully (from page 308) The future is ominous if the charges are true. Your child's denial is a sign that there is a problem. (An innocent child would be worried about the misperception instead of categorically denying that any problem exists.) You might ask the teacher what the school is doing about bullying. Family counseling might help. Because bullies often have friends who egg them on, you may need to monitor your child's friendships and perhaps befriend the victim. Talk matters over with your child. Ignoring the situation might lead to heartache later on. ●

A VIEW FROM SCIENCE

Developing Moral Values

Many adults wonder how best to instill moral values in children. The first thought is to punish immoral behavior, the authoritarian approach explained in Chapter 6. Unfortunately, that stops overt behavior but not covert actions. Children may become sneaky, which is not at all what the adults intended. Ideally, children internalize standards, doing the right thing even when being caught is unlikely.

On that Kohlberg has a point: It would be good if children could think of the moral way to behave, using their cognitive advances to internalize standards. By middle childhood, children should avoid stealing because they believe it is wrong, not because they will be punished for doing so. How do they learn that?

Parents and other adults sometimes lecture children, sometimes hope children will follow the adults' examples, and sometimes discuss issues, expressing opinions but also listening to their children. What works?

A detailed examination of the effect of conversation on morality began with an update of one of Piaget's moral issues: whether *retribution* (hurting the transgressor) or *restitution* (restoring what was lost) is best when someone does something wrong. Piaget believed that restitution was the more advanced punishment; he also found that between ages 8 and 10, children progress from retribution to restitution (Piaget, 1932).

Following Piaget's hypothesis, researchers asked 133 9-year-olds a question:

> Late one afternoon there was a boy who was playing with a ball on his own in the garden. His dad saw him playing with it and asked him not to play with it so near the house because it might break a window. The boy didn't really listen to his dad, and carried on playing near the house. Then suddenly, the ball bounced up high and broke the window in the boy's room. His dad heard the noise and came to see what had happened. The father wonders what would be the fairest way to punish the boy. He thinks of two punishments. The first is to say: "Now, you didn't do as I asked. You will have to pay for the window to be mended, and I am going to take the money from your pocket money." The second is to say: "Now, you didn't do as I asked. As a punishment you have to go to your room and stay there for the rest of the evening." Which of these punishments do you think is the fairest?
>
> *[Leman & Björnberg, 2010, p. 962]*

The 9-year-olds were split equally, half choosing retribution (go to his room) and half choosing restitution (pay for the window). Then the researchers paired 48 of them with a child who answered the other way, and each pair was asked to talk together to try to reach agreement. Six pairs were boy–boy, six were boy–girl with the boy favoring restitution, six were boy–girl with the girl favoring restitution, and six were girl–girl. As a control, the rest of the children were not paired and did not discuss the dilemma.

The conversations typically took only five minutes, and the retribution side was more often chosen—which Piaget would consider a moral backslide. However, when the children were queried again, two weeks and then eight weeks later, their responses changed toward more advanced, restitution thinking (see Figure 8.3). This occurred even for the children who had not been paired to discuss the problem, but it was particularly true for the children who had engaged in conversation.

In this study, the boy–boy pairs used a discussion style that some adults would consider immature, if not immoral. They had many more hostile interruptions ("That's crazy," "You're stupid") than did the other pairs. However, those interruptions did not impede advancement of thought. Instead, such seeming hostility might have been the boys' conventional way of interacting, expected by their partners and not taken as mean.

The main conclusion from this study was that children's "conversation on a topic may stimulate a process of individual reflection that triggers developmental advances" (Leman & Björnberg, 2010, p. 969). Parents and teachers take note: Raising moral issues, and letting children talk about them, may advance morality—not immediately, but soon.

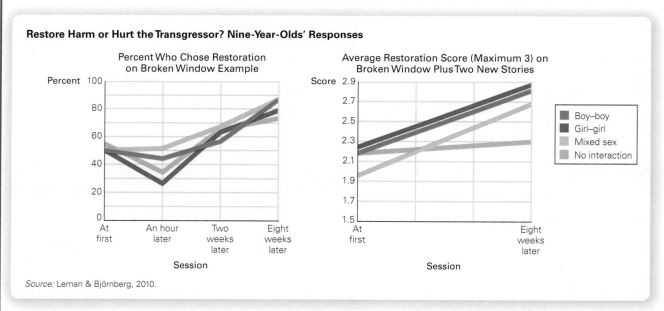

Restore Harm or Hurt the Transgressor? Nine-Year-Olds' Responses

Source: Leman & Björnberg, 2010.

FIGURE 8.3 Benefits of Time and Talking The graph on the left shows that most children, immediately after their initial punitive response, became even more likely to seek punishment rather than to repair damage. However, after some time and reflection, they affirmed the response Piaget would consider more mature. The graph on the right indicates that children who had talked about the broken window example moved toward restorative justice even in examples they had not heard before, which was not true for those who had not talked about the first story.

The Morality of Child Labor

Now consider the tire-changing boy from the opening story of this chapter. Child labor is deemed immoral by the United Nations, but that international body has found it hard to educate children about their rights or to convince nations to enforce child labor standards (Print et al., 2008). Some child labor is clearly hazardous, such as working in mines with cancer-causing pollutants or becoming sex workers with no opportunity for escape. Even for these occupations, nations do not always protect children as they should (Diallo et al., 2010).

Apparently, work done by children is judged as immoral in some places and at some times yet moral in others. A shocking U.S. example comes from the early twentieth century, when moral crusaders took children from their impoverished urban families and sent them to farm families as child labor. The thought was that hard work and fresh air would help them become upright, moral adults—unlike their parents.

The phrase "put up for adoption" came from the practice of making them stand up on railroad platforms at towns in the Midwest, where farmers could choose which child to adopt. No questions were asked or background checks performed: It was assumed that the children would be better off on the Midwestern farms than in the East Coast cities (Kahan, 2006).

Thankfully, that practice stopped by about 1917, but obviously the morality of child labor varies from culture to culture and cohort to cohort. Even today, some children have extensive chores to do around the house, while others have none. Parents on both sides contend that the others are cruel, or at least misguided.

To decide whether that young tire-changer should be helping his father would require finding out whether his life situation satisfies the five needs that are thought to be universal during middle childhood. Are his material needs met, is he learning in school, does he have friends, is he proud of himself, is his work keeping his family harmonious and stable? If the answer to these questions is yes, then my student Tiffany's understandable shock, or the father's acceptance of child labor, may reflect their respective cultures, not the boy's welfare.

The moral lesson of this chapter, then, is that the psychosocial development of children must be carefully assessed, child by child. As you have seen, self-esteem is a positive attribute that may become destructive if it is too high; married-couple families are usually good for children but not always; friends protect victims, but sometimes they encourage bullies. As with all of development, individual children, families, and cultures vary, and that must be taken into account before conclusions are drawn.

Protecting His Brain? No. That lump on his head makes it easier to balance the heavy rocks this boy carries to the stone crusher in Gauhati, India. Such child labor not only "interferes with education" but also is directly "hazardous" to the head—and is thus forbidden by the United Nations on two counts.

KEY points

- During middle childhood, children are intensely concerned about moral issues.
- Kohlberg believed that cognition and morality advance together, as children gradually become less self-centered and more concerned about universal principles.
- Children learn from the morality and customs of their peers and may choose loyalty to friends over cultural or familial values.
- Ongoing conversation and discussion seems to be the best way for children to internalize a moral perspective.

SUMMARY

The Nature of the Child

1. All theories of development acknowledge that school-age children become more independent and capable in many ways.

2. Erikson emphasized industry, when children busily strive to master various tasks. If they are unable to do so, they feel inferior. Freud described a latency period, when psychosexual needs are quiet.

3. Children develop their self-concept during middle childhood, basing it on a more realistic assessment of their competence than they had in earlier years.

4. Children need to develop pride in themselves and in their background, although high self-esteem is not valued in every culture.

5. Both daily hassles and major stresses take a toll on children, with accumulated stresses more likely to impair development than any single event on its own. The child's interpretation of the situation and the availability of supportive adults, peers, and institutions aid resilience.

Families and Children

6. Families influence children in many ways, as do genes and peers. Although most siblings share a childhood home and parents, each sibling experiences different (nonshared) circumstances within the family.

7. The five functions of a supportive family are to satisfy children's physical needs; to encourage learning; to nurture friendships; to foster self-respect; and to provide a safe, stable, and harmonious home.

8. The most common family structure worldwide is the nuclear family, usually with other relatives nearby. Other two-parent families include adoptive, same-sex, grandparent, and stepfamilies, each of which sometimes functions well for children. However, each also has vulnerabilities.

9. Generally, it seems better for children to live with two parents rather than one because a parental alliance can support children's development. Single-parent families tend to be less stable, with changes in where they live and who belongs to the family.

10. Income affects family function. Poor children are at greater risk for emotional and behavioral problems because the stresses that often accompany poverty hinder effective parenting. High income may be stressful as well. No matter what the family SES, instability and conflict are harmful.

The Peer Group

11. Peers teach crucial social skills during middle childhood. Each cohort of children has a culture, passed down from slightly older children. Close friends are wanted and needed.

12. Popular children may be cooperative and easy to get along with or may be competitive and aggressive. Much depends on the age and culture of the children.

13. Rejected children may be neglected, aggressive, or withdrawn. Aggressive and withdrawn children have difficulty with social cognition; their interpretation of the normal give-and-take of childhood is impaired.

14. Bullying of all sorts—physical, verbal, relational, and cyber— is common, with long-term consequences for both bullies and victims. Bullies themselves may be admired, which makes their behavior more difficult to stop.

15. Overall, a multifaceted, long-term, whole-school approach, with parents, teachers, and bystanders working together, seems the best way to halt bullying. Careful evaluation is needed to discover if a particular strategy changes the school culture.

Children's Moral Values

16. School-age children seek to differentiate right from wrong. Peer values, cultural standards, and family practices are all part of their personal morality.

17. Kohlberg described three levels of moral reasoning, each related to cognitive maturity. His theory has been criticized for focusing too much on abstractions.

18. When values conflict, children often choose loyalty to peers over adult standards of behavior. When children discuss moral issues with other children, they develop more thoughtful answers to moral questions.

KEY TERMS

aggressive-rejected (p. 305)
bullying (p. 306)
bully-victim (p. 307)
child culture (p. 304)
conventional moral reasoning (p. 309)
extended family (p. 294)
family function (p. 292)
family structure (p. 292)
industry versus inferiority (p. 284)
latency (p. 285)
nuclear family (p. 294)
polygamous family (p. 294)
postconventional moral reasoning (p. 309)
preconventional moral reasoning (p. 309)
resilience (p. 287)
single-parent family (p. 294)
social comparison (p. 286)
withdrawn-rejected (p. 305)

WHAT HAVE YOU LEARNED?

1. How do Erikson's stages of cognition for school-age children and for preschool children differ?

2. How does a school-age child develop a sense of self?

3. Why is social comparison particularly powerful during middle childhood?

4. What factors help a child become resilient?

5. Why and when might minor stresses be more harmful than major stresses?

6. How might a child's interpretation of events help him or her cope with repeated stress?

7. Give examples of how siblings raised together may not share the same environment.

8. What is the difference between family structure and family function?

9. Why is a harmonious, stable home particularly important during middle childhood?

10. Describe the characteristics of four different family structures.

11. What are the advantages for children in a nuclear family structure?

12. What are the advantages and disadvantages of a stepparent family?

13. List three reasons why the single-parent structure might function less well than other family structures.

14. In what ways are family structure and family function affected by culture?

15. Using the family-stress model, explain how low family income might affect family function.

16. How does what children wear reflect the culture of children?

17. In what ways are friendships at the end of middle childhood different from those at the beginning of middle childhood?

18. How is a child's popularity affected by culture and the child's age?

19. What are the similarities and differences between boy bullies and girl bullies?

20. List at least three causes and three consequences of bullying.

21. How might bullying be reduced?

22. Using Kohlberg's levels of moral reasoning, explain how cognition advances morality.

23. What are the main criticisms of Kohlberg's theory of moral development?

24. What three values are common among school-age children?

25. How could you use the information about the five needs of school-age children to judge whether child labor, or any other situation involving children, is moral?

APPLICATIONS

1. Go someplace where school-age children congregate (such as a schoolyard, a park, or a community center) and use naturalistic observation for at least half an hour. Describe what popular, average, withdrawn, and rejected children do. Note at least one potential conflict. Describe the sequence and the outcome.

2. Focusing on verbal bullying, describe at least two times when someone said something hurtful to you and two times when you said something that might have been hurtful to someone else. What are the differences between the two types of situations?

3. How would your childhood have been different if your family structure had been different, such as if you had (or had not) lived with your grandparents, if your parents had (or had not) gotten divorced, if you had (or had not) been adopted?

>>ONLINE CONNECTIONS

To accompany your textbook, you have access to a number of online resources, including quizzes for every chapter of the book, flashcards (in English and Spanish), critical-thinking questions, and case studies. For access to any of these links, go to www. worthpublishers.com/bergerinvitation2e. In addition to these free resources, you'll also find links to podcasts, video clips, diagnostic quizzing with personalized study advice, and an ebook. Some of the videos and activities available online include:

- *Effects of Divorce and Remarriage on Children.* Learn three factors that affect a child's adjustment and what parents can do to avoid potential problems.

- *Moral Reasoning.* This activity reviews Kohlberg's theory of age-related changes in moral reasoning. Was he right? You can decide as you watch footage of people solving the famous Heinz dilemma.

Adolescence

One observer said adolescence is like "starting turbo-charged engines with an unskilled driver" (Dahl, 2004, p. 17). Would you ride with an unskilled driver? I did. When my daughter Bethany had her learner's permit, I sought to convey confidence. Not until I heard a terrified "Mom! Help!" did I grab the wheel to avoid hitting a subway kiosk. I should have intervened sooner, but it is hard to know when adult-sized children need their mothers. Bethany was an adolescent, neither child nor adult, sometimes wanting independence, sometimes not.

It used to be easier to parent a teenager. A century ago, puberty didn't begin until age 15 or so. Soon after that, most girls married and most boys found work. It is said that *adolescence begins with biology and ends with society*. If so, then 100 years ago adolescence lasted a few months. Currently, it lasts a decade or more. Indeed, the period that was once considered late adolescence (from age 18 to adulthood) is now considered a separate period, called *emerging adulthood* in this book and others.

Understanding adolescence is more than an abstract challenge: Those turbo-charged engines need skilled guidance. Get ready to grab the wheel.

CHAPTER OUTLINE

ADOLESCENCE
Body and Mind

chapter 9

WHAT WILL YOU KNOW?

- What makes a particular child reach puberty early or late?
- Why would any adolescent starve herself to death?
- How can teenagers be both logical and impulsive?
- Why does bullying increase in middle school?

overheard a conversation among three teenagers, including my daughter Rachel, all past their awkward years, now becoming beautiful young women. They were discussing the imperfections of their bodies. One spoke of her fat stomach (what stomach? I could not see it), another of her long neck (hidden by her silky, shoulder-length hair). Rachel complained not only about her bent pinky finger but also about her feet!

The reality that children grow into men and women is no shock to any adult. But for teenagers, their cognitive advances often lead to surprise or even horror, joy or despair, at details of their physical growth. These three were typical. ●

- -

THIS CHAPTER DESCRIBES GROWING BODIES AND CHANGING MINDS. It all begins with hormones, but other invisible changes may be even more potent—such as the timing of neurological maturation that does not yet allow adolescents to realize that their minor imperfections are insignificant.

Puberty

Puberty refers to the years of rapid physical growth and sexual maturation that end childhood, producing a person of adult size, shape, and sexuality. The forces of puberty are unleashed by a cascade of hormones that produce external growth and internal changes, including heightened emotions and sexual desires.

This process normally starts between ages 8 and 14 and follows the sequence outlined in At About This Time. Most physical growth and maturation ends about four years after the first signs appear, though some individuals add height, weight, and muscle until age 20 or so.

For girls, the observable changes of puberty usually begin with nipple growth. Soon a few pubic hairs are visible, then peak growth spurt, widening of the hips, the first menstrual period (**menarche**), full pubic-hair pattern, and breast maturation (Susman et al., 2010). The average age of menarche among normal-weight

puberty
The time between the first onrush of hormones and full adult physical development. Puberty usually lasts three to five years. Many more years are required to achieve psychosocial maturity.

menarche
A girl's first menstrual period, signaling that she has begun ovulation. Pregnancy is biologically possible, but ovulation and menstruation are often irregular for years after menarche.

AT ABOUT THIS TIME
The Sequence of Puberty

Girls	Approximate Average Age*	Boys
Ovaries increase production of estrogen and progesterone**	9	
Uterus and vagina begin to grow larger	9½	Testes increase production of testosterone**
Breast "bud" stage	10	Testes and scrotum grow larger
Pubic hair begins to appear; weight spurt begins	11	
Peak height spurt	11½	Pubic hair begins to appear
Peak muscle and organ growth; hips become noticeably wider	12	Penis growth begins
Menarche (first menstrual period)	12½	Spermarche (first ejaculation); weight spurt begins
First ovulation	13	Peak height spurt
Voice lowers	14	Peak muscle and organ growth; shoulders become noticeably broader
Final pubic-hair pattern	15	Voice lowers; visible facial hair
Full breast growth	16	
	18	Final pubic-hair pattern

*Average ages are rough approximations, with many perfectly normal, healthy adolescents as much as three years ahead of or behind these ages.

**Estrogens and testosterone influence sexual characteristics, including reproduction. Charted here are the increases produced by the gonads (sex glands). The ovaries produce estrogens and the testes produce androgens, especially testosterone. Adrenal glands produce some of both kinds of hormones (not shown).

spermarche
A boy's first ejaculation of sperm. Erections can occur as early as infancy, but ejaculation signals sperm production. Spermarche may occur during sleep (in a "wet dream") or via direct stimulation.

hormone
An organic chemical substance that is produced by one body tissue and conveyed via the bloodstream to another to affect some physiological function.

pituitary
A gland in the brain that responds to a signal from the hypothalamus by producing many hormones, including those that regulate growth and that control other glands, among them the adrenal and sex glands.

adrenal glands
Two glands, located above the kidneys, that produce hormones (including the "stress hormones" epinephrine [adrenaline] and norepinephrine).

HPA (hypothalamus–pituitary–adrenal) axis
A sequence of hormone production that originates in the hypothalamus, moves to the pituitary, and then to the adrenal glands.

HPG (hypothalamus–pituitary–gonad) axis
A sequence of hormone production that originates in the hypothalamus, moves to the pituitary, and then to the gonads.

girls is about 12 years, 8 months (Rosenfield et al., 2009), although variation in timing is quite normal.

For boys, the usual sequence is growth of the testes, initial pubic-hair growth, growth of the penis, first ejaculation of seminal fluid (**spermarche**), appearance of facial hair, peak growth spurt, deepening of the voice, and final pubic-hair growth (Biro et al., 2001; Herman-Giddens et al., 2001; Susman et al., 2010). The typical age of spermarche is just under 13 years, close to the age for menarche.

Unseen Beginnings

Just described are the visible changes of puberty, but the entire process begins with an invisible event, a marked hormonal increase. Throughout adolescence, hormone levels correlate with physiological changes and self-reported development (Shirtcliff et al., 2009).

Hormones are body chemicals that regulate hunger, sleep, moods, stress, sexual desire, immunity, reproduction, and many other bodily reactions, including puberty. The process begins deep within the brain when biochemical signals from the hypothalamus signal another brain structure, the **pituitary.**

The pituitary produces hormones that stimulate the **adrenal glands,** located above the kidneys, which produce more hormones. Many hormones that regulate puberty follow this route, known as the **HPA (hypothalamus–pituitary–adrenal) axis** (see Figure 9.1).

Another hormonal sequence is called the **HPG (hypothalamus–pituitary–gonad) axis.** In adolescence, gonadotropin-releasing hormone (GnRH) is released

```
Hypothalamus ──Hormones──▶ Pituitary ────────▶ Adrenal glands
                                      ────────▶ Gonads
                                                (ovaries or
                                                 testicles)
```

Increase in many hormones, including testosterone and estrogen

Growth spurt

Primary sex characteristics

Secondary sex characteristics

HPA axis and HPG axis

FIGURE 9.1 Biological Sequence of Puberty Puberty begins with a hormonal signal from the hypothalamus to the pituitary gland. The pituitary, in turn, signals the adrenal glands and the ovaries or testes to produce more of their hormones.

by the hypothalamus, causing the pituitary to release gonadotropins (LH & FSH), which in turn activate the gonads. As a result, the gonads enlarge and increase their production of sex hormones, chiefly **estradiol** in girls and **testosterone** in boys.

These sex hormones affect the body's shape and function, producing additional hormones that regulate stress and immunity (E. A. Young et al., 2008). *Estrogens* (including estradiol) are female hormones and *androgens* (including testosterone) are male hormones, although the adrenal glands produce both hormones in both sexes.

A dramatic increase in estrogens or androgens at puberty produces mature ova or sperm, released in menarche or spermarche. This same hormonal rush awakens interest in sex and makes reproduction biologically possible, although peak fertility occurs four to six years later. Sexual interest leads to joyful actions and emotions, as well as many potential problems for the person and society. Sex is powerfully influenced by family and culture; for that reason, it is discussed in the next chapter.

Hormonal increases affect psychopathology in sex-specific ways (Naninck et al., 2011; Steiner & Young, 2008). Psychological disorders in both sexes increase at adolescence, but males are twice as likely as females to become schizophrenic, whereas females are twice as likely to become depressed.

estradiol
A sex hormone, considered the chief estrogen. Females produce much more estradiol than males do.

testosterone
A sex hormone, the best known of the androgens (male hormones); secreted in far greater amounts by males than by females.

✦ **ESPECIALLY FOR Parents of Teenagers** Why would parents blame adolescent moods on hormones? (see response, page 324) ➡

Same Situation, Far Apart: Eye Openers Nature grows eyelashes straight, but adolescent girls want them curly. The main difference between these two settings is not the goal but the equipment. Girls in Pinellas Park, Florida, have large mirrors and metal tools designed for lash curling—both are rare in Beijing, China.

PURESTOCK/ GETTY IMAGES

circadian rhythm
A day–night cycle of biological activity that occurs approximately every 24 hours (*circadian* means "about a day").

I Covered That Teachers everywhere complain that students don't remember what they were taught. Maybe schedules, not dreamers, are to blame.

Body Rhythms

The brain of every living creature responds to the environment with natural rhythms that rise and fall by the hours, days, and seasons. Some *biorhythms* are on a day–night cycle of biological activity that occurs approximately every 24 hours; this cycle is called the **circadian rhythm** (*circadian* means "about a day").

The hypothalamus and the pituitary regulate the hormones that affect the biorhythms of stress, appetite, sleep, and so on. Hormones of the HPA axis at puberty cause a *phase delay* in sleep–wake cycles, making many teens wide awake and hungry at midnight but half asleep with little appetite or energy all morning. By contrast, many older adults are naturally alert in the morning and sleepy at night because of their circadian rhythms.

Biology (circadian rhythms) and culture (parties and technology) work to make teenagers increasingly sleep-deprived with each year of high school (Carskadon, 2011). Not only does insufficient sleep decrease learning and well-being, but so does an uneven sleep schedule (more sleep on weekends, erratic bedtimes) (Fuligni & Hardway, 2006; Holm et al., 2009).

Parents who yell at their wide-awake teenagers to turn off the bedroom lights at midnight often must also drag those same children out of bed at 6 A.M. to get ready for school. Many high schools begin before 8 A.M., even though the evidence finds that a later start time improves adolescent learning (Kirby et al., 2011).

Sleepy teenagers are more likely to have many problems. They doze in school (see Figure 9.2), fall asleep while driving, develop eating and mood disorders (depression, conduct disorder, anxiety), have poor relationships with their parents, and abuse substances (partly to wake up or to sleep), thereby jeopardizing their health (risking future obesity, diabetes, and heart disease) (Mueller et al., 2011; Patrick & Schulenberg, 2011; Roenneberg et al., 2012).

Fatigue Among Middle and High School Students

Percent

(Grades 6–8, Grades 9–12; Too tired to exercise, Asleep in school)

Source: National Sleep Foundation, 2006.

FIGURE 9.2 Dreaming and Learning? This graph shows the percentage of U.S. students who, once a week or more, fall asleep in class or are too tired to exercise. Not shown are those who are too tired overall (59 percent for high school students) or who doze in class "almost every day" (8 percent).

Age and Puberty

Parents have a very practical concern: "When will adolescence begin?" Some fear *precocious puberty* (sexual development before age 8) or very late puberty (after age 16), but both are rare (Cesario & Hughes, 2007). Quite normal are increased hormones any time from ages 8 to 14, with the precise age affected by genes, gender, body fat, and stress.

GENES AND GENDER About two-thirds of the variation in age of puberty is genetic, evident not only in families but also in ethnic groups (Ge et al., 2007; Susman et al., 2010; van den Berg & Boomsma, 2007). African Americans reach puberty about seven months earlier than European or Hispanic Americans, whereas Chinese Americans average several months later (see Figures 9.3 and 9.4).

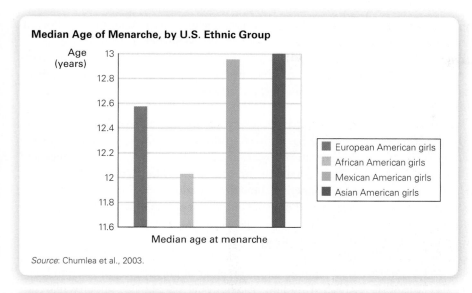

Median Age of Menarche, by U.S. Ethnic Group

Age (years)

Median age at menarche

European American girls
African American girls
Mexican American girls
Asian American girls

Source: Chumlea et al., 2003.

FIGURE 9.3 Usually by Age 13 The median age of menarche (when half the girls have begun to menstruate) differs somewhat among ethnic groups in the United States. (The best signal of puberty is menarche in girls, but similar timing variability is apparent in boys of these ethnic groups.) This data is a decade old, but more recent data is similar, with one exception: Mexican American girls who were born in the U.S. now reach puberty at about 12.4, not 12.9 years of age. The reason is probably more body fat.

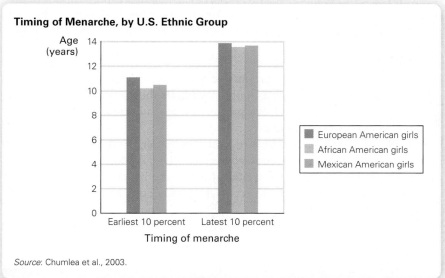

Timing of Menarche, by U.S. Ethnic Group

Age (years)

Earliest 10 percent   Latest 10 percent

Timing of menarche

European American girls
African American girls
Mexican American girls

Source: Chumlea et al., 2003.

FIGURE 9.4 Almost Always by Age 14 This graph shows the age of menarche for the earliest and latest 10 percent of girls in three U.S. ethnic groups. Note that, especially for the slow developers (those in the 90th percentile), ethnic differences are very small.

Both 12 The ancestors of these two Minnesota 12-year-olds came from northern Europe and West Africa, respectively. Their genes have dictated some differences between them, including the timing of puberty, but these differences do not determine their friendship.

Ethnic differences are apparent on other continents as well. For instance, northern European girls reach menarche at 13 years, 4 months, on average; southern European girls do so at 12 years, 5 months (Alsaker & Flammer, 2006).

Genes on the sex chromosomes have a marked effect. In height, the average girl is about two years ahead of the average boy. However, the female height spurt occurs before menarche, whereas for boys, the increase in height is relatively late, occurring after spermarche (Hughes & Gore, 2007).

Thus, when it comes to hormonal and sexual changes, girls are only a few months ahead of boys. The sixth-grade boy with sexual fantasies about the taller girls in his class is neither perverted nor precocious; his hormones are simply ahead of his visible growth.

BODY FAT Another major influence on the onset of puberty is body fat, at least in girls. Heavy girls reach menarche years earlier than malnourished ones do. Most girls must weigh at least 100 pounds (45 kilograms) before they experience their first period (Berkey et al., 2000).

Worldwide, urban children are more often overfed and underexercised than rural children. That is probably why puberty starts earlier in the cities of India and China

RESPONSE FOR Parents of Teenagers (from page 321) If something causes an adolescent to shout "I hate you," to slam doors, or to cry inconsolably, the parents may decide that hormones are the problem. This makes it easy to disclaim personal responsibility for the teenager's anger. However, research on stress and hormones suggests that this comforting attribution is too simplistic. ●

leptin
A hormone that affects appetite and is believed to affect the onset of puberty. Leptin levels increase during childhood and peak at around age 12.

✦ **ESPECIALLY FOR Parents Worried About Early Puberty** Suppose your cousin's 9-year-old daughter has just had her first period, and your cousin blames hormones in the food supply for this "precocious" puberty. Should you change your young daughter's diet? (see response, page 326) ➜

than it does in more remote villages, a year earlier in Warsaw than in rural Poland, and earlier in Athens than in other parts of Greece (Malina et al., 2004).

Body fat also explains why youth reach puberty at age 15 or later in some parts of Africa, although their genetic relatives in North America mature much earlier. Similarly, malnutrition may explain why puberty began at about age 17 in sixteenth-century Europe.

Puberty has occurred at younger ages every century since then. This is one result of the *secular trend*: More food has allowed biological advances. Over most of the twentieth century, each generation experienced puberty a few weeks earlier and grew a centimeter or so taller than did the preceding one (Floud et al., 2011). Not so, currently; the secular trend stopped at about 1990 in developed nations.

One hormone causes increased body fat and then triggers puberty: **leptin,** which stimulates the appetite (Terasawa et al., 2012). Leptin levels in the blood show a natural increase over childhood, peaking at puberty (Rutters et al., 2008). Curiously, leptin affects appetite in females more than it does in males (Geary & Lovejoy, 2008), and body fat is more closely connected to the onset of puberty in girls than in boys.

In fact, the well-established finding that body fat precipitates puberty may not be true for boys in nations where malnutrition is rare: One study found that, unlike girls, U.S. boys who are heavy in childhood reach puberty later, not earlier, than others (J. M. Lee et al., 2010).

STRESS Stress affects the sexual-reproductive system by making reproduction more difficult in adulthood and by *hastening* (not delaying) the hormonal onset of puberty. Thus, puberty arrives earlier if a child's parents are sick, addicted, or divorced, or if the neighborhood is violent and impoverished.

Why would stress trigger puberty? It would be better if stress *delayed* puberty. Then stressed young teens would look and act childlike, evoking adult protection, not lust or anger. Delayed puberty would be especially beneficial in conflicted or single-parent homes. But the opposite occurs—a paradox that has puzzled many scientists, as the following explains.

A VIEW FROM SCIENCE

Stress and Puberty

The connection between stress and puberty is provocative. Is stress really a cause of earlier puberty? Perhaps it is only a correlate, and a third variable is the underlying reason that children under stress experience earlier puberty.

A logical third variable would be genes. For instance, women who are genetically programmed for early menarche are also likely to have early sex. That makes them vulnerable to teenage pregnancy, and if they marry while they are immature, the marriages are likely to be turbulent. The fact that their children experience early puberty would then be the result not of the conflicted marriage, but of genes, inherited from their mother.

However, although genes affect age of puberty, careful research finds that stress is a cause, not merely a correlate, of early menarche. For example, a group of sexually abused

girls began puberty seven months earlier, on average, than did a matched comparison group (Trickett et al., 2011).

It seems that stress hormones, particularly cortisol, cause puberty. One longitudinal study followed 756 children from infancy to adolescence. Those who were harshly treated (rarely hugged, often spanked) in childhood also experienced earlier puberty.

This study found that harsh parenting correlated with earlier puberty for daughters, not sons—especially daughters who cried a lot as infants, which suggests that they were sensitive to stress (Belsky et al., 2007). This means that genes probably have some impact, via differential sensitivity (see Chapter 1). In this study, nature influenced earlier puberty only for some children, and only when nurture was stressful.

A follow-up study of the same girls at age 15, controlled for genetic inheritance, found that harsh treatment in childhood not only speeded up puberty but also increased sexual risk. Those girls had more sex partners, pregnancies, and sexual infections, but they did *not* take more risks overall: They were not more likely to use drugs or commit crimes (Belsky et al., 2010), which suggests that stress targets sexual hormones more than other genetic or environmental factors that increase adolescent rebellion.

If stress is a cause of early puberty, there must be some reason. One explanation comes from evolutionary theory:

Maturing quickly and breeding promiscuously would enhance reproductive fitness more than would delaying development, mating cautiously, and investing heavily in parenting. The latter strategy, in contrast, would make biological sense, for virtually the same reproductive-fitness-enhancing reasons, under conditions of contextual support and nurturance.

[Belsky et al., 2010, p. 121]

This evolutionary explanation seems in accord with the facts (Ellis et al., 2011). In past stressful times, for species survival, stressed adolescents needed to replace themselves before they died. Of course, natural selection would postpone puberty during extreme famine (so that pregnant girls or their newborns would not die of malnutrition).

However, natural selection would favor genes that hastened puberty for well-fed girls whose families and tribes were in conflict. In that case, a new generation could be born before too many young adults were killed. By contrast, in more peaceful times and families, puberty could occur later, allowing children to benefit from years of nurturance from their parents and grandparents. For that reason, genes could have evolved to respond differentially to war and peace—again, differential sensitivity.

Of course, this evolutionary rationale no longer applies. Today, early sexuality and reproduction are more likely to destroy societies than to protect them. However, the genome has been shaped over millennia; the timing of puberty takes centuries to change.

Too Early, Too Late

Few adolescents care about speculation regarding hormones or evolution. Only one aspect of pubertal timing matters to them: their friends' schedules. No one wants to be first or last.

GIRLS Sympathize with the early-maturing girl. If she has visible breasts at age 10, boys tease her. She must fit her developing body into a school chair designed for smaller children; she might hide her breasts in bulky sweaters; she might refuse to undress for gym. Early-maturing girls tend to have lower self-esteem, more depression, and poorer body image than do other girls (Compian et al., 2009).

Some early-maturing girls have older boyfriends, attracted by their womanly shape and girlish innocence. Having an older boyfriend boosts status—but also increases the risk of drug and alcohol use, eating disorders, and relational bullying, as well as the chances of becoming a victim of physical violence (often from that same boyfriend) (DeRose et al., 2011; Schreck et al., 2007).

BOYS There was a time when early-maturing boys became leaders in high school and successful men (M. C. Jones, 1965; Taga et al., 2006). Since about 1960, however, the risks associated with early male maturation have outweighed the benefits.

For the past few decades, early-maturing boys have been more aggressive, law-breaking, and alcohol-abusing than later-maturing boys (Biehl et al., 2007; Lynne et al., 2007). As a result, they have more trouble with parents, schools, and the police. For both sexes, early puberty correlates with sexual activity and teenage parenthood, which lead to depression and other psychosocial problems (B. B. Brown, 2004; Siebenbruner et al., 2007).

Not only is early puberty stressful for boys, but the speed of change adds to the problems. If puberty is both early and quick, boys are especially likely to become depressed (Mendle et al., 2010). In adolescence, male depression may appear as anger: That fuming, flailing 12-year-old boy may actually be more sad than mad.

Is She Ready? For what? Her face and body are developed, but her mind is not. This Australian girl is 13 years old.

SHARONLEIGHTPHOTOGRAPHY.BLOGSPOT.COM / GETTY IMAGES

Boys who reach puberty late also have problems, becoming more anxious, depressed, and afraid of sex than are other boys (Lindfors et al., 2007). Every adolescent wants to hit puberty "on time," and that is a wise hope. For both sexes, early and late puberty increase the rate of almost every adolescent problem.

Growing Bigger and Stronger

growth spurt
The relatively sudden and rapid physical growth that occurs during puberty. Each body part increases in size on a schedule: Weight usually precedes height, and growth of the limbs precedes growth of the torso.

For every child, puberty begins a **growth spurt**—an uneven jump in the size of almost every body part. Growth proceeds from the extremities to the core (the opposite of the earlier proximodistal growth). Thus, fingers and toes lengthen before hands and feet, hands and feet before arms and legs, arms and legs before the torso. Many pubescent children are temporarily big-footed, long-legged, and short-waisted.

SEQUENCE: WEIGHT, HEIGHT, MUSCLES As the bones lengthen and harden (visible on X-rays) children eat more and gain weight. Exactly when, where, and how much they gain depends on heredity, hormones, diet, exercise, and gender. For instance, at age 17, the average girl has twice the percentage of body fat as her male classmate, whose increased weight is mostly muscle (Roche & Sun, 2003).

A height spurt follows the weight spurt. Then, a year or two later, a muscle spurt occurs. Thus, the pudginess and clumsiness of early puberty are usually gone by late adolescence. (The young teen who took nutritional supplements or lifted weights could have simply waited a year or two.)

Lungs triple in weight; consequently, adolescents breathe more deeply and slowly. The heart doubles in size and the heartbeat slows, decreasing the pulse rate while increasing blood pressure (Malina et al., 2004). Red blood cells increase in both sexes, but dramatically more so in boys, which aids oxygen transport during intense exercise. Endurance improves: Some teenagers can run for miles or dance for hours.

Both weight and height increase *before* muscles and internal organs do: Athletic training and weight lifting should be tailored to an adolescent's size the previous year, to protect immature muscles and organs. Sports injuries are the most common school accidents. Injuries increase at puberty, partly because the height spurt precedes increases in bone mass, making young adolescents particularly vulnerable to fractures (Mathison & Agrawal, 2010).

Only one organ system, the lymphoid system (which includes the tonsils and adenoids), *decreases* in size; thus, teenagers are less susceptible to respiratory ailments. Consequently, mild asthma often disappears at puberty (Busse & Lemanske, 2005), and teenagers have fewer colds than younger children do. This is aided by growth of the larynx, which gives deeper voices to both sexes, dramatically noticeable in boys.

SKIN AND HAIR Another organ system, the skin, becomes oilier, sweatier, and more prone to acne. Thus, the child who, a year earlier, resisted every bath often washes and scrubs several times a day.

Hair also changes. During puberty, hair on the head and limbs becomes coarser and darker. New hair grows under arms, on faces, and over sex organs. Visible facial and chest hair is sometimes considered a sign of manliness, even though hairiness in either sex depends on genes as well as on hormones.

RESPONSE FOR Parents Worried About Early Puberty (from page 324) Probably not. If she is overweight, her diet should change, but the hormone hypothesis is speculative. Genes are the main factor; she shares only one-eighth of her genes with her cousin. ●

Although everyone's hair changes texture at puberty, many teenagers fashion their head hair to indicate gender and autonomy. To become more attractive, many adolescents spend considerable time, money, and thought on their visible hair—growing, gelling, shaving, curling, straightening, highlighting, brushing, combing, styling, dyeing, wetting, drying, etc. In many ways, hair is more than a growth characteristic; it becomes a display of sexuality. And if parents dislike the styling choices their teens make, it also becomes a sign of independence.

Sexual Maturation

The body characteristics that are directly involved in conception and pregnancy are called **primary sex characteristics.** During puberty, every primary sex organ (the ovaries, the uterus, the penis, and the testes) increases dramatically in size and matures in function. By the end of the process, reproduction is possible.

At the same time as maturation of the primary sex characteristics, secondary sex characteristics develop. **Secondary sex characteristics** are bodily features that do not directly affect fertility (hence, they are called secondary) but that visually signify masculinity or femininity.

One secondary characteristic is shape. At puberty, males widen at the shoulders and grow about 5 inches taller than females, while girls develop breasts and a wider pelvis. Breasts and broad hips are often considered signs of womanhood, but neither is required for conception; thus, they are secondary, not primary, sex characteristics.

Secondary sex characteristics are important psychologically, if not biologically. Consider breasts. Many adolescent girls buy "minimizer," "maximizer," "training," or "shaping" bras in the hope that they can conform their breasts to an idealized body image. During the same years, many boys are horrified to notice a swelling around their nipples—a normal and temporary result of the erratic hormones of early puberty.

primary sex characteristics
The parts of the body that are directly involved in reproduction, including the vagina, uterus, ovaries, testicles, and penis.

secondary sex characteristics
Physical traits that are not directly involved in reproduction but that indicate sexual maturity, such as a man's beard and a woman's breasts.

KEY points

- Hormones begin the sequence of biological changes known as puberty, affecting every body function, including appetite, sleep, and reproductive potential.
- Although many similarities are evident in how boys and girls experience puberty, timing differs, with girls beginning between 6 months and 2 years ahead of boys, depending on the specific pubertal characteristic.
- The onset of puberty depends on genes, gender, body fat, and stress, with the normal hormonal changes beginning at any time from 8 to 14 years.
- Puberty changes every part of the body and every aspect of sexuality; weight gain precedes increases in height, muscles, and sexuality.

Nutrition

All the changes of puberty depend on adequate nourishment, yet many adolescents do not consume enough vitamins or minerals. Teenagers often skip breakfast; eat at midnight; guzzle down soda; and munch on salty, processed snacks. One reason is that their hormones affect their diurnal rhythms, including their appetites; another reason is that they seek independence, which may mean refusing to sit down to a family dinner.

Cohort and age are crucial factors. In the United States, each new generation seems to eat worse than the previous one, and each 18-year-old consumes a more unbalanced diet than he or she did at age 10 (N. I. Larson et al., 2007). In 2011, only 15 percent of high school seniors ate the recommended three or more servings of vegetables a day (MMWR, June 8, 2012).

Diet Deficiencies

Deficiencies of iron, calcium, zinc, and other minerals are especially common after puberty. Because menstruation depletes iron, anemia is more likely among adolescent

Diet Worldwide, adolescent obesity is increasing. However, parental responses differ. These girls eat breakfast at Wellspring, a California boarding school for overweight teenagers. Tuition is $6,250 a month, exercise is more than 10,000 steps a day (tracked with a pedometer), and fat consumption is less than 20 grams a day (normal is more than 60 grams).

girls than among people of any other age or gender. This is true everywhere, especially in South Asia and sub-Saharan Africa, where teenage girls rarely eat iron-rich meat and green vegetables.

Specific data on young women in developing nations is not available because no large-scale studies have been done that include laboratory analysis of blood iron. However, research in Saudi Arabia involving 18- to 23-year-old college women (usually in good health, never pregnant, and from wealthy families), found that, despite these advantages, half had insufficient iron, and many of them were clinically anemic (Al-Sayes et al., 2011).

Boys may also be iron deficient if they push their bodies in physical labor or sports: Muscles need iron for growth and strength. The cutoff for anemia is higher for boys than for girls because males require more iron to be healthy (Morón & Viteri, 2009). Many adolescents of both sexes in every nation spurn iron-rich foods in favor of iron-poor chips, sweets, and fries. Coffee, tea, and soda reduce iron absorption.

Similarly, although the daily recommended intake of calcium for teenagers is 1,300 milligrams, the average North American teen consumes fewer than 500 milligrams a day. In 2011, only 15 percent of U.S. twelfth graders drank even three glasses of milk daily (MMWR, June 8, 2012).

In the twenty-first century, the beverage most often consumed by U.S. 2- to 18-year-olds is soda (Dietary Guidelines for Americans, 2010), with 11 percent of high school students drinking three or more glasses of soda each day (MMWR, June 8, 2012)! About half of adult bone mass is acquired from ages 10 to 20, which means many contemporary teenagers will develop osteoporosis (fragile bones) because of too little calcium and too much soda, day in and day out. Osteoporosis is a major cause of disability in late adulthood.

Body Image

body image
A person's idea of how his or her body looks.

One reason for poor nutrition among teenagers is anxiety about **body image**—that is, a person's idea of how his or her body looks. Few teenagers welcome every physical change in their bodies. Instead, they exaggerate imperfections (as did the three girls in the anecdote that opened this chapter) and sacrifice future health to improve current body image. For example, much of the soda consumed every day is diet soda—low on calories but high in ingredients that correlate with poor health later on (Gardner et al., 2012).

Girls diet because they want to be thinner, partly because boys tend to prefer thin girls (Halpern et al., 2005). Boys want to look taller and stronger, a concern that increases from ages 12 to 17, partly because girls value well-developed muscles in males (D. Jones & Crawford, 2005). In both sexes and in adolescents of all ethnicities, dissatisfaction with body image correlates strongly with low self-esteem (van den Berg et al., 2010).

Thus, as the hormones of puberty awaken sexual interest, both sexes become less happy with their own bodies and more superficial in what they admire in the other sex. This is true worldwide. A longitudinal study in Korea found that, as in the West, body image dissatisfaction began in early adolescence and increased until age 15 or so (Kim & Kim, 2009).

In many nations, the ideal body type is tall and thin, and the ideal facial appearance is Anglo-Saxon. Of course, few Anglo-Saxon youth achieve the media ideal, but the discrepancy is particularly cruel far from England. A longitudinal study in China found that adolescents in that country had anxieties about weight gain similar to those of U.S. teenagers (Chen & Jackson, 2009).

Eating Disorders

One result of dissatisfaction with body image is that many teenagers, mostly girls, eat erratically or ingest drugs (especially diet pills) to lose weight; others, mostly boys, take steroids to increase muscle mass. Eating disorders are rare in childhood but increase dramatically at puberty, accompanied by distorted body image, food obsession, and depression (Bulik et al., 2008; Hrabosky & Thomas, 2008).

Individuals sometimes switch from obsessive dieting to overeating and back again. Obesity, which is a problem at every age, is discussed primarily in other chapters. Here we describe two other eating disorders that are common in adolescence and early adulthood.

ANOREXIA According to DSM-IV (the fourth edition of the *Diagnostic and Statistical Manual of Mental Disorders*), about 1 percent of all women in late adolescence suffer from **anorexia nervosa,** a disorder characterized by voluntary starvation; it leads to death by organ failure or suicide for between 5 and 20 percent of sufferers. If someone's body mass index (BMI) is 18 or lower, or if she (or, less often, he) loses more than 10 percent of body weight within a month or two, anorexia is suspected.

Anorexia is officially diagnosed when four symptoms are evident:

1. Refusal to maintain a weight that is at least 85 percent of normal BMI
2. Intense fear of weight gain
3. Disturbed body perception and denial of the problem
4. Absence of menstruation (in adolescent and adult females)

Although anorexia existed in earlier centuries, the disease was undiagnosed until about 1950, when some high-achieving, upper-class, young women became so emaciated that they died. Soon anorexia became evident among younger women (the rate spikes at puberty and again in emerging adulthood), among men (especially wrestlers, runners, and dancers), and in every nation and ethnic group (Chao et al., 2008).

Certain alleles increase the risk of anorexia (J. K. Young, 2010), but context is crucial. The disorder seems related to cultural pressure to be thin.

BULIMIA About three times as common as anorexia is **bulimia nervosa,** sometimes called the *binge–purge syndrome.* People with bulimia overeat compulsively, wolfing down thousands of calories within an hour or two, and then purge via vomiting or laxatives.

Girl or Woman? Hannah, here age 16, has been suffering from anorexia since she was 9. Some clinicians suggest that starving oneself is a destructive way to avoid the womanly body that develops at puberty.

anorexia nervosa
An eating disorder characterized by self-starvation. Affected individuals voluntarily undereat and often overexercise, depriving their vital organs of nutrition. Anorexia can be fatal.

bulimia nervosa
An eating disorder characterized by binge eating and subsequent purging, usually by induced vomiting and/or use of laxatives.

● **UNDERSTANDING THE NUMBERS**
You read that anorexia is diagnosed when a person's BMI is 18 or lower, or when a person loses 10 percent of her body weight in two months. According to the BMI chart in the appendix, this means that a 4′10″ person who weighs 90 pounds is anorexic, as is a 4′10″ person weighing 150 pounds (obese) who loses 15 pounds in 9 weeks. However, someone 6′4″ weighing only 156 pounds is not anorexic. In all three cases, the diagnosis may be wrong. Why?

Answer Since muscle weighs more than fat, if that 6′4″ person is muscular, he or she may indeed be anorexic. Genes and body fat may exempt the other two. These numbers all raise alarms; individual factors need to be considered before a diagnosis can be confirmed.

Most are close to normal in weight and therefore unlikely to starve. However, they risk serious health problems, including damage to their gastrointestinal systems and cardiac arrest from electrolyte imbalance (Shannon, 2007). They also risk compulsive disorders and depression, including thoughts of suicide (Parylak et al., 2011).

According to DSM-IV, 1 to 3 percent of female teenagers and young adults in the United States are clinically bulimic. They have the following three symptoms:

1. Binging and purging at least once a week for three months

2. Uncontrollable urges to overeat

3. A distorted perception of body size

Many experts think that eating disorders are much more widespread than DSM statistics portray. For instance, in 2011 among U.S. high school students, 17 percent of the girls had eaten nothing for at least one 24-hour period in the past month, as had 7 percent of the boys (MMWR, June 8, 2012).

KEY𝒫oints

- Adolescent diets are often deficient, especially in calcium and iron.
- Body-image worries are common, leading many adolescent girls to skip eating for a day and many boys to take steroids.
- Some adolescents develop serious eating disorders, starving themselves (anorexia nervosa) or binging and purging (bulimia nervosa).

Thinking, Fast and Slow

The body changes just reviewed are dramatic, but even more life-changing are the intellectual advances during adolescence. Teenagers no longer think like children, but they do not yet think like adults. We begin with the neurological changes of adolescence and then explore the cognitive ones that maturation brings.

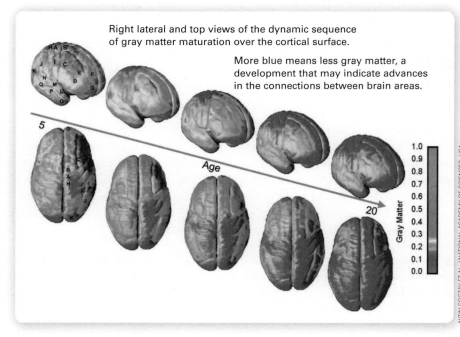

Right lateral and top views of the dynamic sequence of gray matter maturation over the cortical surface.

More blue means less gray matter, a development that may indicate advances in the connections between brain areas.

Same People, But Not the Same Brain
These brain scans are part of a longitudinal study that repeatedly compares the proportion of gray matter from childhood through adolescence. Gray matter is reduced as white matter increases, in part because pruning during the teen years (the last two pairs of images here) allows intellectual connections to build. As the authors of one study that included this chart explain, teenagers may "look like an adult, but cognitively they are not there yet" (K. Powell, 2006, p. 865).

NITIN GOGTAY ET AL. / NATIONAL ACADEMY OF SCIENCES, USA

Brain Development

Like the other parts of the body, different parts of the brain grow at different rates (Blakemore, 2008). The limbic system, including the amygdala (where intense fear and excitement originate) matures before the prefrontal cortex (where planning, emotional regulation, and impulse control occur).

As a result, the instinctual and emotional areas of the adolescent brain develop ahead of the reflective, analytic areas. Furthermore, pubertal hormones target the amygdala directly, whereas the cortex responds more to age and experience than to hormones. Thus, early puberty means emotional rushes, unchecked by caution.

This is evident via brain scans. Emotional control, revealed by fMRI studies, is not fully developed until adulthood (Luna et al., 2010). When compared with 18- to 23-year-olds, 14- to 15-year-olds show heightened arousal in the brain's reward centers, making them seek excitement and pleasure (Van Leijenhorst et al., 2010).

CAUTION NEEDED The fact that the prefrontal cortex is the last to mature may explain something that has long bewildered adults: Many adolescents are driven by the excitement of new experiences and sensations—forgetting the caution that their parents have tried to instill (Steinberg, 2008).

Laurence Steinberg is a noted expert on adolescent thinking. He is also a father.

> When my son, Benjamin, was 14, he and three of his friends decided to sneak out of the house where they were spending the night and visit one of their girl-friends at around two in the morning. When they arrived at the girl's house, they positioned themselves under her bedroom window, threw pebbles against her windowpanes, ... The boys set off the house's burglar alarm, which activated a siren and simultaneously sent a direct notification to the local police station, which dispatched a patrol car. When the siren went off, the boys ran down the street and right smack into the police car, which was heading to the girl's home. . . . One of the boys was caught by the police and taken back to his home, where his parents were awakened and the boy questioned.
>
> . . . . After his near brush with the local police, Ben had returned to the house out of which he had snuck, where he slept soundly until I awakened him with an angry telephone call, telling him to gather his clothes and wait for me in front of his friend's house. On our drive home, after delivering a long lecture about what he had done and about the dangers of running from armed police in the dark when they believe they may have interrupted a burglary, I paused.
>
> "What were you thinking?" I asked.
>
> "That's the problem, Dad," Ben replied, "I wasn't."
>
> *[Steinberg, 2004, pp. 51, 52]*

Steinberg agrees with his son. As he expresses it, "The problem is not that Ben's decision-making was deficient. The problem is that it was nonexistent" (Steinberg, 2004, p. 52). He points out a characteristic of adolescent thought: When emotions are intense, especially when friends are nearby, the logical part of the brain shuts down.

This neurological shutdown in certain contexts is not reflected in questionnaires that ask teenagers to respond to hypothetical dilemmas. On those tests, most teenagers think carefully and answer correctly. They have been taught the risks of sex and drugs in biology or health classes in school, and they circle the right answers on multiple-choice tests. However,

> the prospect of visiting a hypothetical girl from class cannot possibly carry the excitement about the possibility of surprising someone you have a crush on with a visit in the middle of the night. It is easier to put on a hypothetical condom during an act of hypothetical sex than it is to put on a real one when one is in the throes of passion. It is easier to just say no to a hypothetical beer than it is to a cold frosty one on a summer night.
>
> *[Steinberg, 2004, p. 53]*

◆ **ESPECIALLY FOR Parents Worried About Their Teenager's Risk Taking** You remember the risky things you did at the same age, and you are alarmed by the possibility that your child will follow in your footsteps. What should you do? (see response, page 334) ➞

Same Situation, Far Apart: Danger Ahead They may be far apart in SES, but both think like the teenagers they are. He ignores the risk and she ignores the road.

Ben reached adulthood safely. Some other teenagers, with less cautious police or less diligent parents, do not. Ideally, research on adolescent brains will help protect teens from their dangerous impulses (Monastersky, 2007). Brain immaturity is not the origin of every "troublesome adolescent behavior," but it is true that teenage brains have underdeveloped "response inhibition, emotional regulation, and organization" (Sowell et al., 2007, p. 59) because their prefrontal cortexes are immature.

The normal sequence of brain maturation (limbic system at puberty, then prefrontal cortex by the early 20s) combined with the early onset of puberty means that, for contemporary teenagers, emotions rule behavior for years (Blakemore, 2008). The limbic system, unchecked by the slower-maturing prefrontal cortex, makes powerful sensations—loud music, speeding cars, strong drugs—compelling.

It is not that the prefrontal cortex shuts down completely. In fact, it continues to mature throughout childhood and adolescence, and, when they think about it, adolescents are able to assess risks better than children are (Pfeifer et al., 2011). However, *when they think about it* is crucial. The thoughtful parts of the adolescent brain are less synchronized with the limbic system than they were earlier in life, and thus emotions from the amygdala are less modulated than they once were (Pfeifer et al., 2011). The balance and coordination among the various parts of the brain is off kilter, not the brain itself (Casey et al., 2011).

When stress, arousal, passion, sensory bombardment, drug intoxication, or deprivation is extreme, the adolescent brain is flooded with impulses that might shame adults. Teenagers brag about being so drunk they were "wasted," "bombed," "smashed"—a state most adults try to avoid and would be ashamed to admit. Unlike adults, some teenagers choose to spend a night without sleep, go through a day without eating, exercise in pain, or play football after a mild concussion.

RISK AND REWARD Every decision, from whether to eat a peach to where to enroll in college, requires balancing risk and reward, caution and attraction. For everyone, experiences, memories, emotions, and the prefrontal cortex help us choose to avoid some actions and perform others. Neurological research finds that the reward parts of adolescents' brains (the parts that respond to excitement and pleasure) are far stronger than the inhibition parts (the parts that urge caution) (Van Leijenhorst et al., 2010).

The parts of the brain dedicated to analysis may be immature until years after the first hormonal rushes and sexual urges, while teenagers have access to fast cars, lethal weapons, and dangerous drugs. Adults do not realize the risks that their children take, not only because the teenagers do not confide in their parents, but also because they themselves are sometimes illogical (Kahneman, 2011). My friend asked her next-door neighbor, who gave his son a red convertible for high school graduation, "Why didn't you just give him a loaded gun?"

One example of the cautious part of the brain being overwhelmed by the emotions of the moment comes from teens sending text messages while they are driving. In a survey, 64 percent of U.S. 16- to 17-year-olds said they had been in a car when the driver was texting—a practice that occurs in every state and nation even though it is illegal in many of them (Madden & Lenhart, 2009).

More generally, despite faster reflexes and better vision than at later ages, by far the most common cause of teenage death is motor-vehicle crashes. Thoughtless impulses and poor decisions are almost always to blame.

Extensive research finds that four measures have saved hundreds of lives of teenage drivers: (1) requiring more time between issuing a learner's permit and granting a full license, (2) no driving at night, (3) no teenage passengers, and (4) zero tolerance for alcohol and driving (Fell et al., 2011). Note that it is problems in the brain—not the reflexes, senses, or muscles—that cause adolescent injuries: Teenagers are usually quicker and stronger than adults.

Thinking About Oneself

During puberty, young people center many of their thoughts on themselves, in part because maturation of the brain heightens self-consciousness (Sebastian et al., 2008). It is typical for young adolescents to think deeply (but not always realistically) about their own emotions regarding adults, education, friends, and the future. One reason adolescents spend so much time talking on the phone, e-mailing, and texting is that they like to ruminate about each nuance of whatever they have done, might have done, and could do. "He said, she said, and I should've said."

EGOCENTRISM Young adolescents not only think intensely about themselves but also think about what others think of them. Together these two aspects of thought are called **adolescent egocentrism,** first described by David Elkind (1967). Egocentrism dominates in early adolescence, but it appears at times throughout the teen years, especially when the young person enters a new school or new peer group or goes off to college.

In egocentrism, adolescents regard themselves as unique, special, and much more socially significant (i.e., noticed by everyone) than they actually are. For example, it is unlikely that adolescent girls are especially attracted to boys with pimples and braces, but Edgar did not realize this, according to his older sister:

> Now in the 8th grade, Edgar has this idea that all the girls are looking at him in school. He got his first pimple about three months ago. I told him to wash it with my face soap but he refused, saying, "Not until I go to school to show it off." He called the dentist, begging him to approve his braces now instead of waiting for a year. The perfect gifts for him have changed from action figures to a bottle of cologne, a chain, and a fitted baseball hat like the rappers wear.

[adapted from Eva, personal communication, 2007]

Egocentrism leads adolescents to interpret everyone else's behavior as if it were a judgment on them. A stranger's frown or a teacher's critique could make a teenager conclude that "No one likes me" and then deduce that "I am unlovable" or even claim that "I can't leave the house."

More positive casual reactions—a smile from a sales clerk or an extra-big hug from a younger brother—could lead to "I am great" or "Everyone loves me" or similarly distorted self-perception. Given the rapid mood changes of adolescence, such conclusions are usually short-lived, susceptible to reversal with another offhand remark.

FANTASY Elkind named several aspects of adolescent egocentrism, among them the **personal fable** and the **invincibility fable,** which often appear together (Alberts et al., 2007). The *personal fable* is the belief that one is unique, destined to have a heroic, fabled, even legendary life. Some 12-year-olds plan to star in the NBA, or become billionaires, or cure cancer.

In some adolescent minds, there is no contradiction between the personal fable and *invincibility,* the idea that, unless fate wills it, they will not be hurt by fast driving, unprotected sex, or addictive drugs. If they take risks and survive without harm, they feel invincible, not relieved.

In every nation, those who volunteer for military service—knowing or even hoping that they will be sent into combat—are more likely to be under age 20 than over it. Young recruits take risks more often than older, more experienced soldiers (Killgore et al., 2006). Another example comes from online chat rooms. Young teenagers reveal personal information to electronic "friends," oblivious to the dangers inherent in such revelations (McCarty et al., 2011).

Egocentrism creates an **imaginary audience** in the minds of many adolescents. They believe they are at center stage, with all eyes on them, and they imagine how others might react to their appearance and behavior.

PICTURE PARTNERS / ALAMY

Every Detail Appearance has always been significant to young adolescents, but each cohort is distinct. Thin, waxed eyebrows, blue hair and nails, and a checkered shirt over stripes would all have been anathema to this girl's grandmother at age 15, who might have examined her rosy cheeks in a large, living room mirror.

adolescent egocentrism
A characteristic of adolescent thinking that leads young people (ages 10 to 13) to focus on themselves to the exclusion of others.

personal fable
An aspect of adolescent egocentrism characterized by an adolescent's belief that his or her thoughts, feelings, and experiences are unique, more wonderful or awful than anyone else's.

invincibility fable
An adolescent's egocentric conviction that he or she cannot be overcome or even harmed by anything that might defeat a normal mortal, such as unprotected sex, drug abuse, or high-speed driving.

imaginary audience
The other people who, in an adolescent's egocentric belief, are watching and taking note of his or her appearance, ideas, and behavior. This belief makes many teenagers very self-conscious.

The imaginary audience can cause teenagers to enter a crowded room as if they are the most attractive human beings alive. They might put studs in their lips or blast music for all to hear, calling attention to themselves. The reverse is also possible: Unlike Edgar, they might avoid scrutiny lest someone notice a blemish on their chin or make fun of their braces. Many a 12-year-old balks at going to school with a bad haircut or the wrong shoes.

Formal Operational Thought

Adolescents move past concrete operational thinking (discussed in Chapter 7) and consider abstractions. Jean Piaget described a shift to what he called **formal operational thought,** including "assumptions that have no necessary relation to reality" (Piaget, 1972, p. 148).

One way to distinguish formal from concrete thinking is to compare curricula in primary school and high school. For example, in math, younger children multiply real numbers, such as $4 \times 3 \times 8$; adolescents multiply unreal numbers, such as $(2x)$ $(3y)$ or even $(25xy^2)(3zy^3)$.

In social studies, younger children learn about other cultures by reading about daily life or experiencing aspects of the culture themselves—drinking goat's milk or building an igloo, for instance. Adolescents can hypothesize how gross national product and fertility rate might affect global politics.

PIAGET'S EXPERIMENTS Piaget and his colleagues devised a number of tasks to assess formal operational thought (Inhelder & Piaget, 1958). In one experiment (diagrammed in Figure 9.5), children of many ages balance a scale by hooking weights onto the scale's arms. To master this task, they must realize that the weights' heaviness and distance from the center interact reciprocally to affect balance.

The concept of balancing (that a heavy weight close to the center could be balanced by a lighter weight farther from the center on the other side) was completely beyond the 3- to 5-year-olds. By age 7, children could balance the scale by putting the same amount of weight on each arm, but they didn't realize that the distance from the center mattered.

formal operational thought In Piaget's theory, the fourth and final stage of cognitive development, characterized by more systematic logical thinking and by the ability to understand and systematically manipulate abstract concepts.

RESPONSE FOR Parents Worried About Their Teenager's Risk Taking (from page 332) You are right to be concerned, but you cannot keep your child locked up for the next decade or so. Since you know that some rebellion and irrationality are likely, try to minimize them by not boasting about your own youthful exploits, by reacting sternly to minor infractions to nip worse behavior in the bud, and by making allies of your child's teachers. ●

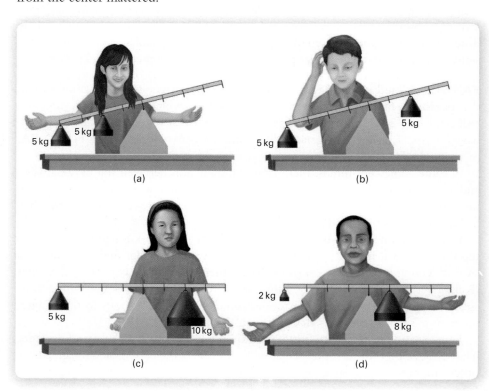

FIGURE 9.5 How to Balance a Scale Piaget's balance-scale test of formal reasoning, as it is attempted by (a) a 4-year-old, (b) a 7-year-old, (c) a 10-year-old, and (d) a 14-year-old. The key to balancing the scale is to make weight times distance from the center equal on both sides of the center; the realization of that principle requires formal operational thought.

By age 10, children thought about location, but used trial and error, not logic. Finally, by about age 13 or 14, some children hypothesized and tested the reciprocal relationship between weight and distance and developed the correct formula (Piaget & Inhelder, 1969).

In all of Piaget's experiments, "in contrast to concrete operational children, formal operational adolescents imagine all possible determinants . . . [and] systematically vary the factors one by one, observe the results correctly, keep track of the results, and draw the appropriate conclusions" (P. H. Miller, 2011, p. 57).

HYPOTHETICAL-DEDUCTIVE REASONING One hallmark of formal operational thought is the capacity to think of possibility, not just reality. "Here and now" is only one of many alternatives, including "there and then," "long, long ago," "nowhere," "not yet," and "never." As Piaget said:

> The adolescent . . . thinks beyond the present and forms theories about everything, delighting especially in considerations of that which is not . . .
>
> *[Piaget, 1972, p. 148]*

Adolescents are primed to engage in **hypothetical thought,** reasoning about *if–then* propositions that do not reflect reality. For example, consider this question (adapted from De Neys & Van Gelder, 2009):

> If all mammals can walk,
> And whales are mammals,
> Can whales walk?

Younger adolescents often answer "No!" They know that whales swim, not walk, so the logic escapes them. Some adolescents answer "Yes." They understand the concept of *if.*

> *Possibility* no longer appears merely as an extension of an empirical situation or of action actually performed. Instead, it is *reality* that is now secondary to *possibility.*
>
> *[Inhelder & Piaget, 1958, p. 251; emphasis in original]*

Because of this new ability, many adolescents sharply criticize their parents, their school, their society. They "naively underestimate the practical problems involved in achieving an ideal future for themselves or for society" (P. H. Miller, 2011, p. 59).

In developing the capacity to think hypothetically, adolescents gradually become capable of **deductive reasoning,** or *top-down reasoning.* Deductive reasoning begins with an abstract idea or premise and then uses logic to draw specific conclusions (Galotti, 2002; Keating, 2004).

A Proud Teacher "Is it possible to train a cockroach?" This hypothetical question, an example of formal operational thought, was posed by 15-year-old Tristan Williams of New Mexico. In his award-winning science project, he succeeded in conditioning Madagascar cockroaches to hiss at the sight of a permanent marker. (His parents' logical reasoning about having 600 cockroaches living in their home is not known.)

hypothetical thought
Reasoning that includes propositions and possibilities that may not reflect reality.

deductive reasoning
Reasoning from a general statement, premise, or principle, through logical steps, to figure out (deduce) specifics. (Also called *top-down reasoning.*)

Impressive Thinking "Correlating Genetic Signature with Surface Sugar Expression in Vibrio vulnificus" is the title of Shilpa Argade's winning science project about a sometimes deadly bacteria. Like many other high school seniors, she is capable of deductive reasoning, but she does not always think that way.

inductive reasoning
Reasoning from one or more specific experiences or facts to reach (induce) a general conclusion. (Also called *bottom-up reasoning*.)

✦ **ESPECIALLY FOR Natural Scientists** Some ideas that were once universally accepted, such as the belief that the sun moved around the Earth, have been disproved. Is it a failure of inductive or deductive reasoning that leads to false conclusions? (see response, page 338) ➞

By contrast, during the primary school years, children accumulate facts and personal experiences (the knowledge base), asking what and why. The result is **inductive reasoning,** or *bottom-up reasoning,* with many specific examples leading to general conclusions.

RACISM: AN EXAMPLE By adolescence, almost every American knows that racism exists—and opposes it. However, children tend to think the core problem is the prejudice of individuals. Using inductive reasoning, they think that the remedy is to reduce racism among those people who express it, believing there will be less prejudice as individuals become more tolerant.

By contrast, as children become adolescents, they think, deductively, that racism is a society-wide problem that requires policy solutions. That is formal operational thinking.

This interpretation arises from a study of adolescent agreement or disagreement with policies to remedy racial discrimination (Hughes & Bigler, 2011). Not surprisingly, most (not all) students in an interracial U.S. high school recognized disparities between African and European Americans and believed that racism was a major cause. What was surprising to the researchers is that age made a difference.

Among those who believed there were marked inequalities, more older adolescents (age 16 to 17) supported systemic solutions (e.g., affirmative action and desegregation) than did younger adolescents (age 14 to 15). The authors of the study wrote that "during adolescence, cognitive development facilitates the understanding that discrimination exists at the social-systemic level . . . [and that] racial awareness begins to inform views of race-conscious policies during middle adolescence" (Hughes & Bigler, 2011, p. 489).

In thinking about race and many other examples, many adults do not reason at the formal operational level. Piaget probably overestimated the prevalence of this fourth period of intelligence in adulthood. Many contemporary scholars believe there are two modes of thinking, and that most people, most of the time, do not use formal operational thought (Barrouillet, 2011).

Two Modes of Thinking

The fact that adolescents and adults *can* use hypothetical-deductive reasoning does not necessarily mean that they *do* use it (Kuhn & Franklin, 2006). Adolescents particularly find it much easier and quicker to forget about logic and instead to follow their impulses. For adults as well as adolescents, at least two modes characterize thought.

In adolescence, abstract logic is counterbalanced by the increasing power of intuitive thinking. A **dual-process model** of adolescent cognition has been formulated (Albert & Steinberg, 2011). (See Infographic 9, page 337.)

dual-process model
The notion that two networks exist within the human brain, one for emotional and one for analytical processing of stimuli.

Various scholars choose different terms and sometimes distinct definitions of the two processes of thinking. These two processes have been called: intuitive/analytic, implicit/explicit, creative/factual, contextualized/decontextualized, unconscious/conscious, hot/cold, gist/quantitative, emotional/intellectual, experiential/rational, or system 1/system 2.

The thinking described by the first of each paired term (intuitive, implicit, creative, contextualized, unconscious, hot, gist, emotional, experiential, system 1) is preferred in everyday life. Sometimes, however, circumstances and experience compel people to use the second mode, when deeper thought is demanded. Because of the discrepancy between the maturation of the limbic system and the prefrontal cortex, adolescents are particularly likely to use intuition, not analysis (Gerrard et al., 2008).

intuitive thought
Thought that arises from an emotion or a hunch, beyond rational explanation, and is influenced by past experiences and cultural assumptions.

● **Intuitive thought** begins with a belief, assumption, or general rule (called a *heuristic*) rather than with logic. Intuition is quick and powerful; it feels "right."

Thinking in Adolescence

There are two ways to use logic—deductively and inductively. Younger children, as concrete operational thinkers, make conclusions on the basis of their own experiences and what they have been told. This is called inductive, or bottom-up, reasoning. Adolescents can also think deductively, from the top down.

INDUCTIVE vs. DEDUCTIVE REASONING

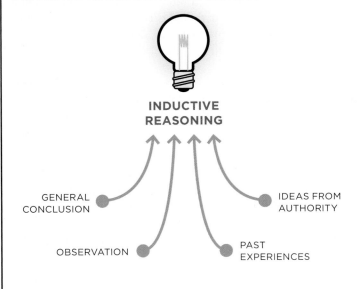

INDUCTIVE REASONING

GENERAL CONCLUSION

OBSERVATION

PAST EXPERIENCES

IDEAS FROM AUTHORITY

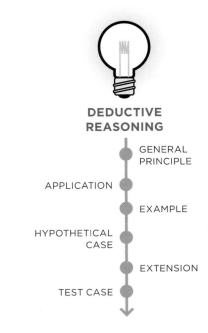

DEDUCTIVE REASONING

GENERAL PRINCIPLE

APPLICATION

EXAMPLE

HYPOTHETICAL CASE

EXTENSION

TEST CASE

CHANGES IN AGE

As people age, their thinking tends to move from intuitive processing to more analytical processing—that is, from inductive to deductive reasoning.

But, except for academics, adolescents tend to use intuitive rather than analytical thinking. Here is an example.

INTUITIVE THINKING

ANALYTICAL THINKING

AGE

YOUNGER

OLDER

INTUITIVE

S/he's cute and sexy = I'll talk to her/him

ANALYTICAL

S/he's not smart in math ✗

S/he's sometimes mean to her/his friends ✗

S/he had a turbulent relationship with her/his girlfriend/boyfriend = I'll ignore her/him

analytic thought
Thought that results from analysis, such as a systematic ranking of pros and cons, risks and consequences, possibilities and facts. Analytic thought depends on logic and rationality.

- **Analytic thought** is the formal, logical, hypothetical–deductive thinking described by Piaget. It involves rational analysis of many factors whose interactions must be calculated, as in the scale-balancing problem.

When the two modes of thinking conflict, people sometimes use one mode and sometimes the other. Experiences and role models influence the choice. For example, one study found that when adolescents enter a multicultural high school, some rely on old stereotypes and others reassess their thoughts to consider new perspectives. Which of these two modes of thinking predominates depends on their specific experiences and on the attitudes of the adults in the school (Crisp & Turner, 2011).

COMPARING INTUITION AND ANALYSIS Paul Klaczynski has conducted dozens of studies comparing the thinking of children, young adolescents, and older adolescents (usually 9-, 12-, and 15-year-olds) (Holland & Klaczynski, 2009; Klaczynski, 2001, 2011; Klaczynski et al., 2009). In one, he presented 19 logical problems. For example:

> Timothy is very good-looking, strong, and does not smoke. He likes hanging around with his male friends, watching sports on TV, and driving his Ford Mustang convertible. He's very concerned with how he looks and with being in good shape. He is a high school senior now and is trying to get a college scholarship.
>
> Based on this [description], rank each statement in terms of how likely it is to be true. . . . The most likely statement should get a 1. The least likely statement should get a 6.
>
> _____ Timothy has a girlfriend.
>
> _____ Timothy is an athlete.
>
> _____ Timothy is popular and an athlete.
>
> _____ Timothy is a teacher's pet and has a girlfriend.
>
> _____ Timothy is a teacher's pet.
>
> _____ Timothy is popular.

In ranking these statements, most adolescents (73 percent) made at least one analytic error, ranking a double statement (e.g., popular _and_ an athlete) as more likely than a single statement included in it (popular _or_ an athlete). They intuitively jumped to the more inclusive statement, rather than sticking to logic. In many other studies, adults often make the same mistake, called the _conjunction fallacy_ (Kahneman, 2011).

Klaczynski found that almost all adolescents were analytical and logical on some of the 19 problems but not on others. Logical thinking improved with age and education, although not with IQ.

In other words, being smarter as measured by an intelligence test did not advance logic as much as did having more experience, in school and in life. Klaczynski (2001) concluded that, even though teenagers _can_ use logic, "most adolescents do not demonstrate a level of performance commensurate with their abilities" (p. 854).

PREFERRING EMOTIONS What would motivate adolescents to use—or fail to use—their formal operational thinking? Klaczynski's participants had all learned the scientific method in school, and they knew that scientists use empirical evidence and deductive reasoning. But they did not always think like scientists. Why not?

Dozens of experiments and extensive theorizing have found some answers (Albert & Steinberg, 2011; Kahneman, 2011). Essentially, analytic thought is more difficult than intuition, and it requires examination of comforting, familiar prejudices.

Once people of any age reach an emotional conclusion (sometimes called a "gut feeling"), they resist changing their minds. As people gain experience in making

RESPONSE FOR Natural Scientists (from page 336) Probably both. Our false assumptions are not logically tested because we do not realize that they need testing. ●

AP PHOTO / GREGORY SMITH

Impressive Connections This robot is about to compete in the Robotics Competition in Atlanta, Georgia. Much more impressive are the brains of the Oregon high school team (including Melissa, shown here) who designed the robot.

OBSERVATION QUIZ
She is alone here, but what sign do you see that suggests she is part of a team who built this robot? (see answer, page 342) ➡

decisions and thinking things through, they become better at knowing when analysis is needed (Milkman et al., 2009).

For example, in contrast to younger students, older adolescents are more suspicious of authority and more likely to consider mitigating circumstances when judging the legitimacy of a rule (Klaczynski, 2011). Both suspicion of authority and awareness of context signify advances in reasoning, but both also complicate simple issues.

KEYpoints

- Uneven brain development characterizes adolescence, with the limbic system developing faster than the prefrontal cortex.
- Young adolescents are often egocentric, thinking of themselves as invincible, and performing for an imaginary audience.
- Adolescents are also capable of logical, hypothetical thought, what Piaget described as formal operational thinking.
- Both emotional intuition and logical analysis are stronger in adolescence than earlier in life. Adolescents usually prefer the former because it's faster and easier.

Teaching and Learning

What does our knowledge of adolescent thought imply about education? Which curricula and school structures (single-sex or co-ed, large or small, public or private) are best for 11- to 18-year-olds? Since adolescents differ, "some students thrive at school, enjoying and benefitting from most of their experiences there; others muddle along and cope as best they can with the stress and demands of the moment; and still others find school an alienating and unpleasant place to be . . ." (Eccles & Roeser, 2011, p. 225).

Given personal and cultural variations, no specific school curriculum, structure, or teaching method is best for everyone. Various scientists, nations, schools, and teachers try many strategies, some based on opposite, but logical, hypotheses. To analyze these, we begin with definitions and facts.

Definitions and Facts

Each year of schooling advances human potential, as recognized by leaders and scholars in every nation and discipline. As you have read, adolescents are capable of deep and wide-ranging thought, no longer limited by personal experience; yet they are often egocentric, impulsive, and intuitive. The quality of education matters: A year can propel thinking forward or can have little impact (Hanushek & Woessmann, 2010).

Secondary education—traditionally grades 7 through 12—denotes the school years after elementary or grade school (known as *primary education*) and before college or university (known as *tertiary education*). Adults are healthier and wealthier if they complete secondary and tertiary education.

Even such a seemingly unrelated condition as serious hearing loss in late adulthood is twice as common among those who never graduated from high school as it is among high school graduates (National Center for Health Statistics, 2010). This statistic comes from the United States, but data on almost every ailment, from every nation and ethnic group, confirm that high school graduation correlates with better health. Some of the reasons are indirectly related to education (e.g., income and place of residence), but even when such factors are taken into account, health improves with education.

More important for nations is another fact: Global economic growth depends on highly educated workers. Partly because political leaders recognize that educated adults advance national wealth and health, every nation is increasing the number of students in secondary schools. Education is compulsory until at least age 12 almost everywhere (UNESCO, 2008), and several national leaders (including President Obama in 2012) advocate compulsory education until age 18 or high school graduation, whichever comes first.

Often two levels of secondary education are provided. As the age of puberty has decreased, junior high schools have been replaced by **middle schools,** created to educate 10- to 13-year-olds (grades 6, 7, and 8), followed by high schools, grades 9 to 12. Each level grapples with particular problems.

Middle School

Many developmentalists find middle schools to be "developmentally regressive" (Eccles & Roeser, 2010, p. 13); that is, they push children's intellectual growth backwards. The average grades on report cards fall, achievement tests show less learning each year, and students are less motivated to study and learn.

Does this matter for later achievement? One team believes so: "Long-term academic trajectories—the choice to stay in school or to drop out and the selection in high school of academic college-prep courses versus basic-level courses—are strongly influenced by experience in grades 6–8" (Snow et al., 2007, p. 72).

As achievement slows down, behavioral problems rise. Puberty itself is part of the problem. Evidence shows that for non-human animals, especially when under stress, learning slows down at puberty (McCormick et al., 2010). The same is probably true for humans.

However, many experts do not believe the biological or psychological stresses of puberty are the main reasons learning suffers in early adolescence. Instead, they blame the organizational structure of many middle schools (Meece & Eccles, 2010).

To be specific, unlike in primary school, in which each teacher is responsible for one classroom of children, middle school teachers are not connected to any small group. Instead they specialize in an academic subject, taught to hundreds of students each year. This makes them impersonal and distant: Their students learn less and risk more because no single teacher is aware of their actions (Crosnoe et al., 2004).

---

secondary education
Literally, the period after primary education (elementary or grade school) and before tertiary education (college). It usually occurs from about age 12 to 18, although there is some variation by school and by nation.

middle school
A school for children in the grades between elementary and high school. Middle school usually begins with grade 6 and ends with grade 8.

✦ **ESPECIALLY FOR Middle School Teachers** You think your lectures are interesting and you know you care about your students, yet many of them cut class, come late, or sleep through it. What do you do? (see response, page 343) →

Same Situation, Far Apart: No Romance Here Young adolescents around the globe, such as these in California *(left)* and Pakistan *(right)*, attend middle school, but what they learn differs. Many North American schools encourage collaboration and hands-on learning (these girls are dissecting a squid), whereas many south Asian schools stress individual writing. Note that both classrooms are single sex—unusual in the United States but standard in many developing nations. What do students learn from that?

It is ironic that just when egocentrism leads young people to feelings of shame or fantasies of stardom (the imaginary audience), many middle schools require them to change rooms, teachers, and classmates every 40 minutes or so. That makes public acclaim and personal recognition difficult.

Since public acclaim is elusive, many middle school students seek acceptance from their peers. Bullying increases, appearance becomes important, status symbols are displayed (from gang colors to expensive shoes), and sexual conquests are flaunted, with boys bragging and girls gaining status if they have older boyfriends.

Values change: In fourth grade, the "coolest" peers are good students; by eighth grade, cool peers are not involved in school but likely to be antisocial (unkind, antagonistic to adults) (Galván, et al., 2011). Of course, much depends on the cultural context, but almost every middle school student seeks peer approval in ways that adults disapprove of (Véronneau & Dishion, 2010).

MOTIVATION A cognitive perspective on development highlights the academic disengagement typical of middle school students, trying to uncover causes and effective prevention. Several causes have already been suggested: puberty, alienation from teachers, reliance on peers. But an additional reason may be an adolescent's assumptions about his or her potential.

Some students prevent feelings of failure by avoiding effort. They blame a low grade on "I didn't study," rather than on "I am stupid." The students' understanding of their own ability and how to achieve what they wish is key.

If they believe in the **entity approach to intelligence** (i.e., that ability is innate, a fixed quantity present at birth), then they think it hopeless to study, especially in subjects that do not come easily. All they can do is accept their deficiencies, whether in math, or writing, or languages. They are convinced that they are innately stupid in some ways and always will be. This entity belief reduces stress but also reduces achievement.

By contrast, if students believe in the **incremental approach to intelligence** (i.e., that ability increases if they work on it), then they will pay attention, participate in class, study, complete their homework, and so on. That is called *mastery motivation*.

This is not just a hypothesis. In the first year of middle school, students with entity beliefs do not achieve much, whereas those with mastery motivation show achievement gains (Blackwell et al., 2007). In one study, some students in their first year of middle school took part in a program in which they were taught eight lessons designed

entity approach to intelligence
An approach to understanding intelligence that sees ability as innate, a fixed quantity present at birth; those who hold this view do not believe that effort enhances achievement.

incremental approach to intelligence
An approach to understanding intelligence that holds that intelligence can be directly increased by effort; those who subscribe to this view believe they can master whatever they seek to learn if they pay attention, participate in class, study, complete their homework, and so on.

ANSWER TO **OBSERVATION QUIZ**
(from page 339) The flag on the robot matches her T-shirt. Often teenagers wear matching shirts to signify their joint identity. ●

to convey the idea that being smart was incremental. For instance, they were taught ways to "Grow Your Intelligence," as one segment of the program was called. Especially if they had formerly held the entity theory of intelligence, those students showed achievement gains while students in other classes did not (Blackwell et al., 2007).

Teachers themselves were surprised at the effect. Among the typical comments was a teacher explaining that a boy

> who never puts in any extra effort and doesn't turn in homework on time, actually stayed up late working for hours to finish an assignment early so I could review it and give him a chance to revise it. He earned a B+ . . . he had been getting C's and lower.
>
> *[quoted in Blackwell et al., 2007, p. 256]*

The concept that skills and intelligence can be mastered motivates the learning of social skills as well as academic subjects (Olson & Dweck, 2008). This makes it particularly important in adolescence, when peers are so important.

The contrast between the entity and incremental approaches is apparent not only for individual adolescents, but also for teachers, parents, schools, and cultures. If a school is structured so that children individually compete with each another rather than work in cooperative groups, then individuals who score low are likely to cope by endorsing the entity theory (Eccles & Roeser, 2011). By contrast, when teachers and students believe in mastery, they are supportive of each other's learning (Patrick et al., 2011).

According to international comparisons, educational systems that track students into higher or lower classes, that expel students who are not learning, and that allow competition between schools for the brightest students (all reflecting entity, not incremental, theory) are also school systems with lower average achievement and a larger gap between student scores at the highest and lowest quartiles (OECD, 2011).

Before condemning all middle schools, however, remember that adolescents vary in every aspect of development, including motivation. A study of student emotional and academic engagement from the fifth to the eighth grade found that, as expected, the overall direction was less engagement. Yet, a distinct group (about 18 percent) was highly engaged throughout, and only a few (about 5 percent) decreased drastically in engagement from grades 5 to 8. The disengaged students were often minority boys from low-income families (Li & Lerner, 2011). That finding should alert teachers to choose those young boys for various roles and responsibilities—engaging them before they have a chance to disengage.

School Transitions

Every transition is stressful. The most difficult times are the first year of middle school, the first year of high school, and the first year of college. The larger and less personal the new institution is, and the more egocentric the student is, the more difficult the transition.

STRANGERS IN SCHOOL When students enter a new school with classmates and customs unlike those in their old school, minority students (who may have been the majority in their neighborhood or nation) often feel alienated, fearing failure (Benner & Graham, 2007). It is not diversity per se that is difficult; it is the sudden unfamiliar circumstances.

One particular problem is *stereotype threat,* the anxiety-producing idea that other people are judging you in stereotyped ways (Aronson & Dee, 2012). Stereotype threat may be disconnected from actual stereotyping, as it describes a person's own perceived fear that other people are judging him or her as deficient for being Black or White, male or female, rich or poor. This idea is further explained in Chapter 11.

A study of the transition from middle to high school confirmed that personal relationships are crucial. Students are less likely to drop out if they have friends in the new school and teachers who encourage learning (Langenkamp, 2010). School policies (e.g., class placement, group discussions) can facilitate such relationships.

Students already at risk of emotional problems may be pushed over the edge by the transition; anxiety, depression, and quitting may result. Worse psychological disorders may occur. As one expert notes:

> Depression, self-injury behavior, substance abuse, eating disorders, bipolar disorder, and schizophrenia have striking developmental patterns corresponding to transitions in early and late adolescence.
>
> *[Masten, 2004, p. 310]*

Of course, transitions are not the only cause of adolescent pathology; hormones, body changes, sexual experiences, family conflict, and cultural expectations also contribute. In addition, puberty may activate genes that predispose a person to mental disorders (Erath et al., 2009), and the sequence of brain development may cause emotional difficulties. Nonetheless, for many reasons, adolescent newcomers to a school community need extra support to learn well.

To eliminate one transition, some school systems and even some nations (e.g., Finland) have children attend the same institution from first through eighth or ninth grade. In the United States, the timing of when children leave primary school varies by school district. When the change occurs early, after fourth grade (but not after fifth, sixth, or seventh) or not until after eighth grade, children seem to learn more (Schwartz et al., 2011).

Some small private schools eliminate transitions by having one school from kindergarten through twelfth grade. This may facilitate learning, or it may make it more difficult for graduates to adjust to college, to the workplace, to a new community.

A school that is too large might also pose difficulties, especially for students entering from more intimate schools. Some research suggests that school enrollment should be 600 or fewer students, although many urban high schools boast more than a thousand students. When schools are that large, many students are strangers to each other, and the principal cannot know everyone by name. For most (though not all) students, engagement decreases as school size increases (Weiss et al., 2010). However, school size may be less problematic than school organization, such as having many different students for each teacher (too impersonal) and weak school norms, loyalty, and spirit (a problem for large schools) (Gottfredson & DiPietro, 2011).

CYBER DANGER Bullying decreases each year of elementary school, perhaps because students learn from classmates and teachers that there are better ways to interact with other children. However, many studies find that bullying increases in the first year of middle school and again in the first year of high school. Puberty itself increases sexual interest and impulses, as you just read, yet many adolescents are uncertain about their urges. One result is an increase in teasing and harassment, sometimes bullying. This occurs between the sexes as well as within them, with girls likely to bully other girls they perceive as sexual rivals, and boys likely to bully other boys they perceive as gay.

Beyond that, many students new to a larger school feel they need to assert themselves. Furthermore, contemporary students are digital natives, having grown up with iPods, cell phones, and high-speed broadband. However, some students, especially bully-victims (see Chapter 8), engage in, and suffer from, **cyberbullying** (Tokunaga, 2010)—that is, any bullying that uses technology. Usually, those most involved are already bullies or victims or both.

RESPONSE FOR Middle School Teachers (from page 341) Students need both challenge and involvement; avoid lessons that are too easy or too passive. Create small groups; assign oral reports, debates, role-plays, and so on. Remember that adolescents like to hear each other's thoughts and their own voices. ●

cyberbullying
Bullying that occurs when one person spreads insults or rumors about another by means of technology (e.g., e-mails, text messages, or cell phone videos).

Suicide Device The social media capabilities of high schooler Yuriko and his cell phone (shown here) drove him to thoughts of suicide. Fortunately, he got help to stop the mental torture he suffered from cyberbullying—a problem that may be worse in Japan because social reputation is crucial. For the same reason, young adolescents are particularly vulnerable to cyberbullying.

In many ways, cyberbullying is similar to other forms of harassment—harmful to everyone, as it undermines learning in bullies, bystanders, and particularly in victims (Marsh et al., 2010; P. K. Smith et al., 2008; Schneider et al., 2012). It is another form of relational bullying, designed to harm social interactions, with girls being cyberbullies as often as boys.

Although the causes of all forms of bullying seem similar, each carries its own sting. For example, the impact of cyberbullying is worse when the self-image is forming, the imaginary audience is looming, and impulsive thinking often supersedes analytic thinking in early adolescence. With technology, rumors and insults spread far and wide, with immediate reach, day and night, and impulses can be actualized at the touch of a button (Englander et al., 2009). The ease of posting photos makes it even worse: It is hard to deny visual evidence of oneself drunk, naked, or crying.

All forms of bullying are affected by the school climate. When students consider their school a good place to be—with supportive teachers, friendly students, opportunities for growth (clubs, sports, theater, music), and so on—those with high self-esteem are not only less likely to engage in cyberbullying, but they also disapprove of it (Gendron et al., 2011). That reduces the incidence overall.

However, when the school climate is negative, those with high self-esteem are often bullies (Gendron et al., 2011). As with other forms of bullying, the victim and bystanders can stop cyberbullying, in this case by deleting messages unread and thus unspread (Parris et al., 2012).

High School

As we have seen, adolescents can think abstractly, analytically, hypothetically, and logically—as well as personally, emotionally, intuitively, and experientially. The curriculum and teaching style in high school often require the former mode of thinking. Students who need more individualized, personal attention may struggle.

Same Situation, Far Apart: How to Learn Although developmental psychologists find that adolescents learn best when they are actively engaged with ideas, many school systems find that teenagers are easier to control when they are taking tests (left, Winston-Salem, United States) or reciting scripture (right, Kabul, Afghanistan).

THE COLLEGE-BOUND From a developmental perspective, the fact that high schools emphasize analytic, deductive thinking makes sense since many 15- to 18-year-olds are capable of abstract logic. Instead of teaching their pupils formal operational thinking, high school teachers typically assume that the students have already mastered it (Kuhn & Franklin, 2006).

The United States is trying to raise standards so that all high school graduates will be college-ready. One way to accomplish this has been to increase the number of students who take classes that are assessed by externally scored exams, either the

IB (International Baccalaureate) or the AP (Advanced Placement). Such classes have high standards and satisfy some college requirements.

Unfortunately, merely taking such classes does not necessarily lead to college readiness (Sadler et al., 2010). In 2010, although 17 percent of U.S. students took AP exams, about one-third of them failed. Far fewer take the IB exams, and very few of them are granted the highest scores. In 2010, only one graduate in nine earned college credit based on an AP or IB exam—and that was an improvement over prior years (Gewertz, 2011).

Most U.S. high school students are required to pass a **high-stakes test** in order to graduate. (Any exam for which the consequences of failing are severe is called a high-stakes test.) No state required such tests for graduation two decades ago.

high-stakes test
An evaluation that is critical in determining success or failure. If a single test determines whether a student will graduate or be promoted, it is a high-stakes test.

OPPOSING PERSPECTIVES

Testing

Students in the United States take many more tests than they did even a decade ago. This includes several high-stakes tests—not only the tests to earn a high school diploma, but also tests to get into college (the SAT and ACT, achievement and aptitude); tests to earn college credits while in high school; and tests to get into high school, middle school, fourth grade, and even gifted kindergarten classes.

These tests often carry high stakes not only for the students who repeat a grade if they fail, but also for teachers and schools. Teachers sometimes earn extra pay or tenure, or are fired, based on what their students have learned in a year, and schools are sometimes granted more resources, or are shut down, because of test scores.

The impact of these tests on learning is controversial, with data supporting both sides. Some argue that adolescents study harder and learn more if they know a high-stakes test is coming. From 2000 to 2008, some states have seen an increase in the percentage of students who pass high-stakes tests, but other states have decreasing graduation rates (Zhang, 2009).

Overall, high school graduation rates in the United States are inching upwards, with 72 percent of ninth-grade students staying in school to graduate four years later (see Figure 9.6) (Swanson, 2011). Some say that tests and standards are part of the reason.

However, many fear that students who do not graduate are discouraged, and that some students leave before twelfth grade because they fear failure. According to the U.S. Center for Education Policy, high-stakes tests have "a negative impact on . . . low-performing students, students of color, or students from low-income families" (2010, p. 1). One such negative impact is that students who experience stereotype threat, especially minorities, avoid taking high-stakes tests in order to protect their identity (Syed et al., 2011). This may be racist on their part, or on the part of the test advocates.

Even those who pass may be less excited about education. Overall, a panel of experts in education found that too

much testing reduces learning rather than advances it (Hout & Elliot, 2011). But how much is "too much"?

Polls of United States citizens consistently find more people in favor of accountability, standards, and tests than opposed to them (Phelps, 2005). Presidents of the United States—first in No Child Left Behind (instituted by George W. Bush, a Republican) and then in Race to the Top (instituted by Barack Obama, a Democrat), for example—use test scores to entice states to raise school standards.

As reviewed in Chapter 7, two international tests, the TIMSS (Trends in International Mathematics and Science Study) and the PIRLS (Progress in International Reading Literacy Study), find that the United States is only middling among developed nations in student learning. A third international test, the PISA (Programme for International Student Assessment), explained toward the end of this chapter, places U.S. students even lower (see Appendix A).

In many nations, scores on those three international tests compel reexamination of school policies and practices. Although the United States' scores have not improved because of more testing, one critic commends such tests for revealing deficiencies in U.S. education that previously were hard to measure (Walberg, 2011).

International data do not provide clear answers on this controversial topic. One nation whose children generally score well is South Korea, where high-stakes tests have resulted in extensive studying. To be specific, many South Korean parents spend substantial sums on "shadow education," hiring tutors to teach their children after school and on weekends to improve their test scores (Lee & Shouse, 2011).

On the opposite side, students in Finland also score very well on international tests, and yet they have no national tests until the end of high school. Nor do they spend much time on homework or after-school education. A Finnish expert proudly states that "schoolteachers teach in order to help their students learn, not to pass tests" (Sahlberg, 2011, p. 26). He believes that teachers are motivated to do their best with each child because there is no external standard that makes them "teach to the test."

Many educators fear that overtesting is sapping the energy and creativity of teachers and students. In Finland, teaching is a prestigious profession, with 10 times as many applicants as acceptances to the university programs that offer a teaching degree (Sahlberg, 2011). However, since developmentalists are scientists, they try not to be swayed by public opinion. Instead, data are needed, but the data can be interpreted in many ways.

Some people argue that tests add stress and decrease learning, with one American asking educators to "make this fight against standardized tests our top priority until we have chased this monster from our schools" (Kohn, 2001, p. 350). Others recommend "using tests to motivate students and teachers for better performance" (Walberg, 2011, p. 7). The expert just cited believes that well-constructed tests benefit everyone—teachers, students, and the taxpayers who fund public education. Poorly designed tests are destructive, he says, but that fact should not be used to condemn testing.

Ironically, just when more U.S. schools are raising standards and requirements, many East Asian nations, including China, Singapore, and Japan (all with high scores on international tests), are moving in the opposite direction. Particularly in Singapore, national high-stakes tests are being phased out, and local autonomy is increasing (Hargreaves, 2012).

Soon more international data will provide some answers, we hope. If Finland and Singapore continue to do well, and improvement lags in North America, it may indicate that tests are not helping. On the other hand, many factors besides tests could explain those results, and political leaders can interpret scores in opposite ways. Ideally, each developmentalist will consider the data objectively, and half the people will change their minds—not easy for anyone.

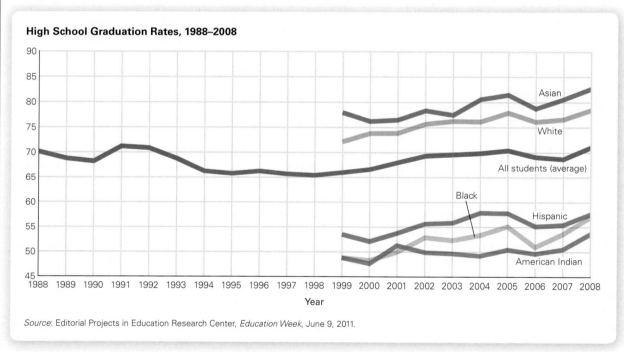

High School Graduation Rates, 1988–2008

Source: Editorial Projects in Education Research Center, *Education Week*, June 9, 2011.

FIGURE 9.6 Graduation Rates on the Rebound The U.S. graduation rate has reached its highest point thus far. Every racial and ethnic group posted solid gains for the class of 2008, marking the second straight year of across-the-board improvements—and more recent data (not shown because ethnic breakdown not yet available) show even greater gains. These data are based on the most conservative and probably the most accurate estimate of graduation; that is, the percentage of new ninth-grade students who earn a diploma four years later. The gap between Asian/White and the three other groups is almost always the result of differences in SES—poor families often live in communities with poor schools.

✦ **ESPECIALLY FOR High School Teachers** You are much more interested in the nuances and controversies than in the basic facts of your subject, but you know that your students will take high-stakes tests on the basics and that their scores will have a major impact on their futures. What should you do? (see response, page 348) ➞

THOSE WHO DO NOT GO TO COLLEGE In the United States, one result of pushing an academic curriculum is that most students hope to attend college, most enroll, and . . . most leave without the bachelor's degree they seek. Many high school graduates (70 percent) enter college. However, a decade later, only 32 percent of U.S. young adults, aged 25–34, have earned a bachelor's degree (Snyder & Dillow, 2011). Some may still earn a degree later in life, but most leave feeling they have failed, never to return.

That fuels a debate among educators. Should students be encouraged to "dream big" early in high school, aspiring for tertiary learning? This suggestion originates from studies finding a correlation between dreaming big in early adolescence and going to college years later (Domina et al., 2011a, 2011b). Others suggest that college is a "fairy tale dream" that may lead to low self-esteem (Rosenbaum, 2011). If adolescents fail academic classes, will they feel bored, stupid, and disengaged?

In the United States, some 2,500 *Career Academies* (small institutions of about 300 students each) prepare students for specific jobs. Seven years after graduation, students who were in these alternative programs earn about $100 more a month than do other students who applied but could not enroll because there was no room (Kemple, 2008). They are also more likely to be married (38 percent versus 34 percent) and living with their children (51 percent versus 44 percent).

In another example, in Italy, vocational education succeeded when the learning included "hands-on" practical education (rare in academic courses that prepare students for college) and a personal commitment by the teachers to their students (relationships again) (Bonica & Sappa, 2010). Why are vocational schools not more popular? Preparing students for jobs instead of college may seem—or may be—racist, classist, sexist, or otherwise stereotyping.

Teachers also favor the college-bound adolescents. If they find themselves teaching vocational students, they may themselves feel like failures. In the United States, the most qualified teachers gravitate away from vocational schools and toward schools with more able students (where salaries are higher and class sizes are smaller).

Within schools, the most experienced teachers are often assigned classes full of college-bound students. All students learn best when a master teacher guides active discussion, debate, and exposition, but those who most need such teaching are least likely to receive it (Slavin et al., 2009).

Nor do teachers necessarily know how to relate to students who are unlike them. Secondary school teachers are hired for their academic expertise, not for their ability to engage adolescents. They model formal operational thinking—answering questions about the intricacies of theoretical physics, advanced calculus, and iambic pentameter—but they may not connect with students or understand practical vocational requirements.

Some nations provide equally qualified and equally paid teachers for every school and encourage teachers to mentor one another. The disparity in teacher quality between wealthy and impoverished schools is much greater in the United States than in nations that score high on the PISA (e.g., Finland and Canada) (Cavanagh, 2007). Not surprisingly, the SES achievement disparity is lowest in Finland (Sahlberg, 2011).

However, it is too simple to conclude that teacher quality, preparation, and prestige are the only reason some nations and schools score higher than others. Finland also has free early-childhood education (98 percent of the children attend) as well as national health care. Those factors help all children reach their potential, but some learn much more than others. Variation of achievement scores within schools is as high in Finland as in the United States and many other nations.

CHOOSING VOCATIONS "What will you be when you grow up?" is a question often asked of children. Younger children often aspire to vocations that fewer than one in a million will obtain—rock star, sports hero, U.S. President—and adults smile at such fantasies. By the teen years, however, more practical concerns arise, specifically what jobs are available and how enjoyable, remunerative, and demanding each is. The question becomes hard to answer.

Adults provide little help. Parents usually know only their particular employment or lack of it, not labor-market projections. Few parents are able to connect their child's interests and abilities with vocational possibilities 20 years hence.

● **UNDERSTANDING THE NUMBERS**
Note that these statistics say that 70 percent of high school *graduates* enter college—a number that does not include students who never graduate from high school. Why?

Answer High school graduation statistics are notoriously varied: Some count only those who formally leave, others include those who disappear (who might be at another school), and still others include everyone who has not graduated after four years of high school. However, the proportion of young adults without a BA (68 percent) is considered a reliable statistic, which makes it particularly troubling that more than a dozen nations (including Australia, Korea, Sweden, and the United Kingdom) do better than the United States on this measure.

RESPONSE FOR High School Teachers (from page 346) It would be nice to follow your instincts, but the appropriate response depends partly on pressures within the school and on the expectations of the parents and administration. A comforting fact is that adolescents can think about and learn almost anything if they feel a personal connection to it. Look for ways to teach the facts your students need for the tests as the foundation for the exciting and innovative topics you want to teach. Everyone will learn more, and the tests will be less intimidating for your students. ●

PISA (Programme for International Student Assessment)
An international test taken by 15-year-olds in 50 nations that is designed to measure problem solving and cognition in daily life.

In theory, adults in high schools guide students toward vocations. But teachers know only their discipline, and guidance counselors in the United States have an *average* caseload of 270 students. Of those 270, many want to apply to a dozen colleges and require recommendations and suggestions; some need immediate and multifaceted emotional support to prevent violence, suicide, or drug addiction. Few counselors have either time or expertise to provide vocational guidance (Zehr, 2011).

Some ambitious adolescents begin to think about careers on their own. Many use John Holland's description (1997) of six possible interests, which is discussed in Chapter 11. If students develop a vision of their future and then realize that particular high school courses might advance their preferred career, they may choose those courses. Few students have such a vision; drifting is the more common pattern.

MEASURING PRACTICAL COGNITION Employers usually provide on-the-job training, which is much more specific and current than what high schools provide. They hope their future employees will have learned in secondary school how to think, explain, write, concentrate, and get along with other people. Similar skills are necessary for the college-bound, especially if they hope to gain enough credits to earn a degree. Those skills are hard to measure, though, especially on national high-stakes tests or on the two international tests explained in Chapter 7, the PIRLS and the TIMSS.

The **PISA,** mentioned earlier, was designed to measure the cognitive abilities needed in adult life, not necessarily the ones that help students in college classes. The PISA is taken by 15-year-olds, an age chosen because many students that age are close to the end of their formal school career. On this test, the questions are written to be practical, measuring knowledge that might apply at home or on the job. As a PISA report described it:

> The tests are designed to generate measures of the extent to which students can make effective use of what they have learned in school to deal with various problems and challenges they are likely to experience in everyday life.
>
> *[PISA, 2009, p. 12]*

For example, among the math questions is this one:

> Robert's mother lets him pick one candy from a bag. He can't see the candies. The number of candies of each color in the bag is shown in the following graph.

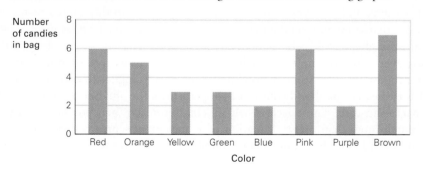

> What is the probability that Robert will pick a red candy?
>
> A. 10%   B. 20%   C. 25%   D. 50%

For that and the other questions on the PISA, the calculations are quite simple—most 10-year-olds can do them; no calculus, calculators, or complex formulas are required. However, the reasoning may be challenging, and many students do not know how to read a graph. Half of the 15-year-olds worldwide got that question wrong (the answer is B), as did more than half of the students from the United States.

TABLE 9.1 Math Scores on the PISA, 2009/2006

Nation	Score	Nation	Score	Nation	Score
China Shanghai	600/n/a	Denmark	503/513	Greece	466/459
Singapore	562/n/a	Norway	498/490	Israel	447/442
Hong Kong	555/547	France	497/496	Turkey	445/424
South Korea	546/547	Austria	496/505	Uruguay	427/427
Chinese Taipei	543/549	Poland	495/495	Romania	427/415
Finland	541/548	Sweden	494/502	Chile	421/411
Switzerland	534/530	Czech Republic	493/510	Thailand	419/417
Japan	529/523	United Kingdom	492/495	Mexico	419/406
Canada	527/527	Hungary	490/491	Argentina	388/381
Netherlands	526/531	Ireland	487/501	Jordan	387/384
New Zealand	519/522	United States	487/474	Brazil	386/370
Belgium	515/520	Portugal	487/466	Colombia	381/370
Australia	514/520	Spain	483/480	Indonesia	371/391
Germany	513/504	Italy	483/462	Tunisia	371/365
Iceland	507/506	Russia	468/476		

Source: PISA, 2009.

Not Geography The PISA is taken by 15-year-olds in many nations. Questions are designed to measure practical applications of school knowledge in science, reading, and math. National variations are more closely tied to educational practices and values at school and home, not to geography, genes, or immigration. For instance, the Netherlands and Norway are close on the map but not in math achievement, and, although most East Asian nations do very well, Thailand scores low. Also note that nations with a higher proportion of immigrants than the United States (e.g., Canada) or very few immigrants (e.g., Japan) seem to do equally well.

Overall, the U.S. students did worse on the PISA than on the PIRLS or TIMSS. On the PISA overall (reading, science, and math), China, Finland, and South Korea were at the top; Canada was close to the top; and the United States scored near average or below average in math, reading, and science (see Table 9.1). Analysis of nations and scores on the PISA finds four factors that correlate with high achievement (OECD, 2010, p. 6):

1. Leaders, parents, and citizens overall value education, with individualized approaches to learning so that all students learn what they need.

2. Standards are high and clear, so every student knows what he or she must do, with a "focus on the acquisition of complex, higher-order thinking skills."

3. Teachers and administrators are valued, given "considerable discretion . . . in determining content" and sufficient salary as well as time for collaboration.

4. Learning is prioritized "across the entire system," with high-quality teachers working in the most challenging environments.

Indications from the PISA and from international comparisons of high school dropout rates suggest that secondary education can be improved for those who do not go to college. Surprisingly, students who are capable of passing their classes drop out almost as often as those who are less capable, at least as measured on IQ tests.

Persistence, engagement, and motivation seem more crucial than intellectual ability (Archambault et al., 2009; Tough, 2012). One study that measured engagement and motivation reported developmental differences: Students were most motivated and engaged in primary school, somewhat engaged in college, but least engaged in secondary school (Martin, 2009).

Praising Adolescent Cognition

It is easy to conclude that adolescent thinking is immature and self-absorbed. No wonder secondary schools have difficulty imparting information and students are disengaged. However, we should not close this chapter on that note.

BENEFITS OF ADOLESCENT BRAIN DEVELOPMENT With increased myelination and still-underdeveloped inhibition, reactions become lightning fast; such speed is valuable in cognition as well as in other domains. For instance, adolescent athletes are potential superstars, not only quick but fearless as they steal a base, tackle a fullback, or race even when their lungs feel about to burst. Ideally, coaches have the wisdom to channel such bravery.

Furthermore, as the reward areas of the brain activate and the production of certain mood-enhancing neurotransmitters increases, teenagers become happier. Reaction to a new love, or a first job, or even an A on a term paper can be ecstasy, a joy to be cherished in memory for life.

Before another wave of pruning (at about age 18), and before the brain becomes fully mature (at about age 25), "young brains have both fast-growing synapses and sections that remain unconnected" (Ruder, 2008, p. 8). This allows new connections to facilitate acquisition of new ideas, words, memories, personality patterns, and dance steps.

Synaptic growth enhances moral development as well. Adolescents question their elders and seek to forge their own standards. Values embraced during adolescence are more likely to endure than those acquired later, after brain connections are firmly established. This is an asset if values developed during adolescence are less self-centered than those of children or are more culturally attuned than those of older generations.

Thus, adolescence is an ideal time to question tradition and learn new things. Of course, some members of a community should uphold traditions while others question them, and society as a whole should be neither too quick to abandon the past nor too stuck in it, but everyone benefits if opposite perspectives are advocated.

In short, several aspects of adolescent brain development can be positive. The fact that the prefrontal cortex is still developing "confers benefits as well as risks. It helps explain the creativity of adolescence and early adulthood, before the brain becomes set in its ways" (Monastersky, 2007, p. A-17). As a practical application, those who care about the next generation must attend to the life lessons that adolescents are learning.

BETTER THINKING Adults are understandably critical when egocentrism leads an impulsive teenager to risk addiction by experimenting with drugs or to risk pregnancy and AIDS by rejecting a condom. Wisdom, to adults, means caution.

But adults may themselves be egocentric in making such judgments. Adults want teenagers to have long and productive lives, and they conclude that adolescents use faulty reasoning when they choose to party instead of study, or do something that risks their health. Adolescents, however, value social warmth and friendship. A 15-year-old who is offered a cigarette might rationally choose camaraderie over the distant risk of cancer (Engels et al., 2006).

Research on how adults make complex decisions, such as who to marry or which investment to make, finds that sometimes intuitive decisions are best and sometimes not (Dijksterhuis & Aarts, 2010). At every age, the best thinking may be "fast and frugal" (Gigerenzer, 2008). Weighing alternatives, and thinking of possibilities, is sometimes paralyzing. Few adolescents have that problem.

Even egocentrism has its advantages, protecting the self "each time an individual enters into a new environmental context or dramatically new life situation" (Schwartz et al., 2008, p. 447). Young adolescents who feel psychologically invincible (not harmed by others' judgments) tend to be resilient, less likely to be depressed (Hill et al., 2012).

Of course, if a criticism from a peer cuts too deep, friends and family need to help the young person gain perspective, but difficult experiences build resilience as long as they are not overwhelming (Seery, 2011). All the sudden and erratic body changes of puberty that we described are easier to handle if a person feels special and strong.

WHAT ADULTS CAN DO Does learning during adolescence matter when considering the entire life span? For individuals, the answer is a resounding yes. Not only health but also most every other indicator of a good life—high income, stable marriage, successful children, satisfying work—correlates with education.

For society, the answer is yes as well. Nations gain from the improved quality of secondary education. A detailed calculation found that *if* the United States' average PISA score increased by a mere 25 points (up to the scores for Belgium, Australia, and Germany; still far below those of South Korea or Chinese Taipei), that would result in an increase of *$40 trillion* in the nation's GDP (gross domestic product, which measures economic production) between 2010 and 2090 (Hanushek & Woessmann, 2010). How could this be?

The cognitive skills that boost economic development are creativity, flexibility, and analytic ability; they allow for innovation and mastery of new technology. When nations raise their human capital by developing more adults with those skills, their economies prosper (Cohen & Soto, 2007). The scores of various nations on the PISA and other tests predict later economic development (Hanushek & Woessmann, 2010).

The cognitive abilities that nations need to succeed in the twenty-first century are exactly what adolescents can develop—with proper education and guidance. The potential is there; what will we do about it?

KEY points

- Secondary education is crucial for personal health and for national economic development.

- Many students become alienated from learning during middle school; middle schools are not usually organized to encourage relationships between teachers and students.

- Transitions to new schools are always challenging, as illustrated by the increase in bullying, especially cyberbullying, as middle school begins.

- High-stakes national tests required for high school graduation, and international tests such as the PISA, raise questions about the quality of secondary education in the United States.

- Adolescents are capable of intense learning of new ideas and of questioning traditional beliefs.

SUMMARY

Puberty

1. Puberty refers to the various changes that transform a child's body into an adult one. A sequence of biochemical signals from the hypothalamus to the pituitary gland to the adrenal glands (the HPA axis) increases production of testosterone, estrogen, and various other hormones, which in turn causes the body to develop.

2. Hormones regulate daily and seasonal body rhythms. In adolescence, these may result in sleep deprivation because high schools open early and the natural circadian rhythm keeps teenagers wide awake at night.

3. Puberty most often begins between ages 10 and 13. Genes, gender, body fat, and family stress all contribute to this variation in timing, with girls generally beginning puberty before boys.

4. Adolescents who reach puberty earlier or later than their friends experience additional stresses. Generally (depending on culture, community, and cohort), early-maturing girls have a particularly difficult time.

5. The growth spurt is an acceleration of growth in every part of the body. Peak weight usually precedes peak height, which is then followed by peak muscle growth.

6. Sexual characteristics differentiate males from females at adolescence, not only in reproductive potential but also in body shape, breasts, voice, body hair, and so on.

Nutrition

7. Many adolescents are very concerned about body image, especially how they think they look to other adolescents. They may diet irrationally instead of eating a balanced diet, which can often result in calcium and iron deficiency.

8. Although anorexia and bulimia are often not diagnosed until early adulthood, their precursors are evident during puberty. The origins are genetic and familial as well as cultural.

Thinking, Fast and Slow

9. Various parts of the brain mature during puberty and in the following decade. The regions dedicated to emotional arousal (including the limbic system) mature before those that regulate and rationalize emotion (the prefrontal cortex). Consequently, many adolescents are quick to react, take risks, and learn.

10. Cognition in early adolescence may be egocentric, a kind of self-centered thinking. Adolescent egocentrism gives rise to the personal fable, the invincibility fable, and the imaginary audience.

11. *Formal operational thought* is Piaget's term for the last of his four periods of cognitive development, in which adolescents are no longer earthbound and concrete in their thinking. They prefer to speculate instead of focusing on reality. They develop hypotheses and explore, using deductive reasoning.

12. Intuitive thinking also becomes stronger during adolescence. Few teenagers always use logic, although they are capable of doing so. Dual processing is evident.

Teaching and Learning

13. Secondary education—after primary education (grade school) and before tertiary education (college)—correlates with the health and wealth of individuals and nations.

14. In middle school, many students tend to be bored, difficult to teach, and hurtful to one another. One reason may be that middle schools are not structured to accommodate egocentrism or intuitive thinking.

15. Cyberbulling and many forms of psychopathology increase during school transitions, which are particularly difficult in adolescence, when young people must also adjust to biological and family changes.

16. Education in high school emphasizes formal operational thinking, sometimes to the detriment of applied cognition as measured by the PISA, an international test. In the United States, the demand for high standards has led to high-stakes tests. These may undercut creativity, innovation, and learning for students who do not earn college degrees.

KEY TERMS

adolescent egocentrism (p. 333)
adrenal glands (p. 320)
analytic thought (p. 338)
anorexia nervosa (p. 329)
body image (p. 328)
bulimia nervosa (p. 329)
circadian rhythm (p. 322)
cyberbullying (p. 343)
deductive reasoning (p. 335)
dual-process model (p. 336)
entity approach to intelligence (p. 341)

estradiol (p. 321)
formal operational thought (p. 334)
growth spurt (p. 326)
high-stakes test (p. 345)
hormone (p. 320)
HPA (hypothalamus–pituitary–adrenal) axis (p. 320)
HPG (hypothalamus–pituitary–gonad) axis (p. 320)
hypothetical thought (p. 335)
imaginary audience (p. 333)

incremental approach to intelligence (p. 341)
inductive reasoning (p. 336)
intuitive thought (p. 336)
invincibility fable (p. 333)
leptin (p. 324)
menarche (p. 319)
middle school (p. 340)
personal fable (p. 333)
PISA (Programme for International Student Assessment) (p. 348)

pituitary (p. 320)
primary sex characteristics (p. 327)
puberty (p. 319)
secondary education (p. 340)
secondary sex characteristics (p. 327)
spermarche (p. 320)
testosterone (p. 321)

WHAT HAVE YOU LEARNED?

1. What visible changes take place in puberty?

2. How do hormones affect the physical and psychological aspects of puberty?

3. Why might some high schools decide to adopt later start times?

4. What are the gender differences in the growth spurt?

5. What is the connection between body fat and onset of puberty in girls? In boys?

6. Why might early puberty be difficult for girls?

7. What problems are common among early-maturing boys?

8. What problems result from the growth spurt sequence (weight, then height, then muscles)?

9. How do the skin and hair change during puberty?

10. What is the crucial difference between primary sex characteristics and secondary sex characteristics? Give examples of each.

11. What problems might occur if adolescents do not get enough iron or calcium?

12. Why is body image often distorted in adolescence?

13. List the symptoms of anorexia and of bulimia.

14. Why does the limbic system develop before the prefrontal cortex, and what are the consequences?

15. How does adolescent egocentrism differ from early childhood egocentrism?

16. How might the invincibility fable explain why adolescents reveal personal information on social media websites?

17. What are the characteristics of formal operational thinking?

18. What is the difference between inductive reasoning and deductive reasoning?

19. How might intuition and analysis lead to opposite conclusions?

20. What mode of thinking—intuitive or analytic—do most people prefer, and why?

21. Why have most junior high schools disappeared?

22. What characteristics of middle schools make them more difficult for students than elementary schools?

23. What is the connection between school climate and bullying?

24. How might a school that believes in the incremental approach to intelligence structure itself to increase student motivation?

25. Why are transitions from one school to another a particular concern for educators? What steps can they take to ease transitions?

26. How does the PISA differ from other international tests?

27. List five benefits of adolescent brain development.

28. Why is high school achievement likely to advance the national economy?

APPLICATIONS

1. Visit a fifth-, sixth-, or seventh-grade class. Note variations in the size and maturity of the students. Do you see any patterns related to gender, ethnicity, body fat, or self-confidence?

2. Interview two to four of your friends who are in their late teens or early 20s about their memories of menarche or spermarche, including their memories of others' reactions. Analyze the connections between body changes and emotional reactions.

3. Talk to a teenager about politics, families, school, religion, or any other topic that might reveal the way that young person thinks. Do you hear any characteristics of adolescent cognition, such as egocentrism, intuitive thinking, or formal thought? Cite examples.

4. Think of a life-changing decision you have made. How did logic and emotion interact? What might have changed if you had given the matter more thought—or less?

>>ONLINE CONNECTIONS

To accompany your textbook, you have access to a number of online resources, including quizzes for every chapter of the book, flashcards (in English and Spanish), critical thinking questions, and case studies. For access to any of these links, go to www.worthpublishers.com/bergerinvitation2e. In addition to these free resources, you'll also find links to podcasts, video clips, diagnostic quizzing with personalized study advice, and an ebook. Some of the videos and activities available online include:

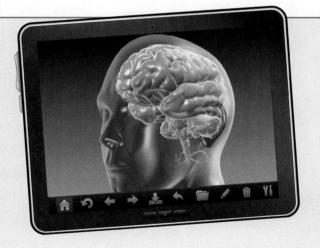

- *The Timing of Puberty.* Too early? Too late? Teens tell their own stories about the impact of pubertal timing. The video also reviews physical changes and gender differences in maturation.

- *Brain Development: Adolescence.* There's a lot going on in a teenager's brain! Animations and illustrations highlight that development and its effect on behavior.

CHAPTER OUTLINE

ADOLESCENCE
Psychosocial Development

WHAT WILL YOU KNOW?

- Why do many teenagers find it hard to achieve sexual identity?
- How could adolescent rebellion be considered a good sign?
- Who is the best source for sex education during adolescence?
- Is adolescent suicide rare, common, or an epidemic?
- When does drug use become drug abuse?

"What does your mother do?" Emil, the head of Town Security, asked my daughter Bethany, whose summer job was security deputy.

"She writes books."

"How does she do that?"

"She spends a lot of time in the library, reading and writing."

"Oh, your poor mother!"

No need for pity, Emil. I enjoy my work.

Each of us has our own preferences, habits, and interests—things we explored when we began to find our identity. Emil liked riding around town, responding to emergencies, searching for "perps." I do not pity him, but I would hate that. Even as a teenager, I enjoyed reading, writing, and explaining. I chose classes that let me find solutions with paper and pencil. Advanced math was a favorite, even though I was the only girl in the class.

In some ways, I was a rebel in high school: I told my friends that I would never be a teacher (too conventional), and I refused to attend the college my parents wanted for me. Instead I ventured 3,000 miles from home, where I knew no one. In other ways, I was typical. I was thrilled when Bill invited me to his college weekend. His roommate said, "That's not the kind of girl you date; that's the kind you marry." That was my plan, too. ●

THIS CHAPTER DESCRIBES THE SEARCH FOR IDENTITY, often a mixture of personal preferences, parental pressure, and teenage rebellion, always within cultural contexts. Adults and peers influence adolescents, who resist parts of their familial and cultural heritage while accepting other parts. One important topic is romance; many adolescents try to discern and express their gender identity via partners, aspirations, and sexuality. That college weekend with Bill would be far less formal today.

Dangers lurk during these years as well. A few adolescents plunge into despair and attempt suicide; most experiment with drugs and defy rules. Details are covered in this chapter, tracing the journey of 11- to 18-year-olds through the psychosocial maze from childhood to adulthood.

Identity

Psychosocial development during adolescence is often considered the search for self-understanding. Self-expression and self-concept become increasingly important, as the egocentrism described in Chapter 9 illustrates. Each young person wants to know, "Who am I?"

identity versus role confusion
Erikson's term for the fifth stage of development, in which the person tries to figure out "Who am I?" but is confused as to which of many possible roles to adopt.

identity achievement
Erikson's term for the attainment of identity, or the point at which a person understands who he or she is as a unique individual, in accord with past experiences and future plans.

According to Erik Erikson, life's fifth psychosocial crisis is **identity versus role confusion:** Negotiating the complexities of finding one's own identity is the primary task of adolescence (Erikson, 1968). He said this crisis is resolved with **identity achievement,** when adolescents have reconsidered the goals and values of their parents and culture, accepting some and discarding others, discerning their own identity.

The result is neither wholesale rejection nor unquestioning acceptance of social norms (Côté, 2009). With their new autonomy, teenagers maintain continuity with the past so they can move into the future.

Not Yet Achieved

Erikson's insights have inspired thousands of researchers. Notable among them was James Marcia, who described and measured four specific ways young people cope with this stage of life: (1) role confusion, (2) foreclosure, (3) moratorium, and finally (4) identity achievement (Marcia, 1966). The opening three will be described here.

First, however, you need to know about an historical change. Over the past half-century, major psychosocial shifts have lengthened the duration of adolescence and made identity achievement more complex (Côté, 2006; Kroger et al., 2010; Meeus, 2011). Although Marcia's way stations on the road to identity achievement still seem evident, the path is longer and more circuitous.

Indeed, several aspects of the search for identity, especially for sexual and vocational identity, have become more arduous than when Erikson wrote about them. Adolescents still seek identity, but developmentalists believe that this crisis is rarely resolved by age 18: "Studies among adults revealed that identity is a life-long process" (Meeus, 2011, p. 88).

role confusion
A situation in which an adolescent does not seem to know or care what his or her identity is. (Sometimes called *identity* or *role diffusion*.)

Role confusion is the opposite of identity achievement. Characterized by lack of commitment to any goals or values, role confusion is sometimes called *identity diffusion,* to emphasize that some adolescents seem diffuse, unfocused, unconcerned about their future (Phillips & Pittman, 2007).

Even the usual social demands—such as putting away clothes, making friends, completing school assignments, and thinking about college or career—are beyond role-confused adolescents. Instead, they might sleep too much, immerse themselves in video games or mind-numbing television, and turn from one flirtation to another. Their thinking is disorganized, they procrastinate, they avoid issues and actions (Côté, 2009).

Identity **foreclosure** occurs when young people accept traditional values (Marcia, 1966; Marcia et al., 1993). They might follow roles and customs transmitted from their parents or culture, never having explored alternatives. Or they might foreclose on an oppositional, *negative identity*—the direct opposite of whatever their parents want—again without thoughtful questioning. Foreclosure is comfortable. For many, it is a temporary shelter, a time for commitment to a particular identity, which might be followed by more exploration (Meeus, 2011).

A more mature shelter is **moratorium,** a time-out that includes some exploration, either in breadth (trying many things) or in depth (examining a single path after making a tentative commitment that may change) (Meeus, 2011). Societies provide many opportunities for moratoria, such as college or military service, allowing adolescents to postpone identity achievement. Moratorium is most common at about age 19, although it can occur earlier or later (Kroger et al., 2010).

Four Arenas of Identity Formation

Erikson (1968) highlighted four aspects of identity: religious, political, vocational, and sexual. Terminology and timing have changed, yet each still merits elaboration.

RELIGIOUS IDENTITY Few adolescents totally reject religion if they've grown up following a particular faith, partly because religion provides meaning as well as coping skills (King & Roeser, 2009).

Religion was considered "very" or "pretty" important by 55 percent of U.S. high school seniors in 2009, with another 20 percent considering religion not important (Aud et al., 2011b). Past parental practices influence religious identity, although some adolescents express that identity in ways that their parents did not anticipate.

Not Just a Uniform Adolescents in moratorium adopt temporary roles to postpone achieving their final identity. High school students like these have signed up for an ROTC (Reserve Officers Training Corps) class, but few of them go on to enlist in the United States Marine Corps.

foreclosure
Erikson's term for premature identity formation, which occurs when an adolescent adopts his or her parents' or society's roles and values wholesale, without questioning or analysis.

moratorium
An adolescent's choice of a socially acceptable way to postpone making identity-achievement decisions. Going to college is a common example.

Same Situation, Far Apart: Chosen, Saved, or Just Another Teenager? An Orthodox Jewish boy lighting Hanukkah candles in Israel and an evangelical Christian girl at a religious rally in Michigan are much alike, despite distance and appearance. Many teenagers express such evident religious devotion that outsiders consider them fanatics.

A Religious Life These young adolescents in Ethiopia are studying to be monks. Their monastery is a haven in the midst of civil strife. Will the rituals and beliefs also provide them with a way to achieve identity?

For example, a Muslim girl might start to wear a headscarf, or a Catholic boy might study for the priesthood, or a Baptist teenager might join a Pentecostal youth group. Although parents might object, in the broad perspective, these initiatives are relatively minor: Almost no young Muslim converts to Judaism, and almost no Baptist teenager becomes Hindu.

Adolescents question specific beliefs as their cognitive processes allow more reflection, but few have a crisis of faith unless unusual circumstances propel it (King & Roeser, 2009). Usually, religious questioning is part of the search for identity, although the process currently lasts long past the teen years (Alisat & Pratt, 2012).

POLITICAL IDENTITY Parents are also influential in the development of political identity. In the twenty-first century in the United States, party identification is weakening among adults, with more saying they are independents rather than Republicans or Democrats (Pew Research Center, 2009b). Their teenage children reflect this; some proudly say they do not care about politics, in which case their apolitical stance is likely to continue in adulthood (Côté, 2009). That itself is a political identity, although not one Erikson anticipated.

A word here about terrorism and extremism. People who are relatively young (under age 30) are often on the front lines of revolutions or are disciples within groups that their elders consider cults. Fanatical political and religious movements have much in common: The age range of most new adherents is one of them (L. L. Dawson, 2010).

However, adolescents are rarely drawn to these groups unless personal loneliness or family background (such as a parent's death caused by an opposing group) compels them. It is a myth that every teenager is potentially a suicide bomber or willing martyr.

This topic also brings up *identity politics,* the tendency to identify with and vote for people of one's own race, religion, ethnicity, or sex (Bernstein, 2005; McClain et al., 2009). Identity politics is more like foreclosure than achievement because it precludes questioning and rational analysis. Although identity politics can be observed at any age, especially when a candidate is the first of one's own group to run for office, youth seem less swayed by ethnic loyalties than are their elders.

For example, younger North Americans are more likely to approve of interracial dating, to welcome neighbors of other groups, to favor gay marriage, and to oppose any law that results in economic inequality. One type of identity politics, however, does seem attractive to the young: generational. They might reject an older member of their ethnic group in favor of a candidate of a different background who is younger than 30.

This does not mean that adolescents ignore ethnicity entirely. Especially in a multicultural society such as the United States, most adolescents identify proudly with their background, often claiming that several labels describe them (such as African, Black, and American). One study found that the typical adolescent endorsed three such labels, with bicultural adolescents considering ethnic identities more central to themselves than monocultural adolescents did (Marks et al., 2011). Ethnic and generational identity overlap with political identity, but they do not determine it. Few adolescents proudly label themselves as members of a political party, as their parents might do.

Same Situation, Far Apart: And If They Were Boys? Signs of gender identity vary from place to place, evident in the bare arms and uncovered heads of these girls in Randolph, New Jersey *(left)*, which would horrify the girls in Sarabaya, Indonesia *(right)*. By contrast, signs of sexual identity may be universal: Girls everywhere laugh together and hold each other in ways their male classmates do not.

VOCATIONAL IDENTITY Vocational identity originally meant envisioning oneself as a worker in a particular occupation. This made sense a century ago, when most girls became wives and mothers, not employees, and most men became farmers, small businessmen, or factory workers. Those few in professions were generalists (doctors were general practitioners, lawyers handled all kinds of cases, teachers were usually unmarried women who taught all subjects). Decades ago, adolescents needed to establish a vocational identity so they could decide whether to stay in high school and aim for college.

Obviously, definitive early vocational identity is no longer needed. No one is expected to be prepared for a lifetime career by age 16. In the United States, the proportion of 16- to 19-year-old males in the labor force (employed or looking for a job) declined from 61 to 35 percent between 1980 and 2010 (Aud et al., 2011a). No teenager can make a wise, permanent choice among the tens of thousands of possible future careers.

This does not mean that future goals are irrelevant, however. As explained in Chapter 9, adolescents are more likely to be engaged in their education if they believe they are learning valuable, necessary skills. A specific vocational identity takes years to establish, but wanting to become a self-sufficient adult with a steady job motivates many young people.

Although some adults hope that part-time employment during high school will keep teenagers out of trouble, the opposite is more likely. Specifics depend on the time commitment and work tasks (Staff & Schulenberg, 2010). Working during vacations or for a few hours during the school week is harmless, but adolescents who work more than 20 hours a week during the school year tend to quit school, fight with parents, smoke cigarettes, and hate their jobs—in adulthood as well as adolescence (see Figure 10.1).

Typically, employed teens spend their wages on clothes, cars, drugs, and concerts, not family support or college savings. Grades fall: Work hours interfere with homework, after-school activities, and school attendance. Only a tiny and shrinking minority—alienated from school but appreciated, mentored, and promoted at work—benefit from intense teenage employment.

SEXUAL IDENTITY Achieving sexual identity is also a lifelong task, in part because norms and attitudes shift over time (see Figure 10.2). Increasing numbers of young adults are single, gay, or cohabiting, providing teenagers with new role models. A half-century ago, Erikson and other theorists thought the two sexes were opposites

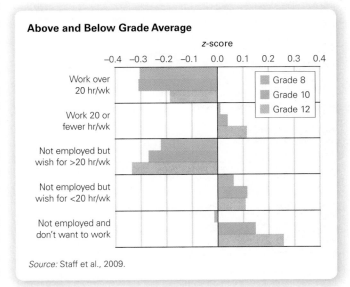

Above and Below Grade Average

z-score

	−0.4	−0.3	−0.2	−0.1	0.0	0.1	0.2	0.3	0.4

Work over 20 hr/wk

Work 20 or fewer hr/wk

Not employed but wish for >20 hr/wk

Not employed but wish for <20 hr/wk

Not employed and don't want to work

Grade 8
Grade 10
Grade 12

Source: Staff et al., 2009.

FIGURE 10.1 Don't Think About It There was a time when high school employment correlated with saving for college and lifetime success. No longer. The surprise is that even wanting a full-time job (and the extra income that would bring) reduces achievement—or is it the other way around? These are *z*-scores, or standard scores, which show the difference from the group average. A *z*-score of 2 is a dramatic difference; a *z*-score of 3 is extreme.

Who and Where? As Erikson explained in 1968, the pride of self-discovery is universal for adolescents: These could be teenagers anywhere. But a closer look reveals gay teenagers in Atlanta, Georgia, where this march could not have occurred 50 years ago.

Changing Attitudes on Gay Marriage (By Birth Year)

Percent who favor same-sex marriage

Millennials (1981 or later)
Generation X (1965–1980)
Baby boomers (1946–1964)
Silent generation (1928–1945)

Year

Source: Pew Forum on Religion & Public Life, July 31, 2012.

FIGURE 10.2 Young and Old Everyone knows that attitudes about same-sex relationships are changing. Less well known is that cohort differences are greater than the shift over the first decade of the twenty-first century.

gender identity
A person's acceptance of the roles and behaviors that society associates with the biological categories of male and female.

(P. Y. Miller & Simon, 1980). Adolescence was once a time for "gender intensification," when people increasingly identified either as male or female. No longer (Priess et al., 2009).

As you remember from Chapter 6, for social scientists *sex* and *sexual* refer to biological characteristics, whereas *gender* refers to cultural and social attributes. The distinction between biology and culture is not always obvious, since the body is affected by behavior and vice versa. Nonetheless, Erikson's term *sexual identity* has been replaced by **gender identity** (Denny & Pittman, 2007), which refers primarily to a person's self-definition as male or female.

Gender identity often (but not always) begins with the person's biological sex and leads to a gender role, one that society considers appropriate for that gender. Gender roles once meant that only men were employed; they were called *breadwinners* (good providers) and women were called *housewives* (married to their houses).

When women entered the labor market in big numbers in about 1970, gender roles expanded but remained distinct, as with secretary/businessman, nurse/doctor, pink collar/blue collar). Now vocational roles are increasingly unisex, although debate still rages as to whether one sex is better suited for certain roles.

One controversy is whether the male/female ratio of engineers (about 10:1) is the result of sex or gender. During childhood, both sexes seem similar in math and science performance. A shift occurs during adolescence such that far fewer girls study math, physics, or engineering in college. There are dozens of plausible explanations, from hormones to role models, from social prejudice to personal preference (Eccles, 2010).

In every chosen profession, traditional gender roles are becoming less rigid. For example, currently in the United States about 20 percent of engineering degrees are earned by women (Chronicle of Higher Education, 2011a). That is double the past ratio, although still far from equal.

It is apparent that gender identity and gender roles are much more complicated than once thought (Perry & Pauletti, 2011). Adolescents still experience strong sexual drives as their hormone levels increase, yet each generation holds different conceptions of appropriate gender identity (Bussey, 2011).

As Erikson recognized, many adolescents are understandably confused regarding when, how, and with whom to express their sexual drives. This complicates achievement of gender identity. Some adolescents foreclose by exaggerating male or female roles; others seek a moratorium by avoiding all sexual contact. Complexities of sexual and gender experiences are further discussed later in this chapter.

KEY points

- As Erikson famously recognized, adolescents experience an identity crisis, asking, "Who am I?"

- Identity achievement is arduous and takes years. Many adolescents experience role confusion or sidestep the anxiety via foreclosure or moratoria.

- In establishing religious and political identity, adolescents usually follow parental examples.

- Achieving vocational identity and sexual identity is more complicated than 50 years ago, partly because the number of careers and the variety of gender identities has increased.

Relationships with Others

Adolescence is often characterized as a time for personal rebellion and raging hormones. That perspective overlooks the reality that most teenagers are powerfully influenced by many people. Social influences include teachers, grandparents, and other relatives, as well as popular musicians, actors and actresses, sports stars, and other luminaries. Here we focus on the two most important powerful influences, parents and peers.

Not only are these impactful social influences, but each also affects the other. When adolescents have a supportive, affectionate relationship with their parents, they tend to have similar relationships with their peers; when they fight with their parents, they are likely to fight with peers. This anger spillover is reciprocal; a conflict with a friend makes it likely that a teen will soon conflict with a parent. The direction is more often reversed—a fight at home typically precedes a fight with friends (Chung et al., 2011).

Parents

Parent–adolescent relationships affect every aspect of adolescent development. Disputes are common because the adolescent's drive for independence, arising from biological as well as psychological impulses, clashes with the parents' desire to maintain control (Eisenberg et al., 2008; Laursen & Collins, 2009).

Normally, parent–adolescent conflict, especially between mothers and daughters, peaks in early adolescence. It usually manifests as **bickering**—repeated, petty arguments (more nagging than fighting) about routine, day-to-day concerns such as cleanliness, clothes, chores, and schedules (Eisenberg et al., 2008).

Some bickering may indicate a healthy family, since close relationships almost always include conflict (Smetana et al., 2004). One of the reasons for conflict is that

bickering
Petty, peevish arguing, usually repeated and ongoing.

THE NEW YORKER COLLECTION 2001 BARBARA SMALLER FROM CARTOONBANK.COM. ALL RIGHTS RESERVED

"So I blame you for everything—whose fault is that?"

both generations misjudge the other: Parents think their off-spring have more negative thoughts than the children have, and adolescents imagine much more intrusive control than the parents intend (Sillars et al., 2010).

Both generations would benefit if they were more explicit. For instance, if the argument is only about the dirty socks on the floor, the solution is easy: The teenager can put them in the laundry. However, if the fight is not really about socks but about parents dictating personal habits, of course the child resists.

With time, parents gradually grant more autonomy, and "friendship and positive affect [emotional state] typically rebound to preadolescent levels" (Collins & Laursen, 2004, p. 337). By age 18, many teenagers appreciate their parents, who have learned to allow more independence (Masche, 2010).

In Chapter 6, you learned that authoritative parenting is usually best for children and that uninvolved parenting is worst. This holds true for adolescents. Although teenagers may say they no longer need their parents, neglect is always destructive.

One example is Joy. When she was 16, her stepfather said: "Teens all around here [are] doing booze and doing drugs. . . . But my Joy here ain't into that stuff" (quoted in C. Smith, 2005, p. 10). In fact, however, Joy was smoking pot, drinking alcohol, and having sex with her boyfriend. She said she

> overdosed on a bunch of stuff once, pills or some prescription of my mom's—I took the whole bottle. It didn't work. I just went to sleep for a long time. . . . They never found out . . . pretty pitiful.
>
> *[quoted in C. Smith, 2005, p. 12]*

OPPOSING PERSPECTIVES

Adolescent Rebellion

Some cultures value social harmony above all else. In those places, adolescents virtually never contradict their parents. Bickering is rare. That raises a question: Could the adolescent rebellion that Western developmentalists and parents take for granted be a social construction, a cultural artifact (Russell et al., 2010)? Might teenage rebellion result from a competitive economy, or U.S. admiration of rugged individualism, rather than a universal consequence of the pubertal hormones (Larson & Wilson, 2004)?

A multicultural perspective has shown that what adolescents and parents expect from one another varies by culture (Brown & Bakken, 2011). For example, Japanese youth expect autonomy in their musical choices but want parents to help them with romance (Hasebe et al., 2004), whereas U.S. teenagers resent parental interference in selecting friends or lovers (Kakihara & Tilton-Weaver, 2009).

In Chile, adolescents usually obey their parents even when they disagree, but if they do something their parents might not like, they keep it secret (Darling et al., 2008). By contrast, some U.S. adolescents provoke an argument by boldly proclaiming ideas that they know their parents disapprove of (Cumsille et al., 2010).

The belief that adolescents *must* rebel in order to become healthy adults was expressed by Anna Freud (Sigmund's daughter, herself a prominent psychoanalyst), who wrote that adolescent resistance to parental authority was "welcome . . . beneficial . . . inevitable." She explained:

> We all know individual children who, as late as the ages of fourteen, fifteen or sixteen, show no such outer evidence of inner unrest. They remain, as they have been during the latency period, "good" children, wrapped up in their family relationships, considerate sons of their mothers, submissive to their fathers, in accord with the atmosphere, idea and ideal of their childhood background. Convenient as this may be, it signifies a delay of their normal development and is, as such, a sign to be taken seriously.
>
> *[A. Freud, 1958/2000, p. 263]*

Contrary to Freud's views, many psychologists, most teachers, and almost all parents are quite happy with well-behaved, considerate teenagers. In many Asian cultures, *filial devotion* (a child's feeling of obligation to his or her parents) is assumed, which curbs adolescent rebellion (Russell et al., 2010). Open disagreement is considered a sign of disrespect, and thus bad parenting.

Perhaps expecting teenagers to rebel creates a generation gap, making life more difficult for both generations. A young person might try drugs, for instance, believing "you're only young once," and a parent might accept uncontrolled behavior as an instance of "sowing wild oats." Both generations might follow those aphorisms when, instead, stricter guidelines and expected cooperation would better protect teenagers and create a happy home.

The opposing perspective also makes sense. Those cultures that value family harmony, in which parents expect acquiescence instead of rebellion, might undermine teenagers rather than help them. If parents punish the first signs of independence, the young person might leave home and suffer the dangers of the street. Or the opposite might occur, with adolescents so docile that they never grow up but instead continue to live at home at age 30, still expecting Mother to do laundry, monitor activities, give permission.

When a 15-year-old comes home past midnight, is it time for the parents to ease up or to punish? The answer depends partly on whether rebellion is healthy, necessary for an independent adulthood . . . or not.

CLOSENESS WITHIN THE FAMILY More important than either family conflict or personal independence may be family closeness, which has four aspects:

1. Communication (Do family members talk openly with one another?)
2. Support (Do they rely on one another?)
3. Connectedness (How emotionally close are they?)
4. Control (Do parents encourage or limit adolescent autonomy?)

No developmentalist doubts that the first two aspects—communication and support—are helpful, perhaps even essential. Patterns set in place during childhood continue, ideally buffering some of the turbulence of adolescence (Cleveland et al., 2005; Laursen & Collins, 2009). As you saw in earlier chapters, discussion leads to more ethical behavior and supportive families, aiding development at every age. Regarding the other two aspects, connectedness and control, consequences vary and observers differ in what they see.

How do you react to this example, written by one of my students?

> I got pregnant when I was sixteen years old, and if it weren't for the support of my parents, I would probably not have my son. And if they hadn't taken care of him, I wouldn't have been able to finish high school or attend college. My parents also helped me overcome the shame that I felt when . . . my aunts, uncles, and especially my grandparents found out that I was pregnant.
>
> *[I., personal communication]*

My student is grateful to her parents, but others might wonder whether her early motherhood gave her parents too much control, requiring dependency instead of autonomy. Indeed, might they unconsciously have created conditions (inadequate supervision and unfamiliarity with contraception) that encouraged her to become pregnant?

If so, the emotional closeness that seems helpful may in fact not be. A longitudinal study of pregnant adolescents found that most (but not all) young mothers and their children fared best if the adolescents' parents did not take over child care (Borkowski et al., 2007). Taking over meant taking too much control and implied that the mother was incapable of mothering.

A related issue is **parental monitoring**—that is, parental knowledge about each child's whereabouts, activities, and companions. When parental knowledge is the result of a warm, supportive relationship, children are likely to become confident, well-educated adults, avoiding drugs and risky sex (G. M. Barnes et al., 2006; Fletcher et al., 2004). However, monitoring is more complex than the broadcast question, "Do you know where your teenager is?"

parental monitoring
Parents' ongoing awareness of what their children are doing, where, and with whom.

The complexity is that some adolescents happily tell parents about their activities, whereas others are secretive (Vieno et al., 2009). Most are selective, omitting things their parents would not approve of (Brown & Bakken, 2011). Thus, monitoring is a good sign if it indicates mutual trust (Kerr et al., 2010). However, monitoring may be harmful when it derives from suspicion.

Too much criticism and control might stop dialogue instead of improve the first crucial items in the list above, communication and support (Tilton-Weaver et al., 2010). Overly restrictive and controlling parenting correlates with many adolescent problems, including depression (Brown & Bakken, 2011).

Finding the right balance between freedom and control has the added complication of the particular personality of the child. As one scholar notes, "deft parental steering" is useful, but if "an adolescent is engaged in more than minor delinquent behavior, a much more structured and rule-based approach may be needed" (Capaldi, 2003, pp. 175–176).

Peer Power

Adolescents rely on peers to help them navigate the physical changes of puberty, the intellectual challenges of high school, and the social adjustments of leaving childhood. Peers are much more useful for those three challenges than parents are. Friendships are important at every stage, but during early adolescence peers have increased power because popularity is also coveted (LaFontana & Cillessen, 2010).

Adults are sometimes unaware of adolescents' desire for respect from their contemporaries. I did not recognize this at the time with my own children, when the following scenarios played out in our home:

- Our oldest daughter wore the same pair of jeans to tenth grade, day after day. She washed them each night by hand and asked me to put them in the dryer early each morning. My husband was bewildered. "Is this some weird female ritual?" he asked. Years later, she explained that she was afraid that if she wore different pants each day, her classmates would think she cared about her clothes and then criticize her choices.

- Our second daughter, at 16, pierced her ears for the third time. When I asked if this meant she would do drugs, she laughed at my naïveté. I later noticed that many of her friends had multiple holes in their earlobes.

- At age 15, our third daughter was diagnosed with cancer. My husband and I weighed conflicting opinions from four physicians; each explained how a particular course of treatment would minimize the risk of death. She had her own priorities: "I don't care what you choose, as long as I keep my hair."

- Our youngest, in sixth grade, refused to wear her jacket (it was new; she had chosen it), even in midwinter. Not until high school did she tell me her reason: She wanted her classmates to think she was tough.

All of my daughters, each in her own way, sought her peers' acceptance. That led them to care about their appearance in ways I did not understand. Another aspect of peer interaction that adults might not realize is how often friends connect with each other. Social interaction was once obvious—teenagers would "hang out" at the local park or tie up the telephone line. Now, texting has become the favorite way to communicate, with the average texter sending or receiving 60 messages a day (Pew Research Center, 2012a).

PEER PRESSURE Peers have power during adolescence—power that can lead to constructive, destructive, or neutral behavior, as evident in the examples above. More generally, adults sometimes fear **peer pressure,** that is, that peers will push an ado-

✦ **ESPECIALLY FOR** Parents of a Teenager Your 13-year-old comes home after a sleepover at a friend's house with a new, weird hairstyle—perhaps cut or colored in a bizarre manner. What do you say and do? (see response, page 366) →

peer pressure
Encouragement to conform to one's friends or contemporaries in behavior, dress, and attitude; usually considered a negative force, as when adolescent peers encourage one another to defy adult authority.

Same Situation, Far Apart: Friends Together Teenagers in the middle of the United States (Illinois) and in the middle of Sudan (Khartoum) prefer to spend their free time with peers (these are all 15- to 17-year-olds), not with adults. Generational loyalty is stronger during these years than during any other stage of life.

OBSERVATION QUIZ

There are dramatic differences among teenagers in these two nations as well. What three can you see? (see answer, page 366) →

lescent to try drugs, break the law, or do other things the child would never do alone. This fear ignores the fact that "friends generally encourage socially desirable behaviors" (Berndt & Murphy, 2002, p. 281), such as playing sports, studying, quitting cigarettes, applying to college.

Peers are probably more helpful than harmful (Audrey et al., 2006; Nelson & DeBacker, 2008), especially in early adolescence, when biological and social stresses can be overwhelming. In later adolescence, teenagers are less susceptible to peer pressure, either positive or negative (Monahan et al., 2009).

To understand the role of peers, it is useful to understand how adolescents organize themselves. A cluster of close friends who are loyal to one another and who exclude outsiders is called a **clique.** A larger group of adolescents who share common interests but who are not necessarily friends is a **crowd.** Cliques and crowds provide control, guidance, and support via comments, exclusion, and admiration (B. Brown & Larson, 2009).

A crowd may exhibit small signs of identity (a certain brand of backpack, a particular greeting) that adults do not notice but that members of other crowds do (Strouse, 1999). Crowds—such as the "brains," "jocks," "skaters," or "goths"—may be based on ethnicity or on some personal characteristic or activity.

Crowds encourage certain values. For instance, one U.S. study found that "tough" and "alternative" crowds felt that teenagers should question every adult rule, whereas the "prep" crowd thought that parental authority was usually legitimate (Daddis, 2010). One European study found that students with the highest grades were dismissive of those who devoted themselves to sports or those who were disaffected from school, who reciprocated by disliking the honors crowd (Laursen et al., 2010).

Peers facilitate romance. Partners, especially in early adolescence, are selected partly because having that partner increases one's status with friends. If the leader of a girls' clique pairs with the leader of a boys' clique, the unattached members of the two cliques may pair with each other as well. That allows easy double or triple dating but also explains why adolescent romantic partners often have less in common, in personality and attitudes, than adult couples do (Zimmer-Gembeck & Ducat, 2010).

Peers are also helpful when romances end. Adolescents may despair at rejection, contemplating revenge or suicide (Fisher, 2006). In such cases, peer support can be a lifesaver. Adolescents rely on friends to hear every detail of a romantic interaction, to provide audience and advice, to soften breakups and encourage new loves (Mehta & Strough, 2009). Friends are usually of the same sex and same sexual orientation but not necessarily so; the crucial factor is that the friend is willing to listen and encourage.

clique
A group of adolescents made up of close friends who are loyal to one another while excluding outsiders.

crowd
A larger group of adolescents who have something in common but who are not necessarily friends.

Instant Connections Ignoring the rides at Coney Island, these two girls lean on each other; both have blue bracelets, tight jeans, sleeveless shirts, and, most important, texts to read and send. As with their use of the car and the telephone, teens have taken an adult invention (the Internet was originally developed for military use) and turned it into a tool for increasing peer support.

deviancy training
Destructive peer support in which one person shows another how to rebel against authority or social norms.

RESPONSE FOR Parents of a Teenager (from page 364) Remember: Communicate, do not control. Let your child talk about the meaning of the hairstyle. Remind yourself that a hairstyle in itself is harmless. Don't say "What will people think?" or "Are you on drugs?" or anything that might give your child reason to stop communicating. ●

ANSWER TO OBSERVATION QUIZ
(from page 365) (1) The U.S. friends are of both sexes; it's all boys in Sudan. (2) Recreational use of inner tubes in the United States; inner tubes are used only for tires in Sudan. (3) The boys in Sudan are comparing cell phones, which would be unlikely in the United States. There are also many differences in clothing—too many to enumerate. ●

SELECTING FRIENDS Because friends need to be sympathetic to the intricacies of one another's relationships to each parent, peer, and partner, friends typically share values and background. For instance, family loyalty is a core value for teenagers from some backgrounds but not for others: In order to be a receptive listener when teenagers complain about their parents, a confidant should have the same core values.

One specific example is *ethnic identity,* the formation of which is a major task for adolescents. The larger society promotes stereotypes and prejudice, and parents may counter with racial socialization (Umana-Taylor et al., 2010). Yet each young person needs to find his or her own ethnic identity, distinct from social stereotypes and from his or her parents' self-concept (A. J. Fuligni et al., 2009). To accomplish that, it is useful to have friends from the same ethnicity. For example, if a teen is dating someone from another group and needs to vent about a particular incident, a friend of the same ethnicity already understands the historical, social, and practical complications.

For many other aspects of ethnic identity, peers are pivotal (Whitehead et al., 2009). In large schools with many ethnic groups, ethnic crowds attract those who seek to avoid isolation while establishing their identity—a difficult process (Kiang et al., 2010). At the same time, students of all groups explore relationships with other groups. Ideally, the adults encourage appreciation of each group and also model interethnic friendships.

The fact that peers are often beneficial does not mean that friends always encourage good behavior, though. Young people *can* lead one another into trouble.

Collectively, peers sometimes provide **deviancy training,** whereby one person shows another how to circumvent adult restrictions (Dishion et al., 2001). However, innocent teens are not routinely corrupted by deviant friends. Adolescents *choose* their friends and models—not always wisely, but never randomly.

There is a developmental progression here: The combination of "problem behavior, school marginalization, and low academic performance" at age 11 leads to gang involvement two years later, deviancy training two years after that, and violent behavior at age 18 or 19 (Dishion et al., 2010, p. 603). But this cascade is not inevitable; adults can help disengaged 11-year-olds instead of blaming their friends years later.

To further understand the impact of peers, two concepts are helpful: *selection* and *facilitation.* Teenagers *select* a clique whose values and interests they share, abandoning former friends who follow other paths. Peers then *facilitate* destructive or constructive behaviors. It is easier to do the wrong thing ("Let's all skip school on Friday") or the right thing ("Let's study together for the chem exam") if close friends are doing it, too.

Both selection and facilitation can work in any direction. One teenager joins a clique whose members smoke cigarettes and drink beer, and together they take the next step, perhaps sharing a joint. Another teenager chooses friends who enjoy math puzzles, and they might all enroll in AP calculus together. As one student explains:

[Companionship] makes me excited about calculus. That is a hard class, but when you need help with calculus, you go to your friends. You may think no one could be excited about calculus, but I am. Having friends in class with you definitely makes school more enjoyable.

[Hamm & Faircloth, 2005, p. 72]

Thus, adolescents select and then facilitate, choose and are chosen. Happy, energetic, and successful teens have close friends who themselves are high achievers, with no major emotional problems. The opposite also holds: Those who are drug users, sexually active, and alienated from school choose compatible friends and support one another in continuing on that path (Crosnoe & Needham, 2004; Kiuru et al., 2010).

KEY points

- Adolescents are influenced by many other people, especially in the years right after puberty begins, when independence is particularly difficult.

- Parents and their adolescents often bicker, mutual communication and support are always helpful. Closeness and control are more controversial.

- Parental monitoring is usually an element of a close, involved parent–child relationship, but may be a sign of suspicion and secrecy.

- Peer influences are typically positive, although peers sometimes provide training and encouragement for deception and deviancy.

Sexual Interactions

As explained in Chapter 9, the hormones of puberty awaken sexual interest. Teenage romance can increase despair, and early sex can be problematic, as soon described. But we also need to remember that adolescent sexual impulses are normal and that they can be joyous and instructive, preparing young people for healthy adult relationships. In several ways, teenagers today are sexually healthier than teenagers once were:

- *Teen births have decreased in every nation.* For example, between 1960 and 2010, the adolescent birth rate in China was cut in half (reducing the United Nations' projections of the world's population in 2050 by about 1 billion). In the United States, the birth rate per thousand 15- to 17-year-old girls was 39 in 1991; it was 15.4 in 2011, about one birth per 65 girls that age (Hamilton et al., 2012). The birth rate for older teens of every ethnic group has also decreased (see Figure 10.3).

- *The use of protection has risen.* Contraception, particularly condom use among adolescent boys, has increased markedly worldwide since 1990 (Santelli & Melnikas, 2010). The U.S. Youth Risk Behavior Survey found that 67 percent of sexually active ninth-grade boys used a condom during their most recent intercourse (MMWR, June 8, 2012). Rates are even higher in most European nations.

- *Teen abortions are less common.* In the United States, the abortion rate for women younger than 20 is about half the rate it was two decades earlier (MMWR, February 25, 2011).

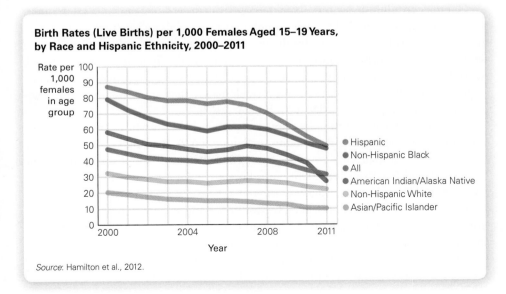

Birth Rates (Live Births) per 1,000 Females Aged 15–19 Years, by Race and Hispanic Ethnicity, 2000–2011

Rate per 1,000 females in age group

- Hispanic
- Non-Hispanic Black
- All
- American Indian/Alaska Native
- Non-Hispanic White
- Asian/Pacific Islander

Year

Source: Hamilton et al., 2012.

COURTESY RICHARD RODNAY

Watch Me Fall Adolescent boys in a skate park were videotaped in two circumstances: with an attractive female stranger sitting on a bench nearby and with no one watching. (The camera was hidden.) The boys took more risks, and fell more often, with the female observer present (Ronay & von Hippel, 2010).

FIGURE 10.3 More Education, Fewer Births In some developing nations, women are still expected to have a baby before age 20. However, in most developed nations, including the United States, young women of every ethnic group are expected to begin college—hard to do with a baby. Other data find that the most marked decline in U.S. teenage pregnancy is among immigrant women, who now aspire to jobs and degrees, not housework and babies.

For all these, cohort and culture are crucial. For most of the twentieth century, North American youth reported sexual activity at younger and younger ages. This trend has reversed. In 1991, 54 percent of U.S. high school students said they had had intercourse, but in 2011 only 47 percent did. Rates varied by state culture: from 37 percent in Hawaii to 58 percent in Mississippi (MMWR, June 8, 2012).

During the same period, the double standard (with boys expected to be more sexually active than girls) decreased, and today boys and girls are quite similar in reported sexual activity. Both sexes are much more knowledgeable about sexual matters, which may be the underlying reason for all the trends above.

Romance

Decades ago, an Australian named Dexter Dunphy (1963) described the sequence of male–female relationships during childhood and adolescence:

1. Groups of friends, exclusively one sex or the other
2. A loose association of girls and boys, with public interactions within a crowd
3. Small mixed-sex groups of the advanced members of the crowd
4. Formation of couples, with private intimacies

Dunphy recognized, and later data from many nations confirm, that culture affects the timing and manifestation of each step, but not the sequence. Youth worldwide (and even the young of other primates) avoid the other sex in childhood and are attracted to them after puberty, with romantic partnerships gradually forming. This universal pattern suggests that physiological maturation governs this sequence.

In modern developed nations, where puberty begins with hormones at about age 10 and enduring partnerships occur much later, each of Dunphy's four stages typically lasts several years. Early, exclusive romances are more often a sign of social trouble than of maturity, especially for girls (Eklund et al., 2010, Hipwell et al., 2010).

SEXUAL INTERCOURSE Early intercourse presages psychosocial problems later on. A study of 3,923 adult women in the United States found that those who *voluntarily* had sex before age 16 were more likely to divorce later on, whether or not that early sex resulted in pregnancy and whether or not they married their first sexual partner. The same study found that adolescents of any age whose first sexual experience was unwanted (either "really didn't want" or "had mixed feelings about") were also more likely to later divorce (Paik, 2011).

Contrary to adult suspicions, many teenage romances do not include intercourse. In the United States in 2011, even though one-third of all high school students said they were sexually experienced by the tenth grade, another one-third of graduating seniors were virgins (see Figure 10.4). Norms vary markedly from crowd to crowd, school to school, city to city, nation to nation. For instance, less than half as many high schoolers in San Francisco as in Philadelphia say they are currently sexually active (20 versus 45 percent) (MMWR, June 8, 2012).

Regarding sex-related impulses, some experts believe that boys are more influenced by hormones and girls by culture (Baumeister & Blackhart, 2007). Perhaps. It does seem true that girls are more concerned than boys about the depth of the romance (Zani & Cicognani, 2006). Girls hope their partners say, "I'll love you forever"; boys like to hear, "I want you now."

However, everyone is influenced by hormones and society, biology and culture. All adolescents have sexual interests (biology), which produce behaviors that teenagers in other nations would not engage in (culture) (Moore & Rosenthal, 2006).

Since only girls can become pregnant, and since they fare better as mothers if the fathers are supportive, their wish for long-term commitment may be a consequence

JIM WEST

Pin It on Him Boutonniere, corsage, formal shirt with matching tie, bare arms—all are common at U.S. high school proms. Yet these sights are unknown to most 17-year-olds in other nations. Despite such cultural oddities and this once-in-a-lifetime moment, Mariel West and John Felczak are evidence of a worldwide phenomenon: sexual attraction in late adolescence.

● UNDERSTANDING THE NUMBERS
Sometimes people say that "numbers do not lie," but exactly what do the numbers reflect?

Answer When it comes to teen sex, they may reflect shame, pride, and norms, which might affect adolescents' answers on even confidential questionnaires. A 2011 survey (MMWR, June 8, 2012) reports that most high school boys in Philadelphia have had sex (69 percent overall) while in San Francisco many boys say they have not (28 percent overall). However, the range from place to place for sex is almost twice as great as the range for having been offered illegal drugs in school. Perhaps social desirability is less likely to affect drug offering than sex. For drugs, Philadelphia (29 percent) and San Francisco (32 percent) are closer to the median of 32 percent. Might social norms affect adolescents' answers on sex, making Philadelphia artificially high and San Francisco artificially low?

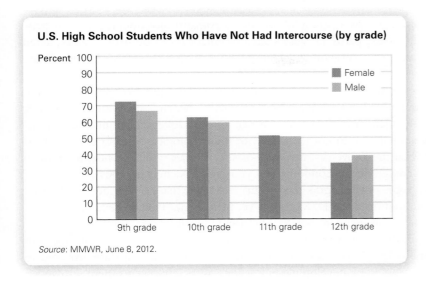

U.S. High School Students Who Have Not Had Intercourse (by grade)

Percent

- Female
- Male

9th grade   10th grade   11th grade   12th grade

Source: MMWR, June 8, 2012.

FIGURE 10.4 Many Virgins For 30 years, the Youth Risk Behavior Survey has asked high school students from all over the United States dozens of confidential questions about their behavior. As you can see, about one-third of all students have already had sex by the ninth grade, and about one-third have not yet had sex by their senior year—a group whose ranks have been increasing in recent years. Other research finds that sexual behaviors are influenced by peers, with some groups all sexually experienced by age 14 and others not until age 18 or older.

of that social reality. If this is so, the gender difference (girls' wanting love versus boys' seeking sex) may disappear as contraception makes unwanted pregnancy rare. On the other hand, the reason for that male–female difference may be rooted in genes and hormones: If so, it will continue, no matter how foolproof contraception becomes.

SAME-SEX ROMANCES Selecting a sexual partner is also a combination of biology and culture. This is obvious in **sexual orientation**, which refers to the direction of a person's erotic desires. One meaning of *orient* is to "turn toward"; thus, sexual orientation refers to whether a person is romantically attracted to (turned on by) people of the other sex, the same sex, or both sexes. That basic orientation seems primarily biological, but culture is involved as well.

sexual orientation
A term that refers to whether a person is sexually and romantically attracted to others of the same sex, the opposite sex, or both sexes.

Same Situation, Far Apart: Shared Joy Adults sometimes call teenage romances "puppy love," as if couples were too immature and playful to experience true affection. Some adults assume that lust, not love, connects teen boys and girls. But as these couples in Los Angeles *(left)* and Estonia *(right)* show, strong emotional connections supersede sexual contact.

It is not known how many adolescents are romantically oriented toward people of their own sex, partly because sexual orientation can be strong, weak, acted upon, secretive, or unconscious. Relying on self-reports is bound to underestimate prevalence.

Currently in North America and western Europe, not just two gender roles and sexual orientations (homosexual and heterosexual) but many are evident (Denny & Pittman, 2007). Gender identity itself has become controversial; an increasing number of early adolescents do not identify with their biological sex and may be diagnosed with what the DSM-IV calls *gender-identity disorder,* which was the focus of an international conference in London a few years ago (Asscheman, 2009).

However, some psychologists and psychiatrists argue that gender-identity disorder should be omitted from the DSM-5 (not yet published). They believe that gender-identity problems originate in society, not in individuals (Ross, 2009).

Research in the United States indicates that boys who identify as male and girls who identify as female (no issue with gender identity) and who are attracted to people of their same sex, develop happily as long as society accepts them. However, well-being is diminished and drug use increases in those adolescents who are bisexual or are confused about their sexuality (Rieger & Savin-Williams, 2012). That may be cultural; adolescents who are uncertain about their sexuality may, someday, no longer be distressed. Gender identity seems to be cognitive, not simply biological, which complicates it for adolescents (Perry & Pauletti, 2011).

Same-sex behaviors are considered criminal and pathological in most nations of Africa and the Middle East. By contrast, people in India who identify as neither male nor female (called *hijras*) have been accepted there for centuries: The 2010 India census asks people to indicate whether they are male, female, or other.

Obviously, for every aspect of teen sexuality, culture and cohort are powerful. This is particularly true for those who are not heterosexual. Many gay youth date members of the other sex to hide their true orientation. Binge drinking, drug addiction, and suicidal thoughts are more common among them, with bisexual youth particularly vulnerable (MMWR, June 10, 2011).

Behavior does not always conform to identity. Among sexually active teenagers in New York City, 10 percent had had same-sex partners—but many of those teenagers (38 percent) identified as straight (Pathela & Schillinger, 2010). In that study, those most at risk of sexual violence and sexually transmitted infections were neither those whose sexual experiences were exclusively same-sex nor exclusively other-sex, but those who had had partners of both sexes.

Adults who care about adolescent health are advised to ask about sexual behavior—which may differ from sexual identity or orientation (Pathela & Schillinger, 2010). When and with whom a person becomes sexually active depends on a cascade of factors, including age at puberty, parenting practices, peer pressure, culture, and dating relationships (Longmore et al., 2009). Sexual impulses are normal and healthy during adolescence, but, as explained next, they may lead to trouble as well.

Possible Problems

As you read, teen births and abortions are declining worldwide. Furthermore, adolescents are more informed about sexuality than they were a few generations ago, and, at least in the United States, fewer teenagers are sexually active in the twenty-first century than at the end of the twentieth. However, several problems are apparent.

ADOLESCENT PREGNANCY The U.S. rate of adolescent pregnancy is lower than it was, but it is still higher than that of any other developed nation. If a pregnant teenager is younger than 16 (most are not), complications—including spontaneous or induced abortion, high blood pressure, stillbirth, preterm birth, and a low-birthweight newborn—are more likely.

The risks to the mother decrease after age 16, but children of young parents (even as "old" as 17 or 18) have more medical, educational, and social problems. From a developmental perspective, each child is born not only to the mother but also to the family. In former generations, more family support was forthcoming. Since most teen mothers were married (more than 80 percent in 1960, about 6 percent in the United States in 2009), most fathers were legally committed to the children of teenage mothers. Furthermore, unlike in the current job market, most such fathers could find employment. In addition, 50 years ago few grandmothers on either side of the family were in the labor force; they often helped with child care. Currently, some unmarried fathers and some employed grandmothers are committed to the children of teenage mothers, but on average family support is much less available than it once was.

Many reasons for the problems faced by babies born to adolescents arise from the society, not the physical immaturity of the mother. Poverty and lack of education correlate with teenage pregnancy and with every problem just mentioned (Santelli & Melnikas, 2010). Beyond that, no matter what their SES, younger pregnant teenagers are often malnourished and postpone prenatal care (Borkowski et al., 2007).

AP TONY DEJAK

What Next? Monica, here with her dog Rosie, is a mom-to-be—as are 13 percent of her female classmates at Timkin High School in Canton, Ohio. She is one of the fortunate ones; already a senior, she will probably graduate. Her child may not be as fortunate. Teenagers typically welcome their unplanned babies but tend to have trouble raising them. This child will reach puberty before Monica is 30; their mutual immaturity will increase the child's risk of depression, delinquency, and another teen pregnancy.

SEXUAL ABUSE Sexual abuse is another hazard, given that puberty occurs at younger ages than a century ago, yet preteens are limited in their mental maturity. Sexual abuse is particularly likely if the parent–child relationship is strained. In that case, adolescents do not ask for help and parents doubt that a relative or family friend could be an abuser—even though child sexual abusers are often family members (Kinnear, 2007).

Child sexual abuse is defined as any activity (including fondling and photographing) that sexually stimulates an adult and that involves a juvenile. The most common time for sexual abuse is when the first signs of puberty occur, with girls particularly vulnerable—although boys are also at risk.

child sexual abuse
Any erotic activity that arouses an adult and excites, shames, or confuses a child, whether or not the victim protests and whether or not genital contact is involved.

Child sexual abuse is often rationalized by the abuser as relatively harmless, especially if it does not include intercourse or if a young teenager does not object. Yet research finds that the victims may be affected for many years.

Prevalence studies find national variations in rates. For instance, relatively low child sexual abuse rates are reported from Asia, and relatively high rates are reported for girls in Australia and boys in Africa (Stoltenborgh et al., 2011). International differences are affected by definitions and by the cultural willingness of adults to report past abuse (Hillberg et al., 2011). However, researchers worldwide agree that sexual abuse is not rare, that it is more likely than other forms of maltreatment to occur across the SES spectrum, and that rates increase at puberty. (See Table 10.1 for U.S. sexual abuse data.)

For example, a careful study of the general population in England found that 2.8 percent of the women and 0.8 percent of the men experienced unwanted intercourse before adulthood; an additional 8.3 percent of the women and 4.5 percent of the men were abused via sexual contact that did not include intercourse (Bebbington et al., 2011). The former were more likely to have psychological disorders as adults, but even those with nonpenetrating abuse later experienced increased rates of psychological problems.

TABLE 10.1 Age and Sex Abuse: United States, 2007

Age	Number of Sex-Abuse Victims	Percent of Malreatment That Is Sex Abuse
Less than 1 year	315	0.3%
1–3	3,249	2.2
4–7	13,137	7.4
8–11	13,459	9.5
12–15	19,848	14.5
16–17	6,084	13.5

Source: U.S. Department of Health and Human Services, 2010.

As with other studies, this research found that sexual abuse was equally prevalent among all ethnic and income groups, but not among all age groups. The experience was more likely to occur in adolescence than earlier, and it was more likely to occur for those born after 1940 (Bebbington et al., 2011). Again, this may not reflect actual rates of past abuse: Older adults may be less likely to recognize, remember, or report sexual abuse.

No matter what criteria are used, developmentalists conclude that the long-term harm from child sexual abuse is worse than the harm from other forms of maltreatment that are more obvious. Since good research on this topic is difficult, and since some adults tend to minimize the effects, the following may help explain this conclusion.

A VIEW FROM SCIENCE

Consequences of Sexual Abuse

Puberty not only increases the odds of sexual abuse, but it can also make the emotional consequences worse because young adolescents experience some sexual impulses and responses (even to unwanted sex), but they have not yet developed a firm sense of their sexual identity (Graber et al., 2010). For example, an 11-year-old girl who is sexually abused might conclude that she is a bad person because she attracts sexual attention, or that all men are abusive, or that her value as a human being depends on her sexuality.

The long-term harm from abuse varies depending on the victim, the family, and the community, as well as on whether the abuse was an isolated instance or continued for years (more common). Nonetheless, virtually every adolescent problem—including early pregnancy, drug abuse, eating disorders, and suicide—is more frequent in those who have been sexually abused.

Consider what you have just read about the importance of supportive family and helpful peers, and then think of how sexual abuse undercuts those connections. Typically, abuse occurs at home, is perpetrated by an adult, and is allowed to continue by people who are supposed to protect the child.

For example, two sisters, La Tanya and Tichelle, were repeatedly sexually abused by their mother's live-in boyfriend. When they told their mother, she turned him out—only to let him back in again and again. The mother bought a lock for the girls' bedroom door, but the abuser broke the lock, not once but three times. Rescue finally came when a school social worker suspected that something was wrong, and La Tanya told her. The abuser was arrested, convicted, and sentenced to 85 years in prison. Later, the mother said that not making him leave permanently was the greatest mistake of her life (Bazelon, 2006).

The consequences extend far beyond the event. Young people who are sexually exploited typically fear sex and devalue themselves lifelong. Those two girls did manage to find outside help, but even as adults they are plagued by their for-

mer abuse. La Tanya has nightmares that cause her to wake up and compulsively check all the locks, all the while recalling her abuser's "black shotgun with a light brown barrel."

La Tanya and Tichelle are just two cases. In other instances, no long-term consequences are apparent, especially when the abuse stopped quickly and the child felt protected. Remember from Chapter 1 that a single case is not conclusive. Scientific research is needed on a group of victims, ideally over several years, with a control group.

Fortunately, at least one such study has been conducted—a 23-year study of 84 reported victims (aged 6 to 16, all girls) of child sex abuse (Trickett et al., 2011). In order to isolate the effects of abuse, the researchers also traced the development of girls from similar backgrounds (SES, ethnicity, etc.) who were not sexually abused.

Sadly, after confidential interviews, 14 of those initially selected for the control group were found to have been sexually abused, although that had not been reported to authorities. Other studies also find that sexual abuse often goes unreported. Those participants who had not reported their abuse were excluded from the final comparison group.

Although both victims and controls moved residences frequently in adolescence and adulthood (including some who went to homeless shelters and some who moved in with distant relatives in other states, leaving no forwarding addresses), the researchers were extraordinarily dedicated. They maintained contact with almost all the participants, keeping in touch (e.g., sending them birthday cards) even when funding temporarily stopped (Trickett et al., 2011).

Thus, because many guidelines for good longitudinal research were followed, the results of this study are probably valid—and definitely tragic. Although prosecutors often center on immediate biological harm (infections, pregnancy, physical abuse), this study found that the long-term cognitive and psychosocial effects of sex abuse were much worse.

To be specific, school achievement and language development were impaired lifelong. Intellectual problems were apparent throughout adolescence (often years after police action stopped the abuse). In adulthood, many former victims suffered new physical and sexual abuse, severe depression, drug addiction, and obesity. Since these women were compared with a control group from families with similar structures, incomes, and neighborhood, the conclusions were not confounded by environmental variables.

This study also found that harm extended to the next generation. Some of the 84 women had children, who also experienced cognitive and emotional problems. Of their 78 babies, 3 died in infancy, and 9 were permanently re-moved from their mothers. These rates were many times higher than those for the control group, who themselves had higher rates of child death or foster care than the national averages—probably because they and the abuse victims were often from dysfunctional neighborhoods.

Only the most severely abused or neglected children are removed from their parents. Many others suffer while remaining with their mothers. Thus, the fact that 9 of the surviving children were removed indicates that many of the other 66 children were also impaired by having mothers who had been sexually abused.

Remember that the HPA (hypothalamus–pituitary–adrenal) system regulates puberty and many other physiological responses. Many abuse victims show signs of a breakdown in the HPA regulatory system, which alters their cortisol responses. That produces heightened stress reactions in early adolescence but then abnormally low stress responses in adulthood (Trickett et al., 2011).

Other research finds that girls who have been sexually abused tend to experience earlier puberty, partly because of the dysregulation of the HPA axis (Mendle et al., 2011). As you remember from Chapter 9, early puberty for girls often leads to many other problems. Another study also finds that childhood sexual abuse correlates, in adulthood, with difficulty recognizing and expressing emotions, yet feeling depressed overall (Thomas et al., 2011).

Many studies indicate that the emotional consequences of childhood sexual abuse—night terrors, dangerous risk-taking, serious addiction, suicidal depression—may linger lifelong. This may be the worst consequence of all: The brains of sex abuse victims may be forever changed, causing distressing flashbacks (such as nightmares of a man suddenly entering the bedroom), impulses (such as the urge to suffocate a lover), and fears (such as fear of being alone) that never disappear.

INFECTIONS AND DISEASES Teen pregnancy, abortions, intercourse, and sexual abuse are less common than they were a decade ago, perhaps because sex education happens earlier and is more interactive than previously. However, one major problem of teenage sex shows no signs of abating: **sexually transmitted infections (STIs).**

STIs were earlier called *sexually transmitted diseases* (STDs) or *venereal disease* (VD), terms that refer to any infection transmitted through sexual contact. One reason for the name change is that diseases may be long-lasting, caused partly by factors that are hard to avoid (such as cancer or heart disease), whereas infections are transmitted from one person to another and are more likely to be cured if treated promptly. There are hundreds of STIs, each with distinct symptoms, treatment, and consequences (James, 2007) (see Appendix A). By calling them infections, perhaps people will be more likely to seek diagnosis and treatment.

sexually transmitted infection (STI) An infection spread by sexual contact; includes syphilis, gonorrhea, genital herpes, chlamydia, and HIV.

Those who have sexual intercourse before age 16 are twice as likely to become infected as are those who begin sexual activity after age 19 (Ryan et al., 2008). One reason is biological. Fully developed women have some natural biological defenses against STIs; this is less true for pubescent girls (World Health Organization, 2005). In addition, if symptoms appear, teens are reluctant to seek diagnosis or alert their partners. Infections continue and spread as a result.

In cultures or families in which teenage sex is forbidden, adolescents avoid treatment for STIs until pain requires it. Adolescents with same-sex partners are especially reluctant to carry condoms or find treatment if their community considers their sexuality shameful.

TABLE 10.2 Condom Use Among 15-Year-Olds (Tenth Grade) in 2009

Country	Sexually Active (% of total)	Used Condom at Last Intercourse (% of those sexually active)
France	20	84
Israel	14	72
Canada	23	78
United States	41	68
England	29	83
Russia	33	75

Sources: MMWR, June 4, 2010; Nic Gabhainn et al., 2009.

Internationally, French teenagers are among the most likely to use condoms, as well as other protective measures simultaneously (called *dual use*), whereas teens in the United States are least likely to do so (Higgins & Cooper, 2012; Nic Gabhainn et al., 2009) (see Table 10.2). One reason may be that most French high schools (including Catholic ones) provide free, confidential medical care and condoms; by contrast, providing either one is illegal at many U.S. schools. The emphasis of sex education in France is on health protection, not sex avoidance.

Worldwide, sexually active teenagers have higher rates of the most common STIs—gonorrhea, genital herpes, and chlamydia—than do sexually active people of any other age group (World Health Organization, 2005). Ominously, the rate of new HIV infections does not seem to be abating among adolescents (Benton, 2011).

Sex Education

Adolescents typically have strong sexual urges but minimal logic when it comes to pregnancy and disease. That might be expected, given the power of intuitive thought and the differential maturation of the limbic system and prefrontal cortex. They do not know what is normal and what is dangerous, and they do not think logically unless they must.

Without guidance, millions of teenagers worry that they are oversexed, undersexed, or deviant, unaware that thousands, maybe millions, of people are just like them. Indeed, "students seem to waffle their way through sexually relevant encounters driven both by the allure of reward and the fear of negative consequences" (Wagner, 2011, p. 193). Obviously, they have much to learn. Where do they learn it?

LEARNING FROM THE MEDIA One source of sex information is the media. Sexual content appears almost seven times per hour on the TV shows most watched by teenagers (Steinberg & Monahan, 2011). That content is almost always enticing: Almost never does a television character develop an STI, deal with an unwanted pregnancy, or mention (much less use) a condom. Print media that teenagers read is no better. One study found that men's magazines convince teenage boys that manliness means many sexual conquests (Ward et al., 2011).

Sex on TV, in film, and in music is controversial (R. L. Collins et al., 2011; Steinberg & Monahan, 2011). Although there is a correlation between adolescent exposure to media sex and adolescent sexual initiation, that correlation may reflect selection, not cause. Perhaps teenagers watch sexy TV because they are sexually active, not vice versa. One analysis concludes that "the most important influences on adolescents' sexual behavior may be closer to home than Hollywood" (Sternberg & Monahan, 2011, p. 575).

LEARNING FROM PARENTS Home is where sex education begins. Every study finds that parental communication is influential (Longmore et al., 2009). Ideally, parents are the best sex educators, because they know their children well and can have private conversations that allow teens to ask personal questions. However, many parents wait too long to discuss sex, are silent about crucial aspects, and know little about their adolescents' romances. Three studies of quite different groups illustrate the problem.

1. Mexican American mothers told their teenagers, "*Cuidate*" ("Take care of yourself"), which their teenagers interpreted as advice about overall health, not

✦ **ESPECIALLY FOR Sex Educators** Suppose adults in your community never talk to their children about sex or puberty. Is that a mistake? (see response, page 376) →

condoms. When teens became pregnant, their mothers wondered why (Moncloa et al., 2010).

2. Parents of 12-year-old girls were asked whether their daughters had hugged or kissed a boy "for a long time" or hung out with older boys (signs that sex information is urgently needed). Only 5 percent of the parents said yes, as did 38 percent of the girls (O'Donnell et al., 2008).

3. African American and Hmong American 14- to 19-year-olds rarely tell their parents about their romances. For example, one girl said she and her girlfriend were going to the movies (true) but omitted that they would meet their boy-friends there (Brown & Bakken, 2011).

What exactly should parents tell their children? That is the wrong question, ac-cording to a longitudinal study of thousands of adolescents. Those teens who be-came sexually active and who were most likely to develop an STI had parents who had told them about sex, warning them to stay away from it. This is not communi-cation; it is the kind of parental lecture that many teenagers ignore. The same study found that adolescents were more likely to remain virgins if they had a warm rela-tionship with their parents—specific information was less important than was open communication, enabling the adolescents to ask questions and get honest answers (Deptula et al., 2010).

LEARNING FROM PEERS Adolescent sexual behavior is strongly influenced by peers, especially when parents are silent, forbidding, or vague. Many younger ado-lescents discuss details of romance and sex with close friends, seeking advice and approval (Laursen & Mooney, 2007).

Often the boys brag and the girls worry. Sometimes two inexperienced partners teach each other. However, the lessons from a sexual partner are more about pleasure and techniques than about consequences and protection. Only about half of U.S. adolescent couples discuss how they will avoid pregnancy and disease before they have sex (Ryan et al., 2007).

LEARNING AT SCHOOL Most northern European nations begin sex education in elementary school. By middle school, students learn about sexual responsibility, masturbation, same-sex romance, oral and anal sex—subjects rarely covered in U.S. classes. Rates of teenage pregnancy in most European nations are less than half those in the United States; perhaps curriculum is the reason.

Many U.S. sex educators wish teachers would be more forthcoming about sex. However, probably the entire culture, not just the curriculum, is relevant. For instance, in Russia, few schools include sex education—and yet their official rate of HIV is far lower than that in the United States (Gevorgyan et al., 2011) (although some reports claim the official rate underestimates actual prevalence).

Within the United States, the timing and content of sex education varies by state and community, a result of local culture expressed via school curriculum. Some high schools provide comprehensive educa-tion, free condoms, and medical treatment; others provide nothing. Some schools begin sex education in the sixth grade; others wait until the end of high school. This is a crucial difference: When sex education precedes sexual experiences, adolescents are more likely to delay sexual activity.

Specific information and attitudes influence the success of the cur-riculum—some programs have no impact (Kirby & Laris, 2009). A mas-sive experiment in sex education involved "abstinence-only" curricula, as was U.S. federal policy until 2009. It is true, of course, that abstaining

"Smirking or non-smirking?"

CARTOONSTOCK.COM

RESPONSE FOR Sex Educators (from page 374) Yes, but forgive them. Ideally, parents should talk to their children about sex, presenting honest information and listening to the child's concerns. However, many parents find it very difficult to do this because they feel embarrassed and ignorant. You might schedule separate sessions for people older than 30, for emerging adults, and for adolescents. ●

from sex (including oral sex) prevents STIs and pregnancy, but longitudinal data four to six years after adolescents had participated in abstinence-only programs revealed that the programs did not succeed.

To be specific, about half the students in both experimental (abstinence-only) and control groups had had sex by age 16. The number of partners and use of contraceptives were the same with and without the special curriculum (Trenholm et al., 2007). Students in the control groups knew slightly more about preventing disease and pregnancy, but that knowledge neither slowed nor hastened their sexual initiation.

Overall, according to a controlled nationwide study of sex education in the United Kingdom, whether an adolescent becomes sexually active depends more on family, peers, and culture than on information from classes (Allen et al., 2007). The success of sex education is measured not by whether adolescents can learn facts (most pass multiple-choice tests) but by whether their knowledge affects their behavior (Kirby & Laris, 2009). Often it does not.

KEYpoints

- Adolescent sexual interactions are healthier than they were a few decades ago, with fewer unwanted pregnancies, fewer abortions, and more contraception use.
- Biological impulses at puberty lead to sexual interest, but culture strongly affects behavior, including whether a teenager becomes sexually active and with whom.
- Sex education varies dramatically from nation to nation and, in the United States, from school to school.
- Adolescents benefit from parental discussion of sexual matters, but many parents are unable or hesitant to talk openly and honestly about sex with their children.

Sadness and Anger

Adolescence is usually a wonderful time, perhaps better for current teenagers than for any prior generation. Nonetheless, troubles plague about 20 percent of today's adolescents. Distinguishing between normal moodiness and serious pathology is complex. Adolescent emotions change day to day, even minute by minute. For a few, negative emotions become intense, chronic, even deadly.

Depression

The general trend from late childhood through adolescence is toward less confidence, with more moments of emotional despair and anger than when younger—as well as more moments of happiness (Neumann et al., 2011).

A dip in self-esteem at puberty is reported in children of every ethnicity and gender (Fredricks & Eccles, 2002; Greene & Way, 2005; Kutob et al., 2009). Some studies report rising self-esteem thereafter (especially for African American girls and European American boys), but variations are many, as are individual differences.

On average, self-esteem is lower in girls than in boys, lower in Asian Americans than African Americans, lower in younger adolescents than older adolescents (Bachman et al., 2011). Many studies report a gradual rise in self-esteem from early adolescence through at least age 30, but all find notable variability as well as some continuity, as you would expect since genes remain the same as age increases. That means that seriously depressed adolescents cannot be promised "you'll feel better soon"—depression may ease, but it rarely disappears completely (Huang, 2010).

All studies find that parents and peers affect self-esteem (Hall-Lande et al., 2007) and that some communities have lower rates of depression because they promote strong and supportive relationships between teenagers and adults. One factor in an individual's level of self-esteem may be the adolescents' own neurological propensity (differential sensitivity again).

Cultural contexts are influential as well. One cultural norm is **familism,** the belief that family members should sacrifice personal freedom and success to care for one another. Familism (in Spanish, *familismo*) is particularly strong among Mexican Americans, for whom family solidarity cushions the strains of poverty, parenthood, and prejudice (Behnke et al., 2008). For Latin American youth, self-esteem and ethnic pride rise after puberty, especially if familism is strong, because their new maturity enables them to contribute to their families. However, if a Latino family is characterized by fighting and fragmentation, adolescents' self-esteem is reduced even more than in similar, non-Latino families (Smokowski et al., 2010).

Especially for gay adolescents, family rejection increases the rate of suicide (Saewyc, 2011). Adolescents of any background with low self-esteem turn to drugs, sex, self-harm, and dieting—all of which deepen depression (Biro et al., 2006; Trzesniewski et al., 2006).

CLINICAL DEPRESSION   Some adolescents sink into **clinical depression,** a deep sadness and hopelessness that disrupts all normal, regular activities. The origins and causes, such as certain alleles of particular genes and early insecure attachment, predate adolescence. Then puberty—with its myriad physical and emotional ups and downs—plunges some into despair. The rate of clinical depression more than doubles during this time, to an estimated 15 percent, affecting about 1 in 5 girls and 1 in 10 boys.

It is not known whether the reasons for these gender differences are primarily biological, psychological, or social (Alloy & Abramson, 2007). Obviously, sex hormones differ, but girls also experience social pressures from their families, peers, and cultures that boys do not. Perhaps the combination of biological and psychosocial stresses causes some to slide into depression.

Genes matter as well. For instance, adolescent girls are especially likely to be depressed if their mothers are belligerent, disapproving, and contemptuous. However, some girls seem genetically protected. They have equally difficult mothers, but they escape depression, probably because they are innately less vulnerable (Whittle et al., 2011).

One study found that the short allele of the serotonin transporter promoter gene (5-HTTLPR) increased the rate of depression among girls everywhere but increased depression among boys only if they lived in communities of low SES (Uddin et al., 2010). It is not surprising that certain genes make depression more likely, but the gender-specific neighborhood correlation is puzzling. Perhaps boys become depressed only if they see no future job prospects, and that is more likely in poor neighborhoods.

The hypothesis that hope for the future relates to teen depression comes from a provocative experiment in India, where depression is much higher in females than in males. Indian villages were randomly chosen to have an unusual requirement: It was mandated that a certain number of women had to be elected to leadership positions in those villages. The results showed that the adolescent girls in those villages had higher aspirations, did less domestic work, and had more education. Apparently, the new female role models changed their image of themselves (Beaman et al., 2012).

A cognitive explanation has been offered for gender differences in depression. **Rumination**—talking about, remembering, and mentally replaying past experiences—is more common among girls than boys. If unpleasant incidents are replayed,

familism
The belief that family members should support one another, sacrificing individual freedom and success, if necessary, in order to preserve family unity and protect the family from outside forces.

clinical depression
Feelings of hopelessness, lethargy, and worthlessness that last two weeks or more.

rumination
Repeatedly thinking and talking about past experiences; can contribute to depression.

rumination may lead to depression (Ayduk & Kross, 2008). In some cases, close mother–daughter relationships may be harmful: When mothers and daughters ruminate about the mother's problems, daughters often become depressed (Waller & Rose, 2010).

Adolescent depression is expressed in many ways, including eating disorders, school alienation, and sexual risk taking, all already discussed. In addition, an increasing number of depressed adolescents turn to self-harm, specifically, cutting themselves to draw blood, or burning themselves to relieve anxiety.

Cutting and burning are not intended as suicide attempts, and they temporarily halt the emotions that triggered self-abuse. However, such actions may become addictive, leading to deeper depression. That deeper depression links to suicide (Asarnow et al., 2011).

SUICIDE Serious depression can lead to thoughts about killing oneself (called **suicidal ideation**), to a specific plan, to an attempt, or to death. The 2011 Youth Risk Behavior Survey revealed that more than one-third (36 percent) of U.S. high school girls felt so hopeless that they stopped doing some usual activities for two weeks or more, and almost one-fifth (19 percent) seriously thought about suicide. The corresponding rates for boys were 22 percent and 13 percent (MMWR, June 8, 2012).

Suicidal ideation can lead to **parasuicide,** also called *attempted suicide* or *failed suicide*. Parasuicide includes any deliberate self-harm that could have been lethal. *Parasuicide* is the best word to use because "failed" implies that death is success! "Attempt" is likewise misleading because, especially in adolescence, the difference between attempted and completed suicide is often luck, timing, and medical response.

As you see in Figure 10.5, parasuicide can be categorized according to those who require medical attention (surgery, pumped stomach, etc.) and those who do not, but any parasuicide needs to be taken seriously. Parasuicide is a flashing warning that, if there is a next time, the person may die. Among U.S. high school students in 2011, 10 percent of the girls and 6 percent of the boys said they had tried to kill themselves in the past year (MMWR, June 8, 2012).

While suicidal ideation during adolescence is common, completed suicides are not. The U.S. annual rate of completed suicide for people aged 15 to 19 (in school or

suicidal ideation
Thinking about suicide, usually with some serious emotional and intellectual or cognitive overtones.

parasuicide
Any potentially lethal action against the self that does not result in death. (Also called *attempted suicide* or *failed suicide*.)

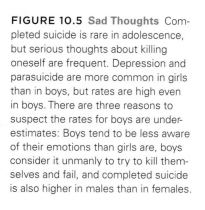

FIGURE 10.5 **Sad Thoughts** Completed suicide is rare in adolescence, but serious thoughts about killing oneself are frequent. Depression and parasuicide are more common in girls than in boys, but rates are high even in boys. There are three reasons to suspect the rates for boys are underestimates: Boys tend to be less aware of their emotions than girls are, boys consider it unmanly to try to kill themselves and fail, and completed suicide is also higher in males than in females.

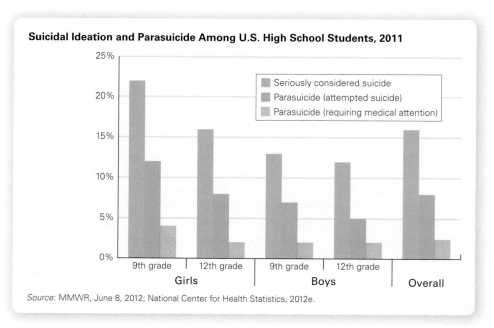

Suicidal Ideation and Parasuicide Among U.S. High School Students, 2011

Legend:
- Seriously considered suicide
- Parasuicide (attempted suicide)
- Parasuicide (requiring medical attention)

Source: MMWR, June 8, 2012; National Center for Health Statistics, 2012e.

not) is less than 8 per 100,000, or 0.008 percent. Rates for those under 15 are much lower. Adolescents are *less* likely to kill themselves than adults are.

Many people mistakenly think suicide is more frequent in adolescence for four reasons:

1. The rate, low as it is, is higher than it appeared to be decades ago (see Appendix A).

2. Statistics on "youth" often include emerging adults, aged 18 to 25, whose suicide rates are higher than those of adolescents.

3. Adolescent suicides capture media attention, and people of all ages make a logical error (called base rate neglect), noticing the published cases and not considering the millions of non-suicidal youth.

4. Parasuicide may be more common in adolescence than later.

Gender differences in suicide are dramatic. Depression and parasuicide are more common among females (see Figure 10.5), but completed suicide is higher for males (except in China). For instance, among U.S. 15- to 19-year-olds, three times as many boys kill themselves as girls (National Center for Health Statistics, 2012e).

A major reason is method: Males typically jump from high places or shoot themselves (immediately lethal), whereas females often swallow pills or cut their wrists (allowing time for possible intervention or second thoughts).

Another explanation is that girls talk about their emotions, allowing friends and families to help them. Rumination may increase depression but decrease suicide. Boys withdraw; their warning signs are less obvious.

Because they are more emotional than analytical, adolescents are particularly affected when they hear about a suicide, either via media reports or from peers (Insel & Gould, 2008). That makes them susceptible to **cluster suicides,** a term for several suicides within a group over a brief span of time—a few weeks or months. If a high school student's "tragic end" is sentimentalized, that elicits suicidal ideation among his or her peers. Media attention increases the risk.

Wealth and education decrease the incidence of many disorders, but *not* of suicide—quite the opposite. The reason may be news reports that typically highlight the lost potential of a suicidal adolescent (e.g., "Honor Student Kills Self"). This may encourage cluster suicides among, say, other honor students. Or adolescents from high-SES families may not know how to cope with a failing grade or a broken relationship.

Since 1990, rates of adolescent suicide have fallen in the United States, especially among high-SES teenagers. One reason may be that parents spot problems and involve their teens in psychotherapy, which often includes antidepressant use—which relieve the desperate sadness that some adolescents feel (Gentile, 2010).

Delinquency and Disobedience

Like low self-esteem and suicidal ideation, bouts of anger are common in adolescence. In fact, the moody adolescent could be both depressed and delinquent because externalizing and internalizing behavior are more closely connected in adolescence than at any other age (Loeber & Burke, 2011). That is why teenagers jailed for assault (externalizing) are suicide risks (internalizing).

Externalizing actions are obvious. Many adolescents slam doors, defy parents, and tell friends exactly how badly other teenagers (or siblings or teachers) have behaved. Some teenagers—particularly boys—"act out" by breaking laws. They steal, damage property, or injure others. Girls who cut or burn themselves also have neurological

Nothing to Do Compared with most other Americans, these three adolescents are at higher risk of diabetes, alcoholism, unemployment, and suicide. They live on the Rosebud Sioux Reservation in South Dakota. The suicide rate among Native American teenagers is more than three times as high as the rate for U.S. adolescents overall.

cluster suicides
Several suicides committed by members of a group within a brief period.

✦ **ESPECIALLY FOR Journalists** You just heard that a teenage cheerleader jumped off a tall building and died. How should you report the story? (see response, page 380) →

Hope and Anger Adolescents and young adults everywhere demonstrate against adult authority, with varied strategies and results. In Cairo's Tahrir Square *(left)*, this young man flashes the peace sign hours before President Mubarak's resignation, but the 2011 "Arab Spring" in other nations was not as successful. French students *(right)* protested cuts in high school staff, but their demands were resisted by the government. Worldwide, social change is fueled by youthful aspirations—sometimes leading to victory, sometimes to despair., and often (as in Egypt) with high emotions that seem unrealistic later on. The French students *(right)* seem to have lost all hope—a sign of political despair.

RESPONSE FOR Journalists (from page 379) Since teenagers seek admiration from their peers, be careful not to glorify the victim's life or death. Facts are needed, as is, perhaps, the inclusion of warning signs that were missed or cautions about alcohol abuse. Avoid prominent headlines or anything that might encourage another teenager to do the same thing. ●

patterns similar to those of externalizing boys: They experience the anger and turn it on themselves (Crowell et al., 2012).

Before further discussing juvenile rebellion, we should emphasize that adolescents who commit serious crimes are unusual. Most teenagers usually obey the law, with moments of hot anger (loud profanity) or minor rebellion (smoking a joint), but nothing more.

Dozens of longitudinal studies confirm that increased anger after puberty is normal, but anger is usually expressed in acceptable ways. For a few, anger explodes: They break something or hurt someone. And a few of that few have been aggressive throughout childhood, becoming worse after puberty.

BREAKING THE LAW Both the prevalence (how widespread) and the incidence (how frequent) of crime increase during adolescence and continue at high levels in emerging adulthood. Arrest statistics in every nation reflect this, although some nations have much higher arrest rates overall than others.

Confidential self-reports reveal that virtually every adolescent boy breaks the law at least once before age 20. If all lawbreaking is considered—including buying cigarettes or beer, having sex with someone underage, skipping school, and breaking a curfew—girls are lawbreakers, too. Only about one-fourth of young lawbreakers are caught, and most of them are released with a warning (Dodge et al., 2006).

Not all adolescent crimes are victimless. One study of 1,559 urban seventh-graders (both sexes, all races, from parochial as well as public schools), found that more than three-fourths had committed at least one harmful offense (stolen something, damaged property, or hurt someone physically). The same study, however, found that less than one-third had committed five or more such acts (Nichols et al., 2006).

Our understanding of statistics on convictions may benefit from research on interrogation of suspects as well as from what we know about teenagers. In the United States, about 20 percent of confessions are false: Innocent people confess to crimes. This is especially likely in adolescence, partly because of brain immaturity and partly because young people want to please adults—including the police (Owen-Kostelnik et al., 2006; Steinberg, 2009). Knowing this, some jurisdictions record all interrogations and train police officers in the special attributes of adolescents (Lassiter & Meissner, 2010). For example, younger teens are more egocentric and thus might take full blame for something they did not actually do.

CAUSES OF DELINQUENCY Two clusters of factors, one from childhood (primarily brain-based) and one from adolescence (primarily contextual), predict delinquency. Knowing this allows prevention to focus on causes.

The first of these clusters includes a short attention span, hyperactivity, inadequate emotional regulation, slow language development, low intelligence, early and severe malnutrition, autistic tendencies, maternal cigarette smoking, and being the victim of severe child abuse, especially if it includes blows to the head. Most of these factors are more common among boys than girls, which may be one reason the male/female ratio in U.S. prisons is 13:1.

Any of these signs of neurological impairment (either inborn or caused by early experiences) increases the risk that a child will become a **life-course-persistent offender** (Moffitt et al., 2001). As the term implies, a life-course-persistent offender is someone who breaks the law before and after adolescence as well as during it.

The second cluster of factors that predict delinquency encompasses risk factors that are primarily psychosocial. They include having deviant friends; having few connections to school; living in a crowded, violent, unstable neighborhood; not having a job; using drugs and alcohol; and having close relatives (especially older siblings) in jail. These factors are more prevalent among low-income, urban adolescents, but certainly not exclusive to them. At any income level, an adolescent who experiences several of these risks is likely to become an **adolescence-limited offender,** someone whose criminal activity starts at puberty and stops by age 21 (Moffitt, 2003).

Adolescence-limited offenders break the law with their friends, facilitated by their chosen antisocial clique. More boys than girls are in this group, but some lawbreaking cliques include both sexes (the gender gap in lawbreaking is narrower in late adolescence than earlier or later) (Moffitt et al., 2001).

The criminal records of both types of teenagers may be similar. However, if adolescence-limited offenders can be protected from various snares (e.g., quitting school, entering prison, drug addiction, early parenthood), they may outgrow their criminal behavior. This is confirmed by other research: Few delinquent youth who are not imprisoned continue breaking the law in early adulthood (Monahan et al., 2009).

This does not mean that adolescence-limited lawbreaking should be ignored. Antisocial behavior is dangerous, especially to other adolescents, who are victimized three times as often as adults (Baum, 2005). Adolescents are more likely to be killed by another adolescent than to kill themselves. Fortunately, maturation puts an end to adolescence-limited lawbreaking.

By contrast, life-course-persistent offending begins in childhood and continues in adulthood with more crime, less education, lower income, unhappy marriages, and violence (Huesmann et al., 2009). It extends to the next generation: If life-course-persistent offenders have children, those children are likely to become lawbreakers themselves, partly for genetic reasons but primarily because they were mistreated by their parents before and after birth.

One way to prevent adolescent crime is to analyze earlier behavior patterns and stop delinquency before the police become involved. Three pathways can be seen (Loeber & Burke, 2011):

1. Stubbornness can lead to defiance, which can lead to running away—runaways are often victims as well as criminals (e.g., prostitutes, petty thieves).

2. Shoplifting can lead to arson and burglary.

3. Bullying can lead to assault, rape, and murder.

Each of these pathways demands a different response. The rebelliousness of the stubborn child can be channeled or limited until more maturation and less impulsive

Some Want Her Dead But Florida law did not allow 15-year-old Morgan Leppert to be executed for murdering a 63-year-old man when she and her 22-year-old boyfriend, Toby, stole the man's car. Instead, she was sentenced to life in prison without parole. Developmentalists agree that teenage criminals are not like adult ones, but they also wonder why Morgan's mother let Toby sleep in Morgan's bedroom when she was just 14.

✦ **ESPECIALLY FOR Police Officers** You see some 15-year-olds drinking beer in a local park when they belong in school. What do you do? (see response, page 382) →

life-course-persistent offender
A person whose criminal activity typically begins in early adolescence and continues throughout life; a career criminal.

adolescence-limited offender
A person whose criminal activity stops by age 21.

RESPONSE FOR Police Officers (from page 381) Avoid both extremes: Don't let them think this situation is either harmless or horrifying. You might take them to the police station and call their parents. These adolescents are probably not life-course-persistent offenders; jailing them or grouping them with other lawbreakers might encourage more crime. ●

anger prevail. Those on the second pathway require stronger human relationships and moral education.

Those on the third pathway present the most serious problem. Bullies need to be stopped and helped in early childhood, as already discussed. If that does not occur, and a teenager is convicted of assault, rape, or murder, then arrest, conviction, and jail might be the only options. In all cases, intervention is more effective earlier than later (Loeber & Burke, 2011).

Adolescent crime in the United States and many other nations has decreased in the past 20 years. Murder statistics provide a solid measure because neither victims nor the police can affect whether an offense is counted. In the United States, only half as many juveniles under age 18 are currently arrested for murder than was the case in 1990.

Although these data are solid, explanations are not. Possibilities include: fewer school dropouts (more education means less crime); wiser judges (using community service and drug treatment to prevent escalation); better policing (arrests for misdemeanors are up, alerting parents); smaller families (parents attend more to each child); better contraception and legal abortion (wanted children less often become criminals); more immigrants (who are more law-abiding); less lead poisoning (reducing impulsivity); stricter drug laws (binge-drinking and use of crack are down).

KEYpoints

- The emotions of adolescents often include marked depression and anger, sometimes pathological, sometimes not.
- Clinical depression is more common in teenage girls than boys; experts disagree as to whether this is primarily caused by hormones, rumination, or society.
- Breaking the law is common among adolescents, with more arrests during these years than later.
- Some offenders are adolescence-limited—they stop breaking the law at adulthood; some are life-course-persistent—they become criminal adults.

Drug Use and Abuse

Adolescents enjoy doing something forbidden. Moreover, their hormonal surges and brain patterns increase the reward sensations produced by drugs. But their developing bodies and brains make drug use particularly hazardous.

Variations in Drug Use

Most teenagers try *psychoactive drugs,* which are drugs that affect the mind. Although a police officer is concerned only with the legal issues of drug use, a developmentalist's concern is that cigarettes, alcohol, and many prescription medicines are as addictive and damaging as illegal drugs like marijuana, cocaine, and heroin.

Both the prevalence and incidence of drug use increase every year from age 10 to 25 and then decrease. Use before age 18 predicts later abuse.

The exception to this developmental pattern is inhalants (fumes from aerosol containers, cleaning fluid, etc.), which are used more by younger adolescents, partly because they can be easily purchased. Sadly, the youngest adolescents are least able, cognitively, to analyze risks, and parents rarely suspect a drug problem until their child dies from breathing toxic vapors.

VARIATIONS BY PLACE Nations vary markedly in drug use. Consider the most common drugs: alcohol and tobacco. In most European nations, alcohol is widely used, even by children. In much of the Middle East, however, alcohol use is illegal, and teenagers almost never drink. In many Asian nations, anyone may smoke anywhere; in the United States, smoking is forbidden in many schools and public places, but advertised widely; in Canada, cigarette advertising is outlawed. Not surprisingly, fewer teens in Canada smoke.

U.S. teens of both sexes smoke fewer cigarettes than do western European teens, and U.S. boys smoke fewer cigarettes than do Asian boys. The specifics of use and abuse vary historically and culturally, partly because each generation develops a distinct pattern that differentiates it from earlier cohorts and other cultures.

Variations within nations are marked as well. In the United States, most high school students have tried alcohol, and almost half have smoked cigarettes and marijuana—but a significant minority (about 20 percent) never use any drugs, especially if their classmates or crowds never use drugs. Regional differences are apparent. For instance, 24.1 percent of high school students in Kentucky have smoked in the past month, but only 5.1 percent of Utah students have (MMWR, June 8, 2012).

VARIATIONS BY GENERATION AND GENDER Cohorts vary, sometimes dramatically, as shown by a study called Monitoring the Future in which thousands of young people, diverse in every way, are asked about their recent and lifetime drug use. Use of most drugs has decreased in the United States since 1976 (as Figure 10.6 shows), but adolescent abuse of synthetic narcotics and prescription drugs has increased. During 2009, 10 percent of U.S. high school seniors used Vicodin and 6 percent used OxyContin (Johnston et al., 2012), both highly addictive and neither known to teenagers two decades ago.

With some exceptions, adolescent boys use more drugs, and use them more often, than girls do, especially outside the United States. An international survey of 13- to 15-year-olds in 131 nations found that more boys are smokers (except in a few European nations), including three times as many boys as girls in Southeast Asia

A Man Now This boy in Tibet is proud to be a smoker—in many Asian nations, smoking is considered manly.

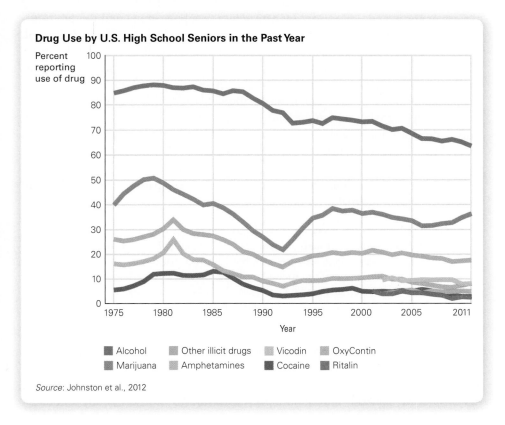

Drug Use by U.S. High School Seniors in the Past Year

Percent reporting use of drug

Year

■ Alcohol ■ Other illicit drugs ■ Vicodin ■ OxyContin
■ Marijuana ■ Amphetamines ■ Cocaine ■ Ritalin

Source: Johnston et al., 2012

FIGURE 10.6 Rise and Fall By asking the same questions year after year, the Monitoring the Future study shows notable historical effects. It is encouraging that something in society, not in the adolescent, makes drug use increase and decrease and that the most recent data show a decline. However, as Chapter 1 emphasized, survey research cannot prove what causes change.

(Warren et al., 2006). According to another international survey of 31 nations, almost twice as many boys as girls have tried marijuana (26 versus 15 percent) (ter Bogt et al., 2006).

These gender differences are reinforced by social constructions about proper male and female behavior. In Indonesia, for instance, 38 percent of the boys smoke cigarettes, but only 5 percent of the girls do. One Indonesian boy explained, "If I don't smoke, I'm not a real man" (quoted in Ng et al., 2007).

In the United States, the two sexes are quite similar in choice of drugs, although girls drink alcohol at younger ages and boys use more illegal drugs (Johnston et al., 2012). The most notable gender difference is that boys use more steroids and girls use more diet drugs.

Harm from Drugs

Many teenagers believe that adults exaggerate the evils of drug use and think it hypocritical that a parent who has cocktails before dinner or beer with lunch would dare prohibit adolescent drug use. Nonetheless, developmentalists see both immediate and long-term harm when teenagers use drugs.

Addiction and brain damage are among "the deleterious consequences of drug use [that] appear to be more pronounced in adolescents than in adults, a difference that has been linked to brain maturation" (Moffitt et al., 2006, p. 12). Few adolescents notice when they move past *use* (experimenting) to *abuse* (experiencing harm) and then to *addiction* (needing the drug to avoid feeling nervous, anxious, or in pain).

An obvious negative effect of *tobacco* is that it impairs digestion and nutrition, slowing down growth. Abuse of tobacco occurs with bidis, cigars, pipes, and chewing tobacco as well as with cigarettes. In India, widespread tobacco abuse is one reason for chronic undernutrition (Warren et al., 2006). Since internal organs continue to mature after the height spurt, cigarette-smoking teenagers who appear full-grown may damage their developing hearts, lungs, brains, and reproductive systems.

Alcohol is the most frequently abused drug in North America. Heavy drinking impairs memory and self-control by damaging the hippocampus and the prefrontal cortex, perhaps distorting the reward circuits of the brain lifelong (Guerri & Pascual, 2010). Although some specifics of the impact of alcohol on the adolescent brain are still unknown, there is no doubt that alcohol affects adolescents more than adults because of their brain immaturity (Chin et al., 2010).

✦ **ESPECIALLY FOR Parents Who Drink Socially** You have heard that parents should allow their children to drink at home, to teach them to drink responsibly and not get drunk elsewhere. Is that wise? (see response, page 387) →

Like many other drugs, alcohol allows momentary denial of problems: Worries seem to disappear when a person is under the influence. When ignored problems get worse, more alcohol is needed—a vicious cycle that often leads to addiction. Denial is a problem for all alcoholics, but particularly for teenagers who have not yet learned that they cannot drive, write, or even think after several drinks.

Similarly, *marijuana* seems harmless to many teenagers, partly because users seem more relaxed than inebriated. A girl named Johanna said:

> I started off using about every other weekend, and pretty soon it increased to three to four times a week. . . . I started skipping classes to get high. I quit soccer because my coach was a jerk. My grades dropped, but I blamed that on my not being into school. . . . Finally, some of my friends cornered me and told me how much I had changed, and they said it started when I started smoking marijuana. They came with me to see the substance-abuse counselor at school.
>
> *[Bell, 1998, p. 199]*

Johanna's future was in jeopardy. Adolescents who regularly smoke marijuana are more likely to drop out of school, become teenage parents, and be unemployed. Marijuana affects memory, language proficiency, and motivation (Lane et al., 2005)—all of which are especially crucial during adolescence. An Australian study found that even occasional marijuana use (once a week) before age 20 affected development up to 10 years later (Degenhardt et al., 2010).

Those are correlations, which, as you know, do not reveal causation. Is it possible that adolescents who are not particularly clever or ambitious choose to smoke marijuana, rather than vice versa? Is some third variable (such as hostile parents) the cause of both academic problems and drug use, rendering the correlation deceptive? This seems plausible because drug-using adolescents often distrust their parents, injure themselves, hate their schools, and break many laws.

These questions led to the hypothesis that the psychic strains of adolescence lead to drug use, not vice versa. In fact, however, longitudinal research suggests that drug use *causes* more problems than it solves, often *preceding* anxiety disorders, depression, and rebellion (Chassin et al., 2009; Meririnne et al., 2010).

Marijuana use is particularly common among wealthier adolescents, who then become less motivated to achieve in school and more likely to develop other problems (Ansary & Luthar, 2009). Rather than lack of ambition leading to marijuana use, marijuana itself destroys ambition.

How to Escape Imagine living where these boys do, on the streets in the capital city (Tegucigalpa) of Honduras, the nation with the highest murder rate in the world. What would stop you from doing what they do—sniff paint thinner for a dangerous moment of joy?

Preventing Drug Abuse: What Works?

Drug abuse is a progression, beginning with a social occasion and ending alone. The first use usually occurs with friends, which leads adolescents to believe that occasional use is an expression of friendship or generational solidarity. Few adolescents are addicts. An early sign of trouble is lower school achievement, but few notice that as early as they should. (See Infographic 10 on page 386 for school dropout rates.)

However, the Monitoring the Future study found that 25 percent of high school seniors had had five drinks in a row in the past two weeks, 11 percent were daily cigarette smokers, and 5 percent were daily marijuana users (Johnston et al., 2012). These figures suggest that addiction is the next step. The younger a person is when beginning occasional drug use, the more likely addiction will eventually occur.

That may not persuade young adolescents, who, as you remember, think they are invulnerable, exceptions to any rule. They do not know or care that every psychoactive drug excites the limbic system and interferes with the prefrontal cortex. That makes drug users more emotional (specifics vary, from ecstasy to terror, paranoia to rage) than they otherwise would be, as well as less reflective. Every hazard of adolescence—including car crashes, unsafe sex, and suicide—is more common among teens who have taken a psychoactive drug.

With harmful drugs, as with many other aspects of life, each generation prefers to learn things for themselves. A common phenomenon is **generational forgetting,** the idea that each new generation forgets what the previous generation knew (Chassin et al., 2009; Johnston et al., 2012). Mistrust of the older generation, added to loyalty to one's peers, leads not only to generational forgetting but also to a backlash. If adults say something is forbidden, that is a reason to try it.

Some antidrug curricula and advertisements that use scare tactics (such as the one showing eggs being broken into a hot frying pan while an announcer intoned, "This is your brain on drugs") have the opposite effect than intended, increasing rather than decreasing drug use. One reason may be that such advertisements make drugs seem exciting; another may be that adolescents recognize the exaggeration. Antismoking announcements produced by cigarette companies (such as one that showed a clean-cut young person advising viewers to think before they started smoking) actually increase use (Strasburger et al., 2009).

An added problem is that many parents are unaware of their children's drug use, so their educational efforts may be too late, too general, or too naive. For instance, in

generational forgetting
The idea that each new generation forgets what the previous generation learned. As used here, the term refers to knowledge about the harm drugs can do.

How Many Adolescents Are in School?

Attendance in secondary school is a psychosocial topic as much as a cognitive one. Whether or not an adolescent is in school reflects every aspect of the social context, including national policies, family support, peer pressures, and employment prospects. Social scientists believe that one reason for political violence, poverty, and teenage pregnancy in developing nations is that many teenagers are not in school.

PERCENTAGE OF ADOLESCENTS NOT IN SCHOOL, AGES 12 TO 15

Sub-Saharan Africa 36.7

South and West Asia 29.5

Arab States 16.6

East Asia and Pacific 10

Central and Eastern Europe 6.8

Latin America and the Caribbean 4.9

Western Europe 1.8

North America 1.8

There are many ways to calculate dropout rates, some of which amount to 2 or 3 times the rates shown here. Nonetheless, these indicate each state's data relative to other states, even when the data are presented in the way states prefer.

World Average 18.4

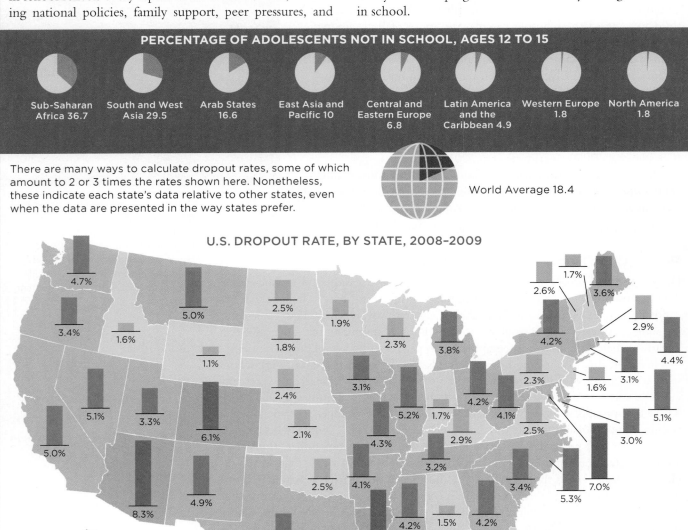

U.S. DROPOUT RATE, BY STATE, 2008–2009

4.7%
3.4%
1.6%
5.0%
2.5%
1.9%
1.7%
2.6%
3.6%
1.1%
1.8%
2.3%
3.8%
4.2%
2.9%
2.4%
3.1%
2.3%
1.6%
3.1%
4.4%
5.1%
3.3%
6.1%
2.1%
5.2%
1.7%
4.2%
4.1%
2.5%
3.0%
5.1%
5.0%
4.3%
2.5%
2.9%
7.0%
8.3%
4.9%
4.1%
3.2%
3.4%
5.3%
3.2%
4.2%
1.5%
4.2%
6.8%
2.6%
7.0%
4.9%

0%–2.9%
3%–5.9%
6%–8.9%

WHEN ADOLESCENTS ARE NOT IN SCHOOL, WHERE ARE THEY?

Some possibilities:

- Working in hazardous conditions with little possibility of advancement
- Living on the streets, involved in petty crime, with worse crime in the future
- Using drugs to get through the day
- Having babies

SOURCES & CREDITS LISTED ON P. SC-1

one U.S. study, less than 1 percent of parents of sixth-graders thought their children had ever had alcohol, but 22 percent of the children said they had (O'Donnell et al., 2008). In general, adolescents follow their parents' example more than their advice.

Changing the social context has had an impact. Throughout the United States, higher prices, targeted warnings, and better law enforcement have led to a marked decline in cigarette smoking among younger adolescents. In 2009, only 6.5 percent of eighth-graders had smoked cigarettes in the past month, compared with 21 percent 10 years earlier (Johnston et al., 2012).

All the research confirms that parents are influential. When parents forbid smoking in their homes, fewer adolescents smoke (Messer et al., 2008); when parents are careful with their own drinking, fewer teenagers abuse alcohol (Van Zundert et al., 2006). When parents provide guidance about drinking, teenagers are less likely to get drunk or use other substances (Miller & Plant, 2010).

Growing up with two married parents reduces cigarette and alcohol use, even when other influences (such as parental smoking and family income) are taken into account (Brown & Rinelli, 2010). The probable reasons include better monitoring: Usually, at least one of the parents is aware of what the child is doing.

As this chapter draws to a close, it is apparent that, although puberty is a universal biological process, its effects vary widely. Sharply declining rates of teenage pregnancy, abortions, suicides, and homicides, and less use of several legal and illegal drugs are evident in many nations. Changing times bring new iterations of the identity crisis. Human growth starts with genes when a single sperm penetrates a single ovum, but it certainly is not wholly determined by biology.

This will be even more apparent in the next five chapters: By the end of adolescence, a person has completed body growth but not development. No adult of any age has been unchanged over the past five years, and no one will be the same five years hence.

RESPONSE FOR Parents Who Drink Socially (from page 384) No. Alcohol is particularly harmful for young brains. It is best to drink only when your children are not around. Children who are encouraged to drink with their parents are more likely to drink when no adults are present. It is true that adolescents are rebellious, and they may drink even if you forbid it. But if you allow alcohol, they might rebel with other drugs. ●

KEY points

- Many adolescents try psychoactive drugs, most commonly alcohol and cigarettes, although nations vary tremendously in whether drugs are legal and available.
- Adolescents are often unaware of the dangers of drugs, which are particularly harmful to the developing brain and body.
- Drug use has declined among U.S. high school students over the past decades, although prescription drugs are abused more often than they once were.
- Some educational measures to halt adolescent drug use are not effective, but parental example and raising the cost of drugs have reduced prevalence.

SUMMARY

Identity

1. Adolescence is a time for self-discovery. According to Erikson, adolescents seek their own identity, sorting through the traditions of their families and cultures.

2. Many young adolescents foreclose on their options without exploring possibilities, experience role confusion, or reach moratorium. Identity achievement takes longer for contemporary adolescents than it did half a century ago, when Erikson first described it.

3. Identity achievement occurs in many domains, including religion, politics, vocation, and sex. Each of these remains important over the life span, but timing, contexts, and terminology have changed.

Relationships with Others

4. Parents continue to influence their growing children, despite bickering over minor issues. Ideally, communication and warmth remain high within the family, while parental control decreases and adolescents develop autonomy.

5. There are cultural differences in the timing of conflicts and particulars of parental monitoring. Too much parental control, with psychological intrusiveness, is harmful, as is neglect. Parents need to find a balance between granting freedom and providing guidance.

6. Peers and peer pressure can be beneficial or harmful, depending on particular friends, cliques, and crowds. Adolescents select their friends, including friends of the other sex, who then facilitate constructive and/or destructive behavior.

7. Crowds and cliques are evident in high schools; they are necessary to help adolescents develop their values and life habits. Peers may be particularly crucial for ethnic-minority and immigrant adolescents, who need to establish their own ethnic identity—one not quite corresponding with the messages they have received from society or their parents.

Sexual Interactions

8. Current youth may have healthier sexual relationships than did youth a generation ago. Teen pregnancy and abortion are lower, contraception use is higher, and sexual intercourse, at least in the United States, occurs at later ages.

9. Puberty triggers sexual interest, but cultures and crowds have a major influence on how, when, and to whom those interests are expressed. Early, exclusive sexual relationships are a sign of emotional immaturity.

10. Some youth are oriented toward same-sex romance; others have sexual relationships with both sexes. Depending on the family, culture, and cohort, sexual-minority youth may experience depression and other problems.

11. Problems with adolescent sexuality include adolescent pregnancy (higher in the United States than elsewhere) and STIs (higher in adolescence than later).

12. Sexual abuse is more likely to occur in early adolescence than at other ages, and it can harm a victim's brain and psychological development lifelong. Girls are most often the victims; the perpetrators are most often family members.

13. Sex education occurs in many ways, with parents the most powerful influence but often the least informed. Schools vary in scope and success of sex education.

Sadness and Anger

14. A few adolescents become seriously depressed. Many adolescents (especially girls) think about suicide, and some attempt it. Few adolescents actually kill themselves; most who do so are boys.

15. Lawbreaking as well as momentary rage are common; boys are more likely to be arrested for violent offenses than are girls. Adolescence-limited offenders should be prevented from hurting themselves or others. Life-course-persistent offenders are aggressive in childhood and may continue to be so in adulthood.

Drug Use and Abuse

16. Most adolescents experiment with drugs, especially alcohol and tobacco, although such substances impair growth of the body and the brain. National culture has a powerful influence on which specific drugs are used as well as on the frequency of use. Age, gender, community, and parental factors are also influential.

17. Prevention and moderation of adolescent drug use and abuse are possible. Antidrug programs and messages need to be carefully designed to avoid a backlash or generational forgetting.

KEY TERMS

adolescence-limited offender (p. 381)
bickering (p. 361)
child sexual abuse (p. 371)
clinical depression (p. 377)
clique (p. 365)
cluster suicides (p. 379)
crowd (p. 365)
deviancy training (p. 366)
familism (p. 377)
foreclosure (p. 357)
gender identity (p. 360)
generational forgetting (p. 385)
identity achievement (p. 356)
identity versus role confusion (p. 356)
life-course-persistent offender (p. 381)
moratorium (p. 357)
parasuicide (p. 378)
parental monitoring (p. 363)
peer pressure (p. 364)
role confusion (p. 356)
rumination (p. 377)
sexual orientation (p. 369)
sexually transmitted infection (STI) (p. 373)
suicidal ideation (p. 378)

WHAT HAVE YOU LEARNED?

1. What are the differences between identity achievement and role confusion?

2. What role do parents play in religious and political identity?

3. What are the pros and cons of teens having part-time jobs while in school?

4. In what crucial way do the terms "sexual identity" and "gender identity" differ?

5. Why do parents and adolescents often bicker?

6. What four factors affect family closeness? Why is each factor important?

7. How and when can peer pressure be helpful and how can it be harmful?

8. What are the roles of parents, peers, and society in helping an adolescent develop an ethnic identity?

9. What evidence is there that teenagers today are sexually healthier than teenagers a few decades ago?

10. What are Dunphy's four stages of male–female relationships?

11. What factors influence sexual activity? Explain.

12. How does culture affect the development of sexual orientation?

13. What risks are associated with teenage pregnancy, for both the mother and the child?

14. Why is it harmful for a young adolescent and an adult to have sex?

15. Why is it difficult to know what influence the media has on adolescents having sex?

16. In terms of learning about sex from parents, what seems to be the most influential factor?

17. Why might peers be an unreliable source of information about sex?

18. What are the variations in sex education in schools, and how does this affect adolescent sexual behavior?

19. Among sexually active people, why do adolescents have more STIs than adults?

20. What gender differences are evident in depression, and why?

21. What gender differences are evident in suicide, and why?

22. What factors make serious delinquency more likely, and what factors decrease the risk?

23. What variations in adolescent drug use are evident? Why?

24. Why are psychoactive drugs particularly destructive in adolescence?

25. What works and doesn't work in reducing adolescent drug use?

APPLICATIONS

1. Teenage cliques and crowds may be more important in large U.S. high schools than elsewhere. Interview people who spent their teenage years in U.S. schools of various sizes, or in another nation, about the peer relationships in their high schools. Describe and discuss any differences you find.

2. Locate a news article about a teenager who committed suicide. Can you find evidence in the article that there were warning signs that were ignored? Does the report inadvertently encourage cluster suicides?

3. Research suggests that most adolescents have broken the law but that few have been arrested or incarcerated. Ask 10 of your fellow students if they ever broke the law when they were younger than 18 and, if so, how often, in what ways, and with what consequences. (Assure them of confidentiality.) What hypothesis arises about lawbreaking in your cohort?

4. Cultures have different standards for drug use among children, adolescents, and adults. Interview three people from different cultures (not necessarily from different nations; each occupation, generation, or religion can be said to have a culture) about their culture's drug-use standards. Ask your respondents to explain the reasons behind the cultural standards.

>>ONLINE CONNECTIONS

To accompany your textbook, you have access to a number of online resources, including quizzes for every chapter of the book, flashcards (in English and Spanish), critical-thinking questions, and case studies. For access to any of these links, go to www. worthpublishers.com/bergerinvitation2e. In addition to these free resources, you'll also find links to podcasts, video clips, diagnostic quizzing with personalized study advice, and an ebook. Some of the videos and activities available online include:

- *Who Am I?* This video reviews pathways to identity achievement and Marcia's dimensions of exploration and commitment. Teens talk about identity. The embedded questionnaire lets you gauge your progress in identity formation.

- *Interview with Anne Petersen.* This expert talks about the role of parents in adolescence and the need for solid community services.

VI

- CHAPTER 11
- CHAPTER 12
- CHAPTER 13

Adulthood

We now begin the sixth part of this text. These three chapters cover 47 years (ages 18 to 65), when bodies mature, minds master new material, and people work productively.

No decade of adulthood is exclusively programmed for any one event: Adults at many ages get stronger and weaker, learn and produce, nurture friendships and marriages, care for children and aging relatives. Many experience hiring and firing, wealth and poverty, births and deaths, weddings and divorces, windfalls and disasters, illness and recovery. Adulthood is a long sweep, punctuated by many events, joyful and sorrowful.

There are some chronological norms, noted in these chapters. Early in adulthood, few people are married or settled in a career; later, most people have partners and offspring. Expertise at a particular job is more likely at age 50 than 20.

Developmental history is always relevant: Adults are guided by their nature and nurture, as they choose partners, activities, communities, and habits. For the most part, these are good years, when each person's goals become more attainable.

The experience of adulthood is not the same everywhere. In some nations and cultures, dominant influences are families, economics, and past history; in others, genetic heritage and personal choice. Of course, it is a matter of degree, but economic forces are particularly strong when governments provide no safety nets, whereas genes and choice are stronger when governments and cultures are less autocratic. For example, virtually everyone marries in some nations, but genetic heritage and the ability to make a broader range of personal choices are stronger influences elsewhere.

The following three chapters describe adulthood: the universals, the usual, and the diverse.

EMERGING ADULTHOOD
Body, Mind, and Social World

WHAT WILL YOU KNOW?

- When is it a problem to be fertile?
- How can imagining other people's stereotypes be harmful?
- Does cohabitation precede, ruin, or substitute for marriage?
- Is independence from parents a sign of healthy adulthood?

The years from ages 18 to 25 were once merely part of adulthood; then were distinguished as late adolescence, youth, or early adulthood; and now are often labeled **emerging adulthood.** In emerging adulthood, many people seek higher education and explore their identity by postponing marriage, parenthood, and career.

I experienced this myself. Between ages 18 and 25, I attended four colleges or universities, changed majors five times, rejected marriage proposals from four young men, lived in ten places, and started several jobs—none lasting more than 18 months. After that period of rapid change, I stayed put for 30 years—one husband, one city, one street, one career.

Similar patterns occur everywhere. Although few have as many options as I did, youth in every nation gain more education and marry later than previous generations did. ●

EMERGING ADULTHOOD IS A STAGE, or a process, worldwide (Arnett et al., 2011). As always, culture, context, and cohort are influential, but few people have settled down by age 18. Although 18-year-olds are no longer adolescents in body, mind, or social context, they are also not yet adults as traditionally defined.

Biosocial Development

Biologically, the years from ages 18 to 25 are prime time for hard physical work and successful reproduction. However, the fact that young adults can carry rocks, plow fields, and reproduce more easily than older adults is no longer universally admired.

Indeed, if a contemporary young couple had a baby every year, their neighbors would be more appalled than approving. Now, during emerging adulthood, societies, families, and young adults themselves expect more education, later marriage,

emerging adulthood
The period of life between the ages of 18 and 25. Emerging adulthood is now widely thought of as a separate developmental stage.

Peak Performance Because this is a soccer match, of course we see skilled feet and strong legs—but also notice the arms, torsos, and feats of balance. Deniz Naki (age 21) and Luis Gustavo (age 23) are German soccer team members in better shape than most emerging adults, but imagine these two a decade earlier (at age 11 and 13) or later (at age 31 and 33) and you will realize why, physiologically, one's early 20s are considered the prime of life.

and fewer children than was true as recently as 50 years ago (see At About This Time).

Sometimes such expectations are thought to be exclusive to the middle class in advanced nations, but the trends are apparent everywhere. For most workers today, desk work and factory jobs have replaced hard labor, and dramatic fertility shifts over the past 50 years have been seen in Iran (average births per woman declined from 7 to 1.5), Kenya (from 8 to 4), South America (from 6 to 2), and East Asia (from 5 to 1.5). For the world as a whole, the birth rate from 1960 to 2010 fell from 4.9 to 2.45 (United Nations, 2011). In the United States, the 2010 rate for every major ethnic group was only half of what it was in the 1960s.

Strong and Active Bodies

Health has not changed, except maybe to improve. As probably has been true for millennia, every human body system—including the digestive, respiratory, circulatory, and sexual-reproductive systems—functions optimally at the beginning of adulthood. In a mammoth survey, 95.8 percent of young adults (aged 18 to 29) in the United States rated their health as good, very good, or excellent (National Center for Health Statistics, 2010).

Specifics confirm the health of emerging adults. Serious diseases are not yet apparent, and some childhood ailments are outgrown. For example, childhood asthma disappears as often as it continues. Although many emerging adults continue the poor health habits they had as adolescents, the trend is toward better diets and regular exercise, and that improves mental as well as physical health (Walsh, 2011).

However, this does not mean that serious health problems from childhood disappear. In the same survey in which only 4.2 percent of young adults rated their health as less than good, 15 percent said they had been told they had a chronic disease or condition—often asthma, arthritis, or high blood pressure (National Center for Health Statistics, 2010). A comprehensive review of many studies finds that low birthweight, undernutrition in infancy, and rapid weight gain in early childhood tend to result in shorter height, reduced body functioning, and higher risk of disease in early adulthood (Victora et al., 2008).

Fortunately, severe health problems are usually kept in check. During early adulthood, the immune system is strong, fighting off everything from the sniffles to cancer

These are norms, which convey the median age for these events, each traditionally considered signs of adulthood. Note that most people do not achieve college graduation and that the median age for family commitment is at the end of emerging adulthood. Furthermore, many people do not follow this normative path.

AT ABOUT THIS TIME

Following Certain Patterns, by Average Age (U.S., 2010)

Age 17–18—Graduate from high school (about 25 percent do not do so)

Age 18–19—Enroll in college (about 30 percent of high school graduates do not)

Age 22—Earn college degree (about half of those who enter college)

Age 25—Steady employment in chosen field (rate fluctuates, depends on economy)

Age 25—Women's first birth* (for those who will have children; about 20 percent will not)

Age 26—Women's first marriage (about 18 percent never marry)

Age 28—Men's first marriage (about 25 percent never marry)

*By ethnicity: Age 23—African American or Hispanic; age 26—European American; age 29—Asian American
Source: U.S. Bureau of the Census, 2011b, and previous years.

and responding well to vaccines (Grubeck-Loebenstein, 2010). In the United States each year, cancer kills 1 in 65 adults older than 85 but only 1 in 25,000 emerging adults. Death from heart disease is equally rare for emerging adults.

For most emerging adults, teeth have no new cavities, heart rate is steady, the brain functions well, and lung capacity is sufficient. Many diagnostic tests, such as PSAs (for prostate cancer), mammograms (for breast cancer), and colonoscopies (for colon cancer) are not usually recommended until decades later—and often not even then unless risk factors are present. Death from any disease is rare (see Table 11.1), although, as discussed later, death from accidents, suicide, and homicide increase, and psychosocial problems may arise.

Fertility, Then and Now

As already mentioned, the sexual-reproductive system is at its strongest during emerging adulthood. Thanks to nature's wonderful mechanism to preserve the human species, young adults experience great joy from sexual interactions. During these years, orgasms are frequent and the sex drive is powerful.

Moreover, fertility is optimal, miscarriage less common, serious birth complications unusual. Historically, most couples had their first child as teenagers. Many had a second and a third child before age 25. These statistics highlight the new reality. Age 25 is now the average age for a *first* birth in the United States, with first births occurring even later in some other countries.

PREMARITAL SEX Reproductive ease has become a burden, not a blessing. The bodies of emerging adults want sex, but their minds know they are not prepared for parenthood (Lefkowitz & Gillen, 2006). When they consider the cost of raising a child, most couples wonder if they can afford a baby.

For many, the solution to this dilemma is sex without pregnancy, made possible by modern contraception. Although no contraception is always successful, long-acting contraception (implant, IUD, Depo-Provera) almost never fails (about 1 failure in 400 women), whereas shorter-acting measures (pill, patch, or ring) fail for 1 in 20 women (Winner et al., 2012). Failure rates are higher in adolescents than in emerging adults.

According to a poll in the beginning of the twenty-first century, most U.S. 18- to 24-year-olds answered that premarital sex is "not wrong at all," but only 18 percent of those over age 65 agree (T. W. Smith, 2005). Those sentiments may be even stronger with the current cohort: Few young adults (27 percent) think living together before marriage is bad for society, even though most older adults (64 percent) think that it is (Pew Research Center, 2010).

Even compared with 1997, fewer of today's young adults are married, but more hope to become good parents (Wang & Taylor, 2011) (see Figure 11.1). Most U.S. women under age 30 who had babies in 2011 were not married—a dramatic contrast with the past—the shift is most evident among European American women without college degrees.

Part of being a good parent, according to emerging adults, is providing financially for each child. For that reason, as the economy has soured, the birth rate has fallen—a trend for all women under age 40, with a particularly strong drop for those aged 20 to 24 (Livingston, 2011). Women in their 20s who have babies often have jobs as well, another shift from earlier times.

Years of Practice, But Not Too Many Years of Life People of any age can begin ballet lessons or any other physical activity, but mastery requires a decade or more. Russian ballerinas begin intensive practice in childhood, hoping for the fame achieved by Yulia Tikka, here at age 23 in her prime. Her solo career will soon end; superstars in almost every demanding athletic activity slow down before age 30.

TABLE 11.1 U.S. Deaths from the Top Three Causes (Heart Disease, Stroke, Cancer)

Age Group	Annual Rate per 100,000
15–24	7
25–34	18
35–44	65
45–54	219
55–64	561
65–74	1,313
75–84	2,971
85+	7,126

Source: National Center for Health Statistics, 2010.

Young and Healthy Young adults rarely die of diseases, including the top three: heart disease, cancer, and stroke. These are annual rates, which means that for each person, the chance of death in that decade is 10 times the yearly rate. Thus, a 15-year-old has less than 1 chance in 1,000 of dying of disease before age 25; a 75-year-old has more than 1 chance in 3 of dying of disease before age 85.

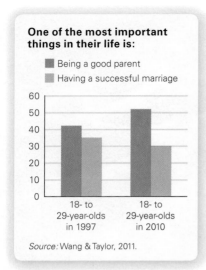

One of the most important things in their life is:

- ■ Being a good parent
- ■ Having a successful marriage

Source: Wang & Taylor, 2011.

FIGURE 11.1 Children Before Partners As you can see from this comparison of emerging adults in the 1990s and in 2010, an increasing number of young adults think parenthood is more important than marriage.

✦ **ESPECIALLY FOR Marriage Counselors** Sex is no longer the main reason for divorce—money is. If you are counseling a cohabiting couple who want to marry, do you still need to ask them about sex? (see response, page 399) ➜

✦ **ESPECIALLY FOR Nurses** When should you suspect that a patient has an untreated STI? (see response, page 399) ➜

Although most emerging adults accept *pre*marital sex, many (80 percent) believe that *extra*marital sex is "always wrong" (T. W. Smith, 2005). For child development, this may be good news: Children fare better if they are wanted and if their parents are committed to each other as well as emotionally ready for child rearing.

SEXUAL DISEASES Premarital sex and single motherhood are controversial. Many older adults and some young adults wish everyone would marry before having sex; others disagree. However, there is no controversy about one consequence of sexual freedom, the rise of sexually transmitted infections (STIs), with half of all new cases worldwide occurring in people younger than 26 (Gewirtzman et al., 2011). Every nation has noted that rise, and every nation is attempting to stop it—with quite different strategies. No single nation can succeed alone.

Globalization accelerates every contagious disease, including STIs (Herring & Swedlund, 2010). In earlier times, prostitution was local, which kept STIs local as well. Now, with international travel, an STI caught from an infected sex worker in one place quickly spreads to young adults thousands of miles away. Sexual freedom among unmarried adults means that many young people who would never engage in prostitution are carriers of STIs, often without their knowledge.

This proliferation is particularly devastating with regard to HIV/AIDS, which probably began in remote parts of the world, then was confined to gay men in major cities, and then to injection drug users who shared needles, or to transfusion recipients before donated blood was screened for the virus. That was tragic, but limited.

Within the past 20 years, primarily because of the sexual activities of emerging adults, HIV has become a worldwide epidemic, with more female than male victims, more heterosexual than homosexual victims (Davis & Squire, 2010). Worldwide, young adults remain the prime STI vectors (those who spread disease).

Since about 2010, the AIDS epidemic has been slowing, largely because "a generation of young people are taking charge of their destinies and are protecting themselves against HIV" (UNAIDS, 2011, p. 17). Protection includes fewer sex partners, later sex, more condom use, and voluntary circumcision among young adult men (with rates as high as 70 percent in some communities) (World Health Organization, 2011).

Another protective measure would be to stop forced sex. That would particularly help young women: About 20 percent of females with AIDS contracted it because of rape (Jewkes et al., 2011).

In strategic measures to halt AIDS, some nations (e.g., South Africa, Brazil, and Cambodia) are making progress, but others (e.g., Nigeria, Russia, and Vietnam) are not (UNAIDS, 2011). Each culture needs to target their prime vectors. For instance, providing sterile needles to intravenous drug users is a proven successful strategy, but some nations have relatively few injection drug addicts. If those nations ignore their prime vectors, who—depending on the culture—might be female sex workers or heterosexual young men, then HIV will spread.

Taking Risks

Remember that each developmental period brings gains and losses, and any specific age-related characteristic can be a blessing or a burden. One example is risk taking, with emerging adults particularly likely (bravely or foolishly) to take risks. In addition to age, risk taking is affected by gender, genes, hormones, and culture. Young North American males who are genetically impulsive are often remarkably brave and foolhardy.

BENEFITS AND LIABILITIES Societies, as well as individuals, benefit from this characteristic of emerging adults. Enrolling in college, moving to a new state or nation, getting married, having a baby—all are risky. So is starting a business, filming a documentary, entering an athletic contest, enlisting in the army, joining the Peace

Corps, rescuing a stranger. Without emerging adults, all those activities would occur less often.

Yet risk taking is often destructive. Although their bodies are strong and their reactions quick, emerging adults have more accidents that send them to emergency rooms than do people of any other age (except for falls in the elderly). Because of their good overall health, usually they are stitched, casted, medicated, stabilized, and discharged in short order.

The low rate of serious disease between ages 18 and 25 is counterbalanced by a high rate of severe injuries (see Figure 11.2) and violent deaths, with males at least twice as vulnerable as females. (Sometimes the ratio is as high as 5:1, not just 2:1, depending on which nation and which type of violent death is analyzed.)

For both sexes, age is always a factor in suicide, homicide, and accidents. More people are murdered during emerging adulthood than at any other period. Many specific types of accidental death are also more frequent during these years, including drug overdose, motor vehicle crashes, and drowning.

Among the destructive risks more common in emerging adulthood are:

- Unprotected sex with a new partner
- Driving fast without a seat belt
- Carrying a loaded gun
- Abusing drugs
- Addictive gambling

People behave this way partly for the rush of adrenalin (Cosgrave, 2010). The high rate of violent death is evident in historical data as well, particularly among young males who experience a so-called accident hump in the death rate at about age 20 (Goldstein, 2011).

Violent deaths are more common than disease deaths during these years even in nations with rampant infection and malnutrition. The only exception has been South Africa, where AIDS kills more young adults than suicide does (but AIDS itself results from risk taking). Ironically, warning emerging adults about the risks may lead to a backlash—some subsequently *increase* their risk taking in order to defy death and aging (Popham et al., 2011a).

RISKY SPORTS Many young adults seek the rush of risk taking in recreation. They climb mountains, swim in oceans, run in pain, play past exhaustion, and so on. Sky-diving, bungee-jumping, pond-swooping, parkour, potholing (in caves), waterfall kayaking, and many more activities have been invented to satisfy the joy of risk. Serious injury is not the goal, of course, but high risk adds to the challenge (Brymer, 2010).

Anywhere In some ways, life in China is radically different from life elsewhere, but universals are also apparent. This emerging-adult couple poses in front of the Beijing stadium.

OBSERVATION QUIZ
One detail in the young man's hands suggests that the setting is Asia, not North America. What is it? (see answer, page 399) →

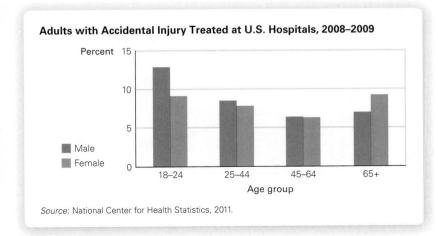

Adults with Accidental Injury Treated at U.S. Hospitals, 2008–2009

Source: National Center for Health Statistics, 2011.

FIGURE 11.2 Send Them Home Accidents, homicides, and suicides occur more frequently during emerging adulthood than later (except for older women, who fall more often). Fewer young adults stay in the hospital, however. They are usually stitched, bandaged, injected, and sent home.

REUTERS /TIM WIMBORNE

Travis Could Crash But he didn't. The possibility of death is what makes thousands watch Travis Pastrana perform his risky stunts, as here in Sidney, Australia.

OBSERVATION QUIZ

Travis added more danger to this motorcycle leap. What is it? (see answer, page 400) →

extreme sports
Forms of recreation that include apparent risk of injury or death and are attractive and thrilling as a result.

drug abuse
The ingestion of a drug to the extent that it impairs the user's biological or psychological well-being.

✦ **ESPECIALLY FOR Substance Abuse Counselors** Can you think of three possible explanations for the more precipitous drop in the use of illegal drugs compared with legal ones? (see response, page 400) →

FIGURE 11.3 Too Old for That
As you can see, emerging adults are the biggest substance abusers, but illegal drug use drops much faster than cigarette use or binge drinking. This depicts drug use in one nation (the United States in 2008), but the same trends are universal.

Competitive **extreme sports** (such as *freestyle motocross*—riding a motorcycle off a ramp, catching "big air," doing tricks while falling, and hoping to land upright) are thrilling for some emerging adults. They find golf, bowling, and so on too tame (Breivik, 2010). As the authors of one study of dirt-bikers (off-road motorcyclists) explain, particularly from ages 18 to 24 there is a "developmental lag between impulse control and cognitive evaluation of risk" (Dwane, 2012, p. 62). The thrill overwhelms reason.

This is clearer with an example. Travis Pastrana won the 2006 X Games MotoX Freestyle event at age 22 with a double backflip because, as he explained, "The two main things are that I've been healthy and able to train at my fullest, and a lot of guys have had major crashes this year" (Higgins, 2006, D7).

Four years later, in 2010, he set a new record for leaping through big air in an automobile, driving over the ocean from a ramp on the California shore to a barge more than 250 feet out. He crashed into a barrier on the boat, emerging, ecstatic and unhurt, to the thunderous cheers of thousands of other young adults (Roberts, 2010). In 2011, a broken foot and ankle made him temporarily halt extreme sports—but soon he was back risking his life to the acclaim of his cohort, winning races rife with flips and other hazards.

DRUG ABUSE The same impulse that is admired in extreme sports leads to behaviors that are clearly destructive, not only for individuals but for the community. The most studied of these is drug abuse, which can involve dozens of substances—both legal and illegal (Maisto et al., 2011).

By definition, **drug abuse** occurs whenever a person uses a drug that harms physical, cognitive, or psychosocial well-being. Occasional smoking can be abuse, as can alcohol bingeing (4 or 5 drinks on one occasion). Even one-time use can be abusive, if, for instance, it leads to driving while drunk, walking into traffic while hallucinating, being arrested for cocaine use, and so on.

More often, abusers are also addicts: They need the drug to feel OK, and they become chronic users. Drug addiction and abuse are more common during emerging adulthood than at any other age (Johnston et al., 2010).

For emerging adults, part of the attraction of drugs is in their abuse, specifically in taking a drug to feel dizzy, out-of-body, or high. It adds to the thrill if authority figures disapprove. Buying, carrying, and using an illegal drug, knowing that arrest is possible, are all exciting. So is selling: Most street sellers of drugs are relatively young— they often quit, go to prison, or are killed before middle age. Illegal drug use peaks at about age 20 and declines sharply after that (see Figure 11.3). The thrill is gone.

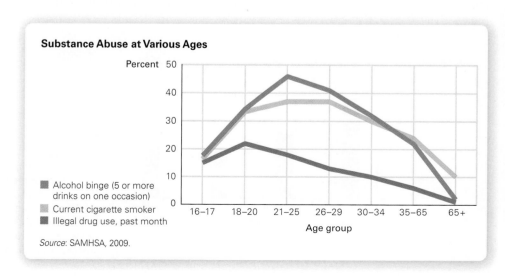

Substance Abuse at Various Ages

Percent

- Alcohol binge (5 or more drinks on one occasion)
- Current cigarette smoker
- Illegal drug use, past month

Age group

Source: SAMHSA, 2009.

Higher Education College provides many benefits, but it also seems to encourage drug use. Everyone at this fraternity party appears to be using alcohol, and one young woman is drinking from a beer bong. Seeking admiration for drinking large quantities in a short time is a sign that a person is at risk for alcoholism.

Surprisingly, drug abuse is more common among college students than among their contemporaries who are not in college. Alcohol abuse is rampant in college, with 25 percent of young men and 5 percent of young women reporting that they consumed 10 or more drinks in a row at least once in the previous two weeks (Johnston et al., 2009). Such excesses arise from the same drive as extreme sports or other risks—with the same potential consequence: death.

RESPONSE FOR Marriage Counselors (from page 396) Yes. The specifics of sex—frequency, positions, preferences—are no longer a taboo topic for most couples, but the couple still needs to discuss exactly what sex means to each of them. Issues of contraception, fidelity, and abortion can drive partners apart, each believing that he or she is right and the other is rigid, loose, immoral, hidebound, irresponsible, or unloving. ●

KEYpoints

- Young adults are usually healthy and at peak reproductive potential.
- Having sex without fear of pregnancy is desired by many emerging adults.
- Sexually transmitted infections are more common with globalization and sexual freedom.
- Emerging adults are risk takers, sometimes risking their life.
- Drug abuse and addiction are more common during emerging adulthood than in any other period.

RESPONSE FOR Nurses (from page 396) Always. In this context, "suspect" refers to a healthy skepticism, not to prejudice or disapproval. Your attitude should be professional rather than judgmental, but be aware that education, gender, self-confidence, and income do not necessarily mean that a given patient is free of an STI. ●

ANSWER TO **OBSERVATION QUIZ** (from page 397) The cigarette (not the camera). Most young men in Canada and the United States do not smoke, especially publicly and casually, as this man does. ●

Cognitive Development

As you remember, each of the four periods of child and adolescent development is characterized by major cognitive advances, each described by Piaget as a new stage. Piaget thought that the fourth stage, *formal operational thought,* continued lifelong.

However, some recent scholars contend that adult thought differs from adolescent thinking: It is more practical, more flexible, better able to coordinate objective and subjective perspectives. This may constitute a major advance, combining a new "ordering of formal operations" with a "necessary subjectivity" (Sinnott, 1998, p. 24).

Postformal Thought

Indeed, many developmentalists believe that Piaget's fourth stage, formal operational thought, is inadequate to describe adult cognition. Some have proposed a fifth stage, called **postformal thought,** characterized by "problem finding," not just "problem solving," wherein a person is more open to ideas and less concerned with absolute right and wrong (Yan & Arlin, 1995).

postformal thought
A proposed adult stage of cognitive development, following Piaget's four stages. Postformal thought goes beyond adolescent thinking by being more practical, more flexible, and more dialectical (i.e., more capable of combining contradictory elements into a comprehensive whole).

Crammed Together Students flock to the Titan Student Union at Cal State Fullerton for the biannual All Night Study before final exams, making cramming a social experience. This is contrary to what scientific evidence has shown is the best way to learn— that is, through *distributed practice,* which means studying consistently throughout the semester, not bunching it all at the end. Is cramming simply the result of poor time management or is it a rational choice?

◆ **ESPECIALLY FOR Someone Who Has to Make an Important Decision** Which is better: to go with your gut feelings or to consider pros and cons as objectively as you can? (see response, page 402) →

ANSWER TO **OBSERVATION QUIZ** (from page 398) That helicopter is hovering, with whirling propellers. ●

RESPONSE FOR Substance Abuse Counselors (from page 398) Legal drugs could be more addictive, or the thrill of illegality may diminish with age, or the fear of arrest may increase. In any case, treatment for young-adult substance abusers may need to differ from that for older ones. ●

As a group of scholars explained, in postformal thought "one can conceive of multiple logics, choices, or perceptions. . . in order to better understand the complexities and inherent biases in 'truth'" (Griffin et al., 2009, p. 173). That is more typical of adult thought than adolescent thought; hence the idea that a fifth stage exists.

COMBINING EMOTIONS AND LOGIC As you remember from Chapter 9, adolescents use two modes of thought (dual-processing, called by various names) but have difficulty combining the two. They use formal analysis to learn science, distill principles, develop arguments, and resolve the world's problems; in the other mode, they think spontaneously and emotionally. However, they rarely coordinate both types of thinking. They prefer the quick, impulsive, intuitive thought.

Postformal thinkers are less impulsive than adolescents. They do not wait for someone to present a problem to solve or for circumstances to require a reaction. They take a more flexible and comprehensive approach, using forethought, noting difficulties, and anticipating problems, not denying, avoiding, or procrastinating.

As a result, postformal thought is more practical as well as more creative and imaginative than thinking in previous cognitive stages (Wu & Chiou, 2008). Investment bankers, corporation heads, surgeons, and police detectives all need both modes of thought, which is why even the smartest young person is not chosen for those roles (Kahneman, 2011).

REALLY A STAGE? Almost every contemporary cognitive scientist finds fault with some aspects of Piaget's theory of child cognition. Piaget's notion that the final, and best, thinking is formal operational, achieved at adolescence, has come under especially heavy criticism, with some data finding that adults do not usually reach formal operations.

However, a similar problem arises with postformal thought. Attempts to measure it empirically are not very successful: Many other variables in addition to intellectual maturation affect how adults think (Cartwright et al., 2009). Some cognitive scientists, especially those who take an information-processing perspective, think that all stage theories of cognition are mistaken; others, especially those influenced by Vygotsky, think that formal and postformal thought are more affected by culture than by maturation.

Certainly, if *stage* means reaching a new set of abilities (such as the verbal explosion that distinguishes sensorimotor from preoperational thought), then adulthood has no cognitive stages. Rather than a fifth stage, adult thinking is like adolescent thinking in many ways. For instance, the same two processes that were described in Chapter 9 (intuitive and analytic, or system 1 and system 2) are evident throughout adulthood (Kahneman, 2011).

Nonetheless, the prefrontal cortex is not fully mature until the early 20s, and new dendrites and even new neurons grow throughout adulthood. This neurological maturation enables adults to think in ways that adolescents do not.

One lead researcher concludes that adult thinking "can be ordered in terms of increasing levels of complexity and integration" (Labouvie-Vief et al., 2009, p. 182). For instance, research on people aged 13 to 45 found that logical skills improved from adolescence to emerging adulthood and then stayed steady, as might be expected, as analytic thought becomes established (Demetriou & Bakracevic, 2009).

That same study found that social understanding continued to advance beyond early adulthood (Demetriou & Bakracevic, 2009). (Social understanding includes

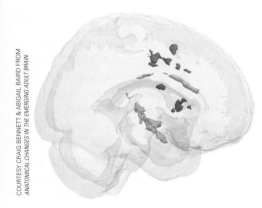

COURTESY CRAIG BENNETT & ABIGAIL BAIRD FROM *ANATOMICAL CHANGES IN THE EMERGING ADULT BRAIN*

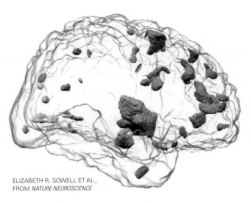

ELIZABETH R. SOWELL ET AL.,
FROM *NATURE NEUROSCIENCE*

Thinking Away from Home Entering a residential college means experiencing new foods, new friends, and new neurons. A longitudinal study of 18-year-old students at the beginning and end of their first year in college (Dartmouth) found increases in the brain areas that integrate emotion and cognition—namely, the cingulate cortex (blue and yellow), caudate nucleus (red), and insula (orange). Researchers also studied one-year changes in the brains of students over age 25 at the same college and found no dramatic growth.

More Purple Means More Planning Shown here are the areas of one person's brain changes from age 14 to age 25. The frontal cortex (purple) demonstrated many changes in particular parts, as did the areas for processing speech (green and blue)—a crucial aspect of young adult learning. Areas for visual processing (yellow) showed less change. Researchers now know that brains mature in many ways between adolescence and adulthood; scientists are not yet sure of the cognitive implications.

knowing how best to interact with other people: making and keeping good friends, responding to social slights, helping others effectively, and so on.) It makes sense that social cognition continues to improve, since cohort changes, cultural variations, and genetic uniqueness combine to make this the most complex type of thought.

Another study found that college students who have friends from other backgrounds are more likely to think in postformal ways (Galupo et al., 2010). The researchers believe that having friends with varied cultural perspectives advances postformal thought. A third study found that students' concepts of God became more complex theologically when they were more capable of postformal thinking (Benovenli et al., 2011).

Overall, many scholars find that thinking changes both qualitatively and quantitatively during adulthood (Bosworth & Hertzog, 2009). The term *fifth stage* may be a misnomer, but emerging adults can, and often do, reach a new cognitive level when their brains and life circumstances allow it.

Countering Stereotypes

Cognitive flexibility, particularly the ability to change one's childhood assumptions, is needed to counter stereotypes. Daily life for young adults shows many signs of such flexibility, as adulthood often requires studying and working with people from various backgrounds, as well as adjusting to historical changes.

The very fact that today's emerging adults marry and become parents later than previous generations suggests that, couple by couple, their thinking processes are not determined by their own childhood experiences or by traditional norms. Of course, early experiences are influential. If you were born when your mother was a teenager, it is more likely that you will have your first child earlier than the cultural norm.

However, for postformal thinkers, background factors and early influences are not determinative. Almost all emerging adults reach some conclusions that conflict with those of their parents, if not in when or whether to have children, then in how to raise them.

RESPONSE FOR Someone Who Has to Make an Important Decision (from page 400) Both are necessary. Mature thinking requires a combination of emotions and logic. Take your time (don't just act on your first impulse) and talk with people you trust. Ultimately, you will have to live with your decision, so do not ignore either intuitive or logical thought. ●

stereotype threat
The possibility that one's appearance or behavior will be misread to confirm another person's oversimplified, prejudiced attitudes.

CORBIS

The Threat of Bias If students fear that others expect them to do poorly in school because of their ethnicity or gender, they might not identify with academic achievement and therefore do worse on exams than they otherwise would have.

OBSERVATION QUIZ

Which of these three college students taking an exam is least vulnerable to stereotype threat? (see answer, page 406) →

Research on racial prejudice is another example. Most Americans say that they are not prejudiced, and their behavior reveals no bias (at least in explicit tests in a research laboratory). This is age-related: Younger adults show less prejudice overall than older adults, on average. However, many U.S. residents of all ethnicities and ages harbor implicit bias against African Americans, detectable in reaction times when viewing photos of African Americans and European Americans (Baron & Banaji, 2006).

Thus, many adults have both unconscious prejudice and conscious tolerance—a combination of emotion and reason that illustrates dual-processing. Ideally, cognitive flexibility allows people to recognize their underlying emotional biases and then to change their behavior to be in accord with their rational thought. This is difficult without the intellectual openness and flexibility that characterize emerging adults.

People are usually unaware of their own stereotypes, even when their false beliefs harm them. However, as the prefrontal cortex matures after age 18, people are able to rethink their stereotypes.

A notable example of implicit prejudice, and then the ability to overcome it, occurs with **stereotype threat,** first named by an African American scholar who called it a "threat in the air" (Steele, 1997). Stereotype threat begins with the thought that other people hold unspoken prejudices against one's social group, and then that thought becomes a threat which produces anxiety. In reality, those other people may not hold those stereotypes (that's why the threat is "in the air"), but the mere possibility that they do undermines cognition (Inzlicht & Schmader, 2012).

For example, if a person imagines that someone else (or even people in general) holds the stereotype that members of a particular group are stupid, lazy, oversexed, or somehow inferior because of ethnicity, sex, age, or appearance, then the mere awareness of the *possibility* of being stereotyped will make that person feel anxious. That anxiety hijacks cognition, disrupting memory, logic, and so on (Schmader, 2010).

Stereotype threat may interfere with emerging adults in many ways. If young people fear that leaving home will expose them to prejudice, they might not attend a residential college. That will limit their exposure to other opinions. If students from a visible minority bravely go away to college, they might be more aware of possible prejudice than majority students are. Indeed, majority students may be unaware of small insults (called microaggressions) unless they understand the sensitivities of their minority friends.

A study of students at a predominantly Black college and a predominantly White college found that in both places, the majority (White or Black) thought everyone should promote assimilation ("This university should treat students from different racial groups the same in all respects"). However, those in the minority (again, whether White or Black) were more likely to endorse pluralist ideas (e.g., "This university should respect the unique situations of students from different racial groups") (Hehman et al., 2012). Note that none of the groups thought their opinions reflected any bias, yet all four groups held opinions that reflected their own situation.

Stereotype threat can create a vicious cycle: Some college admissions personnel wonder if it interferes with college acceptance (Soares, 2012). This is insidious; if applicants fear stereotyping, anxiety may make them too quiet or too talkative in the interview, which may lead to a prejudicial reaction from the admissions officer. If applicants are rejected, they can correctly blame a stereotype, not realizing that they themselves set it in motion. This is not inevitable, however, as the following explains.

A VIEW FROM SCIENCE

Undercutting Stereotype Threat

One statistic has troubled social scientists for decades: African American men have lower grades in high school, drop out more often, and earn only half as many college degrees as their genetic peers, African American women. And African American women themselves do less well than women of other ethnic groups. This disparity has many possible causes, with most scientists blaming the current context and historical past discrimination (Arnett & Brody, 2008).

Claude Steele, the African American man who first described stereotype threat, reasoned that when African American males become aware of the stereotype that they are poor scholars, they become anxious. That anxiety reduces their ability and motivation to focus on schoolwork. Then, if they underachieve, they might dismiss academics in order to protect their pride, which leads to disengagement from studying and even lower achievement (Ogbu, 2008).

Two decades of research have demonstrated that downward trajectory, not only for African American men. Hundreds of studies show that almost all humans can be harmed by stereotype threat: Women underperform in math, older people are more forgetful, bilingual students stumble while speaking English, and every member of a stigmatized minority in every nation performs less well if they think others are judging them unfairly.

Even those sometimes thought to be on top—White men—do less well in math if they think they will be negatively compared with Asian American men (stereotyped as innately skilled in math), and they do less well in basketball if they think they will be compared with African American men (again stereotyped as innately skilled) (Schmader et al., 2008). When athletes of any ethnicity unexpectedly underperform because of stress (called choking), stereotype threat may be the cause (Hill et al., 2010).

Can stereotype threat be eliminated, or at least reduced? One group of researchers developed a hypothesis that stereotype threat will decrease and academic achievement will increase for African American college students if they *internalize* (believe wholeheartedly, not just intellectually) that intelligence is plastic, not the unchangeable product of genes and gender.

Using a clever combination of written materials, mentoring, and video performing, these scientists convinced an experimental group of students at Stanford University that their ability and hence their achievement depended on their personal efforts. Some of the students were African American, some were European American.

The hypothesis: Convincing college students that intellectual ability could be improved by hard work (the incremental, not the entity, theory of intelligence described in Chapter 9) would encourage them to study and prevent choking under pressure (as when taking exams). The intervention succeeded for the African Americans: They earned higher grades. The European American students were not affected; apparently, stereotype threat had not impaired their achievement (Aronson et al., 2002).

This experiment intrigued thousands of researchers. They realized that this study required replication, since the participants were only 79 students at a highly selective university. Might other stereotyped groups respond differently?

Soon this study was replicated with many other groups, often but not always targeting young adults. The results confirm, again and again, that stereotype threat is pervasive and debilitating but that it can be alleviated (Inzlicht & Schmader, 2012; Mangels et al., 2010; Rydell & Boucher, 2010). It is activated especially when someone reminds a person of the stereotype (e.g., "This test will reveal whether women are inferior in math ability"), but it disappears if a person internalizes the notion that the stereotype is irrelevant (e.g., "My math ability depends only on me and is not affected by gender").

The Effects of College

A major reason that emerging adulthood has become a new period of development, when people postpone the usual markers of adult life (marriage, a steady job), is that many older adolescents seek education, choosing to postpone traditional adult responsibilities.

MASSIFICATION Tertiary education improves health and wealth. Although not every young adult enrolls in college, and most do not graduate, U.S. census data confirm that a college degree adds about $20,000 per year to a worker's salary. This is averaged over a lifetime—often more apparent in middle age than right after college.

massification
The idea that establishing higher learning institutions and encouraging college enrollment could benefit everyone (the masses), leading to marked increases in the number of emerging adults in college.

In addition, college graduates are healthier, living about 10 years longer than those without a high school diploma. This is the result of better health habits. For example, among U.S. adults, the rate of obesity is 9 percent for those with a BA degree, 30 percent for those without it (National Center for Health Statistics, 2012f).

To improve health and increase productivity, every nation has increased the number of students enrolled in college. This has led to **massification,** the idea that college could benefit everyone (the masses) (Altbach et al., 2010). The United States was the first major nation to accept that idea, establishing thousands of institutions of higher learning and boasting millions of college students by the middle of the twentieth century.

The United States no longer leads in massification, however. More than half of all 25- to 29-year-olds in Canada, Korea, Russia, and Japan are college graduates. The United States ranks twelfth on that measure, with only one-third (32 percent) of U.S. 25- to 29-year-olds having at least a bachelor's degree (Aud et al., 2012; Montgomery & Williams, 2010; UNESCO, 2009).

Massification has stalled in the United States but not elsewhere (Altbach et al., 2010). Within Asia and Africa, college enrollment has more than tripled in the past several decades. Thirty years ago, many wealthy and capable students in developing nations traveled west to earn college degrees. Such students often returned to their home nations as professors, bringing new perspectives to their classrooms.

A global shift is under way: Hundreds of new universities have opened in Asia, Africa, and the Middle East. Most undergraduates now remain in their own nations to continue their studies. As a result, there are far more college students in China and in India than in the United States. Of course, the total population of those nations is larger than that of the United States, but these numbers are part of a global trend. (See Infographic 11, page 409.)

Education in Process These students, checking the Internet on the steps in San Miguel de Allende in Mexico *(top)* and discussing Pakistan on the quad at Brown University in the United States *(bottom),* illustrate why some scholars claim that college students learn more from each other than from their professors.

COLLEGE AND COGNITION For developmentalists interested in cognition, the crucial question is not about the three issues already mentioned: wealth, health, and massification. Instead, the question is: "Does college education advance critical thinking and postformal thought?" Past research finds that the answer is yes.

According to one classic study (Perry, 1981, 1999), thinking progresses through nine levels of complexity over the four years that lead to a bachelor's degree. A first-year student may think with simplistic dualism (right or wrong, yes or no, success or failure) and gradually progress to recognizing the validity of many perspectives (see Table 11.2).

Other research has confirmed Perry's conclusions. In general, the more years of higher education a person pursues, the deeper and more postformal that person's reasoning becomes (Pascarella & Terenzini, 1991).

Which aspect of college is the primary catalyst for such growth? Is it the challenging academic work, the professors' lectures, the peer discussions, the new setting, living away from home? All are possibilities. Perry found that the college experience itself causes this progression, as peers, professors, books, and class discussion stimulate new thoughts. Every scientist finds that social interaction and intellectual challenge advance thinking.

College students expect classes and conversations to further their intellectual depth—which is exactly what occurs (Kuh et al., 2005). This is not surprising, since colleges were designed to foster intellectual growth.

TABLE 11.2 Perry's Scheme of Cognitive and Ethical Development During College

Freshmen	Position 1	Authorities know, and if we work hard, read every word, and learn Right Answers, all will be well.
Dualism modified	Transition	But what about those Others I hear about? And different opinions? And Uncertainties? Some of our own Authorities disagree with each other or don't seem to know, and some give us problems instead of Answers.
	Position 2	True Authorities must be Right; the others are frauds. We remain Right. Others must be different and Wrong. Good Authorities give us problems so we can learn to find the Right Answer by our own independent thought.
	Transition	But even Good Authorities admit they don't know all the answers yet!
	Position 3	Then some uncertainties and different opinions are real and legitimate temporarily, even for Authorities. They're working on them to get to the Truth.
	Transition	But there are so many things they don't know the Answers to! And they won't for a long time.
Relativism discovered	Position 4a	Where Authorities don't know the Right Answers, everyone has a right to his own opinion; no one is wrong!
	Transition	Then what right have They to grade us? About what?
	Position 4b	In certain courses, Authorities are not asking for the Right Answer. They want us to think about things in a certain way, supporting opinion with data. That's what they grade us on.
	Position 5	Then all thinking must be like this, even for Them. Everything is relative but not equally valid. You have to understand how each context works. Theories are not Truth but metaphors to interpret data with. You have to think about your thinking.
	Transition	But if everything is relative, am I relative, too? How can I know I'm making the Right Choice?
	Position 6	I see I'm going to have to make my own decisions in an uncertain world with no one to tell me I'm Right.
	Transition	I'm lost if I don't. When I decide on my career (or marriage or values), everything will straighten out.
Commitments in relativism developed	Position 7	Well, I've made my first Commitment!
	Transition	Why didn't that settle everything?
	Position 8	I've made several commitments. I've got to balance them—how many, how deep? How certain, how tentative?
	Transition	Things are getting contradictory. I can't make logical sense out of life's dilemmas.
Seniors	Position 9	This is how life will be. I must be wholehearted while tentative, fight for my values yet respect others, believe my deepest values are right yet be ready to learn. I see that I shall be retracing this whole journey over and over—but, I hope, more wisely.

Source: Perry, 1981, 1999.

Professors may also advance in their own thinking as they teach and learn, passing those advances on to their students. For example, one of the leading thinkers in post-formal thought is Jan Sinnott, a professor and former editor of the *Journal of Adult Development*. She describes the first course she taught:

> I did not think in a postformal way. . . . Teaching was good for passing information from the informed to the uninformed. . . . I decided to create a course in the psychology of aging . . . with a fellow graduate student. Being compulsive graduate students had paid off in our careers so far, so my colleague and I continued on that path. Articles and books and photocopies began to take over my house. And having found all this information, we seem to have unconsciously sworn to use all of it. . . .
>
> Each class day, my colleague and I would arrive with reams of notes and articles and lecture, lecture, lecture. Rapidly! . . . The discussion of death and dying came close to the end of the term (naturally). As I gave my usual jam-packed lecture, the sound of note-taking was intense. But toward the end of the class . . . an extremely

✦ **ESPECIALLY FOR Those Considering Studying Abroad** Given the effects of college, would it be better for a student to study abroad in the first year or last year of a college education? (see response, page 406) →

ANSWER TO **OBSERVATION QUIZ**
(from page 402) It depends on what
is being tested and on the students'
backgrounds. White males are generally least vulnerable, but if the test
is about literature and if the male
student believes that men are not as
good as women at understanding
poetry and fiction, his performance
on the exam might be affected by that
stereotype. ●

**RESPONSE FOR Those Considering
Studying Abroad** (from page 405)
Since one result of college is that
students become more open to other
perspectives while developing their
commitment to their own values, foreign study might be most beneficial
after several years of college. If they
study abroad too early, some students
might be either too narrowly patriotic
(they are not yet open) or too quick to
reject everything about their national
heritage (they have not yet developed
their own commitments). ●

**✦ ESPECIALLY FOR High School
Teachers** One of your brightest students doesn't want to go to college.
She would rather keep waitressing in
a restaurant, where she makes good
money in tips. What do you say? (see
response, page 408) →

capable student burst into tears and said she had to drop the class. . . . Unknown to
me, she had been the caretaker of an older relative who had just died in the past
few days. She had not said anything about this significant experience when we
lectured on caretaking. . . . How could she? . . . We never stopped talking. "I wish I
could tell people what it's really like," she said.

[Sinnott, 2008, pp. 54–55]

Sinnott changed her lesson plan. In the next class, the student told her story.

In the end, the students agreed that this was a class when they . . . synthesized material and analyzed research and theory critically.

[Sinnott, 2008, p. 56]

Sinnott still lectures and gives multiple-choice exams, but she also includes personal stories. She combines analysis and emotion; she includes the experiences of her
students. Her teaching became postformal, flexible, and responsive.

CURRENT CONTEXTS But wait. You probably noticed that Perry's study was first
published in 1981. Hundreds of other studies have also found that college education deepens cognition, but most of that research occurred in the twentieth century.
Since cohort and culture are crucial, you may wonder if those conclusions still hold.

Many recent books criticize today's college education on exactly those grounds.
Notably, an impressive twenty-first-century longitudinal study of U.S. college students
found that their growth in critical thinking, analysis, and communication over the
four years of college was only half as much as it was among college students two
decades earlier (Arum et al., 2011).

The results of that study were published in a provocative book titled *Academically
Adrift*. Among the findings is that 45 percent of college students made no significant
advances at all in the first two years (Arum & Roksa, 2011). The reasons are many:
Students study less, academic expectations are reduced, fewer students enroll in classes
that require reading 40 pages a week or writing 20 pages a semester. Administrators
hope for intellectual growth, but rigorous classes are canceled or not required, to the
distress of many faculty members, including the scholars who published that study.

OPPOSING PERSPECTIVES

What Is College For?

Underlying the debate about standards and massification are
opposite opinions about the purpose of higher education.
Developmentalists, most professors, and many college graduates believe that "personal and intellectual growth" is the
goal. However, adults who have never attended college believe that "acquiring specific skills and knowledge" is more
important (see Figure 11.4). Many contemporary students
seem to agree.

Although each person develops his or her own opinions,
the social context is influential. Opposing views of the purpose of college are evident between current students ("Will
that be on the test?") and faculty educated decades ago
("Better to thirst for knowledge than to know the answers"),
and between current political leaders and traditional scholars.

These questions are debated everywhere, even in nations
that seem to regiment higher education. For instance, a new

Chinese university (called South University of Science and
Technology of China, SUSTC) is designed to encourage
analysis and critical thinking, a deliberate contrast to the emphasis on knowledge and skills in other Chinese institutions.

SUSTC does not require prospective students to take the
national exam (*Gao Kao*); instead, "creativity and a passion
for learning" are the admission criteria (Stone, 2011, p. 161).
SUSTC faculty are supposed to nurture curiosity, to evoke
questions, not to lecture. After waiting a year to see how the
first group of students performed, the Chinese government
accredited SUSTC in April 2012 (Huang, 2012).

In a study by Arum and Roksa (2011), students majoring in business and in other career fields were less likely to
gain in critical thinking than those majoring in the liberal
arts. The correlation was strong: Courses that demand more
reading and writing, which often occur in the humanities,

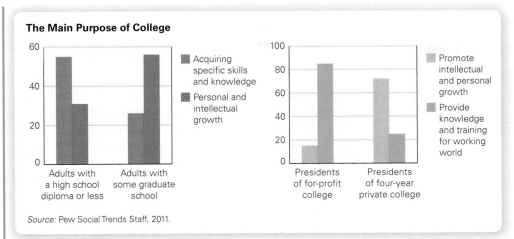

The Main Purpose of College

Source: Pew Social Trends Staff, 2011.

FIGURE 11.4 Intellectual or Practical Skills? As you see, people disagree as to whether a college education should foster intellectual growth or provide useful knowledge and skills. Presented here are the extremes: Students with some college experience and presidents of community colleges fall in between these extremes.

were more likely to advance critical thinking. Such results are used to criticize business education (too narrow, not reflective) but may, instead, mean that business students simply learn what they think their employers want them to know.

Business has become the most popular major in U.S. colleges (Chronicle of Higher Education, 2011b). No matter what their major, many students now attend college primarily for career reasons (see Figure 11.5). They select colleges, majors, and specific classes because they hope to earn more money, not because they seek to advance their ability in reading, writing, and thinking.

Likewise, government officials often use job placement rates to index college success. Employers may want workers with advanced skills, knowledge, and practical experience with technology, not workers who have been encouraged to ask critical questions. Since tuition and government grants are the main sources of college income, institutions that do not stress postformal analysis may be very successful, financially.

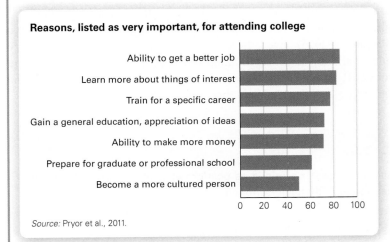

Reasons, listed as very important, for attending college

Source: Pryor et al., 2011.

FIGURE 11.5 Cohort Shift Students in 1980 thought new ideas and a philosophy of life were prime reasons to go to college—they were less interested in jobs, careers, and money than are students in 2011. If this thinking causes a conflict between student motivation and professors' goals, who should adjust?

There may be a generational divide here. Many older professors were undergraduates 50 years ago, when most U.S. colleges were four-year institutions emphasizing the liberal arts. Only 275 junior colleges existed then. In 2010, there were almost 1,500 such colleges (a fivefold increase), now called community colleges, which typically focus on preparation for employment. Some community colleges have extended their reach, offering bachelor's degrees in careers that often have job openings. In Florida alone, there are 19 such colleges.

Another U.S. manifestation of the shift from exploration to employment is the proliferation of for-profit colleges, scarce until about 1980, now numbering more than 1,300 (Chronicle of Higher Education, 2010). These schools promote a direct link between college and jobs, giving credit for life experience or past work skills. That helps recruit students, especially workers who need a degree for a salary increase. But is that the goal of college?

Some instructors give more Fs than As, reducing graduation rates. Are students wise or lazy to avoid such courses? Results from a six-year study of the 14 public colleges in Pennsylvania showed that 24 percent of the incoming students at Cheyney University earned a BA and 65 percent of those at West Chester University did (Selingo, 2012). Which institution produced more learning? Hard to say.

How should learning be measured? If not by graduation rates, then perhaps by national tests, grade-point averages, credit accumulation, retention, transfers, or later employment? None of these indicate advances in postformal thought: One study found no correlation between GPA and postformal thinking (Benovenli et al., 2011). Perhaps prospective graduates should be given data on an unfamiliar topic and required to write an error-free, critical, analytic essay . . . but that might be irrelevant for many legislators, parents, employers, or students themselves. Back to basics: What is college for?

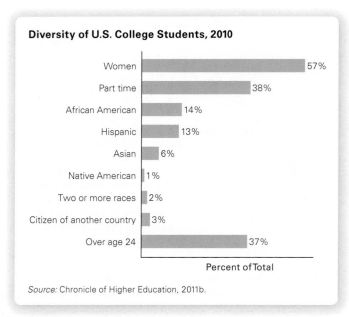

FIGURE 11.6 All Kinds of People If anything, this graph underestimates the diversity of the student body. For example, students who attend school full time for half the year and who work the other half are still considered full-time students. Another statistic summarizes the point: At one time, the typical college student was a full-time, single, European American emerging-adult male. Today, such individuals comprise only about 20 percent of the student body.

THE EFFECTS OF DIVERSITY At least one characteristic of the twenty-first-century college scene bodes well for cognitive growth—the diversity of the student body (see Infographic 11). People learn when they interact with others who disagree with them. Those who are most likely to be postformal thinkers are also those with the most friends from other backgrounds (Galupo et al., 2010).

The most obvious increased diversity is gender: In 1970, two-thirds of the college students were male; now in every developed nation (except Germany), more than half (57 percent in the United States) are female. Moreover, majors that were traditionally male (math, physics) now include many women, and virtually all single-sex colleges (even military academies) are now co-ed. That means almost every college student hears academic insights and opinions from the other sex.

Ethnic, economic, religious, and cultural diversity is also evident (see Figure 11.6). Although in the United States, the modal student is still European American, aged 18 to 22, attending full time, the trend for the past 50 years has been toward more students who are non-European and older than 24, and who attend part time.

Discussion among people of different backgrounds, ages, and experiences leads to intellectual challenge and deeper thought. Thus, the increased diversity of the student body may enhance learning (Bowman, 2011; Loss et al., 2012). Colleges that make use of their diversity—via curriculum, class assignments, discussions, cooperative education, learning communities, and so on—help students stretch their understanding, not only of differences and similarities among people but also of themselves.

College does not automatically produce a leap ahead in cognitive development or in appreciation of differing political, social, and religious views. Skeptical readers might question the data that link college graduation to wealthier, wiser, and happier adults. Such skepticism is warranted since correlation does not equal causation: Student characteristics before college may be a third variable that explains these links.

However, when selection is taken into account, college still seems to aid cognitive development (Pascarella, 2005). Even the critics agree that some students at every institution advance markedly in critical thinking and analysis because of their college experience (Arum & Roksa, 2011). Readers of this text can remember their thinking before college and currently. Have you become a postformal thinker?

RESPONSE FOR High School Teachers (from page 406) Even more than ability, motivation is crucial for college success, so don't insist that she attend college immediately. Since your student has money and a steady job (prime goals for today's college-bound youth), she may not realize what she would be missing. Ask her what she hopes for, in work and lifestyle, over the decades ahead. ●

KEY Points

- Adult cognition has been described as postformal, a fifth stage, although not every scholar agrees with that description.
- As the prefrontal cortex matures, thinking in adulthood becomes more flexible, better able to combine emotions and analysis.
- College attendance is rapidly increasing in developing nations, as it is apparent that tertiary education improves health, productivity, and income.
- College education advances thought, not only through academic work but also via the diversity of the student body.

Why Study?

From a life-span perspective, college graduation is a good investment, for individuals (they become healthier and wealthier) and for nations (national income rises). That long-term perspective is the main reason why nations that control enrollment, such as China, have opened dozens of new colleges in the past two decades. However, when the effort and cost of higher education depend on immediate choices made by students and families, as in the United States, many decide it is not worth it, as illustrated by the number of people who earn BAs.

EDUCATION IN THE U.S.

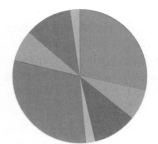 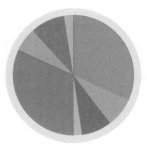 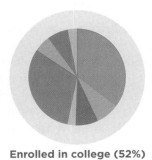 

10-year-olds in school (98.5%) **High school graduates (80%)** **Enrolled in college (52%)** **BA earned (19%)**

- Non-Hispanic White boys
- Non-Hispanic White girls
- African American boys
- African American girls
- Hispanic boys
- Hispanic girls
- Asian boys
- Asian girls

LOCATING COLLEGE ENROLLMENT

This map emphasizes that North America is lagging behind in college enrollment and that Africa is surging ahead, but the numbers suggest a more complex picture. Enrollment in Africa, for instance, was very low in 1990, so even now the overall proportion of college students in Africa remains lower than in North America. Nonetheless, one fact is obvious: Millions more students in developing nations are attending college than were a generation ago.

2007 Enrollments in Millions	
Asia	70.5
Europe	32.8
North America	19.1
Central and South America	17.8
Africa	9.0
World	150.7

Increases in College Enrollment, 1990–2007

22%	144%	74%	217%	203%	116%
North America	Central and South America	Europe	Africa	Asia	Australia

INCOME IMPACT

Over an average of 40 years of employment, someone who completes a master's degree earns $500,000 more than someone who leaves school in eleventh grade. That translates into about $90,000 for each year of education from twelfth grade to a master's. The earnings gap is even wider than those numbers indicate because this chart includes only adults who have jobs, yet finding work is more difficult for those with less education.

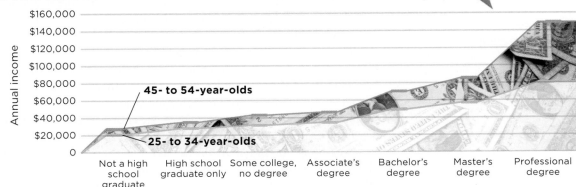

45- to 54-year-olds

25- to 34-year-olds

Annual income: $160,000 / $140,000 / $120,000 / $100,000 / $80,000 / $60,000 / $40,000 / $20,000 / 0

Education: Not a high school graduate | High school graduate only | Some college, no degree | Associate's degree | Bachelor's degree | Master's degree | Professional degree

SOURCE: U.S. BUREAU OF THE CENSUS, 2011

SOURCES & CREDITS LISTED ON P. SC-1

Psychosocial Development

A theme of human development is that continuity and change are evident lifelong. In emerging adulthood, the legacy of early development is apparent amidst new achievement. As you remember, Erikson recognized this ongoing process in describing the fifth of his eight stages, *identity versus role confusion*. The identity crisis begins in adolescence, but it is not usually resolved then.

Identity Achieved

Erikson believed that the outcome of earlier crises provides the foundation for each new stage. The identity crisis is an example (see Table 11.3).

Worldwide, adults ponder all four arenas of identity—religious commitments, sex/gender roles, political/ethnic loyalties, and career options—trying to reconcile plans for the future with beliefs acquired in the past. Their new cognitive abilities, combining emotional and rational thinking, aid in identity integration and achievement.

An interesting recent example is that, against their parents' wishes, many young women in Western nations choose to wear the *hijab*, the headscarf that indicates they are devout Muslims. This may convey their devotion for all to see, and paradoxically may give them the freedom to attend school and go to work with non-Muslims. The headscarf becomes a protective shield against the male advances, advertising that this woman is a student or a worker, not a potential mate. Thus, a traditional religious and gender identity allows for options their unveiled mothers never had (Ahmed, 2011).

Now we will focus specifically on ethnicity and vocation, two identities that were described in Chapter 10 but that are especially significant in emerging adulthood.

TABLE 11.3 Erikson's Eight Stages of Development

Stage	Virtue/Pathology	Possible in Emerging Adulthood If Not Successfully Resolved
Trust vs. mistrust	Hope/withdrawal	Suspicious of others, making close relationships difficult
Autonomy vs. shame and doubt	Will/compulsion	Obsessively driven, single-minded, not socially responsive
Initiative vs. guilt	Purpose/inhibition	Fearful, regretful (e.g., very homesick in college)
Industry vs. inferiority	Competence/inertia	Self-critical of any endeavor, procrastinating, perfectionistic
Identity vs. role diffusion	Fidelity/repudiation	Uncertain and negative about values, lifestyle, friendships
Intimacy vs. isolation	Love/exclusivity	Anxious about close relationships, jealous, lonely
Generativity vs. stagnation	Care/rejection	[In the future] Fear of failure
Integrity vs. despair	Wisdom/disdain	[In the future] No "mindfulness," no life plan

Source: Erikson, 1982.

Past as Prologue In elaborating his eight stages of development, Erikson associated each stage with a particular virtue and a type of psychopathology, as shown here. He also thought that earlier crises could reemerge, taking a specific form at each stage. Listed are some possible problems that could occur in emerging adulthood if earlier crises were not resolved.

ETHNIC IDENTITY Identity development, especially "the development of ethnic and racial identity," now continues long past adolescence (Whitbourne et al., 2009, p. 1328). This extended search is often the result of new challenges that emerging adults face.

The most basic challenge is how to identify oneself amidst a multi-ethnic society. For example, high school senior Natasha Scott "just realized that my race is something I have to think about." Her mother is Asian and her father is African American, which had not been an issue as she was growing up. However, college applications (and the U.S. census) require choices regarding ethnic identity (Saulny & Steinberg, 2011).

Natasha is not alone. In the United States and Canada, almost half of 18- to 25-year-olds are of African, Asian, Latino, or Native American heritage. Many of them identify as Americans or Canadians but also as something else, as they have ancestors of more than one ethnic group. Usually, those ancestors are long dead, but an increasing number have parents who each come from different traditions.

Whether one's heritage is mixed or not, considered minority or not, ethnicity is a significant aspect of American identity (Phinney, 2006). During late adolescence and early adulthood, people are more likely to be proud, or at least accepting, of their ethnic background than younger adolescents are (Worrell, 2008).

More than any other age group, as they leave their childhood homes to enroll in colleges or to find work, emerging adults have friends and acquaintances of many backgrounds. Typically, they have "both positive and negative experiences" related to their ethnic background, developing "a strong sense of ethnic identity"—true for college students of every group (Syed & Azmitia, 2010, p. 218).

It may be a mistake if they either assimilate (blend in) or become alienated (isolated and antagonistic), at least according to a study of Hispanic college students. Those who resisted both assimilation and alienation fared best: They were most likely to maintain their ethnic identity, deflect stereotype threat, and become good students (Rivas-Drake & Mooney, 2009).

College classes (especially in history, ethnic studies, and sociology) attract many emerging adults who want to learn more about their culture. In addition, extracurricular groups help solidify identity because students encounter others of similar backgrounds who confront the same issues, as well as youth of other backgrounds as they join teams, political committees, special interest groups, and so on.

A longitudinal study found that students at four-year colleges were more likely to be involved in extracurricular activities than were students at two-year colleges (57 percent compared with 23 percent). That disparity may explain why there is less ethnic search at two-year colleges and why the adoption of an ethnic label that includes the word *American* (e.g., not Chinese, but Chinese American) is also less common at two-year institutions (58 percent compared to 43 percent). The overall conclusion of this study is that while ethnic identity is important for everyone in high school and college, the specific context (e.g., community college or university) also makes a difference (Tsai & Fuligni, 2012).

VOCATIONAL IDENTITY Establishing a vocational identity is considered part of growing up, not only by developmental psychologists but also by emerging adults themselves (Arnett, 2004). As already noted, many young adults go to college, not primarily as a moratorium but to prepare for work (see Figure 11.5). Emerging adulthood is a "critical stage for the acquisition of resources"—including the education, skills, and experience needed for family and career success lifelong (Tanner et al., 2009, p. 34) (see Table 11.4).

Preparation for lifetime work may include taking temporary jobs. Between ages 18 and 27, the average U.S. worker holds eight jobs, with college-educated workers changing jobs more often than those who are less educated (U.S. Bureau of the Census, 2011). This illustrates the exploration that is part of the identity search. Another way to explore is to take vocational aptitude tests, or a variety of courses, or to use Holland's six categories (first mentioned in Chapter 9) to figure out how one's personal preferences mesh with a considered vocation (Holland, 1997) (see Figure 11.7).

ISSEI KATO / REUTERS

Just Like Me Emerging adults of every ethnicity take pride in their culture. In Japan, adulthood begins with a celebration at age 20, to the evident joy of these young women on Coming of Age Day, a national holiday.

Look Again Vocational identity is difficult for contemporary emerging adults. If projections prove accurate, many of them will not consider themselves "well off financially."

TABLE 11.4 Top Six "Very Important" Objective in Life*

Being well off financially	78%
Raising a family	75%
To make more money	71%
Helping others	69%
Becoming an authority in my field	59%
Obtaining recognition in my special field	56%

*Based on a national survey of students entering four-year colleges in the United States in the fall of 2010.

Source: Chronicle of Higher Education, 2010.

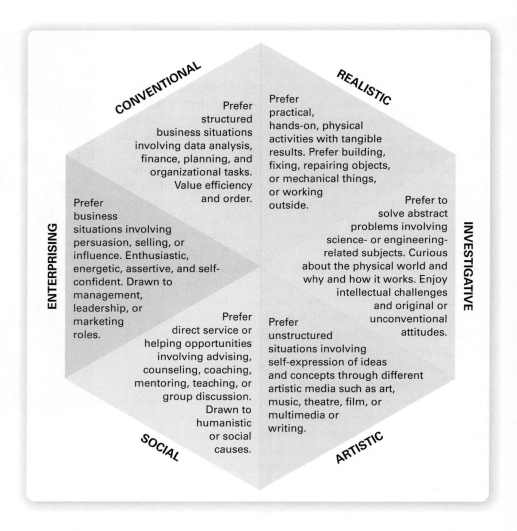

FIGURE 11.7 Happy at Work John Holland's six-part diagram is used to help job seekers realize that income and benefits are not the only goals of employment. Workers have healthier hearts and minds if their job fits their personal preferences.

None of this is guaranteed to make vocational choice easy. For most emerging adults, "the process of identifying with society's work ethic, the core of this issue [identity achievement] in Erikson's scheme, continues to evolve throughout early adulthood" (Whitbourne et al., 2009, p. 1329). The young worker is not yet climbing, rung-by-rung, a chosen career ladder.

Many developmentalists wonder whether achieving a single vocational identity is still possible and desirable. Especially for young people, hiring and firing sometimes seems disconnected from education, skills, or aspirations. Commitment to a particular career may limit rather than increase vocational success.

Flexibility seems especially needed for the current generation. In the United States, the job market for new college graduates collapsed from about 2007 to 2012 when the housing boom burst, the stock market fell, and the entire economy entered a severe recession. That has made development of vocational identity particularly difficult for emerging adults, who cannot flit from job to job as the earlier cohort did. A life-span perspective suggests that young adults may still be affected when the financial picture improves (M. K. Johnson et al., 2011). Experiences, habits, and fears of early adulthood linger.

Personality in Emerging Adulthood

Continuity and change are evident in personality as well (McAdams & Olson, 2010). Of course, the genetic roots of temperament and the early childhood influences on

Same Situation, Far Apart: Connecting with Their Generation Neither of these young women considers her job a vocation, but both use skills and knowledge that few older adults have. The DJ *(left)* mixes music for emerging adults who crowd thousands of clubs in China to drink, dance, and socialize despite regulations that attempt to close down such establishments. More than 10,000 Apple Store "geniuses" *(right)* work at low pay to meet the booming young-adult demand for the latest social networking tools.

personality endure. If self-doubt, anxiety, depression, and so on are present in childhood and adolescence, they are often still evident years later. Traits present at age 5 or 15 do not disappear by age 25.

Yet personality is not static. After adolescence, new characteristics may appear and negative traits diminish. Emerging adults make choices that break with the past. This age period is now characterized by years of freedom from a settled lifestyle, which allows shifts in attitude and personality.

A crucial factor found in many studies is whether the person thrives in high school and college. This is affected *by* personality but also *affects* personality (Klimstra et al., 2012). In other words, college success can improve personality.

RISING SELF-ESTEEM Psychological research finds both continuity and improvement in attitudes. For example, one longitudinal study found that 17-year-olds who saw life in positive terms maintained their outlook as time went on, while those who were negative often changed for the better (Blonigen et al., 2008).

Another team of researchers traced 3,912 U.S. high school seniors until age 23 or 24. Those in college who lived away from home showed the largest gains in well-being; those who had become single parents or who still lived with their own parents showed the least. Even the latter, however, tended to be happier than they had been in high school (Schulenberg et al., 2005). Similarly, 404 young adults in western Canada, repeatedly questioned from ages 18 to 25, reported increasing self-esteem (Galambos et al., 2006).

This positive trend of increasing happiness has become more evident over recent decades, perhaps because young adults are more likely to make their own life decisions (Twenge et al., 2008). Logically, one might expect that the many stresses and transitions of emerging adulthood would reduce self-esteem, but that is not what the research finds. Psychopathology may be increasing, and some emerging adults develop serious disorders that they did not have as children (Twenge et al., 2010), but most do not. Instead, most enjoy their new maturity and independence.

WORRISOME CHILDREN GROW UP The research just cited about rising self-esteem came from several studies of North American youth. However, similar conclusions can be drawn from a European longitudinal study that began with 4-year-olds who were high in one or the other of two traits known to have strong genetic roots: shyness and aggression. These 38 children were extremely shy or aggressive at age 4 and continued to exhibit those undesirable traits throughout childhood. This is not surprising because the same genetic, familial, and cultural influences that were present at age 4 were present every later year (Asendorpf et al., 2008).

By early adulthood, those early traits were still evident, but neither was as extreme nor debilitating as earlier. Continuity could be seen, especially for those who had been aggressive 4-year-olds. At age 25, they had more conflicts with their parents and friends. They were more likely to have quit school—two-thirds had dropped out of high school, as had only one-third of their nonaggressive peers. By age 23, half had been arrested at least once, another sign of their aggressive temperament.

Yet, unexpectedly, these aggressive emerging adults had as many friends as their average peers did. They sought more education and rated themselves as quite conscientious. Their arrests were usually adolescent-limited, for minor offenses: Only one had been sent to prison, and only one other had been arrested several times.

A closer examination of their school records found that behavior, not ability, caused their childhood teachers to fail them. That proved harmful; many had to repeat grades. In high school, they were older than their classmates, often rebelled against restrictions and assumptions, and ultimately quit. But they still enjoyed learning and were intellectually capable.

That explained some seemingly surprising outcomes: As emerging adults, most of the formerly aggressive children were developing well, with social and vocational lives that were normal for their cohort. Many had put their childhood problems behind them; some were employed and others had enrolled in college.

As for those formerly shy 4-year-olds, outcomes were good. Evidence of their earlier temperament was that they were "cautious, reserved adults." For example, they were slower than average to secure a job, choose a career, or find a romance. At age 23, two-thirds had no current partner.

However, there were "few signs of internalizing problems" (Asendorpf et al., 2008, p. 1007). The participants were neither more anxious nor more depressed than their peers, and their self-esteem was similar. They had many friends and saw them often. Their delayed employment and later partnership were in keeping with the patterns of successful emerging adults. The shyness that was considered a handicap in childhood had become an asset in adulthood.

SERIOUS PSYCHOLOGICAL DISORDERS The general trends toward better health and rising self-esteem do not mean that every emerging adult is healthy and happy, however. Indeed, the rate of emotional disorders also rises toward the end of adolescence and in the first years of adulthood (Kessler et al., 2007).

The most troubling increase is in *schizophrenia*, rare before the mid-teens but showing a peak of new cases diagnosed at about age 21, with men more likely to develop schizophrenia than women. Schizophrenia is certainly partly genetic and biochemical, but both physiological maturation and psychological stresses cause this increase in diagnosis in emerging adulthood.

A combination of medical and psychological interventions can reduce the impairment, but consequences of the disorder may remain lifelong. Those who are not diagnosed with schizophrenia but who have schizoid symptoms—such as distorted thinking, lack of energy, and flat affect (i.e., not particularly happy or sad at various experiences)—are at higher risk of later psychological disorders (Rössler et al., 2011). After age 30, however, few people are newly diagnosed with this disorder: Emerging adulthood is the usual time when symptoms become overpowering.

Severe *anxiety* and *depression* are not unusual during adolescence and emerging adulthood, especially for young women. The anxiety that is particularly likely to be diagnosed at about age 20 is social phobia, the fear of other people. Without treatment, anxiety and depression restrict an emerging adult's later development, as they make it much more difficult to succeed in college or to find a mate.

As already noted, the rates of suicide and drug addiction also rise in early adulthood: Many believe that ongoing psychological vulnerability, combined with the need to establish one's own identity apart from the family, is the reason (O'Neil et al., 2011). Family communication and guidelines during adolescence can reduce the rate of these internalizing disorders, though there are certainly biological and social causes as well (Trudeau et al., 2012).

PLASTICITY In the research just discussed as well as in other research, plasticity is evident. Personality is not fixed by age 5, or 15, or 20, as it was once thought to be.

Emerging adults are open to experiences (a reflection of their adventuresome spirit), which allows personality shifts and eagerness for more education (McAdams & Olson, 2010; Tanner et al., 2009). The trend is toward less depression and more joy, along with more insight into the self (Galambos et al., 2006; McAdams et al., 2006).

Going to college, leaving home, paying one's way, stopping drug abuse, moving to a new city, finding satisfying work and performing it well, making new friends, committing to a partner—each of these might alter a person's life course. Each of these is more common from ages 18 to 25 than at any other time of life. The feeling of self-efficacy builds with each successful accomplishment, giving people the confidence and courage to modify whatever destructive traits they may have.

Total transformation does not occur since genes, childhood experiences, and family circumstances affect people lifelong. Nor do new experiences always result in desirable changes. Cohort may be important: Perhaps rising self-esteem as reported in longitudinal research reflects historical conditions at the end of the twentieth century. Perhaps the current economic downturn may soon cause the self-esteem of the average emerging adult to fall. But there is no doubt that personality *can* shift after adolescence.

Increased well-being and maturation may explain another shift: Emerging adults seem to become less self-centered and more caring of others (Eisenberg et al., 2005; Padilla-Walker et al., 2008). This can be seen as the foundation of the next psychosocial stage of development.

Intimacy

In Erikson's theory, after achieving identity, people experience the sixth developmental crisis, **intimacy versus isolation.** This crisis arises from the powerful desire to share one's personal life with someone else. Without intimacy, adults are lonely and isolated. Erikson explains:

> The young adult, emerging from the search for and the insistence on identity, is eager and willing to fuse his identity with others. He is ready for intimacy, that is, the capacity to commit himself to concrete affiliations and partnerships and to develop the ethical strength to abide by such commitments, even though they call for significant sacrifices and compromises.
>
> *[Erikson, 1963, p. 263]*

The urge for social connection is a powerful human impulse, one reason our species has thrived. Other theorists use different words (*affiliation, affection, interdependence, communion, belonging, bonding, love*) for the same human need.

There is no doubt that all adults seek friends, lovers, companions, and partners. Having close friends in early adulthood correlates with close relationships earlier in life and helps in other aspects of current life—including the ability to do well in college (Pettit et al., 2011).

All intimate relationships (friendship, family ties, and romance) have much in common—both in the psychic needs they satisfy and in the behaviors they require (Reis & Collins, 2004). Intimacy progresses from attraction to close connection to

intimacy versus isolation
The sixth of Erikson's eight stages of development. Adults seek someone with whom to share their lives in an enduring and self-sacrificing commitment. Without such commitment they risk profound loneliness and isolation.

ongoing commitment. Each relationship demands some personal sacrifice, including vulnerability that brings deeper self-understanding and shatters the isolation caused by too much self-protection. As Erikson explains, to establish intimacy, the emerging adult must

> face the fear of ego loss in situations which call for self-abandon: in the solidarity of close affiliations [and] sexual unions, in close friendship and in physical combat, in experiences of inspiration by teachers and of intuition from the recesses of the self. The avoidance of such experiences . . . may lead to a deep sense of isolation and consequent self-absorption.
>
> *[Erikson, 1963, pp. 163–164]*

According to a more recent theory, an important aspect of close human connections is "self-expansion," the idea that each of us enlarges our understanding, our experiences, and our resources through our intimate friends and lovers (Aron et al., 2005). Without that, we are not only lonely, we are also likely to get sick, feel tired, and more likely to eat and drink too much (Cacioppo & Cacioppo, 2012; Miller, 2011).

The loneliest group may be college freshmen in residential colleges. They have left behind their family and high school friends and have not yet found new intimate connections (Miller, 2011). For the most part, though, they soon make new friends.

In fact, contemporary emerging adults often gain friends, as they transition from their childhood family and move away from their neighborhood to their adult community. This has led to wider social networks and expanded understanding, one reason for the adult cognition explained earlier. Intimacy needs remain; the way they are satisfied differs.

A specific example is the use of social networking, texting, email, video chatting, and so on. Although older adults once thought that technology would lead to social isolation, the opposite seems more likely: Most emerging adults connect often with many friends, face-to-face and online. The result is emotional health and well-being. As one study concludes, "social networking sites help youth to satisfy enduring human psychosocial needs for permanent relations in a geographically mobile world" (Manago et al., 2012).

ROMANTIC PARTNERS Love, romance, and commitment are all of primary importance for emerging adults, although many specifics have changed. One dramatic change in the United States is that most people in their 20s are not married: The proportion of adults who are single, as well as the average age of marriage, have risen every year for the past 20 years. The average age at first marriage in the United States was 21 in 1960; it was 27 in 2010. Most emerging adults are postponing, not abandoning, marriage.

Observers note two new sexual interaction patterns. One is "hooking up" (when two people have sex without any interpersonal relationship), and the other is "friends with benefits" (when two people are friends, sometimes having sex, but not in a dating relationship). However, a study of college men, of several levels of sexual experience and various ethnic backgrounds, found that although all of them were familiar with the distinctions among hook-ups, friends with benefits, and committed relationships, none of them were "happy beneficiaries of nonrelational or casual sex," as college men are sometimes portrayed (Epstein et al., 2009, p. 414).

Furthermore, of those college men, aged 18 to 21, who said they'd had dating and sexual experience, only a few had had a hook-up that ended well. Casual sex was remembered as disappointing or was a step toward a more serious relationship. For example, Joe said:

> We originally hooked up because I was on vacation basically, and then she was on vacation, too, so we just. . . . I mean we had kinda similar backgrounds like that. We

casually kind of talked a little bit and then after a while, like, the relationship progressed and then we got a little more serious.

[Epstein et al., 2009, p. 421]

Another man had had sex with a girl who later said she did not want a serious relationship with him. He was disappointed, saying, "I am not really looking for casual relationships" (Epstein et al., 2009, p. 421).

As one U.S. sociologist explains, "despite the culture of divorce, Americans remain optimistic about, and even eager to enter, marriages" (Hill, 2007, p. 295). A hot political issue is whether gay and lesbian couples should be allowed to marry. The very fact that this is controversial indicates that, for people of all sexual orientations, marriage matters.

Marriage matters for society as well. Again, this is most obvious in the controversy about same-sex marriage. Gay and lesbian couples argue that many political benefits (in taxes, health insurance, etc.) are unfairly reserved for married couples. As for the opposing perspective, many argue that churches, temples, schools, and the media will be harmed if homosexuals marry.

The relationship between love and marriage is obviously not only a personal one. It reflects era and culture, with three distinct patterns evident (Georgas et al., 2006):

1. In about one-third of the world's families, love does not lead to marriage; parents do. They arrange marriages that will join two families together.

2. In another one-third of families, adolescents meet only a select group (single-sex schools keep them from unsuitable mates). If they decide to marry someone from that preselected group, usually of their same ethnicity, religion, and social class, the man asks the woman's father for "her hand in marriage." For these couples, parents supervise premarital interactions, usually bestowing their blessing. That was a traditional pattern: If parents did not approve, young people parted sorrowfully or eloped.

3. The final pattern is relatively new, although it is the dominant one in developed nations today. Young people socialize with hundreds of other young people, mostly unknown to their parents. They sometimes hook up, they sometimes develop serious relationships, but they often do not marry until they are able, financially and emotionally, to be independent.

Suggesting "one-third" for each of these patterns is a rough approximation. In former times, most marriages were of the first type; young people almost never met anyone unknown to their parents or thought of marrying without advance approval (Apostolou, 2007).

Currently, in developing nations, practice often blends the first two types. For example, most brides in modern India believe they have a choice, but many meet their future husbands shortly before the wedding via parental arrangement. The young man or woman can veto the match, but they rarely do so (Desai & Andrist, 2010).

Parents are peripheral for the last one-third. A young person's choices tilt toward personal qualities observable at the moment—physical appearance, personal hygiene, personality, sexuality, a sense of humor—and not to qualities more important to parents, such as religion, ethnicity, or long-term stability. For instance, a person who has been married and divorced is seen much more negatively by parents than by unpartnered adults (Buunk et al., 2008).

For Western emerging adults, love is considered a prerequisite for marriage. Once love has led to commitment, sexual exclusiveness is expected. A survey asked 14,121 adults of many ethnic groups and sexual orientations to rate (on a scale from 1 to 10, 10 being the highest) how important money, race, commitment, love, and

ABER CPC / ALAMY

Much in Common Emerging adults seek partners who are like them. These two both wear glasses, unlike 95 percent of their classmates, who prefer contacts. And their ancestry is Chinese, unlike 99 percent of the undergraduates at their college, Aberystwyth University in Wales. If they met in China, where glasses and Chinese ancestry are common, would they still be in love?

faithfulness were for a successful marriage or a serious long-term relationship (Meier et al., 2009).

Faithfulness was the most important of all (rated 10 by 89 percent) and love was almost as high (rated 10 by 86 percent). By contrast, most thought being the same race did not matter much (57 percent rated it very low, at 1, 2, or 3). Money, while important to many, was not nearly as crucial as love and fidelity.

This survey was conducted in North America, but emerging adults worldwide now share similar values. Six thousand miles away, emerging adults in Kenya also reported that love was the prime reason for sex and marriage; money was less important (S. Clark et al., 2010). The international question is whether love precedes marriage, as most Westerners believe, or follows it, as was expected in the past.

LOVE AND ETHNICITY In 2008, 15 percent of all U.S. marriages were officially counted as interethnic, a statistic from the American Community Survey. Very broad ethnic categories were used. For example, Black people from Africa, the Caribbean, and America were considered one ethnic group; Asians from more than a dozen nations were another ethnicity; European ancestry was a third category, lumping eastern, western, northern, and southern Europe together.

Thus, a marriage between a Pakistani and a Chinese person would *not* be categorized as interethnic. Nor would a marriage between a person of Greek heritage and one of Norwegian ancestry, even though the couple might be well aware of ethnic differences. Given the reality of cultural differences, far more than 15 percent of U.S. marriages are interethnic—although not officially so.

The survey counted Hispanics as a distinct ethnicity, whether they spoke Spanish or not. In 2008, 26 percent of them who married chose someone non-Hispanic. Interethnic marriages were also entered into by 31 percent of the Asians, 16 percent of the Blacks, and 9 percent of the Whites.

When it comes to sexual intimacy, ethnicity may be a bond. Most young adults are happy to talk with friends of other groups and 93 percent approve of Black–White dating, with college students particularly likely to accept interracial romance (Pew, June 4, 2010). Nonetheless, college students tend to choose sexual partners (from hook-ups to marriage) from within their own group (McClintock, 2010).

This does not contradict the interethnic marriage statistics above. If mating were random, more than half the marriages would be interethnic, not merely 15 percent. Although emerging adults do not usually exclude relationships with people of other ethnicities, their neighborhoods, religious institutions, and colleges make it more likely they will meet others of similar backgrounds.

The reasons for romances within groups involve not rejection of other groups so much as bonding with co-ethnics over matters of daily life—habits of speech, food preferences, jokes, and so on. Therefore, ethnic identity is an example of the emerging adult's ability to combine the personal and the political, the intuitive and the analytic. Interethnic marriages also show this ability, as usually such couples have much in common. Thus, they bond because of political, religious, or economic values, which overcome their ethnic differences.

Thus, emerging adults usually choose mates like themselves. That is particularly true for Asian men and Black women, who tend to marry within their group. Those Asians who marry outside their group are twice as often female as male, and those African Americans who marry outside their group are three times as often male (Passel et al., 2010). Apparently, ethnic differences in gender roles affect marriage.

FINDING EACH OTHER As already explained, the traditional way to find marriage partners was through the parents, or within a very narrow social circle. But many of today's emerging adults range far from home and would resist any parental match-

● **UNDERSTANDING THE NUMBERS**
To estimate how many marriages would be interethnic requires knowing how many U.S. emerging adults are from each ethnic group and then figuring how many pairs, by chance, would be interethnic. Explain how.

Answer In 2010, among U.S. emerging adults, about 60 percent were European, 17 percent Hispanic, 16 percent Black, 4 percent Asian, 2 percent biracial, and 1 percent American Indian. That means, if all the young adults were randomly paired, just by their numbers, most Europeans would end up with another European, but 40 percent would not. By contrast, someone in the smallest group, American Indian, would have only a 1 in 100 chance of marrying another American Indian. Adding all the odds suggests that, if couples were randomly paired, 58 percent of the pairs would be interethnic.

making. Instead, they must find partners among many thousands of possible mates—not an unmixed blessing.

Many Web sites now allow individuals to post their photos and personal information on the Internet, sharing the details of their daily lives and romantic involvement with thousands of others. This seems to be a wonderful innovation, as "the potential to reach out to nearly 2 billion other people offers several opportunities to the relationship-seeker that are unprecedented in human history" (Finkel et al., 2012, p. 4). Most emerging adults use such social networks, some of which preselect potential mates (by religion, age, education, orientation, hobbies, and so on).

One potential problem with this is **choice overload,** when too many options are available. Choice overload increases doubts after a selection is made (people wonder if another choice would have been better). Some people, feeling overloaded, freeze; they are unable to choose (Iyengar & Lepper, 2000; Reutskaja & Hogarth, 2009).

Having many complex options, such as spouse selection, each requiring assessment of future advantages and disadvantages, makes choice overload likely (Scheibehenne et al., 2010). Successful matches require face-to-face interactions over time to discern compatibility, as was the case for couples before the Internet (Finkel et al., 2012).

It is logical that too many choices make marriage commitment difficult, but choice overload studies have not focused scientifically on mate selection. Instead, research has compared having a few choices or many when choosing jams, or cars, or apartments. It is possible that similar doubts might emerge if a person has too many possible mates, but more research needs to be done.

We already know one problem is that having too many choices slows down analysis. If people feel rushed, they are more likely to regret their choice later on (Inbar et al., 2011). This might be why couples slow down the selection process by postponing marriage and living together instead.

LIVING TOGETHER A new form of mating for contemporary emerging adults is **cohabitation,** living together in a romantic partnership without being married. Marked national differences are apparent in acceptance and timing of cohabitation.

Currently, most emerging adults in the United States, Canada, northern Europe, England, and Australia live unmarried with a partner for at least a few months (see Figure 11.8). Some think of their living together as a prelude to marriage, others as a test of compatibility, and still others as a way to have an intimate relationship while saving money.

Matched Online Karen and James met through the Internet and now enjoy a face-to-face connection—as do thousands of other social networking couples.

choice overload
Having so many options that a thoughtful choice becomes difficult, and regret after making a choice is more likely.

cohabitation
An arrangement in which a couple live together in a committed romantic relationship but are not formally married.

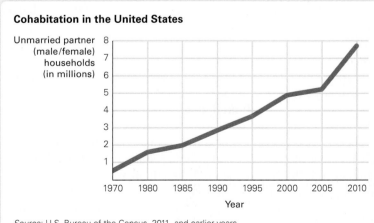

Cohabitation in the United States

Unmarried partner (male/female) households (in millions)

Year

Source: U.S. Bureau of the Census, 2011, and earlier years.

FIGURE 11.8 More Together, Fewer Married As you see, the number of cohabiting male–female households in the United States has increased dramatically over the past decades. These numbers are an underestimate: Couples who do not tell the U.S. census takers that they are living together, or who cohabit within their parents' households, or who are same-sex couples (not tallied until 2000) are not included here. In addition, most emerging adults who are not now cohabiting may begin to do so within a few years.

RICHARD TSONG-TAATARII / MCT / NEWSCOM

Love, Not Marriage Andrew and Jessica decided to raise their daughter together but not to marry. They live in White Bear, Minnesota, a relatively conservative area, but cohabiting couples are increasingly common everywhere.

By contrast, in some regions—Sweden, France, Jamaica, and Puerto Rico among them—cohabitation is more often a substitute for, not merely a prelude to, marriage. In still other nations—including Japan, Ireland, and Italy—cohabitation is not the norm, neither as a prelude nor as an enduring state; in those areas, cohabitation is unusual.

Research from 27 nations finds that acceptance of cohabitation within the nation affects the happiness of those who cohabit. Within those 27 nations, among the married and cohabitants, demographic differences (such as education, income, age, and religion) affect happiness, as one might expect, but it is remarkable that national attitudes permeate such a personal experience (Lee & Ono, 2012).

Past research in the United States finds that people who cohabited have higher rates of divorce and that their children develop less well than children of married couples (Schmeer, 2011; Stanley et al., 2006). Such conclusions may be specific to a particular place or time—in former decades, cohabitants were more often of low SES, which may be the underlying third variable that affects their children, not cohabitation itself.

However, although there are practical reasons for cohabitation—it saves money and postpones commitment—no research from any nation has yet found that it improves psychosocial development later in life. Thus, the research suggests caution—that neither the popularity of cohabitation, nor the immediate happiness of those who move in together, is proof that cohabitation is beneficial over the long term.

Family Forces

It is hard to overestimate the importance of the family at any period of the life span. Although made up of individuals, a family is much more than the individuals who belong to it. In dynamic synergy, children grow, adults find support, and everyone is part of a family ethos that gives meaning to, and provides models for, hope and action.

linked lives
Lives in which the success, health, and well-being of each family member are connected to those of other members, including members of another generation, as in the relationship between parents and children.

LINKED LIVES Emerging adults are said to set out on their own, leaving their parents and childhood home behind. They strive for independence and postpone establishing new family commitments. From that one might conclude that they no longer need family support and guidance. Wrong conclusion.

The data show that parents continue to be crucial for adult children—perhaps even more so now than for previous generations since fewer contemporary young adults have completed their education or have new families and high-paying jobs. They rely on their parents, who often are deeply concerned about their welfare.

All members of each family have **linked lives,** meaning that the experiences and needs of individuals at one stage of life are affected by those at other stages (Macmillan & Copher, 2005). We have seen this in earlier chapters: Each newborn affects every family member of every age, and growing children are affected by their parents' relationship, even if the children are not directly involved in domestic disputes, financial stresses, parental alliances, and so on.

A strong linkage between emerging adults and their parents in the twenty-first century may seem counterintuitive, as emerging adults are striving for independence and cohort changes are notable. Nonetheless, many studies have found family congruence in attitudes, aspirations, and actions. As already noted, political and religious loyalties often link the generations.

For instance, a detailed Dutch study found substantial agreement between parents and their adult children on issues that might, in theory, be contentious—such as cohabitation, same-sex partnerships, and divorce. Some generational differences appeared, but when parents were compared with their own children (not young adults in general), similar attitudes were apparent (Bucx et al., 2010).

Adult children who still lived with their parents (about one-fourth of the sample) were more likely to agree with their parents than were adults who lived apart from them, but all groups showed "intergenerational convergence" (Bucx et al., 2010, p. 131).

Extensive other research confirms that family patterns persist, affecting every adult as well as every child. For example, early attachment between infant and caregiver influences that child's future relationships, including friendships, romantic partnerships, and parenthood (see Infographic 4.1). Securely attached infants are more likely to become happily married adults; avoidant infants hesitate to marry. Some insecure infants marry early, but they are more likely to divorce.

Overall, the quality of adult romantic relationships reflects early attachment styles, both anxious (too clingy and jealous) and avoidant (too distancing and secretive) (Collins & Gillath, 2012; Li & Chan, 2012). Adults who were securely attached infants are more likely to have secure relationships with their own children. Of course, plasticity is evident lifelong; early attachment affects adult relationships, but it does not determine them.

NATIONAL DIFFERENCES Is living with parents the key to strong relationships? Apparently, it depends on the economy and on the culture. Almost all unmarried young adults in Italy and Japan remain in their childhood home, and in those nations both generations seem content with that arrangement. Half of the young adults in England live with their parents, but frictions often arise there (Manzi et al., 2006).

Fewer emerging adults live with parents in the United States if separate households are affordable. If the young adult cannot pay the rent on an apartment, parents often subsidize their child's independent living—as expected by both generations (Furstenberg, 2010). The economic downturn that began in 2007 increased both the number of adult children who cannot find employment and the number of parents who cannot underwrite their child's rent. Not only are more emerging adults living with their parents (see Figure 11.9), but all linked family members are less happy (Stein et al., 2011).

Looking at many cultures, it is apparent that families can be destructive as well as helpful to emerging adults. Cultural expectations are an important variable. Some Westerners believe that dependence on parents is not healthy for young adults.

Not all Westerners agree. As explained earlier, familism is a strong value among many Latino Americans, among others. Closer relationships between parents and their adult children are increasingly common and welcomed among North Americans of all ethnicities. As two experts in human development write, "with delays in marriage, more Americans choosing to remain single, and high divorce rates, a tie to a parent may be the most important bond in a young adult's life" (Fingerman & Furstenberg, 2012).

FIGURE 11.9 No More House Rules? Among emerging adults in the United States, half the women and more than half the men live with their parents. This arrangement is fraught with conflict and resentment, unless expectations about finances, chores, overnight visitors, drug use, meals, and so on are discussed, clarified, and agreed upon.

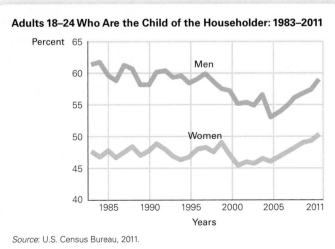

Adults 18–24 Who Are the Child of the Householder: 1983–2011

Source: U.S. Census Bureau, 2011.

Brilliant, Unemployed, and Laughing
This is not an unusual combination for contemporary college graduates. Melissa, in Missoula, Montana, graduated summa cum laude from George Washington University and is one of the many college graduates who live with their parents. The arrangement provides many financial and family benefits, but it is not known who cooked dinner or who will wash the dishes.

✦ **ESPECIALLY FOR Family Therapists**
Emerging-adult children who live with their parents do so primarily for financial reasons, yet you have learned that families often function better when young adults live on their own. What would you advise? (see response, page 423)

This bond may be financial as well as emotional. In many nations, young adults who leave home to find work send most of their salary back home. If they cannot get a job, and hence have no money to send home, they feel they have failed. Personal goals are sacrificed for family concerns, and "collectivism often takes precedence and overrides individual needs and interests," making "family a source of both collective identity and tension" (Wilson & Ngige, 2006, p. 248).

That quotation came from a study of African families, but it applies to many North American families as well. Almost all young adults think adult children should care for a parent who needs help, but the older generations do not necessarily agree, especially if that means living with an adult child (Pew, November 3, 2011).

Familism has advantages. Parents reciprocate by providing support (such as child care for grandchildren) and emotional encouragement. They may also protect their adult child. If an arranged marriage is a disaster (e.g., the husband severely beats the wife, the wife refuses sex, the husband never works, the wife never cooks), then the elders intervene.

Each family member within each culture judges such intervention differently: What is expected in, say, Cambodia, would be unacceptable in, say, Colombia. Chinese young adults expect their parents and friends to comment on their romantic partners; North American adults know they must *not* do so. Compared with their U.S. contemporaries, Chinese emerging adults are about twice as likely to stop dating someone if their parents disapprove (Zhang & Kline, 2009).

Among the developmental advantages of family involvement are that each new baby has many caregivers, so young adults are less burdened by child care. This may be one reason why parenthood begins much earlier in African nations. By contrast, parenthood in the United States is an impediment to education and career success (Osgood et al., 2005), and some family members are reluctant or unable to provide free child care. Partly for that reason, many emerging adults postpone parenthood (Furstenberg, 2010).

Cultural differences aside, parents encourage young adults in every nation to do well in school and to get good jobs, partly to make their families proud, partly so they will be able to care for their relatives when necessary, and partly to help secure their own future. Immigrant young adults tend to be highly motivated to learn and work, and they reciprocate their parents' support. These values help them to become more successful than many native-born young adults (García Coll & Marks, 2012).

Same Situation, Far Apart: Dedication Is Universal It may seem as if the activities and clothing of the Fresno college student in the bookstore *(left)* could not differ more from those of the young mother in the doorway of her Rajastan, India, home *(right)*. However, both are typical emerging adults: active, healthy, and working for their futures within the norms of their culture.

ALL TOGETHER NOW When we look at actual lives, not the cultural ideal of independence or interdependence, all emerging adults have much in common, including close family connections and a new freedom from parental limits (Georgas et al., 2006). It is a mistake to assume that emerging adults in Western nations abandon their parents. Just the opposite: Some studies find that family relationships *improve* when young adults leave home (Smetana et al., 2004).

Family members feel obligated to one another no matter where they live. In fact, far from ignoring the needs of their elders, a Dutch study found that adult children are more likely to believe that their generation should attend to the needs of the older generation than the older generation themselves believe (Bucx et al., 2010).

Regarding the overall experiences of emerging adults, this stage of life has many critical opportunities, since "decisions made during the transition to adulthood have a particularly long-lasting influence on the remainder of the life course because they set individuals on paths that are sometimes difficult to change" (Thornton et al., 2007, p. 13).

Fortunately, most emerging adults, like humans of all ages, have strengths as well as liabilities. Many survive risks, overcome substance abuse, combat loneliness, and deal with other problems through further education, friends, family, and maturation. If they postpone marriage, prevent parenthood, and avoid a set career (all characteristic of 18- to 25-year-olds) until their identity is firmly established and their education complete, they may be ready for joyful adult commitments and responsibilities.

KEY points

- Many emerging adults continue their identity search, especially for vocational and ethnic identity.

- Personality shows continuity and change in emerging adulthood, with many people gradually becoming happier. Another, smaller group develops serious disorders.

- Marriage is often postponed but intimacy needs are met in other ways.

- Computer matches and cohabitation have become the norm in the United States, each with obvious advantages but also troublesome disadvantages.

- Intergenerational bonds continue to be important in every culture, with many parents helping their emerging adult children, financially and emotionally.

RESPONSE FOR Family Therapists (from page 422) Remember that family function is more important than family structure. Sharing a home can work out well if contentious issues—like sexual privacy, money, and household chores—are clarified before resentments arise. You might offer a three-session preparation package to explore assumptions and guidelines.

SUMMARY

Biosocial Development

1. Emerging adults usually have strong and healthy bodies. Death from disease is rare.

2. The sexual-reproductive system reaches a peak during these years, but most current emerging adults postpone childbearing. The results include both increased use of contraception and higher rates of sexually transmitted diseases.

3. Willingness to take risks is characteristic of emerging adults. This allows positive behaviors, such as entering college, meeting new people, volunteering for difficult tasks, and finding new jobs. It also leads to destructive actions, such as unprotected sex, drug use, and an increase in violent deaths.

4. Extreme sports are attractive to some emerging adults, who find the risk of serious injury thrilling.

Cognitive Development

5. Adult thinking is more flexible, better able to coordinate the objective and the subjective. Some scholars consider this development a fifth stage of cognition, referred to as postformal thought.

6. Whether or not a fifth stage exists, there is no doubt that maturation of the prefrontal cortex allows more advanced thought.

7. The flexibility of young-adult cognition allows people to re-examine stereotypes from their childhood. This may decrease stereotype threat, which impairs adult performance if left unchecked.

8. Worldwide there are far more college students, especially in Asia and Africa, than there were a few decades ago, as massification has become an accepted goal.

9. Everywhere students' backgrounds and current situations are more diverse, which advances postformal thinking. Practical, vocational skills are also valued in college, which is one reason business has become the most common U.S. major.

Psychosocial Development

10. Identity continues to be worked out in emerging adulthood. Ethnic identity is particularly important in multiethnic cultures, not only for people of mixed and minority backgrounds, but also for those in the majority.

11. The current economic situation makes achieving vocational identity even more problematic than a decade ago. The average emerging adult changes jobs several times.

12. Personality traits from childhood do not disappear in emerging adulthood, but many people learn to modify or compensate for whatever negative traits they have. New experiences—such as moving away from home and going to college—allow some plasticity in personality.

13. The need for social connections and relationships is lifelong. In earlier times, and in some cultures currently, emerging adults followed their parents' wishes in seeking marriage partners. Today's emerging adults are more likely to choose their own partners and postpone marriage.

14. Cohabitation is the current norm for emerging adults in many nations. Nonetheless, marriage to partners of similar backgrounds still seems to be the goal.

15. Family members continue to be important to emerging adults. Parental support—financial as well as emotional—may be more crucial than in earlier times.

KEY TERMS

choice overload (p. 419)
cohabitation (p. 419)
drug abuse (p. 398)

emerging adulthood
  (p. 393)
extreme sports (p. 398)

intimacy versus isolation
  (p. 415)
linked lives (p. 420)

massification (p. 404)
postformal thought (p. 399)
stereotype threat (p. 402)

WHAT HAVE YOU LEARNED?

1. What advantages do emerging adults have in terms of their health?

2. Biologically, why is emerging adulthood the best time to have a baby?

3. What cohort differences are evident in people's attitudes toward premarital sex?

4. Why has the AIDS epidemic slowed in recent years?

5. What are the pros and cons of risk taking in emerging adulthood?

6. Why are emerging adults more likely than people of other ages to take part in risky sports?

7. Why is drug abuse common among emerging adults?

8. What are the differences between formal operational thought and postformal thought?

9. How is adult thinking different from adolescent thinking?

10. In what ways does cognition continue to change throughout adulthood?

11. How does flexible thinking affect social understanding?

12. How do current college enrollment patterns differ from those of 50 years ago?

13. According to Perry, how does students' thinking change during their college career? What factors explain this change?

14. Why are some current researchers criticizing college education?

15. In what way does diversity affect college students' learning?

16. How does ethnic pride change from early adolescence to adulthood?

17. Why might vocational identity be an outdated social construction?

18. What is the general trend of self-esteem during emerging adulthood?

19. What reassurance might you offer the parents of an aggressive teen and of a shy teen as their children enter emerging adulthood?

20. What factors might explain personality shifts—both positive and negative—after adolescence?

21. In what three main ways do young adults meet their need for intimacy?

22. In what three main ways do emerging adults meet their romantic partners?

23. How has social networking changed the process of mate selection?

24. Why do many emerging adults cohabit instead of marrying?

25. Why do people assume that emerging adults are not influenced by their parents?

26. What surprises have emerged from studies of the attitudes of emerging adults and their parents?

27. What evidence is there that familism is highly valued in many Latino and Asian cultures?

28. Why might family relationships sometimes improve when young adults leave home?

APPLICATIONS

1. Describe an incident during your emerging adulthood when taking a risk could have led to disaster. What were your feelings at the time? What would you do if you knew that a child of yours was about to do the same thing?

2. Read a biography or autobiography that includes information about the person's thinking from adolescence through adulthood. How did personal experiences, education, and maturation affect the person's reactions and analysis?

3. Only a few statistics regarding historical and national changes in the number of students of both sexes and various backgrounds are reported here. Compare your nation, state, or province with another, in current as well as historical date. Discuss causes and implications of differences.

4. Talk to three people you would expect to have contrasting views on love and marriage (differences in age, gender, upbringing, experience, and religion might affect attitudes). Ask each the same questions and then compare their answers.

>>ONLINE CONNECTIONS

To accompany your textbook, you have access to a number of online resources, including quizzes for every chapter of the book, flashcards (in English and Spanish), critical-thinking questions, and case studies. For access to any of these links, go to www.worthpublishers.com/bergerinvitation2e. In addition to these free resources, you'll also find links to podcasts, video clips, diagnostic quizzing with personalized study advice, and an ebook. Some of the videos and activities available online include:

- *Interview with Kurt Fischer.* This noted developmentalist discusses the influence of experience on brain development.

- *Transition to Parenthood.* Videos of couples in various stages of parenthood highlight the physical, emotional, social, household, and vocational changes that accompany this new responsibility.

- *Homosexuality: Genes Versus Environment.* What makes someone gay? This video shows how the nature–nurture debate plays out when applied to this question.

CHAPTER OUTLINE

ADULTHOOD
Body and Mind

WHAT WILL YOU KNOW?

- Why don't people feel as old as they are?
- Why are lung cancer rates decreasing in American men but increasing in American women?
- Do adults get smarter or dumber from age 25 to age 65?
- Is everyone an expert in something?

Jenny was in her early 30s, a star in my human development class long ago, before my first textbook was published. She told the class that she was divorced, raising her son, daughter, and two orphaned nephews in public housing in the south Bronx. She spoke eloquently and enthusiastically about free activities for her children—public parks, museums, the zoo, Fresh Air Fund camp. We were awed by her creativity and energy.

A year later, Jenny came to my office to speak privately. She said she was four weeks pregnant. The father, Billy, was a married man. He had told her he would not leave his wife but that he would pay for an abortion. She loved him and feared he might end their relationship if she did not terminate the pregnancy. She wanted to talk to me first.

I learned more. She was not opposed to abortion on religious grounds; her 7-year-old son needed speech therapy; she thought she was too old to have another infant; she was a carrier for sickle-cell anemia, which had complicated her most recent pregnancy; her crowded apartment was no longer "babyproof" since her youngest child was 7.

Jenny was about to graduate with honors and had found a job that would enable her family to leave their dangerous neighborhood. She was eager to get on with her adult life. After a long conversation, she thanked me profusely—even though I had only asked questions, provided facts, and listened.

Then she surprised me: "I'll have the baby," she said. "Men come and go, but children are always with you." I had thought her narrative was leading to a different conclusion, but her values shaped *her* life, not mine. We all make decisions about our bodies and our futures, ideally after discussing facts and implications with someone we trust. ●

senescence
A gradual physical decline related to aging. Senescence occurs in everyone and in every body part, but the rate of decline is highly variable within and between persons.

organ reserve
The extra capacity built into each organ, such as the heart and lungs, that allows a person to cope with extraordinary demands or to withstand organ strain.

homeostasis
The adjustment of all the body's systems to keep physiological functions in a state of equilibrium, moment by moment. As the body ages, it takes longer for these homeostatic adjustments to occur, so it becomes harder for older bodies to adapt to stress.

allostasis
A dynamic body adjustment, related to homeostasis, that over time affects overall physiology. The main difference is that while homeostasis requires an immediate response, allostasis requires longer-term adjustment.

ADULTHOOD COVERS FOUR DECADES, FROM AGES 25 TO 65. As with my student, questions about childbearing and child rearing arise throughout adulthood, as do concerns about health. This chapter explains facts about sex, reproduction, aging, and more, then goes on to describe adult thinking processes. Cognition helps adults sort through facts, emotions, and values, leading to sometimes unexpected thoughts and personal decisions.

Expertise is described in this chapter. Jenny came to me not for advice, but because she believed I am an expert in human development. I told her about age (she was *not* too old to have a baby) and about genes (the father should be tested for sickle-cell), but Jenny was the expert about her own circumstances—which will become clear at the end of this chapter, when you learn what happened after she left my office.

Senescence

Everyone ages. As soon as growth stops, **senescence,** a gradual physical aging over time, begins. Senescence affects every part of the body, visible and invisible.

In a culture that devalues aging, senescence has a negative connotation, but aging can be positive. From a developmental perspective, every period of life is multidirectional. Our scientific study of life-span development helps us see the gains and losses of adulthood.

The Experience of Aging

Although we are all aging, senescence often goes unacknowledged until late in adulthood. Typically, 30- to 65-year-olds feel 5 to 10 years younger than their chronological age and think that "old" describes people significantly older than they themselves are currently (Pew Research Center, 2009a; see Figure 12.1). Other research confirms that most adults feel strong, capable, healthy, and "in their prime."

At least three aspects of body functioning protect adults from recognizing senescence: organ reserve, homeostasis, and allostasis.

Organ reserve is a characteristic of every organ that allows normal functioning throughout the adult years. Because extra power is built into the human body, people rarely notice that their hearts, lungs, and so on are losing capacity. That reserve power decreases each year, but it usually does not matter because people rarely need to draw on it. Bodies function well throughout middle age unless major stress has caused too much extra strength to ebb away.

Furthermore, all the parts of the body work in harmony. **Homeostasis**—a balance between various parts of the body systems—keeps every physical function connected to every other. The result is that few adults are aware of their aging organs.

For instance, when people exercise, the muscles require more oxygen, so heart rate increases and breathing quickens to bring in more air, first to the lungs and then oxygen to the bloodstream. Age reduces this process: Vital capacity (the amount of air expelled after a deep breath) decreases about 4 percent per decade (faster for smokers). Breathing becomes quicker and shallower as people age, but homeostasis keeps sufficient oxygen in the blood (P. S. Timiras & De Martinis, 2007). Marked shortness of breath is a sign of illness, not aging.

Related to homeostasis is **allostasis**, a dynamic body adjustment over time that affects overall physiology. The main difference between homeostasis and allostasis is time: Homeostasis requires

A Trick Question How old is he? His leg muscles and the angle of his stretch make him comparable to a fit 30-year-old. However, the placement of this photo should give you a clue about his real age—he is 61.

PATRICK FRASER / CORBIS OUTLINE

an immediate response from the body systems whereas allostasis requires longer-term adjustment.

For example, how much a person eats daily is affected by many factors related to appetite—that is the homeostatic set point. An empty stomach triggers hormones, stomach pains, digestion, and so on, that lead a person to eat again. If an overweight person begins a serious diet, rapid weight loss soon triggers short-term, homeostatic reactions, making it harder to lose weight (Tremblay & Chaput, 2012).

Eating is related to a broader set of human needs: how emotionally satisfied or distressed a person is. Many people overeat when they are upset, and eat less when they have recently exercised—those responses could be considered part of homeostasis as well. Our bodies are designed to be comfortable, with many mechanisms to relieve the pain of hunger, low oxygen, thirst, and so on. Those reactions are short term—if a person is hungry for a long time, the body adjusts. Feeding a starving person a heavy meal might result in vomiting or diarrhea, ironically because of homeostasis.

Over the years, allostasis becomes crucial: If a person overeats or starves day after day, the body suffers. In medical terminology, that person has an increased allostatic load; the short-term equilibrium (homeostasis) may impair long-term health. Obesity is one cause of diabetes, heart disease, high blood pressure and so on—all the result of physiological adjustment (allostasis) (Sterling, 2012).

Thus, overeating and underexercising require not just adjustment for each moment (homeostasis) but also adjustment over decades. One heavy meal reduces appetite for the next few hours (homeostasis); years of obesity put increasing pressure on the allostatic system, so a new stress (such as running up three flights of stairs) may cause a major breakdown (such as a heart attack). Both homeostasis and allostasis work to keep adults from realizing that their bodies function less efficiently as they age.

Since momentary stresses that become ongoing habits increase the allostatic load, the solution is to choose patterns that gradually become habits and decrease stress over the years—enjoying nature, or jogging, or socializing, or yoga, or prayer, or simply a beautiful sunset. Homeostasis will make such activities part of the daily rhythm: That is why a runner who is immobilized will feel unhappy. These joys, day after day, will improve long-term health by lightening the allostatic load.

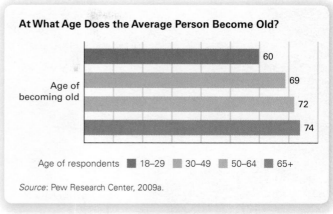

At What Age Does the Average Person Become Old?

Age of becoming old
60
69
72
74

Age of respondents ■ 18–29 ■ 30–49 ■ 50–64 ■ 65+

Source: Pew Research Center, 2009a.

FIGURE 12.1 Not Old Yet When people are asked when someone is "old," answers depend on how old they themselves are. The trend continues—my mother, in her 80s living in a senior residence, complained that she did not belong there because too many of the people were old.

Sex and Fertility

As you just read, 60-year-olds can usually do almost everything 30-year-olds can do, and they are often unaware of doing anything less well. However, they do notice changes in the sexual-reproductive system and sometimes mourn the loss. Arousal, orgasm, fertility, and menopause are all affected by age, with the impact dependent on culture. As one wag said, "The most important human sexual organ is between the . . . ears."

SEXUAL RESPONSIVENESS Sexual arousal occurs more slowly with age, and orgasm takes longer. These slowdowns are counterbalanced, however, by reduced anxiety, longer lovemaking, and better communication, as partners become more familiar with their own bodies and those of their mates. Distress is less connected to age than to troubled relationships, irrational fears, and unrealistic expectations (Duplassie & Daniluk, 2007; L. Siegel & Siegel, 2007).

It is thus a mistake to think of middle-aged adults as sexually deprived. According to a study of Chicago couples conducted in the early 1990s, most adults of all

His Arm Around Her Whether in formal wear (the Akha pair in Thailand) or casual North American clothes, at every adult age couples delight in being close to each other, physically and emotionally.

infertility
The inability to conceive a child after trying for at least a year.

ages enjoy "very high levels of emotional satisfaction and physical pleasure from sex within their relationships" (Laumann & Michael, 2000, p. 250). That study found that men and women were likely to be "extremely satisfied" with sex if they were in a committed, monogamous relationship—a circumstance more likely between ages 25 and 65 than earlier or later. Frequency of intercourse correlated with age, but not necessarily with satisfaction.

REPRODUCTION Bearing many children was crucial for societies and individuals in former centuries. In Chapter 11, you learned that fertility peaks in the late teens and early 20s. Historically, pregnancy was welcomed, partly to compensate for the infants and teenagers who died. Now pregnancy is often dreaded, not desired.

Infertility is not regarded as it once was. Though still defined as the inability to conceive after a year of trying (about 1 in 7 couples today are infertile), reasons for infertility and reactions to it have changed. In earlier eras, almost everyone was married by age 20. If couples did not have a baby within a year or two, it was assumed that something was wrong—either with the relationship or with their bodies. That was a sad situation, sometimes leading to divorce, sometimes to adoption, and sometimes to an intense focus on career that could strain the marital relationship.

Now age is a common factor in fertility because most teenagers and young adults postpone pregnancy, yet conception becomes increasingly difficult with each passing year of adulthood. Age as well as health affects both sexes. For about one-third of infertile couples, the primary source of the problem is the man; for another one-third, it's the woman; for the final one-third, the cause is uncertain.

A common reason for male infertility is a low sperm count. Conception is most likely if a man ejaculates more than 20 million sperm per milliliter of semen, two-thirds of them mobile and viable, because each sperm's journey through the cervix and uterus is aided by millions of fellow travelers. In most men, about 100 million sperm reach maturity each day after about 75 days of development. Anything that impairs body functioning over that 75-day period (e.g., fever, radiation, prescription drugs, time in a sauna, excessive stress, environmental toxins, drug abuse, alcoholism, cigarette smoking) can reduce sperm number, shape, and motility (activity) and make conception less likely.

Age also reduces sperm count. Men older than 45 take five times as many months to impregnate a woman as do men who are younger than 25 (Hassan & Killick, 2003). (This study controlled for frequency of sex and age of the woman.)

Pollution, stress, and sexually transmitted infections (STIs), all of which accumulate with age, reduce sperm count and motility. Those factors may be the reason the number of viable sperm varies by geographic location—higher in southern France than in Paris, higher in New York than in California, higher in Finland than in Sweden—although the interpretation and even the validity of such data are debatable (Merzenich et al., 2010).

Female fertility is also affected by anything that impairs physical functioning—including several diseases, smoking, extreme dieting, and obesity. Many infertile women have had *pelvic inflammatory disease* (PID). Unless properly diagnosed and treated, PID creates scar tissue that blocks fallopian tubes, preventing the sperm from reaching an ovum. Ovulation stops at menopause.

Even more than for men, age slows down every step of female reproduction—ovulation, implantation, fetal growth, labor, and birth. For both sexes, STIs interfere with healthy reproduction: Since the number of past partners increases with age, this may be another reason that age correlates with infertility.

CULTURE AND INFERTILITY Infertility occurs everywhere, but the impact depends on the culture. In some nations, Nigeria among them, a woman is not considered truly female until she bears a child. There, each year of infertility is a sad one (Hollos et al., 2009). In other nations, such as Germany, being childless by choice is an accepted, even admired, condition, and fertility is more often a problem than the goal (Sobotka & Testa, 2008).

Currently in the United States, about 15 percent of all adult couples are infertile, some because they postponed childbearing. Another 15 percent of couples choose not to have children. Among the remaining 70 percent, about half become pregnant as desired and about half become pregnant by mistake (i.e., mistimed, not necessarily unwanted). Wanting a baby is also affected by the economy, which explains why the U.S. birth rate has decreased each year since 2008.

Although birth rates overall have declined in recent years, in many nations the birth rate among older women has increased. Despite the fact that the risk of infertility and birth complications increase with age, in 2008, 115,000 babies were born in the United States to women over age 39 (U.S. Bureau of the Census, 2011b), with most babies and mothers quite healthy. A major reason for the increased birth rate after age 35 is that people no longer accept infertility as a sad reality. Instead, many older infertile couples seek medical assistance. It is no longer odd for a couple to be married and childless for a decade or more, and then to have twins.

FERTILITY RESTORED In the past 40 years, advances in medicine have solved about half of all fertility problems. Surgery can repair male or female reproductive systems, and *assisted reproductive technology* (ART) helps many couples overcome various fertility obstacles (Sharif & Coomarasamy, 2012).

For instance, drugs can precipitate ovulation, often of several ova. Or ova can be surgically removed from an ovary and fertilized in a glass lab dish. This is **in vitro fertilization (IVF)**—*in vitro* literally means "in glass." One standard procedure, called *intra-cytoplasmic sperm injection* (ICSI), is to insert a single sperm into each healthy ovum to overcome low sperm count.

IVF zygotes begin to duplicate in the glass dish, and at the 4- or 8-cell stage, technicians insert one or several of them into the mother's womb. Most do not implant and grow, but some do. To be specific, only about 40 percent of all IVF cycles result in successful births, even when women are healthy, normal weight, and younger than 30. Success rates decrease with age (Centers for Disease Control and Prevention, 2011).

✦ **ESPECIALLY FOR Young Men**
A young man who impregnates a woman is often proud of his manhood. Is this reaction valid? (see response, page 433) →

● **UNDERSTANDING THE NUMBERS**
You read in Chapter 11 that at peak fertility, a newly married woman in her early 20s typically becomes pregnant within three months. That assumes that her husband is about her age. How long would pregnancy take, on average, if her husband is 50 years old?

Answer A year or more.

in vitro fertilization (IVF)
A technique in which ova (egg cells) are surgically removed from a woman and fertilized with sperm in a laboratory. After the original fertilized cells (the zygotes) have divided several times, they are inserted into the woman's uterus.

Her Parents' Love Three-month-old Avery is blessed by having two adoring parents, Jared and Wendy Kennedy. It could even be said that she has a third parent—the woman who donated the ovum. That egg was fertilized through ART, to help this couple realize their dream of parenthood.

Despite this failure rate, since the first "test-tube" baby was born in 1973, IVF has produced 4 million babies worldwide. Between 1 and 3 percent of all newborns in developed nations and thousands more in developing nations are now conceived via IVF.

Millions of formerly childless couples, either infertile or same-sex, are parents. Their children need not be their genetic offspring. Donated sperm have been used for decades, resulting in millions of babies born after *intrauterine insemination* (formerly called *artificial insemination*). Donor ova and donor wombs (when an IVF embryo is implanted in a woman who did not provide the ovum) are increasingly common. (The word *donor* is misleading, though; people are paid for their sperm, ova, or pregnancies.)

Birth defects and later illnesses increase slightly with IVF (Kalra & Barnhart, 2011; C. Williams et al., 2010), but the risk is small: About 97 percent of all IVF newborns have no apparent defects. Not small, however, is the risk of prematurity and low birthweight. In the United States, about half of all IVF babies are low-birthweight twins or triplets (Centers for Disease Control and Prevention, 2011).

The Aging Brain

Like every other part of the body, the brain also slows down with age. Neurons fire more slowly, and messages sent from the axon of one neuron are not picked up as quickly by the dendrites of other neurons. One result is that reaction time lengthens. Multitasking becomes harder, processing takes longer, and complex working-memory tasks (e.g., repeating eight numbers in sequence, adding the first four, deleting the fifth one, subtracting the next two, and multiplying the total by the last one—all in your head) become virtually impossible (Fabiani & Gratton, 2009).

A few individuals (less than 1 percent of those under age 65) experience significant brain loss with age; they "encounter a catastrophic rate of cognitive decline, passing through . . . the dementia threshold" (Dangour et al., 2007, p. 54). But for most adults, brain changes do not correlate with intellectual power (Greenwood & Parasuraman, 2012). Adults can perform the brain equivalent of a marathon—one reason that judges, bishops, and world leaders are usually at least 50 years old. Their thinking has benefited from their experience.

If severe brain loss occurs before late adulthood, the cause is not normal senescence but one of the following:

● *Drug abuse.* All psychoactive drugs harm the brain, especially prolonged, excessive use of alcohol, which can cause Wernicke-Korsakoff syndrome ("wet brain").

● *Poor circulation.* Everything that impairs blood flow—such as hypertension (high blood pressure) and heavy cigarette smoking—also impairs cognition.

● *Viruses.* The blood–brain barrier keeps most viruses away, but a few—including HIV and the prion that causes mad cow disease—can destroy neurons.

● *Genes.* About 1 in 1,000 people inherits a dominant gene for Alzheimer disease, which destroys memory. Other uncommon genes also affect the brain.

Later in this chapter, we will describe adult cognitive development. Intellectual abilities can rise, fall, zigzag, or stay the same, partly dependent on specifics of each individual's life. This again illustrates the life-span perspective: Intelligence is multidirectional, multicultural, multicontextual, and plastic, but overall quite steady.

As a leading researcher on adult intellect wrote, "Decline prior to 60 years of age is almost inevitably a symptom or precursor of pathological age changes" (Schaie, 2005, p. 418).

Sense Organs

Although brain changes are usually insignificant until late adulthood, significant sensory changes occur in almost everyone. Each sense becomes less acute with age. Specifics of which part of vision, hearing, and so on changes depends on genes, experience, and programmed senescence, which vary by particulars.

For example, with sight, peripheral (sidelong) vision ages faster than frontal vision, perception of some colors fades more quickly than that of others, and nearsightedness decreases as farsightedness increases. This explains why, compared with 20-year-olds, 40-year-olds hold their electronic tablets farther away (the print is blurry at a closer reading distance). The eyes take longer to adjust to darkness or glare, making driving at night more dangerous. Note, however, that some people who were previously nearsighted can now see well while driving without glasses—an age-related improvement.

Variable losses also occur in hearing, which is most acute at about age 10. Sounds at high frequencies (e.g., the voice of a small child) become inaudible sooner than do sounds at low frequencies (e.g., a low booming voice).

For contemporary middle-aged adults, hearing loss is rarely problematic before age 65. However, in one recent study of 1,512 teenagers, almost one-third reported early symptoms of hearing loss (ringing, muffled sounds, temporary deafness) after listening to music on their headphones. Most routinely set the volume to decibel levels known to damage the sensitive hairs of the inner ear (Vogel et al., 2010). In future generations, then, middle-aged adults might have significant hearing problems.

The senses of taste and smell, as well as one's balance, are also affected by age throughout adulthood. The variations are usually not noticeable to the individual, but they are detectable in laboratory measurements.

Physical Appearance

As you have just read, the invisible changes of senescence do not affect daily life for most contemporary adults. However, visible changes may be disconcerting. In an age-conscious society, no one wants to look old, yet everyone ages.

SKIN AND HAIR The first visible changes are in the skin, which becomes dryer and rougher. Collagen, a component of the body's connective tissue, decreases by about 1 percent every year after age 20 (M. L. Timiras, 2007). Skin becomes thinner and less flexible; the cells just beneath the surface are more variable; wrinkles appear, particularly around the eyes. Diet has an effect (fat slows down wrinkling), but aging is apparent in every layer of the skin for everyone (Nagata et al., 2010).

Especially on the face (exposed to sun, rain, heat, cold, and pollution), the skin loses "firmness and elasticity, leading to the formation of sagging areas" (Whitbourne, 2008, p. 88). These changes are almost imperceptible, but if you meet a typical pair of siblings, aged 18 and 28, you can tell by their skin which one is older. By age 60, all faces are wrinkled—some much more so than others. The smooth, taut, flexible young face has disappeared.

RESPONSE FOR Young Men (from page 431) The answer depends on a person's definition of what manhood is. No developmentalist would consider manhood simply as high sperm count. ●

DPA / CORBIS

Gains and Losses In his 20s, Phil Collins was the drummer for the band Genesis, becoming a star solo singer and songwriter by age 30. A midlife ear infection and a spinal injury resulted in major sensory loss, making drumming impossible and new harmonies more difficult—but Collins adjusted. He continues to gain fans and make music: His *Going Back* album, released at age 59, reached the top of the charts. Most adults are neither so impaired nor so successful, but a combination of gains and losses occurs between ages 25 and 65 for everyone.

Hair usually turns gray and thins, first at the temples by age 40, and then over the rest of the scalp. This does not affect health, but since hair is a visible sign of aging, adults spend money and time on coloring, thickening, styling, and more. Body hair (on the arms, legs, and pubic area) also becomes thinner and lighter. An occasional thick, unwanted hair may appear on the chin, inside the nose, or in some other place.

SHAPE AND AGILITY The body also changes shape between ages 25 and 65. A "middle-age spread" increases waist circumference; all the muscles weaken; pockets of fat settle on the abdomen, upper arms, buttocks, and chin; people stoop slightly when they stand (Whitbourne et al., 2008).

By late middle age, back muscles, connective tissue, and bones lose density, making the vertebrae in the spine shrink. People lose about an inch (2 to 3 centimeters) of height by age 65. That loss occurs not in leg bones but in the trunk, with compression of the space between spinal disks (Tilling et al., 2006)—another reason that waists widen.

Agility is also reduced. Consequently, rising from sitting on the floor, twisting in a dance, or even walking "with a spring in your step" is harder. The joints lose flexibility; stiffness is more evident; bending is harder, especially by middle age.

The aging of the body is most evident in sports that require strength, agility, and speed: Gymnasts, boxers, and basketball players benefit from youth. Of course, the intellectual and emotional gains of adulthood may compensate for the physiological slowdowns: Some 30-year-olds are better athletes than their younger teammates.

Declining Hormones

Over the decades of adulthood, the level of hormones in the bloodstream decreases, altering sleep patterns, appetite, and the appearance changes just noted. The decline in sex hormones, which occurs suddenly in women and more gradually in men, is the hormonal change that adults notice most, since it affects desire and behavior.

menopause
The time in middle age, usually around age 50, when a woman's menstrual periods cease and the production of estrogen, progesterone, and testosterone drops. Strictly speaking, menopause is dated one year after a woman's last menstrual period, although many months before and after that date are considered part of the period of menopause.

MENOPAUSE For women, ovulation and menstruation stop at **menopause,** when estrogen levels fall. This occurs naturally between ages 42 and 58 (the average age is 51). Genes are an important influence on a woman's age at menopause (Morris et al., 2011). A *hysterectomy* (surgical removal of the uterus) usually includes removal of the ovaries, which causes sudden menopause if the woman has not already experienced it naturally.

About one in four U.S. women has a hysterectomy. Rates vary by cohort, region, and nation: They are higher in Mexico but lower in Canada. Rates are falling in many places as the risks of surgery and the benefits of estrogen, when naturally produced by the ovaries, become better known.

Common menopause symptoms are disturbances of body temperature—hot flashes (feeling hot), hot flushes (looking hot), and cold sweats (feeling chilled). These vary by ethnicity. No marked disturbances are reported by 40 percent of Asian Americans, 25 percent of European and Hispanic Americans, and 15 percent of African Americans.

The psychological consequences vary as well. Some menopausal women find a new zest for life; others become depressed. One woman said menopause is "somewhere between a taboo and a joke" (Duffy et al., 2011, p. 497).

The historical Western notion that menopausal women "temporarily lose their minds" (Neugarten & Neugarten, 1986) contrasts with the traditional view among Hindi women in India that menopause represents liberation (Menon, 2001). The latter reaction is becoming more common in the United States as well, as women typically are less depressed and less anxious five years after menopause than five years before (Gibson et al., 2012).

Pausing, Not Stopping During the years of menopause, these two women experienced more than physiological changes: Jane Goodall *(left)* was widowed and Ellen Johnson-Sirleaf *(right)* was imprisoned. Both, however, are proof that post-menopausal women can be productive. After age 50, Goodall (shown visiting a German zoo at age 70) founded and led several organizations that educate children and protect animals, and Johnson-Sirleaf (shown speaking to the International Labor Organization at age 68) became the President of Liberia.

Over the past 30 years, millions of women undergoing **hormone replacement therapy (HRT)** took hormone supplements, usually estrogen combined with progesterone. Some did so to alleviate menopause symptoms; others, to prevent osteoporosis (fragile bones). Correlational studies originally found that heart disease, strokes, and dementia occurred less often with estrogen, which prompted many women to use HRT for decades.

Researchers now believe that a third variable, SES, was the reason HRT-takers experienced less disease. Women with more education and income were more likely to use HRT and to be healthier overall. In fact, in controlled longitudinal studies, the U.S. Women's Health Initiative found that taking estrogen for 10 years or more *increased* the risk of heart disease, stroke, and breast cancer and had no effect on the most common types of dementia (U.S. Preventive Services Task Force, 2002).

When that result was publicized, millions of women stopped HRT—but that may have been an overreaction. There is no dispute that estrogen replacement reduces hot flashes and decreases osteoporosis, but the fear of increased disease may be greater than the research warrants (Cumming et al., 2011; Powledge, 2007; Sturdee & Pines, 2011).

A medical review stresses the variability of risk, complaining that the early presentation of the Women's Health Initiative may have "disadvantaged nearly a decade of women who may have unnecessarily suffered severe menopausal symptoms" (Sturdee & Pines, 2011, p. 305). Estrogen may aid cognition, if not prevent dementia (Erickson & Korol, 2009; Greenwood & Parasuraman, 2012). On the other hand, the breast-cancer risk has been confirmed. Risks and benefits vary from person to person (Stevenson et al., 2011).

ANDROPAUSE? Hormone replacement for men is likewise controversial. The debate begins by asking whether men undergo anything like menopause. Some suggest that many men experience an age-related reduction of testosterone that decreases sexual desire, erections, and muscle mass (Harrison, 2011).

But many doctors think that the term **andropause** (or *male menopause*) is misleading because it implies a sudden drop in reproductive ability or hormones. That does not occur; many men produce viable sperm throughout their lives.

Sexual inactivity and anxiety cause a reduction in testosterone—a phenomenon similar to menopause but with a psychological, not physiological, cause. As one review explains, "Retirement, financial problems, unresolved anger, and dwindling social relationships can wreak havoc on some men's sense of masculinity and virility" (L. Siegel & Siegel, 2007, p. 239).

hormone replacement therapy (HRT)
Taking hormones (in pills, patches, or injections) to compensate for hormone reduction. HRT is most common in women at menopause or after removal of the ovaries, but it is also used by men to help restore their decreased testosterone level. HRT has some medical uses but also carries health risks.

andropause
A term coined to signify a drop in testosterone levels in older men, which normally results in reduced sexual desire, erections, and muscle mass. (Also called *male menopause*.)

To combat a decline in testosterone, some men choose HRT, in their case taking testosterone (some women also take smaller amounts of testosterone to increase their sexual desire). Widespread use is not recommended, however, as age-related reductions in testosterone are no more pathological than menopause is (Handelsman, 2011).

Doctors are thus understandably cautious; supplemental hormones may be harmful (Bhasin, 2007; Moffat, 2005; Sokol, 2009). Overdoses of testosterone by athletes have led to sudden cardiac arrest. Yet low testosterone correlates with increased risk of heart disease (Kaushik et al., 2010). This debate is not settled, but all the evidence finds that adult health, for both men and women, depends more on habits than on hormones.

KEY points

- Aging is universal, but the meaning of senescence depends on the individual and on cultural factors.

- Fertility decreases with time. Many infertile couples use assisted reproductive technology, especially IVF.

- Brains, muscles, and the senses are notably affected by age, but few adults in developed nations are debilitated by these changes.

- Menopause is universal, but reactions to it vary. Experts do not agree about the existence of andropause or about the use of hormonal supplements.

Health Habits and Age

Each person's routines of daily life powerfully affect their susceptibility to every disease and chronic condition; this applies both to current routines and to those that have been in place since childhood. It is particularly true for problems associated with aging—from arthritis to varicose veins.

Consider cancer, the leading cause of death for adults aged 25 to 65. The rate of cancer increases with every year of life, but lifestyle, not age, is usually the underlying cause. One estimate parcels out the causes at smoking (30 percent), diet (30 percent), and inactivity (5 percent) (Willett & Trichopoulos, 1996).

Of course, the specific lifestyle effects on susceptibility vary with each disease, even each type of cancer, and uncontrollable factors, primarily genetic, play a major role in some diseases and a minor role in others. However, people can cut in half their overall morbidity and mortality during adulthood (ages 25 to 65) if they have healthy habits.

To clarify this, it's important to know the various ways in which health is measured:

- *Mortality* means death.

- *Morbidity* means disease, the rates of which depend partly on diagnosis.

- *Disability,* the usual result of morbidity, is the inability to do something that people usually can do. For example, one form of morbidity is vision loss; this could mean serious disability if a person can see only shapes, but less serious disability if the person cannot read without glasses.

- *Vitality*—also known as life force, or *joie de vivre*—may be the most important, but it is the most difficult to measure. Some people with morbid conditions that increase disability and the risk of mortality are nonetheless happy and active.

The goal of good health habits is not only to reduce illness but also to increase wellness, so that adults can live for decades at full vitality.

✦ **ESPECIALLY FOR Doctors and Nurses** If you had to choose between recommending various screening tests and recommending various lifestyle changes to a 35-year-old, which would you choose? (see response, page 438) ⟶

Tobacco and Alcohol

Many adults, when they were teenagers, believed that smoking and drinking made them cool and signified maturity. Nicotine also provided an energy boost, which seemed to be an indicator of health. Accordingly, many young people picked up those habits as soon as they could, legally or not.

We now know that cancer deaths reflect smoking patterns of years earlier. Because North American men have been quitting for decades, lung cancer deaths for 55- to 64-year-old males are about half what they were in 1970.

Relatively few women smoked at the beginning of the twentieth century, but their smoking has increased over time. Consequently, in the United States, during the same period in which male lung cancer deaths declined, the rates for women increased, in fact doubling from 1980 to 2008 (see Figure 12.2). Even without cancer, the long-term effects of smoking include reduced oxygen intake and thus lower vitality.

Cancer deaths are decreasing in most developed nations, including the United States, yet about one-third of adults in Greece, Turkey, the Netherlands, and Japan still smoke. In China, India, and Indonesia, more than half of the men are smokers, as are less than 10 percent of the women—but rates of smoking and cancer are rising, particularly for women. The World Health Organization calls tobacco "the single largest preventable cause of death and chronic disease in the world" (Blas & Kurup, 2010, p. 199).

The harm from cigarettes is dose-related: Each puff, each day of smoking, each breath of secondhand smoke makes cancer, heart disease, stroke, and emphysema more likely. No such linear harm results from drinking alcohol.

In fact, alcohol can be beneficial: People who drink wine, beer, or spirits *in moderation*—no more than two drinks a day—live longer than abstainers. The primary reason is that alcohol reduces coronary heart disease and strokes. It increases HDL (high-density lipoprotein), the "good" form of cholesterol, and reduces LDL (low-density lipoprotein), the "bad" cholesterol that causes clogged arteries and blood clots. It also lowers blood pressure and glucose (Klatsky, 2009).

Guess His Age A man puffs on a bidi, a flavored cigarette, in Bangalore, India. He looks elderly but is actually middle-aged (about age 40). He is at risk of being among the 1 million Indians who die each year of smoking-related causes.

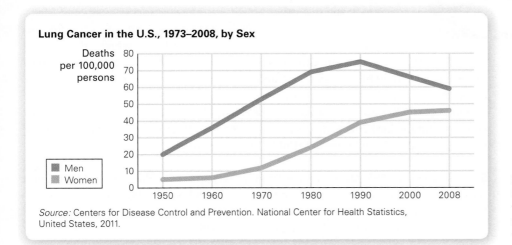

Lung Cancer in the U.S., 1973–2008, by Sex

Source: Centers for Disease Control and Prevention. National Center for Health Statistics, United States, 2011.

FIGURE 12.2 Gender, Not Sex Humans of either sex are more likely to die if they smoke, but gender norms, not biological sex, determine the divergent patterns shown here.

RESPONSE FOR Doctors and Nurses
(from page 436) Obviously, much
depends on the specific patient. Overall, however, far more people develop
disease or die because of years of
poor health habits than because of
various illnesses not spotted in time.
With some exceptions, age 35 is too
early to detect incipient cancers or
circulatory problems, but it's prime
time for stopping cigarette smoking,
curbing alcohol abuse, and improving
exercise and diet ●

However, moderation is impossible for some. Alcoholics find it easier to abstain than to have one, and only one, drink a day. Occasional drinking may be protective, but alcohol destroys brain cells; contributes to osteoporosis; decreases fertility; accompanies many suicides, homicides, and accidents; destroys families; and increases the risk of 60 diseases, not only of the liver but also of the breasts, stomach, and throat (Hampton, 2005).

Alcoholism increases with poverty and "alcohol causes a disproportionate burden of harm in poorer countries" (Gonzalez, quoted in Grimm, 2008, p. 863) because prevention, treatment, and enforcement strategies have not caught up with abuse. In general, low-income nations have more abstainers as well as more abusers, while more affluent nations have more moderate drinkers (Blas & Kurup, 2010).

Homeostasis and allostasis may be factors: Poverty reduces the sources of pleasure and increases stress, so temporary joy comes from smoking and drinking. But then more nicotine and alcohol become needed because of homeostasis, and, over the long term, addiction begins, joy declines, and life ends (Sterling, 2012). Momentary vitality becomes morbidity and then mortality.

Overeating

Metabolism decreases by one-third between ages 20 and 60, which means that adults need to eat less and move more each year. Few adults do so; instead, obesity increases with each decade of adulthood until old age.

A WORLDWIDE PROBLEM Obesity is now recognized as a major health problem in many nations (see Infographic 12, page 439). Cultural solutions—a national diet

that emphasizes less meat and more vegetables as in China, or fewer fast food restaurants and more leisurely dining as in France, or more olive oil and less corn oil as in Greece—are beyond the scope of this book, or probably any book. Although one might hope that globalization would lead to these or other improvements in eating habits in the United States, the opposite seems true. Fast food restaurants are proliferating in every nation.

Likewise, although one might hope that adults develop better eating habits as they mature, the rate of obesity increases with age until late adulthood. In the United States, 65 to 70 percent of adults are overweight, with a body mass index (BMI) above 25. More than half of those overweight people are obese (with a BMI of 30 or more), 6 percent overall are morbidly obese (with a BMI of 40 or more) (Flegal et al., 2012). (See Appendix A for BMI chart.)

Rates in the two other North American nations, Canada and Mexico, are also high. Excess weight increases the risk of every chronic disease, but the most glaring example is diabetes, which affects twice as many North Americans currently as it did 40 years ago (Taubes, 2009). The direct cause is insulin resistance, which, left untreated, can lead to death, but diabetes also causes eye, heart, and foot problems.

Cocaine or Coffee Cake? Could this be as dangerous as shooting up in a crack house? Few people are troubled by an overweight office worker drinking coffee and munching cake made with white flour, butter, and sugar. Yet more adult deaths occur because millions snack unhealthily than because thousands are addicted to cocaine. It is far easier to criticize people with bad habits than it is to change our own behavior.

Sadly, partly because of how they are treated, obese adults avoid socializing, exercising, and medical check-ups: As a result, their morbidity increases far more than their weight alone would predict (Puhl & Heuer, 2010).

SOLUTIONS TO THE OBESITY EPIDEMIC Stopping any addiction is difficult because long-standing habits are embedded in each adult's daily life. Diets—there are hundreds of them—work if they reduce calories and involve exercise, but they need to be maintained for decades, a daunting task. Sustained counseling and encouragement

Adult Overweight Around the Globe

Obesity is on the rise throughout the world. Even more than inactivity, eating calorie-dense foods—fried, sweetened, or salted—increases weight and illness. That is hard to track by nation, but it is the reason obesity is more common among the poor in wealthy nations and among the rich in poor nations.

OVERWEIGHT AND GNP

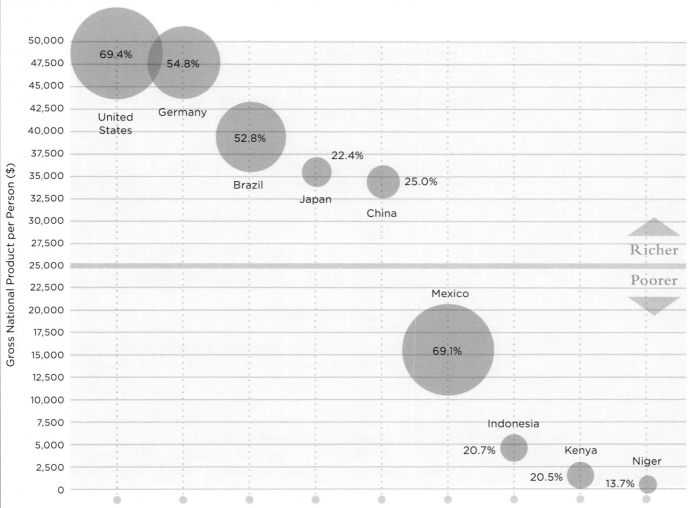

International cutoff weights for overweight and obesity are set at various levels. These numbers show proportions of adults whose BMI is over 25.

Rate of overweight

SOURCE FOR OVERWEIGHT: WHO, 2012.
SOURCE FOR GNP: WORLD BANK, 2013.

WHO RECOMMENDATIONS FOR REDUCING OBESITY IN ADULTHOOD INCLUDE:

Eating a healthy diet

Limit total fat intake and shift fat consumption away from saturated fats to unsaturated fats; increase consumption of fruits, vegetables, whole grains, and nuts.

Limit the intake of sugar and salt.

Regular physical activity

Engage in adequate levels of physical activity throughout life.

At least 30 minutes of regular, moderate-intensity physical activity on most days reduces the risk of disease. Muscle strengthening and balance training reduce falls and improve mobility.

SOURCES & CREDITS LISTED ON P. SC-1

from health practitioners is time-consuming but effective in the long run. Many people seek a quick, effective weight-loss method instead.

In the past, when diet drugs have been approved and mass marketed, the results have not always been positive (Li et al., 2005). Drug addiction is a hazard, as are cardiovascular and digestive problems. These outcomes were not apparent before approval of those diet drugs, however, partly because obese people in experimental groups are particularly likely to drop out when they experience side effects. This left only those participants who completed the study—a biased sample that misrepresented the full effects of a drug (Fabricatore et al., 2009).

Inadequate research up to now has thus resulted in too few approved medical solutions to obesity. Yet effective methods are needed because obesity can make many diseases deadly. One expert who first opposed and then approved a new drug (Qsymia, formerly called Qnexa) acknowledged "an urgent need for better pharmacologic options . . . . [T]here are consequences to nontreatment" (Morrato, quoted in Pollack, 2012).

The same problem is apparent for gastric bypass surgery, which causes dramatic weight loss in many patients but also leads to additional surgery for almost one-fourth of them. That risk may be worth it, though, since morbidly obese people have higher death rates without surgery than with it (Schauer et al., 2010).

The problem with both drugs and surgery is that, if they succeed, patients must change their lifestyle to accommodate new eating habits. People who are highly motivated and long past adolescence and emerging adulthood are much more likely to follow through with those required lifestyle changes. For those morbidly obese teenagers who undergo surgery the adjustments may be particularly difficult (Widhalm et al., 2011).

Developmentalists emphasize that early prevention is more effective than medical remedies. You have already read that babies born underweight often become fat children, who may become overweight adults. At that point, other people and social pressures are crucial—but sometimes they're no help at all (Puhl & Heuer, 2010).

Inactivity

Regular exercise protects against illness even if a person is overweight or a smoker. And when any habit changes for the better, a daily hour of exercise is the best predictor of maintaining the change (Shai & Stampfer, 2009). Specific benefits of exercise include lower blood pressure, stronger hearts and lungs, and reduced risk of almost every disease, including depression, diabetes, osteoporosis, heart disease, arthritis, and even cancer.

By contrast, sitting for long hours correlates with almost every unhealthy condition, especially heart disease and diabetes, both of which carry additional health hazards beyond the disease itself. Even a little movement—gardening, light housework, walking up the stairs or to the bus—helps.

Walking briskly for 30 minutes a day, five days a week, is a reasonable goal. More intense exercise (e.g., swimming, jogging, bicycling) is ideal. It is possible to exercise too much, but almost no adult aged 25 to 65 does. In fact, one study that used objective assessment of adult movement (electronic monitors) found that less than 5 percent of adults in the United States and England exercise even 30 minutes per day (Weiler et al., 2010). Self-reports put the number at about 30 percent (see Figure 12.3).

The close connection between exercise and health, both physical and mental, is well known, as is the influence of family, friends, and neighborhoods. Exercise-friendly communities have lower rates of

Just Give Me the Usual Even bad habits can feel comfortable—that's what makes them habits.

"The fresh mountain air is starting to depress me."

BRUCE ERIC KAPLAN / THE NEW YORKER COLLECTION / CARTOONBANK.COM

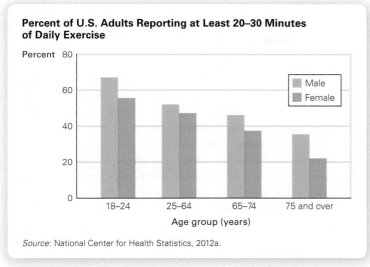

Percent of U.S. Adults Reporting at Least 20–30 Minutes of Daily Exercise

Source: National Center for Health Statistics, 2012a.

FIGURE 12.3 Older and Lazier Exercise is important at every age, but increasingly so as people get older. Why do those who need it most move the least?

Hope It Helps Ideally, this is part of her daily exercise routine, and no one will complain about a fire hazard. More likely, though, her back hurts from hunching over her desk in an uncomfortable chair; her supervisor questions her undignified behavior; no one in the adjoining cubicles asks to borrow her ball. Social norms make exercise difficult.

obesity, hypertension, and depression (Lee et al., 2009). This is not merely a correlation but a cause: People who are more fit are likely to resist disease and to feel healthier as they age (Carnethon et al., 2003; Shirom et al., 2008).

Researchers are now trying to pin down specifics. Does the type of exercise matter (walking, gardening, swimming, running)? Is half an hour each day better than four hours on the weekend (Etnier, 2009)? These are unanswered questions, but no one doubts that adults should be active, year in, year out. Maintaining any healthy habit is the hardest part, as the following explains.

A VIEW FROM SCIENCE

A Habit Is Hard to Break

Every adult knows that smoking cigarettes, abusing alcohol, overeating, and sedentary behavior are harmful, yet many have at least one destructive habit. Why don't we all shape up and live right? Breaking New Year's resolutions; criticizing people whose bad habits are not our own; feeling guilty for consuming sweets, salt, fried foods, cigarettes, or alcohol; buying gym memberships that go unused or exercise equipment that becomes dust-gathering sculptures—these behaviors are common.

Social scientists have focused on this conundrum (Conner, 2008; Shumaker et al., 2009). They have found that changing a habit is a long, multistep process: Ignoring that reality is one reason habits continue, because strategies that work at one stage fail at another. One list of these steps is as follows:

1. Denial
2. Awareness
3. Planning
4. Implementation
5. Maintenance

The first step, *denial,* occurs because all bad habits exist for good reasons. For example, most cigarette smokers begin as teenagers because they seek social acceptance and/or weight control—both especially important to adolescents. Warnings about mortality in the distant future seem irrelevant. Then nicotine creates addiction: Without the drug, smokers become anxious, confused, angry, and depressed—no wonder some smokers deny the harm of smoking since the pain of not smoking is evident to them.

In fact, with many life-threatening addictions, hearing that death might result leads to *more* smoking, drinking, and so on, not less (Ben-Zur & Zeidner, 2009; Martin & Kamins, 2010). A theory, called *terror management theory,* explains that people reduce fear by doing exactly what they have been warned not to do, as explained in the Epilogue.

Denial reduces stress, which leads people to deny what is obvious to others. They say, "I only drink on weekends," or "It's genetic," or "Other people eat more." Ideally, denial crumbles and the person moves to the next stage.

Awareness must be attained by the individual. Others help, not by accusing but by listening, either via *motivational interviewing* (encouraging the individual to describe the reasons why change is needed) or via *acceptance and commitment therapy* (recognizing the emotional aspects of the habit). Both motivational interviewing and commitment therapy begin with the person's own values. This is crucial: Adults rebel when others tell them what to do, think, or believe (Bricker & Tollison, 2011).

Planning occurs only after the person is aware of the problem and wants to solve it. Planning is specific, with a set date for quitting and strategies to overcome obstacles. Care is needed at this step because humans tend to underestimate the power of their own impulses; this is true for smokers, dieters, and addicts of all kinds.

Such underestimating was evident in a particular experiment. Researchers gave students who were entering or leaving a college cafeteria their choice of several packaged snacks, promising them about $10 (and the snack) if they did not eat it for a week. Those who were entering, presumably aware of the demands of hunger, planned to avoid temptation by choosing a less desirable snack. Most of them (61 percent) earned the money.

However, those leaving the cafeteria apparently underestimated the power of hunger. They chose a more desirable snack and later ate it; only 39 percent earned the money (Nordgren et al., 2009). Planning has to take into account a person's weakest moments: Most planners are too optimistic; counselors can help turn awareness into a solid plan.

Implementation is quitting according to plan. One crucial factor is gathering social support, such as (1) letting others know the date and the plan, (2) finding a buddy, and (3) joining a group (e.g., Weight Watchers, Alcoholics Anonymous, or SmokEnders)—or, better yet, *all three*. Private efforts often fail.

Willpower is like a muscle: Putting too much stress on it for too long will make it break, but gradual strengthening is possible (Vohs & Baumeister, 2011). That means implementation is most successful when tackling one habit at a time: Quitting cigarettes when starting a diet is almost impossible; this double-barreled approach is usually short-lived.

Maintenance is the most important step, yet the one that most people ignore. Although quitting may be difficult, many addicts experience the pain of quitting, get past the pain, and then relapse, only to quit again and again. Dieters gain and lose weight so often that this phenomenon has a name—*yo-yo dieting*. That same phenomenon is part of every addiction: Maintaining a good habit requires intense, individualized attention (Ridenour et al., 2012).

Maintenance is destroyed by overconfidence. People forget the power of temptation. The recovered alcoholic goes out with friends who drink, planning to order only juice; the dieter buys ice cream to offer to guests or for the rest of the family; the person who joined the gym skips a day, promising to make up for it the following day. Such actions are far more dangerous than people realize because they add stress. For instance, the dinner guests might not eat all the ice cream, and later, the stress of having resisted it earlier finally makes the ice cream all the more irresistible.

In another study, dieters who were given a stressful task (remembering a nine-digit number) entered a room that had been set, seemingly at random, either with some tempting foods or with a scale and a diet book. They were then asked to taste a milkshake to give their opinion of the particular drink; they were also told they could take a tiny sip or drink as much as they wanted. Those who saw eating clues drank more than those who saw dieting clues (Mann & Ward, 2007), unaware that stress made them vulnerable.

This is an example of *attention myopia,* when resolve (maintenance ability) momentarily fades. Attention myopia occurs with many self-control efforts: People temporarily lose focus on the goal of halting aggression, curbing lust, stopping drug abuse, and so on (Giancola et al., 2010). Many people who restart a bad habit cite a specific stress—from a bitter divorce to a bothersome toothache—that makes them lose focus. Sooner or later every adult is stressed and habits reappear, unless maintenance strategies are ongoing.

Accumulating Stressors

Stress is part of life, from birth to death. Between ages 25 and 65, everyone experiences major stress (e.g., the death of a family member), minor stress (e.g., an unexpected downpour), and daily hassles (e.g., traffic jams).

stressor
Any situation, event, experience, or other stimulus that causes a person to feel stressed. Many circumstances become stressors for some people but not for others.

FROM STRESS TO STRESSOR Not every stress becomes a **stressor,** however. A stressor is any experience, circumstance, or condition that negatively affects a person. How people cope with stresses, making some become stressors and others not, affects their health.

Particularly if organ reserves are depleted or allostatic load is high, the physiological toll of major and minor stressors lowers immunity, increases blood pressure, speeds up the heart, reduces sleep, and produces many other reactions that lead to serious illness. A comprehensive review finds that "stress clearly affects the whole body," but that the best coping measures vary for each illness and each person (Aldwin, 2007, p. 54). For instance, some patients recover from surgery better if they know details of their vital signs and healing; others just need to know that doctors are working to make them better.

For some, reactions to stressors can cause more stressors. For example, a longitudinal study of married couples in their 30s found that, if the husband's health deteriorated, the chance of divorce increased. This was apparent with all couples, but it was particularly evident for well-educated European Americans (Teachman, 2010).

GENDER AND AGE One possible explanation is that these couples were less accustomed to stress and thus less able to cope. Those best able to deal with stress are those who have had some, but not too much, trauma in their lives (Seery, 2011).

Psychologists distinguish two major ways of coping. In **problem-focused coping,** people attack their problems (e.g., confront a difficult boss, move out of a noisy neighborhood). In **emotion-focused coping,** people change their emotions (e.g., from anger to acceptance). In general, younger adults and adults of higher SES are more likely to attack problems while older adults and those of lower SES try to accept them (Aldwin, 2007).

This may indicate that those who are poorer and older believe that there is not much they can do to change their circumstances. A pessimistic attitude about the future is more common the less money one has (Robb et al., 2011).

Sex hormones may also affect responses to stress. Men are inclined to be problem-focused, reacting in a "fight-or-flight" manner. Their sympathetic nervous system (faster heart rate, increased adrenaline) prepares them for attack or escape. Their testosterone rises when they attack and decreases if they fail.

On the other hand, women are more emotion-focused. They "tend and befriend" —that is, seek the reassurance of other people when they are under pressure. In reaction to stress, their bodies produce oxytocin, a hormone that leads them to seek confidential and caring interactions (S. E. Taylor, 2006; S. E. Taylor et al., 2000).

This gender difference explains why a woman might get upset if a man doesn't want to talk about his problems. By contrast, a man might be annoyed if a woman just talks, not appreciating his advice about how to confront and solve the problem.

Adults of both sexes and of every age and income level use both strategies, depending on the situation. None of these group differences is absolute: Most adults sometimes attack stress and sometimes change their attitudes. Worse is having no strategy at all—denying a problem until it escalates and takes a physical toll.

One study found that when both spouses in a marriage avoid either strategy and instead suppress justifiable anger, their death rate is twice as high as when at least one partner expresses anger (Harburg, 2008). With age and experience, adults may learn to respond wisely, as age brings a more positive attitude toward life. Then stresses do not become stressors (Charles & Carstensen, 2010).

Age brings another advantage. Emerging adulthood is "a time of heightened hassles" (Aldwin, 2007, p. 298). Once life settles down, some stresses (dating, job hunting, moving) are less frequent. Adults "are more adept at arranging their lives to minimize the occurrence of stressors" (Aldwin, 2007, p. 298). Even parenthood is more stressful with the first baby than the last.

problem-focused coping
A strategy to deal with stress by tackling a stressful situation directly.

emotion-focused coping
A strategy to deal with stress by changing feelings about the stressor rather than changing the stressor itself.

Love Your Brother Desert life as an ethnic minority in an Arab nation seems extraordinarily difficult. Yet millions of Bedouin in Syria, Saudi Arabia, Israel, Lebanon, and Egypt have survived over the centuries, developing coping practices that make nomadic life possible. Among these are fierce family loyalty, strong religious devotion, respect for camels, and, as shown here, acceptance of physical affection among kinsmen.

NATHAN BENN / CORBIS

SES and Health Habits

Money and education protect health in every nation. According to an economist who analyzed historical U.S. data, after age 35 the average life span increases by 1.7 years for each year of education (Lleras-Muney, 2005).

It is not obvious why this connection is so strong. Does education teach better health habits? Does income result in better medical care? Does high IQ added to high family SES in childhood allow more education followed by living in better neighborhoods, with less pollution and more opportunities to walk, bike, and play outside? Are wealthy people better able to insulate themselves from stressors because they can hire people to help them?

For whatever reason, the differences are dramatic. The 10 million U.S. residents with the highest SES outlive—by an average of about 30 years—the 10 million with the lowest SES (C. J. L. Murray et al., 2006). Recent data find the SES gap widening in the United States (Olshansky et al., 2012).

SES is protective between nations as well as within them: Rich nations have less disease, injury, and death. For example, a baby born in 2010 in northern Europe can expect to live to age 79; in sub-Saharan Africa, to 55 (United Nations, 2012).

DISEASES OF AFFLUENCE Certain diseases, including diabetes, lung cancer, and breast cancer, were once called *diseases of affluence* because they were more common among the rich than the poor (Hu, 2011; Krieger, 2002, 2003) and in wealthier groups within each nation—Japanese Americans more than Filipino Americans, for instance. However, when smoking became cheaper (between 1920 and 1950), fast food more available, and illness better diagnosed, the "diseases of affluence" did not correlate with wealth at all; they were more common among the poor.

Distinguishing the effects of income, education, cohort, and culture is difficult because, as you remember from Chapter 1, all these factors overlap. For example, currently, African American women are more likely to die of breast cancer than are women of other U.S. ethnic groups, but medical researchers are not sure why (DeSantis et al., 2011). The reason could be genetic, but it could also be a lower quality of health care, poorer eating habits, more stress, or an avoidance of doctors.

A recently proposed hypothesis is that low SES in the United States leads to poor health habits—overeating, smoking, drinking—as ways of coping with stress; such practices impair physical health while reducing depression and anxiety. This may begin prenatally: A poor pregnant woman, worried about how she will provide for her baby, is less likely to follow good nutritional and sleep routines. Ironically, avoidance of such poor lifestyle habits means wealthier adults are generally in better physical health, but accumulation of stress may lead to higher rates of mental disorders among them (Jackson, 2012).

This is counterintuitive, but a trade-off between physical and psychological health may explain an odd gender difference: Women are far less likely to be drug addicts, somewhat less likely to be obese, but far more likely to be depressed. Whether it is the case that the wealthy actually have higher rates of depression and anxiety or, rather, that the data merely reflect a higher rate of diagnosis and therapy seeking is not known.

HEALTH OF IMMIGRANTS Data on immigrants adds complications to the connection between SES and health. Immigrants are healthier yet poorer than the native born: They have less heart disease, drug abuse, obesity, and so on than do their wealthier co-ethnics (García Coll & Marks, 2012).

In the United States, children and grandchildren of immigrants tend to surpass their elders in education, income, and English fluency—but as SES rises over the generations, so does virtually every illness, including cardiovascular problems (see

Figure 12.4). Grandchildren of immigrants die at the same rate as grandchildren of the native born (Barger & Gallo, 2008; Bates et al., 2008).

An immigrant's age at arrival and years in the United States make a difference. Adults who arrived within the past year have only one-eleventh the rate of obesity as adults who immigrated in childhood and who have lived in the United States for more than 15 years (Roshania et al., 2008). Heart disease, diabetes, and many other illnesses are likewise affected by those two variables.

One suggested explanation is that healthy people are more likely to emigrate; then their good health protects them even though they may be poor. This may be partly true, as genes that protect health may enable the hazardous journey to another place. However, the data find that this "healthy migrant" theory is not sufficient to explain immigrant health (Bates et al., 2008; García Coll & Marks, 2012). Perhaps psychological or ethnic influences in low-SES cultures foster good health habits that continue after emigration.

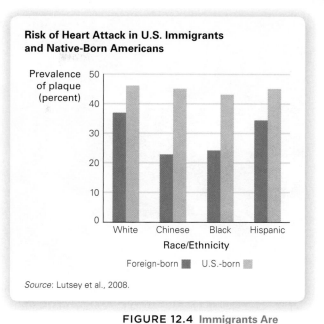

Risk of Heart Attack in U.S. Immigrants and Native-Born Americans

Source: Lutsey et al., 2008.

FIGURE 12.4 Immigrants Are Healthier Members of all these ethnic groups who were born in the United States are more likely to have arterial plaque than are their counterparts who were born elsewhere and emigrated to the United States. Plaque is a buildup of fatty substances (including cholesterol) that constricts blood flow inside an artery, increasing the risk of heart attack.

KEYpoints

- Mortality is increasingly uncommon in adulthood (ages 25 to 65): morbidity, disability, and loss of vitality remain problems.
- Smoking always harms health, but alcohol is more tricky—beneficial in moderation and lethal in excess.
- Obesity and inactivity are increasing worldwide, leading to higher rates of many diseases, especially diabetes.
- People of different ages, genders, and incomes cope with stressors in varying ways.

What Is Adult Intelligence?

You just read that both education and intelligence, measured by IQ tests, might explain why high-SES adults are healthier than those of low SES. But is there such a thing as "intelligence"? You read in Chapter 7 that intelligence in childhood correlates with school achievement, itself controversial. But what about intellectual development over the years of adulthood?

One leading theoretician, Charles Spearman (1927), proposed that there is such a thing as intelligence, a single entity that he called **general intelligence (g)**. Although *g* cannot be measured directly, it can be inferred from various abilities, such as vocabulary, memory, and reasoning.

Most experts who agree with Spearman contend that children gain in ability as they mature, and thus scores on intelligence tests take a child's age into account. Once a person reaches adulthood, an IQ score indicates whether that adult is a genius, average, or slow, no matter what the person's age. The same IQ test is taken at age 18 or 88.

The belief that *g* exists still influences thinking and testing on intelligence. Many neuroscientists seek genetic underpinnings for the intellectual differences among adults. However, efforts to find specific genes or abilities that comprise *g* have not succeeded (Deary et al., 2010; Haier et al., 2009). Some researchers believe *g* does not exist.

general intelligence (g)
The idea of *g* assumes that intelligence is one basic trait, underlying all cognitive abilities. According to this concept, people have varying levels of this general ability.

Smart Enough for the Trenches?
These young men were drafted to fight in World War I. Younger men (about age 17 or 18) did better on the military's intelligence tests than slightly older ones did.

OBSERVATION QUIZ
Beyond the test itself, what conditions of the testing favored the teenage men? (see answer, page 448) ➡

Flynn effect
The rise in average IQ scores that has occurred over the decades in many nations.

✦ **ESPECIALLY FOR Older Brothers and Sisters** If your younger siblings mock your ignorance of current TV shows and beat you at the latest video games, does that mean your intellect is fading? (see response, page 448) ➡

Research on Age and Intelligence

Research on intelligence over the years of adulthood has reached conflicting conclusions (Hertzog, 2011). Cross-sectional studies find that intellectual ability peaks in adolescence and then gradually declines. Typical 50-year-olds score lower on IQ tests than typical 25-year-olds do, and 50-year-olds score higher than typical 75-year-olds do.

However, when longitudinal research is conducted, testing the same people again and again as they age, scores improve—at least until late adulthood. Those 50-year-olds score higher than they themselves did at age 25. How could this be?

THE FLYNN EFFECT The most plausible hypothesis for the divergence between the conclusions of cross-sectional and longitudinal research begins with a fact: For most of the past century, each generation was healthier and better educated than the previous one.

In many nations, the typical 75-year-old had never attended college, but now a typical 25-year-old has some college education. Furthermore, 25-year-olds have had better childhood health (vaccines, nutrition) and more information (television, computers) available to them. That affects intelligence; younger cohorts would therefore have higher IQ scores on cross-sectional research.

The same factors explain the results of longitudinal research. Contemporary 75-year-olds have experienced those advantages as they aged, being better informed about the world than they were as children. For that reason, longitudinal research would find them scoring higher than they themselves did 50 years ago.

Powerful evidence supporting this explanation comes from test scores in many nations (Dickinson & Hiscock, 2010). In every country where data allow a valid comparison, more recent cohorts outscore previous generations tested at the same age. This is called the **Flynn effect.**

That makes it unfair—and scientifically invalid—to compare IQ scores of a cross section of adults of various ages. Older adults will score lower, but that does not mean they have lost intellectual power; quite the opposite is the case (this may not be true for the oldest adults, however; more on that in Chapter 14).

CROSS-SEQUENTIAL RESEARCH Scientists now realize that neither cross-sectional nor longitudinal research is completely accurate to ascertain age changes since historical conditions change as well (Hertzog, 2011). The best way to understand the effects of time without the confounding complications of contextual changes is to combine the two. One scholar famously pioneered this combination.

As an undergraduate in the middle of the twentieth century, K. Warner Schaie began to study adult intelligence. To obtain his PhD, he tested 500 adults, aged 20 to 50, on five standard primary mental abilities thought to be the foundation of intelligence: (1) verbal meaning (vocabulary), (2) spatial orientation, (3) inductive reasoning, (4) number ability, and (5) word fluency (rapid verbal associations).

Schaie's initial cross-sectional results showed a gradual, age-related decline in these five abilities, as others had found before him. He had read that longitudinal research found an increase in IQ, so he planned to retest his population seven years later.

He then had a brilliant idea: He would not only retest his initial participants, he would also test a new young group who were the same age as his earlier sample had been. By comparing the scores of the retested individuals with their own earlier scores *and* with the scores of a new group who were the same age as his first group had been, he hoped to learn more about age and intelligence. His results surprised the experts; he discovered cohort effects that few people had imagined earlier.

For example, each successive cohort scored higher in verbal memory and inductive reasoning but scored lower in number ability than adults who had been tested seven years earlier at the same age. That led to the hypothesis that classroom teaching affected ability: The curriculum in many U.S. schools had shifted by mid-century to emphasize reading, writing, and self-expression, not math.

Schaie found that one correlate of higher ability was intellectual complexity at work and at home, both of which tended to peak in middle age, from ages 39 to 53. Because of complexity, women of earlier cohorts, who often stayed home or had less challenging jobs, lost IQ in midlife, but this did not occur for contemporary women.

Schaie conducted the first massive *cross-sequential research* (see Chapter 1). Cross-age comparisons allowed analysis of potential influences, including retesting, cohort differences, experience, education, and gender. Every seven years for the past four decades, Schaie has tested a new group and retested his earlier participants (Schaie, 2005).

The results of this project, known as the **Seattle Longitudinal Study,** confirmed and extended what others had found: People improve in most mental abilities during adulthood. As Figure 12.5 shows, each particular ability at each age and for each gender has a distinct pattern. All abilities gradually improve and then eventually decline. Men are initially better with numbers and women with words, and that gap narrows with age.

Many other researchers have reported similar results (Alwin, 2009). For example, Paul Baltes (2003) tested hundreds of older Germans in Berlin and found that only at age 80 did every cognitive ability show age-related declines. As noted earlier in this chapter, for some people aging impairs the brain, reducing cognition. But more often adult IQ increases, or at least stays the same.

Components of Intelligence: Many and Varied

Developmentalists are now looking closely at patterns of cognitive gains and losses over the adult years. These patterns vary markedly; intelligence often rises and falls within the same person, as "vast domains of cognitive performance . . . may not follow a common, age-linked trajectory of decline" (Dannefer & Patterson, 2009, p. 116).

Seattle Longitudinal Study The first cross-sequential study of adult intelligence. This study began in 1956; the most recent testing was conducted in 2005.

FIGURE 12.5 Age Differences in Intellectual Abilities Cross-sectional data on intellectual abilities at various ages would show much steeper declines. Longitudinal research, in contrast, would show more notable rises. Because Schaie's research is cross-sequential, the trajectories it depicts are more revealing: None of the average scores for the five abilities at any age are above 55 or below 35. Because the methodology takes into account the cohort and historical effects, the age-related differences from ages 25 to 60 are very small.

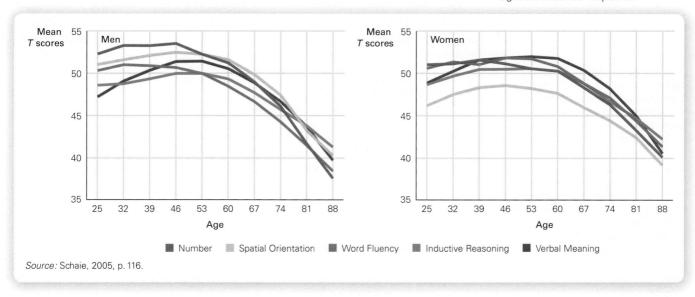

Source: Schaie, 2005, p. 116.

ANSWER TO **OBSERVATION QUIZ**
(from page 446) Sitting on the floor
with no back support, with a test paper
at a distance on your lap, and with
someone standing over you holding
a stopwatch all are enough to rattle
anyone—especially people over 18. ●

fluid intelligence
Those types of basic intelligence that
make learning of all sorts quick and
thorough. Abilities such as short-term
memory, abstract thought, and speed
of thinking are all usually considered
part of fluid intelligence.

**RESPONSE FOR Older Brothers and
Sisters** (from page 446) No. While
it is true that each new cohort might
be smarter than the previous one in
some ways, cross-sequential research
suggests that you are smarter than
you used to be. Knowing that might
help you respond wisely—smiling quietly rather than insisting that you are
superior. ●

crystallized intelligence
Those types of intellectual ability
that reflect accumulated learning.
Vocabulary and general information
are examples. Some developmental
psychologists think crystallized intelligence increases with age, while fluid
intelligence declines.

analytic intelligence
A form of intelligence that involves
such mental processes as abstract
planning, strategy selection, focused
attention, and information processing,
as well as verbal and logical skills.

creative intelligence
A form of intelligence that involves the
capacity to be intellectually flexible and
innovative.

As you remember from Chapter 7, many psychologists envision multiple intellectual abilities (Roberts & Lipnevich, 2012). One influential proposal—Gardner's theory of nine multiple intelligences, with its many implications for childhood education—was explained in Chapter 7. We now consider in detail two other proposals.

FLUID AND CRYSTALLIZED INTELLIGENCE In the 1960s, leading personality researcher Raymond Cattell teamed up with a promising graduate student, John Horn, to study intelligence tests. They concluded that adult intelligence is best understood if various measures are grouped into two categories, called fluid and crystallized.

As its name implies, **fluid intelligence** is like water, flowing to its own level no matter where it happens to be. Fluid intelligence is quick and flexible, enabling people to learn anything, even things that are unfamiliar and unconnected to what they already know. Curiosity, learning for the joy of it, and the thrill of discovering something new are marks of fluid intelligence (Silvia & Sanders, 2010).

People high in fluid abilities can draw inferences, understand relations between concepts, and quickly process new ideas and facts. They are fast and creative with words and numbers and enjoy intellectual puzzles. The kind of question that tests fluid intelligence among Western adults might be:

What comes next in each of these two series?
4 9 1 6 2 5 3
V X Z B D*

Puzzles are often used to measure fluid intelligence, with speedy solutions earning bonus points (as on many IQ tests). Efficient working memory—with immediate recall of nonsense words, of numbers, of a sentence just read—is a crucial aspect of fluid intelligence.

Since fluid intelligence seems disconnected from past learning, is it impractical? No. A study of adults aged 34 to 83 found that stresses and stressors did not vary by age but did vary by fluid intelligence. People high in fluid intelligence were more often exposed to stress but were less likely to suffer from it: They used their intellect to turn potential stressors into positive experiences (Stawski et al., 2010).

The ability to detoxify stress may be one reason that high fluid intelligence in emerging adulthood leads to longer life and higher IQ later in adulthood. Fluid intelligence is associated with openness to new experiences and overall brain health (Batterham et al., 2009; Silvia & Sanders, 2010).

By contrast, the accumulation of facts, information, and knowledge as a result of education and experience is called **crystallized intelligence.** Size of vocabulary, knowledge of chemical formulas, and memory for dates in history all indicate crystallized intelligence. Tests to measure this intelligence might include questions like these:

What is the meaning of the word *misanthrope*?
Who would hold a harpoon?
What was Sri Lanka called in 1950?†

Although questions that test for crystallized intelligence seem to measure education more than aptitude, these two are connected, especially in adulthood. Intelligent adults read widely, think deeply, and remember what they learn: Crystallized intelligence reflects fluid intelligence. Consequently, many researchers consider years of education a rough indication of IQ.

---

*The fluid intelligence answers are 6 and F, dependent on knowledge of the times tables and alphabet, although other answers are possible.

†The answers for crystallized intelligence might be: someone who dislikes people; a fisherman who caught whales or swordfish in the past; Ceylon.

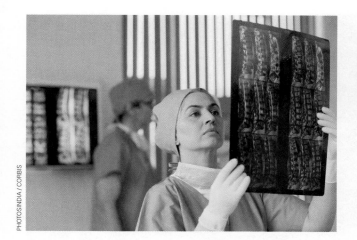

PHOTOSINDIA / CORBIS

JEFF GREENBERG / PHOTOEDIT

Think Before Acting Both these adults need to combine fluid and crystallized intelligence, insight and intuition, logic and experience. One *(left)* is a surgeon, studying X-rays before picking up her scalpel. The other *(right)* is a court reporter for a TV station, jotting notes during a lunch recess before delivering her on-camera report on a trial.

Age complicates the calculation of adult IQ. Scores on items measuring fluid intelligence decrease with age since everything in the brain as well as the body slows down. However, if a person continues to read and think, scores on items measuring crystallized intelligence increase. These two clusters, changing in opposite directions, make a person's IQ score (composed of diverse subtests) fairly steady from ages 30 to 70, even though particular abilities change.

Barring pathology, the brain slowdown is rarely apparent until massive declines in fluid intelligence begin to affect crystallized intelligence, perhaps at age 70 or so. It may be foolish to try to measure *g*, a single omnibus intelligence, because both fluid and crystallized intelligence need to be measured separately.

When thinking about age changes in fluid and crystallized intelligence, note the connection between speed and IQ. Many items that test fluid intelligence are timed, with extra points for quick answers. In a culture that values youth, abilities that favor the young (e.g., fast reaction time, capacious short-term memory) are central to success on psychometric intelligence tests, whereas the strengths of older adults (e.g., emotional regulation and the upholding of traditional values) are not.

Thus, fluid intelligence is valued in a youth-oriented culture more than crystallized intelligence. A word often used to describe a highly intelligent person is *quick,* whereas a stupid person is called *slow*—exactly what happens with age. Perhaps the assumptions that led to the creation of IQ tests are faulty when applied to adults.

THREE FORMS OF INTELLIGENCE: STERNBERG Robert Sternberg (1988, 2003) agrees that the notion of a single intelligence score is misleading. As first mentioned in Chapter 7, Sternberg proposed three fundamental forms of intelligence: analytic, creative, and practical. Each can be tested.

Analytic intelligence includes all the mental processes that foster academic proficiency. It draws on abstract planning, strategy selection, focused attention, memory, and information processing, as well as on verbal and logical skills. Strengths in those areas are particularly valuable for younger adults, in higher education and job training. Multiple-choice tests and brief essays that call forth remembered information, with one and only one right answer, indicate analytic intelligence.

Creative intelligence involves the capacity to be intellectually flexible and innovative. Creative thinking is divergent rather than convergent, valuing unexpected, imaginative, and unusual thoughts rather than standard and conventional ones. Sternberg developed tests of creative intelligence that include writing a short story titled "The Octopus's Sneakers" or planning an advertising campaign for a new doorknob. High scores are earned by those with many unusual ideas.

PHOTO COURTESY OF JESSICA BAYNE / WECHSLER ADULT INTELLIGENCE SCALE, FOURTH EDITION (WAIS-IV). COPYRIGHT © 2008 NCS PEARSON, INC. REPRODUCED WITH PERMISSION. ALL RIGHTS RESERVED.

Quick and Smart Rotate the cubes until they match the picture: The faster you succeed at this task, the higher your IQ. Are speeded tests equally fair at every age? ["Wechsler Adult Intelligence Scale" and "WAIS" are trademarks, in the US and/or other countries, of Pearson Education, Inc. or its affiliate(s).]

Smart Farmer; Smart Teacher This creative field trip is not to a museum or a fire station but to a wheat field, where children study grains that will become bread. Like this teacher, modern farmers use every kind of intelligence. To succeed they need to decide what crops and seed varieties to plant; to anticipate market prices; and to analyze soil, fertilizer, pests, and so on.

practical intelligence
The intellectual skills used in everyday problem solving. (Sometimes called *tacit intelligence*.)

✦ **ESPECIALLY FOR Prospective Parents** In terms of the intellectual challenge, what type of intelligence is most needed for effective parenting? (see response, page 452) →

Practical intelligence involves the capacity to adapt to the demands of a given situation. This includes an accurate grasp of the expectations and needs of the people involved and an awareness of the particular skills that are called for, along with the ability to use these insights effectively. If employers want to assess practical intelligence, they might test workers with a case study or see how they function on the job.

Practical intelligence is sometimes called *tacit intelligence* because it is not obvious on tests. Instead it comes from "the school of hard knocks" and is sometimes called "street smarts," not "book smarts."

Practical intelligence is needed in adulthood. It allows a person to manage the conflicting personalities in a family or to convince members of an organization (e.g., a business, a social group, or a school) to do something. Ideally, practical intelligence gradually builds over the years, as people learn from experience. Flexibility is also needed, as you will soon see in the discussion of expertise (K. Sloan, 2009).

Without practical intelligence, a solution found by analytic intelligence is doomed to fail because people resist academic brilliance as unrealistic and elite. Similarly, a stunningly creative idea may be rejected as ridiculous without practical intelligence.

Sternberg believes that each of these three forms of intelligence is useful; adults ideally deploy the strengths and guard against the limitations of each. Choosing which type of intelligence to use takes wisdom, which Sternberg has added as a fourth ingredient of successful intelligence. He writes:

> One needs creativity to generate novel ideas, analytical intelligence to ascertain whether they are good ideas, practical intelligence to implement the ideas and persuade others of their value, and wisdom to ensure that the ideas help reach a common goal.

[Sternberg, 2012, p. 21]

Think about these intelligences cross-culturally. Each type might be more appreciated in some cultures than in others. For example, analytic individuals would do well in college but might then be seen as arrogant, criticized for being the "elite." Creative individuals are critical of tradition and would be tolerated only in some political environments (Sternberg, 2006b). Practical intelligence might be particularly

FREDRICK ONYANGO

BLUE JEAN IMAGES / GETTY IMAGES

needed when traditional customs and practices no longer seem useful. Wisdom, at least in popular understanding, increases with age, as described in Chapter 14, but some cultures respect the aged more than others do: Wisdom might be devalued as old-fashioned.

The fact that those who do well in college might not adapt well to real life in a developing nation raises the question—what do adults need to do in order to succeed? In a knowledge economy, analytic intelligence may be crucial . . . or may not be. Opposing perspectives on this are illustrated by asking, "What makes a good parent?"

Same Situation, Far Apart: Men at Work The bean merchant in Nairobi, Kenya *(left)*, and the construction supervisor in Beijing, China *(right)*, have much in common: They are high in practical intelligence and they love their jobs. Context is also crucial since, if they traded places, each would be lost at first. However, practical intelligence could save the day—a few months of intensive instruction might enable each to master his new role.

OPPOSING PERSPECTIVES

What Makes a Good Parent?

Tests of good infant care have been developed, based primarily on analytic, not practical, child rearing (e.g., McCall et al., 2010). One of the most common scales is the *Knowledge of Infant Development Inventory* (KIDI) (MacPhee, 1981). KIDI measures how much caregivers know about infant senses, motor skills, and communication—such as at what age an infant is expected to sit up or whether parents should talk to preverbal babies.

Such knowledge seems helpful. For example, mothers and fathers who score higher on the KIDI are less depressed and more likely to provide responsive baby care (Howard, 2010; Zolotor et al., 2008). Many researchers believe that knowledge of infant development causes (not merely correlates with) good care.

Should we worry when mothers do not know about their babies' growth? Perhaps. For instance, in one study only 29 percent of immigrant mothers knew that 2-month-olds can distinguish one speech sound from another, an item on the KIDI. The researchers suggest that those mothers are less able to advance their infants' language and social skills, handicapping the children later on (Bornstein & Cote, 2007).

The opposing perspective suggests that knowledge of infant development does not matter in caregiving. A study supporting this view found that an immigrant child's later cognitive development was best predicted not by KIDI scores or other measures of parenting, but by parents' SES and language use. In this longitudinal study, the mothers' KIDI scores did not predict later school success for Asian American or Latino children, but it did for European American children (Han et al., 2012).

In another study, researchers provided supportive, encouraging visitors to low-income, unmarried mothers—many of whom did not plan or want their babies. Compared with a control group with no visits, and even compared with mothers in the intervention group who had relatively few home visits, mothers who were visited 30 or more times became better infant caregivers. However, both before and after many visits, the KIDI scores of the mothers were low. The authors of the study write:

> A significant impact of this intervention was its effect on the mothers' ability to create home environments more suitable for the needs of their infants . . . despite lack

of measurable change in mothers' knowledge of infant development.

[Katz et al., 2011, p. S81]

In other words, advances in practical skills, not analytic ones, made a difference.

Knowledge may not improve parenting. Instead, warmth and patience, responsiveness (without expecting an infant to reciprocate), mental health, or social support networks may be more critical than knowledge.

Part of the underlying reason why tests of knowledge do not always predict good parenting is that cultures vary in what they believe about infant development. For example, an anthropologist studied the Ache in Paraguay. They were respectful and deferential to her on repeated visits, until she and her husband

> arrived at their study site in the forest of Paraguay with their infant daughter in tow. The Ache greeted her in a whole new way. They took her aside and in friendly and intimate but no-nonsense terms told her all the things she was doing wrong as a mother. . . . "This older woman sat with me and told me I *must* sleep with my daughter. They were horrified that I brought a basket with me for her to sleep in." Here was a group of forest hunter-gatherers, people living in what Westerners would call basic conditions, giving instructions to a highly educated woman from a technologically sophisticated culture.
>
> *[Small, 1998, p. 213]*

How important to quality care is accurate knowledge of child development? I am not neutral on this question; I have devoted much of my life to teaching about child develop-

ment. Yet the most important aspects of good parenting may not be information, and the sign of an intelligent adult may be something other than analytic intelligence. This box raises these issues, but I still believe in teaching. If I become convinced that responsiveness is more important than knowledge, I will try to teach it.

Keep Him Close Mothers everywhere keep their toddlers nearby, but it is particularly important in an environment where poisonous spiders and plants thrive. Thus, you can see why this Ache mother physically protects her son much more than would a typical North American mother—who might instead watch her son play in the house after removing small objects and covering the electric outlets.

TERRY WHITTAKER / ALAMY

RESPONSE FOR Prospective Parents (from page 450) Because parenthood demands flexibility and patience, Sternberg's practical intelligence or Gardner's social understanding is probably most needed. Anything that involves finding a single correct answer, such as analytic intelligence or number ability, would not be much help. ●

KEY points

- Cross-sectional research shows declines in the IQ scores of adults, longitudinal research shows increases, and cross-sequential research shows cohort effects.
- Worldwide improvements in health and education have advanced adult intelligence.
- Fluid intelligence declines with age; crystallized intelligence advances.
- Analytic, creative, and practical intelligence are each more important in certain contexts and cultures than in others.

Selective Gains and Losses

Aging neurons, cultural pressures, historical conditions, and past schooling all affect adult cognition, as just reviewed. None of these is under direct individual control.

However, adults can choose what abilities to nurture. For example, many adults use calculators instead of paper-and-pencil (or mental) calculations to do math. If adults threw out their calculators, would their math skills improve? Probably. But most adults would not choose to do so. They prefer to let their math skills languish.

Optimization with Compensation

Paul and Margret Baltes (1990) developed a theory, called **selective optimization with compensation,** to describe the "general process of systematic function" (P. B. Baltes, 2003, p. 25) as older adults maintain a balance in their lives. The idea is that people seek to *optimize* their development, looking for the best ways to *compensate* for losses and to become more proficient at activities they want to perform well.

Selective optimization helps explain the variations in intellectual abilities just reviewed. As other research has found, when older adults are motivated to do well, few age-related deficits are apparent. However, compared with younger adults, older adults are typically less motivated to put forth their best effort when the task at hand is not particularly engaging (Hess et al., 2009). Quick responses are more valued by the young than the old. Often people prefer the easy way over the way that will challenge their intellect.

SPECIALIZED LEARNING Specialization works as follows. Suppose a man who was interested in one area of the world noticed that aging affected his vision and memory. He might compensate by buying reading glasses, increasing the type size on his computer, and keeping a file or notebook for whatever he reads about that area, sometimes rereading it. He might be selective, skipping over most of the news that he used to read. In that way, he would still know more about his particular specialty (optimization) than anyone else.

Selective optimization with compensation may be particularly crucial on the job, as older workers notice that some tasks now take longer or are more difficult for them to do. If they use compensation strategies, they are more likely to see opportunities for continued growth and improvement, making the job more interesting to them (Zacher & Frese, 2011).

An example that may be familiar to everyone is multitasking, which becomes more difficult with every passing decade (Reuter-Lorenz & Sylvester, 2005). "I can't do everything at once" is more often said by adults than by teenagers because adults have learned to be selective, compensating for slower thinking by concentrating on one task at a time. Resources—of the brain as well as material resources—may be increasingly limited with age, but compensation allows optimal functioning (Freund, 2008).

Selective optimization with compensation applies to every aspect of life, from choosing friends to playing baseball. Each adult seeks to maximize gains and minimize losses, choosing to practice some abilities and ignore others. Choices are critical because every ability can be enhanced or diminished, depending on how, when, and why a person uses it. It is possible to "teach an old dog new tricks," but adults need to choose and practice the tricks.

Particularly relevant may be the selection of cognitive abilities. As Baltes and Baltes (1990) explain, selective optimization means that each person optimizes some intellectual abilities and neglects others. If the ignored abilities are the ones measured by IQ tests, then IQ scores fall. This would occur even though other abilities increase.

SELECTION AND ACTION Selective optimization is the probable explanation for the continued intellectual ability of adults. However, the concept is most easily demonstrated by brain activity that involves the motor system, not disembodied thinking (Beilock, 2010).

For example, experienced typists scan more letters at a time to compensate for slower finger action, chefs prepare more foods in advance to avoid having multiple

selective optimization with compensation
The theory, developed by Paul and Margret Baltes, that people try to maintain a balance in their lives by looking for the best way to compensate for physical and cognitive losses and to become more proficient in activities they can already do well.

RYAN MCGINNIS / ALAMY

Focus It might seem as if Cindy Fay, shown here, has too many distractions to get anything done, but this scene actually depicts her intense, productive focus. She is a meteorologist for the National Weather Service, focused on predicting the weather in the next 24 hours in Hastings, Nebraska. The monitors, phones, keyboards, and notes on her expansive desk are all carefully selected to optimize her forecasting ability.

pots on the stove at once, waitresses use downtime to establish rapport with other employees. Each of these occupations has been studied, with efficiency more apparent in experienced workers because of compensatory moves.

The most frequently studied action-based compensation is that of professional sports players, probably because optimal performance is worth millions (Ajemian et al., 2010). Apparently, athletes need to practice and warm up to activate the neurological connections in their brains that allow the quick and precise movements to hit a baseball, throw a basketball, kick a football, and so on. If they are not selective in their neurological activity, and they allow interference from memory or emotion, they risk failure.

Thus, when star athletes are asked the secret of their success, they often do not know or remember because memory and emotion must shut down in order for professional expertise to focus solely on performance. According to a cognitive psychologist, "That's why they usually thank God or their moms. They don't know what they did, so they don't know what else to say" (Beilock, quoted in Bascom, 2012, p. 22).

Expert Cognition

Another way to express this idea is to say that everyone can develop expertise, specializing in activities that are personally meaningful—whether that be car repair, gourmet cooking, illness diagnosis, or fly fishing. As people develop expertise in some areas, they pay less attention to others. For example, adults tune out most channels on the TV, and some never go to events that others pay hundreds of dollars to attend.

Culture and context guide all of us in selecting areas of expertise. Many adults born 60 years ago are much better than more recent cohorts at writing letters with distinctive but legible handwriting. Because of their childhood culture, they selected and practiced penmanship, became expert in it, and maintained that expertise.

Today's schools and children make other choices: Reading, for instance, is now crucial for every child, unlike a century ago when adult illiteracy was common. Younger adults grew up with various technological devices; some older adults are still cautious in programming everything from smart phones to video screens.

Experts, as cognitive scientists define them, are not necessarily those with rare and outstanding proficiency. Although sometimes the term *expert* connotes an extraordinary genius, to researchers it means more—and less—than that. An **expert** is notably more accomplished, proficient, and knowledgeable in a

Experts All Every adult is an expert. Shown here (clockwise from top left): a Borek (a Turkish delicacy) baker at the market, a connoisseur evaluating the bouquet of a costly red wine, a musician playing the didgeridoo, and a professor in her biology lab. Most of us would be inept and bewildered in those roles. However, when I asked my students about their expertise, each knew a great deal about something unfamiliar to others—bluegrass music, artistic makeup, Nigerian cuisine, police procedures, professional baseball, and more.

particular skill, topic, or task than the average person (Charness & Krampe, 2008; Ericsson, 2009).

Expertise is not innate, nor does it always correlate with basic abilities (such as the five abilities measured in the Seattle Longitudinal Study). However, genetic predispositions may incline a person to be better at some skills than others. Expert language interpreters, for instance, might have been born with brain capacity to understand dialect, but they also need years of training and experience to become expert (Golestani et al., 2011).

An expert is not simply someone who knows more about something, or who has done it often. At a certain tipping point, accumulated knowledge, practice, and experience become transformative, changing the brain, putting the expert in a different league (Ericsson, 2009; Wan et al., 2011). The quality as well as the quantity of cognition is advanced. Expert thought is (1) intuitive, (2) automatic, (3) strategic, and (4) flexible, as we now describe.

INTUITIVE Novices follow formal procedures and rules. Experts rely more on their past experiences and on immediate contexts. Their actions are therefore more intuitive and less stereotypic. The role of experience and intuition is evident, for example, during surgery. Outsiders might think medicine is straightforward, but experts understand the reality:

> Hospitals are filled with varieties of knives and poisons. Every time a medication is prescribed, there is potential for an unintended side effect. In surgery, collateral damage is inherent. External tissue must be cut to allow internal access so that a diseased organ may be removed, or some other manipulation may be performed to return the patient to better health.
>
> *[Dominguez, 2001, p. 287]*

In one study, many surgeons saw the same videotape of a gallbladder operation and were asked to talk about it. The experienced surgeons anticipated and described problems twice as often as did the residents (who had also removed gallbladders, just not as many) (Dominguez, 2001). Data on physicians indicate that the single most important question to ask a surgeon is, "How often have you performed this operation?" The novice, even with the best, most recent training, is less skilled than the expert.

On the other hand, motivation and training are crucial. Another study found that the number of years since a doctor was in medical school correlated *negatively* with proficiency (Choudhry, 2005). Obviously, when experience leads to habits that should change because of more recent advances, then simply having done something the same old way a thousand times does not mean that the task is performed better than someone who uses a better technique, learned recently, and performed only 50 times. Intuition arises from practice, but practice does not always lead to intuition.

A different experiment that studied the relationship between expertise and intuition centered on predicting winners of several soccer matches, either instantly or after two minutes. College students who were avid fans made more accurate predictions when they had two minutes of unconscious thought (they were required to perform difficult math calculations and then give their answer) compared with when they had two minutes to mull over their choice (see Figure 12.6). In this, intuition trumped conscious thought.

When given the same task, college students who didn't care much about soccer (the nonexperts) did worse overall, as expected, but the surprising result is that intuition didn't help at all: They did

expert
One who is notably more accomplished, proficient, and/or knowledgeable in a particular skill, topic, or task than the average person.

expertise
A person's ability to be more accomplished at a particular skill, or to have better knowledge of a particular subject, than the average person.

FIGURE 12.6 If You Don't Know, Don't Think! Undergraduates at the University of Amsterdam were asked to predict winners of four World Cup soccer matches in one of three conditions: (1) immediate—as soon as they saw the names of the nations that were competing in each of the contests, (2) conscious—after thinking for two minutes about their answers, and (3) unconscious—after two minutes of solving distracting math tasks. As you can see, the experts were better at predicting winners after unconscious processing, but the nonexperts became less accurate when they thought about their answers, either consciously or unconsciously.

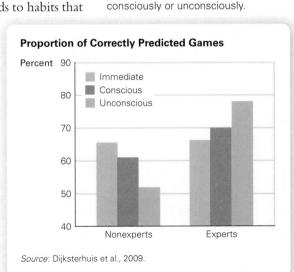

Proportion of Correctly Predicted Games

Source: Dijksterhuis et al., 2009.

worst of all when they had two minutes of the same math problems that helped the experts (Dijksterhuis et al., 2009).

This experiment suggests that intuition, here occurring unconsciously, helps experts but not those who are nonexperts. The latter gain nothing from thinking it over, either consciously or not.

automatic processing
Thinking that occurs without deliberate, conscious thought. Experts process most tasks automatically, saving conscious thought for unfamiliar challenges.

AUTOMATIC **Automatic processing** is thought to be a crucial reason why expert chess and Go players are much better at the game than are novices. They see a configuration of game pieces and automatically encode it as a whole, rather than analyzing it bit by bit.

A study of expert chess players (aged 17 to 81) found minor age-related declines, but expertise was much more important than age. This was particularly apparent for speedy recognition that the king was threatened: Older experts did it almost as quickly (within a fraction of a second) as younger experts despite far steeper, age-related declines on standard tests of memory and speed (Jastrzembski et al., 2006).

Many elements of expert performance are automatic. The complex action and thought required for performance have become routine, making it appear that most aspects of the task are performed instinctively. Experts process incoming information more quickly and analyze it more efficiently than do nonexperts. They then act in well-rehearsed ways that make their efforts appear unconscious.

In fact, some automatic actions are no longer accessible to the conscious mind. For example, adults are much better at tying their shoelaces than children are (adults can do it in the dark), but they are much worse at describing how they do it (McLeod et al., 2005). When experts think, they engage in "automatic weighting" of various unverbalized factors (Dijksterhuis et al., 2009, p. 1382).

This is apparent if you are an experienced driver and have attempted to teach someone else to drive. Excellent drivers who are inexperienced instructors find it hard to recognize or verbalize things that have become automatic—such as noticing pedestrians and cyclists on the far side of the road, or feeling the car shift gears as it heads up an incline, or hearing the tires lose traction on a bit of sand. Yet such factors differentiate the expert from the novice.

This may explain why, despite powerful motivation, quicker reactions, and better vision, teenagers have far more car accidents than middle-aged drivers do. Sometimes teenage drivers deliberately take risks (speeding, running a red light, etc.), but more often they simply misjudge and misperceive conditions that a more experienced driver would automatically notice.

Automaticity is particularly crucial if a person's conscious mind is focused on something else, which is why many U.S. states do not allow a teenager to drive with other teen passengers in the car (Zernike, 2012). By contrast, adult drivers automatically ignore passengers when their unconscious alert system signals that focused attention is needed.

The relationship among expertise, age, and automaticity is not straightforward. Time is only one of the essential requirements for expertise. Not everyone becomes an expert over time (depending on the task), but everyone needs months—or even years—of deliberate practice to develop expertise (Ericsson et al., 2006).

Some researchers think practice must be extensive—several hours a day for at least 10 years (Charness et al., 1996; Ericsson, 1996)—but that may be true in only some areas, not all. Circumstances, training, talent, ability, practice, and age all affect expertise, which means that experts in one specific field are often quite inexpert in other areas.

STRATEGIC The third characteristic of experts is that they have more and better strategies, especially when problems are unexpected (Ormerod, 2005). Indeed, strategy may be the most crucial difference between a skilled person and an unskilled one. Expert chess players not only have general strategies for winning, but they also have specific plans for the possibilities after a move—that is their specialty (Bilalić et al., 2009).

Similarly, a strategy used by expert team leaders in the military and in civilian life is ongoing communication and reminders, especially during slow times. Consequently, when stress builds, no team member misinterprets the rehearsed plans, commands, and requirements. You have likely witnessed the same phenomenon in expert professors: They put well-developed strategies in place during the early weeks to avoid problems later on.

An intriguing study of age and strategy in job effectiveness comes from an occupation most everyone is familiar with: driving a taxi. In major cities, taxi drivers must find the best route (factoring in traffic, construction, time of day, and many other details), all while knowing where new passengers are likely to be found, as well as how to relate to customers, some of whom might want to chat, others not.

Research in England—where taxi drivers "have to learn the layout of 25,000 streets in London and the locations of thousands of places of interest, and pass stringent examinations" (Woollett et al., 2009, p. 1407)—found not only that the drivers became more expert with time, but also that their brains adjusted to the need for particular knowledge.

In fact, some regions of English taxi drivers' brains (areas thought to help with spatial representation) were more extensive and active than those of an average person (Woollett et al., 2009). On ordinary IQ tests, their scores were typical, but in navigating London, expertise was apparent. Other studies also show that people become more expert, and that their brains adapt, as they practice various skills (Park & Reuter-Lorenz, 2009).

Of course, strategies themselves need to be updated as situations change—and no chess game, or battle, or class is exactly like another. The monthly fire drill required by some schools, the standard lecture given by some professors, and the pat safety instructions read by airline attendants before takeoff become less effective than when they were first used. People tune them out.

I recently heard a flight attendant precede his standard talk with, "For those of you who have not ridden in an automobile since 1960, this is how you buckle a seat belt." That was one of the few times I actually listened to all the words.

In one study of pilots, the older ones were as proficient as the younger ones in following flight instructions because they compensated by taking better notes. In fact, these researchers found no differences in the read-back proficiency among experienced pilots of three age groups: 22 to 40, 50 to 59, and 60 to 76 (Morrow et al., 2003).

This does not mean, of course, that strategy always overcomes age deficits. In another study of airplane pilots (aged 19 to 79) conducted with a flight simulator, the decision of whether to land in the fog involved more risk with increasing age, not the other way around. Older adult pilots had some strengths—they were quicker to begin necessary actions needed for a safe landing in difficult weather—but the older pilots had slower processing skills. When confronted with many indicators of weather and flight, they were less skilled than their younger colleagues at the necessary split-second judgments required in this simulation (Kennedy et al., 2010).

FLEXIBLE Finally, perhaps because they are intuitive, automatic, and strategic thinkers, experts are also more flexible. The expert artist, musician, or scientist is creative and curious, deliberately experimenting, enjoying the challenge when things do not go according to plan (Csikszentmihalyi, 1996).

Consider the expert surgeon, who takes the most complex cases and prefers unusual patients over typical ones because operating on them might bring sudden, unexpected complications. Compared with the novice, the expert surgeon is not only more likely to notice telltale signs (an unexpected lesion, an oddly shaped organ, a rise or drop in a vital sign) that may signal a problem, but is also more flexible and more willing to deviate from standard textbook procedures if those procedures prove ineffective (Patel et al., 1999).

In the same way, experts in all walks of life adapt to individual cases and exceptions—like an expert chef who adjusts ingredients, temperature, technique, and timing as a dish develops, tasting to see if a little more ginger is needed, seldom following a recipe exactly. Standards are high: Some chefs throw food in the garbage rather than serve a dish that many people would happily eat. Expert chess players, auto mechanics, and violinists are similarly aware of nuances that might escape the novice.

Jenny, Again

The research on expertise focuses on job-related learning, but the most important aspect of adult life may be responding to other people—especially children and partners. Years of experience in human relationships may sometimes make adults more intuitive, automatic, strategic, and flexible. For example, many parents find themselves less anxious about their second or third baby than their first, and grandparents may be more responsive and patient with children than they were as parents.

A dispassionate analysis of Jenny's situation when she consulted me would conclude that another baby—with no marriage, no job, and an apartment in the south Bronx—would doom her to poor health, poor prospects, and a depressing life. This is not a stereotype: The data show that lifelong poverty is the usual future for low-income mothers who have another child, out-of-wedlock, with another man.

But statistics do not reflect Jenny's intelligence, creativity, and practical expertise. She already had a habit of gathering social support, evident by her seeking me out. She was not daunted by her poverty; remember, she found many free activities for her children to enjoy, including sending them on vacation in the country. She was exceptional, but not unique: Some low-income people overcome the potential stressors of poverty (Chen & Miller, 2012).

Jenny used her knowledge well. She asked Billy to be tested for sickle-cell anemia (it was negative), and she knew she should be honest with him. She told him she would have the baby, which was not his choice but one he admired. She continued to encourage her children in public school and established friendships with some of their teachers, who in turn gave them special attention.

After she had the baby (a healthy, full-term girl), she interviewed for a city job tutoring children in her home; that way, she could earn money while caring for her newborn. I brought baby clothes to her railroad apartment in the projects one day and noticed her framed Bronx Community College associate's degree diploma wasn't displayed anywhere; she explained that she took it off the wall, fearing that the job agency might think she was overqualified. That was expertise: She got the tutoring job.

When her baby was a little older, Jenny headed back to college, earning her BA on a full scholarship. Her professors recognized her intelligence: She was chosen to give the student speech at graduation. She then found work as a receptionist in a city hospital, a job that provided day care and health benefits. That allowed her to move her family to a better neighborhood of the Bronx.

Billy would sometimes visit Jenny and the daughter he had not wanted. His wife became suspicious and hired a detective to follow him—and then gave him an ultimatum: Stop seeing Jenny or obtain a divorce. At that point, it was very obvious that Jenny had some insight into human relations that I did not recognize in my office years earlier—because Billy chose divorce and then married her. Within a few years, Jenny, Billy, and the children moved to Florida, where she got a master's degree (she phoned me to say she was assigned my textbook to read) and then a professional job in the school system.

The last time I saw her, I learned that she bikes, swims, and gardens every day. I met her speech-impaired son: He not only overcame his speech problem, he earned a PhD in psychology. Both her daughters are also college graduates.

Not everyone becomes an expert in human relations. But one lesson from this chapter is that health, intelligence, and even wisdom may improve over the years of adulthood. As further explained in Chapter 13, adult choices made, and relationships tended, make a difference—true for Jenny and for us all.

KEY points

- Adults compensate for deficits, selecting what particular skills and abilities to optimize.
- Expertise is developed over the years as adults become more intuitive, automatic, strategic, and flexible in their thinking and actions regarding what task they have chosen as their specialty.
- Some people become experts in human relations, able to accurately assess their own abilities and the motivations of other people.

SUMMARY

Senescence

1. Senescence causes a universal slowdown during adulthood, but aging is often imperceptible because organ reserve maintains capacity. The entire body adjusts to changes in the short term (homeostasis) and the long term (allostasis).

2. Sexual satisfaction may improve with age, but infertility becomes more common. Sperm count gradually decreases in men, and every step of female reproduction—ovulation, implantation, fetal growth, labor, and birth—slows down. For both sexes, STIs interfere with healthy reproduction. Overall good health, especially sexual health, correlates with fertility.

3. A number of assisted reproductive technology (ART) procedures, including in vitro fertilization (IVF), offer potential answers to infertility. Donor sperm, donor ova, and/or donor wombs have helped millions of infertile couples become parents.

4. The brain slows down and begins a gradual decline. The brain benefits from measures to improve overall health, especially exercise, and is harmed by most psychoactive drugs.

5. Senescence is apparent in the senses, notably vision and hearing. Everyone becomes more farsighted and less able to hear high-frequency sounds as they age.

6. Appearance also changes with age, as evident in less elastic skin, more wrinkles, less hair, and more fat. Ease of movement decreases as people become less agile.

7. At menopause, ovulation ceases and estrogen is markedly reduced. Hormone production declines more gradually in men. For both sexes, hormone replacement therapy (HRT) should be used cautiously, if at all.

Health Habits and Age

8. Mortality, morbidity, disability, and vitality are all measures of health, each overlapping but distinct. During adulthood (ages 25 to 65), mortality is unusual in developed nations, unless drug abuse (including smoking and drinking) is severe.

9. Adults in North America smoke cigarettes much less often than they once did, and rates of lung cancer and other diseases are falling, largely for that reason. Alcohol abuse remains a major health problem worldwide.

10. Good health habits include exercising regularly and not gaining weight. On both these counts, today's adults are less healthy than prior generations. This is especially true in the United States.

11. People experience many stresses over the 40 years of adulthood. They use various coping measures, both problem-focused

and emotion-focused, to prevent stresses from becoming stressors. Low income correlates with many measures of poor health.

What Is Adult Intelligence?

12. It was traditionally assumed that there is one general intelligence (*g*), measurable by IQ tests. Cross-sectional research found that *g* decreased over adulthood. However, longitudinal research found that IQ scores increased in adulthood, particularly in tests of vocabulary. In addition, James Flynn found that average IQ scores increased over the twentieth century, perhaps due to education and health.

13. Much depends on how intelligence is defined and measured. Crystallized intelligence, reflecting accumulated knowledge, increases, but fluid, flexible reasoning declines in adults.

14. Sternberg proposed three fundamental forms of intelligence: analytic, creative, and practical. Cultural values encourage development of some cognitive abilities more than others. Each person responds to these cultural priorities, which may not be reflected in IQ scores.

Selective Gains and Losses

15. As people grow older, they select certain aspects of their lives to focus on, optimizing development in those areas and compensating for declines in others. Applied to cognition, this means that people become selective experts in whatever intellectual skills they choose to develop. Meanwhile, abilities that are not exercised may fade.

16. In addition to being more experienced, experts are better thinkers than novices because they are more intuitive; their cognitive processes are automatic, often seeming to require little conscious thought; they use more and better strategies to perform whatever task is required; and they are more flexible in their thinking.

17. Experienced adults may surpass younger adults if they specialize and harness their efforts, compensating for any deficits that may appear. According to a study of taxi drivers in London, brains grow to support selective expertise.

KEY TERMS

allostasis (p. 428)
analytic intelligence (p. 449)
andropause (p. 435)
automatic processing (p. 456)
creative intelligence (p. 449)
crystallized intelligence (p. 448)
emotion-focused coping (p. 443)

expert (p. 454)
expertise (p. 455)
fluid intelligence (p. 448)
Flynn effect (p. 446)
general intelligence (*g*) (p. 445)
homeostasis (p. 428)
hormone replacement therapy (HRT) (p. 435)

in vitro fertilization (IVF) (p. 431)
infertility (p. 430)
menopause (p. 434)
organ reserve (p. 428)
practical intelligence (p. 450)
problem-focused coping (p. 443)

Seattle Longitudinal Study (p. 447)
selective optimization with compensation (p. 453)
senescence (p. 428)
stressor (p. 442)

WHAT HAVE YOU LEARNED?

1. How often and why do people lose significant brain function before age 65?

2. How do vision and hearing change during adulthood?

3. What visible changes take place in the skin and hair between ages 25 and 65?

4. What visible changes take place in body shape between ages 25 and 65?

5. What aspects of body functioning keep adults from recognizing that their bodies are working less well over time?

6. How are men and women affected by the changes in sexual responsiveness with age?

7. What are some of the factors that diminish fertility?

8. How have advances in medicine helped people with fertility problems?

9. What are the advantages and disadvantages of HRT for women?

10. Why do many doctors consider the term *andropause* misleading?

11. What changes in tobacco use have occurred, where, and with what consequences?

12. How does obesity affect health and well-being?

13. What are some solutions to obesity? What drawbacks are there to these solutions?

14. What diseases and conditions are less likely in people who exercise every day?

15. In what different ways do men and women deal with stress? What biological factors help explain these differences?

16. Why have traditional diseases of affluence become more common among the poor?

17. Why does health vary between and within SES and ethnic groups?

18. What differing opinions exist about *g*?

19. What does cross-sectional research on IQ scores throughout adulthood usually find? What does longitudinal research on IQ scores throughout adulthood usually find?

20. Why do cross-sectional and longitudinal studies of intelligence reach different conclusions?

21. How does cross-sequential research control for cohort effects?

22. How is fluid intelligence different from crystallized intelligence?

23. What are Sternberg's three fundamental forms of intelligence?

24. What is the basic idea of selective optimization with compensation?

25. What might a person do to optimize ability in some area not discussed in the book, such as playing the flute, growing tomatoes, or building a cabinet?

26. How do athletes compensate for the physical losses that come with age?

27. What factors contribute to expertise?

28. Using a specific example, demonstrate how an expert's intuition might aid ability.

29. How does automatic thinking lead to expert performance?

30. Why might strategy be the most important difference between a skilled person and an unskilled one?

31. Give an example of how an expert in a profession of your choice might think flexibly.

APPLICATIONS

1. Guess the ages of five people you know and then ask them how old they are. Analyze the clues you used for your guesses and the people's reactions to your question.

2. Find a speaker willing to come to your class who is an expert on weight loss, adult health, smoking, or drinking. Write a one-page proposal explaining why you think this speaker would be good and what topics he or she should address. Give this proposal to your instructor, with contact information for your speaker. The instructor can call the potential speakers, thank them for their willingness, and decide whether to actually invite them to speak.

3. The importance of context and culture is illustrated by the things that people think are basic knowledge. Choose a partner, and each of you write four questions that you think are hard but fair as measures of general intelligence. Then give your test to your partner and answer the four questions that person has prepared for you. What did you learn from the results?

4. Skill at video games is sometimes thought to reflect intelligence. Interview three or four people who play such games. What abilities do they think video games require? What do you think these games reflect in terms of experience, age, and motivation?

>>ONLINE CONNECTIONS

To accompany your textbook, you have access to a number of online resources, including quizzes for every chapter of the book, flashcards (in English and Spanish), critical-thinking questions, and case studies. For access to any of these links, go to www.worthpublishers.com/bergerinvitation2e. In addition to these free resources, you'll also find links to podcasts, video clips, diagnostic quizzing with personalized study advice, and an ebook. Some of the videos and activities available online include:

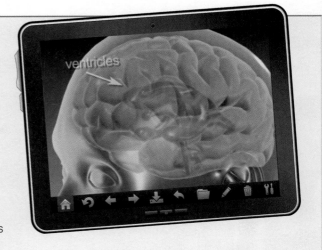

- *Brain Development: Middle Adulthood.* Animations show age-related loss of brain volume and compensatory increase in size of the ventricles and volume of cerebrospinal fluid.

- *Development of Expertise.* Expertise involves analytic, creative, and practical intelligence, but what makes it happen? Research shows that talent is not enough—practice, practice, practice!

CHAPTER OUTLINE

ADULTHOOD:
Psychosocial Development

WHAT WILL YOU KNOW?

- Do adults still have the personality they had as infants?
- When is it better to divorce than to stay married?
- When is it better to be unemployed than to have a job?

broke two small bones in my pelvis—a mishap I caused myself: I was rushing, wearing smooth-soled shoes, carrying papers, in the rain, after dark, stepping up a curb. I fell hard on the sidewalk. That led to a 911 call, an ambulance, five hospital days, five rehab days, heartfelt admiration for the physical therapists who got me walking, and deep appreciation of colleagues who taught my classes for two weeks.

I mention that minor event because it spotlights generativity. My four children, adults now, cared for me far beyond what I thought I needed. The two nearby daughters, Elissa and Sarah, got to the emergency room within an hour; Rachel flew in from Minnesota and bought me new shoes with slip-proof treads; Bethany drove down from Connecticut with planters, dirt, flowers, and trees to beautify my home. They did much more: brought me books and a computer; questioned nurses and doctors; phoned insurance companies; filled prescriptions; arranged taxis; pushed my wheelchair; did laundry, shopping, cooking, cleaning.

It is hard for me to accept help. I'd told my friends that I wanted no visitors. One said, "You can't move, you are stuck in bed, I am coming." I'd planned to immediately return to the classroom because I thought my students needed me. But after several days in the hospital, I realized I needed them as much as, or more than, they needed me. ●

AGAIN AND AGAIN I WAS REMINDED that generativity is mutual: People need to receive as well as to give. That is a theme of this chapter, which focuses on the many interactions that mark adult lives: partnering and parenting, mating and mentoring. Each individual is unique, charting his or her own path, but always aided by everyone else. We begin, then, with the personality traits that endure, we continue with some of the ways people support each other, and we end with the complexities of combining work and family.

Personality Development in Adulthood

A mixture of genes, experiences, and contexts results in personality, which includes each person's unique actions and attitudes. Continuity is evident: Few people develop characteristics that are the opposite of their childhood temperament. But personality can change, usually for the better, as people overcome earlier adversity and confusion.

Theories of Adult Personality

To organize this mix of embryonic beginnings, childhood experiences, and adult-hood contexts, we begin with theories.

ERIKSON AND MASLOW Erikson originally envisioned eight stages of development, three after adolescence. He is praised as "the one thinker who changed our minds about what it means to live as a person who has arrived at a chronologically mature position and yet continues to grow, to change, and to develop" (Hoare, 2002, p. 3).

Erikson's early stages, already explained, are each tied to a particular chronological period. But late in his life, Erikson stressed that adult stages do not occur in lock-step. Adults of many ages can be in the fifth stage, *identity versus role confusion*, or in any of the three adult stages—*intimacy versus isolation, generativity versus stagnation*, and *integrity versus despair* (McAdams, 2006) (see Table 13.1). He saw adulthood as the continuation of identity seeking via exploration of intimacy and generativity, a vision confirmed by current research (Beaumont & Pratt, 2011).

Similarly, Abraham Maslow (1954) refused to link chronological age and adult development when he described a *hierarchy of needs* with five stages achieved in sequence (see Chapter 1, Figure 1.11). Completion of each stage allows a person to move ahead.

As an example, people who are in Maslow's third level (*love and belonging*, similar to Erikson's *intimacy versus isolation*) seek to be loved and accepted by partners, family

---

TABLE 13.1 Erikson's Stages of Adulthood

Unlike Freud or other early theorists who thought adults simply worked through the legacy of their childhood, Erikson described psychosocial needs after puberty in half of his eight stages. His most famous book, *Childhood and Society* (1963), devoted only two pages to each adult stage, but published and unpublished elaborations in later works led to a much richer depiction (Hoare, 2002).

Identity Versus Role Confusion

Although Erikson originally situated the identity crisis during adolescence, he realized that identity concerns could be lifelong. Identity combines values and traditions from childhood with the current social context. Since contexts keep evolving, many adults reassess all four types of identity (sexual/gender, vocational/work, religious/spiritual, and political/ethnic).

Intimacy Versus Isolation

Adults seek intimacy—a close, reciprocal connection with another human being. Intimacy is mutual, not self-absorbed, which means that adults need to devote time and energy to one another. This process begins in emerging adulthood and continues lifelong. Isolation is especially likely when divorce or death disrupts established intimate relationships.

Generativity Versus Stagnation

Adults need to care for the next generation, either by raising their own children or by mentoring, teaching, and helping others. Erikson's first description of this stage focused on parenthood, but later he included other ways to achieve generativity. Adults extend the legacy of their culture and their generation with ongoing care, creativity, and sacrifice.

Integrity Versus Despair

When Erikson himself was in his 70s, he decided that integrity, with the goal of combating prejudice and helping all humanity, was too important to be left to the elderly. He also thought that each person's entire life could be directed toward connecting a personal journey with the historical and cultural purpose of human society, the ultimate achievement of integrity.

Same Situation, Far Apart: Caution to the Winds Generally, risk taking decreases with age, but modern technology allows older adults to put their bodies on the line. This 80-year-old Israeli woman *(left)* has just skydived and this man in his 50s *(right)* chases tornados with a "Doppler on wheels."

✦ **ESPECIALLY FOR People in Their 20s** Will future "decade" birthdays —30, 40, 50, and so on—be major turning points in your life? (see response, page 466) →

members, and friends. Without affection, people might stay stuck, needing love but never feeling satisfied that they have enough of it. By contrast, those who experience abundant love are able to move to the next level, *success and esteem.* The dominant need at this fourth stage is to be respected and admired.

For humanists like Maslow, these five drives characterize all people, with most adults seeking love or respect (levels three and four). Unless mired in poverty or war, people move past Maslow's lower two stages (safety and basic needs) by adulthood.

Other theorists agree, sometimes describing *affiliation* and *achievement,* sometimes using other labels. We will soon use Erikson's terms, intimacy and generativity, as a scaffold to describe these two universal needs. Every theory of adult personality recognizes that both are important in adulthood.

midlife crisis
A supposed period of unusual anxiety, radical self-reexamination, and sudden transformation that was once widely associated with middle age but that actually had more to do with developmental history than with chronological age.

THE MIDLIFE CRISIS No current theorist sets chronological boundaries for specific stages of adult development. Middle age, if it exists, can begin at age 35 or 50.

This contradicts the theory of the **midlife crisis**, thought to be a time of anxiety and radical change as age 40 approaches. Men, in particular, were said to leave their wives, buy red sports cars, and quit their jobs because of midlife panic. The midlife crisis was popularized by Gail Sheehy (1976), who called it "the age 40 crucible," and by Daniel Levinson (1978), who said men experienced

> tumultuous struggles within the self and with the external world. . . . Every aspect of their lives comes into question, and they are horrified by much that is revealed. They are full of recriminations against themselves and others.
>
> *[Levinson, 1978, p. 199]*

The midlife crisis continues to be referenced in popular movies, books, and songs. A 2012 Google search found more than 3 million citations for "midlife crisis," including an article in the *Wall Street Journal* about successful middle-aged men in crisis (Clements, 2005) and a title song by the rock band Faith No More. However, no large study over the past three decades has found any normative midlife crisis (Austrian, 2008). How could earlier observers have been so wrong?

In hindsight, it is easy to see where they went astray. Levinson studied just 40 men, all from one cohort. The data were then analyzed by men who were also middle-aged. That would no longer be considered good science. Sheehy is not a scientist; she summarized Levinson's research and then supplemented it by interviewing people she chose. Neither Sheehy nor Levinson used replicated, multimethod, longitudinal research, now the bedrock of developmental science.

RESPONSE FOR People in Their 20s (from page 465) Probably not. While many younger people associate certain ages with particular attitudes or accomplishments, few people find those ages significant when they actually live through them. ●

Big Five
The five basic clusters of personality traits that remain quite stable throughout adulthood: openness, conscientiousness, extroversion, agreeableness, and neuroticism.

ecological niche
The particular lifestyle and social context that adults settle into because it is compatible with their individual personality needs and interests.

Personality Endures Fearfulness is one of the personality traits that is most likely to endure from childhood through late adulthood. Some children are terrified even by Disney movies and fairy tales and thus might become adults who always lock their doors. Others enjoy the thrill of fear.

Young Stephen King

Of course, even imperfect and limited data, such as that of Levinson and Sheehy, might contain clues for new trends. Case studies and personal experiences sometimes start scientists on a path of discovery. With the midlife crisis, however, every attempt at replication has failed. Why?

It is now apparent that cohort effects were misleading. Middle-class men in the United States who reached age 40 in about 1970 were affected by historic upheavals in their own families. Many began marriages and careers in the 1950s, expecting grateful children, wives, employers, and coworkers. When they reached middle age, their wives were in the first wave of feminism (some called their husbands "sexist pigs") and their teenagers thought their fathers were rigid and irrelevant (some said, "Don't trust anyone over 30").

No wonder many men were troubled. But their crisis was caused by personal reflections, family pressures, and historical circumstances, not by chronological age. Most men who reach age 40 do not have a midlife crisis.

Personality Traits

Remember from Chapter 4 that each baby has a distinct temperament. Some are shy, others outgoing; some are frightened, others fearless. Such traits are affected by experiences, but they begin with genes.

THE BIG FIVE Temperament does not vanish: Researchers find substantial, even astonishing, coherence in personality throughout life. There are hundreds of examples. One recent study found, for instance, that temperament at age 3 predicted gambling problems at age 32 (Slutske et al., 2012).

Longitudinal, cross-sectional, and multicultural research has identified five clusters of personality traits that appear in every culture and era, called the **Big Five:**[1]

- *Openness:* imaginative, curious, artistic, creative, open to new experiences
- *Conscientiousness:* organized, deliberate, conforming, self-disciplined
- *Extroversion:* outgoing, assertive, active
- *Agreeableness:* kind, helpful, easygoing, generous
- *Neuroticism:* anxious, moody, self-punishing, critical

Each person's personality is somewhere between extremely high and extremely low on each of these five. The low end might be described, in the same order as above, with these five adjectives: *closed, careless, introverted, hard to please,* and *placid.*

These five clusters not only affect career choices and health habits, as expected, but also much more. Adults choose their social context, or **ecological niche,** selecting vocations, hobbies, mates, and neighborhoods at least in part because of personality traits. Even the decision to retire and the reaction to retirement are related to the Big Five (Robinson et al., 2010).

Among the factors linked to the Big Five are education (conscientious people have higher rates of college graduation), marriage (extroverts are more likely to marry), divorce (more often for neurotics), fertility (lower for women in recent cohorts who are more conscientious), IQ (higher in people who are more open), verbal fluency (again, openness and extroversion), and even political views (conservatives are less open) (Duckworth et al., 2007; Gerber et al., 2011; Jokela, 2012; Pedersen et al., 2005; Silvia & Sanders, 2010).

---

[1]To remember the Big Five, the acronym OCEAN is useful.

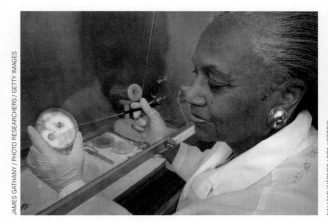

International research confirms that all human personality traits (there are hundreds of them) can be grouped in the Big Five. Of course, personality and behavior are influenced by many other factors, not only gender and cohort as seen above, but also culture. It would be foolish to predict college graduation or voting behavior or anything else *solely* on a person's rank on the Big Five.

Indeed, anyone might act in uncharacteristic ways if circumstances are dramatically altered—perhaps by unexpected divorce, recovery from addiction, forced emigration, treated depression, a sudden disabling disease (Mroczek et al., 2006). Events influence traits, although the specific impact is always affected by personality (Specht et al., 2011). Nature and nurture interact, each affecting the other.

Thus, new events sometimes bring out old personality patterns. People might divorce and then remarry someone like the old partner, for instance, or find a new job that reflects their personality rather than change their personality to fit the job. In general, people are most comfortable when their personality fits with their partners, their neighbors, their careers. For instance, one study found that people high in neuroticism tend to work in hazardous conditions—and then complain about it (Sutin & Costa, 2010).

Even happiness seems a matter of personality more than circumstances. Adults who experience things that temporarily make them overjoyed (e.g., winning a lottery) or depressed (e.g., losing a leg) often revert to the level of happiness they had before that event. Personality trumps experience (Gilbert, 2006).

CULTURE, AGE, AND CONTEXT Many researchers who study personality find that people adapt to their culture, expressing personality traits differently in, say, Egypt or Ecuador (Church, 2010). Traits that are considered pathological in one place (such as neuroticism in the United States) tend to be modified as people mature within that community (L. A. Clark, 2009). By contrast, traits that are valued (such as conscientiousness) endure.

That is exactly what was found in a massive study of midlife North Americans (called MIDUS). Agreeableness and conscientiousness increased slightly overall while neuroticism decreased, as did openness and extroversion (which may be more appreciated in the young than the old) (Lachman & Bertrand, 2001) (see Figure 13.1). This pattern was also found in other research (Allemand et al., 2008; Donnellan & Lucas, 2008).

Since cultural values interact with personality traits, it should also be noted that the terms used to describe personality are not neutral. For instance, "open" seems a positive trait and "closed" seems negative. But instead of closed, perhaps another term, such as *traditional,* might be a more accurate descriptor.

Same Situation, Far Apart: Scientists at Work Most scientists are open-minded and conscientious (two of the Big Five personality traits), as both these women are. Culture and social context are crucial, however. If she were in Tanzania, would the woman on the left be a doctor surrounded by patients in the open air, as the woman on the right is? Or is she so accustomed to her North American laboratory, protected by gloves and a screen, that she could not adjust?

✦ **ESPECIALLY FOR Immigrants and Children of Immigrants** Poverty and persecution are the main reasons some people leave their home for another country, but personality is also influential. Which of the Big Five personality traits do you think is most characteristic of immigrants? (see response, page 468) →

FIGURE 13.1 Trends, Not Rules Overall stability, and some marked individual variation, is the main story for the Big Five over the decades of adulthood. In addition, each of the traits tends to shift slightly, as depicted here.

Adult Personality: Stability Within Change

Personality →

Quite stable overall, but with minor ups and downs:

Openness ↘

Conscientiousness ↗

Extroversion ↘

Agreeableness ↗

Neuroticism ↘

**RESPONSE FOR Immigrants and
Children of Immigrants** (from page
467) Extroversion and neuroticism,
according to one study (Silventoinen
et al., 2008). Because these traits
decrease over adulthood, fewer older
adults migrate. ●

The relationship between enduring personality and changing context was evident in a longitudinal study that tracked women in the United States from ages 20 to 70 (George et al., 2011). When they were in college, the female role was limited. These young women expected to be wives and mothers, not employees. In the 1960s, the culture shifted; so did the women. Most entered the workforce, displaying abilities submerged when they were young, learning new skills, gaining confidence. Nonetheless, personality endured, evident in the jobs they found. How could this be? Those high in extroversion might work in sales and management; those high in conscientiousness might become nurses or accountants.

The study previously mentioned on fertility and the Big Five found that, for both men and women born in 1920, those high in openness had about the same number of children as those low in that trait. Presumably, their openness was expressed in other ways. For those born in 1960, however, the more open a person was, the fewer children he or she had. They were open to nontraditional life patterns, which for some meant having no children (Jokela, 2012).

OPPOSING PERSPECTIVES

Local Context Versus Genes

Some people believe that personality is powerfully shaped by regional culture, so that a baby will have a quite different personality if born and raised in, say, Mexico or Canada. The opposite hypothesis is that personality is innate, fixed at birth and impervious to social pressures with only minor, temporary impact from culture.

Evidence for the second hypothesis includes the fact that the same Big Five traits are found in many nations, with similar age-related trends. Supposed national differences in personality may be "unfounded stereotypes" (McCrae & Terracciano, 2006, p. 156).

Further evidence that personality is inborn, not made by context, is the stability of personality throughout adulthood (B. W. Roberts et al., 2006; Specht et al., 2011). Extroverted emerging adults become outgoing grandmothers, with many friends from early adulthood and with more new friends along the way. Other traits likewise endure, in new forms.

Other research, however, finds that culture and events change personality. For example, according to some social scientists, Asian cultures encourage a sixth personality dimension, called *dependence on others,* which should be added to the Big Five when studying Asians (Hofstede, 2007; Okazaki et al., 2009; Suh et al., 2008).

Asian children who seem low on this trait are encouraged by their culture to increase it, so cooperation is more common among Asian adults than among children. Since we now know that brain structures respond to experience, the childhood context—such as a preschool that teaches sharing and group cohesion—may cause an enduring, neurological change.

When Asian adults emigrate to a culture in which that trait is less valued, they may be considered too docile, overly concerned with blending in. This would not be true for Asians who emigrated as babies and were raised in the individualistic culture, unless their parents were strongly opposed to new cultural influences and raised their children as they themselves had been raised. Clinicians find that personality tests developed for native-born North Americans do not properly assess the personality traits of Asian Americans who grew up in Asia (Okasaki et al., 2009).

Another example of personality change is in the Big Five trait of openness. Cultures differ in whether they consider openness desirable. In some cultures, openness is prized as an indication of intelligence and willingness to learn. Children who ask questions in class, without raising their hands, are appreciated.

However, in some places interpersonal harmony is more valued than individual initiative (Church, 2010). One team concluded: "Openness is not commonly used as a distinct dimension in the taxonomy of personality traits in Chinese culture" (Cheung et al., 2008, p. 103). Children are discouraged from impulsively "interrupting" with questions.

The idea that context shapes personality comes from the finding that the Big Five scores differ among adults in the 50 U.S. states (Rentfrow et al., 2008). According to the answers of 619,397 respondents to an Internet survey that asked questions about their traits, New Yorkers are highest in openness, New Mexicans highest in conscientiousness, North Dakotans highest in both extroversion and agreeableness, and West Virginians highest in neuroticism. Lowest in these five are, in order, residents of North Dakota, Alaska, Maryland, Alaska (again), and Utah.

This suggests that local norms, institutions, history, and geography have an impact. For example, residents of Utah are surrounded by Mormons (no drugs, large families, generally good health) and awesome mountains. That might make them less anxious and more serene, hence low in neuroticism. New York is multiethnic because it has always been an international arrival city (Ellis Island and the Statue of Liberty are in the harbor), which might encourage openness. The authors of this study suggest that many aspects of adults' lives, including criminal behavior, morbidity, education, and political preference, spring from regional differences in personality (Rentfrow, 2010).

Before concluding that environment shapes personality, however, consider the opposite idea—that personality is innate. This could also spring from the same U.S. data. Perhaps adults move to wherever they feel appreciated for who they are. For example, a North Dakotan who, unlike his neighbors, is high in openness might relocate to New York. If many people moved because of their personality, then regional or national differences would appear as people go where their inborn temperament is valued.

A decades-long study in Finland indeed found that personality often leads to relocation (Jokela et al., 2008; Silventoinen et al., 2008). Finns with an outgoing personality (high in extroversion, or sociability) were likely to move from isolated rural areas to urban ones.

A consensus regarding the relationship between culture, geography, genes, and personality has not yet emerged (Church, 2010). As you see, both opposing views make sense: More longitudinal research is needed.

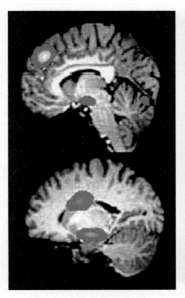
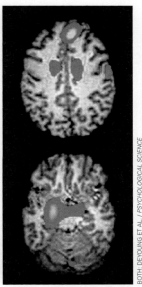

BOTH: DEYOUNG ET AL. / PSYCHOLOGICAL SCIENCE

Active Brains, Active Personality
The hypothesis that individual personality traits originate in the brain was tested by scientists who sought correlates between brain activity (shown in red) and personality traits. People high in four of the Big Five (conscientiousness, extroversion, agreeableness, neuroticism—but not openness) activated brain regions known for comparable characteristics. Here are two side views *(left)* and a top and bottom view *(right)* of brains of people high in neuroticism. Regions sensitive to stress, depression, threat, and punishment (yellow bullseyes) were more active than in the low neurotic individuals (DeYoung et al., 2010).

KEY Points

- Adults seek intimacy and generativity (Erikson) or love and respect (Maslow).
- The Big Five personality traits (openness, conscientiousness, extroversion, agreeableness, neuroticism) are evident worldwide.
- Adult personality shows both continuity with childhood temperament and change in reaction to life circumstances.
- Personality traits affect adults' choices of partners, jobs, and life patterns.

Intimacy

Every adult experiences the crisis Erikson called **intimacy versus isolation**, seeking to connect with other people. Specifics vary. Some adults are distant from their parents but close to partners and friends; others rely on family members but not on nonrelatives. The need for intimacy is universal yet dynamic: Each adult regulates closeness and reciprocity, combining friends, acquaintances, and relatives (Lang et al., 2009).

Everyone is part of a **social convoy,** a group of people who "provide a protective layer of social relations to guide, encourage, and socialize individuals as they go through life" (Antonucci et al., 2001, p. 572). The term *convoy* originally referred to

intimacy versus isolation
The sixth of Erikson's eight stages of development. Adults seek someone with whom to share their lives in an enduring and self-sacrificing commitment. Without such commitment, they risk profound aloneness and isolation.

social convoy
Collectively, the family members, friends, acquaintances, and even strangers who move through life with an individual.

a group of travelers in hostile territory, such as the pioneers in ox-drawn wagons headed for California or soldiers marching across unfamiliar terrain. Individuals were strengthened by the convoy, sharing difficult conditions and defending one another.

As people move through life, their social convoy metaphorically functions as those earlier convoys did (Crosnoe & Elder, 2002; Lang et al., 2009). Paradoxically, current changes in the historical context (globalization, longevity, and ethnic and sexual diversity), make intimacy more vital. Humans need social convoys (Antonucci et al., 2007).

Friends and Acquaintances

Friends are crucial members of the social convoy, partly because they are chosen for the traits that make them reliable fellow travelers. They are usually about the same age, with similar experiences and values. Mutual loyalty and aid are expected from friends: A relationship that is imbalanced (one person always giving, the other always taking) over the years is likely to end because both parties are uneasy.

Of course, sometimes a friend needs care and cannot reciprocate at the time. Friends provide practical help and useful advice when serious problems—death of a family member, personal illness, job loss—arise. The underlying connection is more mundane: Friends offer companionship, information, and laughter in daily life—how to get a child to eat his carrots; whether to remodel or replace the kitchen cabinets; when to ask for a raise; why a particular person is ludicrous, unreasonable, or both.

Shared Genes, Different History
These four generations of one family in rural China illustrate historical shifts in nutrition and fashion. More significant changes are less visible. The great-grandmother's social convoy was confined to close family members, a marked contrast to her great-granddaughter, who has many friends from work and school.

OBSERVATION QUIZ
Do you see any differences in facial expressions and posture? (see answer, page 472) →

consequential strangers
People who are not in a person's closest friendship circle but nonetheless have an impact.

FRIENDSHIP AND HUMAN DEVELOPMENT A comprehensive study found that friendships improve with age. To be specific, adolescents and young adults consider a significant minority of their friendships *ambivalent* or *problematic.* By adulthood, most friendships are rated *close,* few are ambivalent, and almost none are problematic (Fingerman et al., 2004).

For those reasons, friendship helps with mental health: One reason depression seems to decrease with age is that friends are more carefully selected, and friendships more nourished, so that friends become more supportive over time.

Friends help with details of physical health as well, encouraging one another to eat better, to quit smoking, to exercise, and so on. The reverse is also true: If someone gains weight over the years of adulthood, his or her best friend is likely to do so as well. In fact, although most adults keep their friends for decades, health habits are one reason some adults change friends (O'Malley & Christakis, 2011). For instance, a friendship between a chain smoker and someone who quit smoking is likely to fray.

If an adult has no friends, health suffers (Couzin, 2009). This seems as true in poor nations as in rich ones: Universally, humans are healthier with supportive friends and relatives, and sicker when they are socially isolated (Kumar et al., 2012).

ACQUAINTANCES In addition to friends, hundreds of other acquaintances provide information, support, social integration, and new ideas (Fingerman, 2009). Neighbors, coworkers, store clerks, the local police officer, members of a religious or community group, and so on are **consequential strangers,** defined as people who are not in a person's closest convoy but who nonetheless have an impact.

Among the consequential strangers in your life might be:

- Several other dog owners if you walk your dog
- Your barber or beautician if you regularly get your hair cut
- The street vendor from whom you buy a muffin every day
- The parent of your child's friend

A consequential stranger may be literally a stranger: someone who sits next to you on an airplane, or directs you when you are lost, or gives you a seat on the bus.

Such acquaintances differ from most close friends and family members in that they include people of diverse religions, ethnic groups, ages, and political opinions—and that diversity is one reason they are consequential, particularly in current times (Fingerman, 2009). The Internet has strengthened friendships and added more consequential strangers to many lives (Stern & Adams, 2010; Wang & Wellman, 2010).

Regular acquaintances are part of each person's peripheral social network. With age, the number of such peripheral friends decreases. For example, one study found that the average emerging adult had 16 peripheral friends but that the average middle-aged adult had 12 (Zhang et al., 2011).

The same study also found, however, that people who were high in the temperamental characteristic of interdependence (suggested as a sixth trait, added to the Big Five) did not follow the usual pattern of having fewer peripheral friends as they aged. In fact, they were likely to add people to their social network, not lose them (Zhang et al., 2011).

The composition of social networks varies by culture. In many African nations, everyone in the community is in the peripheral network. They might stop by, unannounced, to visit. In other cultures, that might be considered rude.

Another cultural difference is whether family members are considered friends. For example, one study found that in both Germany and Hong Kong, adults had about the same number of intimates, but the Germans tended to include more nonfamily friends, whereas the Chinese included more family members (Fung et al., 2008).

In high-fertility regions where everyone has many siblings and cousins, almost all close companions are relatives. Since family size has been decreasing in the past few decades, nonrelatives increasingly meet intimacy needs. Nonetheless, as we now describe, family connections remain significant.

Strangers No More Leanne Kennedy *(right)* was dying from kidney failure, barely surviving with daily dialysis, four years on the waiting list for a donor kidney. Nonetheless, she accepted Shawn Stefanovic's marriage proposal. He offered his kidney—no match. Then Stuart Kilgannan *(left)*, a consequential stranger to Leanne but Shawn's best man, offered his. A match! How could the new couple repay him? "Name a baby after me," he said.

Family Bonds

Everywhere close friends are referred to as being "like a sister" or "my brother." Such terms reflect the assumption that family connections are intimate. As just mentioned, this is truer in some cultures than others, but family relationships are crucial for many adults, usually more so as they age.

Which particular family members become intimates varies for many reasons, as one might expect. One intriguing study of the population of Denmark found that twins married less often than single-born adults. However, if they married, they typically stayed married. According to the researchers, twins may be less likely to need another close companion (no spouse needed since they have each other), but if they married, they were less likely to divorce because they knew how to get along with another person (Petersen et al., 2011).

ADULT CHILDREN AND THEIR PARENTS Although most adults in modern societies leave their parents' homes to establish their own households, a study of 7,578 adults in seven nations found that physical separation did not necessarily weaken family ties.

Family Harmony It is not easy to craft and sell stringed instruments, especially if you are a Black man in the mountains of Northern Italy, as these two are. But they are successful, partly because they support each other. They are father and son.

DIEGO CERVO / BLEND IMAGES RM / GETTY IMAGES

ANSWER TO **OBSERVATION QUIZ**
(from page 470) The great-grand-daughter and her mother seem proud and happy; the two older women seem tired and resigned. Of course, one snapshot is not conclusive. However, their attitudes may be affected by the cultural revolution and counter-revolution. ●

In fact, these authors concluded that intergenerational relationships are becoming stronger, not weaker, as more adult children live apart from their parents (Treas & Gubernskaya, 2012).

Other research draws the same conclusion. The relationship between parents and adult children tends to be less affectionate if they live together (Ward & Spitze, 2007). This may be correlation rather than cause, since intergenerational living may come about when either the parents or the children are unable to live independently.

Nonetheless, household composition is a poor measure of family closeness, and not only in developed nations. In rural Thailand, for example, income, not affection, determines whether a young married couple lives with the wife's parents (the traditional custom) or establishes their own household (Piotrowski, 2008). Remittances voluntarily sent back by adult children employed far from home are an important source of income; family loyalty leads some adult children to underwrite independent households for their siblings, a sign of closeness despite geographical distance.

SIBLINGS AND OTHER RELATIVES With adulthood often comes "marriage and childbearing, both of which have the potential to enhance closeness in sibling relationships or exacerbate previous difficulties" (Conger & Little, 2010, p. 89). This potential usually leads to closer relationships, especially when nieces and nephews are born. Parents want their children to know their aunts, uncles, and cousins, and that reduces sibling distance. Furthermore, adulthood frees siblings from forced cohabitation and rivalry, allowing them to differ without fighting.

Adult siblings often help one another, providing practical support (especially between brothers) and emotional support (especially between sisters) (Voorpostel & van der Lippe, 2007) (see Figure 13.2). For example, a middle-aged woman who lived thousands of miles from her four siblings said:

> I have a good relationship with my brothers. . . . Every time I come, they are very warm and loving, and I stayed with my brother for a week. . . . Sisters is another story. Sisters are best friends. Sisters is like forever. When I have a problem, I phone my sisters. When I'm feeling down, I phone my sisters. And they always pick me up.

[quoted in Connidis, 2007, p. 488]

FIGURE 13.2 From Rival to Friend
Adolescents are not usually close to their siblings, but that often changes with time. By late adulthood, brothers and sisters usually consider each other among their best friends.

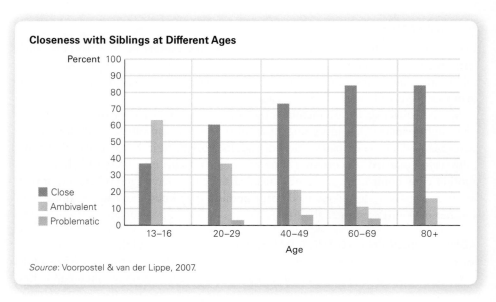

Closeness with Siblings at Different Ages

Source: Voorpostel & van der Lippe, 2007.

In several South Asian nations, brothers are obligated to bestow gifts on their sisters, who are expected to cook for and nurture their brothers (Conger & Little, 2010). Such patterns may impede individual growth, but they reduce poverty and strengthen family bonds. By encouraging siblings to care for one another, they satisfy intimacy needs.

A large study in the Netherlands found a curious relationship between closeness to parents and closeness among siblings. As expected, when adult women were close to their parents, they also were close to their siblings. To some extent, this was true for the men as well. However, those brothers who were distant from their parents tended to be closer than average to their siblings, as if to compensate. One family link became stronger because another one was weak (Voorpostel & Blieszner, 2008).

MIXED EMOTIONS In assessing intimacy, it should be noted that whenever adult children have serious financial, legal, or marital problems, parents try to help. This has always been evident for young, single adults, but the economic recession has led to an increasing number of 25- to 34-year-olds living with their parents. Specifically, in the United States the percentage of adults living with parents increased from 11 percent to 20 percent between 1980 and 2008 (Pew Social Trends Staff, 2010).

Overall, parents provide more financial and emotional support to their adult children than vice versa, although children rally if necessary (as did my four daughters when I fractured my pelvis).

Time and again researchers find that adults who have separate households from other adults in their family are nevertheless profoundly affected by their relationships. Such relationships can be destructive or supportive. Often they are both; ambivalence in parent–child relationships is more likely than placid harmony (Bojczyk et al., 2011; Reid & Reczek, 2011). Parental satisfaction is strongly affected by the adult lives of their children, with the most troubled children having more impact on parental well-being than the happy, successful ones (Fingerman et al., 2012).

In one international study, older adults (average age 77) were asked how they got along with a particular child (average age 53) (Silverstein et al., 2010). Answers clustered into four groups: *amicable* (close, got along well, high communication), *detached* (distant, low on communication), *disharmonious* (conflict, critical, arguing), and *ambivalent* (both close and critical, high on communication).

Every nation had some elders in each of the four clusters, with amicable relationships the most common. Ironically, frail and dependent elders were more likely to experience friction, even though they often lived with their children.

National differences appeared in how common each cluster was, with England and Norway most amicable, Germany and Spain most detached, and Israel most ambivalent. No nation had many disharmonious relationships, but the United States had more (20 percent) than the other five nations (Silverstein et al., 2010).

Close and affectionate family relations were most likely when the government provided many services (e.g., health care, senior residences). This suggests again that emotional intimacy is a distinct need for adults, independent of practical necessity.

Back to the interplay of friends and relatives: In every nation, most family members support each other. However, some adults stay distant from their blood relatives because they find them toxic. Such adults may become **fictive kin** in another family. They are not technically related (hence fictive) but accepted and treated like a family member (hence kin).

Especially if adults are rejected by their original family (perhaps because of their sexual orientation) or they are far from home (perhaps immigrants), or changing

Arch Rivals or Blood Brothers? Both. Fernando and Humberto Campana are designers, shown here at an exhibit of their work in Spain, far from their native Brazil. As with many siblings, competition and collaboration have inspired them all their lives.

fictive kin
Someone who becomes accepted as part of a family to which he or she has no blood relation.

Same Situation, Far Apart: Happily Married Nebraska *(top)* and Siberia *(bottom)* are at opposite ends of the globe, but both places have much in common: sparse population, many farms, cold winters, and enduring marriages. In every nation, couples in rural areas are less likely to divorce.

their habits (such as stopping addiction), fictive kin can be a lifeline (Ebaugh & Curry, 2000; Heslin et al., 2011; Kim, 2009; Muraco, 2006). Adults benefit from kin, fictive or not.

Committed Partners

As detailed earlier, people in every nation take longer than previous generations did to publicly commit to one long-term sexual partner. Nonetheless, although specifics differ (marriage at age 20 is late in some cultures and far too early in others), adults everywhere seek long-term partners to help meet their needs for intimacy as well as to raise children, share resources, and provide care when needed.

Although adults marry later in life than earlier generations did, this is more a shift in timing and formality than a rejection of partnership. Recent data suggest that less than 10 percent of contemporary U.S. adults will *never* make a marriage-like commitment, i.e., a partnership that is expected to last.

In some other nations, less than 2 percent stay single lifelong. Cohort matters. Almost all U.S. residents born before 1940 married (96 percent). Fewer of those born between 1940 and 1960 married (89 percent) and a significant number of them are now divorced and not remarried (16 percent) (U.S. Bureau of the Census, 2011a).

MARRIAGE AND HAPPINESS From a developmental perspective, marriage is a useful institution. Adults thrive if another person is committed to their well-being; children benefit when they have two parents who are legally as well as emotionally dedicated to them; societies are stronger if individuals sort themselves into families.

From an individual perspective, the consequences are more mixed. There is no doubt that a satisfying marriage improves health, wealth, and happiness, but some marriages are not satisfying at all (Fincham & Beach, 2010). Generally, married people are a little happier, healthier, and richer than never-married ones—but not by much.

A 16-nation survey 20 years ago found one nation (Portugal) where single people were happier than married ones, another (France) where both groups were equally content, and several where married adults were only slightly more often "very happy" than never-married adults. The largest differences were in the United States, where more married than single adults were "very happy" (37 versus 26 percent) (Inglehart, 1990).

Another large longitudinal study of married adults found that

> there were as many people who ended up less happy than they started as there were people who ended up happier than they started (a fact that is particularly striking given that we restricted the sample to people who stayed married).
>
> *[Lucas et al., 2003, p. 536]*

Thus, most adults marry and expect ongoing happiness because of it, but some will be disappointed (Coontz, 2005). Those who never marry can be quite happy as well, at least in North America (DePaulo, 2006).

Cohabitation historically has led to less happy adults than has marriage, especially for women. However, this also is changing by cohort and varies by culture, with some places finding few significant differences between cohabiting and married couples, or between men and women (Stavrova et al., 2012).

Researchers now realize cohabiters who expect to marry are quite different from those who slide into living together because of convenience. If the latter couple eventually marries, their chances of a happy marriage are less than average. The same is true for couples who have sex within the first month of being together (Sassler et al., 2012).

Others cohabit as the first step in commitment and mutual trust. For them, the next step is the wedding, and then each year of marriage increases their public and personal commitment to each other. As divorce becomes less likely, many signs are evident that they are a couple, not just two individuals. For instance, they have more children than cohabiters who drifted into marriage, the man earns more than comparable unmarried men, the wife spends more time on household tasks (Kuperberg, 2012).

A sizable number of adults have found a third way to have a steady romantic partner, called *living apart together* (LAT). They have separate residences, but especially when the partners are older than 30, LATs may be committed to each other, perhaps functioning as a couple for decades (Duncan & Phillips, 2010).

There are many ways to understand love, cross-culturally and over time (Sternberg & Weis, 2006). Robert Sternberg developed one useful one when he wrote that love has three parts: passion, intimacy, and commitment. Among twenty-first-century Westerners, passion is usually first, then shared confidences create intimacy, and finally commitment leads to an enduring relationship. When all three are evident, that is consummate love—an ideal sometimes, but not always, attained in marriage (Sternberg, 2006a).

FRANK BARON / CAMERA PRESS / GUARDIAN / REDUX

One Love, Two Homes Their friends and family know that Jonathan and Diana are a couple, happy together day and night, year after year. But one detail distinguishes them from most couples: Each owns a house. They commute 10 miles to be LAT, living apart together.

PARTNERSHIPS OVER THE YEARS Not surprisingly, a meta-analysis of 93 studies found that personal well-being is affected by the quality of the marriage as well as vice versa, especially for people married eight years or longer (Proulx et al., 2007). The long-term nature of a relationship is affected by many factors, including the childhood experiences of both partners (Overbeek et al., 2007), economic instability (decreasing happiness), and the partners' personalities (agreeable people are usually happy; neurotic ones usually not).

The passage of time also makes a difference. For instance, the honeymoon period tends to be happy, but soon frustration increases because conflicts arise (see At About This Time). However, domestic violence is more likely in the first years of a relationship than later on (H. K. Kim et al., 2008). Partnerships (including heterosexual married couples, committed cohabiters, same-sex couples, LAT couples) tend to be less happy when the first child is born, and again when children reach puberty (Umberson et al., 2010). Divorce risk rises and then falls (see Infographic 13, page 476).

✦ **ESPECIALLY FOR Young Couples**
Suppose you are one-half of a turbulent relationship in which moments of intimacy alternate with episodes of abuse. Should you break up? (see response, page 477) →

AT ABOUT THIS TIME
Marital Happiness Over the Years

Interval After Wedding	Characterization
First 6 months	Honeymoon period—happiest of all
6 months to 5 years	Happiness dips; divorce is more common now than later in marriage
5 to 10 years	Happiness holds steady
10 to 20 years	Happiness dips as children reach puberty
20 to 30 years	Happiness rises when children leave the nest
30 to 50 years	Happiness is high and steady, barring serious health problems

Not Always These are trends, often masked by more pressing events. For example, some couples stay together because of the children, so the empty nest stage becomes a time of conflict or divorce.

VISUALIZING DEVELOPMENT

Partners or Not

Adults seek committed partners, but do not always find them—age, cohort, and culture are always influential. Some choose to avoid marriage, more commonly in northern Europe and less commonly in North Africa than in the United States. As you see, in 2010, U.S. emerging adults were unlikely to marry, middle-aged adults had the highest rates of separation or divorce, and widows often chose to stay alone while widowers often remarried.

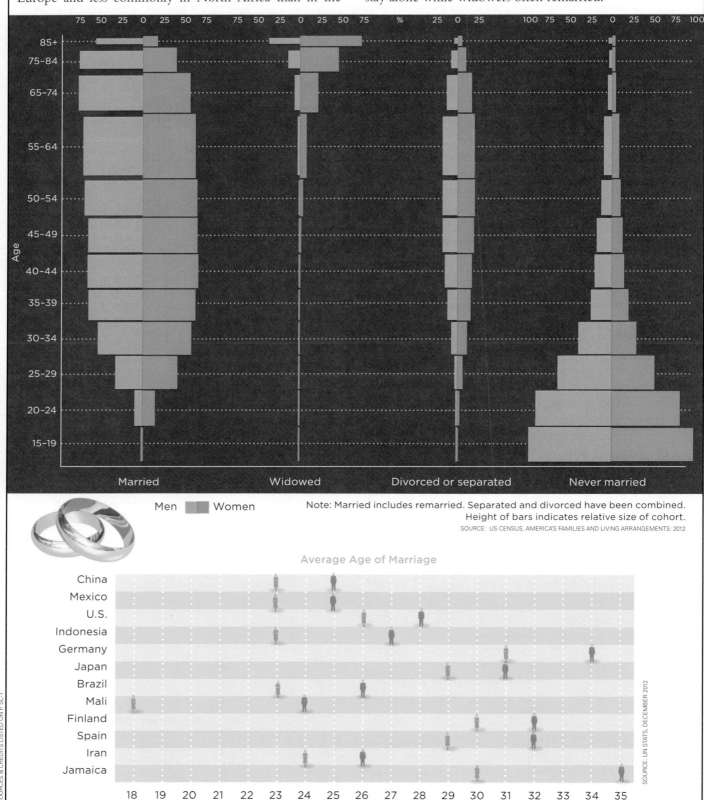

Men Women

Note: Married includes remarried. Separated and divorced have been combined. Height of bars indicates relative size of cohort.

SOURCE: US CENSUS, AMERICA'S FAMILIES AND LIVING ARRANGEMENTS: 2012

Average Age of Marriage

SOURCES & CREDITS LISTED ON P. SC-1

SOURCE: UN STATS, DECEMBER 2012

Gradually, after a decade or two of declining satisfaction, partnerships improve (Scarf, 2008). Part of the explanation is that many unhappy relationships end after a few years; this is particularly true for cohabiters, who have fewer barriers to separation. Generally, those who continue to be committed learn to appreciate each other, avoiding the flash points that caused earlier fights.

Contrary to outdated impressions, the **empty nest** (the time when parents are alone again after their children have moved out and launched their own lives) often improves a relationship (Gorchoff et al., 2008). Simply spending time together, without interruptions from infants, demands from children, or rebellions from teenagers, improves intimacy as partners can focus on each other's needs.

empty nest
The time in the lives of parents when their children have left the family home to pursue their own lives.

We have already noted that many parents (the so-called helicopter parents) are intensively involved with their emerging-adult children, and many young adults live with their parents when they cannot afford independent homes. Here we should reiterate that this does not necessarily make life better for the parents (Fingerman et al., 2012).

Even in nations where living with parents is the norm (e.g., Italy), adult children eventually move out, sometimes living nearby and helping the parents who helped them for so long (Leopold, 2012).

When all the children have become independent, long-term partnerships often benefit financially. The money spent on child care is reduced when adult children become self-supporting. Many middle-aged couples finally have fewer expenses, so they can afford to be generous in supporting their offspring, and such generosity is appreciated, unlike the money spent on the children earlier. Another financial advantage is seniority: If one or both have a steady job, income and security are likely to increase over time. Contemporary couples fight more about money than anything else; middle age reduces that friction.

Aside from the impact of freedom and income, some troubled relationships rebound to earlier levels of satisfaction as mates learn to understand and forgive one another (Fincham et al., 2007). Much depends on context: "[F]orgiveness is a process that can be either beneficial or harmful depending on characteristics of the relationship in which it occurs" (McNulty & Fincham, 2012). Shared backgrounds, values, and interests (homogamy) reduce conflict, while different backgrounds (heterogamy) raise issues that were not expected.

Marriages among people of different ethnic groups "soared more than 20-fold . . . from 1960 to 2000" (Lee & Bean, 2007, p. 562), but such marriages have a higher risk of divorce, not only because of tensions from the outside culture but also because of clashes in assumptions and habits between the partners (Burton et al., 2010; Fu & Wolfinger, 2011). As you learned in Chapter 1, SES may be more crucial than race: If a couple have ancestors from different continents, but have similar levels of education and family income and are acculturated to the same culture, they may be more compatible than some same-race couples.

Time does not fix every relationship, of course, and new stressors may occur. Economic stress causes marital friction no matter how many years a couple has been together (Conger et al., 2010), and contextual factors can undermine a couple's willingness to communicate and compromise (Karney & Bradbury, 2005). A long-standing relationship might crumble, especially under the weight of major crises—particularly financial (such as a foreclosed home, a stretch of unemployment) or relational (such as demanding in-laws or an extramarital affair).

Every generality obscures specifics. Some long-term marriages are blissful; others are horrible. Marriage has never been magical: It does not always make adults joyful or children successful (Acs, 2007; Foster & Kalil, 2007). As you remember from the discussion of family structure in Chapter 8, correlation is not causation. Some husbands and wives consider each other best friends; others do not.

RESPONSE FOR Young Couples
(from page 475) There is no simple answer, but you should bear in mind that, while abuse usually decreases with age, breakups become more difficult with every year, especially if children are involved. ●

ARISTIDE ECONOMOPOULOS / STAR LEDGER / CORBIS

Why Marry? Because many young people question the need for a wedding, marriage rates are down overall, but states that allow same-sex couples to wed find a sudden increase. Miriam Brown and Carol Anastasio were among the 16,046 people to marry in New York City on July 24, 2011, the first day such marriages were legal. Extra judges and court rooms were pressed into service.

GAY AND LESBIAN PARTNERS Almost everything just described applies to gay and lesbian partners as well as to heterosexual ones (Biblarz & Savci, 2010; Herek, 2006). Some same-sex couples are faithful and supportive of each other; their emotional well-being thrives on their intimacy. Others are conflicted, with problems of finances, communication, and domestic abuse resembling those in heterosexual marriages.

Political and cultural contexts for same-sex couples are changing markedly. As of this writing, many nations, including Canada and Spain, and nine U.S. states (Connecticut, Iowa, Maine, Maryland, Massachusetts, New Hampshire, New York, Vermont, and Washington) recognize same-sex marriage. Many other nations and U.S. states are ambivalent, and most countries, as well as about 25 states, explicitly outlaw same-sex marriage. Attitudes are fluid; research even a few years old may be inaccurate.

Current research with a large, randomly selected sample of people in gay or lesbian marriages in the United States is not yet available. Many studies are designed to prove that same-sex marriage is, or is not, beneficial. That makes it difficult to draw objective conclusions. A review of 15 years of same-sex marriages in Denmark, Sweden, and Norway finds that neither the greatest fears nor the greatest hopes for such unions are realized (Biblarz & Stacey, 2010).

It is not known how many committed same-sex couples there are. According to the U.S. Bureau of the Census (2010), only 0.6 percent of U.S. households are headed by unmarried same-sex couples. All gay and lesbian groups, and most social scientists, consider this an underestimate because many such couples are reluctant to proclaim their status.

Before 2000, the U.S. census defined an *unmarried couple* as a "cohabiting man and woman." Now *unmarried partners* are allowed to specify male–female, male–male, or female–female. The data show a 31 percent increase in the number of total same-sex couples between 2000 and 2006, probably because more such couples openly declared themselves as such (see Table 13.2). Beginning in 2004, and increasing each year, several states have allowed marriage between same-sex partners, so the number of unmarried same-sex partners has decreased as the number of other-sex cohabitants has continued to climb.

DIVORCE AND SEPARATION Throughout this text, developmental events that seem isolated, personal, and transitory are shown to be interconnected, socially mediated, and with enduring consequences. Relationships never improve or end in a vacuum; they are influenced by the social and political context (Fine & Harvey, 2006). Divorce, separation, and the end of a cohabiting relationship are all affected by time and circumstances (see Table 13.3).

TABLE 13.2 Unmarried-Partner Households in the United States, 2000, 2006, 2010*

	Male–Female	Male–Male	Female–Female	Total Same-Sex
2000	4,881,377	301,026	293,365	594,391
2006	5,237,595	417,044	362,823	779,867
2010	6,174,759	287,687	305,637	593,324
Change from 2000 to 2006: Number and Percent				
	+356,218 (7%)	+116,018 (39%)	+69,458 (24%)	+185,476 (31%)
Change from 2006 to 2010: Number and Percent				
	+937,164 (18%)	−129,357 (31%)	−57,186 (16%)	−186,543 (24%)

*Officially declared
Source: U.S. Bureau of the Census, 2002, 2008, 2012.

Divorce occurs because at least one half of a couple believes that he or she would be happier not married. That conclusion is reached fairly often in the United States: Since 1980, almost half as many divorces or permanent separations have occurred as marriages. (More than one-third of first marriages end in divorce and with each subsequent marriage the odds of divorce increase.)

Typically, people divorce because some aspects of the marriage have become difficult to endure; often they are unaware of the future impact on other aspects of their lives. Among these aspects are reduced income; lost friendships (many couples have only other couples as friends); and weakened relationships with the children, not only immediately but also when the children become adults (Kalmijn, 2010; Mustonen et al., 2011).

Family problems arise not only with children (usually custodial parents become stricter and noncustodial parents feel excluded) but also with other relatives. The divorced adult's parents may be financially supportive, but often they are emotionally critical that their child's marriage did not work out. Some married adults have good relationships with some of their in-laws; this almost always disappears when the couple splits, a loss of part of the social convoy.

For all these reasons, intimacy is often diminished when couples separate. Sometimes adults then confide their troubles to their children, which may help the adults with intimacy needs but does not help the children. Even if adults avoid that attractive trap, children need more parental help than before (H. S. Kim, 2011).

Although divorce is finalized on a particular day, from a developmental perspective it is a process that begins years before the official decree and reverberates for decades after (Amato, 2010). Income, family welfare, and self-esteem are lower among the formerly married than among people of the same age who are still married or who have always been single.

Some research finds that women suffer from divorce more than men do (their income, in particular, is lower), but men's intimacy needs are especially at risk. Some husbands rely on their wives for companionship and social interaction; they are unaccustomed to inviting friends over or chatting on the phone. Divorced fathers are often lonely, alienated from their adult children and grandchildren (Lin, 2008a).

This research on divorce is sobering. As with all of adult development, the shifting social context may have improved life for the formerly married, and even without that some people escape the usual patterns. If divorce ends an abusive, destructive relationship (as it does about one-third of the time), it usually benefits at least one spouse and the children (Amato, 2010). Furthermore, developing stronger and warmer mother–child relationships after a divorce helps children cope, not only immediately but also for years later (Vélez et al., 2011). This can occur, but it is not the usual outcome.

> **TABLE 13.3 Factors That Make Divorce More Likely**
>
> **Before Marriage**
> Divorced parents
> Either partner under age 21
> Family opposed
> Cohabitation before marriage
> Previous divorce of either partner
> Large discrepancy in age, background, interests, values (heterogamy)
>
> **During Marriage**
> Divergent plans and practices regarding childbearing and child rearing
> Financial stress, unemployment
> Substance abuse
> Communication difficulties
> Lack of time together
> Emotional or physical abuse
> Unsupportive relatives
>
> **In the Culture**
> High divorce rate in cohort
> Weak religious values
> Laws that make divorce easier
> Approval of remarriage
> Acceptance of single parenthood

"But you knew I was addicted to bad men when you married me."

TOM CHENEY / THE NEW YORKER COLLECTION / CARTOONBANK.COM

Surprised? Many brides and grooms hope to rescue and reform their partners, but they should know better. Changing another person's habits, values, or addictions is very difficult.

REPARTNERING Divorce is most likely within the first five years after a wedding, and cohabitation usually ends even sooner, with half of cohabiting relationships ending before two years (Kennedy & Bumpass, 2008). (These data are for the United States; intimate partnerships typically last longer elsewhere.)

Usually, both former partners in a severed relationship attempt to reestablish friendships and resume dating. Often they marry again, especially if they are young men. Women with children are less likely to remarry, but when they do, often their new husbands also have children from a previous marriage (Goldscheider & Sassler, 2006). About half of all U.S. marriages are remarriages for at least one partner.

Divorced adults who do not plan to remarry often develop new sexual partnerships, on average within two years of divorce. Rates of repartnering vary depending on several factors: Rates are higher among those with more education, higher among those with more income, and lower among those who are already parents. Ethnicity is also a factor—in the United States, African Americans, especially those with less than a high school education, are least likely to remarry (McNamee & Raley, 2011).

Initially, remarriage restores intimacy, health, and financial security. For remarried fathers, bonds with their new stepchildren or with a new baby may replace strained relationships with their children from the earlier marriage. Divorce usually increases depression and loneliness; repartnering brings relief. Most remarried adults are quite happy immediately after the wedding (Blekesaune, 2008).

However, their happiness may not endure. Remember that personality tends to change only slightly over the life span; people who were chronically unhappy in their first marriage may also become unhappy in their second. Stepchildren add unexpected stresses (Sweeney, 2010), and stepparents have difficulty letting the spouse's former mate continue to care for their own children (Gold, 2010). One theory is that because laws and norms are not clear about the proper role of stepparents, adults fight about what they expect each other to do or not do (Pollet, 2010).

Remember, however, that each cohort develops in a distinct historical period and the context of divorce has changed over the past decades. As more people separate or divorce, more people find suitable new partners and more stepchildren and stepparents have friends who have experienced the same problems, and who can help with adjustment.

One specific cohort change is that contemporary adults have more friends of both sexes than was true 50 years ago. If they get divorced, that friendship network may buffer them from the loneliness and loss of intimacy that divorced adults once experienced. Research on older adults who are divorced makes staying married seem best, on average, but that research may not predict the future for 30-year-olds who cohabit, marry, divorce, or remarry.

● **UNDERSTANDING THE NUMBERS**
It is often said that half the marriages in the United States end in divorce, and that is roughly true. However, the more times a person has married, not only is there a higher likelihood of divorce for each marriage (evidence of continuity), but remarriage also affects divorce statistics. How?

Answer For instance, if one person marries once and never divorces, and another person is married three times, divorcing each time, then the total is four marriages and three divorces—a divorce rate of 75%! It is not true that each marriage has a 50/50 chance of divorce: A first marriage of college graduates who are at least 25 years old is likely to endure.

> ## KEY ℘oints
>
> - Friends and consequential strangers are part of the social convoy that helps adults navigate happily through the years.
> - Family connections remain important, especially between parent and adult child and between siblings.
> - Happiness in marriage ebbs and flows, with highs in the first months of a new relationship and lows when children are very young.
> - Divorce is almost always difficult; remarriage can bring new happiness and new problems.

Generativity

According to Erikson, after the stage of *intimacy versus isolation* comes that of **generativity versus stagnation,** when adults seek to be productive in a caring way. Without generativity, adults experience "a pervading sense of stagnation and personal impoverishment" (Erikson, 1963, p. 267).

Adults satisfy their need to be generative in many ways, especially through art, caregiving, and employment. Of these three, the link between artistic expression and generativity has been least studied (although creativity is recognized as an avenue for self-expression, as we will see in the next chapter). Here we explore what has been learned about the two other generative activities: caregiving and employment. Balancing care and employment to achieve generativity is not easy, as we also discuss.

generativity versus stagnation
The seventh of Erikson's eight stages of development. Adults seek to be productive in a caring way, perhaps through art, caregiving, and employment.

Parenthood

Although generativity can take many forms, its chief form is "establishing and guiding the next generation," usually through parenthood (Erikson, 1963, p. 267). Many adults pass along their values as they respond to the hundreds of requests and unspoken needs of their children each day, thus becoming generative.

Parenting has been discussed many times in this text, primarily with a focus on its impact on children. Now we concentrate on the adult half of this interaction—the impact of parenting on the parents themselves. Bearing and rearing children are labor-intensive expressions of generativity, "a transformative experience" with more costs than benefits when children are young (Umberson et al., 2010). Indeed, "having a child is perhaps the most stressful experience in a family's life" (LeMasters, cited in McClain, 2011).

Because adults seek to be generative, many choose parenthood, willingly coping with the many stresses that come with that role. As Erikson (1963) says, "The fashionable insistence on dramatizing the dependence of children on adults often blinds us to the dependence of the older generation on the younger one" (p. 266).

Four Generations of Caregiving
These four women, from the great-grandmother to her 17-year-old great-granddaughter, all care for one another. Help flows to whoever needs it, not necessarily to the oldest or the youngest—although everyone cares for the youngest family member, the boy in front.

Children sometimes reorder adult perspectives, as adults become less focused on their personal identity or intimate relationships. One sign of a good parent is the parent's realization that the infant's cries are communicative, not selfish, and that adults need to care for children more than vice versa (Katz et al., 2011). This generative response does not always happen in the way that developmentalists would prefer. For example, a study of 91 gang members who became fathers found that almost all of them expressed new pride and priorities, but few quit their gangs and law-breaking ways (Moloney et al., 2009).

Every parent is tested by the dynamic experience of raising children. As experienced parents know, just when adults think they have mastered the art of parenting, children become older, thus presenting new challenges. Over the decades of family life, babies arrive and older children grow up, financial burdens shift, income almost never seems adequate, and, if the family includes several children, seldom is every child thriving. Illness and disability require extra care.

Problems and stresses increase as family size does. This is true worldwide, at least until the children are grown (Margolis & Myrskylä, 2011). As already mentioned, adult children usually bring their parents more joy than distress, but if even only one of them is troubled, middle-aged and older parents are less happy (Fingerman et al., 2012).

An added joy and burden occurs when adult children have children themselves. Grandparenthood begins, on average, when adults are about age 50, and it continues

Same Situation, Far Apart: Caregiving Dads Fathers are often caregivers for their young children, as shown here in Indonesia *(above)* and the United States *(below)*. Most developmentalists think that men have always nurtured their children, although in modern times employed mothers, plastic bottles, and sturdy baby carriers are among the specifics that have made caregiving easier as well as more crucial for men.

for decades. This topic is discussed in detail in Chapter 15, which presents the experiences of many older adults who have grandchildren of various ages and needs.

Here we should note that, worldwide, grandparents believe their work includes helping their grandchildren, especially if the middle generation is in crisis, such as divorce or illness (Herlofson & Hagestad, 2012). Grandparenthood can be another source of generativity and intimacy, depending on national policies and customs, gender, parent–child relationships, and the financial resources of both adult generations.

Chapter 8 explained that children can develop well in any family structure—nuclear or extended; heterosexual or same-sex; single-parent, two-parent, or grandparent. Can adults also thrive in any kind of parenting relationship?

Roughly one-third of all North American adults become stepparents, adoptive parents, or foster parents. These nonbiological parents have abundant opportunities for generativity, but they also experience distinct vulnerabilities as they meet the challenges of each of these routes to parenthood.

FOSTER CHILDREN Although parent–child attachment does not depend on biology, many foster children spent their early years with their birth parents and remain attached to them. This is part of human bonding to familiar caregivers, and normally it is mutually beneficial for parent and child. Intimacy needs may be met, even if the parent is not ideally generative.

However, if birth parents are so neglectful or abusive that the children are seriously harmed by their care, the children may be sent to foster care and their early attachment to their birth parents can impede connection to the foster parent. Furthermore, a secure new attachment is hampered if both adult and child know that their connection can be severed for reasons unrelated to caregiving quality or relationship strength. Such separations often occur with foster children who may be moved from one foster home to another, or back to the birth parent, for reasons unrelated to the adequacy of the foster parents (Pew Commission on Children in Foster Care, 2004).

As a result, adults who are not the birth parents face the dilemma of "whether to 'love' the children or maintain a cool, aloof posture with minimal sensitive or responsive interactions" (St. Petersburg–USA Orphanage Research Team, 2008, p. 15). A loving bond is better for both the foster parent and the child, but if that forms, separation is painful to both.

Generative caring does not occur in the abstract; it involves a particular caregiver and care receiver, so everything needs to be done to encourage attachment between the foster parent and child. Adults who recognize developmental norms are more likely to delight in their foster children, and this bodes well for the relationship (Bernard & Dozier, 2011).

All the details already explained in this text, from the Brazelton Neonatal Behavioral Assessment Scale (Chapter 2) to the first words (Chapter 3), from theory of mind (Chapter 5) to learning to read (Chapter 7), are accomplishments celebrated by an astute parent—no matter how parenting came about. For this, continuity of care is crucial because knowing a particular child well is essential in interpreting those first mispronounced words, understanding early emotional expressions, and knowing when to help with schoolwork. In many ways, good foster parents are intensely committed to a particular, unique human being—and from that commitment both the joys and the concerns of parenting arise.

STEPPARENTING Parents of stepchildren face some of the same challenges as foster parents, with additional complications. One is that many stepchildren have been adequately cared for in early childhood. The average age of new stepchildren is 9 years old, which means that they may be strongly connected to their biological

SYLWIA KAPUSCINSKI / NEWSCOM

Mother/Stepmother Remarriage gave Susan Heise *(far right)* a husband and stepchildren, joining her two biological progeny, both shown here. Erika, 16, converses with her at the table while Richard, 10, plays his trumpet, and Annie, 8, exercises in the doorway.

OBSERVATION QUIZ

Which one is a stepchild? (see answer, page 484) ➞

parents. This is normal and beneficial for the children, but hinders new connections to the stepparents.

Stepmothers may hope to heal a broken family through love and understanding, whereas stepfathers may think their new children will welcome a benevolent disciplinarian. Often they were chosen partly because their new spouse thought they would be a better father or mother than the original one.

Such expectations may be unrealistic, partly because stepchildren resist but also because few adults are able to live up to the generative ideal, day after day (Ganong, 2011). Some stepparents go to the other extreme, remaining distant from the children. One reason they do so may be that they know their connection to their stepchildren depends on the strength of their relationship with their spouse, the biological parent.

Young stepchildren often are hurt, sick, lost, or disruptive; teenage stepchildren may get pregnant, drunk, or arrested. These are all signs that the child needs special attention—and are conditions that may make stepparents angry and resentful rather than caring and patient. If the adults overreact to, or are indifferent to, such situations, the two generations become further alienated (Coleman et al., 2007).

The personality of the adults and the nature of the new marriage affect whether a family will weather such storms (Ganong & Coleman, 2004). On the positive side, many men become "social fathers," providing fatherly care to children who are not their genetic progeny, benefitting both generations (Bzostek, 2008).

ADOPTION Compared with foster parents and stepparents, adoptive parents have several advantages: They are legally connected to their child for life, and they desperately wanted the child. Current adoptions are usually "open," which means that the biological parents decided that someone else would be a better parent for the child, and the child is aware of this—an advantage for both sets of adults.

Strong parent–child bonds often develop, especially when children are adopted as infants. Secure attachments can also develop if adoption occurs when the children are older (ages 4 to 7), especially when the adopting mother was strongly attached to her own mother (Pace et al., 2011). However, children who spend their early years in an institution may never have been attached to anyone, and that makes it more difficult for the adoptive parent. Such children are mistrustful of all adults and fearful of loving anyone (St. Petersburg–USA Orphanage Research Team, 2008).

ANSWER TO **OBSERVATION QUIZ**
(from page 483) Erika. There are two clues: The ages of the children make it more likely that the eldest is from the father's first marriage, and biological children often try to grab their mother's attention if she seems to focus on another child. ●

As you remember, adolescence, when teenagers seek their own identity, can stress any family. This can be particularly problematic with adoptive families, as all teenagers want to know their genetic and ethnic roots. One college student who feels well loved and cared for by her adoptive parents explains:

> In attempts to upset my parents sometimes I would (foolishly) say that I wish I was given to another family, but I never really meant it. Still when I did meet my birth family I could definitely tell we were related—I fit in with them so well. I guess I have a very similar attitude and make the same faces as my birth mother! It really makes me consider nature to be very strong in personality.
>
> *[April, 2012, personal communication]*

A longitudinal study of parent–adoptive child relationships found that the parents' response to adolescent behavior was crucial. Neither overly strict nor overly permissive parenting helps the adopted teenager; consistent, supportive parenting does (Klahr et al., 2011).

Attitudes in the larger culture often increase tensions between adoptive parents and children. For example, the mistaken notion that the "real" parents are the biological ones is a common social construction that hinders a secure attachment.

Adoptive parents who undergo the complications of international adoption are usually intensely dedicated to their children, as are parents of domestic adoptees of another ethnicity. They are very much "real" parents, as is evident as they fight the discrimination experienced by children of minority heritage that they might have been unaware of before it affected their child.

Despite all the stresses and complications associated with foster, step-, or adoptive parenting, most adults cherish the experience. For instance, most adults who adopt seek a second child. As Erikson realized, adults want to be needed, and children offer their parents an opportunity to be generative every day.

Caregiving

Erikson (1963) wrote that a mature adult "needs to be needed" (p. 266). Some caregiving requires meeting physical needs—feeding, cleaning, and so on—but much of it involves fulfilling another person's psychological needs. As one study concludes:

> The time and energy required to provide emotional support to others must be reconceptualized as an important aspect of the *work* that takes place in families. . . . Caregiving, in whatever form, does not just emanate from within, but must be managed, focused, and directed so as to have the intended effect on the care recipient.
>
> *[Erickson, 2005, p. 349]*

Thus, caregiving includes responding to the emotions of people who need a confidant, a cheerleader, a counselor, a close friend. Parents and children care for one another, as do partners. Often neighbors, friends, and more distant relatives are caregivers as well.

kinkeeper
A caregiver who takes responsibility for maintaining communication among family members.

Most extended families include a **kinkeeper,** a caregiver who takes responsibility for maintaining communication. The kinkeeper gathers everyone for holidays; spreads the word about anyone's illness, relocation, or accomplishments; buys gifts for special occasions; and reminds family members of one another's birthdays and anniversaries (Sinardet & Mortelmans, 2009). Guided by their kinkeeper, all the family members become more generative.

Fifty years ago, kinkeepers were almost always women, usually the mother or grandmother of a large family. Now families are smaller and gender equity is more apparent, so some men or young women are kinkeepers. Generally, however, the kinkeeper is still a middle-aged or older mother with several adult children. This role may seem burdensome, but caregiving provides both satisfaction and power (Mitchell, 2010). The best caregivers share the work; shared kinkeeping is an example of generativity.

CARING FOR AGING PARENTS Because of their position in the generational hierarchy, many middle-aged adults are expected to help both the older and younger generations. They have been called the **sandwich generation,** a term that evokes an image of a layer of filling pressed between two slices of bread. This analogy suggests that the middle generation is squeezed between the needs of younger and older relatives. This sandwich metaphor is vivid, but it gives a false impression (Grundy & Henretta, 2006).

Caregiving is beneficial because people feel useful when they help one another. Far from being squeezed, older adults are *less* likely to be depressed if they are supporting their adult children than when they are distant from them (Byers et al., 2008). On their part, many grown children get pleasure from helping their parents.

I have seen this many times, including in my own life. My children were cheerful and insisted on caring for me when I broke those small bones in my pelvis; they enjoy advising me about fashion, social media, and celebrities. Researchers find that young adults often help their parents understand current culture and technological change, providing information and insight as well as programming their cell phones.

Because of better health and vitality throughout life, many adults do not need to provide extensive physical care for older generations. As explained in detail in Chapter 15, in developed nations when elders need care, it is typically provided by a spouse or a paid caregiver. Adult children and grandchildren are part of the caregiving team, but not the major providers. Few middle-aged adults are stuck in the middle of a sandwich.

This is not to deny that, for a minority of adults—usually middle-aged women—providing care for an elderly relative affects sibling relationships, marriages, or employment. For example, although siblings usually become closer in adulthood, a caregiving burden can disrupt that. If an elderly parent needs care, one sibling usually becomes the chief caregiver, to the resentment of everyone else.

This was apparent in a particular family. A caregiving sister described one sibling as "real immature . . . a little slow" and the other as "very irresponsible," adding that "when it came right down to having to bathe and having to take care of physical tasks, neither of them would be able to handle it." A brother in another family resented his caregiving sister: "My sister reminds me all the time that she's taking care of [our parents]. They're actually pretty self-sufficient" (quotes from Ingersoll-Dayton et al., 2003, pp. 208–209).

Specifics of elder care differ (see Table 13.4). Husbands and wives can become resentful, too, if care of one spouse's elderly relatives is not what the other spouse anticipated. As explained next, cultures differ radically on caregiving expectations, and husbands may have been raised with opposite assumptions from those of their wives, and vice versa.

sandwich generation
The generation of middle-aged people who are supposedly "squeezed" by the needs of the younger and older members of their families. In reality, some adults do feel pressured by these obligations, but most are not burdened by them, either because they enjoy fulfilling them or because they choose to take on only some of them or none of them.

TABLE 13.4 Contacts and Help Provided by Middle-Aged Couples to Parents and In-Laws

	Phone Calls per Month	Visits per Month	Minutes of Help per Week
Wife to own parents	11	6	120
Husband to wife's parents	8	5	70
Total to wife's parents	19	11	190
Husband to own parents	7	4	100
Wife to husband's parents	5	4	58
Total to husband's parents	12	8	158

Source: E. Lee et al., 2003

Hi, Mom Connections between middle-aged adults and their parents vary a great deal from family to family, cohort to cohort, and place to place. These data are from the United States. In many Asian nations, connections are stronger to the husband's parents than the wife's. Geographical distance also reduces visits. However, phone calls and Internet messages remain high over the distance; according to some studies, even higher than the numbers shown here.

CULTURE AND FAMILY CAREGIVING Specifics of family bonds depend on many factors, including childhood attachments, cultural norms, and the financial and practical resources of each generation. Some cultures assume that elderly parents should live with their children; others believe that elders should live alone as long as possible and then enter some care-providing residence (Parveen, 2009; Ron, 2009). Cultures also differ as to whether sons or daughters should provide more help and whether divorced, step-, or distant parents deserve care.

In North America, Western Europe, and Australia, older adults cherish their independence and dread burdening their children. Even frail parents seek to maintain autonomy, feeling that moving in with their children is a sign of failure. By contrast, in nations where dependence on others is a desirable personality trait, living with family does not necessarily signify a problem (Harvey & Yoshino, 2006).

For instance, one study of 549 Latino families found that those who were high in *familismo* had little conflict between the husbands and wives, both of whom were very proud and nurturing of the children. That led, in turn, to children liking school and doing well there. Thus, every family member tried to please the other ones, with good results (Taylor et al., 2012). In such families, when elders need care, everyone realizes they must do their share.

Familism may lead relatives to help one another, even if someone is addicted to drugs, abusive, or wanted by the police. Some families consider it betrayal for a family member to report a child-abusing relative; instead of calling the authorities, other family members are expected to take over child care.

A contrasting value is individualism. Some families expect all adults to be self-supporting and law-abiding. They would not subsidize a cousin who could not pay her bills or protect a nephew who broke the law.

Two dramatic examples make the point: One of my students shot someone (he said it was justified) and then hid in his cousin's house. To his shock and anger, she called the police. Likewise, Theodore Kaczynski (the "Unabomber") mailed letter bombs that killed three people and wounded 23 others. He escaped detection for 17 years until his suspicious younger brother alerted the authorities.

More mundane examples occur for everyone: Some people are expected to baby-sit for their siblings' children, quit college in a family emergency, or provide housing for distant relatives. Other people would consider that wrong.

Ethnic variations are evident in how close family members are expected to be. Generally, ethnic minorities are more closely connected to family members than are ethnic majorities in that they see each other more often and share food, money, and so on. However, although people may assume that closeness means affection, for minorities particularly, closeness sometimes increases conflict (Voorpostel & Schans, 2011).

As you might imagine, if a husband and wife have different assumptions about what should become of elderly relatives, or how indulgent parents should be of their grown children, or whether citizens should be intensely involved in community organizations or national politics, then clashes about generativity result.

The expectations even of spouses who come from the same ethnic group may differ. For instance, most elderly Chinese have their own homes; however, if they live with an adult child, in mainland China it is usually with a son but in Taiwan it is usually with a daughter (Chu et al., 2011). What would happen in a marriage if the husband expected his elderly parents to move in but the wife thought the husband's sisters should take on that burden?

Employment

Besides family caregiving, the other major avenue for generativity is employment. Most of the social science research on jobs has focused on economic productivity, an important issue but not central to our study of human development. Social scientists, in economics and in other disciplines, are beginning to put "thinking about working into the broader fabric of psychological theory and practice" (Blustein, 2006, p. xiv). To understand life-span development, a multidisciplinary approach is needed (as explained in Chapter 1); appreciating the importance of work in adulthood is a prime example.

As is evident from many of the terms used to describe healthy adult development —*generativity, success and esteem, instrumental,* and *achievement*—adults have many psychosocial needs that employment can fill. The converse is also true: Unemployment is associated with higher rates of child abuse, alcoholism, depression, and many other social and mental health problems (Freisthler et al., 2006; Wanberg, 2012). Indeed, adults who can't find work are 60 percent more likely to die than other people their age, especially if they are younger than 40 (Roelfs et al., 2011).

WAGES AND BENEFITS Income pays living expenses, and it also does far more than that. Beginning with Thorstein Veblen (1899/2008), sociologists have described *conspicuous consumption,* whereby people buy things—such as expensive cars, hip sunglasses, and MP3 players—primarily to show them off. Families move to more affluent neighborhoods not only for safety but also for status. People buy more when they are depressed; money is a mood-changer (Cryder et al., 2008).

Given this human characteristic, it is not surprising that raises and bonuses increase motivation. Surprisingly, though, the absolute income (whether a person earns $30,000 or $33,000 or $40,000 a year, for instance) matters less to many people than how their income compares with others in their profession or neighborhood, or to their own salary a year or two ago. Salary cuts have emotional, not just financial, effects.

This might explain why even though average household income has doubled in the United States over the past 50 years, happiness has not increased. Worldwide, extreme poverty correlates with unhappiness, but most people are mildly happy. Some people at every income level are depressed (E. Diener & Biswas-Diener, 2008).

The sense of unfairness is innate and universal, encoded in the human brain (Hsu et al., 2008). Awareness of this helps explain some of the attitudes of adults about their pay. English workers in one study were less happy and more likely to quit if they thought the salary ranking in their company was unfair, especially if the higher ranks were paid much more than the lower ones (G. D. A. Brown et al., 2008).

In the United States, many are offended by the extremely high salaries of corporate executives, which is why the slogan "We are the 99 percent" has such power. Indeed, it is part of human nature to notice when other people seem advantaged. Women complain that men are better paid, each ethnic group resents the other groups for their income or benefits, younger workers resent the seniority of older workers, older workers complain that the young are less dedicated, and so on. This is not to deny that discrimination exists: All these complaints arise from reality as well as from human nature.

However, much of the resentment arises not directly from wages, benefits, and working conditions per se but from the way they are determined: If workers have a role in setting fair wages, they are more satisfied (Choshen-Hillel & Yaniv, 2011).

A wish for fairness is also evident when benefits are compared. Consider health insurance. Globalization has made more Americans aware of the Canadian and European health care systems, which provide care for everyone; as a result, pressure

©THE NEW YORKER COLLECTION 1992 DANA FRADON FROM CARTOONBANK.COM. ALL RIGHTS RESERVED.

Lowered Expectations It was once realistic, a "secular trend," for adults to expect to be better off than their parents had been, but hard times have reduced the socioeconomic status of many adults.

for the United States to switch to a similarly all-inclusive system has been growing. In nations where family health care is provided primarily through employment, "health care coverage may be key to understanding who remains employed in the face of overwhelming caregiving demands" (Bianchi & Milkie, 2010. p. 719).

A related problem is that people are much more likely to want to hold on to whatever they have than to risk losing it to get something better (Kahneman, 2011). This characteristic, called *risk aversion,* explains why seniors who receive medical care paid by the government (Medicare) are fiercely protective of that benefit yet do not want the same benefits to extend to younger adults. Any change in employment conditions that benefits many people but harms a few is likely to be resisted by the few more than welcomed by the many.

WORKING FOR MORE THAN MONEY To understand human development, we must go beyond income and consider the generative aspects of work—and there are many. Work provides a structure for daily life, a setting for human interaction, a source of social status and fulfillment. In addition, work meets generativity needs by allowing people to do the following:

- Develop and use their personal skills
- Express their creative energy
- Aid and advise coworkers, as mentor or friend
- Support the education and health of their families
- Contribute to the community by providing goods or services

The pleasure of "a job well done" is universal, as is the joy of having supportive supervisors and friendly coworkers. Job satisfaction correlates more strongly with challenge, creativity, productivity, and relationships among employees than with high pay or easy work (Pfeffer, 2007). Workers quit their jobs more often because of unpleasant social interactions at the workplace than because of dissatisfaction with wages or benefits (LeBlanc & Barling, 2004).

These facts highlight the distinction between the **extrinsic rewards of work**—which are the tangible benefits such as salary, health insurance, and pension—and the **intrinsic rewards of work**—which are the intangible gratifications of actually doing the job. Generativity is intrinsic.

A developmental view finds that extrinsic rewards tend to be more important at first, when young people enter the workforce and begin to establish their careers (Kooij et al, 2011). After a few years, in a developmental shift, the "intrinsic rewards of work—satisfaction, relationships with coworkers, and a sense of participation in meaningful activity—become more important as an individual ages" (Sterns & Huyck, 2001, p. 452).

The power of intrinsic rewards explains why older employees display, on average, less absenteeism, less lateness, and more job commitment than do younger workers (Landy & Conte, 2007). A crucial factor may be that in many jobs, older workers have more control over what they do, as well as when and how they do it. Autonomy reduces strain and increases dedication and vitality.

In a demonstration of this effect, one study began with 972 men who went back to work after a mild heart attack. Their work was categorized as high strain (with many psychological demands but little personal control), low strain (fewer demands but more control), or mixed (moderate demands and some control). After taking into account age, high blood pressure, and 24 other factors that make heart attacks more likely, the researchers found that new heart problems (including death) were twice as common among those with high work strain (Aboa-Éboulé et al., 2007).

extrinsic rewards of work
The tangible benefits, usually in the form of compensation (e.g., salary, health insurance, pension), that one receives for doing a job.

intrinsic rewards of work
The intangible gratifications (e.g., job satisfaction, self-esteem, pride) that come from within oneself as a result of doing a job.

Another crucial factor is family support. Family members being appreciative and helpful regarding a worker's job requirements benefits the person's health. Satisfaction at work spills over to satisfaction at home and vice versa: When health impairs a husband's ability to work, divorce is more likely (Teachman, 2010).

The Changing Workplace

Obviously, work is changing in many ways. Globalization means that each nation exports what it does best (and cheapest) and imports what it needs. Specialization, interdependency, and international trade are increasing. Advanced nations are shifting from industry-based economies to information and service economies; poorer nations are shifting from subsistence agriculture to industry.

Multinational corporations are replacing small, local businesses; employees are hired for competency, not family connections; work goes on every hour of the day and every day of the week. Although every change has implications for human development, we focus here on only three—diversity among workers, job changes, and alternate schedules.

DIVERSITY Dramatic changes have occurred in who has a job and what they do. This is true in every nation, but we provide statistics for the United States as an obvious example. Fifty years ago, the labor force was 36 percent women, 11 percent non-White (as all minorities were then called). In 2012, 47 percent of the employed civilians were female and 35 percent were non-White (nearly 16 percent Hispanic, 12 percent African American, 5 percent Asian, and 2 percent more than one race) (see Figure 13.3).

Specific occupations were far more segregated by sex and ethnicity; male nurses and female police officers were very rare in 1960. Employment discrimination in gender and ethnicity is still present—but to a much smaller degree.

This benefits people who would not have been hired in previous decades, but also requires employers to be sensitive to differences they might not have noticed.

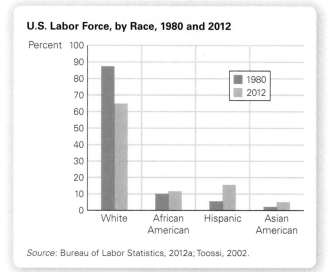

U.S. Labor Force, by Race, 1980 and 2012

Source: Bureau of Labor Statistics, 2012a; Toossi, 2002.

FIGURE 13.3 Diversity at Work The U.S. labor force is increasingly non-White, even according to Labor Department statistics (which exclude some low-wage workers). Ideally, all adults would have jobs that complement their individual abilities, but that is not yet the case. The next challenge is for women and people of all ethnic groups to be proportionally distributed in various vocations, management positions, and workplaces.

If You Had to Choose These hundreds of trainees in India *(left)* hope for a steady job, responding to North American callers who are confused about their computers, their bills, or their online orders. For millions of educated but unemployed Indians, this aspect of the global labor market may be their best hope. However, their hourly salary is less than one-fifth the salary of the two men at the right, skilled technicians on an offshore oil rig. Despite high pay, their jobs are hard to fill because they must spend days and even years far from their homes and families.

✦ **ESPECIALLY FOR** Entrepreneurs
Suppose you are starting a business. In what ways would middle-aged adults be helpful to you? (see response, page 492)➔

Younger adults may have an advantage here, since they more often have grown up with people of many backgrounds. Older people have their own advantage if their life experience has helped them understand ethnic and other differences. As the following explains, research finds that each group may be troubled by actions and attitudes that well-intentioned people of other groups do not notice.

A VIEW FROM SCIENCE

Accommodating Diversity

Accommodating the various sensitivities and needs of a diverse workforce requires far more than reconsidering the cafeteria menu and the holiday schedule. Private rooms for breast-feeding, revised uniform guidelines, better office design, and new management practices may be required. Exactly what is needed depends on the particular culture of the workers: Some are satisfied with conditions that others would reject.

For example, one study found that U.S. employees were stressed when they had little control over their work or when they had direct confrontations with their supervisors, whereas employees in China are most stressed by the possibility of negative job evaluations and indirect conflicts with coworkers (C. Liu et al., 2007).

Some words, policies, jokes, or mannerisms may seem innocuous to people of one group but toxic to people of another group. Researchers have begun to explore *micro-aggressions*—small things unnoticed by the majority person that seem aggressive to the minority person (Sue, 2010).

Micro-aggressions can be detected by anyone, not only by people who identify with a particular ethnic group but also by people of a particular age, sexual orientation, or religion. For example, one research group found that older workers were particularly likely to experience micro-aggression at their workplace, but that some young men also noticed micro-aggressions aimed at them (Chou & Choi, 2011). Comments about "senior moments" or being "color blind" or the "fair sex" or "the model minority" can be perceived as aggressive, even though the person making such comments is convinced that they are helpful, not hurtful.

Consider one study in detail. African Americans and European Americans read transcripts of discussions among hiring teams who were supposedly analyzing job applicants (Salvatore & Shelton, 2007). The applicants listed experiences or memberships that alerted the readers about their race. The transcripts were designed to show one of three possibilities: (1) that the hiring teams judged applicants fairly, regardless of race; (2) that the teams were clearly racist; or (3) that a minority applicant was rejected with reasons that seemed plausible though not entirely convincing.

After reading the transcripts, the participants took a test that required mental concentration. The performance of the European Americans was impaired after they read the blatantly racist responses but not after they read the more subtle ones. The opposite was true for the African Americans—their intellectual sharpness was not affected by the clearly racist responses but was hindered by the ambiguous ones.

The experimenters believe that this result shows that the African Americans were not surprised by overt racism, so processing the racist transcripts did not require much mental energy. However, more subtle prejudice did trouble them because considerable mental effort was required for them to decide whether racism was a factor. That result alerts every worker and employer to be aware not only of racist or sexist remarks but also of inadvertent comments or behaviors that might be interpreted as prejudicial.

CHANGING JOBS One recent change in the labor market is that resignations, firings, and hirings occur more often. Temporary employees are more common. Between the ages of 23 and 44, the average worker in the United States has seven different employers, with men somewhat more likely to change jobs than women (U.S. Bureau of the Census, 2011b). Sometimes jobs are lost because employers downsize, reorganize, relocate, outsource, or merge. Sometimes adults choose to quit because of dissatisfaction or frustration.

Either way, social connections to consequential strangers are broken and workers suffer. These human costs are confirmed by longitudinal research: People who frequently changed jobs by age 36 were three times more likely to have various health problems by age 42 (Kinnunen et al., 2005). This study controlled for smoking and drinking; if it had not, the health impact would have been even greater since poor health habits correlate with job instability.

As adults grow older, job changes become increasingly stressful, for several reasons (Rix, 2011):

1. Seniority brings higher salaries, more respect, and greater expertise; workers who leave a job they have had for years lose these advantages.

2. Many skills required for employment were not taught decades ago, and many employers are reluctant to hire and train older workers.

3. Age discrimination is illegal, but workers are convinced that it is common, especially after age 50. Even if this is not true, we know from stereotype threat that it undercuts success in job searches.

4. Relocation reduces both intimacy and generativity.

From a developmental perspective, this last factor is crucial. Imagine that you are a middle-aged adult who has always lived in Michigan, and your employer goes out of business. You try to find work, but no one hires you, partly because unemployment in Michigan is high since many industrial employers have moved overseas. Would you move a thousand miles to North Dakota, where the unemployment rate is only one-fourth that of Michigan?

If you were unemployed and in debt, and a new job was guaranteed, you might leave your friends and your community. But would your spouse and children quit their jobs, schools, and social networks to move with you? For you and everyone in your family, moving means losing intimacy.

Such difficulties are magnified for immigrants, who make up about 15 percent of the U.S. adult workforce and more than 20 percent of Canada's. Many depend on other immigrants for housing, work, and social support (García Coll & Marks, 2012). That meets some intimacy and generativity needs, but obviously any move decreases a person's chance to have friends, family, and employment that enhance psychological and physical health.

WORK SCHEDULES No longer does work always follow a 9-to-5, Monday-through-Friday schedule. In the United States, only about half of all employees work on that traditional schedule. The service part of the economy often includes work during evenings, nights, and weekends, and service jobs are increasing as manufacturing and agriculture jobs decrease. In Europe, the proportion of employees on nonstandard work schedules varies from 25 percent in Sweden to 40 percent in Italy (Presser et al., 2008) (see Figure 13.4).

One crucial variable for job satisfaction is whether employees can choose their own hours. Workers who volunteer for paid overtime are usually satisfied, but workers who are required to work overtime are not (Beckers et al., 2008). This is true no matter how experienced the workers are, what their occupation is, or where they live.

For instance, a nationwide study of 53,851 nurses, ages 20 to 59, found that *required* overtime was one of the few factors that reduced job satisfaction in every cohort (Klaus et al., 2012). Similarly, a study of office workers in China also found that the extent of required overtime correlated with less satisfaction and poorer health (Houdmont et al., 2011). Apparently, although work (paid or unpaid) is satisfying to every adult, working too long and not by choice undercuts the psychological and physical benefits.

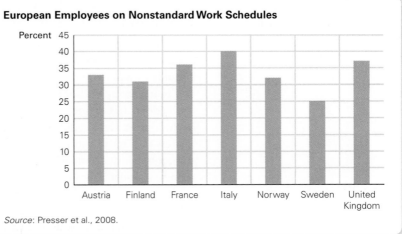

European Employees on Nonstandard Work Schedules

Source: Presser et al., 2008.

FIGURE 13.4 In Whose Favor? The traditional work schedule—Monday to Friday, 9:00 A.M. to 5:00 P.M.—is best for workers and their families. Employers and consumers, however, would prefer to have workers on the job on weekends and during evening and night shifts. European nations tilt toward the standard schedule. In the United States, about half of all workers have nonstandard schedules. In developing nations, most workers have nonstandard hours.

Barefoot Commuting Straddling home and work has many advantages: A person's visible half can be dressed to impress, while his bottom half relaxes. Yet if this telecommuter is torn between demands of job and family, this setup is more stressful than it appears.

flextime
An arrangement in which work schedules are flexible so that employees can balance personal and occupational responsibilities.

telecommuting
Working at home and keeping in touch with the office via computer, telephone, and scanner.

RESPONSE FOR Entrepreneurs
(from page 490) As employees and as customers. Middle-aged workers are steady, with few absences and good "people skills," and they like to work. In addition, household income is likely to be higher at about age 50 than at any other time, so middle-aged adults will probably be able to afford your products or services. ●

Weekend work, especially with mandatory overtime, is particularly difficult for father–child relationships, because "normal rhythms of family life are impinged upon by irregular schedules" (Hook, 2012, p. 631). Some nations impose limits on what employers can demand of employees who are parents; this is not true of the United States (Gornick & Meyers, 2003).

One attempt to provide more worker choice is **flextime,** now offered by some employers and available to about one-fourth of U.S. employees, who have some choice in the particular hours they work. **Telecommuting,** whereby an employee can work from home and use videoconferencing, online communication, and scanning to keep in touch with the office, is also becoming more common. These options are offered primarily for office and professional jobs and thus are not available for most young parents.

Such schedules have many advantages for employees and employers. However, while they allow workers to "experience the benefits of greater family enrichment," the concurrent demands of family life and work can increase stress (Bianchi & Milkie, 2010; Golden et al., 2006, p. 1348).

In theory, part-time work and self-employment might allow adults to balance conflicting demands. But reality does not conform to the theory. In many nations (except the Netherlands, where half the workers are part time), part-time work is typically underpaid, without benefits such as health care (in the United States) or pensions (in many nations). Thus, workers avoid it if possible.

About one-third of all working couples who have young children and nonstandard schedules choose to have one parent at home while the other is at work. Mothers, particularly, are likely to rearrange meal and sleeping schedules so that they spend time with their children (Hook et al., 2012). However, night work and other nonstandard work schedules, especially when combined with overwork, correlate with personal, relational, and child-rearing difficulties (K.D. Davis et al., 2008; H. Liu et al., 2011).

Combining Intimacy and Generativity

Adult development depends on particulars of job, home, and personality that affect the ability to balance intimacy and generativity (Voydanoff, 2007). Employment contributes to adult psychosocial health, but other factors are important as well: Some adults are happy without a job, especially if others in their household are employed, with adequate income.

A large study of adult Canadians found that about half of the variation in their distress was related to employment (working conditions, support at work, occupation, job security), but at least as much was related to family (having children younger than 5, support at home) and feeling personally competent (Marchand et al., 2012).

To find an ideal balance, at least three factors are helpful: adequate income, chosen schedules, and social support. Some employers consider the psychosocial needs of their workers, but most do not (Breaugh & Frye, 2008). Indeed, it can be argued that worker satisfaction does not predict worker productivity and that the latter should be the goal of employers (Ajzen, 2011).

Fortunately, research on linked lives shows that husbands and wives adjust to each other's work, which helps them as a unit (Abele & Volmer, 2011). For instance, husbands spend more hours working after marriage, and wives spend more hours maintaining the home, so that five years after marriage the man's salary is notably higher than it would have been if he were single, while their shared home is notably more accommodating (Kuperberg, 2012).

If they have children, they adjust their work and child-care hours, usually with the mother cutting back on employment, but not always—sometimes the father has fewer labor market hours and the mother has more. When mothers work full time,

often fathers spend far more time with their children, and mothers do less housework (Abele & Volmer, 2011). If job loss threatens, both partners often prepare for their changed lives (Sweet & Moen, 2012). These factors reduce adult depression, especially in women.

In many ways, family members adjust to one another's employment, helping everyone cope. Perhaps men, women, and children are better off with today's dual-income families, variable schedules, and so on (Bianchi & Milkie, 2010).

However, whether psychosocial development in adulthood is getting better or worse is debatable. Because personality is enduring and variable, the stance on this issue depends on personal perspective. Some people are optimists—high in extroversion and agreeableness—and they tend to believe that adulthood is better now than it used to be. Others are pessimists—high in neuroticism and low in openness—and they are likely to conclude that life was better before the rise of cohabitation, LATs, and divorce, when almost all couples married, had children, and mothers stayed home.

The data support both perspectives—suicide is less common, for instance, but poverty is increasing. From a developmental perspective, it is clear that intimacy and generativity continue to be important to adults, as they always have been. As you will see in Chapters 14 and 15, many perspectives are possible on late adulthood as well. Some view the last years of life with horror, others consider them the golden years. Neither view is quite accurate.

Mothers at Work Mothers have always worked while tending their babies—be it in the fields, as this Hmong woman *(left)* still does, or at home *(right)*, before stoves, dishwashers, freezers, microwaves, washer-dryers, and vacuum cleaners lightened the load. Now work is less physical and more cognitive, allowing many mothers to enter the labor market. That raises a controversial question: Which mother and child have a better life?

KEY points

- Adults strive to meet their generativity needs, primarily through raising children, caring for others, and being productive members of society.
- Parenthood of all kinds is difficult yet rewarding, with foster, step-, and adoptive parents facing special challenges.
- Caregivers are generative, with each adult caring for other family members.
- Employment ideally aids generativity, via productivity and social networks.
- Many parents seek to combine child rearing and employment, with mixed success, depending on the specifics of employment and family life.

SUMMARY

Personality Development in Adulthood

1. The personality of adults remains quite stable, although many adults become more mature, as described by Erikson and Maslow. The midlife crisis is more myth than fact, more a cohort effect than a universal experience.

2. The Big Five personality traits—openness, conscientiousness, extroversion, agreeableness, and neuroticism—characterize personality at every age, with each person relatively high or low on each of these five. Adults choose their particular ecological niche based partly on personality. Culture and context affect everyone.

3. Although chosen careers and partners typically reinforce existing personality traits, unexpected events (e.g., a major illness or financial windfall) can temporarily disrupt personality.

Intimacy

4. Intimacy is a universal human need, satisfied in diverse ways, with friends and family, romantic partners, and consequential strangers. Each person has a social convoy of other people with whom he or she travels through life.

5. Friends are crucial for buffering stress and sharing secrets, for everyday companionship and guidance. This is true for both sexes.

6. Family members have linked lives, continuing to affect one another as they all grow older. Parents and adult children are less likely to live together than in earlier times, but family members are often mutually supportive, emotionally and financially.

7. Marriage typically occurs later now than it did in earlier decades, and cohabitation and living apart together are sometimes alternatives to, sometimes preludes to, marriage. Most adults still seek a romantic partner (same sex or other sex) with whom to share life.

8. Divorce is difficult for both partners and their family members, not only immediately but for years before and after the event.

9. Remarriage is common, especially for men. This solves some of the problems (particularly financial and intimacy troubles) of divorced adults, but the success of second marriages varies.

Generativity

10. Adults seek to feel generative, achieving, successful, instrumental—all words used to describe a major psychosocial need that each adult meets in various ways.

11. Parenthood is a common expression of generativity. Even wanted and planned-for biological children pose challenges; foster children, stepchildren, and adoptive children bring additional stresses and joys.

12. Caregiving is more likely to flow from the older generations to the younger ones, so the "sandwich generation" metaphor is misleading. Many families have a kinkeeper, who aids generativity within the family.

13. Employment brings many rewards to adults, particularly intrinsic benefits such as pride and friendship. Changes in employment patterns—including job switches, shift work, and the diversity of fellow workers—can affect other aspects of adult development.

14. Combining work schedules, caregiving requirements, and intimacy needs is not easy; consequences are mixed. Some adults benefit from new patterns within the labor market; others find that the demands of work impair family well-being.

KEY TERMS

Big Five (p. 466)
consequential strangers (p. 470)
ecological niche (p. 466)
empty nest (p. 477)
extrinsic rewards of work (p. 488)
fictive kin (p. 473)
flextime (p. 492)
generativity versus stagnation (p. 481)
intimacy versus isolation (p. 469)
intrinsic rewards of work (p. 488)
kinkeeper (p. 484)
midlife crisis (p. 465)
sandwich generation (p. 485)
social convoy (p. 469)
telecommuting (p. 492)

WHAT HAVE YOU LEARNED?

1. Describe the two basic needs of adulthood.

2. Explain how the midlife crisis might reflect cohort rather than maturational changes.

3. Give examples to demonstrate how each of the Big Five personality traits might influence an adult's choice of jobs, mates, and neighborhoods.

4. Explain the concept of "social convoy."

5. What roles do friends play in a person's life?

6. What are the differences between friends and consequential strangers?

7. What is the usual relationship between adult children and their parents? What factors might explain this relationship?

8. What usually happens to sibling relationships over the course of adulthood?

9. Why do people have fictive kin?

10. What needs do long-term partners meet?

11. How and why does marital happiness change from the wedding to old age?

12. What evidence is there that political and cultural attitudes toward same-sex partnerships are changing?

13. What are the usual consequences of divorce?

14. Many people who repartner are happy at first, but their happiness may not last. Why might this be the case?

15. What is the basic idea of generativity?

16. In what ways does parenthood satisfy an adult's need to be generative?

17. What factors might make it difficult for foster children and foster parents to bond?

18. How might each of the Big Five personality traits make it easier or more difficult to develop positive relationships with stepchildren?

19. What advantages do adoptive parents have over foster parents or stepparents?

20. Women are more often kinkeepers and caregivers than are men. How is this role both a blessing and a burden?

21. Why are middle-aged adults sometimes called the "sandwich generation"? Why might this metaphor create a false impression?

22. What are the advantages and disadvantages of familism? Of individualism?

23. What are some extrinsic and intrinsic rewards of work?

24. What are the advantages of greater ethnic diversity at work?

25. List four reasons why changing jobs is stressful.

26. What innovations in work scheduling have helped families? What innovations have hurt families?

27. Why, overall, might men and women be happier with current employment patterns than earlier ones?

APPLICATIONS

1. Describe a relationship that you know of in which a middle-aged person and a younger adult learned from each other.

2. Did your parents' marital and employment status affect you? How would you have fared if they had chosen other marriage or work patterns?

3. Imagine becoming a foster or adoptive parent yourself. What do you see as the personal benefits and costs?

4. Ask several people how their personalities have changed in the past decade. The research suggests that changes are usually minor. Is that what you found?

>>ONLINE CONNECTIONS

To accompany your textbook, you have access to a number of online resources, including quizzes for every chapter of the book, flashcards (in English and Spanish), critical-thinking questions, and case studies. For access to any of these links, go to www.worthpublishers.com/bergerinvitation2e. In addition to these free resources, you'll also find links to podcasts, video clips, diagnostic quizzing with personalized study advice, and an ebook. Some of the videos and activities available online include:

- *Romantic Love and the Brain.* Explores neural and hormonal activity as the foundations of love and relationships and looks at the evolutionary benefit of pairing.

- *Caregivers Between Generations: What Is the "Sandwich Generation"?* In this short video, two experts discuss the realities and stresses of caring for impaired elders.

Late Adulthood

What emotions do you anticipate as you read about late adulthood? Sadness, depression, resignation, sympathy, sorrow? Expect instead surprise and joy. You will learn that many older adults are active, alert, and self-sufficient; that marked intellectual decline ("senility") is unusual; and that even at age 90 or 100 people are quite happy. That does not mean mindless contentment. Earlier personality and social patterns continue; the complexities of human life are evident. Joy is mixed with sorrow, and poverty, loneliness, and chronic illness are always difficult. However, most older adults, most of the time, are active and independent.

Unfortunately, late adulthood, more than any other part of life, is a magnet for misinformation and prejudice. If your first thought was a sad one as you approached these chapters, you are one of many. Why? Think about that as you read.

CHAPTER OUTLINE

LATE ADULTHOOD
Body and Mind

WHAT WILL YOU KNOW?

- What percentage of older people are in nursing homes?
- At what age is it no longer possible to learn new things?
- Is forgetting names the first sign of dementia?
- Is wisdom always, sometimes, or never characteristic of the elderly? The young?

I took Asa, age 1, to the playground. One mother, watching her son, warned me that the sandbox would be crowded before long because the children from a nearby daycare center would soon arrive. I asked questions, and to my delight she explained details of the center's curriculum, staffing, scheduling, and tuition as if I were Asa's mother, weighing my options for next year.

Soon I realized she probably was merely being polite, because a girl too young to be graciously ageist glanced at me and asked:

"Is that your grandchild?"

I nodded.

"Where is the mother?" was her next question.

Later that afternoon came the final blow. As I opened the gate for a middle-aged man, he said, "Thank you, young lady." I don't think I look old, but no one would imagine I was young. That "young lady" was benevolent, but it made me realize that my pleasure at the first woman's words was a sign of my own, self-deceptive, prejudice. ●

- -

NOW WE BEGIN OUR STUDY of the last phase of life, from age 65 or so until death. This chapter starts by exploring the prejudices that surround aging. Then we describe biosocial changes—in the senses, the vital organs, and especially the mind.

Prejudice and Predictions

Prejudice about late adulthood is common among people of all ages, including young children and older adults. That is a reflection of **ageism**, the idea that age determines who you are. Stereotyping makes ageism "a social disease, much like racism and sexism . . . [causing] needless fear, waste, illness, and misery" (Palmore, 2005, p. 90).

ageism
A prejudice whereby people are categorized and judged solely on the basis of their chronological age.

Same Situation, Far Apart: Agile, Balanced, and Old Not every older adult can spin wool or traverse a tight rope, like this Moroccan woman *(left)* and Korean man *(right).* Arthritic fingers or unsteady feet may render this impossible. But these two prove that stereotypes and generalities are false.

Ageism can target people of any age, as with curfew laws that require every teenager to be off the streets by 10 P.M. Ageism is not recognized as readily as racism or sexism: Imagine the outcry if a curfew targeted all non-Whites, or all males. Why do people accept ageism, especially in regard to the old?

One expert contends that "there is no other group like the elderly about which we feel free to openly express stereotypes and even subtle hostility. . . . [M]ost of us . . . believe that we aren't really expressing negative stereotypes or prejudice, but merely expressing true statements about older people when we utter our stereotypes" (Nelson, 2011, p. 40). This author believes a major problem is that ageism is institutionalized in our culture, evident in television, employment, and retirement communities.

Another reason people accept ageism is that it often seems complimentary ("young lady") or solicitous (Bugental & Hehman, 2007). However, the effects of ageism, whether benevolent or not, are insidious, seeping into the older person's feelings of competence. The resulting self-doubt fosters anxiety, morbidity, and even mortality.

Believing the Stereotype

With racism or sexism, parents teach their minority or female children to recognize and counter bias, while encouraging them to be proud of who they are. However, when children believe an ageist idea, few people teach them otherwise. Later on, their long-standing prejudice is "extremely resistant to change," undercutting their own health and intellect (Golub & Langer, 2007, pp. 12–13).

For example, in one study, adults younger than 50 expressed opinions about the elderly. Those who were most ageist initially were twice as likely to have serious heart disease 30 years later, compared with those who were least ageist (Levy, 2009).

AGEIST ELDERS Ageism thus becomes a self-fulfilling prophecy. Most people older than 70 think they are doing better than other people their age—who, they believe, have worse problems and are too self-absorbed (Cruikshank, 2009; Townsend et al., 2006). If an older person forgets something, he or she might claim a "senior moment," not realizing the ageism of that reaction. When hearing an ageist phrase—not only "dirty old man" or "second childhood," but also patronizing compliments such as "spry" or "having all her marbles"—elders themselves miss the insult.

✦ **ESPECIALLY FOR Young Adults**
Should you always speak louder and slower when talking to a senior citizen? (see response, page 502) →

Asked how old they feel, typical 80-year-olds lop a decade or more off their age (Pew Research, 2009). Yet if most 80-year-olds feel like they imagine the average 70-year-old feels, then that feeling is, in fact, typical for 80-year-olds. In this example, old people reject their own ageist stereotype of 80-year-olds, although they feel the same way most 80-year-olds actually do. This is illogical, but in an ageist culture, thinking you feel younger than your chronological age is self-protective. Indeed "feeling youthful is more strongly predictive of health than any other factors including commonly noted ones like chronological age, gender, marital status and socioeconomic status" (Barrett, 2012, p. 3).

Stereotype threat (discussed in Chapter 11) can be as debilitating for the aged as for other groups (Hummert, 2011). If the elderly fear they are losing their minds, that fear itself may undermine cognitive competence (Hess et al., 2009).

The effect of internalized ageism was apparent in a classic study (Levy & Langer, 1994). The researchers selected three groups. Two were chosen because they might have been less exposed to ageism: residents of China, where the old were traditionally venerated, and North Americans who had been deaf lifelong. The third group was composed of North Americans with typical hearing, who presumably had listened to ageist comments all their lives. In each of these three groups, half the participants were young and half were old.

Memory tests were given to everyone, six clusters in all. Elders in all three groups (Chinese, deaf Americans, and hearing Americans) scored lower than their younger counterparts. This was expected; age differences are common in laboratory tests of memory.

The purpose of this study, however, was not to replicate earlier research, but to see if ageism affected memory. It did. The gap in scores between younger and older hearing North Americans (most exposed to ageism) was double that between younger and older deaf North Americans and five times wider than the age gap in the Chinese. Ageism undercut ability, a conclusion also found in many later studies (Levy, 2009). Sadly, later studies have found that many Asian cultures, with modernization, have become more ageist than they were when this earlier research occurred (Nelson, 2011).

When older people believe that they are independent and in control of their own life, despite the ageist assumptions of others, they are likely to be healthier—mentally, as well as physically—than other people their age. Of course, some elders need special care. If an older person struggling with a heavy bag is offered a helping hand, it might be appreciated. But do not assume help is needed.

Elders must find "a delicate balance . . . knowing when to persist and when to switch gears . . . some aspects of aging are out of one's control" (Lachman et al., 2011, p. 186). For instance, at a restaurant, older people should feel no shame in asking a younger dinner companion to read the fine print of a menu, but that younger person should not spontaneously offer to cut the elder's steak.

AGEISM LEADING TO ILLNESS Ageism impairs daily life. It prevents depressed older people from seeking help because they resign themselves to infirmity. Could that be why elderly European American men have the highest suicide rate of any age, gender, or ethnic group (CDC, 2009)?

Ageism also leads others to undermine the vitality and health of the aged. For instance, health professionals are less aggressive in treating disease in older patients, researchers testing new prescription drugs enroll few older adults (who are most likely to use those drugs), and caregivers diminish independence by helping the elderly too much (Cruikshank, 2009; Herrera, 2010; Peron & Ruby, 2011–2012).

Not Yet When should aging rock stars retire? In her younger years, Tina Turner won a Grammy and entered the Rock and Roll Hall of Fame. Here she begins a new European tour at age 69, with millions of fans less than half her age.

WOLFGANG RATTAY / REUTERS / CORBIS

RESPONSE FOR Young Adults (from page 500) No. Some seniors hear quite well, and they would resent it. ●

elderspeak
A condescending way of speaking to older adults that resembles baby talk, with simple and short sentences, exaggerated emphasis, repetition, and a slower rate and a higher pitch than used in normal speech.

Speed Demon? Road rage? No. Neither his bike nor his garb is designed for speed, and anger is far more common in the young than in those over age 75, as this man is. He seems faster and happier than the drivers on his right, stuck in traffic in central London.

ASHLEY COOPER / CORBIS

One specific example is sleep. The day–night circadian rhythm diminishes with age: Many older people wake before dawn and are sleepy during the day. Older adults spend more time in bed, take longer to fall asleep, wake frequently (about 10 times per night) (Ayalon & Ancoli-Israel, 2009). They also are more likely to nap. All this is normal: If they choose their own sleep schedules, elders are less likely to feel tired than are young adults.

However, ageism not only results in stereotypes, it also makes people think that the patterns of the young are ideal. That makes every age difference a deficit. If such ageism leads to distress over normal elderly sleep patterns, doctors might prescribe narcotics, or elders might drink alcohol to put themselves to sleep. These can overwhelm an aging body, causing heavy sleep, confusion, nausea, depression, and unsteadiness.

A similar downward spiral is apparent in exercise. In the United States, only 30 percent of those over age 64 meet recommended guidelines for exercise (2½ hours a week of moderate activity), compared with 55 percent for adults aged 18 to 44 (CDC, 2011). An ageist culture does not expect the elderly to move vigorously or often, again thinking that the patterns of the young are ideal. For that reason, team sports are organized for the young; traditional dancing assumes a balanced sex ratio; many yoga, aerobic, and other classes are paced and designed for young adults.

Added to that, self-imposed ageism leads the elderly to exercise less, which increases stiffness and reduces range of motion while impairing circulation, digestion, and thinking. Balance is decreased, necessitating a slower gait, a cane, or a walker (Newell et al., 2006). Thus, internalized as well as externalized ageism makes people sick.

None of the normal changes of senescence require that exercise stop, although some adjustments may be needed (more walking, less sprinting). Health is protected by activity, but ageism in the culture, in the caregivers, and in the elderly themselves leads to inaction, then stagnation, and then poor health. Indeed, the passive, immobile elder is at increased risk of virtually every illness.

ELDERSPEAK Many people who think they are compassionate tend to infantilize the elderly, regarding them as if they are children ("so cute," "second childhood") (Albert & Freedman, 2010). One reason is that nurses, doctors, and other care workers are accustomed to treat elderly people who are, at that moment, sick and dependent (Williams et al., 2009). The danger is that these caregivers generalize their professional experiences and impressions and treat all elderly as if they were feeble.

Consequently, ageism is evident in many caregivers: Efforts to reduce that prejudice are not always successful, perhaps because they attempt to counteract a common stereotype (Eymard & Douglas, 2012).

A specific example is **elderspeak,** the way people talk to the old (Nelson, 2011). Like baby talk, elderspeak uses simple and short sentences, slower talk, higher pitch, louder volume, and frequent repetition. Elderspeak is especially patronizing when people call an older person "honey" or "dear," or use a nickname instead of a surname ("Billy," not "Mr. White").

Ironically, elderspeak reduces communication. Higher frequencies are harder for the elderly to hear, stretching out words makes comprehension worse, shouting causes stress and anxiety, and simplified vocabulary reduces the precision of language.

DESTRUCTIVE PROTECTION Some younger adults and the media discourage the elderly from leaving home. For example, whenever an older person is robbed, raped, or assaulted, sensational headlines add to fear and consequently add to ageism. In fact, street crime targets young adults, not old ones (see Figure 14.1). The homicide rate (the most reliable indicator of violent crime, since reluctance to report is not an issue) of those over age 65 is only one-tenth the rate for those aged 20 to 24. To protect our relatives, perhaps we should insist that young adults never leave the house alone—a ridiculous suggestion that makes it obvious why telling older adults to stay home is shortsighted.

The truth is that although advertisements induce younger adults to buy medical-alert devices for older relatives, they might do better to go walking or biking with them. Lest you think that bikes are only for children, an extensive study of five European nations (Germany, Italy, Finland, Hungary, the Netherlands) found that 15 percent of Europeans *older than 75* ride their bicycles every day (Tacken & van Lamoen, 2005). In other nations, few elderly ride bikes, partly because bike paths are scarce and many bikes are designed for speed, not stability. Laws requiring bike helmets often apply only to children—another example of ageism.

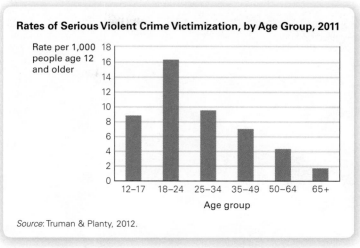

Rates of Serious Violent Crime Victimization, by Age Group, 2011

Source: Truman & Planty, 2012.

FIGURE 14.1 Victims of Crime As people grow older, they are less likely to be crime victims. These figures come from personal interviews in which respondents were asked whether they had been the victim of a violent crime—assault, sexual assault, rape, or robbery—in the past several months. This approach yields more accurate results than official crime statistics because many crimes are never reported to the police.

The Demographic Shift

Demography is the science that describes populations, including population by cohort, age, gender, or region. Demographers describe "the greatest demographic upheaval in human history" (Bloom, 2011, p. 562), a **demographic shift** in the proportions of the population of various ages. In an earlier era, there were 20 times more children than older people, and only 50 years ago, the world had 7 times more people under age 15 than over age 64. No longer.

THE WORLD'S AGING POPULATION The United Nations estimates that nearly 8 percent of the world's population in 2010 was 65 or older, compared with only 2 percent a century earlier. This number is expected to double by the year 2050. Already 13 percent in the United States are that old, as are 14 percent in Canada and Australia, 20 percent in Italy, and 23 percent in Japan (United Nations, 2012).

As you saw in Chapter 1, demographers often depict the age structure of a population as a series of stacked bars, one bar for each age group, with the bar for the youngest at the bottom and the bar for the oldest at the top (refer to Infographic 1.1). Historically, the shape was a *demographic pyramid*. Like a wedding cake, it was widest at the base, and each higher level was narrower than the one beneath it, for three reasons—none currently true:

1. More children were born than the replacement rate of one per adult, so each new generation had more people than the previous one.

2. Many babies died, which made the bottom bar much wider than later ones.

3. Serious illness was usually fatal, reducing the size of each older group.

Sometimes unusual events caused a deviation from this wedding-cake pattern. For example, the Great Depression and World War II reduced births. Then postwar prosperity and the soldiers' return caused a baby boom between 1946 and 1964, just when infant survival increased. The mushrooming birth and survival rates led many demographers to predict a population explosion, with mass starvation by 2000 (Ehrlich, 1968).

That fear evaporated as new data emerged. Birth rates fell and a "green revolution" doubled the food supply. Now people worry about another demographic

demographic shift A shift in the proportions of the populations of various ages.

Same Situation, Far Apart: Keep Smiling Good humor seems to be a cause of longevity, and vice versa. This is true for both sexes, including the British men on Founder's Day *(left)*, and the two Indian women on an ordinary sunny day in Dwarka *(right)*.

● **UNDERSTANDING THE NUMBERS**
In 2050 in the United States, among every 100 people, how many will be younger than 65 and how many will be older than 65?

Answer Although the absolute numbers are increasing rapidly, the proportions are rising more slowly. In 2050, the aged will still be outnumbered: 80 people in every 100 will be younger than 65 and only 20 will be older than that age.

dependency ratio
A calculation of the number of self-sufficient, productive adults compared with the number of dependents (children and the elderly) in a given population.

shift: fewer babies and more elders, affecting world health and politics (Albert & Freedman, 2010). Early death is uncommon; demographic stacks have become rectangles, not pyramids.

The demographic revolution is ongoing, although not yet starkly evident everywhere. Most nations still have more people under age 15 than over age 64. Worldwide, children outnumber elders more than 3 to 1, but not 20 to 1. United Nations predictions for 2015 are for 1,877,551,000 people younger than 15 and 602,332,000 older than 64. Not until 2065 is the ratio projected to be 1 to 1 (United Nations, 2012).

STATISTICS THAT FRIGHTEN Unfortunately, demographic data are sometimes reported in ways designed to alarm. For instance, have you heard that people aged 80 and up are the fastest-growing age group? That is true but misleading.

In 2010 in the United States, there were more than 4 times as many people 80 and older than there were 50 years earlier (11.8 million compared with 2.7 million). Stating the numbers that way triggers ageist fears of a nation burdened by hungry hoards of frail and confused elders.

But stop and think. The U.S. population has also grown. The percent of residents 80 and older has more than doubled, but not quadrupled (increasing between 1960 and 2010 from 1.6 percent to 3.8 percent). That proportion is far from overwhelming the other 96.2 percent. What percent of the population 80 years and older are in nursing homes or hospitals? (Guess—the answer will be presented soon.)

Demographers and politicians sometimes report the **dependency ratio,** estimating the proportion of the population that *depends* on care from others. This ratio is calculated by dividing the number of dependents (defined as those under age 15 or over 64) by the number of people in the middle, aged 15 to 64. The highest dependency ratio is in Uganda, with more than one dependent per adult (1:1); the lowest in Bahrain, with one dependent per three adults (1:3). Most nations, including the United States, are about 1:2, that is, one child or elder for every two adults (United Nations, 2012).

But the calculation of the dependency ratio assumes that older adults are dependent. This mistake is echoed in dire predictions of what will happen when baby boomers age. Supposedly, they will force a shrinking number of working adults to carry a crushing burden of senility and fragility. Social Security, Medicare, and public hospitals will all go bankrupt, according to some. That specter is false.

Most elders are fiercely independent, care*givers* not care receivers. Only 10 percent of those over age 64 are dependent on others for basic care, and those "others" are usually relatives, not taxpaying strangers. In the United States, only 4 percent of people over 64 (less than one-half of 1 percent of the total population) are in nursing homes or hospitals. (Is that what you predicted?). Most are living completely independently, alone or with an aging spouse; only a minority are living with adult children.

The rate of dependency increases with age, but many very old people remain independent. The United States has a higher rate than most nations of people in hospitals and nursing homes, yet even after age 80, only 10 percent of U.S. residents are in such facilities. The average person 80 years or older spends two weeks per year in a hospital (CDC, 2011, 2009). These rates are actually lower than 20 years ago; now more people stay in their homes, with visiting nurses, home health aides, and so on, if needed.

YOUNG, OLD, AND OLDEST Almost everyone overestimates the population in nursing homes because people tend to notice only the frail, not recognizing the rest. This is a characteristic of human thought—the memorable case is thought to be typical—that feeds ageism rather than reflecting reality.

Gerontologists distinguish among the *young-old*, the *old-old*, and the *oldest-old*. The **young-old** are the largest group of older adults. They are healthy, active, financially secure, and independent. Few people notice them or realize their age. The **old-old** suffer some losses in body, mind, or social support, but they proudly care for themselves. Only the **oldest-old** are dependent, and they are the most noticeable.

Many of the young-old are aged 65 to 75, old-old 75 to 85, and oldest-old over 85, but age itself does not indicate dependency. An old-old person can be 65 or 100. For well-being and independence, attitude is more important than age (O'Rourke et al., 2010a).

Ongoing Senescence

The reality that most people over age 64 are quite capable of caring for themselves does not mean that they are unaffected by time. The processes of senescence, described in Chapter 12, continue lifelong. Good health habits slow down aging but do not stop it.

THEORIES OF AGING Why don't people stay young? Hundreds of theories and thousands of scientists have sought to understand why aging occurs. To simplify, these theories can be understood in three clusters: wear and tear, genetic adaptation, and cellular aging.

The oldest, most general theory of aging is known as **wear and tear.** This theory contends that the body wears out, part by part, after years of use. Organ reserve and repair processes are exhausted as the decades pass (Gavrilov & Gavrilova, 2006).

Is this true? For some body parts, yes. Athletes who put repeated stress on their shoulders or knees often have chronically painful joints by middle adulthood; workers who inhale asbestos and smoke cigarettes destroy their lungs.

However, many body functions benefit from use. Exercise improves heart and lung functioning; tai chi improves balance; weight training increases muscles; sexual activity stimulates the sexual-reproductive system; foods that require intestinal activity benefit the digestive system. In many ways, people are more likely to "rust out" from disuse than to wear out. Thus, although the wear-and-tear theory applies to some body parts, it does not explain aging overall.

A second cluster of theories focuses on genes (Sutphin & Kaeberlein, 2011). Humans may have a **genetic clock,** a mechanism in the DNA of cells that regulates

young-old
Healthy, vigorous, financially secure older adults (generally, those aged 60 to 75) who are well integrated into the lives of their families and communities.

old-old
Older adults (generally, those older than 75) who suffer from physical, mental, or social deficits.

oldest-old
Elderly adults (generally, those older than 85) who are dependent on others for almost everything, requiring supportive services such as nursing homes and hospital stays.

wear and tear
A view of aging as a process by which the human body wears out because of the passage of time and exposure to environmental stressors.

✦ **ESPECIALLY FOR Biologists** What are some immediate practical uses for research on the causes of aging? (see response, page 506) →

genetic clock
A purported mechanism in the DNA of cells that regulates the aging process by triggering hormonal changes and controlling cellular reproduction and repair.

RESPONSE FOR Biologists (from page 505) Although ageism and ambivalence limit the funding of research on the causes of aging, many scientists believe that research on cell aging and on the immune system will benefit people of all ages. Such applications include prevention of AIDS, cancer, senility, and physical damage from pollution. ●

cellular aging
The ways in which molecules and cells are affected by age. Many theories aim to explain how and why aging causes cells to deteriorate.

Hayflick limit
The number of times a human cell is capable of dividing into two new cells. The limit for most human cells is approximately 50 divisions, an indication that the life span is limited by our genetic program.

life, growth, and aging. Just as genes start puberty at about age 10, genes may switch on aging. For instance, when a person is injured, aging genes spread the damage, so that an infection spreads rather than being halted and healed (Borgens & Liu-Snyder, 2011).

Evidence for genetic aging comes from premature aging. For example, children born with Hutchinson-Gilford syndrome (a genetic disease also called *progeria*) stop growing at about age 5 and begin to look old, with wrinkled skin and balding heads. These children die in their teens of heart diseases typically found in people five times their age.

Other genes seem to allow an extraordinarily long and healthy life. People who live far longer than the average usually have alleles that other people do not (Halaschek-Wiener et al., 2009; Sierra et al., 2009).

Hundreds of genes hasten aging of one body part or another, such as genes for hypertension or many forms of cancer. Certain alleles—SIR2, def-2, among them—directly accelerate aging and death (Finch, 2010).

Other alleles are protective. For instance, allele 2 of ApoE is protective, aiding survival. Of men in their 70s, 12 percent have ApoE2, but of men older than 85, 17 percent have it. This suggests that men with allele 2 are, for some reason, more likely to survive. Another common allele of the same gene, ApoE4, increases the risk of death by heart disease, stroke, dementia, and—if a person is HIV-positive—by AIDS (Kuhlmann et al., 2010).

Why would human genes promote human aging? Evolutionary theory provides an explanation (Hughes, 2010). Societies need young adults to reproduce the next generation and then need the elders to die (leaving their genes behind) so that the new generation can thrive. Thus, genetic aging may seem harsh to older individuals, but it is actually benevolent for communities.

The third cluster of theories examines **cellular aging,** focusing on molecules and cells (Sedivy et al., 2008). Toxins damage cells over time, so minor errors in copying accumulate (remember, cells replace themselves many times). Over time, imperfections proliferate. The job of the cells of the immune system is to recognize pathogens and destroy them, but the immune system weakens with age as well as with repeated stresses and infections (Wolf, 2010).

Eventually, the organism can no longer repair every cellular error, resulting in senescence. This process is first apparent in the skin, an organ that replaces itself often. The skin becomes wrinkled and rough, eventually developing "age spots" as cell rejuvenation slows down. Cellular aging also occurs inside the body, notably in cancer, which involves duplication of rogue cells. Every type of cancer becomes more common with age because the body is increasingly less able to control the cells.

Even without specific infections, healthy cells stop replicating at a certain point, referred to as the **Hayflick limit,** named after the scientist who discovered this phenomenon. One such cellular change over time occurs with telomeres—material at the ends of the chromosome that become shorter with each duplication. Eventually, at the Hayflick limit, the telomere is gone, duplication stops, and the creature dies (Aviv, 2011).

Hayflick himself believes that the Hayflick limit, and therefore aging, is caused by a natural loss of molecular fidelity—that is, by inevitable errors in transcription as each cell reproduces itself. He believes that aging is a natural process built into the very cells of our species, affected by stress, drugs, and so on (Hayflick, 2004).

For example, telomere length is about the same in newborns of both sexes and all ethnic groups; but by late adulthood, telomeres are longer in women than in men, and longer in European Americans than in African Americans (Aviv, 2011). There are many possible explanations, but cellular aging theorists consider this one reason that women outlive men and European Americans outlive African Americans.

CALORIE RESTRICTION Aging slows down in most living organisms with **calorie restriction,** which is drastically reducing daily calories while maintaining ample vitamins, minerals, and other important nutrients. The benefits of calorie restriction have been demonstrated by careful research with dozens of creatures, from fruit flies to chimpanzees. Generally, compared with no restrictions, feeding less than usual reduces many of the diseases of aging and extends the life span. However, specifics of diet and timing may be crucial. Some research on monkeys finds that calorie restriction extends life, but other studies do not (Mattison et al., 2012). Much remains to be understood; application to humans is controversial.

Less aging and longer life (sometimes twice as long), as well as stronger hearts, less disease, and better cognition, result from keeping nonhuman animals on a restricted diet after puberty (Bendlin et al., 2010). Calorie restriction is a fact in search of a theory, as "the molecular mechanisms by which such a simple intervention has such a stunning effect has eluded researchers for decades" (Masoro & Austad, 2011, p. xi).

Controlled experiments with people would be unethical as well as impossible since researchers would have to find hundreds of people, half of whom would be randomly assigned to eat much less than usual, while the other half would eat normally. For both groups, periodic checks would ascertain whether they were sticking to their diets and would measure dozens of biomarkers in the blood, urine, heart rate, breathing, and so on.

The researchers would exclude anyone younger than 21 or potentially pregnant since undereating would be particularly harmful to them. They would warn the participants that calorie restriction reduces the sex drive, causes temporary infertility, weakens bones and muscles, affects moods, decreases energy, and probably affects other body functions.

Given all that, it would be difficult to recruit even a dozen people from the general population. However, in several places (e.g., Okinawa, Denmark, Norway), wartime brought severe calorie reduction plus healthy diets (mostly fresh vegetables) to entire populations. The result was a markedly lower death rate (Fontana et al., 2011).

Human research in this case requires volunteers (not random participants) who choose to reduce their calories. Currently, more than 1,000 North Americans belong to the Calorie Restriction Society, voluntarily eating only 1,000 nutritious calories a day, none of them buttered or fried. Preliminary data find some health improvements but also find somewhat different responses than for nonhuman animals.

One leader of this group is Michael Rae, from Calgary, Canada. He explained:

> Aging is a horror and it's got to stop right now. People are popping antioxidants, getting face-lifts, and injecting Botox, but none of that is working. At the moment, C.R. [calorie restriction] is the only tool we have to stay younger longer.
>
> [quoted in Hochman, 2003, p. A9]

A newspaper reporter notes, "Mr. Rae is 6 feet tall, weighs just 115 pounds, and is often very hungry." The implication is that Rea is foolish. Scientists are trying to find some easier way—perhaps a drug or nutrient—that would achieve the same result as calorie restriction, halting genetic or cellular aging (Barzilai & Bartke, 2009; Beil, 2011), although "it is important to note that thus far none of the DR [dietary restriction] mimetics extends life as effectively as DR itself" even with flies, worms, and mice (the usual research subjects) (Greer & Brunet, 2011, p. 17).

All the theories of aging, and all the research on calorie restriction, have not led to any simple way to stop senescence. Most scientists are skeptical, not only of calorie restriction but of what people are willing to give up for a longer life. More than ever, scientists recommend exercise, a moderate diet, and staying away from harmful drugs (especially cigarettes). Many people seem unready to follow that advice.

calorie restriction
The practice of limiting dietary energy intake (while consuming sufficient quantities of vitamins, minerals, and other important nutrients) for the purpose of improving health and slowing down the aging process.

"If you give up alcohol, cigarettes, sex, red meat, cakes and chocolate, and don't get too excited, you can enjoy life for a few more years yet."

Selective Optimization

Social scientists have another goal, not about adding years to life but adding life to years. One method is called *selective optimization with compensation* (see Chapter 12). The hope is that the elderly will compensate for any impairments of senescence and will excel (optimize) at whatever specific tasks they select. We will look at three examples: sex, driving, and the senses. All three involve personal choice, societal practices, and technological options, but here each is used to illustrate one of these three dimensions of the compensation process.

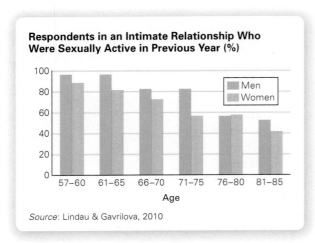

Respondents in an Intimate Relationship Who Were Sexually Active in Previous Year (%)

Source: Lindau & Gavrilova, 2010

FIGURE 14.2 Your Reaction Older adults who consider their health good (most of them) were asked if they had had sexual intercourse within the past year. If they answered yes, they were considered sexually active. What is your reaction to the data? Some young adults might be surprised that many adults, aged 60 to 80, still experience sexual intercourse. Other people might be saddened that most healthy adults over age 80 do not. However, neither reaction may be appropriate. For many elders, sexual affection is expressed in many more ways than intercourse, and it continues lifelong.

OBSERVATION QUIZ

What are the male/female differences and how can they be explained, since all of these respondents had partners of the other sex? (see answer, page 511) ➞

INDIVIDUAL COMPENSATION: SEX Most people are sexually active throughout adulthood. Some continue to have intercourse long past age 65 (Lindau & Gavrilova, 2010) (see Figure 14.2). However, on average, intercourse becomes less frequent than it was earlier, often stopping completely. Nonetheless, sexual satisfaction within long-term relationships increases past middle age (Heiman et al., 2011). How could that be?

Many older adults reject the idea that intercourse is the only or even the optimal measure of sexual activity. Instead, if sexual desire remains, then cuddling, kissing, caressing, and fantasizing become more important. Is that optimization, compensation, or both? Desire correlates with sexual satisfaction and quality of life in late adulthood more than frequency of intercourse does (Chao et al., 2011). Indeed, a five-nation (United States, Germany, Japan, Brazil, Spain) study found that kissing and hugging, not intercourse, predicted happiness in long-lasting romances (Heiman et al., 2011).

The research finds that older women, more often than older men, say they have no sexual desire. This may be nature's way of adjusting to the reality that there are more older women than older men. However, elders who feel sexual desire tend to be happier and healthier than those who do not (Ambler et al., 2012), so the women with diminished sexual desire may be impaired by ageism and sexism.

Alternatively, it may be ageist and sexist to think that women should feel desire when they say they do not. On this, researchers disagree. There is no disagreement that women, on average, stop intercourse earlier than men, primarily because of partner availability, not biology.

After divorce or death of a partner, selectivity is evident. Some of the elderly prefer to consider sex a thing of the past, some cohabit, some begin LAT (living apart together) with a new partner but without marriage or leaving their own home, and some remarry. That is selective optimization—each older person choosing whether and how to be sexual. Of course, social factors make some options easier than others, which leads to the next topic.

SOCIAL COMPENSATION: DRIVING A life-span perspective reminds us that "aging is a process, socially constructed to be a problem" (Cruikshank, 2009, p. 8). The process is biological, but the problem begins in the social world. That means selective optimization with compensation is needed by families and societies, too.

One example is driving. With age, sign reading takes longer, head turning is reduced, reaction time slows, and night vision worsens. The elderly compensate: Many drive slowly and avoid night driving. As a result, elderly drivers have fewer accidents than do younger adults (although not when calculated per mile driven). (See Infographic 14, page 509.)

But although drivers compensate, few societies do. If an older adult causes a crash, age is blamed but not the family or the law (Satariano, 2006). Laws are often lax; many jurisdictions renew licenses without testing, even at age 80. If testing is required, it

Social Comparison: Elders Behind the Wheel

Older people often change their driving habits in order to compensate for their slowing reaction time. Contrary to popular perception, elderly adults have fewer accidents than young people (although not when calculated per mile driven). Many states have initiated restrictions, including requiring older drivers to renew their licenses in person, to make sure older drivers stay safe. Because most older drivers limit themselves (they avoid night, rainy, and distance driving), their crash rate is low overall, but not when measured by the rate per miles driven.

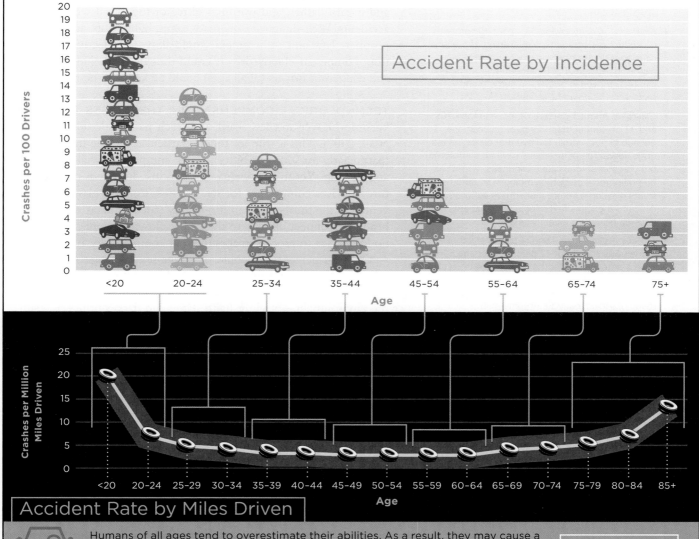

Accident Rate by Incidence

Crashes per 100 Drivers

Age: <20, 20-24, 25-34, 35-44, 45-54, 55-64, 65-74, 75+

Accident Rate by Miles Driven

Crashes per Million Miles Driven

Age: <20, 20-24, 25-29, 30-34, 35-39, 40-44, 45-49, 50-54, 55-59, 60-64, 65-69, 70-74, 75-79, 80-84, 85+

Humans of all ages tend to overestimate their abilities. As a result, they may cause a kitchen fire, or fall on ice, or ignore a lump or a chest pain until it is too late.
Especially after age 65, adults who want to drive need to answer six questions:

Self-Check

1. Is your vision fading? [Ask your optometrist if any visual losses affect driving.]

2. Do your medications affect reaction time or alertness? [Ask both doctor and pharmacist.]

3. Do your physical limitations affect neck-turning, foot-pushing, wheel-turning?

4. Do you get lost more easily now than in earlier years?

5. Do other drivers honk at you? [Don't just get angry, consider the reason.]

6. Have you had any minor accidents? [Even a scrape or a fender bender signify something.]

If your answers are all no, review them with someone who will be honest with you. Some of the elderly are very safe drivers whereas others can be a risk to themselves and to those around them. Before you step on the accelerator, make sure you are one of the safe ones.

SOURCES & CREDITS LISTED ON P. SC-1

often focuses on knowing the rules of the road or being able to read with glasses, not on the characteristics that correlate with accidents. For instance, when vision is tested, it is usually to gauge a person's face-front reading ability, yet peripheral vision is a stronger predictor of accidents (Johnson & Wilkinson, 2010; Wood, 2002).

Beyond retesting, there is much else that societies can do. Larger-print signs before an exit, mirrors that replace the need to turn the neck, illuminated side streets and driveways, nonglaring headlights and hazard flashes, and warnings of ice or fog ahead would reduce accidents. Well-designed cars, roads, signs, lights, tests, as well as appropriate laws and enforcement would allow for selective optimization; competent elderly drivers could thus maintain independence, and dangerous drivers (of all ages) could be kept off the road.

TECHNOLOGICAL COMPENSATION: THE SENSES Every sense becomes slower and less sharp with each passing decade (Meisami et al., 2007). This is true for touch (particularly in the fingers), taste (particularly for sour and bitter), smell, and pain, as well as for sight and hearing. Yet in the twenty-first century, hundreds of manufactured devices compensate for sensory loss, from eyeglasses (first invented in the thirteenth century) to tiny video cameras worn on the head that connect directly to the brain, allowing people whose eyes no longer see to process images (not yet commercially available).

Only 10 percent of people of either sex over age 65 see well without glasses (see Table 14.1), but selective compensation allows almost everyone to use their remaining sight quite well. Changing the environment—brighter lights, large and darker print—is a simple first step. Corrective lenses and magnifying glasses can also help. For those who are totally blind, dogs, canes, and audio devices have for decades allowed mobility and cognition.

TABLE 14.1 Common Vision Impairments Among the Elderly

- *Cataracts.* As early as age 50, about 10 percent of adults have cataracts, a thickening of the lens, causing vision to become cloudy, opaque, and distorted. By age 70, 30 percent do. Cataracts can be removed in outpatient surgery and replaced with an artificial lens.

- *Glaucoma.* About 1 percent of those in their 70s and 10 percent in their 90s have glaucoma, a buildup of fluid within the eye that damages the optic nerve. The early stages have no symptoms, but the later stages cause blindness, which can be prevented if an ophthalmologist or optometrist treats glaucoma before it becomes serious. African Americans and people with diabetes may develop glaucoma as early as age 40.

- *Macular degeneration.* About 4 percent of those in their 60s and about 12 percent over age 80 have a deterioration of the retina, called macular degeneration. An early warning occurs when vision is spotty (e.g., some letters missing when reading). Again, early treatment—in this case, medication—can restore some vision, but without treatment, macular degeneration is progressive, causing blindness about five years after it starts.

Through Different Eyes These photographs depict the same scene as it would be perceived by a person with *(a)* normal vision, *(b)* cataracts, *(c)* glaucoma, or *(d)* macular degeneration. Thinking about how difficult it would be to find your own car if you had one of these disorders may help you remember to have your vision checked regularly.

(a) (b) (c) (d)

ALL: PHOTODISC / GETTY IMAGES

Similarly, by age 90, the average man is almost deaf, as are about half the women. For all sensory deficits, an active effort to compensate—not accept—is needed. Unfortunately, ageism leads elders to avoid bifocals and hearing aids, squinting and mishearing, until blindness or deafness is imminent (Meisami et al., 2007).

Ageism also affects the use or nonuse of technological possibilities by society. Few designers and engineers compensate for sensory losses, although the technology is available. Just about everything, from airplane seats to fashionable shoes, is designed for able-bodied, sensory-acute adults. Many disabilities would disappear with better design (Satariano, 2006).

Look around at the built environment (stores, streets, colleges, and homes); notice the print on medicine bottles; listen to the public address systems in train stations; ask why most homes have entry stairs and narrow bathrooms, why most buses and cars require a big step up to enter, why smelling remains the usual way to detect a gas leak.

Sensory loss need not lead to morbidity or senility, but without compensation, isolation and depression result in less movement and reduced intellectual stimulation. Consequently, illness increases and cognition declines as the senses become less acute.

No Quitter When hearing fades, many older people avoid social interaction. Not so for Don Shula, former head coach of the Miami Dolphins, who led his team to two Super Bowl victories. He kept his players fighting, often surging ahead from behind. Here he proudly displays his hearing aid.

KEY points

- Ageism is stereotyping based on age, a prejudice that leads to less competent and less confident elders.

- Demographic changes have resulted in more elders and fewer children in every nation.

- There are many theories of aging, but beyond good health habits, calorie restriction is the only way proven to extend life for some creatures—but not yet proven in humans.

- Elders need not be dependent if they themselves, and others, compensate for whatever difficulties they have.

- Every sense becomes less acute with age, but technology provides many remedies—if individuals and societies take advantage of them.

ANSWER TO **OBSERVATION QUIZ** (from page 508) Overall, older men are about 15 percent more likely to be sexually active than older women. Why? One explanation is that, among this cohort, brides were about five years younger than grooms, so some of those older married women had partners who were no longer "sexually active." Another explanation is that, just as the high school students described in Chapter 1, men are still more likely to brag and women to demur—actual rates may be more unisex than this figure depicts. ●

Cognition

Ageism impairs elders in many ways, but the most insidious, and most feared, involves the mind, not the body. As with many stereotypes, it begins with a half-truth and stops there. In fact, "although many 70- to 80-year-old adults show evidence of age-related decline, some continue to maintain very high levels of cognitive performance" (Nyberg & Bäckman, 2011). The fear is worse than the facts, but the fear itself makes compensation less likely.

The Aging Brain

New neurons form and dendrites grow in adulthood—a fact that 10 years ago surprised many scientists who thought brain growth stopped in childhood. However, that good news is tempered by another fact—growth is slow. Just like the legs, the heart, and every other part of the body, the brain becomes less efficient as people grow older (Park & Reuter-Lorenz, 2009).

Mind Over Matter Federal Judge Wesley Brown, age 103, compensates for diminished lung capacity by taking supplemental oxygen. He optimizes by no longer taking cases that might drag on, saying, "At my age, I no longer buy green bananas." Retired judges collect generous pensions, but Brown continues to work, hearing a full load of criminal cases—to the admiration of colleagues, lawyers, and defendants. Given what is known about cognitive variations in old age, he surely functions a bit more slowly than when President Kennedy first appointed him in 1962, but he may judge as well as ever.

SLOWER AND SMALLER Senescence reduces production of neurotransmitters—glutamate, acetylcholine, serotonin, and especially dopamine—that allow a nerve impulse to jump quickly across the synaptic gap from one neuron to another. Neural fluid decreases, myelination thins, cerebral blood circulates more slowly. The result is an overall brain slowdown, evident in reaction time, moving, talking, and thinking.

This slowdown can be a severe drain on the intellect because speed is crucial for many aspects of cognition. In fact, some experts believe that speed is the *g* mentioned in Chapter 12, the intellectual ability that underlies all other aspects of intelligence.

Deterioration of cognition correlates with slower walking as well as with almost every kind of physical disability (Kuo et al., 2007; Salthouse, 2010). However, although all scientists agree that reduced speed is a component of late-life cognition, other factors may be more important, especially when individuals, not group averages, are examined (Zimprich & Martin, 2009).

Brain aging is evident not only in speed but also in size. Some areas shrink more than others, among them the hippocampus (crucial for memory) and the prefrontal cortex (necessary for planning, inhibiting unwanted responses, and coordinating thoughts) (Kramer et al., 2006; Rodrigue & Kennedy, 2011).

In every part of the brain, the volume of gray matter (crucial for processing new experiences) is reduced; as a consequence, many people must use their cognitive reserve to understand events (Park & Reuter-Lorenz, 2009). White matter typically is reduced overall as well, but white matter increases in an odd way: Bright white spots appear on MRIs after age 50 or so. These markedly increase the time it takes for a thought to be processed in the brain (Rodrigue & Kennedy, 2011).

VARIATION IN BRAIN EFFICIENCY As is the case with every other organ, all these aspects of brain senescence vary markedly from individual to individual. Although variability is obvious, the reasons are not. Higher education and vocational challenge correlate with less decline, either because keeping the mind active is protective or because such people began late adulthood with more robust and flexible minds (Gow et al., 2011; Salthouse, 2010).

Exercise, nutrition, and normal blood pressure are powerful influences on brain health, and all predict intelligence in old age. In fact, some experts contend that with good health habits and favorable genes, no intellectual decrement will occur (Greenwood & Parasuraman, 2012).

USING MORE OF THE BRAIN A curious finding from PET and fMRI scans is that, compared with younger adults, older adults use more parts of their brains, including both hemispheres, to solve problems. This may be selective compensation: Using only one brain region may be inadequate, so the older brain automatically activates more parts.

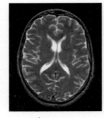 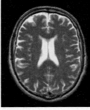 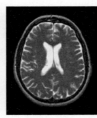 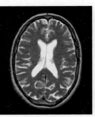 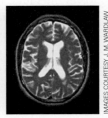

Lowest · 25th Percentile · Median · 75th Percentile · Highest

Atrophy Ranking

Not All Average A team of neuroscientists in Scotland (Farrell et al., 2009) published these images of the brains of healthy 65- to 70-year-olds. The images show normal brain loss (the white areas) from the lowest (5th percentile) to the highest (95th percentile). Some atrophy is inevitable (even younger brains atrophy), but few elders are merely average.

Consequently, on many tasks, older adults are as intellectually sharp as they always were. However, in performing difficult tasks that require younger adults to use all their cognitive resources, older adults are less proficient, perhaps because they already are using their brains to the max (Cappell et al., 2010).

Brain shrinkage interferes with multitasking. No one is intellectually as efficient with two tasks as with one, but young children and older adults are particularly affected when they are given several tasks at once (Krampe et al., 2011) (see Figure 14.3). Recognizing this, many elders are selective.

In daily life, suppose that a grandfather is interrupted by a grandchild's questions while reading the newspaper, or that a grandmother is getting dressed when someone asks her to choose which bus to take. Most likely the grandfather will put the newspaper down and then answer, and the grandmother will first dress and then decide on transportation (avoiding mismatched shoes).

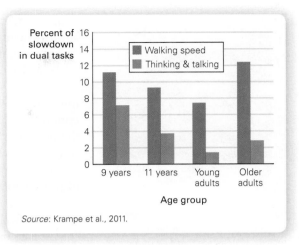

Source: Krampe et al., 2011.

FIGURE 14.3 One Task at a Time Doing two things at once impairs performance. In this study, researchers compared the speed of a sensorimotor task (walking) and a cognitive task (naming objects within a category—e.g., colors, spices, insects, crimes, four-legged animals). The participants did each task separately first, and then they did both at once. The latter resulted in performance losses across the board. Note, however, that the eldest seemed to safeguard verbal fluency (only a 3 percent slowdown) at the expense of significantly slower walking.

OBSERVATION QUIZ
How much were the 9-year-olds affected by doing both tasks at once? (see answer, page 515) →

Information Processing After Age 65

Given the complexity and diversity of late life cognition, we need to examine specifics to combat general stereotypes. For this, the information-processing approach is useful, with details of input (sensing), memory (storage), programming (control), and output.

INPUT Processing information requires that sensations precede perception, yet as you just read, no sense is as sharp at age 65 as at age 15. Glasses and hearing aids mitigate most severe sensory losses, but more subtle deficits impair cognition as well. Information must cross the *sensory threshold,* the divide between what is sensed and what is not, in order to be perceived.

Sensory losses may not be recognized because the brain automatically fills in missed sights and sounds. People of all ages believe they look at the eyes of their conversation partner, yet a study that examined gaze following found that older adults were less adept at knowing where someone was looking (Slessor et al., 2008). That creates a disadvantage in social interactions. Another study found that already by age 50, adults were less adept at reading emotions by looking at the eyes (Pardini & Nichelli, 2009).

Acute hearing is also needed to detect nuances of emotion. Older adults are less able to decipher the emotional content in speech, even when they hear the words correctly (Dupuis & Pichora-Fuller, 2010). Similarly, for older adults, understanding speech is impaired when vision is impaired (Tye-Murray et al., 2011), probably because we all watch lips and facial expressions to assist in understanding. Thus, small sensory losses—not noticed by the person or family but inevitable with age—impair cognition.

MEMORY The second step of information processing is memory. Remember stereotype threat: If older people suspect their memory is fading, anxiety itself impairs memory, a phenomenon more apparent among those with more education (Hess et al., 2009), probably because they are quicker to notice it.

Here again, specifics are important to fight stereotypes. Some aspects of memory remain strong throughout late adulthood, including vocabulary, while others do not, such as memory for names. Thus, a person who cannot recall a name should not conclude that memory, overall, is fading.

One memory deficit is *source amnesia*—forgetting the origin of a fact, idea, or snippet of conversation. Source amnesia is particularly problematic with the information

Recognition At every age, recognition memory is much better than recall. Chances are that few of my high school classmates could describe how I looked back then, but all of them could point out my picture among the hundreds of photos in our yearbook.

ecological validity
The idea that cognition should be measured in settings that are as realistic as possible and that the abilities measured should be those needed in real life.

✦ **ESPECIALLY FOR Students** If you want to remember something you learn in class for the rest of your life, what should you do? (see response, page 516) →

bombardment of television, radio, and print. Elders may believe a rumor or political advertisement if they forget the source (Jacoby & Rhodes, 2006). Compensation would mean deliberate attention to the reason behind the message before accepting a televised ad or a con man's promises.

Working memory, the memory of information held in the brain for a moment before processing (evaluating, calculating, and inferring), shrinks with age. Speed is critical here: Older individuals take longer to perceive and process sensations, and this reduces working memory because some items fade before they can be evaluated.

For example, a common test of working memory is repeating a string of digits backwards, but if the digits are said quickly, a slow-thinking person may not be able to process each number and properly hold them all in memory. Speed of processing would explain why memory for vocabulary (especially recognition memory, not recall) is often unaffected by age. For instance, speed is irrelevant in deciding if *chartreuse* is a color or an animal.

Some research finds that when older people take their time and concentrate, their working memory may be as good as ever. For example, a study of reading ability found that although older people reread phrases more than younger people did, when allowed ample time the old and young were equally accurate in reading comprehension (Stine-Morrow et al., 2010). For testing memory, not only time but also motivation and context are crucial. Almost invariably, realistic circumstances (as when people are quizzed at home instead of in a university laboratory) result in better results on memory tests.

IN DAILY LIFE Ecological validity is the idea that ability should be measured in everyday tasks and circumstances, not as laboratory tests assess it. Ecological validity is particularly significant for the elderly, who are handicapped by traditional testing (Marsiske & Margrett, 2006).

Ecological validity in measuring the intellect begins with arranging the testing conditions so that optimal performance is assessed. For example, older adults are at their best in the early morning, when adolescents are half asleep. If both groups are tested at 8 A.M., or at 2 P.M., comparisons would reflect time of day, not just mental ability. Similarly, if basic intellectual ability is assessed via a timed test, then faster thinkers (usually young) would seem more capable than slower thinkers (usually old), even if the slower ones were more accurate, given a few more seconds to think.

A more fundamental ecological issue regards what should be assessed: pure, abstract thinking or practical, contextual thought. Traditional tests measure fluid cognitive abilities that are valued by the young, but the elderly are more adept at problem solving and emotional regulation. Those practical abilities may improve with age but are not traditionally measured.

Awareness of the need for ecological validity has helped scientists restructure research on memory, finding fewer deficits than originally thought. However, some tests may still overestimate or underestimate ability. For instance, how should we test long-term memory? We know that people of all ages misremember and that few early memories are verifiable. Many older people recount vivid and detailed memories of events that occurred decades ago. That is an impressive intellectual feat—if the memories are accurate.

Unfortunately, "there is no objective way to evaluate the degree of ecological validity . . . because ecological validity is a subjective concept" (Salthouse, 2010, p. 77). It is impossible to be totally objective in assessing memory. We know, at least, that stereotypes must be avoided, and global assessments are too simplistic. Not only do individuals vary, but some kinds of memory show marked age-related loss, and other kinds do not. Names are harder to recall than actions: Grandpa can still swim, ride a bike, and drive a car, even if he cannot name both state senators.

The final ecological question is, "What is memory for?" Older adults usually think they remember well enough. Fear of memory loss is more typical at age 60 than at age 80. Unless they develop a brain condition such as Alzheimer disease (soon to be described), elders are correct: They remember how to live their daily lives, happily and independently.

CONTROL PROCESSES Instead of the analysis and forethought that characterize executive function, the elderly tend to rely on prior knowledge, general principles, familiarity, and rules of thumb in their decision making (Peters et al., 2011). They are less likely to use analytic reasoning and more likely to base conclusions on personal and emotional experience. As you remember from the discussion of dual processing in Chapter 9, experiential thinking is not always faulty, but sometimes analytical thinking is needed to control the impulses that arise from past experience.

Thus, the underlying impairment of cognition in late adulthood may be in **control processes,** the various methods used to regulate the analysis and flow of information from all the parts of the brain. These include memory and retrieval strategies, selective attention, and rules or strategies for problem solving, all part of what is called *executive function.* Control processes depend on the prefrontal cortex, which shrinks with age.

One control process is retrieval. Some developmentalists believe retrieval is crucial because elders may have many thoughts and memories that they cannot access. Analysis includes recognizing the similarities and differences in each new challenge. Without retrieval of past instances, the benefits of past experiences fade.

Inadequate control processes may explain why many older adults have extensive vocabularies (measured by written tests) but limited fluency (when they write or talk), why they are much better at recognition than recall, why tip-of-the-tongue forgetfulness is common, and why spelling is poorer than pronunciation.

In a study that illustrated strategic retrieval, adults of varying ages were given props for 30 odd and memorable actions, such as kissing an artificial frog or stepping into a large plastic bag (Thomas & Bulevich, 2006). They were asked to perform 15 of these actions (and they did them), and they were told to *imagine* doing the other 15. Two weeks later, participants read a list of 45 actions (15 done, 15 imagined, and 15 new). They were asked which were performed, which were imagined, and which were new. Half the participants just read the list and answered performed/imagined/new; the other half were first guided in memory strategies that might help (asked to remember sensations, such as the feel of the frog as they kissed it).

Among the half who merely read the list, the younger adults assigned 78 percent of the items to the correct categories, whereas the older adults got only 52 percent correct. As for the half who were taught memory strategies, the younger adults still got 78 percent correct, but the older ones got 66 percent right (Thomas & Bulevich, 2006). Thus, guidance in retrieval strategies was more helpful to the old than to the young.

Many gerontologists think elders would benefit from using control strategies, as in this example. Unfortunately, even though "a high sense of control is associated with being happy, healthy, and wise," many older adults resist suggested strategies because they believe that declines are "inevitable or irreversible" and that no strategy could help (Lachman et al., 2009, p. 144). Efforts to improve their use of control strategies are often discouraging (McDaniel & Bugg, 2012).

ANSWER TO **OBSERVATION QUIZ**
(from page 513) Nine-year-olds were the only group to slow down significantly in both tasks. Impairment was about 11 percent in walking and 7 percent in naming within a category. ●

control processes
The part of the information-processing system that regulates the analysis and flow of information. Memory and retrieval strategies, selective attention, and rules or strategies for problem solving are all useful control processes.

Don't Forget As a retrieval strategy, this Maryland shop owner posts dozens of reminders for herself on the wall.

AP PHOTO / SALISBURY DAILY TIMES, BRICE STUMP

RESPONSE FOR Students (from page 514) Learn it very well now, and you will probably remember it in 50 years, with a little review. ●

✦ **ESPECIALLY FOR People Who Are Proud of Their Intellect** What can you do to keep your mind sharp all your life? (see response, page 518) →

OUTPUT The final step in information processing is output. In the Seattle Longitudinal Study (described in Chapter 12), the measured output of all five primary mental abilities—verbal meaning, spatial orientation, inductive reasoning, number ability, and word fluency—declined, beginning at about age 60. This was particularly notable in the subtests affected by spatial perception and processing speed (Schaie, 2005).

Similar results are found in many tests of cognition: Thus, the usual path of cognition in late adulthood is gradual decline, at least in output (Salthouse, 2010).

Overall, note that output is usually measured by various tests of production, validated by comparing the output of younger adults. As detailed in Chapters 7 and 12, intelligence tests were initially designed to measure success in school. Many of the questions are quite abstract, and many are timed, since speed of thinking correlates with intelligence for younger adults. A smart person is said to be a "quick" thinker, the opposite of someone who is "slow."

But abstractions and speed are exactly the aspects of cognition that fade most with age. Perhaps ecological validity, already described regarding memory tests, is especially crucial for output. Perhaps training that considers individual interests and abilities can increase the intellect. This possibility is being explored by many scientists, as the following describes.

A VIEW FROM SCIENCE

Learning Late in Life

Many people have tried to improve the intellectual abilities of older adults by teaching, or training them in various tasks (Lustig et al., 2009; Stine-Morrow & Basak, 2011). Success has been reported in specific abilities. In one part of the Seattle Longitudinal Study, 60-year-olds who had lost some spatial understanding had five sessions of personalized training and practice. They returned to the skill level of 14 years earlier (Schaie, 2005).

Another group of researchers (Basak et al., 2008) targeted control processes. Volunteers, with an average age of 69 and no signs of dementia, were divided into an experimental group and a control group (all similar in cognition before the study began). None were video-game players. They took a battery of cognitive tests to measure executive function.

The experimental group was taught to play a video game, set to begin at the easiest level. They enjoyed the game and tried to improve. After each game, they were told their score, and another game began—more challenging in pace and memory if the earlier game was too easy. After 20 hours of training over several weeks, the original battery of tests was given again. The experimental group improved, compared with the control group, in mental activities that were *not* exactly the ones taught by the video game.

Similar results have been found in many other training programs involving the young-old who are taught a specific skill. This has led to a conclusion now accepted by almost all researchers: People younger than 80 can learn almost any cognitive skill if the educational process is carefully targeted to the individual's motivation and ability.

JOSE LUIS PELAEZ, INC. / CORBIS

Screen to Brain Although elders are least likely to have Internet connection at home, they may be most likely to benefit from it, as video games seem to improve cognition in late adulthood. Even better than game playing may be videoconferencing with a grandchild, as shown here. Mental flexibility and family joy correlate with a long and happy life.

What about the old-old? Learning is more difficult, but possible. One careful experiment improved visual working memory in healthy people in their 80s (Buschkuehl et al., 2008). However, the benefits were no longer apparent a year later. Apparently, ongoing practice is particularly important for the old-old (Buschkuehl et al., 2008). From this and other research, it seems that learning is possible in late adulthood, but the older a person is, the more difficult and less comprehensive that learning will be (Stine-Morrow & Basak, 2011).

Many developmentalists are suspicious of the simple "use it or lose it" hypothesis, especially when it leads to many of the elderly doing newspaper puzzles (crosswords, mazes, Sudoku) to supposedly prevent dementia. However, they are not about to tell older people to stop trying to learn new skills. One researcher concluded, "[A]lthough my professional opinion is that . . . the mental-exercise hypothesis is more of an optimistic hope than an empirical reality, my personal recommendation is that people should behave as if it is true" (Salthouse, 2006, p. 84).

Excited Neurons As you see, this nursing home in New Mexico has a large, impersonal assembly room, where some residents sit in isolation. However, that deficit may be offset for others by the energetic Activities Director (Cyndi Bolen, left), who provided Wii Sports bowling on a wide screen. At least one of the oldest-old (Mildred Secrest, right) was thrilled in body and mind when she got a spare.

KEY Points

- The brain slows down in late adulthood, which impairs cognition.
- Variation is evident in late-life intellectual ability, not only among people but also among abilities, with vocabulary particularly likely to stay or increase, and speed of thought and spatial abilities particularly likely to decrease.
- Memory for names and places fades more quickly than memory overall.
- Impairment in control processes—especially retrieval strategies—may underlie the cognitive deficits of old age.

Aging and Disease

As you read in Chapter 12, with each passing decade reaction time slows, the senses become less acute, organ reserves are depleted, and homeostasis takes longer. Skin, hair, and body shape show unmistakable senescence, while every internal organ—especially the heart and the brain—ages.

Primary and Secondary Aging

Gerontologists distinguish between **primary aging,** which involves universal changes that occur with the passage of time, and **secondary aging,** the consequences of particular inherited weaknesses, chosen health habits, and environmental conditions. One explains:

> Primary aging is defined as the universal changes occurring with age that are not caused by diseases or environmental influences. Secondary aging is defined as changes involving interactions of primary aging processes with environmental influences and disease processes.
>
> [Masoro, 2006, p. 46]

primary aging
The universal and irreversible physical changes that occur in all living creatures as they grow older.

secondary aging
The specific physical illnesses or conditions that become more common with aging but are caused by health habits, genes, and other influences that vary from person to person.

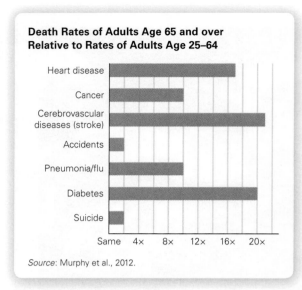

Death Rates of Adults Age 65 and over Relative to Rates of Adults Age 25–64

Source: Murphy et al., 2012.

FIGURE 14.4 More Years to Live Even compared with a decade ago, fewer people die before age 65, which means that, for many causes, death is far more likely in old age. Most of the underlying conditions for these diseases were present in middle age.

RESPONSE FOR People Who Are Proud of Their Intellect (from page 516) If you answered, "Use it or lose it" or "Do crossword puzzles," you need to read more carefully. No specific brain activity has been proved to prevent brain slowdown. Overall health is good for the brain as well as for the body, so exercise, a balanced diet, and well-controlled blood pressure are some smart answers. ●

compression of morbidity
A shortening of the time a person spends ill or infirm, accomplished by postponing illness.

Primary aging does not directly cause illness, but it makes almost every disease more likely.

For example, with age the heart pumps more slowly and the vascular network is less flexible, increasing the risk of stroke and heart attack. The lungs take in and expel less air with each breath so that blood oxygen is reduced and chronic obstructive pulmonary disease is more common. Digestion slows and the kidneys are less efficient, risking problems if people become dehydrated because they drink less to reduce incontinence, which itself is caused by an aging renal/urinary system.

Furthermore, healing takes longer if an illness or an accident occurs (Arking, 2006). For example, young adults who contract pneumonia usually recover in a few weeks, but in the very old the strain of pneumonia over several days can overwhelm a weakened body. Indeed, pneumonia is a leading cause of death for the oldest-old. Primary aging increases the impact of every secondary factor—cigarette smoking, viruses, obesity, stress.

Medical intervention affects the old differently than the young, reducing the effectiveness of drugs, surgery, and so on. For example, anesthesia may damage an older person's brain or may cause the heart to stop. Temporary hallucinations and delirium after surgery are far more common for the old than for the young (Strauss, 2013).

A surprising example of the effects of age comes from medication that reduces hypertension. If systolic blood pressure is above 140, and diet and exercise do not lower it, drugs not only reduce it but also make strokes and heart attacks less likely for middle-aged adults. However, the same drugs for the same blood pressure are counterproductive for the oldest-old. For them, mild hypertension (140–160) may be protective because their slower homeostasis does not quickly respond to a sudden dip in blood pressure. That can be fatal (Beckett et al., 2008).

A developmental view of the relationship between primary and secondary aging harkens back to the lifelong toll of stress, as explained in Chapter 12. *Allostatic load* is measured by 10, or even 16, biomarkers—including cortisol, C-reactive protein, systolic and diastolic blood pressure, waste-hip ratio, and insulin resistance. All of these indicate stress on the body, and such stress, if ongoing, harms health.

Thus, measurement of allostatic load assesses the combined, long-term effect of many indicators, none necessarily dangerous alone. If many of these biomarkers are outside the normal range, people become sick and die, especially when aging already has reduced organ reserve (see Figure 14.4). Thus, lifelong responses to stress create a biological burden, a load that becomes lethal.

Compression of Morbidity

Ideally, prevention of the diseases of the old begins in childhood and continues lifelong, so "the target of public health and aging efforts is not just the older adults of today but the children and adults who are the future elders" (Albert & Freedman, 2010, pp. 31–32). Illness can be delayed, and its severity can be limited by having established good childhood habits. Delayed illness is an example of **compression of morbidity,** which is reducing (compressing) sickness before death.

There is good news here. In recent years, morbidity has been successfully compressed. For instance, unlike 30 years ago, most people diagnosed with cancer, diabetes, or a heart condition continue to be independent for decades (Hamerman, 2007). As an example, the percentage of U.S. residents over age 65 with a limitation in activity—something that interferes with self-care, work, or socialization—

decreased from 35 percent to 31 percent between 1997 and 2009 (U.S. Census Bureau, 2011).

Compression of morbidity is a social and psychological blessing as well as a personal, biological one. A healthier person remains alert and active—in other words, experiences the optimal aging of the young-old, not the dependence of the oldest-old. Improved prevention, diagnosis, and treatment mean less pain, more mobility, better vision, stronger teeth, sharper hearing, clearer thinking, and enhanced vitality.

The importance of compression of morbidity is apparent with **osteoporosis** (fragile bones), which occurs because primary aging makes bones more porous, especially if a person is at genetic risk (European American women are more vulnerable, genetically, than women of other ethnic groups). A fall that would have merely bruised a young person may result in a broken wrist or hip in an elder. That leads to morbidity, sometimes for months, especially when hospitalization and bed rest cause infections and stress.

How can morbidity from osteoporosis be compressed? First, through better health habits earlier in life. Tobacco and alcohol weaken bones, as does low calcium and insufficient weight-bearing exercise. With strong bones, a fall does not cause a break.

Second, through faster recuperation if a fracture occurs. By old age, the most common liability from a fall is fear. A prospective longitudinal study of Dutch elders (Stel et al., 2004) found that one-third of those who fell became overcautious, reducing their activity. That inactivity made all their organs less efficient. Ironically, only 6 percent of the falls for these elders resulted in serious injury, but the 94 percent with less serious injuries often moved less. That increased their morbidity.

Cognitive impairment increases falling more than physical weakness (Muir et al., 2011). This provides a clue for compression of morbidity. If falling can be reduced with special equipment, such as shoes, canes, and so on—and if the elderly and their caregivers become less fearful and fatalistic—then morbidity will decrease. Ideally, elders strengthen their muscles and improve their balance, so morbidity does not even begin.

This applies to every kind of primary aging. If the elderly selectively remedy whatever challenges their primary aging presents, morbidity will be compressed.

Dementia

The patterns of cognitive aging challenge another assumption: that senility is typical. Actually, *senile* simply means "old," but senility is used to mean severe mental impairment, implying that old age brings intellectual failure—an ageist myth. **Dementia** is a more precise term than *senility* for irreversible, pathological loss of brain functioning.

Traditionally, when dementia occurred before age 60, it was called *presenile dementia;* when it occurred after age 60, it was called *senile dementia* or *senile psychosis.* However, age is a poor marker: A person may develop dementia at age 40 or age 90; the symptoms are the same at every age.

More than 70 diseases can cause dementia, each different in sequence, severity, and particulars, although all are characterized by mental confusion and forgetfulness. Dementia is chronic, which means it is long-lasting, unlike **delirium,** which refers to acute, severe memory loss and confusion that disappears in hours or days (Inouye, 2006).

Memory loss is usually a significant symptom, but people with dementia have other cognitive problems as well. They may easily get lost, or may be confused about

osteoporosis
Fragile bones that result from primary aging, which makes bones more porous, especially if a person is at genetic risk.

AGE FOTOSTOCK / SUPERSTOCK

Moving Along Her stiffening joints have made a walker necessary, but this elderly woman in Gujarat, India, is maintaining her mobility by walking every day.

dementia
Irreversible loss of intellectual functioning caused by organic brain damage or disease. Dementia becomes more common with age, but it is abnormal and pathological even in the very old.

delirium
A temporary loss of memory, often accompanied by hallucinations, terror, grandiosity, and irrational behavior.

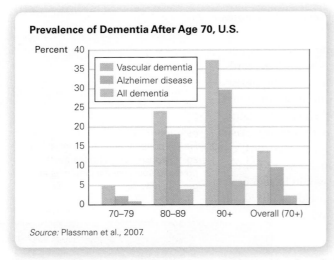

Prevalence of Dementia After Age 70, U.S.

Percent

Source: Plassman et al., 2007.

FIGURE 14.5 Not Everyone Gets It Most elderly people never experience dementia. Among people in their 70s, only 1 person in 20 does, and most of those who reach 90 or 100 are not demented. Presented another way, the prevalence data sound more dire: Almost 4 million people in the United States have dementia.

● **UNDERSTANDING THE NUMBERS** Estimating the number of people with dementia depends on assumptions and goals, not just math. How did researchers arrive at the 4 million reported here?

Answer It is the result of multiplying 0.14 times the number of U.S. residents at least 70 years of age (about 24 million). That's 3,780,000. Added to that is 1 percent of those in their 60s (0.01 × 30 million = 300,000), and about 50,000 of those younger than 60, totaling 4,130,000, or "about 4 million." This is close to the 3.9 million estimated by the World Health Organization, but is lower than the 5.4 million reported by the Alzheimer's Association (WHO and Alzheimer's Disease International, 2012). That discrepancy occurs primarily because the Alzheimer's Association has a higher estimate of people who are not yet diagnosed.

Alzheimer disease (AD)
The most common cause of dementia, characterized by gradual deterioration of memory and personality and marked by the formation of plaques of beta-amyloid protein and tangles of tau in the brain. (Sometimes called *senile dementia of the Alzheimer type.*)

how to use common objects like a telephone or toothbrush, or may have extreme emotional reactions that are unlike their usual personality.

THE PREVALENCE OF DEMENTIA Before discussing specific types of dementia, we should note that many instances of memory loss are not signs of dementia. Older adults who cannot remember names or places as well as they did might have *mild cognitive impairment*. About half of them will be mildly impaired for decades or will regain cognitive abilities (Lopez et al., 2007; Salthouse, 2010). Thus, it is not true that mild impairment means that dementia is inevitable.

To find out how many people are truly demented, researchers selected a representative sample of people 70 years and older from every part of the United States, interviewed and examined each one, and spoke with someone who knew them well (usually an immediate relative). They combined this information with test results, medical records, and clinical judgment, and found that 14 percent had some form of dementia (Plassman et al., 2007) (see Figure 14.5). Although the researchers did not survey people younger than 70, only about 1 percent of people in their 60s have dementia, as do even fewer people younger than 60. Thus, their research indicates that probably about 4 million U.S. residents now have dementia of one type or another.

Rates of dementia among elders vary by nation, from about 2 to 25 percent, with an estimated 35 million people affected worldwide (Kalaria et al., 2008; WHO, 2010). Developing nations have lower rates, but that may be because millions of people in the early stages are not counted or because health care overall is poor.

To understand how poor health care could lead to fewer, not more, people with dementia, you need to realize that nations with many people who live past 80 will have higher rates of dementia than will poor nations where only fortunate and unusual people live that long. Diabetes, for example, increases the rate of dementia, but in some nations most people with diabetes die in middle age.

Health can also make a difference in the opposite direction. If good health habits reduce the underlying factors that increase dementia, then rates will fall. For instance, if exercise increased and obesity decreased overall, then dementia would be less common as well. That is the public health goal: less illness, less dementia, as well as longer lives.

Genetics and social context always affect rates, but it is not known by how much (Bondi et al., 2009). For example, more women than men have dementia, which may be genetic, educational, or stress-related. However, it may be simply that women live longer than men (Alzheimer's Association, 2012).

ALZHEIMER DISEASE The most feared type of dementia is **Alzheimer disease (AD),** also called *senile dementia of the Alzheimer type* (SDAT) (Weiner & Lipton, 2009). Alzheimer disease is characterized by the proliferation of *plaques* and *tangles* in the cerebral cortex. These abnormalities destroy the ability of neurons to communicate with one another, eventually stopping brain function. (See Table 14.2 for the stages of Alzheimer disease.)

Plaques are clumps of a protein called *beta-amyloid,* found in tissues surrounding the neurons; tangles are twisted masses of threads made of a protein called *tau* within the neurons. A normal brain contains some beta-amyloid and some tau, but in brains with AD these plaques and tangles proliferate, especially in the hippocampus (the brain structure that is crucial for memory). Forgetfulness is the dominant symptom; working memory disappears first.

TABLE 14.2 Stages of Alzheimer Disease

Stage 1. People in the first stage forget recent events or new information, particularly names and places. For example, they might forget the name of a famous film star or how to get home from a familiar place. This first stage is similar to mild cognitive impairment—even experts cannot always tell the difference. In retrospect, it seems clear that President Ronald Reagan had early AD while in office, but no doctor diagnosed it.

Stage 2. Generalized confusion develops, with deficits in concentration and short-term memory. Speech becomes aimless and repetitious, vocabulary is limited, words get mixed up. Personality traits are not curbed by rational thought. For example, suspicious people may decide that others have stolen the things that they themselves have mislaid.

Stage 3. Memory loss becomes dangerous. Although people at stage 3 can care for themselves, they might leave a lit stove or hot iron on or might forget whether they took essential medicine and thus take it twice—or not at all.

Stage 4. At this stage, full-time care is needed. People cannot communicate well. They might not recognize their closest loved ones.

Stage 5. Finally, people with AD become unresponsive. Identity and personality have disappeared. When former president Ronald Reagan was at this stage, a longtime friend who visited him was asked, "Did he recognize you?" The friend answered, "Worse than that—I didn't recognize him." Death comes 10 to 15 years after the first signs appear.

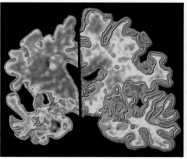

The Alzheimer Brain This computer graphic shows a vertical slice through a brain ravaged by Alzheimer disease *(left)* compared with a similar slice of a normal brain *(right)*. The diseased brain is shrunken as a result of the degeneration of neurons.

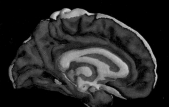 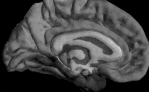 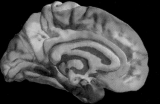 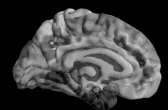

(a) Non-carriers   (b) Pre-symptomatic   (c) Mild symptoms   (d) Dementia

Although finding massive brain plaques and tangles at autopsy proves that a demented person had Alzheimer disease, between 20 and 30 percent of cognitively normal elders have, at autopsy, the same level of plaques in their brains as people who had been diagnosed with probable AD (Jack et al., 2009). Possibly the normal elders had compensated by using other parts of the brain; possibly they were in the early stages, not yet suspected to have AD; possibly plaques are a symptom, not a cause.

Alzheimer disease is partly genetic. If it develops in middle age, the affected person either has trisomy-21 (Down syndrome) or has inherited one of three genes: amyloid precursor protein (APP), presenilin 1, or presenilin 2. For these people, the disease progresses quickly, reaching the last phase within three to five years.

Most cases of AD begin much later, at age 75 or so. Then many genes have some impact, including SORL1 and ApoE4 (i.e., allele 4 of the ApoE gene). People who inherit one copy of ApoE4 (as about one-fifth of all U.S. residents do) have about a 50/50 chance of developing AD. Those who inherit two copies almost always develop the disease if they live long enough, although many die before diagnosis because ApoE4 increases the risk of many other serious ailments (Plassman et al., 2007).

VASCULAR DEMENTIA The second most common cause of dementia is a stroke (a temporary obstruction of a blood vessel in the brain) or a series of strokes, called *transient ischemic attacks* (TIAs, or ministrokes). The interruption in blood flow reduces oxygen, destroying part of the brain. Symptoms (blurred vision, weak or paralyzed limbs, slurred speech, and mental confusion) suddenly appear.

Hopeful Brains Even the brain without symptoms *(a)* might eventually develop Alzheimer disease, but people with a certain dominant gene definitely will. They have no symptoms *(b)* in early adulthood, some symptoms *(c)* in middle adulthood, and stage five Alzheimer disease *(d)* before old age. Research has led to discovery of early markers (such as those shown here) that predict the disease. As scientists detect early signs, they hope to determine a treatment to halt brain destruction before it starts.

✦ **ESPECIALLY FOR Genetic Counselors** Would you order a test for ApoE4 if someone asked for it? (see response, page 523) →

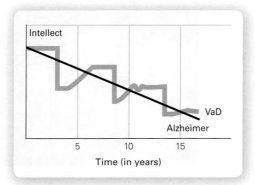

FIGURE 14.6 The Progression of Alzheimer Disease and Vascular Dementia Cognitive decline is apparent in both Alzheimer disease (AD) and vascular dementia (VaD). However, the pattern of decline for each disease is different. Victims of AD show steady, gradual decline, while those who suffer from VaD get suddenly much worse, improve somewhat, and then experience another serious loss.

In a TIA, symptoms may vanish quickly, unnoticed. However, unless recognized and treated, another TIA will occur. Repeated TIAs produce **vascular dementia (VaD)**, also called *multi-infarct dementia*. The progression of VaD is different from the progression of Alzheimer disease, but the result is similar (see Figure 14.6).

In North America and Europe, VaD is not the primary diagnosis for most people with dementia, but in Japan and China, as well as in the oldest-old everywhere, VaD is more common than Alzheimer disease. It correlates with stroke risk, stroke recovery, and with the ApoE4 allele (Cramer & Procaccio, 2012). Vascular dementia is also a risk if an older person undergoes surgery that requires general anesthesia, probably because it can cause a ministroke, which, added to reduced cognitive reserve, damages the brain (Gorelick & Bowler, 2010).

OTHER DEMENTIAS   Several types of dementia are **frontal lobe dementias,** or *frontotemporal lobar degeneration* (Pick disease is the most common form), which causes perhaps 15 percent of all cases of dementia in the United States. Parts of the brain that regulate emotions and social behavior (the amygdala and the frontal lobes) deteriorate, with emotional and personality changes being the main symptoms (Seelaar et al., 2011). A loving mother with a frontal lobe dementia might reject her children or a smart businessman might invest in a hare-brained scheme.

Frontal lobe dementia may be worse than Alzheimer disease or vascular dementia in that compassion, self-awareness, and judgment fade in a person who otherwise seems normal. One wife was furious at her husband, and considering divorce because:

> he threw away tax documents, got a ticket for trying to pass an ambulance, and bought stock in companies that were obviously in trouble. Once a good cook, he burned every pot in the house. He became withdrawn and silent, and no longer spoke to his wife over dinner. That same failure to communicate got him fired from his job.
>
> *[Grady, 2012, p. A1]*

Finally, she learned the diagnosis—frontal lobe dementia—and asked forgiveness for her fury. It is not clear that he understood either her anger or her apology.

Although there are many forms and many causes of frontal lobe dementia—including a dozen or so alleles—it usually begins before age 70 and progresses rapidly, leading to death in about five years. That five-year estimate may be misleading, however: Diagnosis typically occurs years after the first signs, which means frontal lobe dementia could last a decade or more.

Many other dementias begin with impaired motor control (shaking when picking up a coffee cup, falling when trying to walk), not with impaired thinking. The most common of these is **Parkinson disease,** the cause of about 3 percent of all cases of dementia (Aarsland et al., 2005).

Parkinson disease starts with rigidity or tremor of the muscles as dopamine-producing neurons degenerate, affecting movement long before cognition. Younger adults with Parkinson disease usually have sufficient cognitive reserve to avoid dementia unless they live for many years with the disease; older people with Parkinson disease develop dementia sooner (Pfeiffer, 2012).

Another 3 percent of all dementias in the United States are **Lewy body dementia,** named after round deposits of protein (Lewy bodies) in the neurons. Lewy bodies are also present in Parkinson disease, but in Lewy body dementia they are more numerous and dispersed throughout the brain. Motor movements and cognition are both impacted, although the motor effects are less severe than in Parkinson disease and the memory loss is not as dramatic as it is in Alzheimer disease (Bondi

vascular dementia (VaD)
A form of dementia characterized by sporadic, and progressive, loss of intellectual functioning caused by repeated infarcts, or temporary obstructions of blood vessels, which prevent sufficient blood from reaching the brain. (Also called *multi-infarct dementia*.)

frontal lobe dementia
Deterioration of the amygdala and frontal lobes that may be the cause of 15 percent of all dementias. (Also called *frontotemporal lobar degeneration*.)

Parkinson disease
A chronic, progressive disease that is characterized by muscle tremor and rigidity and sometimes dementia; caused by reduced dopamine production in the brain.

Lewy body dementia
A form of dementia characterized by an increase in Lewy body cells in the brain. Symptoms include visual hallucinations, momentary loss of attention, falling, and fainting.

et al., 2009). The main symptom is loss of inhibition: A person might gamble, or become hypersexual.

Comorbidity is common with dementia. For instance, most people with Alzheimer disease also show signs of multi-infarct dementia (Doraiswamy, 2012). Parkinson, Alzheimer, and Lewy body dementias can occur together: People who have all three experience more rapid and severe cognitive loss (Compta et al., 2011).

Some other types of dementia begin in middle age or even earlier, caused by Huntington disease, multiple sclerosis, a severe head injury, repeated concussions as experienced by athletes or soldiers, or the last stages of syphilis, AIDS, or bovine spongiform encephalitis (BSE, or mad cow disease). Symptoms and survival rates vary.

Derek Boogaard, a star National Hockey League enforcer, died of a drug overdose at age 28. His autopsied brain showed traumatic brain damage that would have become full-fledged dementia in a few years. Another hockey player said, "His demeanor, his personality, it just left him. He didn't have a personality anymore" (John Scott, quoted in Branch, 2011, p. B13).

Although the rate of systemic brain disease increases dramatically with every decade after age 60, Boogaard and many dead professional boxers and football stars reveal that brain disease can occur at any age. Obviously, senility and senescence are not synonyms for dementia.

PREVENTING IMPAIRMENT Since aging increases the rate of dementia, slowing down senescence postpones the onset. Because brain plasticity continues throughout life, exercise that improves blood circulation also may build brain capacity and repair damage, not merely prevent loss (Gitler, 2011; Kramer & Erickson, 2007).

Medication to prevent stroke also protects against dementia. In a Finnish study, half of a large group of older Finns were given drugs to reduce lipids (primarily cholesterol). Years later, fewer of them had developed dementia than did a comparable group who were not given the drug (Solomon et al., 2010).

For some dementias, avoiding specific pathogens can prevent the disease. For example, beef can be tested to ensure that it does not have BSE, condoms can protect against AIDS, syphilis can be cured with antibiotics. For most dementias, however, cure and prevention are not known, despite efforts of thousands of scientists and millions of older people. Avoiding toxins (lead, aluminum, copper, and pesticides) or adding supplements (hormones, aspirin, coffee, insulin, antioxidants, red wine, blueberries, and statins) have been tried but not proven effective in controlled, scientific research.

Thousands of scientists seek to halt the production of beta-amyloid, with some success in mice but not yet in humans. One goal is to diagnose Alzheimer disease 10 or 15 years before the first outward signs, to prevent brain damage (G. Miller, 2009). Among professionals, hope is replacing despair. Earlier diagnosis seems possible, and many drug and lifestyle treatments are under review (Hampel et al., 2012; Lane et al., 2011).

Hope comes not only from ongoing research but also from success with other diseases. Heart attacks, for instance, were once the leading cause of death for middle-aged men. No longer. Now risk reduction and surgical intervention make coronary disease rarely fatal until primary aging has weakened the heart.

As with heart disease, the first step in treating dementia is to improve overall health. High blood pressure, diabetes, arteriosclerosis, and emphysema all impair cognition. They disrupt the flow of oxygen to the brain and trigger or worsen the symptoms of dementia. Each type of dementia, each slowdown, and every chronic disease interact, so progress in one area may reduce the incidence of dementia. Healthy diet, social interaction, and especially exercise all decrease cognitive impairment of every kind, changing the chemicals in the brain as well as improving other health habits.

RESPONSE FOR Genetic Counselors (from page 521) A general guideline for genetic counselors is to provide clients with whatever information they seek; but because of both the uncertainty and the devastation of Alzheimer disease, the ApoE4 test is not available at present. This may change (as was the case with the test for HIV) if early methods of prevention and treatment become more effective. ●

Chemical Baby Not directly, of course, but this cuddly doll may affect the chemistry of the brain. Timed to a gentle, recorded voice, itself timed to talk a person to sleep, the eyes of this Japanese doll named Yumel blink and then close as the voice advises that it is time to sleep. Yumel is purchased not only for children but also for the elderly, whose responses to it may slow down dementia.

KURITA KAKU / GAMMA-RAPHO VIA GETTY IMAGES

TREATMENT OF DEMENTIA Early, accurate diagnosis, years before obvious symptoms appear, leads to more effective treatment. Drugs do not cure dementia, but many slow the progression. For some, dementia surgery or stem-cell therapy can be beneficial. The U.S. Pentagon estimates that more than 200,000 U.S. soldiers who were in Iraq or Afghanistan suffered traumatic brain injury, which predisposes them to early-onset dementia (Miller, 2012). Measures to remedy their brain damage may, ironically, help the aged as well.

I Love You, Dad This man, who is in the last stage of Alzheimer disease, no longer remembers his daughter, but she obviously has fond memories of his fatherly affection.

Significant progress in diagnosis is evident: Two decades ago, many people thought senility, dementia, and Alzheimer disease were synonyms. Yet even today, diagnosis is often missed or delayed (Bradford et al., 2009), partly because symptoms are ignored or accepted as mere aging. Tests of behavior, cognition, blood, spinal fluid, and brain can help in specific diagnosis, but they also are expensive, time-consuming, and stressful.

Unfortunately, the major types of dementia, including Alzheimer disease, have several distinct subtypes. Each may have particular symptoms, and varied drug responses, so treatment must be tailored to each person.

Thousands of new professionals are urgently needed to provide individualized medical and psychological care for patients and their families. Few physicians are trained care providers for people with dementia; many avoid telling caregivers when dementia seems likely. That hesitancy is understandable, but wrong in two ways: (1) early treatment might slow the progression, and (2) caregivers are often relieved to know why someone they love is confused, distant, and forgetful (Carpenter et al., 2008).

Mini-Mental State Examination (MMSE)
A test that is used to measure cognitive ability, especially in late adulthood.

REVERSIBLE DEMENTIA? As you have just read, care improves when everyone knows that dementia is occurring and what form it's taking. Accurate diagnosis is even more crucial when memory problems are *not* dementia. True dementias destroy parts of the brain, but many older people are thought to be permanently "losing their minds" when in fact a reversible condition is at fault. One test that can help is the **Mini-Mental State Examination (MMSE),** which reveals whether a person's cognition is worsening because of dementia or whether some nondementia problem is the likely cause.

The most common reversible condition that is mistaken for dementia is depression. If an older person repeatedly despairs at every memory lapse, that despair may signify a treatable mental disorder. Normally, older people tend to be quite happy; frequent sadness or anxiety is not normal. Ongoing depression, untreated, increases the risk of dementia (Sierksma et al., 2010).

Ironically, people with untreated anxiety or depression may exaggerate minor memory losses or refuse to talk. Quite the opposite reaction occurs with early Alzheimer disease, when victims are often surprised when they cannot answer questions, or with Lewy body or frontal lobe dementia, when people talk without thinking.

Specifics provide other clues. People with dementia might forget what they just said, heard, or did because current brain activity is impaired, but they might repeatedly describe details of something that happened long ago. The opposite may be true for emotional disorders, when memory of the past is impaired but short-term memory is not.

Five other conditions—malnutrition, dehydration, brain tumors, physical illness, and overmedication—can also cause symptoms that can mimic dementia (Milosevic et al., 2007). Each is more likely as people grow older, as we now describe.

The aging digestive system needs better nutrition but fewer calories. That requires new habits, less fast food, and more money (which many do not have). Since homeostasis slows with age, malnutrition and dehydration are harder to recognize and remedy (e.g., thirst signals from body to brain are reduced).

Symptoms of brain tumors (headaches, blurred vision) or other serious diseases may not get medical attention if getting to a physician requires considerable effort. In this regard, living alone is a liability: Partners make each other go to the doctor.

The fifth item listed above, overmedication, is a risk for almost every older person and is least likely to be recognized by a partner, friend, or caregiver. At home as well as in the hospital, most elderly people take numerous drugs—not only prescribed medications, but also over-the-counter preparations and herbal remedies—a situation known as **polypharmacy** (Hajjar et al., 2007).

Unfortunately, recommended doses are determined primarily by clinical trials with younger adults, for whom homeostasis usually eliminates excess medication (Herrera et al., 2010). Metabolism and digestion are slower in the old, and thus their bodies take longer to absorb swallowed pills into their bloodstream and then to excrete excess medication. Dosages need adjustment, but the elderly are excluded from most drug research. In addition, people of every age forget when to take which drugs (before, during, or after meals? after dinner or at bedtime?), a problem that's multiplied as more drugs are prescribed (Bosworth & Ayotte, 2009).

Even when medications are taken as prescribed, and a therapeutic dose reaches the bloodstream, drug interactions can cause symptoms that seem like dementia. Cognitive side effects (e.g., confusion and depression) can occur with almost any drug. Many drugs affect the mind, as intended (e.g., to reduce anxiety or depression) but also as unintended (e.g., decreasing memory or reason).

In addition, anesthesia often triggers hallucinations, and pain medication can produce delirium. Risks of polypharmacy increase with transitions: When someone is transferred from a hospital to a nursing home, overmedication and confusion are common (Garcia-Caballos et al., 2010).

The average elderly person in the United States sees a doctor eight times a year (Schiller et al., 2012). Typically, each doctor treats a particular illness, unaware of what other doctors have prescribed. Physicians follow "clinical practice guidelines," recommendations for best practices for each particular condition, not for the comorbid conditions that the typical elderly person has. A "prescribing cascade" (when a drug is prescribed to treat an adverse effect of another drug) is possible.

In one distressing case, a doctor prescribed medication to raise blood pressure, and another doctor, noting the raised blood pressure, prescribed a drug to lower it (McLendon & Shelton, 2011–2012). Usually, doctors ask patients what medications they are taking and why, which could prevent this from happening. However, people who are already sick and confused may not be comprehensive and accurate.

Finally, following recommendations from the radio, friends, and television ads, many of the elderly try supplements, compounds, and herbal preparations that contain mind-altering toxins. Polypharmacy can be dangerous, as the following describes.

polypharmacy
Refers to a situation in which elderly people are prescribed several medications. The various side effects and interactions of those medications can result in dementia symptoms.

OPPOSING PERSPECTIVES

Too Many Drugs or Too Few?

The case for medication is persuasive. Thousands of drugs have been proven effective, many of them responsible for longer and healthier lives. It is estimated that, on doctor's orders, 20 percent of older people take 10 or more drugs on a regular basis (Boyd et al., 2005). Common examples of life-saving drugs are insulin to halt the ravages of diabetes, statins to prevent strokes, and antidepressants to reduce despair.

In addition, many older people take supplements, drink alcohol, and swallow vitamins and other nonprescription drugs daily. The combination of doctor-ordered and self-administered drugs sometimes promotes death, not life. For example, Audrey, a 70-year-old widow:

> was covered with large black bruises and burns from her kitchen stove. Audrey no longer had an appetite, so she ate little and was emaciated. One night she passed out in her driveway and scraped her face. The next morning, her neighbor found her face down on the pavement in her nightgown.
>
> Audrey couldn't be trusted with the grandchildren anymore, so family visits were fewer and farther between. She rarely showered and spent most days sitting in a chair alternating between drinking, sleeping, and watching television. She stopped calling friends, and social invitations had long since ceased.
>
> Audrey obtained prescriptions for Valium, a tranquilizer, and Placidyl, a sleep inducer. Both medications, which are addictive and have more adverse effects in patients over age 60, should only be used for short periods of time. Audrey had taken both medications for years at three to four times the prescribed dosage. She mixed them with large quantities of alcohol. She was a full-fledged addict . . . close to death.
>
> Her children knew she had a problem, but they . . . couldn't agree among themselves on the best way to help her. Over time, they became desensitized to the seriousness of her problem—until it progressed to a dangerously advanced stage. Luckily for Audrey, she was referred to a new doctor who recognized her addiction. . . . Once Audrey was in treatment and weaned off the alcohol and drugs, she bloomed. Audrey's memory improved; her appetite returned; she regained her energy; and she started walking, swimming and exercising every day. Now, a decade later, Audrey plays an important role in her grandchildren's lives, gardens, and she lives creatively and with meaning.
>
> *[Colleran & Jay, 2003, p. 11]*

Audrey is a stunning example of the danger of ageist assumptions as well as of polypharmacy. Her children did not realize that she was capable of an intellectually and socially productive life.

The solution seems simple: Discontinue drugs. However, that may increase both disease and dementia. One expert criticizes polypharmacy but adds that "underuse of medications in older adults can have comparable adverse effects on quality of life" (Miller, 2011–2012, p. 21).

For instance, untreated diabetes and hypertension cause cognitive loss. Lack of drug treatment for those conditions may be one reason why low-income elders experience more illness, more dementia, and earlier death than do high-income elders: The poor are less likely to obtain medical care or to be able to afford drugs that might improve their health.

As with this example, money complicates the issue: Prescription drugs are expensive, which increases profits for drug companies but also reduces surgery and hospital stays, thus saving money. As one observer notes, the war on spending for prescription drugs

> is highly polarized, emotionally loaded, and characterized by very little useful debate. This war is being waged over the cost issues connected with drug treatment and prescribing for older people, and it is a gloves-off, stab-you-in-the-guts struggle to the death.
>
> *[Sloan, 2011–2012, p. 56]*

Which is it—too many drugs or too few? The answer depends not only on careful analysis of the health and values of each elderly person, but also on analysis of the attitudes of the person doing the analysis. Some caregivers are antidrug; others want drugs to control symptoms (e.g., insomnia, anger, sadness) that an elderly person might prefer not to medicate. Is it better to be suspicious of every drug, herb, or supplement or better to hope that drugs will protect health?

The current policy is to let the doctor and the patient decide. But remember Audrey.

KEY points

- The diseases that increase with aging can be the direct result of senescence or the accumulated load from years of destructive habits and circumstances.
- Among the many types of dementia, each with distinct symptoms, are Alzheimer disease, vascular dementia, frontal lobe dementia, and Parkinson disease.
- A cure for dementia has not yet been found, but treatment may slow the progression and sometimes prevent the onset.
- The elderly are sometimes thought to suffer from dementia when in fact they are depressed, alcoholic, or taking too many drugs.

New Cognitive Development

You have learned that most older adults maintain adequate intellectual power. Some losses—in rapid reactions, for instance—are quite manageable, and only a minority of elders become demented. But the life-span perspective holds that gains as well as losses occur at every period. Are there cognitive gains in late adulthood? Yes! New depth, enhanced creativity, and even wisdom are possible.

Erikson and Maslow

Both Erik Erikson and Abraham Maslow were particularly interested in the elderly, interviewing older people to understand their views. Erikson's final book, *Vital Involvement in Old Age* (Erikson et al., 1986), written when he was in his 90s, was based on responses from other 90-year-olds—the cohort who had been studied since they were babies in Berkeley, California.

Erikson found that many older people gained interest in the arts, in children, and in human experience as a whole. He said elders are "social witnesses," aware of the interdependence of the generations as well as of all of human experience. His eighth stage, *integrity versus despair,* is the time when life comes together in a "re-synthesis of all the resilience and strengths already developed" (Erikson et al., 1986, p. 40).

Maslow maintained that older adults are more likely than younger people to reach the highest stage of development, **self-actualization.** Remember that Maslow rejected an age-based sequence of life, refusing to confine self-actualization to the old. Some youth might already be self-actualizers and some elders might still be at earlier steps of his hierarchy, seeking love or success. However, Maslow also believed that life experience helps people move forward, so more of the old reach the final stage.

The stage of self-actualization is characterized by aesthetic, creative, philosophical, and spiritual understanding (Maslow, 1970). A self-actualized person might have a deeper spirituality than ever; or might be especially appreciative of nature; or might find life more amusing, laughing often at himself or herself. Studies of centenarians find that they often have a deep spiritual grounding and a surprising sense of humor—surprising, that is, if one assumes that people with limited sight, poor hearing, and frequent pain have nothing to laugh about.

self-actualization
The final stage in Maslow's hierarchy of needs, characterized by aesthetic, creative, philosophical, and spiritual understanding.

Aesthetic Sense and Creativity

For many, "old age can be a time of emotional sensory awareness and enjoyment" (R. N. Butler et al., 1998, p. 65). For that reason, some of the elderly take up gardening, bird watching, sculpting, painting, or making music, even if they have never done so before.

An example of late creative development is Anna Moses, who was a farm wife in rural New York. For most of her life, she expressed her artistic impulses by stitching quilts and embroidering in winter, when farm work was slow. At age 75, arthritis made needlework impossible, so she took to "dabbling in oil."

Four years later, three of her paintings, displayed in a local drugstore, caught the eye of a New York City art dealer who happened to be driving through town. He bought them, drove to her house, and bought 15 more.

The following year, at age 80, "Grandma Moses" had a one-woman show, receiving international recognition for her unique "primitive" style. She continued to paint, and her work "developed and changed considerably over the course of her twenty-year career" (Cardinal, 2001). Anna Moses died at age 101.

Other well-known artists continue in late adulthood, sometimes producing their best work. Michelangelo painted the awe-inspiring frescoes in the Sistine Chapel at age 75; Verdi composed the opera *Falstaff* when he was 80; Frank Lloyd Wright

Exercise and the Mind Creative activity may improve the intellect, especially when it involves social activity. Both the woman in a French ceramics class *(top)*, subsidized by the government for residents of Grenoble over age 60, and the man playing the tuba in a band in Cuba *(bottom)* are gaining much more than the obvious finger or lung exercise.

life review
An examination of one's own role in the history of human life, engaged in by many elderly people.

completed the design of New York City's Guggenheim Museum when he was 91.

In a study of extraordinarily creative people, almost none felt that their ability, their goals, or the quality of their work had been much impaired by age. The leader of that study observed, "In their seventies, eighties, and nineties, they may lack the fiery ambition of earlier years, but they are just as focused, efficient, and committed as before . . . perhaps more so" (Csikszentmihalyi, 1996, p. 503).

The creative impulse is one that family members and everyone else should encourage in the elderly, according to many professionals. Expressing one's creativity and aesthetic sense is said to aid in social skills, resilience, and even brain health (McFadden & Basting, 2010).

The same can be said for the **life review,** in which elders provide an account of their personal journey by writing or telling their story. They want others to know their history, telling not solely about themselves but also about their family, cohort, or ethnic group. A leading gerontologist wants us to listen:

> We have been taught that this nostalgia represents living in the past and a preoccupation with self and that it is generally boring, meaningless, and time-consuming. Yet as a natural healing process it represents one of the underlying human capacities on which all psychotherapy depends. The life review should be recognized as a necessary and healthy process in daily life as well as a useful tool in the mental health care of older people.
>
> *[R. N. Butler et al., 1998, p. 91]*

Wisdom

The idea that older people are wise is a "hoped-for antidote to views that have cast the process of aging in terms of intellectual deficit and regression" (Labouvie-Vief, 1990, p. 52). One reviewer contends that "wise elders might become a valuable asset for a more just and caring future society" (Ardelt, 2011, p. 287). A massive international survey of 26 nations, at least one on each inhabited continent, found that most people everywhere agree that wisdom is a characteristic of the elderly (Löckenhoff et al., 2009).

However, contrary to these wishes and opinions, most objective research finds that wisdom does not necessarily increase with age. Starting at age 25 or so, some adults of every age are wise, but most, even at age 80, are not (Ardelt, 2011).

An underlying research quandary is that a universal definition of wisdom is elusive: Each culture and each cohort has its own concept, with fools sometimes seeming wise (as in Shakespeare). Older and younger adults differ in how they make decisions; one interpretation of these differences is that the older adults are wiser, but not every younger adult would agree (Worthy et al., 2011).

One summary describes wisdom as an "expert knowledge system dealing with the conduct and understanding of life" (P. B. Baltes & Smith, 2008, p. 58). Several factors just mentioned, including the ability to put aside one's personal needs (as in self-actualization), self-reflective honesty (as in integrity), and perspective on past living (the life review), are considered part of wisdom.

If this is true, the elderly have a head start in becoming wise, particularly if they have dedicated their lives to the "understanding of life," are willing and able to learn from their experiences, and have become more mature and integrated in the process

(Ardelt, 2011, p. 283). Probably for that reason, philosophers, psychologists, and the general public connect wisdom with old age: That may be why Popes and Supreme Court judges are usually quite old.

The popular consensus may be grounded in reality. As two psychologists explain:

> Wisdom is one domain in which some older individuals excel. . . . [They have] a combination of psychosocial characteristics and life history factors, including openness to experience, generativity, cognitive style, contact with excellent mentors, and some exposure to structured and critical life experiences.
>
> *[P. B. Baltes & Smith, 2008, p. 60]*

These researchers posed life dilemmas to adults of various ages and asked others (who had no clue as to how old the participants were) to judge whether the responses were wise. They found that wisdom is rare at any age, but, unlike physical strength and cognitive quickness, wisdom does not fade with maturity. Thus, some people of every age were judged as wise.

Similarly, the author of a detailed longitudinal study of 814 people concludes that wisdom is not reserved for the old, and yet humor, perspective, and altruism increase over the decades, gradually making people wiser. He then wrote:

> To be wise about wisdom we need to accept that wisdom does—and wisdom does not—increase with age. . . . Winston Churchill, that master of wise simplicity and simple wisdom, reminds us, "We are all happier in many ways when we are old than when we are young. The young sow wild oats. The old grow sage."
>
> *[Vaillant, 2002, p. 256]*

The Centenarians

If age brings integrity, creativity, and maybe even wisdom, then the oldest-old should excel in many ways and those who reach age 100 and beyond should be best of all. Is there any evidence that this is true?

OTHER PLACES, OTHER STORIES In the 1970s, three remote places—one in the Republic of Georgia, one in Pakistan, and one in Ecuador—were in the news because many vigorous old people were found to live there, with several over 100 years old. As one researcher described people 90 and older:

> Most of the aged work regularly. . . . Some even continue to chop wood and haul water. Close to 40 percent of the aged men and 30 percent of the aged women report good vision; that is, that they do not need glasses for any sort of work, including reading or threading a needle. Between 40 and 50 percent have reasonably good hearing. Most have their own teeth. Their posture is unusually erect, even into advanced age. Many take walks of more than two miles a day and swim in mountain streams.
>
> *[Benet, 1974]*

A more comprehensive study (Pitskhelauri, 1982) found that the lifestyles in all three of these regions were similar in four ways:

1. *Diet.* People ate mostly fresh vegetables and herbs, with little meat or fat. They thought it better to be a little bit hungry than too full.
2. *Work.* Even the very old did farm work, household tasks, and childcare.
3. *Family and community.* The elderly were well integrated into families of several generations and interacted frequently with friends and neighbors.
4. *Exercise and relaxation.* Most took a walk every morning and evening (often up and down mountains), napped midday, and socialized in the evening.

Perhaps these factors—diet, work, social interaction, and exercise—lengthened life.

That the social context promotes longevity is buttressed by evidence from bumblebees. Genetically, worker bees and queen bees are the same, but worker bees live about three months while queen bees, who are fed special food and treated with deference, live about five years. When a queen dies, a worker bee is chosen to become a queen, thereby living 20 times longer than that bee otherwise would have.

THE TRUTH ABOUT LIFE AFTER 100 Surely your suspicions were raised by the preceding paragraphs. Humans have almost nothing in common with bumblebees, and the information about those long-lived people was published decades ago.

Indeed, the three regions famous for long-lived humans lack verifiable birth or marriage records. Everyone who claimed to be a centenarian was probably exaggerating, and every researcher who believed them was too eager to accept the idea that life would be long and wonderful if only the ills of modern civilization could be avoided (Thorson, 1995).

As for preventing the ills of old age, it does seem that exercise, diet, and social integration add a few years to the average life, but not decades. It is important to distinguish the *average* life span from the *maximum*.

Genes seem to bestow on every species an inherent **maximum life span,** defined as the oldest possible age for members of that species (Wolf, 2010). Under ideal circumstances, the maximum that rats live seems to be 4 years; rabbits, 13; tigers, 26; house cats, 30; brown bats, 34; brown bears, 37; chimpanzees, 55; Indian elephants, 70; finback whales, 80; humans, 122; lake sturgeon, 150; giant tortoises, 180.

Maximum life span is quite different from **average life expectancy,** which is the average life span of individuals in a particular group. In human groups, average life expectancy varies a great deal, depending on historical, cultural, and socioeconomic factors as well as on genes (Sierra et al., 2009). Recent increases in life expectancy are attributed to the reduction in deaths from adult diseases (heart attack, pneumonia, cancer, childbed fever).

In the United States in 2012, average life expectancy at birth was about 76 years for men and 81 years for women. That is four years longer than it was 30 years ago, and it is projected to be another five years longer in 2050 (United Nations, 2012).

These projections are disputed, however: Gerontologists are engaged in a "fiery debate" as to whether the average life span will keep rising and whether the maximum is genetically fixed and our society has just about reached that (Couzin-Frankel, 2011b, p. 549). It is known that the oldest well-documented life ended at age 122, when Jeanne Calment died in southern France in 1997. No one has yet been proven to have outlived her, despite documented birth dates for a billion people who have died since then.

Everyone agrees, however, that the last years of life can be good ones. Those who study centenarians find many quite happy (Jopp & Rott, 2006). Jeanne Calment enjoyed a glass of red wine and some olive oil each day. "I will die laughing," she said.

Disease, disability, depression, and dementia may eventually set in; studies disagree about how common these problems are past age 100. Some studies find a higher rate of physical and mental health problems before age 100 than after. For example, in Sweden, where medical care is free, researchers found that centenarians were less likely to take antidepressants, but more likely to use pain medication, than those who were aged 80 or so (Wastesson et al., 2012).

maximum life span
The oldest possible age that members of a species can live under ideal circumstances. For humans, that age is approximately 122 years.

average life expectancy
The number of years the average newborn in a particular population group is likely to live.

Long Past Warring Many of the oldest men of Mali are revered as the most devout and spiritual Muslims, as this man is. Unfortunately, Mali has experienced violent civil wars and two national coups in recent years, perhaps because men over 70 make up less than 1 percent of the population, whereas 75 percent are under age 30.

SEAN CAFFREY / LONELY PLANET IMAGES / GETTY IMAGES

Could centenarians be happier than octogenarians, as these Swedish data suggest? That is not known. However, it is true that more and more people live past 100, and many of them are energetic, alert, and optimistic (Perls, 2008; Poon, 2008). Social relationships in particular correlate with robust mental health (Margrett et al., 2011). Centenarians tend to be upbeat about life.

Whether their attitude is justified is not clear. Remember, however, that ageism affects all of us. As explained in the beginning of this chapter, ageism shortens life and makes the final years less satisfying. Don't let it. As thousands of centenarians demonstrate, a long life can be a happy one.

Guess Their Age Someone who has not read this chapter would be surprised to learn that Bessie Cooper *(left)* was 114 and Jiroemon Kimura *(right)* was 112 when these photos were taken. The pictures are not the most current, however: She was the oldest woman alive until her death at age 116 in 2012, and he turned 115 the same year—the oldest man to have lived so long. Some of the reasons for longevity are visible: genes (note their smooth skin), caregivers (note her carefully coiffed hair and his pristine white shirt), technology (glasses and hearing aid), and attitude (proud smiles). Not visible is their independence (she lived alone on a Georgia farm from ages 67 to 105) or many descendants (over 60 for Jiroemon, including that infant great-great-grandchild on the right).

KEY points

- Old age may be a time of integrity and self-actualization, although this is not always the case.

- Many older people are more creative than they were earlier in life, enjoying art and music.

- Wisdom is thought to correlate with experience, although research finds that some people are wise long before old age, and most people are never wise.

- The number of centenarians is increasing, as the average but not the maximum life span increases; some of those over age 100 are active, independent, and happy.

SUMMARY

Prejudice and Predictions

1. Contrary to ageist stereotypes, most older adults are happy, quite healthy, and active. Benevolent as well as dismissive ageism reduces health and self-image, as elderspeak illustrates.

2. An increasing percentage of the population is older than 64, but the numbers are sometimes presented in misleading ways.

Currently, about 13 percent of people in the U.S. population are elderly, and most of them are self-sufficient and productive.

3. Gerontologists distinguish the young-old, the old-old, and the oldest-old, according to each age group's relative degree of dependency. In the United States, only 10 percent of the population older than 64 are dependent, and only 4 percent are in nursing homes or hospitals. Numbers are even lower in most other nations.

4. Sexual intercourse occurs less often, driving a car becomes more difficult, and all the senses become less acute with age. However, selective optimization with compensation can mitigate almost any loss. A combination of personal determination, adjustment by society, and technological devices is needed.

Cognition

5. Brain scans and measurements show that the speed of processing slows down, parts of the brain shrink, and more areas of the brain are activated in older people.

6. Memory is affected by aging, but specifics vary. As the senses become dulled, some stimuli never reach the sensory memory. Working memory shows notable declines with age because slower processing means that some thoughts are lost.

7. Control processes are less effective with age, as retrieval strategies become less efficient. Anxiety may prevent older people from using the best strategies for cognitive control. Ecologically valid, real-life measures of cognition are needed.

Aging and Disease

8. Primary aging happens to everyone, reducing organ reserve in body and brain. Secondary aging depends on the individual's past health habits and genes. The combination of primary and secondary aging eventually causes morbidity, disability, and mortality.

9. Dementia, whether it occurs in late adulthood or earlier, is characterized by memory loss—at first minor lapses, then more serious forgetfulness, and, finally, in many cases, such extreme memory losses that recognition of even the closest family members fades.

10. The most common cause of dementia in the United States is Alzheimer disease, an incurable ailment that becomes more prevalent with age and worsens over time.

11. Also common worldwide is vascular dementia (also called multi-infarct dementia), which results from a series of ministrokes (transient ischemic attacks, or TIAs) that occur when impairment of blood circulation destroys portions of brain tissue.

12. Other dementias, including frontal lobe dementia and Lewy body dementia, also become more common with age. Several other types of dementia can occur in early or middle adulthood. One is Parkinson disease, which begins with loss of muscle control. Parkinson disease can also cause dementia, particularly in the old.

13. Dementia is sometimes mistakenly diagnosed when individuals are suffering from a reversible problem, such as anxiety, depression, brain tumors, and polypharmacy.

New Cognitive Development

14. Many people become more interested and adept in creative endeavors, as well as more philosophical, as they grow older. The life review is a personal reflection that many older people undertake, remembering earlier experiences, putting their entire lives into perspective, and achieving integrity or self-actualization.

15. Wisdom does not necessarily increase as a result of age, but some elderly people are unusually wise or insightful.

16. It was once believed that many people in certain parts of the world lived long past 100 as a result of moderate diet, exercise, hard work, and respect for the aged. Such reports turned out to be exaggerated.

17. The number of centenarians is increasing, and many of them are quite healthy and happy. The personality and attitudes of the very old suggest that long-term survival may be welcomed more than feared.

KEY TERMS

ageism (p. 499)
Alzheimer disease (AD) (p. 520)
average life expectancy (p. 530)
calorie restriction (p. 507)
cellular aging (p. 506)
compression of morbidity (p. 518)
control processes (p. 515)

delirium (p. 519)
dementia (p. 519)
demographic shift (p. 503)
dependency ratio (p. 504)
ecological validity (p. 514)
elderspeak (p. 502)
frontal lobe dementia (p. 522)
genetic clock (p. 505)
Hayflick limit (p. 506)

Lewy body dementia (p. 522)
life review (p. 528)
maximum life span (p. 530)
Mini-Mental State Examination (MMSE) (p. 524)
old-old (p. 505)
oldest-old (p. 505)
osteoporosis (p. 519)

Parkinson disease (p. 522)
polypharmacy (p. 525)
primary aging (p. 517)
secondary aging (p. 517)
self-actualization (p. 527)
vascular dementia (VaD) (p. 522)
wear and tear (p. 505)
young-old (p. 505)

WHAT HAVE YOU LEARNED?

1. What are the similarities and differences among ageism, racism, and sexism?

2. In what ways do older adults perpetuate ageism?

3. How does ageism affect older adults' mental and physical health?

4. In what ways does elderspeak reduce communication?

5. Give an example of how protecting older adults might actually lead to more harm.

6. Why is the increasing number of older people less problematic than it was once thought to be?

7. What are the differences among young-old, old-old, and oldest-old?

8. What are the differences in the sleep patterns of the old and the young?

9. What problems associated with aging do older drivers experience? How do they compensate for these problems? What other measures would help them (and all other drivers)?

10. What changes occur in the sense organs in old age, and how can their effects be minimized?

11. What changes in the brain occur with age?

12. Why is multitasking particularly difficult in late adulthood?

13. How does sensory loss affect cognition?

14. Which kinds of things are harder to remember with age? Which kinds of memories seem well preserved with age?

15. How are control processes affected by age?

16. Why is ecological validity especially important for testing cognition and abilities?

17. What is the difference between primary aging and secondary aging?

18. How is compression of morbidity good for society as well as for the individual?

19. Why is falling a serious health problem in old age?

20. What are some signs of dementia?

21. What abnormalities in the brain characterize Alzheimer disease? How do these abnormalities affect brain function?

22. Why are most people unaware of the early stages of vascular dementia?

23. What changes in the brain are associated with Parkinson disease? How are the symptoms of the disease the same and different in younger and older adults?

24. What measures help protect people against dementia? What measures have not been proven effective in controlled scientific research?

25. Why is accurate diagnosis important when older people have cognitive difficulties?

26. Why is overmedication more likely for older people than younger adults?

27. According to Erikson, what gains may be evident in older people? What gains may be evident according to Maslow?

28. What are the purpose and benefits of the life review?

29. What factors are considered part of wisdom, and how do these relate to aging?

30. What lifestyle factors might result in increased energy, alertness, and optimism in centenarians?

APPLICATIONS

1. Analyze Web sites that have information about aging for evidence of ageism, anti-aging measures, and exaggeration of longevity.

2. Ask five people of various ages if they want to live to age 100 and record their responses. Would they be willing to eat half as much, exercise much more, experience weekly dialysis, or undergo other procedures in order to extend life? Analyze the responses.

3. Visit someone in a hospital. Note all the elements in the environment—such as noise, lights, schedules, and personnel—that might cause an elderly patient to seem demented.

>> ONLINE CONNECTIONS

To accompany your textbook, you have access to a number of online resources, including quizzes for every chapter of the book, flashcards (in English and Spanish), critical thinking questions, and case studies. For access to any of these links, go to www.worthpublishers.com/bergerinvitation2e. In addition to these free resources, you'll also find links to podcasts, video clips, diagnostic quizzing with personalized study advice, and an ebook. Some of the videos and activities available online include:

- *Perceptions and Reality in Older Adulthood.* Discusses ageism, demographics, and the gains and losses associated with aging. In video clips, elders tell the real story of what it's like to age.

- *Alzheimer Disease.* Outlines the progressive course of Alzheimer disease, as well as the types and limits of treatments. Includes video about the effects of chronic stress on two caregivers.

CHAPTER OUTLINE

LATE ADULTHOOD
Psychosocial Development

WHAT WILL YOU KNOW?

- Do older people become more depressed as time goes by?
- Do the elderly hope to move to a distant, warm place?
- What do adult children owe their elderly parents?
- Is home care better than nursing home care?

Almost every week I walk with Doris, a widow in her 80s, to a meeting we both attend. The walk is short, through a park. On the way, she greets several people of all backgrounds, including a few homeless men and a woman who owns the nearby hotel. One person she often greets is Colin, who plays his piano (on wheels) in the park on sunny days. Four months ago, the park police ticketed him for not having a permit. Doris organized a protest, and not only was the ticket withdrawn but Community Board 2 passed a resolution about free speech. The Parks Department amended its guidelines.

Doris claims that babies and animals love her, which may well be true. Squirrels scamper up to take the peanuts she offers, and sometimes pigeons perch on her arm. She dresses well, appropriate for the season, but one day in August she wore a long-sleeved blouse. She told me the reason with pride: Her arm was scratched because two pigeons had fought over the same spot.

Often we stop at the mailbox for her to mail a timely greeting card: She corresponds with hundreds of people. I have become one of them. I get various colorful envelopes from Doris—green for St. Patrick's Day, orange for Halloween, gray for Thanksgiving, and festooned with stickers for Christmas, July 4th, my birthday, and so on.

Usually, friends have much in common, but Doris and I are quite different. I never send cards, feed squirrels, or protect pianists (although Doris did get me to help Colin). We are members of opposing political parties. She has no children; I have four.

How did we happen to become friends? Five years ago, Doris had knee surgery and needed volunteers to wheel her to her meetings and appointments. Dozens of people offered their services, including me—

for the weekly meeting on both our calendars. Soon she became quite capable of walking alone, but we have remained in touch ever since. And I have come to appreciate her anecdotes, her outgoing nature, her attitudes. Doris exemplifies the qualities of many of the elderly, who continue to be active, social, and appreciated as the years roll by. ●

THAT IS THE TOPIC OF THIS CHAPTER, which describes the variability and complexity of development in later life. Some of the elderly are frail, lonely, and vulnerable to abuse, either because of private circumstances or public failures. For most, however, psychosocial development includes working and socializing, concern for others as well as self-care. Doris does all this admirably. I hope to be like her when I am in my 80s.

Theories of Late Adulthood

self theories
Theories of late adulthood that emphasize the core self, or the search to maintain one's integrity and identity.

Development in late adulthood may be more diverse than at any other age: Some elderly people run marathons and lead nations, whereas others can no longer walk or talk. Moreover, individuals vary within themselves in almost every measure from day to day, with some days much better than others (Krenk et al., 2009). Many social scientists try to understand the significance and origin of these variations as well as to describe the general course of old age.

Some theories of late adulthood have been called *self theories* because they focus on individuals' perceptions of themselves and their ability to meet challenges to their identity. Other theories are called *stratification theories* because they describe the ways in which societies place people on a particular life path.

Self Theories

It can be said that people become more truly themselves as they grow old, an idea captured by Anna Quindlen:

> It's odd when I think of the arc of my life from child to young woman to aging adult. First I was who I was, then I didn't know who I was, then I invented someone and became her, then I began to like what I'd invented, and finally I was what I was again. It turned out I wasn't alone in that particular progression.
>
> *[Quindlen, 2012, ix]*

AP PHOTO / COLUMBUS DAILY DISPATCH, ERIC ALBRECHT

Still Helping Virginia Ryder, here helping Betty Baldwin put on her coat, is a lifelong helper. She cared for younger children when she was a child, and she has been a senior companion for the past 19 years, again often for younger people. She is 89 years old.

The essential self is protected and rediscovered, despite all the changes that may occur. **Self theories** emphasize "the ways people negotiate challenges to the self" (Sneed & Whitbourne, 2005, p. 380). Such negotiation is particularly crucial when older adults are confronted with multiple challenges like illness, retirement, and the death of loved ones.

A central idea of self theories is that each person ultimately depends on himself or herself. As one woman explained:

> I actually think I value my sense of self more importantly than my family or relationships or health or wealth or wisdom. I do see myself as on my own, ultimately. . . . Statistics certainly show that older women are likely to end up being alone, so I really do value my own self when it comes right down to things in the end.
>
> *[quoted in J. Kroger, 2007, p. 203]*

Studies of personality over the life span confirm the continuity of self. An individual's high or low level on each of the Big Five personality traits (see Chapter 13) tends to remain the same, not only throughout adulthood, but even when people are in their 80s (Mõttus et al., 2012).

INTEGRITY The most comprehensive self theory came from Erik Erikson. His eighth and final stage of development is called **integrity versus despair,** a period in which older adults seek to integrate their unique experiences with their vision of community (Erikson et al., 1986). The word *integrity* is often used to mean honesty, but it also means a feeling of being whole, not scattered, comfortable with oneself. (*Integrity* comes from the same root word as *integer,* a math term meaning "a whole number, not a fraction.")

As an example of integrity, many older people express pride and contentment regarding their personal history. They are proud of their past, even when it includes events that an outsider might not consider worthy of pride—such as skipping school, taking drugs, escaping arrest, or being physically abused. Psychologists sometimes call this the *"sucker to saint" phenomenon*—that is, people interpret their experiences as signs of their nobility (saintly), not their stupidity (Jordan & Monin, 2008).

As Erikson (1963) explains it, such self-glorifying distortions are far better than losing hope, "feeling that the time is now short, too short for the attempt to start another life" (p. 269). As with every crisis described by Erikson, tension occurs between the two opposing aspects of development. Past crises, particularly Erikson's fifth crisis of *identity versus role confusion,* reappear when the usual pillars of the self-concept (such as employment or good looks) crumble. One 70-year-old said, "I know who I've been, but who am I now?" (quoted in J. Kroger, 2007, p. 201).

This tension helps advance the person toward a more complete self-concept. In this last stage,

> life brings many, quite realistic reasons for experiencing despair: aspects of the present that cause unremitting pain; aspects of a future that are uncertain and frightening. And, of course, there remains inescapable death, that one aspect of the future which is both wholly certain and wholly unknowable. Thus, some despair must be acknowledged and integrated as a component of old age.
>
> *[Erikson et al., 1986, p. 72]*

That integration of death and the self is an important accomplishment of this stage. The life review (explained in Chapter 14) and the acceptance of death (to be explained in the Epilogue) are crucial aspects of the integrity envisioned by Erikson (Zimmerman, 2012).

HOLDING ON TO ONE'S SELF Most older people consider their personalities and attitudes quite stable over their life span, even as they acknowledge the physical changes of their bodies (Fischer et al., 2008). One 103-year-old woman observed, "My core has stayed the same. Everything else has changed" (quoted in Troll & Skaff, 1997, p. 166). Sometimes it is a struggle to maintain a strong sense of self. As bodies and social relationships change, adults may need to revise their self theory about their identity.

The need to maintain the self may explain behavior that younger people might consider foolish. For example, many elders hate to give up driving a car because "the loss felt, for men in particular, is deeper than that of simply not being able to get from A to B; it is a loss of a sense of self, of the meaning of manhood" (Davidson, 2008, p. 46). Objects and places become more precious in late adulthood than they were earlier, as people seek a way to hold on to identity (J. Kroger, 2007; Whitmore, 2001).

The tendency to cling to familiar places and possessions may be problematic if it leads to **compulsive hoarding.** The urge to accumulate old papers, furniture, and mementos becomes stronger with age; younger relatives may complain that clutter takes up space and becomes a fire hazard (Thobaben, 2006). However, compulsive hoarding can be seen as maintaining the self: Most elderly hoarders saved things when they were much younger, and want to keep doing so. With time, the problem gets worse, not only because things accumulate, but also because possessions are part of self-expression, and the elderly resist self-destruction (Ayers et al., 2010).

integrity versus despair
The final stage of Erik Erikson's developmental sequence, in which older adults seek to integrate their unique experiences with their vision of community.

compulsive hoarding
The urge to accumulate and hold on to familiar objects and possessions, sometimes to the point of their becoming health and/or safety hazards. This impulse tends to increase with age.

positivity effect
The tendency for elderly people to perceive, prefer, and remember positive images and experiences more than negative ones.

Similarly, many older people refuse to move from drafty and dangerous dwellings into smaller, safer apartments because abandoning familiar places means abandoning personal history. Likewise, they may avoid surgery or reject medicine because they fear anything that might distort their thinking or emotions: Their priority is self-protection, even if it means shortening life (S. W. Miller, 2011–2012).

The need to preserve oneself explains why many of the elderly strive to maintain childhood cultural and religious practices. For instance, grandparents may painstakingly teach a grandchild a language that is rarely used in their current community, or encourage the child to repeat rituals and prayers they themselves learned as children. In cultures that emphasize youth and novelty, the elderly worry that their old values will be lost and thus that they themselves will disappear from memory.

Ideally, younger generations appreciate the elders' traditions. The older generation realizes they could have been raised in other cultures and followed other paths through life, especially if they lived elsewhere, but they appreciate their particular identity, religion, and national origin. As Erikson (1963) wrote, the older person

> knows that an individual life is the accidental coincidence of but one life cycle with but one segment of history and that for him all human integrity stands or falls with the one style of integrity of which he partakes. . . . In such a final consolation, death loses its sting.
>
> *[p. 268]*

The importance of self-validation is particularly apparent among older immigrants. Many grew up with customs unlike those where they and their descendants now live. They may become depressed if they think their culture is not appreciated.

For example, in the United States, older people from India reported to researchers that their grandchildren were disrespectful and that "Indian culture is ignored, compartmentalized, and debased in America" (Kalavar & van Willigen, 2005, p. 228). Similarly, elderly immigrants from the Middle East and from Korea struggle to reconcile their traditional values with those of their children (Abu-Bader et al., 2011; H. Y. Lee et al., 2011).

THE POSITIVITY EFFECT As you remember from Chapter 14, some people cope successfully with the changes of late adulthood through *selective optimization with compensation*. This is central to self theories. Individuals set their personal goals, assess their own abilities, and figure out how to accomplish those goals despite limitations. For some people, simply maintaining identity correlates with well-being (Ebner et al., 2006).

One strategy for selective optimization is known as the **positivity effect.** Elderly people are more likely to perceive, prefer, and remember positive images and experiences than negative ones (Carstensen et al., 2006). Compensation occurs via selective recall: Unpleasant experiences are reinterpreted as inconsequential. For example, with age, stressful events (economic loss; serious illness; the death of friends, family, or, in the future, oneself) are less likely to be considered central to one's identity. That enables the elderly to be unperturbed by whatever happens; they maintain emotional health via positive self-perception (Boals et al., 2012).

The positivity effect is evident in dozens of nations. After taking into account income, education, and gender, adults everywhere report gradually increasing happiness from age 50 on (Blanchflower et al., 2008). This may explain why, in every nation and religion, older people tend to be more patriotic and devout than younger ones. They are more comfortable being themselves—proud to be Canadian, Czech, Chinese, or whatever. Back to Anna Quindlen: "I was what I was again."

Fiercely Independent In the first half of his life, Nelson Mandela led the fight against apartheid in his native South Africa—until he was convicted of sabotage and sentenced to life in prison. Remarkably, he stayed true to his beliefs; released 27 years later to lead once again, he was elected president and served from 1994 to 1999. Still his true self, he next formed The Elders, pledged to be "a fiercely independent force for good." At age 92, he sits with two other Elders, Desmond Tutu (72) and Jimmy Carter (79).

AP PHOTO / JEFF MOORE, POOL

A VIEW FROM SCIENCE

No Regrets

Many researchers have studied the positivity effect. They have found not only that a positive world view usually increases with age but also that it correlates with believing that life is meaningful (Hicks et al., 2012). Those elders who are highest on positivity (e.g., feeling happy, not frustrated or depressed) are likely to agree strongly that their life has a purpose (e.g., "I have a system of values that guides my daily activities" and "I am at peace with my past") (Hicks et al., 2012).

Researchers have measured not only expressed attitudes and memories, but also brain and body reactions to disappointment. When something doesn't happen as you wish, are you likely to take a greater risk the next time, or are you likely to let go of your disappointment? If you are an emerging adult, you might take a greater risk, but not if you are an older adult. The elderly react to disappointment by letting it go, thinking positively about going forward (see Figure 15.1).

In this and many other experiments, older adults are found to be able to let bygones be bygones, with "an increase in emotional well-being from middle age onward, whereas the experience of anger declines" (Brassen et al., 2012, p. 614). In this particular study, the brain activity and heart rate of healthy older adults (average age 66) show a different response to disappointment (Brassen et al., 2012).

This study also included a group of older adults who had been diagnosed with late-life depression. Their brains, bodies, and behavior were more like those of the younger adults. The researchers concluded that "emotionally healthy aging is associated with a reduced responsiveness to regretful events" (Brassen et al., 2012, p. 614).

Other research has also found that depressed older adults are neurologically impaired, particularly in the anterior cingulate cortex, a brain region crucial for processing conflicting emotions and thoughts (Ochsner et al., 2009). Because of the positivity effect, anger, sadness, and disappointment are limited in healthy older people—and they are happier because of it.

The positivity effect is not always dramatic. Consider the details of a different study (Werheid et al., 2010). In four experiments, a total of 132 individuals—60 young (average age 25) and 72 old (average age 66)—looked at photographs of happy, neutral, or angry faces. They

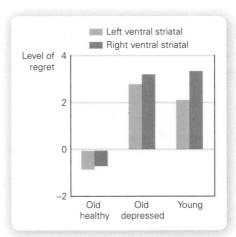

FIGURE 15.1 **Let Bygones Be Bygones** Areas of the brain (the ventral striatal) are activated when a person feels regret. In this experiment, brain activation correlated with past loss and then unwise choices, repeating behavior that had just failed. Older adults were usually wiser, evident in brain activation as well as actions. However, elders who had been diagnosed as depressed seemed to linger on past losses. The positivity effect had passed them by.

were then shown the same faces and an equal number of new faces either one day later (experiments 1, 2, and 3) or two weeks later (experiment 4), and were asked which faces they had seen before.

All four experiments showed the positivity effect somewhat, but not dramatically. For instance, in the first experiment, the older adults were slightly better than the younger ones at recognizing happy faces (74 versus 70 percent), worse at recognizing angry faces (81 versus 84 percent) or neutral faces (65 versus 69 percent). They were also likely to mistakenly claim that the new happy faces were familiar (22 versus 7 percent).

It could be argued that anger and frustration are useful emotions and that the elders' rosy outlook ignores reality. However, having a positive outlook not only makes a person happier, but it may also benefit daily life. For example, adults in one study were asked about recent instances of personal confrontation (Sorkin & Rook, 2006). More than one-third (39 percent) of the adults older than 65 could not think of any negative social exchanges. Of those who remembered unpleasant encounters, most of the elders, unlike the younger participants, said that their primary goal after the event was to maintain goodwill. Only a few sought to change the other person's behavior (see Figure 15.2).

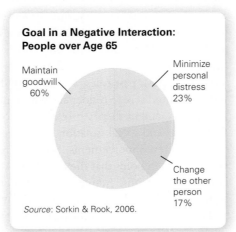

Goal in a Negative Interaction: People over Age 65

Maintain goodwill 60%
Minimize personal distress 23%
Change the other person 17%

Source: Sorkin & Rook, 2006.

FIGURE 15.2 **Keep the Peace** When someone does something mean or unpleasant, what is your goal in your interaction with that person? If your goal is to maintain goodwill, as was the case for a majority of older adults studies, you are likely to be quicker to forgive and forget.

Since their goal was to achieve harmony, the elderly were more likely to compromise instead of insist that they were correct. This led to a happier outcome.

Participants whose primary coping goal was to preserve goodwill reported the highest levels of perceived success and the least intense and shortest duration of distress. In contrast, participants whose . . . goal was to change the other person reported the lowest levels of perceived success and the most intense and longest lasting distress.

[Sorkin & Rook, 2006, p. 723]

Might we all learn from those older than us and avoid "lasting distress" because of it?

Stratification Theories

stratification theories
Theories that emphasize that social forces, particularly those related to a person's social stratum or social category, limit individual choices and affect a person's ability to function in late adulthood because past stratification continues to limit life in various ways.

A second set of theories, called **stratification theories,** emphasizes societal forces that place each person in a social strata or level. Such stratification makes it difficult for a person to earn more income, have better health, or live longer than people of their group. Stratification begins in childhood, as "individuals are born into a society that is already stratified—that is differentiated—along key dimensions, including sex, race, and SES" (Lynch & Brown, 2011, p. 107).

The problem with stratification is that it results in inequality for reasons beyond the individual. As the decades of life go by, stratification by age, gender, ethnicity, and income become increasingly burdensome, causing double, triple, or even quadruple jeopardy. We describe each of these in turn.

Twice Fortunate Ageism takes many forms. Some cultures are youth-oriented, devaluing the old, while others are the opposite. These twin sisters are lucky to be alive: They were born in rural China in 1905, a period when most female twins died. Now, at age 103, they are fortunate again, venerated because they have lived so long.

STRATIFICATION BY AGE Ageism is, of course, stratification by age. Age affects a person's life in many ways, including income and health. For example, seniority builds in the workplace, increasing income up to a certain point, and then employment may stop, perhaps with a pension but never with as much income as before.

This is just one example of the many ways in which industrialized nations segregate elderly people, gradually shutting them out of the mainstream of society as they grow older (Achenbaum, 2005). That harms both generations because it limits social experiences: Younger as well as older people have a narrower perspective on life if they interact only with people their own age.

disengagement theory
The view that aging makes a person's social sphere increasingly narrow, resulting in role relinquishment, withdrawal, and passivity.

activity theory
The view that elderly people want and need to remain active in social spheres—with relatives, friends, and community groups—and become withdrawn only unwillingly, as a result of ageism.

The most controversial version of age-stratification theory is **disengagement theory** (Cumming & Henry, 1961). This theory holds that, as people age, traditional roles become unavailable or unimportant, the social circle shrinks, coworkers stop asking for help, and adult children turn away to focus on their own children.

According to this theory, disengagement is a mutual process, chosen by both older and younger generations. Children want to be with other children, adults with other adults, and older adults with one another or by themselves. Thus, younger people disengage from the old, who themselves voluntarily disengage from younger adults. They relinquish past roles, withdrawing from life's action. If they can afford it, they move to gated senior residences where no young people are allowed.

Disengagement theory provoked a storm of protest because people feared it justified ageism and social isolation. Many gerontologists insisted that older people need and want new involvements. Some developed an opposing theory, called **activity theory,** which holds that the elderly seek to remain active with relatives, friends, and community groups. Activity theorists contend that if the elderly disengage, they do so unwillingly (J. R. Kelly, 1993; Rosow, 1985).

Later research has found that elders who are more active are also happier and intellectually more alert as well as less depressed. This is true at younger ages as well, although some studies find that activity is particularly likely to correlate with high functioning at older ages (Bielak, 2010; Bielak et al., 2012).

Since those who are sick and poorly educated are most likely to disengage, and since generally the happier and healthier elders are quite active—continuing as worker, wife, husband, mother, father, neighbor—it could be argued that disengagement itself is the result of past stratification (Clarke, 2011). Literally being active—bustling around the house, climbing stairs, walking to work—lengthens life and increases satisfaction.

Both disengagement and activity theories need to be applied with caution, however. Disengagement in one aspect of life (e.g., retiring from employment) does not necessarily mean disengagement overall: Many retirees disengage from work but find new roles and activities to participate in (Freund et al., 2009). The positivity effect, just described, may mean that an older person disengages from emotional events that cause anger, regret, and sadness, while actively enjoying other experiences (Brassen et al., 2012).

A cautionary note comes from research in China. One study found that among the Chinese young-old, activity correlated with health, particularly if the activities involved social interactions. But among the oldest-old, activity did not correlate with longevity: For some of the oldest Chinese, disengagement was more closely associated with health (R. Sun & Liu, 2008). Both theories—that all the elderly want to withdraw and that they all should stay active—may arise from cultural stereotypes.

STRATIFICATION BY GENDER Feminist theory draws attention to stratification that puts males and females on separate tracks through life. From pink or blue blankets for newborns' bassinettes to flowers or stripes for nursing home bedsheets, gender is signaled lifelong. These signals alert everyone—caregivers, family members, and strangers—to treat males and females differently. Such stratification, when combined with ageism, makes people expect older women to be either warm and compliant (grandmotherly, providing kindness and cookies) or cold and ugly (hags or crones) (Bugental & Hehman, 2007).

The implications of gender divergence are illustrated by a study of caregiving among older married couples. Both sexes provided care if their spouse became needy, but they did so in opposite ways: Women quit their jobs, whereas men worked longer. To be specific, employed women whose husbands needed care were five times more likely to retire than were other employed women. By contrast, employed husbands whose wife needed care retired only half as often as other men (Dentinger & Clarkberg, 2002).

Note, however, that both partners sacrifice. Men stayed on the job so they could keep insurance and hire household help, and women quit to provide personal care. Both sexes followed the gender stratification of decades earlier: Women were socialized to be caregivers while men's employment patterns (not part-time, more seniority) typically included higher salaries and better insurance than women's patterns (more interruptions, and hence less pay and benefits). In this situation, past stratification disadvantages the older women: Their caregiving response leads to poverty and loneliness.

Irrational, gender-based fear may also limit women's independence. For example, because they want to protect their mothers, adult children are more likely to persuade their widowed mothers to live with them than their widowed fathers. The children's fear for the mother's safety is not based on

Twice-Abandoned Widows Traditionally in India, widows walked into the funeral pyre that cremated their husband's body, a suicide called sati. If they hesitated, his relatives would sometimes push. Currently, sati is outlawed, but many Indian widows experience a social death nonetheless: They are forbidden to meet men and remarry, except sometimes to the dead man's brother. Thus, several venture to the sacred city of Vrindavan, where they are paid a pittance to chant prayers all day, as this woman does.

Memories Older adults often provide links between the past and present. Toni Morrison won a Pulitzer Prize for her novel *Beloved*, published when she was 56. It provided insight into the emotional horror of slavery for women who died long ago. Here, in Paris at age 81, Morrison dedicates a bench commemorating slavery's abolition.

✦ **ESPECIALLY FOR Social Scientists**
The various social science disciplines tend to favor different theories of aging. Can you tell which theories would be more acceptable to psychologists and which to sociologists? (see response, page 545) →

evidence. Men living alone are more likely than women to have a sudden health crisis and are more likely to be the victim of a violent crime (5 percent versus 2 percent) (P. Klaus, 2005).

In another example of stratification, women typically marry men a few years older than they are and then outlive them. Especially if they lived in rural areas (as most Americans did until about 1950), married women often relied on their husbands to drive, to manage money, and to keep up with politics. Then, if the husband died, past gender stratification led to isolation, poverty, and dependence among the oldest-old widows.

Men, too, may be harmed. For instance, boys are taught that males are stoic, repressing emotions and avoiding medical care. Is that why, in every nation, adult women outlive men? This could be biological (protective hormones), but it could result from lifelong stratification, making men more vulnerable in old age.

STRATIFICATION BY ETHNICITY Like age and gender, ethnic background affects every aspect of development lifelong, including education, health, place of residence, and employment. Stratification theory suggests that these factors accumulate, creating large discrepancies by old age. The stress of past discrimination is thought to catch up to African Americans, causing "weathering," an increased allostatic load that shortens life (Thrasher et al., 2012).

Age and gender disparities may be magnified by ethnicity. As one reviewer explains, "[W]omen . . . are much more likely to live in households that fall below the federal poverty line. Black and Hispanic women are particularly vulnerable" (J. S. Jackson et al., 2011, p. 93). One crucial factor is past employment. Many of today's elderly non-White women never worked in jobs that paid social security. For them, unlike for most White men, an important source of income is thus absent.

Another example of how earlier ethnic stratification affects the elderly is home ownership, which provides financial security for many seniors. Fifty years ago, racial stratification prevented many African Americans from buying homes. This was especially true for unmarried women, and one reason for their poverty in old age.

After laws against housing discrimination allowed many African Americans to become homeowners, a disproportionate number of them lost their homes in the foreclosure crisis that began in 2007. This circumstance can be seen as a new example of an old story: Ethnic stratification causes repeated losses (Saegert et al., 2012).

FIGURE 15.3 Older and Poorer This chart underestimates the percentage of U.S. elderly who are poor because medical expenses are not included in determining the poverty line. It seems as if fewer 65- to 74-year-olds than 60- to 64-year-olds are poor because pensions and social security usually begin after age 64.

OBSERVATION QUIZ

Which affects income more, age or ethnicity? (see answer, page 545) →

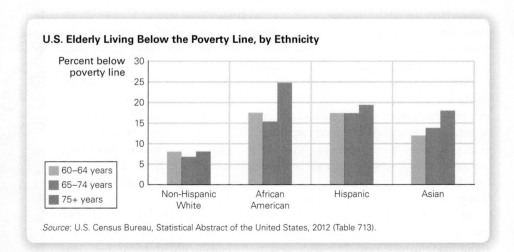

Health disparities also accumulate, such that the elderly of an ethnic minority, especially if they are low SES and immigrant, have far more impairments than European Americans (Haas et al., 2012). The fact that such problems are cumulative "suggests multiple intervention points at which disparities can be reduced," beginning before birth (Haas et al., 2012, p. 238).

Repeated stresses cause hypertension and obesity, as well as the other 8 to 14 indicators of allostatic load, to take a great toll each year. This may be the reason that if two Americans—one White, one Black—reach age 65 and are no longer at risk for the main causes of premature death for African Americans (low birthweight and violence), the Black person will still die two years earlier, on average, at age 82, not 84 (see Figure 15.4).

Stratification may also explain developmental changes in self-esteem. In general, adolescent African Americans have higher self-esteem than European-Americans do, but the oldest-old of all backgrounds have lower self-esteem than they did earlier in life, with a steeper drop that starts earlier (around age 65, not 85) for African Americans (Shaw et al., 2010).

Curiously, although the ethnic disparity in survival and self-esteem is evident for the young-old, it disappears at about age 80 and then reverses by age 100. The average Black centenarian lives seven months longer than does the average non-Black one (U.S. Bureau of the Census, 2011b)—and feels quite happy to have done so.

Elderly Hispanics also seem to have a longevity advantage over elderly non-Hispanics in the United States. One explanation for this *race crossover* is selective survival (perhaps only extremely healthy non-Europeans reach old age), but other interpretations are possible. Perhaps ethnic inequality diminishes because very old age is a powerful "leveler," overwhelming ethnic and gender stratification (Bird et al., 2010; Robert et al., 2009).

A particular form of ethnic stratification may affect immigrant elders raised in another nation who find themselves dependent on their adult children within a culture stratified against both the old and the immigrant (see Infographic 15, page 544). Many traditional cultures expect younger generations to defer to the elderly, but U.S. homes are designed for nuclear families, not extended ones, and workers are expected to retire and are given pensions to support them—which leaves many older immigrants (without U.S. work history) unemployed, poor, and lonely.

Consider the fate of an elderly man born and raised in Russia. His U.S.-born son put him in an assisted-living center for senior citizens on Staten Island. The man hated it and left, to the distress of his son who had searched carefully for an appropriate place. The old man moved to Florida, where he rented a room from an 85-year-old Russian widow, to whom he became attached. But when she became frail and he began taking care of her, his son moved him out. Once again, the father was on his own and unhappy. He said:

> Would I like to live with my kids? Of course. But I know that's impossible. They don't want me . . . not that they don't love me. I understand that. In the old days, a hundred years ago, old people stayed at home.
>
> *[quoted in Koch, 2000, p. 53]*

As a result of this cultural divide, the man's life was described as one of "lonely independence . . . a quintessentially American tragedy" (Koch, 2000, p. 55).

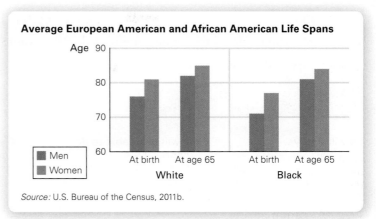

Average European American and African American Life Spans

Source: U.S. Bureau of the Census, 2011b.

FIGURE 15.4 Age As the Equalizer? As you see, once a person survives the hazards of childhood and adolescence, he or she is likely to live until age 80 or older. (The terms Black and White are used here because that is how the data are reported. White includes most Hispanics, and Black includes most Africans; the ethnic differences would be greater if the data compared European and African Americans.)

Life After 65: Living Independently

Most people who reach age 65 not only survive a decade or more, but will also live independently.

AGE 65   Of 100 people

86 will survive.

Most will spend that decade caring for all their basic needs.

7 will be unable to do chores, take care of finances, go shopping, etc. (IADLs).

6 will have difficulty with at least one activity of daily life (ADLs: bathing, dressing, eating, toileting, getting in or out of a bed or chair).

1 will live in a nursing home (many spend a few days in a hospital or rehabilitation center, but only one stays in an institution long term, almost always someone disabled in several IADLS and ADLs).

AGE 75   Of 100 people

73 will survive.

Most will spend that decade caring for all their basic needs.

7 will be unable to do chores, take care of finances, go shopping, etc. (IADLs).

14 will have difficulty with at least one activity of daily life (ADLs).

4 will live in a nursing home (disabled in several IADLS and ADLs).

AGE 85   Of 100 people

68 will survive.

Most will spend that decade caring for all their basic needs.

45 will be unable to do chores, take care of finances, go shopping, etc. (IADLs).

36 will have difficulty with at least one activity of daily life (ADLs).

13 will live in a nursing home (disabled in several IADLS and ADLs).

AGE 95   Of 100 people

Those who reach this age tend to be unusually healthy, living 4 years longer, on average.

About half are still able to care for themselves.

Where?

Not necessarily in a warm state or with caregivers.

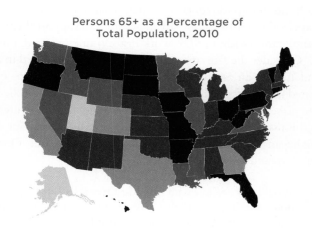

Persons 65+ as a Percentage of Total Population, 2010

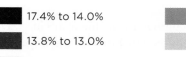

■ 17.4% to 14.0%	■ 11.4% to 10.4%
■ 13.8% to 13.0%	■ 9.0% to 7.7%
■ 12.9% to 12.1%	

(SOURCE: 2010 POPULATION ESTIMATES FROM THE U.S. BUREAU OF CENSUS)

With whom?

Only about 15 percent of those over age 65 move in with an adult child or live in a nursing home or hospital.

Living Arrangements of Persons 65+, 2010

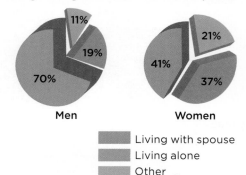

Men: 70%, 19%, 11%
Women: 41%, 37%, 21%

Men   **Women**

■ Living with spouse
■ Living alone
■ Other

SOURCES & CREDITS LISTED ON P. SC-1

STRATIFICATION BY SES Finally, the pivotal influence on the well-being of the elderly may be financial, not directly gender, ethnicity, or age. Income correlates with those three but is not caused by them (Bird et al., 2010).

Sexist and racist practices are harmful lifelong, of course, but a family's low SES leads to less education, worse health, and then poorer work history (and thus more unemployment, fewer benefits, no pensions) for their children. A poor child experiences stress of all kinds, accumulating disadvantages that are increasingly limiting as the years go by (Bowen & González, 2010).

The problem may begin even before birth, since epigenetic factors—themselves affected by maternal health—shape the genetic expression (Shanahan & Hofer, 2011). Those who are born into low-SES families risk late-life diabetes, disability, and death. Obviously, poverty among elders should be alleviated, but mitigating poverty early in life may be critical for well-being in late adulthood (Herd et al., 2011).

Two aspects of current conditions in the United States make low income particularly difficult for the old. One is medical care. Medicare pays for many medical expenses, but there are significant gaps (Marilyn Moon, 2011). For instance, part D of the plan, which is designed to cover medications, indicates that if costs exceed $2,830 in a year (as happened to 27 percent of enrollees in 2007), recipients must pay about $4,000 themselves until drug benefits begin again. Many other medical costs are not covered or require a large co-pay. As a result, low-income seniors often defer health care or cut back on food, phone, and transportation to pay for it.

The second problem is that inflation makes retirement income worth less than half of what it did when that money was first set aside. Those middle-aged adults who have adequate savings for retirement are in the minority: Those who are best prepared are already wealthy, another example of SES stratification.

Internationally, stratification by income for the elderly varies a great deal. Some nations provide free health care and heavily subsidized senior residences for everyone. One of these is Denmark, which also has the highest proportion of happy seniors. By contrast, other nations provide nothing at all, expecting family members to care for the elderly. In several Asian nations, it is illegal for adult children not to provide for their parents.

This is a developmental issue to which applying a cross-cultural approach would be useful. Every nation has had unexpectedly large increases in the number of older adults, and every nation is cutting government assistance to the poor. The resulting dilemma is more poor elders than before. Some nations have found better solutions than others, but nations can learn from one another.

RESPONSE FOR Social Scientists (from page 542) In general, psychologists favor self theories, and sociologists favor stratification theories. Of course, each discipline respects the other, but each believes that its perspective is more honest and accurate. ●

ANSWER TO **OBSERVATION QUIZ** (from page 542) Ethnicity. Not shown is that ethnic differences are even greater for children: 36 percent of African American children live below the poverty line. ●

KEY points

- Self theories of late adulthood stress that people try to remain themselves, achieving integrity and not despairing.

- The positivity effect protects the self, as elders take pleasure and pride in who they are.

- The disengagement theory holds that as people age, they relinquish past roles and withdraw from life's action.

- Activity theory suggests that, if the aged disengage, it is not by choice. Contrary to disengagement theory, it suggests societies should encourage activity in old age.

- Gender, ethnicity, and economic strata all place people on particular paths lifelong: This stratification may be particularly harmful in late adulthood.

Activities in Late Adulthood

Many elders complain that they do not have enough time each day to do all they want to do. This might come as a surprise to younger adults, who see few gray hairs at sports events, political rallies, job sites, or midnight concerts. In fact, most college students consider the elderly to be relatively passive and inactive, with plenty of time on their hands (Wurtele, 2009). Wrong.

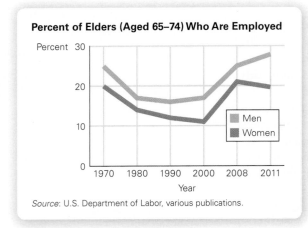

Percent of Elders (Aged 65–74) Who Are Employed

Source: U.S. Department of Labor, various publications.

FIGURE 15.5 Along with Everyone Else Although younger adults might imagine that older people stop work as soon as they can, this is clearly not the case for everyone.

Paid Work

Developmentalists are aware of "a growing body of research that points to the positive physical and psychological impacts, for women as well as men, of employment" (Moen & Spencer, 2006, p. 135). Work provides social support and status, boosting self-esteem. For many people, employment allows generativity and is evidence of "productivity, effectiveness, and independence"—all cherished Western values (Tornstam, 2005, p. 23). Many elders are reluctant to give that up (see Figure 15.5).

Of course, many elders work because they need the money, increasingly so as pensions and investments shrink or disappear in the economic recession. This shrinkage is global. For example, riots and strikes in France, aimed at stopping the government from changing the age at which French citizens are granted government pensions, were unsuccessful. It had been age 60; as of 2011, it is 62. French workers must stay on the job longer now.

Participation in the labor force after age 60 is higher among nonunionized low-wage workers (who need the income) and professionals (who welcome the status) than among those in between. Many older adults who have pensions work part time (Rix, 2011); some employers offer phased retirement (called "bridge work"). Older workers are also more likely to become self-employed, with small businesses or consulting work.

RETIREMENT Are all older adults healthier and happier when they are employed? Not necessarily, although some people thought so, warning about "the presumed traumatic aspects of retirement" (Tornstam, 2005, p. 19). Accordingly, in the 1980s,

Same Situation, Far Apart: Satisfying Work In Nice, France *(left),* two paleontologists examine a skull bone, and in Arizona, the United States *(right),* a great-grandmother prepares wool for weaving. Note their facial expressions: Elders are often happier when they continue working.

SEBASTIEN NOGIER / AFP / GETTY IMAGES

RICHARD NOWITZ / NATIONAL GEOGRAPHIC SOCIETY / CORBIS

U.S. legislators outlawed mandatory retirement (except in special occupations, such as that of jet pilot).

Paradoxically, when older workers in the United States were no longer required to quit at 65, the average age of retirement *decreased*. Rather than working, beginning in about 1970 many older adults retired as soon as they could afford to (Hardy, 2006). On average, they gain in health because of it (Coe & Zamarro, 2011). Retirement is as likely to improve health as it is to precipitate a decline. Only when retirement is precipitated by poor health or fading competence does it correlate with illness (A. Shapiro & Yarborough-Hayes, 2008).

A major problem since 2000 is that private pensions (possessed by about three-fourths of U.S. households) are tied not only to past work history but also to the stock market, which went from boom to bust in the first decade of the twenty-first century. The result is that many baby boomers, now reaching retirement age, calculate that they need their pay (Wolff, 2011). The public pension system, Social Security, is less affected by the recession, but many elders find that their Social Security checks do not cover expenses.

Of course, employment and retirement can both cause distress. Planning and income are often inadequate; married couples may disagree as to who should retire, when retirement should begin, and how their lives should be restructured (Moen et al., 2005). Many retirees live longer than they expected, not having anticipated inflation, lost pensions, and increased health costs. After retirees' initial activities, completing long-postponed projects (anything from traveling to China to painting the porch), their goals need "expanding, reducing, concentrating and diffusing" (Nimrod, 2007, p. 91).

VOLUNTEER WORK Volunteering offers some of the benefits of paid employment (generativity, social connections, less depression). Consequently, "gerontologists have been strongly attracted to the idea that active engagement [volunteering and political activity] in society is related to well-being in later life" (Morrow-Howell & Freedman, 2006–2007, p. 6).

Is the connection between well-being and volunteering merely an "idea"? No; empirical data confirm the benefits. Longitudinal as well as cross-sectional research find a strong link between health and volunteering (Cutler et al., 2011). It is true that volunteers are typically healthy and socially active *before* they volunteer as well as after, but helping other people itself aids well-being.

As self theory would predict, volunteer work attracts older people who always were strongly committed to their community and had more social contacts (Pilkington et al., 2012). Those who volunteered earlier in adulthood are more likely to continue volunteering in old age, becoming "mentors, guides, and repositories of experience" for younger people (Settersten, 2002, p. 65).

Beyond that, volunteering reduces the odds of death. Some of that is correlational, since volunteers tend to have had more education, which predicts longer life. However, the data suggest that volunteering itself adds to life. For example, among people who live in rural areas and do not drive (both correlates of less education), those who volunteer have about half the death rate of those who do not (S. J. Lee et al., 2011).

Culture or national policy affects volunteering: Nordic elders (in Sweden and Norway) volunteer more often than Mediterranean ones (in Italy and Greece), differences that persist when illness is taken into account (Erlinghagen & Hank, 2006). The microsystem also has an effect. Being married to a volunteer makes it more likely that a person will volunteer also. A major reason why volunteering is beneficial to the volunteer is that it fosters social connections, which themselves can lead to more volunteering (Pilkington et al., 2012).

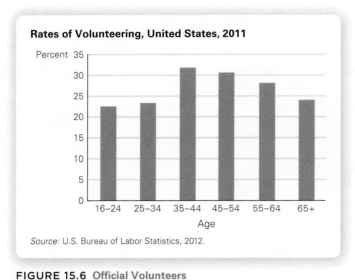

Rates of Volunteering, United States, 2011

Source: U.S. Bureau of Labor Statistics, 2012.

FIGURE 15.6 Official Volunteers
As you can see, older adults volunteer less often than do middle-aged adults, according to official statistics. However, this counts people who volunteer for organizations—schools, churches, social service groups, and so on. Not counted is all the volunteer help that people give to friends, family members, neighbors, and even strangers. If that were counted, would everyone of every age be a volunteer?

✦ ESPECIALLY FOR Social Workers
Your agency needs more personnel but does not have money to hire anyone. Should you go to your local senior-citizen center and recruit volunteers? (see response, page 550) →

The data reveal two areas of concern, however. First, contrary to what most people imagine, older, retired people are *less* likely to volunteer than are middle-aged, employed people; three-fourths of people older than 65 do no volunteer work (see Figure 15.6). Second, less than one-third of all adults of any age volunteer.

Should developmentalists encourage more people to volunteer? Some fear that might be a way for public institutions to avoid hiring paid workers (Minkler & Holstein, 2008). However, most gerontologists wish that more elders were volunteers. Why aren't they? Four possible explanations:

1. *Social culture.* Ageism may discourage meaningful volunteering. Many volunteer opportunities are geared toward the young, who are attracted to intense, short-term experiences. Two weeks of building a house during spring break or two years teaching with the Peace Corps in a developing nation are not designed for older volunteers (Morrow-Howell & Freedman, 2006–2007).

2. *Organizations.* Institutions lack recruitment, training, and implementation strategies for attracting older volunteers. For instance, although most primary school students would benefit from a personal mentor, schools have discouraging barriers (e.g., health exams, lengthy background checks, long flights of stairs).

3. *The elderly themselves.* Older people may be afraid to leave their familiar patterns. This is suggested by other statistics: Almost half of the elderly volunteers do so within their own religious organizations. Only 1 in 12 older volunteers work with youth, compared with about 1 in 3 younger adult volunteers (Bureau of Labor Statistics, 2012b).

4. *The science.* The problem may lie not with the people but with the definitions used in the research. Surveys of volunteer work ignore daily caregiving and informal helping. Babysitting, caring for an ill relative, shopping for an infirm neighbor—are not counted. If they were, the rates of volunteering would be much higher, for the elderly overall and for minority elders in particular.

Indeed, every survey finds that most of the elderly give money and time to help other people. A study of elders who had graduated from Wisconsin high schools in 1957 found that 96 percent of the women and 92 percent of the men provided help to someone else, not including their spouse (Kahn et al., 2011). This study did not include providing financial help; if it did, the rate would be almost 100 percent.

Home Sweet Home

One of the favorite activities of many retirees is caring for their own homes. Typically, both men and women do more housework and meal preparation (less fast food, more fresh ingredients) after retirement (Luengo-Prado & Sevilla, 2012). Both sexes also do yard work, redecorate, build shelves, rearrange furniture.

Gardening is popular: More than half the elderly in the United States cultivate plants each year (see Figure 15.7). Tending flowers, herbs, and vegetables is particularly beneficial during late adulthood because it is a productive activity that not only involves exercise but often promotes social interaction (Schupp & Sharp, 2012). Even the oldest-old benefit from caring for a plant on a windowsill. Better, of course, are more challenging hobbies, home-repair projects, and gardening activities. These correlate with less dementia and longer life (E. Kröger et al., 2008; Paganini-Hill et al., 2011).

In keeping up with household tasks and maintaining their property, many older people demonstrate that they prefer to **age in place,** rather than moving to another residence. That is the preference of most baby boomers as well: 83 percent of those aged 55 to 64 prefer to stay in their own homes when they retire (Koppen, 2009).

If they must move, most want to remain in their familiar neighborhood, perhaps in a smaller apartment with an elevator, but not in a different city or state. In fact, they are wise: Elders fare best when they are surrounded by friends and acquaintances, people who are difficult to replace. Gerontologists recognize that "interrupting social connections . . . might be harmful, especially for women and the frailest" (Berkman et al., 2011, p. 347).

The preference for aging in place is evident in state statistics. Of the 50 states, Florida has the highest proportion of people over age 65, but the next three states highest in that proportion—Maine, West Virginia, and Pennsylvania—are not places where older people move to, but places where they have always lived. Obviously, some people prefer to stay put.

One result is that houses are being built or remodeled to suit people who have problems with mobility or vision. About 4,000 consultants are now certified by the National Association of Homebuilders to advise about **universal design,** which is the design of physical space and common tools (from computer screens to screwdrivers) such that people of all ages and all levels of ability can use them. This includes those with obvious visual, hearing, or motor difficulties as well as those for whom age has made it harder to reach the top shelves, climb steep stairs, or respond to the doorbell.

Sometimes a neighborhood or an apartment complex becomes a **naturally occurring retirement community (NORC),** a neighborhood where people who moved in as young adults never move out. Many elderly people in NORCs are content to live alone. They stay on after their children have moved away or their partners have died, in part because they know the community and have friends there (C. C. Cook et al., 2007). One reason they enjoy home repair, housework, and gardening is that neighbors notice, appreciating the new curtains, the polished door, the blooming rosebush.

To age in place successfully, elderly people need many community services (K. Black, 2008). If an elderly adult remains in dilapidated housing, especially in a rural or high-crime urban community, simply pointing out the danger is not enough. Someone needs to help them move out or remodel. Aging in place does not mean seniors need to be left alone; it means that care should come to them (Golant, 2008).

NORCs can be granted public money to replace after-school karate with senior centers, or piano teachers with visiting nurses, if that is what the community needs (Greenfield et al, 2012). If a low-income elder lives in a high-crime neighborhood (and many do), not only must the residence be made accommodating, but the neighborhood must be fixed as well, with a protective social network. This is possible, especially if the elder has a personality that makes people of all backgrounds watch out for him or her (A. E. Smith, 2009), as does my friend Doris.

Religious Involvement

Older adults attend fewer religious services than do the middle-aged, but faith and praying increase with age. This may be part of a universal developmental process. In his later years, Maslow reassessed his final level, *self-actualization.* He suggested a sixth,

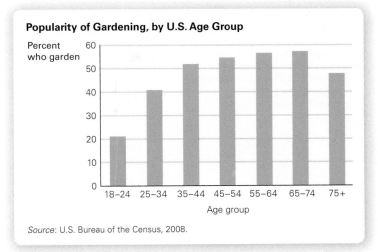

Popularity of Gardening, by U.S. Age Group

Source: U.S. Bureau of the Census, 2008.

FIGURE 15.7 Dirty Fingernails Almost three times as many 60-year-olds as 20-year-olds are gardeners. What is it about dirt, growth, and time that makes gardening an increasingly popular hobby as people age?

age in place
Remaining in the same home and community in later life, adjusting but not leaving when health fades.

universal design
Designing physical space and common tools that are suitable for people of all ages and all levels of ability.

naturally occurring retirement community (NORC)
A neighborhood or apartment complex whose population is mostly retired people who moved to the location as younger adults and never left.

RESPONSE FOR Social Workers (from page 548) Yes, but be careful. If people want to volunteer and are just waiting for an opportunity, you will probably benefit from their help and they will also benefit. But if you convince reluctant seniors to help you, the experience may benefit no one. ●

✦ **ESPECIALLY FOR Religious Leaders** Why might the elderly have strong faith but poor church attendance? (see response, page 552) →

more spiritual level, which he called *self-transcendence* (Koltko-Rivera, 2006)—not usually attained until late in life.

The elderly are more likely than younger adults to believe in God and an afterlife. This benefits their development. Religious practices of all kinds correlate with physical and emotional health (Idler, 2006). Social scientists have found several reasons for this: (1) Religious prohibitions encourage health (e.g., less drug use); (2) joining a faith community increases social relationships; and (3) beliefs give meaning to life and death, thus reducing stress (Atchley, 2009).

Religious identity and religious institutions are especially important for older members of minority groups, many of whom feel a stronger commitment to their religious heritage than to their national or cultural background. For example, although Westerners may note only the national origin of Ethiopians or Iraqis or Turks, elderly people in those groups may focus on their Muslim, or Christian, or Jewish faith (Gelfand, 2003). They may identify more closely with a particular branch of their religion than with their nation—as is evident in Iraq, with its sharp distinctions between the Shiite and Sunni branches of Islam.

Religious institutions fulfill many needs of the elderly, including having a social network of people who care for them (Lim & Putnam, 2010). A nearby house of worship, where not only their volunteer efforts but also their mere presence is valued, is one reason why American elders prefer to age in place.

Particularly for older African Americans, churches may be a cherished spiritual home, providing practical aid and activities (choir, study, meals) as well as close, supportive friends. Many African American churches have extensive social service programs (e.g., feeding the homeless, counseling drug abusers, sponsoring after-school activities). Such programs give members a convenient way to "do the Lord's work" while simultaneously reaping the benefits from volunteering mentioned earlier (Carlton-LaNey, 2006–2007). Pastors consider it an important part of their role to provide mental health services for the elderly who need it (Allen et al., 2010).

Religious faith may explain an oddity in mortality statistics, specifically in suicide data (Chatters et al., 2011). In the United States, suicide after age 65 among elderly European American men occurs 50 times more often than among African American women. A possible explanation is that African American women's religious faith is often very strong, making them less depressed about their daily lives (Colbert et al., 2009).

For all elderly people, no matter what their particular faith or ethnicity, psychological health depends on feeling that they are part of traditions that were handed down by their ancestors and will be carried on by their descendants. At least one gerontologist believes that an "increasing feeling of cosmic communion" comes with age and that older people are better able to see beyond their own immediate needs and to care about other people, ask enduring questions, and emphasize spiritual needs (Tornstam, 2005, p. 41). Every religion helps elders deal with these concerns (Idler, 2006).

Political Activism

Younger adults might be forgiven if they think that elderly people are not politically active. Fewer older people turn out for massive rallies, and only about 2 percent volunteer in political campaigns. When political activity is more broadly defined to include not only elections but also involvement with international organizations (such as UNESCO) or professional groups (such as the American Psychological Association), engagement is still low. In 2011, about 7 percent of U.S. residents older than 65 gave time for any political, civic, international, or professional group (Bureau of Labor Statistics, 2012b).

This is not good news, since democracy depends on involvement. More-over, "gerontologists have been strongly attracted to the idea that active en-gagement in society is related to well-being in later life" (Cutler et al., 2011; Morrow-Howell & Freedman, 2006–2007, p. 6).

By other measures, however, the elderly are more politically active than people of any other age. More of them write letters to their elected represen-tatives, vote, and identify with a political party. Over the past 20 years in off-year (nonpresidential) U.S. elections, an average of 60 percent of those over age 65 voted, compared with 16 percent of those aged 18 to 20 (U.S. Bureau of the Census, 2011b). This difference seems to be more a result of age than of cohort. As Table 15.1 shows, the percent of adults who are registered to vote increases with age, with the eldest having the highest rates, despite some fluctuations over time.

In addition, the elderly are more likely than younger adults to keep up with the news. For example, the Pew Research Center for the People and the Press periodically asks U.S. residents questions on current events, and the elderly always best the young. They also remember political history. In 2011, elders (65 and older) beat the youngest (aged 18 to 30) by a ratio of about 3-to-2 in knowing the political party of Nancy Pelosi, John Boehner, Franklin Roosevelt, and Abraham Lincoln (Pew Research Center, 2012b).

The largest organized interest group in the world, **AARP** (originally the American Association of Retired Persons) advocates for the elderly. In 2010, AARP had nearly 36 million members, many of whom were baby boomers (members must be at least 50 but need not be retired). About 8 percent of AARP's budget goes to research and action regarding politics (Binstock, 2006–2007).

AARP's political influence is thought to be one reason that the U.S. Social Security program is called "the third rail" of domestic politics, named for the high-voltage electrical rail that delivers power to trains and could electrocute a person who touches it. The idea is that advocating changes in Social Security may be fatal to a politician's career—even though most experts believe that some reform is needed.

Many government policies affect the elderly, especially those regarding housing, pensions, prescription drugs, and medical costs. However, members of this age group do not necessarily vote their own economic interests. An estimated 60,000 people canceled their AARP membership because the organization supported President Obama's health care reform, while 10 times that number joined—not necessarily in support of health care, but because they thought they wanted to be part of AARP.

Even in Medicare and Social Security, the elderly do not usu-ally vote as a bloc, although in the 2010 off-year elections those is-sues compelled many elderly swing voters to act (Binstock, 2012). The elderly typically are divided on most issues, including global warming, military conflicts, and public education.

Generally, the political opinions of the elderly reflect national trends and their own personal history more than their chrono-logical age. Even on health care, although most realize the need for reform, in 2008 they were the only age group to vote for the Republican candidate for president. In 2012, again the elderly voted Republican (56 percent) but were outvoted by those under age 40, who voted for Obama (60 percent). Elders are also are more likely to identify with a political party—in the current co-hort, usually Republican.

Some suggest that the selfish political concerns of the old nec-essarily clash with those of the young, but that is not confirmed by the data: Many older people are passionate about the well-being

	TABLE 15.1 U.S. Voter Registration in Nonpresidential Election Years, by Age Group		
Age Group	Registered Voters (%)		
	1974	1990	2010
18–20	36	35	34
21–24	45	43	47
24–34	55	56	50
35–44	67	66	57
45–64	74	71	66
65+	71	77	73

AARP
A U.S. organization of people 50 and older that advocates for the elderly. It was originally called the American Association of Retired Persons, but now only the initials AARP are used, since members need not be retired.

Odd Man Out Most of the elderly avoid political demonstrations and favor the military, unlike this man at St. Paul's Church, rallying as part of Occupy London. He is with his cohort in another way, however: Many are more informed and concerned about global issues than younger adults are.

FRANCESCA MOORE / ALAMY

RESPONSE FOR Religious Leaders (from page 550) There are many possible answers, including the specifics of getting to church (transportation, stairs), physical comfort in church (acoustics, temperature), and content (unfamiliar hymns and language). ●

of future generations. A particular concern is the legacy of the natural environment, whether the "golden pond will be polluted and fresh water will be running out" (Moody, 2009–2010, p. 70).

In fact, some suggest that the idea of "gray power" is a myth, promulgated to reduce support among young adults for programs that benefit the old (A. Walker, 2006, p. 349). Given that ageism zigzags from hostile to benign—and is often based on beliefs that are far from reality—it is not surprising that "older persons [are] attacked as too powerful and, at the same time, as a burdensome responsibility" (Schulz & Binstock, 2008, p. 8). As you know, the aged merit neither compassion nor fury.

KEY points

- The elderly remain active in many ways, sometimes staying in the labor force when it is not financially necessary.
- Volunteering is an example of an activity that benefits individual health as well as the community.
- Retirement sometimes improves health and leads to more active involvement with home, neighborhood, and religion.
- Compared with young adults, the elderly are more likely to be informed about current events and to vote—although not always in their own self-interest.

Same Situation, Far Apart: Partners Whether in the living room of their home in the United States *(left)* or at a senior center in the Philippines *(right)*, elderly people are more likely to smile when they are with one another than when they are alone.

OBSERVATION QUIZ
What does the clothing of the people in these photographs indicate about their economic status? (see answer, page 555) ──→

Friends and Relatives

Humans are social animals, dependent on one another for survival and drawn to one another for joy. This is as true in late life as in infancy and at every stage in between.

Remember from Chapter 13 that every person travels the life course in the company of other people, who make up the social convoy (Antonucci et al., 2007). Given that, it is not surprising that friends are particularly important in old age. Bonds

formed over a lifetime allow people to share triumphs and tragedies with others who understand past victories and defeats. Siblings, old friends, and spouses are ideal convoy members.

Long-Term Partnerships

Spouses buffer each other against the problems of old age, thus extending life. This was one conclusion from a meta-analysis of dozens of studies with a combined total of 250,000 participants (Manzoli et al., 2007). Married older adults are healthier, wealthier, and happier than unmarried people their age. Of course, as self theories contend, the dominant influence on each person's sense of well-being is his or her own past well-being, not that of their partner. However, longitudinal research finds that spouses continue to affect each other, even in late adulthood: One older partner who is healthy and happy improves the other's well-being (Ruthig et al., 2012).

Elderly divorced people are lower in health and happiness than are those who are still married, although some argue that income and personality are the reasons, not marital status (Manzoli et al., 2007). Obviously, not every marriage is good for every older person: About one in every six long-term marriages is not satisfying, in which case the relationship increases neither health nor happiness (Waldinger & Schulz, 2010).

Nonetheless, happiness typically increases with the length as well as the quality of an intimate relationship—an association more apparent in longitudinal than in cross-sectional research (Proulx et al., 2007; Scarf, 2008). A lifetime of shared experiences—living together, raising children, and dealing with financial and emotional crises—brings partners closer. Often couples develop "an exceedingly positive portrayal" (O'Rourke et al., 2010b) of their mate, seeing their partner's personality as better than their own.

In general, older couples have learned how to disagree. They consider their conflicts to be discussions, not fights. I know one example personally.

Irma and Bob are a politically active elderly couple, proud parents of two adult children, as well as devoted grandparents. They seem happily married and I have watched them cooperate well when they babysit together for their 2-year-old grandson. Yet they almost always vote for opposing candidates. That puzzled me until Irma explained: "We sit together on the fence, seeing both perspectives, and then, when it is time to get off the fence and vote, Bob and I fall on opposite sides." I could always predict who would fall on which side, but to this couple, both the discussion and the final choice are productive. Their long-term affection keeps disagreements from becoming fights.

That is not unusual. In one U.S. study of long-lasting marriages, 86 percent of the partners surveyed thought their relationship was about equal in give-and-take (Gurung et al., 2003). Similar results were found in a comparison of couples in various European nations. Objectively, wives were less equal in some nations (e.g., Portugal) than others (e.g., France), but subjectively they felt fairly treated (M. Braun et al., 2008).

Outsiders might judge many long-term marriages as unequal, since one or the other spouse usually provides most of the money, or needs most of the care, or does most of the housework. Yet such disparities do not seem to bother older partners, who typically accept each other's frailties and dependencies, remembering times (perhaps decades ago) when the situation was reversed. This stunned me with my own parents. For the last decades of his life, my father was a devoted caregiver to my mother, who was bedridden. He said he was glad to do it, partly because 50 years earlier he'd gone away to war and left her alone to care for my young brother and me.

One crucial factor is that, over the years, some couples improve their parental alliance, as they weather the challenges of child rearing, home ownership, economic

CHRIS HOWELL / BLOOMINGTON HERALD TIMES / AP PHOTO

A Morning Kiss Ralph Young awakens Ruth with a kiss each day, as he has for most of the 78 years of their marriage. The only major separation occurred when he was a soldier in World War II; then he wrote to her every day. Here they are both 99, sharing a room in their Indiana residence, "more in love than ever." They had no children, so parental alliance did not bring them closer, but they did enjoy many things together—vacations, square dancing, and listening to country music on the radio.

crises, and so on. Evidence for the importance of a history of shared lives comes from research that finds that when older husbands and wives share the same close friends, they are more likely to help each other if special needs arise (Cornwell, 2012).

Given the importance of relationship building over the life span, it is not surprising that elders who are disabled (e.g., have difficulty walking, bathing, and performing other activities of daily life) are less depressed and anxious if they are in a close marital relationship (Mancini & Bonanno, 2006). A couple can achieve selective optimization with compensation: The one who is bedbound but alert can keep track of what the mobile but confused one is supposed to do, for instance.

Besides caregiving, sexual intimacy is another major aspect of long-lasting marriages. As already noted in Chapter 14, younger adults tend to measure sexual activity by frequency of orgasm. By that measure, sexual activity decreases with each decade (Lindau & Gavrilova, 2010). Remember, however, that diversity is common among older adults: Some are no longer interested in sexual intimacy whereas others enjoy frequent sexual interaction, hugging and caressing as well as, for some, having intercourse.

For most older couples, sexual interaction remains important (Johnson, 2007). Fortunately, this is one issue about which public opinion has changed. Recent cohorts of professionals in many nations realize that sexual desire and satisfaction are part of life for many elderly people, although the frequency and specifics of their sexual expression differ from those of younger adults (Helmes & Chapman, 2012).

Sex is also part of life for many older adults who are not married; they may cohabit, or they may live apart together (LAT). Although LAT is often associated with young or gay adults, many elders—especially those who are divorced or widowed—live apart from their sexual partner, not only because they want to age in place but also because they want independent relationships with their own children or parents (Strohm et al., 2009), a topic discussed next.

Relationships with Younger Generations

In past centuries, many adults died before their grandchildren were born. By contrast, some families currently span five generations, consisting of elders and their children, grandchildren, great-grandchildren, and great-great-grandchildren. The result is "longer years of 'shared lives' across generations" (Bengtson, 2001, p. 6).

Since the average couple now has fewer children, the *beanpole family,* representing multiple generations but with only a few members in each, is becoming more common (Murphy, 2011) (see Figure 15.8). Some members of the youngest generation have no cousins, brothers, or sisters but a dozen elderly relatives. Intergenerational relationships are becoming more important as many grandparents have only one or two grandchildren.

Although elderly people's relationships with members of younger generations are usually positive, they can also include tension and conflict. In some families, intergenerational respect and harmony abound whereas in others, members of one generation never see members of another. Each culture and, indeed, each family, have patterns and expectations for how the younger and oldest generations interact (Herlofson & Hagestad, 2011). Some conflict is commonplace.

For the most part, however, family members tend to support one another. As you remember, *familism* prompts siblings, cousins, and even more distant relatives to care for one another as adulthood unfolds. One manifestation of familism is called **filial responsibility,** the obligation of adult children to care for their aging parents. This does not always work out well for either generation, but filial responsibility is a value in every nation, stronger in some cultures than in others (Saraceno, 2010).

filial responsibility
The obligation of adult children to care for their aging parents.

When parents need caregiving, adult children often sacrifice to provide it. More often, though, the older generation gives to their adult children. This can strain a long-lasting marriage. For example:

> When my daughter divorced, they nearly lost the house to foreclosure, so I went on the loan and signed for them. But then again they nearly foreclosed, so my husband and I bought it. . . . So now I have to make the payment on my own house and most of the payment on my daughter's house, and that is hard. . . . I am hoping to get that money back from our daughter, to quell my husband's sense that the kids are all just taking and no one is giving back. He sometimes feels used and abused.
>
> *[quoted in Meyer, 2012, p. 83]*

Emotional support and help with managing life may be more crucial and complex than financial assistance, sometimes increasing when money is less needed (Herlofson & Hagestad, 2012). One complexity is that some elders resent exactly the same supportive behaviors that other elders expect from their children—such as visiting frequently, giving presents, or cleaning the refrigerator—and some children resent help that the parents give. For instance, one grandmother suggested that the baby's bathwater was too hot, and the daughter took it as a global criticism of her ability to care for her child (Roiphe, 2010).

A longitudinal study of attitudes found no evidence that recent changes in family structure (including divorce) reduce the sense of filial responsibility (Gans & Silverstein, 2006). In fact, younger cohorts (born in the 1950s and 1960s) endorsed *more* responsibility toward older generations, "regardless of the sacrifices involved," than did earlier cohorts (born in the 1930s and 1940s). Likewise, almost all elders believe the older generation should help the younger ones, although specifics vary by culture (Herlofson & Hagestad, 2012).

In the United States, every generation values independence. That is why, after midlife and especially after the death of their own parents, members of the older generation are *less* likely to say that children should provide substantial care for their parents and more likely to strive to be helpful to their children. The authors of this study conclude that, as adults become more likely to receive than to give intergenerational care, "reappraisals are likely the result of altruism (growing relevance as a potential receiver) or role loss (growing irrelevance as a provider)" (Gans & Silverstein, 2006, p. 974). Adults of all ages like to be needed, not needy.

This may be less true in Asian cultures. Often the first-born son encourages his elderly parents to move in with him and they expect to do so. Indeed, a study in rural China found depression more common among the elderly people whose daughters took care of them instead of their daughters-in-law (Cong & Silverstein, 2008). Asian daughters-in-law seem to experience similar frustrations and joys in caregiving as European American daughters do (Pinquart & Sörensen, 2011).

TENSIONS BETWEEN OLDER AND YOUNGER ADULTS A good relationship with successful grown children enhances a parent's well-being, especially when both generations do whatever the other generation expects. By contrast, a poor relationship makes life worse for everyone. Ironically, conflict is more likely in emotionally close relationships than in distant ones (Silverstein et al., 2010), especially when either generation becomes dependent on the other (Birditt et al., 2009).

ANSWER TO OBSERVATION QUIZ (from page 552) The U.S. couple is relatively rich (their nightclothes look new, and pajamas are mostly the preference of well-to-do men); the Filipina women are relatively poor (they are wearing identical dresses, a gift from the agency that runs this senior center). ●

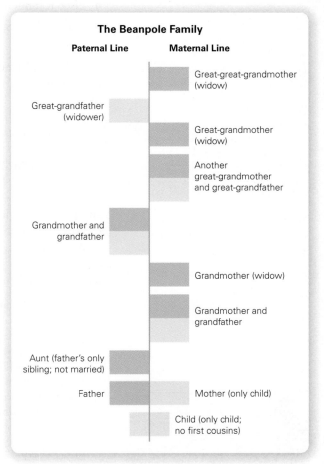

FIGURE 15.8 Many Households, Few Members The traditional nuclear family consists of two parents and their children living together. Today, as couples have fewer children, the beanpole family is becoming more common. This kind of family has many generations, each typically living in its own household, with only a few members in each generation.

It is a mistake to think of the strength of the relationship as merely the middle generation paying back the older one for past sacrifices when they were children or young adults. Although sons seem more supportive of elderly parents if the parents took care of the sons' children, this is not true for daughters. Instead, family norms—either for intergenerational support or for independence—seem to predict how family members interact in late adulthood (Bucx et al., 2012; Henretta et al., 2011).

Extensive research has found that relationships between parents and adult children are affected by many factors:

- Assistance arises both from need and from the ability to provide.
- Frequency of contact is related to geographical proximity, not affection.
- Love is influenced by the interaction remembered from childhood.
- Sons feel stronger obligation; daughters feel stronger affection.

Members of each generation tend to overestimate how much they contribute (Lin, 2008b; Mandemakers & Dykstra, 2008). As already noted, contrary to popular perceptions, financial assistance and emotional support flow more often from the older generation down instead of from the younger generation up, although much depends on who needs what (Silverstein, 2006). Only when elders become frail (discussed later) are they more likely to receive family assistance than to give it.

GRANDCHILDREN Most (85 percent) of those U.S. elders currently older than 65 are grandparents. (The rate was lower in some previous cohorts because the birth rate fell during the 1930s, and it is expected to be lower again.) Personality, background, and past family interactions all influence the nature of the grandparent–grandchild relationship, as does the child's personality.

As with parents and children, the relationship between grandparents and grandchildren depends partly on the age of the grandchildren. One of my college students realized this when she wrote:

> Brian and Brianna are twins and are turning 13 years old this coming June. Over the spring break my family celebrated my grandmother's 80th birthday and I overheard the twins' talking about how important it was for them to still have grandma around because she was the only one who would give them money if they really wanted something their mom wasn't able to give them. . . . I lashed out . . . how lucky we were to have her around and that they were two selfish little brats. . . . Now that I am older, I learned to appreciate her for what she really is. She's the rock of the family and "the bank" is the least important of her attributes now.
>
> [Giovanna, 2010]

"They grow up too fast."

Ignorant? Each generation has much to teach as well as much to learn.

In developed nations, grandparents fill one of four roles:

1. *Remote grandparents* (sometimes called *distant grandparents*) are emotionally distant from their grandchildren. They are esteemed elders who are honored, respected, and obeyed, expecting to get help whenever they need it.

2. *Companionate grandparents* (sometimes called *"fun-loving" grandparents*) entertain and "spoil" their grandchildren—especially in ways, or for reasons, that the parents would not.

3. *Involved grandparents* are active in the day-to-day lives of their grandchildren. They live near them and see them daily.

4. *Surrogate parents* raise their grandchildren, usually because the parents are unable or unwilling to do so.

Currently, in developed nations, most grandparents are companionate, partly because all three generations expect them to be beloved older companions rather than

Same Situation, Far Apart: Happy Grandfathers No matter where they are, grandparents and grandchildren often enjoy each other partly because conflict is less likely, as grandparents are usually not as strict as parents are. Indeed, Sam Levinson quipped, "The reason grandparents and grandchild get along so well is that they have a common enemy."

authority figures. Contemporary elders are usually proud of their grandchildren and care about their well-being but also enjoy their own independence. They provide babysitting and financial help but not advice or discipline (May et al., 2012). If grandparents become too involved and intrusive, parents tend to be forgiving but not appreciative (Pratt et al., 2008).

Such generative distance is not possible for grandparents who become surrogates when the biological parents are incapable of parenting; what results is a family structure called *skipped generation* because the middle generation is absent. Social workers often seek grandparents for kinship foster care, which works for the children as well or better than foster care by strangers, but it may be difficult for the older generation for many reasons.

One reason is that both old and young are sad about the missing middle generation; another is that difficult grandchildren (such as drug-affected infants and rebellious school-age boys) are more likely to live with grandparents; a third is that surrogate grandparents tend to be the most vulnerable elders, almost always grandmothers not grandfathers, already affected by past poverty.

For all these reasons, in North America and Europe, grandparents who are totally responsible for their grandchildren experience more illness, depression, and marital problems than do other elders (Hank & Buber, 2009; S. J. Kelley & Whitley, 2003). Stresses of all kinds abound, including worries about the children under their care (Shakya et al., 2012).

Furthermore, children of skipped-generation families are less likely to graduate from high school than are children from the same SES and ethnic groups who grow up in other family structures (Monserud & Elder, 2011). This has lifelong consequences: The average life span of those in the United States who have not graduated from high school has actually decreased since 1990 (Olshansky et al., 2012) (see Figure 15.9). That makes the trend toward more skipped-generation families a sad one for children as well as adults.

But before concluding that grandparents raising children without the parents is always problematic for all three generations, we need to consider the circumstances. In China, many grandparents become full-time caregivers because the middle generation is working in the cities, unable to bring children with them. The working parents typically make sure the grandparents want the caregiver role and then make sure to send money, as well as to visit when they can. For those grandparents, caring for their grandchildren actually improves their physical and psychological health (Baker & Silverstein, 2012).

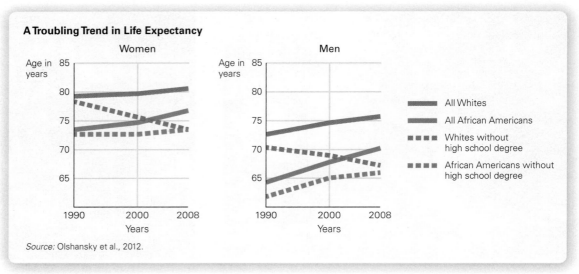

FIGURE 15.9 Too Young to Die
Medical advances and improving health habits mean that most adults live longer than their parents did: The average life span has increased every decade for both sexes, all ethnic groups, in every nation. However, in the United States those without a high school education find that steady work is increasingly scarce, which takes a toll on survival.

The fact that grandparenting is not always wonderful should not obscure the more typical situation: Most grandparents enjoy their role, gain generativity from it, and are appreciated by younger family members (C. L. Kemp, 2005; Thiele & Whelan, 2008). International college students, despite being thousands of miles away from their grandparents, often express warmth, respect, and affection for at least one of them (usually their maternal grandmother) back home (A. C. Taylor et al., 2005). In most conditions, grandparenting benefits all three generations.

Some grandparents are rhapsodic and spiritual about the experience. As one writes:

> Not until my grandson was born did I realize that babies are actually miniature angels assigned to break through our knee-jerk habits of resistance and to remind us that love is the real reason we're here.
>
> *[Golden, 2010, p. 125]*

The animal kingdom may help us see the bigger picture. Wild elephants normally live in multigenerational herds. In one region of Africa, elephant poachers killed most of the oldest generation until strict enforcement put an end to killing mature elephants for their tusks. In those herds, when the younger elephants became adults, without the guidance of their parents, some were infertile and most had more stress (measured physiologically) than elephants normally do (Gobush et al., 2008). Like humans, elephants benefit from multigenerational families.

Friendship

In 2010, 96 percent of people older than 75 in the United States had been married, making this oldest generation the most married cohort in history (U.S. Bureau of the Census, 2011a). Each younger generation has more people who never married: 5 percent for those aged 65 to 74, 8 percent for those 55 to 64, and 12 percent for those 45 to 54. Obviously, the next cohort of elders will include far fewer married people. Furthermore, many middle-aged adults, married and unmarried, have no children, hence more elders will have no grandchildren. Accordingly, this next generation will have many fewer family members. Will they be lonely and lack social support?

Probably not, according to recent data. Members of the current oldest generation who never married are usually quite content, not lonely. Some of them have partners, of the same sex or other sex, and are cohabiting or LAT, seemingly just as happy as traditionally married people (Brown & Kawamura, 2010).

Recent widowhood or divorce is almost always difficult, but elderly people who have spent a lifetime without a spouse or a partner usually have friendships, activities, and social connections that keep them busy and happy (DePaulo, 2006). A study of 85 single elders found that their level of well-being was similar to that of people in long-term equitable marriages, and they were happier than either recent widows or the married adults in unequal marriages (Hagedoorn et al., 2006).

This does not mean that loners are happy, however. All the research finds that older adults need at least one close companion. For many (especially husbands), their intimate friend is also a spouse; for others, the friend is another relative; for still others, it is an unrelated member of their social convoy. The need for a confidant is an important recognition for older adults who may not realize this necessity until a relationship is severed.

For example, one man consulted a therapist because he was unexpectedly depressed after retiring. He quit work when he chose to do so, expecting to be happy. The therapist noted, "For over forty years, he had car-pooled with another man who worked in the same office. They traveled to and from work; an hour's drive each way. They had spent ten hours each week together, for over forty years, sharing their lives, hopes, dreams, and demons" (Rosowsky, 2007, p. 39). Once that problem was recognized, the man initiated get-togethers with his friend, and his depression lifted.

There is a lesson here: Many people do not realize the importance of social relationships until those relationships end. Quality (not quantity) of friendship is crucial, especially among the oldest-old (Krause, 2006). A study of widows found that those who fared best increased their contact with close friends after the death of their spouse (Zettel & Rook, 2004). Successful aging requires that people not be socially isolated. For contemporary elders, does this mean that they should begin social networking on their computers? Maybe, but not everyone agrees, as explained in the following.

Close Friends Late adulthood poses many challenges, from what scarf to wear in a convertible to how to spend one's money and time. Making those decisions with a friend is less stressful than making them alone.

MICHELLE PEDONE / PHOTONICA / GETTY IMAGES

OPPOSING PERSPECTIVES

Social Networking, for Good or Ill

Older people text, tweet, post, and stream less than younger ones. Compared with emerging adults, older adults own fewer computers, are less connected to the Internet, and avoid social networking. One statistic makes the point: In the United States in 2010, 80 percent of all 18- to 29-year-olds had broadband connections *at home,* but only 31 percent of those over age 65 did (A. Smith, 2010).

Older adults may not realize what they are missing: "Seniors are significantly less likely than other age groups to view a lack of broadband access as a major disadvantage across a range of topics—from finding out about job or career opportunities to using government services," with only one elder in nine considering lack of Internet connection "a major disadvantage" (A. Smith, 2010, p. 15).

The digital age gap is particularly apparent for social networking. Facebook, Twitter, MySpace, LinkedIn, online dating, and so on are populated by millions of 15- to 25-year-olds, with fewer participants in every older cohort.

A contrary trend is emerging, however. In one recent year, the rates of social networking among those 65 and older increased 100 percent, while rates for 18- to 29-year-olds rose only 15 percent (see Figure 15.10). As one newspaper reported:

Richard Bosack joined Facebook on Thursday, after his buddy Ray Urbans recommended the ubiquitous social networking site a few days earlier. Bosack is 89. Urbans is 96. . . . The hottest growth segment in online social networking sites is guys like Richard and Ray and their lady friends. That's right. Grampy and Grammy are down with "the Face."

[*Gregory, 2010*]

From a developmental perspective, this may be good news. As the text explains, elders who have strong social networks, close friends, and cognitively stimulating activities tend to live long and healthy lives. Involved, interacting

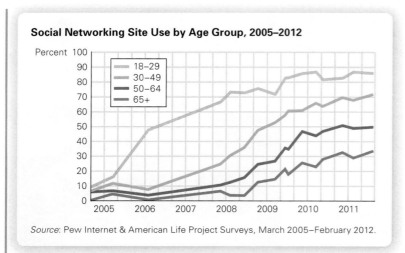

Social Networking Site Use by Age Group, 2005–2012

Percent

- 18–29
- 30–49
- 50–64
- 65+

Source: Pew Internet & American Life Project Surveys, March 2005–February 2012.

FIGURE 15.10 Generation Gap No More Only a few years ago, many older adults warned the young generation about the evil that social networking might bring. Now emerging adults have a new reason to be apprehensive: Their grandparents can see what they do for fun.

elders are more cogent and happier than their relatively lonely and isolated peers. Internet use and social networking correlate with more frequent contact with friends, family, and community organizations (Hogeboom et al., 2010; Lewis & Ariyachandra, 2011).

Analysis of the characteristics of those who are not involved in social networking finds that old age itself is the characteristic they have most in common but that shyness and loneliness are also typical (Sheldon, 2012). Those who are networking are also less shy and less lonely—could that be cause, not merely correlation?

Pause to appreciate the scope of this historical change. A few decades ago, social networks were maintained through direct contact. Neighbors were *neighborly,* a word that means "friendly and helpful." Everyone shopped, worshipped, studied, and played at the same places as everyone else, so they saw one another often. People always answered their phones and doorbells and complained if their friends did not "stay

Looking at Herself Remember self-theory. Rosie Chapman's Facebook page allows her to maintain her identity, aided by other elements of technology—note her glasses, her phone, her printer. Late adulthood is easier for her than it was for her grandparents.

in touch," which once meant literally touching, with a hug or a handshake.

My friend Doris, in the introduction to this chapter, sends cards to hundreds of people. I never do. She is not online; I am. That is as much a cohort difference as a personality one.

Many other elders are like Doris, with dozens of face-to-face friends but no online ones. Are they missing something? Most adults would be upset if a friend stopped by unannounced, but one study found that those over age 80 would not mind (Felmlee & Muraco, 2009).

For younger adults, Internet use correlates with more off-line friends, partly because friendships seem strengthened through online contact (Wang & Wellman, 2010). This could happen for the aged as well.

Then why is social networking a topic for "opposing perspectives" instead of celebration, with suggestions as to how to get more of the elderly online? Three reasons:

1. Older adults' first reaction to social media is negative. They worry especially about privacy.
2. Social networking may increase prejudice.
3. Virtual activism and involvement may decrease community activism.

First, privacy concerns. As you have read, many elders are fiercely independent, and they fear that social networking will make them vulnerable to strangers who want to sell them something, alter their habits, or change their lives (Sheldon, 2012). This concern is also expressed by people of all other ages; perhaps the elders, as a cohort, are more aware of the need for personal privacy than younger adults are.

Second, with wider access, people become more exclusive and selective about their contacts, lists, and news sources—screening out anything that might disagree with their preconceived notions. Yet on blogs, in chat rooms, and on YouTube, much more so than in newspapers and magazines, rumors and prejudices become viral, infecting thousands before anyone discovers a hoax, lie, or distortion.

Reflection, analysis, and contrary opinions are more necessary than ever, yet with aging, the prefrontal cortex that enables such thinking shrinks. Remember that source amnesia is a particular problem with age, so bias might increase as more elderly get online.

Third, although social networking increases the frequency of contact with friends, it may also decrease true intimacy and commitment. As Malcolm Gladwell (2010) explains:

> The platforms of social media are built around weak ties. . . . Facebook is a tool for effectively managing your acquaintances, for keeping up with the people you would not otherwise be able to stay in touch with.
>
> *[p. 42]*

Weak ties, Gladwell contends, do not spur people to action; instead, they encourage comfort, lip service, and passivity—thus maintaining the status quo.

"I used to call people, then I got into e-mailing, then texting, and now I just ignore everyone."

Two eminent scholars, Thomas Sander and Robert Putnam (2010), fear that social networking will weaken social involvement. They hope that "technological innovators may yet master the elusive social alchemy that will enable online behavior to produce real and enduring civic effects" (p. 15), but they do not see it thus far.

Gladwell (2010) reported that the thousands of people who declared their support on Facebook for a group dedicated to ending the violence in Darfur gave an average of only 9 cents each to that cause. Might declaring support online make people less likely to donate, rally, write letters, or do anything else constructive?

Any answer is premature. Sander and Putnam (2010) note that "posts on Twitter (known as 'tweets') convey people's meal and sock choices, instant movie reactions, rush-hour rants, and occasionally even their profound reflections." These two scholars "remain agnostic . . . about whether [these] replace traditional social ties" (p. 15).

Two other social scientists conclude: "Changing social connectivity is, after all, neither a dystopian loss nor a utopian gain but an intricate, multifaceted, fundamental social transformation" (Wang & Wellman, 2010, p. 1164). Apparently all of us—old and young alike—are in the thralls of this transformation. Opinions differ as to the outcome.

KEY points

- Long-term partnerships are beneficial, as research finds that married people tend to have longer, healthier, and happier lives than unmarried ones.
- Adults who have never married tend to have strong social connections with friends, sometimes faring better than those who have been divorced or widowed.
- Children and grandchildren are important parts of the social network for many elders, who more often give care than receive it from the younger generations.
- Familism, not only in filial obligation but also in older parents caring for the younger generations, is apparent in every culture, expressed in divergent ways.

The Frail Elderly

Now that we have dispelled stereotypes by describing aging adults who are active and enjoy supportive friends and family, we can turn to the **frail elderly**—those who are infirm, very ill, seriously disabled, cognitively impaired. They are not the majority, but they are also not rare: Typically, older people are happy and independent, but eventually about one-third will be frail for at least a year before they die.

Activities of Daily Life

The crucial indicator of frailty, according to insurance standards and medical professionals, is the inability to perform the tasks of self-care to maintain independence. Gerontologists often assess five physical **activities of daily life (ADLs):** eating, bathing, toileting, dressing, and moving (transferring) from a bed to a chair.

Equally important may be the **instrumental activities of daily life (IADLs),** which require intellectual competence and forethought. Indeed, problems with IADLs often precede problems with ADLs since planning and problem solving help frail elders maintain self-care.

It is more difficult to list IADLs because they vary from culture to culture. In developed nations, IADLs may include evaluating nutrition, preparing income tax forms, using modern appliances, and keeping appointments (see Table 15.2). In rural areas of other nations, feeding the chickens, cultivating the garden, mending clothes, getting water from the well, and making dinner might be considered IADLs.

Everywhere, the inability to perform IADLs makes people frail, even if they can perform all five ADLs. Fortunately, the trends are encouraging as morbidity is compressed and technology helps with ADLs. Between 1984 and 2004, people older than 65 in the United States were less likely to be disabled in one of the five ADLs, and markedly less likely (by 42 percent) to have difficulty with IADLs (Redfoot & Houser, 2010). As both a cause and a consequence, more of the elderly are living in the community.

WHOSE RESPONSIBILITY? There are marked cultural differences in care for the frail elderly, as already mentioned. As is true in many non-Western cultures, there is

Sidebar

● **UNDERSTANDING THE NUMBERS**
To say "about one-third" will be frail is an estimate, based on data that only about 20 percent of those at age 70 are functionally disabled but more than half of those 85 and older are (Crimmins & Beltrán-Sánchez, 2011). Explain.

Answer The range is vast: Some elders (more men than women) are quite capable until death, and others (more women than men) are frail for a decade or more. Disease rates have not been reduced, but many of the elders function well with conditions (e.g., heart disease) that once meant frailty. One problem with estimating frailty is that often elders believe they are more capable than their children think they are.

frail elderly
People older than 65, and often older than 85, who are physically infirm, very ill, or cognitively disabled.

activities of daily life (ADLs)
Typically identified as five tasks of self-care that are important to independent living: eating, bathing, toileting, dressing, and transferring from a bed to a chair. The inability to perform any of these tasks is a sign of frailty.

instrumental activities of daily life (IADLs)
Actions (e.g., budgeting and preparing food) that are important to independent living and that require some intellectual competence and forethought. The ability to perform these tasks may be even more critical to self-sufficiency than ADL ability.

TABLE 15.2 Instrumental Activities of Daily Life

Domain	Exemplar Task
Managing medical care	Keeping current on check-ups, including teeth and eyes
	Assessing supplements as good, worthless, harmful
Food preparation	Evaluating nutritional information on food labels
	Preparing and storing food to eliminate spoilage
Transportation	Comparing costs of car, taxi, bus, and train
	Determining quick and safe walking routes
Communication	Knowing when and whether to use landline, cell, texting, mail, email
	Programming speed dial for friends, emergencies
Maintaining household	Following instructions for operating an appliance
	Keeping safety devices (fire extinguishers, CO_2 alarms) active
Managing one's finances	Budgeting future expenses (housing, utilities, etc.)
	Completing timely income tax returns

a strong cultural ideology in many African and Asian nations that values filial responsibility. As an example, India passed a law in 2007 making it a crime to neglect one's elderly parents. Other Asian cultures also stress that children should care for the old. Indeed, this was one reason the birth rate was much higher a few generations ago: Parents wanted children as old-age insurance. Filial responsibility arose as a concept when relatively few people reached old age.

Demographics have changed in developed nations. Gerontologists note that one middle-aged couple, neither with siblings, might be responsible for four elderly parents and eight grandparents—fewer if some died, but more if some divorced and remarried. At least one of those 12, and maybe several, are likely to need intense caregiving. If each adult cares for all their needy elders, some will be overburdened. Not fair.

One solution to this inequity is more government aid; another is to prevent frailty from beginning. Governments, families, and aging individuals sometimes blame one another for frailty. The responsibility actually rests with all three.

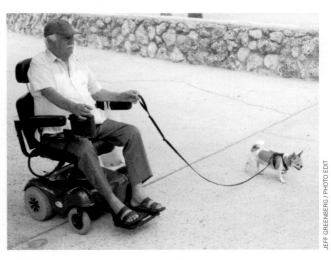

An Odd Couple This tiny short-haired Chihuahua and big, mustached Hispanic man may seem an odd pair, but what you see here is admirable self-protection. The cognitive demands of a mobile wheelchair and the physical demands of a dog are likely to prevent frailty for years to come.

PREVENTING FRAILTY To take a simple example, leg muscles weaken in everyone in old age, but the individual, the social network, and the larger community all influence whether weakened leg muscles lead to frailty. Fear of falling might make the person walk rarely, preferring to stay in bed. Other people might encourage frailty: Perhaps an overly solicitous caregiver brings meals and an adult child buys a large-screen TV with remote control for the bedroom. Because of the macrosystem and exosystem, the physical environment might make walking outside hazardous, the home might have been constructed with many stairs, and the TV news might make violent crime seem common. Thus all three conspire, creating frailty.

To prevent frailty, the person could exercise daily, first in bed, then lying on the floor, then with machines to increase strength and daily excursions. Family members, friends, and volunteers could walk with that leg-weakened person on pathways that the local government has built to be safe and pleasant. Someone could make sure the person has a sturdy walker, and public funds could underwrite the purchase. Personal trainers and/or physical therapists could help, paid by the individual, the family, or public health care.

Thus, all three—the elder, the family, and the community—could prevent or at least postpone frailty. Consider another example, this one not theoretical:

> A 70-year-old Hispanic man came to his family doctor following a visit to his family in Colombia, where he had appeared to be disoriented (he said he believed he was in the United States, and he did not recognize places that were known to be familiar to him) and he was very agitated, especially at night. An interview with the patient and a family member revealed a history that had progressed over the past six years, at least, of gradual worsening cognitive deficit which that family had interpreted as part of normal aging. Recently his symptoms had included difficulty operating simple appliances, misplacement of items, and difficulty finding words, with the latter attributed to his having learned English in his late 20s. . . . [His] family had been very protective and increasingly had compensated for his cognitive problems.
>
> . . . He had a lapse of more than five years without proper control of his medical problems [hypertension and diabetes] because of difficulty gaining access to medical care. . . .
>
> Based on the medical history, a cognitive exam . . . and a magnetic resonance imaging of the brain . . . the diagnosis of moderate Alzheimer's disease was made.

Treatment with ChEI [cholinesterase inhibitors] was started. . . . His family noted that his apathy improved and that he was feeling more connected with the environment.

[Griffith & Lopez, 2009]

In this example, you can see that both the community (those five years without treatment for hypertension and diabetes, both known to impair cognition) and the family (making excuses, protecting him) contributed to his reaching a stage of dementia that could have been delayed, if not prevented altogether. The man himself was not blameless.

If he had recognized his condition, he would have realized that travelling to Colombia was the worst thing he could do: Disorientation of place is an early symptom of dementia, and changing one's physical (or geographic) location can make the problem worse. With many types of dementia, which causes severe IADL disability, as well as with all other kinds of physical and mental impairment, delay, moderation, and sometimes prevention are possible.

Caring for the Frail Elderly

The caregiver of a married frail elderly person is usually the spouse, who is also elderly (Pinquart & Sörensen, 2011). If an impaired person in the United States has no partner, usually siblings or adult daughters become caregivers. Less often, sons and daughters-in-law or adult grandchildren provide care. When home health aides or nursing homes are used, usually the elderly person needs extensive daily care, and families are still needed to coordinate, supplement, and sometimes fund the care. It is not true that professional caregivers are a substitute for family care; instead they are part of a team that is necessary when family members are overwhelmed.

Even with professional help, family caregivers experience substantial stress; without help, they experience less health and more depression. The stress is manifest in various illnesses, in part because the immune system weakens. This is particularly true when caregivers themselves are old, as is usually the case (Lovell & Wetherell, 2011). After listing the problems and frustrations of caring for someone who is mentally incapacitated but physically strong, the authors of one overview note:

> The effects of these stresses on family caregivers can be catastrophic. . . . They may include increased levels of depression and anxiety as well as higher use of psychotropic medicine such as tranquilizers, poorer self-reported health, compromised immune function, and increased mortality.
>
> *[Gitlin et al., 2003, p. 362]*

Remember diversity, however. Some caregivers feel they are repaying past caregiving, and sometimes everyone, including the care receiver, expresses appreciation. In fact, a longitudinal study found that when caregivers feel increasingly supported by family, with practical help as well as emotional encouragement, they experience less stress over time, even though the frail person's needs increase (Roth et al., 2005).

The designated caregiver of a frail elderly person is chosen less for practical reasons (e.g., the relative with the most patience, time, and skill) than for cultural ones. Currently in the United States, the spouse is the usual caregiver—two-thirds of the time it's the wife, one-third of the time, the husband—and they often have had no prior caregiving experience of that kind.

In northern European nations, most elder care is provided through a social safety net of senior day-care centers, senior homes, and skilled nurses. In some cultures, an older person who is dying is taken to a hospital; in other cultures, such intervention is seen as interference with the natural order.

Traditionally in Asian nations, a son's wife provides elder care. In a 1990s study in South Korea, for instance, 80 percent of those with dementia were cared for by daughters-in-law and only 7 percent by spouses. In contrast, among Americans of Korean descent with dementia, 19 percent were cared for by daughters-in-law and 40 percent by spouses, with some of the rest in nursing homes (which almost never happened in Korea) (Youn et al., 1999). That is changing, in Korea and in other Asian nations.

In every culture, emotional and physical needs, as well as expectations, vary because of past experiences and current personalities. Some older people would rather accept help from a paid stranger than from a son or a daughter; others insist on the opposite. Some families admire caregivers and help them often; others isolate and resent them. A tradition of caregiving may explain why at least one study found that caregiving African Americans are less depressed than caregivers of other ethnicities (Roth et al., 2008). As always, ethnic generalities may obscure many individual variations: Some caregivers of every group are abusive and depressed; others are uplifted by the role.

Not What You Think This photo is a stereotype check: What do you think is happening here? In fact, the hairdresser is a volunteer, the place is a nursing home, the country is Haiti. Do any of these surprise you?

Even in ideal circumstances with cultural and community support, family caregiving in the United States often results in many problems:

- If one adult child is the primary caregiver, other siblings feel both relief and jealousy. The caregiver wants sibling help, but the siblings resent being told what to do.
- Care receivers and caregivers disagree about schedules, menus, doctor visits, and so on. Resentments on both sides disrupt mutual affection and appreciation.
- Public agencies rarely provide services unless a crisis arises.

This last item is of particular concern to developmentalists, who are trained to see "change over time," as Chapter 1 explains. From a life-span perspective, frailty should be anticipated and postponed. Caregiver exhaustion and elder abuse are preventable. However, in many nations, public policy and cultural values result in "a system that places inappropriate burdens of elder care upon the family" (Seki, 2001, p. 101).

One cause of this burden is the widespread fear of nursing homes, even though some provide excellent care (as will soon be discussed). Remember that humans tend to focus on the worst, most memorable cases of every kind of problem. Given that, it is not surprising that elderly people often regard living in a nursing home as a fate worse than death, and some families feel shame if they place an elderly relative in an institution.

Developmentalists, concerned about the well-being of people of all ages, advocate more help for families caring for frail elders at home (see Fortinsky et al., 2007; Stone, 2006). Spouses in particular need some relief from full responsibility, including more free time (via professional providers or family members who take over on a regular basis) and better medical attention (usually with visiting nurses who provide medical and psychological care for both caregiver and care receiver).

✦ **ESPECIALLY FOR** Those Uncertain About Future Careers Would you like to work in a nursing home? (see response, page 567) →

Such measures can make home care tolerable, even fulfilling, for caregivers. Fortunately, these developmental concerns are now shared by many members of the public: Elderly people are far more likely to age in place than was true 20 years ago, and help is more available (Lovell & Wetherell, 2010).

ELDER ABUSE When caregiving results in resentment and social isolation, the risk of depression, poor health, and abuse (of either the frail person or the caregiver)

Sweet But Sad Family support is evident here, as an older sister (Lillian, age 75) escorts the younger sister (Julia, age 71) to the doctor. Unseen is how family support wrecked their lives: The sisters lost their life savings and their childhood home because their nephew was addicted to crack.

escalates (Smith et al., 2011). Abuse is likely if the *caregiver* suffers from emotional problems or substance abuse, if the *care receiver* is frail and demanding, and if *care location* is an isolated place where visitors are few and far between.

Ironically, although relatives are less prepared to cope with difficult patients than professionals are, they often provide round-the-clock care with little outside help or supervision. Some resort to overmedication, locked bedroom doors, and physical restraints, all of which are considered elder abuse. The next step may be not feeding properly, or rough treatment.

Extensive public and personal safety nets for the frail elderly are needed. Most social workers and medical professionals are alert to the possibility of elder abuse and are suspicious if an elder is unexpectedly quiet, or losing weight, or injured. Often elder abuse is financial more than physical, yet bankers, lawyers, and investment advisors are not trained to recognize it nor obligated to respond (S. L. Jackson & Hafemeister, 2011).

Typically, abuse begins gradually and can continue for years without anyone realizing it. Political and legal definitions and remedies are not clear-cut (Dong & Simon, 2011).

A major problem is awareness: Professionals and relatives alike hesitate to criticize a family caregiver who is spending the Social Security check, disrespecting the elder, or simply not responding as quickly and carefully as the elder wishes. At what point does this become abuse? This is an issue for all cultures, incomes, and families.

Sometimes the caregiver becomes the victim, cursed at or even attacked by the confused elderly person. As with other forms of abuse, the dependency of the victim makes prosecution difficult (Mellor & Brownell, 2006). This problem gets worse when a family's pride, secrecy, and suspicion keep outsiders away.

Researchers find that about 5 percent of elders say they are abused and that up to one-fourth of all elders are vulnerable but do not report abuse (Cooper et al., 2008). Because elders who are mistreated by family members are ashamed to admit it, the actual rate is probably close to that one-fourth. Accurate incidence data are complicated by lack of consensus regarding standards of care: Some elders feel abused, but caregivers disagree. It is known that elders who are mistreated are more likely to be depressed and ill, but neither of these conditions proves abuse (Dong et al., 2011).

LONG-TERM CARE Many elders and their relatives, horrified by old headlines and photographs of abuse in nursing homes, are convinced that those institutions should be avoided at all costs. And some institutions *are* dehumanizing. One 61-year-old woman with cerebral palsy, who spent time in a nursing home, said:

> I would rather die than have to exist in such a place where residents are neglected, ignored, patronized, infantilized, demeaned; where the environment is chaotic, noisy, cold, clinical, even psychotic.
>
> *[quoted in W. H. Thomas, 2007, p. 159]*

Fortunately, outright abuse is now rare in nursing homes. Laws forbid the use of physical restraints except temporarily in specific, extraordinary circumstances. Some nursing homes provide individualized, humane care, allowing residents to decide what to eat, where to walk, whether to have a pet (W. H. Thomas, 2007). In the United States, nursing homes are frequently visited by government inspectors to "stop dreadful things from happening" (Baker, 2007).

In North America and particularly in western Europe, good private nursing-home care is available for those who can afford it and know what to look for. Some nonprofit homes are subsidized by religious organizations, and these may be excellent as well. Among the signs of a humane setting are provisions for independence, individual choice, and privacy. Activities should not be demeaning. For example, many of today's elderly find Bingo ageist (Baker, 2007). As with day care for young children, continuity of care is crucial: An institution with a high rate of staff turn-over is to be avoided.

The training and the workload of the staff, especially of the aides who provide the most frequent and most personal care, are crucial: Such simple tasks as helping a frail person out of bed can be done clumsily, painfully, or skillfully. The difference depends on proficiency, experience, and patience—all possible with a sufficient number of well-trained and well-paid staff. Currently, however, most front-line workers have little training, low pay, and many patients—and almost half leave each year (Golant, 2011).

Quality care is much more labor-intensive and expensive than most people realize. The average annual nursing home cost in the United States in 2011 was $85,775 for a private room. Variations are dramatic, primarily because of the cost of personnel. In Alaska, it costs $177,755 a year for a room shared with one other person; in Louisiana, it's only $50,370 (John Hancock Life & Health Insurance Company, 2011). Most people think that Medicare, Medicaid, or long-term insurance covers the entire cost—another misconception (Feng et al., 2008).

In the United States, the trend over the past 20 years has been toward fewer nursing-home residents (currently about 1.5 million people nationwide), and those few are usually over 80 years old, frail and confused, with several medical problems (Moore et al., 2012).

Another trend is toward smaller nursing homes with more individualized care—nurses and aides work more closely together, especially in homes designated as Eden Alternative or Green, named after exemplars that stressed the autonomy of the individual (Sharkey et al., 2011). Although 90 percent of elders are independent and community dwelling at any given moment, half of them will need nursing-home care at some point, usually for less than a month as they recuperate from hospitalization. Some need such care for more than a year, and only a few will need it for 10 years or more (Stone, 2006).

Same Situation, Far Apart: Diversity Continues No matter where they live, elders thrive with individualized care and social interaction, as apparent here. Lenore Walker *(left)* celebrates her 100th birthday in a Florida nursing home with her younger sister nearby, and an elderly chess player in a senior residence in Kosovo *(right)* contemplates protecting his king. Both photos show, in tiny details such as the women's earrings and the men's head coverings, that these elders maintain their individuality.

RESPONSE FOR Those Uncertain About Future Careers (from page 565) Why not? The demand for good workers will increase as the population ages, and the working conditions will improve. An important problem is that the quality of nursing homes varies, so you need to make sure you work in one whose policies incorporate the view that the elderly can be quite capable, social, and independent. •

assisted living
A living arrangement for elderly people that combines privacy and independence with medical supervision.

Alternative Care

Most elder-care arrangements that include special services—which could be home care, aging in place, and NORCs—are less costly and more individualized than nursing homes. Another alternative is **assisted living,** an arrangement that combines some of the privacy and independence of home life with some of the medical supervision of a nursing home (Imamoglu, 2007).

An assisted-living residence typically provides a private room or apartment for each person, allowing pets and furnishings just as in a traditional home. Services might include one communal meal per day, special bus trips and activities, and optional arrangements for household cleaning and minor repairs. Usually, medical assistance is readily available—from daily supervision of pill taking to emergency help, with a doctor and ambulance provided when necessary.

Assisted-living facilities range from group homes for three or four elderly people to large apartment or townhouse developments for hundreds of residents (Golant, 2011). Almost every state, province, or nation has its own standards for assisted-living facilities, but many such places are unlicensed. Some regions of the world (e.g., northern Europe) have many assisted living options, while others (e.g., sub-Saharan Africa) have almost none.

Another form is sometimes called *village care.* Although not really a village, it is so named because of the African proverb, "It takes a whole village to raise a child." The idea is that if elderly people who live near one another all pool their resources, they can stay in their homes but also have special assistance when they need it. Such communities require that the elderly contribute financially and that they be relatively competent, so village care is not suited for everyone. However, for some it is ideal (Scharlach et al., 2012).

Overall, as with many other aspects of aging, the emphasis in living arrangements is on selective optimization with compensation. Elders need to live in settings that allow them to be at their best, safe and respected, in control of as much of their own lives as possible. Depending not only on the specifics of ADLs and IADLs, but also on the personality of the elder and the depth of the social network, many housing solutions are possible. One expert explains: "There is no one-size-fits-all set of optimum residential activities, experiences, and situations" (Golant, 2011).

We close with an example of family care and nursing-home care at their best. A young adult named Rob related that his 98-year-old great-grandmother "began to fail. We had no idea why and thought, well, maybe she is growing old" (quoted in L. P. Adler, 1995, p. 242). All three younger generations of the family conferred and reluctantly decided that it was time to move the matriarch from her suburban home, where she had lived for decades, into a nearby nursing home. She reluctantly agreed.

Fortunately, this nursing home encouraged independence and did not assume that decline is always a sign of "final failing." The doctors there discovered that the woman's heart pacemaker was not working properly. Rob tells what happened next:

> We were very concerned to have her undergo surgery at her age, but we finally agreed. . . . Soon she was back to being herself, a strong, spirited, energetic, independent woman. It was the pacemaker that was wearing out, not Great-grandmother.
>
> *[quoted in L. P. Adler, 1995, p. 242]*

This story contains a lesson repeated throughout this book. When a toddler does not talk, or a preschooler grabs a toy, or a teenager gets drunk, or an emerging adult takes dangerous risks, or a newlywed contemplates divorce, or an older person seems to be failing, one might conclude that such problems are normal for that particular age. There is truth in that: Each of these is more common at those stages.

But each of these behaviors should also alert caregivers to encourage talking, sharing, moderation, caution, or self-care. The life-span perspective holds that, at every age, people can be "strong, spirited, and energetic" if all of us do our part.

KEY points

- The frail elderly are unable to perform activities of daily life (ADLs) such as feeding, dressing, and bathing themselves.
- Instrumental activities of daily life (IADLs) require intellectual competence and may be more crucial for independent living than ADLs.
- Caregiving of the frail elderly can be depressing or satisfying, depending partly on support from professionals, family members, and the care receiver.
- Professional help, in assisted-living facilities or nursing homes, can be beneficial or dehumanizing.

SUMMARY

Theories of Late Adulthood

1. Self theories hold that adults make personal choices in ways that allow them to become fully themselves. One such theory arises from Erikson's last stage, integrity versus despair, in which individuals seek integrity that connects them to the human community.

2. Research finds substantial continuity over adulthood in the Big Five personality traits. The positivity effect and a tendency toward self-actualization also can be seen as part of the drive to become more oneself.

3. Compulsive hoarding can be understood as an effort to hold onto the self, keeping objects from the past that others might consider worthless.

4. Stratification theories maintain that social forces—such as ageism, racism, and sexism—limit personal choices throughout the life span, keeping people on a particular level or stratum of society.

5. Age stratification can be blamed for the disengagement of older adults. Activity theory counters disengagement theory, stressing that older people need to be active.

6. Because of earlier discrimination and past experiences—in health, education, and employment—people who are from low-income backgrounds, especially if they are from minority ethnic groups, have a more difficult old age. This does not seem true if they reach very old age, 90 and older.

Activities in Late Adulthood

7. At every age, employment can provide social and personal satisfaction as well as needed income. However, retirement may be welcomed by the elderly, if they remain active in other ways.

8. Some elderly people perform volunteer work and are active politically—writing letters, voting, staying informed. These activities enhance health and well-being and benefit the larger society.

9. Common among retirees are an increase in religious activity (but not church attendance) and a wish to age in place. Many of the elderly engage in home improvement or redecoration, preferring to stay in their own homes and attend their local house of worship.

Friends and Relatives

10. A romantic partner is the most important member of a person's social convoy. Older adults in long-standing marriages tend to be satisfied with their relationships and to safeguard each other's health. As a result, married elders tend to live longer, happier, and healthier lives than unmarried ones.

11. Elders who have never married tend to have many friends. Everyone needs someone who is a close confidant.

12. Relationships with adult children and grandchildren are usually mutually supportive, although conflicts arise as well. Financially, elders more often support the younger generations than vice versa.

13. Most of the elderly prefer to maintain their independence, living alone, but some become surrogate parents, raising their grandchildren. This adds stress to the older generation, especially when it occurs suddenly because the middle generation is unfit or unable to care for the children.

The Frail Elderly

14. Most elderly people are self-sufficient, but some eventually become frail. They need help with their activities of daily life, either with physical tasks (such as eating and bathing) or with instrumental ones (such as completing income taxes and comparing transportation options).

15. Care of the frail elderly is usually undertaken by adult children or spouses, who are often elderly themselves. Most families have a strong sense of filial responsibility, although elder abuse may occur when the stress of care is great and social support is lacking.

16. Nursing homes, assisted living, and professional home care are of varying quality and availability. Each of these arrangements can provide necessary and beneficial care, but they do not always do so. Good care for the frail elderly involves a combination of professional and family support, recognizing diversity in needs and personality.

KEY TERMS

AARP (p. 551)
activities of daily life (ADLs) (p. 562)
activity theory (p. 540)
age in place (p. 549)
assisted living (p. 568)

compulsive hoarding (p. 537)
disengagement theory (p. 540)
filial responsibility (p. 554)
frail elderly (p. 562)
instrumental activities of daily life (IADLs) (p. 562)

integrity versus despair (p. 537)
naturally occurring retirement community (NORC) (p. 549)
positivity effect (p. 538)
self theories (p. 536)

stratification theories (p. 540)
universal design (p. 549)

WHAT HAVE YOU LEARNED?

1. What do self theories seek to explain?

2. Explain Erikson's eighth stage, integrity versus despair, as it relates to late adulthood.

3. How are behaviors such as refusing to give up driving and compulsive hoarding examples of older adults maintaining the self?

4. Explain the connection between the positivity effect and well-being.

5. What do stratification theories seek to explain?

6. Give examples to demonstrate how both the disengagement theory and the activity theory might apply to older adults.

7. How is gender stratification evident in the way that older men and women take care of one another?

8. In what ways might stratification by ethnicity exacerbate the problems that older adults experience?

9. What two government policies make low income particularly difficult for the very old in the United States?

10. Why would a person choose not to retire?

11. What are some benefits of volunteering, and what can be done to encourage more volunteerism among older adults?

12. What are the benefits and liabilities for elders who want to age in place?

13. How do religion and religious institutions fulfill the needs of the elderly?

14. How does the political activism of older and younger adults differ?

15. In what ways might long-term partners protect one another against the problems of old age?

16. In what ways do older and younger generations support one another?

17. Choose one factor that impacts relationships between parents and adult children and explain how it might affect the relationship.

18. Which type of grandparenting seems to benefit both generations the most? Explain.

19. Why is it important for older adults to have close companions?

20. What are ADLs and IADLs? Why is it important to consider both when discussing frailty?

21. What problems might arise in caring for a frail elderly person? What measures might help caregivers?

22. What factors might increase the likelihood of elder abuse?

23. What criteria would you use when evaluating a nursing home?

24. When might assisted living be a good option for elderly people and when might village care be a good option?

APPLICATIONS

1. Attitudes about disabilities are influential. Visit the disability office on your campus, asking both staff and students what they see as the effects of attitude on the performance of all students. How do your findings relate to the elderly?

2. People of different ages, cultures, and experiences vary in their values regarding family caregiving, including the need for safety, privacy, independence, and professional help. Find four people whose backgrounds (age, ethnicity, SES) differ. Ask their opinions on family caregiving and analyze the results.

3. Visit a nursing home or assisted-living residence in your community. Record details about the physical setting, the social interactions of the residents, and the activities of the staff. Would you like to work or live in this place? Why or why not?

>>ONLINE CONNECTIONS

To accompany your textbook, you have access to a number of online resources, including quizzes for every chapter of the book, flashcards (in English and Spanish), critical-thinking questions, and case studies. For access to any of these links, go to www. worthpublishers.com/bergerinvitation2e. In addition to these free resources, you'll also find links to podcasts, video clips, diagnostic quizzing with personalized study advice, and an ebook. Some of the videos and activities available online include:

- *Making the Most of Life During Adulthood.* Explains the keys to successful aging and discusses Erikson's final three stages of development. Video clips show how culture affects the experience of aging.

- *Grandparents as Parents.* In text and video, find out how elders cope with this growing phenomenon and how it affects grandparents and grandchildren.

CHAPTER OUTLINE

Death and Dying

WHAT WILL YOU KNOW?

- Why is death a topic of hope, not despair?
- What is the difference between a good death and a bad one?
- How does mourning help with grief?

M y husband, Martin, died 10 years ago. The immediate cause was an infection, which was exacerbated by steroids, which helped him breathe and which he needed because he had lung cancer, which occurred because he was a lifelong smoker. I blame both of us—me because I never convinced him to quit smoking, him because he never quit. I blame the U.S. Army, too, because they gave him free cigarettes when he was a 17-year-old recruit. And I blame our culture because boys smoke to act like men. I even blame Hitler, already dead when Martin enlisted, but Martin had grown up wanting to join the army to fight him.

My search for causes—steroids, addiction, him, me, the military, machismo, Hitler—arises from anger and guilt, not from acceptance of death as a natural part of the life span. I have kept fresh flowers on our mantle next to his urn for 10 years now: Martin would have laughed at that and insisted that I stop being so foolish. ●

THIS CHAPTER IS ABOUT DEATH. Dying is a process that begins with personal choices (such as smoking cigarettes) and social contexts (such as the army). Culture is always influential. Blame is irrational; bereavement takes many forms. Foolishness is not unusual. When Joan Didion's husband died, she described a "year of magical thinking," including keeping his shoes in the closet because he would need them if he came back (Didion, 2005).

Thanatology is the study of all this. Perhaps surprisingly, thanatology is neither morbid nor gloomy. Rather, as the three sections of this chapter detail, *hope* in death, *choices* in dying, and *affirmation* of life are the themes of thanatology.

Death and Hope

A multicultural life-span perspective reveals that reactions to death are filtered through many cultural prisms and are affected by historical changes and regional variations, as well as by the age of both the dying and the bereaved. We will examine some of these differences.

thanatology
The study of death and dying, especially of the social and emotional aspects.

You will see that one emotion is constant, however: hope. It appears in many ways: hope for life after death, hope that the world is better because someone lived, hope that death occurred for a reason, hope that survivors rededicate themselves.

Cultures, Epochs, and Death

Few people in developed nations have actually witnessed someone die. This was not always the case (see Table EP.1). Those who reached age 50 in 1900 in the United States and who'd had 20 classmates in their high school class would have already seen at least six of those 20 die. The survivors would have visited and reassured several of their friends dying at home, promising to see them in heaven. Shared religious beliefs led almost everyone to believe in life after death.

Now fewer people die before old age, and those who do usually die suddenly and unexpectedly, most often in a motor vehicle accident. Ironically, death has become more feared as it has become less familiar (Carr, 2012). Accordingly, we begin by describing various responses to death, to help each of us find the hope that death can provide.

ANCIENT TIMES One of the signs of a "higher" animal is reacting with sorrow when death occurs. Elephants and chimpanzees have done that for hundreds of thousands of years. Jane Goodall reported that when the chimp Flo died, Flo's older daughter was away, so Flo's youngest son (Flint) did not recover from his grief. Instead, alone, he became "hollow-eyed, gaunt, and utterly depressed, huddled in the vegetation near where Flo had died" (Goodall, 2000, p. 224). Within weeks, he was dead also.

Thus, grief may be innate. Humans have developed ways to deal with that sorrow. Paleontologists believe that 100,000 years ago, the Neanderthals buried their dead with tools, bowls, or jewelry, signifying belief in an afterlife (Hayden, 2012). The date is controversial: Burial could have begun 200,000 years ago or only 20,000 years ago, but it is certain that by 5,000 years ago death had become an occasion for hope, mourning, and remembrance. Two ancient Western civilizations with written records—Egypt and Greece—had elaborate death rituals, described here to help us see what is universal and what is unique about the human response to death.

The ancient Egyptians built magnificent pyramids, refined the science of mummification, and scripted written instructions (called the Book of the Dead) to aid the soul (ka), personality (ba), and shadow (akh) in reuniting after death, blessing and protecting the living (Taylor, 2010).

The fate of a dead Egyptian depended partly on his or her actions while alive, partly on the circumstances of death, and partly on proper burial by the family. That made death a reason to live morally and to honor the past. If a dead person was not appropriately cared for after death, the living would suffer.

The other ancient set of beliefs comes from the Greeks. Again, continuity between life and death was evident, with hope for this world and the next. The fate of a dead person depended on past good or evil deeds. A few would have a blissful afterlife, a few were condemned to torture (in Hades, a form of hell), and most would exist in a shadow world until they were reincarnated to try again.

Three themes are apparent in all the known ancient cultures, not only those of Greece and Egypt, but also in the Mayan, Chinese, and African cultures.

● Actions during life were thought to affect destiny after death.

● An afterlife was more than a hope; it was assumed.

● Mourners responded to death with specific prayers and offerings, in part to prevent the spirit of the dead person from haunting and hurting them.

● **UNDERSTANDING THE NUMBERS**
The only U.S. state that had valid death data for babies born in 1850 was Massachusetts (U.S. Bureau of the Census, 1949). Their life expectancy at birth was 35; if they reached age 20, it increased to 55. How are such statistics determined?

Answer Most early deaths were of infants (hence the initial life expectancy of age 35), but tuberculosis, pneumonia, and accidents killed some young adults, as did childbirth fever for women before age 30 and heart attacks for men before age 50. Since Massachusetts had relatively good public health, and the *average* 20-year-old lived only to age 55, six out of 20 high school classmates' dying (as the text says) is a conservative estimate.

CONTEMPORARY RELIGION AND DEATH Now let us look at contemporary religions. Each faith seems distinct. One review states: "Rituals in the world's religions, especially those for the major tragic and significant events of bereavement and death, have a bewildering diversity" (Idler, 2006, p. 285).

Some details illustrate this diversity. According to many branches of Hinduism, for example, a person should die on the floor, surrounded by family, who neither eat nor wash until the funeral pyre is extinguished. By contrast, among some (but not all) Christians, the very sick should be taken to the hospital; if they die, then mourners gather at their home to eat and drink, often with music and dancing.

In many Muslim and Hindu cultures, the dead person is bathed by the next of kin; among some Native Americans (e.g., the Navajo), no family member touches the dead person. While religions everywhere have specific beliefs and rituals, these vary as much by region as by religion. For instance, there are more than 500 Native American tribes in North America, each with its own heritage: It is a mistake to assume that Native Americans all have the same customs (Cacciatore, 2009).

Buddhism is even older than Christianity and Islam, and perhaps for that reason the diversity of beliefs among Buddhists is especially evident. Some Buddhist rituals help believers accept the death and detach from grieving for the specific person in order to escape the suffering that living without that person entails. Other rituals help people connect to the dead, part of the continuity between life and death (Cuevas & Stone, 2011). Diversity is common in other religions as well. For example, all major religions include opinions for and against organ donation (Bresnahan & Mahler, 2010).

Religious practices change as historical conditions do. One specific example comes from Korea. Traditionally, Koreans were opposed to autopsies because the body is considered a sacred gift from the parents. However, contemporary Koreans value science education, evident in the stellar academic achievements of Korean youth. That creates a dilemma because medical schools need bodies to autopsy in order to teach the next generation. This clash led to a new custom: a special religious service honoring the dead who give their body for medical education (J-T. Park et al., 2011). As medical schools instituted such ceremonies, the number of bodies donated for research in Korea rose dramatically.

Diversity is also evident in descriptions of life after death. Some religions believe in reincarnation—that a dead person is reborn, with the specific new life dependent on the person's past life. Other religions believe that souls are judged and then sent to heaven or hell. Still others contend that the spirits of the dead remain on earth, affecting the life of those still living. And finally, some religions hold that the dead live on only in memory, which leads to customs such as naming a baby after a dead person or honoring the dead on a particular memorial day.

The Western practice of building a memorial, dedicating a plaque, or naming a location for a dead person is antithetical to Eastern cultures, in which all signs of the dead are removed after proper prayers have been said, in order to allow the spirit to leave in peace. This was evident when terrorist bombs in Bali, Indonesia, killed 38 Indonesians and 164 foreigners, mostly Australian and British. The Indonesians prayed intensely and then destroyed all reminders; the Australians raised money to build a memorial (Jonge, 2011). Neither group understood the deep emotions of the other.

TABLE EP.1 How Death Has Changed in the Past 100 Years

Death occurs later. A century ago, the average life span worldwide was less than 40 years (47 in the rapidly industrializing United States). Half of the world's babies died before age 5. Now newborns are expected to live to age 79; in many nations, elderly people age 85 and over are the fastest-growing age group.

Dying takes longer. In the early 1900s, death was usually fast and unstoppable; once the brain, the heart, or other vital organs failed, the rest of the body quickly followed. Now death can often be postponed through medical intervention: Hearts can beat for years after the brain stops functioning, respirators can replace lungs, and dialysis can do the work of failing kidneys. As a result, dying is often a lengthy process.

Death often occurs in hospitals. A hundred years ago, death almost always occurred at home, with the dying person surrounded by familiar faces. Now many deaths occur in hospitals, surrounded by medical personnel and technology.

The main causes of death have changed. People of all ages once died of infectious diseases (tuberculosis, typhoid, smallpox), and many women and infants died in childbirth. Now disease deaths before age 50 are rare, and almost all newborns (99 percent) and their mothers (99.99 percent) live, unless the infant is very frail or medical care of the mother is grossly inadequate.

And after death . . . People once knew about life after death. Some believed in heaven and hell; others, in reincarnation; others, in the spirit world. Many prayers were repeated—some on behalf of the souls of the deceased, some for remembrance, some to the dead asking for protection. Believers were certain that their prayers were heard. Today's young adults are aware of cultural and religious diversity, which makes them question what earlier generations believed, raising doubts that never occurred to their ancestors.

Source: Adapted from Kastenbaum, 2006; data from U.S. Bureau of the Census, 2012.

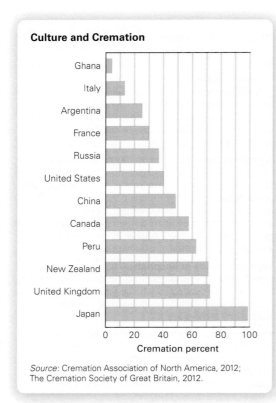

Culture and Cremation

Source: Cremation Association of North America, 2012; The Cremation Society of Great Britain, 2012.

FIGURE EP.1 We All Die . . . But
What happens to the body depends on where we live. If a dead elder in Ghana were cremated, everyone would be shocked, as that practice is considered an insult that might harm the entire community. However, cremation would be assumed in Japan, where anything else would be viewed as disrespectful to the community and to the deceased.

This helps explain variations in what happens to a dead body. An open casket and then burial is traditional in North America. Caskets themselves can be luxurious, silk-lined, and protected from the elements with strong metal, or families can opt for "a plain pine box," as some religions prescribe (Sanders, 2010). Traditionally among North American and western European groups, every churchyard had a cemetery, so parishioners could visit the graves of loved ones.

By contrast, in many Muslim groups, even a pine box is not recommended because the body should return to the earth and thus be buried directly in the soil. In most nations of Asia, from Japan in the east to India in the west, bodies are cremated and returned to the land or water.

Today in North America, hearses may take coffins to distant cemeteries, where people of many faiths are buried. Cremation is more common, with regional variations (see Figure EP.1). Ashes may be interred next to buried coffins or may be scattered. Public health laws often regulate burial and cremation—sometimes in culturally insensitive or antiquated ways. In Texas, for instance, cremation cannot occur until 48 hours after the death, even though some religions require burial, of the body or the ashes, within 24 hours.

In some cultures, a home altar is created, where the living can commune with the spirits of the dead. Spirits not only hover in their special spot, but they also travel—especially during the Hungry Ghost Festival (in many East Asian nations), on the Day of the Dead (in many Latin American nations), or on All Souls Day (in many European nations). All of these beliefs can change as cultures do. For instance, while every Chinese home once had an altar honoring the ancestors, currently most do not (Chan, 2011).

In recent decades, people everywhere have become less devout, evident in surveys of religious beliefs as well as in attendance at religious services. Has death then become a source of despair, not hope? Maybe not. People worldwide become more religious when confronted with their own or someone else's death. This is true even for people who do not consider themselves religious (Heflick & Goldenberg, 2012). Psychologists contend that human cognition naturally leads people to believe in life after death (Pereira et al., 2012).

Consequently, do not get distracted by death customs or beliefs that seem odd to you, such as mummies, hungry ghosts, or hellfire. Instead, notice that death has always inspired strong emotions, often benevolent ones. It is the *denial* of death that leads to despair (Wong & Tomer, 2011). In all faiths and cultures, death is considered a passage, not an endpoint, a reason for families and strangers to come together.

Understanding Death Throughout the Life Span

This entire book reflects the life-span perspective. As you now expect, thoughts about death are influenced by each person's cognitive maturation and past experiences. Here are some of the specifics.

DEATH IN CHILDHOOD Some adults think children are oblivious to death; others believe children should participate in funerals and other rituals, just as adults do (Talwar et al., 2011). You know from your study of childhood cognition that neither view is completely correct.

Children as young as 2 have some understanding of death, but their perspective differs from that of older people. One idea they find particularly incomprehensible is that the dead person or animal cannot come alive again, which means that a child might not be sad initially when someone dies. Later, the child might have moments of profound sorrow, when the reality sinks in.

Each child is affected by the attitudes of other family members. If a child encounters death, adults should listen with full attention, neither ignoring the child's concerns nor expecting adult-like reactions (Doering, 2010). Children are more impulsive than deliberate, as their limbic systems mature more rapidly than their prefrontal cortexes. They may seem happy one day and morbidly depressed the next. Children neither forget nor dwell on the death of a loved one.

Children who themselves are fatally ill typically fear that death means being abandoned by beloved and familiar people (Wolchik et al., 2008). Consequently, parents are advised to stay with a dying child day and night, holding, reading, singing, and sleeping, always ensuring that the child is not alone. Frequent and caring presence is more important than logic.

Sorrow All Around When a 5-day-old baby died in Santa Rosa, Guatemala, the entire neighborhood mourned. Symbols and a procession help with grief: The coffin is white to indicate that the infant was without sin and will therefore be in heaven.

A child who loses a friend, a relative, or a pet typically demonstrates sadness, loneliness, anger, and other signs of mourning, but adults cannot be certain how a particular child might react. For example, one 7-year-old boy seemed to take in stride the loss of three grandparents and an uncle within two years. However, he became extremely upset when his dog, Twick, died.

That boy's parents, each grieving for a dead mother, were taken aback by the depth of the boy's emotions. They regretted that they had not taken him to the animal hospital to say goodbye to the dog. The boy angrily refused to go back to school, saying, "I wanted to see him one more time. . . . You don't understand. . . . I play with Twick every day" (quoted in K. R. Kaufman & Kaufman, 2006, pp. 65–66).

Because the loss of a particular companion is a young child's prime concern, it is not helpful to say that a dog can be replaced. Even a 1-year-old knows that a new puppy is not the same dog and might be upset or confused that an adult would think so. Nor should a child be told that Grandma is sleeping, that God wanted his or her sister in heaven, or that Grandpa went on a trip. The child may take such explanations literally, wanting to wake up Grandma, complain to God, or tell Grandpa to come home.

If a child realizes that adults are afraid to say that death has occurred, the child might conclude that death is so horrible that adults cannot talk about it—a terrifying conclusion. Even worse may be the idea that adults are not to be trusted: They lie about important events (Doering, 2010).

Remember how cognition changes with development. Egocentric preschoolers fear that they, personally, caused death and may be seriously troubled that their unkind words or thoughts killed someone. As children become concrete operational thinkers, they seek specific facts, such as exactly how a person died and where he or she is now. Adolescents may be self-absorbed, philosophical, or analytic—or all three at different moments.

At every age, questions should be answered honestly, in words the child can understand. In a study of 4- to 8-year-olds, those who knew more about the specifics of a loved one's death were less anxious about death and dying (Slaughter & Griffiths, 2007).

In another series of studies in several nations, children saw no contradiction between biological facts of death and spiritual hope for the afterlife, as long as adults were forthcoming about both (Talwar et al., 2011). Even if a parent dies, some children cope well—if their caregiving adult is able to cope well (Melhem et al., 2011).

terror management theory (TMT)
The idea that people adopt cultural values and moral principles in order to cope with their fear of death. This system of beliefs protects individuals from anxiety about their mortality and bolsters their self-esteem, so they react harshly when other people go against any of the moral principles involved.

DEATH IN LATE ADOLESCENCE AND EMERGING ADULTHOOD "Live fast, die young, and leave a good-looking corpse" is advice often attributed to actor James Dean, who died in a car crash at age 24. At what stage would a person be most likely to agree? Emerging adulthood, of course. Worldwide, teenagers and emerging adults control their death anxiety by taking risks and valuing friends, perhaps expecting to die long before old age (de Bruin et al., 2007; Luxmoore, 2012).

Terror management theory explains some illogical responses to death, including why young people take death-defying risks (Mosher & Danoff-Burg, 2007). By surviving, they prove to themselves that they will not die. Especially when people aged 15 to 24 have access to guns and cars, the developmental tendency toward risk taking can be deadly (see Figure EP.2). Cluster suicides, foolish dares, fatal gang fights, and drunk driving are all much more common in those younger than 25 than older. Three attitudes typical of older adolescents correlate with one another: ageism, terror management, and risk taking (Popham et al., 2011b).

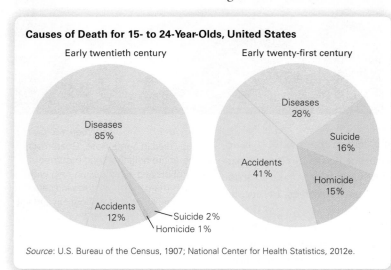

Causes of Death for 15- to 24-Year-Olds, United States

Source: U.S. Bureau of the Census, 1907; National Center for Health Statistics, 2012e.

FIGURE EP.2 Typhoid Versus Driving into a Tree In 1905, most young adults in the United States who died were victims of diseases, usually infectious ones like tuberculosis and typhoid. In 2005, 25 times more died in the most common type of accident (motor vehicle) than died of the most common lethal disease (leukemia).

Many studies have found, as already noted, that "a health promotion message that equates smoking with death may ironically have the exact opposite effect" (Goldenberg & Arndt, 2008, p. 1049); it may increase smoking in teenagers and young adults who want to protect their pride and self-esteem while defying death and adults. Likewise, college students who heard about the fatal risks associated with binge drinking were more willing to binge, not less so (Jessop & Wade, 2008).

Other research in many nations finds that when adolescents and emerging adults think about death, they sometimes "strive to maintain self-esteem and faith in their cultural worldviews, at least in part to protect themselves from death-related anxiety" (Maxfield et al., 2007, p. 342). This makes people more likely to accept stereotypes and to be intolerant of people of other ethnicities because they want to convince themselves that members of their own group (including themselves) are more worthy of life.

Some people distance themselves from people with cancer to avoid anxiety about their own death; others avoid funerals and blame people who died from accidents that occurred through no fault of their own (Hirschberger, 2006; Renkema et al., 2008).

Teenagers who themselves are dying of a fatal disease tend first to be saddened and shocked ("Why me?") and then to try to live life to the fullest, proving that death cannot conquer them. One dying 17-year-old said

> don't be scared of death. Don't go and lock yourself in your little room, under your little bedcovers, and just sit there and cry and cry and cry. Don't do that because you're wasting time, and you're not only hurting yourself, you're hurting the people around you. . . . That's why never ever ever stop doing what you love. Just be yourself. Be normal. Don't shut them out, but bring them in—your loved ones, your friends.

> *[Kellehear & Ritchie, 2003, p. 21]*

DEATH IN ADULTHOOD A shift in attitudes occurs when adults become responsible for work and family. Death is no longer romanticized; it is to be avoided or at least postponed. Fear of death builds in early adulthood, reaching a lifetime peak in middle age.

Many adults quit addictive drugs, start wearing seat belts, and adopt other precautions when they become parents. One of my students eagerly anticipated the thrill of her first skydive. She reserved her spot on the plane and paid in advance. However, the day before the scheduled dive she learned she was pregnant. She forfeited the money and shopped for prenatal vitamins.

To defend themselves against the fear of aging and untimely death, adults do not readily accept the death of others—even others who are ready to die. Thus, when Dylan Thomas was about age 30, he wrote his most famous poem, addressed to his dying father: "Do not go gentle into that good night/Rage, rage against the dying of the light" (D. Thomas, 1957).

Nor do adults readily accept their own death. A woman diagnosed at age 42 with a rare and almost always fatal cancer (a sarcoma) wrote:

> I hate stories about people dying of cancer, no matter how graceful, noble, or beautiful. . . . I refuse to accept that I am dying; I prefer denial, anger, even desperation. . . . I resist the lure of dignity; I refuse to be graceful, beautiful, beloved.
>
> *[Robson, 2010, pp. 19, 27, 28]*

When adults hear about another's death, their reaction is closely connected to the person's age. Death in the prime of life is harder to accept than death in late adulthood. Consider the public reaction to the deaths of two U.S. presidents, Ronald Reagan and John Fitzgerald Kennedy. Reagan was the more popular of the two; he was president for eight years (Kennedy for only three) and was elected twice by a wide margin. Yet Kennedy's violent death at age 46 evoked far more public sorrow than did Reagan's death from Alzheimer disease at age 93. More recently, the deaths of Michael Jackson and Whitney Houston were mourned by millions, in part because they were not yet old.

Reactions to one's own mortality differ depending on developmental stage as well. In adulthood, from ages 25 to 65, terminally ill people worry about leaving something undone or abandoning family members, especially children.

One such adult was Randy Pausch, a 47-year-old professor and father of three young children. Ten months before he died of cancer in 2008, he delivered a famous last lecture, detailing his childhood dreams and saluting those who would continue his work. After advising his students to follow their own dreams, he concluded, "This talk is not for you, it's for my kids" (R. Pausch, 2008). Not surprisingly, that message was embraced by his wife, also in mid-adulthood, who wrote her own book titled *Dream New Dreams*, which deals with overcoming death by focusing on life (J. Pausch, 2012).

Attitudes about death are often irrational. Rationally, adults should work to change social factors that increase the risk of mortality—such as air pollution, junk foods, and unsafe transportation. Instead, many people react more strongly to events that rarely cause death, such as anthrax and avalanches.

Often, when adults hear about someone's death, they want details in order to convince themselves that their situation is different. Sometimes the deceased was much older and had been ailing; in that case, adults do not take the death personally. If the dead person was a contemporary or even younger, then adults seek to explain why that person's genes, or habits, or foolish behavior is unlike their own.

The most feared deaths are the seemingly random ones, such as a freak accident or a mysterious poison. For this reason, many more people are afraid of flying than of driving. The data find that, per mile traveled, a person is 200 times more likely to be killed by a car than by a plane. In 2008, for example, there were only 11 fatal airline crashes in the entire

"For My Kids" Randy Pausch was a brilliant, innovative scientist who specialized in virtual reality research at Pittsburgh's Carnegie Mellon University. When he was diagnosed with terminal pancreatic cancer, he gave a talk titled "The Last Lecture: Really Achieving Your Childhood Dreams" that became famous worldwide. He devoted the final 10 months of his life to his family—his wife Jai and their children Chloë, Dylan, and Logan.

PHOTOGRAPH © JAI PAUSCH. FROM THE BOOK THE LAST LECTURE BY RANDY PAUSCH WITH JEFFREY ZASLOW. COPYRIGHT © 2008 RANDY PAUSCH. REPRINTED BY PERMISSION OF HYPERION. ALL RIGHTS RESERVED.

world, killing 587 people, whereas 84,000 people were killed by motor vehicles in the United States alone (U.S. Bureau of the Census, 2011b).

Thus, the fear of flying is irrational, based on the belief that when people drive or ride in cars they are in control. Ironically, when four airplanes crashed on September 11, 2001, many Americans chose to drive long distances instead of fly. As an indirect result, 2,300 more people died in car crashes than usual (Blalock et al., 2009).

In general, adults ignore their own life-shortening behaviors, such as smoking cigarettes, eating salty snacks, and having unsafe sex. In this book, I tend to focus on risks I never, or no longer, take. For example, I stressed that cigarette smoking is linked to heart attacks, dementia, and many cancers—including the one that killed my husband. Those links are proven, but would my emphasis change if I were a smoker?

As a general example, more people die *each day* of heart disease in the United States than died in the attacks of September 11th, but that has little impact on public policy or private behavior. Intensified airport security measures seem protective, yet Americans eat artery-clogging food and drive instead of walking, maintaining unhealthy weight. Not logical, but very human.

DEATH IN LATE ADULTHOOD In late adulthood, attitudes about death shift again. Anxiety decreases; hope rises (De Raedt et al., 2013). Life-threatening illnesses reduce life satisfaction more among the middle-aged than the elderly (Wurm et al., 2008). The irrational reactions of terror management theory are less prominent in late adulthood (Maxfield et al., 2007) (see Figure EP.3). Some older people are quite happy despite knowing that their remaining time is short.

This shift in attitudes is beneficial. Indeed, many developmentalists believe that one sign of mental health among older adults is acceptance of mortality, increasing altruistic concern about those who will live on after them.

As evidence of the change in attitude, older people write their wills, designate health care proxies, read scriptures, reconcile with estranged family members, and, in general, tie up all the loose ends that most young adults avoid (Kastenbaum, 2012). Sometimes middle-aged adults are troubled when their elderly parents allocate heirlooms, choose funeral music, or buy a burial plot, but all those actions might be developmentally appropriate toward the end of life.

Acceptance of death does not mean that the elderly give up on living. On the contrary, most try to maintain their health and independence. However, priorities shift. In an intriguing series of studies (Carstensen, 2011), people were presented with the following scenario:

> Imagine that in carrying out the activities of everyday life, you find that you have half an hour of free time, with no pressing commitments. You have decided that you'd like to spend this time with another person. Assuming that the following three persons are available to you, whom would you want to spend that time with?

- A member of your immediate family
- The author of a book you have just read
- An acquaintance with whom you seem to have much in common

FIGURE EP.3 A Toothache Worse Than Death? A cohort of young adults (average age 21) and old adults (average age 74) were divided into three groups. One group wrote about death (so that they had overt thoughts about it), another did a puzzle with some words about death (so that their thoughts about death were unconscious), and the third wrote about dental pain (so that they served as the control group). Then they all judged how harshly people should be punished for various moral transgressions. Those who wrote about dental pain are represented by the zero point on this graph. Compared with them, those older adults who thought about death were less punitive, but younger adults were more so. The difference in the ratings of the young and old was more pronounced if their thoughts were unconscious than if they were overt.

Thoughts About Death and Severity of Punishment

Source: Maxfield et al., 2007.

Older adults, more than younger ones, choose the family member. The researchers explain that family becomes more important when death seems near. This is supported by a study of 329 people of various ages who had recently been diagnosed with cancer and a matched group of 170 people (of the same ages) who had no serious illness (Pinquart & Silbereisen, 2006). The most marked difference was between those with and without cancer, regardless of age (see Figure EP.4). Life-threatening illness, more common in late adulthood but not directly caused by age, seems to change attitudes about life, people, and death.

People who think they might die soon are more likely than others to believe in life after death (Vail et al., 2010). This is one reason why the aged in the United States tend to be more religious than the young, praying more—although not necessarily attending church, temple, or mosque more frequently (Pyne, 2010). It may also explain why people in nations with higher death rates tend to be more devout.

Near-Death Experiences

Even coming close to death is often an occasion for hope. This is most obvious in what is called a *near-death experience,* in which a person almost dies but survives and reports having left his or her body and moved toward a bright white light while feeling peacefulness and joy. The following classic report is typical:

> I was in a coma for approximately a week. . . . I felt as though I were lifted right up, just as though I didn't have a physical body at all. A brilliant white light appeared. . . . The most wonderful feelings came over me—feelings of peace, tranquility, a vanishing of all worries.
>
> *[quoted in R. A. Moody, 1975, p. 56]*

Near-death experiences often include religious elements (angels have been seen, celestial music heard), and survivors often adopt a more spiritual, less materialistic view of life as a result (Vaillant, 2008). To some, near-death experiences prove that "Heaven is for real" (Burpo & Vincent, 2010). Most scientists are skeptical, claiming that

> there is no evidence that what happens when a person really dies and "stays dead" has any relationship to the experience reported by those who have recovered from a life-threatening episode. In fact, it is difficult to imagine how there could ever be such evidence.
>
> *[Kastenbaum, 2006, p. 448]*

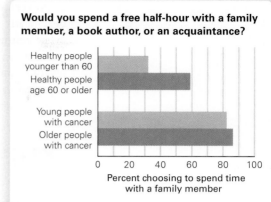

Would you spend a free half-hour with a family member, a book author, or an acquaintance?

Source: Pinquart & Silbereisen, 2006.

FIGURE EP.4 Turning to Family as Death Approaches Both young and old people diagnosed with cancer (one-fourth of whom died within five years) were more likely to prefer to spend a free half-hour with a family member rather than with an interesting person whom they did not know well. Unlike for the sick, for healthy people age differences were significant.

Same Situation, Far Apart: Death of a Holy Man Thousands attend the funeral of a religious leader, offering blessings and confirming their belief in life after death by doing so. That much is universal, but notice the many contrasts between the rituals for the Catholic Archbishop Benoir and Vicar Serge in Haiti *(left)* and the Buddhist monk Young Am in Korea *(right).*

Nevertheless, a reviewer of near-death experiences is struck by the similarity of near-death experiences in many cultures and religious beliefs about death itself. In every culture, "all varieties of the dying experience" move people toward the same realizations: (1) the limitations of social status, (2) the insignificance of material possessions, and (3) the narrowness of self-centeredness (Greyson, 2009). Near-death experiences do this as well: Those who recall such moments seem more loving and hopeful than they were before.

KEY points

- Since the mid-twentieth century, first-hand experience with death has become less common and therefore death less familiar. In the nineteenth century, everyone knew several people who died before age 40.
- Ancient cultures and current world religions have various customs about death, which help people live better lives as they respond to sorrow with hope.
- People react to death differently, depending on their developmental stage, with older adults less anxious than younger ones.
- Near-death experiences seem to make people more spiritual, less materialistic, and more appreciative of others.

Choices in Dying

Do you recoil at the thought of "choices in dying"? If so, you may be living in the wrong century. Every twenty-first-century death involves choices, beginning with risks taken or not. This is very apparent in accidents (the leading cause of death from age 1 to age 50) and also for most diseases.

The most common causes of death (cancer and heart disease account for 23 and 25 percent of all U.S. deaths, respectively) involve a multitude of choices, not only in behaviors that increase risk but also after diagnosis—that is, whether medical treatment is provided and, if so, what, where, and when. Ideally, when confronted with a life-threatening illness, the patient decides. We now describe some of these choices.

A Good Death

People everywhere hope for a good death (Vogel, 2011), one that is:

- At the end of a long life
- Peaceful
- Quick
- In familiar surroundings
- With family and friends present
- Without pain, confusion, or discomfort

Those six characteristics are accepted by almost everyone, but other aspects are less universal. Many would add that *control over circumstances* and *acceptance of the outcome* are also characteristic of a good death, but cultures and individuals differ. Some dying individuals willingly cede control to doctors or caregivers, and some fight every sign that death is near. Since individuals and cultures disagree on what is considered good, "the term [good death] itself can be problematic" (Bauer-Maglin & Perry, 2010, p. 9).

Although aspects of a good death are culturally driven, a *bad death* (lacking the six characteristics above) is universally dreaded, particularly by the elderly. Many of them have known people who died in hospitals, semiconscious and alone.

In some ways, modern medicine makes a good death more likely. The first item on the list has become the norm: Death usually occurs at the end of a long life. Younger people still get sick, but surgery, drugs, radiation, and rehabilitation typically mean that, in developed countries, the ill go to the hospital, are treated, and then return home.

In other ways, however, contemporary advances have made a bad death more likely. When a cure is impossible, physical and emotional comfort may deteriorate (Kastenbaum, 2012). Instead of acceptance, which allows people to die peacefully at home with close friends, people attempt to fight death with surgery and drugs that prolong pain and confusion rather than restore health and comfort. Hospitals may exclude visitors at the most critical stage of patient illness, and patients may become delirious or unconscious, unable to die in peace.

The underlying problem may be medical care itself, so focused on life-saving that dying invites "the dangers of well-intentioned over 'medicalization'" (Ashby, 2009, p. 94). Dying involves emotions, values, and a community—not just a heart that might stop beating. Fortunately, three factors that make a good death more likely have increased: honest conversation, the hospice, and palliative care.

HONEST CONVERSATION In about 1960, researcher Elisabeth Kübler-Ross (1969, 1975) asked the administrator of a large Chicago hospital for permission to speak with dying patients. He informed her that no one in the hospital was dying! Eventually, she found a few terminally ill patients who, to everyone's surprise, wanted very much to talk.

From ongoing interviews, Kübler-Ross identified emotions experienced by dying people, which she divided into a sequence of five stages:

1. Denial ("I am not really dying.")
2. Anger ("I blame my doctors, or my family, or God for my death.")
3. Bargaining ("I will be good from now on if I can live.")
4. Depression ("I don't care about anything; nothing matters anymore.")
5. Acceptance ("I accept my death as part of life.")

Another set of stages of dying is based on Abraham Maslow's hierarchy of needs, discussed in Chapter 1 (Zalenski & Raspa, 2006).

1. Physiological needs (freedom from pain)
2. Safety (no abandonment)
3. Love and acceptance (from close family and friends)
4. Respect (from caregivers)
5. Self-actualization (appreciating one's unique past and present)

Maslow later suggested a possible sixth stage, *self-transcendence* (Koltko-Rivera, 2006), which emphasizes the acceptance of death.

Other researchers have *not* found sequential stages in dying people's approach to death. Remember the woman, cited earlier, who was dying of a sarcoma? She said that she would never accept death and that Kübler-Ross should have included desperation as a stage.

Many thanatologists find that the stages of denial, anger, and depression disappear and reappear, that bargaining is brief because it is fruitless, and that acceptance may never occur. Regarding Maslow, although all of his levels are important throughout the dying process, there is no set sequence.

Nevertheless, both lists remind caregivers that each dying person has emotions and needs that may be unlike those of another—or even unlike that same person's emotions and needs a few days or weeks earlier. Furthermore, a dying person's emotions may not be what family, medical personnel, and others might expect.

It is important for everyone—doctors, nurses, family, friends, and the patient—to know that a person is dying; then, care is more likely to improve rather than degrade (Lundquist et al., 2011). Unfortunately, even if a patient is terminally ill with incurable cancer, most doctors never ask what end-of-life care the patient wants. In one study, compared with similar patients in the same hospital whose doctors did discuss final care (31 percent), those who did *not* have such a conversation (69 percent) endured more pain, procedures, and hospital bills in their final week ($2,917 on average compared with $1,876) but not longer life (Zhang et al., 2009).

As Kübler-Ross and others have discovered, most dying people want to spend time with loved ones and to talk honestly with medical and religious professionals. Human relationships are crucial: People continue to need each other (Planalp & Trost, 2008). Dying patients do not want to be cut off from daily life; they want to know what their relatives and friends are doing and how they are feeling.

However, avoid assumptions. Kübler-Ross also stressed that each person responds to death in his or her own way; some people do *not* want the whole truth, and some do *not* want many visitors. In some cultures, telling people they are dying is thought to destroy hope. Indeed, even maintaining human relationships via long, intimate conversations may be counter to certain religious beliefs (Baugher, 2008)—for instance, when the purpose of death is seen as relinquishing ties to this world.

hospice
An institution or program in which terminally ill patients receive palliative care to reduce suffering; family and friends of the dying are helped as well.

THE HOSPICE In 1950s London, Cecily Saunders opened the first modern **hospice,** where terminally ill people could spend their last days in comfort (Saunders, 1978). Thousands of other such places have opened in many nations, and hundreds of thousands of hospice caregivers bring medication and care to dying people where they live. In the United States, half of all hospice deaths occur at home (National Center for Health Statistics, 2011).

Hospice professionals relieve pain and discomfort, not only with drugs but also with massage, bathing, and so on. They avoid measures that merely delay death; their aim is to make dying easier. There are two principles for hospice care:

● Each patient's autonomy and decisions are respected. For example, pain medication is readily available, not on a strict schedule or at a minimal dosage. In a massive U.S. study of the last week of life, 91 percent of hospice care patients had been given narcotic analgesics.

● Family members and friends are counseled before the death, taught to provide care, and guided in mourning. Hospice personnel believe that the mourners' needs, both before and after the death, are as important as the needs of the patient.

Unfortunately, many dying people never begin hospice care, or they enter it only in the last days before death. The reasons for this delay are detailed in Table EP.2. Currently in the United States, 60 percent of people die without hospice care; of the 40 percent in hospice, one-third die before the first week ends (National Center for Health Statistics, 2011). That is not long enough for the personal medical and emotional needs of a dying person and their loved ones to be assessed and satisfied.

One reason for the delay is that hospice care once meant certain death; a doctor had to certify that the person would die in less than six months. That admission was hard for doctors, patients, and family members. In fact, however, 16 percent of U.S.

✦ **ESPECIALLY FOR Relatives of a Person Who Is Dying** Why would a healthy person want the attention of hospice caregivers? (see response, page 586) →

Same Situation, Far Apart: As It Should Be Dying individuals and their families benefit from physical touch and suffer from medical practices (gowns, tubes, isolation) that restrict movement and prevent contact. A good death is likely for these two patients—a husband with his wife in their renovated hotel/hospital room in North Carolina *(left),* and a man with his family in a Catholic hospice in Andhra Pradesh, India *(right).*

hospice patients are discharged alive. Entering hospice still means that comfort takes precedence over cure, but sometimes that is enough for life to continue longer than expected.

Unfortunately, hospice care is far from universally available, even in wealthy nations, much less in developing ones (Kiernan, 2010). Hospice care is more common in England than in mainland Europe and more common in the western part of the United States than the southeastern part, but it is rare in poor nations. Even in one region (northern California) and among clients of one insurance company (Kaiser), the likelihood that people with terminal cancer will enter hospice depends on exactly where they live (N. L. Keating et al., 2006).

Cost is also a problem if the hospice is a separate institution where many skilled workers—doctors, nurses, psychologists, social workers, clergy, music therapists, and so on—provide individualized care day and night. Until recently, most insurance companies (including Medicare) did not cover hospice care unless the patient agreed to stop all measures that might cure the ailment. That has changed, but now many new hospice programs are for-profit, which may undercut the quality of care.

Home hospice care is less expensive, but caregivers are needed, day and night. Usually, such caregivers are family members, trained by hospice nurses, but not everyone

TABLE EP.2 Barriers to Entering Hospice Care

- Hospice patients must be terminally ill, with death anticipated within, on average, six months, but such predictions are difficult to make. For example, in one study of noncancer patients, physician predictions were 90 percent accurate for those who died within a week but only 13 percent accurate when death was predicted in three to six weeks (usually the patients died sooner) (Brandt et al., 2006).

- Patients and caregivers must accept death. Traditionally, entering a hospice meant the end of curative treatment (chemotherapy, dialysis, and so on). This is no longer true. Now treatment can continue, and death is estimated to occur, on average, at six months without treatment. That means many hospice patients survive for longer than six months, and some get so much better that they are discharged (Salpeter et al., 2012).

- Hospice care is expensive, especially if curative therapy continues. Many skilled workers—doctors, nurses, psychologists, social workers, clergy, music therapists, and so on—provide individualized care day and night.

- Availability varies. Hospice care is more common in England than in mainland Europe and is a luxury in poor nations. In the United States, western states have more hospices than southern states do. Even in one region (northern California) and among clients of one insurance company (Kaiser), the likelihood that people with terminal cancer will enter hospice depends on exactly where they live (N. L. Keating et al., 2006).

has such family members available. Because of hospice, the percentage of U.S. deaths that occur at home has been rising, but it is only 24 percent. Most deaths still occur in hospitals, with many others occurring in nursing homes (National Center for Health Statistics, 2011).

Given all this, it is not surprising that hospice care correlates with ethnicity, education, and income. In the United States, those of higher SES are more likely, and African Americans are less likely, to receive hospice care. When African Americans enter hospice care, they are more often admitted from a hospital than a home and are likely to die relatively quickly (one week, on average) (K.S. Johnson et al., 2011).

PALLIATIVE CARE The same "bad death" conditions that inspired the hospice movement have led to **palliative care,** a medical specialty that focuses on the relief of pain and suffering. Powerful painkillers were once prescribed sparingly until palliative care specialists alerted doctors that drug addiction is not a concern if a person is expected to die soon.

Morphine and other opiates have a **double effect:** They relieve pain (a positive effect), but they also slow down respiration (a negative effect). A painkiller that reduces both pain and breathing is considered acceptable in law, ethics, and medical practice. In England, for instance, although it is illegal to cause the death of a terminally ill patient (even one who repeatedly asks to die), it is legal to prescribe drugs that have a double effect. One-third of all English deaths include such drugs. Indeed, some people fear that heavy doses of narcotics are used to hasten death more than to relieve pain (Billings, 2011).

The continued sedation of someone who is dying is another method that is sometimes used to alleviate pain. Concerns have been raised that this is not prolonging life in any meaningful way (heavy sedation means the person is unconscious, unable to think or feel), but is merely avoiding death (Raus et al., 2011).

Deciding When Death Occurs

As implied in the discussion of palliative care, controversies have emerged because medical care has become more successful. In earlier times, death occurred when an organ shut down, but not now. Breathing continues with respirators, stopped hearts are restarted, stomach tubes provide calories, drugs fight pneumonia. At what point, if ever, should such measures be halted so that death will occur?

Ethical dilemmas arise in almost every life-threatening condition. Treatments are avoided, started, or stopped, prolonging life or hastening dying. This has fostered impassioned arguments about ethics, both between nations (evidenced by radically different laws) and within nations. Family members, religious advisers, doctors, and lawyers disagree among themselves and with one another (Ball, 2012; Engelhardt, 2012; Prado, 2008).

Historically, death was determined by listening to a person's heart: No heartbeat meant death. To make sure, a feather was put to the person's nose to indicate respiration—a person who did not exhale was pronounced dead. Very rarely, but widely publicized when it happened, a person was declared dead when in fact he or she was alive. Modern medicine has changed that: If an individual is still alive, but not capable of breathing on his or her own, respirators can pump air into the lungs and life can continue.

Many other life-support measures and medical interventions now circumvent the diseases and organ failures that once caused death. Checking breathing with feathers is a curiosity, thankfully never used today. But how can we know for sure when death has occurred?

In the late 1970s, a group of Harvard physicians concluded that when brain waves ceased, death occurred. This definition was accepted by a U.S. presidential

palliative care
Care designed not to treat an illness but to provide physical and emotional comfort to the patient and support and guidance to his or her family.

double effect
A situation in which an action (such as administering opiates) has both a positive effect (relieving a terminally ill person's pain) and a negative effect (hastening death by suppressing respiration).

RESPONSE FOR Relatives of a Person Who Is Dying (from page 584) Death affects the entire family, including children and grandchildren. I learned this myself when my mother was dying. A hospice nurse not only gave her pain medication (which made it easier for me to be with her) but also counseled me. At the nurse's suggestion, I asked for forgiveness. My mother indicated that there was nothing to forgive. We both felt a peace that would have eluded us without hospice care. ●

commission in 1981 and is used worldwide (Wijdicks et al., 2010). However, many doctors now suggest that death can occur even if primitive brain waves continue (Kellehear, 2008; Truog, 2007) (see Table EP.3).

Some researchers attempt to distinguish between people who are in a permanent vegetative state (and thus will never regain the ability to think) and those who are in a coma but could recover. Many scientists seek to define death more precisely than was possible even 30 years ago. One crucial factor is whether the person could ever again be expected to breathe without a respirator, but that is hard to guarantee if "ever again" includes the distant future.

In 2008, the American Academy of Neurology gathered experts to conduct a meta-analysis of all the recently published studies regarding end-of-life brain functioning. They found 38 empirical articles. Two experts independently read each one, noting what measures were used to determine death and how much time was required between lack of brain function and the pronouncement of a person's death. They reached no consensus. Only two indicators of death were confirmed: Dead people no longer breathe spontaneously, and their eyes no longer respond to pain.

As this article points out, the dying and those who love them need to know when a person is brain-dead, but there is not yet a definitive, instant test because there are "severe limitations in the current evidence base" (Wijdicks et al., 2010, p. 1914). Thus, family members may spend weeks, sometimes months or years, hoping for life long after medical experts believe no recovery is possible.

ETHICAL QUANDARIES Many elderly people fear being kept alive too long when death is near, and many younger people fear dying too soon. Death can now be postponed with antibiotics and other drugs, surgery, respirators, and stomach tubes, which is partly why the average person today lives twice as long as the average person did a century ago. These measures raise new ethical questions—especially regarding suicide and euthanasia.

In **passive euthanasia,** a person nearing death is simply allowed to die in due course. The chart of a patient may include a **DNR (do not resuscitate)** order, which instructs the medical staff not to restore breathing or restart the heart if breathing or pulsating stops. A DNR usually reflects the expressed wishes of the patient or health care proxy (discussed below).

Passive euthanasia is legal everywhere, but many emergency personnel start artificial respiration and stimulate hearts without taking time to read the chart to ascertain whether DNR has been chosen. Then the issue becomes more complex because removing life support may be considered active euthanasia.

Active euthanasia is deliberately doing something to cause a person's death, such as turning off a respirator before a person has been declared brain dead or giving the person a lethal drug. Some physicians perform active euthanasia when confronted with three conditions: (1) suffering they cannot relieve, (2) illness they cannot cure, and (3) a patient who wants to die. Active euthanasia is legal under some circumstances in the Netherlands, Belgium, Luxembourg, and Switzerland, but it is illegal (yet rarely prosecuted) elsewhere.

Many people see a major moral distinction between active and passive euthanasia, although the final result is the same. A survey of physicians in the United States found that while a majority (69 percent) objected to active euthanasia, few (18 percent) objected to sedation that had a double effect. Even fewer (5 percent) objected

---

TABLE EP.3 Dead or Not? Yes, No, and Maybe

Brain death: Prolonged cessation of all brain activity with complete absence of voluntary movements; no spontaneous breathing; no response to pain, noise, and other stimuli. Brain waves have ceased; the electroencephalogram is flat; *the person is dead.*

Locked-in syndrome: The person cannot move, except for the eyes, but normal brain waves are still apparent; *the person is not dead.*

Coma: A state of deep unconsciousness from which the person cannot be aroused. Some people awaken spontaneously from a coma; others enter a vegetative state; *the person is not yet dead.*

Vegetative state: A state of deep unconsciousness in which all cognitive functions are absent, although eyes may open, sounds may be emitted, and breathing may continue; *the person is not yet dead.* The vegetative state can be *transient, persistent,* or *permanent.* No one has ever recovered after two years; most who recover (about 15 percent) improve within three weeks (Preston & Kelly, 2006). After sufficient time has elapsed, the person may, effectively, be dead, although exactly how many days that requires is not yet determined (Wijdicks et al., 2010).

---

passive euthanasia
A situation in which a seriously ill person is allowed to die naturally, through the cessation of medical intervention.

DNR (do not resuscitate) order
A written order from a physician (sometimes initiated by a patient's advance directive or by a health care proxy's request) that no attempt should be made to revive a patient if he or she suffers cardiac or respiratory arrest.

active euthanasia
A situation in which someone takes action to bring about another person's death, with the intention of ending that person's suffering.

physician-assisted suicide
A form of active euthanasia in which a doctor provides the means for someone to end his or her own life.

to withdrawing life support when a patient was brain-dead (Curlin et al., 2008). A similar survey in seven other nations found wide variations within and among them, with some physicians saying they would never perform active euthanasia and others reporting they had done so (Löfmark et al., 2008).

Between passive and active euthanasia is another end-of-life option: Someone may provide the means for an alert patient to end his or her own life. Some people advocate **physician-assisted suicide,** whereby a doctor provides lethal medication that a patient can then swallow in order to die.

The state of Oregon has legalized physician-assisted suicide, explicitly asserting that such deaths should be called "death with dignity," not suicide. No matter what the name, acceptance varies markedly by culture (Prado, 2008). Reasons have less to do with experience with dying than with religion, education, and local values (Verbakel & Jaspers, 2010).

For example, in some Asian nations, suicides may be noble, as when Buddhist monks publicly burned themselves to death to advocate Tibetan independence from China, or when people choose to die for the honor of their nation or themselves. However, in the United States, physicians of Asian heritage are *less* likely to condone physician-assisted suicide than are non-Asian physicians (Curlin et al., 2008).

This reluctance of doctors to speed death helps explain a practice in Thailand. When everyone agrees that a hospitalized patient will inevitably die soon, an ambulance takes that person back home, where death can occur without medical interference. Then the person, and the family, can benefit from a better understanding of life, suffering, and death (Stonington, 2012).

Radical or Conventional? Since most voters and legislators oppose physician-assisted suicide, this woman advocating death with dignity might seem to be radical. However, she is from Oregon, and she is elderly, which makes her fear of prolonged dying not unusual at all.

WHEN DOCTORS HELP PEOPLE DIE The Netherlands has permitted active euthanasia and physician-assisted suicide since 1980 and refined the law in 2002. The patient must be clear and aware in making the request, and the goal is to halt "unbearable suffering" (Buiting et al., 2009). Consequently, the physician's first response is to make the suffering bearable, usually by increasing or changing medication.

However a qualitative analysis found that "fatigue, pain, decline, negative feelings, loss of self, fear of future suffering, dependency, loss of autonomy, being worn out, being a burden, loneliness, loss of all that makes life worth living, hopelessness, pointlessness and being tired of living were constituent elements of unbearable suffering" (Dees et al., 2011, p. 727). Obviously, medication cannot alleviate all those.

Two other nations near the Netherlands—Belgium and Luxembourg—passed similar laws. One reason is that they saw that Dutch people who choose medical help to die are a tiny minority, perhaps 2 percent of those who die (van Alphen et al., 2010; van der Heide et al., 2007). Likewise, Switzerland has explicitly declined to prosecute doctors who hasten death, although there are no Swiss regulations as to when doctors may, and may not, hasten death.

Oregon voters approved physician-assisted "death with dignity" (but not other forms of active euthanasia) in 1994 and again in 1997. The first such legal deaths occurred in 1998. The law requires the following:

● The dying person must be an adult and an Oregon resident.

● The dying person must request the lethal drugs twice orally and once in writing.

● Fifteen days must elapse between the first request and the prescription.

● Two physicians must confirm that the person is terminally ill, has less than six months to live, and is competent (i.e., not mentally impaired or depressed).

The law also requires record-keeping and annual reporting. About one-third of the requests are granted, and about one-third of those who are approved never take the drugs. They want the deadly drugs in case they need them, but they choose to die naturally.

Between 1998 and 2011, more than 160,000 people in Oregon died. Only 596 of them obtained prescriptions for lethal drugs and used them to die. Note that a diagnosis of terminal illness is required to allow for physician-assisted suicide in Oregon; intense pain itself is not considered a necessary or sufficient reason.

As Table EP.4 shows, Oregon residents requested the drugs primarily for psychological, not biological, reasons—they were more concerned about their autonomy than their pain. In 2011 alone, 114 Oregonians obtained lethal prescriptions, and 65 used them to die. Most of the rest died naturally, but some were still alive at the end of that year and thought they might use the drug in the future (according to data from previous years, about 10 percent of the people who obtain the prescription save it to use in the following year) (Oregon Department of Human Services, 2012).

TABLE EP.4 Oregon Residents' Reasons for Requesting Physician Assistance in Dying, 1998–2011

Reason	Patients Giving Reason (%)
Loss of autonomy	91
Less able to enjoy life	88
Loss of dignity	83
Loss of control over body	54
Burden on others	36
Pain	23

Source: Oregon Public Health Division, 2012.

slippery slope
The argument that a given action will start a chain of events that will culminate in an undesirable outcome.

OPPOSING PERSPECTIVES

The "Right to Die"?

Many people fear that legalizing euthanasia or physician-assisted suicide will create a **slippery slope,** which means that hastening death at the request of the dying will cause society to slide toward killing people who are *not* ready to die—especially the disabled, the old, the minorities, and the poor.

The 2002 revision of the Netherlands law allows euthanasia not only when a person is terminally ill but also when a person is chronically ill and in pain. Is this evidence of a slide? Some people think so, especially those who believe that God alone decides the moment of death, and that anyone who interferes is defying God.

Arguing against that, a cancer specialist writes:

To be forced to continue living a life that one deems intolerable when there are doctors who are willing either to end one's life or to assist one in ending one's own life, is an unspeakable violation of an individual's freedom to live—and to die—as he or she sees fit. Those who would deny patients a legal right to euthanasia or assisted suicide typically appeal to two arguments: a "slippery slope" argument, and an argument about the dangers of abuse. Both are scare tactics, the rhetorical force of which exceeds their logical strength.

[Benatar, 2011, p. 206]

In Oregon the oldest-old, the poor, and those of non-European heritage are *less* likely to use the fatal prescriptions. In fact, in 2011, of those who died with physician-assisted suicide, most were European American (96 percent), had health insurance, were well educated (82 percent had attended college), and had lived a long life (average age was

70)—but not so long that, if it were not for their illness, they were a burden for society. Almost all died at home, with close friends or family nearby.

All these statistics are used to refute both the slippery slope and the social abuse arguments, because these people were not likely to slide anywhere they did not wish to go, nor were they likely to be pushed to die. Nonetheless, even those who agree that people should make their own choices are not sure they will ever, personally, choose death. African Americans are particularly mistrustful of hospices, euthanasia, and physician-assisted suicide (Wicher & Meeker, 2012).

An influential review of 25 years of data, official and unofficial, from Oregon and the Netherlands found

no evidence of heightened risk for the elderly, women, the uninsured (inapplicable in the Netherlands, where all are insured), people with low educational status, the poor, the physically disabled or chronically ill, minors, people with psychiatric illnesses including depression, or racial or ethnic minorities, compared with background populations.

[Battin et al., 2007, p. 591]

Yet not everyone agrees with the conclusions of Battin and others. Might people who decide to die be depressed? As you know, depression is common and usually treatable, but many people do not realize they are depressed. If they are depressed, that should prohibit physicians from prescribing lethal drugs (Finlay & George, 2011). Declining ability to do enjoyable activities is cited by 88 percent of Oregonians who request physician-assisted suicide. Is that a sign of sanity or depression?

Worldwide, most voters and lawmakers do not believe that laws need to be revised to give people freedom to die as they wish. Indeed, those with disabling and painful conditions who choose medical treatments to prolong life are admired. Even where it is legal, few of the terminally ill choose assisted suicide, and no one wants anyone else to choose for them. In a jesting post on the Canadian Broadcasting Company Blog, a young man made that point:

> If I want to commit suicide, and someone wants to help hold the rope or whatever, fine. What are friends for? I do have a problem with someone assisting in my suicide if I wasn't planning on being suicidal that day. There are some people that I would love to assist though. Often I will ask people if I can assist in their suicide, most say no, well, all of them have said no.

> [Twomey, 2011]

In the state of Washington, just north of Oregon, 58 percent of the voters approved a death with dignity law in November 2008; in 2009, Luxembourg joined the Netherlands and Belgium in allowing active euthanasia; in 2011, the Montana senate voted against a bill that would outlaw physician-assisted suicide; and in 2012, a legal scholar contends that the U.S. constitution's defense of liberty includes the freedom to decide how to die (Ball, 2012).

All that might seem like a growing trend, but proposals to legalize physician-assisted suicide have been defeated in several U.S. states and other nations. Most jurisdictions recognize the dilemma, in that they do not prosecute doctors who help people die, as long as it is done privately and quietly. Opposing perspectives, and diametrically opposed individual choices, are evident.

● **UNDERSTANDING THE NUMBERS**
Is the rate of physician-assisted suicide higher in the Netherlands or in Oregon?

Answer The rate is low in both places, but it is higher in the Netherlands—17 physician-assisted deaths per 1,000 deaths, compared with about 4 per 1,000 in Oregon.

living will
A document that indicates what medical intervention an individual prefers if he or she is not conscious when a decision is to be expressed. For example, some do not want to be given mechanical breathing.

health care proxy
A person chosen by another person to make medical decisions if the second person becomes unable to do so.

ADVANCE DIRECTIVES Many people hope to increase personal choice about death, but they stop short of legalizing medical assistance. For example, a massive effort in Hawaii to inform people about end-of-life issues resulted in *less* support for physician-assisted suicide but *more* support for advance directives—an individual's instructions regarding end-of-life medical care, written before such care is needed (K. L. Braun et al., 2005).

Even this is controversial. An original part of the U.S. health care bill passed in 2010 allowed doctors to be paid for informing the dying of their treatment options—a measure that had the support of many physicians (e.g., Kettl, 2010). That provision was labeled "death panels" by some opponents of the bill, a phrase that almost torpedoed the entire package of benefits. As a result, that measure was scrapped: Physicians are not paid for telling a person about palliative care.

Some people try to exert control over their dying by creating a living will and/or assigning a health care proxy. Recognizing that individuals differ dramatically on specifics, hospitals and hospices strongly recommend both of these. Nonetheless, most people resist: A study of cancer patients in a leading hospital found that only 16 percent had living wills and only 48 percent had designated a proxy (Halpern et al., 2011).

A **living will** indicates what sort of medical intervention a person wants or does not want in the event that he or she becomes unable to express those preferences. (If the person is conscious, hospital personnel ask about each specific procedure, often requiring written consent before surgery. Patients who are conscious and lucid can choose to override any instructions they wrote earlier in their living will.)

The reason a person might want to override their own earlier wishes is that living wills include phrases such as "incurable," "reasonable chance of recovery," and "extraordinary measures," and it is difficult to know what those phrases mean until a specific issue arises. Doctors and family members also disagree about what is "extraordinary" or "reasonable."

Some people designate a **health care proxy,** another person to make medical decisions for them if they become unable to do so. That seems logical, but unfortunately neither a living will nor a health care proxy guarantees that medical care will be exactly what a person would choose. For one thing, designated proxies often find it difficult to allow a loved one to die if there is any chance of recovery.

A larger problem is that few people—experts included—understand the risks, benefits, and alternatives to every medical procedure. That makes it difficult to decide for oneself, much less for a family member, exactly when the risks outweigh the benefits. Even people who have been married for years do not necessarily know their partner's wishes; husbands are more likely than wives to believe they know, but are less likely to be accurate (Zettel-Watson et al., 2008). Family members may be on opposite sides when it comes to specifics.

A heartbreaking example occurred in the case of Theresa (Terri) Schiavo, who was 26 years old when her heart suddenly stopped. Emergency personnel restarted her heart, but she fell into a deep coma. Like almost everyone her age, Terri had no advance directives. A court designated Michael, her husband of six years, as her health care proxy.

Michael attempted many measures to bring back his wife, but after 11 years he accepted her doctors' repeated diagnosis: Terri was in a persistent vegetative state. He petitioned to have her feeding tube removed. The court agreed, noting the testimony of witnesses who said that Terri had told them that she never wanted to be on life support. Terri's parents appealed the decision, but lost. They then pleaded with the public.

The Florida legislature responded, passing a law that required that the tube be reinserted. After three more years of legal wrangling, the U.S. Supreme Court ruled that the lower courts were correct. By this point, every North American newspaper and TV station was following the case. Congress passed a law requiring that artificial feeding be continued, but that law, too, was overturned as unconstitutional. The stomach tube was removed, and Terri died on March 31, 2005—although some maintained that she had really died 15 years earlier.

Partly because of the conflicts among family members, and between appointed judges and elected politicians, Terri's case caught media attention, inspiring vigils and protests. Lost in that blitz are the thousands of other mothers and fathers, husbands and wives, sons and daughters, judges and legislators, doctors and nurses who struggle less publicly with similar issues.

One way to help with the specifics of end-of-life decisions is to fill out the Five Wishes, available online as of 2011. Among the many possible choices listed therein are medication to relieve pain as well as to sedate; life support (or not) if in a coma and not expected to recover; life support (or not) with permanent, severe brain damage; warm baths and oils, music, tooth- and hair-brushing, photo displays of loved ones; praying by the bedside, hand-holding, and conversation.

Advance directives are intended to help caregivers avoid conflicts, but in any case, honest conversation is needed long before a crisis occurs (Sabatino, 2010). Dying is hard to talk about, much less accept. Thanatologists wish otherwise.

✦ **ESPECIALLY FOR People Without Advance Directives** Why do very few young adults have advance directives? (see response, page 592) →

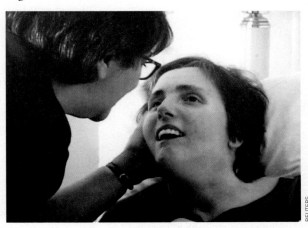

REUTERS

Is She Thinking? This photo of Terri Schiavo with her mother was released by those who believed Terri could recover. Other photos (not released) and other signs told the opposite story. Although autopsy showed that Terri's brain had shrunk markedly, remember that hope is part of being human. It is easy to understand why some people were passionately opposed to removal of Terri's stomach tube.

KEY points

- Modern medicine has made some aspects of a good death more likely but has also added complexities, including the possibility of physician action to hasten death.
- Honest conversation, hospice care, and palliative medicine have all made dying easier than when almost everyone died alone, in hospitals.
- Determining when death has occurred, or when a dying person cannot recover, is not always obvious.
- Living wills, health care proxies, and the Five Wishes form can prevent some family conflicts and help people die as they wish.

grief
The deep sorrow that people feel at the death of another. Grief is personal and unpredictable.

RESPONSE FOR People Without Advance Directives (from page 591) Young adults tend to avoid thinking realistically about their own deaths. This attitude is emotional, not rational. The actual task of preparing the documents is easy (the forms can be downloaded; no lawyer is needed). Young adults have no trouble doing other future-oriented things, such as getting a tetanus shot or enrolling in a pension plan. ●

Affirmation of Life

Grief and mourning are part of living. Humans need relationships with many others in order to survive and thrive, but every person who reaches adulthood experiences the death of someone they know. Grief can turn into depression or can become a reason to live life more deeply.

Grief

Grief is the powerful sorrow that an individual feels at the death of another. It is a highly personal emotion, an anguish that overtakes daily life.

NORMAL GRIEF The first thing to understand about grief is that it is a normal human emotion, even when it leads to unusual actions and thoughts. Grief is manifest in uncontrollable crying, sleeplessness, and irrational and delusional thoughts—the "magical thinking" Joan Didion described:

> Grief has no distance. Grief comes in waves, paroxysms, sudden apprehensions that weaken the knees and blind the eyes and obliterate the dailiness of life. . . . I see now that my insistence on spending that first night alone was more complicated than it seemed, a primitive instinct. . . . There was a level on which I believed that what had happened remained reversible. That is why I needed to be alone. . . . I needed to be alone so that he could come back. This was the beginning of my year of magical thinking.
>
> *[Didion, 2005, pp. 27, 32, 33]*

It is normal to be overtaken by grief when a loved one dies. Loneliness, denial, anger, and sorrow come in rapid waves, and the normal human needs—to sleep, to eat—temporarily give way. Grief usually hits hardest in the first week after death and then lingers—with much dependent on mourning, soon to be discussed. But first, let us recognize that grief is not always normal (Qualls & Kasl-Godley, 2010; van der Houwen et al., 2010).

COMPLICATED GRIEF In recent times, death has become a more private, less religious event. As a result, new complications in the grieving process have emerged.

Protecting the Survivors These young women—Emily Lopez (kneeling), Karina Barba (lighting candle), and Renee Hewlett (standing)—were at the midnight showing of *The Dark Knight Rises* when James Holmes shot and killed 12 people. Their participation in this vigil outside that Colorado movie theater may help them avoid survivor's guilt, an emotion that sometimes cripples people who see someone nearby suffer an untimely death.

Emblematic of this change are funeral trends in the United States: Whereas older generations prefer burial after a traditional funeral, younger generations are likely to prefer small memorial services after cremation.

This may, in the abstract, seem a simpler, more rational way to deal with death, but that is not always the case: Decisions about what to do with the ashes after cremation may be fraught with denial and controversy and thus complicate grief (Cranwell, 2010). About 10 percent of all mourners experience what is known as **complicated grief,** a type of grief that impedes the person's future life (Neimeyer & Currier, 2009).

Perhaps surprisingly, one complication is called **absent grief,** when a bereaved person does not seem to grieve. This may be a first reaction, as some people cannot face the reality of the death, but if it continues, absent grief can trigger physical or psychological symptoms—for instance, trouble breathing or walking, sudden panic attacks, or depression. If such disabilities appear for no reason, the underlying cause might be grief that was never expressed.

Absent grief may be more common in modern society than it was earlier. People who live and work where no one knows their personal lives have no community or recognized customs to help them grieve. Indeed, for workers at large corporations or students in universities, grief becomes "an unwelcome intrusion (or violent intercession) into the normal efficient running of everyday life" (M. Anderson, 2001, p. 141). This leads to isolation—exactly the opposite of what bereaved people need.

Modern life also increases the incidence of **disenfranchised grief,** wherein the bereaved are not allowed to mourn publicly because of cultural customs or social restrictions. Typically, only a current spouse or close blood relative decides on funeral arrangements, disposal of the body, and other matters. This made sense when all adults were closely connected to their relatives, but it may result in "gagged grief and beleaguered bereavement" when, for instance, a long-time but unmarried partner is excluded (L. Green & Grant, 2008, p. 275).

There are many people who are disenfranchised in their grieving, who feel the powerful emotion but cannot express it. The deceased's unmarried lover (of the same or other sex), a divorced spouse, young children, and close friends at work may be excluded (perhaps by the relatives, either deliberately or through ignorance) from saying goodbye to the dying person, viewing the corpse, or participating in the aftermath of death. Parents may grieve the loss of a fetus or newborn, but others may dismiss their sorrow, saying, "You never knew that child; you can have another."

Another possible complication is **incomplete grief.** Murders and suicides often trigger police investigations and press reports, which interfere with the grief process. An autopsy undercuts grieving if someone believes that the body will rise again or that the soul does not leave the body immediately. The inability to recover a body, as happens for soldiers who are missing in action or victims of a major flood or fire, may not allow grief to be expressed and then to dissipate.

Sometimes events interrupt the responses of the community. When death occurs on a major holiday, immediately after another death or disaster, or during wartime, it is harder for the survivors to grieve because the social network is not responsive.

For example, one widow whose husband died of cancer on September 10, 2001, complained, "People who attended the funeral talked only about the terrorist attack of September 11, and my husband wasn't given the respect he deserved"

complicated grief
A type of grief that impedes a person's future life, usually because the person clings to sorrow or is buffeted by contradictory emotions.

absent grief
A situation in which mourners do not grieve, either because other people do not allow grief to be expressed or because the mourners do not allow themselves to feel sadness.

disenfranchised grief
A situation in which certain people, although they are bereaved, are prevented from mourning publicly by cultural customs or social restrictions.

incomplete grief
A situation in which circumstances, such as a police investigation or an autopsy, interfere with the process of grieving.

Empty Boots The body of a young army corporal killed near Baghdad has been shipped home to his family in Mississippi for a funeral and burial, but his fellow soldiers in Iraq also need to express their grief. The custom is to hold an informal memorial service, placing the dead soldier's boots, helmet, and rifle in the middle of a circle of mourners, who weep, pray, and reminisce.

AP PHOTO / JOHN MOORE

(quoted in Schachter, 2003, p. 20). Although she expressed concern for her husband, it is apparent that she herself needed sympathy.

After natural or human-caused disasters, including hurricanes and wars, many people die of causes not directly attributable to the disaster, becoming victims of the indifference of others and of their own diminished self-care. The same thing can happen to an individual after a close family member dies.

I can see this in my own family. My father died 5 months after my mother died, even though my brother and I tried to get him involved in activities he could not participate in when she was alive and bedridden. Although I did not expect his death, it is not uncommon for widows and widowers to die within a year of losing their spouse if they have been married for a long time. Children are also more vulnerable after a parent dies: Caregivers need to be more sensitive and vigilant, because survivors are not as adept at caring for themselves.

In a minor way, I also experienced this with my daughter. Bethany was driving to her father's memorial service when her car spun into a ditch. She was fine (thanks to her seat belt), but the car was disabled. She said she hit a patch of black ice. I am sure that is true, but I also suspect that she was not being as careful as usual.

Mourning

mourning
The ceremonies and behaviors that a religion or culture prescribes for people to employ in expressing their bereavement after a death.

Grief splinters people into jumbled pieces, making them vulnerable. Mourning reassembles them, making them whole again and able to rejoin the larger community. To be more specific, **mourning** is the public and ritualistic expression of bereavement, the ceremonies and behaviors that a religion or culture prescribes to honor the dead.

HOW MOURNING HELPS Mourning is needed because, as we just read, the grief-stricken are vulnerable not only to irrational thoughts but also to self-destructive acts. Physical as well as mental health dips in the recently bereaved, and the rate of suicide increases (Ajdacic-Gross et al., 2008; Elwert & Christakis, 2008).

Same Situation, Far Apart: Gateway to Heaven or Final Rest Many differences are obvious between a Roman Catholic burial in Mbongolwane, South Africa *(left),* and a Buddhist funeral procession before cremation in Bali, Indonesia *(right).* In both places, however, friends and neighbors gather to honor the dead person and to comfort his or her family members.

Mourning customs are designed to move grief from loss toward reaffirmation (Harlow, 2005). For this reason, eulogies emphasize the dead person's good qualities; people who did not personally know the deceased person attend wakes, funerals, or memorial services to help comfort the survivors.

If the dead person was a public figure, mourners may include thousands, even millions. They express their sorrow to one another, weep as they watch funerals on television, and pledge to affirm the best of the deceased, forgetting any criticisms they might have had.

One function of mourning is to allow expression of grief publicly and then to limit acute personal grief. Examples include the Jewish custom of sitting shiva at home for a week, or the three days of active sorrow among some Muslim groups, or 10 days of ceremonies beginning at the next full moon following a death in Hinduism. Memories often return on the anniversary of a death, so many cultures include annual rituals such as visiting a grave or lighting a candle.

Among many people, religious practices such as these have been replaced with memorial services, with less ritual. Some fear that a deficit of mourning may undercut survivors' ability to grasp the meaning of life, grief, and death.

For example, one Christian theologian believes that modern customs and ideology have weakened mourning, making it almost inevitable that

> the dead with their embarrassing bodies would be banned from their own funerals and the living would be condemned to sit motionless, contemplating the meaning of it all and pretending to celebrate life as the nephew of the deceased sings "When Irish Eyes Are Smiling."
>
> *[Long, 2009, p. 76]*

PLACING BLAME AND SEEKING MEANING A common impulse after death is for the survivors to assess blame—for medical measures not taken, laws not enforced, unhealthy habits not changed. The bereaved sometimes blame the dead person, sometimes themselves, and sometimes others. In November 2011, Michael Jackson's personal doctor, Conrad Murray, was found guilty and jailed for prescribing the drugs that led to his death. Many fans and family members cheered at the verdict; Murray was one of the few who blamed Jackson, not himself.

For public tragedies, nations accuse one another. Blame is not rational; for instance, outrage at the assassination of Archduke Francis Ferdinand of Austria by a Serbian terrorist in 1914 provoked a conflict between Austria and Serbia, joined by a dozen other nations, leading to the four years and 16 million deaths of World War I.

As you remember, denial and anger appear first on Kübler-Ross's list of reactions to death; ideally, people move on to acceptance. The need to find meaning may be crucial to the reaffirmation that follows grief. In some cases, this search starts with preserving memories: Displaying photographs and personal effects and telling anecdotes about the dead person are central to many memorial services. Especially when a death is sudden and traumatic, mourners—including those who were agnostic before the death—often find comfort in religious practices and beliefs (Chapple et al., 2011).

Mourners may also be helped by strangers who have experienced a similar loss, especially

Life in the Balance The death of a young child is especially devastating to families. This girl is in a hospital in Bangladesh; she is suffering from cholera, which kills more than 2,000 children a year worldwide, most of them in areas with unsafe water supplies.

OBSERVATION QUIZ
Is this girl likely to die? (see answer, page 597) →

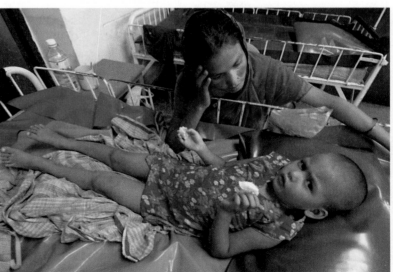

Mommy's Memorial Praying beside the ghost bike at the spot where an 18-wheeler killed cyclist Kathryn Rickson may help these two grieve and then recover. Grief is much less likely to destroy the survivors when markers or rituals are observed.

when friends are unlikely to understand. This explains why groups have been organized for parents of murdered children, mothers whose adolescents were killed by drunk drivers, widows of firefighters who died at the World Trade Center, relatives of passengers who died in the same plane crash, and so on.

Mourners sometimes want strangers to know about a death. Pages of paid obituaries are found in every major newspaper, and spontaneous memorials (graffiti, murals, stuffed animals, flowers) appear in public spaces, such as a spot on a roadside where a fatal crash occurred. This practice was once rare and discouraged, but no longer. Authorities realize that public commemoration aids grief and mourning, building community: Public markers of bouquets and so on are dismantled only when flowers fade and complaints are lodged after time has passed (Dickinson & Hoffmann, 2010).

Organizations devoted to causes such as fighting cancer and banning handguns find their most dedicated supporters among people who have lost a loved one to that particular circumstance. Often when someone dies, the close family designates a charity that is somehow connected to the deceased, inviting other mourners to make contributions.

To make a death meaningful, mourning may lead to public protest:

- When a truck killed a 9-year-old in Germany, neighbors and strangers blocked the street for days until new safeguards were installed.
- When a cyclist was killed by a car, other cyclists erected "ghost bikes" and ritualistically raised their bicycles, leading to a plethora of new bike lanes in New York City (Rulfs, 2011; Dobler, 2011).

Obviously, the impulse to blame and seek meaning are not always constructive. Revenge sometimes arises, even leading to long-standing and often fatal feuds between one family, one gang, or one cultural, ethnic, or religious group and another.

In general, the normal grief reaction is intense and irrational at first, but it gradually eases as time, social support, and traditions help with the initial outpouring of emotion and then with the search for meaning and reaffirmation. The individual may engage in *grief work,* experiencing and expressing strong emotions and then moving toward wholeness, which includes recognizing the larger story of human life and death.

Diversity of Reactions

Bereaved people depend on the customs and attitudes of their community, as well as on their social network, to guide them through their irrational thoughts and grief. Particulars depend on the specific culture. For example, mourners who keep the dead person's possessions, talk to the deceased, and frequently review memories are notably *less* well-adjusted 18 months after the death if they live in the United States but are *better* adjusted if they live in China (Lalande & Bonanno, 2006).

LEGACY OF EARLIER LOSS Childhood experiences also affect bereavement. A child who lost her parents might be more distraught decades later when someone else dies. Attachment history may also be important (Hansson & Stroebe, 2007). Older adults who were securely attached may be more likely to experience normal grief; those whose attachment was insecure-avoidant may have absent grief; and those who were insecure-resistant may become stuck, unable to find meaning in death and thus unable to reaffirm their own lives.

Reaffirmation does not mean forgetting the dead person; many *continuing bonds* are evident years after death (Stroebe et al., 2010). Although in Western nations having hallucinations of the dead person (seeing ghosts, hearing voices) is a sign of complicated grief, continuing bonds such as thinking about memories and seeing the dead person as a role model are "linked to greater personal growth" (Field & Filanosky, 2009, p. 20). Often survivors write letters to the deceased person, or talk to them, or consider events—a sunrise, a butterfly, a rainstorm—as messages of comfort from the dead person.

Bereavement theory once held that mourners should grieve, then move on and realize that the dead person is gone forever. It was thought that if this did not happen, pathological grief could result, with the person either not grieving enough (absent grief) or grieving too long (incomplete grief). Current research finds a much wider variety of reactions.

ANSWER TO **OBSERVATION QUIZ** (from page 595) No. She is in a hospital, where she can receive the oral rehydration that saves almost every cholera patient. She has two additional advantages: an attentive mother and no signs of malnutrition. ●

A VIEW FROM SCIENCE

Resilience After a Death

Earlier studies overestimated the frequency of pathological grief. For obvious reasons, scientists usually began research on mourning with mourners—that is, with people who had recently experienced the death of a loved one. They did not analyze personality before the death, yet we now know that personality traits powerfully affect grief (Boyraz, 2012).

Furthermore, psychiatrists often studied people who needed psychological help, again for obvious reasons. Some patients experienced absent grief; others felt disenfranchised grief; some were overcome by unremitting sadness many months after the loss; still others could not find meaning in a violent, sudden, unexpected death. All these people consulted therapists, who often helped them and described the problems and the solutions.

Such mourners are *not* typical. Almost everyone experiences several deaths over a lifetime—of parents and grandparents, of a spouse or close friend. Most feel sadness at first but then resume their customary activities, functioning as well a few months later as they did before. And only a small subset, about 10 to 15 percent, exhibit extreme or complicated grief (Bonanno & Lilienfeld, 2008).

The variety of grief reactions was evident in a longitudinal study that began by interviewing and assessing married older adults in greater Detroit. Over several years, 319 became widows or widowers. Most were reinterviewed at 6 and 18 months after the death of their spouse, and about one-third were seen again four years later (Boerner et al., 2004, 2005).

General trends were evident. Almost all the widows and widowers idealized their past marriages, a normal phenomenon that other research finds connected to psychological health, not pathology (O'Rourke et al., 2010b). In the Detroit study, recollections after death were rosier than the descriptions they had given of their relationships when their spouse was still alive. Many thought of their spouse several times each day immediately after the death; with time, such thoughts became less frequent.

Reactions to the spouse's death were originally clustered into five categories (Boerner et al., 2004, 2005) and then, using updated statistical techniques, into four final categories (Galatzer-Levy & Bonanno, 2012).

1. Sixty-six percent were resilient. They were sad at first, but 6 months later they were about as happy and productive as they had been before the death.
2. Ten percent were *less* depressed after the death than before, perhaps because they had been caregivers for their seriously ill partners.
3. Nine percent were slow to recover, functioning poorly at 18 months. By four years after the death, however, they functioned almost as well as they had before. This slow recovery suggests that some of them had complicated grief.
4. Fifteen percent were depressed at every assessment, before as well as years after the death. If this research had begun only after the death, it might seem that the loss caused depression. However, the pre-loss assessment suggests that these people were chronically depressed, not stuck in grief.

This research study (and others like it) shows that grief and then recovery are the usual pattern. A person's health, finances, and personality all contribute to postmortem reactions. Crucial are the person's beliefs before the death (Mancini et al., 2011). If a person tends to have a positive perspective, believing that justice will prevail and that life has meaning, then the death of a close family member is likely to deepen, not weaken, those beliefs. Depression is less likely if a person has already accepted the reality of death—one reason this Epilogue is part of this text.

PRACTICAL APPLICATIONS The research suggests that when someone is grieving, it is common to experience powerful, complicated, and unexpected emotions. To help the griever, a friend should listen and sympathize, never implying that the person is too grief-stricken or not grief-stricken enough.

A bereaved person *might or might not* want to visit the grave, light a candle, cherish a memento, pray, or sob. Whatever the action, he or she may want to be alone or may want company. Those who have been taught to bear grief stoically may be doubly distressed if a friend advises them to cry but they cannot. Conversely, those whose cultures expect loud wailing may resent it if they are urged to hush.

Even absent grief—in which the bereaved person refuses to do any of these things— might be appropriate. So might the opposite reaction, when people want to talk again and again about their loss, gathering sympathy, ascribing blame, and finding meaning.

It may help to express emotions through action—by joining a bereavement group; protesting some policy; planting a garden; walking, running, or biking to raise money for a cause. Remember the 7-year-old boy whose grandparents, uncle, and dog (Twick) died? He wrote a memorial poem for Twick, which his parents framed and hung in the living room. That comforted him. He agreed to return to school (K. R. Kaufman & Kaufman, 2006).

No matter what rituals are followed or what pattern is evident, the result may give the living a deeper appreciation of themselves and others. In fact, a theme frequently sounded by those who work with the dying and the bereaved is that death leads to a greater appreciation of life, especially of the value of intimate, caring relationships. In the example of the chimpanzees on page 574, Jane Goodall implied that if Flint's sister had been nearby to help him mourn, he would not have been alone with his grief and would not have died.

George Vaillant is a psychiatrist who studied a group of men from the time they were Harvard students through old age. He writes about funerals: "With tears of remembrance running down our cheeks. . . . Remembered love lives triumphantly today" (Vaillant, 2008, p. 133).

It is fitting to end this Epilogue, and this book, with a reminder of the creative work of living. As first described in Chapter 1, the study of human development is a science, with topics to be researched, understood, and explained. But the process of living is an art as well as a science, with strands of love and sorrow woven into each person's unique tapestry. Death, when it leads to hope; dying, when it is accepted; and grief, when it fosters affirmation—all add meaning to birth, growth, development, and love.

KEYpoints

- Grief is an overpowering and irrational emotion, a normal reaction when a loved one dies.
- Grief can be complicated—continuing too long, absent, or disenfranchised.
- Mourning is a social and cultural process to help people move past grief and reaffirm life.
- Among the common reactions to death are to blame someone and to seek meaning in the death. These can be either helpful or destructive.

SUMMARY

Death and Hope

1. Thanatology is the study of death and dying, a topic that has always led to strong emotions. Currently, fewer people have personally witnessed the dying process than in the past.

2. In ancient times, death was considered a connection between the living, the dead, and the spirit world. People respected the dead and tried to live their lives so that their own death and afterlife would be good.

3. Every religion includes rituals and beliefs about death. These vary a great deal, but all bring hope to the living and strengthen the community.

4. Death has various meanings, depending partly on the age of the person involved and whether that person is dying or mourning. For example, young children are more concerned about being separated from those they see every day whereas adults tend to worry about leaving something undone or abandoning family members, especially children.

5. Terror management theory finds that some emerging adults cope with anxiety about death by defiantly doing whatever is considered risky for their health. Adults are concerned about their own life plans; older adults are more accepting of death.

Choices in Dying

6. Everyone wants a good death—painless, at the end of a long life. This may be more possible today than earlier. However, other aspects of a good death—quick, at home, surrounded by loved ones—may be less likely.

7. The emotions of people who are dying may change over time. Some may move from denial to acceptance, although stages of

dying vary much more than originally proposed. Honest conversation helps many, but not all, dying persons.

8. Hospice caregivers meet the biological and psychological needs of terminally ill people and their families. This can occur at home or at a specific place. Palliative care relieves pain and other uncomfortable aspects of dying.

9. Drugs that reduce pain as well as hasten dying, producing a double effect, are acceptable by many. However, both passive and active euthanasia and physician-assisted suicide are controversial. A few nations and some U.S. states allow some forms of these, but most do not.

10. Since 1980, death has been defined as occurring when brain waves stop; however, many modern measures can prolong life when no conscious thinking occurs. The need for a more precise, updated definition is apparent, but professionals are not sure what that new definition should be.

11. A living will and a health care proxy are recommended for everyone, although it is impossible to anticipate the possible interventions that may occur when someone is dying. Family members as well as professionals often disagree about specifics.

Affirmation of Life

12. Grief is overwhelming sorrow. It may be irrational and complicated, absent or disenfranchised.

13. Mourning rituals channel human grief, helping people move to affirm life. Most people are able to do this. Feelings of continuing bonds with the deceased are no longer thought to be pathological, and many people with lingering depression years after a death are people who were depressed before the death.

KEY TERMS

absent grief (p. 593)
active euthanasia (p. 587)
complicated grief (p. 593)
disenfranchised grief (p. 593)
DNR (do not resuscitate) order (p. 587)

double effect (p. 586)
grief (p. 592)
health care proxy (p. 590)
hospice (p. 584)
incomplete grief (p. 593)
living will (p. 590)

mourning (p. 594)
palliative care (p. 586)
passive euthanasia (p. 587)
physician-assisted suicide (p. 588)
slippery slope (p. 589)

terror management theory (p. 578)
thanatology (p. 573)

WHAT HAVE YOU LEARNED?

1. Why are people less familiar with death than they were 100 years ago? What impact might this have?

2. According to the ancient Egyptians and Greeks, what determined a person's fate after death?

3. What is one example of contrasting rituals about death?

4. What should parents remember when talking with children about death?

5. How does terror management theory explain young people's risk taking?

6. How does parenthood affect people's thoughts about their own death?

7. How do attitudes about death shift in late adulthood? What evidence is there of this shift?

8. In what ways do people change after a near-death experience?

9. What is a good death?

10. According to Kübler-Ross, what are the five stages of emotions associated with dying? Why doesn't everyone agree with Kübler-Ross's stages?

11. What determines whether a dying person will receive hospice care? What are the guiding principles of hospice care, and why is each one important?

12. Why is the double effect legal everywhere, even though it speeds death?

13. What differences of opinion are there with respect to the definition of death?

14. What is the difference between passive and active euthanasia?

15. What are the four conditions of physician-assisted "death with dignity" in Oregon? Why is each condition important?

16. Why would a person who has a living will also need a health care proxy?

17. What is grief, and what are some of its signs?

18. List three types of complicated grief. Why is each type considered "complicated"?

19. What are the differences among grief, mourning, and bereavement?

20. How can a grieving person find meaning in death?

21. How might reactions such as talking to the deceased make it both easier and more difficult to adjust to the death of a loved one?

22. If a person still feels a loss six months after a death, is that pathological?

23. What should friends and relatives remember when helping someone who is grieving?

APPLICATIONS

1. Death is sometimes said to be hidden, even taboo. Ask 10 people if they have ever been with someone who was dying. Note not only the yes and no answers, but also the details and reactions. For instance, how many of the deaths occurred in hospitals?

2. Find quotes about death in *Bartlett's Familiar Quotations* or a similar collection. Do you see any historical or cultural patterns of acceptance, denial, or fear?

3. Every aspect of dying is controversial in modern society. Do an Internet search for a key term such as *euthanasia* or *grief*. An-alyze the information and the underlying assumptions. What is your opinion, and why?

4. People of varying ages have different attitudes toward death. Ask people of different ages (ideally, at least one person younger than 20, one adult between 20 and 60, and one older person) what thoughts they have about their own death. What differences do you find?

>>ONLINE CONNECTIONS

To accompany your textbook, you have access to a number of online resources, including quizzes for every chapter of the book, flashcards (in English and Spanish), critical thinking questions, and case studies. For access to any of these links, go to www.worthpublishers.com/bergerinvitation2e. In addition to these free resources, you'll also find links to podcasts, video clips, diagnostic quizzing with personalized study advice, and an ebook. Some of the videos and activities available online include:

■ *Bereavement.* This in-depth activity covers the four stages of the grieving process and bereavement at different points in the life span. People share their personal experiences of loss.

■ *Preparing to Die.* Experts discuss the process of dying, and dying people tell their stories. Covers death at different ages, palliative and hospice care, and more.

Appendix A

Supplemental Charts, Graphs and Tables

Often, examining specific data is useful, even fascinating, to developmental researchers. The particular numbers reveal trends and nuances not apparent from a more general view. Each chart, graph or table in this appendix contains information that may challenge some of your common assumptions.

The Human Brain

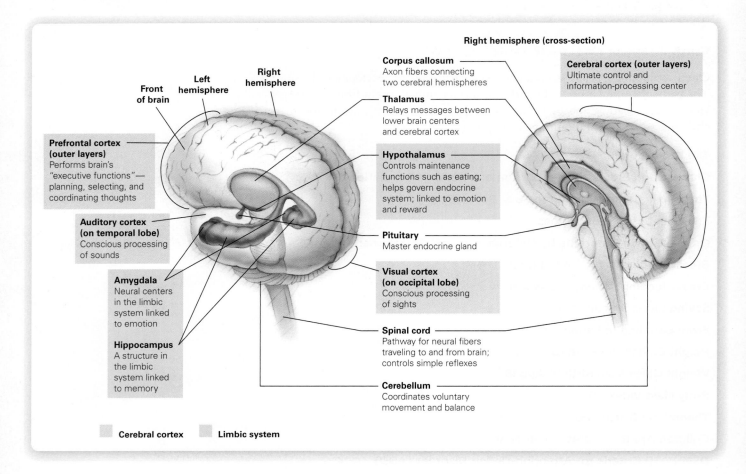

Right hemisphere (cross-section)

Corpus callosum
Axon fibers connecting
two cerebral hemispheres

Cerebral cortex (outer layers)
Ultimate control and
information-processing center

Thalamus
Relays messages between
lower brain centers
and cerebral cortex

**Prefrontal cortex
(outer layers)**
Performs brain's
"executive functions"—
planning, selecting, and
coordinating thoughts

Hypothalamus
Controls maintenance
functions such as eating;
helps govern endocrine
system; linked to emotion
and reward

**Auditory cortex
(on temporal lobe)**
Conscious processing
of sounds

Pituitary
Master endocrine gland

Amygdala
Neural centers
in the limbic
system linked
to emotion

**Visual cortex
(on occipital lobe)**
Conscious processing
of sights

Hippocampus
A structure in
the limbic
system linked
to memory

Spinal cord
Pathway for neural fibers
traveling to and from brain;
controls simple reflexes

Cerebellum
Coordinates voluntary
movement and balance

Front of brain Left hemisphere Right hemisphere

◻ Cerebral cortex   ◻ Limbic system

Children and Elders as a Proportion of a Nation's Population

More Children, Fewer Elders? Nations that have high birth rates also have high death rates, short life spans, and less education. A systems approach suggests that these variables are connected. For example, the Reggio Emilia early-childhood education program, perhaps the best in the world, originated in Italy, and Italy has one of the lowest proportions of children younger than 15. By contrast, the nations of sub-Saharan Africa have almost no government aid for children or the elderly.

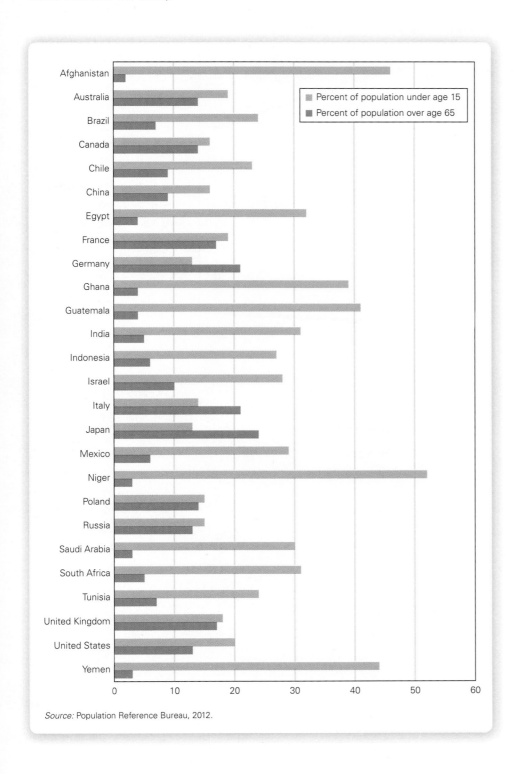

Source: Population Reference Bureau, 2012.

The Ethnic Composition of the U.S. Population

Thinking about the ethnic makeup of the U.S. population helps explain the rising importance of sociocultural theory and the limitations of the concept of race. The traditional bifurcation of "White" and "non-White" is increasingly irrelevant with growing numbers of Latino and Asian Americans. Every one of these broad categories includes many distinct ethnic groups. Furthermore, a growing number consider themselves more than one race.

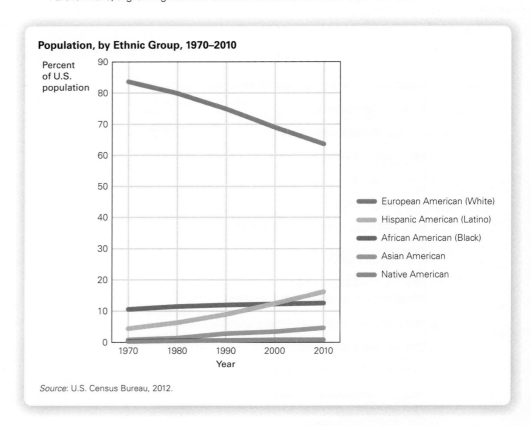

Population, by Ethnic Group, 1970–2010

- European American (White)
- Hispanic American (Latino)
- African American (Black)
- Asian American
- Native American

Source: U.S. Census Bureau, 2012.

OBSERVATION QUIZ
Which ethnic group is growing more rapidly? (see answer, page A-6) →

Percent of U.S. Population					
Ethnic origin	1970	1980	1990	2000	2010
European (White)	83.7	80	75	69.1	63.7
African (Black)	10.6	11.5	12	12.5	16.3
Hispanic (Latino)	4.5	6.4	9	12.3	12.6
Asian	1.0	1.5	3	3.6	4.8
Native American	0.4	0.6	0.7	0.9	0.9

The Genetics of Blood Types

Blood types A and B are dominant traits and type O is recessive. The percentages given in the first column of this chart represent the odds that a child born to parents with the specified combinations of genotypes will have the genotype given in the second column. Note that each of the four blood phenotypes can be the outcome of at least six parental genotypes. Complex as this may seem, it is actually a very simple example. Most inheritance patterns are additive, not dominant/recessive, and even for blood types, many other factors (e.g., Rh negative or positive) may be part of the phenotype.

Genotypes of Parents*	Genotype of Offspring	Phenotype	Can Donate Blood to (Phenotype)	Can Receive Blood from (Phenotype)
AA + AA (100%) AA + AB (50%) AA + AO (50%) AB + AB (25%) AB + AO (25%) AO + AO (25%)	AA (inherits one A from each parent)	A	A or AB	A or O
AA + OO (100%) AB + OO (50%) AO + AO (50%) AO + OO (50%) AB + AO (25%) AB + BO (25%)	AO	A	A or AB	A or O
BB + BB (100%) AB + BB (50%) BB + BO (50%) AB + AB (25%) AB + BO (25%) BO + BO (25%)	BB	B	B or AB	B or O
BB + OO (100%) AB + OO (50%) BO + BO (50%) BO + OO (50%) AB + AO (25%) AB + BO (25%)	BO	B	B or AB	B or O
AA + BB (100%) AA + AB (50%) AA + BO (50%) AB + AB (50%) AB + BB (50%) AO + BB (50%) AB + BO (25%) AO + BO (25%)	AB	AB	AB only	A, B, AB, O ("universal recipient")
OO + OO (100%) AO + OO (50%) BO + OO (50%) AO + AO (25%) AO + BO (25%) BO + BO (25%)	OO	O	A, B, AB, O ("universal donor")	O only

*Blood type is not sex-linked because blood type comes equally from each parent.
Source: Adapted from Hartl & Jones, 1999.

Odds of Down Syndrome by Maternal Age and Gestational Age

The odds of any given fetus, at the end of the first trimester, having three chromosomes at the 21st site (trisomy 21) and thus having Down syndrome are shown in the 10-weeks column. These data were collected before widespread prenatal testing and induced abortion. As you see, almost half of all Down syndrome fetuses are spontaneously aborted. Also note that the odds of Down syndrome increase steadily with the age of the mother. Nonetheless, even for women giving birth in their 40s, most newborns do not have chromosomal abnormalities.

Mother's age (yrs)	Weeks of Gestation		Live Births
	10	35	
20	1/804	1/1,464	1/1,527
21	1/793	1/1,445	1/1,507
22	1/780	1/1,421	1/1,482
23	1/762	1/1,389	1/1,448
24	1/740	1/1,348	1/1,406
25	1/712	1/1,297	1/1,352
26	1/677	1/1,233	1/1,286
27	1/635	1/1,157	1/1,206
28	1/586	1/1,068	1/1,113
29	1/531	1/967	1/1,008
30	1/471	1/858	1/895
31	1/409	1/745	1/776
32	1/347	1/632	1/659
33	1/288	1/525	1/547
34	1/235	1/427	1/446
35	1/187	1/342	1/356
36	1/148	1/269	1/280
37	1/115	1/209	1/218
38	1/88	1/160	1/167
39	1/67	1/122	1/128
40	1/51	1/93	1/97
41	1/38	1/70	1/73
42	1/29	1/52	1/55
43	1/21	1/39	1/41
44	1/16	1/29	1/30

Source: Snijders & Nicolaides, 1996.

ANSWER TO **OBSERVATION QUIZ**
(from page A-4) Asian Americans, whose share of the U.S. population has more than tripled in the past 30 years. Latinos are increasing most rapidly in numbers, but not in proportion. ●

Provisional Breast-Feeding Rates by Sociodemographic Factors, Among Children Born in 2006

	Ever breast-feeding	Breast-feeding at 6 months	Breast-feeding at 12 months
U.S. overall	73.9%	43.4%	22.7%
Race/ethnicity			
Native American	69.9	38.5	21.8
Asian or Pacific islander	83.1	55.1	35.1
Hispanic or Latino	82.1	48.5	27.2
African American (non-Hispanic)	56.5	27.5	12.3
European (non-Hispanic)	73.8	44.3	22.6
Birth order			
First-born	73.6	45.4	23.8
Not first-born	74.4	41.0	21.5
Mother's age			
Less than 20	55.6	24.0	7.8
20–29	69.2	34.1	17.3
30+	78.0	50.4	27.0
Mother's education			
Less than high school	68.3	38.0	21.1
High school graduate	64.9	33.3	16.6
Some college	75.3	41.9	21.8
College graduate	86.3	58.5	30.8
Mother's marital status			
Married	79.9	50.4	26.6
Unmarried*	60.6	27.6	14.0

*Unmarried includes never married, widowed, separated, and divorced.

Source: CDC National Immunization Survey, Department of Health and Human Services, 2012, based on 2006 data for detailed sociodemographic breakdown.

Breast-Feeding in the United States

Differentiating excellent from less optimal mothering is not easy, once the child's basic needs for food and protection are met. However, psychosocial development depends on responsive parent–infant relationships. Breast-feeding is one sign of intimacy between mother and infant, itself one aspect of parenting. In the United States, breastfeeding overall is increasing (see figure on p. 111), but some women are more likely to breast-feed than others, as seen in this detailed breakdown for babies born in 2006.

Regional summaries	Exclusively Breast-fed for 6 months	Still Breast-fed 12–15 months
Africa	34	86
Sub-Saharan Africa	33	88
Eastern and Southern Africa	49	89
West and Central Africa	24	88
Middle East and North Africa	34	70
Asia	38	72
South Asia	45	87
East Asia and Pacific	29	51
Latin America and Caribbean	42	59
Central and Eastern Europe	30	59
Norway	9	46
Italy	2	24
Developing nations	37	75
Least developed nations	42	90
World	37	74

Sources: UNICEF, 2012; European Nutrition and Health Report, 2009 (for Italy and Norway).

Breast-Feeding Around the World

Regions of the world differ dramatically in the rates of breast-feeding, with the highest rates in Southeast Asia, where half of all 2-year-olds are still breast-feeding. Rates vary dramatically. For example, within Europe, Norwegian babies are nearly twice as likely to be breast-fed at 1 year than are Italian babies.

Saving Lives: Immunization

Most immunizations of children are recommended worldwide and have already saved a billion or more lives. Some, however, are controversial, and some nations differ from the U.S. recommendations shown here.

Recommended Childhood Immunization Schedule, Birth to Age 6, United States, 2012

Vaccine	Birth	1 month	2 months	4 months	6 months	9 months	12 months	15 months	18 months	19–23 months	2–3 years	4–6 years
Hepatitis B	Hep B	Hep B			Hep B							
Rotavirus			RV	RV	RV							
Diphtheria, tetanus, pertussis			DTaP	DTaP	DTaP			DTaP				DTaP
Haemophilus influnzae, type B			Hib	Hib	Hib		Hib					
Pneumococcal			PCV	PCV	PCV		PCV					PPSV
Inactivated poliovirus			IPV	IPV	IPV							IPV
Influenza					Influenza (yearly)							
Measles, mumps, rubella							MMR					MMR
Varicella							Varicella					Varicella
Hepatitis A							Dose 1				HepA Series	
Meningococcal							MCV4					

███ Range of recommended ages for all children

███ Range of recommended ages for certain high-risk groups

███ Range of recommended ages for catch-up vaccination

Recommended Immunizations Schedule for U.S. Children Aged 7 Through 18 Years

Vaccine	7–10 years	11–12 years	13–18 years
Tetanus, diphtheria, pertussis	1 dose	1 dose	1 dose
Human papilomavirus		3 doses	Complete 3 dose series
Meningococcal		Dose 1	Booster
Influenza		Influenza (yearly)	
Pneumococcal			
Hepatitis A			
Hepatitis B			
Inactivated poliovirus			
Measles, mumps, rubella			
Varicella			

███ Range of recommended ages for all children

███ Range of recommendations for certain high-risk groups

███ Range of recommended ages for catch-up immunization

Recommended Immunizations for Adults, United States

Vaccine	19–21 years	22–26 years	27–49 years	50–59 years	60–64 years	65+ years
Influenza	Influenza (yearly)					
Tetanus, diphtheria, and pertussis	Get a Tdap vaccine once, then a booster every 10 years					
Varicella	2 doses					
HPV for women	HPV for women					
HPV for men	HPV for men					
Zoster (shingles)					Zoster	
Measles, mumps, rubella	MMR			MMR		
Pneumococcal	Pneumococcal					
Meningococcal						
Hepatitis A						
Hepatatis B						

Source: MMWR, January 28, 2013.

■ Range of recommended ages for all adults

■ Range of recommendations for certain high-risk groups

From Babbling to Language

Every language accommodates the abilities of toddlers. The "the" sound is difficult, so no language expects 1-year-olds to say it.

Baby's word for:		
Language	Mother	Father
English	mama, mommy	dada, daddy
Spanish	mama	papa
French	maman, mama	papa
Italian	mamma	babbo, papa
Latvian	mama	te-te
Syrian Arabic	mama	baba
Bantu	ba-mama	taata
Swahili	mama	baba
Sanskrit	nana	tata
Hebrew	ema	abba
Korean	oma	apa

Height Gains from Birth to Age 18

The range of height (on this page) and weight (see page A-11) of children in the United States. The columns labeled "50th" (the fiftieth percentile) show the average; the columns labeled "90th" (the ninetieth percentile) show the size of children taller and heavier than 90 percent of their contemporaries; and the columns labeled "10th" (the tenth percentile) show the size of children who are taller than only 10 percent of their peers. Note that girls are slightly shorter, on average, than boys.

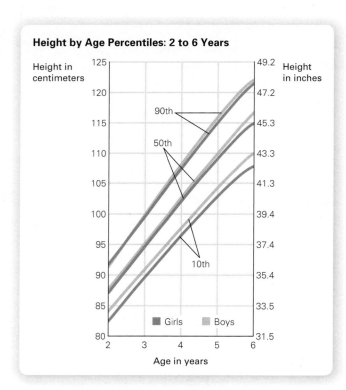

Height by Age Percentiles: 2 to 6 Years

Same Data, Different Form

The columns of numbers in the table at right provide detailed and precise information about height ranges for every year of childhood. The illustration above shows the same information in graphic form for ages 2–6. The same is done for weight ranges on page A-11. Ages 2–6 are singled out because that is the period during which a child's eating habits are set. Which form of data presentation do you think is easier to understand?

Length in Centimeters (and Inches)						
	Boys: percentiles			**Girls: percentiles**		
AGE	10th	50th	90th	10th	50th	90th
Birth	47.5 (18¾)	50.5 (20)	53.5 (21)	46.5 (18¼)	49.9 (19¾)	52.0 (20½)
1 month	51.3 (20¼)	54.6 (21½)	57.7 (22¾)	50.2 (19¾)	53.5 (21)	56.1 (22)
3 months	57.7 (22¾)	61.1 (24)	64.5 (25½)	56.2 (22¼)	59.5 (23½)	62.7 (24¾)
6 months	64.4 (25¼)	67.8 (26¾)	71.3 (28)	62.6 (24¾)	65.9 (26)	69.4 (27¼)
9 months	69.1 (27¼)	72.3 (28½)	75.9 (30)	67.0 (26½)	70.4 (27¾)	74.0 (29¼)
12 months	72.8 (28¾)	76.1 (30)	79.8 (31½)	70.8 (27¾)	74.3 (29¼)	78.0 (30¾)
18 months	78.7 (31)	82.4 (32½)	86.6 (34)	77.2 (30½)	80.9 (31¾)	85.0 (33½)
24 months	83.5 (32¾)	87.6 (34½)	92.2 (36¼)	82.5 (32½)	86.5 (34)	90.8 (35¾)
3 years	90.3 (35½)	94.9 (37¼)	100.1 (39½)	89.3 (35¼)	94.1 (37)	99.0 (39)
4 years	97.3 (38¼)	102.9 (40½)	108.2 (42½)	96.4 (38)	101.6 (40)	106.6 (42)
5 years	103.7 (40¾)	109.9 (43¼)	115.4 (45½)	102.7 (40½)	108.4 (42¾)	113.8 (44¾)
6 years	109.6 (43¼)	116.1 (45¾)	121.9 (48)	108.4 (42¾)	114.6 (45)	120.8 (47½)
7 years	115.0 (45¼)	121.7 (48)	127.9 (50¼)	113.6 (44¾)	120.6 (47½)	127.6 (50¼)
8 years	120.2 (47¼)	127.0 (50)	133.6 (52½)	118.7 (46¾)	126.4 (49¾)	134.2 (52¾)
9 years	125.2 (49¼)	132.2 (52)	139.4 (55)	123.9 (48¾)	132.2 (52)	140.7 (55½)
10 years	130.1 (51¼)	137.5 (54¼)	145.5 (57¼)	129.5 (51)	138.3 (54½)	147.2 (58)
11 years	135.1 (53¼)	143.33 (56½)	152.1 (60)	135.6 (53½)	144.8 (57)	153.7 (60½)
12 years	140.3 (55¼)	149.7 (59)	159.4 (62¾)	142.3 (56)	151.5 (59¾)	160.0 (63)
13 years	145.8 (57½)	156.5 (61½)	167.0 (65¾)	148.0 (58¼)	157.1 (61¾)	165.3 (65)
14 years	151.8 (59¾)	63.1 (64¼)	173.8 (68½)	151.5 (59¾)	160.4 (63¼)	168.7 (66½)
15 years	158.2 (62¼)	169.0 (66½)	178.9 (70½)	153.2 (60¼)	161.8 (63¾)	170.5 (67¼)
16 years	163.9 (64½)	173.5 (68¼)	182.4 (71¾)	154.1 (60¾)	162.4 (64)	171.1 (67¼)
17 years	167.7 (66)	176.2 (69¼)	184.4 (72½)	155.1 (61)	163.1 (64¼)	171.2 (67½)
18 years	168.7 (66½)	176.8 (69½)	185.3 (73)	156.0 (61½)	163.7 (64½)	171.0 (67¼)

Source: These data are those of the National Center for Health Statistics (NCHS), Health Resources Administration, DHHS. They were based on studies of The Fels Research Institute, Yellow Springs, Ohio. These data were first made available with the help of William M. Moore, M.D., of Ross Laboratories, who supplied the conversion from metric measurements to approximate inches and pounds. This help is gratefully acknowledged.

Weight Gains from Birth to Age 18

These height and weight charts present rough guidelines; a child might differ from these norms and be quite healthy and normal. However, if a particular child shows a discrepancy between height and weight (e.g., at the 90th percentile in height but only the 20th percentile in weight) or is much larger or smaller than most children the same age, a pediatrician should see whether disease, malnutrition, or genetic abnormality could be part of the reason.

Weight by Age Percentiles: 2 to 6 Years

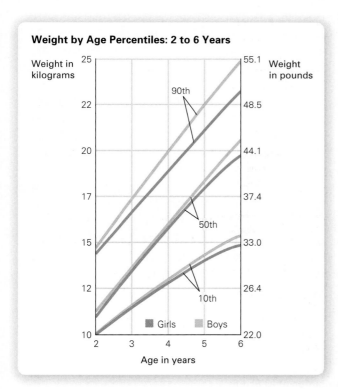

Weight in Kilograms (and Pounds)						
	Boys: percentiles			**Girls: percentiles**		
AGE	10th	50th	90th	10th	50th	90th
Birth	2.78 (6¼)	3.27 (7¼)	3.82 (8½)	2.58 (5¾)	3.23 (7)	3.64 (8)
1 month	3.43 (7½)	4.29 (9½)	5.14 (11¼)	3.22 (7)	3.98 (8¾)	4.65 (10¼)
3 months	4.78 (10½)	5.98 (13¼)	7.14 (15¾)	4.47 (9¾)	5.40 (12)	6.39 (14)
6 months	6.61 (14½)	7.85 (17¼)	9.10 (20)	6.12 (13½)	7.21 (16)	8.38 (18½)
9 months	7.95 (17½)	9.18 (20¼)	10.49 (23¼)	7.34 (16¼)	8.56 (18¾)	9.83 (21¾)
12 months	8.84 (19½)	10.15 (22½)	11.54 (25½)	8.19 (18)	9.53 (21)	10.87 (24)
18 months	9.92 (21¾)	11.47 (25¼)	13.05 (28¾)	9.30 (20½)	10.82 (23¾)	12.30 (27)
24 months	10.85 (24)	12.59 (27¾)	14.29 (31½)	10.26 (22½)	11.90 (26¼)	13.57 (30)
3 years	12.58 (27¾)	14.62 (32¼)	16.95 (37¼)	12.26 (27)	14.10 (31)	16.54 (36½)
4 years	14.24 (31½)	16.69 (36¾)	19.32 (42½)	13.84 (30½)	15.96 (35¼)	18.93 (41¾)
5 years	15.96 (35¼)	18.67 (41¼)	21.70 (47¾)	15.26 (33¾)	17.66 (39)	21.23 (46¾)
6 years	17.72 (39)	20.69 (45½)	24.31 (53½)	16.72 (36¾)	19.52 (43)	23.89 (52¾)
7 years	19.53 (43)	22.85 (50¼)	27.36 (60¼)	18.39 (40½)	21.84 (48¼)	27.39 (60½)
8 years	21.39 (47¼)	25.30 (55¾)	31.06 (68½)	20.45 (45)	24.84 (54¾)	32.04 (70¾)
9 years	23.33 (51½)	28.13 (62)	35.57 (78½)	22.92 (50½)	28.46 (62¾)	37.60 (83)
10 years	25.52 (56¼)	31.44 (69¼)	40.80 (90)	25.76 (56¾)	32.55 (71¾)	43.70 (96¼)
11 years	28.17 (62)	35.30 (77¾)	46.57 (102¾)	28.97 (63¾)	36.95 (81½)	49.96 (110¼)
12 years	31.46 (69¼)	39.78 (87¾)	52.73 (116¼)	32.53 (71¼)	41.53 (91½)	55.99 (123½)
13 years	35.60 (78½)	44.95 (99)	59.12 (130¼)	36.35 (80¼)	46.10 (101¾)	61.45 (135½)
14 years	40.64 (89½)	50.77 (112)	65.57 (144½)	40.11 (88½)	50.28 (110¾)	66.04 (145½)
15 years	46.06 (101½)	56.71 (125)	71.91 (158½)	43.38 (95¾)	53.68 (118¼)	69.64 (153¼)
16 years	51.16 (112¾)	62.10 (137)	77.97 (172)	45.78 (101)	55.89 (123¼)	71.68 (158)
17 years	55.28 (121¾)	66.31 (146¼)	83.58 (184¼)	47.04 (103¾)	56.69 (125)	72.38 (159½)
18 years	57.89 (127½)	68.88 (151¾)	88.41 (195)	47.47 (104¾)	56.62 (124¾)	72.25 (159¼)

Source: Data are those of the National Center for Health Statistics, Health Resources Administration, DHHS, collected in its Health Examination Surveys.

Body Mass Index

BMI is a quick way to indicate weight problems. Too thin is a BMI below 19; the preferred range is 19 to 24, overweight is 25 to 29, obese is more than 30, and very obese is more than 35. However, for some people, mitigating factors need to be considered before a person is advised to change his or her diet. For example, muscle is heavier than fat, so fit adults could have a BMI of 26 and still be quite healthy.

Body Mass Index (BMI)

To find your BMI, locate your height in the first column, then look across that row. Your BMI appears at the top of the column that contains your weight.

BMI	19	20	21	22	23	24	25	26	27	28	29	30	35	40
Height (in feet and inches)							**Weight** (in pounds)							
4'10"	91	96	100	105	110	115	119	124	129	134	138	143	167	191
4'11"	94	99	104	109	114	119	124	128	133	138	143	148	173	198
5'0"	97	102	107	112	118	123	128	133	138	143	148	153	179	204
5'1"	100	106	111	116	122	127	132	137	143	148	153	158	185	211
5'2"	104	109	115	120	126	131	136	142	147	153	158	164	191	218
5'3"	107	113	118	124	130	135	141	146	152	158	163	169	197	225
5'4"	110	116	122	128	134	140	145	151	157	163	169	174	204	232
5'5"	114	120	126	132	138	144	150	156	162	168	174	180	210	240
5'6"	118	124	130	136	142	148	155	161	167	173	179	186	216	247
5'7"	121	127	134	140	146	153	159	166	172	178	185	191	223	255
5'8"	125	131	138	144	151	158	164	171	177	183	190	197	230	262
5'9"	128	135	142	149	155	162	169	176	182	189	196	203	236	270
5'10"	132	139	146	153	160	167	174	181	188	195	202	207	243	278
5'11"	136	143	150	157	165	172	179	186	193	200	208	215	250	286
6'0"	140	147	154	162	169	177	184	191	199	206	213	221	258	294
6'1"	144	151	159	166	174	182	189	197	204	212	219	227	265	302
6'2"	148	155	163	171	179	186	194	202	210	218	225	233	272	311
6'3"	152	160	168	176	184	192	200	208	216	224	232	240	279	319
6'4"	156	164	172	180	189	197	205	213	221	230	238	246	287	328
				Normal				*Overweight*					*Obese*	

Source: National Heart, Lung, and Blood Institute, n.d.

IQ Scores

Almost 70 percent of IQ scores fall within the normal range. Note, however, that this is a norm-referenced test. In fact, actual IQ scores have risen in many nations; 100 is no longer exactly the midpoint. Furthermore, in practice, scores below 50 are slightly more frequent than indicated by the normal curve shown here because severe retardation is the result not of normal distribution but of genetic and prenatal factors.

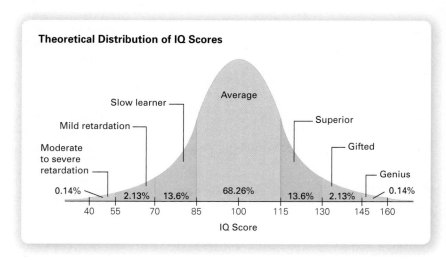

Theoretical Distribution of IQ Scores

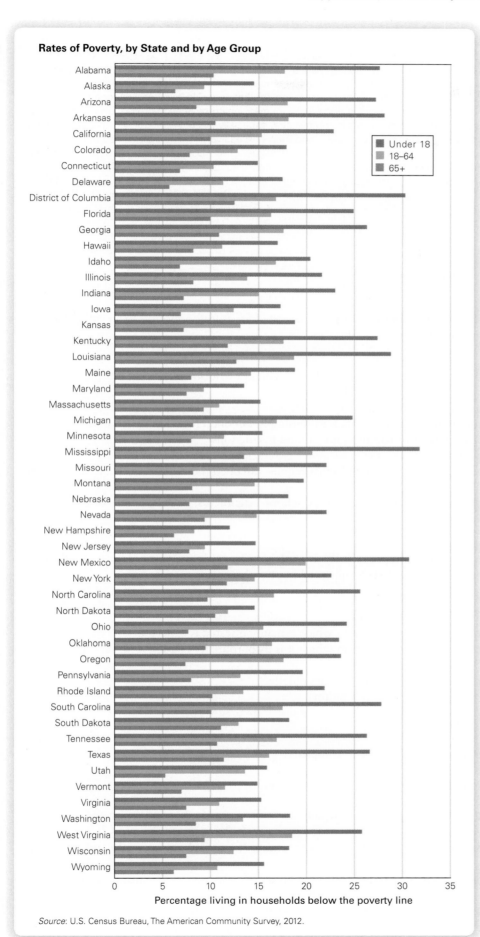

Rates of Poverty, by State and by Age Group

Legend: Under 18 / 18–64 / 65+

Percentage living in households below the poverty line

Source: U.S. Census Bureau, The American Community Survey, 2012.

Children Are the Poorest Americans

It probably comes as no surprise that the rate of poverty is twice as high in some states as in others. What is surprising is how much the rates vary among age groups within the same state.

OBSERVATION QUIZ

As you can see, most states have far more poor children than poor adults, unlike in most European nations. Which seven states have the most balanced poverty rates (i.e., where children are *not* twice as often poor as those over 64)? (see answer, page A-14) →

ANSWER TO **OBSERVATION QUIZ** (from page A-13) Maryland, Massachusetts, Minnesota, New Hampshire, New Jersey, North Dakota, and South Dakota. Note that those states tend to have relatively low poverty overall. ●

DSM-IV-TR Criteria for Attention-Deficit Disorder (ADD)

The Diagnostic and Statistical Manual, the fourth edition (DSM-IV) was written to help clinicians, researchers, and insurance companies distinguish one disorder from another, as well as to know when behavior is normal for that age. This is the criteria for attention deficit disorder, which appears in two types—primarily inattentive and primarily hyperactive. As you read in the text, diagnosis is complicated, especially since childhood bipolar disorder shares some symptoms. For example, "often talks excessively" is characteristic of the manic phase of bipolar—although how frequent qualifies as "often" is a matter of judgment. The DSM-IV is more than 900 pages and includes not only diagnostic criteria as shown here, but also discussion of prevalence, age and gender statistics, cultural aspects, and prognosis for about 400 disorders or subtypes, 40 of which appear primarily in childhood. The DSM-5 is expected in 2013 and some criteria, including Autistic Spectrum Disorders, will change a great deal.

Diagnostic Criteria for Attention-Deficit/Hyperactivity Disorder

A. Either (1) or (2):

(1) Six (or more) of the following symptoms of **inattention** have persisted for at least 6 months to a degree that is maladaptive and inconsistent with developmental level:

INATTENTION

  (a) often fails to give close attention to details or makes careless mistakes in schoolwork, work, or other activities
  (b) often has difficulty sustaining attention in tasks or play activities
  (c) often does not seem to listen when spoken to directly
  (d) often does not follow through on instructions and fails to finish schoolwork, chores, or duties in the workplace (not due to oppositional behavior or failure to understand instructions)
  (e) often has difficulty organizing tasks and activities
  (f) often avoids, dislikes, or is reluctant to engage in tasks that require sustained mental effort (such as schoolwork or homework)
  (g) often loses things necessary for tasks or activities (e.g., toys, school assignments, pencils, books, or tools)
  (h) is often easily distracted by extraneous stimuli
  (i) is often forgetful in daily activities

(2) Six (or more) of the following symptoms of **hyperactivity-impulsivity** have persisted for at least 6 months to a degree that is maladaptive and inconsistent with developmental level:

HYPERACTIVITY

  (a) often fidgets with hands or feet or squirms in seat
  (b) often leaves seat in classroom or in other situations in which remaining seated is expected
  (c) often runs about or climbs excessively in situations in which it is inappropriate (in adolescents or adults, may be limited to subjective feelings of restlessness)
  (d) often has difficulty playing or engaging in leisure activities quietly
  (e) is often "on the go" or often acts as if "driven by a motor"
  (f) often talks excessively

IMPULSIVITY

  (g) often blurts out answers before questions have been completed
  (h) often has difficulty awaiting turn
  (i) often interrupts or intrudes on others (e.g., butts into conversations or games)

B. Some hyperactive-impulsive or inattentive symptoms that caused impairment were present before age 7 years.

C. Some impairment from the symptoms is present in two or more settings (e.g., at school [or work] and at home).

D. There must be clear evidence of clinically significant impairment in social, academic, or occupational functioning.

Motivation or Achievement?

The PISA (Programme for International Student Assessment) is an international test of 15-year-olds' abilities to apply their knowledge. One explanation for the high scores of China and low scores of the United States is motivation of the students: Experts believe that students in the United States are not strongly motivated to learn in school—so they don't.

Science		Reading		Math	
Region	PISA Score	Region	PISA Score	Region	PISA Score
China	575	China	556	China	600
Finland	554	Korea	539	Singapore	562
Hong Kong	549	Finland	536	Hong Kong	555
Singapore	542	Hong Kong	533	Korea	546
Japan	539	Singapore	526	Taiwan	543
Korea	538	Canada	524	Finland	541
New Zealand	532	New Zealand	521	Liechtenstein	536
Canada	529	Japan	520	Switzerland	534
Estonia	528	Australia	515	Japan	529
Australia	527	Netherlands	508	Canada	527
Netherlands	522	Belgium	506	Netherlands	526
Taiwan	520	Norway	503	New Zealand	519
Germany	520	Estonia	501	Belgium	515
Liechtenstein	520	Switzerland	501	Australia	514
Switzerland	517	Poland	500	Germany	513
Britain	514	Iceland	500	Estonia	512
Slovenia	512	**United States**	**500**	Iceland	507
Poland	508	Liechtenstein	499	Denmark	503
Ireland	508	Sweden	497	Slovenia	501
Belgium	507	Germany	497	Norway	498
Hungary	503	Ireland	496	France	497
United States	**502**	France	496	Slovakia	497
AVERAGE SCORE*	501	Taiwan	495	AVERAGE SCORE*	497
Czech Republic	500	Denmark	495	Austria	496
Norway	500	Britain	494	Poland	495
Denmark	499	Hungary	494	Sweden	494
France	498	AVERAGE SCORE*	494	Czech Republic	493
Iceland	496	Portugal	489	Britain	492
Sweden	495	Italy	486	Hungary	490
Austria	494	Latvia	484	Luxembourg	489
Latvia	494	Slovenia	483	**United States**	**487**
Portugal	493	Greece	483	Ireland	487

*Average is based on all the students who took the test, which includes many in low-scoring nations not shown here.
Sources: OECD, 2010a, 2010b.

Major Sexually Transmitted Infections: Some Basics

These and other STIs, if left untreated, may lead to serious reproductive and other health problems or even, as with HIV/AIDS and syphilis, to death. STIs can be avoided by consistently using condoms, having sex only in a relationship with an uninfected partner, or abstaining from sex—oral, anal, and genital.

Sexually Transmitted Infection (and Cause)	Symptoms	Treatment
Chlamydia (bacterium)	The most frequently reported bacterial STI in the United States. In women, abnormal vaginal discharge or burning sensation when urinating; may be followed by pain in low abdomen or low back, nausea, fever, pain during intercourse, or bleeding between menstrual periods. In men, discharge from penis or burning sensation when urinating.	Antibiotics
Genital HPV infection (virus)	One of the most common STIs in the world. Causes no symptoms or health problems in most people, but certain types may cause genital warts and others can cause cervical cancer in women and other cancers of the genitals in both sexes.	A vaccine is now available and is recommended for 11- and 12-year-old girls who are not yet sexually active.
Genital herpes (virus)	Blisters on or around the genitals or rectum that break and leave sores, which may take 2 to 4 weeks to heal; some people may experience fever, swollen glands, and other flu-like symptoms. Later outbreaks are usually less severe and shorter. Many people never have sores and may take years to realize they are infected. May lead to potentially fatal infections in babies and makes infected person more susceptible to HIV infection.	There is no vaccine or cure, but antiviral medications can shorten and prevent outbreaks.
Gonorrhea (bacterium)	Some men and most women have no symptoms. In men, a burning sensation when urinating; a white, yellow, or green discharge from the penis; painful or swollen testicles. In women, symptoms—pain or burning during urination, increased vaginal discharge, vaginal bleeding between periods—may be so mild or nonspecific that they are mistaken for a bladder or vaginal infection. May cause pelvic inflammatory disease (PID) in women and infertility in both sexes. Infected person can more easily contract HIV.	Antibiotics
Pelvic inflammatory disease (PID) (various bacteria)	A common and serious complication in women who have certain other STIs, especially chlamydia and gonorrhea. Pain in lower abdomen, fever, unusual vaginal discharge that may have a foul odor, painful intercourse, painful urination, irregular menstrual bleeding, and (rarely) pain in the right upper abdomen. May lead to blocked fallopian tubes, causing infertility.	Administration of at least two antibiotics that are effective against a wide range of infectious agents. In severe cases, surgery.
HIV/AIDS (virus)	Infection with the human immunodeficiency virus (HIV) eventually leads to acquired immune deficiency syndrome (AIDS). Infection with other STIs increases a person's likelihood of both acquiring and transmitting HIV. Soon after exposure, some people have flu-like symptoms: fever, headache, tiredness, swollen lymph glands. Months or years later, when the virus has weakened the immune system, the person may experience lack of energy, weight loss, frequent fevers and sweats, yeast infections, skin rashes, short-term memory loss. Symptoms of full-blown AIDS include certain cancers (Kaposi's sarcoma and lymphomas), seizures, vision loss, and coma. A leading cause of death among young adults in many nations.	There is no vaccine or cure, but antiretroviral drugs can slow the growth of the virus; antibiotics can cure some secondary infections, and various treatments are available to relieve painful or unpleasant symptoms.
Syphilis (bacterium)	Symptoms may not appear for years. Primary stage: One or more sores (chancres) a few days or weeks after exposure. Secondary stage: Skin rash, lesions of mucous membranes, fever, swollen lymph glands, sore throat, patchy hair loss, headaches, weight loss, muscle aches, fatigue. Latent stage: Primary and secondary symptoms disappear, but infection remains in the body. Late stage (10 to 20 years after first infection): Damage to brain, nerves, eyes, heart, blood vessels, liver, bones, and joints, progressing to difficulty coordinating muscle movements, paralysis, numbness, blindness, dementia.	Penicillin injections will kill the syphilis bacterium and prevent further damage but cannot repair damage already done.
Trichomoniasis (*Trichomonas vaginalis,* a single-celled protozoan parasite)	Most men have no symptoms, but some may temporarily have an irritation inside the penis, mild discharge, or slight burning after urination or ejaculation. Women may have a frothy, yellow-green, strong-smelling vaginal discharge and may experience discomfort during intercourse and urination; irritation and itching of the genital area; and, rarely, lower abdominal pain.	A single oral dose of metronidazole or tinidazole

Source: Centers for Disease Control and Prevention, 2012.

Sexual Behaviors of U.S. High School Students, 2011

These percentages, as high as they may seem, are actually lower than they were in the early 1990s. (States not listed did not participate fully in the survey.) The data in this table reflect responses from students in the 9th to 12th grades. When only high school seniors are surveyed, the percentages are higher: Nationwide, 62 percent of seniors have had sexual intercourse, and 21 percent have had four or more partners.

Percentage of High School Students Who Ever Had Sexual Intercourse and Who Had Sexual Intercourse for the First Time Before Age 13, by Sex — Selected U.S. Sites, Youth Risk Behavior Survey, 2011

Site	Ever had sexual intercourse (%)			Had first sexual intercourse before age 13 years (%)			Had sexual intercourse with four or more persons during their life (%)			Currently sexually active (%)		
State surveys	Female	Male	Total	Female	Male	Total	Female	Male	Total	Female	Male	Total
Alabama	54.4	60.6	**57.6**	5.8	13.9	**10**	19	26.3	**22.8**	44.8	43.1	**44.1**
Alaska	37.3	39.3	**38.3**	2.4	6.2	**4.4**	7.5	11.8	**9.7**	26.2	24.2	**25.2**
Arizona	44.2	49.7	**46.9**	3.1	7.9	**5.4**	11.9	16.6	**14.2**	31.3	35.9	**33.5**
Arkansas	48.6	51.9	**50.3**	4.7	12.1	**8.4**	16	23	**19.5**	39.6	36.4	**38.1**
Colorado	36.1	44.5	**40.8**	2	5.4	**3.6**	11.1	14.8	**13.2**	29.2	33.5	**31.8**
Connecticut	41.8	43.7	**42.7**	3.3	6.5	**4.9**	8.6	12.6	**10.6**	31.9	29.2	**30.5**
Delaware	57.1	60.8	**59**	4.3	13.7	**8.8**	17	26.5	**21.7**	42.9	42.7	**42.9**
Florida	43.9	52.4	**48.2**	3.2	11.8	**7.6**	10.8	21.4	**16.1**	32.2	35.8	**34**
Georgia	—†	—	**—**	—	—	**—**	—§		**—**	—	—	**—**
Hawaii	37.4	36.7	**37**	3	7.5	**5.2**	7.4	8.7	**8**	25.9	21.7	**23.9**
Idaho	39.1	40.8	**40**	2.2	4.9	**3.6**	11	16.5	**13.8**	—	—	**—**
Illinois	45.3	44.4	**44.8**	3.4	9.1	**6.3**	10.4	14.4	**12.4**	35.2	30.3	**32.8**
Indiana	50.5	51.4	**51**	3.6	6.9	**5.2**	15.2	18.4	**16.8**	39.9	37	**38.5**
Iowa	43.5	44.3	**43.9**	2.5	5.6	**4.2**	13.1	13.1	**13.1**	34.3	31.7	**33**
Kansas	43	43.4	**43.2**	1.9	5.5	**3.7**	8.5	10.9	**9.7**	33.6	32.1	**32.8**
Kentucky	51.9	51.7	**51.8**	5.5	8.9	**7.2**	16.3	17	**16.6**	40.9	34.6	**37.7**
Louisiana	—	—	**—**	—	—	**—**	—	—	**—**	—	—	**—**
Maine	45.2	44.6	**45.1**	2.2	5.6	**4**	9.6	11.2	**10.5**	35.6	31.3	**33.6**
Maryland	—	—	**—**	—	—	**—**	—	—	**—**	—	—	**—**
Massachusetts	39.4	44.7	**42**	2.1	6.2	**4.2**	9.5	13.3	**11.4**	30.3	30.7	**30.4**
Michigan	40.4	42.1	**41.2**	2.9	5.9	**4.4**	9	12.2	**10.7**	30.9	27.2	**29.1**
Mississippi	53.3	62.5	**57.9**	4.8	19.1	**11.8**	13.7	30.6	**22.1**	38.6	45.4	**42.1**
Montana	46.6	49.1	**47.9**	2.4	6.3	**4.4**	14.5	15.5	**15**	36.8	32.6	**34.7**
Nebraska	37.2	37.2	**37.1**	2.7	4.8	**3.8**	9.9	11.3	**10.6**	28.5	25.7	**27**
New Hampshire	45.7	49.4	**47.5**	2.4	6.5	**4.5**	11.5	13.4	**12.4**	36.4	37.9	**37.1**
New Jersey	41.4	47.6	**44.6**	2.6	7.5	**5.1**	9.9	17.8	**13.9**	30.6	33.6	**32.2**
New Mexico	—	—	**—**	5.1	10.4	**7.7**	11.5	17.5	**14.5**	31.8	31.9	**31.9**
New York	39.6	44.5	**42**	4	7.6	**5.7**	11.1	15.5	**13.3**	31.1	31	**31**
North Carolina	47.1	51.4	**49.3**	5.3	12	**8.6**	14.6	18.9	**16.8**	36.7	32.9	**34.9**
North Dakota	46.2	43.4	**44.8**	3	4.4	**3.7**	14.7	11.5	**13.2**	—	—	**—**
Ohio	—	—	**—**	4.3	8	**6.1**	15.8	19	**17.5**	43.3	39.8	**41.8**
Oklahoma	50.1	51	**50.5**	2.7	7.2	**5**	14.9	18.6	**16.8**	39.2	36.4	**37.8**
Rhode Island	38.2	45.4	**41.7**	1.7	8	**4.9**	7.2	13.9	**10.5**	28.4	31.2	**29.8**
South Carolina	52	61.3	**56.6**	3.9	17.1	**10.5**	16.7	25.9	**21.3**	38.9	44.6	**41.8**
South Dakota	48.9	46.1	**47.4**	2.5	5.1	**3.8**	15.4	14.5	**14.9**	37.6	33.4	**35.4**
Tennessee	49.4	55.3	**52.4**	4	10.4	**7.2**	13.9	20.5	**17.2**	37.4	36.8	**37.1**
Texas	48.6	54.8	**51.6**	4	10.1	**7**	12.9	20.7	**16.7**	36.8	35.6	**36.2**
Utah	—	—	**—**	—	—	**—**	—	—	**—**	—	—	**—**
Vermont	—	—	**—**	2.6	5.7	**4.2**	10	12.1	**11.1**	32.8	30.7	**31.8**
Virginia	—	—	**—**	—	—	**—**	—	—	**—**	—	—	**—**
West Virginia	50.1	51.8	**50.9**	2.3	7.5	**4.9**	10.2	14.6	**12.4**	39.4	35.9	**37.6**
Wisconsin	41.4	41.7	**41.6**	2.7	6	**4.4**	9.6	10.1	**9.9**	32.9	28.8	**30.8**
Wyoming	47.4	48.5	**47.9**	4.3	7.6	**6**	16.2	18.4	**17.3**	37.8	31.6	**34.7**
Median	**45.3**	**47.6**	**46.9**	**3**	**7.5**	**5**	**11.5**	**15.5**	**13.8**	**35.4**	**33.1**	**33.8**

Source: MMWR, June 8, 2012.

Smoking Behavior Among U.S. High School Students, 1991–2011

The data in these two tables reveal many trends. For example, do you see that African American adolescents are much less likely to smoke than Hispanics or European Americans, but that this racial advantage is decreasing? Are you surprised to see that White females smoke more than White males?

Percentage of High School Students Who Reported Smoking Cigarettes

Smoking Behavior	1991	1995	1999	2003	2005	2007	2009	2011
Lifetime (ever smoked)	70.1	71.3	70.4	58.4	54.3	50.3	46.3	44.7
Current (smoked at least once in past 30 days)	27.5	34.8	34.8	21.9	23.0	20.0	19.5	18.1
Current frequent (smoked 20 or more times in past 30 days)	12.7	16.1	16.8	9.7	9.4	8.1	7.3	6.4

Percentage of High School Students Who Reported Current Smoking, by Sex, Ethnicity, and Grade

Characteristic	1991	1995	1999	2003	2005	2007	2009	2011
Sex								
Female	27.3	34.3	34.9	21.9	23.0	18.7	19.1	16.1
Male	27.6	35.4	34.7	21.8	22.9	21.3	19.8	19.9
Ethnicity								
White, non-Hispanic	30.9	38.3	38.6	24.9	25.9	23.2	22.5	20.3
Female	31.7	39.8	39.1	26.6	27.0	22.5	22.8	18.9
Male	30.2	37.0	38.2	23.3	24.9	23.8	22.3	21.5
Black, non-Hispanic	12.6	19.2	19.7	15.1	12.9	11.6	9.5	10.5
Female	11.3	12.2	17.7	10.8	11.9	8.4	8.4	7.4
Male	14.1	27.8	21.8	19.3	14.0	14.9	10.7	13.7
Hispanic	25.3	34.0	32.7	18.4	22.0	16.7	18.0	17.5
Female	22.9	32.9	31.5	17.7	19.2	14.6	16.7	15.2
Male	27.9	34.9	34.0	19.1	24.8	18.7	19.4	**19.5**
Grade								
9th	23.2	31.2	27.6	17.4	19.7	14.3	13.5	13.0
10th	25.2	33.1	34.7	21.8	21.4	19.6	18.3	15.6
11th	31.6	35.9	36.0	23.6	24.3	21.6	22.3	19.3
12th	30.1	38.2	42.8	26.2	27.6	26.5	25.2	25.1

Source: MMWR, 2012.

Demographic Changes

These numbers show dramatic shifts in family planning, with teenage births continuing to fall and births after age 30 rising again. These data come from the United States, but the same trends are apparent in almost every nation. Can you tell when contraception became widely available?

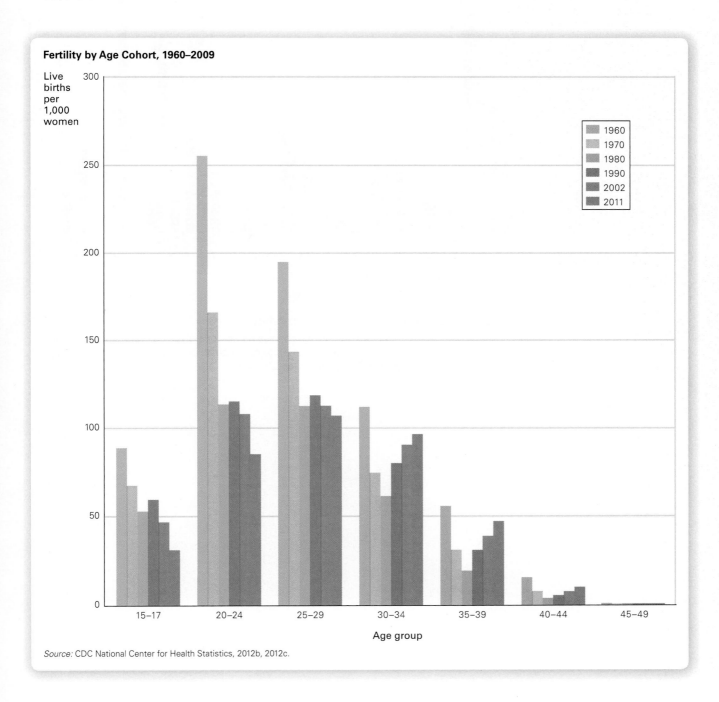

Fertility by Age Cohort, 1960–2009

Live births per 1,000 women

Legend: 1960, 1970, 1980, 1990, 2002, 2011

Age group: 15–17, 20–24, 25–29, 30–34, 35–39, 40–44, 45–49

Source: CDC National Center for Health Statistics, 2012b, 2012c.

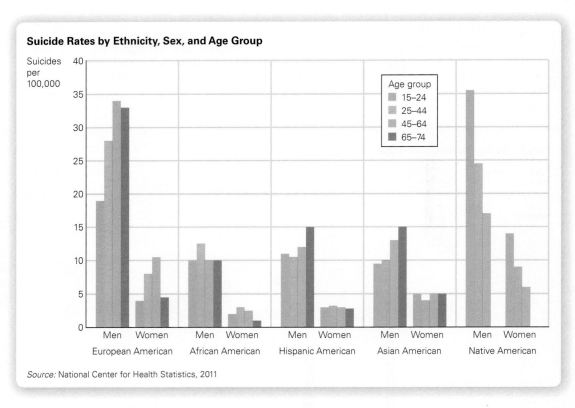

Suicide Rates by Ethnicity, Sex, and Age Group

Source: National Center for Health Statistics, 2011

Suicide Rates in the United States

These are the rates per 100,000. When there is no bar for a given age group, that means there are too few suicides in that age group to calculate an accurate rate. Overall, the highest rates are among older European American men.

Appendix B
More About
Research Methods

This appendix explains how to learn about any topic. It is crucial that you distinguish valid conclusions from wishful thinking. Such learning begins with your personal experience.

Make It Personal

Think about your life, observe your behavior, and watch the people around you. Pay careful attention to details of expression, emotion, and behavior. The more you see, the more fascinated, curious, and reflective you will become. Ask questions and listen carefully and respectfully to what other people say regarding development.

Whenever you ask specific questions as part of an assignment, **remember that observing ethical standards (see Chapter 1) comes first.** *Before* you interview anyone, inform the person of your purpose and assure him or her of confidentiality. Promise not to identify the person in your report (use a pseudonym) and do not repeat any personal details that emerge in the interview to anyone (friends or strangers). Your instructor will provide further ethical guidance. If you might publish what you've learned, get in touch with your college's Institutional Research Board (IRB).

Read the Research

No matter how deeply you think about your own experiences, and no matter how intently you listen to others whose background is unlike yours, you also need to read scholarly published work in order to fully understand any topic that interests you. Be skeptical about magazine or newspaper reports; some are bound to be simplified, exaggerated, or biased.

Professional Journals and Books

Part of the process of science is that conclusions are not considered solid until they are corroborated in many studies, which means that you should consult several sources on any topic. Four **journals in human development** are:

- *Developmental Psychology* (published by the American Psychological Association)
- *Child Development* (Society for Research in Child Development)
- *Developmental Review* (Elsevier)
- *Human Development* (Karger)

These journals differ in the types of articles and studies they publish, but all are well respected and *peer-reviewed,* which means that other scholars review each article submitted and recommend that it be accepted, rejected, or revised. Every article includes references to other recent work.

Beyond these four are literally thousands of other professional journals, each with a particular perspective or topic. To judge them, look for journals that are peer-reviewed. Also consider the following details: the background of the author (research funded by corporations tends to favor their products); the nature of the publisher (professional organizations, as in the first two journals above, protect their reputations); how long the journal has been published (the volume number tells you that). Some interesting work does not meet these criteria, but these are guides to quality.

Many **books** cover some aspect of development. Single-author books are likely to present only one viewpoint. That view may be insightful, but it is limited. You might consult a *handbook,* which is a book that includes many authors and many topics. Two good handbooks in development, both now in their sixth editions (a sign that past scholars have found them useful) are:

- *Handbook of Child Psychology* (2006, Damon & Lerner, eds.), four volumes, published by Wiley
- *Handbook of Aging* (2011), three volumes (biology, psychology, and social sciences), published by Academic Press

Again, dozens of good handbooks are available, many of which focus on a particular age or topic.

The Internet

The **Internet** is a mixed blessing, useful to every novice and experienced researcher but dangerous as well. Every library worldwide and most homes in North America, western Europe, and East Asia have computers that provide access to journals and other information. Ask for help from the librarians; many are highly skilled. In addition, other students, friends, and even strangers can be helpful.

Virtually everything is on the Internet, not only massive national and international statistics but also very personal accounts. Photos, charts, quizzes, ongoing experiments, newspapers from around the world, videos, and much more are available at the click of a mouse. Every journal has a Web site, with tables of contents, abstracts, and sometimes full texts (an abstract gives the key findings; for the full text, you may need to consult the library's copy of the print version).

Unfortunately, you can spend many frustrating hours sifting through information that is useless, trash, or tangential. *Directories* (which list general topics or areas and then move you step by step in the direction you choose) and *search engines* (which give you all the sites that use a particular word or words) can help you select appropriate information. Each directory or search engine provides somewhat different lists; none provides only the most comprehensive and accurate sites. With experience and help, you will find the best sites for you, but you will also encounter some junk no matter how experienced you are.

Anybody can put anything on the Web, regardless of its truth or fairness, so evaluate with a very critical eye everything you find. Make sure you have several divergent sources for every "fact" you find; consider who provided the information and why. Every controversial issue has sites that forcefully advocate opposite viewpoints, sometimes with biased statistics and narrow perspectives.

Here are seven Internet sites that are quite reliable:

- *www.worthpublishers.com/berger* Includes links to Web sites, quizzes, PowerPoint slides, and activities keyed to every chapter of the textbook.
- *embryo.soad.umich.edu* The Multidimensional Human Embryo. Presents MRI images of a human embryo at various stages of development, accompanied by brief explanations.

- *http://childdevelopmentinfo.com/* Child Development Institute. A useful site, with links and articles on child development and information on common childhood psychological disorders.
- *ericeece.org* ERIC Clearinghouse. Provides links to many education-related sites and includes brief descriptions of each.
- *http://portal.education.indiana.edu/cafs/aboutus/AdolescenceDirectoryonLineADOL.aspx* Adolescence Directory online (ADOL) is an electronic guide to information on adolescent issues. It is a service of the Center for Adolescent and Family Studies at Indiana University.
- *http://www.nia.nih.gov/* National Institute on Aging. Includes information about current research on aging.
- *www.cdc.gov/nchs/hus.htm* The National Center for Health Statistics issues an annual report on health trends, called *Health, United States.*

Every source—you, your interviewees, journals, books, and the Internet—is helpful. Do not depend on any particular one. Especially if you use the Web, also check print resources. Avoid plagiarism and prejudice by citing every source and noting objectivity, validity, and credibility. Your own analysis, opinions, words, and conclusions are crucial.

Additional Terms and Concepts

As emphasized throughout this text, the study of development is a science. Social scientists spend years in graduate school, studying methods and statistics. Chapter 1 touches on some of these matters (observation and experiments; correlation and statistical significance; independent and dependent variables; experimental and control groups; cross-sectional, longitudinal, and cross-sequential research), but there is much more. A few additional aspects of research are presented here, to help you evaluate research wherever you find it.

Who Participates?

The entire group of people about whom a scientist wants to learn is called the **population.** Generally, a research population is quite large—not usually the world's entire population of almost 8 billion, but perhaps all the 4 million babies born in the United States last year, or all the 25 million Japanese currently over age 65.

The particular individuals who are studied in a specific research project are called the **participants.** They are used as a **sample** of the larger group. Ideally, a large number of people are used as a **representative sample,** that is, a sample who reflect the entire population. Every peer-reviewed published study reports details on the sample.

Selection of the sample is crucial. Volunteers, or people with telephones, or people treated with some particular condition, are not a *random sample,* in which everyone in that population is equally likely to be selected. To avoid *selection bias,* some studies are *prospective,* beginning with an entire cluster (for instance, every baby born on a particular day) and then tracing the development of some particular characteristic.

For example, prospective studies find the antecedents of heart disease, or child abuse, or high school dropout rates—all of which are much harder to find if the study is *retrospective,* beginning with those who had heart attacks, experienced abuse, or left school. Thus, although retrospective research finds that most high school dropouts say they disliked school, prospective research finds that some who like school still decide to drop out and then later say they hated school, while others dislike school but stay to graduate. Prospective research discovers how many students are in these last two categories; retrospective research on people who have already dropped out does not.

population
The entire group of individuals who are of particular concern in a scientific study, such as all the children of the world or all newborns who weigh less than 3 pounds.

participants
The people who are studied in a research project.

sample
A group of individuals drawn from a specified population. A sample might be the low-birthweight babies born in four particular hospitals that are representative of all hospitals.

representative sample
A group of research participants who reflect the relevant characteristics of the larger population whose attributes are under study.

Research Design

Every researcher begins not only by formulating a hypothesis but also by learning what other scientists have discovered about the topic in question and what methods might be useful and ethical in designing research. Often they include measures to guard against inadvertently finding only the results they expect. For example, the people who actually gather the data may not know the purpose of the research. Scientists say that these data gatherers are **blind** to the hypothesized outcome. Participants are sometimes "blind" as well, because otherwise they might, for instance, respond the way they think they should.

Another crucial aspect of research design is to define exactly what is to be studied. Researchers establish an **operational definition** of whatever phenomenon they will be examining, defining each variable by describing specific, observable behavior. This is essential in quantitative research (see Chapter 1), but it is also useful in qualitative research. For example, if a researcher wants to know when babies begin to walk, does *walking* include steps taken while holding on? Is one unsteady step enough? Some parents say yes, but the usual operational definition of walking is "takes at least three steps without holding on." This operational definition allows comparisons worldwide, making it possible to discover, for example, that well-fed African babies tend to walk earlier than well-fed European babies.

Operational definitions are difficult but essential when personality traits are studied. How should *aggression* or *sharing* or *shyness* be defined? Lack of an operational definition leads to contradictory results. For instance, some say that infant day care makes children more aggressive, but others say it makes them less passive. Similarly, as explained in the Epilogue, the operational definition of death is the subject of heated disputes. For any scientist, operational definitions are crucial.

Reporting Results

You already know that results should be reported in sufficient detail so that another scientist can analyze the conclusions and replicate the research. Various methods, populations, and research designs may produce divergent conclusions. For that reason, handbooks, some journals, and some articles are called *reviews:* They summarize past research. Often, when studies are similar in operational definitions and methods, the review is a **meta-analysis,** combining the findings of many studies to present an overall conclusion.

Table 1.3 describes some statistical measures. One of them is *statistical significance,* which indicates whether or not a particular result could have occurred by chance.

Another statistic that is often crucial is **effect size,** a way of measuring how much impact one variable has on another. Effect size ranges from 0 (no effect) to 1 (total transformation, never found in actual studies). Effect size may be particularly important when the sample size is large, because a large sample often leads to highly "significant" results (unlikely to have occurred by chance) that have only a tiny effect on the variable of interest.

Hundreds of statistical measures are used by developmentalists. Often the same data can be presented in many ways: Some scientists examine statistical analysis intently before they accept conclusions as valid. A specific example involved methods to improve students' writing ability between grades 4 and 12. A meta-analysis found that many methods of writing instruction have a significant impact, but effect size is much larger for some methods (teaching strategies and summarizing) than for others (prewriting exercises and studying models). For teachers, this statistic is crucial, for they want to know what has a big effect, not merely what is better than chance (significant).

blind
The condition of data gatherers (and sometimes participants as well) who are deliberately kept ignorant of the purpose of the research so that they cannot unintentionally bias the results.

operational definition
A description of the specific, observable behavior that will constitute the variable that is to be studied, so that any reader will know whether that behavior occurred or not. Operational definitions may be arbitrary (e.g., an IQ score at or above 130 is operationally defined as "gifted"), but they must be precise.

meta-analysis
A technique of combining results of many studies to come to an overall conclusion. Meta-analysis is powerful, in that small samples can be added together to lead to significant conclusions, although variations from study to study sometimes make combining them impossible.

effect size
A way to indicate, statistically, how much of an impact the independent variable had on the dependent variable.

Numerous articles published in the past decade are meta-analyses that combine similar studies to search for general trends. Often effect sizes are also reported, which is especially helpful for meta-analysis since standard calculations almost always find some significance if the number of participants is in the thousands. Here are three recent examples, to help you grasp the use and implications of meta-analyses and effect size.

- **Twenge, Jean M., Gentile, Brittany, DeWall, C. Nathan, Ma, Debbie, Lacefield, Katharine, & Schurtz, David R.** (2010). Birth cohort increases in psychopathology among young Americans, 1938–2007: A cross-temporal meta-analysis of the MMPI. *Clinical Psychology Review, 30,* 145–154. [Using responses to the Minnesota Multiphasic Personality Inventory (the MMPI, an old chestnut, originally developed to spot psychopathology), this meta-analysis finds increasing prevalence of psychological disorders among adolescents and emerging adults in the United States. The reported effect size is large, 1.05. The authors hypothesize that contemporary culture is too materialistic and selfish, leading youth to ignore the deeper meaning of life. Note, however, that impressive statistics, as shown here, do not prove or disprove a causal explanation.]

- **Grote, Nancy K., Bridge, Jeffrey A., Gavin, Amelia R., Melville, Jennifer L., Iyengar, Satish, & Katon, Wayne J.** (2010). A meta-analysis of depression during pregnancy and the risk of preterm birth, low birthweight, and intrauterine growth restriction. *Archives of General Psychiatry, 67,* 1012–1024. [This meta-analysis confirms that pregnant women who are depressed are more likely to have low-birthweight newborns. The article also shows one of the benefits of meta analysis—the possibility of comparing people in different contexts on the same variables. In this case, depressed women in less developed nations were more at risk, and, within the United States, maternal depression has a more marked effect on low-income women. This meta-analysis makes a very convincing case that maternal mood and fetal growth are connected. Of course, additional variables may cause both the depression and the prenatal complications.]

- **Webb, Thomas L., Joseph, Judith, Yardley, Lucy, & Michie, Susan.** (2010). Using the internet to promote health behavior change: A systematic review and meta-analysis of the impact of theoretical basis, use of behavior change techniques, and mode of delivery on efficacy. *Journal of Medical Internet Research, 12,* e4. [The conclusion this article makes is not surprising: Messages sent via the Internet and texting can effectively promote health. Again, however, the advantages of meta-analyses are notable. In this study, the effect size of electronic messages on health was very small ($d = 0.16$). Such small effects might be ignored in studies with fewer participants, but a meta-analytic study can find them, with useful implications. For instance, if texting health messages annually saves only one life in 100,000, and if cost-benefit analysis finds no negative effects, then universal health texting in the United States would save 3,000 lives per year.]

GLOSSARY

A

AARP A U.S. organization of people 50 and older that advocates for the elderly. It was originally called the American Association of Retired Persons, but now only the initials AARP are used, since members need not be retired.

absent grief A situation in which mourners do not grieve, either because other people do not allow grief to be expressed or because the mourners do not allow themselves to feel sadness.

achievement test A measure of mastery or proficiency in reading, mathematics, writing, science, or some other subject.

active euthanasia A situation in which someone takes action to bring about another person's death, with the intention of ending that person's suffering.

activities of daily life (ADLs) Typically identified as five tasks of self-care that are important to independent living: eating, bathing, toileting, dressing, and transferring from a bed to a chair. The inability to perform any of these tasks is a sign of frailty.

activity theory The view that elderly people want and need to remain active in a variety of social spheres—with relatives, friends, and community groups—and become withdrawn only unwillingly, as a result of ageism.

additive gene A gene that adds something to some aspect of the phenotype. Its contribution depends on additions from the other genes, which may come from either the same or the other parent.

adolescence-limited offender A person whose criminal activity stops by age 21.

adolescent egocentrism A characteristic of adolescent thinking that leads young people (ages 10 to 13) to focus on themselves to the exclusion of others.

adrenal glands Two glands, located above the kidneys, that produce hormones (including the "stress hormones" epinephrine [adrenaline] and norepinephrine).

age in place Remaining in the same home and community in later life, adjusting but not leaving when health fades.

age of viability The age (about 22 weeks after conception) at which a fetus may survive outside the mother's uterus if specialized medical care is available.

ageism A prejudice whereby people are categorized and judged solely on the basis of their chronological age.

aggressive-rejected Rejected by peers because of antagonistic, confrontational behavior.

allele Any of the possible forms in which a gene for a particular trait can occur.

allocare Literally, "other-care"; the care of children by people other than the biological parents.

allostasis A dynamic body adjustment, related to homeostasis, that over time affects overall physiology. The main difference is that while homeostasis requires an immediate response, allostasis requires longer-term adjustment.

Alzheimer disease (AD) The most common cause of dementia, characterized by gradual deterioration of memory and personality and marked by the formation of plaques of beta-amyloid protein and tangles of tau in the brain. (Sometimes called *senile dementia of the Alzheimer type*.)

amygdala A tiny brain structure that registers emotions, particularly fear and anxiety.

analytic intelligence A form of intelligence that involves such mental processes as abstract planning, strategy selection, focused attention, and information processing, as well as verbal and logical skills.

analytic thought Thought that results from analysis, such as a systematic ranking of pros and cons, risks and consequences, possibilities and facts. Analytic thought depends on logic and rationality.

andropause A term coined to signify a drop in testosterone levels in older men, which normally results in reduced sexual desire, erections, and muscle mass. (Also called *male menopause*.)

animism The belief that natural objects and phenomena are alive.

anorexia nervosa An eating disorder characterized by self-starvation. Affected individuals voluntarily undereat and often overexercise, depriving their vital organs of nutrition. Anorexia can be fatal.

anoxia A lack of oxygen that, if prolonged, can cause brain damage or death.

antipathy Feelings of dislike or even hatred for another person.

antisocial behavior Actions that are deliberately hurtful or destructive to another person.

Apgar scale A quick assessment of a newborn's body functioning. The baby's heart rate, respiratory effort, muscle tone, color, and reflexes are given a score of 0, 1, or 2 twice—at one minute and five minutes after birth—and each time the total of all five scores is compared with the ideal score of 10 (which is rarely attained).

aptitude The potential to master a specific skill or to learn a certain body of knowledge.

assisted living A living arrangement for elderly people that combines privacy and independence with medical supervision.

asthma A chronic disease of the respiratory system in which inflammation narrows the airways from the nose and mouth to the lungs, causing difficulty in breathing. Signs and symptoms include wheezing, shortness of breath, chest tightness, and coughing.

attachment According to Ainsworth, "an affectional tie" that an infant forms with a caregiver—a tie that binds them together in space and endures over time.

attention-deficit/hyperactivity disorder (ADHD) A condition in which a person not only has great difficulty concentrating for more than a few moments but also is inattentive, impulsive, and overactive.

authoritarian parenting An approach to child rearing that is characterized by high behavioral standards, strict punishment of misconduct, and little communication.

authoritative parenting An approach to child rearing in which the parents set limits and enforce rules but are flexible and listen to their children.

autism spectrum disorder Any of several disorders characterized by inadequate social skills, impaired communication, and unusual play.

automatic processing Thinking that occurs without deliberate, conscious thought. Experts process most tasks automatically, saving conscious thought for unfamiliar challenges.

autonomy versus shame and doubt Erikson's second crisis of psychosocial development. Toddlers either succeed or fail in gaining a sense of self-rule over their actions and their bodies.

average life expectancy The number of years the average newborn in a particular population group is likely to live.

axon A fiber that extends from a neuron and transmits electrochemical impulses from that neuron to the dendrites of other neurons.

B

babbling The extended repetition of certain syllables, such as *ba-ba-ba,* that begins when babies are between 6 and 9 months old.

balanced bilingual A person who is fluent in two languages, not favoring one over the other.

behavioral teratogens Agents and conditions that can harm the prenatal brain, impairing the future child's intellectual and emotional functioning.

behaviorism A theory of human development that studies observable behavior. Behaviorism is also called *learning theory* because it describes the laws and processes by which behavior is learned.

bickering Petty, peevish arguing, usually repeated and ongoing.

Big Five The five basic clusters of personality traits that remain quite stable throughout adulthood: openness, conscientiousness, extroversion, agreeableness, and neuroticism.

bilingual schooling A strategy in which school subjects are taught in both the learner's original language and the second (majority) language.

binocular vision The ability to focus the two eyes in a coordinated manner in order to see one image.

bipolar disorder A condition characterized by extreme mood swings, from euphoria to deep depression, not caused by outside experiences.

blind The condition of data gatherers (and sometimes participants as well) who are deliberately kept ignorant of the purpose of the research so that they cannot unintentionally bias the results.

body image A person's idea of how his or her body looks.

body mass index (BMI) A person's weight in kilograms divided by the square of height in meters.

Brazelton Neonatal Behavioral Assessment Scale (NBAS) A test often administered to newborns that measures responsiveness and records 46 behaviors, including 20 reflexes.

bulimia nervosa An eating disorder characterized by binge eating and subsequent purging, usually by induced vomiting and/or use of laxatives.

bully-victim Someone who attacks others and who is attacked as well. (Also called *provocative victims* because they do things that elicit bullying.)

bullying aggression Unprovoked, repeated physical or verbal attack, especially on victims who are unlikely to defend themselves.

bullying Repeated, systematic efforts to inflict harm through physical, verbal, or social attack on a weaker person.

C

calorie restriction The practice of limiting dietary energy intake (while consuming sufficient quantities of vitamins, minerals, and other important nutrients) for the purpose of improving health and slowing down the aging process.

carrier A person whose genotype includes a gene that is not expressed in the phenotype. Such an unexpressed gene occurs in half the carrier's gametes and thus is passed on to half the carrier's children, who will most likely be carriers, too. Generally, the characteristic appears in the phenotype only when such a gene is inherited from both parents.

case study An in-depth study of one person, usually requiring personal interviews to collect background information and various follow-up discussions, tests, questionnaires, and so on.

cellular aging The ways in which molecules and cells are affected by age. Many theories aim to explain how and why aging causes cells to deteriorate.

center day care Child care that occurs in a place especially designed for the purpose, where several paid adults care for many children. Usually, the children are grouped by age, the day-care center is licensed, and providers are trained and certified in child development.

centration A characteristic of preoperational thought whereby a young child focuses (centers) on one idea, excluding all others.

cerebral palsy A disorder that results from damage to the brain's motor centers. People with cerebral palsy have difficulty with muscle control, so their speech and/or body movements are impaired.

cesarean section (c-section) A surgical birth, in which incisions through the mother's abdomen and uterus allow the fetus to be removed quickly, instead of being delivered through the vagina.

charter school A public school with its own set of standards that is funded and licensed by the state or local district in which it is located.

child abuse Deliberate action that is harmful to a child's physical, emotional, or sexual well-being.

child culture The particular habits, styles, and values that reflect the set of rules and rituals that characterize children as distinct from adult society.

child maltreatment Intentional harm to or avoidable endangerment of anyone under 18 years of age.

child neglect Failure to meet a child's basic physical, educational, or emotional needs.

child sexual abuse Any erotic activity that arouses an adult and excites, shames, or confuses a child, whether or not the victim protests and whether or not genital contact is involved.

child-directed speech The high-pitched, simplified, and repetitive way adults speak to infants. (Also called *baby talk* or *motherese*.)

childhood obesity In a child, having a BMI above the 95th percentile, according to the U.S. Centers for Disease Control's 1980 standards for children of a given age.

childhood overweight In a child, having a BMI above the 85th percentile, according to the U.S. Centers for Disease Control's 1980 standards for children of a given age.

choice overload Having so many options that a thoughtful choice becomes difficult, and regret after making a choice is more likely.

chromosome One of the 46 molecules of DNA (in 23 pairs) that each cell of the human body contains and that, together, contain all the genes. Other species have more or fewer chromosomes.

circadian rhythm A day–night cycle of biological activity that occurs approximately every 24 hours (*circadian* means "about a day").

classical conditioning A learning process in which a meaningful stimulus (such as the smell of food to a hungry animal) gradually comes to be connected with a neutral stimulus (such as a particular sound) that had no special meaning before the learning process began. (Also called *respondent conditioning*.)

classification The logical principle that things can be organized into groups (or categories or classes) according to some characteristic they have in common.

clinical depression Feelings of hopelessness, lethargy, and worthlessness that last two weeks or more.

clique A group of adolescents made up of close friends who are loyal to one another while excluding outsiders.

cluster suicides Several suicides committed by members of a group within a brief period.

co-sleeping A custom in which parents and their children (usually infants) sleep together in the same bed.

cognitive theory A theory of human development that focuses on changes in how people think over time. According to this theory, our thoughts shape our attitudes, beliefs, and behaviors.

cohabitation An arrangement in which a couple live together in a committed romantic relationship but are not formally married.

cohort A group defined by the shared age of its members, who, because they were born at about the same time, move through life together, experiencing the same historical events and cultural shifts.

comorbid Refers to the presence of two or more disease conditions at the same time in the same person.

complicated grief A type of grief that impedes a person's future life, usually because the person clings to sorrow or is buffeted by contradictory emotions.

compression of morbidity A shortening of the time a person spends ill or infirm, accomplished by postponing illness.

compulsive hoarding The urge to accumulate and hold on to familiar objects and possessions, sometimes to the point of their becoming health and/or safety hazards. This impulse tends to increase with age.

concrete operational thought Piaget's term for the ability to reason logically about direct experiences and perceptions.

conditioning According to behaviorism, the processes by which responses become linked to particular stimuli and learning takes place. The word *conditioning* is used to emphasize the importance of repeated practice, as when an athlete *conditions* his or her body to perform well by training for a long time.

consequential strangers People who are not in a person's closest friendship circle but nonetheless have an impact.

conservation The principle that the amount of a substance remains the same (i.e., is conserved) even when its appearance changes.

control processes Mechanisms (including selective attention, metacognition, and emotional regulation) that combine memory, processing speed, and knowledge to regulate the analysis and flow of information within the information-processing system. (Also called *executive processes*.)

control processes The part of the information-processing system that regulates the analysis and flow of information. Memory and retrieval strategies, selective attention, and rules or strategies for problem solving are all useful control processes.

conventional moral reasoning Kohlberg's second level of moral reasoning, emphasizing social rules.

corpus callosum A long, thick band of nerve fibers that connects the left and right hemispheres of the brain and allows communication between them.

correlation A number that indicates the degree of relationship between two variables, expressed in terms of the likelihood that one variable will (or will not) occur when the other variable does (or does not). A correlation indicates only that two variables are related, not that one variable causes the other to occur.

cortex The outer layers of the brain in humans and other mammals. Most thinking, feeling, and sensing involve the cortex.

cortisol The primary stress hormone; fluctuations in the body's cortisol level affect human emotion.

couvade Symptoms of pregnancy and birth experienced by fathers.

creative intelligence A form of intelligence that involves the capacity to be intellectually flexible and innovative.

critical period A time when a particular type of developmental growth (in body or behavior) must happen if it is ever going to happen.

cross-sectional research A research design that compares groups of people who differ in age but are similar in other important characteristics.

cross-sequential research A hybrid research design in which researchers first study several groups of people of different ages (a cross-sectional approach) and then follow those groups over the years (a longitudinal approach). (Also called *cohort-sequential research* or *time-sequential research*.)

crowd A larger group of adolescents who have something in common but who are not necessarily friends.

crystallized intelligence Those types of intellectual ability that reflect accumulated learning. Vocabulary and general information are examples. Some developmental psychologists think crystallized intelligence increases with age, while fluid intelligence declines.

culture A system of shared beliefs, norms, behaviors, and expectations that persist over time and prescribe social behavior and assumptions.

cyberbullying Bullying that occurs when one person spreads insults or rumors about another by means of technology (e.g., e-mails, text messages, or cell phone videos).

D

deductive reasoning Reasoning from a general statement, premise, or principle, through logical steps, to figure out (deduce) specifics. (Also called *top-down reasoning*.)

deferred imitation A sequence in which an infant first perceives something done by someone else and then performs the same action hours or even days later.

delirium A temporary loss of memory, often accompanied by hallucinations, terror, grandiosity, and irrational behavior.

dementia Irreversible loss of intellectual functioning caused by organic brain damage or disease. Dementia becomes more common with age, but it is abnormal and pathological even in the very old.

demographic shift A shift in the proportions of the populations of various ages.

dendrite A fiber that extends from a neuron and receives electrochemical impulses transmitted from other neurons via their axons.

dependency ratio A calculation of the number of self-sufficient, productive adults compared with the number of dependents (children and the elderly) in a given population.

dependent variable In an experiment, the variable that may change as a result of whatever new condition or situation the experimenter adds. In other words, the dependent variable *depends* on the independent variable.

developmental theory A group of ideas, assumptions, and generalizations that interpret and illuminate the thousands of observations that have been made about human growth. A developmental theory provides a framework for explaining the patterns and problems of development.

deviancy training Destructive peer support in which one person shows another how to rebel against authority or social norms.

difference-equals-deficit error The mistaken belief that a deviation from some norm is necessarily inferior to behavior or characteristics that meet the standard.

differential sensitivity The idea that some people are more vulnerable than others are to certain experiences, usually because of genetic differences.

disenfranchised grief A situation in which certain people, although they are bereaved, are prevented from mourning publicly by cultural customs or social restrictions.

disengagement theory The view that aging makes a person's social sphere increasingly narrow, resulting in role relinquishment, withdrawal, and passivity.

disorganized attachment A type of attachment that is marked by an infant's inconsistent reactions to the caregiver's departure and return.

distal parenting Caregiving practices that involve remaining distant from the baby, providing toys, food, and face-to-face communication with minimal holding and touching.

dizygotic twins Twins who are formed when two separate ova are fertilized by two separate sperm at roughly the same time. (Also called *fraternal twins*.)

DNA (deoxyribonucleic acid) The molecule that contains the chemical instructions for cells to manufacture various proteins.

DNR (do not resuscitate) order A written order from a physician (sometimes initiated by a patient's advance directive or by a health care proxy's request) that no attempt should be made to revive a patient if he or she suffers cardiac or respiratory arrest.

dominant–recessive pattern The interaction of a pair of alleles in such a way that the phenotype reveals the influence of one allele (the dominant gene) more than that of the other (the recessive gene).

double effect A situation in which an action (such as administering opiates) has both a positive effect (relieving a terminally ill person's pain) and a negative effect (hastening death by suppressing respiration).

doula A woman who helps with the birth process. Doulas are trained to offer support to new mothers, including massage and suggestions for breast-feeding positions.

Down syndrome A condition in which a person has 47 chromosomes instead of the usual 46, with three rather than two chromosomes at the 21st position. People with Down syndrome typically have distinctive characteristics, including unusual facial features (thick tongue, round face, slanted eyes), heart abnormalities, and language difficulties. (Also called *trisomy-21*.)

drug abuse The ingestion of a drug to the extent that it impairs the user's biological or psychological well-being.

dual-process model The notion that two networks exist within the human brain, one for emotional and one for analytical processing of stimuli.

dynamic-systems approach A view of human development as an ongoing, ever-changing interaction between a person's physical and emotional being and between the person and every aspect of his or her environment, including the family and society.

dyscalculia Unusual difficulty with math, probably originating from a distinct part of the brain.

dyslexia Unusual difficulty with reading; thought to be the result of some neurological underdevelopment.

E

ecological niche The particular lifestyle and social context that adults settle into because it is compatible with their individual personality needs and interests.

ecological validity The idea that cognition should be measured in settings that are as realistic as possible and that the abilities measured should be those needed in real life.

ecological-systems approach The view that in the study of human development, the person should be considered in all the contexts and interactions that constitute a life. (Later renamed *bioecological theory*.)

effect size A way to indicate, statistically, how much of an impact the independent variable had on the dependent variable.

egocentrism Piaget's term for young children's tendency to think about the world entirely from their own personal perspective.

elderspeak A condescending way of speaking to older adults that resembles baby talk, with simple and short sentences, exaggerated emphasis, repetition, and a slower rate and a higher pitch than used in normal speech.

Electra complex The unconscious desire of girls to replace their mothers and win their fathers' exclusive love.

embryo The name for a developing human organism from about the third through the eighth week after conception.

embryonic period The stage of prenatal development from approximately the third through the eighth week after conception, during which the basic forms of all body structures, including internal organs, develop.

emerging adulthood The period of life between the ages of 18 and 25. Emerging adulthood is now widely thought of as a separate developmental stage.

emotion-focused coping A strategy to deal with stress by changing feelings about the stressor rather than changing the stressor itself.

emotional regulation The ability to control when and how emotions are expressed.

empathy The ability to understand the emotions and concerns of another person, especially when they differ from one's own.

empirical evidence Evidence based on data from scientific observation or experiments; not theoretical.

empty nest The time in the lives of parents when their children have left the family home to pursue their own lives.

entity approach to intelligence An approach to understanding intelligence that sees ability as innate, a fixed quantity present at birth; those who hold this view do not believe that effort enhances achievement.

epigenetic Referring to the effects of environmental forces on the expression of an individual's, or a species', genetic inheritance.

equifinality A basic principle of developmental psychopathology that holds that one symptom can have many causes.

ESL (English as a second language) An approach to teaching English in which all children who do not speak English are placed together in an intensive course to learn basic English so that they can be educated in the same classroom as native English speakers.

estradiol A sex hormone, considered the chief estrogen. Females produce much more estradiol than males do.

ethnic group People whose ancestors were born in the same region and who often share a language, culture, and religion.

experiment A research method in which the researcher tries to determine the cause-and-effect relationship between two variables by manipulating one (called the *independent variable*) and then observing and recording the ensuing changes in the other (called the *dependent variable*).

expert One who is notably more accomplished, proficient, and/or knowledgeable in a particular skill, topic, or task than the average person.

expertise A person's ability to be more accomplished at a particular skill, or to have better knowledge of a particular subject, than the average person.

extended family A family of three or more generations living in one household.

externalizing problems Difficulty with emotional regulation that involves expressing powerful feelings through uncontrolled physical or verbal outbursts, as by lashing out at other people or breaking things.

extreme sports Forms of recreation that include apparent risk of injury or death and are attractive and thrilling as a result.

extremely low birthweight (ELBW) A body weight at birth of less than 2 pounds, 3 ounces (1,000 grams).

extrinsic motivation A drive, or reason to pursue a goal, that arises from the need to have one's achievements rewarded from outside, perhaps by receiving material possessions or another person's esteem.

extrinsic rewards of work The tangible benefits, usually in the form of compensation (e.g., salary, health insurance, pension), that one receives for doing a job.

F

familism The belief that family members should support one another, sacrificing individual freedom and success, if necessary, in order to preserve family unity and protect the family from outside forces.

family day care Child care that includes several children of various ages and usually occurs in the home of a woman who is paid to provide it.

family function The way a family works to meet the needs of its members. Children need families to provide basic material necessities, to encourage learning, to help them develop self-respect, to nurture friendships, and to foster harmony and stability.

family structure The legal and genetic relationships among relatives living in the same home; includes nuclear family, extended family, stepfamily, and so on.

fast-mapping The speedy and sometimes imprecise way in which children learn new words by tentatively placing them in mental categories according to their perceived meaning.

fetal alcohol syndrome (FAS) A cluster of birth defects, including abnormal facial characteristics, slow physical growth, and intellectual disabilities, that may occur in the child of a woman who drinks alcohol while pregnant.

fetal period The stage of prenatal development from the ninth week after conception until birth, during which the fetus grows in size and matures in functioning.

fetus The name for a developing human organism from the start of the ninth week after conception until birth.

fictive kin Someone who becomes accepted as part of a family to which he or she has no blood relation.

filial responsibility The obligation of adult children to care for their aging parents.

fine motor skills Physical abilities involving small body movements, especially of the hands and fingers, such as drawing and picking up a coin. (The word *fine* here means "small.")

flextime An arrangement in which work schedules are flexible so that employees can balance personal and occupational responsibilities.

fluid intelligence Those types of basic intelligence that make learning of all sorts quick and thorough. Abilities such as short-term memory, abstract thought, and speed of thinking are all usually considered part of fluid intelligence.

Flynn effect The rise in average IQ scores that has occurred over the decades in many nations.

focus on appearance A characteristic of preoperational thought whereby a young child ignores all attributes that are not apparent.

foreclosure Erikson's term for premature identity formation, which occurs when an adolescent adopts his or her parents' or society's roles and values wholesale, without questioning or analysis.

formal operational thought In Piaget's theory, the fourth and final stage of cognitive development, characterized by more systematic logical thinking and by the ability to understand and systematically manipulate abstract concepts.

frail elderly People older than 65, and often older than 85, who are physically infirm, very ill, or cognitively disabled.

frontal lobe dementia Deterioration of the amygdala and frontal lobes that may be the cause of 15 percent of all dementias. (Also called *frontotemporal lobar degeneration*.)

G

gamete A reproductive cell; that is, a sperm or an ovum that can produce a new individual if it combines with a gamete from the other sex to form a zygote.

gender differences Differences in the roles and behaviors that are prescribed by a culture for males and females.

gender identity A person's acceptance of the roles and behaviors that society associates with the biological categories of male and female.

gender schema A child's cognitive concept or general belief about sex differences, which is based on his or her observations and experiences.

gene A small section of a chromosome; the basic unit for the transmission of heredity. A gene consists of a string of chemicals that provide instructions for the cell to manufacture certain proteins.

general intelligence (g) The idea of g assumes that intelligence is one basic trait, underlying all cognitive abilities. According to this concept, people have varying levels of this general ability.

generational forgetting The idea that each new generation forgets what the previous generation learned. As used here, the term refers to knowledge about the harm drugs can do.

generativity versus stagnation The seventh of Erikson's eight stages of development. Adults seek to be productive in a caring way, perhaps through art, caregiving, and employment.

genetic clock A purported mechanism in the DNA of cells that regulates the aging process by triggering hormonal changes and controlling cellular reproduction and repair.

genome The full set of genes that are the instructions to make an individual member of a certain species.

genotype An organism's entire genetic inheritance, or genetic potential.

germinal period The first two weeks of prenatal development after conception, characterized by rapid cell division and the beginning of cell differentiation.

grammar All the methods—word order, verb forms, and so on—that languages use to communicate meaning, apart from the words themselves.

grief The deep sorrow that people feel at the death of another. Grief is personal and unpredictable.

gross motor skills Physical abilities involving large body movements, such as walking and jumping. (The word *gross* here means "big.")

growth spurt The relatively sudden and rapid physical growth that occurs during puberty. Each body part increases in size on a schedule: Weight usually precedes height, and growth of the limbs precedes growth of the torso.

H

Hayflick limit The number of times a human cell is capable of dividing into two new cells. The limit for most human cells is approximately 50 divisions, an indication that the life span is limited by our genetic program.

Head Start The most widespread early-childhood-education program in the United States, begun in 1965 and funded by the federal government.

head-sparing A biological mechanism that protects the brain when malnutrition disrupts body growth. The brain is the last part of the body to be damaged by malnutrition.

health care proxy A person chosen by another person to make medical decisions if the second person becomes unable to do so.

heritability A statistic that indicates what percentage of the variation in a particular trait within a particular population, in a particular context and era, can be traced to genes.

hidden curriculum The unofficial, unstated, or implicit rules and priorities that influence the academic curriculum and every other aspect of learning in a school.

high-stakes test An evaluation that is critical in determining success or failure. If a single test determines whether a student will graduate or be promoted, it is a high-stakes test.

hippocampus A brain structure that is a central processor of memory, especially memory for locations.

Hispanic paradox The surprising discovery that, although low SES usually correlates with poor health, this is not true for Hispanics in the United States. For example, when compared with the U.S. average LBW rate, Hispanic newborns are less often of low birthweight.

holophrase A single word that is used to express a complete, meaningful thought.

home schooling Education in which children are taught at home, usually by their parents, instead of attending any school, public or private.

homeostasis The adjustment of all the body's systems to keep physiological functions in a state of equilibrium, moment by moment. As the body ages, it takes longer for these homeostatic adjustments to occur, so it becomes harder for older bodies to adapt to stress.

hormone An organic chemical substance that is produced by one body tissue and conveyed via the bloodstream to another to affect some physiological function.

hormone replacement therapy (HRT) Taking hormones (in pills, patches, or injections) to compensate for hormone reduction. HRT is most common in women at menopause or after removal of the ovaries, but it is also used by men to help restore their decreased testosterone level. HRT has some medical uses but also carries health risks.

hospice An institution or program in which terminally ill patients receive palliative care to reduce suffering; family and friends of the dying are helped as well.

HPA (hypothalamus–pituitary–adrenal) axis A sequence of hormone production that originates in the hypothalamus, moves to the pituitary, and then to the adrenal glands.

HPG (hypothalamus–pituitary–gonad) axis A sequence of hormone production that originates in the hypothalamus, moves to the pituitary, and then to the gonads.

humanism A theory that stresses the potential of all human beings for good and the belief that all people have the same basic needs, regardless of culture, gender, or background.

hybrid theory A perspective that combines various aspects of different theories to explain how language, or any other developmental phenomenon, occurs.

hypothalamus A brain area that responds to the amygdala and the hippocampus to produce hormones that activate other parts of the brain and body.

hypothesis A specific prediction that can be tested.

hypothetical thought Reasoning that includes propositions and possibilities that may not reflect reality.

I

identification An attempt to defend one's self-concept by taking on the behaviors and attitudes of someone else.

identity achievement Erikson's term for the attainment of identity, or the point at which a person understands who he or she is as a unique individual, in accord with past experiences and future plans.

identity versus role confusion Erikson's term for the fifth stage of development, in which the person tries to figure out "Who am I?" but is confused as to which of many possible roles to adopt.

imaginary audience The other people who, in an adolescent's egocentric belief, are watching and taking note of his or her appearance, ideas, and behavior. This belief makes many teenagers very self-conscious.

imaginary friends Make-believe friends who exist only in a child's imagination; increasingly common from ages 3 through 7, they combat loneliness and aid emotional regulation.

immersion A strategy in which instruction in all school subjects occurs in the second (usually the majority) language that a child is learning.

immunization A process that stimulates the body's immune system to defend against attack by a particular contagious disease. Immunization may be accomplished either naturally (by having the disease) or through vaccination (often by having an injection). (Also called *vaccination*.)

implantation The process, beginning about 10 days after conception, in which the developing organism burrows into the tissue that lines the uterus, where it can be nourished and protected as it continues to develop.

in vitro fertilization (IVF) A technique in which ova (egg cells) are surgically removed from a woman and fertilized with sperm in a laboratory. After the original fertilized cells (the zygotes) have divided several times, they are inserted into the woman's uterus.

incomplete grief A situation in which circumstances, such as a police investigation or an autopsy, interfere with the process of grieving.

incremental approach to intelligence An approach to understanding intelligence that holds that intelligence can be directly increased by effort; those who subscribe to this view believe they can master whatever they seek to learn if they pay attention, participate in class, study, complete their homework, and so on.

independent variable In an experiment, the variable that is introduced to see what effect it has on the dependent variable. (Also called *experimental variable*.)

individual education plan (IEP) A document that specifies educational goals and plans for a child with special needs.

inductive reasoning Reasoning from one or more specific experiences or facts to reach (induce) a general conclusion. (Also called *bottom-up reasoning*.)

industry versus inferiority The fourth of Erikson's eight psychosocial crises, during which children attempt to master many skills, developing a sense of themselves as either industrious or inferior, competent or incompetent.

infertility The inability to conceive a child after trying for at least a year.

information-processing theory A perspective that compares human thinking processes, by analogy, to computer analysis of data, including sensory input, connections, stored memories, and output.

initiative versus guilt Erikson's third psychosocial crisis, in which children undertake new skills and activities and feel guilty when they do not succeed at them.

injury control/harm reduction Practices that are aimed at anticipating, controlling, and preventing dangerous activities; these practices reflect the beliefs that accidents are not random and that injuries can be made less harmful if proper controls are in place.

insecure-avoidant attachment A pattern of attachment in which an infant avoids connection with the caregiver, as when the infant seems not to care about the caregiver's presence, departure, or return.

insecure-resistant/ambivalent attachment A pattern of attachment in which an infant's anxiety and uncertainty are evident, as when the infant becomes very upset at separation from the caregiver and both resists and seeks contact on reunion.

instrumental activities of daily life (IADLs) Actions (e.g., budgeting and preparing food) that are important to independent living and that require some intellectual competence and forethought. The ability to perform these tasks may be even more critical to self-sufficiency than ADL ability.

instrumental aggression Hurtful behavior that is intended to get something that another person has and to keep it.

integrity versus despair The final stage of Erik Erikson's developmental sequence, in which older adults seek to integrate their unique experiences with their vision of community.

internalizing problems Difficulty with emotional regulation that involves turning one's emotional distress inward, as by feeling excessively guilty, ashamed, or worthless.

intimacy versus isolation The sixth of Erikson's eight stages of development. Adults seek someone with whom to share their lives in an enduring and self-sacrificing commitment. Without such commitment, they risk profound loneliness and isolation.

intrinsic motivation A drive, or reason to pursue a goal, that comes from inside a person, such as the need to feel smart or competent.

intrinsic rewards of work The intangible gratifications (e.g., job satisfaction, self-esteem, pride) that come from within oneself as a result of doing a job.

intuitive thought Thought that arises from an emotion or a hunch, beyond rational explanation, and is influenced by past experiences and cultural assumptions.

invincibility fable An adolescent's egocentric conviction that he or she cannot be overcome or even harmed by anything that might defeat a normal mortal, such as unprotected sex, drug abuse, or high-speed driving.

IQ (intelligence quotient) test A test designed to measure intellectual aptitude, or ability to learn in school. Originally, intelligence was defined as mental age divided by chronological age, times 100—hence the term *intelligence quotient,* or *IQ.*

irreversibility A characteristic of preoperational thought whereby a young child thinks that nothing can be undone. A thing cannot be restored to the way it was before a change occurred.

J

just right The tendency of children to insist on having things done in a particular way. This can include clothes, food, bedtime routines, and so on.

K

kangaroo care A child-care technique in which a new mother holds the baby between her breasts, like a kangaroo that carries her immature newborn in a pouch on her abdomen.

kinkeeper A caregiver who takes responsibility for maintaining communication among family members.

kinship care A form of foster care in which a relative of a maltreated child, usually a grandparent, becomes the approved caregiver.

knowledge base A body of knowledge in a particular area that makes it easier to master new information in that area.

kwashiorkor A disease of chronic malnutrition during childhood, in which a protein deficiency makes the child more vulnerable to other diseases, such as measles, diarrhea, and influenza.

L

language acquisition device (LAD) Chomsky's term for a hypothesized mental structure that enables humans to learn language, including the basic aspects of grammar, vocabulary, and intonation.

latency Freud's term for middle childhood, during which children's emotional drives and psychosexual needs are quiet (latent). Freud thought that sexual conflicts from earlier stages are only temporarily submerged, bursting forth again at puberty.

lateralization Literally, "sidedness," referring to the specialization in certain functions by each side of the brain, with one side dominant for each activity. The left side of the brain controls the right side of the body, and vice versa.

learning disability A marked delay in a particular area of learning that is not caused by an apparent physical disability, by another disorder, or by an unusually stressful home environment.

least restrictive environment (LRE) A legal requirement that children with special needs be assigned to the most general educational context in which they can be expected to learn.

leptin A hormone that affects appetite and is believed to affect the onset of puberty. Leptin levels increase during childhood and peak at around age 12.

Lewy body dementia A form of dementia characterized by an increase in Lewy body cells in the brain. Symptoms include visual hallucinations, momentary loss of attention, falling, and fainting.

life review An examination of one's own role in the history of human life, engaged in by many elderly people.

life-course-persistent offender A person whose criminal activity typically begins in early adolescence and continues throughout life; a career criminal.

life-span perspective An approach to the study of human development that takes into account all phases of life, not just childhood or adulthood.

limbic system The major brain region crucial to the development of emotional expression and regulation; its three main areas are the amygdala, the hippocampus, and the hypothalamus, although recent research has found that many other areas of the brain are involved with emotions.

linked lives Lives in which the success, health, and well-being of each family member are connected to those of other members, including members of another generation, as in the relationship between parents and children.

little scientist The stage-five toddler (age 12 to 18 months) who experiments without anticipating the results, using trial and error in active and creative exploration.

living will A document that indicates what medical intervention an individual prefers if he or she is not conscious when a decision is to be expressed. For example, some do not want to be given mechanical breathing.

long-term memory The component of the information-processing system in which virtually limitless amounts of information can be stored indefinitely.

longitudinal research A research design in which the same individuals are followed over time and their development is repeatedly assessed.

low birthweight (LBW) A body weight at birth of less than 5½ pounds (2,500 grams).

M

marasmus A disease of severe protein-calorie malnutrition during early infancy, in which growth stops, body tissues waste away, and the infant eventually dies.

massification The idea that establishing higher learning institutions and encouraging college enrollment could benefit everyone (the masses), leading to marked increases in the number of emerging adults in college.

maximum life span The oldest possible age that members of a species can live under ideal circumstances. For humans, that age is approximately 122 years.

menarche A girl's first menstrual period, signaling that she has begun ovulation. Pregnancy is biologically possible, but ovulation and menstruation are often irregular for years after menarche.

menopause The time in middle age, usually around age 50, when a woman's menstrual periods cease and the production of estrogen, progesterone, and testosterone drops. Strictly speaking, menopause is dated one year after a woman's last menstrual period, although many months before and after that date are considered part of the period of menopause.

meta-analysis A technique of combining results of many studies to come to an overall conclusion. Meta-analysis is powerful, in that small samples can be added together to lead to significant conclusions, although variations from study to study sometimes make combining them impossible.

metacognition "Thinking about thinking," or the ability to evaluate a cognitive task in order to determine how best to accomplish it, and then to monitor and adjust one's performance on that task.

middle childhood The period between early childhood and early adolescence, approximately from ages 6 to 11.

middle school A school for children in the grades between elementary and high school. Middle school usually begins with grade 6 and ends with grade 8.

midlife crisis A supposed period of unusual anxiety, radical self-reexamination, and sudden transformation that was once widely associated with middle age but that actually had more to do with developmental history than with chronological age.

Mini–Mental State Examination (MMSE) A test that is used to measure cognitive ability, especially in late adulthood.

mirror neurons Cells in an observer's brain that respond to an action performed by someone else in the same way they would if the observer had actually performed that action.

monozygotic twins Twins who originate from one zygote that splits apart very early in development. (Also called *identical twins*.)

Montessori schools Schools that offer early-childhood education based on the philosophy of Maria Montessori (an Italian educator more than a century ago); it emphasizes careful work and tasks that each young child can do.

moratorium An adolescent's choice of a socially acceptable way to postpone making identity-achievement decisions. Going to college is a common example.

motor skills The learned abilities to move some part of the body, in actions ranging from a large leap to a flicker of the eyelid. (The word *motor* here refers to movement of muscles.)

mourning The ceremonies and behaviors that a religion or culture prescribes for people to employ in expressing their bereavement after a death.

multifinality A basic principle of developmental psychopathology that holds that one cause can have many (multiple) final manifestations.

multiple intelligences The idea that human intelligence is comprised of a varied set of abilities rather than a single, all-encompassing one.

myelination The process by which axons become coated with myelin, a fatty substance that speeds the transmission of nerve impulses from neuron to neuron.

N

National Assessment of Educational Progress (NAEP) An ongoing and nationally representative measure of U.S. children's achievement in reading, mathematics, and other subjects over time; nicknamed "the Nation's Report Card."

naturally occurring retirement community (NORC) A neighborhood or apartment complex whose population is mostly retired people who moved to the location as younger adults and never left.

nature A general term for the traits, capacities, and limitations that each individual inherits genetically from his or her parents at the moment of conception.

neglectful/uninvolved parenting An approach to child rearing in which the parents are indifferent toward their children and unaware of what is going on in their children's lives.

neuron One of billions of nerve cells in the central nervous system, especially in the brain.

neurotransmitter A brain chemical that carries information from the axon of a sending neuron to the dendrites of a receiving neuron.

No Child Left Behind Act A U.S. law enacted in 2001 that was intended to increase accountability in education by requiring states to qualify for federal educational funding by administering standardized tests to measure school achievement.

norm An average, or standard, measurement, calculated from the measurements of many individuals within a specific group or population.

nuclear family A family that consists of a father, a mother, and their biological children under age 18.

nurture A general term for all the environmental influences that affect development after an individual is conceived.

O

object permanence The realization that objects (including people) still exist even if they can no longer be seen, touched, or heard.

Oedipus complex The unconscious desire of young boys to replace their fathers and win their mothers' exclusive love.

old-old Older adults (generally, those older than 75) who suffer from physical, mental, or social deficits.

oldest-old Elderly adults (generally, those older than 85) who are dependent on others for almost everything, requiring supportive services such as nursing homes and hospital stays.

operant conditioning A learning process in which a particular action is followed either by something desired (which makes the person or animal more likely to repeat the action) or by something unwanted (which makes the action less likely to be repeated). (Also called *instrumental conditioning.*)

operational definition A description of the specific, observable behavior that will constitute the variable that is to be studied, so that any reader will know whether that behavior occurred or not. Operational definitions may be arbitrary (e.g., an IQ score at or above 130 is operationally defined as "gifted"), but they must be precise.

organ reserve The extra capacity built into each organ, such as the heart and lungs, that allows a person to cope with extraordinary demands or to withstand organ strain.

osteoporosis Fragile bones that result from primary aging, which makes bones more porous, especially if a person is at genetic risk.

overimitation The tendency of children to copy an action that is not a relevant part of the behavior to be learned; common among 2- to 6-year-olds when they imitate adult actions that are irrelevant and inefficient.

overregularization The application of rules of grammar even when exceptions occur, making the language seem more "regular" than it actually is.

P

palliative care Care designed not to treat an illness but to provide physical and emotional comfort to the patient and support and guidance to his or her family.

parasuicide Any potentially lethal action against the self that does not result in death. (Also called *attempted suicide* or *failed suicide.*)

parent–infant bond The strong, loving connection that forms as parents hold, examine, and feed their newborn.

parental monitoring Parents' ongoing awareness of what their children are doing, where, and with whom.

Parkinson disease A chronic, progressive disease that is characterized by muscle tremor and rigidity and sometimes dementia; caused by reduced dopamine production in the brain.

parochial school Non-public schools organized by a religious group, often Roman Catholic but sometimes Jewish, Muslim, and so on. The curriculum, discipline, and many instructors in parochial schools reflect the beliefs of the religious body, which often provides substantial financial support.

participants The people who are studied in a research project.

passive euthanasia A situation in which a seriously ill person is allowed to die naturally, through the cessation of medical intervention.

peer pressure Encouragement to conform to one's friends or contemporaries in behavior, dress, and attitude; usually considered a negative force, as when adolescent peers encourage one another to defy adult authority.

perception The mental processing of sensory information when the brain interprets a sensation.

permanency planning An effort by child-welfare authorities to find a long-term living situation that will provide stability and support for a maltreated child. A goal is to avoid repeated changes of caregiver or school, which can be particularly harmful to the child.

permissive parenting An approach to child rearing that is characterized by high nurturance and communication but little discipline, guidance, or control.

perseveration The tendency to persevere in, or stick to, one thought or action for a long time.

personal fable An aspect of adolescent egocentrism characterized by an adolescent's belief that his or her thoughts, feelings, and experiences are unique, more wonderful or awful than anyone else's.

phallic stage Freud's third stage of development, when the penis becomes the focus of concern and pleasure.

phenotype The observable characteristics of a person, including appearance, personality, intelligence, and all other traits.

physician-assisted suicide A form of active euthanasia in which a doctor provides the means for someone to end his or her own life.

PISA (Programme for International Student Assessment) An international test taken by 15-year-olds in 50 nations that is designed to measure problem solving and cognition in daily life.

pituitary A gland in the brain that responds to a signal from the hypothalamus by producing many hormones, including those that regulate growth and that control other glands, among them the adrenal and sex glands.

polygamous family A family consisting of one man, several wives, and their children.

polypharmacy Refers to a situation in which elderly people are prescribed several medications. The various side effects and interactions of those medications can result in dementia symptoms.

population The entire group of individuals who are of particular concern in a scientific study, such as all the children of the world or all newborns who weigh less than 3 pounds.

positivity effect The tendency for elderly people to perceive, prefer, and remember positive images and experiences more than negative ones.

postconventional moral reasoning Kohlberg's third level of moral reasoning, emphasizing moral principles.

postformal thought A proposed adult stage of cognitive development, following Piaget's four stages. Postformal thought goes beyond adolescent thinking by being more practical, more flexible, and more dialectical (i.e., more capable of combining contradictory elements into a comprehensive whole).

postpartum depression The sadness and inadequacy felt by some new mothers in the days and weeks after giving birth.

practical intelligence The intellectual skills used in everyday problem solving. (Sometimes called *tacit intelligence*.)

pragmatics The practical use of language that includes the ability to adjust language communication according to audience and context.

preconventional moral reasoning Kohlberg's first level of moral reasoning, emphasizing rewards and punishments.

prefrontal cortex The area of the cortex at the front of the brain that specializes in anticipation, planning, and impulse control.

prefrontal cortex The area of the cortex at the very front of the brain that specializes in anticipation, planning, and impulse control.

preoperational intelligence Piaget's term for cognitive development between the ages of about 2 and 6; it includes language and imagination (which involve symbolic thought), but logical, operational thinking is not yet possible.

preterm birth A birth that occurs three or more weeks before the full 38 weeks of the typical pregnancy have elapsed—that is, at 35 or fewer weeks after conception.

primary aging The universal and irreversible physical changes that occur in all living creatures as they grow older.

primary prevention Actions that change overall background conditions to prevent some unwanted event or circumstance, such as injury, disease, or abuse.

primary sex characteristics The parts of the body that are directly involved in reproduction, including the vagina, uterus, ovaries, testicles, and penis.

private school A school funded by parents and sponsoring institutions. Such schools have control over admissions, hiring, and specifics of curriculum, although some regulations apply.

problem-focused coping A strategy to deal with stress by tackling a stressful situation directly.

Progress in International Reading Literacy Study (PIRLS) Inaugurated in 2001, a planned five-year cycle of international trend studies in the reading ability of fourth-graders.

prosocial behavior Actions that are helpful and kind but that are of no obvious benefit to the person doing them.

protein-calorie malnutrition A condition in which a person does not consume sufficient food of any kind. This deprivation can result in several illnesses, severe weight loss, and even death.

proximal parenting Caregiving practices that involve being physically close to the baby, with frequent holding and touching.

pruning When applied to brain development, the process by which unused connections in the brain atrophy and die.

psychoanalytic theory A theory of human development that holds that irrational, unconscious drives and motives, often originating in childhood, underlie human behavior.

psychological control A disciplinary technique that involves threatening to withdraw love and support and that relies on a child's feelings of guilt and gratitude to the parents.

psychopathology An illness or disorder of the mind.

puberty The time between the first onrush of hormones and full adult physical development. Puberty usually lasts three to five years. Many more years are required to achieve psychosocial maturity.

Q

qualitative research Research that considers qualities instead of quantities. Descriptions of particular conditions and participants' expressed ideas are often part of qualitative studies.

quantitative research Research that provides data that can be expressed with numbers, such as ranks or scales.

R

race A group of people regarded as distinct from other groups on the basis of appearance, typically skin color. Social scientists think race is a misleading concept, as biological differences are not signified by outward appearance.

reaction time The time it takes to respond to a stimulus, either physically (with a reflexive movement such as an eyeblink) or cognitively (with a thought).

reactive aggression An impulsive retaliation for another person's intentional or accidental action, verbal or physical.

reflex An unlearned, involuntary action or movement in response to a stimulus. A reflex occurs without conscious thought.

Reggio Emilia A famous program of early-childhood education that originated in the town of Reggio Emilia, Italy; it encourages each child's creativity in a carefully designed setting.

reinforcement A technique for conditioning a particular behavior in which that behavior is followed by something desired, such as food for a hungry animal or a welcoming smile for a lonely person.

relational aggression Nonphysical acts, such as insults or social rejection, aimed at harming the social connection between the victim and other people.

REM (rapid eye movement) sleep A stage of sleep characterized by flickering eyes behind closed lids, dreaming, and rapid brain waves.

reminder session A perceptual experience that is intended to help a person recollect an idea, a thing, or an experience, without testing whether the person remembers it at the moment.

replication The repetition of a study, using different participants.

reported maltreatment Harm or endangerment about which someone has notified the authorities.

representative sample A group of research participants who reflect the relevant characteristics of the larger population whose attributes are under study.

resilience The capacity to adapt well to significant adversity and to overcome serious stress.

response to intervention (RTI) An educational strategy that uses early intervention to help children who demonstrate below-average achievement. Only children who are not helped are designated for more intense measures.

role confusion A situation in which an adolescent does not seem to know or care what his or her identity is. (Sometimes called *identity* or *role diffusion*.)

rough-and-tumble play Play that mimics aggression through wrestling, chasing, or hitting, but in which there is no intent to harm.

rumination Repeatedly thinking and talking about past experiences; can contribute to depression.

S

sample A group of individuals drawn from a specified population. A sample might be the low-birthweight babies born in four particular hospitals that are representative of all hospitals.

sandwich generation The generation of middle-aged people who are supposedly "squeezed" by the needs of the younger and older members of their families. In reality, some adults do feel pressured by these obligations, but most are not burdened by them, either because they enjoy fulfilling them or because they choose to take on only some of them or none of them.

scaffolding Temporary support that is tailored to a learner's needs and abilities and aimed at helping the learner master the next task in a given learning process.

science of human development The science that seeks to understand how and why people of all ages and circumstances change or remain the same over time.

scientific method A way to answer questions that requires empirical research and data-based conclusions.

scientific observation A method of testing a hypothesis by unobtrusively watching and recording participants' behavior in a systematic and objective manner—in a natural setting, in a laboratory, or in searches of archival data.

Seattle Longitudinal Study The first cross-sequential study of adult intelligence. This study began in 1956; the most recent testing was conducted in 2005.

secondary aging The specific physical illnesses or conditions that become more common with aging but are caused by health habits, genes, and other influences that vary from person to person.

secondary education Literally, the period after primary education (elementary or grade school) and before tertiary education (college). It usually occurs from about age 12 to 18, although there is some variation by school and by nation.

secondary prevention Actions that avert harm in a high-risk situation, such as stopping a car before it hits a pedestrian or installing traffic lights at dangerous intersections.

secondary sex characteristics Physical traits that are not directly involved in reproduction but that indicate sexual maturity, such as a man's beard and a woman's breasts.

secure attachment A relationship in which an infant obtains both comfort and confidence from the presence of his or her caregiver.

selective attention The ability to concentrate on some stimuli while ignoring others.

selective optimization with compensation The theory, developed by Paul and Margret Baltes, that people try to maintain a balance in their lives by looking for the best way to compensate for physical and cognitive losses and to become more proficient in activities they can already do well.

self theories Theories of late adulthood that emphasize the core self, or the search to maintain one's integrity and identity.

self-actualization The final stage in Maslow's hierarchy of needs, characterized by aesthetic, creative, philosophical, and spiritual understanding.

self-awareness A person's realization that he or she is a distinct individual whose body, mind, and actions are separate from those of other people.

self-concept A person's understanding of who he or she is, incorporating self-esteem, physical appearance, personality, and various personal traits, such as gender and size.

self-righting The inborn drive to remedy a developmental deficit; literally, to return to sitting or standing upright after being tipped over. People of all ages have self-righting impulses, for emotional as well as physical imbalance.

senescence A gradual physical decline related to aging. Senescence occurs in everyone and in every body part, but the rate of decline is highly variable within and between persons.

sensation The response of a sensory system (eyes, ears, skin, tongue, nose) when it detects a stimulus.

sensitive period A time when a certain type of development is most likely to happen or happens most easily, although it may still happen later with more difficulty. For example, early childhood is considered a sensitive period for language learning.

sensorimotor intelligence Piaget's term for the way infants think—by using their senses and motor skills—during the first period of cognitive development.

sensory memory The component of the information-processing system in which incoming stimulus information is stored for a split second to allow it to be processed. (Also called the *sensory register*.)

separation anxiety An infant's distress when a familiar caregiver leaves, most obvious between 9 and 14 months.

sex differences Biological differences between males and females, in organs, hormones, and body shape.

sexual orientation A term that refers to whether a person is sexually and romantically attracted to others of the same sex, the opposite sex, or both sexes.

sexually transmitted infection (STI) An infection spread by sexual contact; includes syphilis, gonorrhea, genital herpes, chlamydia, and HIV.

shaken baby syndrome A life-threatening injury that occurs when an infant is forcefully shaken back and forth, a motion that ruptures blood vessels in the brain and breaks neural connections.

single-parent family A family that consists of only one parent and his or her biological children under age 18.

slippery slope The argument that a given action will start a chain of events that will culminate in an undesirable outcome.

small for gestational age (SGA) Having a body weight at birth that is significantly lower than expected, given the time since conception. For example, a 5-pound (2,265-gram) newborn is considered SGA if born on time but not SGA if born two months early. (Also called *small-for-dates*.)

social comparison The tendency to assess one's abilities, achievements, social status, and other attributes by measuring them against those of other people, especially one's peers.

social construction An idea that is based on shared perceptions, not on objective reality. Many age-related terms, such as *childhood, adolescence, yuppie,* and *senior citizen,* are social constructions.

social convoy Collectively, the family members, friends, acquaintances, and even strangers who move through life with an individual.

social learning The acquisition of behavior patterns by observing the behavior of others.

social learning theory An extension of behaviorism that emphasizes that other people influence each person's behavior. The theory's basic principle is that even without specific reinforcement, every individual learns many things through observation and imitation of other people.

social referencing Seeking information about how to react to an unfamiliar or ambiguous object or event by observing someone else's expressions and reactions. That other person becomes a social reference.

social smile A smile evoked by a human face, normally first evident in infants about 6 weeks after birth.

sociodramatic play Pretend play in which children act out various roles and themes in stories that they create.

socioeconomic status (SES) A person's position in society as determined by income, wealth, occupation, education, and place of residence. (Sometimes called *social class*.)

spermarche A boy's first ejaculation of sperm. Erections can occur as early as infancy, but ejaculation signals sperm production. Spermarche may occur during sleep (in a "wet dream") or via direct stimulation.

static reasoning A characteristic of preoperational thought whereby a young child thinks that nothing changes. Whatever is now has always been and always will be.

stem cells Cells from which any other specialized type of cell can form.

stereotype threat The possibility that one's appearance or behavior will be misread to confirm another person's oversimplified, prejudiced attitudes.

still-face technique An experimental practice in which an adult keeps his or her face unmoving and expressionless in face-to-face interaction with an infant.

Strange Situation A laboratory procedure for measuring attachment by evoking infants' reactions to the stress of various adults' comings and goings in an unfamiliar playroom.

stranger wariness An infant's expression of concern—a quiet stare when clinging to a familiar person, or a look of sadness—when a stranger appears.

stratification theories Theories that emphasize that social forces, particularly those related to a person's social stratum or social category, limit individual choices and affect a person's ability to function in late adulthood because past stratification continues to limit life in various ways.

stressor Any situation, event, experience, or other stimulus that causes a person to feel stressed. Many circumstances become stressors for some people but not for others.

stunting The failure of children to grow to a normal height for their age due to severe and chronic malnutrition.

substantiated maltreatment Harm or endangerment that has been reported, investigated, and verified.

sudden infant death syndrome (SIDS) The term used to describe an infant's unexpected death; when a seemingly healthy baby, usually between 2 and 6 months old, suddenly stops breathing and dies unexpectedly while asleep.

suicidal ideation Thinking about suicide, usually with some serious emotional and intellectual or cognitive overtones.

superego In psychoanalytic theory, the judgmental part of the personality that internalizes the moral standards of the parents.

survey A research method in which information is collected from a large number of people by interviews, written questionnaires, or some other means.

symbolic thought The concept that an object or word can stand for something else, including something pretend or something not seen. Once symbolic thought is possible, language becomes much more useful.

synapses The intersection between the axon of one neuron and the dendrites of other neurons.

synaptic gap The pathway across which neurotransmitters carry information from the axon of the sending neuron to the dendrites of the receiving neuron.

synchrony A coordinated, rapid, and smooth exchange of responses between a caregiver and an infant.

T

telecommuting Working at home and keeping in touch with the office via computer, telephone, and scanner.

temperament Inborn differences between one person and another in emotions, activity, and self-regulation. It is measured by the person's typical responses to the environment.

teratogen Any agent or condition, including viruses, drugs, and chemicals, that can impair prenatal development, resulting in birth defects or complications.

terror management theory (TMT) The idea that people adopt cultural values and moral principles in order to cope with their fear of death. This system of beliefs protects individuals from anxiety about their mortality and bolsters their self-esteem, so they react harshly when other people go against any of the moral principles involved.

tertiary prevention Actions, such as immediate and effective medical treatment, that are taken after an adverse event (such as illness, injury, or abuse) occurs and that are aimed at reducing the harm or preventing disability.

testosterone A sex hormone, the best known of the androgens (male hormones); secreted in far greater amounts by males than by females.

thanatology The study of death and dying, especially of the social and emotional aspects.

theory of mind A person's theory of what other people might be thinking. In order to have a theory of mind, children must realize that other people are not necessarily thinking the same thoughts that they themselves are. That realization is seldom achieved before age 4.

theory-theory The idea that children attempt to explain everything they see and hear.

threshold effect A situation in which a certain teratogen is relatively harmless in small doses but becomes harmful once exposure reaches a certain level (the threshold).

time-out A disciplinary technique in which a child is separated from other people and activities for a specified time.

transient exuberance The great but temporary increase in the number of dendrites that develop in an infant's brain during the first two years of life.

Trends in Math and Science Study (TIMSS) An international assessment of the math and science skills of fourth- and eighth-graders. Although the TIMSS is very useful, different countries' scores are not always comparable because sample selection, test administration, and content validity are hard to keep uniform.

trust versus mistrust Erikson's first crisis of psychosocial development. Infants learn basic trust if the world is a secure place where their basic needs (for food, comfort, attention, and so on) are met.

U

ultrasound An image of a fetus (or an internal organ) produced by using high-frequency sound waves. (Also called *sonogram*.)

universal design Designing physical space and common tools that are suitable for people of all ages and all levels of ability.

V

vascular dementia (VaD) A form of dementia characterized by sporadic, and progressive, loss of intellectual functioning caused by repeated infarcts, or temporary obstructions of blood vessels, which prevent sufficient blood from reaching the brain. (Also called *multi-infarct dementia*.)

very low birthweight (VLBW) A body weight at birth of less than 3 pounds, 5 ounces (1,500 grams).

voucher A monetary commitment by the government to pay for the education of a child. Vouchers vary a great deal from place to place, not only in amount and availability, but in restrictions as to who gets them and what schools accept them. Typically, the voucher goes to whatever school the child attends.

W

wasting The tendency for children to be severely underweight for their age as a result of malnutrition.

wear and tear A view of aging as a process by which the human body wears out because of the passage of time and exposure to environmental stressors.

withdrawn-rejected Rejected by peers because of timid, withdrawn, and anxious behavior.

working memory The component of the information-processing system in which current conscious mental activity occurs. (Formerly called *short-term memory*.)

working model In cognitive theory, a set of assumptions that the individual uses to organize perceptions and experiences. For example, a person might assume that other people are trustworthy and be surprised by an incident that this working model of human behavior was erroneous.

X

X-linked A gene carried on the X chromosome. If a male inherits an X-linked recessive trait from his mother, he expresses that trait because the Y from his father has no counteracting gene. Females are more likely to be carriers of X-linked traits but are less likely to express them.

XX A 23rd chromosome pair that consists of two X-shaped chromosomes, one each from the mother and the father. XX zygotes become females.

XY A 23rd chromosome pair that consists of an X-shaped chromosome from the mother and a Y-shaped chromosome from the father. XY zygotes become males.

Y

young-old Healthy, vigorous, financially secure older adults (generally, those aged 60 to 75) who are well integrated into the lives of their families and communities.

Z

zone of proximal development (ZPD) Vygotsky's term for the skills—cognitive as well as physical—that a person can exercise only with assistance, not yet independently.

zygote The single cell that is formed from the fusing of two gametes, a sperm and an ovum.

REFERENCES

Aarnoudse-Moens, Cornelieke S. H., Smidts, Diana P., Oosterlaan, Jaap, Duivenvoorden, Hugo J., & Weisglas-Kuperus, Nynke. (2009). Executive function in very preterm children at early school age. *Journal of Abnormal Child Psychology, 37*, 981–993.

Aarsland, Dag, Zaccai, Julia, & Brayne, Carol. (2005). A systematic review of prevalence studies of dementia in Parkinson's disease. *Movement Disorders, 20*, 1255–1263.

Abel, Ernest L. (2009). Fetal alcohol syndrome: Same old, same old. *Addiction, 104*, 1274–1275.

Abele, Andrea E., & Volmer, Judith. (2011). Dual-career couples: Specific challenges for work-life integration. In Stephan Kaiser, Max Josef Ringlstetter, Doris Ruth Eikhof, & Miguel Pina e Cunha (Eds.), *Creating balance? International perspectives on the work-life integration of professionals* (pp. 173–189). Heidelberg, Germany: Springer Berlin Heidelberg.

Aboa-Éboulé, Corine, Brisson, Chantal, Maunsell, Elizabeth, Mâsse, Benoît, Bourbonnais, Renée, Vézina, Michel,... Dagenais, Gilles R. (2007). Job strain and risk of acute recurrent coronary heart disease events. *Journal of the American Medical Association, 298*, 1652–1660.

Abrams, Dominic, Rutland, Adam, Ferrell, Jennifer M., & Pelletier, Joseph. (2008). Children's judgments of disloyal and immoral peer behavior: Subjective group dynamics in minimal intergroup contexts. *Child Development, 79*, 444–461.

Abu-Bader, Soleman H., Tirmazi, M. Taqi, & Ross-Sheriff, Fariyal. (2011). The impact of acculturation on depression among older Muslim immigrants in the United States. *Journal of Gerontological Social Work, 54*, 425–448.

Achenbaum, W. Andrew. (2005). *Older Americans, vital communities: A bold vision for societal aging.* Baltimore, MD: Johns Hopkins University Press.

Acs, Gregory. (2007). Can we promote child well-being by promoting marriage? *Journal of Marriage and Family, 69*, 1326–1344.

Adam, Emma K., Klimes-Dougan, Bonnie, & Gunnar, Megan R. (2007). Social regulation of the adrenocortical response to stress in infants, children, and adolescents: Implications for mental health and education. In Donna Coch, Geraldine Dawson, & Kurt W. Fischer (Eds.), *Human behavior, learning, and the developing brain: Atypical development* (pp. 264–304). New York, NY: Guilford Press.

Adamson, Lauren B., & Bakeman, Roger. (2006). Development of displaced speech in early mother-child conversations. *Child Development, 77*, 186–200.

Adler, Lynn Peters. (1995). *Centenarians: The bonus years.* Santa Fe, NM: Health Press.

Adolph, Karen E., & Berger, Sarah E. (2005). Physical and motor development. In Marc H. Bornstein & Michael E. Lamb (Eds.), *Developmental science: An advanced textbook* (5th ed., pp. 223–281). Mahwah, NJ: Erlbaum.

Adolph, Karen E., Vereijken, Beatrix, & Shrout, Patrick E. (2003). What changes in infant walking and why. *Child Development, 74*, 475–497.

Afifi, Tracie O., Enns, Murray W., Cox, Brian J., Asmundson, Gordon J. G., Stein, Murray B., & Sareen, Jitender. (2008). Population attributable fractions of psychiatric disorders and suicide ideation and attempts associated with adverse childhood experiences. *American Journal of Public Health, 98*, 946–952.

Ahmed, Leila. (2011). *A quiet revolution: The veil's resurgence, from the Middle East to America.* New Haven, CT: Yale University Press.

Ahmed, Parvez, & Jaakkola, Jouni J. K. (2007). Maternal occupation and adverse pregnancy outcomes: A Finnish population-based study. *Occupational Medicine, 57*, 417–423.

Ainsworth, Mary D. (1967). *Infancy in Uganda: Infant care and the growth of love.* Oxford, England: Johns Hopkins Press.

Ainsworth, Mary D. Salter. (1973). The development of infant-mother attachment. In Bettye M. Caldwell & Henry N. Ricciuti (Eds.), *Review of child development research* (Vol. 3, pp. 1–94). Chicago, IL: University of Chicago Press.

Ajdacic-Gross, Vladeta, Ring, Mariann, Gadola, Erika, Lauber, Christoph, Bopp, Matthias, Gutzwiller, Felix, Rössler, Wulf. (2008). Suicide after bereavement: An overlooked problem. *Psychological Medicine, 38*, 673–676.

Ajemian, Robert, D'Ausilio, Alessandro, Moorman, Helene, & Bizzi, Emilio. (2010). Why professional athletes need a prolonged period of warm-up and other peculiarities of human motor learning. *Journal of Motor Behavior, 42*, 381–388.

Ajzen, Icek. (2011). Job satisfaction, effort, and performance: A reasoned action perspective. *Contemporary Economics, 5*, 32.

Akinbami, Lara J., Lynch, Courtney D., Parker, Jennifer D., & Woodruff, Tracey J. (2010). The association between childhood asthma prevalence and monitored air pollutants in metropolitan areas, United States, 2001–2004. *Environmental Research, 110*, 294–301.

Al-Namlah, Abdulrahman S., Meins, Elizabeth, & Fernyhough, Charles. (2012). Self-regulatory private speech relates to children's recall and organization of autobiographical memories. *Early Childhood Research Quarterly, 27*, 441–446.

Al-Sayes, Fatin, Gari, Mamdooh, Qusti, Safaa, Bagatian, Nadiah, & Abuzenadah, Adel. (2011). Prevalence of iron deficiency and iron deficiency anemia among females at university stage. *Journal of Medical Laboratory and Diagnosis, 2*, 5–11.

Alasuutari, Pertti, Bickman, Leonard, & Brannen, Julia. (2008). Introduction: Social research in changing social conditions. In Pertti Alasuutari, Leonard Bickman, & Julia Brannen

(Eds.), *The SAGE Handbook of Social Research Methods* (pp. 1–8). London: Sage.

Albert, Dustin, & Steinberg, Laurence. (2011). Judgment and decision making in adolescence. *Journal of Research on Adolescence, 21*, 211–224.

Albert, Steven M., & Freedman, Vicki A. (2010). *Public health and aging: Maximizing function and well-being* (2nd ed.). New York, NY: Springer.

Alberts, Amy, Elkind, David, & Ginsberg, Stephen. (2007). The personal fable and risk-taking in early adolescence. *Journal of Youth and Adolescence, 36*, 71–76.

Aldwin, Carolyn M. (2007). *Stress, coping, and development: An integrative perspective* (2nd ed.). New York, NY: Guilford Press.

Alegre, Alberto. (2011). Parenting styles and children's emotional intelligence: What do we know? *The Family Journal, 19*, 56–62.

Alisat, Susan, & Pratt, Michael W. (2012). Characteristics of young adults' personal religious narratives and their relation with the identity status model: A longitudinal, mixed methods study. *Identity, 12*, 29–52.

Allemand, Mathias, Zimprich, Daniel, & Martin, Mike. (2008). Long-term correlated change in personality traits in old age. *Psychology and Aging, 23*, 545–557.

Allen, Argie, Davey, Maureen, & Davey, Adam. (2010). Being examples to the flock: The role of church leaders and African American families seeking mental health care services. *Contemporary Family Therapy, 32*, 117–134.

Allen, Elizabeth, Bonell, Chris, Strange, Vicki, Copas, Andrew, Stephenson, Judith, Johnson, Anne, & Oakley, Ann. (2007). Does the UK government's teenage pregnancy strategy deal with the correct risk factors? Findings from a secondary analysis of data from a randomised trial of sex education and their implications for policy. *Journal of Epidemiology & Community Health, 61*, 20–27.

Allen, Kathleen P. (2010). A bullying intervention system in high school: A two-year school-wide follow-up. *Studies in Educational Evaluation, 36*, 83–92.

Allen, Shanley. (2007). The future of Inuktitut in the face of majority languages: Bilingualism or language shift? *Applied Psycholinguistics, 28*, 515–536.

Alloy, Lauren B., & Abramson, Lyn Y. (2007). The adolescent surge in depression and emergence of gender differences: A biocognitive vulnerability-stress model in developmental context. In Daniel Romer & Elaine F. Walker (Eds.), *Adolescent psychopathology and the developing brain: Integrating brain and prevention science* (pp. 284–312). New York, NY: Oxford University Press.

Alm, Bernt. (2007). To co-sleep or not to sleep. *Acta Pædiatrica, 96*, 1385–1386.

Almeida, Leandro S., Prieto, Maria Dolores, Ferreira, Aristides I., Bermejo, Maria Rosario, Ferrando, Mercedes, & Ferrandiz, Carmen. (2010). Intelligence assessment: Gardner multiple intelligence theory as an alternative. *Learning and Individual Differences, 20*, 225–230.

Alsaker, Françoise D., & Flammer, August (2006). Pubertal development. In Sandy Jackson & Luc Goossens (Eds.),

Handbook of adolescent development (pp. 30–50). Hove, East Sussex, UK: Psychology Press.

Altbach, Philip G., Reisberg, Liz, & Rumbley, Laura E. (2010, March/April). Tracking a global academic revolution. *Change: The Magazine of Higher Learning, 42*, 30–39.

Alwin, Duane F. (2009). History, cohorts, and patterns of cognitive aging. In Hayden B. Bosworth & Christopher Hertzog (Eds.), *Aging and cognition: Research methodologies and empirical advances* (pp. 9–38). Washington, DC: American Psychological Association.

Alzheimer's Association. (2012). 2012 Alzheimer's disease facts and figures. *Alzheimer's & Dementia: The Journal of the Alzheimer's Association, 8*, 131–168.

Amato, Paul R. (2005). The impact of family formation change on the cognitive, social, and emotional well-being of the next generation. *Future of Children, 15*(2), 75–96.

Amato, Paul R. (2010). Research on divorce: Continuing trends and new developments. *Journal of Marriage and Family, 72*, 650–666.

Ambady, Nalini, & Bharucha, Jamshed. (2009). Culture and the brain. *Current Directions in Psychological Science, 18*, 342–345.

Ambler, Dana R., Bieber, Eric J., & Diamond, Michael P. (2012). Sexual function in elderly women: A review of current literature. *Reviews in Obstetrics and Gynecology, 5*, 16–27.

American Psychological Association. (2010). *Ethical principles of psychologists and code of conduct 2002: 2010 amendments.* Retrieved from http://www.apa.org/ethics/code/index.aspx

Anderson, Craig A., Gentile, Douglas A., & Buckley, Katherine E. (2007). *Violent video game effects on children and adolescents: Theory, research, and public policy.* New York, NY: Oxford University Press.

Anderson, Craig A., Sakamoto, Akira, Gentile, Douglas A., Ihori, Nobuko, Shibuya, Akiko, Yukawa, Shintaro, . . . Kobayashi, Kumiko. (2008). Longitudinal effects of violent video games on aggression in Japan and the United States. *Pediatrics, 122*, e1067–1072. doi:10.1542/peds.2008–1425

Anderson, Michael. (2001). 'You have to get inside the person' or making grief private: Image and metaphor in the therapeutic reconstruction of bereavement. In Jenny Hockey, Jeanne Katz, & Neil Small (Eds.), *Grief, mourning, and death ritual* (pp. 135–143). Buckingham, England: Open University Press.

Anderson, Robert N., Kochanek, Kenneth D., & Murphy, Sherry L. (1997). *Report of final mortality statistics, 1995.* Hyattsville, MD: National Center for Health Statistics.

Ansary, Nadia S., & Luthar, Suniya S. (2009). Distress and academic achievement among adolescents of affluence: A study of externalizing and internalizing problem behaviors and school performance. *Development and Psychopathology, 21*, 319–341.

Antonucci, Toni C., Akiyama, Hiroko, & Merline, Alicia. (2001). Dynamics of social relationships in midlife. In Margie E. Lachman (Ed.), *Handbook of midlife development* (pp. 571–598). New York, NY: Wiley.

Antonucci, Toni C., Jackson, James S., & Biggs, Simon. (2007). Intergenerational relations: Theory, research, and policy. *Journal of Social Issues, 63*, 679–693.

Aouizerat, Bradley, Pearce, C. Leigh, & Miaskowski, Christine. (2011). The search for host genetic factors of HIV/AIDS pathogenesis in the post-genome era: Progress to date and new avenues for discovery. *Current HIV/AIDS Reports, 8,* 38–44.

Apgar, Virginia. (1953). A proposal for a new method of evaluation of the newborn infant. *Current Researches in Anesthesia and Analgesia, 32,* 260–267.

Apostolou, Menelaos. (2007). Sexual selection under parental choice: The role of parents in the evolution of human mating. *Evolution and Human Behavior, 28,* 403–409.

Applegate, Anthony J., Applegate, Mary DeKonty, McGeehan, Catherine M., Pinto, Catherine M., & Kong, Ailing. (2009). The assessment of thoughtful literacy in NAEP: Why the states aren't measuring up. *Reading Teacher, 62,* 372–381.

Arber, Sara, & Timonen, Virpi (Eds.). (2012). *Contemporary grandparenting: Changing family relationships in global contexts.* Chicago, IL: Policy Press.

Archambault, Isabelle, Janosz, Michel, Fallu, Jean-Sebastien, & Pagani, Linda S. (2009). Student engagement and its relationship with early high school dropout. *Journal of Adolescence, 32,* 651–670.

Ardelt, Monika. (2011). Wisdom, age, and well-being. In K. Warner Schaie & Sherry L. Willis (Eds.), *Handbook of the psychology of aging* (7th ed., pp. 279–291). San Diego, CA: Academic Press.

Arking, Robert. (2006). *The biology of aging: Observations and principles* (3rd ed.). New York, NY: Oxford University Press.

Armstrong, Thomas. (2009). *Multiple intelligences in the classroom* (3rd ed.). Alexandria, VA: Association for Supervision and Curriculum Development.

Arnett, Jeffrey Jensen. (2004). *Emerging adulthood: The winding road from the late teens through the twenties.* New York, NY: Oxford University Press.

Arnett, Jeffrey Jensen, & Brody, Gene H. (2008). A fraught passage: The identity challenges of African American emerging adults. *Human Development, 51,* 291–293.

Arnett, Jeffrey Jensen, Kloep, Marion, Hendry, Leo B., & Tanner, Jennifer L. (2011). *Debating emerging adulthood: Stage or process?* New York, NY: Oxford University Press.

Arnold, L. Eugene, Farmer, Cristan, Kraemer, Helena Chmura, Davies, Mark, Witwer, Andrea, Chuang, Shirley, . . . Swiezy, Naomi B. (2010). Moderators, mediators, and other predictors of risperidone response in children with autistic disorder and irritability. *Journal of Child and Adolescent Psychopharmacology, 20,* 83–93.

Aron, Arthur, McLaughlin-Volpe, Tracy, Mashek, Debra, Lewandowski, Gary, Wright, Stephen C., & Aron, Elaine N. (2005). Including others in the self. *European Review of Social Psychology, 15,* 101–132.

Aronson, Joshua, & Dee, Thomas. (2012). Stereotype threat in the real world. In Michael Inzlicht & Toni Schmader (Eds.), *Stereotype threat: Theory, process, and application* (pp. 264–279). New York, NY: Oxford University Press.

Aronson, Joshua, Fried, Carrie B., & Good, Catherine. (2002). Reducing the effects of stereotype threat on African American college students by shaping theories of intelligence. *Journal of Experimental Social Psychology, 38,* 113–125.

Arum, Richard, & Roksa, Josipa. (2011). *Academically adrift: Limited learning on college campuses.* Chicago, IL: University of Chicago Press.

Arum, Richard, Roksa, Josipa, & Cho, Esther. (2011). *Improving undergraduate learning: Findings and policy recommendations from the SSRC-CLA Longitudinal Project.* New York, NY: Social Science Research Council.

Asarnow, Joan Rosenbaum, Porta, Giovanna, Spirito, Anthony, Emslie, Graham, Clarke, Greg, Wagner, Karen Dineen, . . . Brent, David A. (2011). Suicide attempts and nonsuicidal self-injury in the treatment of resistant depression in adolescents: Findings from the TORDIA study. *Journal of the American Academy of Child and Adolescent Psychiatry, 50,* 772–781.

Asendorpf, Jens B., Denissen, Jaap J. A., & van Aken, Marcel A. G. (2008). Inhibited and aggressive preschool children at 23 years of age: Personality and social transitions into adulthood. *Developmental Psychology, 44,* 997–1011.

Ashby, Michael. (2009). The dying human: A perspective from palliative medicine. In Allan Kellehear (Ed.), *The study of dying: From autonomy to transformation* (pp. 76–98). New York, NY: Cambridge University Press.

Ashman, Sharon B., Dawson, Geraldine, & Panagiotides, Heracles. (2008). Trajectories of maternal depression over 7 years: Relations with child psychophysiology and behavior and role of contextual risks. *Development and Psychopathology, 20,* 55–77.

Asscheman, Henk. (2009). Gender identity disorder in adolescents. *Sexologies, 18,* 105–108.

Atchley, Robert C. (2009). *Spirituality and aging.* Baltimore, MD: Johns Hopkins University Press.

Atkinson, Janette, & Braddick, Oliver. (2003). Neurobiological models of normal and abnormal visual development. In Michelle De Haan & Mark H. Johnson (Eds.), *The cognitive neuroscience of development* (pp. 43–71). New York, NY: Psychology Press.

Atladóttir, Hjördís Ó., Henriksen, Tine B., Schendel, Diana E., & Parner, Erik T. (2012). Using maternally reported data to investigate the association between early childhood infection and autism spectrum disorder: The importance of data source. *Paediatric and Perinatal Epidemiology, 26,* 373–385.

Aud, Susan, Hussar, William, Johnson, Frank, Kena, Grace, Roth, Erin, Manning, Eileen, . . . Jijun Zhang. (2011a). *The condition of education 2011* (NCES 2011-033). Washington, DC: U.S. Department of Education, National Center for Education Statistics.

Aud, Susan, Hussar, William, Johnson, Frank, Kena, Grace, Roth, Erin, Manning, Eileen, . . . Jijun Zhang. (2012). *The condition of education 2012* (NCES 2012-045). Washington, DC: U.S. Department of Education, National Center for Education Statistics.

Aud, Susan, Hussar, William, Planty, Michael, Snyder, Thomas, Bianco, Kevin, Fox, Mary Ann, . . . Lauren Drake. (2010). *The condition of education 2010.* Washington, DC: National Center for Education Statistics, Institute of Education Sciences, U.S. Department of Education.

Aud, Susan, KewalRamani, Angelina, & Frohlich, Lauren. (2011b). *America's youth: Transitions to adulthood* (NCES 2012-026). Washington, DC: U.S. Department of Education, National Center for Education Statistics.

Audrey, Suzanne, Holliday, Jo, & Campbell, Rona. (2006). It's good to talk: Adolescent perspectives of an informal, peer-led intervention to reduce smoking. *Social Science & Medicine, 63,* 320–334.

Aunola, Kaisa, & Nurmi, Jari-Erik. (2004). Maternal affection moderates the impact of psychological control on a child's mathematical performance. *Developmental Psychology, 40,* 965–978.

Australian Bureau of Statistics. (2009). *Australian social trends 2009: Using statistics to paint a picture of Australian society,* Catalogue No. 4102.0. Author: Canberra.

Austrian, Sonia G. (Ed.) (2008). *Developmental theories through the life cycle* (2nd ed.). New York, NY: Columbia University Press.

Aviv, Abraham. (2011). Leukocyte telomere dynamics, human aging and life span. In Edward J. Masoro & Steven N. Austad (Eds.), *Handbook of the biology of aging* (7th ed., pp. 163–176). San Diego, CA: Academic Press.

Ayalon, Liat, & Ancoli-Israel, Sonia. (2009). Normal sleep in aging. In Teofilo L. Lee-Chiong (Ed.), *Sleep medicine essentials* (pp. 173–176). Hoboken, NJ: Wiley-Blackwell.

Ayduk, Özlem, & Kross, Ethan. (2008). Enhancing the pace of recovery. *Psychological Science, 19,* 229–231.

Ayers, Catherine R., Saxena, Sanjaya, Golshan, Shahrokh, & Wetherell, Julie Loebach. (2010). Age at onset and clinical features of late life compulsive hoarding. *International Journal of Geriatric Psychiatry, 25,* 142–149.

Bachman, Jerald G., O'Malley, Patrick M., Freedman-Doan, Peter, Trzesniewski, Kali H., & Donnellan, M. Brent. (2011). Adolescent self-esteem: Differences by race/ethnicity, gender, and age. *Self Identity, 10,* 445–473.

Bagner, Daniel M., Pettit, Jeremy W., Lewinsohn, Peter M., & Seeley, John R. (2010). Effect of maternal depression on child behavior: A sensitive period? *Journal of the American Academy of Child and Adolescent Psychiatry, 49,* 699–707.

Bailey, Kira, West, Robert, & Anderson, Craig A. (2010). A negative association between video game experience and pro-active cognitive control. *Psychophysiology, 47,* 34–42.

Baker, Beth. (2007). *Old age in a new age: The promise of transformative nursing homes.* Nashville, TN: Vanderbilt University Press.

Baker, Jeffrey P. (2000). Immunization and the American way: 4 childhood vaccines. *American Journal of Public Health, 90,* 199–207.

Baker, Lindsey, & Silverstein, Merril. (2012). The wellbeing of grandparents caring for grandchildren in rural China and the United States. In Sara Arber & Virpi Timonen (Eds.), *Contemporary grandparenting: Changing family relationships in global contexts* (pp. 51–70). Bristol, UK: Policy Press.

Baker, Lindsey A., & Mutchler, Jan E. (2010). Poverty and material hardship in grandparent-headed households. *Journal of Marriage and Family, 72,* 947–962.

Bakermans-Kranenburg, Marian J., Bos, Karen, Bunkers, Kelley McCreery, Dobrova-Krol, Natasha A., Engle, Patrice L., Fox, Nathan A., . . . Zeanah, Charles H. (2011). Children without permanent parents: Research, practice, and policy. *Monographs of the Society for Research in Child Development, 76*(4, Serial No. 301), 1–318.

Baldry, Anna C., & Farrington, David P. (2007). Effectiveness of programs to prevent school bullying. *Victims & Offenders, 2,* 183–204.

Ball, Howard. (2012). *At liberty to die: The battle for death with dignity in America.* New York, NY: New York University Press.

Baltes, Paul B. (2003). On the incomplete architecture of human ontogeny: Selection, optimization and compensation as foundation of developmental theory. In Ursula M. Staudinger & Ulman Lindenberger (Eds.), *Understanding human development: Dialogues with lifespan psychology* (pp. 17–43). Dordrecht, The Netherlands: Kluwer.

Baltes, Paul B., & Baltes, Margret M. (1990). Psychological perspectives on successful aging: The model of selective optimization with compensation. In Paul B. Baltes & Margret M. Baltes (Eds.), *Successful aging: Perspectives from the behavioral sciences* (pp. 1–34). New York, NY: Cambridge University Press.

Baltes, Paul B., Lindenberger, Ulman, & Staudinger, Ursula M. (2006). Life span theory in developmental psychology. In William Damon & Richard M. Lerner (Series Eds.) & Richard M. Lerner (Vol. Ed.), *Handbook of child psychology: Vol. 1. Theoretical models of human development* (6th ed., pp. 569–664). Hoboken, NJ: Wiley.

Baltes, Paul B., & Smith, Jacqui. (2008). The fascination of wisdom: Its nature, ontogeny, and function. *Perspectives on Psychological Science, 3,* 56–64.

Bamford, Christi, & Lagattuta, Kristin Hansen. (2010). A new look at children's understanding of mind and emotion: The case of prayer. *Developmental Psychology, 46,* 78–92.

Bandura, Albert. (1977). *Social learning theory.* Englewood Cliffs, NJ: Prentice Hall.

Bandura, Albert. (2006). Toward a psychology of human agency. *Perspectives on Psychological Science, 1,* 164–180.

Banerjee, Robin, & Lintern, Vicki. (2000). Boys will be boys: The effect of social evaluation concerns on gender-typing. *Social Development, 9,* 397–408.

Barbarin, Oscar, Downer, Jason T., Head, Darlene, & Odom, Erica. (2010). Home-school differences in beliefs, support, and control during public pre-kindergarten and their link to children's kindergarten readiness. *Early Childhood Research Quarterly, 25,* 358–372.

Barber, Brian K. (Ed.). (2002). *Intrusive parenting: How psychological control affects children and adolescents.* Washington, DC: American Psychological Association.

Barger, Steven D., & Gallo, Linda C. (2008). Ability of ethnic self-identification to partition modifiable health risk among US residents of Mexican ancestry. *American Journal of Public Health, 98,* 1971–1978.

Barkin, Shari, Scheindlin, Benjamin, Ip, Edward H., Richardson, Irma, & Finch, Stacia. (2007). Determinants of parental discipline practices: A national sample from primary care practices. *Clinical Pediatrics, 46,* 64–69.

Barkley, Russell A. (2006). *Attention-deficit hyperactivity disorder: A handbook for diagnosis and treatment* (3rd ed.). New York, NY: Guilford Press.

Barlow, Sarah E., & the Expert Committee. (2007). Expert committee recommendations regarding the prevention, assessment, and treatment of child and adolescent overweight and obesity: Summary report. *Pediatrics, 120*(Suppl. 4), S164–S192.

Barnes, Grace M., Hoffman, Joseph H., Welte, John W., Farrell, Michael P., & Dintcheff, Barbara A. (2006). Effects of parental monitoring and peer deviance on substance use and delinquency. *Journal of Marriage and Family, 68,* 1084–1104.

Barnett, Mark, Watson, Ruth, & Kind, Peter. (2006). Pathways to barrel development. In Reha Erzurumlu, William Guido, & Zoltán Molnár (Eds.), *Development and plasticity in sensory thalamus and cortex* (pp. 138–157). New York, NY: Springer.

Barnett, W. Steven. (2007). The importance of demographic, social, and political context for estimating policy impacts: Comment on "Implementing New York's universal pre-kindergarten program." *Early Education and Development, 18,* 609–616.

Barnett, W. Steven, Epstein, Dale J., Carolan, Megan E., Fitzgerald, Jen, Ackerman, Debra J., & Friedman, Allison H. (2010). *The state of preschool 2010.* New Brunswick, NJ: National Institute for Early Education Research.

Baron, Andrew Scott, & Banaji, Mahzarin R. (2006). The development of implicit attitudes: Evidence of race evaluations from ages 6 and 10 and adulthood. *Psychological Science, 17,* 53–58.

Barrett, Anne E. (2012). Feeling young—A prescription for growing older? *Aging Today, 33,* 3–4.

Barros, Romina M., Silver, Ellen J., & Stein, Ruth E. K. (2009). School recess and group classroom behavior. *Pediatrics, 123,* 431–436.

Barrouillet, Pierre. (2011). Dual-process theories and cognitive development: Advances and challenges. *Developmental Review, 31,* 79–85.

Barzilai, Nir, & Bartke, Andrzej. (2009). Biological approaches to mechanistically understand the healthy life span extension achieved by calorie restriction and modulation of hormones. *The Journals of Gerontology Series A: Biological Sciences and Medical Sciences, 64A,* 187–191.

Basak, Chandramallika, Boot, Walter R., Voss, Michelle W., & Kramer, Arthur F. (2008). Can training in a real-time strategy video game attenuate cognitive decline in older adults? *Psychology and Aging, 23,* 765–777.

Bascom, Nick. (2012, January 14). Brainy ballplayers: Elite athletes get their heads in the game. *Science News, 181,* 22–25.

Bates, Lisa M., Acevedo-Garcia, Dolores, Alegria, Margarita, & Krieger, Nancy. (2008). Immigration and generational trends in body mass index and obesity in the United States: Results of the National Latino and Asian American Survey, 2002–2003. *American Journal of Public Health, 98,* 70–77.

Bateson, Patrick. (2005, February 4). Desirable scientific conduct. *Science, 307,* 645.

Batterham, Philip J., Christensen, Helen, & Mackinnon, Andrew J. (2009). Fluid intelligence is independently associated with all-cause mortality over 17 years in an elderly community sample: An investigation of potential mechanisms. *Intelligence, 37,* 551–560.

Battin, Margaret P., van der Heide, Agnes, Ganzini, Linda, van der Wal, Gerrit, & Onwuteaka-Philipsen, Bregje. D. (2007). Legal physician-assisted dying in Oregon and the Netherlands: Evidence concerning the impact on patients in "vulnerable" groups. *Journal of Medical Ethics, 33,* 591–597.

Bauer, Patricia J., San Souci, Priscilla, & Pathman, Thanujeni. (2010). Infant memory. *Wiley Interdisciplinary Reviews: Cognitive Science, 1,* 267–277.

Bauer-Maglin, Nan, & Perry, Donna Marie (Eds.). (2010). *Final acts: Death, dying, and the choices we make.* New Brunswick, NJ: Rutgers University Press.

Baugher, John Eric. (2008). Facing death: Buddhist and western hospice approaches. *Symbolic Interaction, 31,* 259–284.

Baum, Katrina. (2005). *Juvenile victimization and offending, 1993–2003* (NCJ 209468). Washington, DC: U.S. Department of Justice, Office of Justice Programs.

Baumeister, Roy F., & Blackhart, Ginnette C. (2007). Three perspectives on gender differences in adolescent sexual development. In Rutger C. M. E. Engels, Margaret Kerr, & Håkan Stattin (Eds.), *Friends, lovers, and groups: Key relationships in adolescence* (pp. 93–104). Hoboken, NJ: Wiley.

Baumrind, Diana. (1967). Child care practices anteceding three patterns of preschool behavior. *Genetic Psychology Monographs, 75,* 43–88.

Baumrind, Diana. (1971). Current patterns of parental authority. *Developmental Psychology, 4*(1, Pt. 2), 1–103.

Baumrind, Diana. (2005). Patterns of parental authority and adolescent autonomy. *New Directions for Child and Adolescent Development, 2005,* 61–69.

Baumrind, Diana, Larzelere, Robert E., & Owens, Elizabeth B. (2010). Effects of preschool parents' power assertive patterns and practices on adolescent development. *Parenting: Science and Practice, 10,* 157–201.

Bayer, Jordana K., Hiscock, Harriet, Hampton, Anne, & Wake, Melissa. (2007). Sleep problems in young infants and maternal mental and physical health. *Journal of Paediatrics and Child Health, 43,* 66–73.

Bazelon, Emily. (2006, April 30). A question of resilience. *New York Times Magazine.* Retrieved from http://www.nytimes.com/2006/04/30/magazine/30abuse.html?pagewanted=all

Beal, Susan. (1988). Sleeping position and sudden infant death syndrome. *Medical Journal of Australia, 149,* 562.

Beaman, Lori, Duflo, Esther, Pande, Rohini, & Topalova, Petia. (2012, February 3). Female leadership raises aspirations and educational attainment for girls: A policy experiment in India. *Science, 335,* 582–586.

Beauchaine, Theodore P., Klein, Daniel N., Crowell, Sheila E., Derbidge, Christina, & Gatzke-Kopp, Lisa. (2009). Multifinality in the development of personality disorders: A Biology × Sex × Environment interaction model of antisocial and borderline traits. *Development and Psychopathology,* *21,* 735–770.

Beaumont, Sherry, & Pratt, Michael. (2011). Identity processing styles and psychosocial balance during early and middle adulthood: The role of identity in intimacy and generativity. *Journal of Adult Development, 18,* 172–183.

Bebbington, Paul, Jonas, Sarah, Brugha, Terry, Meltzer, Howard, Jenkins, Rachel, Cooper, Claudia,... McManus, S. (2011). Child sexual abuse reported by an English national sample: Characteristics and demography. *Social Psychiatry and Psychiatric Epidemiology, 46,* 255–262.

Beck, Melinda. (2009, May 26). How's your baby? Recalling the Apgar score's namesake. *Wall Street Journal,* p. D1.

Beckers, Debby G. J., van der Linden, Dimitri, Smulders, Peter G. W., Kompier, Michiel A. J., Taris, Toon W., & Geurts, Sabine A. E. (2008). Voluntary or involuntary? Control over overtime and rewards for overtime in relation to fatigue and work satisfaction. *Work & Stress, 22,* 33–50.

Beckett, Nigel S., Peters, Ruth, Fletcher, Astrid E., Staessen, Jan A., Liu, Lisheng, Dumitrascu, Dan,... Bulpitt, Christopher J. (2008). Treatment of hypertension in patients 80 years of age or older. *New England Journal of Medicine, 358,* 1887–1898.

Behnke, Andrew O., MacDermid, Shelley M., Coltrane, Scott L., Parke, Ross D., Duffy, Sharon, & Widaman, Keith F. (2008). Family cohesion in the lives of Mexican American and European American parents. *Journal of Marriage and Family, 70,* 1045–1059.

Beil, Laura. (2011, June 4). Healthy aging in a pill. *Science News, 179,* 22–25.

Beilin, Lawrence, & Huang, Rae-Chi. (2008). Childhood obesity, hypertension, the metabolic syndrome and adult cardiovascular disease. *Clinical and Experimental Pharmacology and Physiology, 35,* 409–411.

Beilock, Sian. (2010). *Choke: What the secrets of the brain reveal about getting it right when you have to* (1st Free Press hardcover ed.). New York, NY: Free Press.

Beise, Jan, & Voland, Eckart. (2002). A multilevel event history analysis of the effects of grandmothers on child mortality in a historical German population: Krummhörn, Ostfriesland, 1720–1874. *Demographic Research, 7,* 469–498.

Belfield, Clive R., Nores, Milagros, Barnett, Steve, & Schweinhart, Lawrence. (2006). The High/Scope Perry Preschool Program: Cost benefit analysis using data from the age-40 followup. *Journal of Human Resources, 41,* 162–190.

Bell, Aleeca F., White-Traut, Rosemary, & Medoff-Cooper, Barbara. (2010). Neonatal neurobehavioral organization after exposure to maternal epidural analgesia in labor. *Journal of Obstetric, Gynecologic, & Neonatal Nursing, 39,* 178–190.

Bell, Alison M., & Robinson, Gene E. (2011, June 3). Behavior and the dynamic genome. *Science, 332,* 1161–1162.

Bell, Martha Ann, & Calkins, Susan D. (2012). Attentional control and emotion regulation in early development. In Michael I. Posner (Ed.), *Cognitive neuroscience of attention* (2nd ed., pp. 322–330). New York, NY: Guilford Press.

Bell, Ruth. (1998). *Changing bodies, changing lives: A book for teens on sex and relationships* (Expanded 3rd ed.). New York, NY: Times Books.

Belsky, Jay, Bakermans-Kranenburg, Marian J., & Van IJzendoorn, Marinus H. (2007). For better and for worse: Differential susceptibility to environmental influences. *Current Directions in Psychological Science, 16,* 300–304.

Belsky, Jay, & de Haan, Michelle. (2011). Parenting and children's brain development: The end of the beginning. *Journal of Child Psychology and Psychiatry, 52,* 409–428.

Belsky, Jay, & Pluess, Michael. (2009). Beyond diathesis stress: Differential susceptibility to environmental influences. *Psychological Bulletin, 135,* 885–908.

Belsky, Jay, Schlomer, Gabriel L., & Ellis, Bruce J. (2012). Beyond cumulative risk: Distinguishing harshness and unpredictability as determinants of parenting and early life history strategy. *Developmental Psychology, 48,* 662–673.

Belsky, Jay, Steinberg, Laurence, Houts, Renate M., Halpern-Felsher, Bonnie L., & The NICHD Early Child Care Research Network. (2010). The development of reproductive strategy in females: Early maternal harshness → earlier menarche → increased sexual risk taking. *Developmental Psychology, 46,* 120–128.

Ben-Zur, Hasida, & Zeidner, Moshe. (2009). Threat to life and risk-taking behaviors: A review of empirical findings and explanatory models. *Personality and Social Psychology Review, 13,* 109–128.

Benatar, David. (2011). A legal right to die: Responding to slippery slope and abuse arguments. *Current Oncology, 18,* 206–207.

Bendlin, Barbara B., Canu, Elisa, Willette, Auriel A., Kastman, Erik K., McLaren, Donald G., Kosmatka, K. J.,... Johnson, Sterling C. (2011). Effects of aging and calorie restriction on white matter in rhesus macaques. *Neurobiology of Aging, 32,* 2319.e1–2319.e11. doi:10.1016/j.neurobiolaging .2010.04.008

Benet, Sula. (1974). *Abkhasians: The long-living people of the Caucasus.* New York, NY: Holt, Rinehart & Winston.

Bengtson, Vern L. (2001). Beyond the nuclear family: The increasing importance of multigenerational bonds (The Burgess Award Lecture). *Journal of Marriage & the Family, 63,* 1–16.

Benjamin, Georges C. (2004). The solution is injury prevention. *American Journal of Public Health, 94,* 521.

Benner, Aprile D., & Graham, Sandra. (2007). Navigating the transition to multi-ethnic urban high schools: Changing ethnic congruence and adolescents' school-related affect. *Journal of Research on Adolescence, 17,* 207–220.

Benovenli, Liza, Fuller, Elizabeth, Sinnott, Jan, & Waterman, Sarah. (2011). Three applications of the theory of postformal thought: Wisdom, concepts of God, and success in college. In Ralph L. Piedmont & Andrew Village (Eds.), *Research in the social scientific study of religion* (Vol. 22, pp. 141–154). Leiden, The Netherlands: Brill.

Bentley, Gillian R., & Mascie-Taylor, C. G. Nicholas. (2000). Introduction. In Gillian R. Bentley & C. G. Nicholas Mascie-Taylor (Eds.), *Infertility in the modern world: Present* *and future prospects* (pp. 1–13). Cambridge, England: Cambridge University Press.

Benton, Tami D. (2011). Psychiatric considerations in children and adolescents with HIV/AIDS. *Pediatric Clinics of North America, 58,* 989–1002.

Berenbaum, Sheri A., Martin, Carol Lynn, Hanish, Laura D., Briggs, Phillip T., & Fabes, Richard A. (2008). Sex differences in children's play. In Jill B. Becker, Karen J. Berkley, Nori Geary, Elizabeth Hampson, James P. Herman, & Elizabeth Young (Eds.), *Sex differences in the brain: From genes to behavior* (pp. 275–290). New York, NY: Oxford University Press.

Berg, Sandra J., & Wynne-Edwards, Katherine E. (2002). Salivary hormone concentrations in mothers and fathers becoming parents are not correlated. *Hormones & Behavior, 42,* 424–436.

Berger, Kathleen Stassen. (2007). Update on bullying at school: Science forgotten? *Developmental Review, 27,* 90–126.

Berger, Lawrence M., Paxson, Christina, & Waldfogel, Jane. (2009). Income and child development. *Children and Youth Services Review, 31,* 978–989.

Berkey, Catherine S., Gardner, Jane D., Frazier, A. Lindsay, & Colditz, Graham A. (2000). Relation of childhood diet and body size to menarche and adolescent growth in girls. *American Journal of Epidemiology, 152,* 446–452.

Berkman, Lisa F., Ertel, Karen A., & Glymour, Maria M. (2011). Aging and social intervention: Life course perspectives. In Robert H. Binstock & Linda K. George (Eds.), *Handbook of aging and the social sciences* (7th ed., pp. 337–351). San Diego, CA: Academic Press.

Bernard, Kristin, & Dozier, Mary. (2010). Examining infants' cortisol responses to laboratory tasks among children varying in attachment disorganization: Stress reactivity or return to baseline? *Developmental Psychology, 46,* 1771–1778.

Bernard, Kristin, & Dozier, Mary. (2011). This is my baby: Foster parents' feelings of commitment and displays of delight. *Infant Mental Health Journal, 32,* 251–262.

Berndt, Thomas J., & Murphy, Lonna M. (2002). Influences of friends and friendships: Myths, truths, and research recommendations. In Robert V. Kail (Ed.), *Advances in child development and behavior* (Vol. 30, pp. 275–310). San Diego, CA: Academic Press.

Bernstein, Mary. (2005). Identity politics. *Annual Review of Sociology, 31,* 47–74.

Bhasin, Shalender. (2007). Approach to the infertile man. *Journal of Clinical Endocrinology & Metabolism, 92,* 1995–2004.

Bhattacharjee, Yudhijit. (2008, February 8). Choking on fumes, Kolkata faces a noxious future. *Science, 319,* 749.

Bialystok, Ellen. (2010). Global-local and trail-making tasks by monolingual and bilingual children: Beyond inhibition. *Developmental Psychology, 46,* 93–105.

Bialystok, Ellen, & Barac, Raluca. (2012). Emerging bilingualism: Dissociating advantages for metalinguistic awareness and executive control. *Cognition, 122,* 67–73.

Bialystok, Ellen, & Viswanathan, Mythili. (2009). Components of executive control with advantages for bilingual children in two cultures. *Cognition, 112,* 494–500.

Bianchi, Suzanne M., & Milkie, Melissa A. (2010). Work and family research in the first decade of the 21st century. *Journal of Marriage and Family, 72,* 705–725.

Biblarz, Timothy J., & Savci, Evren. (2010). Lesbian, gay, bisexual, and transgender families. *Journal of Marriage and Family, 72,* 480–497.

Biblarz, Timothy J., & Stacey, Judith. (2010). How does the gender of parents matter? *Journal of Marriage and Family, 72,* 3–22.

Biederman, Joseph, Monuteaux, Michael C., Spencer, Thomas, Wilens, Timothy E., & Faraone, Stephen V. (2009). Do stimulants protect against psychiatric disorders in youth with ADHD? A 10-year follow-up study. *Pediatrics, 124,* 71–78.

Biederman, Joseph, Spencer, Thomas J., Monuteaux, Michael C., & Faraone, Stephen V. (2010). A naturalistic 10-year prospective study of height and weight in children with attention-deficit hyperactivity disorder grown up: Sex and treatment effects. *The Journal of Pediatrics, 157,* 635–640.e1. doi:10.1016/j.jpeds.2010.04.025

Biehl, Michael C., Natsuaki, Misaki N., & Ge, Xiaojia. (2007). The influence of pubertal timing on alcohol use and heavy drinking trajectories. *Journal of Youth and Adolescence, 36,* 153–167.

Bielak, Allison A. M. (2010). How can we not 'lose it' if we still don't understand how to 'use it'? Unanswered questions about the influence of activity participation on cognitive performance in older age—A mini-review. *Gerontology, 56,* 507–519.

Bielak, Allison A. M., Anstey, Kaarin J., Christensen, Helen, & Windsor, Tim D. (2012). Activity engagement is related to level, but not change in cognitive ability across adulthood. *Psychology and Aging, 27,* 219–228.

Bilali , Merim, McLeod, Peter, & Gobet, Fernand. (2009). Specialization effect and its influence on memory and problem solving in expert chess players. *Cognitive Science, 33,* 1117–1143.

Billings, J. Andrew. (2011). Double effect: A useful rule that alone cannot justify hastening death. *Journal of Medical Ethics, 37,* 437–440.

Binstock, Robert. (2006–2007). Older people and political engagement: From avid voters to 'cooled-out marks'. *Generations, 30*(4), 24–30.

Binstock, Robert H. (2012). Older voters and the 2010 U.S. election: Implications for 2012 and beyond? *The Gerontologist, 52,* 408–417.

Birch, Susan A. J., & Bloom, Paul. (2003). Children are cursed: An asymmetric bias in mental-state attribution. *Psychological Science, 14,* 283–286.

Bird, Chloe E., Seeman, Teresa, Escarce, José J., Basurto-Dávila, Ricardo, Finch, Brian K., Dubowitz, Tamara, . . . Lurie, Nicole. (2010). Neighbourhood socioeconomic status and biological 'wear and tear' in a nationally representative sample of US adults. *Journal of Epidemiology and Community Health, 64,* 860–865.

Birditt, Kira S., Miller, Laura M., Fingerman, Karen L., & Lefkowitz, Eva S. (2009). Tensions in the parent and adult child relationship: Links to solidarity and ambivalence. *Psychology and Aging, 24,* 287–295.

Birdsong, David. (2006). Age and second language acquisition and processing: A selective overview. *Language Learning, 56*(Suppl. 1), 9–49.

Birney, Damian P., Citron-Pousty, Jill H., Lutz, Donna J., & Sternberg, Robert J. (2005). The development of cognitive and intellectual abilities. In Marc H. Bornstein & Michael E. Lamb (Eds.), *Developmental science: An advanced textbook* (5th ed., pp. 327–358). Mahwah, NJ: Erlbaum.

Biro, Frank M., McMahon, Robert P., Striegel-Moore, Ruth, Crawford, Patricia B., Obarzanek, Eva, Morrison, John A., . . . Falkner, Frank. (2001). Impact of timing of pubertal maturation on growth in black and white female adolescents: The National Heart, Lung, and Blood Institute Growth and Health Study. *Journal of Pediatrics, 138,* 636–643.

Biro, Frank M., Striegel-Moore, Ruth H., Franko, Debra L., Padgett, Justina, & Bean, Judy A. (2006). Self-esteem in adolescent females. *Journal of Adolescent Health, 39,* 501–507.

Bitensky, Susan H. (2006). *Corporal punishment of children: A human rights violation.* Boston, MA: Brill.

Bjorklund, David F., Dukes, Charles, & Brown, Rhonda Douglas. (2009). The development of memory strategies. In Mary L. Courage & Nelson Cowan (Eds.), *The development of memory in infancy and childhood* (2nd ed., pp. 145–175). New York, NY: Psychology Press.

Black, Kathy. (2008). Health and aging-in-place: Implications for community practice. *Journal of Community Practice, 16,* 79–95.

Blackwell, Lisa S., Trzesniewski, Kali H., & Dweck, Carol Sorich. (2007). Implicit theories of intelligence predict achievement across an adolescent transition: A longitudinal study and an intervention. *Child Development, 78,* 246–263.

Blair, Clancy, & Dennis, Tracy. (2010). An optimal balance: The integration of emotion and cognition in context. In Susan D. Calkins & Martha Ann Bell (Eds.), *Child development at the intersection of emotion and cognition* (pp. 17–36). Washington, DC: American Psychological Association.

Blakemore, Sarah-Jayne. (2008). Development of the social brain during adolescence. *The Quarterly Journal of Experimental Psychology, 61,* 40–49.

Blalock, Garrick, Kadiyali, Vrinda, & Simon, Daniel H. (2009). Driving fatalities after 9/11: A hidden cost of terrorism. *Applied Economics, 41,* 1717–1729.

Blanchflower, David G., & Oswald, Andrew J. (2008). Is well-being U-shaped over the life cycle? *Social Science & Medicine, 66,* 1733–1749.

Blandon, Alysia Y., Calkins, Susan D., & Keane, Susan P. (2010). Predicting emotional and social competence during early childhood from toddler risk and maternal behavior. *Development and Psychopathology, 22,* 119–132.

Blas, Erik, & Kurup, Anand Sivasankara (Eds.). (2010). *Equity, social determinants, and public health programmes.* Geneva, Switzerland: World Health Organization.

Blekesaune, Morten. (2008). Partnership transitions and mental distress: Investigating temporal order. *Journal of Marriage and Family, 70,* 879–890.

Blonigen, Daniel M., Carlson, Marie D., Hicks, Brian M., Krueger, Robert F., & Iacono, William G. (2008). Stability and change in personality traits from late adolescence to early adulthood: A longitudinal twin study. *Journal of Personality, 76,* 229–266.

Bloom, Barbara, Cohen, Robin A., & Freeman, Gulnur. (2009). Summary health statistics for U.S. children: National Health Interview Survey, 2008. *Vital and Health Statistics, 10*(244).

Bloom, David E. (2011, July 29). 7 billion and counting. *Science, 333,* 562–569.

Blum, Deborah. (2002). *Love at Goon Park: Harry Harlow and the science of affection.* Cambridge, MA: Perseus.

Blurton-Jones, Nicholas G. (1976). Rough-and-tumble play among nursery school children. In Jerome S. Bruner, Alison Jolly, & Kathy Sylva (Eds.), *Play: Its role in development and evolution* (pp. 352–363). New York, NY: Basic Books.

Blustein, David Larry. (2006). *The psychology of working: A new perspective for career development, counseling, and public policy.* Mahwah, NJ: Erlbaum.

Boals, Adriel, Hayslip, Bert, Knowles, Laura R., & Banks, Jonathan B. (2012). Perceiving a negative event as central to one's identity partially mediates age differences in post-traumatic stress disorder symptoms. *Journal of Aging and Health, 24,* 459–474.

Bodrova, Elena, & Leong, Deborah J. (2005). High quality preschool programs: What would Vygotsky say? *Early Education and Development, 16,* 435–444.

Boerner, Kathrin, Schulz, Richard, & Horowitz, Amy. (2004). Positive aspects of caregiving and adaptation to bereavement. *Psychology and Aging, 19,* 668–675.

Boerner, Kathrin, Wortman, Camille B., & Bonanno, George A. (2005). Resilient or at risk? A 4-year study of older adults who initially showed high or low distress following conjugal loss. *The Journals of Gerontology Series B: Psychological Sciences and Social Sciences, 60B,* 67–73.

Bojczyk, Kathryn E., Lehan, Tara J., McWey, Lenore M., Melson, Gail F., & Kaufman, Debra R. (2011). Mothers' and their adult daughters' perceptions of their relationship. *Journal of Family Issues, 32,* 452–481.

Boles, David B., Barth, Joan M., & Merrill, Edward C. (2008). Asymmetry and performance: Toward a neurodevelopmental theory. *Brain and Cognition, 66,* 124–139.

Bonanno, George A., & Lilienfeld, Scott O. (2008). Let's be realistic: When grief counseling is effective and when it's not. *Professional Psychology: Research and Practice, 39,* 377–378.

Bondi, Mark W., Salmon, David P., & Kaszniak, Alfred W. (2009). The neuropsychology of dementia. In Igor Grant & Kenneth M. Adams (Eds.), *Neuropsychological assessment of neuropsychiatric and neuromedical disorders* (3rd ed., pp. 159–198). New York, NY: Oxford University Press.

Bonica, Laura, & Sappa, Viviana. (2010). Early school-leavers' microtransitions: Towards a competent self. *Education + Training, 52,* 368–380.

Borgens, Richard Ben, & Liu-Snyder, Peishan. (2012). Understanding secondary injury. *The Quarterly Review of Biology, 87,* 89–127.

Borke, Jörn, Lamm, Bettina, Eickhorst, Andreas, & Keller, Heidi. (2007). Father-infant interaction, paternal ideas about early child care, and their consequences for the development of children's self-recognition. *Journal of Genetic Psychology, 168,* 365–379.

Borkowski, John G., Farris, Jaelyn Renee, Whitman, Thomas L., Carothers, Shannon S., Weed, Keri, & Keogh, Deborah A. (2007). *Risk and resilience: Adolescent mothers and their children grow up.* Mahwah, NJ: Erlbaum.

Borland, James H. (Ed.). (2003). *Rethinking gifted education.* New York, NY: Teachers College Press.

Bornstein, Marc H., Arterberry, Martha E., & Mash, Clay. (2005). Perceptual development. In Marc H. Bornstein & Michael E. Lamb (Eds.), *Developmental science: An advanced textbook* (5th ed., pp. 283–325). Mahwah, NJ: Erlbaum.

Bornstein, Marc H., & Cote, Linda R. (2007). Knowledge of child development and family interactions among immigrants to America: Perspectives from developmental science. In Jennifer E. Lansford, Kirby Deater-Deckard, & Marc H. Bornstein (Eds.), *Immigrant families in contemporary society* (pp. 121–136). New York, NY: Guilford Press.

Bornstein, Marc H., Mortimer, Jeylan T., Lutfey, Karen, & Bradley, Robert. (2011). Theories and processes in life-span socialization. In Karen Fingerman, Cynthia Berg, Jacqui Smith, & Toni Antonucci (Eds.), *Handbook of life-span development* (pp. 27–56). New York, NY: Springer.

Borrelli, Belinda, McQuaid, Elizabeth L., Novak, Scott P., Hammond, S. Katharine, & Becker, Bruce. (2010). Motivating Latino caregivers of children with asthma to quit smoking: A randomized trial. *Journal of Consulting and Clinical Psychology, 78,* 34–43.

Boseovski, Janet J. (2010). Evidence for "rose-colored glasses": An examination of the positivity bias in young children's personality judgments. *Child Development Perspectives, 4,* 212–218.

Bossé, Yohan, & Hudson, Thomas J. (2007). Toward a comprehensive set of asthma susceptibility genes. *Annual Review of Medicine, 58,* 171–184.

Bosworth, Hayden B., & Ayotte, Brian J. (2009). The role of cognitive and social function in an applied setting: Medication adherence as an example. In H. B. Bosworth & C. Hertzog (Eds.), *Aging and cognition: Research methodologies and empirical advances* (pp. 219–239). Washington, DC: American Psychological Association.

Bosworth, Hayden B., & Hertzog, Christopher (Eds.). (2009). *Aging and cognition: Research methodologies and empirical advances.* Washington, DC: American Psychological Association.

Bowen, Mary Elizabeth, & González, Hector M. (2010). Childhood socioeconomic position and disability in later life: Results of the Health and Retirement Study. *American Journal of Public Health, 100*(Suppl. 1), S197–S203.

Bowes, Lucy, Maughan, Barbara, Caspi, Avshalom, Moffitt, Terrie E., & Arseneault, Louise. (2010). Families promote emotional and behavioural resilience to bullying: Evidence of an environmental effect. *Journal of Child Psychology and Psychiatry, 51,* 809–817.

Bowman, Nicholas A. (2011). Promoting participation in a diverse democracy: A meta-analysis of college diversity experiences and civic engagement. *Review of Educational Research, 81,* 29–68.

Boyce, W. Thomas, Essex, Marilyn J., Alkon, Abbey, Goldsmith, H. Hill, Kraemer, Helena C., & Kupfer, David J. (2006). Early father involvement moderates biobehavioral susceptibility to mental health problems in middle childhood. *Journal of the American Academy of Child and Adolescent Psychiatry, 45,* 1510–1520.

Boyd, Cynthia M., Darer, Jonathan, Boult, Chad, Fried, Linda P., Boult, Lisa, & Wu, Albert W. (2005). Clinical practice guidelines and quality of care for older patients with multiple comorbid diseases: Implications for pay for performance. *Journal of the American Medical Association, 294,* 716–724.

Boyd, William L. (2007). The politics of privatization in American education. *Educational Policy, 21,* 7–14.

Boyraz, Guler, Horne, Sharon G., & Sayger, Thomas V. (2012). Finding meaning in loss: The mediating role of social support between personality and two construals of meaning. *Death Studies, 36,* 519–540.

Bracken, Bruce A., & Crawford, Elizabeth. (2010). Basic concepts in early childhood educational standards: A 50-state review. *Early Childhood Education Journal, 37,* 421–430.

Bradford, Andrea, Kunik, Mark E., Schulz, Paul, Williams, Susan P., & Singh, Hardeep. (2009). Missed and delayed diagnosis of dementia in primary care: Prevalence and contributing factors. *Alzheimer Disease and Associated Disorders, 23,* 306–314.

Bradley, Robert H., & Corwyn, Robert F. (2005). Productive activity and the prevention of behavior problems. *Developmental Psychology, 41,* 89–98.

Branca, Francesco, Nikogosian, Haik, & Lobstein, Tim (Eds.). (2007). *The challenge of obesity in the WHO European Region and the strategies for response.* Copenhagen, Denmark: WHO Regional Office for Europe.

Branch, John. (2011, December 5). Derek Boogaard: A brain 'going bad'. *New York Times,* p. B13.

Brandt, Hella E., Ooms, Marcel E., Ribbe, Miel W., Wal, Gerrit van der, & Deliens, Luc. (2006). Predicted survival vs. actual survival in terminally ill noncancer patients in Dutch nursing homes. *Journal of Pain and Symptom Management, 32,* 560–566.

Brassen, Stefanie, Gamer, Matthias, Peters, Jan, Gluth, Sebastian, & Büchel, Christian. (2012, May 4). Don't look back in anger! Responsiveness to missed chances in successful and nonsuccessful aging. *Science, 336,* 612–614.

Braun, Kathryn L., Zir, Ana, Crocker, Joanna, & Seely, Marilyn R. (2005). Kokua Mau: A statewide effort to improve end-of-life care. *Journal of Palliative Medicine, 8,* 313–323.

Braun, Michael, Lewin-Epstein, Noah, Stier, Haya, & Baumgärtner, Miriam K. (2008). Perceived equity in the gendered division of household labor. *Journal of Marriage and Family, 70,* 1145–1156.

Breaugh, James, & Frye, N. Kathleen. (2008). Work-family conflict: The importance of family-friendly employment practices and family-supportive supervisors. *Journal of Business and Psychology, 22,* 345–353.

Breivik, Gunnar. (2010). Trends in adventure sports in a postmodern society. *Sport in Society: Cultures, Commerce, Media, Politics, 13,* 260–273.

Brendgen, Mara, Lamarche, Véronique, Wanner, Brigitte, & Vitaro, Frank. (2010). Links between friendship relations and early adolescents' trajectories of depressed mood. *Developmental Psychology, 46,* 491–501.

Brennan, Arthur, Ayers, Susan, Ahmed, Hafez, & Marshall-Lucette, Sylvie. (2007). A critical review of the Couvade syndrome: The pregnant male. *Journal of Reproductive and Infant Psychology, 25,* 173–189.

Brenner, Samantha, Kleinhaus, Karine, Kursmark, Meredith, & Weitzman, Michael. (2009). Increased paternal age and child health and development. *Current Pediatric Reviews, 5,* 135–146.

Bresnahan, Mary Jiang, & Mahler, Kevin. (2010). Ethical debate over organ donation in the context of brain death. *Bioethics, 24,* 54–60.

Bretherton, Inge. (2010). Fathers in attachment theory and research: A review. *Early Child Development and Care, 180,* 9–23.

Bricker, Jonathan, & Tollison, Sean. (2011). Comparison of motivational interviewing with acceptance and commitment therapy: A conceptual and clinical review. *Behavioural and Cognitive Psychotherapy, 39,* 541–559.

Brickhouse, Tegwyn H., Rozier, R. Gary, & Slade, Gary D. (2008). Effects of enrollment in Medicaid versus the State Children's Health Insurance Program on kindergarten children's untreated dental caries. *American Journal of Public Health, 98,* 876–881.

Britto, Pia Rebello, Boller, Kimberley, & Yoshikawa, Hirokazu. (2011). Quality of early childhood development programs in global contexts: Rationale for investment, conceptual framework and implications for equity. *Social Policy Report, 25*(2), 1–30.

Brody, Gene H., Beach, Steven R. H., Philibert, Robert A., Chen, Yi-fu, & Murry, Velma McBride. (2009). Prevention effects moderate the association of 5-HTTLPR and youth risk behavior initiation: Gene × environment hypotheses tested via a randomized prevention design. *Child Development, 80,* 645–661.

Bronfenbrenner, Urie, & Morris, Pamela A. (2006). The bioecological model of human development. In William Damon & Richard M. Lerner (Eds.), *Handbook of child psychology: Vol. 1. Theoretical models of human development* (6th ed., pp. 793–828). Hoboken, NJ: Wiley.

Bronte-Tinkew, Jacinta, Moore, Kristin A., Matthews, Gregory, & Carrano, Jennifer. (2007). Symptoms of major depression in a sample of fathers of infants: Sociodemographic correlates and links to father involvement. *Journal of Family Issues, 28,* 61–99.

Brotman, Melissa A., Guyer, Amanda E., Lawson, Evin S., Horsey, Sarah E., Rich, Brendan A., Dickstein, Daniel P., . . . Leibenluft, Ellen. (2008). Facial emotion labeling deficits in children and adolescents at risk for bipolar disorder. *American Journal of Psychiatry, 165,* 385–389.

Brotman, Melissa A., Rich, Brendan A., Guyer, Amanda E., Lunsford, Jessica R., Horsey, Sarah E., Reising, Michelle M., . . . Leibenluft, Ellen. (2010). Amygdala activation during emotion processing of neutral faces in children with severe mood dysregulation versus ADHD or bipolar disorder. *American Journal of Psychiatry, 167,* 61–69.

Brown, B. Bradford. (2004). Adolescents' relationships with peers. In Richard M. Lerner & Laurence D. Steinberg (Eds.), *Handbook of adolescent psychology* (2nd ed., pp. 363–394). Hoboken, NJ: Wiley.

Brown, B. Bradford, & Bakken, Jeremy P. (2011). Parenting and peer relationships: Reinvigorating research on family–peer linkages in adolescence. *Journal of Research on Adolescence, 21,* 153–165.

Brown, B. Bradford, & Larson, James. (2009). Peer relationships in adolescence. In Richard M. Lerner & Laurence Steinberg (Eds.), *Handbook of adolescent psychology: Vol. 2. Contextual influences on adolescent development* (3rd ed., pp. 74–103). Hoboken, NJ: Wiley.

Brown, Christia Spears, Alabi, Basirat O., Huynh, Virginia W., & Masten, Carrie L. (2011). Ethnicity and gender in late childhood and early adolescence: Group identity and awareness of bias. *Developmental Psychology, 47,* 463–471.

Brown, Gordon D. A., Gardner, Jonathan, Oswald, Andrew J., & Qian, Jing. (2008). Does wage rank affect employees well-being? *Industrial Relations, 47,* 355–389.

Brown, Susan L. (2010). Marriage and child well-being: Research and policy perspectives. *Journal of Marriage and Family, 72,* 1059–1077.

Brown, Susan L., & Kawamura, Sayaka. (2010). Relationship quality among cohabitors and marrieds in older adulthood. *Social Science Research, 39,* 777–786.

Brown, Susan L., & Rinelli, Lauren N. (2010). Family structure, family processes, and adolescent smoking and drinking. *Journal of Research on Adolescence, 20,* 259–273.

Brown, Tony N., Tanner-Smith, Emily E., Lesane-Brown, Chase L., & Ezell, Michael E. (2007). Child, parent, and situational correlates of familial ethnic/race socialization. *Journal of Marriage and Family, 69,* 14–25.

Bruce, Susan, & Muhammad, Zayyad. (2009). The development of object permanence in children with intellectual disability, physical disability, autism, and blindness. *International Journal of Disability, Development and Education, 56,* 229–246.

Bryant, Allison S., Worjoloh, Ayaba, Caughey, Aaron B., & Washington, A. Eugene. (2010). Racial/ethnic disparities in obstetric outcomes and care: Prevalence and determinants. *American Journal of Obstetrics and Gynecology, 202,* 335–343.

Bryant, Brenda K., & Donnellan, M. Brent. (2007). The relation between socio-economic status concerns and angry peer conflict resolution is moderated by pet provisions of support. *Anthrozoös, 20,* 213–223.

Bryant, Gregory A., & Barrett, H. Clark. (2007). Recognizing intentions in infant-directed speech: Evidence for universals. *Psychological Science, 18,* 746–751.

Brymer, Eric. (2010). Risk and extreme sports: A phenomenological perspective. *Annals of Leisure Research, 13,* 218–239.

Buckley, Maureen, & Saarni, Carolyn. (2009). Emotion regulation: Implications for positive youth development. In Rich Gilman, E. Scott Huebner, & Michael J. Furlong (Eds.), *Handbook of positive psychology in schools* (pp. 107–118). New York, NY: Routledge/Taylor & Francis.

Bucx, Freek, Raaijmakers, Quinten, & van Wel, Frits. (2010). Life course stage in young adulthood and intergenerational congruence in family attitudes. *Journal of Marriage and Family, 72,* 117–134.

Bucx, Freek, van Wel, Frits, & Knijn, Trudie. (2012). Life course status and exchanges of support between young adults and parents. *Journal of Marriage and Family, 74,* 101–115.

Bugental, Daphne Blunt, & Grusec, Joan E. (2006). Socialization theory. In William Damon & Richard M. Lerner (Series Eds.) & Nancy Eisenberg (Vol. Ed.), *Handbook of child psychology: Vol. 3. Social, emotional, and personality development* (6th ed., pp. 366–428). Hoboken, NJ: Wiley.

Bugental, Daphne Blunt, & Hehman, Jessica A. (2007). Ageism: A review of research and policy implications. *Social Issues and Policy Review, 1,* 173–216.

Buiting, Hilde, van Delden, Johannes, Onwuteaka-Philpsen, Bregje, Rietjens, Judith, Rurup, Mette, van Tol, Donald,... van der Heide, Agnes. (2009). Reporting of euthanasia and physician-assisted suicide in the Netherlands: Descriptive study. *BMC Medical Ethics, 10,* 18.

Bulik, Cynthia M., Thornton, Laura, Pinheiro, Andréa Poyastro, Plotnicov, Katherine, Klump, Kelly L., Brandt, Harry,... Kaye, Walter H. (2008). Suicide attempts in anorexia nervosa. *Psychosomatic Medicine, 70,* 378–383.

Burd-Sharps, Sarah, Lewis, Kristen, & Martins, Eduardo Borges (Eds.). (2008). *The measure of America: American human development report, 2008–2009.* New York, NY: Columbia University Press.

Bureau of Labor Statistics. (2011). *The employment situation—November 2011* [News release]. Retrieved from http://www.bls.gov/news.release/archives/empsit_12022011.pdf

Bureau of Labor Statistics. (2012a, October 5). *The employment situation—September 2012* [News release]. Retrieved from http://www.bls.gov/news.release/archives/empsit_10052012.htm

Bureau of Labor Statistics. (2012b, February 22). *Volunteering in the United States—2011.* Washington, DC: U.S. Department of Labor.

Burpo, Todd, & Vincent, Lynn. (2011). *Heaven is for real: A little boy's astounding story of his trip to heaven and back.* Nashville, TN: Thomas Nelson.

Burt, S. Alexandra. (2009). Rethinking environmental contributions to child and adolescent psychopathology: A meta-analysis of shared environmental influences. *Psychological Bulletin, 135,* 608–637.

Burton, Linda M., Bonilla-Silva, Eduardo, Ray, Victor, Buckelew, Rose, & Hordge Freeman, Elizabeth. (2010). Critical race theories, colorism, and the decade's research on families of color. *Journal of Marriage and Family, 72,* 440–459.

Buschkuehl, Martin, Jaeggi, Susanne M., Hutchison, Sara, Perrig-Chiello, Pasqualina, Dapp, Christoph, Muller, Matthias,... Perrig, Walter J. (2008). Impact of working memory training on memory performance in old-old adults. *Psychology and Aging, 23,* 743–753.

Busse, William W., & Lemanske, Robert F. (Eds.). (2005). *Lung biology in health and disease: Vol. 195. Asthma prevention.* Boca Raton, FL: Taylor & Francis.

Bussey, Kay. (2011). Gender identity development. In Seth J. Schwartz, Koen Luyckx, & Vivian L. Vignoles (Eds.), *Handbook of identity theory and research* (pp. 603–628). New York, NY: Springer.

Butler, Robert N., Lewis, Myrna I., & Sunderland, Trey. (1998). *Aging and mental health: Positive psychosocial and biomedical approaches* (5th ed.). Boston, MA: Allyn & Bacon.

Butterworth, Brian, Varma, Sashank, & Laurillard, Diana. (2011, May 27). Dyscalculia: From brain to education. *Science, 332,* 1049–1053.

Buunk, Abraham P., Park, Justin H., & Dubbs, Shelli L. (2008). Parent-offspring conflict in mate preferences. *Review of General Psychology, 12,* 47–62.

Byers, Amy L., Levy, Becca R., Allore, Heather G., Bruce, Martha L., & Kasl, Stanislav V. (2008). When parents matter to their adult children: Filial reliance associated with parents' depressive symptoms. *The Journals of Gerontology Series B: Psychological Sciences and Social Sciences, 63B,* 33–40.

Byers-Heinlein, Krista, Burns, Tracey C., & Werker, Janet F. (2010). The roots of bilingualism in newborns. *Psychological Science, 21,* 343–348.

Byng-Hall, John. (2008). The significance of children fulfilling parental roles: Implications for family therapy. *Journal of Family Therapy, 30,* 147–162.

Bzostek, Sharon H. (2008). Social fathers and child well-being. *Journal of Marriage and Family, 70,* 950–961.

Cacciatore, Joanne. (2009). Appropriate bereavement practice after the death of a Native American child. *Families in Society, 90,* 46–50.

Cacioppo, John T., & Cacioppo, Stephanie. (2012). The phenotype of loneliness. *European Journal of Developmental Psychology, 9,* 446–452.

Cain, Daphne S., & Combs-Orme, Terri. (2005). Family structure effects on parenting stress and practices in the African American family. *Journal of Sociology & Social Welfare, 32,* 19–40.

Cairns, Robert B., & Cairns, Beverley D. (2006). The making of developmental psychology. In William Damon & Richard M. Lerner (Series Eds.) & Richard M. Lerner (Vol. Ed.), *Handbook of child psychology: Vol. 1. Theoretical models of human development* (6th ed., pp. 89–165). Hoboken, NJ: Wiley.

Calkins, Susan D., & Keane, Susan P. (2009). Developmental origins of early antisocial behavior. *Development and Psychopathology, 21,* 1095–1109.

Cameron, Judy, & Pierce, W. David. (2002). *Rewards and intrinsic motivation: Resolving the controversy.* Westport, CT: Bergin & Garvey.

Camilli, Gregory, Vargas, Sadako, Ryan, Sharon, & Barnett, W. Steven. (2010). Meta-analysis of the effects of early education interventions on cognitive and social development. *Teachers College Record, 112,* 579–620.

Camos, Valérie, & Barrouillet, Pierre. (2011). Developmental change in working memory strategies: From passive maintenance to active refreshing. *Developmental Psychology, 47,* 898–904.

Campbell, Frances A., Pungello, Elizabeth P., Miller-Johnson, Shari, Burchinal, Margaret, & Ramey, Craig T. (2001). The development of cognitive and academic abilities: Growth curves from an early childhood educational experiment. *Developmental Psychology, 37,* 231–242.

Camras, Linda A., & Shutter, Jennifer M. (2010). Emotional facial expressions in infancy. *Emotion Review, 2,* 120–129.

Canadian Psychological Association. (2000). *Canadian code of ethics for psychologists* (3rd ed.). Ottawa, Ontario, Canada: Author.

Capaldi, Deborah M. (2003). Parental monitoring: A person-environment interaction perspective on this key parenting skill. In Ann C. Crouter & Alan Booth (Eds.), *Children's influence on family dynamics: The neglected side of family relationships* (pp. 171–179). Mahwah, NJ: Lawrence Erlbaum.

Cappell, Katherine A., Gmeindl, Leon, & Reuter-Lorenz, Patricia A. (2010). Age differences in prefontal recruitment during verbal working memory maintenance depend on memory load. *Cortex, 46,* 462–473.

Caravita, Simona C. S., Di Blasio, Paola, & Salmivalli, Christina. (2010). Early adolescents' participation in bullying: Is ToM involved? *The Journal of Early Adolescence, 30,* 138–170.

Cardinal, Roger. (2001). The sense of time and place. In Jane Kallir (Ed.), *Grandma Moses in the 21st century* (pp. 79–102). Alexandria, VA: Art Services International.

Carey, Susan. (2010). Beyond fast mapping. *Language Learning and Development, 6,* 184–205.

Carlson, Susan A., Fulton, Janet E., Lee, Sarah M., Maynard, L. Michele, Brown, David R., Kohl, Harold W., III, & Dietz, William H. (2008). Physical education and academic achievement in elementary school: Data from the Early Childhood Longitudinal Study. *American Journal of Public Health, 98,* 721–727.

Carlson, Stephanie M. (2003). Executive function in context: Development, measurement, theory and experience. *Monographs of the Society for Research in Child Development, 68*(3, Serial No. 274), 138–151.

Carlton-LaNey, Iris. (2006–2007). 'Doing the lord's work': African American elders' civic engagement. *Generations, 30*(4), 47–50.

Carnethon, Mercedes R., Gidding, Samuel S., Nehgme, Rodrigo, Sidney, Stephen, Jacobs, David R., Jr., & Liu, Kiang. (2003). Cardiorespiratory fitness in young adulthood and the development of cardiovascular disease risk factors. *Journal of the American Medical Association, 290,* 3092–3100.

Carpendale, Jeremy I. M., & Lewis, Charlie. (2004). Constructing an understanding of mind: The development of children's social understanding within social interaction. *Behavioral and Brain Sciences, 27,* 79–96.

Carpenter, Brian D., Xiong, Chengjie, Porensky, Emily K., Lee, Monica M., Brown, Patrick J., Coats, Mary, … Morris, John C. (2008). Reaction to a dementia diagnosis in individuals with Alzheimer's disease and mild cognitive impairment. *Journal of the American Geriatrics Society, 56,* 405–412.

Carpenter, Siri. (2012, March 30). Psychology's bold initiative. *Science, 335,* 1558–1561.

Carr, Deborah. (2012). Death and dying in the contemporary United States: What are the psychological implications of anticipated death? *Social and Personality Psychology Compass, 6,* 184–195.

Carskadon, Mary A. (2011). Sleep in adolescents: The perfect storm. *Pediatric Clinics of North America, 58,* 637–647.

Carstensen, Laura. (2011). *A long bright future: Happiness, health, and financial security in an age of increased longevity.* New York, NY: PublicAffairs.

Carstensen, Laura L., Mikels, Joseph A., & Mather, Mara. (2006). Aging and the intersection of cognition, motivation, and emotion. In James E. Birren & K. Warner Schaie (Eds.), *Handbook of the psychology of aging* (6th ed., pp. 343–362). Amsterdam, The Netherlands: Elsevier.

Cartwright, Kelly, Galupo, M., Tyree, Seth, & Jennings, Jennifer. (2009). Reliability and validity of the complex postformal thought questionnaire: Assessing adults' cognitive development. *Journal of Adult Development, 16,* 183–189.

Case-Smith, Jane, & Kuhaneck, Heather Miller. (2008). Play preferences of typically developing children and children with developmental delays between ages 3 and 7 years. *OTJR: Occupation, Participation and Health, 28,* 19–29.

Casey, B. J., Jones, Rebecca M., & Somerville, Leah H. (2011). Braking and accelerating of the adolescent brain. *Journal of Research on Adolescence, 21,* 21–33.

Caspi, Avshalom, Moffitt, Terrie E., Morgan, Julia, Rutter, Michael, Taylor, Alan, Arseneault, Louise, … Polo-Tomas, Monica. (2004). Maternal expressed emotion predicts children's antisocial behavior problems: Using monozygotic-twin differences to identify environmental effects on behavioral development. *Developmental Psychology, 40,* 149–161.

Caspi, Avshalom, & Shiner, Rebecca L. (2006). Personality development. In William Damon & Richard M. Lerner (Series Eds.) & Nancy Eisenberg (Vol. Ed.), *Handbook of child psychology: Vol. 3. Social, emotional, and personality development* (6th ed., pp. 300–365). Hoboken, NJ: Wiley.

Cassia, Viola Macchi, Kuefner, Dana, Picozzi, Marta, & Vescovo, Elena. (2009). Early experience predicts later plasticity for face processing: Evidence for the reactivation of dormant effects. *Psychological Science, 20,* 853–859.

Catani, Claudia, Gewirtz, Abigail H., Wieling, Elizabeth, Schauer, Elizabeth, Elbert, Thomas, & Neuner, Frank. (2010). Tsunami, war, and cumulative risk in the lives of Sri Lankan schoolchildren. *Child Development, 81,* 1176–1191.

Cavanagh, Sean. (2007, December 13). Poverty's effect on U.S. scores greater than for other nations. *Education Week,* pp. 1, 13.

Cave, Damien. (2012, June 19). American children, now struggling to adjust to life in Mexico. *New York Times,* p. A1.

CBS News. (2005, Feb 8). *World's smallest baby goes home: Cellphone-sized baby is discharged from hospital.* Retrieved from http://www.cbsnews.com/stories/2005/02/08/health/main672488.shtml

Center on Education Policy. (2010). *State high school tests: Exit exams and other assessments.* Washington, DC: Author.

Centers for Disease Control and Prevention (CDC) (Ed.). (2007). *Epidemiology and prevention of vaccine-preventable diseases* (10th ed.). Washington, DC: Public Health Foundation.

Centers for Disease Control and Prevention. (2009). Sexually transmitted diseases: Health communication: Fact cheets. Retrieved July 14, 2009, from http://www.cdc.gov/std/healthcomm/fact_sheets.htm

Centers for Disease Control and Prevention. (2011). *Deaths: Preliminary data for 2011.* Atlanta, GA: Author.

Centers for Disease Control and Prevention. (2012a). *Breastfeeding among U.S. children born 2000–2009, CDC National Immunization Survey.* Retrieved from http://www.cdc.gov/breastfeeding/data/nis_data/

Centers for Disease Control and Prevention. (2012b, August 1). *Breastfeeding report card—United States, 2012.* Retrieved from http://www.cdc.gov/breastfeeding/data/reportcard.htm

Centers for Disease Control and Prevention (CDC). (2012c). Disability health and data system. Atlanta, GA: Author.

Centers for Disease Control and Prevention. (2012d, June 27). *Lead—CDC's National Surveillance Data (1997–2010).* Retrieved from http://www.cdc.gov/nceh/lead/data/national.htm

Centers for Disease Control and Prevention. (2012e). *Sexually transmitted disease surveillance 2011.* Atlanta, GA: U.S. Department of Health and Human Services.

Centers for Disease Control and Prevention, American Society for Reproductive Medicine, Society for Assisted Reproductive Technology. (2011). *2009 assisted reproductive technology success rates: National summary and fertility clinic reports.* Atlanta, GA: U.S. Department of Health and Human Services.

Centers for Disease Control and Prevention, National Center for Health Statistics. (2009). The National Nursing Home Survey: 2004 overview. *Vital and Health Statistics, 13*(167).

Centers for Disease Control and Prevention, National Immunization Survey, Department of Health and Human Services. (2012). Breastfeeding among U.S. children born 2006, CDC National Immunization Survey. Retrieved February 1, 2012, from http://www.cdc.gov/breastfeeding/data/NIS_data/2006/socio-demographic_any.htm

Centre for Community Child Health and Telethon Institute for Child Health Research. (2009). *A snapshot of early childhood development in Australia: Australian Early Development Index (AEDI) national report 2009.* Retrieved from http://www.rch.org.au/aedi/media/Snapshot_of_Early_Childhood_DevelopmentinAustralia_AEDI_National_Report.pdf

Cesario, Sandra K., & Hughes, Lisa A. (2007). Precocious puberty: A comprehensive review of literature. *Journal of Obstetric, Gynecologic, & Neonatal Nursing, 36,* 263–274.

Chafen, Jennifer J. Schneider, Newberry, Sydne J., Riedl, Marc A., Bravata, Dena M., Maglione, Margaret, Suttorp, Marika J., . . . Shekelle, Paul G. (2010). Diagnosing and managing common food allergies. *Journal of the American Medical Association, 303,* 1848–1856.

Chakravarti, Aravinda. (2011, October 7). Genomics is not enough. *Science, 334,* 15.

Chambers, Bette, Cheung, Alan C., Slavin, Robert E., Smith, Dewi, & Laurenzano, Mary. (2010). *Effective early childhood education programs: A systematic review.* Baltimore, MD: Johns Hopkins University, Center for Research and Reform in Education.

Champagne, Frances A., & Curley, James P. (2010). Maternal care as a modulating influence on infant development. In Mark S. Blumberg, John H. Freeman, & Scott R. Robinson (Eds.), *Oxford handbook of developmental behavioral neuroscience* (pp. 323–341). New York, NY: Oxford University Press.

Chan, Cheri C. Y., Brandone, Amanda C., & Tardif, Twila. (2009). Culture, context, or behavioral control? English- and Mandarin-speaking mothers' use of nouns and verbs in joint book reading. *Journal of Cross-Cultural Psychology, 40,* 584–602.

Chan, Siu Mui, Bowes, Jennifer, & Wyver, Shirley. (2009). Parenting style as a context for emotion socialization. *Early Education & Development, 20,* 631–656.

Chan, Tak Wing, & Koo, Anita. (2011). Parenting style and youth outcomes in the UK. *European Sociological Review, 27,* 385–399.

Chan, Wing-hoi. (2011). Reviving sociability in contemporary cultural practices and concepts of death in Hong Kong. In Stephen Conway (Ed.), *Governing death and loss: Empowerment, involvement and participation* (pp. 63–70). New York, NY: Oxford University Press.

Chao, Jian-Kang, Lin, Yen-Chin, Ma, Mi-Chia, Lai, Chin-Jen, Ku, Yan-Chiou, Kuo, Wu-Hsien, . . . Chao, I. Chen. (2011). Relationship among sexual desire, sexual satisfaction, and quality of life in middle-aged and older adults. *Journal of Sex & Marital Therapy, 37,* 386–403.

Chao, Ruth K. (2001). Extending research on the consequences of parenting style for Chinese Americans and European Americans. *Child Development, 72,* 1832–1843.

Chao, Y. May, Pisetsky, Emily M., Dierker, Lisa C., Dohm, Faith-Anne, Rosselli, Francine, May, Alexis M., . . . Striegel-Moore, Ruth H. (2008). Ethnic differences in weight control practices among U.S. adolescents from 1995 to 2005. *International Journal of Eating Disorders, 41,* 124–133.

Chaplin, Lan Nguyen, & John, Deborah Roedder. (2007). Growing up in a material world: Age differences in materialism in children and adolescents. *Journal of Consumer Research, 34,* 480–493.

Chapple, Alison, Swift, Chris, & Ziebland, Sue. (2011). The role of spirituality and religion for those bereaved due to a traumatic death. *Mortality, 16,* 1–19.

Charles, Susan T., & Carstensen, Laura L. (2010). Social and emotional aging. *Annual Review of Psychology, 61,* 383–409.

Charness, Neil, Krampe, Ralf, & Mayr, Ulrich. (1996). The role of practice and coaching in entrepreneurial skill domains: An international comparison of life-span chess skill acquisition. In Karl Anders Ericsson (Ed.), *The road to excellence: The acquisition of expert performance in the arts and sciences, sports, and games* (pp. 51–80). Hillsdale, NJ: Erlbaum.

Charness, Neil, & Krampe, Ralf T. (2008). Expertise and knowledge. In Scott M. Hofer & Duane F. Alwin (Eds.), *Handbook of cognitive aging: Interdisciplinary perspectives* (pp. 244–258). Thousand Oaks, CA: Sage.

Chassin, Laurie, Hussong, Andrea, & Beltran, Iris. (2009). Adolescent substance use. In Richard M. Lerner & Laurence Steinberg (Eds.), *Handbook of adolescent psychology: Vol. 1. Individual bases of adolescent development* (3rd ed., pp. 723–763). Hoboken, NJ: Wiley.

Chatters, Linda M., Taylor, Robert Joseph, Lincoln, Karen D., Nguyen, Ann, & Joe, Sean. (2011). Church-based social support and suicidality among African Americans and Black Caribbeans. *Archives of Suicide Research, 15,* 337–353.

Chaux, Enrique, Molano, Andrés, & Podlesky, Paola. (2009). Socio-economic, socio-political and socio-emotional variables explaining school bullying: A country-wide multilevel analysis. *Aggressive Behavior, 35,* 520–529.

Chen, Edith, Cohen, Sheldon, & Miller, Gregory E. (2010). How low socioeconomic status affects 2-year hormonal trajectories in children. *Psychological Science, 21,* 31–37.

Chen, Edith, & Miller, Gregory E. (2012). "Shift-and-persist" strategies: Why low socioeconomic status isn't always bad for health. *Perspectives on Psychological Science, 7,* 135–158.

Chen, Hong, & Jackson, Todd. (2009). Predictors of changes in weight esteem among mainland Chinese adolescents: A longitudinal analysis. *Developmental Psychology, 45,* 1618–1629.

Chen, Xinyin (2011). Culture and children's socioemotional functioning: A contextual-developmental perspective. In Xinyin Chen & Kenneth H. Rubin (Eds.), *Socioemotional development in cultural context* (pp. 29–52). New York, NY: Guilford Press.

Chen, Xinyin, Rubin, Kenneth H., & Sun, Yuerong. (1992). Social reputation and peer relationships in Chinese and Canadian children: A cross-cultural study. *Child Development, 63,* 1336–1343.

Cheng, Yi-Chia, & Yeh, Hsin-Te. (2009). From concepts of motivation to its application in instructional design: Reconsidering motivation from an instructional design perspective. *British Journal of Educational Technology, 40,* 597–605.

Cherlin, Andrew J. (2009). *The marriage-go-round: The state of marriage and the family in America today.* New York, NY: Knopf.

Chernoff, Jodi Jacobson, Flanagan, Kristin Denton, McPhee, Cameron, & Park, Jennifer. (2007). *Preschool: First findings from the preschool follow-up of the Early Childhood Longitudinal Study, Birth Cohort (ECLS-B)* (NCES 2008-025). Washington, DC: National Center for Education Statistics.

Cheslack-Postava, Keely, Liu, Kayuet, & Bearman, Peter S. (2011). Closely spaced pregnancies are associated with increased odds of autism in California sibling births. *Pediatrics, 127,* 246–253.

Cheung, Fanny M., Shu Fai Cheung, Jianxin Zhang, Leung, Kwok, Leong, Frederick, & Kuang Huiyeh. (2008). Relevance of openness as a personality dimension in Chinese culture. *Journal of Cross-Cultural Psychology, 39,* 81–108.

Chiao, Joan Y., & Blizinsky, Katherine D. (2010). Culture-gene coevolution of individualism-collectivism and the serotonin transporter gene. *Proceedings of the Royal Society B: Biological Sciences, 277,* 529–537.

Child Trends. (2012, March). *Low and very low birthweight infants.* Retrieved from www.childtrendsdatabank.org/alphalist?q=node/67

Children's Bureau. (2010). *Child maltreatment 2008.* Washington, DC: U.S. Department of Health and Human Services, Administration for Children and Families, Administration on Children, Youth and Families.

Chin, Vivien S., Skike, Candice E. Van, & Matthews, Douglas B. (2010). Effects of ethanol on hippocampal function during adolescence: A look at the past and thoughts on the future. *Alcohol, 44,* 3–14.

Chomsky, Noam. (1968). *Language and mind.* New York, NY: Harcourt Brace & World.

Chomsky, Noam. (1980). *Rules and representations.* New York, NY: Columbia University Press.

Choshen-Hillel, Shoham, & Yaniv, Ilan. (2012). Agency and the construction of social preference: Between inequality aversion and prosocial behavior. *Journal of Personality and Social Psychology, 101,* 1253–1261.

Chou, Rita Jing-Ann, & Choi, Namkee G. (2011). Prevalence and correlates of perceived workplace discrimination among older workers in the United States of America. *Ageing and Society, 31,* 1051–1070.

Choudhry, Niteesh K., Fletcher, Robert H., & Soumerai, Stephen B. (2005). Systematic review: The relationship between clinical experience and quality of health care. *Annals of Internal Medicine, 142,* 260–273.

Christian, Cindy W., Block, Robert, & the Committee on Child Abuse and Neglect. (2009). Abusive head trauma in infants and children. *Pediatrics, 123,* 1409–1411.

Chronicle of Higher Education. (2010). *Almanac of higher education 2010–11.* Washington, DC: Author.

Chronicle of Higher Education. (2011a). *Almanac of higher education 2011–12.* Washington, DC: Author.

Chronicle of Higher Education. (2011b, August 26). Business was the most common major among bachelor's degree recipients in 2008–9. *Chronicle of Higher Education,* p. 39.

Chu, C. Y. Cyrus, Xie, Yu, & Yu, Ruoh Rong. (2011). Coresidence with elderly parents: A comparative study of southeast China and Taiwan. *Journal of Marriage and Family, 73,* 120–135.

Chudacoff, Howard P. (2011). The history of children's play in the United States. In Anthony D. Pellegrini (Ed.), *The Oxford handbook of the development of play* (pp. 101–109). New York, NY: Oxford University Press.

Chumlea, William Cameron, Schubert, Christine M., Roche, Alex F., Kulin, Howard E., Lee, Peter A., Himes, John H., & Sun, Shumei S. (2003). Age at menarche and racial comparisons in US girls. *Pediatrics, 111,* 110–113.

Chung, Grace H., Flook, Lisa, & Fuligni, Andrew J. (2011). Reciprocal associations between family and peer conflict in adolescents' daily lives. *Child Development, 82,* 1390–1396.

Church, A. Timothy (2010). Current perspectives in the study of personality across cultures. *Perspectives on Psychological Science, 5,* 441–449.

Cicchetti, Dante, & Toth, Sheree L. (2009). The past achievements and future promises of developmental psychopathology: The coming of age of a discipline. *Journal of Child Psychology and Psychiatry, 50,* 16–25.

Cillessen, Antonius H. N., & Mayeux, Lara. (2004). From censure to reinforcement: Developmental changes in the association between aggression and social status. *Child Development, 75,* 147–163.

Cipriano, Elizabeth A., & Stifter, Cynthia A. (2010). Predicting preschool effortful control from toddler temperament and parenting behavior. *Journal of Applied Developmental Psychology, 31,* 221–230.

Claas, Marieke J., de Vries, Linda S., Bruinse, Hein W., van Haastert, Ingrid C., Uniken Venema, Monica M. A., Peelen, Linda M., & Koopman, Corine. (2011). Neurodevelopmental outcome over time of preterm born children ≤750g at birth. *Early Human Development, 87,* 183–191.

Clark, Lee Anna. (2009). Stability and change in personality disorder. *Current Directions in Psychological Science, 18,* 27–31.

Clark, Nina Annika, Demers, Paul A., Karr, Catherine J., Koehoorn, Mieke, Lencar, Cornel, Tamburic, Lillian, & Brauer, Michael. (2010). Effect of early life exposure to air pollution on development of childhood asthma. *Environmental Health Perspectives, 118,* 284–290.

Clark, Shelley, Kabiru, Caroline, & Mathur, Rohini. (2010). Relationship transitions among youth in urban Kenya. *Journal of Marriage and Family, 72,* 73–88.

Clarke, Philippa, Marshall, Victor, House, James, & Lantz, Paula. (2011). The social structuring of mental health over the adult life course: Advancing theory in the sociology of aging. *Social Forces, 89,* 1287–1313.

Clements, Jonathan. (2005, October 5). Rich, successful— and miserable: New research probes mid-life angst. *Wall Street Journal.* Retrieved from http://online.wsj.com/public/article/SB112846380547659946.html

Cleveland, Michael J., Gibbons, Frederick X., Gerrard, Meg, Pomery, Elizabeth A., & Brody, Gene H. (2005). The impact of parenting on risk cognitions and risk behavior: A study of mediation and moderation in a panel of African American adolescents. *Child Development, 76,* 900–916.

Coe, Norma B., & Zamarro, Gema. (2011). Retirement effects on health in Europe. *Journal of Health Economics, 30,* 77–86.

Cohen, David. (2006). *The development of play* (3rd ed.). New York, NY: Routledge.

Cohen, Daniel, & Soto, Marcelo. (2007). Growth and human capital: Good data, good results. *Journal of Economic Growth, 12,* 51–76.

Cohen, Joel E., & Malin, Martin B. (Eds.). (2010). *International perspectives on the goals of universal basic and secondary education.* New York, NY: Routledge.

Cohen, Jon. (2007a, September 7). DNA duplications and deletions help determine health. *Science, 317,* 1315–1317.

Cohen, Jon. (2007b, March 9). Hope on new AIDS drugs, but breast-feeding strategy backfires. *Science, 315,* 1357.

Cohen, Larry, Chávez, Vivian, & Chehimi, Sana. (Eds.) (2010). *Prevention is primary: Strategies for community well-being* (2nd ed.). San Francisco, CA: Jossey-Bass.

Cohen, Leslie B., & Cashon, Cara H. (2006). Infant cognition. In William Damon & Richard M. Lerner (Series Eds.) & Deanna Kuhn & Robert S. Siegler (Vol. Eds.), *Handbook of child psychology: Vol. 2. Cognition, perception, and language* (6th ed., pp. 214–251). Hoboken, NJ: Wiley.

Colbert, Linda, Jefferson, Joseph, Gallo, Ralph, & Davis, Ronnie. (2009). A study of religiosity and psychological well-being among African Americans: Implications for counseling and psychotherapeutic processes. *Journal of Religion and Health, 48,* 278–289.

Cole, Claire, & Winsler, Adam. (2010). Protecting children from exposure to lead: Old problem, new data, and new policy needs. *Social Policy Report, 24,* 3–29.

Cole, Pamela M., Armstrong, Laura Marie, & Pemberton, Caroline K. (2010). The role of language in the development of emotion regulation. In Susan D. Calkins & Martha Ann Bell (Eds.), *Child development at the intersection of emotion and cognition* (pp. 59–78). Washington, DC: American Psychological Association.

Cole, Pamela M., Tan, Patricia Z., Hall, Sarah E., Zhang, Yiyun, Crnic, Keith A., Blair, Clancy B., & Li, Runze. (2011). Developmental changes in anger expression and attention focus: Learning to wait. *Developmental Psychology, 47,* 1078–1089.

Coleman, Marilyn, Ganong, Lawrence H., & Warzinik, Kelly. (2007). *Family life in 20th-century America.* Westport, CT: Greenwood Press.

Coles, Robert. (1997). *The moral intelligence of children: How to raise a moral child.* New York, NY: Random House.

Colleran, Carol, & Jay, Debra. (2003). Surviving addiction: Audrey's story. *Aging Today, 24*(1).

Collins, Pamela Y., Patel, Vikram, Joestl, Sarah S., March, Dana, Insel, Thomas R., Daar, Abdallah S.,… Walport, Mark. (2011). Grand challenges in global mental health. *Nature, 475,* 27–30.

Collins, Rebecca L., Martino, Steven C., Elliott, Marc N., & Miu, Angela. (2011). Relationships between adolescent sexual outcomes and exposure to sex in media: Robustness to propensity-based analysis. *Developmental Psychology, 47,* 585–591.

Collins, Tara J., & Gillath, Omri. (2012). Attachment, breakup strategies, and associated outcomes: The effects of security enhancement on the selection of breakup strategies. *Journal of Research in Personality, 46,* 210–222.

Collins, W. Andrew, & Laursen, Brett. (2004). Parent-adolescent relationships and influences. In Richard M. Lerner & Laurence D. Steinberg (Eds.), *Handbook of adolescent psychology* (2nd ed., pp. 331–361). Hoboken, NJ: Wiley.

Compian, Laura J., Gowen, L. Kris, & Hayward, Chris. (2009). The interactive effects of puberty and peer victimization on weight concerns and depression symptoms among early adolescent girls. *The Journal of Early Adolescence, 29,* 357–375.

Compta, Yaroslau, Parkkinen, Laura, O'Sullivan, Sean S., Vandrovcova, Jana, Holton, Janice L., Collins, Catherine,… Revesz, Tamas. (2011). Lewy- and Alzheimer-type pathologies in Parkinson's disease dementia: Which is more important? *Brain, 134,* 1493–1505.

Conboy, Barbara T., & Thal, Donna J. (2006). Ties between the lexicon and grammar: Cross-sectional and longitudinal studies of bilingual toddlers. *Child Development, 77,* 712–735.

Cong, Zhen, & Silverstein, Merril. (2008). Intergenerational support and depression among elders in rural China: Do daughters-in-law matter? *Journal of Marriage and Family, 70,* 599–612.

Conger, Katherine J., & Little, Wendy M. (2010). Sibling relationships during the transition to adulthood. *Child Development Perspectives, 4,* 87–94.

Conger, Rand D., Conger, Katherine J., & Martin, Monica J. (2010). Socioeconomic status, family processes, and individual development. *Journal of Marriage and Family, 72,* 685–704.

Conger, Rand D., Wallace, Lora Ebert, Sun, Yumei, Simons, Ronald L., McLoyd, Vonnie C., & Brody, Gene H. (2002). Economic pressure in African American families: A replication and extension of the family stress model. *Developmental Psychology, 38,* 179–193.

Conner, Mark (2008). Initiation and maintenance of health behaviors. *Applied Psychology, 57,* 42–50.

Connidis, Ingrid Arnet. (2007). Negotiating inequality among adult siblings: Two case studies. *Journal of Marriage and Family, 69,* 482–499.

Cook, Christine C., Martin, Peter, Yearns, Mary, & Damhorst, Mary Lynn. (2007). Attachment to "place" and coping with losses in changed communities: A paradox for aging adults. *Family & Consumer Sciences Research Journal, 35,* 201–214.

Cooke, Lynn Prince, & Baxter, Janeen. (2010). "Families" in international context: Comparing institutional effects across Western societies. *Journal of Marriage and Family, 72,* 516–536.

Coon, Carleton S. (1962). *The origin of races.* New York, NY: Knopf.

Coontz, Stephanie. (2005). *Marriage, a history: From obedience to intimacy or how love conquered marriage.* New York, NY: Viking.

Cooper, Claudia, Selwood, Amber, & Livingston, Gill. (2008). The prevalence of elder abuse and neglect: A systematic review. *Age and Ageing, 37,* 151–160.

Coovadia, Hoosen M., & Wittenberg, Dankwart F. (Eds.). (2004). *Paediatrics and child health: A manual for health professionals in developing countries* (5th ed.). New York, NY: Oxford University Press.

Copen, Casey, Daniels, Kimberly, Vespa, Jonathan, & Moshen, William. (2012, March 2012). First marriages in the United States: Data from the 2006-2010 National Survey of Family growth. *National Center for Health Statistics, 49.*

Coplan, Robert J., & Weeks, Murray. (2009). Shy and soft-spoken: Shyness, pragmatic language, and socio-emotional adjustment in early childhood. *Infant and Child Development, 18,* 238–254.

Corballis, Michael C. (2011). *The recursive mind: The origins of human language, thought, and civilization.* Princeton, NJ: Princeton University Press.

Corda, Larisa, Khanapure, Amita, & Karoshi, Mahantesh. (2012). Biopanic, advanced maternal age and fertility outcomes. In Mahantesh Karoshi, Sandra Newbold, Christopher B. Lynch, & Louis Keith (Eds.), *A textbook of preconceptional medicine and management* (pp. 3–18). Carlisle, UK: Sapiens.

Cornwell, Benjamin. (2012). Spousal network overlap as a basis for spousal support. *Journal of Marriage and Family, 74,* 229–238.

Cosgrave, James F. (2010). Embedded addiction: The social production of gambling knowledge and the development of gambling markets. *Canadian Journal of Sociology, 35,* 113–134.

Côté, James E. (2006). Emerging adulthood as an institutionalized moratorium: Risks and benefits to identity formation. In Jeffrey Jensen Arnett & Jennifer Lynn Tanner (Eds.), *Emerging adults in America: Coming of age in the 21st century* (pp. 85–116). Washington, DC: American Psychological Association.

Côté, James E. (2009). Identity formation and self-development in adolescence. In Richard M. Lerner & Laurence Steinberg (Eds.), *Handbook of adolescent psychology: Vol. 1. Individual bases of adolescent development* (3rd ed., pp. 266–304). Hoboken, NJ: Wiley.

Côté, Sylvana M., Borge, Anne I., Geoffroy, Marie-Claude, Rutter, Michael, & Tremblay, Richard E. (2008). Nonmaternal care in infancy and emotional/behavioral difficulties at 4 years old: Moderation by family risk characteristics. *Developmental Psychology, 44,* 155–168.

Couzin, Jennifer. (2009, January 23). Friendship as a health factor. *Science, 323,* 454–457.

Couzin-Frankel, Jennifer. (2010, November 26). Bacteria and asthma: Untangling the links. *Science, 330,* 1168–1169.

Couzin-Frankel, Jennifer. (2011a, January 14). New high-tech screen takes carrier testing to the next level. *Science, 331,* 130–131.

Couzin-Frankel, Jennifer. (2011b, July 29). A pitched battle over life span. *Science, 333,* 549–550.

Cowan, Nelson (Ed.). (1997). *The development of memory in childhood.* Hove, East Sussex, UK: Psychology Press.

Cowan, Nelson, & Alloway, Tracy. (2009). Development of working memory in childhood. In Mary L. Courage & Nelson Cowan (Eds.), *The development of memory in infancy and childhood* (2nd ed., pp. 303–342). New York, NY: Psychology Press.

Crain, William C. (2005). *Theories of development: Concepts and applications* (5th ed.). Upper Saddle River, NJ: Prentice Hall.

Cramer, Steven C., & Procaccio, Vincent. (2012). Correlation between genetic polymorphisms and stroke recovery: Analysis of the GAIN Americas and GAIN International Studies. *European Journal of Neurology, 19,* 718–724.

Cranwell, Brian. (2010). Care and control: What motivates people's decisions about the disposal of ashes. *Bereavement Care, 29*(2), 10–12.

Crawford, Emily, Wright, Margaret O'Dougherty, & Masten, Ann S. (2006). Resilience and spirituality in youth. In Eugene C. Roehlkepartain, Pamela Ebstyne King, Linda Wagener, & Peter L. Benson (Eds.), *The handbook of spiritual development in childhood and adolescence* (pp. 355–370). Thousand Oaks, CA: Sage.

Creswell, John W. (2009). *Research design: Qualitative, quantitative, and mixed methods approaches* (3rd ed.). Thousand Oaks, CA: Sage.

Crimmins, Eileen M., & Beltrán-Sánchez, Hiram. (2011). Mortality and morbidity trends: Is there compression of morbidity? *The Journals of Gerontology Series B: Psychological Sciences and Social Sciences, 66B,* 75–86.

Crinion, Jenny, Turner, R., Grogan, Alice, Hanakawa, Takashi, Noppeney, Uta, Devlin, Joseph T.,... Price, C. J. (2006, June 9). Language control in the bilingual brain. *Science, 312,* 1537–1540.

Crisp, Richard J., & Turner, Rhiannon N. (2011). Cognitive adaptation to the experience of social and cultural diversity. *Psychological Bulletin, 137,* 242–266.

Crone, Eveline A., & Westenberg, P. Michiel. (2009). A brain-based account of developmental changes in social decision making. In Michelle de Haan & Megan R. Gunnar (Eds.), *Handbook of developmental social neuroscience* (pp. 378–396). New York, NY: Guilford Press.

Crosnoe, Robert, & Elder, Glen H., Jr. (2002). Successful adaptation in the later years: A life course approach to aging. *Social Psychology Quarterly, 65,* 309–328.

Crosnoe, Robert, & Johnson, Monica Kirkpatrick. (2011). Research on adolescence in the twenty-first century. *Annual Review of Sociology, 37,* 439–460.

Crosnoe, Robert, Johnson, Monica Kirkpatrick, & Elder, Glen H., Jr. (2004). Intergenerational bonding in school: The behavioral and contextual correlates of student–teacher relationships. *Sociology of Education, 77,* 60–81.

Crosnoe, Robert, Leventhal, Tama, Wirth, Robert John, Pierce, Kim M., Pianta, Robert C., & NICHD Early Child Care Research Network. (2010). Family socioeconomic status and consistent environmental stimulation in early childhood. *Child Development, 81,* 972–987.

Crosnoe, Robert, & Needham, Belinda. (2004). Holism, contextual variability, and the study of friendships in adolescent development. *Child Development, 75,* 264–279.

Cross, Donna, Monks, Helen, Hall, Marg, Shaw, Thérèse, Pintabona, Yolanda, Erceg, Erin,... Lester, Leanne. (2010). Three-year results of the Friendly Schools whole-of-school intervention on children's bullying behaviour. *British Educational Research Journal, 37,* 105–129.

Crowell, Sheila, Beauchaine, Theodore, Hsiao, Ray, Vasilev, Christina, Yaptangco, Mona, Linehan, Marsha, & McCauley, Elizabeth. (2012). Differentiating adolescent self-injury from adolescent depression: Possible implications for borderline personality development. *Journal of Abnormal Child Psychology, 40,* 45–57.

Cruikshank, Margaret. (2009). *Learning to be old: Gender, culture, and aging* (2nd ed.). Lanham, MD: Rowman & Littlefield.

Cruz, Alvaro A., Bateman, Eric D., & Bousquet, Jean. (2010). The social determinants of asthma. *European Respiratory Journal, 35,* 239–242.

Cryder, Cynthia E., Lerner, Jennifer S., Gross, James J., & Dahl, Ronald E. (2008). Misery is not miserly: Sad and self-focused individuals spend more. *Psychological Science, 19,* 525–530.

Csikszentmihalyi, Mihaly. (1996). *Creativity: Flow and the psychology of discovery and invention.* New York, NY: HarperCollins.

Cuevas, Bryan J., & Stone, Jacqueline Ilyse. (Eds.) (2007). *The Buddhist dead: Practices, discourses, representations.* Honolulu, HI: University of Hawaii Press.

Cuijpers, Pim, Brännmark, Jessica G., & van Straten, Annemieke. (2008). Psychological treatment of postpartum depression: A meta-analysis. *Journal of Clinical Psychology, 64,* 103–118.

Cumming, Elaine, & Henry, William Earl. (1961). *Growing old: The process of disengagement.* New York, NY: Basic Books.

Cumming, Grant P., Currie, Heather D., Panay, Nick, Moncur, Rik, & Lee, Amanda J. (2011). Stopping hormone replacement therapy: Were women ill advised? *Menopause International, 17,* 82–87.

Cumsille, Patricio, Darling, Nancy, & Martínez, M. Loreto. (2010). Shading the truth: The patterning of adolescents' decisions to avoid issues, disclose, or lie to parents. *Journal of Adolescence, 33,* 285–296.

Curlin, Farr A., Nwodim, Chinyere, Vance, Jennifer L., Chin, Marshall H., & Lantos, John D. (2008). To die, to sleep: US physicians' religious and other objections to physician-assisted suicide, terminal sedation, and withdrawal of life support. *American Journal of Hospice and Palliative Medicine, 25,* 112–120.

Currie, Janet, & Widom, Cathy Spatz. (2010). Long-term consequences of child abuse and neglect on adult economic well-being. *Child Maltreatment, 15,* 111–120.

Cutler, Stephen J., Hendricks, Jon, & O'Neill, Greg. (2011). Civic engagement and aging. In Robert H. Binstock & Linda K. George (Eds.), *Handbook of aging and the social sciences* (7th ed., pp. 221–233). San Diego, CA: Academic Press.

D'Angelo, Denise, Williams, Letitia, Morrow, Brian, Cox, Shanna, Harris, Norma, Harrison, Leslie,... Zapata, Lauren. (2007). Preconception and interconception health status of women who recently gave birth to a live-born infant—Pregnancy Risk Assessment Monitoring System (PRAMS), United States, 26 reporting areas, 2004. *Morbidity and Mortality Weekly Report Surveillance Summaries, 56*(SS10), 1–35.

Daddis, Christopher. (2010). Adolescent peer crowds and patterns of belief in the boundaries of personal authority. *Journal of Adolescence, 33,* 699–708.

Dahl, Ronald E. (2004). Adolescent brain development: A period of vulnerabilities and opportunities. Keynote address. In Ronald E. Dahl & Linda Patia Spear (Eds.), *Adolescent brain development: Vulnerabilities and opportunities* (Vol. 1021, pp. 1–22). New York, NY: New York Academy of Sciences.

Dai, David Yun. (2010). *The nature and nurture of giftedness: A new framework for understanding gifted education.* New York, NY: Teachers College Press.

Dalman, Christina, Allebeck, Peter, Gunnell, David, Harrison, Glyn, Kristensson, Krister, Lewis, Glyn,... Karlsson, Håkan. (2008). Infections in the CNS during childhood and the risk of subsequent psychotic illness: A cohort study of more than one million Swedish subjects. *American Journal of Psychiatry, 165,* 59–65.

Danel, Isabella, Berg, Cynthia, Johnson, Christopher H., & Atrash, Hani. (2003). Magnitude of maternal morbidity during labor and delivery: United States, 1993–1997. *American Journal of Public Health, 93,* 631–634.

Dangour, Alan D., Fletcher, Astrid E., & Grundy, Emily, M. D. (Eds.) (2007). *Ageing well: Nutrition, health, and social interventions.* Boca Raton, FL: CRC Press/Taylor & Francis.

Dannefer, Dale, & Patterson, Robin Shura. (2008). The missing person: Some limitations in the contemporary study of cognitive aging. In Scott M. Hofer & Duane F. Alwin (Eds.), *Handbook of cognitive aging: Interdisciplinary perspectives* (pp. 105–119). Thousand Oaks, CA: Sage.

Darling, Nancy, Cumsille, Patricio, & Martinez, M. Loreto. (2008). Individual differences in adolescents' beliefs about the legitimacy of parental authority and their own obligation to obey: A longitudinal investigation. *Child Development, 79,* 1103–1118.

Daro, Deborah. (2009). The history of science and child abuse prevention: A reciprocal relationship. In Kenneth A. Dodge & Doriane Lambelet Coleman (Eds.), *Preventing child maltreatment: Community approaches* (pp. 9–28). New York, NY: Guilford Press.

Darwin, Charles. (1859). *On the origin of species by means of natural selection.* London, England: J. Murray.

David, Barbara, Grace, Diane, & Ryan, Michelle K. (2004). The gender wars: A self-categorization perspective on the development of gender identity. In Mark Bennett & Fabio Sani (Eds.), *The development of the social self* (pp. 135–157). Hove, East Sussex, England: Psychology Press.

Davidovitch, Michael, Hemo, Beatriz, Manning-Courtney, Patricia, & Fombonne, Eric. (2012). Prevalence and incidence of autism spectrum disorder in an Israeli population. *Journal of Autism and Developmental Disorders,* 1–9. Advance online publication. doi:10.1007/s10803-012-1611-z

Davidson, Kate. (2008). Declining health and competence: Men facing choices about driving cessation. *Generations, 32*(1), 44–47.

Davis, Kelly D., Goodman, W. Benjamin, Pirretti, Amy E., & Almeida, David M. (2008). Nonstandard work schedules, perceived family well-being, and daily stressors. *Journal of Marriage and Family, 70,* 991–1003.

Davis, Linell (1999). *Doing culture: Cross-cultural communication in action.* Beijing, China: Foreign Language Teaching & Research Press.

Davis, Mark, & Squire, Corinne (Eds.). (2010). *HIV treatment and prevention technologies in international perspective.* New York, NY: Palgrave Macmillan.

Davis, R. Neal, Davis, Matthew M., Freed, Gary L., & Clark, Sarah J. (2011). Fathers' depression related to positive and negative parenting behaviors with 1-year-old children. *Pediatrics, 127,* 612–618.

Davis-Kean, Pamela E., Jager, Justin, & Collins, W. Andrew (2009). The self in action: An emerging link between self-beliefs and behaviors in middle childhood. *Child Development Perspectives, 3,* 184–188.

Dawson, Lorne L. (2010). The study of new religious movements and the radicalization of home-grown terrorists: Opening a dialogue. *Terrorism and Political Violence, 22,* 1–21.

Dawson, Michelle, Soulières, Isabelle, Gernsbacher, Morton Ann, & Mottron, Laurent. (2007). The level and nature of autistic intelligence. *Psychological Science, 18,* 657–662.

de Bruin, Wändi Bruine, Parker, Andrew M., & Fischhoff, Baruch. (2007). Can adolescents predict significant life events? *The Journal of Adolescent Health, 41,* 208–210.

de Castro, Bram Orobio, Brendgen, Mara, Boxtel, Herman, Vitaro, Frank, & Schaepers, Linda. (2007). "Accept me, or else…": Disputed overestimation of social competence predicts increases in proactive aggression. *Journal of Abnormal Child Psychology, 35,* 165–178.

De Cock, Kevin M. (2011). Trends in global health and CDC's international role, 1961–2011. *Morbidity and Mortality Weekly Report, 60*(Suppl. 4), 104–111.

de Heering, Adelaide, de Liedekerke, Claire, Deboni, Malorie, & Rossion, Bruno. (2010). The role of experience during childhood in shaping the other-race effect. *Developmental Science, 13,* 181–187.

de Jonge, Ank, van der Goes, Birgit Y., Ravelli, Anita C. J., Amelink-Verburg, Marianne P., Mol, Ben Willem, Nijhuis, Jan G.,… Buitendijk, Simone E. (2009). Perinatal mortality and morbidity in a nationwide cohort of 529,688 low-risk planned home and hospital births. *BJOG: An International Journal of Obstetrics & Gynaecology, 116,* 1177–1184.

De Neys, Wim, & Van Gelder, Elke. (2009). Logic and belief across the lifespan: The rise and fall of belief inhibition during syllogistic reasoning. *Developmental Science, 12,* 123–130.

De Raedt, Rudi, Koster, Ernst H. W., & Ryckewaert, Ruben. (2013). Aging and attentional bias for death related and general threat-related information: Less avoidance in older as compared with middle-aged adults. *The Journals of Gerontology Series B: Psychological Sciences and Social Sciences, 68B,* 41–48.

de Schipper, Elles J., Riksen-Walraven, J. Marianne, & Geurts, Sabine A. E. (2006). Effects of child-caregiver ratio on the interactions between caregivers and children in child-care centers: An experimental study. *Child Development, 77,* 861–874.

Dean, Angela J., Walters, Julie, & Hall, Anthony. (2010). A systematic review of interventions to enhance medication adherence in children and adolescents with chronic illness. *Archives of Disease in Childhood, 95,* 717–723.

Dearing, Eric, Wimer, Christopher, Simpkins, Sandra D., Lund, Terese, Bouffard, Suzanne M., Caronongan, Pia,… Weiss, Heather. (2009). Do neighborhood and home contexts help explain why low-income children miss opportunities to participate in activities outside of school? *Developmental Psychology, 45,* 1545–1562.

Deary, Ian J., Penke, Lars, & Johnson, Wendy. (2010). The neuroscience of human intelligence differences. *Nature Reviews Neuroscience, 11,* 201–211.

Deci, Edward L., Koestner, Richard, & Ryan, Richard M. (1999). A meta-analytic review of experiments examining the effects of extrinsic rewards on intrinsic motivation. *Psychological Bulletin, 125,* 627–668.

Dees, Marianne K., Vernooij-Dassen, Myrra J., Dekkers, Wim J., Vissers, Kris C., & van Weel, Chris. (2011). 'Unbearable suffering': A qualitative study on the perspectives of patients who request assistance in dying. *Journal of Medical Ethics, 37,* 727–734.

Degenhardt, Louisa, Coffey, Carolyn, Carlin, John B., Swift, Wendy, Moore, Elya, & Patton, George C. (2010). Outcomes of occasional cannabis use in adolescence: 10-year follow-up study in Victoria, Australia. *The British Journal of Psychiatry, 196,* 290–295.

Delaunay-El Allam, Maryse, Soussignan, Robert, Patris, Bruno, Marlier, Luc, & Schaal, Benoist. (2010). Long-lasting memory for an odor acquired at the mother's breast. *Developmental Science, 13,* 849–863.

Demetriou, Andreas, & Bakracevic, Karin. (2009). Reasoning and self-awareness from adolescence to middle age: Organization and development as a function of education. *Learning and Individual Differences, 19,* 181–194.

Denham, Susanne A., Blair, Kimberly A., DeMulder, Elizabeth, Levitas, Jennifer, Sawyer, Katherine, Auerbach-Major, Sharon, & Queenan, Patrick. (2003). Preschool emotional competence: Pathway to social competence. *Child Development, 74,* 238–256.

Denny, Dallas, & Pittman, Cathy. (2007). Gender identity: From dualism to diversity. In Mitchell S. Tepper & Annette Fuglsang Owens (Eds.), *Sexual health: Vol. 1. Psychological foundations* (pp. 205–229). Westport, CT: Praeger/Greenwood.

Dentinger, Emma, & Clarkberg, Marin. (2002). Informal caregiving and retirement timing among men and women: Gender and caregiving relationships in late midlife. *Journal of Family Issues, 23,* 857–879.

DePaulo, Bella M. (2006). *Singled out: How singles are stereotyped, stigmatized, and ignored and still live happily ever after.* New York, NY: St. Martin's Press.

Deptula, Daneen P., Henry, David B., & Schoeny, Michael E. (2010). How can parents make a difference? Longitudinal associations with adolescent sexual behavior. *Journal of Family Psychology, 24,* 731–739.

DeRose, Laura M., Shiyko, Mariya P., Foster, Holly, & Brooks-Gunn, Jeanne. (2011). Associations between menarcheal timing and behavioral developmental trajectories for girls from age 6 to age 15. *Journal of Youth and Adolescence, 40,* 1329–1342.

Desai, Sonalde, & Andrist, Lester. (2010). Gender scripts and age at marriage in India. *Demography, 47,* 667–687.

DeSantis, Carol, Siegel, Rebecca, Bandi, Priti, & Jemal, Ahmedin. (2011). Breast cancer statistics, 2011. *CA: A Cancer Journal for Clinicians, 61,* 408–418.

Devi, Sharmila. (2008). Progress on childhood obesity patchy in the USA. *Lancet, 371,* 105–106.

DeYoung, Colin G., Hirsh, Jacob B., Shane, Matthew S., Papademetris, Xenophon, Rajeevan, Nallakkandi, & Gray, Jeremy R. (2010). Testing predictions from personality neuroscience. *Psychological Science, 21,* 820–828.

Diallo, Yacouba, Hagemann, Frank, Etienne, Alex, Gurbuzer, Yonca, & Mehran, Farhad (2010). *Global child labour developments: Measuring trends from 2004 to 2008.* Geneva, Switzerland: International Labour Office, International Programme on the Elimination of Child Labour.

Diamond, Adele, & Amso, Dima. (2008). Contributions of neuroscience to our understanding of cognitive development. *Current Directions in Psychological Science, 17,* 136–141.

Diamond, Lisa M., & Fagundes, Christopher P. (2010). Psychobiological research on attachment. *Journal of Social and Personal Relationships, 27,* 218–225.

Diamond, Mathew E. (2007). Neuronal basis of perceptual intelligence. In Flavia Santoianni & Claudia Sabatano (Eds.), *Brain development in learning environments: Embodied and perceptual advancements* (pp. 98–108). Newcastle, UK: Cambridge Scholars.

Dick, Danielle M. (2011). Developmental changes in genetic influences on alcohol use and dependence. *Child Development Perspectives, 5,* 223–230.

Dickinson, George E., & Hoffmann, Heath C. (2010). Roadside memorial policies in the United States. *Mortality, 15,* 154–167.

Dickinson, Mercedes D., & Hiscock, Merrill. (2010). Age-related IQ decline is reduced markedly after adjustment for the Flynn effect. *Journal of Clinical and Experimental Neuropsychology, 32,* 865–870.

Didion, Joan. (2005). *The year of magical thinking.* New York, NY: Knopf.

Diener, Ed, & Biswas-Diener, Robert. (2008). *Happiness: Unlocking the mysteries of psychological wealth.* Malden, MA: Blackwell.

Dietrich, Anne. (2008). *When the hurting continues: Revictimization and perpetration in the lives of childhood maltreatment survivors.* Saarbrücken, Germany: VDM Verlag.

DiGirolamo, Ann, Thompson, Nancy, Martorell, Reynaldo, Fein, Sara, & Grummer-Strawn, Laurence. (2005). Intention or experience? Predictors of continued breast-feeding. *Health Education & Behavior, 32,* 208–226.

Dijksterhuis, Ap, & Aarts, Henk. (2010). Goals, attention, and (un)consciousness. *Annual Review of Psychology, 61,* 467–490.

Dijksterhuis, Ap, Bos, Maarten W., van der Leij, Andries, & van Baaren, Rick B. (2009). Predicting soccer matches after unconscious and conscious thought as a function of expertise. *Psychological Science, 20,* 1381–1387.

Dijksterhuis, Ap, & Nordgren, Loran F. (2006). A theory of unconscious thought. *Perspectives on Psychological Science, 1,* 95–109.

Dilworth-Bart, Janean E., & Moore, Colleen F. (2006). Mercy mercy me: Social injustice and the prevention of environmental pollutant exposures among ethnic minority and poor children. *Child Development, 77,* 247–265.

Dishion, Thomas J., & Bullock, Bernadette Marie. (2002). Parenting and adolescent problem behavior: An ecological analysis of the nurturance hypothesis. In John G. Borkowski, Sharon Landesman Ramey, & Marie Bristol-Power (Eds.), *Parenting and the child's world: Influences on academic, intellectual, and social-emotional development* (pp. 231–249). Mahwah, NJ: Erlbaum.

Dishion, Thomas J., Poulin, François, & Burraston, Bert. (2001). Peer group dynamics associated with iatrogenic effects in group interventions with high-risk young adolescents. In William Damon (Series Ed.) & Douglas W. Nangle & Cynthia

A. Erdley (Vol. Eds.), *New directions for child and adolescent development: No. 91. The role of friendship in psychological adjustment* (pp. 79–92). San Francisco, CA: Jossey-Bass.

Dishion, Thomas J., Véronneau, Marie-Hélène, & Myers, Michael W. (2010). Cascading peer dynamics underlying the progression from problem behavior to violence in early to late adolescence. *Development and Psychopathology, 22,* 603–619.

Dobler, Robert Thomas. (2011). Ghost bikes: Memorialization and protest on city streets. In Peter Jan Margry & Cristina Sanchez-Carretero (Eds.), *Grassroots memorials: The politics of memorializing traumatic death* (pp. 169–187). New York, NY: Berghahn Books.

Dobson, Velma, Candy, T. Rowan, Hartmann, E. Eugenie, Mayer, D. Luisa, Miller, Joseph M., & Quinn, Graham E. (2009). Infant and child vision research: Present status and future directions. *Optometry & Vision Science, 86,* 559–560.

Dodge, Kenneth A., Coie, John D., & Lynam, Donald R. (2006). Aggression and antisocial behavior in youth. In William Damon & Richard M. Lerner (Series Eds.) & Nancy Eisenberg (Vol. Ed.), *Handbook of child psychology: Vol. 3. Social, emotional, and personality development* (6th ed., pp. 719–788). New York, NY: Wiley.

Doering, Katie. (2010). Death: The unwritten curriculum. *Encounter: Education for Meaning and Social Justice, 23,* 57–62.

Domina, Thurston, Conley, AnneMarie, & Farkas, George. (2011a). The case for dreaming big. *Sociology of Education, 84,* 118–121.

Domina, Thurston, Conley, AnneMarie, & Farkas, George. (2011b). The link between educational expectations and effort in the college-for-all era. *Sociology of Education, 84,* 93–112.

Dominguez, Cynthia O. (2001). Expertise in laparoscopic surgery: Anticipation and affordances. In Eduardo Salas & Gary Klein (Eds.), *Linking expertise and naturalistic decision making* (pp. 287–301). Mahwah, NJ: Erlbaum.

Dominguez, Ximena, Vitiello, Virginia E., Maier, Michelle F., & Greenfield, Daryl B. (2010). A longitudinal examination of young children's learning behavior: Child-level and classroom-level predictors of change throughout the preschool year. *School Psychology Review, 39,* 29–47.

Dong, XinQi, & Simon, Melissa A. (2011). Enhancing national policy and programs to address elder abuse. *Journal of the American Medical Association, 305,* 2460–2461.

Dong, XinQi, Simon, Melissa A., Beck, T. T., Farran, Carol, McCann, Judith J., Mendes de Leon, Carlos F., . . . Evans, Denis A. (2011). Elder abuse and mortality: The role of psychological and social wellbeing. *Gerontology, 57,* 549–558.

Donnellan, M. Brent, & Lucas, Richard E. (2008). Age differences in the Big Five across the life span: Evidence from two national samples. *Psychology and Aging, 23,* 558–566.

Doraiswamy, P. Murali. (2012). Silent cerebrovascular events and Alzheimer's disease: An overlooked opportunity for prevention? *American Journal of Psychiatry, 169,* 251–254.

dosReis, Susan, Mychailyszyn, Matthew P., Evans-Lacko, Sara E., Beltran, Alicia, Riley, Anne W., & Myers, Mary Anne. (2009). The meaning of attention-deficit/hyperactivity disorder medication and parents' initiation and continuity of treatment for their child. *Journal of Child and Adolescent Psychopharmacology, 19,* 377–383.

dosReis, Susan, & Myers, Mary Anne. (2008). Parental attitudes and involvement in psychopharmacological treatment for ADHD: A conceptual model. *International Review of Psychiatry, 20,* 135–141.

Doumbo, Ogobara K. (2005, February 4). It takes a village: Medical research and ethics in Mali. *Science, 307,* 679–681.

Dowling, John E. (2004). *The great brain debate: Nature or nurture?* Washington, DC: Joseph Henry Press.

Downs, Danielle Symons, & Hausenblas, Heather A. (2007). Pregnant women's third trimester exercise behaviors, body mass index, and pregnancy outcomes. *Psychology & Health, 22,* 545–559.

Drover, James, Hoffman, Dennis R., Castañeda, Yolanda S., Morale, Sarah E., & Birch, Eileen E. (2009). Three randomized controlled trials of early long-chain polyunsaturated fatty acid supplementation on means-end problem solving in 9-month-olds. *Child Development, 80,* 1376–1384.

Duckworth, Angela L., Peterson, Christopher, Matthews, Michael D., & Kelly, Dennis R. (2007). Grit: Perseverance and passion for long-term goals. *Journal of Personality and Social Psychology, 92,* 1087–1101.

Duffy, Oonagh, Iversen, Lisa, & Hannaford, Philip C. (2011). The menopause: 'It's somewhere between a taboo and a joke.' A focus group study. *Climacteric, 14,* 497–505.

Duncan, Greg J., & Magnuson, Katherine. (2007). Penny wise and effect size foolish. *Child Development Perspectives, 1,* 46–51.

Duncan, Greg J., Ziol-Guest, Kathleen M., & Kalil, Ariel. (2010). Early-childhood poverty and adult attainment, behavior, and health. *Child Development, 81,* 306–325.

Duncan, Simon, & Phillips, Miranda. (2010). People who live apart together (LATs)—How different are they? *The Sociological Review, 58,* 112–134.

Dunning, David. (Ed.) (2011). *Social motivation.* New York, NY: Psychology Press.

Dunphy, Dexter C. (1963). The social structure of urban adolescent peer groups. *Sociometry, 26,* 230–246.

Duplassie, Danielle, & Daniluk, Judith C. (2007). Sexuality: Young and middle adulthood. In Mitchell S. Tepper & Annette Fuglsang Owens (Eds.), *Sexual health: Vol. 1. Psychological foundations* (pp. 263–289). Westport, CT: Praeger/Greenwood.

Dupuis, Kate, & Pichora-Fuller, M. Kathleen. (2010). Use of affective prosody by young and older adults. *Psychology and Aging, 25,* 16–29.

Dwane, H. Dean. (2012). Self-control and perceived physical risk in an extreme sport. *Young Consumers: Insight and Ideas for Responsible Marketers, 13,* 62–73.

Dweck, Carol S. (2007). Is math a gift? Beliefs that put females at risk. In Stephen J. Ceci & Wendy M. Williams (Eds.), *Why aren't more women in science: Top researchers debate the evidence* (pp. 47–55). Washington, DC: American Psychological Association.

Earth Policy Institute. (2011). *Two stories of disease: Smallpox and polio.* Retrieved from http://www.earth-policy.org/data_highlights/2011/highlights19

Ebaugh, Helen Rose, & Curry, Mary. (2000). Fictive kin as social capital in new immigrant communities. *Sociological Perspectives, 43,* 189–209.

Ebner, Natalie C., Freund, Alexandra M., & Baltes, Paul B. (2006). Developmental changes in personal goal orientation from young to late adulthood: From striving for gains to maintenance and prevention of losses. *Psychology and Aging, 21,* 664–678.

Eccles, Jacquelynne. (2011). Gendered educational and occupational choices: Applying the Eccles et al. model of achievement-related choices. *International Journal of Behavioral Development, 35,* 195–201.

Eccles, Jacquelynne S., & Roeser, Robert W. (2010). An ecological view of schools and development. In Judith L. Meece & Jacquelynne S. Eccles (Eds.), *Handbook of research on schools, schooling, and human development* (pp. 6–22). New York, NY: Routledge.

Eccles, Jacquelynne S., & Roeser, Robert W. (2011). Schools as developmental contexts during adolescence. *Journal of Research on Adolescence, 21,* 225–241.

Eddleman, Keith A., Malone, Fergal D., Sullivan, Lisa, Dukes, Kim, Berkowitz, Richard L., Kharbutli, Yara, . . . D'Alton, Mary E. (2006). Pregnancy loss rates after midtrimester amniocentesis. *Obstetrics & Gynecology, 108,* 1067–1072.

Editorial Projects in Education Research Center. (2011, June 9). Diplomas count 2011: Beyond high school, before baccalaureate [Special issue]. *Education Week, 30*(34).

Edwards, Judge Leonard P. (2007). Achieving timely permanency in child protection courts: The importance of frontloading the court process. *Juvenile and Family Court Journal, 58,* 1–37.

Eggum, Natalie D., Eisenberg, Nancy, Kao, Karen, Spinrad, Tracy L., Bolnick, Rebecca, Hofer, Claire, . . . Fabricius, William V. (2011). Emotion understanding, theory of mind, and prosocial orientation: Relations over time in early childhood. *The Journal of Positive Psychology, 6,* 4–16.

Ehrlich, Paul R. (1968). *The population bomb.* New York, NY: Ballantine Books.

Einstein, Albert. (1994). *Ideas and opinions* (Carl Seelig, Ed., and Sonja Bargmann, Trans.). New York, NY: Modern Library. (Originally published 1954.)

Eisenberg, Nancy, Cumberland, Amanda, Guthrie, Ivanna K., Murphy, Bridget C., & Shepard, Stephanie A. (2005). Age changes in prosocial responding and moral reasoning in adolescence and early adulthood. *Journal of Research on Adolescence, 15,* 235–260.

Eisenberg, Nancy, Fabes, Richard A., & Spinrad, Tracy L. (2006). Prosocial development. In William Damon & Richard M. Lerner (Series Eds.) & Nancy Eisenberg (Vol. Ed.), *Handbook of child psychology: Vol. 3. Social, emotional, and personality development* (6th ed., pp. 646–718). Hoboken, NJ: Wiley.

Eisenberg, Nancy, Hofer, Claire, Spinrad, Tracy L., Gershoff, Elizabeth T., Valiente, Carlos, Losoya, Sandra, . . . Maxon, Elizabeth. (2008). Understanding mother-adolescent conflict discussions: Concurrent and across-time prediction from youths' dispositions and parenting. *Monographs of the Society for Research in Child Development, 73*(2, Serial No. 290), vii–viii, 1–160.

Eisenberg, Nancy, Spinrad, Tracy L., Fabes, Richard A., Reiser, Mark, Cumberland, Amanda, Shepard, Stephanie A., . . . Thompson, Marilyn. (2004). The relations of effortful control and impulsivity to children's resiliency and adjustment. *Child Development, 75,* 25–46.

Eisenberg, N., Valiente, C., Spinrad, T. L., Cumberland, A., Liew, J., Reiser, M., Zhou, Q., & Losoya, S. H. (2009). Longitudinal relations of children's effortful control, impulsivity, and negative emotionality to their externalizing, internalizing, and co-occurring behavior problems. *Developmental Psychology, 45,* 988–1008.

Eklund, Jenny M., Kerr, Margaret, & Stattin, Håkan. (2010). Romantic relationships and delinquent behaviour in adolescence: The moderating role of delinquency propensity. *Journal of Adolescence, 33,* 377–386.

Elder, Glen H., Jr,, & Shanahan, Michael J. (2006). *The life course and human development* (6th ed.). Hoboken, NJ: Wiley.

Elkind, David. (1967). Egocentrism in adolescence. *Child Development, 38,* 1025–1034.

Elkind, David. (2007). *The power of play: How spontaneous, imaginative activities lead to happier, healthier children.* Cambridge, MA: Da Capo Press.

Ellis, Bruce J., & Boyce, W. Thomas. (2008). Biological sensitivity to context. *Current Directions in Psychological Science, 17,* 183–187.

Ellis, Bruce J., Shirtcliff, Elizabeth A., Boyce, W. Thomas, Deardorff, Julianna, & Essex, Marilyn J. (2011). Quality of early family relationships and the timing and tempo of puberty: Effects depend on biological sensitivity to context. *Development and Psychopathology, 23,* 85–99.

Ellison, Christopher G., Musick, Marc A., & Holden, George W. (2011). Does conservative Protestantism moderate the association between corporal punishment and child outcomes? *Journal of Marriage and Family, 73,* 946–961.

Else-Quest, Nicole M., Hyde, Janet Shibley, Goldsmith, H. Hill, & Van Hulle, Carol A. (2006). Gender differences in temperament: A meta-analysis. *Psychological Bulletin, 132,* 33–72.

Elwert, Felix, & Christakis, Nicholas A. (2008). The effect of widowhood on mortality by the causes of death of both spouses. *American Journal of Public Health, 98,* 2092–2098.

Engelberts, Adèle C., & de Jonge, Guus A. (1990). Choice of sleeping position for infants: Possible association with cot death. *Archives of Disease in Childhood, 65,* 462–467.

Engelhardt, H. Tristram, Jr. (2012). Why clinical bioethics so rarely gives morally normative guidance. In H. Tristram Engelhardt, Jr. (Ed.), *Bioethics critically reconsidered* (pp. 151–174). New York, NY: Springer.

Engels, Rutger C. M. E., Scholte, Ron H. J., van Lieshout, Cornelis F. M., de Kemp, Raymond, & Overbeek, Geertjan. (2006). Peer group reputation and smoking and alcohol consumption in early adolescence. *Addictive Behaviors, 31,* 440–449.

Englander, Elizabeth, Mills, Elizabeth, & McCoy, Meghan. (2009). Cyberbullying and information exposure: User-generated content in post-secondary education. *International Journal of Contemporary Sociology, 46*, 213–230.

Enserink, Martin. (2011, February 18). Can this DNA sleuth help catch criminals? *Science, 331*, 838–840.

Epps, Chad, & Holt, Lynn. (2011). The genetic basis of addiction and relevant cellular mechanisms. *International Anesthesiology Clinics, 49*, 3–14.

Epstein, Jeffery N., Langberg, Joshua M., Lichtenstein, Philip K., Altaye, Mekibib, Brinkman, William B., House, Katherine, & Stark, Lori J. (2010). Attention-deficit/hyperactivity disorder outcomes for children treated in community-based pediatric settings. *Archives of Pediatrics & Adolescent Medicine, 164*, 160–165.

Epstein, Marina, Calzo, Jerel P., Smiler, Andrew P., & Ward, L. Monique. (2009). "Anything from making out to having sex": Men's negotiations of hooking up and friends with benefits scripts. *Journal of Sex Research, 46*, 414–424.

Epstein, Steven. (2007). *Inclusion: The politics of difference in medical research.* Chicago, IL: University of Chicago Press.

Erath, Stephen A., Keiley, Margaret K., Pettit, Gregory S., Lansford, Jennifer E., Dodge, Kenneth A., & Bates, John E. (2009). Behavioral predictors of mental health service utilization in childhood through adolescence. *Journal of Developmental & Behavioral Pediatrics, 30*, 481–488.

Erdman, Phyllis, & Ng, Kok-Mun (Eds.). (2010). *Attachment: Expanding the cultural connections.* New York, NY: Routledge.

Erickson, Kirk I., & Korol, Donna L. (2009). Effects of hormone replacement therapy on the brains of postmenopausal women: A review of human neuroimaging studies. In Wojtek Chodzko-Zajko, Arthur F. Kramer, & Leonard W. Poon (Eds.), *Enhancing cognitive functioning and brain plasticity* (pp. 133–158). Champaign, IL: Human Kinetics.

Erickson, Rebecca J. (2005). Why emotion work matters: Sex, gender, and the division of household labor. *Journal of Marriage and Family, 67*, 337–351.

Ericsson, K. Anders. (1996). The acquisition of expert performance: An introduction to some of the issues. In Karl Anders Ericsson (Ed.), *The road to excellence: The acquisition of expert performance in the arts and sciences, sports, and games* (pp. 1–50). Hillsdale, NJ: Erlbaum.

Ericsson, K. Anders (Ed.). (2009). *Development of professional expertise: Toward measurement of expert performance and design of optimal learning environments.* New York, NY: Cambridge University Press.

Ericsson, K. Anders, Charness, Neil, Feltovich, Paul J., & Hoffman, Robert R. (Eds.). (2006). *The Cambridge handbook of expertise and expert performance.* New York, NY: Cambridge University Press.

Erikson, Erik H. (1963). *Childhood and society* (2nd ed.). New York, NY: Norton.

Erikson, Erik H. (1968). *Identity: Youth and crisis.* New York, NY: Norton.

Erikson, Erik H. (1982). *The life cycle completed: A review.* New York, NY: Norton.

Erikson, Erik H., Erikson, Joan M., & Kivnick, Helen Q. (1986). *Vital involvement in old age.* New York, NY: Norton.

Erlinghagen, Marcel, & Hank, Karsten. (2006). The participation of older Europeans in volunteer work. *Ageing & Society, 26*, 567–584.

Ertesvåg, Sigrun K. (2011). Measuring authoritative teaching. *Teaching and Teacher Education, 27*, 51–61.

Ertmer, David J., Young, Nancy M., & Nathani, Suneeti. (2007). Profiles of vocal development in young cochlear implant recipients. *Journal of Speech, Language, and Hearing Research, 50*, 393–407.

Etchu, Koji. (2007). Social context and preschoolers' judgments about aggressive behavior: Social domain theory. *Japanese Journal of Educational Psychology, 55*, 219–230.

Etnier, Jennifer L. (2009). Physical activity programming to promote cognitive function: Are we ready for prescription? In Wojtek Chodzko-Zajko, Arthur F. Kramer, & Leonard W. Poon (Eds.), *Enhancing cognitive functioning and brain plasticity* (pp. 159–175). Champaign, IL: Human Kinetics.

European Nutrition and Health Report. (2009). *European nutrition and health report, 2009: Forum of nutrition* (Vol. 62, Ed. Ibrahim Elmadfa). Basel: Karger.

Evans, Angela D., & Lee, Kang. (2011). Verbal deception from late childhood to middle adolescence and its relation to executive functioning skills. *Developmental Psychology, 47*, 1108–1116.

Evans, Angela D., Xu, Fen, & Lee, Kang. (2011). When all signs point to you: Lies told in the face of evidence. *Developmental Psychology, 47*, 39–49.

Evans, David W., & Leckman, James F. (2006). Origins of obsessive-compulsive disorder: Developmental and evolutionary perspectives. In Dante Cicchetti & Donald J. Cohen (Eds.), *Developmental psychopathology: Vol. 3. Risk, disorder, and adaptation* (2nd ed., pp. 404–435). Hoboken, NJ: Wiley.

Evans, David W., Leckman, James F., Carter, Alice, Reznick, J. Steven, Henshaw, Desiree, King, Robert A., & Pauls, David. (1997). Ritual, habit, and perfectionism: The prevalence and development of compulsive-like behavior in normal young children. *Child Development, 68*, 58–68.

Eyer, Diane E. (1992). *Mother-infant bonding: A scientific fiction.* New Haven, CT: Yale University Press.

Eymard, Amanda Singleton, & Douglas, Dianna Hutto. (2012). Ageism among health care providers and interventions to improve their attitudes toward older adults: An integrative review. *Journal of Gerontological Nursing, 38*, 26–35.

Fabiani, Monica, & Gratton, Gabriele. (2009). Brain imaging probes into the cognitive and physiological effects of aging. In Wojtek Chodzko-Zajko, Arthur F. Kramer, & Leonard W. Poon (Eds.), *Enhancing cognitive functioning and brain plasticity* (pp. 1–13). Champaign, IL: Human Kinetics.

Fabricatore, Anthony N., Wadden, Thomas A., Moore, Reneé H., Butryn, Meghan L., Gravallese, Elizabeth A., Erondu, Ngozi E., . . . Nguyen, Allison Martin. (2009). Attrition from randomized controlled trials of pharmacological weight loss agents: A systematic review and analysis. *Obesity Reviews, 10*, 333–341.

Farahani, Mansour, Subramanian, S. V., & Canning, David. (2009). The effect of changes in health sector resources on infant mortality in the short-run and the long-run: A longitudinal econometric analysis. *Social Science & Medicine, 68,* 1918–1925.

Faraone, Stephen V., & Wilens, Timothy. (2003). Does stimulant treatment lead to substance use disorders? *Journal of Clinical Psychiatry, 64,* 9–13.

Farrar, Ruth D., & Al-Qatawneh, Khalil S. (2010). Interdisciplinary theoretical foundations for literacy teaching and learning. *European Journal of Social Sciences, 13,* 56–66.

Farrell, C., Chappell, F., Armitage, P. A., Keston, P., MacLullich, A., Shenkin, S.,... Wardlaw, J. M. (2009). Development and initial testing of normal reference MR images for the brain at ages 65–70 and 75–80 years. *European Radiology, 19,* 177–183.

Fazzi, Elisa, Signorini, Sabrina Giovanna, Bomba, Monica, Luparia, Antonella, Lanners, Josée, & Balottin, Umberto. (2011). Reach on sound: A key to object permanence in visually impaired children. *Early Human Development, 87,* 289–296.

Feinberg, Andrew P. (2008). Epigenetics at the epicenter of modern medicine. *Journal of the American Medical Association, 299,* 1345–1350.

Feldman, Ruth. (2007). Parent-infant synchrony and the construction of shared timing; Physiological precursors, developmental outcomes, and risk conditions. *Journal of Child Psychology and Psychiatry, 48,* 329–354.

Feldman, Ruth, Gordon, Ilanit, & Zagoory-Sharon, Orna. (2011). Maternal and paternal plasma, salivary, and urinary oxytocin and parent–infant synchrony: Considering stress and affiliation components of human bonding. *Developmental Science, 14,* 752–761.

Fell, James C., Todd, Michael, & Voas, Robert B. (2011). A national evaluation of the nighttime and passenger restriction components of graduated driver licensing. *Journal of Safety Research, 42,* 283–290.

Felmlee, Diane, & Muraco, Anna. (2009). Gender and friendship norms among older adults. *Research on Aging, 31,* 318–344.

Feng, Zhanlian, Grabowski, David C., Intrator, Orna, Zinn, Jacqueline, & Mor, Vincent. (2008). Medicaid payment rates, case-mix reimbursement, and nursing home staffing—1996–2004. *Medical Care, 46,* 33–40.

Fergusson, Emma, Maughan, Barbara, & Golding, Jean. (2008). Which children receive grandparental care and what effect does it have? *Journal of Child Psychology and Psychiatry, 49,* 161–169.

Fewtrell, Mary, Wilson, David C., Booth, Ian, & Lucas, Alan. (2011). Six months of exclusive breast feeding: How good is the evidence? *BMJ, 342.* doi:10.1136/bmj.c5955

Field, Nigel P., & Filanosky, Charles. (2009). Continuing bonds, risk factors for complicated grief, and adjustment to bereavement. *Death Studies, 34,* 1–29.

Finch, Caleb E. (2010). Evolution of the human lifespan and diseases of aging: Roles of infection, inflammation, and nutrition. *Proceedings of the National Academy of Sciences, 107*(Suppl. 1), 1718–1724.

Fincham, Frank D., & Beach, Steven R. H. (2010). Of memes and marriage: Toward a positive relationship science. *Journal of Family Theory & Review, 2,* 4–24.

Fincham, Frank D., Stanley, Scott M., & Beach, Steven R. H. (2007). Transformative processes in marriage: An analysis of emerging trends. *Journal of Marriage and Family, 69,* 275–292.

Fine, Mark A., & Harvey, John H. (Eds.) (2006). *Handbook of divorce and relationship dissolution.* Mahwah, NJ: Erlbaum.

Fingerman, Karen L. (2009). Consequential strangers and peripheral ties: The importance of unimportant relationships. *Journal of Family Theory & Review, 1,* 69–86.

Fingerman, Karen L., Berg, Cynthia, Smith, Jacqui, & Antonucci, Toni C. (Eds.) (2011). *Handbook of lifespan development.* New York, NY: Springer.

Fingerman, Karen L., Cheng, Yen-Pi, Birditt, Kira, & Zarit, Steven. (2012). Only as happy as the least happy child: Multiple grown children's problems and successes and middle-aged parents' well-being. *The Journals of Gerontology Series B: Psychological Sciences and Social Sciences, 67B,* 184–193.

Fingerman, Karen L., & Furstenberg, Frank F. (2012, May 30). You can go home again. *New York Times,* p. A29.

Fingerman, Karen L., Hay, Elizabeth L., & Birditt, Kira S. (2004). The best of ties, the worst of ties: Close, problematic, and ambivalent social relationships. *Journal of Marriage and Family, 66,* 792–808.

Finkel, Eli J., Eastwick, Paul W., Karney, Benjamin R., Reis, Harry T., & Sprecher, Susan. (2012). Online dating: A critical analysis from the perspective of psychological science. *Psychological Science in the Public Interest, 13,* 3–66.

Finlay, Ilora G., & George, R. (2011). Legal physician-assisted suicide in Oregon and The Netherlands: Evidence concerning the impact on patients in vulnerable groups—Another perspective on Oregon's data. *Journal of Medical Ethics, 37,* 171–174.

Fischer, Regina Santamäki, Norberg, Astrid, & Lundman, Berit. (2008). Embracing opposites: Meanings of growing old as narrated by people aged 85. *International Journal of Aging and Human Development, 67,* 259–271.

Fisher, Helen E. (2006). Broken hearts: The nature and risks of romantic rejection. In Ann C. Crouter & Alan Booth (Eds.), *Romance and sex in adolescence and emerging adulthood: Risks and opportunities* (pp. 3–28). Mahwah, NJ: Erlbaum.

Flegal, Katherine M., Carroll, Margaret D., Kit, Brian K., & Ogden, Cynthia L. (2012). Prevalence of obesity and trends in the distribution of body mass index among US adults, 1999–2010. *Journal of the American Medical Association, 307,* 491–497.

Flensborg-Madsen, Trine, Bay von Scholten, Mikael, Flachs, Esben Meulengracht, Mortensen, Erik Lykke, Prescott, Eva, & Tolstrup, Janne Schurmann. (2011). Tobacco smoking as a risk factor for depression. A 26-year population-based follow-up study. *Journal of Psychiatric Research, 45,* 143–149.

Fletcher, Anne C., Steinberg, Laurence, & Williams-Wheeler, Meeshay. (2004). Parental influences on adolescent problem behavior: Revisiting Stattin and Kerr. *Child Development, 75,* 781–796.

Fletcher, Jack M., & Vaughn, Sharon. (2009). Response to intervention: Preventing and remediating academic difficulties. *Child Development Perspectives, 3*, 30–37.

Floud, Roderick, Fogel, Robert W., Harris, Bernard, & Hong, Sok Chul. (2011). *The changing body: Health, nutrition, and human development in the western world since 1700.* Cambridge, UK: Cambridge University Press.

Flynn, James R. (1999). Searching for justice: The discovery of IQ gains over time. *American Psychologist, 54*, 5–20.

Flynn, James R. (2007). *What is intelligence? Beyond the Flynn effect.* New York, NY: Cambridge University Press.

Fontana, Luigi, Colman, Ricki J., Holloszy, John O., & Weindruch, Richard. (2011). Calorie restriction in nonhuman and human primates. In J. Masoro Edward & N. Austad Steven (Eds.), *Handbook of the biology of aging* (7th ed., pp. 447–461). San Diego, CA: Academic Press.

Forget-Dubois, Nadine, Dionne, Ginette, Lemelin, Jean-Pascal, Pérusse, Daniel, Tremblay, Richard E., & Boivin, Michel. (2009). Early child language mediates the relation between home environment and school readiness. *Child Development, 80*, 736–749.

Fortinsky, Richard H., Tennen, Howard, Frank, Natalie, & Affleck, Glenn. (2007). Health and psychological consequences of caregiving. In Carolyn M. Aldwin, Crystal L. Park, & Avron Spiro, III (Eds.), *Handbook of health psychology and aging* (pp. 227–249). New York, NY: Guilford Press.

Fortuna, Keren, & Roisman, Glenn I. (2008). Insecurity, stress, and symptoms of psychopathology: Contrasting results from self-reports versus interviews of adult attachment. *Attachment & Human Development, 10*, 11–28.

Foster, E. Michael, & Kalil, Ariel. (2007). Living arrangements and children's development in low-income White, Black, and Latino families. *Child Development, 78*, 1657–1674.

Fox, Nathan A., Henderson, Heather A., Marshall, Peter J., Nichols, Kate E., & Ghera, Melissa M. (2005). Behavioral inhibition: Linking biology and behavior within a developmental framework. *Annual Review of Psychology, 56*, 235–262.

Fox, Nathan A., Henderson, Heather A., Rubin, Kenneth H., Calkins, Susan D., & Schmidt, Louis A. (2001). Continuity and discontinuity of behavioral inhibition and exuberance: Psychophysiological and behavioral influences across the first four years of life. *Child Development, 72*, 1–21.

Frankenburg, William K., Dodds, Josiah, Archer, Philip, Shapiro, Howard, & Bresnick, Beverly. (1992). The Denver II: A major revision and restandardization of the Denver Developmental Screening Test. *Pediatrics, 89*, 91–97.

Frayling, Timothy M., Timpson, Nicholas J., Weedon, Michael N., Zeggini, Eleftheria, Freathy, Rachel M., Lindgren, Cecilia M.,... McCarthy, Mark I. (2007, May 11). A common variant in the FTO gene is associated with body mass index and predisposes to childhood and adult obesity. *Science, 316*, 889–894.

Frazier, Thomas W., & Hardan, Antonio Y. (2009). A meta-analysis of the corpus callosum in autism. *Biological Psychiatry, 66*, 935–941.

Fredricks, Jennifer A., & Eccles, Jacquelynne S. (2002). Children's competence and value beliefs from childhood through adolescence: Growth trajectories in two male-sex-typed domains. *Developmental Psychology, 38*, 519–533.

Fredrickson, Barbara L., & Carstensen, Laura L. (1990). Choosing social partners: How old age and anticipated endings make people more selective. *Psychology and Aging, 5*, 335–347.

Freeman, Joan. (2010). *Gifted lives: What happens when gifted children grow up?* New York, NY: Routledge.

Freisthler, Bridget, Merritt, Darcey H., & LaScala, Elizabeth A. (2006). Understanding the ecology of child maltreatment: A review of the literature and directions for future research. *Child Maltreatment, 11*, 263–280.

Freud, Anna. (2000). Adolescence. In James B. McCarthy (Ed.), *Adolescent development and psychopathology* (Vol. 13, pp. 29–52). Lanham, MD: University Press of America. (Reprinted from *Psychoanalytic Study of the Child*, pp. 255–278, 1958, New Haven, CT: Yale University Press)

Freud, Sigmund. (1935). *A general introduction to psychoanalysis* (Joan Riviere, Trans.). New York, NY: Liveright.

Freud, Sigmund. (1938). *The basic writings of Sigmund Freud* (A. A. Brill, Ed. and Trans.). New York, NY: Modern Library.

Freud, Sigmund. (1964). An outline of psycho-analysis. In James Strachey (Ed. and Trans.), *The standard edition of the complete psychological works of Sigmund Freud* (Vol. 23, pp. 144–207). London, England: Hogarth Press. (Original work published 1940)

Freund, Alexandra M. (2008). Successful aging as management of resources: The role of selection, optimization, and compensation. *Research in Human Development, 5*, 94–106.

Freund, Alexandra M., Nikitin, Jana, & Ritter, Johannes O. (2009). Psychological consequences of longevity: The increasing importance of self-regulation in old age. *Human Development, 52*, 1–37.

Fries, Alison B. Wismer, & Pollak, Seth D. (2007). Emotion processing and the developing brain. In Donna Coch, Kurt W. Fischer, & Geraldine Dawson (Eds.), *Human behavior, learning, and the developing brain. Typical development* (pp. 329–361). New York, NY: Guilford Press.

Frost, Joe L. (2009). *A history of children's play and play environments: Toward a contemporary child-saving movement.* New York, NY: Routledge.

Fu, Vincent Kang, & Wolfinger, Nicholas H. (2011). Broken boundaries or broken marriages? Racial intermarriage and divorce in the United States. *Social Science Quarterly, 92*, 1096–1117.

Fuligni, Andrew J., & Hardway, Christina. (2006). Daily variation in adolescents' sleep, activities, and psychological well-being. *Journal of Research on Adolescence, 16*, 353–378.

Fuligni, Andrew J., Hughes, Diane L., & Way, Niobe. (2009). Ethnicity and immigration. In Richard M. Lerner & Laurence Steinberg (Eds.), *Handbook of adolescent psychology: Vol. 2. Contextual influences on adolescent development* (3rd ed., pp. 527–569). Hoboken, NJ: Wiley.

Fuligni, Allison Sidle, Howes, Carollee, Lara-Cinisomo, Sandraluz, & Karoly, Lynn A. (2009). Diverse pathways in early childhood professional development: An exploration of early educators in public preschools, private preschools, and family child care homes. *Early Education and Development, 20,* 507–526.

Fung, Helene H., Stoeber, Franziska S., Yeung, Dannii Yuen-lan, & Lang, Frieder R. (2008). Cultural specificity of socioemotional selectivity: Age differences in social network composition among Germans and Hong Kong Chinese. *The Journals of Gerontology Series B: Psychological Sciences and Social Sciences, 63B,* 156–164.

Fung, Joey J., & Lau, Anna S. (2009). Punitive discipline and child behavior problems in Chinese-American immigrant families: The moderating effects of indigenous child-rearing ideologies. *International Journal of Behavioral Development, 33,* 520–530.

Furnham, Adrian. (2012). Intelligence and intellectual styles. In Li-fang Zhang, Robert J. Sternberg, & Stephen Rayner (Eds.), *Handbook of intellectual styles: Preferences in cognition, learning, and thinking* (pp. 173–192). New York, NY: Springer.

Furstenberg, Frank F., Jr. (2010). On a new schedule: Transitions to adulthood and family change. *Future of Children, 20,* 67–87.

Gabrieli, John D. E. (2009, July 17). Dyslexia: A new synergy between education and cognitive neuroscience. *Science, 325,* 280–283.

Gaertner, Bridget M., Spinrad, Tracy L., Eisenberg, Nancy, & Greving, Karissa A. (2007). Parental childrearing attitudes as correlates of father involvement during infancy. *Journal of Marriage and Family, 69,* 962–976.

Galambos, Nancy L., Barker, Erin T., & Krahn, Harvey J. (2006). Depression, self-esteem, and anger in emerging adulthood: Seven-year trajectories. *Developmental Psychology, 42,* 350–365.

Galatzer-Levy, Isaac R., & Bonanno, George A. (2012). Beyond normality in the study of bereavement: Heterogeneity in depression outcomes following loss in older adults. *Social Science & Medicine, 74,* 1987–1994.

Gallese, Vittorio, Fadiga, Luciano, Fogassi, Leonardo, & Rizzolatti, Giacomo. (1996). Action recognition in the premotor cortex. *Brain, 119,* 593–609.

Galotti, Kathleen M. (2002). *Making decisions that matter: How people face important life choices.* Mahwah, NJ: Erlbaum.

Galupo, M. Paz, Cartwright, Kelly, & Savage, Lanya. (2010). Cross-category friendships and postformal thought among college students. *Journal of Adult Development, 17,* 208–214.

Galván, Adriana, Spatzier, Agnieszka, & Juvonen, Jaana. (2011). Perceived norms and social values to capture school culture in elementary and middle school. *Journal of Applied Developmental Psychology, 32,* 346–353.

Gandara, Patricia, & Rumberger, Russell W. (2009). Immigration, language, and education: How does language policy structure opportunity? *Teachers College Record, 111,* 750–782.

Gandini, Leila, Hill, Lynn, Cadwell, Louise, & Schwall, Charles (Eds.). (2005). *In the spirit of the studio: Learning from the atelier of Reggio Emilia.* New York, NY: Teachers College Press.

Gangestad, Steven W., & Simpson, Jeffry A. (Eds.) (2007). *The evolution of mind: Fundamental questions and controversies.* New York, NY: Guilford Press.

Ganong, Lawrence H., & Coleman, Marilyn. (2004). *Stepfamily relationships: Development, dynamics, and interventions.* New York, NY: Kluwer Academic/Plenum.

Ganong, Lawrence H., Coleman, Marilyn, & Jamison, Tyler. (2011). Patterns of stepchild–stepparent relationship development. *Journal of Marriage and Family, 73,* 396–413.

Gans, Daphna, & Silverstein, Merril. (2006). Norms of filial responsibility for aging parents across time and generations. *Journal of Marriage and Family, 68,* 961–976.

García, Fernando, & Gracia, Enrique. (2009). Is always authoritative the optimum parenting style? Evidence from Spanish families. *Adolescence, 44,* 101–131.

Garcia-Caballos, Marta, Ramos-Diaz, Francisco, Jimenez-Moleon, José Juan, & Bueno-Cavanillas, Aurora. (2010). Drug-related problems in older people after hospital discharge and interventions to reduce them. *Age and Ageing, 39,* 430–438.

García Coll, Cynthia T., & Marks, Amy Kerivan. (2009). *Immigrant stories: Ethnicity and academics in middle childhood.* New York, NY: Oxford University Press.

García Coll, Cynthia T., & Marks, Amy Kerivan (Eds.). (2012). *The immigrant paradox in children and adolescents: Is becoming American a developmental risk?* Washington, DC: American Psychological Association.

Gardner, Christopher, Wylie-Rosett, Judith, Gidding, Samuel S., Steffen, Lyn M., Johnson, Rachel K., Reader, Diane, & Lichtenstein, Alice H. (2012). Nonnutritive sweeteners: Current use and health perspectives. *Circulation, 126,* 509–519.

Gardner, Howard. (1983). *Frames of mind: The theory of multiple intelligences.* New York, NY: Basic Books.

Gardner, Howard. (1999). Are there additional intelligences? The case for naturalist, spiritual, and existential intelligences. In Jeffrey Kane (Ed.), *Education, information, and transformation: Essays on learning and thinking* (pp. 111–131). Upper Saddle River, NJ: Merrill.

Gardner, Howard. (2006). *Multiple intelligences: New horizons in theory and practice* (Completely rev. and updated ed.). New York, NY: Basic Books.

Gardner, Howard, & Moran, Seana. (2006). The science of multiple intelligences theory: A response to Lynn Waterhouse. *Educational Psychologist, 41,* 227–232.

Gaskins, Suzanne. (1999). Children's daily lives in a Mayan village: A case study of culturally constructed roles and activities. In Artin Goncu (Ed.), *Children's engagement in the world: Sociocultural perspectives* (pp. 25–60). New York, NY: Cambridge University Press.

Gauvain, Mary, Beebe, Heidi, & Zhao, Shuheng. (2011). Applying the cultural approach to cognitive development. *Journal of Cognition and Development, 12,* 121–133.

Gavrilov, Leonid A., & Gavrilova, Natalia S. (2006). Reliability theory of aging and longevity. In Edward J. Masoro &

Steven N. Austad (Eds.), *Handbook of the biology of aging* (6th ed., pp. 3–42). Amsterdam, The Netherlands: Elsevier Academic Press.

Ge, Xiaojia, Natsuaki, Misaki N., Neiderhiser, Jenae M., & Reiss, David. (2007). Genetic and environmental influences on pubertal timing: Results from two national sibling studies. *Journal of Research on Adolescence, 17,* 767–788.

Geary, Nori, & Lovejoy, Jennifer. (2008). Sex differences in energy metabolism, obesity, and eating behavior. In Jill B. Becker, Karen J. Berkley, Nori Geary, Elizabeth Hampson, James P. Herman, & Elizabeth Young (Eds.), *Sex differences in the brain: From genes to behavior* (pp. 253–274). New York, NY: Oxford University Press.

Geelhoed, Elizabeth, Harris, Anthony, & Prince, Richard. (1994). Cost-effectiveness analysis of hormone replacement therapy and lifestyle intervention for hip fracture. *Australian Journal of Public Health, 18,* 153–160.

Gelfand, Donald E. (2003). *Aging and ethnicity: Knowledge and services* (2nd ed.). New York, NY: Springer.

Geller, Barbara, Tillman, Rebecca, Bolhofner, Kristine, & Zimerman, Betsy. (2008). Child bipolar I disorder: Prospective continuity with adult bipolar I disorder; characteristics of second and third episodes; predictors of 8-year outcome. *Archives of General Psychiatry, 65,* 1125–1133.

Gendron, Brian P., Williams, Kirk R., & Guerra, Nancy G. (2011). An analysis of bullying among students within schools: Estimating the effects of individual normative beliefs, self-esteem, and school climate. *Journal of School Violence, 10,* 150–164.

Genesee, Fred. (2008). Early dual language learning. *Zero to Three, 29,* 17–23.

Genesee, Fred, & Nicoladis, Elena. (2007). Bilingual first language acquisition. In Erika Hoff & Marilyn Shatz (Eds.), *Blackwell handbook of language development* (pp. 324–342). Malden, MA: Blackwell.

Gentile, Brittany, Grabe, Shelly, Dolan-Pascoe, Brenda, Wells, Brooke E., Maitino, Alissa, & Twenge, Jean M. (2009). Gender differences in domain-specific self-esteem: A meta-analysis. *Review of General Psychology, 13,* 34–45.

Gentile, Douglas. (2009). Pathological video-game use among youth ages 8 to 18. *Psychological Science, 20,* 594–602.

Gentile, Douglas A., Saleem, Muniba, & Anderson, Craig A. (2007). Public policy and the effects of media violence on children. *Social Issues and Policy Review, 1,* 15–61.

Georgas, James, Berry, John W., van de Vijver, Fons J. R., Kagitçibasi, Çigdem, & Poortinga, Ype H. (Eds.) (2006). *Families across cultures: A 30-nation psychological study.* Cambridge, UK: Cambridge University Press.

George, Linda G., Helson, Ravenna, & John, Oliver P. (2011). The "CEO" of women's work lives: How Big Five Conscientiousness, Extraversion, and Openness predict 50 years of work experiences in a changing sociocultural context. *Journal of Personality and Social Psychology, 101,* 812–830.

Gerber, Alan S., Huber, Gregory A., Doherty, David, & Dowling, Conor M. (2011). The Big Five personality traits in the political arena. *Annual Review of Political Science, 14,* 265–287.

Gerrard, Meg, Gibbons, Frederick X., Houlihan, Amy E., Stock, Michelle L., & Pomery, Elizabeth A. (2008). A dual-process approach to health risk decision making: The prototype willingness model. *Developmental Review, 28,* 29–61.

Gershkoff-Stowe, Lisa, & Hahn, Erin R. (2007). Fast mapping skills in the developing lexicon. *Journal of Speech, Language, and Hearing Research, 50,* 682–696.

Gershoff, Elizabeth T., Grogan-Kaylor, Andrew, Lansford, Jennifer E., Chang, Lei, Zelli, Arnaldo, Deater-Deckard, Kirby, & Dodge, Kenneth A. (2010). Parent discipline practices in an international sample: Associations with child behaviors and moderation by perceived normativeness. *Child Development, 81,* 487–502.

Gettler, Lee T., & McKenna, James J. (2010). Never sleep with baby? Or keep me close but keep me safe: Eliminating inappropriate safe infant sleep rhetoric in the United States. *Current Pediatric Reviews, 6,* 71–77.

Gevorgyan, Ruzanna, Schmidt, Elena, Wall, Martin, Garnett, Geoffrey, Atun, Rifat, Maksimova, Svetlana, ... Renton, Adrian. (2011). Does Russia need sex education? The views of stakeholders in three Russian regions. *Sex Education, 11,* 213–226.

Gewertz, Catherine. (2011, February 22). AP passing rates rose for last year's seniors. *Education Week,* p. 5.

Gewirtzman, Aron, Bobrick, Laura, Conner, Kelly, & Tyring, Stephen K. (2011). Epidemiology of sexually transmitted infections. In Gerd Gross & Stephen K. Tyring (Eds.), *Sexually transmitted infections and sexually transmitted diseases* (pp. 13–34). New York, NY: Springer.

Giancola, Peter R., Josephs, Robert A., Parrott, Dominic J., & Duke, Aaron A. (2010). Alcohol myopia revisited: Clarifying aggression and other acts of disinhibition through a distorted lens. *Perspectives on Psychological Science, 5,* 265–278.

Giardino, Angelo P., & Alexander, Randell (Eds.). (2011). *Child maltreatment* (4th ed., Vol. 1–2). St. Louis, MO: G. W. Medical.

Gibson, Carolyn J., Joffe, Hadine, Bromberger, Joyce T., Thurston, Rebecca C., Lewis, Tene T., Khalil, Naila, & Matthews, Karen A. (2012). Mood symptoms after natural menopause and hysterectomy with and without bilateral oophorectomy among women in midlife. *Obstetrics and Gynecology, 119,* 935–941.

Gibson-Davis, Christina. (2011). Mothers but not wives: The increasing lag between nonmarital births and marriage. *Journal of Marriage and Family, 73,* 264–278.

Gibson-Davis, Christina M., & Gassman-Pines, Anna. (2010). Early childhood family structure and mother–child interactions: Variation by race and ethnicity. *Developmental Psychology, 46,* 151–164.

Gigerenzer, Gerd. (2008). Why heuristics work. *Perspectives on Psychological Science, 3,* 20–29.

Gilbert, Daniel. (2006). *Stumbling on happiness.* New York, NY: Knopf.

Giles, Amy, & Rovee-Collier, Carolyn. (2011). Infant long-term memory for associations formed during mere exposure. *Infant Behavior and Development, 34,* 327–338.

Gillen-O'Neel, Cari, Ruble, Diane N., & Fuligni, Andrew J. (2011). Ethnic stigma, academic anxiety, and intrinsic motivation in middle childhood. *Child Development, 82,* 1470–1485.

Gilles, Floyd H., & Nelson, Marvin D. (2012). *The developing human brain: Growth and adversities.* London, UK: Mac Keith Press.

Gillespie, Michael Allen. (2010). Players and spectators: Sports and ethical training in the American university. In Elizabeth Kiss & J. Peter Euben (Eds.), *Debating moral education: Rethinking the role of the modern university* (pp. 293–316). Durham, NC: Duke University Press.

Gilligan, Carol. (1982). *In a different voice: Psychological theory and women's development.* Cambridge, MA: Harvard University Press.

Gillis, John R. (2008). The islanding of children: Reshaping the mythical landscapes of childhood. In Marta Gutman & Ning De Coninck-Smith (Eds.), *Designing modern childhoods: History, space, and the material culture of children* (pp. 316–329). New Brunswick, NJ: Rutgers University Press.

Gitler, Aaron D. (2011, November 4). Another reason to exercise. *Science, 334,* 606–607.

Gitlin, Laura N., Belle, Steven H., Burgio, Louis D., Czaja, Sara J., Mahoney, Diane, Gallagher-Thompson, Dolores,... Ory, Marcia G. (2003). Effect of multicomponent interventions on caregiver burden and depression: The REACH multisite initiative at 6-month follow-up. *Psychology & Aging, 18,* 361–374.

Gladwell, Malcolm. (2010, October 4). Small change: Why the revolution will not be tweeted. *The New Yorker, 86,* 42–49.

Gluckman, Peter D., & Hanson, Mark A. (Eds.) (2006). *Developmental origins of health and disease.* Cambridge, England: Cambridge University Press.

Gobush, Kathleen S., Mutayoba, Benezeth M., & Wasser, Samuel K. (2008). Long-term impacts of poaching on relatedness, stress physiology, and reproductive output of adult female African elephants. *Conservation Biology, 22,* 1590–1599.

Golant, Stephen M. (2008). Commentary: Irrational exuberance for the aging in place of vulnerable low-income older homeowners. *Journal of Aging & Social Policy, 20,* 379–397.

Golant, Stephen M. (2011). The changing residential environments of older people. In Robert H. Binstock & Linda K. George (Eds.), *Handbook of aging and the social sciences* (7th ed., pp. 207–220). San Diego, CA: Academic Press.

Gold, Joshua M. (2010). Helping stepfathers "step away" from the role of "father": Directions for family intervention. *The Family Journal, 18,* 208–214.

Goldberg, Wendy A., Prause, JoAnn, Lucas-Thompson, Rachel, & Himsel, Amy. (2008). Maternal employment and children's achievement in context: A meta-analysis of four decades of research. *Psychological Bulletin, 134,* 77–108.

Golden, Marita. (2009). Angel baby. In Barbara Graham (Ed.), *Eye of my heart: 27 writers reveal the hidden pleasures and perils of being a grandmother* (pp. 125–133). New York, NY: HarperCollins.

Golden, Timothy D., Veiga, John F., & Simsek, Zeki. (2006). Telecommuting's differential impact on work-family conflict: Is there no place like home? *Journal of Applied Psychology, 91,* 1340–1350.

Goldenberg, Jamie L., & Arndt, Jamie. (2008). The implications of death for health: A terror management health model for behavioral health promotion. *Psychological Review, 115,* 1032–1053.

Goldin-Meadow, Susan. (2006). Nonverbal communication: The hand's role in talking and thinking. In William Damon & Richard M. Lerner (Series Eds.) & Deanna Kuhn & Robert S. Siegler (Vol. Eds.), *Handbook of child psychology: Vol. 2. Cognition, perception, and language* (6th ed., pp. 336–369). Hoboken, NJ: Wiley.

Goldin-Meadow, Susan. (2009). How gesture promotes learning throughout childhood. *Child Development Perspectives, 3,* 106–111.

Goldscheider, Frances, & Sassler, Sharon. (2006). Creating stepfamilies: Integrating children into the study of union formation. *Journal of Marriage and Family, 68,* 275–291.

Goldstein, Joshua R. (2011). A secular trend toward earlier male sexual maturity: Evidence from shifting ages of male young adult mortality. *PLoS ONE, 6*(8), e14826. doi:10.1371/journal.pone.0014826w

Goldstein, Michael H., Schwade, Jennifer A., & Bornstein, Marc H. (2009). The value of vocalizing: Five-month-old infants associate their own noncry vocalizations with responses from caregivers. *Child Development, 80,* 636–644.

Golestani, Narly, Price, Cathy J., & Scott, Sophie K. (2011). Born with an ear for dialects? Structural plasticity in the expert phonetician brain. *The Journal of Neuroscience, 31,* 4213–4220.

Golinkoff, Roberta Michnick, & Hirsh-Pasek, Kathy. (2008). How toddlers begin to learn verbs. *Trends in Cognitive Sciences, 12,* 397–403.

Golub, Sarit A., & Langer, Ellen J. (2007). Challenging assumptions about adult development: Implications for the health of older adults. In Carolyn M. Aldwin, Crystal L. Park, & Avron Spiro, III (Eds.), *Handbook of health psychology and aging* (pp. 9–29). New York, NY: Guilford Press.

Göncü, Artin, & Gaskins, Suzanne. (2011). Comparing and extending Piaget's and Vygotsky's understandings of play: Symbolic play as individual, sociocultural, and educational interpretation. In Anthony D. Pellegrini (Ed.), *The Oxford handbook of the development of play* (pp. 48–57). New York, NY: Oxford University Press.

Gonzales, Patrick, Williams, Trevor, Jocelyn, Leslie, Roey, Stephen, Kastberg, David, & Brenwald, Summer. (2009). *Highlights From TIMSS 2007: Mathematics and science achievement of U.S. fourth- and eighth-grade students in an international context.* Washington, DC: National Center for Education Statistics, U.S. Department of Education.

Goodall, Jane. (2000). *Through a window: My thirty years with the chimpanzees of Gombe* (1st Mariner Books ed.). Boston, MA: Houghton Mifflin.

Goodman, Judith C., Dale, Philip S., & Li, Ping. (2008). Does frequency count? Parental input and the acquisition of vocabulary. *Journal of Child Language, 35,* 515–531.

Goodman, Sherryl H., & Gotlib, Ian H. (Eds.). (2002). *Children of depressed parents: Mechanisms of risk and implications for treatment.* Washington, DC: American Psychological Association.

Gopnik, Alison. (2001). Theories, language, and culture: Whorf without wincing. In Melissa Bowerman & Stephen C. Levinson (Eds.), *Language acquisition and conceptual development* (pp. 45–69). Cambridge, UK: Cambridge University Press.

Gorchoff, Sara M., John, Oliver P., & Helson, Ravenna. (2008). Contextualizing change in marital satisfaction during middle age: An 18-year longitudinal study. *Psychological Science, 19,* 1194–1200.

Gordis, Elana B., Granger, Douglas A., Susman, Elizabeth J., & Trickett, Penelope K. (2008). Salivary alpha amylase-cortisol asymmetry in maltreated youth. *Hormones and Behavior, 53,* 96–103.

Gorelick, Philip B., & Bowler, John V. (2010). Advances in vascular cognitive impairment. *Stroke, 41,* e93–e98. Advance online publication. doi:10.1161/strokeaha.109.569921

Gormley, William T., Jr., Phillips, Deborah, & Gayer, Ted. (2008, June 27). Preschool programs can boost school readiness. *Science, 320,* 1723–1724.

Gornick, Janet C., & Meyers, Marcia. (2003). *Families that work: Policies for reconciling parenthood and employment.* New York, NY: Russell Sage Foundation.

Gosso, Yumi. (2010). Play in different cultures. In Peter K. Smith (Ed.), *Children and play: Understanding children's worlds* (pp. 80–98). Chichester, West Sussex, UK: Wiley-Blackwell.

Gottfredson, Denise C., & DiPietro, Stephanie M. (2011). School size, social capital, and student victimization. *Sociology of Education, 84,* 69–89.

Gottfried, Adele Eskeles, Marcoulides, George A., Gottfried, Allen W., & Oliver, Pamella H. (2009). A latent curve model of parental motivational practices and developmental decline in math and science academic intrinsic motivation. *Journal of Educational Psychology, 101,* 729–739.

Gottlieb, Gilbert. (2002). *Individual development and evolution: The genesis of novel behavior.* Mahwah, NJ: Erlbaum. (Original work published 1992)

Gottlieb, Gilbert. (2007). Probabilistic epigenesis. *Developmental Science, 10,* 1–11.

Gottlieb, Gilbert. (2010). Normally occurring environmental and behavioral influences on gene activity. In Kathryn E. Hood, Carolyn Tucker Halpern, Gary Greenberg, & Richard M. Lerner (Eds.), *Handbook of developmental science, behavior, and genetics* (pp. 13–37). Malden, MA: Wiley-Blackwell.

Gottman, John Mordechai, Murray, James D., Swanson, Catherine, Tyson, Rebecca, & Swanson, Kristin R. (2002). *The mathematics of marriage: Dynamic nonlinear models.* Cambridge, MA: MIT Press.

Gough, Margaret, & Killewald, Alexandra. (2011). Unemployment in families: The case of housework. *Journal of Marriage and Family, 73,* 1085–1100.

Gow, Alan J., Johnson, Wendy, Pattie, Alison, Brett, Caroline E., Roberts, Beverly, Starr, John M., & Deary, Ian J. (2011). Stability and change in intelligence from age 11 to ages 70, 79, and 87: The Lothian Birth Cohorts of 1921 and 1936. *Psychology and Aging, 26,* 232–240.

Graber, Julia A., Nichols, Tracy R., & Brooks-Gunn, Jeanne. (2010). Putting pubertal timing in developmental context: Implications for prevention. *Developmental Psychobiology, 52,* 254–262.

Grady, Denise. (2007, February 6). Girl or boy? As fertility technology advances, so does an ethical debate. *New York Times,* pp. F5, F10.

Grady, Denise. (2012, May 5). When illness makes a spouse a stranger. *New York Times,* p. A1.

Gräff, Johannes, Kim, Dohoon, Dobbin, Matthew M., & Tsai, Li-Huei. (2011). Epigenetic regulation of gene expression in physiological and pathological brain processes. *Physiological Reviews, 91,* 603–649.

Graham, Steve, & Perin, Dolores. (2007). A meta-analysis of writing instruction for adolescent students. *Journal of Educational Psychology, 99,* 445–476.

Grandin, Temple, & Johnson, Catherine. (2009). *Animals make us human: Creating the best life for animals.* Boston, MA: Houghton Mifflin Harcourt.

Granic, Isabela, & Patterson, Gerald R. (2006). Toward a comprehensive model of antisocial development: A dynamic systems approach. *Psychological Review, 113,* 101–131.

Granpeesheh, Doreen, Tarbox, Jonathan, & Dixon, Dennis R. (2009). Applied behavior analytic interventions for children with autism: A description and review of treatment research. *Annals of Clinical Psychiatry, 21,* 162–173.

Granpeesheh, Doreen, Tarbox, Jonathan, Dixon, Dennis R., Wilke, Arthur E., Allen, Michael S., & Bradstreet, James Jeffrey. (2010). Randomized trial of hyperbaric oxygen therapy for children with autism. *Research in Autism Spectrum Disorders, 4,* 268–275.

Green, James A., Whitney, Pamela G., & Potegal, Michael. (2011). Screaming, yelling, whining, and crying: Categorical and intensity differences in vocal expressions of anger and sadness in children's tantrums. *Emotion, 11,* 1124–1133.

Green, Lorraine, & Grant, Victoria. (2008). "Gagged grief and beleaguered bereavements?" An analysis of multidisciplinary theory and research relating to same sex partnership bereavement. *Sexualities, 11,* 275–300.

Greenberg, Saadia. (2011). *A profile of older Americans, 2011.* United States Department of Health and Human Services, Administration on Aging.

Greene, Melissa L., & Way, Niobe. (2005). Self-esteem trajectories among ethnic minority adolescents: A growth curve analysis of the patterns and predictors of change. *Journal of Research on Adolescence, 15,* 151–178.

Greenfield, Emily A., Scharlach, Andrew, Lehning, Amanda J., & Davitt, Joan K. (2012). A conceptual framework for examining the promise of the NORC program and Village models to promote aging in place. *Journal of Aging Studies, 26,* 273–284.

Greenhalgh, Susan. (2008). *Just one child: Science and policy in Deng's China.* Berkeley, CA: University of California Press.

Greenwood, Pamela M., & Parasuraman, R. (2012). *Nurturing the older brain and mind*. Cambridge, MA: MIT Press.

Greer, Eric, & Brunet, Anne. (2011). The genetic network of life-span extension by dietary restriction. In J. Masoro Edward & N. Austad Steven (Eds.), *Handbook of the biology of aging* (7th ed., pp. 3–23). San Diego, CA: Academic Press.

Gregory, Ted. (2010, August 28). Grampy down with 'the Face': Social networking by seniors doubles over last year, survey says. *Chicago Tribune*. Retrieved from http://articles.chicagotribune.com/2010-08-28/news/ct-talk-social-media-older-adults-08220100827_1_social-networking-facebook-sites

Greyson, Bruce. (2009). Near-death experiences and deathbed visions. In Allan Kellehear (Ed.), *The study of dying: From autonomy to transformation* (pp. 253–275). New York, NY: Cambridge University Press.

Griffin, James, Gooding, Sarah, Semesky, Michael, Farmer, Brittany, Mannchen, Garrett, & Sinnott, Jan. (2009). Four brief studies of relations between postformal thought and non-cognitive factors: Personality, concepts of god, political opinions, and social attitudes. *Journal of Adult Development, 16*, 173–182.

Griffith, Patrick, & Lopez, Oscar. (2009). Disparities in the diagnosis and treatment of Alzheimer's disease in African American and Hispanic patients: A call to action. *Generations, 33*(1), 37–46.

Grimm, David. (2008, May 16). Staggering toward a global strategy on alcohol abuse. *Science, 320*, 862–863.

Grissom, Robert J., & Kim, John J. (2005). *Effect sizes for research: A broad practical approach*. Mahwah, NJ: Erlbaum.

Grivell, Rosalie M., Reilly, Aimee J., Oakey, Helena, Chan, Annabelle, & Dodd, Jodie M. (2012). Maternal and neonatal outcomes following induction of labor: A cohort study. *Acta Obstetricia et Gynecologica Scandinavica, 91*, 198–203.

Grobman, Kevin H. (2008). *Learning & teaching developmental psychology: Attachment theory, infancy, & infant memory development*. Retrieved from http://www.devpsy.org/questions/attachment_theory_memory.html

Grolnick, Wendy S., McMenamy, Jannette M., & Kurowski, Carolyn O. (2006). Emotional self-regulation in infancy and toddlerhood. In Lawrence Balter & Catherine S. Tamis-LeMonda (Eds.), *Child psychology: A handbook of contemporary issues* (2nd ed., pp. 3–25). New York, NY: Psychology Press.

Grossmann, Klaus E., Grossmann, Karin, & Waters, Everett (Eds.). (2005). *Attachment from infancy to adulthood: The major longitudinal studies*. New York, NY: Guilford Press.

Grosvenor, Theodore. (2003). Why is there an epidemic of myopia? *Clinical and Experimental Optometry, 86*, 273–275.

Grubeck-Loebenstein, Beatrix. (2010). Fading immune protection in old age: Vaccination in the elderly. *Journal of Comparative Pathology, 142*(Suppl. 1), S116–S119.

Grundy, Emily, & Henretta, John C. (2006). Between elderly parents and adult children: A new look at the intergenerational care provided by the 'sandwich generation.' *Ageing & Society, 26*, 707–722.

Guerra, Nancy G., & Williams, Kirk R. (2010). Implementing bullying prevention in diverse settings: Geographic, economic, and cultural influences. In Eric M. Vernberg & Bridget K. Biggs (Eds.), *Preventing and treating bullying and victimization* (pp. 319–336). New York, NY: Oxford University Press.

Guerra, Nancy G., Williams, Kirk R., & Sadek, Shelly. (2011). Understanding bullying and victimization during childhood and adolescence: A mixed methods study. *Child Development, 82*, 295–310.

Guerri, Consuelo, & Pascual, María. (2010). Mechanisms involved in the neurotoxic, cognitive, and neurobehavioral effects of alcohol consumption during adolescence. *Alcohol, 44*, 15–26.

Gummerum, Michaela, Keller, Monika, Takezawa, Masanori, & Mata, Jutta. (2008). To give or not to give: Children's and adolescents' sharing and moral negotiations in economic decision situations. *Child Development, 79*, 562–576.

Guo, Sufang, Padmadas, Sabu S., Zhao, Fengmin, Brown, James J., & Stones, R. William. (2007). Delivery settings and caesarean section rates in China. *Bulletin of the World Health Organization, 85*, 755–762.

Gupta, Ramesh C. (Ed.) (2011). *Reproductive and developmental toxicology*. Boston, MA: Elsevier/Academic Press.

Gurung, Regan A. R., Taylor, Shelley E., & Seeman, Teresa E. (2003). Accounting for changes in social support among married older adults: Insights from the MacArthur Studies of Successful Aging. *Psychology & Aging, 18*, 487–496.

Haas, Steven A., Krueger, Patrick M., & Rohlfsen, Leah. (2012). Race/ethnic and nativity disparities in later life physical performance: The role of health and socioeconomic status over the life course. *The Journals of Gerontology Series B: Psychological Sciences and Social Sciences, 67B*, 238–248.

Hagedoorn, Mariët, Van Yperen, Nico W., Coyne, James C., van Jaarsveld, Cornelia H. M., Ranchor, Adelita V., van Sonderen, Eric, & Sanderman, Robbert. (2006). Does marriage protect older people from distress? The role of equity and recency of bereavement. *Psychology and Aging, 21*, 611–620.

Haier, Richard J., Colom, Roberto, Schroeder, David H., Condon, Christopher A., Tang, Cheuk, Eaves, Emily, & Head, Kevin. (2009). Gray matter and intelligence factors: Is there a neuro-g? *Intelligence, 37*, 136–144.

Hajjar, Emily R., Cafiero, Angela C., & Hanlon, Joseph T. (2007). Polypharmacy in elderly patients. *American Journal of Geriatric Pharmacotherapy, 5*, 345–351.

Halaschek-Wiener, Julius, Amirabbasi-Beik, Mahsa, Monfared, Nasim, Pieczyk, Markus, Sailer, Christian, Kollar, Anita, . . . Brooks-Wilson, Angela R. (2009). Genetic variation in healthy oldest-old. *PLoS One, 4*(8), e6641. doi:10.1371/journal.pone.0006641

Hall, Lynn K. (2008). *Counseling military families: What mental health professionals need to know*. New York, NY: Taylor and Francis.

Hall-Lande, Jennifer A., Eisenberg, Marla E., Christenson, Sandra L., & Neumark-Sztainer, Dianne. (2007). Social isolation, psychological health, and protective factors in adolescence. *Adolescence, 42*, 265–286.

Halpern, Carolyn Tucker, King, Rosalind Berkowitz, Oslak, Selene G., & Udry, J. Richard. (2005). Body mass index, dieting, romance, and sexual activity in adolescent girls: Relationships over time. *Journal of Research on Adolescence, 15,* 535–559.

Halpern, Diane F., Benbow, Camilla P., Geary, David C., Gur, Ruben C., Hyde, Janet Shibley, & Gernsbacher, Morton Ann. (2007). The science of sex differences in science and mathematics. *Psychological Science in the Public Interest, 8,* 1–51.

Halpern, Neil A., Pastores, Stephen M., Chou, Joanne F., Chawla, Sanjay, & Thaler, Howard T. (2011). Advance directives in an oncologic intensive care unit: A contemporary analysis of their frequency, type, and impact. *Journal of Palliative Medicine, 14,* 483–489.

Hamerman, David. (2007). *Geriatric bioscience: The link between aging and disease.* Baltimore, MD: Johns Hopkins University Press.

Hamerton, John L., & Evans, Jane A. (2005). Sex chromosome anomalies. In Merlin Gene Butler & F. John Meaney (Eds.), *Genetics of developmental disabilities* (pp. 585–650). Boca Raton, FL: Taylor & Francis.

Hamilton, Alice. (1914). Lead poisoning in the United States. *American Journal of Public Health, 4,* 477–480.

Hamilton, Brady E., Martin, Joyce A., & Ventura, Stephanie J. (2011). Births: Preliminary data for 2010. *National Vital Statistics Reports, 60*(2).

Hamilton, Brady E., Martin, Joyce A., & Ventura, Stephanie J. (2012). Births: Preliminary data for 2011. *National Vital Statistics Reports, 61*(5).

Hamm, Jill V., & Faircloth, Beverly S. (2005). The role of friendship in adolescents' sense of school belonging. *New Directions for Child and Adolescent Development, 107,* 61–78.

Hammer, Carol Scheffner, Jia, Gisela, & Uchikoshi, Yuuko. (2011). Language and literacy development of dual language learners growing up in the United States: A call for research. *Child Development Perspectives, 5,* 4–9.

Hammond, Christopher J., Andrew, Toby, Mak, Ying Tat, & Spector, Tim D. (2004). A susceptibility locus for myopia in the normal population is linked to the PAX6 gene region on chromosome 11: A genomewide scan of dizygotic twins. *American Journal of Human Genetics, 75,* 294–304.

Hampel, Harald, Lista, Simone, & Khachaturian, Zaven S. (2012). Development of biomarkers to chart all Alzheimer's disease stages: The royal road to cutting the therapeutic Gordian Knot. *Alzheimer's & Dementia, 8,* 312–336.

Hampton, Tracy. (2005). Alcohol and cancer. *Journal of the American Medical Association, 294,* 1481.

Han, Euna, Norton, Edward C., & Powell, Lisa M. (2011). Direct and indirect effects of body weight on adult wages. *Economics & Human Biology, 9,* 381–392.

Han, Wen-Jui, Lee, RaeHyuck, & Waldfogel, Jane. (2012). School readiness among children of immigrants in the US: Evidence from a large national birth cohort study. *Children and Youth Services Review, 34,* 771–782.

Handelsman, David J. (2011). Androgen misuse and abuse. *Best Practice & Research Clinical Endocrinology & Metabolism, 25,* 377–389.

Hane, Amie Ashley, Cheah, Charissa, Rubin, Kenneth H., & Fox, Nathan A. (2008). The role of maternal behavior in the relation between shyness and social reticence in early childhood and social withdrawal in middle childhood. *Social Development, 17,* 795–811.

Hank, Karsten, & Buber, Isabella. (2009). Grandparents caring for their grandchildren: Findings from the 2004 Survey of Health, Ageing, and Retirement in Europe. *Journal of Family Issues, 30,* 53–73.

Hannan, Claire, Buchanan, Anna DeBlois, & Monroe, Judy. (2009). Maintaining the vaccine safety net. *Pediatrics, 124*(Suppl. 5), S571–572.

Hansson, Robert O., & Stroebe, Margaret S. (2007). *Bereavement in late life: Coping, adaptation, and developmental influences.* Washington, DC: American Psychological Association.

Hanushek, Eric A. (2009, November 6). Building on No Child Left Behind. *Science, 326,* 802–803.

Hanushek, Eric A., & Woessmann, Ludger. (2009). *Do better schools lead to more growth? Cognitive skills, economic outcomes, and causation* (IZA Discussion Paper 4575). Bonn, Germany: Institute for the Study of Labor.

Hanushek, Eric A., & Woessmann, Ludger. (2010). *The high cost of low educational performance: The long-run economic impact of improving PISA outcomes.* Paris, France: OECD.

Harburg, Ernest, Kaciroti, Niko, Gleiberman, Lillian, Julius, Mara, & Schork, M. Anthony. (2008). Marital pair anger-coping types may act as an entity to affect mortality: Preliminary findings from a prospective study (Tecumseh, Michigan, 1971–1988). *Journal of Family Communication, 8,* 44–61.

Hardy, Melissa. (2006). Older workers. In Robert H. Binstock & Linda K. George (Eds.), *Handbook of aging and the social sciences* (6th ed., pp. 201–218). Amsterdam, The Netherlands: Elsevier.

Hargreaves, Andy. (2012). Singapore: The Fourth Way in action? *Educational Research for Policy and Practice, 11,* 7–17.

Harjes, Carlos E., Rocheford, Torbert R., Bai, Ling, Brutnell, Thomas P., Kandianis, Catherine Bermudez, Sowinski, Stephen G.,... Buckler, Edward S. (2008, January 18). Natural genetic variation in lycopene epsilon cyclase tapped for maize biofortification. *Science, 319,* 330–333.

Harkness, Sara, Super, Charles M., & Mavridis, Caroline Johnston. (2011). Parental ethnotheories about children's socio-emotional development. In Xinyin Chen & Kenneth H. Rubin (Eds.), *Socioemotional development in cultural context* (pp. 73–98). New York, NY: Guilford Press.

Harknett, Kristen S., & Hartnett, Caroline Sten. (2011). Who lacks support and why? An examination of mothers' personal safety nets. *Journal of Marriage and the Family, 73,* 861–875.

Harlow, Ilana. (2005). Shaping sorrow: Creative aspects of public and private mourning. In Samuel Heilman (Ed.), *Death, bereavement, and mourning* (pp. 33–52). New Brunswick, NJ: Transaction.

Harris, Judith Rich. (1998). *The nurture assumption: Why children turn out the way they do.* New York, NY: Free Press.

Harris, Judith Rich. (2002). Beyond the nurture assumption: Testing hypotheses about the child's environment. In John

G. Borkowski, Sharon Landesman Ramey, & Marie Bristol-Power (Eds.), *Parenting and the child's world: Influences on academic, intellectual, and social-emotional development* (pp. 3–20). Mahwah, NJ: Erlbaum.

Harrison, Denise, Bueno, Mariana, Yamada, Janet, Adams-Webber, Thomasin, & Stevens, Bonnie. (2010). Analgesic effects of sweet-tasting solutions for infants: Current state of equipoise. *Pediatrics, 126*, 894–902.

Harrison, Janet. (2011). 'Talking about my generation': A state-of-the-art review of health information for men in the andropause. *Health Information & Libraries Journal, 28*, 161–170.

Harrison, Kristen, Bost, Kelly K., McBride, Brent A., Donovan, Sharon M., Grigsby-Toussaint, Diana S., Kim, Juhee,... Jacobsohn, Gwen Costa. (2011). Toward a developmental conceptualization of contributors to overweight and obesity in childhood: The Six-Cs model. *Child Development Perspectives, 5*, 50–58.

Harrison, Linda J., & McLeod, Sharynne. (2010). Risk and protective factors associated with speech and language impairment in a nationally representative sample of 4- to 5-year-old children. *Journal of Speech, Language, and Hearing Research, 53*, 508–529.

Harrist, Amanda W., Topham, Glade L., Hubbs-Tait, Laura, Page, Melanie C., Kennedy, Tay S., & Shriver, Lenka H. (2012). What developmental science can contribute to a transdisciplinary understanding of childhood obesity: An interpersonal and intrapersonal risk model. *Child Development Perspectives, 6*, 445–455.

Hart, Chantelle N., Cairns, Alyssa, & Jelalian, Elissa. (2011). Sleep and obesity in children and adolescents. *Pediatric Clinics of North America, 58*, 715–733.

Harter, Susan. (2006). The self. In William Damon & Richard M. Lerner (Series Eds.) & Nancy Eisenberg (Vol. Ed.), *Handbook of child psychology: Vol. 3. Social, emotional, and personality development* (6th ed., pp. 505–570). Hoboken, NJ: Wiley.

Hartl, Daniel L., & Jones, Elizabeth W. (1999*). Essential genetics* (2nd ed.). Sudbury, MA: Jones and Bartlett.

Harvey, Carol D. H., & Yoshino, Satomi. (2006). Social policy for family caregivers of elderly: A Canadian, Japanese, and Australian comparison. *Marriage & Family Review, 39*, 143–158.

Hasebe, Yuki, Nucci, Larry, & Nucci, Maria S. (2004). Parental control of the personal domain and adolescent symptoms of psychopathology: A cross-national study in the United States and Japan. *Child Development, 75*, 815–828.

Hassan, Mohamed A. M., & Killick, Stephen R. (2003). Effect of male age on fertility: Evidence for the decline in male fertility with increasing age. *Fertility and Sterility, 79*, 1520–1527.

Hassett, Janice M., Siebert, Erin R., & Wallen, Kim. (2008). Sex differences in rhesus monkey toy preferences parallel those of children. *Hormones and Behavior, 54*, 359–364.

Hawthorne, Joanna. (2009). Promoting development of the early parent-infant relationship using the Neonatal Behavioural Assessment Scale. In Jane Barlow & P. O. Svanberg (Eds.), *Keeping the baby in mind: Infant mental health in practice* (pp. 39–51). New York, NY: Routledge/Taylor & Francis Group.

Hayden, Brian. (2012). Neandertal social structure? *Oxford Journal of Archaeology, 31*, 1–26.

Hayes, Rachel A., & Slater, Alan. (2008). Three-month-olds' detection of alliteration in syllables. *Infant Behavior & Development, 31*, 153–156.

Hayflick, Leonard. (2004). "Anti-aging" is an oxymoron. *The Journals of Gerontology Series A: Biological Sciences and Medical Sciences, 59A*, 573–578.

Hayne, Harlene, & Simcock, Gabrielle. (2009). Memory development in toddlers. In Mary L. Courage & Nelson Cowan (Eds.), *The development of memory in infancy and childhood* (2nd ed., pp. 43–68). New York, NY: Psychology Press.

Hayward, Diane W., Gale, Catherine M., & Eikeseth, Svein. (2009). Intensive behavioural intervention for young children with autism: A research-based service model. *Research in Autism Spectrum Disorders, 3*, 571–580.

Hazlett, Heather Cody, Poe, Michele D., Gerig, Guido, Styner, Martin, Chappell, Chad, Smith, Rachel Gimpel, ... Piven, Joseph. (2011). Early brain overgrowth in autism associated with an increase in cortical surface area before age 2 years. *Archives of General Psychiatry, 68*, 467–476.

Heaton, Tim B., & Darkwah, Akosua. (2011). Religious differences in modernization of the family: Family demographics trends in Ghana. *Journal of Family Issues*. Advance online publication. doi:10.1177/0192513x11398951

Heflick, Nathan A., & Goldenberg, Jamie L. (2012). No atheists in foxholes: Arguments for (but not against) afterlife belief buffers mortality salience effects for atheists. *British Journal of Social Psychology, 51*, 385–392.

Hehman, Eric, Gaertner, Samuel L., Dovidio, John F., Mania, Eric W., Guerra, Rita, Wilson, David C., & Friel, Brian M. (2012). Group status drives majority and minority integration preferences. *Psychological Science, 23*, 46–52.

Heiman, Julia R., Long, J. Scott, Smith, Shawna N., Fisher, William A., Sand, Michael S., & Rosen, Raymond C. (2011). Sexual satisfaction and relationship happiness in midlife and older couples in five countries. *Archives of Sexual Behavior, 40*, 741–753.

Helmes, Edward, & Chapman, Joanne. (2012). Education about sexuality in the elderly by healthcare professionals: A survey from the Southern Hemisphere. *Sex Education: Sexuality, Society and Learning, 12*, 95–107.

Henretta, John C., Soldo, Beth J., & Van Voorhis, Matthew F. (2011). Why do families differ? Children's care for an unmarried mother. *Journal of Marriage and Family, 73*, 383–395.

Herd, Pamela, Robert, Stephanie A., & House, James S. (2011). Health disparities among older adults: Life course influences and policy solutions. In Robert H. Binstock & Linda K. George (Eds.), *Handbook of aging and the social sciences* (7th ed., pp. 121–134). San Diego, CA: Academic Press.

Herek, Gregory M. (2006). Legal recognition of same-sex relationships in the United States: A social science perspective. *American Psychologist, 61*, 607–621.

Herlofson, Katharina, & Hagestad, Gunhild. (2011). Challenges in moving from macro to micro: Population and family structures in ageing societies. *Demographic Research, 25*, 337–370.

Herlofson, Katharina, & Hagestad, Gunhild O. (2012). Transformations in the role of grandparents across welfare states. In Sara Arber & Virpi Timonen (Eds.), *Contemporary grandparenting: Changing family relationships in global contexts* (pp. 27–49). Bristol, UK: Policy Press.

Herman, Khalisa N., Paukner, Annika, & Suomi, Stephen J. (2011). Gene × environment interactions and social play: Contributions from rhesus macaques. In Anthony D. Pellegrini (Ed.), *The Oxford handbook of the development of play* (pp. 58–69). New York, NY: Oxford University Press.

Herman-Giddens, Marcia E., Wang, Lily, & Koch, Gary. (2001). Secondary sexual characteristics in boys: Estimates from the National Health and Nutrition Examination Survey III, 1988–1994. *Archives of Pediatrics & Adolescent Medicine, 155,* 1022–1028.

Herrera, Angelica P., Snipes, Shedra Amy, King, Denae W., Torres-Vigil, Isabel, Goldberg, Daniel S., & Weinberg, Armin D. (2010). Disparate inclusion of older adults in clinical trials: Priorities and opportunities for policy and practice change. *American Journal of Public Health, 100*(Suppl. 1), S105–S112.

Herring, Ann, & Swedlund, Alan C. (Eds.). (2010). *Plagues and epidemics: Infected spaces past and present.* New York, NY: Berg.

Herrmann, Esther, Call, Josep, Hernàndez-Lloreda, María Victoria, Hare, Brian, & Tomasello, Michael. (2007, September 7). Humans have evolved specialized skills of social cognition: The cultural intelligence hypothesis. *Science, 317,* 1360–1366.

Herschensohn, Julia Rogers. (2007). *Language development and age.* New York, NY: Cambridge University Press.

Hertzog, Christopher. (2011). Intelligence in adulthood. In Robert J. Sternberg & Scott Barry Kaufman (Eds.), *The Cambridge handbook of intelligence* (pp. 174–190). New York, NY: Cambridge University Press.

Heslin, Kevin C., Hamilton, Alison B., Singzon, Trudy K., Smith, James L., Lois, Nancy, & Anderson, Ruth. (2011). Alternative families in recovery: Fictive kin relationships among residents of sober living homes. *Qualitative Health Research, 21,* 477–488.

Hess, Thomas, Hinson, Joey, & Hodges, Elizabeth. (2009). Moderators of and mechanisms underlying stereotype threat effects on older adults' memory performance. *Experimental Aging Research, 35,* 153–177.

Hess, Thomas M., Leclerc, Christina M., Swaim, Elizabeth, & Weatherbee, Sarah R. (2009). Aging and everyday judgments: The impact of motivational and processing resource factors. *Psychology and Aging, 24,* 735–740.

Hicks, Joshua A., Trent, Jason, Davis, William E., & King, Laura A. (2012). Positive affect, meaning in life, and future time perspective: An application of socioemotional selectivity theory. *Psychology and Aging, 27,* 181–189.

Higgins, Jenny A., & Cooper, Anne D. (2012). Dual use of condoms and contraceptives in the USA. *Sexual Health, 9,* 73–80.

Higgins, Matt. (2006, August 7). A series of flips creates some serious buzz. *New York Times,* p. D7.

Higuchi, Susumu, Matsushita, Sachio, Muramatsu, Taro, Murayama, Masanobu, & Hayashida, Motoi. (1996). Alcohol and aldehyde dehydrogenase genotypes and drinking behavior in Japanese. *Alcoholism: Clinical and Experimental Research, 20,* 493–497.

Hill, Denise M., Hanton, Sheldon, Matthews, Nic, & Fleming, Scott. (2010). Choking in sport: A review. *International Review of Sport and Exercise Psychology, 3,* 24–39.

Hill, Nancy E., Bush, Kevin R., & Roosa, Mark W. (2003). Parenting and family socialization strategies and children's mental health: Low-income, Mexican-American and Euro-American mothers and children. *Child Development, 74,* 189–204.

Hill, Patrick L., Duggan, Peter M., & Lapsley, Daniel K. (2012). Subjective invulnerability, risk behavior, and adjustment in early adolescence. *The Journal of Early Adolescence, 32,* 489–501.

Hill, Shirley A. (2007). Transformative processes: Some sociological questions. *Journal of Marriage and Family, 69,* 293–298.

Hillberg, Tanja, Hamilton-Giachritsis, Catherine, & Dixon, Louise. (2011). Review of meta-analyses on the association between child sexual abuse and adult mental health difficulties: A systematic approach. *Trauma, Violence, & Abuse, 12,* 38–49.

Hindman, Annemarie H., Skibbe, Lori E., Miller, Alison, & Zimmerman, Marc. (2010). Ecological contexts and early learning: Contributions of child, family, and classroom factors during Head Start, to literacy and mathematics growth through first grade. *Early Childhood Research Quarterly, 25,* 235–250.

Hinds, David A., Stuve, Laura L., Nilsen, Geoffrey B., Halperin, Eran, Eskin, Eleazar, Ballinger, Dennis G., . . . Cox, David R. (2005, February 18). Whole-genome patterns of common DNA variation in three human populations. *Science, 307,* 1072–1079.

Hines, Melissa. (2004). *Brain gender.* Oxford, England: Oxford University Press.

Hines, Melissa. (2010). Sex-related variation in human behavior and the brain. *Trends in Cognitive Sciences, 14,* 448–456.

Hipwell, Alison E., Keenan, Kate, Loeber, Rolf, & Battista, Deena. (2010). Early predictors of sexually intimate behaviors in an urban sample of young girls. *Developmental Psychology, 46,* 366–378.

Hirschberger, Gilad. (2006). Terror management and attributions of blame to innocent victims: Reconciling compassionate and defensive responses. *Journal of Personality and Social Psychology, 91,* 832–844.

Hirsh-Pasek, Kathy, Golinkoff, Roberta Michnick, Berk, Laura E., & Singer, Dorothy G. (2009). *A mandate for playful learning in preschool: Presenting the evidence.* New York, NY: Oxford University Press.

Ho, Caroline, Bluestein, Deborah N., & Jenkins, Jennifer M. (2008). Cultural differences in the relationship between parenting and children's behavior. *Developmental Psychology, 44,* 507–522.

Ho, Emily S. (2010). Measuring hand function in the young child. *Journal of Hand Therapy, 23,* 323–328.

Hoare, Carol Hren. (2002). *Erikson on development in adulthood: New insights from the unpublished papers.* New York, NY: Oxford University Press.

Hochman, David. (2003, November 23). Food for holiday thought: Eat less, live to 140? *The New York Times,* p. A9.

Hochschild, Jennifer L., & Powell, Brenna Marea. (2008). Racial reorganization and the United States census 1850–1930: Mulattoes, half-breeds, mixed parentage, Hindoos, and the Mexican race. *Studies in American Political Development, 22,* 59–96.

Hoffmann, Rasmus. (2008). *Socioeconomic difference in old age mortality.* New York, NY: Springer.

Hofstede, Geert. (2007). A European in Asia. *Asian Journal of Social Psychology, 10,* 16–21.

Hogeboom, David L., McDermott, Robert J., Perrin, Karen M., Osman, Hana, & Bell-Ellison, Bethany A. (2010). Internet use and social networking among middle aged and older adults. *Educational Gerontology, 36,* 93–111.

Holland, James D., & Klaczynski, Paul A. (2009). Intuitive risk taking during adolescence. *Prevention Researcher, 16,* 8–11.

Holland, John L. (1997). *Making vocational choices: A theory of vocational personalities and work environments* (3rd ed.). Odessa, FL: Psychological Assessment Resources.

Hollich, George J., Hirsh-Pasek, Kathy, Golinkoff, Roberta Michnick, Brand, Rebecca J., Brown, Ellie, Chung, He Len, . . . Rocroi, Camille. (2000). Breaking the language barrier: An emergentist coalition model for the origins of word learning. *Monographs of the Society for Research in Child Development, 65*(3, Serial No. 262), v–123.

Hollos, Marida, Larsen, Ulla, Obono, Oka, & Whitehouse, Bruce. (2009). The problem of infertility in high fertility populations: Meanings, consequences and coping mechanisms in two Nigerian communities. *Social Science & Medicine, 68,* 2061–2068.

Holm, Stephanie M., Forbes, Erika E., Ryan, Neal D., Phillips, Mary L., Tarr, Jill A., & Dahl, Ronald E. (2009). Reward-related brain function and sleep in pre/early pubertal and mid/late pubertal adolescents. *The Journal of Adolescent Health, 45,* 326–334.

Holmboe, Karla, Nemoda, Z., Fearon, R. M. P., Sasvari-Szekely, M., & Johnson, M. H. (2011). Dopamine D4 receptor and serotonin transporter gene effects on the longitudinal development of infant temperament. *Genes, Brain, and Behavior, 10,* 513–522.

Holsti, Liisa, Grunau, Ruth E., & Shany, Eilon. (2011). Assessing pain in preterm infants in the neonatal intensive care unit: Moving to a brain-oriented approach. *Pain Management, 1,* 171–179.

Holtzman, Jennifer. (2009). Simple, effective—and inexpensive—strategies to reduce tooth decay in children. *ICAN: Infant, Child, & Adolescent Nutrition, 1,* 225–231.

Holtzworth-Munroe, Amy. (2011). Controversies in divorce mediation and intimate partner violence: A focus on the children. *Aggression and Violent Behavior, 16,* 319–324.

Hook, Jennifer L. (2010). Gender inequality in the welfare state: Sex segregation in housework, 1965–2003. *American Journal of Sociology, 115,* 1480–1523.

Hook, Jennifer L. (2012). Working on the weekend: Fathers' time with family in the United Kingdom. *Journal of Marriage and Family, 74,* 631–642.

Houdmont, Jonathan, Zhou, Jieming, & Hassard, Juliet. (2011). Overtime and psychological well-being among Chinese office workers. *Occupational Medicine, 61,* 270–273.

Hougaard, Karin S., & Hansen, Åse M. (2007). Enhancement of developmental toxicity effects of chemicals by gestational stress. A review. *Neurotoxicology and Teratology, 29,* 425–445.

Hout, Michael, & Elliott, Stuart W. (Eds.). (2011). *Incentives and test-based accountability in education.* Washington, DC: National Academies Press.

Howard, Kimberly S. (2010). Paternal attachment, parenting beliefs and children's attachment. *Early Child Development and Care, 180,* 157–171.

Howlin, Patricia, Magiati, Iliana, Charman, Tony, & MacLean, William E., Jr. (2009). Systematic review of early intensive behavioral interventions for children with autism. *American Journal on Intellectual and Developmental Disabilities, 114,* 23–41.

Hoyert, Donna L., & Xu, Jiaquan. (2012). Deaths: Preliminary data for 2011. *National Vital Statistics Reports, 61*(6).

Hrabosky, Joshua I., & Thomas, Jennifer J. (2008). Elucidating the relationship between obesity and depression: Recommendations for future research. *Clinical Psychology: Science and Practice, 15,* 28–34.

Hrdy, Sarah Blaffer. (2009). *Mothers and others: The evolutionary origins of mutual understanding.* Cambridge, MA: Harvard University Press.

Hsia, Yingfen, & Maclennan, Karyn. (2009). Rise in psychotropic drug prescribing in children and adolescents during 1992–2001: A population-based study in the UK. *European Journal of Epidemiology, 24,* 211–216.

Hsu, Ming, Anen, Cedric, & Quartz, Steven R. (2008, May 23). The right and the good: Distributive justice and neural encoding of equity and efficiency. *Science, 320,* 1092–1095.

Hu, Frank B. (2011). Globalization of diabetes: The role of diet, lifestyle, and genes. *Diabetes Care, 34,* 1249–1257.

Huang, Chien-Chung. (2009). Mothers' reports of nonresident fathers' involvement with their children: Revisiting the relationship between child support payment and visitation. *Family Relations, 58,* 54–64.

Huang, Chiungjung. (2010). Mean-level change in self-esteem from childhood through adulthood: Meta-analysis of longitudinal studies. *Review of General Psychology, 14,* 251–260.

Huang, Yuli. (2012, May 30). SUSTC enrolls 180 scholarship students. *China Daily.* Retrieved from http://www.chinadaily.com.cn/china/2012-05/30/content_15427093.htm

Hubbard, Raymond, & Lindsay, R. Murray. (2008). Why *p* values are not a useful measure of evidence in statistical significance testing. *Theory and Psychology, 18,* 69–88.

Huberty, Thomas J. (2012). *Anxiety and depression in children and adolescents: Assessment, intervention, and prevention.* New York, NY: Springer.

Huesmann, L. Rowell, Dubow, Eric F., & Boxer, Paul. (2009). Continuity of aggression from childhood to early adulthood as a predictor of life outcomes: Implications for the adolescent-limited and life-course-persistent models. *Aggressive Behavior, 35,* 136–149.

Hugdahl, Kenneth, & Westerhausen, René. (Eds.) (2010). *The two halves of the brain: Information processing in the cerebral hemispheres.* Cambridge, MA: MIT Press.

Hughes, Julie Milligan, & Bigler, Rebecca S. (2011). Predictors of African American and European American adolescents' endorsement of race-conscious social policies. *Developmental Psychology, 47,* 479–492.

Hughes, Kimberly A. (2010). Mutation and the evolution of ageing: From biometrics to system genetics. *Philosophical Transactions of the Royal Society B: Biological Sciences, 365,* 1273–1279.

Hughes, Sonya M., & Gore, Andrea C. (2007). How the brain controls puberty, and implications for sex and ethnic differences. *Family & Community Health, 30*(Suppl. 1), S112–S114.

Huh, Susanna Y., Rifas-Shiman, Sheryl L., Taveras, Elsie M., Oken, Emily, & Gillman, Matthew W. (2011). Timing of solid food introduction and risk of obesity in preschool-aged children. *Pediatrics, 127,* e544-e551. doi:10.1542/peds.2010-0740.

Huijbregts, Sanne K., Tavecchio, Louis, Leseman, Paul, & Hoffenaar, Peter. (2009). Child rearing in a group setting: Beliefs of Dutch, Caribbean Dutch, and Mediterranean Dutch caregivers in center-based child care. *Journal of Cross-Cultural Psychology, 40,* 797–815.

Hummert, Mary Lee. (2011). Age stereotypes and aging. In K. Warner Schaie & Sherry L. Willis (Eds.), *Handbook of the psychology of aging* (7th ed., pp. 249–262). Boston, MA: Elsevier/Academic Press.

Husain, Nusrat, Chaudhry, Nasim, Tomenson, Barbara, Jackson, Judy, Gater, Richard, & Creed, Francis. (2011). Depressive disorder and social stress in Pakistan compared to people of Pakistani origin in the UK. *Social Psychiatry and Psychiatric Epidemiology, 46,* 1153–1159.

Hussey, Jon M., Chang, Jen Jen, & Kotch, Jonathan B. (2006). Child maltreatment in the United States: Prevalence, risk factors, and adolescent health consequences. *Pediatrics, 118,* 933–942.

Huston, Aletha C., & Aronson, Stacey Rosenkrantz. (2005). Mothers' time with infant and time in employment as predictors of mother-child relationships and children's early development. *Child Development, 76,* 467–482.

Huston, Aletha C., & Ripke, Marika N. (2006). Middle childhood: Contexts of development. In Aletha C. Huston & Marika N. Ripke (Eds.), *Developmental contexts in middle childhood: Bridges to adolescence and adulthood* (pp. 1–22). New York, NY: Cambridge University Press.

Huver, Rose M. E., Otten, Roy, de Vries, Hein, & Engels, Rutger C. M. E. (2010). Personality and parenting style in parents of adolescents. *Journal of Adolescence, 33,* 395–402.

Hvistendahl, Mara. (2011, May 6). China's population growing slowly, changing fast. *Science, 332,* 650–651.

Hyde, Janet S., Lindberg, Sara M., Linn, Marcia C., Ellis, Amy B., & Williams, Caroline C. (2008, July 25). Gender similarities characterize math performance. *Science, 321,* 494–495.

Hyson, Marilou, Copple, Carol, & Jones, Jacqueline. (2006). Early childhood development and education. In William Damon & Richard M. Lerner (Series Eds.) & K. Ann Renninger & Irving E. Sigel (Vol. Eds.), *Handbook of child psychology: Vol. 4. Child psychology in practice* (6th ed., pp. 3–47). Hoboken, NJ: Wiley.

Iacovidou, Nicoletta, Varsami, Marianna, & Syggellou, Angeliki. (2010). Neonatal outcome of preterm delivery. In George Creatsas & George Mastorakos (Eds.), *Annals of the New York Academy of Sciences: Vol. 1205. Women's health and disease* (pp. 130–134). Malden, MA: Blackwell.

Idler, Ellen. (2006). Religion and aging. In Robert H. Binstock & Linda K. George (Eds.), *Handbook of aging and the social sciences* (6th ed., pp. 277–300). Amsterdam, The Netherlands: Elsevier.

ILO. (2012). *Database of conditions of work and employment laws.* Retrieved from http://www.ilo.org/dyn/travail/travmain.home

Imai, Mutsumi, Kita, Sotaro, Nagumo, Miho, & Okada, Hiroyuki. (2008). Sound symbolism facilitates early verb learning. *Cognition, 109,* 54–65.

Imamoglu, Çagri. (2007). Assisted living as a new place schema: A comparison with homes and nursing homes. *Environment and Behavior, 39,* 246–268.

Inan, Hatice Zeynep, Trundle, Kathy Cabe, & Kantor, Rebecca. (2010). Understanding natural sciences education in a Reggio Emilia-inspired preschool. *Journal of Research in Science Teaching, 47,* 1186–1208.

Inbar, Yoel, Botti, Simona, & Hanko, Karlene. (2011). Decision speed and choice regret: When haste feels like waste. *Journal of Experimental Social Psychology, 47,* 533–540.

Ingersoll-Dayton, Berit, Neal, Margaret B., Ha, Jung-Hwa, & Hammer, Leslie B. (2003). Redressing inequity in parent care among siblings. *Journal of Marriage & Family, 65,* 201–212.

Inglehart, Ronald. (1990). *Culture shift in advanced industrial society.* Princeton, NJ: Princeton University Press.

Inhelder, Bärbel, & Piaget, Jean. (1958). *The growth of logical thinking from childhood to adolescence: An essay on the construction of formal operational structures.* New York, NY: Basic Books.

Inhelder, Bärbel, & Piaget, Jean. (1964). *The early growth of logic in the child.* New York, NY: Harper & Row.

Inouye, Sharon K. (2006). Delirium in older persons. *New England Journal of Medicine, 354,* 1157–1165.

Insel, Beverly J., & Gould, Madelyn S. (2008). Impact of modeling on adolescent suicidal behavior. *Psychiatric Clinics of North America, 31,* 293–316.

Institute of Medicine, Committee on Food Marketing and the Diets of Children and Youth. (2006). *Food marketing to children and youth: Threat or opportunity?* (J. Michael McGinnis, Jennifer Appleton Gootman, & Vivica I. Kraak, Eds.) Washington, DC: National Academies Press.

International Monetary Fund (2012). *World economic outlook: October 2012.* Washington DC: Author. Retrieved January 2013 from http://www.imf.org/external/pubs/ft/weo/2012/02/weodata/groups.htm

Inzlicht, Michael, & Schmader, Toni (Eds.). (2012). *Stereotype threat: Theory, process, and application.* New York, NY: Oxford University Press.

Irwin, Scott, Galvez, Roberto, Weiler, Ivan Jeanne, Beckel-Mitchener, Andrea, & Greenough, William. (2002). Brain structure and the functions of FMR1 protein. In Randi Jenssen Hagerman & Paul J. Hagerman (Eds.), *Fragile X syndrome: Diagnosis, treatment, and research* (3rd ed., pp. 191–205). Baltimore, MD: Johns Hopkins University Press.

Ispa, Jean M., Fine, Mark A., Halgunseth, Linda C., Harper, Scott, Robinson, JoAnn, Boyce, Lisa, ... Brady-Smith, Christy. (2004). Maternal intrusiveness, maternal warmth, and mother-toddler relationship outcomes: Variations across low-income ethnic and acculturation groups. *Child Development, 75,* 1613–1631.

Issa, Jean-Pierre. (2011). Epigenetic variation and cellular Darwinism. *Nature Genetics, 43,* 724–726.

Iyengar, Sheena S., & Lepper, Mark R. (2000). When choice is demotivating: Can one desire too much of a good thing? *Journal of Personality and Social Psychology, 79,* 995–1006.

Izard, Carroll E. (2009). Emotion theory and research: Highlights, unanswered questions, and emerging issues. *Annual Review of Psychology, 60,* 1–25.

Izard, Carroll E., Fine, Sarah, Mostow, Allison, Trentacosta, Christopher, & Campbell, Jan. (2002). Emotion processes in normal and abnormal development and preventive intervention. *Development & Psychopathology, 14,* 761–787.

Jack, Clifford R., Jr., Lowe, Val J., Weigand, Stephen D., Wiste, Heather J., Senjem, Matthew L., Knopman, David S., ... Petersen, Ronald C. (2009). Serial PIB and MRI in normal, mild cognitive impairment and Alzheimer's disease: Implications for sequence of pathological events in Alzheimer's disease. *Brain, 132*(5), 1355–1365.

Jackson, James S. (2012, May). *The masquerade of racial group differences in psychological sciences.* Keynote address delivered at the 24th Annual Convention of the Association for Psychological Science, Chicago, IL.

Jackson, James S., Govia, Ishtar O., & Sellers, Sherrill L. (2011). Racial and ethnic influences over the life course. In Robert H. Binstock & Linda K. George (Eds.), *Handbook of aging and the social sciences* (7th ed., pp. 91–103). San Diego, CA: Academic Press.

Jackson, Shelly L., & Hafemeister, Thomas L. (2011). Risk factors associated with elder abuse: The importance of differentiating by type of elder maltreatment. *Violence and Victims, 26,* 738–757.

Jacob, Jenet I. (2009). The socio-emotional effects of non-maternal childcare on children in the USA: A critical review of recent studies. *Early Child Development and Care, 179,* 559–570.

Jacoby, Larry L., & Rhodes, Matthew G. (2006). False remembering in the aged. *Current Directions in Psychological Science, 15,* 49–53.

Jaffee, Sara R., Caspi, Avshalom, Moffitt, Terrie E., Polo-Tomás, Monica, & Taylor, Alan. (2007). Individual, family, and neighborhood factors distinguish resilient from non-resilient maltreated children: A cumulative stressors model. *Child Abuse & Neglect, 31,* 231–253.

James, Raven. (2007). Sexually transmitted infections. In Annette Fuglsang Owens & Mitchell S. Tepper (Eds.), *Sexual health: Vol. 4. State-of-the-art treatments and research* (pp. 235–267). Westport, CT: Praeger/Greenwood.

James, Stephanie, Simmons, Cameron P., & James, Anthony A. (2011, November 11). Mosquito trials. *Science, 334,* 771–772.

Jasny, Barbara R., Chin, Gilbert, Chong, Lisa, & Vignieri, Sacha. (2011, December 2). Again, and again, and again ... *Science, 334,* 1225.

Jastrzembski, Tiffany S., Charness, Neil, & Vasyukova, Catherine. (2006). Expertise and age effects on knowledge activation in chess. *Psychology and Aging, 21,* 401–405.

Jenson, Jeffrey M., & Fraser, Mark W. (Eds.). (2006). *Social policy for children & families: A risk and resilience perspective.* Thousand Oaks, CA: Sage.

Jessop, Donna C., & Wade, Jennifer. (2008). Fear appeals and binge drinking: A terror management theory perspective. *British Journal of Health Psychology, 13,* 773–788.

Jewkes, Rachel K., Dunkle, Kristin, Nduna, Mzikazi, & Shai, Nwabisa. (2010). Intimate partner violence, relationship power inequity, and incidence of HIV infection in young women in South Africa: A cohort study. *The Lancet, 376,* 41–48.

John Hancock Life & Health Insurance Company. (2011). *John Hancock 2011 Cost of Care Survey.* Boston, MA: Author.

Johnson, Chris A., & Wilkinson, Mark E. (2010). Vision and driving: The United States. *Journal of Neuro-Ophthalmology, 30,* 170–176.

Johnson, Elizabeth K., & Tyler, Michael D. (2010). Testing the limits of statistical learning for word segmentation. *Developmental Science, 13,* 339–345.

Johnson, Kimberly S., Kuchibhatla, Maragatha, & Tulsky, James A. (2011). Racial differences in location before hospice enrollment and association with hospice length of stay. *Journal of the American Geriatrics Society, 59,* 732–737.

Johnson, Mary. (2007). Our guest editors talk about couples in later life. *Generations, 31*(3), 4–5.

Johnson, Mark H., & Fearon, R. M. Pasco. (2011). Commentary: Disengaging the infant mind: Genetic dissociation of attention and cognitive skills in infants—Reflections on Leppänen et al. (2011). *Journal of Child Psychology and Psychiatry, 52,* 1153–1154.

Johnson, Mark H., Grossmann, Tobias, & Kadosh, Kathrin Cohen. (2009). Mapping functional brain development: Building a social brain through interactive specialization. *Developmental Psychology, 45,* 151–159.

Johnson, Mark H., with Michelle de Haan. (2011). *Developmental cognitive neuroscience: An introduction* (3rd ed.). Malden, MA: Wiley-Blackwell.

Johnson, Monica Kirkpatrick, Crosnoe, Robert, & Elder, Glen H. (2011). Insights on adolescence from a life course perspective. *Journal of Research on Adolescence, 21,* 273–280.

Johnson, Susan C., Dweck, Carol S., Chen, Frances S., Stern, Hilarie L., Ok, Su-Jeong, & Barth, Maria. (2010). At the intersection of social and cognitive development: Internal working models of attachment in infancy. *Cognitive Science, 34,* 807–825.

Johnson, Teddi Dineley. (2011). Report calls for examination of chemical safety: National coalition notes difficulty determining exposures. *The Nation's Health, 41,* 9.

Johnson, Wendy. (2010). Understanding the genetics of intelligence: Can height help? Can corn oil? *Current Directions in Psychological Science, 19,* 177–182.

Johnston, Lloyd D., O'Malley, Patrick M., Bachman, Jerald G., & Schulenberg, John E. (2008). *Monitoring the Future national results on adolescent drug use: Overview of key findings, 2007* (NIH Publication No. 08-6418). Bethesda, MD: National Institute on Drug Abuse.

Johnston, Lloyd D., O'Malley, Patrick M., Bachman, Jerald G., & Schulenberg, John E. (2009). *Monitoring the Future national survey results on drug use, 1975–2008: Vol. II. College students and adults ages 19–50* (NIH Publication No. 09-7403). Bethesda, MD: National Institute on Drug Abuse.

Johnston, Lloyd D., O'Malley, Patrick M., Bachman, Jerald G., & Schulenberg, John E. (2010). *Monitoring the Future national results on adolescent drug use: Overview of key findings, 2009* (NIH Publication No. 10-7583). Bethesda, MD: National Institute on Drug Abuse.

Johnston, Lloyd D., O'Malley, Patrick M., Bachman, Jerald G., & Schulenberg, John E. (2012). *Monitoring the Future national results on adolescent drug use: Overview of key findings, 2011.* Ann Arbor, MI: Institute for Social Research, The University of Michigan.

Jokela, Markus. (2012). Birth-cohort effects in the association between personality and fertility. *Psychological Science, 12,* 835–841.

Jokela, Markus, Elovainio, Marko, Kivimäki, Mika, & Keltikangas-Järvinen, Liisa. (2008). Temperament and migration patterns in Finland. *Psychological Science, 19,* 831–837.

Jones, Diane, & Crawford, Joy. (2005). Adolescent boys and body image: Weight and muscularity concerns as dual pathways to body dissatisfaction. *Journal of Youth and Adolescence, 34,* 629–636.

Jones, Lisa A., Sinnott, Loraine T., Mutti, Donald O., Mitchell, Gladys L., Moeschberger, Melvin L., & Zadnik, Karla. (2007). Parental history of myopia, sports and outdoor activities, and future myopia. *Investigative Ophthalmology & Visual Science, 48,* 3524–3532.

Jones, Mary Cover. (1965). Psychological correlates of somatic development. *Child Development, 36,* 899–911.

Jones, Randall M. (2011). Psychosocial development and first substance use in third and fourth grade students: A short-term longitudinal study. *Child Development Research, 2011.* doi:10.1155/2011/916020

Jong, Jyh-Tsorng, Kao, Tsair, Lee, Liang-Yi, Huang, Hung-Hsuan, Lo, Po-Tsung, & Wang, Hui-Chung. (2010). Can temperament be understood at birth? The relationship between neonatal pain cry and their temperament: A preliminary study. *Infant Behavior and Development, 33,* 266–272.

Jonge, Huub de. (2011). Purification and remembrance: Eastern and western ways to deal with the Bali bombing. In Peter Jan Margry & Cristina Sanchez-Carretero (Eds.), *Grassroots memorials: The politics of memorializing traumatic death* (pp. 262–284). New York, NY: Berghahn Books.

Jopp, Daniela, & Rott, Christoph. (2006). Adaptation in very old age: Exploring the role of resources, beliefs, and attitudes for centenarians' happiness. *Psychology and Aging, 21,* 266–280.

Jordan, Alexander H., & Monin, Benoît. (2008). From sucker to saint: Moralization in response to self-threat. *Psychological Science, 19,* 809–815.

Jordan-Young, Rebecca M. (2010). *Brain storm: The flaws in the science of sex differences.* Cambridge, MA: Harvard University Press.

Juan, Shan. (2010, January 14). C-section epidemic hits China. *China Daily.* Retrieved from http://www.chinadaily.com.cn/index.html

Kachel, A. Friederike, Premo, Luke S., & Hublin, Jean-Jacques. (2011). Modeling the effects of weaning age on length of female reproductive period: Implications for the evolution of human life history. *American Journal of Human Biology, 23,* 479–487.

Kagan, Jerome. (2008). In defense of qualitative changes in development. *Child Development, 79,* 1606–1624.

Kagan, Jerome, & Herschkowitz, Norbert (with Herschkowitz, Elinore Chapman). (2005). *A young mind in a growing brain.* Mahwah, NJ: Erlbaum.

Kagan, Jerome, Snidman, Nancy, Kahn, Vali, & Towsley, Sara. (2007). The preservation of two infant temperaments into adolescence. *Monographs of the Society for Research in Child Development, 72*(2, Serial No. 287), 1–95.

Kahan, Michelle. (2006). "Put up" on platforms: A history of twentieth century adoption policy in the United States. *Journal of Sociology & Social Welfare, 33,* 51–72.

Kahn, Joan R., McGill, Brittany S., & Bianchi, Suzanne M. (2011). Help to family and friends: Are there gender differences at older ages? *Journal of Marriage and Family, 73,* 77–92.

Kahneman, Daniel. (2011). *Thinking, fast and slow.* New York, NY: Farrar, Straus and Giroux.

Kakihara, Fumiko, & Tilton-Weaver, Lauree. (2009). Adolescents' interpretations of parental control: Differentiated by domain and types of control. *Child Development, 80,* 1722–1738.

Kalambouka, Afroditi, Farrell, Peter, Dyson, Alan, & Kaplan, Ian. (2007). The impact of placing pupils with special educational needs in mainstream schools on the achievement of their peers. *Educational Research, 49,* 365–382.

Kalaria, Raj N., Maestre, Gladys E., Arizaga, Raul, Friedland, Robert P., Galasko, Doug, Hall, Kathleen, … Antuono, Piero. (2008). Alzheimer's disease and vascular dementia in developing countries: Prevalence, management, and risk factors. *The Lancet Neurology, 7,* 812–826.

Kalavar, Jyotsna, & van Willigen, John. (2005). Older Asian Indians resettled in America: Narratives about households, culture and generation. *Journal of Cross-Cultural Gerontology, 20,* 213–230.

Kalliala, Marjatta. (2006). *Play culture in a changing world.* Maidenhead, England: Open University Press.

Kalmijn, Matthijs. (2010). Country differences in the effects of divorce on well-being: The role of norms, support, and selectivity. *European Sociological Review, 26*, 475–490.

Kalra, Suleena Kansal, & Barnhart, Kurt T. (2011). In vitro fertilization and adverse childhood outcomes: What we know, where we are going, and how we will get there. A glimpse into what lies behind and beckons ahead. *Fertility and Sterility, 95*, 1887–1889.

Kanner, Andres M. (Ed.) (2012). *Depression in neurologic disorders: Diagnosis and management.* Chichester, West Sussex, UK: John Wiley & Sons.

Kapornai, Krisztina, & Vetró, Ágnes. (2008). Depression in children. *Current Opinion in Psychiatry, 21*, 1–7.

Kärnä, Antti, Voeten, Marinus, Little, Todd D., Poskiparta, Elisa, Kaljonen, Anne, & Salmivalli, Christina. (2011). A large-scale evaluation of the KiVa antibullying program: Grades 4–6. *Child Development, 82*, 311–330.

Karney, Benjamin R., & Bradbury, Thomas N. (2005). Contextual influences on marriage: Implications for policy and intervention. *Current Directions in Psychological Science, 14*, 171–174.

Kärtner, Joscha, Borke, Jörn, Maasmeier, Kathrin, Keller, Heidi, & Kleis, Astrid. (2011). Sociocultural influences on the development of self-recognition and self-regulation in Costa Rican and Mexican toddlers. *Journal of Cognitive Education and Psychology, 10*, 96–112.

Kärtner, Joscha, Keller, Heidi, & Yovsi, Relindis D. (2010). Mother–infant interaction during the first 3 months: The emergence of culture-specific contingency patterns. *Child Development, 81*, 540–554.

Kastenbaum, Robert. (2006). *Death, society, and human experience* (9th ed.). Boston, MA: Allyn and Bacon.

Kastenbaum, Robert. (2012). *Death, society, and human experience* (11th ed.). Boston, MA: Pearson.

Katz, Kathy S., Jarrett, Marian, El-Mohandes, Ayman, Schneider, Susan, McNeely-Johnson, Doris, & Kiely, Michele. (2011). Effectiveness of a combined home visiting and group intervention for low income African American mothers: The Pride in Parenting Program. *Maternal and Child Health Journal, 15*(Suppl. 1), S75–S84.

Kaufman, Kenneth R., & Kaufman, Nathaniel D. (2006). And then the dog died. *Death Studies, 30*, 61–76.

Kaushik, Manu, Sontineni, Siva P., & Hunter, Claire. (2010). Cardiovascular disease and androgens: A review. *International Journal of Cardiology, 142*, 8–14.

Kavanaugh, Robert D. (2011). Origins and consequences of social pretend play. In Anthony D. Pellegrini (Ed.), *The Oxford handbook of the development of play* (pp. 296–307). New York, NY: Oxford University Press.

Keating, Daniel P. (2004). Cognitive and brain development. In Richard M. Lerner & Laurence D. Steinberg (Eds.), *Handbook of adolescent psychology* (2nd ed., pp. 45–84). Hoboken, NJ: Wiley.

Keating, Nancy L., Herrinton, Lisa J., Zaslavsky, Alan M., Liu, Liyan, & Ayanian, John Z. (2006). Variations in hospice use among cancer patients. *Journal of the National Cancer Institute, 98*, 1053–1059.

Kegel, Cornelia A. T., Bus, Adriana G., & van IJzendoorn, Marinus H. (2011). Differential susceptibility in early literacy instruction through computer games: The role of the dopamine D4 receptor gene (DRD4). *Mind, Brain, and Education, 5*, 71–78.

Keil, Frank C. (2011, February 25). Science starts early. *Science, 331*, 1022–1023.

Kelemen, Deborah, Callanan, Maureen A., Casler, Krista, & Perez-Granados, Deanne R. (2005). Why things happen: Teleological explanation in parent-child conversation. *Developmental Psychology, 41*, 251–264.

Kellehear, Allan. (2008). Dying as a social relationship: A sociological review of debates on the determination of death. *Social Science & Medicine, 66*, 1533–1544.

Kellehear, Allan, & Ritchie, David. (2003). *Seven dying Australians.* Bendigo, Victoria, Australia: St. Luke's Innovative Resources.

Keller, Heidi, Borke, Jörn, Chaudhary, Nandita, Lamm, Bettina, & Kleis, Astrid. (2010). Continuity in parenting strategies: A cross-cultural comparison. *Journal of Cross-Cultural Psychology, 41*, 391–409.

Keller, Heidi, & Otto, Hiltrud. (2011). Different faces of autonomy. In Xinyin Chen & Kenneth H. Rubin (Eds.), *Socioemotional development in cultural context* (pp. 164–185). New York, NY: Guilford Press.

Keller, Heidi, Yovsi, Relindis, Borke, Joern, Kärtner, Joscha, Jensen, Henning, & Papaligoura, Zaira. (2004). Developmental consequences of early parenting experiences: Self-recognition and self-regulation in three cultural communities. *Child Development, 75*, 1745–1760.

Kelley, Susan J., & Whitley, Deborah M. (2003). Psychological distress and physical health problems in grandparents raising grandchildren: Development of an empirically-based intervention model. In Bert Hayslip, Jr., & Julie Hicks Patrick (Eds.), *Working with custodial grandparents* (pp. 127–144). New York, NY: Springer.

Kellman, Philip J., & Arterberry, Martha E. (2006). Infant visual perception. In William Damon & Richard M. Lerner (Series Eds.) & Deanna Kuhn & Robert S. Siegler (Vol. Eds.), *Handbook of child psychology: Vol. 2. Cognition, perception, and language* (6th ed., pp. 109–160). Hoboken, NJ: Wiley.

Kelly, Daniel, Faucher, Luc, & Machery, Edouard. (2010). Getting rid of racism: Assessing three proposals in light of psychological evidence. *Journal of Social Philosophy, 41*, 293–322.

Kelly, John R. (Ed.) (1993). *Activity and aging: Staying involved in later life.* Newbury Park, CA: Sage.

Kemp, Candace L. (2005). Dimensions of grandparent-adult grandchild relationships: From family ties to intergenerational friendships. *Canadian Journal on Aging, 24*, 161–177.

Kempe, Ruth S., & Kempe, C. Henry. (1978). *Child abuse.* Cambridge, MA: Harvard University Press.

Kemple, James J. (with Cynthia J. Willner). (2008). *Career academies: Long-term impacts on labor market outcomes, educational attainment, and transitions to adulthood.* New York, NY: MDRC.

Kempner, Joanna, Perlis, Clifford S., & Merz, Jon F. (2005, February 11). Forbidden knowledge. *Science, 307*, 854.

Kendler, Kenneth S., Eaves, Lindon J., Loken, Erik K., Pedersen, Nancy L., Middeldorp, Christel M., Reynolds, Chandra, ... Gardner, Charles O. (2011). The impact of environmental experiences on symptoms of anxiety and depression across the life span. *Psychological Science, 22*, 1343–1352.

Kennedy, Quinn, Taylor, Joy L., Reade, Gordon, & Yesavage, Jerome A. (2010). Age and expertise effects in aviation decision making and flight control in a flight simulator. *Aviation, Space, and Environmental Medicine, 81*, 489–497.

Kennedy, Sheela, & Bumpass, Larry. (2008). Cohabitation and children's living arrangements: New estimates from the United States. *Demographic Research, 19*, 1663–1692.

Kéri, Szabolcs. (2009). Genes for psychosis and creativity. *Psychological Science, 20*, 1070–1073.

Kerns, Kathryn A., Brumariu, Laura E., & Seibert, Ashley. (2011). Multi-method assessment of mother-child attachment: Links to parenting and child depressive symptoms in middle childhood. *Attachment & Human Development, 13*, 315–333.

Kerr, Margaret, Stattin, Håkan, & Burk, William J. (2010). A reinterpretation of parental monitoring in longitudinal perspective. *Journal of Research on Adolescence, 20*, 39–64.

Kesselring, Thomas, & Müller, Ulrich. (2011). The concept of egocentrism in the context of Piaget's theory. *New Ideas in Psychology, 29*, 327–345.

Kessler, Ronald C., Amminger, G. Paul, Aguilar-Gaxiola, Sergio, Alonso, Jordi, Lee, Sing, & Üstün, T. Bedirhan. (2007). Age of onset of mental disorders: A review of recent literature. *Current Opinion in Psychiatry, 20*, 359–364.

Kettl, Paul. (2010). One vote for death panels. *Journal of the American Medical Association, 303*, 1234–1235.

Keysers, Christian, & Gazzola, Valeria. (2010). Social neuroscience: Mirror neurons recorded in humans. *Current Biology, 20*, R353–R354.

Khaleque, Abdul, & Rohner, Ronald P. (2002). Perceived parental acceptance-rejection and psychological adjustment: A meta-analysis of cross-cultural and intracultural studies. *Journal of Marriage & the Family, 64*, 54–64.

Khan, Laura Kettel, Sobush, Kathleen, Keener, Dana, Goodman, Kenneth, Lowry, Amy, Kakietek, Jakub, & Zaro, Susan. (2009, July 24). Recommended community strategies and measurements to prevent obesity in the United States. *Morbidity and Mortality Weekly Report Recommendations and Reports, 58*(RR07), 1–26.

Khoury-Kassabri, Mona. (2009). The relationship between staff maltreatment of students and bully-victim group membership. *Child Abuse & Neglect: The International Journal, 33*, 914–923.

Kiang, Lisa, & Harter, Susan. (2008). Do pieces of the self-puzzle fit? Integrated/fragmented selves in biculturally-identified Chinese Americans. *Journal of Research in Personality, 42*, 1657–1662.

Kiang, Lisa, Witkow, Melissa, Baldelomar, Oscar, & Fuligni, Andrew. (2010). Change in ethnic identity across the high school years among adolescents with Latin American, Asian, and European backgrounds. *Journal of Youth and Adolescence, 39*, 683–693.

Kiernan, Stephen P. (2010). The transformation of death in America. In Nan Bauer Maglin & Donna Marie Perry (Eds.), *Final acts: Death, dying, and the choices we make* (pp. 163–182). New Brunswick, NJ: Rutgers University Press.

Killen, Melanie. (2007). Children's social and moral reasoning about exclusion. *Current Directions in Psychological Science, 16*, 32–36.

Killen, Melanie, Lee-Kim, Jennie, McGlothlin, Heidi, & Stangor, Charles. (2002). How children and adolescents evaluate gender and racial exclusion. *Monographs of the Society for Research in Child Development, 67*(4, Serial No. 271).

Killen, Melanie, Margie, Nancy Geyelin, & Sinno, Stefanie. (2006). Morality in the context of intergroup relationships. In Melanie Killen & Judith G. Smetana (Eds.), *Handbook of moral development* (pp. 155–183). Mahwah, NJ: Erlbaum.

Killen, Melanie, & Smetana, Judith. (2007). The biology of morality: Human development and moral neuroscience. *Human Development, 50*, 241–243.

Killgore, William D. S., Vo, Alexander H., Castro, Carl A., & Hoge, Charles W. (2006). Assessing risk propensity in American soldiers: Preliminary reliability and validity of the Evaluation of Risks (EVAR) scale—English version. *Military Medicine, 171*, 233–239.

Kilmer, Ryan P., & Gil-Rivas, Virginia. (2010). Exploring posttraumatic growth in children impacted by Hurricane Katrina: Correlates of the phenomenon and developmental considerations. *Child Development, 81*, 1211–1227.

Kim, Dong-Sik, & Kim, Hyun-Sun. (2009). Body-image dissatisfaction as a predictor of suicidal ideation among Korean boys and girls in different stages of adolescence: A two-year longitudinal study. *The Journal of Adolescent Health, 45*, 47–54.

Kim, Esther Chihye. (2009). "Mama's family": Fictive kinship and undocumented immigrant restaurant workers. *Ethnography, 10*, 497–513.

Kim, Hyoun K., Laurent, Heidemarie K., Capaldi, Deborah M., & Feingold, Alan. (2008). Men's aggression toward women: A 10-year panel study. *Journal of Marriage and Family, 70*, 1169–1187.

Kim, Hyun Sik. (2011). Consequences of parental divorce for child development. *American Sociological Review, 76*, 487–511.

Kim, Heejung S., & Chu, Thai Q. (2011). Cultural variation in the motivation of self-expression. In David Dunning (Ed.), *Social motivation* (pp. 57–78). New York, NY: Psychology Press.

Kim, Heejung S., Sherman, David K., & Taylor, Shelley E. (2008). Culture and social support. *American Psychologist, 63*, 518–526.

Kim, Joon Sik. (2011). Excessive crying: Behavioral and emotional regulation disorder in infancy. *Korean Journal of Pediatrics, 54*, 229–233.

Kim-Cohen, Julia, Moffitt, Terrie E., Caspi, Avshalom, & Taylor, Alan. (2004). Genetic and environmental processes in young children's resilience and vulnerability to socioeconomic deprivation. *Child Development, 75*, 651–668.

Kimbro, Rachel Tolbert, Brooks-Gunn, Jeanne, & McLanahan, Sara. (2011). Young children in urban areas: Links among neighborhood characteristics, weight status, outdoor play, and television watching. *Social Science & Medicine, 72,* 668–676.

King, Pamela Ebstyne, & Roeser, Robert W. (2009). Religion and spirituality in adolescent development. In Richard M. Lerner & Laurence Steinberg (Eds.), *Handbook of adolescent psychology: Vol. 1. Individual bases of adolescent development* (3rd ed., pp. 435–478). Hoboken, NJ: Wiley.

King, Sara, Waschbusch, Daniel A., Pelham, William E., Frankland, Bradley W., Corkum, Penny V., & Jacques, Sophie. (2009). Subtypes of aggression in children with attention deficit hyperactivity disorder: Medication effects and comparison with typical children. *Journal of Clinical Child and Adolescent Psychology, 38,* 619–629.

Kinnear, Karen L. (2007). *Childhood sexual abuse: A reference handbook* (2nd ed.). Santa Barbara, CA: ABC-CLIO.

Kinney, Hannah C., & Thach, Bradley T. (2009). The sudden infant death syndrome. *New England Journal of Medicine, 361,* 795–805.

Kinnunen, Marja-Liisa, Kaprio, Jaakko, & Pulkkinen, Lea. (2005). Allostatic load of men and women in early middle age. *Journal of Individual Differences, 26,* 20–28.

Kirby, Douglas, & Laris, B. A. (2009). Effective curriculum-based sex and STD/HIV education programs for adolescents. *Child Development Perspectives, 3,* 21–29.

Kirby, Matthew, Maggi, Stefania, & D'Angiulli, Amedeo. (2011). School start times and the sleep–wake cycle of adolescents. *Educational Researcher, 40,* 56–61.

Kirkorian, Heather L., Pempek, Tiffany A., Murphy, Lauren A., Schmidt, Marie E., & Anderson, Daniel R. (2009). The impact of background television on parent–child interaction. *Child Development, 80,* 1350–1359.

Kiuru, Noona, Burk, William J., Laursen, Brett, Salmela-Aro, Katariina, & Nurmi, Jari-Erik. (2010). Pressure to drink but not to smoke: Disentangling selection and socialization in adolescent peer networks and peer groups. *Journal of Adolescence, 33,* 801–812.

Klaczynski, Paul, Daniel, David B., & Keller, Peggy S. (2009). Appearance idealization, body esteem, causal attributions, and ethnic variations in the development of obesity stereotypes. *Journal of Applied Developmental Psychology, 30,* 537–551.

Klaczynski, Paul A. (2001). Analytic and heuristic processing influences on adolescent reasoning and decision-making. *Child Development, 72,* 844–861.

Klaczynski, Paul A. (2011). Age differences in understanding precedent-setting decisions and authorities' responses to violations of deontic rules. *Journal of Experimental Child Psychology, 109,* 1–24.

Klahr, Ashlea M., McGue, Matt, Iacono, William G., & Burt, S. Alexandra. (2011). The association between parent-child conflict and adolescent conduct problems over time: Results from a longitudinal adoption study. *Journal of Abnormal Psychology, 120,* 46–56.

Klatsky, Arthur L. (2009). Alcohol and cardiovascular diseases. *Expert Review of Cardiovascular Therapy, 7,* 499–506.

Klaus, Marshall H., & Kennell, John H. (1976). *Maternal-infant bonding: The impact of early separation or loss on family development.* St. Louis, MO: Mosby.

Klaus, Patsy. (2005). *Crimes against persons age 65 or older, 1993–2002* (NCJ 206154). Washington, DC: Bureau of Justice Statistics.

Klaus, Susan F., Ekerdt, David J., & Gajewski, Byron. (2012). Job satisfaction in birth cohorts of nurses. *Journal of Nursing Management, 20,* 461–471.

Klimstra, Theo A., Hale, William W., III, Raaijmakers, Quinten A. W., Branje, Susan J. T., & Meeus, Wim H. J. (2009). Maturation of personality in adolescence. *Journal of Personality and Social Psychology, 96,* 898–912.

Kline, Kathleen Kovner. (Ed.) (2008). *Authoritative communities: The scientific case for nurturing the whole child.* New York, NY: Springer.

Koch, Tom. (2000). *Age speaks for itself: Silent voices of the elderly.* Westport, CT: Praeger.

Kochanska, Grazyna, Aksan, Nazan, Prisco, Theresa R., & Adams, Erin E. (2008). Mother-child and father-child mutually responsive orientation in the first 2 years and children's outcomes at preschool age: Mechanisms of influence. *Child Development, 79,* 30–44.

Kochanska, Grazyna, Barry, Robin A., Jimenez, Natasha B., Hollatz, Amanda L., & Woodard, Jarilyn. (2009). Guilt and effortful control: Two mechanisms that prevent disruptive developmental trajectories. *Journal of Personality and Social Psychology, 97,* 322–333.

Kohlberg, Lawrence. (1963). The development of children's orientations toward a moral order: I. Sequence in the development of moral thought. *Vita Humana, 6,* 11–33.

Kohlberg, Lawrence, Levine, Charles, & Hewer, Alexandra. (1983). *Moral stages: A current formulation and a response to critics.* New York, NY: Karger.

Kohn, Alfie. (2001). Fighting the tests: A practical guide to rescuing our schools. *Phi Delta Kappan, 82,* 348–357.

Kohyama, Jun, Mindell, Jodi A., & Sadeh, Avi. (2011). Sleep characteristics of young children in Japan: Internet study and comparison with other Asian countries. *Pediatrics International, 53,* 649–655.

Kolb, Bryan, & Whishaw, Ian Q. (2008). *Fundamentals of human neuropsychology* (6th ed.). New York, NY: Worth.

Koltko-Rivera, Mark E. (2006). Rediscovering the later version of Maslow's hierarchy of needs: Self-transcendence and opportunities for theory, research, and unification. *Review of General Psychology, 10,* 302–317.

Konner, Melvin. (2007). Evolutionary foundations of cultural psychology. In Shinobu Kitayama & Dov Cohen (Eds.), *Handbook of cultural psychology* (pp. 77–105). New York, NY: Guilford Press.

Konner, Melvin. (2010). *The evolution of childhood: Relationships, emotion, mind.* Cambridge, MA: Harvard University Press.

Kooij, Dorien T. A. M., Annet, H. D. E., Lange, Paul G. W., Jansen, Ruth Kanfer, & Dikkers, Josje S. E. (2011). Age and work-related motives: Results of a meta-analysis. *Journal of Organizational Behavior, 225,* 197–225.

Kopp, Claire B. (2011). Development in the early years: Socialization, motor development, and consciousness. *Annual Review of Psychology, 62,* 165–187.

Koppen, Jean. (2009). *Effect of the economy on housing choices.* Washington, DC: AARP.

Koretz, Daniel. (2009, November 6). Moving past No Child Left Behind. *Science, 326,* 803–804.

Kossowsky, Joe, Wilhelm, Frank H., Roth, Walton T., & Schneider, Silvia. (2012). Separation anxiety disorder in children: Disorder-specific responses to experimental separation from the mother. *Journal of Child Psychology and Psychiatry, 53,* 178–187.

Kovacs, Maria, Joormann, Jutta, & Gotlib, Ian H. (2008). Emotion (dys)regulation and links to depressive disorders. *Child Development Perspectives, 2,* 149–155.

Kovas, Yulia, Hayiou-Thomas, Marianna E., Oliver, Bonamy, Dale, Philip S., Bishop, Dorothy V. M., & Plomin, Robert. (2005). Genetic influences in different aspects of language development: The etiology of language skills in 4.5-year-old twins. *Child Development, 76,* 632–651.

Kramer, Arthur F., & Erickson, Kirk I. (2007). Capitalizing on cortical plasticity: Influence of physical activity on cognition and brain function. *Trends in Cognitive Sciences, 11,* 342–348.

Kramer, Arthur F., Fabiani, Monica, & Colcombe, Stanley J. (2006). Contributions of cognitive neuroscience to the understanding of behavior and aging. In James E. Birren & K. Warner Schaie (Eds.), *Handbook of the psychology of aging* (6th ed., pp. 57–83). Amsterdam, The Netherlands: Elsevier.

Krampe, Ralf Th., Schaefer, Sabine, Lindenberger, Ulman, & Baltes, Paul B. (2011). Lifespan changes in multitasking: Concurrent walking and memory search in children, young, and older adults. *Gait & Posture, 33,* 401–405.

Krause, Neal. (2006). Social relationships in late life. In Robert H. Binstock & Linda K. George (Eds.), *Handbook of aging and the social sciences* (6th ed., pp. 181–200). Amsterdam, The Netherlands: Elsevier.

Krebs, Dennis L. (2008). Morality: An evolutionary account. *Perspectives on Psychological Science, 3,* 149–172.

Krebs, John R. (2009). The gourmet ape: Evolution and human food preferences [Keynote address]. *American Journal of Clinical Nutrition, 90,* 707S–711S. doi:10.3945/ajcn.2009.27462B

Krenk, Lene, Rasmussen, Lars S., Siersma, Volkert D., & Kehlet, Henrik. (2012). Short-term practice effects and variability in cognitive testing in a healthy elderly population. *Experimental Gerontology, 47,* 432–436.

Krieger, Nancy. (2002). Is breast cancer a disease of affluence, poverty, or both? The case of African American women. *American Journal of Public Health, 92,* 611–613.

Krieger, Nancy. (2003). Does racism harm health? Did child abuse exist before 1962? On explicit questions, critical science, and current controversies: An ecosocial perspective. *American Journal of Public Health, 93,* 194–199.

Kröger, Edeltraut, Andel, Ross, Lindsay, Joan, Benounissa, Zohra, Verreault, René, & Laurin, Danielle. (2008). Is complexity of work associated with risk of dementia?

The Canadian Study of Health and Aging. *American Journal of Epidemiology, 167,* 820–830.

Kroger, Jane. (2007). *Identity development: Adolescence through adulthood* (2nd ed.). Thousand Oaks, CA: Sage.

Kroger, Jane, Martinussen, Monica, & Marcia, James E. (2010). Identity status change during adolescence and young adulthood: A meta-analysis. *Journal of Adolescence, 33,* 683–698.

Kronenberg, Mindy E., Hansel, Tonya Cross, Brennan, Adrianne M., Osofsky, Howard J., Osofsky, Joy D., & Lawrason, Beverly. (2010). Children of Katrina: Lessons learned about postdisaster symptoms and recovery patterns. *Child Development, 81,* 1241–1259.

Kruger, Daniel J., & Polanski, Stephen P. (2011). Sex differences in mortality rates have increased in China following the single-child law. *Letters on Evolutionary Behavioral Science, 2,* 1–4.

Kryzer, Erin M., Kovan, Nikki, Phillips, Deborah A., Domagall, Lindsey A., & Gunnar, Megan R. (2007). Toddlers' and preschoolers' experience in family day care: Age differences and behavioral correlates. *Early Childhood Research Quarterly, 22,* 451–466.

Kübler-Ross, Elisabeth. (1969). *On death and dying.* New York, NY: Macmillan.

Kübler-Ross, Elisabeth (Ed.). (1975). *Death: The final stage of growth.* Englewood Cliffs, NJ: Prentice-Hall.

Kuczmarski, R. J., Ogden, C. L., Guo, S. S., et al. (2002). 2000 CDC growth charts for the United States: Methods and development. National Center for Health Statistics, *Vital Health Statistics, 11*(246). Retrieved from: http://www.cdc.gov/growthcharts/zscore.htm

Kuehn, Bridget M. (2011). Scientists find promising therapies for fragile X and Down syndromes. *The Journal of the American Medical Association, 305,* 344–346.

Kuh, George D., Gonyea, Robert M., & Williams, Julie M. (2005). What students expect from college and what they get. In Thomas E. Miller, Barbara E. Bender, John H. Schuh, & Associates (Eds.), *Promoting reasonable expectations: Aligning student and institutional views of the college experience* (pp. 34–64). San Francisco, CA: Jossey-Bass.

Kuhlmann, Inga, Minihane, Anne, Huebbe, Patricia, Nebel, Almut, & Rimbach, Gerald. (2010). Apolipoprotein E genotype and hepatitis C, HIV and herpes simplex disease risk: A literature review. *Lipids in Health and Disease, 9,* 8.

Kuhn, Deanna, & Franklin, Sam. (2006). The second decade: What develops (and how). In William Damon & Richard M. Lerner (Series Eds.) & Deanna Kuhn & Robert Siegler (Vol. Eds.), *Handbook of child psychology: Vol. 2. Cognition, perception, and language* (6th ed., pp. 953–993). Hoboken, NJ: Wiley.

Kuhn, Louise, Sinkala, Moses, Thea, Don, Kankasa, Chipepo, & Aldrovandi, Grace. (2009). HIV prevention is not enough: Child survival in the context of prevention of mother to child HIV transmission. *Journal of the International AIDS Society, 12,* 36.

Kumar, Santosh, Calvo, Rocio, Avendano, Mauricio, Sivaramakrishnan, Kavita, & Berkman, Lisa F. (2012). Social support, volunteering and health around the world:

Cross-national evidence from 139 countries. *Social Science & Medicine, 74,* 696–706.

Kun, Jürgen F. J., May, Jürgen, & Noedl, Harald. (2010). Surveillance of malaria drug resistance: Improvement needed? *Future Medicine, 7,* 3–6.

Kuo, Hsu-Ko, Leveille, Suzanne G., Yu, Yau-Hua, & Milber, William P. (2007). Cognitive function, habitual gait speed, and late-life disability in the National Health and Nutrition Examination Survey (NHANES) 1999–2002. *Gerontology, 53,* 102–110.

Kuperberg, Arielle. (2012). Reassessing differences in work and income in cohabitation and marriage. *Journal of Marriage and Family, 74,* 688–707.

Kuppens, Sofie, Grietens, Hans, Onghena, Patrick, & Michiels, Daisy. (2009). Associations between parental control and children's overt and relational aggression. *British Journal of Developmental Psychology, 27,* 607–623.

Kutob, Randa M., Senf, Janet H., Crago, Marjorie, & Shisslak, Catherine M. (2010). Concurrent and longitudinal predictors of self-esteem in elementary and middle school girls. *Journal of School Health, 80,* 240–248.

LaBar, Kevin S. (2007). Beyond fear: Emotional memory mechanisms in the human brain. *Current Directions in Psychological Science, 16,* 173–177.

Labouvie-Vief, Gisela. (1990). Wisdom as integrated thought: Historical and developmental perspectives. In Robert J. Sternberg (Ed.), *Wisdom: Its nature, origins, and development* (pp. 52–83). Cambridge, England: Cambridge University Press.

Labouvie-Vief, Gisela, Grühn, Daniel, & Mouras, Harold. (2009). Dynamic emotion-cognition interactions in adult development: Arousal, stress, and the processing of affect. In Hayden B. Bosworth & Christopher Hertzog (Eds.), *Aging and cognition: Research methodologies and empirical advances* (pp. 181–196). Washington, DC: American Psychological Association.

Lachman, Margie E., & Bertrand, Rosanna M. (2001). Personality and the self in midlife. In Margie E. Lachman (Ed.), *Handbook of midlife development* (pp. 279–309). New York, NY: Wiley.

Lachman, Margie E., Neupert, Shevaun D., & Agrigoroaei, Stefan. (2011). The relevance of control beliefs for health and aging. In K. Warner Schaie & Sherry L. Willis (Eds.), *Handbook of the psychology of aging* (7th ed., pp. 175–190). Boston, MA: Elsevier/Academic Press.

Lachman, Margie E., Rosnick, Christopher B., & Röcke, Christina. (2009). The rise and fall of control beliefs and life satisfaction in adulthood: Trajectories of stability and change over ten years. In H. B. Bosworth & C. Hertzog (Eds.), *Aging and cognition: Research methodologies and empirical advances* (pp. 143–160). Washington, DC: American Psychological Association.

LaFontana, Kathryn M., & Cillessen, Antonius H. N. (2010). Developmental changes in the priority of perceived status in childhood and adolescence. *Social Development, 19,* 130–147.

Laible, Deborah, Panfile, Tia, & Makariev, Drika. (2008). The quality and frequency of mother-toddler conflict: Links with attachment and temperament. *Child Development, 79,* 426–443.

Lalande, Kathleen M., & Bonanno, George A. (2006). Culture and continuing bonds: A prospective comparison of bereavement in the United States and the People's Republic of China. *Death Studies, 30,* 303–324.

Lam, Raymond W. (2012). *Depression* (2nd ed.). Oxford, UK: Oxford University Press.

Lamb, Michael E. (1982). Maternal employment and child development: A review. In Michael E. Lamb (Ed.), *Nontraditional families: Parenting and child development* (pp. 45–69). Hillsdale, NJ: Erlbaum.

Lamb, Michael E. (Ed.). (2010). *The role of the father in child development* (5th ed.). Hoboken, NJ: Wiley.

Lambert, Nathaniel M., Fincham, Frank D., Stillman, Tyler F., Graham, Steven M., & Beach, Steven R. H. (2010). Motivating change in relationships. *Psychological Science, 21,* 126–132.

Landis, Story, & Insel, Thomas R. (2008, November 7). The "neuro" in neurogenetics. *Science, 322,* 821.

Landy, Frank J., & Conte, Jeffrey M. (2007). *Work in the 21st century: An introduction to industrial and organizational psychology* (2nd ed.). Malden, MA: Blackwell.

Lane, Rachel F., Shineman, Diana W., & Fillit, Howard M. (2011). Beyond amyloid: A diverse portfolio of novel drug discovery programs for Alzheimer's disease and related dementias. *Alzheimer's Research & Therapy, 3,* 36.

Lane, Scott D., Cherek, Don R., Pietras, Cynthia J., & Steinberg, Joel L. (2005). Performance of heavy marijuana-smoking adolescents on a laboratory measure of motivation. *Addictive Behaviors, 30,* 815–828.

Lang, Frieder R., Wagner, Jenny, & Neyer, Franz J. (2009). Interpersonal functioning across the lifespan: Two principles of relationship regulation. *Advances in Life Course Research, 14,* 40–51.

Langenkamp, Amy G. (2010). Academic vulnerability and resilience during the transition to high school. *Sociology of Education, 83,* 1–19.

Långström, Niklas, Rahman, Qazi, Carlström, Eva, & Lichtenstein, Paul. (2010). Genetic and environmental effects on same-sex sexual behavior: A population study of twins in Sweden. *Archives of Sexual Behavior, 39,* 75–80.

Lara, Marielena, Akinbami, Lara, Flores, Glenn, & Morgenstern, Hal. (2006). Heterogeneity of childhood asthma among Hispanic children: Puerto Rican children bear a disproportionate burden. *Pediatrics, 117,* 43–53.

Lara-Cinisomo, Sandraluz, Fuligni, Allison Sidle, & Karoly, Lynn A. (2011). Preparing preschoolers for kindergarten. In DeAnna M. Laverick & Mary Renck Jalongo (Eds.), *Transitions to early care and education* (Vol. 4, pp. 93–105). New York, NY: Springer.

Laraway, Kelly A., Birch, Leann L., Shaffer, Michele L., & Paul, Ian M. (2010). Parent perception of healthy infant and toddler growth. *Clinical Pediatrics, 49,* 343–349.

Larson, Nicole I., Neumark-Sztainer, Dianne, Hannan, Peter J., & Story, Mary. (2007). Trends in adolescent fruit and vegetable consumption, 1999–2004: Project EAT. *American Journal of Preventive Medicine, 32,* 147–150.

Larson, Reed, & Wilson, Suzanne. (2004). Adolescence across place and time: Globalization and the changing pathways to adulthood. In Richard M. Lerner & Laurence D. Steinberg (Eds.), *Handbook of adolescent psychology* (2nd ed., pp. 299–330). Hoboken, NJ: Wiley.

Larzelere, Robert, Cox, Ronald, & Smith, Gail. (2010). Do nonphysical punishments reduce antisocial behavior more than spanking? A comparison using the strongest previous causal evidence against spanking. *BMC Pediatrics, 10,* 10.

Lassiter, G. Daniel, & Meissner, Christian A. (Eds.). (2010). *Police interrogations and false confessions: Current research, practice, and policy recommendations.* Washington, DC: American Psychological Association.

Laumann, Edward O., & Michael, Robert T. (Eds.) (2000). *Sex, love, and health in America: Private choices and public policies.* Chicago, IL: University of Chicago Press.

Laurino, Mercy Y., Bennett, Robin L., Saraiya, Devki S., Baumeister, Lisa, Doyle, Debra Lochner, Leppig, Kathleen,... Raskind, Wendy H. (2005). Genetic evaluation and counseling of couples with recurrent miscarriage: Recommendations of the National Society of Genetic Counselors. *Journal of Genetic Counseling, 14,* 165–181.

Laursen, Brett, Bukowski, William M., Nurmi, Jari-Eri, Marion, Donna, Salmela-Aro, Katariina, & Kiuru, Noona. (2010). Opposites detract: Middle school peer group antipathies. *Journal of Experimental Child Psychology, 106,* 240–256.

Laursen, Brett, & Collins, W. Andrew. (2009). Parent-child relationships during adolescence. In Richard M. Lerner & Laurence Steinberg (Eds.), *Handbook of adolescent psychology: Vol. 2. Contextual influences on adolescent development* (3rd ed., pp. 3–42). Hoboken, NJ: Wiley.

Laursen, Brett, & Mooney, Karen S. (2007). Individual differences in adolescent dating and adjustment. In Rutger C. M. E. Engels, Margaret Kerr, & Håkan Stattin (Eds.), *Friends, lovers, and groups: Key relationships in adolescence* (pp. 81–92). Hoboken, NJ: Wiley.

Lavelli, Manuela, & Fogel, Alan. (2005). Developmental changes in the relationship between the infant's attention and emotion during early face-to-face communication: The 2-month transition. *Developmental Psychology, 41,* 265–280.

Layden, Tim. (2004, November 15). Get out and play! *Sports Illustrated, 101,* 80–93.

Leach, Penelope. (1997). *Your baby & child: From birth to age five* (3rd ed.). New York, NY: Knopf.

Leach, Penelope. (2009). *Child care today: Getting it right for everyone.* New York, NY: Knopf.

Leadbeater, Bonnie J., & Hoglund, Wendy L. G. (2009). The effects of peer victimization and physical aggression on changes in internalizing from first to third grade. *Child Development, 80,* 843–859.

LeBlanc, Manon Mireille, & Barling, Julian. (2004). Workplace aggression. *Current Directions in Psychological Science, 13,* 9–12.

Lee, Eunju, Spitze, Glenna, & Logan, John R. (2003). Social support to parents-in-law: The interplay of gender and kin hierarchies. *Journal of Marriage and Family, 65,* 396–403.

Lee, Hee Yun, Gibson, Priscilla, & Chaisson, Rebecca. (2011). Elderly Korean immigrants' socially and culturally constructed definitions of elder neglect. *Journal of Aging Studies, 25,* 126–134.

Lee, I-Min, Ewing, Reid, & Sesso, Howard D. (2009). The built environment and physical activity levels: The Harvard Alumni Health Study. *American Journal of Preventive Medicine, 37,* 293–298.

Lee, Jennifer, & Bean, Frank D. (2007). Reinventing the color line: Immigration and America's new racial/ethnic divide. *Social Forces, 86,* 561–586.

Lee, Joyce M., Kaciroti, Niko, Appugliese, Danielle, Corwyn, Robert F., Bradley, Robert H., & Lumeng, Julie C. (2010). Body mass index and timing of pubertal initiation in boys. *Archives of Pediatric and Adolescent Medicine, 164,* 139–144.

Lee, Kristen Schultz, & Ono, Hiroshi. (2012). Marriage, cohabitation, and happiness: A cross-national analysis of 27 countries. *Journal of Marriage and Family, 74,* 953–972.

Lee, Soojeong, & Shouse, Roger C. (2011). The impact of prestige orientation on shadow education in South Korea. *Sociology of Education, 84,* 212–224.

Lee, Sei J., Steinman, Michael A., & Tan, Erwin J. (2011). Volunteering, driving status, and mortality in U.S. retirees. *Journal of the American Geriatrics Society, 59,* 274–280.

Lefkowitz, Eva S., & Gillen, Meghan M. (2006). "Sex is just a normal part of life": Sexuality in emerging adulthood. In Jeffrey Jensen Arnett & Jennifer Lynn Tanner (Eds.), *Emerging adults in America: Coming of age in the 21st century* (pp. 235–255). Washington, DC: American Psychological Association.

Leman, Patrick J., & Björnberg, Marina. (2010). Conversation, development, and gender: A study of changes in children's concepts of punishment. *Child Development, 81,* 958–971.

Leopold, Thomas. (2012). The legacy of leaving home: Long-term effects of coresidence on parent–child relationships. *Journal of Marriage and Family, 74,* 399–412.

Lepper, Mark R., Greene, David, & Nisbett, Richard E. (1973). Undermining children's intrinsic interest with extrinsic reward: A test of the "overjustification" hypothesis. *Journal of Personality & Social Psychology, 28,* 129–137.

Lerner, Claire, & Dombro, Amy Laura. (2004). Finding your fit: Some temperament tips for parents. *Zero to Three, 24,* 42–45.

Lerner, Richard M. (Ed.). (2010). *The handbook of life-span development* (Vol. 1–2). Hoboken, NJ: Wiley.

Lesane-Brown, Chase L., Brown, Tony N., Tanner-Smith, Emily E., & Bruce, Marino A. (2010). Negotiating boundaries and bonds: Frequency of young children's socialization to their ethnic/racial heritage. *Journal of Cross-Cultural Psychology, 41,* 457–464.

Leslie, Mitch. (2012, March 23). Gut microbes keep rare immune cells in line. *Science, 335,* 1428.

Lester, Patricia, Leskin, Gregory, Woodward, Kirsten, Saltzman, William, Nash, William, Mogil, Catherine,... Beardslee, William. (2011). Wartime deployment and military children: Applying prevention science to enhance family resilience. In Shelley MacDermid & David S. Riggs (Eds.), *Risk and resilience in U.S. military families* (pp. 149–174). New York, NY: Springer.

Levinson, Daniel J. (1978). *The seasons of a man's life.* New York, NY: Knopf.

Levy, Becca. (2009). Stereotype embodiment: A psychosocial approach to aging. *Current Directions in Psychological Science, 18,* 332–336.

Levy, Becca, & Langer, Ellen. (1994). Aging free from negative stereotypes: Successful memory in China among the American deaf. *Journal of Personality & Social Psychology, 66,* 989–997.

Lewallen, Lynne Porter. (2011). The importance of culture in childbearing. *Journal of Obstetric, Gynecologic, & Neonatal Nursing, 40,* 4–8.

Lewin, Kurt. (1943). Psychology and the process of group living. *Journal of Social Psychology, 17,* 113–131.

Lewin-Benham, Ann. (2008). *Powerful children: Understanding how to teach and learn using the Reggio approach.* New York, NY: Teachers College Press.

Lewis, Charlotte W., Linsenmayer, Kristi A., & Williams, Alexis. (2010). Wanting better: A qualitative study of low-income parents about their children's oral health. *Pediatric Dentistry, 32,* 518–524.

Lewis, Kristen, & Burd-Sharps, Sarah. (2010). *The measure of America 2010–2011: Mapping risks and resilience.* New York, NY: New York University Press.

Lewis, Michael. (2011). Inside and outside: The relation between emotional states and expressions. *Emotion Review, 3,* 189–196.

Lewis, Michael, & Brooks, Jeanne. (1978). Self-knowledge and emotional development. In Michael Lewis & L. A. Rosenblum (Eds.), *Genesis of behavior: Vol. 1. The development of affect* (pp. 205–226). New York, NY: Plenum Press.

Lewis, Michael, & Kestler, Lisa. (Eds.) (2012). *Gender differences in prenatal substance exposure.* Washington, DC: American Psychological Association.

Lewis, Michael, & Ramsay, Douglas. (2005). Infant emotional and cortisol responses to goal blockage. *Child Development, 76,* 518–530.

Lewis, Sam, & Ariyachandra, Thilini. (2011). Seniors and social networking. *Journal of Information Systems Applied Research, 4,* 4–18.

Lewkowicz, David J. (2010). Infant perception of audio-visual speech synchrony. *Developmental Psychology, 46,* 66–77.

Li, Qing, & Keith, Louis G. (2011). The differential association between education and infant mortality by nativity status of Chinese American mothers: A life-course perspective. *American Journal of Public Health, 101,* 899–908.

Li, Tianyuan, & Chan, Darius K. S. (2012). How anxious and avoidant attachment affect romantic relationship quality differently: A meta-analytic review. *European Journal of Social Psychology, 42,* 406–419.

Li, Yibing, & Lerner, Richard M. (2011). Trajectories of school engagement during adolescence: Implications for grades, depression, delinquency, and substance use. *Developmental Psychology, 47,* 233–247.

Li, Zhaoping, Maglione, Margaret, Tu, Wenli, Mojica, Walter, Arterburn, David, Shugarman, Lisa R., ... Morton, Sally C. (2005). Meta-analysis: Pharmacologic treatment of obesity. *Annals of Internal Medicine, 142,* 532–546.

Libertus, Klaus, & Needham, Amy. (2010). Teach to reach: The effects of active vs. passive reaching experiences on action and perception. *Vision Research, 50,* 2750–2757.

Libertus, Melissa E., & Brannon, Elizabeth M. (2009). Behavioral and neural basis of number sense in infancy. *Current Directions in Psychological Science, 18,* 346–351.

Lichter, Daniel T., Qian, Zhenchao, & Mellott, Leanna M. (2006). Marriage or dissolution? Union transitions among poor cohabiting women. *Demography, 43,* 223–240.

Lillard, Angeline, & Else-Quest, Nicole. (2006, September 29). Evaluating Montessori education. *Science, 313,* 1893–1894.

Lillard, Angeline Stoll. (2005). *Montessori: The science behind the genius.* New York, NY: Oxford University Press.

Lim, Boo Yeun. (2004). The magic of the brush and the power of color: Integrating theory into practice of painting in early childhood settings. *Early Childhood Education Journal, 32,* 113–119.

Lim, Chaeyoon, & Putnam, Robert D. (2010). Religion, social networks, and life satisfaction. *American Sociological Review, 75,* 914–933.

Limber, Susan P. (2011). Development, evaluation, and future directions of the Olweus Bullying Prevention Program. *Journal of School Violence, 10,* 71–87.

Lin, I-Fen. (2008a). Consequences of parental divorce for adult children's support of their frail parents. *Journal of Marriage and Family, 70,* 113–128.

Lin, I-Fen. (2008b). Mother and daughter reports about upward transfers. *Journal of Marriage and Family, 70,* 815–827.

Lincove, Jane A., & Painter, Gary (2006). Does the age that children start kindergarten matter? Evidence of long-term educational and social outcomes. *Educational Evaluation and Policy Analysis, 28,* 153–179.

Lindau, Stacy Tessler, & Gavrilova, Natalia. (2010). Sex, health, and years of sexually active life gained due to good health: Evidence from two US population based cross sectional surveys of ageing. *British Medical Journal, 340,* c810.

Lindau, Stacy Tessler, Schumm, L. Philip, Laumann, Edward O., Levinson, Wendy, O'Muircheartaigh, Colm A., & Waite, Linda J. (2007). A study of sexuality and health among older adults in the United States. *New England Journal of Medicine, 357,* 762–774.

Lindfors, Kaj, Elovainio, Marko, Wickman, Sanna, Vuorinen, Risto, Sinkkonen, Jari, Dunkel, Leo, & Raappana, Aleksi. (2007). Brief report: The role of ego development in psychosocial adjustment among boys with delayed puberty. *Journal of Research on Adolescence, 17,* 601–612.

Linn, Susan, & Novosat, Courtney L. (2008). Calories for sale: Food marketing to children in the twenty-first century. In Amy B. Jordan (Ed.), *Annals of the American Academy of Political and Social Science: Vol. 615. Overweight and obesity in America's children: Causes, consequences, solutions* (pp. 133–155). Thousand Oaks, CA: Sage.

Lipton, Jennifer S., & Spelke, Elizabeth S. (2003). Origins of number sense: Large-number discrimination in human infants. *Psychological Science, 14*, 396–401.

Liszkowski, Ulf, Schäfer, Marie, Carpenter, Malinda, & Tomasello, Michael. (2009). Prelinguistic infants, but not chimpanzees, communicate about absent entities. *Psychological Science, 20*, 654–660.

Liu, Cong, Spector, Paul E., & Shi, Lin. (2007). Cross-national job stress: A quantitative and qualitative study. *Journal of Organizational Behavior, 28*, 209–239.

Liu, David, Wellman, Henry M., Tardif, Twila, & Sabbagh, Mark A. (2008). Theory of mind development in Chinese children: A meta-analysis of false-belief understanding across cultures and languages. *Developmental Psychology, 44*, 523–531.

Liu, Hui, Wang, Qiu, Keesler, Venessa, & Schneider, Barbara. (2011). Non-standard work schedules, work-family conflict and parental well-being: A comparison of married and cohabiting unions. *Social Science Research, 40*, 473–484.

Livas-Dlott, Alejandra, Fuller, Bruce, Stein, Gabriela L., Bridges, Margaret, Mangual Figueroa, Ariana, & Mireles, Laurie. (2010). Commands, competence, and *cariño*: Maternal socialization practices in Mexican American families. *Developmental Psychology, 46*, 566–578.

Livingston, Gretchen. (2011, October 12). *In a down economy, fewer births.* Washington, DC: Pew Social & Demographic Trends.

Lleras-Muney, Adriana. (2005). The relationship between education and adult mortality in the United States. *Review of Economic Studies, 72*, 189–221.

Lloyd-Fox, Sarah, Blasi, Anna, Volein, Agnes, Everdell, Nick, Elwell, Claire E., & Johnson, Mark H. (2009). Social perception in infancy: A near infrared spectroscopy study. *Child Development, 80*, 986–999.

Lobstein, Tim, & Dibb, Sue. (2005). Evidence of a possible link between obesogenic food advertising and child overweight. *Obesity Reviews, 6*, 203–208.

LoBue, Vanessa, & DeLoache, Judy S. (2011). Pretty in pink: The early development of gender-stereotyped colour preferences. *British Journal of Developmental Psychology, 29*, 656–667.

Löckenhoff, Corinna E., De Fruyt, Filip, Terracciano, Antonio, McCrae, Robert R., De Bolle, Marleen, Costa, Paul T., Jr., … Yik, Michelle. (2009). Perceptions of aging across 26 cultures and their culture-level associates. *Psychology and Aging, 24*, 941–954.

Loe, Irene M., & Feldman, Heidi M. (2007). Academic and educational outcomes of children with ADHD. *Journal of Pediatric Psychology, 32*, 643–654.

Loeber, Rolf, & Burke, Jeffrey D. (2011). Developmental pathways in juvenile externalizing and internalizing problems. *Journal of Research on Adolescence, 21*, 34–46.

Loes, Chad, Pascarella, Ernest, & Umbach, Paul. (2012). Effects of diversity experiences on critical thinking skills: Who benefits? *Journal of Higher Education, 83*, 1–25.

Löfmark, Rurik, Nilstun, Tore, Cartwright, Colleen, Fischer, Susanne, van der Heide, Agnes, Mortier, Freddy, … The EURELD Consortium. (2008). Physicians' experiences with end-of-life decision-making: Survey in 6 European countries and Australia. *BMC Medicine, 6*(4). doi:10.1186/1741-7015-6-4

Long, Thomas G. (2009, October 6). The good funeral: Recovering Christian practices. *The Christian Century, 126.*

Longmore, Monica, Eng, Abbey, Giordano, Peggy, & Manning, Wendy. (2009). Parenting and adolescents' sexual initiation. *Journal of Marriage and Family, 71*, 969–982.

Lopez, Oscar L., Kuller, Lewis H., Becker, James T., Dulberg, Corinne, Sweet, Robert A., Gach, H. Michael, & Dekosky, Steven T. (2007). Incidence of dementia in mild cognitive impairment in the cardiovascular health study cognition study. *Archives of Neurology, 64*, 416–420.

Lorber, Michael F., & Egeland, Byron. (2011). Parenting and infant difficulty: Testing a mutual exacerbation hypothesis to predict early onset conduct problems. *Child Development, 82*, 2006–2020.

Lord, Catherine, & Bishop, Somer L. (2010). Autism spectrum disorders: Diagnosis, prevalence, and services for children and families. *Social Policy Report, 24*(2), 1–26.

Lovecky, Deirdre V. (2009). Moral sensitivity in young gifted children. In Tracy Cross & Don Ambrose (Eds.), *Morality, ethics, and gifted minds* (pp. 161–176). New York, NY: Springer.

Lovell, Brian, & Wetherell, Mark A. (2011). The cost of caregiving: Endocrine and immune implications in elderly and non elderly caregivers. *Neuroscience & Biobehavioral Reviews, 35*, 1342–1352.

Lowell, Darcy I., Carter, Alice S., Godoy, Leandra, Paulicin, Belinda, & Briggs-Gowan, Margaret J. (2011). A randomized controlled trial of Child FIRST: A comprehensive home-based intervention translating research into early childhood practice. *Child Development, 82*, 193–208.

Lucas, Richard E., Clark, Andrew E., Georgellis, Yannis, & Diener, Ed. (2003). Reexamining adaptation and the set point model of happiness: Reactions to changes in marital status. *Journal of Personality and Social Psychology, 84*, 527–539.

Ludington-Hoe, Susan. (2011). Thirty years of kangaroo care science and practice. *Neonatal Network: The Journal of Neonatal Nursing, 30*, 357–362.

Luengo-Prado, María José, & Sevilla, Almudena. (2012). Time to cook: Expenditure at retirement in Spain. *The Economic Journal.* Advance online publication. doi:10.1111/j.1468-0297.2012.02546.x

Luking, Katherine R., Repovs, Grega, Belden, Andy C., Gaffrey, Michael S., Botteron, Kelly N., Luby, Joan L., & Barch, Deanna M. (2011). Functional connectivity of the amygdala in early-childhood-onset depression. *Journal of the American Academy of Child & Adolescent Psychiatry, 50*, 1027–1041 .e3. doi:10.1016/j.jaac.2011.07.019

Luna, Beatriz, Padmanabhan, Aarthi, & O'Hearn, Kirsten. (2010). What has fMRI told us about the development of cognitive control through adolescence? *Brain and Cognition, 72*, 101–113.

Lundquist, Gunilla, Rasmussen, Birgit H., & Axelsson, Bertil. (2011). Information of imminent death or not: Does it make a difference? *Journal of Clinical Oncology, 29*, 3927–3931.

Lupien, Sonia J., McEwen, Bruce S., Gunnar, Megan R., & Heim, Christine. (2009). Effects of stress throughout the lifespan on the brain, behaviour and cognition, *Nature Reviews Neuroscience, 10*, 434–445.

Lustig, Cindy, Shah, Priti, Seidler, Rachael, & Reuter-Lorenz, Patricia A. (2009). Aging, training, and the brain: A review and future directions. *Neuropsychology Review, 19*, 504–522.

Luthar, Suniya S., Cicchetti, Dante, & Becker, Bronwyn. (2000). The construct of resilience: A critical evaluation and guidelines for future work. *Child Development, 71*, 543–562.

Luthar, Suniya S., D'Avanzo, Karen, & Hites, Sarah. (2003). Maternal drug abuse versus other psychological disturbances: Risks and resilience among children. In Suniya S. Luthar (Ed.), *Resilience and vulnerability: Adaptation in the context of childhood adversities* (pp. 104–129). New York, NY: Cambridge University Press.

Lutsey, Pamela L., Diez Roux, Ana V., Jacobs, David R., Jr., Burke, Gregory L., Harman, Jane, Shea, Steven, & Folsom, Aaron R. (2008). Associations of acculturation and socioeconomic status with subclinical cardiovascular disease in the Multi-Ethnic Study of Atherosclerosis. *American Journal of Public Health, 98*, 1963–1970.

Lutz, Wolfgang, & K. C., Samir. (2011, July 29). Global human capital: Integrating education and population. *Science, 333*, 587–592.

Luxmoore, Nick. (2012). *Young people, death, and the unfairness of everything.* London, England: Jessica Kingsley.

Lynch, Scott M., & Brown, J. Scott. (2011). Stratification and inequality over the life course. In Robert H. Binstock & Linda K. George (Eds.), *Handbook of aging and the social sciences* (7th ed., pp. 105–117). San Diego, CA: Academic Press.

Lynn, Richard, & Mikk, Jaan. (2007). National differences in intelligence and educational attainment. *Intelligence, 35*, 115–121.

Lynne, Sarah D., Graber, Julia A., Nichols, Tracy R., Brooks-Gunn, Jeanne, & Botvin, Gilbert J. (2007). Links between pubertal timing, peer influences, and externalizing behaviors among urban students followed through middle school. *Journal of Adolescent Health, 40*(2), 181.e7–181.e13. doi:10.1016/j.jadohealth.2006.09.008

Lyons-Ruth, Karlen, Bronfman, Elisa, & Parsons, Elizabeth. (1999). IV. Maternal frightened, frightening, or atypical behavior and disorganized infant attachment patterns. *Monographs of the Society for Research in Child Development, 64*(3, Serial No. 258), 67–96.

Ma, Lang, Phelps, Erin, Lerner, Jacqueline V., & Lerner, Richard M. (2009). Academic competence for adolescents who bully and who are bullied: Findings from the 4-H Study of Positive Youth Development. *The Journal of Early Adolescence, 29*, 862–897.

Macgregor, Stuart, Lind, Penelope A., Bucholz, Kathleen K., Hansell, Narelle K., Madden, Pamela A. F., Richter, Melinda M., . . . Whitfield, John B. (2009). Associations of ADH and ALDH2 gene variation with self report alcohol reactions, consumption and dependence: An integrated analysis. *Human Molecular Genetics, 18*, 580–593.

Macmillan, Ross, & Copher, Ronda. (2005). Families in the life course: Interdependency of roles, role configurations, and pathways. *Journal of Marriage and Family, 67*, 858–879.

MacPhee, David. (1981). *Knowledge of Infant Development Inventory (KIDI).* Unpublished manuscript, Educational Testing Service, Ewing, NJ.

Madden, Mary, & Lenhart, Amanda. (2009). *Teens and distracted driving: Texting, talking and other uses of the cell phone behind the wheel.* Washington, DC: Pew Internet & American Life Project.

Magnuson, Katherine, & Berger, Lawrence M. (2009). Family structure states and transitions: Associations with children's well-being during middle childhood. *Journal of Marriage and Family, 71*, 575–591.

Maguire, Kathleen. (2010). *Sourcebook of criminal justice statistics.* Washington, DC: U.S. Department of Justice.

Mahler, Margaret S., Pine, Fred, & Bergman, Anni. (1975). *The psychological birth of the human infant: Symbiosis and individuation.* New York, NY: Basic Books.

Maisto, A. Stephen, Galizio, Mark, & Connors, Gerard J. (2011). *Drug use and abuse* (6th ed.). Belmont, CA: Wadsworth/Cengage Learning.

Majercsik, Eszter. (2005). Hierachy of needs of geriatric patients. *Gerontology, 51*, 170–173.

Makimoto, Kiyoko. (1998). Drinking patterns and drinking problems among Asian-Americans and Pacific Islanders. *Alcohol Health and Research World, 22*, 270–275.

Malina, Robert M., Bouchard, Claude, & Bar-Or, Oded. (2004). *Growth, maturation, and physical activity* (2nd ed.). Champaign, IL: Human Kinetics.

Malloy, Michael H. (2009). Impact of cesarean section on intermediate and late preterm births: United States, 2000–2003. *Birth: Issues in Perinatal Care, 36*, 26–33.

Malone, Fergal D., Canick, Jacob A., Ball, Robert H., Nyberg, David A., Comstock, Christine H., Bukowski, Radek, . . . D'Alton, Mary E. (2005). First-trimester or second-trimester screening, or both, for Down's syndrome. *New England Journal of Medicine, 353*, 2001–2011.

Manago, Adriana M., Taylor, Tamara, & Greenfield, Patricia M. (2012). Me and my 400 friends: The anatomy of college students' Facebook networks, their communication patterns, and well-being. *Developmental Psychology, 48*, 369–380.

Mancini, Anthony D., & Bonanno, George A. (2006). Marital closeness, functional disability, and adjustment in late life. *Psychology and Aging, 21*, 600–610.

Mancini, Anthony D., Prati, Gabriele, & Bonanno, George A. (2011). Do shattered worldviews lead to complicated grief? Prospective and longitudinal analyses. *Journal of Social and Clinical Psychology, 30*, 184–215.

Mandemakers, Jornt J., & Dykstra, Pearl A. (2008). Discrepancies in parent's and adult child's reports of support and contact. *Journal of Marriage and Family, 70,* 495–506.

Mangels, Jennifer A., Good, Catherine, Whiteman, Ronald C., Maniscalco, Brian, & Dweck, Carol S. (2012). Emotion blocks the path to learning under stereotype threat. *Social Cognitive and Affective Neuroscience, 7,* 230–241.

Mann, Joshua R., McDermott, Suzanne, Bao, Haikun, & Bersabe, Adrian. (2009). Maternal genitourinary infection and risk of cerebral palsy. *Developmental Medicine & Child Neurology, 51,* 282–288.

Mann, Ronald D., & Andrews, Elizabeth B. (Eds.). (2007). *Pharmacovigilance* (2nd ed.). Hoboken, NJ: Wiley.

Mann, Traci, & Ward, Andrew. (2007). Attention, self-control, and health behaviors. *Current Directions in Psychological Science, 16,* 280–283.

Manzi, Claudia, Vignoles, Vivian L., Regalia, Camillo, & Scabini, Eugenia. (2006). Cohesion and enmeshment revisited: Differentiation, identity, and well-being in two European cultures. *Journal of Marriage and Family, 68,* 673–689.

Manzoli, Lamberto, Villari, Paolo, Pironec, Giovanni M., & Boccia, Antonio. (2007). Marital status and mortality in the elderly: A systematic review and meta-analysis. *Social Science & Medicine, 64,* 77–94.

Mar, Raymond A. (2011). The neural bases of social cognition and story comprehension. *Annual Review of Psychology, 62,* 103–134.

Mar, Raymond A., Tackett, Jennifer L., & Moore, Chris. (2010). Exposure to media and theory-of-mind development in preschoolers. *Cognitive Development, 25,* 69–78.

Marazita, John M., & Merriman, William E. (2010). Verifying one's knowledge of a name without retrieving it: A u-shaped relation to vocabulary size in early childhood. *Language Learning and Development, 7,* 40–54.

March, John S., Franklin, Martin E., Leonard, Henrietta L., & Foa, Edna B. (2004). Obsessive-compulsive disorder. In Tracy L. Morris & John S. March (Eds.), *Anxiety disorders in children and adolescents* (2nd ed., pp. 212–240). New York, NY: Guilford Press.

Marchand, Alain, Drapeau, Aline, & Beaulieu-Prévost, Dominic. (2011). Psychological distress in Canada: The role of employment and reasons for non-employment. *International Journal of Social Psychiatry, 58,* 596–604.

Marcia, James E. (1966). Development and validation of ego-identity status. *Journal of Personality & Social Psychology, 3,* 551–558.

Marcia, James E., Waterman, Alan S., Matteson, David R., Archer, Sally L., & Orlofsky, Jacob L. (1993). *Ego identity: A handbook for psychosocial research.* New York, NY: Springer-Verlag.

Marcovitch, Stuart, Boseovski, Janet J., Knapp, Robin J., & Kane, Michael J. (2010). Goal neglect and working memory capacity in 4- to 6-year-old children. *Child Development, 81,* 1687–1695.

Marcus, Gary F., & Rabagliati, Hugh. (2009). Language acquisition, domain specificity, and descent with modification.

In John Colombo, Peggy McCardle, & Lisa Freund (Eds.), *Infant pathways to language: Methods, models, and research disorders* (pp. 267–285). New York, NY: Psychology Press.

Margolis, Rachel, & Myrskylä, Mikko. (2011). A global perspective on happiness and fertility. *Population and Development Review, 37,* 29–56.

Margrett, Jennifer A., Daugherty, Kate, Martin, Peter, MacDonald, Maurice, Davey, Adam, Woodard, John L., . . . Poon, Leonard W. (2011). Affect and loneliness among centenarians and the oldest old: The role of individual and social resources. *Aging & Mental Health, 15,* 385–396.

Marks, Amy K., Patton, Flannery, & García Coll, Cynthia. (2011). Being bicultural: A mixed-methods study of adolescents' implicitly and explicitly measured multiethnic identities. *Developmental Psychology, 47,* 270–288.

Marlow-Ferguson, Rebecca (Ed.). (2002). *World education encyclopedia: A survey of educational systems worldwide* (2nd ed.). Detroit, MI: Gale Group.

Marschark, Marc, & Spencer, Patricia Elizabeth. (Eds.) (2003). *Oxford handbook of deaf studies, language, and education.* New York, NY: Oxford University Press.

Marsh, Louise, McGee, Rob, Nada-Raja, Shyamala, & Williams, Sheila. (2010). Text bullying and traditional bullying among New Zealand secondary school students. *Journal of Adolescence, 33,* 237–240.

Marsiske, Michael, & Margrett, Jennifer A. (2006). Everyday problem solving and decision making. In James E. Birren & K. Warren Schaie (Eds.), *Handbook of the psychology of aging* (6th ed., pp. 315–342). Burlington, MA: Elsevier Academic Press.

Martin, Andrew J. (2009). Motivation and engagement across the academic life span: A developmental construct validity study of elementary school, high school, and university/college students. *Educational and Psychological Measurement, 69,* 794–824.

Martin, Carol, Fabes, Richard, Hanish, Laura, Leonard, Stacie, & Dinella, Lisa. (2011). Experienced and expected similarity to same-gender peers: Moving toward a comprehensive model of gender segregation. *Sex Roles, 65,* 421–434.

Martin, Carol Lynn, & Ruble, Diane N. (2010). Patterns of gender development. *Annual Review of Psychology, 61,* 353–381.

Martin, Ingrid M., & Kamins, Michael A. (2010). An application of terror management theory in the design of social and health-related anti-smoking appeals. *Journal of Consumer Behaviour, 9,* 172–190.

Marvasti, Amir B., & McKinney, Karyn D. (2011). Does diversity mean assimilation? *Critical Sociology, 37,* 631–650.

Masche, J. Gowert. (2010). Explanation of normative declines in parents' knowledge about their adolescent children. *Journal of Adolescence, 33,* 271–284.

Mascolo, Michael F., Fischer, Kurt W., & Li, Jin. (2003). Dynamic development of component systems of emotions: Pride, shame, and guilt in China and the United States. In Richard J. Davidson, Klaus R. Scherer, & H. Hill Goldsmith (Eds.), *Handbook of affective sciences* (pp. 375–408). Oxford, England: Oxford University Press.

Mashburn, Andrew J., Justice, Laura M., Downer, Jason T., & Pianta, Robert C. (2009). Peer effects on children's language achievement during pre-kindergarten. *Child Development, 80,* 686–702.

Maslow, Abraham H. (1954). *Motivation and personality.* New York, NY: Harper.

Maslow, Abraham H. (1970). *Motivation and personality* (2nd ed.). New York, NY: Harper & Row.

Masoro, Edward J. (2006). Are age-associated diseases an integral part of aging? In Edward J. Masoro & Steven N. Austad (Eds.), *Handbook of the biology of aging* (6th ed., pp. 43–62). Amsterdam, The Netherlands: Elsevier Academic Press.

Masoro, Edward J., & Austad, Steven N. (2011). Forward. In Edward J. Masoro & Steven N. Austad (Eds.), *Handbook of the biology of aging* (7th ed., pp. xi–xii). San Diego, CA: Academic Press.

Masten, Ann S. (2004). Regulatory processes, risk, and resilience in adolescent development. In Ronald E. Dahl & Linda Patia Spear (Eds.), *Annals of the New York Academy of Sciences: Vol. 1021. Adolescent brain development: Vulnerabilities and opportunities* (pp. 310–319). New York, NY: New York Academy of Sciences.

Masten, Carrie L., Guyer, Amanda E., Hodgdon, Hilary B., McClure, Erin B., Charney, Dennis S., Ernst, Monique, . . . Monk, Christopher S. (2008). Recognition of facial emotions among maltreated children with high rates of post-traumatic stress disorder. *Child Abuse & Neglect, 32,* 139–153.

Mathison, David J., & Agrawal, Dewesh. (2010). An update on the epidemiology of pediatric fractures. *Pediatric Emergency Care, 26,* 594–603.

Matsumoto, David. (2004). Reflections on culture and competence. In Robert J. Sternberg & Elena L. Grigorenko (Eds.), *Culture and competence: Contexts of life success* (pp. 273–282). Washington, DC: American Psychological Association.

Mattis, Jacqueline S., & Mattis, Jacob H. (2011). Religiosity and spirituality in the lives of African American children. In Nancy E. Hill, Tammy L. Mann, & Hiram E. Fitzgerald (Eds.), *African American children and mental health* (pp. 125–149). Santa Barbara, CA: Praeger.

Mattison, Julie A., Roth, George S., Beasley, T. Mark, Tilmont, Edward M., Handy, April M., Herbert, Richard L., . . . de Cabo, Rafael. (2012). Impact of caloric restriction on health and survival in rhesus monkeys from the NIA study. *Nature, 489,* 318–321.

Maxfield, Molly, Pyszczynski, Tom, Kluck, Benjamin, Cox, Cathy R, Greenberg, Jeff, Solomon, Sheldon, & Weise, David. (2007). Age-related differences in responses to thoughts of one's own death: Mortality salience and judgments of moral transgressions. *Psychology and Aging, 22,* 341–353.

Maxwell, Lesli A. (2012, March 7). Achievement gaps tied to income found widening. *Education Week,* pp. 1, 22.

May, Vanessa, Mason, Jennifer, & Clarke, Lynda. (2012). Being there, yet not interfering: The paradoxes of grandparenting. In Sara Arber & Virpi Timonen (Eds.), *Contemporary grandparenting: Changing family relationships in global contexts* (pp. 139–158). Bristol, UK: Policy Press.

Mazzocco, Michèle M. M., & Ross, Judith L. (Eds.) (2007). *Neurogenetic developmental disorders: Variation of manifestation in childhood.* Cambridge, MA: MIT Press.

McAdams, Dan P. (2006). The redemptive self: Generativity and the stories Americans live by. *Research in Human Development, 3,* 81–100.

McAdams, Dan P., Bauer, Jack J., Sakaeda, April R., Anyidoho, Nana Akua, Machado, Mary Anne, Magrino-Failla, Katie, . . . Pals, Jennifer L. (2006). Continuity and change in the life story: A longitudinal study of autobiographical memories in emerging adulthood. *Journal of Personality, 74,* 1371–1400.

McAdams, Dan P., & Olson, Bradley D. (2010). Personality development: Continuity and change over the life course. *Annual Review of Psychology, 61,* 517–542.

McCabe, Janice. (2011). Doing multiculturalism: An interactionist analysis of the practices of a multicultural sorority. *Journal of Contemporary Ethnography, 40,* 521–549.

McCall, Robert B., Groark, Christina J., & Fish, Larry. (2010). A caregiver–child socioemotional and relationship rating scale. *Infant Mental Health Journal, 31,* 201–219.

McCartney, Kathleen, Burchinal, Margaret, Clarke-Stewart, Alison, Bub, Kristen L., Owen, Margaret T., Belsky, Jay, & The NICHD Early Child Care Research Network. (2010). Testing a series of causal propositions relating time in child care to children's externalizing behavior. *Developmental Psychology, 46,* 1–17, 17a.

McCarty, Cheryl, Prawitz, Aimee D., Derscheid, Linda E., & Montgomery, Bette. (2011). Perceived safety and teen risk taking in online chat sites. *Cyberpsychology, Behavior, and Social Networking, 14,* 169–174.

McClain, Lauren Rinelli. (2011). Better parents, more stable partners: Union transitions among cohabiting parents. *Journal of Marriage and Family, 73,* 889–901.

McClain, Paula D., Johnson Carew, Jessica D., Walton, Eugene, Jr., & Watts, Candis S. (2009). Group membership, group identity, and group consciousness: Measures of racial identity in American politics? *Annual Review of Political Science, 12,* 471–485.

McClintock, Elizabeth Aura. (2010). When does race matter? Race, sex, and dating at an elite university. *Journal of Marriage and Family, 72,* 45–72.

McCormick, Cheryl M., Mathews, Iva Z., Thomas, Catherine, & Waters, Patti. (2010). Investigations of HPA function and the enduring consequences of stressors in adolescence in animal models. *Brain and Cognition, 72,* 73–85.

McCrae, Robert R., & Terracciano, Antonio. (2006). National character and personality. *Current Directions in Psychological Science, 15,* 156–161.

McCright, Aaron M., & Dunlap, Riley E. (2011). The politicization of climate change and polarization in the American public's views of global warming, 2001–2010. *Sociological Quarterly, 52,* 155–194.

McDaniel, Mark A., & Bugg, Julie M. (2012). Memory training interventions: What has been forgotten? *Journal of Applied Research in Memory and Cognition, 1,* 45–50.

McFadden, Susan H., & Basting, Anne D. (2010). Healthy aging persons and their brains: Promoting resilience through creative engagement. *Clinics in Geriatric Medicine, 26*, 149–161.

McGrath, Susan K., & Kennell, John H. (2008). A randomized controlled trial of continuous labor support for middle-class couples: Effect on cesarean delivery rates. *Birth, 35*, 92–97.

McIntyre, Donald A. (2002). *Colour blindness: Causes and effects.* Chester, UK: Dalton.

McKinley, Jesse. (2010, June 24). Whooping cough kills 5 in California; State declares an epidemic. *New York Times*, p. A15.

McKown, Clark, & Strambler, Michael J. (2009). Developmental antecedents and social and academic consequences of stereotype-consciousness in middle childhood. *Child Development, 80*, 1643–1659.

McLanahan, Sara. (2009). Fragile families and the reproduction of poverty. *The ANNALS of the American Academy of Political and Social Science, 621*, 111–131.

McLendon, Amber, & Shelton, Penny. (2011–2012). New symptoms in older adults: Disease or drug? *Generations, 35*(4), 25–30.

McLeod, Bryce D., Wood, Jeffrey J., & Weisz, John R. (2007). Examining the association between parenting and childhood anxiety: A meta-analysis. *Clinical Psychology Review, 27*, 155–172.

McLeod, Jane D., Pescosolido, Bernice A., Takeuchi, David T., & Falkenberg White, Terry (2004). Public attitudes toward the use of psychiatric medications for children. *Journal of Health and Social Behavior, 45*, 53–67.

McLeod, Peter, Sommerville, Peter, & Reed, Nick. (2005). Are automated actions beyond conscious access? In John Duncan, Peter McLeod, & Louise H. Phillips (Eds.), *Measuring the mind: Speed, control, and age* (pp. 359–372). New York, NY: Oxford University Press.

McLoyd, Vonnie C., Aikens, Nikki L., & Burton, Linda M. (2006). Childhood poverty, policy, and practice. In William Damon & Richard M. Lerner (Series Eds.) & K. Ann Renninger & Irving E. Sigel (Vol. Eds.), *Handbook of child psychology: Vol. 4. Child psychology in practice* (6th ed., pp. 700–775). Hoboken, NJ: Wiley.

McLoyd, Vonnie C., Kaplan, Rachel, Hardaway, Cecily R., & Wood, Dana. (2007). Does endorsement of physical discipline matter? Assessing moderating influences on the maternal and child psychological correlates of physical discipline in African American families. *Journal of Family Psychology, 21*, 165–175.

McManus, I. Chris, Moore, James, Freegard, Matthew, & Rawles, Richard. (2010). Science in the making: Right Hand, Left Hand. III: Estimating historical rates of left-handedness. *Laterality: Asymmetries of Body, Brain and Cognition, 15*, 186–208.

McNally, Richard J., & Geraerts, Elke. (2009). A new solution to the recovered memory debate. *Perspectives on Psychological Science, 4*, 126–134.

McNamee, Catherine, & Raley, Kelly. (2011). A note on race, ethnicity and nativity differentials in remarriage in the United States. *Demographic Research, 24*, 293–231.

McNulty, James K., & Fincham, Frank D. (2012). Beyond positive psychology? Toward a contextual view of psychological processes and well-being. *American Psychologist, 67*, 101–110.

McShane, Kelly E., & Hastings, Paul D. (2009). The New Friends Vignettes: Measuring parental psychological control that confers risk for anxious adjustment in preschoolers. *International Journal of Behavioral Development, 33*, 481–495.

Meadows, Sara. (2006). *The child as thinker: The development and acquisition of cognition in childhood* (2nd ed.). New York, NY: Routledge.

Meaney, Michael J. (2010). Epigenetics and the biological definition of gene × environment interactions. *Child Development, 81*, 41–79.

Meece, Judith L., & Eccles, Jacquelynne S. (Eds.) (2010). *Handbook of research on schools, schooling, and human development.* New York, NY: Routledge.

Meeus, Wim. (2011). The study of adolescent identity formation 2000–2010: A review of longitudinal research. *Journal of Research on Adolescence, 21*, 75–94.

Mehta, Clare M., & Strough, JoNell. (2009). Sex segregation in friendships and normative contexts across the life span. *Developmental Review, 29*, 201–220.

Meier, Ann, Hull, Kathleen E., & Ortyl, Timothy A. (2009). Young adult relationship values at the intersection of gender and sexuality. *Journal of Marriage and Family, 71*, 510–525.

Meisami, Esmail, Brown, Chester M., & Emerle, Henry F. (2007). Sensory systems: Normal aging, disorders, and treatments of vision and hearing in humans. In Paola S. Timiras (Ed.), *Physiological basis of aging and geriatrics* (4th ed., pp. 109–136). New York, NY: Informa Healthcare.

Melhem, Nadine M., Porta, Giovanna, Shamseddeen, Wael, Payne, Monica Walker, & Brent, David A. (2011). Grief in children and adolescents bereaved by sudden parental death. *Archives of General Psychiatry, 68*, 911–919.

Mellor, M. Joanna, & Brownell, Patricia J. (Eds.). (2006). *Elder abuse and mistreatment: Policy, practice, and research.* New York, NY: Haworth Press.

Menacker, Fay, & Hamilton, Brady E. (2010, March). *Recent trends in cesarean delivery in the United States* (NCHS Data Brief No. 35). Hyattsville, MD: National Center for Health Statistics.

Mendle, Jane, Harden, K. Paige, Brooks-Gunn, Jeanne, & Graber, Julia A. (2010). Development's tortoise and hare: Pubertal timing, pubertal tempo, and depressive symptoms in boys and girls. *Developmental Psychology, 46*, 1341–1353.

Mendle, Jane, Leve, Leslie D., Van Ryzin, Mark, Natsuaki, Misaki N., & Ge, Xiaojia. (2011). Associations between early life stress, child maltreatment, and pubertal development among girls in foster care. *Journal of Research on Adolescence, 21*, 871–880.

Menon, Madhavi, Tobin, Desiree D., Corby, Brooke C., Menon, Meenakshi, Hodges, Ernest V. E., & Perry, David G. (2007). The developmental costs of high self-esteem for antisocial children. *Child Development, 78*, 1627–1639.

Menon, Usha. (2001). Middle adulthood in cultural perspectives: The imagined and the experienced in three cultures. In Margie E. Lachman (Ed.), *Handbook of midlife development* (pp. 40–74). New York, NY: Wiley.

Meririnne, Esa, Kiviruusu, Olli, Karlsson, Linnea, Pelkonen, Mirjami, Ruuttu, Titta, Tuisku, Virpi, & Marttunen, Mauri. (2010). Brief report: Excessive alcohol use negatively affects the course of adolescent depression—One year naturalistic follow-up study. *Journal of Adolescence, 33,* 221–226.

Merriam, Sharan B. (2009). *Qualitative research: A guide to design and implementation.* San Francisco, CA: Jossey-Bass.

Merriman, William E. (1999). Competition, attention, and young children's lexical processing. In Brian MacWhinney (Ed.), *The emergence of language* (pp. 331–358). Mahwah, NJ: Erlbaum.

Mervis, Jeffrey. (2008, March 21). Expert panel lays out the path to algebra—And why it matters. *Science, 319,* 1605.

Merz, Emily C., & McCall, Robert B. (2011). Parent ratings of executive functioning in children adopted from psychosocially depriving institutions. *Journal of Child Psychology and Psychiatry, 52,* 537–546.

Merzenich, Hiltrud, Zeeb, Hajo, & Blettner, Maria. (2010). Decreasing sperm quality: A global problem? *BMC Public Health, 10,* 24.

Mesquita, Batja, & Leu, Janxin. (2007). The cultural psychology of emotion. In Shinobu Kitayama & Dov Cohen (Eds.), *Handbook of cultural psychology* (pp. 734–759). New York, NY: Guilford Press.

Messer, Karen, Trinidad, Dennis R., Al-Delaimy, Wael K., & Pierce, John P. (2008). Smoking cessation rates in the United States: A comparison of young adult and older smokers. *American Journal of Public Health, 98,* 317–322.

Messing, Jacqueline. (2007). Multiple ideologies and competing discourses: Language shift in Tlaxcala, Mexico. *Language in Society, 36,* 555–577.

Messinger, Daniel M., Ruvolo, Paul, Ekas, Naomi V., & Fogel, Alan. (2010). Applying machine learning to infant interaction: The development is in the details. *Neural Networks, 23,* 1004–1016.

Meteyer, Karen, & Perry-Jenkins, Maureen. (2010). Father involvement among working-class, dual-earner couples. *Fathering, 8,* 379–403.

Meyer, Daniel R., Skinner, Christine, & Davidson, Jacqueline. (2011). Complex families and equality in child support obligations: A comparative policy analysis. *Children and Youth Services Review, 33,* 1804–1812.

Meyer, Madonna Harrington. (2012). Grandmothers juggling work and grandchildren in the United States. In Sara Arber & Virpi Timonen (Eds.), *Contemporary grandparenting: Changing family relationships in global contexts* (pp. 71–90). Bristol, UK: Policy Press.

Miklowitz, David Jay, & Cicchetti, Dante (Eds.). (2010). *Understanding bipolar disorder: A developmental psychopathology perspective.* New York, NY: Guilford Press.

Milkman, Katherine L., Chugh, Dolly, & Bazerman, Max H. (2009). How can decision making be improved? *Perspectives on Psychological Science, 4,* 379–383.

Miller, Greg. (2009, October 16). Alzheimer's biomarker initiative hits its stride. *Science, 326,* 386–389.

Miller, Greg. (2010, November 26). New clues about what makes the human brain special. *Science, 330,* 1167.

Miller, Greg. (2012, January 6). Engineering a new line of attack on a signature war injury. *Science, 335,* 33–35.

Miller, Gregory E., Lachman, Margie E., Chen, Edith, Gruenewald, Tara L., Karlamangla, Arun S., & Seeman, Teresa E. (2011). Pathways to resilience: Maternal nurturance as a buffer against the effects of childhood poverty on metabolic syndrome at midlife. *Psychological Science, 22,* 1591–1599.

Miller, Joan G. (2004). The cultural deep structure of psychological theories of social development. In Robert J. Sternberg & Elena L. Grigorenko (Eds.), *Culture and competence: Contexts of life success* (pp. 111–138). Washington, DC: American Psychological Association.

Miller, Judith S., Bilder, Deborah, Farley, Megan, Coon, Hilary, Pinborough-Zimmerman, Judith, Jenson, William, . . . McMahon, William M. (2013). Autism spectrum disorder reclassified: A second look at the 1980s Utah/UCLA Autism Epidemiologic Study. *Journal of Autism and Developmental Disorders, 43,* 200–210.

Miller, Patrick, & Plant, Martin. (2010). Parental guidance about drinking: Relationship with teenage psychoactive substance use. *Journal of Adolescence, 33,* 55–68.

Miller, Patricia H. (2011). *Theories of developmental psychology* (5th ed.). New York, NY: Worth.

Miller, Patricia Y., & Simon, William. (1980). The development of sexuality in adolescence. In Joseph Adelson (Ed.), *Handbook of adolescent psychology* (pp. 383–407). New York, NY: Wiley.

Miller, Susan. (2011–2012). Medications and elders: Quality of care or quality of life? *Generations, 35*(4), 19–24.

Miller, Torri W., Nigg, Joel T., & Miller, Robin L. (2009). Attention deficit hyperactivity disorder in African American children: What can be concluded from the past ten years? *Clinical Psychology Review, 29,* 77–86.

Mills-Koonce, W. Roger, Garrett-Peters, Patricia, Barnett, Melissa, Granger, Douglas A., Blair, Clancy, & Cox, Martha J. (2011). Father contributions to cortisol responses in infancy and toddlerhood. *Developmental Psychology, 47,* 388–395.

Milosevic, Dragoslav P., Kostic, S., Potic, B., Kalašić, A., Svorcan, Petar, Bojic, Daniela, . . . Davidovic, M. (2007). Is there such thing as "reversible dementia" (RD)? *Archives of Gerontology and Geriatrics, 44,* 271–277.

Minagawa-Kawai, Yasuyo, van der Lely, Heather, Ramus, Franck, Sato, Yutaka, Mazuka, Reiko, & Dupoux, Emmanuel. (2011). Optical brain imaging reveals general auditory and language-specific processing in early infant development. *Cerebral Cortex, 21,* 254–261.

Mindell, Jodi A., Sadeh, Avi, Wiegand, Benjamin, How, Ti Hwei, & Goh, Daniel Y. T. (2010). Cross-cultural differences in infant and toddler sleep. *Sleep Medicine, 11,* 274–280.

Minkler, Meredith, & Holstein, Martha B. (2008). From civil rights to . . . civic engagement? Concerns of two older critical gerontologists about a "new social movement" and what it portends. *Journal of Aging Studies, 22,* 196–204.

Mintz, Toben H. (2005). Linguistic and conceptual influences on adjective acquisition in 24- and 36-month-olds. *Developmental Psychology, 41,* 17–29.

Mishra, Ramesh C., Singh, Sunita, & Dasen, Pierre R. (2009). Geocentric dead reckoning in Sanskrit- and Hindi-medium school children. *Culture & Psychology, 15,* 386–408.

Misra, Dawn P., Caldwell, Cleopatra, Young, Alford A., & Abelson, Sara. (2010). Do fathers matter? Paternal contributions to birth outcomes and racial disparities. *American Journal of Obstetrics and Gynecology, 202,* 99–100.

Mitchell, Barbara A. (2010). Happiness in midlife parental roles: A contextual mixed methods analysis. *Family Relations, 59,* 326–339.

Mitchell, Edwin A. (2009). SIDS: Past, present and future. *Acta Pædiatrica, 98,* 1712–1719.

MMWR. (2002, September 13). Folic acid and prevention of spina bifida and anencephaly: 10 years after the U.S. public health service recommendation. *Morbidity and Mortality Weekly Report Recommendations and Reports, 51*(RR13), 1–3.

MMWR. (2005, January 14). Reducing childhood asthma through community-based service delivery—New York City, 2001–2004. *Morbidity and Mortality Weekly Report, 54,* 11–14.

MMWR. (2008, July 11). Disparities in secondhand smoke exposure—United States, 1988–1994 and 1999–2004. *Morbidity and Mortality Weekly Report, 57,* 744–747.

MMWR. (2010, June 4). Youth risk behavior surveillance—United States, 2009. *Morbidity and Mortality Weekly Report Surveillance Summaries, 59*(SS5), 1–142.

MMWR. (2011, February 25). Abortion surveillance—United States, 2007. *Morbidity and Mortality Weekly Report Surveillance Summaries, 60*(SS1), 1–39.

MMWR. (2011, January 7). Notifiable diseases and mortality tables. *Morbidity and Mortality Weekly Report, 59,* 1704–1717.

MMWR. (2011, June 10). Sexual identity, sex of sexual contacts, and health-risk behaviors among students in grades 9–12—Youth risk behavior surveillance, selected sites, United States, 2001–2009. *Morbidity and Mortality Weekly Report Surveillance Summaries, 60*(SS07), 1–133.

MMWR. (2012, June 8). Youth risk behavior surveillance—United States, 2011. *Morbidity and Mortality Weekly Report, 61,* 4–162.

MMWR. (2013, January 28). Advisory committee on immunization practices (ACIP) recommended immunization schedules for persons aged 0 through 18 years and adults aged 19 years and older—United States, 2013. CDC, U.S. Department of Health and Human Services, MMWR; 62(Suppl1): Atlanta.

Moen, Phyllis, & Spencer, Donna. (2006). Converging divergences in age, gender, health, and well-being: Strategic selection in the third age. In Robert H. Binstock & Linda K. George (Eds.), *Handbook of aging and the social sciences* (6th ed., pp. 127–144). Amsterdam, The Netherlands: Elsevier.

Moen, Phyllis, Sweet, Stephen, & Swisher, Raymond. (2005). Embedded career clocks: The case of retirement planning. In Ross Macmillan (Ed.), *The structure of the life course: Standardized? Individualized? Differentiated?* (pp. 237–265). Greenwich, CT: Elsevier/JAI Press.

Moffat, Scott D. (2005). Effects of testosterone on cognitive and brain aging in elderly men. In Richard G. Cutler, S. Mitchell Harman, Chris Heward, & Mike Gibbons (Eds.), *Longevity health sciences: The Phoenix conference* (Vol. 1055, pp. 80–92). New York, NY: New York Academy of Sciences.

Moffitt, Terrie E. (2003). Life-course-persistent and adolescence-limited antisocial behavior: A 10-year research review and a research agenda. In Benjamin B. Lahey, Terrie E. Moffitt, & Avshalom Caspi (Eds.), *Causes of conduct disorder and juvenile delinquency* (pp. 49–75). New York, NY: Guilford Press.

Moffitt, Terrie E., Caspi, Avshalom, & Rutter, Michael. (2006). Measured gene-environment interactions in psychopathology: Concepts, research strategies, and implications for research, intervention, and public understanding of genetics. *Perspectives on Psychological Science, 1,* 5–27.

Moffitt, Terrie E., Caspi, Avshalom, Rutter, Michael, & Silva, Phil A. (2001). *Sex differences in antisocial behaviour: Conduct disorder, delinquency, and violence in the Dunedin Longitudinal Study.* New York, NY: Cambridge University Press.

Mofidi, Mahyar, Zeldin, Leslie P., & Rozier, R. Gary. (2009). Oral health of Early Head Start children: A qualitative study of staff, parents, and pregnant women. *American Journal of Public Health, 99,* 245–251.

Molina, Brooke S. G., Hinshaw, Stephen P., Swanson, James W., Arnold, L. Eugene, Vitiello, Benedetto, Jensen, Peter S., . . . Houck, Patricia R. (2009). The MTA at 8 years: Prospective follow-up of children treated for combined-type ADHD in a multisite study. *Journal of the American Academy of Child & Adolescent Psychiatry, 48,* 484.

Molitor, Adriana, & Hsu, Hui-Chin. (2011). Child development across cultures. In Kenneth D. Keith (Ed.), *Cross-cultural psychology: Contemporary themes and perspectives* (pp. 75–109). Malden, MA: Wiley-Blackwell.

Møller, Signe J., & Tenenbaum, Harriet R. (2011). Danish majority children's reasoning about exclusion based on gender and ethnicity. *Child Development, 82,* 520–532.

Moloney, Molly, MacKenzie, Kathleen, Hunt, Geoffrey, & Joe-Laidler, Karen. (2009). The path and promise of fatherhood for gang members. *British Journal of Criminology, 49,* 305–325.

Monahan, Kathryn C., Steinberg, Laurence, & Cauffman, Elizabeth. (2009). Affiliation with antisocial peers, susceptibility to peer influence, and antisocial behavior during the transition to adulthood. *Developmental Psychology, 45,* 1520–1530.

Monastersky, Richard. (2007, January 12). Who's minding the teenage brain? *Chronicle of Higher Education,* pp. A14–A18.

Moncloa, Fe, Wilkinson-Lee, Ada M., & Russell, Stephen T. (2010). Cuídate sin pena: Mexican mother-adolescent sexuality communication. *Journal of Ethnic and Cultural Diversity in Social Work, 19,* 217–234.

Monks, Claire P., & Coyne, Iain. (2011). *Bullying in different contexts.* New York, NY: Cambridge University Press.

Monserud, Maria A., & Elder, Glen H. (2011). Household structure and children's educational attainment: A perspective on coresidence with grandparents. *Journal of Marriage and Family, 73,* 981–1000.

Monteiro, Carlos A., Conde, Wolney L., & Popkin, Barry M. (2004). The burden of disease from undernutrition and overnutrition in countries undergoing rapid nutrition transition: A view from Brazil. *American Journal of Public Health, 94*, 433–434.

Monteiro, Carlos A., Conde, Wolney L., & Popkin, Barry M. (2007). Income-specific trends in obesity in Brazil: 1975–2003. *American Journal of Public Health, 97*, 1808–1812.

Montgomery, Leigh, & Williams, Stacie. (2010). *Countries with the highest college graduation rates*. Retrieved from http://www.csmonitor.com/USA/Education/2010/0809/Countries-with-the-highest-college-graduation-rates/Ireland-43.9-percent

Moody, H. R. (2009). Eco-elders: Legacy and environmental advocacy. *Generations, 33*(4), 70–74.

Moody, Raymond A. (1975). *Life after life: The investigation of a phenomenon—Survival of bodily death*. Atlanta, GA: Mockingbird Books.

Moon, Marilyn. (2011). Organization and financing of health care. In Robert H. Binstock & Linda K. George (Eds.), *Handbook of aging and the social sciences* (7th ed., pp. 295–307). San Diego, CA: Academic Press.

Moon, Michelle. (2011). The effects of divorce on children: Married and divorced parents' perspectives. *Journal of Divorce & Remarriage, 52*, 344–349.

Moore, Ginger A., & Calkins, Susan D. (2004). Infants' vagal regulation in the still-face paradigm is related to dyadic coordination of mother-infant interaction. *Developmental Psychology, 40*, 1068–1080.

Moore, Keith L., & Persaud, Trivedi V. N. (2003). *The developing human: Clinically oriented embryology* (7th ed.). Philadelphia, PA: Saunders.

Moore, Keith L., & Persaud, Trivedi V. N. (2007). *The developing human: Clinically oriented embryology* (8th ed.). Philadelphia, PA: Saunders/Elsevier.

Moore, Kelly L., Boscardin, W. John, Steinman, Michael A., & Schwartz, Janice B. (2012). Age and sex variation in prevalence of chronic medical conditions in older residents of U.S. nursing homes. *Journal of the American Geriatrics Society, 60*, 756–764.

Moore, Susan, & Rosenthal, Doreen. (2006). *Sexuality in adolescence: Current trends* (2nd ed.). New York, NY: Routledge.

Morasch, Katherine C., & Bell, Martha Ann. (2009). Patterns of brain-electrical activity during declarative memory performance in 10-month-old infants. *Brain and Cognition, 71*, 215–222.

Morelli, Gilda A., & Rothbaum, Fred. (2007). Situating the child in context: Attachment relationships and self-regulation in different cultures. In Shinobu Kitayama & Dov Cohen (Eds.), *Handbook of cultural psychology* (pp. 500–527). New York, NY: Guilford Press.

Moreno, Carmen, Laje, Gonzalo, Blanco, Carlos, Jiang, Huiping, Schmidt, Andrew B., & Olfson, Mark. (2007). National trends in the outpatient diagnosis and treatment of bipolar disorder in youth. *Archives of General Psychiatry, 64*, 1032–1039.

Moreno, Luis A., Pigeot, Iris, & Ahrens, Wolfgang. (2011). *Epidemiology of obesity in children and adolescents: Prevalence and etiology*. New York: Springer.

Morgan, Ian G. (2003). The biological basis of myopic refractive error. *Clinical and Experimental Optometry, 86*, 276–288.

Morning, Ann. (2008). Ethnic classification in global perspective: A cross-national survey of the 2000 census round. *Population Research and Policy Review, 27*, 239–272.

Morón, Cecilio, & Viteri, Fernando E. (2009). Update on common indicators of nutritional status: Food access, food consumption, and biochemical measures of iron and anemia. *Nutrition Reviews, 67*(Suppl. 1), S31–S35.

Morris, Amanda Sheffield, Silk, Jennifer S., Steinberg, Laurence, Myers, Sonya S., & Robinson, Lara Rachel. (2007). The role of the family context in the development of emotion regulation. *Social Development, 16*, 361–388.

Morris, Danielle H., Jones, Michael E., Schoemaker, Minouk J., Ashworth, Alan, & Swerdlow, Anthony J. (2011). Familial concordance for age at natural menopause: Results from the Breakthrough Generations Study. *Menopause, 18*, 956–961.

Morris, John A., Jordan, Cynthia L., & Breedlove, S. Marc. (2004). Sexual differentiation of the vertebrate nervous system. *Nature Neuroscience, 7*, 1034–1039.

Morrison, Frederick J., Ponitz, Claire Cameron, & McClelland, Megan M. (2010). Self-regulation and academic achievement in the transition to school. In Susan D. Calkins & Martha Ann Bell (Eds.), *Child development at the intersection of emotion and cognition* (pp. 203–224). Washington, DC: American Psychological Association.

Morrison, Mike, Tay, Louis, & Diener, Ed. (2011). Subjective well-being and national satisfaction. *Psychological Science, 22*, 166–171.

Morrissey, Taryn. (2009). Multiple child-care arrangements and young children's behavioral outcomes. *Child Development, 80*, 59–76.

Morrow, Daniel G., Ridolfo, Heather E., Menard, William E., Sanborn, Adam, Stine-Morrow, Elizabeth A. L., Magnor, Cliff, . . . Bryant, David. (2003). Environmental support promotes expertise-based mitigation of age differences on pilot communication tasks. *Psychology & Aging, 18*, 268–284.

Morrow-Howell, Nancy, & Freedman, Marc. (2006–2007). Bringing civic engagement into sharper focus. *Generations, 30*(4), 6–9.

Mosher, Catherine E., & Danoff-Burg, Sharon. (2007). Death anxiety and cancer-related stigma: A terror management analysis. *Death Studies, 31*, 885–907.

Mõttus, René, Johnson, Wendy, & Deary, Ian J. (2012). Personality traits in old age: Measurement and rank-order stability and some mean-level change. *Personality and Aging, 27*, 243–249.

Moulson, Margaret C., Westerlund, Alissa, Fox, Nathan A., Zeanah, Charles H., & Nelson, Charles A. (2009). The effects of early experience on face recognition: An event-related potential study of institutionalized children in Romania. *Child Development, 80*, 1039–1056.

Mroczek, Daniel K., Spiro, Avion, III, & Griffin, Paul W. (2006). Personality and aging. In James E. Birren & K. Warner Schaie (Eds.), *Handbook of the psychology of aging* (6th ed., pp. 363–377). Amsterdam, NL: Elsevier.

Mrozek-Budzyn, Dorota, Kieltyka, Agnieszka, & Majewska, Renata. (2010). Lack of association between measles-mumps-rubella vaccination and autism in children: A case-control study. *The Pediatric Infectious Disease Journal, 29,* 397–400.

Mueller, Christian E., Bridges, Sara K., & Goddard, Michelle S. (2011). Sleep and parent-family connectedness: Links, relationships and implications for adolescent depression. *Journal of Family Studies, 17,* 9–23.

Muir, Susan W., Gopaul, Karen, & Montero Odasso, Manuel M. (2012). The role of cognitive impairment in fall risk among older adults: A systematic review and meta-analysis. *Age and Ageing, 41,* 299–308.

Mulder, Pamela J., & Johnson, Teresa S. (2010). The Beginning Breastfeeding Survey: Measuring mothers' perceptions of breastfeeding effectiveness during the postpartum hospitalization. *Research in Nursing & Health, 33,* 329–344.

Müller, Ulrich, Dick, Anthony Steven, Gela, Katherine, Overton, Willis F., & Zelazo, Philip David. (2006). The role of negative priming in preschoolers' flexible rule use on the dimensional change card sort task. *Child Development, 77,* 395–412.

Mullis, Ina V. S., Martin, Michael O., Foy, Pierre, & Drucker, Kathleen T. (2012). *PIRLS 2011 international results in reading.* Chestnut Hill, MA: TIMSS & PIRLS International Study Center, Boston College.

Munck, Hanne. (2009). Early intervention and fatherhood: Denmark. In Kevin J. Nugent, Bonnie J. Petrauskas, & T. Berry Brazelton (Eds.), *The newborn as a person: Enabling healthy infant development worldwide* (pp. 101–111). Hoboken, NJ: Wiley.

Muñoz, Carmen, & Singleton, David. (2011). A critical review of age-related research on L2 ultimate attainment. *Language Teaching, 44,* 1–35.

Munroe, Robert L., & Romney, A. Kimbal. (2006). Gender and age differences in same-sex aggregation and social behavior: A four-culture study. *Journal of Cross-Cultural Psychology, 37,* 3–19.

Muraco, Anna. (2006). Intentional families: Fictive kin ties between cross-gender, different sexual orientation friends. *Journal of Marriage and Family, 68,* 1313–1325.

Murphy, Michael. (2011). Long-term effects of the demographic transition on family and kinship networks in Britain. *Population and Development Review, 37*(Suppl. 1), 55–80.

Murphy, Sherry L., Xu, Jiaquan, & Kochanek, Kenneth D. (2012). Deaths: Preliminary data for 2010. *National Vital Statistics Reports, 60*(4).

Murray, Christopher J. L., Kulkarni, Sandeep C., Michaud, Catherine, Tomijima, Niels, Bulzacchelli, Maria T., Iandiorio, Terrell J., & Ezzati, Majid. (2006). Eight Americas: Investigating mortality disparities across races, counties, and race-counties in the United States. *PLoS Medicine, 3,* e260.

Musick, Kelly, & Bumpass, Larry. (2012). Reexamining the case for marriage: Union formation and changes in well-being. *Journal of Marriage and Family, 74,* 1–18.

Mustonen, Ulla, Huurre, Taina, Kiviruusu, Olli, Haukkala, Ari, & Aro, Hillevi. (2011). Long-term impact of parental divorce on intimate relationship quality in adulthood and the mediating role of psychosocial resources. *Journal of Family Psychology, 25,* 615–619.

Mutti, Donald. (2010, January 1). Myopia out of control. *Science, 327,* 17.

Mutti, Donald O., & Zadnik, Karla. (2009). Has near work's star fallen? *Optometry & Vision Science, 86,* 76–78.

Nadeau, Joseph H., & Dudley, Aimée M. (2011, February 25). Systems genetics. *Science, 331,* 1015–1016.

NAEYC (National Association for the Education of Young Children). (2012). *All criteria document.* Retrieved from http://www.naeyc.org/files/academy/file/AllCriteriaDocument.pdf

Nagata, Chisato, Nakamura, Kozue, Wada, Keiko, Oba, Shino, Hayashi, Makoto, Takeda, Noriyuki, & Yasuda, Keigo. (2010). Association of dietary fat, vegetables and antioxidant micronutrients with skin ageing in Japanese women. *British Journal of Nutrition, 103,* 1493–1498.

Nagda, Biren A., Gurin, Patricia, & Johnson, Shawnti M. (2005). Living, doing and thinking diversity: How does pre-college diversity experience affect first-year students' engagement with college diversity? In Robert S. Feldman (Ed.), *Improving the first year of college: Research and practice* (pp. 73–108). Mahwah, NJ: Erlbaum.

Naninck, Eva F. G., Lucassen, Paul J., & Bakker, Julie. (2011). Sex differences in adolescent depression: Do sex hormones determine vulnerability? *Journal of Neuroendocrinology, 23,* 383–392.

Narayan, Chandan R., Werker, Janet F., & Beddor, Patrice Speeter. (2010). The interaction between acoustic salience and language experience in developmental speech perception: Evidence from nasal place discrimination. *Developmental Science, 13,* 407–420.

Narvaez, Darcia, & Lapsley, Daniel K. (2009). Moral identity, moral functioning, and the development of moral character. In H. Ross Brian (Series Ed.) & Daniel Bartels, Christopher Bauman, Linda Skitka, & Douglas Medin (Vol. Eds.), *Psychology of learning and motivation* (Vol. 50, pp. 237–274). San Diego, CA: Academic Press.

National Center for Environmental Health. (2012). *Tested and confirmed elevated blood lead levels by state, year and blood lead level group for children <72 months.* Atlanta, GA: Centers for Disease Control and Prevention.

National Center for Health Statistics. (2010). *Health, United States, 2009: With special feature on medical technology.* Hyattsville, MD: Author.

National Center for Health Statistics. (2011). *Health, United States, 2010: With special feature on death and dying.* Hyattsville, MD: Author.

National Center for Health Statistics. (2012a, June). *2011 National Health Interview Survey (NHIS).* Hyattsville, MD: Author.

National Center for Health Statistics. (2012b). Anthropometric reference data for children and adults: United States, 2007–2010. Vital Health Statistics, 11.

National Center for Health Statistics. (2012c, August). Births: Final data for 2010. *Vital Health Statistics, 61*(1).

National Center for Health Statistics. (2012d, June). Births: Preliminary data for 2011. *Vital Health Statistics, 61*(5).

National Center for Health Statistics. (2012e). Deaths: Leading causes for 2009. *National Vital Statistics Reports, 61*(7).

National Center for Health Statistics. (2012f). *Health, United States, 2011: With special feature on socioeconomic status and health.* Hyattsville, MD: Author.

National Governors Association Center for Best Practices (NGA Center) and the Council of Chief State School Officers (CCSSO). (2010). *Common Core State Standards Initiative.* Retrieved from http://corestandards.org/

National Heart, Lung, and Blood Institute. (n.d.). Body mass index table. Retrieved September 14, 2009, from http://www.nhlbi.nih.gov/guidelines/obesity/bmi_tbl.htm

National Highway Traffic Safety Administration. (1993). *Addressing the safety issues related to younger and older drivers.* Washington, DC: Author. Retrieved from: www.nhtsa.gov/people/injury/olddrive/pub/Chapter1.html

National Safety Council. (2011). *Injury facts.* Itasca, IL: Author. Retrieved from: www.nsc.org/Documents/Injury_Facts/Injury_Facts_2011_w.pdf

National Sleep Foundation. (2006). *Summary findings of the 2006 Sleep in America poll.* Retrieved from http://www.sleepfoundation.org/atf/cf/%7BF6BF2668-A1B4-4FE8-8D1A-A5D39340D9CB%7D/2006_summary_of_findings.pdf

Neave, Nick. (2008). *Hormones and behaviour: A psychological approach.* New York, NY: Cambridge University Press.

Needleman, Herbert L., & Gatsonis, Constantine A. (1990). Low-level lead exposure and the IQ of children: A meta-analysis of modern studies. *Journal of the American Medical Association, 263*, 673–678.

Needleman, Herbert L., Schell, Alan, Bellinger, David, Leviton, Alan, & Allred, Elizabeth N. (1990). The long-term effects of exposure to low doses of lead in childhood. *New England Journal of Medicine, 322*, 83–88.

Neimeyer, Robert A., & Currier, Joseph M. (2009). Grief therapy: Evidence of efficacy and emerging directions. *Current Directions in Psychological Science, 18*, 352–356.

Nelson, Charles A., III, Zeanah, Charles H., Fox, Nathan A., Marshall, Peter J., Smyke, Anna T., & Guthrie, Donald. (2007, December 21). Cognitive recovery in socially deprived young children: The Bucharest Early Intervention Project. *Science, 318*, 1937–1940.

Nelson, Larry J., Hart, Craig H., & Evans, Cortney A. (2008). Solitary-functional play and solitary-pretend play: Another look at the construct of solitary-active behavior using playground observations. *Social Development, 17*, 812–831.

Nelson, R. Michael, & DeBacker, Teresa K. (2008). Achievement motivation in adolescents: The role of peer climate and best friends. *Journal of Experimental Education, 76*, 170–189.

Nelson, Todd D. (2011). Ageism: The strange case of prejudice against the older you. In Richard L. Wiener & Steven

L. Willborn (Eds.), *Disability and aging discrimination: Perspectives in law and psychology* (pp. 37–47). New York, NY: Springer.

Neugarten, Bernice L., & Neugarten, Dail A. (1986). Changing meanings of age in the aging society. In Alan J. Pifer & Lydia Bronte (Eds.), *Our aging society: Paradox and promise* (pp. 33–52). New York, NY: Norton.

Neumann, Anna, van Lier, Pol, Frijns, Tom, Meeus, Wim, & Koot, Hans. (2011). Emotional dynamics in the development of early adolescent psychopathology: A one-year longitudinal study. *Journal of Abnormal Child Psychology, 39*, 657–669.

Nevin, Rick. (2007). Understanding international crime trends: The legacy of preschool lead exposure. *Environmental Research, 104*, 315–336.

Nevin, Rick, Jacobs, David E., Berg, Michael, & Cohen, Jonathan. (2008). Monetary benefits of preventing childhood lead poisoning with lead-safe window replacement. *Environmental Research, 106*, 410–419.

Newell, Karl M., Vaillancourt, David E., & Sosnoff, Jacob J. (2006). Aging, complexity, and motor performance. In James E. Birren & K. Warner Schaie (Eds.), *Handbook of the psychology of aging* (6th ed., pp. 163–182). Amsterdam, The Netherlands: Elsevier.

Newnham, Carol A., Milgrom, Jeannette, & Skouteris, Helen. (2009). Effectiveness of a modified mother-infant transaction program on outcomes for preterm infants from 3 to 24 months of age. *Infant Behavior and Development, 32*, 17–26.

Ng, Nawi, Weinehall, Lars, & Öhman, Ann. (2007). 'If I don't smoke, I'm not a real man'—Indonesian teenage boys' views about smoking. *Health Education Research, 22*, 794–804.

Ngui, Emmanuel, Cortright, Alicia, & Blair, Kathleen. (2009). An investigation of paternity status and other factors associated with racial and ethnic disparities in birth outcomes in Milwaukee, Wisconsin. *Maternal and Child Health Journal, 13*, 467–478.

Nic Gabhainn, Saoirse, Baban, Adriana, Boyce, William, Godeau, Emmanuelle, & The HBSC Sexual Health Focus Group. (2009). How well protected are sexually active 15-year olds? Cross-national patterns in condom and contraceptive pill use 2002–2006. *International Journal of Public Health, 54*, 209–215.

Niccols, Alison. (2007). Fetal alcohol syndrome and the developing socio-emotional brain. *Brain and Cognition, 65*, 135–142.

NICHD Early Child Care Research Network (Ed.). (2005). *Child care and child development: Results from the NICHD Study of Early Child Care and Youth Development.* New York, NY: Guilford Press.

NICHD Early Child Care Research Network. (2007). Age of entry to kindergarten and children's academic achievement and socioemotional development. *Early Education and Development, 18*, 337–368.

Nichols, Tracy R., Graber, Julia A., Brooks-Gunn, Jeanne, & Botvin, Gilbert J. (2006). Sex differences in overt aggression and delinquency among urban minority middle school students. *Journal of Applied Developmental Psychology, 27*, 78–91.

Nicholson, Barbara, & Parker, Lysa. (2009). *Attached at the heart: 8 proven parenting principles for raising connected and compassionate children.* Bloomington, IN: iUniverse.com.

Nielsen, Mark. (2006). Copying actions and copying outcomes: Social learning through the second year. *Developmental Psychology, 42,* 555–565.

Nielsen, Mark, & Tomaselli, Keyan. (2010). Overimitation in Kalahari Bushman children and the origins of human cultural cognition. *Psychological Science, 21,* 729–736.

Niji, Rie, Arita, Kenji, Abe, Yoko, Lucas, Milanita E., Nishino, Mizuho, & Mitome, Masato. (2010). Maternal age at birth and other risk factors in early childhood caries. *Pediatric Dentistry, 32,* 493–498.

Nimrod, Galit. (2007). Expanding, reducing, concentrating and diffusing: Post retirement leisure behavior and life satisfaction. *Leisure Sciences, 29,* 91–111.

Nishida, Tracy K., & Lillard, Angeline S. (2007). The informative value of emotional expressions: 'Social referencing' in mother-child pretense. *Developmental Science, 10,* 205–212.

Nishina, Adrienne, & Juvonen, Jaana. (2005). Daily reports of witnessing and experiencing peer harassment in middle school. *Child Development, 76,* 435–450.

Nobles, Jenna. (2011). Parenting from abroad: Migration, non-resident father involvement, and children's education in Mexico. *Journal of Marriage and Family, 73,* 729–746.

Nordgren, Loran F., van Harreveld, Frenk, & van der Pligt, Joop. (2009). The restraint bias: How the illusion of self-restraint promotes impulsive behavior. *Psychological Science, 20,* 1523–1528.

Norris, Deborah J. (2010). Raising the educational requirements for teachers in infant toddler classrooms: Implications for institutions of higher education. *Journal of Early Childhood Teacher Education, 31,* 146–158.

Nsamenang, A. Bame. (2004). *Cultures of human development and education: Challenge to growing up African.* New York, NY: Nova Science.

Nucci, Larry, & Turiel, Elliot. (2009). Capturing the complexity of moral development and education. *Mind, Brain, and Education, 3,* 151–159.

Nugent, J. Kevin, Petrauskas, Bonnie J., & Brazelton, T. Berry. (Eds.) (2009). *The newborn as a person: Enabling healthy infant development worldwide.* Hoboken, NJ: Wiley.

Nyberg, Lars, & Bäckman, Lars. (2011). Memory changes and the aging brain: A multimodal imaging approach. In K. Warner Schaie & Sherry L. Willis (Eds.), *Handbook of the psychology of aging* (7th ed., pp. 121–131). San Diego, CA: Academic Press.

O'Donnell, Lydia, Stueve, Ann, Duran, Richard, Myint-U, Athi, Agronick, Gail, Doval, Alexi San, & Wilson-Simmons, Renée. (2008). Parenting practices, parents' underestimation of daughters' risks, and alcohol and sexual behaviors of urban girls. *Journal of Adolescent Health, 42,* 496–502.

O'Leary, Colleen M., Nassar, Natasha, Zubrick, Stephen R., Kurinczuk, Jennifer J., Stanley, Fiona, & Bower, Carol. (2010). Evidence of a complex association between dose, pattern and timing of prenatal alcohol exposure and child behaviour problems. *Addiction, 105,* 74–86.

O'Malley, A. James, & Christakis, Nicholas A. (2011). Longitudinal analysis of large social networks: Estimating the effect of health traits on changes in friendship ties. *Statistics in Medicine, 30,* 950–964.

O'Neil, Kelly A., Conner, Bradley T., & Kendall, Philip C. (2011). Internalizing disorders and substance use disorders in youth: Comorbidity, risk, temporal order, and implications for intervention. *Clinical Psychology Review, 31,* 104–112.

O'Rahilly, Ronan R., & Müller, Fabiola. (2001). *Human embryology & teratology* (3rd ed.). New York, NY: Wiley-Liss.

O'Rourke, Norm, Cappeliez, Philippe, & Claxton, Amy. (2010a). Functions of reminiscence and the psychological well-being of young-old and older adults over time. *Aging & Mental Health, 15,* 272–281.

O'Rourke, Norm, Neufeld, Eva, Claxton, Amy, & Smith, JuliAnna Z. (2010b). Knowing me-knowing you: Reported personality and trait discrepancies as predictors of marital idealization between long-wed spouses. *Psychology and Aging, 25,* 412–421.

Oakes, Lisa M., Cashon, Cara H., Casasola, Marianella, & Rakison, David H. (Eds.). (2011). *Infant perception and cognition: Recent advances, emerging theories, and future directions.* New York, NY: Oxford University Press.

Ochsner, Kevin N., Hughes, Brent, Robertson, Elaine R., Cooper, Jeffrey C., & Gabrieli, John D. E. (2009). Neural systems supporting the control of affective and cognitive conflicts. *Journal of Cognitive Neuroscience, 21,* 1842–1855.

OECD. (2010a). *PISA 2009 results: Learning to learn: Vol. 3. Student engagement, strategies and practices.* Retrieved from http://www.oecd-ilibrary.org/education/pisa-2009-results-learning-to-learn_9789264083943-en

OECD. (2010b). *PISA 2009 results: What students know and can do: Vol. 1. Student performance in reading, mathematics and science.* Retrieved from http://www.oecd.org/dataoecd/10/61/48852548.pdf

OECD. (2011). *Education at a glance 2011: OECD indicators.* Paris, France: OECD.

Offit, Paul A. (2008). *Autism's false prophets: Bad science, risky medicine, and the search for a cure.* New York, NY: Columbia University Press.

Ogbu, John U. (Ed.) (2008). *Minority status, oppositional culture, and schooling.* New York, NY: Routledge.

Ogden, Cynthia L., Carroll, Margaret D., Kit, Brian K., & Flegal, Katherine M. (2012). Prevalence of obesity and trends in body mass index among US children and adolescents, 1999–2010. *Journal of the American Medical Association, 307,* 483–490.

Ogden, Cynthia L., Gorber, Sarah Connor, Dommarco, Juan A. Rivera, Carroll, Margaret, Shields, Margot, & Flegal, Katherine. (2011). The epidemiology of childhood obesity in Canada, Mexico and the United States. In Luis A. Moreno, Iris Pigeot, & Wolfgang Ahrens (Eds.), *Epidemiology of obesity in children and adolescents* (Vol. 2, pp. 69–93). New York, NY: Springer.

Okazaki, Sumie, Okazaki, Mimi, & Sue, Stanley. (2012). Clinical personality assessment with Asian Americans. In James N. Butcher (Ed.), *Oxford handbook of personality assessment* (pp. 377–395). New York, NY: Oxford University Press.

Olatunji, Bunmi O., Cisler, Josh M., & Tolin, David F. (2007). Quality of life in the anxiety disorders: A meta-analytic review. *Clinical Psychology Review, 2,* 572–581.

Oldershaw, Lynn. (2002). *A national survey of parents of young children.* Toronto, Ontario, Canada: Invest in Kids.

Olds, Tim, Maher, Carol, Zumin, Shi, Peneau, Sandrine, Lioret, Sandrine, Castetbon, Katia, et al. (2011). Evidence that the prevalence of childhood overweight is plateauing: Data from nine countries. *International Journal of Pediatric Obesity 6,* 342–360.

Olfson, Mark, Crystal, Stephen, Huang, Cecilia, & Gerhard, Tobias. (2010). Trends in antipsychotic drug use by very young, privately insured children. *Journal of the American Academy of Child and Adolescent Psychiatry, 49,* 13–23.

Olshansky, S. Jay. (2011). Trends in longevity and prospects for the future. In Robert H. Binstock & Linda K. George (Eds.), *Handbook of aging and the social sciences* (7th ed., pp. 47–56). San Diego, CA: Academic Press.

Olshansky, S. Jay, Antonucci, Toni, Berkman, Lisa, Binstock, Robert H., Boersch-Supan, Axel, Cacioppo, John T.,... Rowe, John. (2012). Differences in life expectancy due to race and educational differences are widening, and many may not catch up. *Health Affairs, 31,* 1803–1813.

Olson, Kristina R., & Dweck, Carol S. (2008). A blueprint for social cognitive development. *Perspectives on Psychological Science, 3,* 193–202.

Olson, Kristina R., & Dweck, Carol S. (2009). Social cognitive development: A new look. *Child Development Perspectives, 3,* 60–65.

Olson, Sheryl L., Lopez-Duran, Nestor, Lunkenheimer, Erika S., Chang, Hyein, & Sameroff, Arnold J. (2011). Individual differences in the development of early peer aggression: Integrating contributions of self-regulation, theory of mind, and parenting. *Development and Psychopathology, 23,* 253–266.

Olweus, Dan, Limber, Sue, & Mahalic, Sharon F. (1999). *Bullying prevention program.* Boulder, CO: Center for the Study and Prevention of Violence, Institute of Behavioral Science, University of Colorado at Boulder.

Omariba, D. Walter Rasugu, & Boyle, Michael H. (2007). Family structure and child mortality in sub-Saharan Africa: Cross-national effects of polygyny. *Journal of Marriage and Family, 69,* 528–543.

Ontai, Lenna L., & Thompson, Ross A. (2008). Attachment, parent-child discourse and theory-of-mind development. *Social Development, 17,* 47–60.

Oosterman, Mirjam, Schuengel, Carlo, & Slot, N. Wim. (2007). Disruptions in foster care: A review and meta-analysis. *Children and Youth Services Review, 29,* 53–76.

Oregon Public Health Division. (2012). *Table 1. Characteristics and end-of-life care of 596 DWDA patients who have died from ingesting a lethal dose of medication as of February 29, 2012, by year, Oregon, 1998–2011.* Retrieved from http://public.health. oregon.gov/ProviderPartnerResources/EvaluationResearch/DeathwithDignityAct/Documents/year14-tbl-1.pdf

Ormerod, Thomas C. (2005). Planning and ill-defined problems. In Robin Morris & Geoff Ward (Eds.), *The cognitive psychology of planning* (pp. 53–70). New York, NY: Psychology Press.

Osgood, D. Wayne, Ruth, Gretchen, Eccles, Jacquelynne S., Jacobs, Janis E., & Barber, Bonnie L. (2005). Six paths to adulthood: Fast starters, parents without careers, educated partners, educated singles, working singles, and slow starters. In Richard A. Settersten, Jr., Frank F. Furstenberg, Jr., & Rubén G. Rumbaut (Eds.), *On the frontier of adulthood: Theory, research, and public policy* (pp. 320–355). Chicago, IL: University of Chicago Press.

Osorio, Snezana Nena. (2011). Reconsidering Kwashiorkor. *Topics in Clinical Nutrition, 26,* 10–13.

Ostfeld, Barbara M., Esposito, Linda, Perl, Harold, & Hegyi, Thomas. (2010). Concurrent risks in sudden infant death syndrome. *Pediatrics, 125,* 447–453.

Over, Harriet, & Gattis, Merideth. (2010). Verbal imitation is based on intention understanding. *Cognitive Development, 25,* 46–55.

Overbeek, Geertjan, Stattin, Håkan, Vermulst, Ad, Ha, Thao, & Engels, Rutger C. M. E. (2007). Parent-child relationships, partner relationships, and emotional adjustment: A birth-to-maturity prospective study. *Developmental Psychology, 43,* 429–437.

Owen-Kostelnik, Jessica, Reppucci, N. Dickon, & Meyer, Jessica R. (2006). Testimony and interrogation of minors: Assumptions about maturity and morality. *American Psychologist, 61,* 286–304.

Oyekale, Abayomi Samuel, & Oyekale, Tolulope Olayemi. (2009). Do mothers' educational levels matter in child malnutrition and health outcomes in Gambia and Niger? *The Social Sciences, 4,* 118–127.

Pace, Cecilia Serena, Zavattini, Giulio Cesare, & D'Alessio, Maria. (2011). Continuity and discontinuity of attachment patterns: A short-term longitudinal pilot study using a sample of late-adopted children and their adoptive mothers. *Attachment & Human Development, 14,* 45–61.

Padilla-Walker, Laura M., Barry, Carolyn McNamara, Carroll, Jason S., Madsen, Stephanie D., & Nelson, Larry J. (2008). Looking on the bright side: The role of identity status and gender on positive orientations during emerging adulthood. *Journal of Adolescence, 31,* 451–467.

Pagani, Linda S., Japel, Christa, Girard, Alain, Farhat, Abdeljelil, Cote, Sylvana, & Tremblay, Richard E. (2006). Middle childhood life course trajectories: Links between family dysfunction and children's behavioral development. In Aletha C. Huston & Marika N. Ripke (Eds.), *Developmental contexts in middle childhood: Bridges to adolescence and adulthood* (pp. 130–149). New York, NY: Cambridge University Press.

Paganini-Hill, Annlia, Kawas, Claudia H., & Corrada, María M. (2011). Activities and mortality in the elderly: The Leisure World Cohort Study. *The Journals of Gerontology Series A: Biological Sciences and Medical Sciences, 66A,* 559–567.

Paik, Anthony. (2011). Adolescent sexuality and the risk of marital dissolution. *Journal of Marriage and Family, 73,* 472–485.

Painter, Jodie N., Willemsen, Gonneke, Nyholt, Dale, Hoekstra, Chantal, Duffy, David L., Henders, Anjali K.,... Montgomery, Grant W. (2010). A genome wide linkage scan for dizygotic twinning in 525 families of mothers of dizygotic twins. *Human Reproduction, 25,* 1569–1580.

Palagi, Elisabetta. (2011). Playing at every age: Modalities and potential functions in non-human primates. In Anthony D. Pellegrini (Ed.), *The Oxford handbook of the development of play* (pp. 70–82). New York, NY: Oxford University Press.

Palmore, Erdman. (2005). Three decades of research on ageism. *Generations, 29*(1), 87–90.

Pardini, Matteo, & Nichelli, Paolo F. (2009). Age-related decline in mentalizing skills across adult life span. *Experimental Aging Research, 35,* 98–106.

Park, Denise C., & Reuter-Lorenz, Patricia. (2009). The adaptive brain: Aging and neurocognitive scaffolding. *Annual Review of Psychology, 60,* 173–196.

Park, D. J. J., & Congdon, Nathan G. (2004). Evidence for an "epidemic" of myopia. *Annals, Academy of Medicine, Singapore, 33,* 21–26.

Park, Hyun, Bothe, Denise, Holsinger, Eva, Kirchner, H. Lester, Olness, Karen, & Mandalakas, Anna. (2011). The impact of nutritional status and longitudinal recovery of motor and cognitive milestones in internationally adopted children. *International Journal of Environmental Research and Public Health, 8,* 105–116.

Park, Jong-Tae, Jang, Yoonsun, Park, Min Sun, Pae, Calvin, Park, Jinyi, Hu, Kyung-Seok,... Kim, Hee-Jin. (2011). The trend of body donation for education based on Korean social and religious culture. *Anatomical Sciences Education, 4,* 33–38.

Parke, Ross D., & Buriel, Raymond. (2006). Socialization in the family: Ethnic and ecological perspectives. In William Damon & Richard M. Lerner (Series Eds.) & Nancy Eisenberg (Vol. Ed.), *Handbook of child psychology: Vol. 3. Social, emotional, and personality development* (6th ed., pp. 429–504). Hoboken, NJ: Wiley.

Parke, Ross D., Coltrane, Scott, Duffy, Sharon, Buriel, Raymond, Dennis, Jessica, Powers, Justina,... Widaman, Keith F. (2004). Economic stress, parenting, and child adjustment in Mexican American and European American families. *Child Development, 75,* 1632–1656.

Parladé, Meaghan V., & Iverson, Jana M. (2011). The interplay between language, gesture, and affect during communicative transition: A dynamic systems approach. *Developmental Psychology, 47,* 820–833.

Parris, Leandra, Varjas, Kris, Meyers, Joel, & Cutts, Hayley. (2012). High school students' perceptions of coping with cyberbullying. *Youth & Society, 44,* 284–306.

Parveen, Sahdia, & Morrison, Val. (2009). Predictors of familism in the caregiver role: A pilot study. *Journal of Health Psychology, 14,* 1135–1143.

Parylak, Sarah L., Koob, George F., & Zorrilla, Eric P. (2011). The dark side of food addiction. *Physiology & Behavior, 104,* 149–156.

Pascarella, Ernest T., & Terenzini, Patrick T. (1991). *How college affects students: Findings and insights from twenty years of research.* San Francisco, CA: Jossey-Bass.

Pashler, Harold, McDaniel, Mark, Rohrer, Doug, & Bjork, Robert. (2008). Learning styles: Concepts and evidence. *Psychological Science in the Public Interest, 9,* 105–119.

Passel, Jeffrey S. (2011). Demography of immigrant youth: Past, present, and future. *The Future of Children, 21,* 19–41.

Patel, Vimla L., Arocha, José F., & Kaufman, David R. (1999). Expertise and tacit knowledge in medicine. In Robert J. Sternberg & Joseph A. Horvath (Eds.), *Tacit knowledge in professional practice: Researcher and practitioner perspectives* (pp. 75–99). Mahwah, NJ: Erlbaum.

Pathela, Preeti, & Schillinger, Julia A. (2010). Sexual behaviors and sexual violence: Adolescents with opposite-, same-, or both-sex partners. *Pediatrics, 126,* 879–886.

Patrick, Megan E., & Schulenberg, John E. (2011). How trajectories of reasons for alcohol use relate to trajectories of binge drinking: National panel data spanning late adolescence to early adulthood. *Developmental Psychology, 47,* 311–317.

Pausch, Jai. (2012). *Dream new dreams: Reimagining my life after loss.* New York, NY: Crown Archetype.

Pausch, Randy [CarnegieMellonU]. (2007, December 20). *Randy Pausch last lecture: Achieving your childhood dreams* [Video file]. Retrieved from http://www.youtube.com/watch?v=ji5_MqicxSo

Pearson, Barbara Zurer. (2008). *Raising a bilingual child: A step-by-step guide for parents.* New York, NY: Living Language.

Pedersen, Nancy L., Spotts, Erica, & Kato, Kenji. (2005). Genetic influences on midlife functioning. In Sherry L. Willis & Mike Martin (Eds.), *Middle adulthood: A lifespan perspective* (pp. 65–98). Thousand Oaks, CA: Sage.

Peffley, Mark, & Hurwitz, Jon. (2010). *Justice in America: The separate realities of blacks and whites.* New York, NY: Cambridge University Press.

Pellegrini, Anthony D. (2009). Research and policy on children's play. *Child Development Perspectives, 3,* 131–136.

Pellegrini, Anthony D. (2011). Introduction. In Anthony D. Pellegrini (Ed.), *The Oxford handbook of the development of play* (pp. 3–6). New York, NY: Oxford University Press.

Pellegrini, Anthony D., Dupuis, Danielle, & Smith, Peter K. (2007). Play in evolution and development. *Developmental Review, 27,* 261–276.

Pellegrini, Anthony D., & Smith, Peter K. (Eds.). (2005). *The nature of play: Great apes and humans.* New York, NY: Guilford Press.

Pellis, Sergio M., & Pellis, Vivien C. (2011). Rough-and-tumble play: Training and using the social brain. In Anthony D. Pellegrini (Ed.), *The Oxford handbook of the development of play* (pp. 245–259). New York, NY: Oxford University Press.

Peng, Duan, & Robins, Philip K. (2010). Who should care for our kids? The effects of infant child care on early child development. *Journal of Children and Poverty, 16,* 1–45.

Pennisi, Elizabeth. (2007, May 25). Working the (gene count) numbers: Finally, a firm answer? *Science, 316,* 1113.

Pereira, Vera, Faísca, Luís, & de Sá-Saraiva, Rodrigo. (2012). Immortality of the soul as an intuitive idea: Towards a psychological explanation of the origins of afterlife beliefs. *Journal of Cognition and Culture, 12,* 101–127.

Perfetti, Jennifer, Clark, Roseanne, & Fillmore, Capri-Mara. (2004). Postpartum depression: Identification, screening, and treatment. *Wisconsin Medical Journal, 103,* 56–63.

Pergament, Eugene, Alamillo, Christina, Sak, Katrin, & Fiddler, Morris. (2011). Genetic assessment following increased nuchal translucency and normal karyotype. *Prenatal Diagnosis, 31,* 307–310.

Perls, Thomas T. (2008). Centenarians and genetics. In Catherine Y. Read, Robert C. Green, & Michael A. Smyer (Eds.), *Aging, biotechnology, and the future* (pp. 89–99). Baltimore, MD: Johns Hopkins University Press.

Perner, Josef. (2000). About + belief + counterfactual. In Peter Mitchell & Kevin John Riggs (Eds.), *Children's reasoning and the mind* (pp. 367–401). Hove, England: Psychology Press.

Peron, Emily P., & Ruby, Christine M. (2011–2012). A primer on medication use in older adults for the non-clinician. *Generations, 35*(4), 12–18.

Perron, Andreann, Brendgen, Mara, Boivin, Michel, Vitaro, Frank, & Tremblay, Richard E. (2011, March–April). *Playing sports improves academic performances for victimized children.* Poster presented at the SRCD 2011 Biennial Meeting, Montreal, Quebec, Canada.

Perry, David G., & Pauletti, Rachel E. (2011). Gender and adolescent development. *Journal of Research on Adolescence, 21,* 61–74.

Perry, William G., Jr. (1981). Cognitive and ethical growth: The making of meaning. In A. Chickering (Ed.), *The modern American college: Responding to the new realities of diverse students and a changing society* (pp. 76–116). San Francisco, CA: Jossey-Bass.

Perry, William G. (1999). *Forms of intellectual and ethical development in the college years: A scheme.* San Francisco, CA: Jossey-Bass.

Peters, Ellen, Dieckmann, Nathan F., & Weller, Joshua. (2011). Age differences in complex decision making. In K. Warner Schaie & Sherry L. Willis (Eds.), *Handbook of the psychology of aging* (7th ed., pp. 133–151). San Diego, CA: Academic Press.

Petersen, Inge, Martinussen, Torben, McGue, Matthew, Bingley, Paul, & Christensen, Kaare. (2011). Lower marriage and divorce rates among twins than among singletons in Danish birth cohorts 1940–1964. *Twin Research and Human Genetics, 14,* 150–157.

Peterson, Jane W., & Sterling, Yvonne M. (2009). Children's perceptions of asthma: African American children use metaphors to make sense of asthma. *Journal of Pediatric Health Care, 23,* 93–100.

Peterson, Jordan B., & Flanders, Joseph L. (2005). Play and the regulation of aggression. In Richard Ernest Tremblay, Willard W. Hartup, & John Archer (Eds.), *Developmental origins of aggression* (pp. 133–157). New York, NY: Guilford Press.

Pettit, Gregory S., Erath, Stephen A., Lansford, Jennifer E., Dodge, Kenneth A., & Bates, John E. (2011). Dimensions of social capital and life adjustment in the transition to early adulthood. *International Journal of Behavioral Development, 35,* 482–489.

Pew Commission on Children in Foster Care. (2004). *Fostering the future: Safety, permanence and well-being for children in foster care.* Retrieved from http://pewfostercare.org/research/docs/FinalReport.pdf

Pew Forum on Religion & Public Life. (2012, July 31). *Two-thirds of democrats now support gay marriage.* Retrieved from http://www.pewforum.org/Politics-and-Elections/2012-opinions-on-for-gay-marriage-unchanged-after-obamas-announcement.aspx

Pew Research Center. (2009a, June 29). *Growing old in America: Expectations vs. reality.* Retrieved from http://www.pewsocialtrends.org/2009/06/29/growing-old-in-america-expectations-vs-reality/

Pew Research Center. (2009b). *Independents take center stage in Obama era.* Washington, DC: Author.

Pew Research Center. (2010). *Millennials: A portrait of "Generation Next." Confident. Connected. Open to change.* Retrieved from http://pewsocialtrends.org/files/2010/10/millennials-confident-connected-open-to-change.pdf

Pew Research Center. (2010, November 18). *The decline of marriage and rise of new families.* Washington, DC: Pew Social and Demographic Trends.

Pew Research Center. (2011, November 3). *The generation gap and the 2012 election: Angry silents, disengaged millennials.* Washington, DC: Author.

Pew Research Center. (2012a, March 19). *Teens, smartphones, and texting.* Washington, DC: Author.

Pew Research Center. (2012b, April 11). *What the public knows about the political parties: Pew Research News IQ quiz.* Retrieved from http://www.people-press.org/2012/04/11/what-the-public-knows-about-the-political-parties/

Pew Social Trends Staff. (2010, March 18). *The return of the multi-generational family household.* Washington, DC: Pew Research Center, Social & Demographic Trends.

Pew Social Trends Staff. (2011). *Is college worth it? College presidents, public assess, value, quality and mission of higher education.* Washington, DC: Pew Research Center.

Peyser, James A. (2011). Unlocking the secrets of high-performing charters. *EducationNext, 11,* 36–43.

Pfeffer, Jeffrey. (2007). Human resources from an organizational behavior perspective: Some paradoxes explained. *Journal of Economic Perspectives, 21,* 115–134.

Pfeifer, Jennifer H., Dapretto, Mirella, & Lieberman, Matthew D. (2010). The neural foundations of evaluative self-knowledge in middle childhood, early adolescence, and adulthood. In Philip David Zelazo, Michael J. Chandler, & Eveline Crone (Eds.), *Developmental social cognitive neuroscience* (pp. 141–164). New York, NY: Psychology Press.

Pfeifer, Jennifer H., Masten, Carrie L., Moore, William E., Oswald, Tasha M., Mazziotta, John C., Iacoboni, Marco, . . . Dapretto, Mirella. (2011). Entering adolescence: Resistance to peer influence, risky behavior, and neural changes in emotion reactivity. *Neuron, 69,* 1029–1036.

Pfeiffer, Ronald E. (2012). *Parkinson's disease and nonmotor dysfunction.* New York, NY: Springer.

Phelps, Richard P. (2005). Persistently positive: Forty years of public opinion on standardized testing. In Richard P. Phelps (Ed.), *Defending standardized testing* (pp. 1–22). Mahwah, NJ: Erlbaum.

Phillips, Deborah A., Fox, Nathan A., & Gunnar, Megan R. (2011). Same place, different experiences: Bringing individual differences to research in child care. *Child Development Perspectives, 5,* 44–49.

Phillips, Deborah A., Gormley, William T., Jr., & Lowenstein, Amy E. (2009). Inside the pre-kindergarten door: Classroom climate and instructional time allocation in Tulsa's pre-K programs. *Early Childhood Research Quarterly, 24,* 213–362.

Phillips, Mary L. (2010). Coming of age? Neuroimaging biomarkers in youth. *American Journal of Psychiatry, 167,* 4–7.

Phillips, Tommy M., & Pittman, Joe F. (2007). Adolescent psychological well-being by identity style. *Journal of Adolescence, 30,* 1021–1034.

Phinney, Jean S. (2006). Ethnic identity exploration in emerging adulthood. In Jeffrey Jensen Arnett & Jennifer Lynn Tanner (Eds.), *Emerging adults in America: Coming of age in the 21st century* (pp. 117–134). Washington, DC: American Psychological Association.

Piaget, Jean. (1932). *The moral judgment of the child* (Marjorie Gabain, Trans.). London, England: K. Paul, Trench, Trubner & Co.

Piaget, Jean. (1954). *The construction of reality in the child* (Margaret Cook, Trans.). New York, NY: Basic Books.

Piaget, Jean. (1962). *Play, dreams and imitation in childhood* (C. Gattegno & F. M. Hodgson, Trans.). New York, NY: Norton. (Original work published 1945)

Piaget, Jean. (1972). *The psychology of intelligence.* Totowa, NJ: Littlefield. (Original work published 1950)

Piaget, Jean. (1997). *The moral judgment of the child* (Marjorie Gabain, Trans.). New York, NY: Simon & Schuster. (Original work published 1932)

Piaget, Jean, & Inhelder, Bärbel. (1969). *The psychology of the child.* New York, NY: Basic Books.

Piaget, Jean, Voelin-Liambey, Daphne, & Berthoud-Papandropoulou, Ioanna. (2001). *Problems of class inclusion and logical implication* (Robert L. Campbell, Ed. and Trans.). Hove, East Sussex, England: Psychology Press. (Original work published 1977)

Pianta, Robert C., Barnett, W. Steven, Burchinal, Margaret, & Thornburg, Kathy R. (2009). The effects of preschool education. *Psychological Science in the Public Interest, 10,* 49–88.

Pietrefesa, Ashley S., & Evans, David W. (2007). Affective and neuropsychological correlates of children's rituals and compulsive-like behaviors: Continuities and discontinuities with obsessive-compulsive disorder. *Brain and Cognition, 65,* 36–46.

Pignotti, Maria Serenella. (2010). The definition of human viability: A historical perspective. *Acta Pædiatrica, 99,* 33–36.

Pilkington, Pamela D., Windsor, Tim D., & Crisp, Dimity A. (2012). Volunteering and subjective well-being in midlife and older adults: The role of supportive social networks. *The Journals of Gerontology Series B: Psychological Sciences and Social Sciences, 67B,* 249–260.

Pin, Tamis, Eldridge, Beverley, & Galea, Mary P. (2007). A review of the effects of sleep position, play position, and equipment use on motor development in infants. *Developmental Medicine & Child Neurology, 49,* 858–867.

Pinborg, Anja, Loft, Anne, & Nyboe Andersen, Anders. (2004). Neonatal outcome in a Danish national cohort of 8602 children born after in vitro fertilization or intracytoplasmic sperm injection: The role of twin pregnancy. *Acta Obstetricia et Gynecologica Scandinavica, 83,* 1071–1078.

Pinker, Steven. (2007). *The stuff of thought: Language as a window into human nature.* New York, NY: Viking.

Pinker, Steven. (2011). *The better angels of our nature: Why violence has declined.* New York, NY: Viking.

Pinquart, Martin, & Silbereisen, Rainer K. (2006). Socioemotional selectivity in cancer patients. *Psychology and Aging, 21,* 419–423.

Pinquart, Martin, & Sörensen, Silvia. (2011). Spouses, adult children, and children-in-law as caregivers of older adults: A meta-analytic comparison. *Psychology and Aging, 26,* 1–14.

Piotrowski, Martin. (2008). Migrant remittances and household division: The case of Nang Rong, Thailand. *Journal of Marriage and Family, 70,* 1074–1087.

PISA. (2009). *Learning mathematics for life: A perspective from PISA.* Paris, France: OECD.

Pitskhelauri, G. Z. (1982). *The longliving of Soviet Georgia* (Gari Lesnoff-Caravaglia, Ed. & Trans.). New York, NY: Human Sciences Press.

Planalp, Sally, & Trost, Melanie R. (2008). Communication issues at the end of life: Reports from hospice volunteers. *Health Communication, 23,* 222–233.

Plassman, Brenda L., Langa, Kenneth M., Fisher, Gwenith G., Heeringa, Steven G., Weir, David R., Ofstedal, Mary Beth, . . . Wallace, R. B. (2007). Prevalence of dementia in the United States: The Aging, Demographics, and Memory Study. *Neuroepidemiology, 29,* 125–132.

Plaut, Victoria C., Thomas, Kecia M., & Goren, Matt J. (2009). Is multiculturalism or color blindness better for minorities? *Psychological Science, 20,* 444–446.

Pluess, Michael, & Belsky, Jay. (2009). Differential susceptibility to rearing experience: The case of childcare. *Journal of Child Psychology and Psychiatry and Allied Disciplines, 50,* 396–404.

Pluess, Michael, & Belsky, Jay. (2010). Differential susceptibility to parenting and quality child care. *Developmental Psychology, 46,* 379–390.

Pogrebin, Abigail. (2009). *One and the same: My life as an identical twin and what I've learned about everyone's struggle to be singular.* New York, NY: Doubleday.

Poldrack, Russell A., Wagner, Anthony D., Gotlib, Ian H., & Hamilton, J. Paul. (2008). Neuroimaging and depression: Current status and unresolved issues. *Current Directions in Psychological Science, 17,* 159–163.

Pollack, Andrew. (2012, February 23). In reversal, F.D.A. panel endorses a diet pill. *New York Times,* p. B1.

Pollet, Susan L. (2010). Still a patchwork quilt: A nationwide survey of state laws regarding stepparent rights and obligations. *Family Court Review, 48,* 528–540.

Poon, Leonard W. (2008). What can we learn from centenarians? In Catherine Y. Read, Robert C. Green, & Michael A. Smyer (Eds.), *Aging, biotechnology and the future* (pp. 100–110). Baltimore, MD: Johns Hopkins University.

Popham, Lauren E., Kennison, Shelia M., & Bradley, Kristopher I. (2011a). Ageism and risk-taking in young adults: Evidence for a link between death anxiety and ageism. *Death Studies, 35,* 751–763.

Popham, Lauren E., Kennison, Shelia M., & Bradley, Kristopher I. (2011b). Ageism, sensation-seeking, and risk-taking behavior in young adults. *Current Psychology, 30,* 184–193.

Population Reference Bureau. (2012a). Population age < 15. Retrieved January 29, 2013, from http://www.prb.org/ DataFinder/Topic/Rankings.aspx?ind=10.

Population Reference Bureau. (2012b). Population ages 65 and older. Retrieved January 29, 2013, from http://www.prb. org/DataFinder/Topic/Rankings.aspx?ind=11.

Poropat, Arthur E. (2009). A meta-analysis of the five-factor model of personality and academic performance. *Psychological Bulletin, 135,* 322–338.

Posner, Michael I., Rothbart, Mary K., Sheese, Brad E., & Tang, Yiyuan. (2007). The anterior cingulate gyrus and the mechanism of self-regulation. *Cognitive, Affective & Behavioral Neuroscience, 7,* 391–395.

Potter, Daniel. (2010). Psychosocial well-being and the relationship between divorce and children's academic achievement. *Journal of Marriage and Family, 72,* 933–946.

Poulin-Dubois, Diane, & Chow, Virginia. (2009). The effect of a looker's past reliability on infants' reasoning about beliefs. *Developmental Psychology, 45,* 1576–1582.

Poulsen, Pernille, Esteller, Manel, Vaag, Allan, & Fraga, Mario F. (2007). The epigenetic basis of twin discordance in age-related diseases. *Pediatric Research, 61*(5, Pt. 2), 38R–42R.

Powell, Kendall. (2006). Neurodevelopment: How does the teenage brain work? *Nature, 442,* 865–867.

Powell, Shaun, Langlands, Stephanie, & Dodd, Chris. (2011). Feeding children's desires? Child and parental perceptions of food promotion to the "under 8s." *Young Consumers: Insight and Ideas for Responsible Marketers, 12,* 96–109.

Powledge, Tabitha M. (2007, October). Easing hormone anxiety. *Scientific American, 297,* 32, 34.

Powlishta, Kimberly. (2004). Gender as a social category: Intergroup processes and gender-role development. In Mark Bennett & Fabio Sani (Eds.), *The development of the social self* (pp. 103–133). Hove, East Sussex, England: Psychology Press.

Prado, Carlos G. (2008). *Choosing to die: Elective death and multiculturalism.* New York, NY: Cambridge University Press.

Pratt, Michael W., Norris, Joan E., Cressman, Kate, Lawford, Heather, & Hebblethwaite, Shannon. (2008). Parents' stories of grandparenting concerns in the three-generational family: Generativity, optimism, and forgiveness. *Journal of Personality, 76,* 581–604.

Presser, Harriet B., Gornick, Janet C., & Parashar, Sangeeta. (2008). Gender and nonstandard work hours in 12 European countries. *Monthly Labor Review, 131,* 83–103.

Preston, Tom, & Kelly, Michael. (2006). A medical ethics assessment of the case of Terri Schiavo. *Death Studies, 30,* 121–133.

Priess, Heather A., Lindberg, Sara M., & Hyde, Janet Shibley. (2009). Adolescent gender-role identity and mental health: Gender intensification revisited. *Child Development, 80,* 1531–1544.

Print, Murray, Ugarte, Carolina, Naval, Concepción, & Mihr, Anja. (2008). Moral and human rights education: The contribution of the United Nations. *Journal of Moral Education, 37,* 115–132.

Proulx, Christine M., Helms, Heather M., & Buehler, Cheryl. (2007). Marital quality and personal well-being: A meta-analysis. *Journal of Marriage and Family, 69,* 576–593.

Provasnik, Stephen, Kastberg, David, Ferraro, David, Lemanski, Nita, Roey, Stephen, & Jenkins, Frank. (2012). *Highlights from TIMSS 2011: Mathematics and science achievement of U.S. fourth- and eighth-grade students in an international context* (NCES 2013-009). Washington, DC: National Center for Education Statistics, Institute of Education Sciences, U.S. Department of Education.

Pryor, John H., DeAngelo, Linda, Blake, Laura Palucki, Hurtado, Sylvia, & Tran, Serge. (2011). *The American freshman: National norms fall 2011.* Los Angeles, CA: Higher Education Research Institute, UCLA.

Puhl, Rebecca M., & Heuer, Chelsea A. (2010). Obesity stigma: Important considerations for public health. *American Journal of Public Health, 100,* 1019–1028.

Pullmann, Helle, & Allik, Jüri. (2008). Relations of academic and general self-esteem to school achievement. *Personality and Individual Differences, 45,* 559–564.

Pulvermüller, Friedemann, & Fadiga, Luciano. (2010). Active perception: Sensorimotor circuits as a cortical basis for language. *Nature Reviews Neuroscience, 11,* 351–360.

Puri, Sunita, & Nachtigall, Robert D. (2010). The ethics of sex selection: A comparison of the attitudes and experiences of primary care physicians and physician providers of clinical sex selection services. *Fertility and Sterility, 93,* 2107–2114.

Pyne, Derek. (2010). A model of religion and death. *The Journal of Socio-Economics, 39,* 46–54.

Qualls, Sara Honn, & Kasl-Godley, Julia E. (2010). *End-of-life issues, grief, and bereavement: What clinicians need to know.* Hoboken, NJ: Wiley.

Quindlen, Anna. (2012). *Lots of candles, plenty of cake.* New York, NY: Random House.

Rabin, Roni Caryn. (2011, October 24). Drugs to treat A.D.H.D. reach the preschool set. *New York Times,* p. D5.

Rabkin, Nick, & Hedberg, Eric Christopher. (2011). *Arts education in America: What the declines mean for arts participation* (Research Report #52). Washington, DC: National Endowment for the Arts.

Race, Ethnicity, and Genetics Working Group of the National Human Genome Research Institute. (2005). The use of racial, ethnic, and ancestral categories in human genetics research. *American Journal of Human Genetics, 77,* 519–532.

Rajaratnam, Julie Knoll, Marcus, Jake R., Flaxman, Abraham D., Wang, Haidong, Levin-Rector, Alison, Dwyer, Laura, ... Murray, Christopher J. L. (2010). Neonatal, postneonatal, childhood, and under-5 mortality for 187 countries, 1970–2010: A systematic analysis of progress towards Millennium Development Goal 4. *Lancet, 375,* 1988–2008.

Ramakrishnan, Usha, Goldenberg, Tamar, & Allen, Lindsay H. (2011). Do multiple micronutrient interventions improve child health, growth, and development? *Journal of Nutrition, 141,* 2066–2075.

Ramani, Geetha B., Brownell, Celia A., & Campbell, Susan B. (2010). Positive and negative peer interaction in 3- and 4-year-olds in relation to regulation and dysregulation. *Journal of Genetic Psychology, 171,* 218–250.

Ramscar, Michael, & Dye, Melody. (2011). Learning language from the input: Why innate constraints can't explain noun compounding. *Cognitive Psychology, 62,* 1–40.

Raus, Kasper, Sterckx, Sigrid, & Mortier, Freddy. (2011). Is continuous sedation at the end of life an ethically preferable alternative to physician-assisted suicide? *The American Journal of Bioethics, 11,* 32–40.

Raymond, Neil, Beer, Charlotte, Glazebrook, Cristine, & Sayal, Kapil. (2009). Pregnant women's attitudes towards alcohol consumption. *BMC Public Health, 9,* 175–183.

Reche, Marta, Valbuena, Teresa, Fiandor, Ana, Padial, Antonia, Quirce, Santiago, & Pascual, Cristina. (2011). Induction of tolerance in children with food allergy. *Current Nutrition & Food Science, 7,* 33–39.

Redfoot, Donald L., & Houser, Ari. (2010). *More older people with disabilities living in the community: Trends from the National Long-Term Care Survey, 1984–2004.* Washington, DC: AARP Public Policy Institute.

Reece, E. Albert, & Hobbins, John C. (Eds.). (2007). *Handbook of clinical obstetrics: The fetus & mother handbook* (2nd ed.). Malden, MA: Blackwell.

Reese, Elaine, Bird, Amy, & Tripp, Gail. (2007). Children's self-esteem and moral self: Links to parent-child conversations regarding emotion. *Social Development, 16,* 460–478.

Reeskens, Tim, & Wright, Matthew. (2011). Subjective well-being and national satisfaction: Taking seriously the "Proud of what?" question. *Psychological Science, 22,* 1460–1462.

Reid, Megan, & Reczek, Corinne. (2011). Stress and support in family relationships after hurricane Katrina. *Journal of Family Issues, 32,* 1397–1418.

Reis, Harry T., & Collins, W. Andrew. (2004). Relationships, human behavior, and psychological science. *Current Directions in Psychological Science, 13,* 233–237.

Renk, Kimberly, Donnelly, Reesa, McKinney, Cliff, & Agliata, Allison Kanter. (2006). The development of gender identity: Timetables and influences. In Kam-Shing Yip (Ed.), *Psychology of gender identity: An international perspective* (pp. 49–68). Hauppauge, NY: Nova Science.

Renkema, Lennart J., Stapel, Diederik A., Maringer, Marcus, & van Yperen, Nico W. (2008). Terror management and stereotyping: Why do people stereotype when mortality is salient? *Personality and Social Psychology Bulletin, 34,* 553–564.

Rentfrow, Peter Jason. (2010). Statewide differences in personality: Toward a psychological geography of the United States. *American Psychologist, 65,* 548–558.

Rentfrow, Peter J., Gosling, Samuel D., & Potter, Jeff. (2008). A theory of the emergence, persistence, and expression of geographic variation in psychological characteristics. *Perspectives on Psychological Science, 3,* 339–369.

Rettig, Michael. (2005). Using the multiple intelligences to enhance instruction for young children and young children with disabilities. *Early Childhood Education Journal, 32,* 255–259.

Reuter-Lorenz, Patricia A., & Sylvester, Ching-Yune C. (2005). The cognitive neuroscience of working memory and aging. In Roberto Cabeza, Lars Nyberg, & Denise C. Park (Eds.), *Cognitive neuroscience of aging: Linking cognitive and cerebral aging* (pp. 186–217). New York, NY: Oxford University Press.

Reutskaja, Elena, & Hogarth, Robin M. (2009). Satisfaction in choice as a function of the number of alternatives: When "goods satiate." *Psychology and Marketing, 26,* 197–203.

Reynolds, Arthur J. (2000). *Success in early intervention: The Chicago child-parent centers.* Lincoln, NE: University of Nebraska Press.

Reynolds, Arthur J., & Ou, Suh-Ruu. (2011). Paths of effects from preschool to adult well-being: A confirmatory analysis of the child-parent center program. *Child Development, 82,* 555–582.

Reynolds, Arthur J., Temple, Judy A., White, Barry A. B., Ou, Suh-Ruu, & Robertson, Dylan L. (2011). Age 26 cost–benefit analysis of the child-parent center early education program. *Child Development, 82,* 379–404.

Rhee, Kyung. (2008). Childhood overweight and the relationship between parent behaviors, parenting style, and family functioning. In Amy B. Jordan (Ed.), *Annals of the American Academy of Political and Social Science: Vol. 615. Overweight and obesity in America's children: Causes, consequences, solutions* (pp. 12–37). San Diego, CA: Sage.

Riccio, Cynthia A., & Rodriguez, Olga L. (2007). Integration of psychological assessment approaches in school psychology. *Psychology in the Schools, 44,* 243–255.

Riccio, Cynthia A., Sullivan, Jeremy R., & Cohen, Morris J. (2010). *Neuropsychological assessment and intervention for childhood and adolescent disorders.* Hoboken, NJ: Wiley.

Ridenour, Ty A., Meyer-Chilenski, Sarah, & Reid, Erin E. (2012). Developmental momentum toward substance dependence: Natural histories and pliability of risk factors in youth experiencing chronic stress. *Drug and Alcohol Dependence, 123*(Suppl. 1), S87–S98.

Rieger, Gerulf, & Savin-Williams, Ritch. (2012). Gender nonconformity, sexual orientation, and psychological well-being. *Archives of Sexual Behavior, 41,* 611–621.

Riggs, Shelley A., & Riggs, David S. (2011). Risk and resilience in military families experiencing deployment: The role of the family attachment network. *Journal of Family Psychology, 25*, 675–687.

Riordan, Jan (Ed.). (2005). *Breastfeeding and human lactation* (3rd ed.). Sudbury, MA: Jones and Bartlett.

Riordan, Jan, & Wambach, Karen (Eds.). (2009). *Breastfeeding and human lactation* (4th ed.). Sudbury, MA: Jones and Bartlett.

Ripke, Marika N., Huston, Aletha C., & Casey, David M. (2006). Low-income children's activity participation as a predictor of psychosocial and academic outcomes in middle childhood and adolescence. In Aletha C. Huston & Marika N. Ripke (Eds.), *Developmental contexts in middle childhood: Bridges to adolescence and adulthood* (pp. 260–282). New York, NY: Cambridge University Press.

Rivas-Drake, Deborah, & Mooney, Margarita. (2009). Neither colorblind nor oppositional: Perceived minority status and trajectories of academic adjustment among Latinos in elite higher education. *Developmental Psychology, 45*, 642–651.

Rivers, Ian, Poteat, V. Paul, Noret, Nathalie, & Ashurst, Nigel. (2009). Observing bullying at school: The mental health implications of witness status. *School Psychology Quarterly, 24*, 211–223.

Rix, Sara E. (2011). Employment and aging. In Robert H. Binstock & Linda K. George (Eds.), *Handbook of aging and the social sciences* (7th ed., pp. 193–206). San Diego, CA: Academic Press.

Robb, Kathryn, Simon, Alice, & Wardle, Jane. (2009). Socioeconomic disparities in optimism and pessimism. *International Journal of Behavioral Medicine, 16*, 331–338.

Robelen, Erik W. (2011, April 5). Study finds more students learning Mandarin Chinese. *Education Week*, p. 5.

Robert, Stephanie A., Cherepanov, Dasha, Palta, Mari, Dunham, Nancy Cross, Feeny, David, & Fryback, Dennis G. (2009). Socioeconomic status and age variations in health-related quality of life: Results from the National Health Measurement Study. *The Journals of Gerontology Series B: Psychological Sciences and Social Sciences, 64B*, 378–389.

Roberts, Brent W., Walton, Kate E., & Viechtbauer, Wolfgang. (2006). Patterns of mean-level change in personality traits across the life course: A meta-analysis of longitudinal studies. *Psychological Bulletin, 132*, 1–25.

Roberts, Karen C., Shields, Margot, de Groh, Margaret, Aziz, Alfred, & Gilbert, Jo-Anne. (2012). Overweight and obesity in children and adolescents: Results from the 2009 to 2011 Canadian Health Measures survey: Health Reports,23(3). Statistics Canada: Catalogue no. 82-003-XPE.

Roberts, Leslie. (2007, October 26). Battling over bed nets. *Science, 318*, 556–559.

Roberts, Richard D., & Lipnevich, Anastasiya A. (2012). From general intelligence to multiple intelligences: Meanings, models, and measures. In Karen R. Harris, Steve Graham, & Tim Urdan (Series Eds.) & Sandra Graham, James M. Royer, & Moshe Zeidner (Vol. Eds.), *APA educational psychology handbook: Vol. 2. Individual differences and cultural and contextual factors* (pp. 33–57). Washington, DC: American Psychological Association.

Roberts, Soraya. (2010, January 1). Travis Pastrana breaks world record for longest rally car jump on New Year's Eve. *New York Daily News.* Retrieved from http://www.nydailynews.com

Robinson, Oliver C., Demetre, James D., & Corney, Roslyn. (2010). Personality and retirement: Exploring the links between the Big Five personality traits, reasons for retirement and the experience of being retired. *Personality and Individual Differences, 48*, 792–797.

Robson, Ruthann. (2010). Notes on my dying. In Nan Bauer Maglin & Donna Marie Perry (Eds.), *Final acts: Death, dying, and the choices we make* (pp. 19–28). New Brunswick, NJ: Rutgers University Press.

Rochat, Roger W., Heath, Clark W., Chu, Susan Y., & Marchbanks, Polly A. (2011). Maternal and child health epidemic-assistance investigations, 1946–2005. *American Journal of Epidemiology, 174*(Suppl. 11), S80–S88.

Roche, Alex F., & Sun, Shumei S. (2003). *Human growth: Assessment and interpretation.* Cambridge, UK: Cambridge University Press.

Rodkin, Philip C., & Roisman, Glenn I. (2010). Antecedents and correlates of the popular-aggressive phenomenon in elementary school. *Child Development, 81*, 837–850.

Rodrigue, Karen M., & Kennedy, Kristen M. (2011). The cognitive consequences of structural changes to the aging brain. In K. Warner Schaie & Sherry L. Willis (Eds.), *Handbook of the psychology of aging* (7th ed., pp. 73–91). San Diego, CA: Academic Press.

Roebers, Claudia M., Schmid, Corinne, & Roderer, Thomas. (2009). Metacognitive monitoring and control processes involved in primary school children's test performance. *British Journal of Educational Psychology, 79*, 749–767.

Roelfs, David J., Shor, Eran, Davidson, Karina W., & Schwartz, Joseph E. (2012). Losing life and livelihood: A systematic review and meta-analysis of unemployment and all-cause mortality. *Social Science Medicine, 72*, 840–854.

Roenneberg, Till, Allebrandt, Karla, Merrow, Martha, & Vetter, Céline. (2012). Social jetlag and obesity. *Current Biology, 22*, 939–943.

Rogoff, Barbara. (2003). *The cultural nature of human development.* New York, NY: Oxford University Press.

Roiphe, Anne. (2009). Grandmothers should be seen and not heard. In Barbara Graham (Ed.), *Eye of my heart: 27 writers reveal the hidden pleasures and perils of being a grandmother* (pp. 241–250). New York, NY: HarperCollins.

Ron, Pnina. (2009). Daughters as caregivers of aging parents: The shattering myth. *Journal of Gerontological Social Work, 52*, 135–153.

Ronay, R., & von Hippel, W. (2010). The presence of an attractive woman elevates testosterone and physical risk taking in young men. *Social Psychological and Personality Science, 1*, 57–64.

Rondal, Jean A. (2010). Language in Down syndrome: A lifespan perspective. In Marcia A. Barnes (Ed.), *Genes, brain, and development: The neurocognition of genetic disorders* (pp. 122–142). New York, NY: Cambridge University Press.

Roopnarine, Jaipaul L. (2011). Cultural variations in beliefs about play, parent-child play, and children's play: Meaning for childhood development. In Anthony D. Pellegrini (Ed.), *The Oxford handbook of the development of play* (pp. 19–39). New York, NY: Oxford University Press.

Rose, Amanda J., & Asher, Steven R. (2004). Children's strategies and goals in response to help-giving and help-seeking tasks within a friendship. *Child Development, 75*, 749–763.

Rose, Steven. (2008, January 31). Drugging unruly children is a method of social control [Correspondence]. *Nature, 451*, 521.

Roseberry, Sarah, Hirsh-Pasek, Kathy, Parish-Morris, Julia, & Golinkoff, Roberta M. (2009). Live action: Can young children learn verbs from video? *Child Development, 80*, 1360–1375.

Rosenbaum, James E. (2011). The complexities of college for all. *Sociology of Education, 84*, 113–117.

Rosenberg, Rebecca, Mandell, David, Farmer, Janet, Law, J., Marvin, Alison, & Law, Paul. (2010). Psychotropic medication use among children with autism spectrum disorders enrolled in a national registry, 2007–2008. *Journal of Autism and Developmental Disorders, 40*, 342–351.

Rosenfield, Robert L., Lipton, Rebecca B., & Drum, Melinda L. (2009). Thelarche, pubarche, and menarche attainment in children with normal and elevated body mass index. *Pediatrics, 123*, 84–88.

Roshania, Reshma, Narayan, K. M. Venkat, & Oza-Frank, Reena. (2008). Age at arrival and risk of obesity among US immigrants. *Obesity, 16*, 2669–2675.

Rosow, Irving. (1985). Status and role change through the life cycle. In Robert H. Binstock & Ethel Shanas (Eds.), *Handbook of aging and the social sciences* (2nd ed., pp. 62–93). New York, NY: Van Nostrand Reinhold.

Rosowsky, Erlene. (2007). Loss of the 'supplementary spouse' in marriages in later life. *Generations, 31*(3), 38–40.

Ross, Colin A. (2009). Ethics of gender identity disorder. *Ethical Human Psychology and Psychiatry, 11*, 165–170.

Rossi, Eleonora, Schippers, Marleen, & Keysers, Christian. (2011). Broca's area: Linking perception and production in language and actions. In Shihui Han & Ernst Pöppel (Eds.), *Culture and neural frames of cognition and communication* (pp. 169–184). New York, NY: Springer Berlin Heidelberg.

Rossignol, Daniel, Rossignol, Lanier, Smith, Scott, Schneider, Cindy, Logerquist, Sally, Usman, Anju,... Mumper, Elizabeth. (2009). Hyperbaric treatment for children with autism: A multicenter, randomized, double-blind, controlled trial. *BMC Pediatrics, 9*, 21.

Rössler, Wulf, Hengartner, Michael P., Ajdacic-Gross, Vladeta, Haker, Helene, Gamma, Alex, & Angst, Jules. (2011). Sub-clinical psychosis symptoms in young adults are risk factors for subsequent common mental disorders. *Schizophrenia Research, 131*, 18–23.

Roth, David L., Ackerman, Michelle L., Okonkwo, Ozioma C., & Burgio, Louis D. (2008). The four-factor model of depressive symptoms in dementia caregivers: A structural equation model of ethnic differences. *Psychology and Aging, 23*, 567–576.

Roth, David L., Mittelman, Mary S., Clay, Olivio J., Madan, Alok, & Haley, William E. (2005). Changes in social support as mediators of the impact of a psychosocial intervention for spouse caregivers of persons with Alzheimer's disease. *Psychology and Aging, 20*, 634–644.

Rothbart, Mary K., & Bates, John E. (2006). Temperament. In William Damon & Richard M. Lerner (Series Eds.) & Nancy Eisenberg (Vol. Ed.), *Handbook of child psychology: Vol. 3. Social, emotional, and personality development* (6th ed., pp. 99–166). Hoboken, NJ: Wiley.

Rothbaum, Fred, Morelli, Gilda, & Rusk, Natalie. (2011). Attachment, learning and coping: The interplay of cultural similarities and differences. In Michele J. Gelfand, Chi-yue Chiu, & Ying-yi Hong (Eds.), *Advances in culture and psychology* (Vol. 1, pp. 153–216). New York, NY: Oxford University Press.

Rothrauff, Tanja C., Cooney, Teresa M., & An, Jeong Shin. (2009). Remembered parenting styles and adjustment in middle and late adulthood. *The Journals of Gerontology Series B: Psychological Sciences and Social Sciences, 64B*, 137–146.

Rovee-Collier, Carolyn. (1987). Learning and memory in infancy. In Joy Doniger Osofsky (Ed.), *Handbook of infant development* (2nd ed., pp. 98–148). New York, NY: Wiley.

Rovee-Collier, Carolyn. (1990). The "memory system" of prelinguistic infants. In Adele Diamond (Ed.), *The development and neural bases of higher cognitive functions* (Vol. 608, pp. 517–542). New York, NY: New York Academy of Sciences.

Rovee-Collier, Carolyn, & Cuevas, Kimberly. (2009). The development of infant memory. In Mary L. Courage & Nelson Cowan (Eds.), *The development of memory in infancy and childhood* (2nd ed., pp. 11–41). New York, NY: Psychology Press.

Rovi, Sue, Chen, Ping-Hsin, & Johnson, Mark S. (2004). The economic burden of hospitalizations associated with child abuse and neglect. *American Journal of Public Health, 94*, 586–590.

Rubin, Kenneth H., Coplan, Robert J., & Bowker, Julie C. (2009). Social withdrawal in childhood. *Annual Review of Psychology, 60*, 141–171.

Ruble, Diane N., Martin, Carol Lynn, & Berenbaum, Sheri. (2006). Gender development. In William Damon & Richard M. Lerner (Series Eds.) & Nancy Eisenberg (Vol. Ed.), *Handbook of child psychology: Vol. 3. Social, emotional, and personality development* (6th ed., pp. 858–932). Hoboken, NJ: Wiley.

Ruder, Debra Bradley. (2008, September-October). The teen brain. *Harvard Magazine, 111*, 8–10.

Rueda, M. Rosario, Rothbart, Mary K., Saccomanno, Lisa, & Posner, Michael I. (2007). Modifying brain networks underlying self regulation. In Daniel Romer & Elaine F. Walker (Eds.), *Adolescent psychopathology and the developing brain: Integrating brain and prevention science* (pp. 401–419). Oxford, UK: Oxford University Press.

Rulfs, Monika. (2011). Marking death: Grief, protest and politics after a fatal traffic accident. In Peter Jan Margry & Cristina Sanchez-Carretero (Eds.), *Grassroots memorials: The politics of memorializing traumatic death* (pp. 145–168). New York, NY: Berghahn Books.

Russell, Stephen T., Crockett, Lisa J., & Chao, Ruth K. (2010). Conclusions: The role of Asian American culture in parenting and parent-adolescent relationships. In Stephen Thomas Russell, Lisa J. Crockett, & Ruth K. Chao (Eds.), *Asian American parenting and parent-adolescent relationships* (pp. 117–128). New York, NY: Springer.

Ruthig, Joelle C., Trisko, Jenna, & Stewart, Tara L. (2012). The impact of spouse's health and well-being on own well-being: A dyadic study of older married couples. *Journal of Social and Clinical Psychology, 31*, 508–529.

Rutter, Michael, Colvert, Emma, Kreppner, Jana, Beckett, Celia, Castle, Jenny, Groothues, Christine, . . . Sonuga-Barke, Edmund J. S. (2007). Early adolescent outcomes for institutionally-deprived and non-deprived adoptees: I. Disinhibited attachment. *Journal of Child Psychology and Psychiatry, 48*, 17–30.

Rutter, Michael, Sonuga-Barke, Edmund J., Beckett, Celia, Castle, Jennifer, Kreppner, Jana, Kumsta, Robert, . . . Gunnar, Megan R. (2010). Deprivation-specific psychological patterns: Effects of institutional deprivation. *Monographs of the Society for Research in Child Development, 75*(1, Serial No. 295), 1–252.

Rutters, Femke, Nieuwenhuizen, Arie G., Vogels, Neeltje, Bouwman, Freek, Mariman, Edwin, & Westerterp-Plantenga, Margriet S. (2008). Leptin-adiposity relationship changes, plus behavioral and parental factors, are involved in the development of body weight in a Dutch children cohort. *Physiology & Behavior, 93*, 967–974.

Ruys, Jan H., de Jonge, Guus A., Brand, Ronald, Engelberts, Adèle, C., & Semmekrot, Ben A. (2007). Bed-sharing in the first four months of life: A risk factor for sudden infant death. *Acta Pædiatrica, 96*, 1399–1403.

Ryan, Suzanne, Franzetta, Kerry, Manlove, Jennifer, & Holcombe, Emily. (2007). Adolescents' discussions about contraception or STDs with partners before first sex. *Perspectives on Sexual and Reproductive Health, 39*, 149–157.

Ryan, Suzanne, Franzetta, Kerry, Manlove, Jennifer S., & Schelar, Erin. (2008). Older sexual partners during adolescence: Links to reproductive health outcomes in young adulthood. *Perspectives on Sexual and Reproductive Health, 40*, 17–26.

Rydell, Robert J., & Boucher, Kathryn L. (2010). Capitalizing on multiple social identities to prevent stereotype threat: The moderating role of self-esteem. *Personality and Social Psychology Bulletin, 36*, 239–250.

Saarni, Carolyn, Campos, Joseph J., Camras, Linda A., & Witherington, David. (2006). Emotional development: Action, communication, and understanding. In William Damon & Richard M. Lerner (Series Eds.) & Nancy Eisenberg (Vol. Ed.), *Handbook of child psychology: Vol. 3. Social, emotional, and personality development* (6th ed., pp. 226–299). Hoboken, NJ: Wiley.

Sabatino, Charles P. (2010). The evolution of health care advance planning law and policy. *Milbank Quarterly, 88*, 211–239.

Sacks, Oliver W. (1995). *An anthropologist on Mars: Seven paradoxical tales.* New York, NY: Knopf.

Sadeh, Avi, Mindell, Jodi A., Luedtke, Kathryn, & Wiegand, Benjamin. (2009). Sleep and sleep ecology in the first 3 years: A web-based study. *Journal of Sleep Research, 18*, 60–73.

Sadeh, Avi, Tikotzky, Liat, & Scher, Anat. (2010). Parenting and infant sleep. *Sleep Medicine Reviews, 14*, 89–96.

Sadler, Philip M., Sonnert, Gerhard, Tai, Robert H., & Klopfenstein, Kristin (Eds.). (2010). *AP: A critical examination of the Advanced Placement program.* Cambridge, MA: Harvard Education Press.

Sadler, Thomas W. (2009). *Langman's medical embryology* (11th ed.). Baltimore, MD: Lippincott Williams & Wilkins.

Sadler, Thomas W. (2012). *Langman's medical embryology* (12th ed.). Baltimore, MD: Lippincott Williams & Wilkins.

Saegert, Susan, Fields, Desiree, & Libman, Kimberly. (2011). Mortgage foreclosure and health disparities: Serial displacement as asset extraction in African American populations. *Journal of Urban Health, 88*, 390–402.

Saewyc, Elizabeth M. (2011). Research on adolescent sexual orientation: Development, health disparities, stigma, and resilience. *Journal of Research on Adolescence, 21*, 256–272.

Saey, Tina Hesman. (2008, May 24). Epic genetics: Genes' chemical clothes may underlie the biology behind mental illness. *Science News, 173*, 14–19.

Safe Kids USA. (2008). *Report to the nation: Trends in unintentional childhood injury mortality and parental views on child safety.* Washington, DC: Safe Kids Worldwide.

Saffran, Jenny R., Werker, Janet F., & Werner, Lynne A. (2006). The infant's auditory world: Hearing, speech, and the beginnings of language. In William Damon & Richard M. Lerner (Eds.), *Handbook of child psychology: Vol. 2. Cognition, perception, and language* (pp. 58–108). Hoboken, NJ: Wiley.

Sahlberg, Pasi. (2011). *Finnish lessons: What can the world learn from educational change in Finland?* New York, NY: Teachers College Press.

Sakai, Christina, Lin, Hua, & Flores, Glenn. (2011). Health outcomes and family services in kinship care: Analysis of a national sample of children in the child welfare system. *Archives of Pediatrics & Adolescent Medicine, 165*, 159–165.

Salkind, Neil J. (2004). *An introduction to theories of human development.* Thousand Oaks, CA: Sage.

Salmivalli, Christina. (2010). Bullying and the peer group: A review. *Aggression and Violent Behavior, 15*, 112–120.

Salpeter, Shelley R., Luo, Esther J., Malter, Dawn S., & Stuart, Brad. (2012). Systematic review of noncancer presentations with a median survival of 6 months or less. *The American Journal of Medicine, 125*, 512.e1–512.e16. doi:10.1016/j.amjmed.2011.07.028

Salthouse, Timothy A. (2006). Mental exercise and mental aging: Evaluating the validity of the "use it or lose it" hypothesis. *Perspectives on Psychological Science, 1*, 68–87.

Salthouse, Timothy A. (2010). *Major issues in cognitive aging.* New York, NY: Oxford University Press.

Salvatore, Jessica, & Shelton, J. Nicole. (2007). Cognitive costs of exposure to racial prejudice. *Psychological Science, 18*, 810–815.

SAMHSA (Substance Abuse and Mental Health Services Administration). (2009). *Results from the 2008 National Survey* *on Drug Use and Health: National findings* (Office of Applied Studies, NSDUH Series H-36, HHS Publication No. SMA 09-4434). Rockville, MD: U.S. Department of Health and Human Services.

Sander, Thomas H., & Putnam, Robert David. (2010). Still bowling alone? The post-9/11 split. *Journal of Democracy, 21*(1), 9–16.

Sanders, George. (2010). The dismal trade as culture industry. *Poetics, 38*, 47–68.

Sandstrom, Marlene J., & Zakriski, Audrey L. (2004). Understanding the experience of peer rejection. In Janis B. Kupersmidt & Kenneth A. Dodge (Eds.), *Children's peer relations: From development to intervention* (pp. 101–118). Washington, DC: American Psychological Association.

Sanson, Ann, Smart, Diana, & Misson, Sebastian. (2011). Children's socio-emotional, physical, and cognitive outcomes: Do they share the same drivers? *Australian Journal of Psychology, 63*, 56–74.

Santelli, John S., & Melnikas, Andrea J. (2010). Teen fertility in transition: Recent and historic trends in the United States. *Annual Review of Public Health, 31*, 371–383.

Santosh, Paramala J., & Canagaratnam, Myooran. (2008). Paediatric bipolar disorder—An update. *Psychiatry, 7*, 349–352.

Saraceno, Chiara. (2010). Social inequalities in facing old-age dependency: A bi-generational perspective. *Journal of European Social Policy, 20*, 32–44.

Sassler, Sharon, Addo, Fenaba R., & Lichter, Daniel T. (2012). The tempo of sexual activity and later relationship quality. *Journal of Marriage and Family, 74*, 708–725.

Satariano, William. (2006). *Epidemiology of aging: An ecological approach.* Sudbury, MA: Jones and Bartlett.

Saul, Stephanie. (2008, July 26). Weight drives the young to adult pills, data says. *New York Times.* Retrieved from http://www.nytimes.com/2008/07/26/business/26kidmed.html?pagewanted=all

Saulny, Susan, & Steinberg, Jacques. (2011, June 13). On college forms, a question of race, or races, can perplex. *New York Times,* p. A1.

Saunders, Cicely M. (Ed.) (1978). *The management of terminal disease.* London, England: Arnold.

Savic, Ivanka (Ed.). (2010). *Progress in Brain Research: Vol. 186. Sex differences in the human brain, their underpinnings and implications.* Amsterdam, The Netherlands: Elsevier.

Saw, Seang-Mei, Cheng, Angela, Fong, Allan, Gazzard, Gus, Tan, Donald T. H., & Morgan, Ian. (2007). School grades and myopia. *Ophthalmic and Physiological Optics, 27*, 126–129.

Saxton, Matthew. (2010). *Child language: Acquisition and development.* Thousand Oaks, CA: SAGE.

Saylor, Megan M., & Sabbagh, Mark A. (2004). Different kinds of information affect word learning in the preschool years: The case of part-term learning. *Child Development, 75*, 395–408.

Scannapieco, Maria, & Connell-Carrick, Kelli. (2005). *Understanding child maltreatment: An ecological and developmental perspective.* New York, NY: Oxford University Press.

Scarf, Maggie. (2008). *September songs: The good news about marriage in the later years.* New York, NY: Riverhead Books.

Scarr, Sandra. (1985). Constructing psychology: Making facts and fables for our times. *American Psychologist, 40*, 499–512.

Schachter, Sherry R. (2003). 9/11: A grief therapist's journal. In Marcia Lattanzi-Licht & Kenneth J. Doka (Eds.), *Living with grief: Coping with public tragedy* (pp. 15–25). New York, NY: Brunner-Routledge.

Schafer, Graham. (2005). Infants can learn decontextualized words before their first birthday. *Child Development, 76*, 87–96.

Schaie, K. Warner. (2005). *Developmental influences on adult intelligence: The Seattle longitudinal study* (Rev. ed.). New York, NY: Oxford University Press.

Schanler, Richard J. (2011). Outcomes of human milk-fed premature infants. *Seminars in Perinatology, 35*, 29–33.

Scharlach, Andrew, Graham, Carrie, & Lehning, Amanda. (2012). The "Village" model: A consumer-driven approach for aging in place. *The Gerontologist, 52*, 418–427.

Schauer, Daniel P., Arterburn, David E., Livingston, Edward H., Fischer, David, & Eckman, Mark H. (2010). Decision modeling to estimate the impact of gastric bypass surgery on life expectancy for the treatment of morbid obesity. *Archives of Surgery, 145*, 57–62.

Scheffler, Richard M., Brown, Timothy T., Fulton, Brent D., Hinshaw, Stephen P., Levine, Peter, & Stone, Susan. (2009). Positive association between attention-deficit/hyperactivity disorder medication use and academic achievement during elementary school. *Pediatrics, 123*, 1273–1279.

Scheibehenne, Benjamin, Greifeneder, Rainer, & Todd, Peter M. (2010). Can there ever be too many options? A meta-analytic review of choice overload. *Journal of Consumer Research, 37*, 409–425.

Schermerhorn, Alice C., D'Onofrio, Brian M., Turkheimer, Eric, Ganiban, Jody M., Spotts, Erica L., Lichtenstein, Paul, . . . Neiderhiser, Jenae M. (2011). A genetically informed study of associations between family functioning and child psychosocial adjustment. *Developmental Psychology, 47*, 707–725.

Schiller, Jeannine S., Lucas, Jacqueline W., Ward, Brian W., & Peregoy, Jennifer A. (2012). Summary health statistics for U.S. adults: National Health Interview Survey, 2010. *Vital and Health Statistics, 10*(252).

Schmader, Toni. (2010). Stereotype threat deconstructed. *Current Directions in Psychological Science, 19*, 14–18.

Schmader, Toni, Johns, Michael, & Forbes, Chad. (2008). An integrated process model of stereotype threat effects on performance. *Psychological Review, 115*, 336–356.

Schmeer, Kammi K. (2011). The child health disadvantage of parental cohabitation. *Journal of Marriage and Family, 73*, 181–193.

Schneider, Shari Kessel, O'Donnell, Lydia, Stueve, Ann, & Coulter, Robert W. S. (2011). Cyberbullying, school bullying, and psychological distress: A regional census of high school students. *American Journal of Public Health, 102*, 171–177.

Schneider, Wolfgang, & Lockl, Kathrin. (2008). Procedural metacognition in children: Evidence for developmental trends. In John Dunlosky & Robert A. Bjork (Eds.), *Handbook of metamemory and memory* (pp. 391–409). New York, NY: Psychology Press.

Schofield, Thomas J., Martin, Monica J., Conger, Katherine J., Neppl, Tricia M., Donnellan, M. Brent, & Conger, Rand D. (2011). Intergenerational transmission of adaptive functioning: A test of the interactionist model of SES and human development. *Child Development, 82,* 33–47.

Schön, Daniele, Boyer, Maud, Moreno, Sylvain, Besson, Mireille, Peretz, Isabelle, & Kolinsky, Régine. (2008). Songs as an aid for language acquisition. *Cognition, 106,* 975–983.

Schore, Allan, & McIntosh, Jennifer. (2011). Family law and the neuroscience of attachment, part I. *Family Court Review, 49,* 501–512.

Schreck, Christopher J., Burek, Melissa W., Stewart, Eric A., & Miller, J. Mitchell. (2007). Distress and violent victimization among young adolescents: Early puberty and the social interactionist explanation. *Journal of Research in Crime and Delinquency, 44,* 381–405.

Schulenberg, John, O'Malley, Patrick M., Bachman, Jerald G., & Johnston, Lloyd D. (2005). Early adult transitions and their relation to well-being and substance use. In Richard A. Settersten, Jr., Frank F. Furstenberg, Jr., & Rubén G. Rumbaut (Eds.), *On the frontier of adulthood: Theory, research, and public policy* (pp. 417–453). Chicago, IL: University of Chicago Press.

Schulz, James H., & Binstock, Robert H. (2008). *Aging nation: The economics and politics of growing older in America* (Paperback ed.). Baltimore, MD: Johns Hopkins University Press.

Schupp, Justin, & Sharp, Jeff. (2012). Exploring the social bases of home gardening. *Agriculture and Human Values, 29,* 93–105.

Schwartz, Amy Ellen, Stiefel, Leanna, Rubenstein, Ross, & Zabel, Jeffrey. (2011). The path not taken: How does school organization affect eighth-grade achievement? *Educational Evaluation and Policy Analysis, 33,* 293–317.

Schwartz, Paul D., Maynard, Amanda M., & Uzelac, Sarah M. (2008). Adolescent egocentrism: A contemporary view. *Adolescence, 43,* 441–448.

Schweinhart, Lawrence J., Montie, Jeanne, Xiang, Zongping, Barnett, W. Steven, Belfield, Clive R., & Nores, Milagros. (2005). *Lifetime effects: The High/Scope Perry Preschool Study through age 40.* Ypsilanti, MI: High/Scope Press.

Schweinhart, Lawrence J., & Weikart, David P. (1997). *Lasting differences: The High/Scope Preschool Curriculum Comparison Study through age 23.* Ypsilanti, MI: High/Scope Educational Research Foundation.

Schytt, Erica, & Waldenström, Ulla. (2010). Epidural analgesia for labor pain: Whose choice? *Acta Obstetricia et Gynecologica Scandinavica, 89,* 238–242.

Scott, Lisa S., & Monesson, Alexandra. (2010). Experience-dependent neural specialization during infancy. *Neuropsychologia, 48,* 1857–1861.

Scott, Lisa S., Pascalis, Olivier, & Nelson, Charles A. (2007). A domain-general theory of the development of perceptual discrimination. *Current Directions in Psychological Science, 16,* 197–201.

Sear, Rebecca, & Mace, Ruth. (2008). Who keeps children alive? A review of the effects of kin on child survival. *Evolution and Human Behavior, 29,* 1–18.

Sebastian, Catherine, Burnett, Stephanie, & Blakemore, Sarah-Jayne. (2008). Development of the self-concept during adolescence. *Trends in Cognitive Sciences, 12,* 441–446.

Sebastián-Gallés, Núria. (2007). Biased to learn language. *Developmental Science, 10,* 713–718.

Sedivy, John M., Munoz-Najar, Ursula M., Jeyapalan, Jessie C., & Campisi, Judith. (2008). Cellular senescence: A link between tumor suppression and organismal aging? In Leonard Guarente, Linda Partridge, & Douglas C. Wallace (Eds.), *Molecular biology of aging* (pp. 185–214). Cold Spring Harbor, NY: Cold Spring Harbor Laboratory Press.

Seelaar, Harro, Rohrer, Jonathan D., Pijnenburg, Yolande A. L., Fox, Nick C., & van Swieten, John C. (2011). Clinical, genetic and pathological heterogeneity of frontotemporal dementia: A review. *Journal of Neurology, Neurosurgery & Psychiatry, 82,* 476–486.

Seery, Mark D. (2011). Resilience: A silver lining to experiencing adverse life events? *Current Directions in Psychological Science, 20,* 390–394.

Seifer, Ronald, LaGasse, Linda L., Lester, Barry, Bauer, Charles R., Shankaran, Seetha, Bada, Henrietta S.,... Liu, Jing. (2004). Attachment status in children prenatally exposed to cocaine and other substances. *Child Development, 75,* 850–868.

Seki, Fusako. (2001). The role of the government and the family in taking care of the frail elderly: A comparison of the United States and Japan. In David N. Weisstub, David C. Thomasma, Serge Gauthier, & George F. Tomossy (Eds.), *Aging: Caring for our elders* (pp. 83–105). Dordrecht, The Netherlands: Kluwer.

Seligman, Hilary K., & Schillinger, Dean. (2010). Hunger and socioeconomic disparities in chronic disease. *New England Journal of Medicine, 363,* 6–9.

Selingo, Jeff. (2012, March 9). Do graduation rates matter? *The Chronicle of Higher Education,* pp. A1, A10–A12.

Senju, Atsushi, Southgate, Victoria, Miura, Yui, Matsui, Tomoko, Hasegawa, Toshikazu, Tojo, Yoshikuni,... Csibra, Gergely. (2010). Absence of spontaneous action anticipation by false belief attribution in children with autism spectrum disorder. *Development and Psychopathology, 22,* 353–360.

Setlik, Jennifer, Bond, G. Randall, & Ho, Mona. (2009). Adolescent prescription ADHD medication abuse is rising along with prescriptions for these medications. *Pediatrics, 124,* 875–880.

Settersten, Richard A. (2002). Social sources of meaning in later life. In Robert S. Weiss & Scott A. Bass (Eds.), *Challenges of the third age: Meaning and purpose in later life* (pp. 55–79). London, England: Oxford University Press.

Shai, Iris, & Stampfer, Meir J. (2008). Weight-loss diets—Can you keep it off? *American Journal of Clinical Nutrition, 88,* 1185–1186.

Shakya, Holly Baker, Usita, Paula M., Eisenberg, Christina, Weston, Joanna, & Liles, Sandy. (2012). Family well-being concerns of grandparents in skipped generation families. *Journal of Gerontological Social Work, 55,* 39–54.

Shanahan, Michael J., & Hofer, Scott M. (2011). Molecular genetics, aging, and well-being: Sensitive period, accumulation, and pathway models. In Robert H. Binstock & Linda K. George (Eds.), *Handbook of aging and the social sciences* (7th ed., pp. 135–147). San Diego, CA: Academic Press.

Shanahan, Timothy, & Lonigan, Christopher J. (2010). The National Early Literacy Panel: A summary of the process and the report. *Educational Researcher, 39,* 279–285.

Shannon, Joyce Brennfleck (Ed.). (2007). *Eating disorders sourcebook: Basic consumer health information about anorexia nervosa, bulimia nervosa, binge eating, compulsive exercise, female athlete triad, and other eating disorders* (2nd ed.). Detroit, MI: Omnigraphics.

Shapiro, Adam, & Yarborough-Hayes, Raijah. (2008). Retirement and older men's health. *Generations, 32*(1), 49–53.

Shapiro, Edward S., Zigmond, Naomi, Wallace, Teri, & Marston, Doug (Eds.). (2011). *Models for implementing response to intervention: Tools, outcomes, and implications.* New York, NY: Guilford Press.

Shapiro, James A. (2009). Revisiting the central dogma in the 21st century. In Günther Witzany (Ed.), *Annals of the New York Academy of Sciences: Vol. 1178. Natural genetic engineering and natural genome editing* (pp. 6–28). Malden, MA: Wiley.

Shapiro, Melanie Freedberg. (2011). *Mothers' feelings about physical and emotional intimacy twelve to fifteen months after the birth of a first child* (Master's thesis). Retrieved from https://dspace.smith.edu/handle/11020/23004

Sharif, Khaldoun W., & Coomarasamy, Arri (Eds.). (2012). *Assisted reproduction techniques: Challenges and management options.* Chichester, West Sussex, UK: Wiley-Blackwell.

Sharkey, Siobhan S., Hudak, Sandra, Horn, Susan D., James, Bobbie, & Howes, Jessie. (2011). Frontline caregiver daily practices: A comparison study of traditional nursing homes and the green house project sites. *Journal of the American Geriatrics Society, 59,* 126–131.

Shattuck, Paul T. (2006). The contribution of diagnostic substitution to the growing administrative prevalence of autism in US special education. *Pediatrics, 117,* 1028–1037.

Shaw, Benjamin A., Liang, Jersey, & Krause, Neal (2010). Age and race differences in the trajectories of self-esteem. *Psychology and Aging, 25,* 84–94.

Sheehy, Gail. (1976). *Passages: Predictable crises of adult life.* New York, NY: Dutton.

Sheldon, Pavica. (2012). Profiling the non-users: Examination of life-position indicators, sensation seeking, shyness, and loneliness among users and non-users of social network sites. *Computers in Human Behavior, 28,* 1960–1965.

Shepard, Thomas H., & Lemire, Ronald J. (2004). *Catalog of teratogenic agents* (11th ed.). Baltimore, MD: Johns Hopkins University Press.

Sherblom, Stephen. (2008). The legacy of the "Care challenge": Re-envisioning the outcome of the justice-care debate. *Journal of Moral Education, 37,* 81–98.

Shields, Margot, & Tremblay, Mark S. (2010). Canadian childhood obesity estimates based on WHO, IOTF and CDC cut-points. *International Journal of Pediatric Obesity, 5,* 265–273.

Shirom, Arie, Toker, Sharon, Berliner, Shlomo, Shapira, Itzhak, & Melamed, Samuel. (2008). The effects of physical fitness and feeling vigorous on self-rated health. *Health Psychology, 27,* 567–575.

Shirtcliff, Elizabeth A., Dahl, Ronald E., & Pollak, Seth D. (2009). Pubertal development: Correspondence between hormonal and physical development. *Child Development, 80,* 327–337.

Short, Kathleen. (2011). *The Research Supplemental Poverty Measure: 2010* (Current Population Reports P60-241). Washington, DC: U.S. Census Bureau.

Shumaker, Sally A., Ockene, Judith K., & Riekert, Kristin A. (Eds.). (2009). *The handbook of health behavior change* (3rd ed.). New York, NY: Springer.

Siebenbruner, Jessica, Zimmer-Gembeck, Melanie J., & Egeland, Byron. (2007). Sexual partners and contraceptive use: A 16-year prospective study predicting abstinence and risk behavior. *Journal of Research on Adolescence, 17,* 179–206.

Siegel, Lawrence A., & Siegel, Richard M. (2007). Sexual changes in the aging male. In Annette Fuglsang Owens & Mitchell S. Tepper (Eds.), *Sexual health: Vol. 2. Physical foundations* (pp. 223–255). Westport, CT: Praeger/Greenwood.

Siegler, Robert S. (2009). Improving the numerical understanding of children from low-income families. *Child Development Perspectives, 3,* 118–124.

Siegler, Robert S., & Chen, Zhe. (2008). Differentiation and integration: Guiding principles for analyzing cognitive change. *Developmental Science, 11,* 433–448.

Sierksma, Annerieke S. R., van den Hove, Daniel L. A., Steinbusch, Harry W. M., & Prickaerts, Jos. (2010). Major depression, cognitive dysfunction and Alzheimer's disease: Is there a link? *European Journal of Pharmacology, 626,* 72–82.

Sierra, Felipe, Hadley, Evan, Suzman, Richard, & Hodes, Richard. (2009). Prospects for life span extension. *Annual Review of Medicine, 60,* 457–469.

Silk, Timothy J., & Wood, Amanda G. (2011). Lessons about neurodevelopment from anatomical magnetic resonance imaging. *Journal of Developmental & Behavioral Pediatrics, 32,* 158–168.

Sillars, Alan, Smith, Traci, & Koerner, Ascan. (2010). Misattributions contributing to empathic (in)accuracy during parent-adolescent conflict discussions. *Journal of Social and Personal Relationships, 27,* 727–747.

Silton, Nava R., Flannelly, Laura T., Flannelly, Kevin J., & Galek, Kathleen. (2011). Toward a theory of holistic needs and the brain. *Holistic Nursing Practice, 25,* 258–265.

Silva, Katie G., Correa-Chávez, Maricela, & Rogoff, Barbara. (2010). Mexican-heritage children's attention and learning from interactions directed to others. *Child Development, 81,* 898–912.

Silventoinen, Karri, Hammar, Niklas, Hedlund, Ebba, Koskenvuo, Markku, Ronnemaa, Tapani, & Kaprio, Jaakko. (2008). Selective international migration by social position, health behaviour and personality. *European Journal of Public Health, 18,* 150–155.

Silverstein, Merril. (2006). Intergenerational family transfers in social context. In Robert H. Binstock & Linda K. George (Eds.),

Handbook of aging and the social sciences (6th ed., pp. 165–180). Amsterdam, The Netherlands: Elsevier.

Silverstein, Merril, Gans, Daphna, Lowenstein, Ariela, Giarrusso, Roseann, & Bengtson, Vern L. (2010). Older parent–child relationships in six developed nations: Comparisons at the intersection of affection and conflict. *Journal of Marriage and Family, 72,* 1006–1021.

Silvia, Paul J., & Sanders, Camilla E. (2010). Why are smart people curious? Fluid intelligence, openness to experience, and interest. *Learning and Individual Differences, 20,* 242–245.

Simmons, Joseph P., Nelson, Leif D., & Simonsohn, Uri. (2011). False-positive psychology: Undisclosed flexibility in data collection and analysis allows presenting anything as significant. *Psychological Science, 22,* 1359–1366.

Simon, Viktória, Czobor, Pál, Bálint, Sára, Bitter, István, & Mészáros, Ágnes. (2009). Prevalence and correlates of adult attention-deficit hyperactivity disorder: Meta-analysis. *British Journal of Psychiatry, 194,* 204–211.

Simpkins, Sandra D., Fredricks, Jennifer A., Davis-Kean, Pamela E., & Eccles, Jacquelynne S. (2006). Healthy mind, healthy habits: The influence of activity involvement in middle childhood. In Aletha C. Huston & Marika N. Ripke (Eds.), *Developmental contexts in middle childhood: Bridges to adolescence and adulthood* (pp. 283–302). New York, NY: Cambridge University Press.

Simpson, Jeffry A., & Rholes, W. Steven. (2010). Attachment and relationships: Milestones and future directions. *Journal of Social and Personal Relationships, 27,* 173–180.

Sinardet, Dave, & Mortelmans, Dimitri. (2009). The feminine side to Santa Claus. Women's work of kinship in contemporary gift-giving relations. *The Social Science Journal, 46,* 124–142.

Singh, Amika, Uijtdewilligen, Léonie, Twisk, Jos W. R., van Mechelen, Willem, & Chinapaw, Mai J. M. (2012). Physical activity and performance at school: A systematic review of the literature including a methodological quality assessment. *Archives of Pediatrics & Adolescent Medicine, 166,* 49–55.

Singh, Gopal K., & Siahpush, Mohammad. (2006). Widening socioeconomic inequalities in US life expectancy, 1980–2000. *International Journal of Epidemiology, 35,* 969–979.

Singleton, David, & Muñoz, Carmen. (2011). Around and beyond the critical period hypothesis. In Eli Hinkel (Ed.), *Handbook of research in second language teaching and learning* (Vol. 2, pp. 407–425). Mahwah, NJ: Erlbaum.

Sinnott, Jan D. (1998). *The development of logic in adulthood: Postformal thought and its applications.* New York, NY: Plenum Press.

Siu, Angela F. Y. (2007). Using friends to combat internalizing problems among primary school children in Hong Kong. *Journal of Cognitive and Behavioral Psychotherapies, 7,* 11–26.

Skinner, B. F. (1957). *Verbal behavior.* New York, NY: Appleton-Century-Crofts.

Skipper, Magdalena. (2011). Epigenomics: Epigenetic variation across the generations. *Nature Reviews Genetics, 12,* 740.

Slack, Jonathan M. W. (2012). *Stem cells: A very short introduction.* New York, NY: Oxford University Press.

Slaughter, Virginia, & Griffiths, Maya. (2007). Death understanding and fear of death in young children. *Clinical Child Psychology and Psychiatry, 12,* 525–535.

Slavin, Robert E., Lake, Cynthia, & Groff, Cynthia. (2009). Effective programs in middle and high school mathematics: A best-evidence synthesis. *Review of Educational Research, 79,* 839–911.

Slessor, Gillian, Phillips, Louise H., & Bull, Rebecca. (2008). Age-related declines in basic social perception: Evidence from tasks assessing eye-gaze processing. *Psychology and Aging, 23,* 812–822.

Slining, Meghan, Adair, Linda S., Goldman, Barbara Davis, Borja, Judith B., & Bentley, Margaret. (2010). Infant overweight is associated with delayed motor development. *The Journal of Pediatrics, 157,* 20–25.e1. doi:10.1016/j.jpeds.2009.12.054

Sloan, John. (2011–2012). Medicating elders in the evidence-free zone. *Generations, 35*(4), 56–61.

Sloan, Ken. (2009). The role of personality in a manager's learning effectiveness. *European Journal of Social Sciences, 12,* 31–42.

Sloan, Mark. (2009). *Birth day: A pediatrician explores the science, the history, and the wonder of childbirth.* New York, NY: Ballantine Books.

Sloane, Stephanie, Baillargeon, Renée, & Premack, David. (2012). Do infants have a sense of fairness? *Psychological Science, 23,* 196–204.

Slobin, Dan I. (2001). Form-function relations: How do children find out what they are? In Melissa Bowerman & Stephen C. Levinson (Eds.), *Language acquisition and conceptual development* (pp. 406–449). Cambridge, UK: Cambridge University Press.

Slutske, Wendy S., Moffitt, Terrie E., Poulton, Richie, & Caspi, Avshalom. (2012). Undercontrolled temperament at age 3 predicts disordered gambling at age 32: A longitudinal study of a complete birth cohort. *Psychological Science, 23,* 510–516.

Small, Meredith F. (1998). *Our babies, ourselves: How biology and culture shape the way we parent.* New York, NY: Anchor Books.

Smetana, Judith G., Metzger, Aaron, & Campione-Barr, Nicole. (2004). African American late adolescents' relationships with parents: Developmental transitions and longitudinal patterns. *Child Development, 75,* 932–947.

Smith, Aaron. (2010, August 11). *Home broadband 2010.* Retrieved from http://pewinternet.org/Reports/2010/Home-Broadband-2010.aspx

Smith, Allison E. (2009). *Ageing in urban neighbourhoods: Place attachment and social exclusion.* Bristol, UK: Policy.

Smith, Chris M. M. (Ed.) (2006). *Including the gifted and talented: Making inclusion work for more gifted and able learners.* New York, NY: Routledge.

Smith, Christian (with Denton, Melinda Lundquist). (2005). *Soul searching: The religious and spiritual lives of American teenagers.* Oxford, UK: Oxford University Press.

Smith, G. Rush, Williamson, Gail M., Miller, L. Stephen, & Schulz, Richard. (2011). Depression and quality of informal care: A longitudinal investigation of caregiving stressors. *Psychology and Aging, 26,* 584–591.

Smith, Peter K. (2010). *Children and play: Understanding children's worlds.* Chichester, West Sussex, UK: Wiley-Blackwell.

Smith, Peter K., Mahdavi, Jess, Carvalho, Manuel, Fisher, Sonja, Russell, Shanette, & Tippett, Neil. (2008). Cyberbullying: Its nature and impact in secondary school pupils. *Journal of Child Psychology and Psychiatry, 49,* 376–385.

Smith, Peter K., Pepler, Debra J., & Rigby, Ken. (Eds.) (2004). *Bullying in schools: How successful can interventions be?* New York, NY: Cambridge University Press.

Smith, Tom W. (2005). Generation gaps in attitudes and values from the 1970s to the 1990s. In Richard A. Settersten, Jr., Frank F. Furstenberg, Jr., & Rubén G. Rumbaut (Eds.), *On the frontier of adulthood: Theory, research, and public policy* (pp. 177–221). Chicago, IL: University of Chicago Press.

Smokowski, Paul Richard, Rose, Roderick, & Bacallao, Martica. (2010). Influence of risk factors and cultural assets on Latino adolescents' trajectories of self-esteem and internalizing symptoms. *Child Psychiatry & Human Development, 41,* 133–155.

Smyth, Joshua M. (2007). Beyond self-selection in video game play: An experimental examination of the consequences of massively multiplayer online role-playing game play. *CyberPsychology & Behavior, 10,* 717–727.

Sneed, Joel R., & Whitbourne, Susan Krauss. (2005). Models of the aging self. *Journal of Social Issues, 61,* 375–388.

Snijders, Rosalinde J. M., & Nicolaides, Kypros H. (1996). Ultrasound markers for fetal chromosomal defects. New York: Parthenon.

Snow, Catherine E., & Kang, Jennifer Yusun. (2006). Becoming bilingual, biliterate, and bicultural. In William Damon & Richard M. Lerner (Series Eds.) & K. Ann Renninger & Irving E. Sigel (Vol. Eds.), *Handbook of child psychology: Vol. 4. Child psychology in practice* (6th ed., pp. 75–102). Hoboken, NJ: Wiley.

Snow, Catherine E., Porche, Michelle V., Tabors, Patton O., & Harris, Stephanie Ross. (2007). *Is literacy enough? Pathways to academic success for adolescents.* Baltimore, MD: Brookes.

Snow, David. (2006). Regression and reorganization of intonation between 6 and 23 months. *Child Development, 77,* 281–296.

Snyder, James, Schrepferman, Lynn, Oeser, Jessica, Patterson, Gerald, Stoolmiller, Mike, Johnson, Kassy, & Snyder, Abigail. (2005). Deviancy training and association with deviant peers in young children: Occurrence and contribution to early-onset conduct problems. *Development & Psychopathology, 17,* 39–413.

Snyder, Thomas D., & Dillow, Sally A. (2010). *Digest of education statistics, 2009* (NCES 2010-013). Washington, DC: National Center for Education Statistics.

Snyder, Thomas D., & Dillow, Sally A. (2011). *Digest of education statistics, 2010* (NCES 2011-015). Washington, DC: National Center for Education Statistics.

Snyder, Thomas D., & Dillow, Sally A. (2012). *Digest of Education Statistics 2011* (NCES 2012-001). Washington, DC: National Center for Education Statistics, Institute of Education Sciences, U.S. Department of Education.

Soares, Joseph A. (2012). The future of college admissions: Discussion. *Educational Psychologist, 47,* 66–70.

Sobal, Jeffery, & Hanson, Karla L. (2011). Marital status, marital history, body weight, and obesity. *Marriage & Family Review, 47,* 474–504.

Sobotka, Tomáš, & Testa, Maria Rita. (2008). Attitudes and intentions toward childlessness in Europe. In Charlotte Höhn, Dragana Avramov, & Irena E. Kotowska (Eds.), *European Studies of Population: Vol. 16. People, population change and policies* (Vol. 1, pp. 177–211). The Hague, Netherlands: Springer.

Social Trends Institute. (2012). *The sustainable demographic dividend.* Charlottesville, VA: Author. Retrieved from: http://sustaindemographicdividend.org/wp-content/uploads/2012/07/SDD-2011-Final.pdf

Soenens, Bart, & Vansteenkiste, Maarten. (2010). A theoretical upgrade of the concept of parental psychological control: Proposing new insights on the basis of self-determination theory. *Developmental Review, 30,* 74–99.

Sokol, Rebecca Z. (2009). Is androgen therapy indicated for aging men? *Sexuality, Reproduction & Menopause, 7,* 27–30.

Soley, Gaye, & Hannon, Erin E. (2010). Infants prefer the musical meter of their own culture: A cross-cultural comparison. *Developmental Psychology, 46,* 286–292.

Solomon, Alina, Sippola, R., Soininen, H., Wolozin, B., Tuomilehto, J., Laatikainen, T., & Kivipelto, Miia. (2010). Lipid-lowering treatment is related to decreased risk of dementia: A population-based study (FINRISK). *Neuro-Degenerative Diseases, 7,* 180–182.

Sonnenschein, Susan, Stapleton, Laura M., & Benson, Amy. (2010). The relation between the type and amount of instruction and growth in children's reading competencies. *American Educational Research Journal, 47,* 358–389.

Sorkin, Dara H., & Rook, Karen S. (2006). Dealing with negative social exchanges in later life: Coping responses, goals, and effectiveness. *Psychology and Aging, 21,* 715–725.

Soska, Kasey C., Adolph, Karen E., & Johnson, Scott P. (2010). Systems in development: Motor skill acquisition facilitates three-dimensional object completion. *Developmental Psychology, 46,* 129–138.

Sowell, Elizabeth R., Thompson, Paul M., & Toga, Arthur W. (2007). Mapping adolescent brain maturation using structural magnetic resonance imaging. In Daniel Romer & Elaine F. Walker (Eds.), *Adolescent psychopathology and the developing brain: Integrating brain and prevention science* (pp. 55–84). Oxford, UK: Oxford University Press.

Sparks, Sarah D. (2012, July 16). Form meets function in Finland's new schools. *Education Week,* p. 9.

Spear, Linda Patia. (2011). Adolescent neurobehavioral characteristics, alcohol sensitivities, and intake: Setting the stage for alcohol use disorders? *Child Development Perspectives, 5,* 231–238.

Spearman, Charles Edward. (1927). *The abilities of man, their nature and measurement.* New York, NY: Macmillan.

Specht, Jule, Egloff, Boris, & Schmukle, Stefan C. (2011). Stability and change of personality across the life course: The impact of age and major life events on mean-level and rank-order stability of the Big Five. *Journal of Personality and Social Psychology, 101,* 862–882.

Spencer, John P., Blumberg, Mark S., McMurray, Bob, Robinson, Scott R., Samuelson, Larissa K., & Tomblin, J. Bruce. (2009). Short arms and talking eggs: Why we should no longer abide the nativist–empiricist debate. *Child Development Perspectives, 3,* 79–87.

Spinillo, Arsenio, Montanari, Laura, Gardella, Barbara, Roccio, Marianna, Stronati, Mauro, & Fazzi, Elisa. (2009). Infant sex, obstetric risk factors, and 2-year neurodevelopmental outcome among preterm infants. *Developmental Medicine & Child Neurology, 51,* 518–525.

Spittle, Alicia J., Treyvaud, Karli, Doyle, Lex W., Roberts, Gehan, Lee, Katherine J., Inder, Terrie E.,... Anderson, Peter J. (2009). Early emergence of behavior and social-emotional problems in very preterm infants. *Journal of the American Academy of Child and Adolescent Psychiatry, 48,* 909–918.

Sroufe, L. Alan. (2012, January 28). Ritalin gone wrong. *New York Times,* p. SR1.

Sroufe, L. Alan, Egeland, Byron, Carlson, Elizabeth A., & Collins, W. Andrew. (2005). *The development of the person: The Minnesota study of risk and adaptation from birth to adulthood.* New York, NY: Guilford Press.

St. Petersburg-USA Orphanage Research Team. (2008). The effects of early social-emotional and relationship experience on the development of young orphanage children. *Monographs of the Society for Research in Child Development, 73*(3, Serial No. 291), 1–262.

Staff, Jeremy, Messersmith, Emily E., & Schulenberg, John E. (2009). Adolescents and the world of work. In Richard Lerner & Laurence Steinberg (Eds.), *Handbook of adolescent psychology: Vol. 2. Contextual influences on adolescent development* (pp. 270–313). Hoboken, NJ: Wiley.

Staff, Jeremy, & Schulenberg, John. (2010). Millennials and the world of work: Experiences in paid work during adolescence. *Journal of Business and Psychology, 25,* 247–255.

Stanley, Scott M., Rhoades, Galena Kline, & Markman, Howard J. (2006). Sliding versus deciding: Inertia and the premarital cohabitation effect. *Family Relations, 55,* 499–509.

Staudinger, Ursula M., & Lindenberger, Ulman. (2003). Why read another book on human development? Understanding human development takes a metatheory and multiple disciplines. In Ursula M. Staudinger & Ulman E. R. Lindenberger (Eds.), *Understanding human development: Dialogues with lifespan psychology* (pp. 1–13). Boston, MA: Kluwer.

Stavrova, Olga, Fetchenhauer, Detlef, & Schlösser, Thomas. (2012). Cohabitation, gender, and happiness: A cross-cultural study in thirty countries. *Journal of Cross-Cultural Psychology, 43,* 1063–1081.

Stawski, Robert S., Almeida, David M., Lachman, Margie E., Tun, Patricia A., & Rosnick, Christopher B. (2010). Fluid cognitive ability is associated with greater exposure and smaller reactions to daily stressors. *Psychology and Aging, 25,* 330–342.

Steele, Claude M. (1997). A threat in the air: How stereotypes shape intellectual identity and performance. *American Psychologist, 52,* 613–629.

Steemers, Jeanette. (2010). *Creating preschool television: A story of commerce, creativity and curriculum.* New York, NY: Palgrave Macmillan.

Stein, Arlene. (2006). *Shameless: Sexual dissidence in American culture.* New York, NY: New York University Press.

Stein, Catherine H., Abraham, Kristen M., Bonar, Erin E., Leith, Jaclyn E., Kraus, Shane W., Hamill, Alexis C., ... Fogo, Wendy R. (2011). Family ties in tough times: How young adults and their parents view the U.S. economic crisis. *Journal of Family Psychology, 25,* 449–454.

Steinberg, Laurence. (2001). We know some things: Parent-adolescent relationships in retrospect and prospect. *Journal of Research on Adolescence, 11,* 1–19.

Steinberg, Laurence. (2004). Risk taking in adolescence: What changes, and why? In Ronald E. Dahl & Linda Patia Spear (Eds.), *Adolescent brain development: Vulnerabilities and opportunities* (Vol. 1021, pp. 51–58). New York, NY: New York Academy of Sciences.

Steinberg, Laurence. (2008). A social neuroscience perspective on adolescent risk-taking. *Developmental Review, 28,* 78–106.

Steinberg, Laurence. (2009). Should the science of adolescent brain development inform public policy? *American Psychologist, 64,* 739–750.

Steinberg, Laurence, & Monahan, Kathryn C. (2011). Adolescents' exposure to sexy media does not hasten the initiation of sexual intercourse. *Developmental Psychology, 47,* 562–576.

Steiner, Meir, & Young, Elizabeth A. (2008). Hormones and mood. In Jill B. Becker, Karen J. Berkley, Nori Geary, Elizabeth Hampson, James P. Herman, & Elizabeth Young (Eds.), *Sex differences in the brain: From genes to behavior* (pp. 405–426). New York, NY: Oxford University Press.

Stel, Vianda S., Smit, Johannes H., Pluijm, Saskia M. F., & Lips, Paul. (2004). Consequences of falling in older men and women and risk factors for health service use and functional decline. *Age and Ageing, 33,* 58–65.

Sterck, Elisabeth H. M., & Begeer, Sander. (2010). Theory of mind: Specialized capacity or emergent property? *European Journal of Developmental Psychology, 7,* 1–16.

Sterling, Peter. (2012). Allostasis: A model of predictive regulation. *Physiology & Behavior, 106,* 5–15.

Stern, Michael J., & Adams, Alison E. (2010). Do rural residents really use the internet to build social capital? An empirical investigation. *American Behavioral Scientist, 53,* 1389–1422.

Sternberg, Robert J. (1988). Triangulating love. In Robert J. Sternberg & Michael L. Barnes (Eds.), *The psychology of love* (pp. 119–138). New Haven, CT: Yale University Press.

Sternberg, Robert J. (1996). *Successful intelligence: How practical and creative intelligence determine success in life.* New York, NY: Simon & Schuster.

Sternberg, Robert J. (2003). *Wisdom, intelligence, and creativity synthesized.* New York, NY: Cambridge University Press.

Sternberg, Robert J. (2006a). A duplex theory of love. In Robert J. Sternberg & Karin Weis (Eds.), *The new psychology of love* (pp. 184–199). New Haven, CT: Yale University Press.

Sternberg, Robert J. (2006b). Introduction. In James C. Kaufman & Robert J. Sternberg (Eds.), *The international handbook of creativity* (pp. 1–9). New York, NY: Cambridge University Press.

Sternberg, Robert J. (2012). Why I became an administrator … and why you might become one too. *Observer, 25*(2), 21–22.

Sternberg, Robert J., Jarvin, Linda, & Grigorenko, Elena L. (2011). *Explorations in giftedness.* New York, NY: Cambridge University Press.

Sternberg, Robert J., & Weis, Karin. (Eds.) (2006). *The new psychology of love.* New Haven, CT: Yale University Press.

Sterns, Harvey L., & Huyck, Margaret Hellie. (2001). The role of work in midlife. In Margie E. Lachman (Ed.), *Handbook of midlife development* (pp. 447–486). New York, NY: Wiley.

Stevenson, John C., Hodis, Howard N., Pickar, James H., & Lobo, Rogerio A. (2011). HRT and breast cancer risk: A realistic perspective. *Climacteric, 14*, 633–636.

Stevenson, Olive. (2007). *Neglected children and their families* (2nd ed.). Malden, MA: Blackwell.

Stevenson, Richard J., Oaten, Megan J., Case, Trevor I., Repacholi, Betty M., & Wagland, Paul. (2010). Children's response to adult disgust elicitors: Development and acquisition. *Developmental Psychology, 46*, 165–177.

Stigler, James W., & Hiebert, James. (2009). *The teaching gap: Best ideas from the world's teachers for improving education in the classroom* (1st Free Press trade paperback ed.). New York, NY: Free Press. (Original work published 1999)

Stiles, Joan, & Jernigan, Terry. (2010). The basics of brain development. *Neuropsychology Review, 20*, 327–348.

Stine-Morrow, Elizabeth A. L., & Basak, Chandramallika. (2011). Cognitive interventions. In K. Warner Schaie & Sherry L. Willis (Eds.), *Handbook of the psychology of aging* (7th ed., pp. 153–171). San Diego, CA: Academic Press.

Stine-Morrow, Elizabeth A. L., Noh, Soo Rim, & Shake, Matthew C. (2010). Age differences in the effects of conceptual integration training on resource allocation in sentence processing. *Quarterly Journal of Experimental Psychology, 63*, 1430–1455.

Stoltenborgh, Marije, van IJzendoorn, Marinus H., Euser, Eveline M., & Bakermans-Kranenburg, Marian J. (2011). A global perspective on child sexual abuse: Meta-analysis of prevalence around the world. *Child Maltreatment, 16*, 79–101.

Stone, Richard. (2011, April 8). Daring experiment in higher education opens its doors. *Science, 332*, 161.

Stone, Robyn I. (2006). Emerging issues in long-term care. In Robert H. Binstock & Linda K. George (Eds.), *Handbook of aging and the social sciences* (6th ed., pp. 397–418). Amsterdam, The Netherlands: Elsevier.

Stonington, Scott D. (2012). On ethical locations: The good death in Thailand, where ethics sit in places. *Social Science & Medicine, 75*, 836–844.

Strasburger, Victor C., Wilson, Barbara J., & Jordan, Amy B. (2009). *Children, adolescents, and the media* (2nd ed.). Los Angeles, CA: Sage.

Straus, Murray A., & Paschall, Mallie J. (2009). Corporal punishment by mothers and development of children's cognitive ability: A longitudinal study of two nationally representative age cohorts. *Journal of Aggression, Maltreatment & Trauma, 18*, 459–483.

Strauss, Jason. (2012). Psychotropic medications in the elderly. In Sheila Ryan Barnett (Ed.), *Manual of geriatric anesthesia* (pp. 399–418). New York, NY: Springer.

Streissguth, Ann P., & Connor, Paul D. (2001). Fetal alcohol syndrome and other effects of prenatal alcohol: Developmental cognitive neuroscience implications. In Charles A. Nelson & Monica Luciana (Eds.), *Handbook of developmental cognitive neuroscience* (pp. 505–518). Cambridge, MA: MIT Press.

Stroebe, Margaret, Schut, Henk, & Boerner, Kathrin. (2010). Continuing bonds in adaptation to bereavement: Toward theoretical integration. *Clinical Psychology Review, 30*, 259–268.

Strohm, Charles, Seltzer, Judith, Cochran, Susan, & Mays, Vickie. (2009). "Living Apart Together" relationships in the United States. *Demographic Research, 21*, 177–214.

Strouse, Darcy L. (1999). Adolescent crowd orientations: A social and temporal analysis. In Jeffrey A. McLellan & Mary Jo V. Pugh (Eds.), *The role of peer groups in adolescent social identity: Exploring the importance of stability and change* (pp. 37–54). San Francisco, CA: Jossey-Bass.

Stubben, Jerry D. (2001). Working with and conducting research among American Indian families. *American Behavioral Scientist, 44*, 1466–1481.

Stupica, Brandi, Sherman, Laura J., & Cassidy, Jude. (2011). Newborn irritability moderates the association between infant attachment security and toddler exploration and sociability. *Child Development, 82*, 1381–1389.

Sturdee, David W., & Pines, Amos (on behalf of the International Menopause Society Writing Group). (2011). Updated IMS recommendations on postmenopausal hormone therapy and preventive strategies for midlife health. *Climacteric, 14*, 302–320.

Subcommittee on Attention-Deficit/Hyperactivity Disorder, Steering Committee on Quality Improvement Management. (2011). ADHD: Clinical practice guideline for the diagnosis, evaluation, and treatment of attention-deficit/hyperactivity disorder in children and adolescents. *Pediatrics, 128*, 1007–1022.

Sue, Derald Wing. (Ed.) (2010). *Microaggressions and marginality: Manifestation, dynamics, and impact.* Hoboken, NJ: Wiley.

Suellentrop, Katherine, Morrow, Brian, Williams, Letitia, & D'Angelo, Denise. (2006, October 6). Monitoring progress toward achieving maternal and infant Healthy People 2010 objectives—19 states, Pregnancy Risk Assessment Monitoring System (PRAMS), 2000–2003. *Morbidity and Mortality Weekly Report Surveillance Summaries, 55*(SS09), 1–11.

Suh, Eunkook M., Diener, Ed, & Updegraff, John A. (2008). From culture to priming conditions: Self-construal influences on life satisfaction judgments. *Journal of Cross-Cultural Psychology, 39*, 3–15.

Sun, Rongjun, & Liu, Yuzhi. (2008). The more engagement, the better? A study of mortality of the oldest old in China. In Zeng Yi, Dudley L. Poston, Jr., Denese Ashbaugh Vlosky, & Danan Gu (Eds.), *Healthy longevity in China* (pp. 177–192). Dordrecht, The Netherlands: Springer.

Suris, Joan-Carles, Michaud, Pierre-André, Akre, Christina, & Sawyer, Susan M. (2008). Health risk behaviors in adolescents with chronic conditions. *Pediatrics, 122,* e1113-1118. doi:10.1542/peds.2008-1479

Susman, Elizabeth J., Houts, Renate M., Steinberg, Laurence, Belsky, Jay, Cauffman, Elizabeth, DeHart, Ganie,... The Eunice Kennedy Shriver NICHD Early Child Care Research Network. (2010). Longitudinal development of secondary sexual characteristics in girls and boys between ages 9-1/2 and 15-1/2 years. *Archives of Pediatrics & Adolescent Medicine, 164,* 166–173.

Sutin, Angelina R., & Costa, Paul T., Jr. (2010). Reciprocal influences of personality and job characteristics across middle adulthood. *Journal of Personality, 78,* 257–288.

Sutphin, George L., & Kaeberlein, Matt. (2011). Comparative genetics of aging. In Edward J. Masoro & Steven N. Austad (Eds.), *Handbook of the biology of aging* (7th ed., pp. 215–242). San Diego, CA: Academic Press.

Sutton-Smith, Brian. (2011). The antipathies of play. In Anthony D. Pellegrini (Ed.), *The Oxford handbook of the development of play* (pp. 110–115). New York, NY: Oxford University Press.

Swanson, Christopher B. (2011, June 9). Analysis finds graduation rates moving up: Strong signs of improvement on graduation. *Education Week,* p. 23.

Sweeney, Megan M. (2010). Remarriage and stepfamilies: Strategic sites for family scholarship in the 21st century. *Journal of Marriage and Family, 72,* 667–684.

Sweet, Stephen, & Moen, Phyllis. (2011). Dual earners preparing for job loss: Agency, linked lives, and resilience. *Work and Occupations, 39,* 35–70.

Syed, Moin, & Azmitia, Margarita. (2010). Narrative and ethnic identity exploration: A longitudinal account of emerging adults' ethnicity-related experiences. *Developmental Psychology, 46,* 208–219.

Syed, Moin, Azmitia, Margarita, & Cooper, Catherine R. (2011). Identity and academic success among underrepresented ethnic minorities: An interdisciplinary review and integration. *Journal of Social Issues, 67,* 442–468.

Szaflarski, Magdalena, Cubbins, Lisa A., & Ying, Jun. (2011). Epidemiology of alcohol abuse among US immigrant populations. *Journal of Immigrant and Minority Health, 13,* 647–658.

Tacken, Mart, & van Lamoen, Ellemieke. (2005). Transport behaviour and realised journeys and trips. In Heidrun Mollenkopf, Fiorella Marcellini, Isto Ruoppila, Zsuzsa Széman, & Mart Tacken (Eds.), *Enhancing mobility in later life: Personal coping, environmental resources and technical support. The out-of-home mobility of older adults in urban and rural regions of five European countries* (pp. 105–139). Amsterdam, The Netherlands: IOS Press.

Taga, Keiko A., Markey, Charlotte N., & Friedman, Howard S. (2006). A longitudinal investigation of associations between boys' pubertal timing and adult behavioral health and well-being. *Journal of Youth and Adolescence, 35,* 401–411.

Takahashi, Hidehiko, Kato, Motoichiro, Matsuura, Masato, Mobbs, Dean, Suhara, Tetsuya, & Okubo, Yoshiro. (2009, February 13). When your gain is my pain and your pain is my gain: Neural correlates of envy and schadenfreude. *Science, 323,* 937–939.

Talwar, Victoria, Harris, Paul L., & Schleifer, Michael. (Eds.) (2011). *Children's understanding of death: From biological to religious conceptions.* New York, NY: Cambridge University Press.

Tamay, Zeynep, Akcay, Ahmet, Ones, Ulker, Guler, Nermin, Kilic, Gurkan, & Zencir, Mehmet. (2007). Prevalence and risk factors for allergic rhinitis in primary school children. *International Journal of Pediatric Otorhinolaryngology, 71,* 463–471.

Tamis-LeMonda, Catherine S., Bornstein, Marc H., & Baumwell, Lisa. (2001). Maternal responsiveness and children's achievement of language milestones. *Child Development, 72,* 748–767.

Tamis-LeMonda, Catherine S., Way, Niobe, Hughes, Diane, Yoshikawa, Hirokazu, Kalman, Ronit Kahana, & Niwa, Erika Y. (2008). Parents' goals for children: The dynamic coexistence of individualism and collectivism in cultures and individuals. *Social Development, 17,* 183–209.

Tanaka, Hiroko, Black, Jessica M., Hulme, Charles, Stanley, Leanne M., Kesler, Shelli R., Whitfield-Gabrieli, Susan,... Hoeft, Fumiko. (2011). The brain basis of the phonological deficit in dyslexia is independent of IQ. *Psychological Science, 22,* 1442–1451.

Tanaka, Yuko, & Nakazawa, Jun. (2005). Job-related temporary father absence (Tanshinfunin) and child development. In David W. Shwalb, Jun Nakazawa, & Barbara J. Shwalb (Eds.), *Applied developmental psychology: Theory, practice, and research from Japan* (pp. 241–260). Greenwich, CT: Information Age.

Tandon, Pooja S., Zhou, Chuan, & Christakis, Dimitri A. (2012). Frequency of parent-supervised outdoor play of US preschool-aged children. *Archives of Pediatrics & Adolescent Medicine, 166,* 707–712.

Tanner, Jennifer L., Arnett, Jeffrey J., & Leis, Julie A. (2009). Emerging adulthood: Learning and development during the first stage of adulthood. In M. Cecil Smith (Ed.), *Handbook of research on adult learning and development* (pp. 34–67). New York, NY: Routledge/Taylor & Francis Group.

Tarullo, Amanda R., Garvin, Melissa C., & Gunnar, Megan R. (2011). Atypical EEG power correlates with indiscriminately friendly behavior in internationally adopted children. *Developmental Psychology, 47,* 417–431.

Tarullo, Amanda R., & Gunnar, Megan R. (2006). Child maltreatment and the developing HPA axis. *Hormones and Behavior, 50,* 632–639.

Taubes, Gary. (2009, July 17). Prosperity's plague. *Science, 325,* 256–260.

Tay, Marc Tze-Hsin, Au Eong, Kah Guan, Ng, C. Y., & Lim, M. K. (1992). Myopia and educational attainment in 421,116 young Singaporean males. *Annals, Academy of Medicine, Singapore, 21,* 785–791.

Taylor, Alan C., Robila, Mihaela, & Lee, Hae Seung. (2005). Distance, contact, and intergenerational relationships: Grandparents and adult grandchildren from an international perspective. *Journal of Adult Development, 12,* 33–41.

Taylor, John H. (Ed.). (2010). *Journey through the afterlife: Ancient Egyptian book of the dead.* London, England: British Museum Press.

Taylor, Marjorie, Carlson, Stephanie M., Maring, Bayta L., Gerow, Lynn, & Charley, Carolyn M. (2004). The characteristics and correlates of fantasy in school-age children: Imaginary companions, impersonation, and social understanding. *Developmental Psychology, 40,* 1173–1187.

Taylor, Marjorie, Shawber, Alison B., & Mannering, Anne M. (2009). Children's imaginary companions: What is it like to have an invisible friend? In Keith D. Markman, William M. P. Klein, & Julie A. Suhr (Eds.), *Handbook of imagination and mental simulation* (pp. 211–224). New York, NY: Psychology Press.

Taylor, Ronald D., Seaton, Eleanor, & Dominguez, Antonio. (2008). Kinship support, family relations, and psychological adjustment among low-income African American mothers and adolescents. *Journal of Research on Adolescence, 18,* 1–22.

Taylor, Shelley E. (2006). Tend and befriend: Biobehavioral bases of affiliation under stress. *Current Directions in Psychological Science, 15,* 273–277.

Taylor, Shelley E., Klein, Laura Cousino, Lewis, Brian P., Gruenewald, Tara L., Gurung, Regan A. R., & Updegraff, John A. (2000). Biobehavioral responses to stress in females: Tend-and-befriend, not fight-or-flight. *Psychological Review, 107,* 411–429.

Taylor, Zoe E., Larsen-Rife, Dannelle, Conger, Rand D., & Widaman, Keith F. (2012). Familism, interparental conflict, and parenting in Mexican-origin families: A cultural–contextual framework. *Journal of Marriage and Family, 74,* 312–327.

Teachman, Jay. (2008). Complex life course patterns and the risk of divorce in second marriages. *Journal of Marriage and Family, 70,* 294–305.

Teachman, Jay. (2010). Work-related health limitations, education, and the risk of marital disruption. *Journal of Marriage and Family, 72,* 919–932.

ter Bogt, Tom, Schmid, Holger, Nic Gabhainn, Saoirse, Fotiou, Anastasios, & Vollebergh, Wilma. (2006). Economic and cultural correlates of cannabis use among mid-adolescents in 31 countries. *Addiction, 101,* 241–251.

Terasawa, Ei, Kurian, Joseph R., Keen, Kim L., Shiel, Nicholas A., Colman, Ricki J., & Capuano, Saverio V. (2012). Body weight impact on puberty: Effects of high-calorie diet on puberty onset in female rhesus monkeys. *Endocrinology, 153,* 1696–1705.

The EXPRESS Group. (2009). One-year survival of extremely preterm infants after active perinatal care in Sweden. *Journal of the American Medical Association, 301,* 2225–2233.

Thelen, Esther, & Smith, Linda B. (2006). Dynamic systems theories. In William Damon & Richard M. Lerner (Series Eds.) & Richard M. Lerner (Vol. Ed.), *Handbook of child psychology: Vol. 1. Theoretical models of human development* (6th ed., pp. 258–312). Hoboken, NJ: Wiley.

Thiele, Dianne M., & Whelan, Thomas A. (2008). The relationship between grandparent satisfaction, meaning, and generativity. *International Journal of Aging and Human Development, 66,* 21–48.

Thobaben, Marshelle. (2006). Understanding compulsive hoarding. *Home Health Care Management Practice, 18,* 152–154.

Thomaes, Sander, Reijntjes, Albert, Orobio de Castro, Bram, Bushman, Brad J., Poorthuis, Astrid, & Telch, Michael J. (2010). I like me if you like me: On the interpersonal modulation and regulation of preadolescents' state self-esteem. *Child Development, 81,* 811–825.

Thomas, Alexander, & Chess, Stella. (1977). *Temperament and development.* Oxford, England: Brunner/Mazel.

Thomas, Ayanna K., & Bulevich, John B. (2006). Effective cue utilization reduces memory errors in older adults. *Psychology and Aging, 21,* 379–389.

Thomas, Dylan. (1957). *The collected poems of Dylan Thomas* (6th ed.). New York, NY: New Directions.

Thomas, Michael S. C., & Johnson, Mark H. (2008). New advances in understanding sensitive periods in brain development. *Current Directions in Psychological Science, 17,* 1–5.

Thomas, Nigel. (2011). Care planning and review for looked after children: Fifteen years of slow progress? *British Journal of Social Work, 41,* 387–398.

Thomas, Renu, DiLillo, David, Walsh, Kate, & Polusny, Melissa A. (2011). Pathways from child sexual abuse to adult depression: The role of parental socialization of emotions and alexithymia. *Psychology of Violence, 1,* 121–135.

Thomas, William H. (2007). *What are old people for? How elders will save the world* (Paperback ed.). Acton, MA: VanderWyk & Burnham.

Thompson, Clarissa A., & Siegler, Robert S. (2010). Linear numerical-magnitude representations aid children's memory for numbers. *Psychological Science, 21,* 1274–1281.

Thompson, Elisabeth Morgan, & Morgan, Elizabeth M. (2008). "Mostly straight" young women: Variations in sexual behavior and identity development. *Developmental Psychology, 44,* 15–21.

Thompson, Ross A. (2006). The development of the person: Social understanding, relationships, conscience, self. In William Damon & Richard M. Lerner (Series Eds.) & Nancy Eisenberg (Vol. Ed.), *Handbook of child psychology: Vol. 3. Social, emotional, and personality development* (6th ed., pp. 24–98). Hoboken, NJ: Wiley.

Thompson, Ross A., & Raikes, H. Abigail. (2003). Toward the next quarter-century: Conceptual and methodological challenges for attachment theory. *Development & Psychopathology, 15,* 691–718.

Thompson, Ross A., & Wyatt, Jennifer M. (1999). Values, policy, and research on divorce: Seeking fairness for children. In Ross A. Thompson & Paul R. Amato (Eds.), *The postdivorce family: Children, parenting, and society* (pp. 191–232). Thousand Oaks, CA: Sage.

Thornton, Arland, Axinn, William G., & Xie, Yu. (2007). *Marriage and cohabitation.* Chicago, IL: University of Chicago Press.

Thorson, James A. (1995). *Aging in a changing society.* Belmont, CA: Wadsworth.

Thrasher, Angela D., Clay, Olivio J., Ford, Chandra L., & Stewart, Anita L. (2012). Theory-guided selection of discrimination measures for racial/ethnic health disparities research among older adults. *Journal of Aging and Health, 24,* 1018–1043.

Thurber, James. (1999). The secret life of James Thurber. In James Thurber (Ed.), *The Thurber carnival* (pp. 35–41). New York, NY: Harper Perennial.

Tikotzky, Liat, Sharabany, Ruth, Hirsch, Idit, & Sadeh, Avi. (2010). "Ghosts in the Nursery:" Infant sleep and sleep-related cognitions of parents raised under communal sleeping arrangements. *Infant Mental Health Journal, 31,* 312–334.

Tilling, Kate, Lawlor, Debbie A., Davey Smith, George, Chambless, Lloyd, & Szklo, Moyses. (2006). The relation between components of adult height and intimal-medial thickness in middle age: The Atherosclerosis Risk in Communities Study. *American Journal of Epidemiology, 164,* 136–142.

Tilton-Weaver, Lauree, Kerr, Margaret, Pakalniskeine, Vilmante, Tokic, Ana, Salihovic, Selma, & Stattin, Håkan. (2010). Open up or close down: How do parental reactions affect youth information management? *Journal of Adolescence, 33,* 333–346.

Timiras, Mary L. (2007). The skin. In Paola S. Timiras (Ed.), *Physiological basis of aging and geriatrics* (4th ed., pp. 345–352). New York, NY: Informa Healthcare.

Timiras, Paola S., & De Martinis, Massimo. (2007). The pulmonary respiration, hematopoiesis, and erythrocytes. In Paola S. Timiras (Ed.), *Physiological basis of aging and geriatrics* (4th ed., pp. 277–296). New York, NY: Informa Healthcare.

Tishkoff, Sarah A., Reed, Floyd A., Friedlaender, Françoise R., Ehret, Christopher, Ranciaro, Alessia, Froment, Alain, … Williams, Scott M. (2009, May 22). The genetic structure and history of Africans and African Americans. *Science, 324,* 1035–1044.

Titus, Dale N. (2007). Strategies and resources for enhancing the achievement of mobile students. *NASSP Bulletin, 91,* 81–97.

Tokunaga, Robert S. (2010). Following you home from school: A critical review and synthesis of research on cyberbullying victimization. *Computers in Human Behavior, 26,* 277–287.

Tomalski, Przemyslaw, & Johnson, Mark H. (2010). The effects of early adversity on the adult and developing brain. *Current Opinion in Psychiatry, 23,* 233–238.

Tomasello, Michael. (2006). Acquiring linguistic constructions. In William Damon & Richard M. Lerner (Series Eds.) & Deanna Kuhn & Robert S. Siegler (Vol. Eds.), *Handbook of child psychology: Vol. 2. Cognition, perception, and language* (6th ed., pp. 255–298). Hoboken, NJ: Wiley.

Tomasello, Michael, & Herrmann, Esther. (2010). Ape and human cognition. *Current Directions in Psychological Science, 19,* 3–8.

Toossi, Mitra. (2002). A century of change: The U.S. labor force from 1950 to 2050. *Monthly Labor Review, 125*(5), 15–28.

Toporek, Bryan. (2012, February 29). Sports rules shift in light of concussion research. *Education Week,* p. 8.

Tornstam, Lars. (2005). *Gerotranscendence: A developmental theory of positive aging.* New York, NY: Springer.

Tough, Paul. (2012). *How children succeed: Grit, curiosity, and the hidden power of character.* Boston, MA: Houghton Mifflin Harcourt.

Toutain, Stéphanie. (2010). What women in France say about alcohol abstinence during pregnancy. *Drug and Alcohol Review, 29,* 184–188.

Townsend, Jean, Godfrey, Mary, & Denby, Tracy. (2006). Heroines, villains and victims: Older people's perceptions of others. *Ageing & Society, 26,* 883–900.

Tracy, Erin E. (2009, August). Does home birth empower women, or imperil them and their babies? *OBG Management, 21,* 45–52.

Trautmann-Villalba, Patricia, Gschwendt, Miriam, Schmidt, Martin H., & Laucht, Manfred. (2006). Father-infant interaction patterns as precursors of children's later externalizing behavior problems: A longitudinal study over 11 years. *European Archives of Psychiatry and Clinical Neuroscience, 256,* 344–349.

Treas, Judith, & Gubernskaya, Zoya. (2012). Farewell to moms? Maternal contact for seven countries in 1986 and 2001. *Journal of Marriage and Family, 74,* 297–311.

Tremblay, Angelo, & Chaput, Jean-Philippe. (2012). Obesity: The allostatic load of weight loss dieting. *Physiology & Behavior, 106,* 16–21.

Trenholm, Christopher, Devaney, Barbara, Fortson, Ken, Quay, Lisa, Wheeler, Justin, & Clark, Melissa. (2007). *Impacts of four Title V, Section 510 abstinence education programs final report.* Retrieved from http://www.mathematica-mpr.com/publications/PDFs/impactabstinence.pdf

Trickett, Penelope K., Negriff, Sonya, Ji, Juye, & Peckins, Melissa. (2011). Child maltreatment and adolescent development. *Journal of Research on Adolescence, 21,* 3–20.

Troll, Lillian E., & Skaff, Marilyn McKean. (1997). Perceived continuity of self in very old age. *Psychology & Aging, 12,* 162–169.

Trommsdorff, Gisela, & Cole, Pamela M. (2011). Emotion, self-regulation, and social behavior in cultural contexts. In Xinyin Chen & Kenneth H. Rubin (Eds.), *Socioemotional development in cultural context* (pp. 131–163). New York, NY: Guilford Press.

Tronick, Edward. (2007). *The neurobehavioral and social-emotional development of infants and children.* New York, NY: Norton.

Tronick, Ed, & Beeghly, Marjorie. (2011). Infants' meaning-making and the development of mental health problems. *American Psychologist, 66,* 107–119.

Tronick, Edward Z. (1989). Emotions and emotional communication in infants. *American Psychologist, 44,* 112–119.

Tronick, Edward Z., & Weinberg, M. Katherine. (1997). Depressed mothers and infants: Failure to form dyadic states of consciousness. In Lynne Murray & Peter J. Cooper (Eds.), *Postpartum depression and child development* (pp. 54–81). New York, NY: Guilford Press.

Trudeau, Linda, Spoth, Richard, Randall, G., Mason, W., & Shin, Chungyeol. (2012). Internalizing symptoms: Effects of a preventive intervention on developmental pathways from early adolescence to young adulthood. *Journal of Youth and Adolescence, 41,* 788–801.

Truman, Jennifer L., & Planty, Michael. (2012). *Criminal victimization, 2011* (NCJ 239437). Washington, DC: U.S. Department of Justice.

Truog, Robert D. (2007). Brain death—Too flawed to endure, too ingrained to abandon. *The Journal of Law, Medicine & Ethics, 35,* 273–281.

Trzesniewski, Kali H., Donnellan, M. Brent, Moffitt, Terrie E., Robins, Richard W., Poulton, Richie, & Caspi, Avshalom. (2006). Low self-esteem during adolescence predicts poor health, criminal behavior, and limited economic prospects during adulthood. *Developmental Psychology, 42,* 381–390.

Tsai, James, Floyd, R. Louise, & Bertrand, Jacquelyn. (2007). Tracking binge drinking among U.S. childbearing-age women. *Preventive Medicine: An International Journal Devoted to Practice and Theory, 44,* 298–302.

Tsai, Kim M., & Fuligni, Andrew J. (2012). Change in ethnic identity across the college transition. *Developmental Psychology, 48,* 56–64.

Tsao, Feng-Ming, Liu, Huei-Mei, & Kuhl, Patricia K. (2004). Speech perception in infancy predicts language development in the second year of life: A longitudinal study. *Child Development, 75,* 1067–1084.

Tudge, Jonathan. (2008). *The everyday lives of young children: Culture, class, and child rearing in diverse societies.* New York, NY: Cambridge University Press.

Tudge, Jonathan R. H., Doucet, Fabienne, Odero, Dolphine, Sperb, Tania M., Piccinini, Cesar A., & Lopes, Rita S. (2006). A window into different cultural worlds: Young children's everyday activities in the United States, Brazil, and Kenya. *Child Development, 77,* 1446–1469.

Turiel, Elliot. (2006). The development of morality. In William Damon & Richard M. Lerner (Series Eds.) & Nancy Eisenberg (Vol. Ed.), *Handbook of child psychology: Vol. 3. Social, emotional, and personality development* (6th ed., pp. 789–857). Hoboken, NJ: Wiley.

Turiel, Elliot. (2008). Thought about actions in social domains: Morality, social conventions, and social interactions. *Cognitive Development, 23,* 136–154.

Turley, Ruth N. López, & Desmond, Matthew. (2011). Contributions to college costs by married, divorced, and remarried parents. *Journal of Family Issues, 32,* 767–790.

Turner, Val D., & Berkowitz, Marvin W. (2005). Scaffolding morality: Positioning a socio-cultural construct. *New Ideas in Psychology, 23,* 174–184.

Twenge, Jean M., Gentile, Brittany, DeWall, C. Nathan, Ma, Debbie, Lacefield, Katharine, & Schurtz, David R. (2010). Birth cohort increases in psychopathology among young Americans, 1938–2007: A cross-temporal meta-analysis of the MMPI. *Clinical Psychology Review, 30,* 145–154.

Twenge, Jean M., Konrath, Sara, Foster, Joshua D., Campbell, W. Keith, & Bushma, Brad J. (2008). Egos inflating over time: A cross-temporal meta-analysis of the narcissistic personality inventory. *Journal of Personality, 76,* 875–902.

Twomey, Sean. (2012, June 15). Re: Should Canadians have the legal right to assisted suicide? [Web log comment]. Retrieved from http://www.cbc.ca/news/yourcommunity/2012/06/should-canadians-have-the-legal-right-to-assisted-suicide-1.html

Tye-Murray, Nancy, Spehar, Brent, Myerson, Joel, Sommers, Mitchell S., & Hale, Sandra. (2011). Cross-modal enhancement of speech detection in young and older adults: Does signal content matter? *Ear and Hearing, 32,* 650–655.

U.S. Bureau of the Census. (1907). *Statistical Abstract of the United States 1906.* Washington, DC: U.S. Government Printing Office.

U.S. Bureau of the Census. (1975). *Historical statistics of the United States, colonial times to 1970, Bicentennial edition.* Washington, DC: U.S Government Printing Office.

U.S. Bureau of the Census. (2002). *Statistical abstract of the United States, 2001: The national data book* (121st ed.). Washington, DC: U.S. Department of Commerce.

U.S. Bureau of the Census. (2008). *Statistical abstract of the United States: 2009* (128th ed.). Washington, DC: U.S. Department of Commerce.

U.S. Bureau of the Census. (2010a). *America's families and living arrangements: 2009.* Retrieved from http://www.census.gov/population/www/socdemo/hh-fam/cps2009.html

U.S. Bureau of the Census. (2010b). *Statistical abstract of the United States: 2011* (130th ed.). Washington, DC: U.S. Government Printing Office.

U.S. Bureau of the Census. (2011a). *America's families and living arrangements: 2011.* Retrieved from http://www.census.gov/population/www/socdemo/hh-fam/cps2011.html

U.S. Bureau of the Census. (2011b). *Statistical abstract of the United States: 2012* (131st ed.). Washington, DC: U.S. Government Printing Office.

U.S. Census Bureau. (2012). Statistical abstract of the United States: 2012 (131st edition). Washington, DC, 2011; http://www.census.gov/compendia/statab/

U.S. Census Bureau, American Community Survey. (2012). Income, poverty, and health insurance coverage in the United States: 2011. *Current Population Reports, P60–243,* U.S. Government Printing Office: Washington DC.

U.S. Census Bureau, Population Division. (2010). *Annual estimates of the resident population by sex, race, and Hispanic origin for the United States: April 1, 2000 to July 1, 2009* (NC-EST2009-03). Washington, DC: Government Printing Office.

U.S. Consumer Product Safety Commission. (2011, December). *Pediatric poisoning fatalities from 1972 through 2008.* Retrieved from http://www.cpsc.gov/library/foia/foia12/os/pppa2011.pdf

U.S. Department of Education. (2012). *National Indian Education Study 2011* (NCES 2012–466). Washington, DC: Institute of Education Sciences, U.S. Department of Education.

U.S. Department of Education, National Center for Education Statistics. (2011). Public school graduates and dropouts from the Common Core of Data: School year 2008–09 (NCES 2011-31). Washington, DC: National Center for Education Statistics.

U.S. Department of Health and Human Services. (2011). *The Surgeon General's call to action to support breastfeeding.* Washington, DC: U.S. Department of Health and Human Services, Office of the Surgeon General.

U.S. Department of Health and Human Services, Administration on Children, Youth and Families. (2008). *Child maltreatment 2006*. Washington, DC: U.S. Government Printing Office.

U.S. Department of Health and Human Services, Administration for Children and Families. (2010). *Head Start impact study: Final report*. Washington, DC: Author.

U.S. Department of Health and Human Services, Administration for Children and Families, Administration on Children, Youth and Families, Children's Bureau. (2011). *Child maltreatment 2010*. Retrieved from http://www.acf.hhs.gov/programs/cb/stats_research/index.htm#can.

U.S. Department of Health and Human Services, Administration on Children, Youth and Families. (2003). *Child maltreatment 2001*. Washington, DC: U.S. Government Printing Office.

U.S. Preventive Services Task Force. (2002). Postmenopausal hormone replacement therapy for primary prevention of chronic conditions: Recommendations and rationale. *Annals of Internal Medicine, 137*, 834–839.

Uchida, Shusaku, Hara, Kumiko, Kobayashi, Ayumi, Otsuki, Koji, Yamagata, Hirotaka, Hobara, Teruyuki, … Watanabe, Yoshifumi. (2011). Epigenetic status of Gdnf in the ventral striatum determines susceptibility and adaptation to daily stressful events. *Neuron, 69*, 359–372.

Uddin, Monica, Koenen, Karestan C., de los Santos, Regina, Bakshis, Erin, Aiello, Allison E., & Galea, Sandro. (2010). Gender differences in the genetic and environmental determinants of adolescent depression. *Depression and Anxiety, 27*, 658–666.

Umana-Taylor, Adriana J., & Guimond, Amy B. (2010). A longitudinal examination of parenting behaviors and perceived discrimination predicting Latino adolescents' ethnic identity. *Developmental Psychology, 46*, 636–650.

Umberson, Debra, Pudrovska, Tetyana, & Reczek, Corinne. (2010). Parenthood, childlessness, and well-being: A life course perspective. *Journal of Marriage and Family, 72*, 612–629.

UNAIDS. (2011). *UNAIDS World AIDS Day report*. Geneva, Switzerland: Author.

UNESCO. (2008). *Global education digest 2008: Comparing education statistics across the world*. Montreal, Quebec, Canada: UNESCO Institute for Statistics.

UNESCO. (2009). *Global education digest 2009: Comparing education statistics across the world*. Montreal, Quebec, Canada: UNESCO Institute for Statistics.

UNESCO Institute for Statistics. (2013: data collected at various times). UNESCO eAtlas of out-of-school children. Retrieved from http://www.app.collinsindicate.com/uis-atlas-out-of-school-children/en-us on January 18, 2013.

UNICEF (United Nations Children's Fund). (2008). *The state of the world's children 2009: Maternal and newborn health*. New York, NY: Author.

UNICEF (United Nations Children's Fund). (2012). *The state of the world's children 2012: Children in an urban world*. New York, NY: United Nations.

UNICEF. (2012). Childinfo: Monitoring the situation of children and women: Infant and young child feeding. Retrieved January 29, 2013 from: http://www.childinfo.org/breastfeeding_iycf.php

United Nations. (2011). *The millennium development goals report 2011* (11-31339). New York, NY: Author.

United Nations. (2012). *World population prospects: The 2010 revision*. New York, NY: Population Division of the United Nations Department of Economic and Social Affairs of the United Nations Secretariat.

United Nations, Department of Economic and Social Affairs, Population Division. (2009). *World marriage data 2008*. Retrieved from: http://www.un.org/esa/population/publications/WMD2008/Main.html

United Nations, Department of Economic and Social Affairs. (2011). *Population and Vital Statistics Report: Statistical Papers, Series A, Vol. 64* (ST/ESA/STAT/SER.A/256-257). New York, NY: United Nations.

United Nations, Department of Economic and Social Affairs, Population Division. (2011). *World population prospects, the 2010 revision, highlights and advance tables* (Working Paper No. ESA/P/WP.220). New York, NY: Author.

Unnever, James D. (2005). Bullies, aggressive victims, and victims: Are they distinct groups? *Aggressive Behavior, 31*, 153–171.

Utendale, William T., & Hastings, Paul D. (2011). Developmental changes in the relations between inhibitory control and externalizing problems during early childhood. *Infant and Child Development, 20*, 181–193.

Uttal, William R. (2000). *The war between mentalism and behaviorism: On the accessibility of mental processes*. Mahwah, NJ: Erlbaum.

Vail, Kenneth E., Rothschild, Zachary K., Weise, Dave R., Solomon, Sheldon, Pyszczynski, Tom, & Greenberg, Jeff. (2010). A terror management analysis of the psychological functions of religion. *Personality and Social Psychology Review, 14*, 84–94.

Vaillant, George E. (2002). *Aging well: Surprising guideposts to a happier life from the landmark Harvard Study of Adult Development*. Boston, MA: Little, Brown.

Vaillant, George E. (2008). *Spiritual evolution: A scientific defense of faith*. New York, NY: Broadway Books.

Valentino, Kristin, Cicchetti, Dante, Rogosch, Fred A., & Toth, Sheree L. (2008). True and false recall and dissociation among maltreated children: The role of self-schema. *Development and Psychopathology, 20*, 213–232.

van Alphen, Jojanneke E., Donker, Ge A., & Marquet, Richard L. (2010). Requests for euthanasia in general practice before and after implementation of the Dutch Euthanasia Act. *The British Journal of General Practice, 60*, 263–267.

van den Akker, Alithe, Dekovi, Maja, Prinzie, Peter, & Asscher, Jessica. (2010). Toddlers' temperament profiles: Stability and relations to negative and positive parenting. *Journal of Abnormal Child Psychology, 38*, 485–495.

van den Ban, Els, Souverein, Patrick, Swaab, Hanna, van Engeland, Herman, Heerdink, Rob, & Egberts, Toine. (2010). Trends in incidence and characteristics of children, adolescents, and adults initiating immediate- or extended-release methylphenidate or atomoxetine in the Netherlands during 2001–2006. *Journal of Child and Adolescent Psychopharmacology, 20*, 55–61.

van den Berg, Patricia A., Mond, Jonathan, Eisenberg, Marla, Ackard, Diann, & Neumark-Sztainer, Dianne. (2010). The link between body dissatisfaction and self-esteem in adolescents: Similarities across gender, age, weight status, race/ethnicity, and socioeconomic status. *The Journal of Adolescent Health, 47*, 290–296.

van den Berg, Stéphanie M., & Boomsma, Dorret I. (2007). The familial clustering of age at menarche in extended twin families. *Behavior Genetics, 37*, 661–667.

van der Heide, Agnes, Onwuteaka-Philipsen, Bregje D., Rurup, Mette L., Buiting, Hilde M., van Delden, Johannes J.M., Hanssen-de Wolf, Johanna E.,... van der Wal, Gerrit. (2007). End-of-life practices in the Netherlands under the euthanasia act. *New England Journal of Medicine, 356*, 1957–1965.

van der Houwen, Karolijne, Stroebe, Margaret, Schut, Henk, Stroebe, Wolfgang, & Van den Bout, Jan. (2010). Mediating processes in bereavement: The role of rumination, threatening grief interpretations, and deliberate grief avoidance. *Social Science & Medicine, 71*, 1669–1676.

van IJzendoorn, Marinus H., & Bakermans-Kranenburg, Marian J. (2010). Invariance of adult attachment across gender, age, culture, and socioeconomic status? *Journal of Social and Personal Relationships, 27*, 200–208.

van IJzendoorn, Marinus H., Bakermans-Kranenburg, Marian J., Pannebakker, Fieke, & Out, Dorothée. (2010). In defence of situational morality: Genetic, dispositional and situational determinants of children's donating to charity. *Journal of Moral Education, 39*, 1–20.

van IJzendoorn, Marinus H., Belsky, Jay, & Bakermans-Kranenburg, Marian J. (2012). Serotonin transporter genotype 5HTTLPR as a marker of differential susceptibility? A meta-analysis of child and adolescent gene-by-environment studies. *Translational Psychiatry, 2*, e147.

Van Leijenhorst, Linda, Zanolie, Kiki, Van Meel, Catharina S., Westenberg, P. Michiel, Rombouts, Serge A. R. B., & Crone, Eveline A. (2010). What motivates the adolescent? Brain regions mediating reward sensitivity across adolescence. *Cerebral Cortex, 20*, 61–69.

van Praag, Herman M., de Kloet, E. Ron, & van Os, Jim (2004). *Stress, the brain and depression.* New York, NY: Cambridge University Press.

Van Puyvelde, Martine, Vanfleteren, Pol, Loots, Gerrit, Deschuyffeleer, Sara, Vinck, Bart, Jacquet, Wolfgang, & Verhelst, Werner. (2010). Tonal synchrony in mother-infant interaction based on harmonic and pentatonic series. *Infant Behavior and Development, 33*, 387–400.

van Soelen, Inge L. C., Brouwer, Rachel M., Peper, Jiska S., van Beijsterveldt, Toos C. E. M., van Leeuwen, Marieke, de Vries, Linda S.,... Boomsma, Dorret I. (2010). Effects of gestational age and birth weight on brain volumes in healthy 9 year-old children. *The Journal of Pediatrics, 156*, 896–901.

Van Zundert, Rinka M. P., Van Der Vorst, Haske, Vermulst, Ad A., & Engels, Rutger C. M. E. (2006). Pathways to alcohol use among Dutch students in regular education and education for adolescents with behavioral problems: The role of parental alcohol use, general parenting practices, and alcohol-specific parenting practices. *Journal of Family Psychology, 20*, 456–467.

Vaughan, Ashley M., & Kappe, Stefan H. I. (2012). Malaria vaccine development: Persistent challenges. *Current Opinion in Immunology, 24*, 324–331.

Veenstra, René, Lindenberg, Siegwart, Munniksma, Anke, & Dijkstra, Jan Kornelis. (2010). The complex relation between bullying, victimization, acceptance, and rejection: Giving special attention to status, affection, and sex differences. *Child Development, 81*, 480–486.

Vélez, Clorinda E., Wolchik, Sharlene A., Tein, Jenn-Yun, & Sandler, Irwin. (2011). Protecting children from the consequences of divorce: A longitudinal study of the effects of parenting on children's coping processes. *Child Development, 82*, 244–257.

Verbakel, Ellen, & Jaspers, Eva. (2010). A comparative study on permissiveness toward euthanasia: Religiosity, slippery slope, autonomy, and death with dignity. *Public Opinion Quarterly, 74*, 109–139.

Vered, Karen Orr. (2008). *Children and media outside the home: Playing and learning in after-school care.* Houndmills, Basingstoke, Hampshire, England: Palgrave Macmillan.

Verona, Sergiu. (2003). Romanian policy regarding adoptions. In Victor Littel (Ed.), *Adoption update* (pp. 5–10). New York, NY: Nova Science.

Véronneau, Marie-Hélène, & Dishion, Thomas. (2010). Predicting change in early adolescent problem behavior in the middle school years: A mesosystemic perspective on parenting and peer experiences. *Journal of Abnormal Child Psychology, 38*, 1125–1137.

Véronneau, Marie-Hélène, Vitaro, Frank, Brendgen, Mara, Dishion, Thomas J., & Tremblay, Richard E. (2010). Transactional analysis of the reciprocal links between peer experiences and academic achievement from middle childhood to early adolescence. *Developmental Psychology, 46*, 773–790.

Viadero, Debra. (2007, April 5). Long after Katrina, children show symptoms of psychological distress. *Education Week*, p. 7.

Victora, Cesar G., Adair, Linda, Fall, Caroline, Hallal, Pedro C., Martorell, Reynaldo, Richter, Linda, & Sachdev, Harshpal Singh. (2008). Maternal and child undernutrition: Consequences for adult health and human capital. *Lancet, 371*, 340–357.

Vieno, Alessio, Nation, Maury, Pastore, Massimiliano, & Santinello, Massimo. (2009). Parenting and antisocial behavior: A model of the relationship between adolescent self-disclosure, parental closeness, parental control, and adolescent antisocial behavior. *Developmental Psychology, 45*, 1509–1519.

Virji-Babul, Naznin, Rose, A., Moiseeva, N., & Makan, N. (2012). Neural correlates of action understanding in infants: Influence of motor experience. *Brain and Behavior, 2*, 237–242.

Vitale, Susan, Sperduto, Robert D., & Ferris, Frederick L., III. (2009). Increased prevalence of myopia in the United States between 1971–1972 and 1999–2004. *Archives of Ophthalmology, 127,* 1632–1639.

Vittrup, Brigitte, & Holden, George W. (2010). Children's assessments of corporal punishment and other disciplinary practices: The role of age, race, SES, and exposure to spanking. *Journal of Applied Developmental Psychology, 31,* 211–220.

Vogel, Ineke, Verschuure, Hans, van der Ploeg, Catharina P. B., Brug, Johannes, & Raat, Hein. (2010). Estimating adolescent risk for hearing loss based on data from a large school-based survey. *American Journal of Public Health, 100,* 1095–1100.

Vogel, Lauren. (2011). Dying a "good death." *Canadian Medical Association Journal, 183,* 2089–2090.

Vohs, Kathleen D., & Baumeister, Roy F. (Eds.) (2010). *Handbook of self-regulation research, theory, and applications* (2nd ed.). New York, NY: Guilford Press.

von dem Knesebeck, Olaf, Pattyn, Elise, & Bracke, Piet. (2011). Education and depressive symptoms in 22 European countries. *International Journal of Public Health, 56,* 107–110.

von Mutius, Erika, & Vercelli, Donata. (2010). Farm living: Effects on childhood asthma and allergy. *Nature Reviews Immunology, 10,* 861–868.

Vonderheid, Susan C., Kishi, Rieko, Norr, Kathleen F., & Klima, Carrie. (2011). Group prenatal care and doula care for pregnant women. In Arden Handler, Joan Kennelly, & Nadine Peacock (Eds.), *Reducing racial/ethnic disparities in reproductive and perinatal outcomes: The evidence from population-based interventions* (pp. 369–400). New York, NY: Springer.

Voorpostel, Marieke, & Blieszner, Rosemary. (2008). Intergenerational solidarity and support between adult siblings. *Journal of Marriage and Family, 70,* 157–167.

Voorpostel, Marieke, & Schans, Djamila. (2011). Sibling relationships in Dutch and immigrant families. *Ethnic and Racial Studies, 34,* 2027–2047.

Voorpostel, Marieke, & van der Lippe, Tanja. (2007). Support between siblings and between friends: Two worlds apart? *Journal of Marriage and Family, 69,* 1271–1282.

Vouloumanos, Athena, & Werker, Janet F. (2007). Listening to language at birth: Evidence for a bias for speech in neonates. *Developmental Science, 10,* 159–164.

Voydanoff, Patricia. (2007). *Work, family, and community: Exploring interconnections.* Mahwah, NJ: Erlbaum.

Vygotsky, Lev S. (1987). Thinking and speech (Norris Minick, Trans.). In R. W. Rieber & Aaron S. Carton (Eds.), *The collected works of L. S. Vygotsky* (Vol. 1, pp. 39–285). New York, NY: Plenum Press. (Original work published 1934)

Vygotsky, Lev S. (1994). The development of academic concepts in school aged children (Theresa Prout, Trans.). In Rene van der Veer & Jaan Valsiner (Eds.), *The Vygotsky reader* (pp. 355–370). Cambridge, MA: Blackwell. (Original work published 1934)

Wagner, Laura, & Lakusta, Laura. (2009). Using language to navigate the infant mind. *Perspectives on Psychological Science, 4,* 177–184.

Wagner, Paul A. (2011). Socio-sexual education: A practical study in formal thinking and teachable moments. *Sex Education: Sexuality, Society and Learning, 11,* 193–211.

Wahlstrom, Dustin, Collins, Paul, White, Tonya, & Luciana, Monica. (2010). Developmental changes in dopamine neurotransmission in adolescence: Behavioral implications and issues in assessment. *Brain and Cognition, 72,* 146–159.

Walberg, Herbert J. (2011). *Tests, testing, and genuine school reform.* Stanford, CA: Education Next Books.

Waldinger, Robert J., & Schulz, Marc S. (2010). What's love got to do with it? Social functioning, perceived health, and daily happiness in married octogenarians. *Psychology and Aging, 25,* 422–431.

Walker, Alan. (2006). Aging and politics: An international perspective. In Robert H. Binstock & Linda K. George (Eds.), *Handbook of aging and the social sciences* (6th ed., pp. 339–359). Amsterdam, The Netherlands: Elsevier.

Waller, Erika M., & Rose, Amanda J. (2010). Adjustment trade-offs of co-rumination in mother-adolescent relationships. *Journal of Adolescence, 33,* 487–497.

Walsh, Bridget A., & Petty, Karen. (2007). Frequency of six early childhood education approaches: A 10-year content analysis of early childhood education journal. *Early Childhood Education Journal, 34,* 301–305.

Walsh, Roger. (2011). Lifestyle and mental health. *American Psychologist, 66,* 579–592.

Wan, Xiaohong, Nakatani, Hironori, Ueno, Kenichi, Asamizuya, Takeshi, Cheng, Kang, & Tanaka, Keiji. (2011, January 21). The neural basis of intuitive best next-move generation in board game experts. *Science, 331,* 34–346.

Wanberg, Connie R. (2012). The individual experience of unemployment. *Annual Review of Psychology, 63,* 369–396.

Wang, Hua, & Wellman, Barry. (2010). Social connectivity in America: Changes in adult friendship network size from 2002 to 2007. *American Behavioral Scientist, 53,* 1148–1169.

Wang, Jingyun, & Candy, T. Rowan. (2010). The sensitivity of the 2- to 4-month-old human infant accommodation system. *Investigative Ophthalmology and Visual Science, 51,* 3309–3317.

Wang, Wendy, & Taylor, Paul. (2011, March 9). *For millennials, parenthood trumps marriage.* Washington, DC: Pew Social and Demographic Trends.

Wang, Youfa, & Lim, Hyunjung. (2012). The global childhood obesity epidemic and the association between socioeconomic status and childhood obesity. *International Review of Psychiatry 24,* 176–188.

Ward, L. Monique, Epstein, Marina, Caruthers, Allison, & Merriwether, Ann. (2011). Men's media use, sexual cognitions, and sexual risk behavior: Testing a mediational model. *Developmental Psychology, 47,* 592–602.

Ward, Russell A., & Spitze, Glenna D. (2007). Nestleaving and coresidence by young adult children: The role of family relations. *Research on Aging, 29,* 257–277.

Warneken, Felix, & Tomasello, Michael. (2009). The roots of human altruism. *British Journal of Psychology, 100,* 455–471.

Warren, Charles W., Jones, Nathan R., Eriksen, Michael P., & Asma, Samira. (2006). Patterns of global tobacco use in young people and implications for future chronic disease burden in adults. *Lancet, 367,* 749–753.

Washington, Harriet A. (2006). *Medical apartheid: The dark history of medical experimentation on Black Americans from colonial times to the present.* New York, NY: Doubleday.

Wastesson, Jonas W., Parker, Marti G., Fastbom, Johan, Thorslund, Mats, & Johnell, Kristina. (2012). Drug use in centenarians compared with nonagenarians and octogenarians in Sweden: A nationwide register-based study. *Age and Ageing, 41,* 218–224.

Watson, John B. (1998). *Behaviorism.* New Brunswick, NJ: Transaction. (Original work published 1924)

Watson, John B. (1928). *Psychological care of infant and child.* New York, NY: Norton.

Waxman, Sandra R., & Lidz, Jeffrey L. (2006). Early word learning. In William Damon & Richard M. Lerner (Series Eds.) & Deanna Kuhn & Robert S. Siegler (Vol. Eds.), *Handbook of child psychology: Vol. 2. Cognition, perception, and language* (6th ed., pp. 299–335). Hoboken, NJ: Wiley.

Weikum, Whitney M., Vouloumanos, Athena, Navarra, Jordi, Soto-Faraco, Salvador, Sebastian-Galles, Nuria, & Werker, Janet F. (2007, May 25). Visual language discrimination in infancy. *Science, 316,* 1159.

Weiler, Richard, Stamatakis, Emmanuel, & Blair, Steven. (2010). Should health policy focus on physical activity rather than obesity? Yes. *British Medical Journal, 340,* c2603. doi:10.1136/bmj.c2603

Weiner, Myron F., & Lipton, Anne M. (Eds.). (2009). *The American Psychiatric Publishing textbook of Alzheimer disease and other dementias.* Washington, DC: American Psychiatric Publishing.

Weis, Robert, & Cerankosky, Brittany C. (2010). Effects of video-game ownership on young boys' academic and behavioral functioning. *Psychological Science, 21,* 463–470.

Weisgram, Erica S., Bigler, Rebecca S., & Liben, Lynn S. (2010). Gender, values, and occupational interests among children, adolescents, and adults. *Child Development, 81,* 778–796.

Weiss, Christopher C., Carolan, Brian V., & Baker-Smith, E. Christine. (2010). Big school, small school: (Re)testing assumptions about high school size, school engagement and mathematics achievement. *Journal of Youth and Adolescence, 39,* 163–176.

Wellman, Henry M., Cross, David, & Watson, Julanne. (2001). Meta-analysis of theory-of-mind development: The truth about false belief. *Child Development, 72,* 655–684.

Wendelken, Carter, Baym, Carol L., Gazzaley, Adam, & Bunge, Silvia A. (2011). Neural indices of improved attentional modulation over middle childhood. *Developmental Cognitive Neuroscience, 1,* 175–186.

Wenner, Melinda. (2009, February). The serious need for play. *Scientific American Mind, 20,* 23–29.

Werheid, Katja, Gruno, Maria, Kathmann, Norbert, Fischer, Håkan, Almkvist, Ove, & Winblad, Bengt. (2010). Biased recognition of positive faces in aging and amnestic mild cognitive impairment. *Psychology and Aging, 25,* 1–15.

Werner, Emmy E. (1979). *Cross-cultural child development: A view from the planet Earth.* Monterey, CA: Brooks/Cole.

Werner, Emmy E., & Smith, Ruth S. (1992). *Overcoming the odds: High risk children from birth to adulthood.* Ithaca, NY: Cornell University Press.

Werner, Emmy E., & Smith, Ruth S. (2001). *Journeys from childhood to midlife: Risk, resilience, and recovery.* Ithaca, NY: Cornell University Press.

Werner, Nicole E., & Hill, Laura G. (2010). Individual and peer group normative beliefs about relational aggression. *Child Development, 81,* 826–836.

Wertsch, James V., & Tulviste, Peeter. (2005). L. S. Vygotsky and contemporary developmental psychology. In Harry Daniels (Ed.), *An introduction to Vygotsky* (2nd ed., pp. 57–78). New York, NY: Routledge.

Whelchel, Lisa. (2005). *Creative correction: Extraordinary ideas for everyday discipline.* Wheaton, IL: Tyndale House.

Whitbourne, Susan Krauss. (2008). *Adult development & aging: Biopsychosocial perspectives* (3rd ed.). Hoboken, NJ: John Wiley & Sons.

Whitbourne, Susan Krauss, Sneed, Joel R., & Sayer, Aline. (2009). Psychosocial development from college through midlife: A 34-year sequential study. *Developmental Psychology, 45,* 1328–1340.

White, Rebecca M. B., & Roosa, Mark W. (2012). Neighborhood contexts, fathers, and Mexican American young adolescents' internalizing symptoms. *Journal of Marriage and Family, 74,* 152–166.

Whitehead, Kevin A., Ainsworth, Andrew T., Wittig, Michele A., & Gadino, Brandy. (2009). Implications of ethnic identity exploration and ethnic identity affirmation and belonging for intergroup attitudes among adolescents. *Journal of Research on Adolescence, 19,* 123–135.

Whitfield, Keith E., & McClearn, Gerald. (2005). Genes, environment, and race: Quantitative genetic approaches. *American Psychologist, 60,* 104–114.

Whitmore, Heather. (2001). Value that marketing cannot manufacture: Cherished possessions as links to identity and wisdom. *Generations, 25*(3), 57–63.

Whittle, Sarah, Yap, Marie B. H., Sheeber, Lisa, Dudgeon, Paul, Yücel, Murat, Pantelis, Christos, . . . Allen, Nicholas B. (2011). Hippocampal volume and sensitivity to maternal aggressive behavior: A prospective study of adolescent depressive symptoms. *Development and Psychopathology, 23,* 115–129.

WHO and Alzheimer's Disease International. (2012). *Dementia: A public health priority.* Geneva, Switzerland: World Health Organization.

WHO, UNAIDS. (2011). *Progress in scale-up of male circumcision for HIV prevention in Eastern and Southern Africa: Focus on service delivery.* Geneva, Switzerland: World Health Organization.

Wicher, Camille P., & Meeker, Mary Ann. (2012). What influences African American end-of-life preferences? *Journal of Health Care for the Poor and Underserved, 23,* 28–58.

Wicherts, Jelte M., Dolan, Conor V., & van der Maas, Han L. J. (2010). The dangers of unsystematic selection methods and the representativeness of 46 samples of African test-takers. *Intelligence, 38,* 30–37.

Widhalm, Kurt, Fritsch, Maria, Widhalm, Harald, Silberhumer, Gerd, Dietrich, Sabine, Helk, Oliver, & Prager, Gerhard. (2011). Bariatric surgery in morbidly obese adolescents: Long-term follow-up. *International Journal of Pediatric Obesity, 6*(Suppl. 1), 65–69.

Wijdicks, Eelco F. M., Varelas, Panayiotis N., Gronseth, Gary S., & Greer, David M. (2010). Evidence-based guideline update: Determining brain death in adults: Report of the Quality Standards Subcommittee of the American Academy of Neurology. *Neurology, 74,* 1911–1918.

Wilcox, W. Bradford, & Dew, Jeffrey. (2010). Is love a flimsy foundation? Soulmate versus institutional models of marriage. *Social Science Research, 39,* 687–699.

Willett, Walter C., & Trichopoulos, Dimitrios. (1996). Nutrition and cancer: A summary of the evidence. *Cancer Causes Control, 7,* 178–180.

Williams, Cath, Sutcliffe, Alastair, & Sebire, Neil J. (2010). Congenital malformations after assisted reproduction: Risks and implications for prenatal diagnosis and fetal medicine. *Ultrasound in Obstetrics and Gynecology, 35,* 255–259.

Williams, Kristine N., Herman, Ruth, Gajewski, Byron, & Wilson, Kristel. (2009). Elderspeak communication: Impact on dementia care. *American Journal of Alzheimer's Disease and Other Dementias, 24,* 11–20.

Williams, Lela Rankin, Fox, Nathan A., Lejuez, C. W., Reynolds, Elizabeth K., Henderson, Heather A., Perez-Edgar, Koraly E.,... Pine, Daniel S. (2010). Early temperament, propensity for risk-taking and adolescent substance-related problems: A prospective multi-method investigation. *Addictive Behaviors, 35,* 1148–1151.

Williamson, Rebecca A., Meltzoff, Andrew N., & Markman, Ellen M. (2008). Prior experiences and perceived efficacy influence 3-year-olds' imitation. *Developmental Psychology, 44,* 275–285.

Wilmshurst, Linda. (2011). *Child and adolescent psychopathology: A casebook* (2nd ed.). Thousand Oaks, CA: Sage.

Wilson, Stephan M., & Ngige, Lucy W. (2006). Families in sub-Saharan Africa. In Bron B. Ingoldsby & Suzanna D. Smith (Eds.), *Families in global and multicultural perspective* (2nd ed., pp. 247–273). Thousand Oaks, CA: Sage.

Winner, Brooke, Peipert, Jeffrey F., Zhao, Qiuhong, Buckel, Christina, Madden, Tessa, Allsworth, Jenifer E., & Secura, Gina M. (2012). Effectiveness of long-acting reversible contraception. *New England Journal of Medicine, 366,* 1998–2007.

Winter, Suzanne M. (2011). Culture, health, and school readiness. In DeAnna M. Laverick & Mary Renck Jalongo (Eds.), *Transitions to early care and education* (Vol. 4, pp. 117–133). New York, NY: Springer.

Witherington, David C., Campos, Joseph J., & Hertenstein, Matthew J. (2004). Principles of emotion and its development in infancy. In Gavin Bremner & Alan Fogel (Eds.), *Blackwell handbook of infant development* (Paperback ed., pp. 427–464). Malden, MA: Blackwell.

Wittassek, Matthias, Koch, Holger Martin, Angerer, Jürgen, & Brüning, Thomas. (2011). Assessing exposure to phthalates—The human biomonitoring approach. *Molecular Nutrition & Food Research, 55,* 7–31.

Wittrock, Merlin C. (2010). Learning as a generative process. *Educational Psychologist, 45,* 40–45.

Wolchik, Sharlene A., Ma, Yue, Tein, Jenn-Yun, Sandler, Irwin N., & Ayers, Tim S. (2008). Parentally bereaved children's grief: Self-system beliefs as mediators of the relations between grief and stressors and caregiver-child relationship quality. *Death Studies, 32,* 597–620.

Wolf, Norman S. (Ed.). (2010). *Comparative biology of aging.* New York, NY: Springer.

Wolff, Edward N. (2011). *The transformation of the American pension system: Was it beneficial for workers?* Kalamazoo, MI: W.E. Upjohn Institute for Employment Research.

Wolfinger, Nicholas H. (2005). *Understanding the divorce cycle: The children of divorce in their own marriages.* New York, NY: Cambridge University Press.

Wong, Paul T. P., & Tomer, Adrian. (2011). Beyond terror and denial: The positive psychology of death acceptance. *Death Studies, 35,* 99–106.

Wood, Joanne M. (2002). Aging, driving and vision. *Clinical and Experimental Optometry, 85,* 214–220.

Woods, Douglas W., Piacentini, John, & Walkup, John T. (Eds.) (2007). *Treating Tourette syndrome and tic disorders: A guide for practitioners.* New York, NY: Guilford Press.

Woodward, Amanda L., & Markman, Ellen M. (1998). Early word learning. In William Damon (Series Ed.) & Deanna Kuhn & Robert S. Siegler (Vol. Eds.), *Handbook of child psychology: Vol. 2. Cognition, perception and language* (5th ed., pp. 371–420). New York, NY: Wiley.

Woollett, Katherine, Spiers, Hugo J., & Maguire, Eleanor A. (2009). Talent in the taxi: A model system for exploring expertise. *Philosophical Transactions of the Royal Society of London, 364,* 1407–1416.

World Bank. (2010). *What can we learn from nutrition impact evaluations?* Washington, DC: The International Bank for Reconstruction and Development.

World Health Organization. (2005). *Sexually transmitted infections among adolescents: Issues in adolescent health and development.* Geneva, Switzerland: Author.

World Health Organization. (2010). *Global recommendations on physical activity for health.* Geneva: Author. Retrieved from: http://whqlibdoc.who.int/publications/2010/9789241599979_eng.pdf

World Health Organization. (2010). Global strategy on diet, physical activity, and health. Geneva: Author. From the WHO website at: http://www.who.int/dietphysicalactivity/diet/en/index.html

World Health Organization. (2010, October 5). *WHO global infobase: NCD indicators.* Retrieved from https://apps.who.int/infobase/Indicators.aspx

World Health Organization. (2012). WHO global info-base: Prevalence of overweight and obesity. Geneva: Author. Retrieved from: https://apps.who.int/infobase/

World Health Organization. (2012, February). *Poliomyelitis* [Fact sheet]. Retrieved from http://www.who.int/mediacentre/factsheets/fs114/en/

Worrell, Frank C. (2008). Nigrescence attitudes in adolescence, emerging adulthood, and adulthood. *Journal of Black Psychology, 34,* 156–178.

Worthy, Darrell A., Gorlick, Marissa A., Pacheco, Jennifer L., Schnyer, David M., & Maddox, W. Todd. (2011). With age comes wisdom: Decision making in younger and older adults. *Psychological Science, 22,* 1375–1380.

Wosje, Karen S., Khoury, Philip R., Claytor, Randal P., Copeland, Kristen A., Hornung, Richard W., Daniels, Stephen R., & Kalkwarf, Heidi J. (2010). Dietary patterns associated with fat and bone mass in young children. *American Journal of Clinical Nutrition, 92,* 294–303.

Wright, Mathew W., & Bruford, Elispeth A. (2011). Naming 'junk': Human non-protein coding RNA (ncRNA) gene nomenclature. *Human Genomics, 5,* 90–98.

Wu, Pai-Lu, & Chiou, Wen-Bin. (2008). Postformal thinking and creativity among late adolescents: A post-Piagetian approach. *Adolescence, 43,* 23–251.

Wurm, Susanne, Tomasik, Martin, & Tesch-Römer, Clemens. (2008). Serious health events and their impact on changes in subjective health and life satisfaction: The role of age and a positive view on ageing. *European Journal of Ageing, 5,* 117–127.

Wurtele, Sandy K. (2009). "Activities of Older Adults" survey: Tapping into student views of the elderly. *Educational Gerontology, 35,* 1026–1031.

Xu, Yaoying. (2010). Children's social play sequence: Parten's classic theory revisited. *Early Child Development and Care, 180,* 489–498.

Yamaguchi, Susumu, Greenwald, Anthony G., Banaji, Mahzarin R., Murakami, Fumio, Chen, Daniel, Shiomura, Kimihiro, . . . Krendl, Anne. (2007). Apparent universality of positive implicit self-esteem. *Psychological Science, 18,* 498–500.

Yan, Bernice, & Arlin, Patricia. (1995). Nonabsolute/relativistic thinking: A common factor underlying models of postformal reasoning? *Journal of Adult Development, 2,* 223–240.

Yang, Dahe, Sidman, Jason, & Bushnell, Emily W. (2010). Beyond the information given: Infants' transfer of actions learned through imitation. *Journal of Experimental Child Psychology, 106,* 62–81.

Yerys, Benjamin E., & Munakata, Yuko. (2006). When labels hurt but novelty helps: Children's perseveration and flexibility in a card-sorting task. *Child Development, 77,* 1589–1607.

Yeung, W. Jean, & Conley, Dalton. (2008). Black-White achievement gap and family wealth. *Child Development, 79,* 303–324.

Youn, Gahyun, Knight, Bob G., Jeong, Hyun-Suk, & Benton, Donna. (1999). Differences in familism values and caregiving outcomes among Korean, Korean American, and White American dementia caregivers. *Psychology & Aging, 14,* 355–364.

Young, Elizabeth A., Korszun, Ania, Figueiredo, Helmer F., Banks-Solomon, Matia, & Herman, James P. (2008). Sex differences in HPA axis regulation. In Jill B. Becker, Karen J. Berkley, Nori Geary, Elizabeth Hampson, James P. Herman, & Elizabeth Young (Eds.), *Sex differences in the brain: From genes to behavior* (pp. 95–105). New York, NY: Oxford University Press.

Young, John K. (2010). Anorexia nervosa and estrogen: Current status of the hypothesis. *Neuroscience & Biobehavioral Reviews, 34,* 1195–1200.

Young-Wolff, Kelly C., Enoch, Mary-Anne, & Prescott, Carol A. (2011). The influence of gene-environment interactions on alcohol consumption and alcohol use disorders: A comprehensive review. *Clinical Psychology Review, 31,* 800–816.

Zacher, Hannes, & Frese, Michael. (2011). Maintaining a focus on opportunities at work: The interplay between age, job complexity, and the use of selection, optimization, and compensation strategies. *Journal of Organizational Behavior, 32,* 291–318.

Zachry, Anne H., & Kitzmann, Katherine M. (2011). Caregiver awareness of prone play recommendations. *The American Journal of Occupational Therapy, 65,* 101–105.

Zahn-Waxler, Carolyn, Park, Jong-Hyo, Usher, Barbara, Belouad, Francesca, Cole, Pamela, & Gruber, Reut. (2008). Young children's representations of conflict and distress: A longitudinal study of boys and girls with disruptive behavior problems. *Development and Psychopathology, 20,* 99–119.

Zalenski, Robert J., & Raspa, Richard. (2006). Maslow's hierarchy of needs: A framework for achieving human potential in hospice. *Journal of Palliative Medicine, 9,* 1120–1127.

Zani, Bruna, & Cicognani, Elvira. (2006). Sexuality and intimate relationships in adolescence. In Sandy Jackson & Luc Goossens (Eds.), *Handbook of adolescent development* (pp. 200–222). Hove, East Sussex, UK: Psychology Press.

Zapf, Jennifer A., & Smith, Linda B. (2007). When do children generalize the plural to novel nouns? *First Language, 27,* 53–73.

Zeanah, Charles H., Berlin, Lisa J., & Boris, Neil W. (2011). Practitioner review: Clinical applications of attachment theory and research for infants and young children. *Journal of Child Psychology and Psychiatry, 52,* 819–833.

Zehr, Mary Ann. (2011, April 6). Study stings KIPP on attrition rates. *Education Week,* pp. 1, 24–25.

Zentall, Shannon R., & Morris, Bradley J. (2010). "Good job, you're so smart": The effects of inconsistency of praise type on young children's motivation. *Journal of Experimental Child Psychology, 107,* 155–163.

Zentner, Marcel, & Bates, John E. (2008). Child temperament: An integrative review of concepts, research programs, and measures. *European Journal of Developmental Science, 2,* 7–37.

Zernike, Kate. (2012, August 14). Youth driving laws limit even the double date. *New York Times,* pp. A1, A3.

Zettel, Laura A., & Rook, Karen S. (2004). Substitution and compensation in the social networks of older widowed women. *Psychology and Aging, 19,* 433–443.

Zettel-Watson, Laura, Ditto, Peter H., Danks, Joseph H., & Smucker, William D. (2008). Actual and perceived gender differences in the accuracy of surrogate decisions about life-sustaining medical treatment among older spouses. *Death Studies, 32,* 273–290.

Zhang, Baohui, Wright, Alexi A., Huskamp, Haiden A., Nilsson, Matthew E., Maciejewski, Matthew L., Earle, Craig C., . . . Prigerson, Holly G. (2009). Health care costs in the last week of life: Associations with end-of-life conversations. *Archives of Internal Medicine, 169,* 480–488.

Zhang, Donghui. (2010). Language maintenance and language shift among Chinese immigrant parents and their second-generation children in the U.S. *Bilingual Research Journal, 33,* 42–60.

Zhang, Shuangyue, & Kline, Susan L. (2009). Can I make my own decision? A cross-cultural study of perceived social network influence in mate selection. *Journal of Cross-Cultural Psychology, 40,* 3–23.

Zhang, Xin, Yeung, Dannii Y., Fung, Helene H., & Lang, Frieder R. (2011). Changes in peripheral social partners and loneliness over time: The moderating role of interdependence. *Psychology and Aging, 26,* 823–829.

Zhang, Ying. (2009). *State high school exit exams: Trends in test programs, alternate pathways, and pass rates.* Washington, DC: Center on Education Policy.

Zhu, Qi, Song, Yiying, Hu, Siyuan, Li, Xiaobai, Tian, Moqian, Zhen, Zonglei, . . . Liu, Jia. (2010). Heritability of the specific cognitive ability of face perception. *Current Biology, 20,* 137–142.

Zhu, Ying, Zhang, Li, Fan, Jin, & Han, Shihui. (2007). Neural basis of cultural influence on self-representation. *NeuroImage, 34,* 1310–1316.

Zimmer-Gembeck, Melanie J., & Ducat, Wendy. (2010). Positive and negative romantic relationship quality: Age, familiarity, attachment and well-being as correlates of couple agreement and projection. *Journal of Adolescence, 33,* 879–890.

Zimmerman, Ryan D., & Darnold, Todd C. (2009). The impact of job performance on employee turnover intentions and the voluntary turnover process: A meta-analysis and path model. *Personnel Review, 38*(2): 142–158.

Zimmermann, Camilla. (2012). Acceptance of dying: A discourse analysis of palliative care literature. *Social Science & Medicine, 75,* 217–224.

Zimprich, Daniel, & Martin, Mike. (2009). A multilevel factor analysis perspective on intellectual development in old age. In H. B. Bosworth & C. Hertzog (Eds.), *Aging and cognition: Research methodologies and empirical advances* (pp. 53–76). Washington, DC: American Psychological Association.

Zolotor, Adam J., Burchinal, Margaret, Skinner, Debra, Rosenthal, Marjorie, & The Key Family Life Project Investigators. (2008). Maternal psychological adjustment and knowledge of infant development as predictors of home safety practices in rural low-income communities. *Pediatrics, 121,* e1668-e1675. doi:10.1542/peds.2007-1255

Zosuls, Kristina M., Martin, Carol Lynn, Ruble, Diane N., Miller, Cindy F., Gaertner, Bridget M., England, Dawn E., & Hill, Alison P. (2011). "It's not that we hate you": Understanding children's gender attitudes and expectancies about peer relationships. *British Journal of Developmental Psychology, 29,* 288–304.

Zuvekas, Samuel H., Vitiello, Benedetto, & Norquist, Grayson S. (2006). Recent trends in stimulant medication use among U.S. children. *American Journal of Psychiatry, 163,* 579–585.

SOURCES AND CREDITS

Sources for data and photos in the Visualizing Development feature in each chapter:

Chapter 1:
Top:
International Monetary Fund (2012). *World economic outlook: October 2012.* Washington DC: International Monetary Fund. Retrieved January 2013 from: http://www.imf.org/external/pubs/ft/weo/2012/02/weodata/groups.htm
Middle and bottom:
United Nations, Department of Economic and Social Affairs, Population Division. (2011). *World population prospects, the 2010 revision, highlights and advance tables* (Working Paper No. ESA/P/WP.220). New York, NY: Author.

Chapter 2:
Photo of twins, left: Thinkstock
Photo of baby, center: Photodisk/Thinkstock
Photo of girl and boy, bottom right: Thinkstock

Chapter 3:
Photo of mother/baby: Thinkstock
Photo of mice: Thinkstock
Information on neural pathways in mice from:
Lupien, Sonia J., McEwen, Bruce S., Gunnar, Megan R., & Heim, Christine (2009). Effects of stress throughout the lifespan on the brain, behaviour and cognition, *Nature Reviews Neuroscience, 10,* 434–445.

Chapter 4:
Top photo: George Doyle/Thinkstock
Second photo: Pixland/Thinkstock
Third photo: Thinkstock
Bottom photo: Jupiterimages/Thinkstock

Chapter 6:
"Males and Females" data (weight graph at top): Kuczmarski, R. J., Ogden, C. L., Guo, S. S., et al. (2002). 2000 CDC growth charts for the United States: Methods and development. National Center for Health Statistics, *Vital Health Statistics,* 11(246). Retrieved from: http://www.cdc.gov/growthcharts/zscore.htm
"Some Complications," part 1: Zahn-Waxler, Carolyn, Park, Jong-Hyo, Usher, Barbara, Belouad, Francesca, Cole, Pamela, & Gruber, Reut. (2008). Young children's representations of conflict and distress: A longitudinal study of boys and girls with disruptive behavior problems. *Development and Psychopathology,* 20, 99–119.
"Some Complications," part 2: Eisenberg, N., Valiente, C., Spinrad, T. L., Cumberland, A., Liew, J., Reiser, M., Zhou, Q., & Losoya, S. H. (2009). Longitudinal relations of children's effortful control, impulsivity, and negative emotionality to their externalizing, internalizing, and co-occurring behavior problems. *Developmental Psychology,* 45, 988–1008.

Chapter 7:
Obesity map sources:
Data on Algeria, Seychelles, South Africa, Brazil, Chile, Mexico, Egypt, Iran, Kuwait, Sri Lanka, Japan, South Korea from: Wang, Youfa, & Lim, Hyunjung. (2012). The global childhood obesity epidemic and the association between socio-economic status and childhood obesity. *International Review of Psychiatry 24,* 176–188.
Data on New Zealand: Olds, Tim, Maher, Carol, Zumin, Shi, Peneau, Sandrine, Lioret, Sandrine, Castetbon, Katia, et al. (2011). Evidence that the prevalence of childhood overweight is plateauing: Data from nine countries. *International Journal of Pediatric Obesity 6,* 342–360.

Data on Australia: Australian Bureau of Statistics. (2009). *Australian social trends 2009: Using statistics to paint a picture of Australian society,* Catalogue No. 4102.0. Author: Canberra.
Data on Canada: Roberts, Karen C., Shields, Margot, de Groh, Margaret, Aziz, Alfred, & Gilbert, Jo-Anne. (2012). Overweight and obesity in children and adolescents: Results from the 2009 to 2011 Canadian Health Measures survey: Health Reports,23(3). Statistics Canada: Catalogue no. 82-003-XPE. 5.
All other data on map from: Moreno, Luis A., Pigeot, Iris, & Ahrens, Wolfgang (2011). *Epidemiology of obesity in children and adolescents: Prevalence and etiology.* New York: Springer.
"Ads and Obesity" data: Lobstein, Tim, & Dibb, Sue. (2005). Evidence of a possible link between obesogenic food advertising and child overweight. *Obesity Reviews,* 6, 203–208.
Photo of computer screen: Thinkstock
"WHO Recommendation for Physical Activity" information from: World Health Organization. (2010). *Global recommendations on physical activity for health.* Geneva: Author. Retrieved from: http://whqlibdoc.who.int/publications/2010/9789241599979_eng.pdf

Chapter 8:
"Rates of Single Parenthood" data from: Social Trends Institute. (2012). *The sustainable demographic dividend.* Charlottesville, VA Author. Retrieved from: http://sustaindemographicdividend.org/wp-content/uploads/2012/07/SDD-2011-Final.pdf
"A Young Couple in Love" information from: Copen, Casey, Daniels, Kimberly, Vespa, Jonathan, & Moshen, William. (2012, March 2012). First marriages in the United States: Data from the 2006-2010 National Survey of Family growth. *National Center for Health Statistics,* 49.
U.S. Census Bureau. (2012). *Statistical abstract of the United States: 2012* (131st edition). Washington, DC, 2011; http://www.census.gov/compendia/statab/ United Nations, Department of Economic and Social Affairs, Population Division (2009).*World marriage data 2008.* Retrieved from: http://www.un.org/esa/population/publications/WMD2008/Main.html

Chapter 9:
Photo: Jupiterimages/Thinkstock

Chapter 10:
Photo of students: Thinkstock
"Percentage of Adolescents Not in School, Ages 12 to 15" data from: UNESCO Institute for Statistics. (2013: data collected at various times). UNESCO eAtlas of out-of-school children. Retrieved from http://www.app.collinsindicate.com/uis-atlas-out-of-school-children/en-us on January 18, 2013.
"U.S. Dropout Rate, by State, 2008–2009" data from: U.S. Department of Education, National Center for Education Statistics. (2011). Public school graduates and dropouts from the Common Core of Data: School year 2008–09 (NCES 2011-31). Washington DC: National Center for Education Statistics.

Chapter 11:
Photo of money: Jupiterimages/Thinkstock
Photo of graduation cap: Stockbyte/Thinkstock
"Education in the U.S." and "Income Impact" data from: U.S. Census Bureau, American Community Survey. (2012). Data on educational attainment: 2011. U.S. Government Printing Office: Washington DC.
"Locating College Enrollment" data from: UNESCO. (2009). *Global education digest 2009:*

Comparing education statistics across the world. Montreal, Quebec, Canada: UNESCO Institute for Statistics.

Chapter 12:
"Overweight and GNP" data from:
World Health Organization (2012). WHO global infobase: Prevalence of overweight and obesity. Geneva: Author. Retrieved from: https://apps.who.int/infobase/
The World Bank. (2013). GNI per capita, Atlas method. Washington DC: Author.
"WHO Recommendations for Reducing Obesity" from:
World Health Organization. (2010). Global strategy on diet, physical activity, and health. Geneva: Author. From the WHO website at: http://www.who.int/dietphysicalactivity/diet/en/index.html
World Health Organization. (2010). Global recommendations for physical activity for health. Geneva: Author. From the WHO website at: http://whqlibdoc.who.int/publications/2010/9789241599979_eng.pdf

Chapter 13:
Photo of rings: iStockphoto/Thinkstock
"Partners or Not" data (top graph) from: U.S. Bureau of the Census. (2012). *America's families and living arrangements: 2012.* Retrieved from http://www.census.gov/hhes/families/data/cps2012.html, January 2013.
"Average Age of Marriage" data from:
United Nations, Department of Economic and Social Affairs, Population Division (2009).*World marriage data 2008.* Retrieved from: http://www.un.org/esa/population/publications/WMD2008/Main.html

Chapter 14:
"Accidents Rate by Incidence" data from:
National Safety Council. (2011). *Injury facts.* Itasca, IL: Author. Retrieved from: www.nsc.org/Documents/Injury_Facts/Injury_Facts_2011_w.pdf
"Accidents Rate by Miles Driven" data from:
National Highway Traffic Safety Administration. (1993). *Addressing the safety issues related to younger and older drivers.* Washington, DC: Author. Retrieved from: www.nhtsa.gov/people/injury/olddrive/pub/Chapter1.html

Chapter 15:
Graphics information calculated by the author based on data from:
CDC (Centers for Disease Control and Prevention). (2011). *Deaths: Preliminary data for 2011.* Atlanta: Author.
CDC (Centers for Disease Control and Prevention). (2012). *Disability health and data system.* Atlanta: Author.
Greenberg, Saadia. (2011). *A profile of older Americans, 2011.* United States Department of Health and Human Services, Administration on Aging.
National Center for Health Statistics. (2012a). *2011 National Health Interview Survey (NHIS).* Hyattsville, MD: Author.
U.S. Census Bureau. (2012). *Statistical abstract of the United States: 2012* (131st edition). Washington, DC, 2011; http://www.census.gov/compendia/statab/
U.S. Bureau of the Census. (2011). *America's families and living arrangements: 2011.* Retrieved from http://www.census.gov/population/www/socdemo/hh-fam/cps2011.html

Geary, Nori, 324
Gelfand, Donald E., 550
Geller, Barbara, 274
Gendron, Brian P., 308, 344
Genesee, Fred, 192
Gentile, Douglas, 379
Gentile, Douglas A., 220
Georgas, James, 294, 417, 423
George, Linda G., 468
George, R., 589
Geraerts, Elke, 234
Gerber, Alan S., 466
Gerrard, Meg, 338
Gershkoff-Stowe, Lisa, 190
Gershoff, Elizabeth T., 229, 230, 235
Gettler, Lee T., 99, 100
Gevorgyan, Ruzanna, 375
Gewertz, Catherine, 345
Gewirtzman, Aron, 396
Giancola, Peter R., 442
Giardino, Angelo P., 236
Gibson, Carolyn J., 434
Gibson-Davis, Christina, 301
Gibson-Davis, Christina M., 300
Gigerenzer, Gerd, 350
Gilbert, Daniel, 467
Giles, Amy, 119
Gillath, Omri, 421
Gillen, Meghan M., 395
Gillen-O'Neel, Cari, 289
Gilles, Floyd H., 93
Gillespie, Michael Alen, 245
Gilligan, Carol, 310
Gillis, John R., 304
Gil-Rivas, Virginia, 288
Gitler, Aaron D., 523
Gitlin, Laura N., 564
Gladwell, Malcolm, 561
Glick, Jennifer E., 160
Gluckman, Peter D., 248
Gobush, Kathleen S., 558
Golant, Stephen M., 549, 567, 568
Gold, Joshua M., 480
Golden, Marita, 558
Golden, Timothy D., 492
Goldenberg, Jamie L., 576, 578
Goldin-Meadow, Susan, 121, 184
Goldscheider, Frances, 480
Goldstein, Joshua R., 397
Goldstein, Michael H., 142
Golestani, Narly, 455
Golinkoff, Roberta Michnick, 126
Golub, Sarit A., 500
Göncü, Artin, 212
Gonzales, Patrick, 265
González, Hector M., 545
Goodall, Jane, 435, 574, 598
Goodman, Judith C., 126
Gopnik, Alison, 186
Gorchoff, Sara M., 477
Gordis, Elana B., 137
Gore, Andrea C., 323
Gorelick, Philip B., 522
Gormley, William T., 200
Gornick, Janet C., 492
Gosso, Yumi, 212
Gottfredson, Denise C., 343
Gottfried, Adele Askeles, 208
Gottlieb, Gilbert, 5, 18, 58

Gould, Madelyn S., 379
Gow, Alan J., 512
Graber, Julia A., 372
Gracia, Enrique, 218
Grady, Denise, 53, 522
Gräff, Johannes, 18
Graham, Sandra, 342
Grandin, Temple, 275
Granic, Isabela, 307
Granpeesheh, Doreen, 276
Grant, Victoria, 593
Gratton, Gabriele, 432
Green, James A., 134
Green, Lorraine, 593
Greene, Melissa L., 376
Greenfield, Emily A., 549
Greenhalgh, Susan, 53
Greenwood, Pamela M., 435, 512
Greer, Eric, 507
Gregory, Ted, 559
Greyson, Bruce, 582
Griffin, James, 400
Griffith, Patrick, 563–564
Griffiths, Maya, 577
Grimm, David, 438
Grivell, Rosalie M., 65
Grobman, Kevin H., 143
Grolnick, Wendy S., 207
Grossmann, Klaus E., 142
Grosvenor, Theodore, 83
Grubeck-Loebenstein, Beatrix, 395
Grundy, Emily, 485
Grusec, Joan E., 230
Gubernskaya, Zonya, 472
Guerra, Nancy G., 306, 307
Guerri, Consuelo, 384
Gummerum, Michaela, 310
Gunnar, Megan R., 181
Guo, Sufang, 65
Gupta, Ramesh C., 77
Gurung, Regan A. R., 553
Gustavo, Luis, 394

Haas, Steven A., 543
Hafemeister, Thomas L., 566
Hagedoorn, Mariët, 559
Hagestad, Gunhild O., 482, 554, 555
Hahn, Erin R., 190
Haier, Richard J., 445
Hajjar, Emily R., 525
Halaschek-Wiener, Julius, 506
Hall, Lynn K., 293
Hall-Lande, Jennifer A., 377
Halpern, Carolyn Tucker, 329
Halpern, Diane F., 265
Halpern, Neil A., 590
Hamerman, David, 518
Hamerton, John L., 71
Hamilton, Alice, 172
Hamilton, Brady E., 65, 367
Hamm, Jill V., 366
Hammer, Carol Scheffner, 14, 193, 198
Hammond, Christopher J., 83
Hampel, Harald, 523
Hampton, Tracy, 438
Han, Euna, 247
Han, Wen-Jui, 451
Handelsman, David J., 436
Hane, Amie Ashley, 139

Hank, Karsten, 547, 557
Hannan, Claire, 109
Hannon, Erin E., 121
Hansen, Åse M., 78
Hanson, Karla L., 247
Hanson, Mark A., 248
Hansson, Robert O., 596
Hanushek, Eric A., 264, 266, 351
Harburg, Ernest, 443
Hardan, Antonio Y., 179
Hardway, Christina, 322
Hardy, Melissa, 547
Hargreaves, Andy, 346
Harjes, Carlos E., 83
Harkness, Sara, 208, 209, 231
Harknett, Kristen S., 299
Harlow, Ilana, 595
Harris, Judith Rich, 290
Harrison, Denise, 103
Harrison, Janet, 435
Harrison, Kristen, 247, 248, 250
Harrison, Linda J., 192
Harrist, Amanda W., 247
Hart, Chantelle N., 248
Harter, Susan, 135, 136, 153, 286
Hartnett, Caroline Sten, 299
Hartney, Hannah, 329
Hartl, Daniel L., A5
Harvey, Carol D. H., 486
Harvey, John H., 478
Hasebe, Yuki, 362
Hassan, Mohamed A. M., 431
Hassett, Janice M., 214
Hastings, Paul D., 218, 227
Hausenblas, Heather A., 79
Hawthorne, Joanna, 67
Hayden, Brian, 574
Hayes, Rachel A., 121
Hayflick, Leonard, 506
Hayne, Harlene, 119
Hayward, Diane W., 276
Hazlett, Heather Cody, 96
Heaton, Tim B., 295
Hedberg, Eric Christopher, 262
Heflick, Nathan A., 576
Hehman, Eric, 402
Hehman, Jessica A., 500, 541
Heiman, Julia R., 508
Heise, Susan, 483
Helmes, Edward, 554
Hendrix, Jimi, 180
Henretta, John C., 485, 556
Henry, William Earl, 540
Henry VIII, 52
Herd, Pamela, 545
Herek, Gregory M., 478
Herlofson, Katharina, 482, 554, 555
Herman, Khalisa N., 214
Herman-Giddens, Marcia E., 320
Herrera, Angelica P., 501, 525
Herring, Ann, 396
Herrmann, Esther, 125, 178
Herschensohn, Julia Rogers, 189
Herschkowitz, Elinore Chapman, 178
Herschkowitz, Norbert, 207, 255
Hertzog, Christopher, 401, 446
Heslin, Kevin C., 474
Hess, Thomas, 501, 513
Hess, Thomas M., 453